JIST's *Best Jobs* Series

Best Jobs for the 21st Century

Third Edition

Developed by Michael Farr

With database work by Laurence Shatkin, Ph.D.

Also in JIST's *Best Jobs* Series

▲ *300 Best Jobs Without a Four-Year Degree*

▲ *200 Best Jobs for College Graduates*

JIST *Works*
America's Career Publisher

Best Jobs for the 21st Century, Third Edition

© 2004 by JIST Publishing, Inc.

Published by JIST Works, an imprint of JIST Publishing, Inc.
8902 Otis Avenue
Indianapolis, IN 46216-1033

Phone: 1-800-648-JIST   Fax: 1-800-JIST-FAX   E-mail: info@jist.com

Visit our Web site at www.jist.com for information on JIST, free job search information, book excerpts, and ordering information on our many products. For free information on 14,000 job titles, visit www.careeroink.com.

Some Other Books by the Author

Michael Farr and LaVerne L. Ludden

300 Best Jobs Without a Four-Year Degree
200 Best Jobs for College Graduates
Enhanced Occupational Outlook Handbook
Guide for Occupational Exploration

Michael Farr

Seven Steps to Getting a Job Fast
The Quick Resume & Cover Letter Book
America's Top Resumes for America's Top Jobs
Getting the Job You Really Want
The Very Quick Job Search

Quantity discounts are available for JIST books. Please call our sales department at 1-800-648-JIST for a free catalog and more information.

Editors: Stephanie Koutek, Susan Pines
Cover and Interior Designer: Aleata Howard
Page Layout Coordinator: Carolyn J. Newland
Proofreader: Jeanne Clark

Printed in Canada

08 07 06 05 04   9 8 7 6 5 4 3 2

ISBN 1-56370-961-9

This Is a Big Book, But It Is Very Easy to Use

This book is designed to help you explore career options in a variety of interesting ways. The nice thing about it is that you don't have to read it all. Instead, we designed it to allow you to browse and find information that most interests you.

The Table of Contents will give you a good idea of what's inside and how to use the book, so we suggest you start there. Part I of the book is made up of interesting lists that will help you explore jobs based on pay, interests, education level, personality type, and many other criteria. Part II provides descriptions for each job included in the book. Just find a job that interests you in one of the lists in Part I and look up its description in Part II. Simple.

How We Selected the Best Jobs for the 21st Century

Deciding on the "best" job is a choice that only you can make, but objective criteria can help you identify jobs that are, for example, better paying than other jobs with similar duties. Here is an explanation of the process we used to determine which jobs to include in this book.

We sorted 1027 major jobs from highest to lowest in terms of earnings, growth rate through 2010, and number of annual openings. We then assigned a number to their relative position on each list, doubling the weight for the earnings score. The job position numbers on the three lists were then combined, and jobs with the lowest total scores were put on top, followed by jobs with higher total scores on down the list. We included the 500 jobs with the lowest scores in the book. The first list in Part I is called "The 500 Best Jobs Overall," and it contains the 500 jobs with the lowest scores in order of their combined score on all three measures (earnings, growth rate, and openings).

Of the 1027 major jobs, more than 30 were for specialized postsecondary teaching jobs. We collapsed these jobs into one title: Teachers, Postsecondary. A list of these specialized job titles is provided in Part I's introduction.

You can find descriptions for all 500 best jobs in Part II, along with descriptions of the various specialized postsecondary teaching jobs, for a total of 537 descriptions in all.

(continued)

(continued)

We are not suggesting that the 500 jobs with the best overall scores for earnings, growth, and number of openings are all good ones for you to consider—some will not be. But the 500 jobs that met our criteria present such a wide range of jobs that you are likely to find one or more that will interest you. The jobs that met our "best jobs" criteria are also more likely than average to have higher pay, faster projected growth, and a larger number of openings than other jobs at similar levels of education and training.

Some Things You Can Do with This Book

▲ Identify more-interesting or better-paying jobs that don't require additional training or education.

▲ Develop long-term plans that may require additional training, education, or experience.

▲ Explore and select a college major or a training or educational program that relates to a career objective.

▲ Find reliable earnings information to negotiate pay.

▲ Prepare for interviews and the job search.

These are a few of the many ways you can use this book. We hope you find it as interesting to browse as we did to put together. We have tried to make it easy to use and as interesting as occupational information can be.

When you are done with this book, pass it along or tell someone else about it. We wish you well in your career and in your life.

Credits and Acknowledgments: While the authors created this book, it is based on the work of many others. The occupational information is based on data obtained from the U.S. Department of Labor and the U.S. Census Bureau. These sources provide the most authoritative occupational information available. The job titles and their related descriptions are from the O*NET database, which was developed by researchers and developers under the direction of the U.S. Department of Labor. They, in turn, were assisted by thousands of employers who provided details on the nature of work in the many thousands of job samplings used in the database's development. We used the most recent version of the O*NET database, release 4.0. We appreciate and thank the staff of the U.S. Department of Labor for their efforts and expertise in providing such a rich source of data.

Table of Contents

Summary of Major Sections

Introduction. A short overview to help you better understand and use the book. *Starts on Page 1.*

Part I—The Best Jobs Lists. Very useful for exploring career options! Lists are arranged into easy-to-use groups. The first group of lists presents the best overall jobs–jobs with the highest earnings, projected growth, and number of openings. More specialized lists follow, presenting the best jobs for workers age 16–24, workers 55 and over, part-time workers, self-employed workers, women, and men. Other lists present the best jobs at various levels of education, by interest, and by personality type. The column starting at right presents all the list titles within the groups. *Starts on Page 11.*

Part II—The Job Descriptions. Provides complete descriptions of the 500 jobs that met our criteria for high pay, fast growth, or large number of openings plus the more specialized jobs included in the Teachers, Postsecondary job title. Each description contains information on earnings, projected growth, job duties, skills, related job titles, education and training required, related knowledge and courses, and many other details. *Starts on Page 157.*

Part I—The Best Jobs Lists................. 11

The many interesting lists in this book are organized into the major groupings below. Simply find the lists that interest you, turn to the page number indicated, and browse the lists to find jobs that interest you. Then look up job descriptions in Part II. Easy!

Best Jobs Overall: Lists of Jobs with the Highest Pay, Fastest Growth, and Most Openings ... 15

Best Jobs Lists with High Percentages of Workers Age 16–24, Workers Age 55 and Over, Part-Time Workers, Self-Employed Workers, Women, and Men 41

Best Jobs with a High Percentage of Workers Age 16–24 42

Best Jobs Lists Based on Interests 115

Best Jobs Lists Based on Personality Types 141

Part II—The Job Descriptions 157

Descriptions for all the jobs in this book are included in this part in alphabetical order. The titles are presented below, along with the page numbers where each description begins. We suggest that you use the lists in Part I to identify job titles that interest you and then locate their descriptions in Part II.

Introduction

We kept this introduction short to encourage you to actually read it. For this reason, we don't provide many details on the technical issues involved in creating the job lists or descriptions. Instead, we give you short explanations to help you understand and use the information the book provides for career exploration or planning. We think this brief and user-oriented approach makes sense for most people who will use this book.

Who This Book Is For and What It Covers

We created this book to help students and adults explore their career, education, training, and life options. Employers, educators, program planners, career counselors, and others will also find this book to be of value.

To create it, we started with more than 1,000 major jobs at all levels of training and education. From these, we selected those with the highest earnings, projected growth rate, and number of job openings. Part I contains lists that rank the jobs according to many criteria, including earnings, growth, openings, education level, and interest area. Part II contains job descriptions for all of the jobs.

We think you will find many of the job lists in Part I interesting—and useful for identifying career options to consider. The job descriptions are also packed with useful information.

Where the Information Comes From

The information we used in creating this book comes from three major government sources:

▲ **The U.S. Department of Labor:** We used a variety of data sources to construct the information we used in this book. We started with the jobs included in the U.S. Department of Labor's O*NET database. The O*NET includes information on more than 1,000 occupations and is now the primary source of detailed information on occupations. The Labor Department updates the O*NET on a regular basis, and we used the most recent one available.

▲ **The U.S. Census Bureau:** Because we wanted to include earnings, growth, number of openings, and other data not included in the O*NET, we used information on earnings from the U.S. Department of Labor's Bureau of Labor Statistics (BLS). Some of this data came from the Current Population Survey, conducted by the U.S. Census Bureau, and other data came from the BLS's own Occupational Employment Statistics survey. The information on earnings is the most reliable information we could obtain. The BLS uses a slightly different system of job titles than the O*NET does, but we were able to link the BLS data to most of the O*NET job titles we used to develop this book. The Current Population Survey also provided information about the proportion of workers in each job who are self employed or work part time.

▲ **The U.S. Department of Education:** We used the Classification of Instructional Programs, a system developed by the U.S. Department of Education, to cross-reference the education or training programs related to each job.

Data Complexities

For those of you who like details, we present some of the complexities inherent in our sources of information and what we did to make sense of them here. You don't need to know this to use the book, so jump to the next section of the Introduction if you are bored with details.

Earnings, Growth, and Number of Openings

We include information on earnings, projected growth, and number of job openings for each job throughout this book. We think this information is important to most people, but getting it for each job is not a simple task.

Earnings

The employment security agency of each state gathers information on earnings for various jobs and forwards this to the U.S. Bureau of Labor Statistics. This information is organized in standardized ways by a BLS program called the Occupational Employment Statistics, or OES. To keep the earnings for the various jobs and regions comparable, the OES screens out certain types of earnings and includes others, so the OES earnings we use in this book represent straight-time, gross pay, exclusive of premium pay. More specifically, the OES earnings include the job's base rate; cost-of-living allowances; guaranteed pay; hazardous-duty pay; incentive pay, including commissions and production bonuses; on-call pay; and tips. They do not include back pay, jury duty pay, overtime pay, severance pay, shift differentials, non-production bonuses, or tuition reimbursements. Also, self-employed workers are not included in the earnings estimates, and they can be a significant segment in certain occupations.

The OES earnings data uses a system of job titles called the Standard Occupational Classification system, or SOC. Most of these jobs can be cross-referenced to the O*NET job titles we use in this book, so we can attach earnings information to most job titles and descriptions. But a small number of the O*NET jobs simply do not have earnings data available for them from the sources we used and were not included.

Projected Growth and Number of Job Openings

This information comes from the Office of Occupational Statistics and Employment Projections, a program within the Bureau of Labor Statistics that develops information about projected trends in the nation's labor market for the next ten years. The most recent projections available cover the ten-year period through 2010. The projections are based on information about people moving into and out of occupations. The BLS uses data from various sources in projecting the growth and number of openings for each job title—some data comes from the Census Bureau's Current Population Survey, and some comes from an OES survey. The projections assume that there will be no major war, depression, or other economic upheaval. Like the earnings figures, the figures on projected growth and job openings are reported according to the SOC classification. As with earnings, the relatively few jobs that could not be crosswalked to include projected growth or number of openings were not included in this book.

Information in the Job Descriptions

We used a variety of government and other sources to compile the job descriptions we provide in Part II. Details on these various sources are mentioned later in this Introduction in "Part II: The Job Descriptions."

How the 500 Best Jobs Were Selected

The "This Is a Big Book…" section at the beginning of this book gives a brief description of how we selected the jobs we include in this book. Here are a few more details:

1. We began by creating our own database of information from the O*NET, Census Bureau, and other sources to include the information we wanted. This database covered 1,027 job titles at all levels of education and training.

2. We created three lists that ranked all 1,027 jobs based on three major criteria: median annual earnings, projected growth through 2010, and number of job openings projected per year. Each of these lists was then sorted from highest to lowest and assigned a score based on its position on each list, from 1 to 1027.

3. We then created a new list that doubled the weight of the earnings score and added the number scores for all three lists. The higher a job landed on each list, the lower its score was, so we sorted the total scores from lowest to highest total score. We then assigned a position number from 1 to 1027 to each job. Job titles with lower total scores were listed first. For example, the job of Computer Software Engineers, Applications has the lowest total combined score, so Computer Software Engineers, Applications is listed first in our 500 Best Jobs Overall list, even though this job is not the highest-paying job (which is Anesthesiologists) or the job with the most openings (which is Cashiers). Coincidentally, Computer Software Engineers, Applications does happen to be the fastest-growing job in the list. Only those 500 jobs with the lowest or "best" total scores were selected to be included in this book.

Why This Book Has More Than 500 Jobs

We didn't think you would mind that this book actually provides information on more than 500 jobs. Among the jobs it includes are 38 specialized postsecondary education jobs that we combined into one job called Teachers, Postsecondary. We use this one job title throughout the lists but provide descriptions for all 38 of these specialized postsecondary jobs in Part II. This means that we used 500 job titles to construct the lists, but we have a total of 537 job descriptions in Part II. You can find a list of the 38 specialized postsecondary teaching jobs in the "Some Details on the Lists" section at the beginning of Part I.

The Data in This Book Can Be Misleading

We use the most reliable data we can obtain for the earnings, projected growth, number of openings, and other information to create this book, but keep in mind that this information may or may not be accurate for your situation. This is because the information is true on the average. But just as there is no precisely average person, there is no such thing as a statistically average example of a particular job. We say this because data, while helpful, can also be misleading.

Take, for example, the yearly earnings information in this book. This is highly reliable data obtained from a very large U.S. working population sample by the Bureau of Labor Statistics. It tells us the median annual pay received by people in various job titles. This sounds very useful until you consider that half of all people in that occupation earned less than that amount, and half earn more. (We often use "average" instead of "median" elsewhere in this book for ease of explanation).

For example, people just entering the occupation or people with a few years of work experience will often earn much less than the average. People who live in rural areas or who work for smaller employers typically earn less than those who do similar work in cities, where the cost of living is higher, or for larger employers.

So, in reviewing the information in this book, please understand the limitations of the data it presents. You need to use common sense in career decision-making as in most other things in life. Even so, we hope that you find the information helpful and interesting.

Part I: The Best Jobs Lists

There are 65 separate lists in Part I of this book—look in the Table of Contents for a complete list of them. The lists are not difficult to understand because they have clear titles and are organized into groupings of related lists.

Depending on your situation, some of the jobs lists in Part I will interest you more than others. For example, if you are young, you may be interested to learn the highest-paying jobs that employ high percentages of workers age 16–24. Other lists show jobs within interest groupings, by personality type, by level of education, and in other ways that you might find helpful in exploring your career options.

Whatever your situation, we suggest that you use the lists that make sense for you to help explore career options. Following are the names of each group of lists along with short comments on each group. You will find additional information in a brief introduction provided at the beginning of each group of lists in Part I.

Here is an overview of each major group of lists you will find in Part I.

Best Jobs Overall: Lists of Jobs with the Highest Pay, Fastest Growth, and Most Openings

Four lists are in this group, and they are the ones that most people want to see first. The first list presents all 500 job titles in order of their combined scores for earnings, growth, and number of job openings (with the earnings rankings given twice the weight). Three more lists in this group present the 100 jobs with the highest earnings, the 100 jobs projected to grow most rapidly, and the 100 jobs with the most openings.

Best Jobs Lists with High Percentages of Workers Age 16–24, Workers Age 55 and Over, Part-Time Workers, Self-Employed Workers, Women, and Men

This group of lists presents interesting information for a variety of types of people based on data from the U.S. Census Bureau. The lists are arranged into groups for workers age 16–24, workers age 55 and older, part-time workers, self-employed workers, women, and men. We created five lists for each group, basing the last four on the information in the first list:

▲ The 100 jobs having the highest percentage of people of each type

▲ The 25 jobs with the best combined scores for earnings, growth, and number of openings (with earnings information given double the weight)

▲ The 25 jobs with the highest earnings

▲ The 25 jobs with the highest growth rates

▲ The 25 jobs with the largest number of openings

Best Jobs Lists Based on Levels of Education and Experience

We created separate lists for each level of education and training as defined by the U.S. Department of Labor. We put each of the 500 job titles into one of the lists based on the education and training required for entry. Jobs within these lists are presented in order of their total combined scores for earnings, growth, and number of openings. The lists include jobs in these groupings:

▲ Short-term on-the-job training

▲ Moderate-term on-the-job training

▲ Long-term on-the-job training

▲ Work experience in a related job

▲ Postsecondary vocational training

▲ Associate's degree

▲ Bachelor's degree

▲ Work experience plus degree

▲ Master's degree

▲ Doctoral degree

▲ First professional degree

Best Jobs Lists Based on Interests

These lists organize the 500 jobs into groups based on interests. Within each list, jobs are presented in order of their total scores for earnings, growth, and number of openings. Here are the 14 interest areas used in these lists: Arts, Entertainment, and Media; Science, Math, and Engineering; Plants and Animals; Law, Law Enforcement, and Public Safety; Mechanics, Installers, and Repairers; Construction, Mining, and Drilling; Transportation; Industrial Production; Business Detail; Sales and Marketing; Recreation, Travel, and Other Personal Services; Education and Social Service; General Management and Support; and Medical and Health Services.

Best Jobs Lists Based on Personality Types

These lists organize the 500 jobs into six personality types described in the introduction to the lists: Realistic, Investigative, Artistic, Social, Enterprising, and Conventional. The jobs within each list are presented in order of their total scores for earnings, growth, and number of openings.

Part II: The Job Descriptions

This part of the book provides a brief but information-packed description for each of the 537 jobs that met our criteria for this book. The descriptions in Part II are presented in alphabetical order. This makes it easy to look up any job you identify in a list from Part I that you want to learn more about.

We used the most current information from a variety of government sources to create the descriptions. We designed the descriptions to be easy to understand, and the sample that follows—with an explanation of each of its component parts—will help you better understand and use the descriptions.

▲ **Job Title:** This is the job title for the job as defined by the U.S. Department of Labor and used in its O*NET database.

▲ **Data Elements:** The information on education, earnings, growth, annual openings, percentage of self-employed workers, and percentage of part-time workers comes from various government databases, as we explain earlier in this Introduction.

▲ **Summary Description and Tasks:** The first part of each job description provides a summary of the occupation in bold type. It is followed by a listing of tasks that are generally performed by people who work in the job. This information comes from the O*NET database.

▲ **Skills:** The O*NET database provides data on 46 skills, and we used this source to provide helpful information on the most important skills needed for each job. To make the descriptions useful, we list only skills with a higher-than-average rating for each job. If a job has more than five such skills, we include only those five with the highest ratings and present them from highest to lowest score. We include up to seven skills if scores were tied for fifth place. Finally, at least one skill is listed for each job, even if the rating for that skill is lower than the average for all jobs. Each listed skill is followed by a brief description of that skill.

▲ **GOE Information:** We included information that cross-references the *Guide for Occupational Exploration* (or the *GOE*), a system developed by the U.S. Department of Labor that organizes jobs based on interests. This is very helpful information for exploring job options based on your interests. Our descriptions include the major *GOE* Interest Area number and name and *GOE* Work Group and name, as well as a list of other job titles within that Work Group. This information will help you identify other job titles that

Data Elements ◄—

Job Title ↗

Residential Advisors

- ▲ Education/Training Required: Moderate-term on-the-job training
- ▲ Annual Earnings: $19,680
- ▲ Growth: 24.0%
- ▲ Annual Job Openings: 9,000
- ▲ Self-Employed: 0%
- ▲ Part-Time: 18.0%

Summary Description ↗

GOE Information →

Personality Type →

Education/ Training Programs →

Tasks ◄—

Coordinate activities for residents of boarding schools, college fraternities or sororities, college dormitories, or similar establishments. Order supplies and determine need for maintenance, repairs, and furnishings. May maintain household records and assign rooms. May refer residents to counseling resources if needed. Assigns room, assists in planning recreational activities, and supervises work and study programs. Orders supplies and determines need for maintenance, repairs, and furnishings. Ascertains need for and secures service of physician. Chaperons group-sponsored trips and social functions. Plans menus of meals for residents of establishment. Sorts and distributes mail. Answers telephone. Hires and supervises activities of housekeeping personnel. Escorts individuals on trips outside establishment for shopping or to obtain medical or dental services. Compiles records of daily activities of residents. Counsels residents in identifying and resolving social and other problems. **SKILLS—Social Perceptiveness:** Being aware of others' reactions and understanding why they react as they do. **Active Listening:** Giving full attention to what other people are saying, taking time to understand the points being made, asking questions as appropriate, and not interrupting at inappropriate times. **Coordination:** Adjusting actions in relation to others' actions. **Speaking:** Talking to others to convey information effectively. **Critical Thinking:** Using logic and reasoning to identify the strengths and weaknesses of alternative solutions, conclusions, or approaches to problems.

Skills ↑

GOE Information ◄—

GOE INFORMATION—**Interest Area:** 12. Education and Social Service. **Work Group:** 12.02. Social Services. **Other Job Titles in This Work Group:** Child, Family, and School Social Workers; Clergy; Clinical Psychologists; Clinical, Counseling, and School Psychologists; Community and Social Service Specialists, All Other; Counseling Psychologists; Counselors, All Other; Directors, Religious

Activities and Education; Marriage and Family Therapists; Medical and Public Health Social Workers; Mental Health and Substance Abuse Social Workers; Mental Health Counselors; Probation Officers and Correctional Treatment Specialists; Rehabilitation Counselors; Religious Workers, All Other; Social and Human Service Assistants; Social Workers, All Other; Substance Abuse and Behavioral Disorder Counselors. **PERSONALITY TYPE**—Social. Social occupations frequently involve working with, communicating with, and teaching people. These occupations often involve helping or providing service to others.

EDUCATION/TRAINING PROGRAM(S)—Hotel/ Motel Administration/Management. RELATED KNOWLEDGE/COURSES—**Customer and Personal Service:** Knowledge of principles and processes for providing customer and personal services. This includes customer needs assessment, meeting quality standards for services, and evaluation of customer satisfaction. **Psychology:** Knowledge of human behavior and performance; individual differences in ability, personality, and interests; learning and motivation; psychological research methods; and the assessment and treatment of behavioral and affective disorders. **Therapy and Counseling:** Knowledge of principles, methods, and procedures for diagnosis, treatment, and rehabilitation of physical and mental dysfunctions and for career counseling and guidance. **Administration and Management:** Knowledge of business and management principles involved in strategic planning, resource allocation, human resources modeling, leadership technique, production methods, and coordination of people and resources. **Personnel and Human Resources:** Knowledge of principles and procedures for personnel recruitment, selection, training, compensation and benefits, labor relations and negotiation, and personnel information systems.

Related Knowledge/ Courses ◄—

relate to similar interests or require similar skills. We used the newest *GOE* Interest Areas and Work Groups as presented in the *Guide for Occupational Exploration,* Third Edition (JIST Publishing). You can find more information on the *GOE* and its Interest Areas in the introduction to the lists of jobs based on interests in Part I.

▲ **Personality Type:** The O*NET database assigns each job to its most closely related personality type. Our job descriptions include the name of the related personality type as well as a brief definition of this personality type. You can find more information on the personality types in the introduction to the lists of jobs based on personality types in Part I.

▲ **Education/Training Programs:** This part of the job description provides the name of the educational or training program or programs for the job. It will help you identify sources of formal or informal training for a job that interests you. To get this information, we used a crosswalk created by the National Crosswalk Service Center to connect information in the Classification of Instruction Programs (CIP) to the O*NET job titles we use in this book. We made various changes to connect the O*NET job titles to the education or training programs related to them and also modified the names of some education and training programs so they would be more easily understood.

▲ **Related Knowledge/Courses:** This entry in the job description will help you understand the most important knowledge areas that are required for the job and the types of courses or programs you will likely need to take to prepare for it. We used information in the Department of Labor's O*NET database for this entry. We went through a process similar to the one described for the skills (noted earlier) to end up with entries that are most important for each job.

Getting all the information we used in the job descriptions was not a simple process, and it is not always perfect. Even so, we used the best and most recent sources of data we could find, and we think that our efforts will be helpful to many people.

Sources of Additional Information

Hundreds of sources of career information exist, so here are a few we consider most helpful in getting additional information on the jobs listed in this book.

Print References

▲ *O*NET Dictionary of Occupational Titles:* Revised on a regular basis, this book provides good descriptions for all jobs listed in the U.S. Department of Labor's O*NET database. There are about 1,000 job descriptions at all levels of education and training, plus lists of related job titles in other major career information sources, educational programs, and other information. Published by JIST.

▲ *Guide for Occupational Exploration,* **Third Edition:** The new edition of the *GOE* is cross-referenced in the descriptions in Part II. The *GOE* provides helpful information to consider on each of the Interest Areas and Work Groups, descriptions of all O*NET jobs within each *GOE* group, and many other features useful for exploring career options. This most recent edition is published by JIST.

▲ *Enhanced Occupational Outlook Handbook:* Updated regularly, this book provides thorough descriptions for all major jobs in the current *Occupational Outlook Handbook,* brief descriptions for the O*NET jobs that are related to each, brief descriptions of thousands of more-specialized jobs from the *Dictionary of Occupational Titles,* and other information. Published by JIST.

Internet Resources

▲ **The U.S. Department of Labor Bureau of Labor Statistics Web site:** The Department of Labor Bureau of Labor Statistics Web site (http://www.bls.gov) provides a lot of career information, including links to other Web pages that provide information on the jobs covered in this book. This Web site is a bit formal and, well, confusing, but it will take you to the major sources of government career information if you explore its options.

▲ **O*NET site:** Go to http://www.onetcenter.org for a variety of information on the O*NET database, including links to sites that provide detailed information on the O*NET job titles presented in Part II of this book.

▲ **CareerOINK.com:** This site (http://www.careeroink.com) is operated by JIST and includes free information on thousands of jobs (including all O*NET jobs included in *Best Jobs for the 21ˢᵗ Century*), easy-to-use crosswalks between major career information systems, links from military to civilian jobs, sample resumes, and many other features. A link at http://www.jist.com will also take you to the CareerOINK Web site.

Thanks

Thanks for reading this introduction. You are surely a more thorough person than those who jumped into the book without reading it, and you will probably get more out of the book as a result.

We wish you a satisfying career and, more importantly, a good life.

Part I

The Best Jobs Lists

Tips on Using These Lists

We've tried to make the Best Jobs lists in this section both fun to use and informative. You can use the Table of Contents at the front of the book to find a complete listing of all the list titles in this section. You can then review the lists that most interest you or simply browse the lists in this section. Most, such as the list of highest-paying jobs, are easy to understand and require little explanation. We provide comments on each group of related lists to inform you of the selection criteria or other details we think you may want to know.

As you review the lists, mark job titles that appeal to you (or, if someone else will be using this book, write them on a separate sheet of paper) so that you can look up their descriptions later in Part II.

Understand the Limitations of the Information

Many of the lists emphasize jobs with high pay, high growth, or large numbers of openings. Most people consider these factors important in selecting a desirable job, and they are also easily quantifiable. While these measures are important, we think you should also think about other factors in considering your career options. For example, location, liking the people you work with, having an opportunity to serve others, and enjoying your work are just a few of the many factors that may define the ideal job for you. These measures are difficult or impossible to objectively quantify and are not, therefore, presented in this book. For this reason, we suggest that you consider the importance of these issues yourself and that you thoroughly research any job before making a firm decision.

(continued)

(continued)

For example, of the 500 jobs in our Best Jobs Overall list, the last job is First-Line Supervisors and Manager/Supervisors—Agricultural Crop Workers. It has annual earnings of $33,330, a 13.0 percent growth rate, and 8,000 job openings per year. Is this a "bad" job, one you should avoid? No, of course not. It all depends on what you like or want to do. Another example is the job that had the very best overall score for earnings, growth, and number of openings, Computer Software Engineers, Applications. Is this job a great job to consider? Many people (the authors included) would not want to work in this job or may not have the skills or interest needed to do it well. It would be a great job for someone who was good at it and who would enjoy doing it, but it would simply not be right for someone else. On the other hand, the perfect job for some people would be First-Line Supervisors and Manager/Supervisors—Agricultural Crop Workers because they enjoy it and are good at it.

So, as you look at the lists that follow, keep in mind that earnings, growth, and number of openings are just some things to consider. Also consider that half of all people in a given job earn more than the earnings you will see in this book—and half earn less. If a job really appeals to you, you should consider it even if it is not among the highest paying. And you should also consider jobs not among the fastest growing and jobs with few openings for similar reasons, because openings are always available, even for jobs with slow or negative growth projections or with small numbers of openings.

Some Details on the Lists

The sources of the information we used in constructing these lists are presented in this book's Introduction. Here are some additional details on how we created the lists:

▲ We collapsed a number of specialized postsecondary education jobs into one title. The government database we used for the job titles and descriptions included 38 job titles for postsecondary educators, yet the data source we used for growth and number of openings provided data only for the more general job of Teachers, Postsecondary. To make our lists more useful, we included only one listing—Teachers, Postsecondary—rather than separate listings for each specialized postsecondary education job. We did, however, include descriptions for all the specific postsecondary teaching jobs in Part II. Should you wonder, here are the more specialized titles: Agricultural Sciences Teachers, Postsecondary; Anthropology and Archeology Teachers, Postsecondary; Architecture Teachers, Postsecondary; Area, Ethnic, and Cultural Studies Teachers, Postsecondary; Art, Drama, and Music Teachers, Postsecondary; Atmospheric, Earth, Marine, and Space Sciences Teachers,

Postsecondary; Biological Science Teachers, Postsecondary; Business Teachers, Postsecondary; Chemistry Teachers, Postsecondary; Communications Teachers, Postsecondary; Computer Science Teachers, Postsecondary; Criminal Justice and Law Enforcement Teachers, Postsecondary; Economics Teachers, Postsecondary; Education Teachers, Postsecondary; Engineering Teachers, Postsecondary; English Language and Literature Teachers, Postsecondary; Environmental Science Teachers, Postsecondary; Foreign Language and Literature Teachers, Postsecondary; Forestry and Conservation Science Teachers, Postsecondary; Geography Teachers, Postsecondary; Graduate Teaching Assistants; Health Specialties Teachers, Postsecondary; History Teachers, Postsecondary; Home Economics Teachers, Postsecondary; Law Teachers, Postsecondary; Library Science Teachers, Postsecondary; Mathematical Science Teachers, Postsecondary; Nursing Instructors and Teachers, Postsecondary; Philosophy and Religion Teachers, Postsecondary; Physics Teachers, Postsecondary; Political Science Teachers, Postsecondary; Postsecondary Teachers, All Other; Psychology Teachers, Postsecondary; Recreation and Fitness Studies Teachers, Postsecondary; Social Sciences Teachers, Postsecondary, All Other; Social Work Teachers, Postsecondary; Sociology Teachers, Postsecondary; and Vocational Education Teachers, Postsecondary.

▲ We excluded some jobs from some lists due to a lack of available data. There were 9 jobs that did not have data available for us to use in the Best Jobs with High Percentages of Workers Age 16–24, Workers Age 55 and Over, Part-Time Workers, Self-Employed Workers, Women, and Men section. The reason was that the government information source we used did not collect this data for these jobs. As a result, we had to exclude these jobs from those lists, even though some would likely be included in those lists if we could get accurate data for them. The excluded jobs are Aircraft Cargo Handling Supervisors; Bakers; Computer Support Specialists; First-Line Supervisors/Managers of Correctional Officers; Gaming Cage Workers; Network Systems and Data Communications Analysts; Survey Researchers; Tax Preparers; and Truck Drivers, Heavy and Tractor-Trailer.

▲ Many jobs have tied scores. Some jobs have the same scores for one or more data elements. For example, in the category of jobs with the highest percentage of workers age 16 to 24, there are ten jobs in which 16.6 percent of the workers are between the ages of 16 and 24. Yet, because these jobs were at the lower end of the list, only nine of them could be listed among the 100 with the highest percentage of workers age 16 to 24. In other cases, jobs with the same numbers are listed one after another, making it appear that those listed first have a better rating when that is not the case. There was no way to avoid these issues, so simply understand that the difference of several positions on a list may not mean as much as it seems.

▲ Some jobs have similar titles. We merged two databases of information, and some titles are similar. For example, the job title "Accountants and Auditors" cross-references to two separate job titles in another database, "Accountants" and "Auditors." These entries are not errors; they just reflect the imperfect cross-referencing we had to use to attach data from one source to the job description information in another.

Best Jobs Overall: Lists of Jobs with the Highest Pay, Fastest Growth, and Most Openings

The four lists that follow are this book's premier lists. They are the lists that are most often mentioned in the media and the ones that most readers want to see.

To create these lists, we ranked 1,027 major jobs according to a combination of their earnings (given twice the weight), growth, and openings. We then selected the 500 jobs with the best total scores for use in this book. (The process for ranking the jobs is explained in more detail in the Introduction.)

The first list presents all 500 best jobs according to these combined rankings for pay, growth, and number of openings. Three additional lists present the 100 jobs with the top scores in each of three measures: annual earnings, projected percentage growth through 2010, and number of annual openings. Descriptions for all the jobs in these lists are included in Part II.

The 500 Best Jobs Overall—Jobs with the Best Combination of Pay, Growth, and Openings

This list arranges all 500 jobs that were selected for this book in order of their overall scores for pay, growth, and number of openings. To obtain this list, we sorted 1,027 jobs into three lists based on pay, growth, and number of openings. We sorted each of these lists from highest to lowest and then assigned a number to each entry. For example, the job with the highest pay was given a score of 1, the one with the next highest pay was given a score of 2, and so on. This scoring process was continued for each job on each of the three lists. Since earnings are important to most people, we doubled the weight of the earnings ranking in computing the total scores. We then combined the three scores for each job and sorted the new list based on the total score for all three measures.

The job with the best overall score was Computer Software Engineers, Applications. Other jobs follow in order of their total scores for pay, growth, and openings. These 500 jobs are the ones we use throughout this book: in the other lists in Part I and in the descriptions found in Part II.

As you look over the list, remember that jobs near the top of the list are not necessarily "good" jobs—nor are jobs towards the end of the list necessarily "bad" ones for you to consider. Their position in the list is simply a result of their total scores based on pay, growth, and number of openings. This means, for example, that some jobs with low pay, modest growth, but a high number of openings appear higher on the list, while some jobs with higher pay, modest growth, but a low number of openings appear towards the end of the list. The "right" job for you could be anywhere on this list.

The 500 Best Jobs Overall

Job	Annual Earnings	Percent Growth	Annual Openings
1. Computer Software Engineers, Applications	$70,210	100.0%	28,000
2. Computer Systems Analysts	$61,990	59.7%	34,000
3. Computer and Information Systems Managers	$82,480	47.9%	28,000
4. Teachers, Postsecondary	$52,115	23.5%	184,000
5. Management Analysts	$57,970	28.9%	50,000
6. Registered Nurses	$46,670	25.6%	140,000
7. Computer Software Engineers, Systems Software	$73,280	89.7%	23,000
8. Medical and Health Services Managers	$59,220	32.3%	27,000
9. Sales Agents, Financial Services	$59,690	22.3%	55,000
10. Sales Agents, Securities and Commodities	$59,690	22.3%	55,000
11. Securities, Commodities, and Financial Services Sales Agents	$59,690	22.3%	55,000
12. Computer Support Specialists	$38,560	97.0%	40,000
13. Sales Managers	$71,620	32.8%	21,000
14. Computer Security Specialists	$53,770	81.9%	18,000
15. Network and Computer Systems Administrators	$53,770	81.9%	18,000
16. Financial Managers	$70,210	18.5%	53,000
17. Financial Managers, Branch or Department	$70,210	18.5%	53,000
18. Treasurers, Controllers, and Chief Financial Officers	$70,210	18.5%	53,000
19. Accountants	$45,380	18.5%	100,000
20. Accountants and Auditors	$45,380	18.5%	100,000
21. Auditors	$45,380	18.5%	100,000
22. General and Operations Managers	$65,010	15.2%	235,000
23. Adjustment Clerks	$25,430	32.4%	359,000
24. Customer Service Representatives	$25,430	32.4%	359,000
25. Customer Service Representatives, Utilities	$25,430	32.4%	359,000
26. Pharmacists	$74,890	24.3%	20,000
27. Chief Executives	$120,450	17.2%	48,000
28. Government Service Executives	$120,450	17.2%	48,000
29. Private Sector Executives	$120,450	17.2%	48,000
30. Financial Analysts	$55,120	25.5%	20,000
31. Lawyers	$88,760	18.0%	35,000
32. Administrative Services Managers	$49,810	20.4%	31,000
33. Tractor-Trailer Truck Drivers	$32,580	19.8%	240,000
34. Truck Drivers, Heavy	$32,580	19.8%	240,000

The 500 Best Jobs Overall

Job	Annual Earnings	Percent Growth	Annual Openings
35. Truck Drivers, Heavy and Tractor-Trailer	$32,580	19.8%	240,000
36. Secondary School Teachers, Except Special and Vocational Education	$43,280	18.6%	60,000
37. Personal Financial Advisors	$57,710	34.0%	13,000
38. Public Relations Specialists	$41,010	36.1%	19,000
39. Anesthesiologists	greater than $145,600	17.9%	27,000
40. Internists, General	greater than $145,600	17.9%	27,000
41. Obstetricians and Gynecologists	greater than $145,600	17.9%	27,000
42. Surgeons	greater than $145,600	17.9%	27,000
43. Psychiatrists	$126,460	17.9%	27,000
44. Pediatricians, General	$126,430	17.9%	27,000
45. Graphic Designers	$36,020	26.7%	28,000
46. Family and General Practitioners	$118,390	17.9%	27,000
47. Correctional Officers and Jailers	$32,010	32.4%	30,000
48. Educational, Vocational, and School Counselors	$43,470	25.3%	22,000
49. Child, Family, and School Social Workers	$32,950	26.9%	35,000
50. Paralegals and Legal Assistants	$36,670	33.2%	23,000
51. Marketing Managers	$74,370	29.1%	12,000
52. Caption Writers	$42,450	28.4%	18,000
53. Copy Writers	$42,450	28.4%	18,000
54. Creative Writers	$42,450	28.4%	18,000
55. Poets and Lyricists	$42,450	28.4%	18,000
56. Writers and Authors	$42,450	28.4%	18,000
57. Advertising Sales Agents	$36,560	26.3%	25,000
58. Security Guards	$18,600	35.4%	242,000
59. Special Education Teachers, Preschool, Kindergarten, and Elementary School	$42,110	36.8%	15,000
60. Network Systems and Data Communications Analysts	$57,470	77.5%	9,000
61. Musicians and Singers	$40,320	20.1%	33,000
62. Musicians, Instrumental	$40,320	20.1%	33,000
63. Singers	$40,320	20.1%	33,000
64. Computer Programmers	$60,120	16.2%	36,000
65. Home Health Aides	$17,590	47.3%	120,000
66. Social and Human Service Assistants	$23,070	54.2%	45,000
67. Electricians	$40,770	17.3%	66,000

(continued)

(continued)

The 500 Best Jobs Overall

Job	Annual Earnings	Percent Growth	Annual Openings
68. Legal Secretaries	$34,610	20.3%	36,000
69. Bill and Account Collectors	$25,960	25.3%	71,000
70. Combined Food Preparation and Serving Workers, Including Fast Food	$14,120	30.5%	737,000
71. Landscaping and Groundskeeping Workers	$19,120	29.0%	193,000
72. Licensed Practical and Licensed Vocational Nurses	$30,670	20.3%	58,000
73. Highway Patrol Pilots	$40,970	23.2%	21,000
74. Police and Sheriff's Patrol Officers	$40,970	23.2%	21,000
75. Police Patrol Officers	$40,970	23.2%	21,000
76. Sheriffs and Deputy Sheriffs	$40,970	23.2%	21,000
77. Instructional Coordinators	$46,600	25.0%	15,000
78. First-Line Supervisors and Manager/Supervisors—Construction Trades Workers	$46,570	16.5%	43,000
79. First-Line Supervisors and Manager/Supervisors—Extractive Workers	$46,570	16.5%	43,000
80. First-Line Supervisors/Managers of Construction Trades and Extraction Workers	$46,570	16.5%	43,000
81. Market Research Analysts	$53,450	24.4%	13,000
82. Nuclear Equipment Operation Technicians	$59,690	20.7%	15,000
83. Nuclear Monitoring Technicians	$59,690	20.7%	15,000
84. Personal and Home Care Aides	$16,140	62.5%	84,000
85. Property, Real Estate, and Community Association Managers	$36,290	22.7%	24,000
86. Interviewers, Except Eligibility and Loan	$21,880	33.4%	53,000
87. Receptionists and Information Clerks	$20,650	23.7%	269,000
88. Database Administrators	$54,850	65.9%	8,000
89. Construction Managers	$61,050	16.3%	26,000
90. Industrial-Organizational Psychologists	$66,010	18.1%	18,000
91. Nursing Aides, Orderlies, and Attendants	$19,290	23.5%	268,000
92. First-Line Supervisors/Managers of Mechanics, Installers, and Repairers	$46,320	16.0%	38,000
93. Hotel, Motel, and Resort Desk Clerks	$16,920	33.4%	73,000
94. Teacher Assistants	$18,070	23.9%	256,000
95. Automotive Master Mechanics	$29,510	18.0%	104,000
96. Automotive Service Technicians and Mechanics	$29,510	18.0%	104,000
97. Automotive Specialty Technicians	$29,510	18.0%	104,000

The 500 Best Jobs Overall

Job	Annual Earnings	Percent Growth	Annual Openings
98. Cost Estimators	$46,960	16.5%	28,000
99. Storage and Distribution Managers	$57,240	20.2%	13,000
100. Transportation Managers	$57,240	20.2%	13,000
101. Transportation, Storage, and Distribution Managers	$57,240	20.2%	13,000
102. Education Administrators, Elementary and Secondary School	$69,240	13.4%	35,000
103. Public Relations Managers	$57,200	36.3%	7,000
104. Painters, Construction and Maintenance	$28,420	19.1%	67,000
105. Directors—Stage, Motion Pictures, Television, and Radio	$45,090	27.1%	11,000
106. Heating and Air Conditioning Mechanics	$34,020	22.3%	21,000
107. Heating, Air Conditioning, and Refrigeration Mechanics and Installers	$34,020	22.3%	21,000
108. Producers	$45,090	27.1%	11,000
109. Producers and Directors	$45,090	27.1%	11,000
110. Program Directors	$45,090	27.1%	11,000
111. Refrigeration Mechanics	$34,020	22.3%	21,000
112. Talent Directors	$45,090	27.1%	11,000
113. Technical Directors/Managers	$45,090	27.1%	11,000
114. Education Administrators, Postsecondary	$61,700	13.4%	35,000
115. Medical and Public Health Social Workers	$36,410	31.6%	13,000
116. Training and Development Specialists	$41,780	19.4%	20,000
117. Brazers	$28,490	19.3%	51,000
118. Clinical Psychologists	$50,420	18.1%	18,000
119. Clinical, Counseling, and School Psychologists	$50,420	18.1%	18,000
120. Counseling Psychologists	$50,420	18.1%	18,000
121. Educational Psychologists	$50,420	18.1%	18,000
122. Solderers	$28,490	19.3%	51,000
123. Welder-Fitters	$28,490	19.3%	51,000
124. Welders and Cutters	$28,490	19.3%	51,000
125. Welders, Cutters, Solderers, and Brazers	$28,490	19.3%	51,000
126. Welders, Production	$28,490	19.3%	51,000
127. Amusement and Recreation Attendants	$14,600	32.4%	62,000
128. Advertising and Promotions Managers	$55,940	34.3%	7,000
129. Roofers	$29,460	19.4%	38,000
130. Social and Community Service Managers	$41,260	24.8%	13,000

(continued)

(continued)

The 500 Best Jobs Overall

Job	Annual Earnings	Percent Growth	Annual Openings
131. Elementary School Teachers, Except Special Education	$41,080	13.2%	144,000
132. Probation Officers and Correctional Treatment Specialists	$38,780	23.8%	14,000
133. Physician Assistants	$63,970	53.5%	5,000
134. Telemarketers	$19,210	22.2%	145,000
135. Truck Drivers, Light or Delivery Services	$23,330	19.2%	153,000
136. Cooks, Restaurant	$18,480	21.7%	158,000
137. Production, Planning, and Expediting Clerks	$32,420	17.9%	36,000
138. Physical Therapists	$56,570	33.3%	6,000
139. Editors	$39,960	22.6%	14,000
140. First-Line Supervisors/Managers of Transportation and Material-Moving Machine and Vehicle Operators	$41,140	19.9%	17,000
141. Physical Therapist Assistants	$35,280	44.8%	9,000
142. Food Service Managers	$33,630	15.0%	55,000
143. Dental Hygienists	$54,700	37.1%	5,000
144. Fitness Trainers and Aerobics Instructors	$23,340	40.3%	19,000
145. Dental Assistants	$26,720	37.2%	16,000
146. Medical Assistants	$23,610	57.0%	18,700
147. Pharmacy Technicians	$21,630	36.4%	22,000
148. Segmental Pavers	$26,170	26.7%	21,000
149. Claims Adjusters, Examiners, and Investigators	$42,440	15.1%	25,000
150. Claims Examiners, Property and Casualty Insurance	$42,440	15.1%	25,000
151. Insurance Adjusters, Examiners, and Investigators	$42,440	15.1%	25,000
152. Radiologic Technicians	$37,680	23.1%	13,000
153. Radiologic Technologists	$37,680	23.1%	13,000
154. Radiologic Technologists and Technicians	$37,680	23.1%	13,000
155. Self-Enrichment Education Teachers	$28,880	18.5%	34,000
156. Human Resources Assistants, Except Payroll and Timekeeping	$29,470	19.3%	25,000
157. Packers and Packagers, Hand	$16,280	19.3%	242,000
158. Telecommunications Line Installers and Repairers	$39,200	27.6%	9,000
159. Construction Laborers	$24,070	17.0%	236,000
160. Demonstrators and Product Promoters	$20,690	24.9%	34,000
161. Medical and Clinical Laboratory Technologists	$42,240	17.0%	19,000

The 500 Best Jobs Overall

Job	Annual Earnings	Percent Growth	Annual Openings
162. Mental Health and Substance Abuse Social Workers	$32,080	39.1%	10,000
163. Counter and Rental Clerks	$16,750	19.4%	150,000
164. Gaming Dealers	$13,680	32.4%	28,000
165. Taxi Drivers and Chauffeurs	$17,920	24.4%	37,000
166. Emergency Medical Technicians and Paramedics	$23,170	31.3%	19,000
167. Waiters and Waitresses	$13,720	18.3%	596,000
168. Medical Secretaries	$24,670	19.0%	40,000
169. Commercial and Industrial Designers	$49,820	23.8%	7,000
170. Employment Interviewers, Private or Public Employment Service	$38,010	17.6%	19,000
171. Employment, Recruitment, and Placement Specialists	$38,010	17.6%	19,000
172. Personnel Recruiters	$38,010	17.6%	19,000
173. Sheet Metal Workers	$33,210	23.0%	13,000
174. Medical Transcriptionists	$26,460	29.8%	15,000
175. Technical Writers	$49,360	29.6%	5,000
176. First-Line Supervisors/Managers of Farming, Fishing, and Forestry Workers	$33,330	13.0%	89,000
177. Preschool Teachers, Except Special Education	$18,640	20.0%	55,000
178. Special Education Teachers, Secondary School	$42,780	24.6%	8,000
179. Occupational Therapists	$51,370	33.9%	4,000
180. Medical Records and Health Information Technicians	$23,530	49.0%	14,000
181. Office Clerks, General	$21,780	15.9%	676,000
182. Speech-Language Pathologists	$48,520	39.2%	4,000
183. Hazardous Materials Removal Workers	$31,800	32.8%	9,000
184. Irradiated-Fuel Handlers	$31,800	32.8%	9,000
185. Architectural and Civil Drafters	$37,010	20.8%	12,000
186. Architectural Drafters	$37,010	20.8%	12,000
187. Civil Drafters	$37,010	20.8%	12,000
188. Executive Secretaries and Administrative Assistants	$32,380	11.5%	185,000
189. Art Directors	$59,800	21.1%	6,000
190. Library Technicians	$23,790	19.5%	29,000
191. Cleaners of Vehicles and Equipment	$16,490	18.8%	86,000
192. First-Line Supervisors/Managers of Helpers, Laborers, and Material Movers, Hand	$36,090	18.9%	14,000
193. Fitters, Structural Metal—Precision	$28,000	19.5%	20,000
194. Metal Fabricators, Structural Metal Products	$28,000	19.5%	20,000

(continued)

(continued)

The 500 Best Jobs Overall

Job	Annual Earnings	Percent Growth	Annual Openings
195. Structural Metal Fabricators and Fitters	$28,000	19.5%	20,000
196. First-Line Supervisors, Administrative Support	$37,990	9.4%	146,000
197. First-Line Supervisors, Customer Service	$37,990	9.4%	146,000
198. First-Line Supervisors/Managers of Office and Administrative Support Workers	$37,990	9.4%	146,000
199. Actors	$20,540	26.7%	20,000
200. Medical and Clinical Laboratory Technicians	$28,810	19.0%	19,000
201. Multi-Media Artists and Animators	$42,270	22.2%	8,000
202. Computer and Information Scientists, Research	$75,130	40.3%	2,000
203. Kindergarten Teachers, Except Special Education	$38,740	14.5%	23,000
204. Adult Literacy, Remedial Education, and GED Teachers and Instructors	$35,220	19.4%	12,000
205. Food Preparation Workers	$15,910	16.9%	231,000
206. Surgical Technologists	$30,090	34.7%	8,000
207. Structural Iron and Steel Workers	$38,950	18.4%	12,000
208. Bus Drivers, Transit and Intercity	$28,060	17.4%	24,000
209. Helpers—Installation, Maintenance, and Repair Workers	$21,210	18.5%	35,000
210. Biochemists	$57,100	21.0%	5,000
211. Biochemists and Biophysicists	$57,100	21.0%	5,000
212. Biophysicists	$57,100	21.0%	5,000
213. Middle School Teachers, Except Special and Vocational Education	$41,220	9.6%	54,000
214. Computer Hardware Engineers	$71,560	24.9%	3,000
215. Environmental Engineers	$61,250	26.0%	3,000
216. Recreation Workers	$17,850	20.1%	32,000
217. Pipe Fitters	$38,710	10.2%	49,000
218. Pipelaying Fitters	$38,710	10.2%	49,000
219. Plumbers	$38,710	10.2%	49,000
220. Plumbers, Pipefitters, and Steamfitters	$38,710	10.2%	49,000
221. Education Administrators, Preschool and Child Care Center/Program	$31,860	13.4%	35,000
222. Purchasing Agents, Except Wholesale, Retail, and Farm Products	$43,230	12.3%	23,000
223. Respiratory Therapists	$39,370	34.8%	4,000
224. Substance Abuse and Behavioral Disorder Counselors	$29,870	35.0%	7,000

The 500 Best Jobs Overall

Job	Annual Earnings	Percent Growth	Annual Openings
225. Computer-Controlled Machine Tool Operators, Metal and Plastic	$28,390	19.7%	15,000
226. Numerical Control Machine Tool Operators and Tenders, Metal and Plastic	$28,390	19.7%	15,000
227. Special Education Teachers, Middle School	$40,010	24.4%	6,000
228. Automatic Teller Machine Servicers	$32,890	14.2%	24,000
229. Computer, Automated Teller, and Office Machine Repairers	$32,890	14.2%	24,000
230. Data Processing Equipment Repairers	$32,890	14.2%	24,000
231. Office Machine and Cash Register Servicers	$32,890	14.2%	24,000
232. Coaches and Scouts	$29,020	17.6%	19,000
233. Chiropractors	$68,420	23.4%	3,000
234. Microbiologists	$49,880	21.0%	5,000
235. Veterinarians	$62,000	31.8%	2,000
236. Compensation and Benefits Managers	$61,880	12.7%	14,000
237. Human Resources Managers	$61,880	12.7%	14,000
238. Training and Development Managers	$61,880	12.7%	14,000
239. Freight, Stock, and Material Movers, Hand	$19,440	13.9%	519,000
240. Gaming Change Persons and Booth Cashiers	$18,990	36.1%	13,000
241. Grips and Set-Up Workers, Motion Picture Sets, Studios, and Stages	$19,440	13.9%	519,000
242. Laborers and Freight, Stock, and Material Movers, Hand	$19,440	13.9%	519,000
243. Stevedores, Except Equipment Operators	$19,440	13.9%	519,000
244. Chemists	$51,860	19.1%	6,000
245. Library Assistants, Clerical	$18,580	19.7%	26,000
246. Cashiers	$14,950	14.5%	1,125,000
247. Desktop Publishers	$31,200	66.7%	5,000
248. Health Educators	$35,230	23.5%	7,000
249. First-Line Supervisors/Managers of Correctional Officers	$44,640	29.6%	3,000
250. Biological Technicians	$32,280	26.4%	7,000
251. Refuse and Recyclable Material Collectors	$23,850	16.6%	34,000
252. Zoologists and Wildlife Biologists	$46,220	21.0%	5,000
253. Engineering Managers	$87,490	8.0%	24,000
254. First-Line Supervisors and Manager/Supervisors —Landscaping Workers	$32,100	20.1%	10,000

(continued)

(continued)

The 500 Best Jobs Overall

Job	Annual Earnings	Percent Growth	Annual Openings
255. First-Line Supervisors/Managers of Landscaping, Lawn Service, and Groundskeeping Workers	$32,100	20.1%	10,000
256. Lawn Service Managers	$32,100	20.1%	10,000
257. Rehabilitation Counselors	$25,610	23.6%	12,000
258. Boat Builders and Shipwrights	$33,470	8.2%	161,000
259. Brattice Builders	$33,470	8.2%	161,000
260. Carpenter Assemblers and Repairers	$33,470	8.2%	161,000
261. Carpenters	$33,470	8.2%	161,000
262. Construction Carpenters	$33,470	8.2%	161,000
263. Food Servers, Nonrestaurant	$15,310	16.4%	85,000
264. Rough Carpenters	$33,470	8.2%	161,000
265. Ship Carpenters and Joiners	$33,470	8.2%	161,000
266. Diagnostic Medical Sonographers	$46,980	26.1%	3,000
267. Bus and Truck Mechanics and Diesel Engine Specialists	$33,570	14.2%	20,000
268. Biologists	$44,770	21.0%	5,000
269. Aircraft Body and Bonded Structure Repairers	$41,990	16.7%	11,000
270. Aircraft Engine Specialists	$41,990	16.7%	11,000
271. Aircraft Mechanics and Service Technicians	$41,990	16.7%	11,000
272. Airframe-and-Power-Plant Mechanics	$41,990	16.7%	11,000
273. Janitors and Cleaners, Except Maids and Housekeeping Cleaners	$17,900	13.5%	507,000
274. Environmental Scientists and Specialists, Including Health	$47,330	22.3%	4,000
275. Agents and Business Managers of Artists, Performers, and Athletes	$55,550	27.9%	2,000
276. Private Detectives and Investigators	$28,380	23.5%	9,000
277. Electrical and Electronics Drafters	$40,070	23.3%	5,000
278. Electrical Drafters	$40,070	23.3%	5,000
279. Electronic Drafters	$40,070	23.3%	5,000
280. Counter Attendants, Cafeteria, Food Concession, and Coffee Shop	$14,760	14.4%	216,000
281. Occupational Therapist Assistants	$35,840	39.7%	3,000
282. Nonfarm Animal Caretakers	$16,570	21.6%	20,000
283. Reservation and Transportation Ticket Agents	$24,090	14.5%	39,000
284. Reservation and Transportation Ticket Agents and Travel Clerks	$24,090	14.5%	39,000

The 500 Best Jobs Overall

Job	Annual Earnings	Percent Growth	Annual Openings
285. Travel Clerks	$24,090	14.5%	39,000
286. First-Line Supervisors/Managers of Food Preparation and Serving Workers	$23,600	12.7%	136,000
287. Massage Therapists	$28,050	30.4%	7,000
288. Directors, Religious Activities and Education	$27,420	15.9%	23,000
289. Flight Attendants	$40,600	18.4%	8,000
290. Medical Scientists, Except Epidemiologists	$55,960	26.5%	2,000
291. First-Line Supervisors/Managers of Non-Retail Sales Workers	$51,490	5.8%	41,000
292. Calibration and Instrumentation Technicians	$42,130	10.8%	22,000
293. Electrical and Electronic Engineering Technicians	$42,130	10.8%	22,000
294. Electrical Engineering Technicians	$42,130	10.8%	22,000
295. Electronics Engineering Technicians	$42,130	10.8%	22,000
296. Brickmasons and Blockmasons	$41,590	12.5%	18,000
297. Epidemiologists	$52,710	26.5%	2,000
298. Cardiovascular Technologists and Technicians	$35,010	34.9%	3,000
299. Packaging and Filling Machine Operators and Tenders	$20,760	14.4%	56,000
300. Semiconductor Processors	$26,480	32.4%	7,000
301. Sales Representatives, Wholesale and Manufacturing, Except Technical and Scientific Products	$41,520	5.7%	86,000
302. Architects, Except Landscape and Naval	$55,470	18.5%	4,000
303. Industrial Truck and Tractor Operators	$25,350	11.3%	91,000
304. Sales Representatives, Agricultural	$54,360	7.5%	24,000
305. Sales Representatives, Chemical and Pharmaceutical	$54,360	7.5%	24,000
306. Sales Representatives, Electrical/Electronic	$54,360	7.5%	24,000
307. Sales Representatives, Instruments	$54,360	7.5%	24,000
308. Sales Representatives, Mechanical Equipment and Supplies	$54,360	7.5%	24,000
309. Sales Representatives, Medical	$54,360	7.5%	24,000
310. Sales Representatives, Wholesale and Manufacturing, Technical and Scientific Products	$54,360	7.5%	24,000
311. Respiratory Therapy Technicians	$33,840	34.6%	3,000
312. Chemical Technicians	$36,190	15.0%	13,000
313. Dispatchers, Except Police, Fire, and Ambulance	$30,070	22.2%	8,000
314. Retail Salespersons	$17,150	12.4%	1,124,000
315. Bakers	$20,440	16.8%	25,000

(continued)

(continued)

The 500 Best Jobs Overall

Job	Annual Earnings	Percent Growth	Annual Openings
316. Bakers, Bread and Pastry	$20,440	16.8%	25,000
317. Bakers, Manufacturing	$20,440	16.8%	25,000
318. Economists	$67,050	18.5%	3,000
319. Mapping Technicians	$28,210	25.3%	7,000
320. Surveying and Mapping Technicians	$28,210	25.3%	7,000
321. Surveying Technicians	$28,210	25.3%	7,000
322. Athletes and Sports Competitors	$43,730	22.5%	3,000
323. First-Line Supervisors/Managers of Police and Detectives	$59,300	13.1%	9,000
324. Signal and Track Switch Repairers	$42,390	11.5%	16,000
325. Combination Machine Tool Operators and Tenders, Metal and Plastic	$27,910	14.7%	21,000
326. Combination Machine Tool Setters and Set-Up Operators, Metal and Plastic	$27,910	14.7%	21,000
327. Multiple Machine Tool Setters, Operators, and Tenders, Metal and Plastic	$27,910	14.7%	21,000
328. Sales Engineers	$59,720	17.7%	4,000
329. Makeup Artists, Theatrical and Performance	$30,240	11.4%	27,000
330. First-Line Supervisors/Managers of Retail Sales Workers	$28,590	8.1%	206,000
331. Budget Analysts	$50,510	14.6%	8,000
332. Audiologists	$46,900	44.7%	1,000
333. Compensation, Benefits, and Job Analysis Specialists	$43,330	15.7%	8,000
334. Industrial Production Managers	$64,510	6.2%	22,000
335. Clergy	$33,840	15.0%	12,000
336. Forest Fire Fighting and Prevention Supervisors	$53,420	16.7%	5,000
337. Municipal Fire Fighting and Prevention Supervisors	$53,420	16.7%	5,000
338. Mental Health Counselors	$29,050	21.7%	7,000
339. Interior Designers	$39,580	17.4%	7,000
340. Helpers—Production Workers	$18,990	11.9%	143,000
341. Production Helpers	$18,990	11.9%	143,000
342. Production Laborers	$18,990	11.9%	143,000
343. Physical Therapist Aides	$20,300	46.3%	7,000
344. Geologists	$58,280	18.1%	3,000
345. Bartenders	$14,610	13.4%	84,000
346. Veterinary Technologists and Technicians	$22,430	39.3%	6,000
347. Appraisers and Assessors of Real Estate	$38,950	18.0%	6,000

The 500 Best Jobs Overall

Job	Annual Earnings	Percent Growth	Annual Openings
348. Appraisers, Real Estate	$38,950	18.0%	6,000
349. Assessors	$38,950	18.0%	6,000
350. Veterinary Assistants and Laboratory Animal Caretakers	$17,470	39.8%	8,000
351. Hairdressers, Hairstylists, and Cosmetologists	$18,260	13.0%	78,000
352. Parking Lot Attendants	$15,690	19.8%	17,000
353. Bus Drivers, School	$21,990	11.6%	63,000
354. Environmental Science and Protection Technicians, Including Health	$34,690	24.5%	3,000
355. Hydrologists	$56,400	25.7%	1,000
356. Weighers, Measurers, Checkers, and Samplers, Recordkeeping	$24,690	17.9%	13,000
357. Hosts and Hostesses, Restaurant, Lounge, and Coffee Shop	$14,920	13.0%	84,000
358. Landscape Architects	$46,710	31.1%	1,000
359. Agricultural Technicians	$27,530	15.2%	15,000
360. Food Science Technicians	$27,530	15.2%	15,000
361. Machinists	$32,090	9.1%	28,000
362. Meeting and Convention Planners	$36,550	23.3%	3,000
363. Credit Analysts	$41,650	16.0%	7,000
364. Child Care Workers	$16,030	10.6%	370,000
365. Mechanical Engineers	$61,440	13.1%	7,000
366. Mechanical Drafters	$39,620	15.4%	8,000
367. Environmental Engineering Technicians	$36,590	29.1%	2,000
368. Fashion Designers	$49,530	20.3%	2,000
369. First-Line Supervisors/Managers of Housekeeping and Janitorial Workers	$27,200	14.2%	18,000
370. Housekeeping Supervisors	$27,200	14.2%	18,000
371. Janitorial Supervisors	$27,200	14.2%	18,000
372. Residential Advisors	$19,680	24.0%	9,000
373. Chemical Equipment Controllers and Operators	$36,810	14.9%	9,000
374. Chemical Equipment Operators and Tenders	$36,810	14.9%	9,000
375. Chemical Equipment Tenders	$36,810	14.9%	9,000
376. Refractory Materials Repairers, Except Brickmasons	$35,130	11.5%	16,000
377. Extruding and Drawing Machine Setters, Operators, and Tenders, Metal and Plastic	$25,170	13.5%	23,000
378. Biomedical Engineers	$59,790	31.4%	fewer than 500

(continued)

(continued)

The 500 Best Jobs Overall

Job	Annual Earnings	Percent Growth	Annual Openings
379. Painters, Transportation Equipment	$32,330	17.5%	8,000
380. Commercial Pilots	$47,420	26.9%	1,000
381. Shipping, Receiving, and Traffic Clerks	$22,710	9.3%	133,000
382. Helpers—Electricians	$22,160	13.3%	27,000
383. Child Support, Missing Persons, and Unemployment Insurance Fraud Investigators	$50,960	16.4%	4,000
384. Criminal Investigators and Special Agents	$50,960	16.4%	4,000
385. Detectives and Criminal Investigators	$50,960	16.4%	4,000
386. Immigration and Customs Inspectors	$50,960	16.4%	4,000
387. Police Detectives	$50,960	16.4%	4,000
388. Police Identification and Records Officers	$50,960	16.4%	4,000
389. Loan Officers	$43,210	4.9%	28,000
390. Security and Fire Alarm Systems Installers	$30,490	23.4%	4,000
391. Mobile Heavy Equipment Mechanics, Except Engines	$35,190	14.0%	11,000
392. First-Line Supervisors/Managers of Production and Operating Workers	$42,000	1.0%	71,000
393. Electrical Engineers	$66,890	11.3%	8,000
394. Real Estate Sales Agents	$28,570	9.5%	28,000
395. Film and Video Editors	$36,910	25.8%	2,000
396. Water and Liquid Waste Treatment Plant and System Operators	$32,560	18.1%	6,000
397. Interpreters and Translators	$32,000	23.8%	3,000
398. Commercial Divers	$32,770	11.5%	16,000
399. Gaming Managers	$53,450	30.0%	fewer than 500
400. Billing and Posting Clerks and Machine Operators	$25,350	8.5%	69,000
401. Billing, Cost, and Rate Clerks	$25,350	8.5%	69,000
402. Billing, Posting, and Calculating Machine Operators	$25,350	8.5%	69,000
403. Marriage and Family Therapists	$32,720	29.9%	2,000
404. Statement Clerks	$25,350	8.5%	69,000
405. Geoscientists, Except Hydrologists and Geographers	$58,280	18.1%	2,000
406. Insurance Sales Agents	$38,890	3.3%	43,000
407. Marking Clerks	$19,060	8.5%	467,000
408. Order Fillers, Wholesale and Retail Sales	$19,060	8.5%	467,000
409. Stock Clerks and Order Fillers	$19,060	8.5%	467,000
410. Stock Clerks, Sales Floor	$19,060	8.5%	467,000
411. Stock Clerks—Stockroom, Warehouse, or Storage Yard	$19,060	8.5%	467,000

The 500 Best Jobs Overall

Job	Annual Earnings	Percent Growth	Annual Openings
412. Exhibit Designers	$33,460	27.0%	2,000
413. Set and Exhibit Designers	$33,460	27.0%	2,000
414. Set Designers	$33,460	27.0%	2,000
415. Gaming Cage Workers	$21,540	25.2%	7,000
416. Photographers	$23,040	17.0%	13,000
417. Photographers, Scientific	$23,040	17.0%	13,000
418. Professional Photographers	$23,040	17.0%	13,000
419. Laundry and Dry-Cleaning Workers	$16,360	11.4%	62,000
420. Laundry and Drycleaning Machine Operators and Tenders, Except Pressing	$16,360	11.4%	62,000
421. Precision Dyers	$16,360	11.4%	62,000
422. Spotters, Dry Cleaning	$16,360	11.4%	62,000
423. Political Scientists	$81,350	17.2%	2,000
424. Automotive Body and Related Repairers	$32,490	10.2%	18,000
425. Ceiling Tile Installers	$33,000	9.4%	19,000
426. Drywall and Ceiling Tile Installers	$33,000	9.4%	19,000
427. Drywall Installers	$33,000	9.4%	19,000
428. Vocational Education Teachers, Secondary School	$43,590	13.4%	7,000
429. Radiation Therapists	$49,050	22.8%	1,000
430. Camera Operators, Television, Video, and Motion Picture	$28,980	25.8%	3,000
431. Materials Scientists	$62,750	19.8%	1,000
432. Chefs and Head Cooks	$26,800	9.0%	35,000
433. Pest Control Workers	$23,150	22.1%	7,000
434. Recreational Vehicle Service Technicians	$26,410	25.4%	4,000
435. Nuclear Medicine Technologists	$47,400	22.4%	1,000
436. Grader, Bulldozer, and Scraper Operators	$34,160	6.9%	25,000
437. Operating Engineers	$34,160	6.9%	25,000
438. Operating Engineers and Other Construction Equipment Operators	$34,160	6.9%	25,000
439. Urban and Regional Planners	$48,530	16.4%	3,000
440. Optometrists	$85,650	18.7%	1,000
441. Maintenance and Repair Workers, General	$28,740	4.7%	103,000
442. Casting Machine Set-Up Operators	$22,340	9.8%	38,000
443. Metal Molding, Coremaking, and Casting Machine Operators and Tenders	$22,340	9.8%	38,000

(continued)

(continued)

The 500 Best Jobs Overall

Job	Annual Earnings	Percent Growth	Annual Openings
444. Metal Molding, Coremaking, and Casting Machine Setters and Set-Up Operators	$22,340	9.8%	38,000
445. Molding, Coremaking, and Casting Machine Setters, Operators, and Tenders, Metal and Plastic	$22,340	9.8%	38,000
446. Plastic Molding and Casting Machine Operators and Tenders	$22,340	9.8%	38,000
447. Plastic Molding and Casting Machine Setters and Set-Up Operators	$22,340	9.8%	38,000
448. Sociologists	$54,880	17.2%	2,000
449. Dietitians and Nutritionists	$40,410	15.2%	5,000
450. Tax Preparers	$27,680	17.4%	8,000
451. Arbitrators, Mediators, and Conciliators	$46,660	27.2%	fewer than 500
452. Aircraft Cargo Handling Supervisors	$37,330	27.7%	1,000
453. Survey Researchers	$23,230	34.5%	3,000
454. Costume Attendants	$23,570	19.1%	8,000
455. Elevator Installers and Repairers	$51,630	17.2%	2,000
456. Composers	$33,720	13.1%	9,000
457. Music Arrangers and Orchestrators	$33,720	13.1%	9,000
458. Music Directors	$33,720	13.1%	9,000
459. Music Directors and Composers	$33,720	13.1%	9,000
460. Paperhangers	$31,330	20.2%	3,000
461. Team Assemblers	$22,260	5.9%	283,000
462. Pharmacy Aides	$18,010	19.5%	9,000
463. Soldering and Brazing Machine Operators and Tenders	$28,220	15.1%	9,000
464. Soldering and Brazing Machine Setters and Set-Up Operators	$28,220	15.1%	9,000
465. Welding Machine Operators and Tenders	$28,220	15.1%	9,000
466. Welding Machine Setters and Set-Up Operators	$28,220	15.1%	9,000
467. Welding, Soldering, and Brazing Machine Setters, Operators, and Tenders	$28,220	15.1%	9,000
468. Civil Engineering Technicians	$37,410	11.9%	9,000
469. Reinforcing Iron and Rebar Workers	$34,750	17.5%	4,000
470. Farmers and Ranchers	$42,170	−25.4%	146,000
471. Electronics Engineers, Except Computer	$68,350	10.4%	6,000
472. Insulation Workers, Floor, Ceiling, and Wall	$28,000	13.6%	12,000
473. Insulation Workers, Mechanical	$28,000	13.6%	12,000

The 500 Best Jobs Overall

Job	Annual Earnings	Percent Growth	Annual Openings
474. Geographers	$48,410	17.2%	2,000
475. Real Estate Brokers	$51,370	9.6%	8,000
476. File Clerks	$19,490	9.1%	49,000
477. Helpers—Brickmasons, Blockmasons, Stonemasons, and Tile and Marble Setters	$23,620	14.1%	14,000
478. Bookkeeping, Accounting, and Auditing Clerks	$26,540	2.0%	298,000
479. Coating, Painting, and Spraying Machine Operators and Tenders	$24,710	11.9%	18,000
480. Coating, Painting, and Spraying Machine Setters and Set-Up Operators	$24,710	11.9%	18,000
481. Coating, Painting, and Spraying Machine Setters, Operators, and Tenders	$24,710	11.9%	18,000
482. Tile and Marble Setters	$35,390	15.6%	5,000
483. Tree Trimmers and Pruners	$23,950	16.3%	11,000
484. Nuclear Technicians	$59,690	20.7%	fewer than 500
485. Floral Designers	$19,280	14.9%	15,000
486. Court Clerks	$27,090	12.0%	14,000
487. Court, Municipal, and License Clerks	$27,090	12.0%	14,000
488. License Clerks	$27,090	12.0%	14,000
489. Municipal Clerks	$27,090	12.0%	14,000
490. Manicurists and Pedicurists	$16,700	26.5%	5,000
491. Mechanical Engineering Technicians	$40,910	13.9%	5,000
492. Cooks, Institution and Cafeteria	$17,750	7.6%	110,000
493. Gaming Supervisors	$39,240	18.4%	2,000
494. Stonemasons	$32,470	20.8%	2,000
495. Historians	$42,940	17.2%	2,000
496. First-Line Supervisors/Managers of Personal Service Workers	$28,040	15.1%	8,000
497. Dietetic Technicians	$21,790	27.6%	3,000
498. Ambulance Drivers and Attendants, Except Emergency Medical Technicians	$18,890	33.7%	3,000
499. Helpers—Pipelayers, Plumbers, Pipefitters, and Steamfitters	$21,830	11.5%	20,000
500. First-Line Supervisors and Manager/Supervisors —Agricultural Crop Workers	$33,330	13.0%	8,000

The 100 Best-Paying Jobs

We sorted all 500 jobs based on their annual median earnings from highest to lowest. *Median earnings* means that half of all workers in these jobs earn more than that amount and half earn less. We then selected the 100 jobs with the highest earnings to create the list that follows.

It shouldn't be a big surprise that most of the highest-paying jobs require advanced levels of education, training, and experience. For example, most of the 20 jobs with the highest earnings require a doctoral or professional degree, and others, such as Chief Executives and Marketing Managers, require extensive training and experience. Although the top 20 jobs may not appeal to you for a variety of reasons, you are likely to find others that will among the top 100 jobs with the highest earnings. Keep in mind that the earnings reflect the national average for all workers in the occupation. This is an important consideration, because starting pay in the job is usually a lot less than the pay that workers can earn with several years of experience. Earnings also vary significantly by region of the country, so actual pay in your area could be substantially different.

The 100 Best-Paying Jobs

Job	Annual Earnings
1. Anesthesiologists	greater than $145,600
2. Internists, General	greater than $145,600
3. Obstetricians and Gynecologists	greater than $145,600
4. Surgeons	greater than $145,600
5. Psychiatrists	$126,460
6. Pediatricians, General	$126,430
7. Chief Executives	$120,450
8. Government Service Executives	$120,450
9. Private Sector Executives	$120,450
10. Family and General Practitioners	$118,390
11. Lawyers	$88,760
12. Engineering Managers	$87,490
13. Optometrists	$85,650
14. Computer and Information Systems Managers	$82,480
15. Political Scientists	$81,350
16. Computer and Information Scientists, Research	$75,130
17. Pharmacists	$74,890
18. Marketing Managers	$74,370
19. Computer Software Engineers, Systems Software	$73,280
20. Sales Managers	$71,620
21. Computer Hardware Engineers	$71,560
22. Computer Software Engineers, Applications	$70,210
23. Financial Managers	$70,210

The 100 Best-Paying Jobs

Job	Annual Earnings
24. Financial Managers, Branch or Department	$70,210
25. Treasurers, Controllers, and Chief Financial Officers	$70,210
26. Education Administrators, Elementary and Secondary School	$69,240
27. Chiropractors	$68,420
28. Electronics Engineers, Except Computer	$68,350
29. Economists	$67,050
30. Electrical Engineers	$66,890
31. Industrial-Organizational Psychologists	$66,010
32. General and Operations Managers	$65,010
33. Industrial Production Managers	$64,510
34. Physician Assistants	$63,970
35. Materials Scientists	$62,750
36. Veterinarians	$62,000
37. Computer Systems Analysts	$61,990
38. Compensation and Benefits Managers	$61,880
39. Human Resources Managers	$61,880
40. Training and Development Managers	$61,880
41. Education Administrators, Postsecondary	$61,700
42. Mechanical Engineers	$61,440
43. Environmental Engineers	$61,250
44. Construction Managers	$61,050
45. Computer Programmers	$60,120
46. Art Directors	$59,800
47. Biomedical Engineers	$59,790
48. Sales Engineers	$59,720
49. Nuclear Equipment Operation Technicians	$59,690
50. Nuclear Monitoring Technicians	$59,690
51. Nuclear Technicians	$59,690
52. Sales Agents, Financial Services	$59,690
53. Sales Agents, Securities and Commodities	$59,690
54. Securities, Commodities, and Financial Services Sales Agents	$59,690
55. First-Line Supervisors/Managers of Police and Detectives	$59,300
56. Medical and Health Services Managers	$59,220
57. Geologists	$58,280
58. Geoscientists, Except Hydrologists and Geographers	$58,280
59. Management Analysts	$57,970
60. Personal Financial Advisors	$57,710
61. Network Systems and Data Communications Analysts	$57,470

(continued)

(continued)

The 100 Best-Paying Jobs

Job	Annual Earnings
62. Storage and Distribution Managers	$57,240
63. Transportation Managers	$57,240
64. Transportation, Storage, and Distribution Managers	$57,240
65. Public Relations Managers	$57,200
66. Biochemists	$57,100
67. Biochemists and Biophysicists	$57,100
68. Biophysicists	$57,100
69. Physical Therapists	$56,570
70. Hydrologists	$56,400
71. Medical Scientists, Except Epidemiologists	$55,960
72. Advertising and Promotions Managers	$55,940
73. Agents and Business Managers of Artists, Performers, and Athletes	$55,550
74. Architects, Except Landscape and Naval	$55,470
75. Financial Analysts	$55,120
76. Sociologists	$54,880
77. Database Administrators	$54,850
78. Dental Hygienists	$54,700
79. Sales Representatives, Agricultural	$54,360
80. Sales Representatives, Chemical and Pharmaceutical	$54,360
81. Sales Representatives, Electrical/Electronic	$54,360
82. Sales Representatives, Instruments	$54,360
83. Sales Representatives, Mechanical Equipment and Supplies	$54,360
84. Sales Representatives, Medical	$54,360
85. Sales Representatives, Wholesale and Manufacturing, Technical and Scientific Products	$54,360
86. Computer Security Specialists	$53,770
87. Network and Computer Systems Administrators	$53,770
88. Gaming Managers	$53,450
89. Market Research Analysts	$53,450
90. Forest Fire Fighting and Prevention Supervisors	$53,420
91. Municipal Fire Fighting and Prevention Supervisors	$53,420
92. Epidemiologists	$52,710
93. Teachers, Postsecondary	$52,115
94. Chemists	$51,860
95. Elevator Installers and Repairers	$51,630
96. First-Line Supervisors/Managers of Non-Retail Sales Workers	$51,490
97. Occupational Therapists	$51,370
98. Real Estate Brokers	$51,370
99. Child Support, Missing Persons, and Unemployment Insurance Fraud Investigators	$50,960
100. Criminal Investigators and Special Agents	$50,960

The 100 Fastest-Growing Jobs

We created this list by sorting all 500 best jobs by their projected growth over a ten-year period. Growth rates are one measure to consider in exploring career options, as jobs with higher growth rates tend to provide more job opportunities.

Jobs in the computer and medical fields dominate the 20 fastest-growing jobs. Computer Software Engineers, Applications is the job with the highest growth rate—the number employed is projected to double during this time. You can find a wide range of rapidly growing jobs in a variety of fields and at different levels of training and education among the jobs in this list.

The 100 Fastest-Growing Jobs

Job	Percent Growth
1. Computer Software Engineers, Applications	100.0%
2. Computer Support Specialists	97.0%
3. Computer Software Engineers, Systems Software	89.7%
4. Computer Security Specialists	81.9%
5. Network and Computer Systems Administrators	81.9%
6. Network Systems and Data Communications Analysts	77.5%
7. Desktop Publishers	66.7%
8. Database Administrators	65.9%
9. Personal and Home Care Aides	62.5%
10. Computer Systems Analysts	59.7%
11. Medical Assistants	57.0%
12. Social and Human Service Assistants	54.2%
13. Physician Assistants	53.5%
14. Medical Records and Health Information Technicians	49.0%
15. Computer and Information Systems Managers	47.9%
16. Home Health Aides	47.3%
17. Physical Therapist Aides	46.3%
18. Physical Therapist Assistants	44.8%
19. Audiologists	44.7%
20. Computer and Information Scientists, Research	40.3%
21. Fitness Trainers and Aerobics Instructors	40.3%
22. Veterinary Assistants and Laboratory Animal Caretakers	39.8%
23. Occupational Therapist Assistants	39.7%
24. Veterinary Technologists and Technicians	39.3%
25. Speech-Language Pathologists	39.2%
26. Mental Health and Substance Abuse Social Workers	39.1%

(continued)

(continued)

The 100 Fastest-Growing Jobs

Job	Percent Growth
27. Dental Assistants	37.2%
28. Dental Hygienists	37.1%
29. Special Education Teachers, Preschool, Kindergarten, and Elementary School	36.8%
30. Pharmacy Technicians	36.4%
31. Public Relations Managers	36.3%
32. Gaming Change Persons and Booth Cashiers	36.1%
33. Public Relations Specialists	36.1%
34. Security Guards	35.4%
35. Substance Abuse and Behavioral Disorder Counselors	35.0%
36. Cardiovascular Technologists and Technicians	34.9%
37. Respiratory Therapists	34.8%
38. Surgical Technologists	34.7%
39. Respiratory Therapy Technicians	34.6%
40. Survey Researchers	34.5%
41. Advertising and Promotions Managers	34.3%
42. Personal Financial Advisors	34.0%
43. Occupational Therapists	33.9%
44. Ambulance Drivers and Attendants, Except Emergency Medical Technicians	33.7%
45. Hotel, Motel, and Resort Desk Clerks	33.4%
46. Interviewers, Except Eligibility and Loan	33.4%
47. Physical Therapists	33.3%
48. Paralegals and Legal Assistants	33.2%
49. Hazardous Materials Removal Workers	32.8%
50. Irradiated-Fuel Handlers	32.8%
51. Sales Managers	32.8%
52. Adjustment Clerks	32.4%
53. Amusement and Recreation Attendants	32.4%
54. Correctional Officers and Jailers	32.4%
55. Customer Service Representatives	32.4%
56. Customer Service Representatives, Utilities	32.4%
57. Gaming Dealers	32.4%
58. Semiconductor Processors	32.4%
59. Medical and Health Services Managers	32.3%
60. Veterinarians	31.8%
61. Medical and Public Health Social Workers	31.6%
62. Biomedical Engineers	31.4%

The 100 Fastest-Growing Jobs

Job	Percent Growth
63. Emergency Medical Technicians and Paramedics	31.3%
64. Landscape Architects	31.1%
65. Combined Food Preparation and Serving Workers, Including Fast Food	30.5%
66. Massage Therapists	30.4%
67. Gaming Managers	30.0%
68. Marriage and Family Therapists	29.9%
69. Medical Transcriptionists	29.8%
70. First-Line Supervisors/Managers of Correctional Officers	29.6%
71. Technical Writers	29.6%
72. Environmental Engineering Technicians	29.1%
73. Marketing Managers	29.1%
74. Landscaping and Groundskeeping Workers	29.0%
75. Management Analysts	28.9%
76. Caption Writers	28.4%
77. Copy Writers	28.4%
78. Creative Writers	28.4%
79. Poets and Lyricists	28.4%
80. Writers and Authors	28.4%
81. Agents and Business Managers of Artists, Performers, and Athletes	27.9%
82. Aircraft Cargo Handling Supervisors	27.7%
83. Dietetic Technicians	27.6%
84. Telecommunications Line Installers and Repairers	27.6%
85. Arbitrators, Mediators, and Conciliators	27.2%
86. Directors—Stage, Motion Pictures, Television, and Radio	27.1%
87. Producers	27.1%
88. Producers and Directors	27.1%
89. Program Directors	27.1%
90. Talent Directors	27.1%
91. Technical Directors/Managers	27.1%
92. Exhibit Designers	27.0%
93. Set and Exhibit Designers	27.0%
94. Set Designers	27.0%
95. Child, Family, and School Social Workers	26.9%
96. Commercial Pilots	26.9%
97. Actors	26.7%
98. Graphic Designers	26.7%
99. Segmental Pavers	26.7%
100. Epidemiologists	26.5%

The 100 Jobs with the Most Openings

We created this list by sorting all 500 best jobs by the number of job openings that each is expected to have per year. Jobs that employ lots of people are also likely to have more job openings in a given year. Many of these occupations, such as Cashiers, are not among the highest-paying jobs. But jobs with large numbers of openings often provide easier entry for new workers, make it easier to move from one position to another, or are attractive for other reasons. Some of these jobs may also appeal to people re-entering the labor market, part-time workers, and workers who want to move from one employer to another. And some of these jobs pay quite well, offer good benefits, or have other advantages.

The 100 Jobs with the Most Openings

Job	Annual Openings
1. Cashiers	1,125,000
2. Retail Salespersons	1,124,000
3. Combined Food Preparation and Serving Workers, Including Fast Food	737,000
4. Office Clerks, General	676,000
5. Waiters and Waitresses	596,000
6. Freight, Stock, and Material Movers, Hand	519,000
7. Grips and Set-Up Workers, Motion Picture Sets, Studios, and Stages	519,000
8. Laborers and Freight, Stock, and Material Movers, Hand	519,000
9. Stevedores, Except Equipment Operators	519,000
10. Janitors and Cleaners, Except Maids and Housekeeping Cleaners	507,000
11. Marking Clerks	467,000
12. Order Fillers, Wholesale and Retail Sales	467,000
13. Stock Clerks and Order Fillers	467,000
14. Stock Clerks, Sales Floor	467,000
15. Stock Clerks—Stockroom, Warehouse, or Storage Yard	467,000
16. Child Care Workers	370,000
17. Adjustment Clerks	359,000
18. Customer Service Representatives	359,000
19. Customer Service Representatives, Utilities	359,000
20. Bookkeeping, Accounting, and Auditing Clerks	298,000
21. Team Assemblers	283,000
22. Receptionists and Information Clerks	269,000
23. Nursing Aides, Orderlies, and Attendants	268,000
24. Teacher Assistants	256,000
25. Packers and Packagers, Hand	242,000
26. Security Guards	242,000
27. Tractor-Trailer Truck Drivers	240,000

The 100 Jobs with the Most Openings

Job	Annual Openings
28. Truck Drivers, Heavy	240,000
29. Truck Drivers, Heavy and Tractor-Trailer	240,000
30. Construction Laborers	236,000
31. General and Operations Managers	235,000
32. Food Preparation Workers	231,000
33. Counter Attendants, Cafeteria, Food Concession, and Coffee Shop	216,000
34. First-Line Supervisors/Managers of Retail Sales Workers	206,000
35. Landscaping and Groundskeeping Workers	193,000
36. Executive Secretaries and Administrative Assistants	185,000
37. Teachers, Postsecondary	184,000
38. Boat Builders and Shipwrights	161,000
39. Brattice Builders	161,000
40. Carpenter Assemblers and Repairers	161,000
41. Carpenters	161,000
42. Construction Carpenters	161,000
43. Rough Carpenters	161,000
44. Ship Carpenters and Joiners	161,000
45. Cooks, Restaurant	158,000
46. Truck Drivers, Light or Delivery Services	153,000
47. Counter and Rental Clerks	150,000
48. Farmers and Ranchers	146,000
49. First-Line Supervisors, Administrative Support	146,000
50. First-Line Supervisors, Customer Service	146,000
51. First-Line Supervisors/Managers of Office and Administrative Support Workers	146,000
52. Telemarketers	145,000
53. Elementary School Teachers, Except Special Education	144,000
54. Helpers—Production Workers	143,000
55. Production Helpers	143,000
56. Production Laborers	143,000
57. Registered Nurses	140,000
58. First-Line Supervisors/Managers of Food Preparation and Serving Workers	136,000
59. Shipping, Receiving, and Traffic Clerks	133,000
60. Home Health Aides	120,000
61. Cooks, Institution and Cafeteria	110,000
62. Automotive Master Mechanics	104,000
63. Automotive Service Technicians and Mechanics	104,000
64. Automotive Specialty Technicians	104,000

(continued)

(continued)

The 100 Jobs with the Most Openings

Job	Annual Openings
65. Maintenance and Repair Workers, General	103,000
66. Accountants	100,000
67. Accountants and Auditors	100,000
68. Auditors	100,000
69. Industrial Truck and Tractor Operators	91,000
70. First-Line Supervisors/Managers of Farming, Fishing, and Forestry Workers	89,000
71. Cleaners of Vehicles and Equipment	86,000
72. Sales Representatives, Wholesale and Manufacturing, Except Technical and Scientific Products	86,000
73. Food Servers, Nonrestaurant	85,000
74. Bartenders	84,000
75. Hosts and Hostesses, Restaurant, Lounge, and Coffee Shop	84,000
76. Personal and Home Care Aides	84,000
77. Hairdressers, Hairstylists, and Cosmetologists	78,000
78. Hotel, Motel, and Resort Desk Clerks	73,000
79. Bill and Account Collectors	71,000
80. First-Line Supervisors/Managers of Production and Operating Workers	71,000
81. Billing and Posting Clerks and Machine Operators	69,000
82. Billing, Cost, and Rate Clerks	69,000
83. Billing, Posting, and Calculating Machine Operators	69,000
84. Statement Clerks	69,000
85. Painters, Construction and Maintenance	67,000
86. Electricians	66,000
87. Bus Drivers, School	63,000
88. Amusement and Recreation Attendants	62,000
89. Laundry and Dry-Cleaning Workers	62,000
90. Laundry and Drycleaning Machine Operators and Tenders, Except Pressing	62,000
91. Precision Dyers	62,000
92. Spotters, Dry Cleaning	62,000
93. Secondary School Teachers, Except Special and Vocational Education	60,000
94. Licensed Practical and Licensed Vocational Nurses	58,000
95. Packaging and Filling Machine Operators and Tenders	56,000
96. Food Service Managers	55,000
97. Preschool Teachers, Except Special Education	55,000
98. Sales Agents, Financial Services	55,000
99. Sales Agents, Securities and Commodities	55,000
100. Securities, Commodities, and Financial Services Sales Agents	55,000

Best Jobs Lists with High Percentages of Workers Age 16–24, Workers Age 55 and Over, Part-Time Workers, Self-Employed Workers, Women, and Men

We decided that it would be interesting to include lists in this section that show what sorts of jobs different types of people are most likely to have. For example, what jobs have the highest percentage of men or younger workers? We're not saying that men or younger workers should consider these jobs over others, but it is interesting information to know.

In some cases, the lists can give you ideas for jobs to consider that you might otherwise overlook. For example, perhaps women should consider some jobs that traditionally have high percentages of men in them. Older workers might consider some jobs typically held by younger ones. Although these are not obvious ways of using these lists, the lists may give you some good ideas on jobs to consider. The lists may also help you identify jobs that work well for others in your situation (for example, jobs with plentiful opportunities for part-time work, if that is something you want to do).

All of the lists in this section were created using a similar process. We began with all 500 best jobs and then sorted those jobs in order of the primary criteria for each set of lists. For example, we sorted all 500 jobs based on the percentage of workers age 16 to 24. We then selected the 100 jobs with the highest percentage of workers age 16 to 24 and listed them along with their earnings, growth, and number of openings data. From the list of 100 jobs for each type of worker, we created four more-specialized lists:

▲ 25 Best Jobs Overall (jobs with the best total score for earnings, growth rate, and number of openings)

▲ 25 Best-Paying Jobs

▲ 25 Fastest-Growing Jobs

▲ 25 Jobs with the Most Openings

Again, each of these four lists only includes jobs from among those with the 100 highest percentages of different types of workers. The same basic process was used to create all the lists in this section. The lists are interesting, and we hope you find them helpful.

Best Jobs with a High Percentage of Workers Age 16–24

From our list of 500 jobs used in this book, this list contains jobs with the highest percentage of workers age 16 to 24, presented in order of the percentage of these young workers in each job. Younger workers are found in all jobs, but jobs with higher percentages of younger workers may present more opportunities for initial entry or upward mobility. Many jobs with the highest percentages of younger workers are those that don't require extensive training or education, and there is a wide variety of jobs in different fields among the top 100.

The 100 Jobs with the Highest Percentage of Workers Age 16–24

Job	Percent Age 16–24	Annual Earnings	Percent Growth	Annual Openings
1. Cashiers	51.8%	$14,950	14.5%	1,125,000
2. Gaming Change Persons and Booth Cashiers	51.8%	$18,990	36.1%	13,000
3. Counter Attendants, Cafeteria, Food Concession, and Coffee Shop	51.1%	$14,760	14.4%	216,000
4. Waiters and Waitresses	47.2%	$13,720	18.3%	596,000
5. Freight, Stock, and Material Movers, Hand	46.4%	$19,440	13.9%	519,000
6. Laborers and Freight, Stock, and Material Movers, Hand	46.4%	$19,440	13.9%	519,000
7. Amusement and Recreation Attendants	46.1%	$14,600	32.4%	62,000
8. Gaming Dealers	46.1%	$13,680	32.4%	28,000
9. Gaming Supervisors	46.1%	$39,240	18.4%	2,000
10. Counter and Rental Clerks	44.8%	$16,750	19.4%	150,000
11. Helpers—Brickmasons, Blockmasons, Stonemasons, and Tile and Marble Setters	43.9%	$23,620	14.1%	14,000
12. Helpers—Electricians	43.9%	$22,160	13.3%	27,000
13. Helpers—Pipelayers, Plumbers, Pipefitters, and Steamfitters	43.9%	$21,830	11.5%	20,000
14. Combined Food Preparation and Serving Workers, Including Fast Food	40.1%	$14,120	30.5%	737,000
15. Food Preparation Workers	40.1%	$15,910	16.9%	231,000
16. File Clerks	39.4%	$19,490	9.1%	49,000
17. Food Servers, Nonrestaurant	39.4%	$15,310	16.4%	85,000
18. Hosts and Hostesses, Restaurant, Lounge, and Coffee Shop	39.3%	$14,920	13.0%	84,000
19. Cleaners of Vehicles and Equipment	38.9%	$16,490	18.8%	86,000
20. Library Assistants, Clerical	38.4%	$18,580	19.7%	26,000

The 100 Jobs with the Highest Percentage of Workers Age 16–24

Job	Percent Age 16–24	Annual Earnings	Percent Growth	Annual Openings
21. Bakers, Bread and Pastry	38.2%	$20,440	16.8%	25,000
22. Cooks, Institution and Cafeteria	38.2%	$17,750	7.6%	110,000
23. Cooks, Restaurant	38.2%	$18,480	21.7%	158,000
24. Demonstrators and Product Promoters	33.1%	$20,690	24.9%	34,000
25. Retail Salespersons	33.1%	$17,150	12.4%	1,124,000
26. Nonfarm Animal Caretakers	30.7%	$16,570	21.6%	20,000
27. Veterinary Assistants and Laboratory Animal Caretakers	30.7%	$17,470	39.8%	8,000
28. Grips and Set-Up Workers, Motion Picture Sets, Studios, and Stages	30.1%	$19,440	13.9%	519,000
29. Helpers—Installation, Maintenance, and Repair Workers	30.1%	$21,210	18.5%	35,000
30. Helpers—Production Workers	30.1%	$18,990	11.9%	143,000
31. Production Helpers	30.1%	$18,990	11.9%	143,000
32. Production Laborers	30.1%	$18,990	11.9%	143,000
33. Stevedores, Except Equipment Operators	30.1%	$19,440	13.9%	519,000
34. Landscaping and Groundskeeping Workers	29.6%	$19,120	29.0%	193,000
35. Tree Trimmers and Pruners	29.4%	$23,950	16.3%	11,000
36. Receptionists and Information Clerks	29.0%	$20,650	23.7%	269,000
37. Hotel, Motel, and Resort Desk Clerks	27.9%	$16,920	33.4%	73,000
38. Costume Attendants	26.8%	$23,570	19.1%	8,000
39. Reservation and Transportation Ticket Agents	26.8%	$24,090	14.5%	39,000
40. Reservation and Transportation Ticket Agents and Travel Clerks	26.8%	$24,090	14.5%	39,000
41. Travel Clerks	26.8%	$24,090	14.5%	39,000
42. Interviewers, Except Eligibility and Loan	24.3%	$21,880	33.4%	53,000
43. Dental Assistants	23.8%	$26,720	37.2%	16,000
44. Ambulance Drivers and Attendants, Except Emergency Medical Technicians	22.4%	$18,890	33.7%	3,000
45. Physical Therapist Aides	22.4%	$20,300	46.3%	7,000
46. Physical Therapist Assistants	22.4%	$35,280	44.8%	9,000
47. Roofers	22.4%	$29,460	19.4%	38,000
48. Metal Molding, Coremaking, and Casting Machine Operators and Tenders	22.0%	$22,340	9.8%	38,000
49. Metal Molding, Coremaking, and Casting Machine Setters and Set-Up Operators	22.0%	$22,340	9.8%	38,000

(continued)

(continued)

The 100 Jobs with the Highest Percentage of Workers Age 16–24

Job	Percent Age 16–24	Annual Earnings	Percent Growth	Annual Openings
50. Molding, Coremaking, and Casting Machine Setters, Operators, and Tenders, Metal and Plastic	22.0%	$22,340	9.8%	38,000
51. Office Clerks, General	22.0%	$21,780	15.9%	676,000
52. Plastic Molding and Casting Machine Operators and Tenders	22.0%	$22,340	9.8%	38,000
53. Plastic Molding and Casting Machine Setters and Set-Up Operators	22.0%	$22,340	9.8%	38,000
54. Packers and Packagers, Hand	21.8%	$16,280	19.3%	242,000
55. Insulation Workers, Floor, Ceiling, and Wall	21.7%	$28,000	13.6%	12,000
56. Insulation Workers, Mechanical	21.7%	$28,000	13.6%	12,000
57. Marking Clerks	21.5%	$19,060	8.5%	467,000
58. Packaging and Filling Machine Operators and Tenders	21.5%	$20,760	14.4%	56,000
59. Teacher Assistants	21.3%	$18,070	23.9%	256,000
60. Production, Planning, and Expediting Clerks	20.7%	$32,420	17.9%	36,000
61. Shipping, Receiving, and Traffic Clerks	20.1%	$22,710	9.3%	133,000
62. Bartenders	20.0%	$14,610	13.4%	84,000
63. Bill and Account Collectors	20.0%	$25,960	25.3%	71,000
64. Bakers, Manufacturing	19.6%	$20,440	16.8%	25,000
65. Private Detectives and Investigators	19.3%	$28,380	23.5%	9,000
66. Security Guards	19.3%	$18,600	35.4%	242,000
67. Signal and Track Switch Repairers	18.5%	$42,390	11.5%	16,000
68. Brazers	18.2%	$28,490	19.3%	51,000
69. Solderers	18.2%	$28,490	19.3%	51,000
70. Soldering and Brazing Machine Operators and Tenders	18.2%	$28,220	15.1%	9,000
71. Soldering and Brazing Machine Setters and Set-Up Operators	18.2%	$28,220	15.1%	9,000
72. Kindergarten Teachers, Except Special Education	17.4%	$38,740	14.5%	23,000
73. Order Fillers, Wholesale and Retail Sales	17.4%	$19,060	8.5%	467,000
74. Preschool Teachers, Except Special Education	17.4%	$18,640	20.0%	55,000
75. Stock Clerks, Sales Floor	17.4%	$19,060	8.5%	467,000
76. Stock Clerks—Stockroom, Warehouse, or Storage Yard	17.4%	$19,060	8.5%	467,000
77. Adjustment Clerks	17.2%	$25,430	32.4%	359,000

The 100 Jobs with the Highest Percentage of Workers Age 16–24

Job	Percent Age 16–24	Annual Earnings	Percent Growth	Annual Openings
78. Customer Service Representatives	17.2%	$25,430	32.4%	359,000
79. Drywall and Ceiling Tile Installers	17.2%	$33,000	9.4%	19,000
80. Drywall Installers	17.2%	$33,000	9.4%	19,000
81. Home Health Aides	17.2%	$17,590	47.3%	120,000
82. Nursing Aides, Orderlies, and Attendants	17.2%	$19,290	23.5%	268,000
83. Child Care Workers	17.0%	$16,030	10.6%	370,000
84. Laundry and Dry-Cleaning Workers	16.8%	$16,360	11.4%	62,000
85. Laundry and Drycleaning Machine Operators and Tenders, Except Pressing	16.8%	$16,360	11.4%	62,000
86. Spotters, Dry Cleaning	16.8%	$16,360	11.4%	62,000
87. Automotive Body and Related Repairers	16.7%	$32,490	10.2%	18,000
88. Coating, Painting, and Spraying Machine Operators and Tenders	16.7%	$24,710	11.9%	18,000
89. Coating, Painting, and Spraying Machine Setters and Set-Up Operators	16.7%	$24,710	11.9%	18,000
90. Coating, Painting, and Spraying Machine Setters, Operators, and Tenders	16.7%	$24,710	11.9%	18,000
91. Painters, Transportation Equipment	16.7%	$32,330	17.5%	8,000
92. Advertising Sales Agents	16.6%	$36,560	26.3%	25,000
93. Sales Representatives, Agricultural	16.6%	$54,360	7.5%	24,000
94. Sales Representatives, Chemical and Pharmaceutical	16.6%	$54,360	7.5%	24,000
95. Sales Representatives, Electrical/Electronic	16.6%	$54,360	7.5%	24,000
96. Sales Representatives, Instruments	16.6%	$54,360	7.5%	24,000
97. Sales Representatives, Mechanical Equipment and Supplies	16.6%	$54,360	7.5%	24,000
98. Sales Representatives, Medical	16.6%	$54,360	7.5%	24,000
99. Sales Representatives, Wholesale and Manufacturing, Except Technical and Scientific Products	16.6%	$41,520	5.7%	86,000
100. Sales Representatives, Wholesale and Manufacturing, Technical and Scientific Products	16.6%	$54,360	7.5%	24,000

Best Jobs Overall for Workers Age 16–24

Job	Percent Age 16–24	Annual Earnings	Percent Growth	Annual Openings
1. Adjustment Clerks	17.2%	$25,430	32.4%	359,000
2. Customer Service Representatives	17.2%	$25,430	32.4%	359,000
3. Advertising Sales Agents	16.6%	$36,560	26.3%	25,000
4. Security Guards	19.3%	$18,600	35.4%	242,000
5. Home Health Aides	17.2%	$17,590	47.3%	120,000
6. Bill and Account Collectors	20.0%	$25,960	25.3%	71,000
7. Combined Food Preparation and Serving Workers, Including Fast Food	40.1%	$14,120	30.5%	737,000
8. Landscaping and Groundskeeping Workers	29.6%	$19,120	29.0%	193,000
9. Interviewers, Except Eligibility and Loan	24.3%	$21,880	33.4%	53,000
10. Receptionists and Information Clerks	29.0%	$20,650	23.7%	269,000
11. Nursing Aides, Orderlies, and Attendants	17.2%	$19,290	23.5%	268,000
12. Hotel, Motel, and Resort Desk Clerks	27.9%	$16,920	33.4%	73,000
13. Teacher Assistants	21.3%	$18,070	23.9%	256,000
14. Brazers	18.2%	$28,490	19.3%	51,000
15. Solderers	18.2%	$28,490	19.3%	51,000
16. Amusement and Recreation Attendants	46.1%	$14,600	32.4%	62,000
17. Roofers	22.4%	$29,460	19.4%	38,000
18. Cooks, Restaurant	38.2%	$18,480	21.7%	158,000
19. Production, Planning, and Expediting Clerks	20.7%	$32,420	17.9%	36,000
20. Physical Therapist Assistants	22.4%	$35,280	44.8%	9,000
21. Dental Assistants	23.8%	$26,720	37.2%	16,000
22. Packers and Packagers, Hand	21.8%	$16,280	19.3%	242,000
23. Demonstrators and Product Promoters	33.1%	$20,690	24.9%	34,000
24. Counter and Rental Clerks	44.8%	$16,750	19.4%	150,000
25. Gaming Dealers	46.1%	$13,680	32.4%	28,000

Best-Paying Jobs for Workers Age 16–24

Job	Percent Age 16–24	Annual Earnings	Percent Growth	Annual Openings
1. Sales Representatives, Agricultural	16.6%	$54,360	7.5%	24,000
2. Sales Representatives, Chemical and Pharmaceutical	16.6%	$54,360	7.5%	24,000
3. Sales Representatives, Electrical/Electronic	16.6%	$54,360	7.5%	24,000
4. Sales Representatives, Instruments	16.6%	$54,360	7.5%	24,000
5. Sales Representatives, Mechanical Equipment and Supplies	16.6%	$54,360	7.5%	24,000
6. Sales Representatives, Medical	16.6%	$54,360	7.5%	24,000
7. Sales Representatives, Wholesale and Manufacturing, Technical and Scientific Products	16.6%	$54,360	7.5%	24,000
8. Signal and Track Switch Repairers	18.5%	$42,390	11.5%	16,000
9. Sales Representatives, Wholesale and Manufacturing, Except Technical and Scientific Products	16.6%	$41,520	5.7%	86,000
10. Gaming Supervisors	46.1%	$39,240	18.4%	2,000
11. Kindergarten Teachers, Except Special Education	17.4%	$38,740	14.5%	23,000
12. Advertising Sales Agents	16.6%	$36,560	26.3%	25,000
13. Physical Therapist Assistants	22.4%	$35,280	44.8%	9,000
14. Drywall and Ceiling Tile Installers	17.2%	$33,000	9.4%	19,000
15. Drywall Installers	17.2%	$33,000	9.4%	19,000
16. Automotive Body and Related Repairers	16.7%	$32,490	10.2%	18,000
17. Production, Planning, and Expediting Clerks	20.7%	$32,420	17.9%	36,000
18. Painters, Transportation Equipment	16.7%	$32,330	17.5%	8,000
19. Roofers	22.4%	$29,460	19.4%	38,000
20. Brazers	18.2%	$28,490	19.3%	51,000
21. Solderers	18.2%	$28,490	19.3%	51,000
22. Private Detectives and Investigators	19.3%	$28,380	23.5%	9,000
23. Soldering and Brazing Machine Operators and Tenders	18.2%	$28,220	15.1%	9,000
24. Soldering and Brazing Machine Setters and Set-Up Operators	18.2%	$28,220	15.1%	9,000
25. Insulation Workers, Floor, Ceiling, and Wall	21.7%	$28,000	13.6%	12,000

Fastest-Growing Jobs for Workers Age 16–24

Job	Percent Age 16–24	Annual Earnings	Percent Growth	Annual Openings
1. Home Health Aides	17.2%	$17,590	47.3%	120,000
2. Physical Therapist Aides	22.4%	$20,300	46.3%	7,000
3. Physical Therapist Assistants	22.4%	$35,280	44.8%	9,000
4. Veterinary Assistants and Laboratory Animal Caretakers	30.7%	$17,470	39.8%	8,000
5. Dental Assistants	23.8%	$26,720	37.2%	16,000
6. Gaming Change Persons and Booth Cashiers	51.8%	$18,990	36.1%	13,000
7. Security Guards	19.3%	$18,600	35.4%	242,000
8. Ambulance Drivers and Attendants, Except Emergency Medical Technicians	22.4%	$18,890	33.7%	3,000
9. Hotel, Motel, and Resort Desk Clerks	27.9%	$16,920	33.4%	73,000
10. Interviewers, Except Eligibility and Loan	24.3%	$21,880	33.4%	53,000
11. Adjustment Clerks	17.2%	$25,430	32.4%	359,000
12. Amusement and Recreation Attendants	46.1%	$14,600	32.4%	62,000
13. Customer Service Representatives	17.2%	$25,430	32.4%	359,000
14. Gaming Dealers	46.1%	$13,680	32.4%	28,000
15. Combined Food Preparation and Serving Workers, Including Fast Food	40.1%	$14,120	30.5%	737,000
16. Landscaping and Groundskeeping Workers	29.6%	$19,120	29.0%	193,000
17. Advertising Sales Agents	16.6%	$36,560	26.3%	25,000
18. Bill and Account Collectors	20.0%	$25,960	25.3%	71,000
19. Demonstrators and Product Promoters	33.1%	$20,690	24.9%	34,000
20. Teacher Assistants	21.3%	$18,070	23.9%	256,000
21. Receptionists and Information Clerks	29.0%	$20,650	23.7%	269,000
22. Nursing Aides, Orderlies, and Attendants	17.2%	$19,290	23.5%	268,000
23. Private Detectives and Investigators	19.3%	$28,380	23.5%	9,000
24. Cooks, Restaurant	38.2%	$18,480	21.7%	158,000
25. Nonfarm Animal Caretakers	30.7%	$16,570	21.6%	20,000

Jobs with the Most Openings for Workers Age 16–24

Job	Percent Age 16–24	Annual Earnings	Percent Growth	Annual Openings
1. Cashiers	51.8%	$14,950	14.5%	1,125,000
2. Retail Salespersons	33.1%	$17,150	12.4%	1,124,000
3. Combined Food Preparation and Serving Workers, Including Fast Food	40.1%	$14,120	30.5%	737,000
4. Office Clerks, General	22.0%	$21,780	15.9%	676,000
5. Waiters and Waitresses	47.2%	$13,720	18.3%	596,000
6. Freight, Stock, and Material Movers, Hand	46.4%	$19,440	13.9%	519,000
7. Grips and Set-Up Workers, Motion Picture Sets, Studios, and Stages	30.1%	$19,440	13.9%	519,000
8. Laborers and Freight, Stock, and Material Movers, Hand	46.4%	$19,440	13.9%	519,000
9. Stevedores, Except Equipment Operators	30.1%	$19,440	13.9%	519,000
10. Marking Clerks	21.5%	$19,060	8.5%	467,000
11. Order Fillers, Wholesale and Retail Sales	17.4%	$19,060	8.5%	467,000
12. Stock Clerks, Sales Floor	17.4%	$19,060	8.5%	467,000
13. Stock Clerks—Stockroom, Warehouse, or Storage Yard	17.4%	$19,060	8.5%	467,000
14. Child Care Workers	17.0%	$16,030	10.6%	370,000
15. Adjustment Clerks	17.2%	$25,430	32.4%	359,000
16. Customer Service Representatives	17.2%	$25,430	32.4%	359,000
17. Receptionists and Information Clerks	29.0%	$20,650	23.7%	269,000
18. Nursing Aides, Orderlies, and Attendants	17.2%	$19,290	23.5%	268,000
19. Teacher Assistants	21.3%	$18,070	23.9%	256,000
20. Packers and Packagers, Hand	21.8%	$16,280	19.3%	242,000
21. Security Guards	19.3%	$18,600	35.4%	242,000
22. Food Preparation Workers	40.1%	$15,910	16.9%	231,000
23. Counter Attendants, Cafeteria, Food Concession, and Coffee Shop	51.1%	$14,760	14.4%	216,000
24. Landscaping and Groundskeeping Workers	29.6%	$19,120	29.0%	193,000
25. Cooks, Restaurant	38.2%	$18,480	21.7%	158,000

Best Jobs with a High Percentage of Workers Age 55 and Over

Older workers don't change careers as often as younger ones do, and on the average, they tend to have been in their jobs for quite some time. Many of the jobs with the highest percentages of workers age 55 and over—and those with the highest earnings—require considerable preparation, either through experience or through education and training. These are not the sort of jobs most younger workers could easily get. That should not come as a big surprise, as many of these folks have been in the workforce for a long time and therefore have lots of experience.

But go down the list of the 100 jobs with the highest percentage of older workers and you will find a variety of jobs that many older workers could more easily enter if they were changing careers. Some would make good "retirement" jobs, particularly if they allowed for part-time work or self-employment.

The 100 Jobs with the Highest Percentage of Workers Age 55 and Over

Job	Percent Age 55 and Over	Annual Earnings	Percent Growth	Annual Openings
1. Farmers and Ranchers	40.6%	$42,170	−25.4%	146,000
2. First-Line Supervisors and Manager/Supervisors —Agricultural Crop Workers	36.1%	$33,330	13.0%	8,000
3. First-Line Supervisors and Manager/Supervisors —Landscaping Workers	36.1%	$32,100	20.1%	10,000
4. First-Line Supervisors/Managers of Farming, Fishing, and Forestry Workers	36.1%	$33,330	13.0%	89,000
5. First-Line Supervisors/Managers of Landscaping, Lawn Service, and Groundskeeping Workers	35.2%	$32,100	20.1%	10,000
6. Lawn Service Managers	35.2%	$32,100	20.1%	10,000
7. Clergy	31.2%	$33,840	15.0%	12,000
8. Property, Real Estate, and Community Association Managers	27.0%	$36,290	22.7%	24,000
9. Appraisers and Assessors of Real Estate	26.8%	$38,950	18.0%	6,000
10. Appraisers, Real Estate	26.8%	$38,950	18.0%	6,000
11. Assessors	26.8%	$38,950	18.0%	6,000
12. Real Estate Brokers	26.8%	$51,370	9.6%	8,000
13. Real Estate Sales Agents	26.8%	$28,570	9.5%	28,000
14. Bus Drivers, School	23.3%	$21,990	11.6%	63,000
15. Bus Drivers, Transit and Intercity	23.3%	$28,060	17.4%	24,000

The 100 Jobs with the Highest Percentage of Workers Age 55 and Over

Job	Percent Age 55 and Over	Annual Earnings	Percent Growth	Annual Openings
16. Management Analysts	22.3%	$57,970	28.9%	50,000
17. Personal and Home Care Aides ✎	21.7%	$16,140	62.5%	84,000
18. Private Detectives and Investigators	21.7%	$28,380	23.5%	9,000
19. Security Guards	21.7%	$18,600	35.4%	242,000
20. Social and Human Service Assistants ✎	21.7%	$23,070	54.2%	45,000
21. Taxi Drivers and Chauffeurs	21.6%	$17,920	24.4%	37,000
22. First-Line Supervisors/Managers of Housekeeping and Janitorial Workers	20.4%	$27,200	14.2%	18,000
23. Housekeeping Supervisors	20.4%	$27,200	14.2%	18,000
24. Janitorial Supervisors	20.4%	$27,200	14.2%	18,000
25. Composers	19.4%	$33,720	13.1%	9,000
26. Music Arrangers and Orchestrators	19.4%	$33,720	13.1%	9,000
27. Music Directors	19.4%	$33,720	13.1%	9,000
28. Music Directors and Composers	19.4%	$33,720	13.1%	9,000
29. Musicians and Singers	19.4%	$40,320	20.1%	33,000
30. Musicians, Instrumental	19.4%	$40,320	20.1%	33,000
31. Singers	19.4%	$40,320	20.1%	33,000
32. Teachers, Postsecondary ✎	19.0%	$52,115	23.5%	184,000
33. Insurance Sales Agents	18.7%	$38,890	3.3%	43,000
34. Government Service Executives	18.5%	$120,450	17.2%	48,000
35. Weighers, Measurers, Checkers, and Samplers, Recordkeeping	18.4%	$24,690	17.9%	13,000
36. Bookkeeping, Accounting, and Auditing Clerks	18.3%	$26,540	2.0%	298,000
37. Anesthesiologists	18.0%	greater than $146,500	17.9%	27,000
38. Family and General Practitioners	18.0%	$118,390	17.9%	27,000
39. Internists, General	18.0%	greater than $146,500	17.9%	27,000
40. Obstetricians and Gynecologists	18.0%	greater than $146,500	17.9%	27,000
41. Pediatricians, General	18.0%	$126,430	17.9%	27,000
42. Psychiatrists	18.0%	$126,460	17.9%	27,000
43. Surgeons	18.0%	greater than $146,500	17.9%	27,000
44. Pest Control Workers ✎	17.7%	$23,150	22.1%	7,000

(continued)

(continued)

The 100 Jobs with the Highest Percentage of Workers Age 55 and Over

Job	Percent Age 55 and Over	Annual Earnings	Percent Growth	Annual Openings
45. Janitors and Cleaners, Except Maids and Housekeeping Cleaners	17.6%	$17,900	13.5%	507,000
46. Chiropractors	17.3%	$68,420	23.4%	3,000
47. Directors, Religious Activities and Education	17.3%	$27,420	15.9%	23,000
48. Optometrists	17.3%	$85,650	18.7%	1,000
49. Recreation Workers	17.3%	$17,850	20.1%	32,000
50. Veterinarians	17.3%	$62,000	31.8%	2,000
51. Library Assistants, Clerical	17.0%	$18,580	19.7%	26,000
52. Automatic Teller Machine Servicers	16.4%	$32,890	14.2%	24,000
53. Child Support, Missing Persons, and Unemployment Insurance Fraud Investigators	16.4%	$50,960	16.4%	4,000
54. Police and Sheriff's Patrol Officers	16.4%	$40,970	23.2%	21,000
55. Dietitians and Nutritionists	15.3%	$40,410	15.2%	5,000
56. Education Administrators, Elementary and Secondary School	15.3%	$69,240	13.4%	35,000
57. Education Administrators, Postsecondary	15.3%	$61,700	13.4%	35,000
58. Education Administrators, Preschool and Child Care Center/Program	15.3%	$31,860	13.4%	35,000
59. Instructional Coordinators	15.3%	$46,600	25.0%	15,000
60. Immigration and Customs Inspectors	15.2%	$50,960	16.4%	4,000
61. Health Educators	15.0%	$35,230	23.5%	7,000
62. Administrative Services Managers	14.7%	$49,810	20.4%	31,000
63. Chief Executives	14.7%	$120,450	17.2%	48,000
64. Computer and Information Systems Managers	14.7%	$82,480	47.9%	28,000
65. Construction Managers	14.7%	$61,050	16.3%	26,000
66. Engineering Managers	14.7%	$87,490	8.0%	24,000
67. Industrial Production Managers	14.7%	$64,510	6.2%	22,000
68. Private Sector Executives	14.7%	$120,450	17.2%	48,000
69. Storage and Distribution Managers	14.7%	$57,240	20.2%	13,000
70. Transportation Managers	14.7%	$57,240	20.2%	13,000
71. Transportation, Storage, and Distribution Managers	14.7%	$57,240	20.2%	13,000
72. Gaming Managers	14.6%	$53,450	30.0%	fewer than 500
73. General and Operations Managers	14.6%	$65,010	15.2%	235,000

The 100 Jobs with the Highest Percentage of Workers Age 55 and Over

Job	Percent Age 55 and Over	Annual Earnings	Percent Growth	Annual Openings
74. Medical and Health Services Managers	14.6%	$59,220	32.3%	27,000
75. Network and Computer Systems Administrators	14.6%	$53,770	81.9%	18,000
76. Signal and Track Switch Repairers	14.6%	$42,390	11.5%	16,000
77. Social and Community Service Managers	14.6%	$41,260	24.8%	13,000
78. Office Clerks, General	14.5%	$21,780	15.9%	676,000
79. Mechanical Engineers	14.4%	$61,440	13.1%	7,000
80. Parking Lot Attendants	14.4%	$15,690	19.8%	17,000
81. Demonstrators and Product Promoters	14.3%	$20,690	24.9%	34,000
82. Retail Salespersons	14.3%	$17,150	12.4%	1,124,000
83. First-Line Supervisors/Managers of Non-Retail Sales Workers	14.2%	$51,490	5.8%	41,000
84. First-Line Supervisors/Managers of Retail Sales Workers	14.2%	$28,590	8.1%	206,000
85. Grader, Bulldozer, and Scraper Operators	14.2%	$34,160	6.9%	25,000
86. Bakers, Manufacturing	14.0%	$20,440	16.8%	25,000
87. Child Care Workers	14.0%	$16,030	10.6%	370,000
88. Landscaping and Groundskeeping Workers	13.9%	$19,120	29.0%	193,000
89. Laundry and Dry-Cleaning Workers	13.9%	$16,360	11.4%	62,000
90. Laundry and Drycleaning Machine Operators and Tenders, Except Pressing	13.9%	$16,360	11.4%	62,000
91. Maintenance and Repair Workers, General	13.9%	$28,740	4.7%	103,000
92. Precision Dyers	13.9%	$16,360	11.4%	62,000
93. Spotters, Dry Cleaning	13.9%	$16,360	11.4%	62,000
94. Legal Secretaries	13.8%	$34,610	20.3%	36,000
95. Medical Secretaries	13.8%	$24,670	19.0%	40,000
96. Adult Literacy, Remedial Education, and GED Teachers and Instructors	13.7%	$35,220	19.4%	12,000
97. Fitness Trainers and Aerobics Instructors	13.7%	$23,340	40.3%	19,000
98. Self-Enrichment Education Teachers	13.7%	$28,880	18.5%	34,000
99. Vocational Education Teachers, Secondary School	13.7%	$43,590	13.4%	7,000
100. Caption Writers	13.6%	$42,450	28.4%	18,000

Best Jobs Overall for Workers Age 55 and Over

Job	Percent Age 55 and Over	Annual Earnings	Percent Growth	Annual Openings
1. Computer and Information Systems Managers	14.7%	$82,480	47.9%	28,000
2. Teachers, Postsecondary	19.0%	$52,115	23.5%	184,000
3. Management Analysts	22.3%	$57,970	28.9%	50,000
4. Medical and Health Services Managers	14.6%	$59,220	32.3%	27,000
5. Network and Computer Systems Administrators	14.6%	$53,770	81.9%	18,000
6. General and Operations Managers	14.6%	$65,010	15.2%	235,000
7. Chief Executives	14.7%	$120,450	17.2%	48,000
8. Government Service Executives	18.5%	$120,450	17.2%	48,000
9. Private Sector Executives	14.7%	$120,450	17.2%	48,000
10. Administrative Services Managers	14.7%	$49,810	20.4%	31,000
11. Anesthesiologists	18.0%	greater than $146,500	17.9%	27,000
12. Internists, General	18.0%	greater than $146,500	17.9%	27,000
13. Obstetricians and Gynecologists	18.0%	greater than $146,500	17.9%	27,000
14. Surgeons	18.0%	greater than $146,500	17.9%	27,000
15. Psychiatrists	18.0%	$126,460	17.9%	27,000
16. Pediatricians, General	18.0%	$126,430	17.9%	27,000
17. Family and General Practitioners	18.0%	$118,390	17.9%	27,000
18. Caption Writers ◆	13.6%	$42,450	28.4%	18,000
19. Security Guards	21.7%	$18,600	35.4%	242,000
20. Musicians and Singers	19.4%	$40,320	20.1%	33,000
21. Musicians, Instrumental	19.4%	$40,320	20.1%	33,000
22. Singers	19.4%	$40,320	20.1%	33,000
23. Social and Human Service Assistants	21.7%	$23,070	54.2%	45,000
24. Legal Secretaries	13.8%	$34,610	20.3%	36,000
25. Landscaping and Groundskeeping Workers	13.9%	$19,120	29.0%	193,000

Best-Paying Jobs for Workers Age 55 and Over

Job	Percent Age 55 and Over	Annual Earnings	Percent Growth	Annual Openings
1. Anesthesiologists	18.0%	greater than $146,500	17.9%	27,000
2. Internists, General	18.0%	greater than $146,500	17.9%	27,000
3. Obstetricians and Gynecologists	18.0%	greater than $146,500	17.9%	27,000
4. Surgeons	18.0%	greater than $146,500	17.9%	27,000
5. Psychiatrists	18.0%	$126,460	17.9%	27,000
6. Pediatricians, General	18.0%	$126,430	17.9%	27,000
7. Chief Executives	14.7%	$120,450	17.2%	48,000
8. Government Service Executives	18.5%	$120,450	17.2%	48,000
9. Private Sector Executives	14.7%	$120,450	17.2%	48,000
10. Family and General Practitioners	18.0%	$118,390	17.9%	27,000
11. Engineering Managers	14.7%	$87,490	8.0%	24,000
12. Optometrists	17.3%	$85,650	18.7%	1,000
13. Computer and Information Systems Managers	14.7%	$82,480	47.9%	28,000
14. Education Administrators, Elementary and Secondary School	15.3%	$69,240	13.4%	35,000
15. Chiropractors	17.3%	$68,420	23.4%	3,000
16. General and Operations Managers	14.6%	$65,010	15.2%	235,000
17. Industrial Production Managers	14.7%	$64,510	6.2%	22,000
18. Veterinarians	17.3%	$62,000	31.8%	2,000
19. Education Administrators, Postsecondary	15.3%	$61,700	13.4%	35,000
20. Mechanical Engineers	14.4%	$61,440	13.1%	7,000
21. Construction Managers	14.7%	$61,050	16.3%	26,000
22. Medical and Health Services Managers	14.6%	$59,220	32.3%	27,000
23. Management Analysts	22.3%	$57,970	28.9%	50,000
24. Storage and Distribution Managers	14.7%	$57,240	20.2%	13,000
25. Transportation Managers	14.7%	$57,240	20.2%	13,000

Fastest-Growing Jobs for Workers Age 55 and Over

Job	Percent Age 55 and Over	Annual Earnings	Percent Growth	Annual Openings
1. Network and Computer Systems Administrators	14.6%	$53,770	81.9%	18,000
2. Personal and Home Care Aides	21.7%	$16,140	62.5%	84,000
3. Social and Human Service Assistants	21.7%	$23,070	54.2%	45,000
4. Computer and Information Systems Managers	14.7%	$82,480	47.9%	28,000
5. Fitness Trainers and Aerobics Instructors	13.7%	$23,340	40.3%	19,000
6. Security Guards	21.7%	$18,600	35.4%	242,000
7. Medical and Health Services Managers	14.6%	$59,220	32.3%	27,000
8. Veterinarians	17.3%	$62,000	31.8%	2,000
9. Gaming Managers	14.6%	$53,450	30.0%	fewer than 500
10. Landscaping and Groundskeeping Workers	13.9%	$19,120	29.0%	193,000
11. Management Analysts	22.3%	$57,970	28.9%	50,000
12. Caption Writers	13.6%	$42,450	28.4%	18,000
13. Instructional Coordinators	15.3%	$46,600	25.0%	15,000
14. Demonstrators and Product Promoters	14.3%	$20,690	24.9%	34,000
15. Social and Community Service Managers	14.6%	$41,260	24.8%	13,000
16. Taxi Drivers and Chauffeurs	21.6%	$17,920	24.4%	37,000
17. Health Educators	15.0%	$35,230	23.5%	7,000
18. Private Detectives and Investigators	21.7%	$28,380	23.5%	9,000
19. Teachers, Postsecondary	19.0%	$52,115	23.5%	184,000
20. Chiropractors	17.3%	$68,420	23.4%	3,000
21. Police and Sheriff's Patrol Officers	16.4%	$40,970	23.2%	21,000
22. Property, Real Estate, and Community Association Managers	27.0%	$36,290	22.7%	24,000
23. Pest Control Workers	17.7%	$23,150	22.1%	7,000
24. Administrative Services Managers	14.7%	$49,810	20.4%	31,000
25. Legal Secretaries	13.8%	$34,610	20.3%	36,000

Jobs with the Most Openings for Workers Age 55 and Over

Job	Percent Age 55 and Over	Annual Earnings	Percent Growth	Annual Openings
1. Retail Salespersons	14.3%	$17,150	12.4%	1,124,000
2. Office Clerks, General	14.5%	$21,780	15.9%	676,000
3. Janitors and Cleaners, Except Maids and Housekeeping Cleaners	17.6%	$17,900	13.5%	507,000
4. Child Care Workers	14.0%	$16,030	10.6%	370,000
5. Bookkeeping, Accounting, and Auditing Clerks	18.3%	$26,540	2.0%	298,000
6. Security Guards	21.7%	$18,600	35.4%	242,000
7. General and Operations Managers	14.6%	$65,010	15.2%	235,000
8. First-Line Supervisors/Managers of Retail Sales Workers	14.2%	$28,590	8.1%	206,000
9. Landscaping and Groundskeeping Workers	13.9%	$19,120	29.0%	193,000
10. Teachers, Postsecondary	19.0%	$52,115	23.5%	184,000
11. Farmers and Ranchers	40.6%	$42,170	−25.4%	146,000
12. Maintenance and Repair Workers, General	13.9%	$28,740	4.7%	103,000
13. First-Line Supervisors/Managers of Farming, Fishing, and Forestry Workers	36.1%	$33,330	13.0%	89,000
14. Personal and Home Care Aides	21.7%	$16,140	62.5%	84,000
15. Bus Drivers, School	23.3%	$21,990	11.6%	63,000
16. Laundry and Dry-Cleaning Workers	13.9%	$16,360	11.4%	62,000
17. Laundry and Drycleaning Machine Operators and Tenders, Except Pressing	13.9%	$16,360	11.4%	62,000
18. Precision Dyers	13.9%	$16,360	11.4%	62,000
19. Spotters, Dry Cleaning	13.9%	$16,360	11.4%	62,000
20. Management Analysts	22.3%	$57,970	28.9%	50,000
21. Chief Executives	14.7%	$120,450	17.2%	48,000
22. Government Service Executives	18.5%	$120,450	17.2%	48,000
23. Private Sector Executives	14.7%	$120,450	17.2%	48,000
24. Social and Human Service Assistants	21.7%	$23,070	54.2%	45,000
25. Insurance Sales Agents	18.7%	$38,890	3.3%	43,000

Best Jobs with a High Percentage of Part-Time Workers

Look over the list of 100 jobs with high percentages of part-time workers and you will find some interesting things. For example, seven of the top twenty involve music, which leads one to think that many people working in the music business do so less than full time. In some cases, people work part time in these jobs because they want the freedom of time this arrangement can provide, but others may do so because they can't find full-time employment in these areas. These folks may work in other full- or part-time jobs to make ends meet. If you want to work part time now or in the future, these lists will help you identify jobs that are more likely to provide that opportunity. If you want full-time work, the lists may also help you identify jobs for which such opportunities are more difficult to find. In either case, it's good information to know in advance.

The 100 Jobs with the Highest Percentage of Part-Time Workers

Job	Percent Part-Time Workers	Annual Earnings	Percent Growth	Annual Openings
1. Counter Attendants, Cafeteria, Food Concession, and Coffee Shop	62.9%	$14,760	14.4%	216,000
2. Library Assistants, Clerical	61.7%	$18,580	19.7%	26,000
3. Food Servers, Nonrestaurant	58.2%	$15,310	16.4%	85,000
4. Combined Food Preparation and Serving Workers, Including Fast Food	57.4%	$14,120	30.5%	737,000
5. Food Preparation Workers	57.4%	$15,910	16.9%	231,000
6. Cashiers	57.2%	$14,950	14.5%	1,125,000
7. Gaming Change Persons and Booth Cashiers	57.2%	$18,990	36.1%	13,000
8. Waiters and Waitresses	57.0%	$13,720	18.3%	596,000
9. Composers	53.5%	$33,720	13.1%	9,000
10. Music Arrangers and Orchestrators	53.5%	$33,720	13.1%	9,000
11. Music Directors	53.5%	$33,720	13.1%	9,000
12. Music Directors and Composers	53.5%	$33,720	13.1%	9,000
13. Musicians and Singers	53.5%	$40,320	20.1%	33,000
14. Musicians, Instrumental	53.5%	$40,320	20.1%	33,000
15. Singers	53.5%	$40,320	20.1%	33,000
16. Counter and Rental Clerks	50.8%	$16,750	19.4%	150,000
17. Amusement and Recreation Attendants	48.8%	$14,600	32.4%	62,000
18. Gaming Dealers	48.8%	$13,680	32.4%	28,000
19. Gaming Supervisors	48.8%	$39,240	18.4%	2,000

The 100 Jobs with the Highest Percentage of Part-Time Workers

Job	Percent Part-Time Workers	Annual Earnings	Percent Growth	Annual Openings
20. Teacher Assistants	46.8%	$18,070	23.9%	256,000
21. Flight Attendants	45.7%	$40,600	18.4%	8,000
22. Child Care Workers	43.4%	$16,030	10.6%	370,000
23. Bus Drivers, School	43.3%	$21,990	11.6%	63,000
24. Bus Drivers, Transit and Intercity	43.3%	$28,060	17.4%	24,000
25. Bartenders	43.1%	$14,610	13.4%	84,000
26. Adult Literacy, Remedial Education, and GED Teachers and Instructors	42.5%	$35,220	19.4%	12,000
27. Fitness Trainers and Aerobics Instructors	42.5%	$23,340	40.3%	19,000
28. Self-Enrichment Education Teachers	42.5%	$28,880	18.5%	34,000
29. Vocational Education Teachers, Secondary School	42.5%	$43,590	13.4%	7,000
30. Personal and Home Care Aides	42.4%	$16,140	62.5%	84,000
31. Social and Human Service Assistants	42.4%	$23,070	54.2%	45,000
32. Demonstrators and Product Promoters	40.2%	$20,690	24.9%	34,000
33. Retail Salespersons	40.2%	$17,150	12.4%	1,124,000
34. Costume Attendants	40.1%	$23,570	19.1%	8,000
35. Dental Assistants	39.7%	$26,720	37.2%	16,000
36. Health Educators	39.7%	$35,230	23.5%	7,000
37. Bakers, Bread and Pastry	38.5%	$20,440	16.8%	25,000
38. Cooks, Institution and Cafeteria	38.5%	$17,750	7.6%	110,000
39. Cooks, Restaurant	38.5%	$18,480	21.7%	158,000
40. Freight, Stock, and Material Movers, Hand	38.4%	$19,440	13.9%	519,000
41. Laborers and Freight, Stock, and Material Movers, Hand	38.4%	$19,440	13.9%	519,000
42. Hosts and Hostesses, Restaurant, Lounge, and Coffee Shop	38.3%	$14,920	13.0%	84,000
43. Nonfarm Animal Caretakers	38.1%	$16,570	21.6%	20,000
44. Veterinary Assistants and Laboratory Animal Caretakers	38.1%	$17,470	39.8%	8,000
45. Hairdressers, Hairstylists, and Cosmetologists	36.5%	$18,260	13.0%	78,000
46. Makeup Artists, Theatrical and Performance	36.5%	$30,240	11.4%	27,000
47. Manicurists and Pedicurists	36.5%	$16,700	26.5%	5,000
48. File Clerks	36.1%	$19,490	9.1%	49,000

(continued)

(continued)

The 100 Jobs with the Highest Percentage of Part-Time Workers

Job	Percent Part-Time Workers	Annual Earnings	Percent Growth	Annual Openings
49. Receptionists and Information Clerks	35.1%	$20,650	23.7%	269,000
50. Ambulance Drivers and Attendants, Except Emergency Medical Technicians	34.5%	$18,890	33.7%	3,000
51. Physical Therapist Aides	34.5%	$20,300	46.3%	7,000
52. Physical Therapist Assistants	34.5%	$35,280	44.8%	9,000
53. Bookkeeping, Accounting, and Auditing Clerks	32.8%	$26,540	2.0%	298,000
54. Interviewers, Except Eligibility and Loan	32.5%	$21,880	33.4%	53,000
55. Kindergarten Teachers, Except Special Education	32.4%	$38,740	14.5%	23,000
56. Preschool Teachers, Except Special Education	32.4%	$18,640	20.0%	55,000
57. Janitors and Cleaners, Except Maids and Housekeeping Cleaners	32.3%	$17,900	13.5%	507,000
58. Teachers, Postsecondary	32.3%	$52,115	23.5%	184,000
59. Reservation and Transportation Ticket Agents	31.7%	$24,090	14.5%	39,000
60. Reservation and Transportation Ticket Agents and Travel Clerks	31.7%	$24,090	14.5%	39,000
61. Travel Clerks	31.7%	$24,090	14.5%	39,000
62. Office Clerks, General	30.7%	$21,780	15.9%	676,000
63. Pest Control Workers	30.4%	$23,150	22.1%	7,000
64. Dietitians and Nutritionists	29.1%	$40,410	15.2%	5,000
65. Landscaping and Groundskeeping Workers	28.5%	$19,120	29.0%	193,000
66. Farmers and Ranchers	27.7%	$42,170	–25.4%	146,000
67. Home Health Aides	26.4%	$17,590	47.3%	120,000
68. Nursing Aides, Orderlies, and Attendants	26.4%	$19,290	23.5%	268,000
69. Laundry and Dry-Cleaning Workers	26.3%	$16,360	11.4%	62,000
70. Laundry and Drycleaning Machine Operators and Tenders, Except Pressing	26.3%	$16,360	11.4%	62,000
71. Registered Nurses	26.3%	$46,670	25.6%	140,000
72. Spotters, Dry Cleaning	26.3%	$16,360	11.4%	62,000
73. Hotel, Motel, and Resort Desk Clerks	25.8%	$16,920	33.4%	73,000
74. First-Line Supervisors and Manager/Supervisors —Agricultural Crop Workers	25.6%	$33,330	13.0%	8,000
75. First-Line Supervisors and Manager/Supervisors —Landscaping Workers	25.6%	$32,100	20.1%	10,000

The 100 Jobs with the Highest Percentage of Part-Time Workers

Job	Percent Part-Time Workers	Annual Earnings	Percent Growth	Annual Openings
76. First-Line Supervisors/Managers of Farming, Fishing, and Forestry Workers	25.6%	$33,330	13.0%	89,000
77. Tree Trimmers and Pruners	25.4%	$23,950	16.3%	11,000
78. Actors	25.3%	$20,540	26.7%	20,000
79. Athletes and Sports Competitors	25.3%	$43,730	22.5%	3,000
80. Coaches and Scouts	25.3%	$29,020	17.6%	19,000
81. Directors—Stage, Motion Pictures, Television, and Radio	25.3%	$45,090	27.1%	11,000
82. Film and Video Editors	25.3%	$36,910	25.8%	2,000
83. Producers	25.3%	$45,090	27.1%	11,000
84. Producers and Directors	25.3%	$45,090	27.1%	11,000
85. Program Directors	25.3%	$45,090	27.1%	11,000
86. Public Relations Specialists	25.3%	$41,010	36.1%	19,000
87. Talent Directors	25.3%	$45,090	27.1%	11,000
88. Technical Directors/Managers	25.3%	$45,090	27.1%	11,000
89. Occupational Therapist Assistants	24.9%	$35,840	39.7%	3,000
90. Pharmacy Aides	24.9%	$18,010	19.5%	9,000
91. Pharmacists	24.6%	$74,890	24.3%	20,000
92. Physician Assistants	24.6%	$63,970	53.5%	5,000
93. First-Line Supervisors/Managers of Landscaping, Lawn Service, and Groundskeeping Workers	24.5%	$32,100	20.1%	10,000
94. Lawn Service Managers	24.5%	$32,100	20.1%	10,000
95. Signal and Track Switch Repairers	24.3%	$42,390	11.5%	16,000
96. Graphic Designers	24.0%	$36,020	26.7%	28,000
97. Multi-Media Artists and Animators	24.0%	$42,270	22.2%	8,000
98. Clinical Psychologists	23.4%	$50,420	18.1%	18,000
99. Clinical, Counseling, and School Psychologists	23.4%	$50,420	18.1%	18,000
100. Counseling Psychologists	23.4%	$50,420	18.1%	18,000

Best Overall Part-Time Jobs

Job	Percent Part-Time Workers	Annual Earnings	Percent Growth	Annual Openings
1. Teachers, Postsecondary	32.3%	$52,115	23.5%	184,000
2. Registered Nurses	26.3%	$46,670	25.6%	140,000
3. Pharmacists	24.6%	$74,890	24.3%	20,000
4. Public Relations Specialists	25.3%	$41,010	36.1%	19,000
5. Graphic Designers	24.0%	$36,020	26.7%	28,000
6. Musicians and Singers	53.5%	$40,320	20.1%	33,000
7. Musicians, Instrumental	53.5%	$40,320	20.1%	33,000
8. Singers	53.5%	$40,320	20.1%	33,000
9. Home Health Aides	26.4%	$17,590	47.3%	120,000
10. Social and Human Service Assistants	42.4%	$23,070	54.2%	45,000
11. Combined Food Preparation and Serving Workers, Including Fast Food	57.4%	$14,120	30.5%	737,000
12. Landscaping and Groundskeeping Workers ✎	28.5%	$19,120	29.0%	193,000
13. Personal and Home Care Aides	42.4%	$16,140	62.5%	84,000
14. Interviewers, Except Eligibility and Loan	32.5%	$21,880	33.4%	53,000
15. Receptionists and Information Clerks	35.1%	$20,650	23.7%	269,000
16. Nursing Aides, Orderlies, and Attendants	26.4%	$19,290	23.5%	268,000
17. Hotel, Motel, and Resort Desk Clerks	25.8%	$16,920	33.4%	73,000
18. Teacher Assistants	46.8%	$18,070	23.9%	256,000
19. Directors—Stage, Motion Pictures, Television, and Radio	25.3%	$45,090	27.1%	11,000
20. Producers	25.3%	$45,090	27.1%	11,000
21. Producers and Directors	25.3%	$45,090	27.1%	11,000
22. Program Directors	25.3%	$45,090	27.1%	11,000
23. Talent Directors	25.3%	$45,090	27.1%	11,000
24. Technical Directors/Managers	25.3%	$45,090	27.1%	11,000
25. Clinical Psychologists	23.4%	$50,420	18.1%	18,000

Best-Paying Part-Time Jobs

Job	Percent Part-Time Workers	Annual Earnings	Percent Growth	Annual Openings
1. Pharmacists	24.6%	$74,890	24.3%	20,000
2. Physician Assistants	24.6%	$63,970	53.5%	5,000
3. Teachers, Postsecondary	32.3%	$52,115	23.5%	184,000
4. Clinical Psychologists	23.4%	$50,420	18.1%	18,000
5. Clinical, Counseling, and School Psychologists	23.4%	$50,420	18.1%	18,000
6. Counseling Psychologists	23.4%	$50,420	18.1%	18,000
7. Registered Nurses	26.3%	$46,670	25.6%	140,000
8. Directors—Stage, Motion Pictures, Television, and Radio	25.3%	$45,090	27.1%	11,000
9. Producers	25.3%	$45,090	27.1%	11,000
10. Producers and Directors	25.3%	$45,090	27.1%	11,000
11. Program Directors	25.3%	$45,090	27.1%	11,000
12. Talent Directors	25.3%	$45,090	27.1%	11,000
13. Technical Directors/Managers	25.3%	$45,090	27.1%	11,000
14. Athletes and Sports Competitors	25.3%	$43,730	22.5%	3,000
15. Vocational Education Teachers, Secondary School	42.5%	$43,590	13.4%	7,000
16. Signal and Track Switch Repairers	24.3%	$42,390	11.5%	16,000
17. Multi-Media Artists and Animators	24.0%	$42,270	22.2%	8,000
18. Farmers and Ranchers	27.7%	$42,170	−25.4%	146,000
19. Public Relations Specialists	25.3%	$41,010	36.1%	19,000
20. Flight Attendants	45.7%	$40,600	18.4%	8,000
21. Dietitians and Nutritionists	29.1%	$40,410	15.2%	5,000
22. Musicians and Singers	53.5%	$40,320	20.1%	33,000
23. Musicians, Instrumental	53.5%	$40,320	20.1%	33,000
24. Singers	53.5%	$40,320	20.1%	33,000
25. Gaming Supervisors	48.8%	$39,240	18.4%	2,000

Fastest-Growing Part-Time Jobs

Job	Percent Part-Time Workers	Annual Earnings	Percent Growth	Annual Openings
1. Personal and Home Care Aides	42.4%	$16,140	62.5%	84,000
2. Social and Human Service Assistants	42.4%	$23,070	54.2%	45,000
3. Physician Assistants	24.6%	$63,970	53.5%	5,000
4. Home Health Aides	26.4%	$17,590	47.3%	120,000
5. Physical Therapist Aides	34.5%	$20,300	46.3%	7,000
6. Physical Therapist Assistants	34.5%	$35,280	44.8%	9,000
7. Fitness Trainers and Aerobics Instructors	42.5%	$23,340	40.3%	19,000
8. Veterinary Assistants and Laboratory Animal Caretakers	38.1%	$17,470	39.8%	8,000
9. Occupational Therapist Assistants	24.9%	$35,840	39.7%	3,000
10. Dental Assistants	39.7%	$26,720	37.2%	16,000
11. Gaming Change Persons and Booth Cashiers	57.2%	$18,990	36.1%	13,000
12. Public Relations Specialists	25.3%	$41,010	36.1%	19,000
13. Ambulance Drivers and Attendants, Except Emergency Medical Technicians	34.5%	$18,890	33.7%	3,000
14. Hotel, Motel, and Resort Desk Clerks	25.8%	$16,920	33.4%	73,000
15. Interviewers, Except Eligibility and Loan	32.5%	$21,880	33.4%	53,000
16. Amusement and Recreation Attendants	48.8%	$14,600	32.4%	62,000
17. Gaming Dealers	48.8%	$13,680	32.4%	28,000
18. Combined Food Preparation and Serving Workers, Including Fast Food	57.4%	$14,120	30.5%	737,000
19. Landscaping and Groundskeeping Workers	28.5%	$19,120	29.0%	193,000
20. Directors—Stage, Motion Pictures, Television, and Radio	25.3%	$45,090	27.1%	11,000
21. Producers	25.3%	$45,090	27.1%	11,000
22. Producers and Directors	25.3%	$45,090	27.1%	11,000
23. Program Directors	25.3%	$45,090	27.1%	11,000
24. Talent Directors	25.3%	$45,090	27.1%	11,000
25. Technical Directors/Managers	25.3%	$45,090	27.1%	11,000

Part-Time Jobs with the Most Openings

Job	Percent Part-Time Workers	Annual Earnings	Percent Growth	Annual Openings
1. Cashiers	57.2%	$14,950	14.5%	1,125,000
2. Retail Salespersons	40.2%	$17,150	12.4%	1,124,000
3. Combined Food Preparation and Serving Workers, Including Fast Food	57.4%	$14,120	30.5%	737,000
4. Office Clerks, General	30.7%	$21,780	15.9%	676,000
5. Waiters and Waitresses	57.0%	$13,720	18.3%	596,000
6. Freight, Stock, and Material Movers, Hand	38.4%	$19,440	13.9%	519,000
7. Laborers and Freight, Stock, and Material Movers, Hand	38.4%	$19,440	13.9%	519,000
8. Janitors and Cleaners, Except Maids and Housekeeping Cleaners	32.3%	$17,900	13.5%	507,000
9. Child Care Workers	43.4%	$16,030	10.6%	370,000
10. Bookkeeping, Accounting, and Auditing Clerks	32.8%	$26,540	2.0%	298,000
11. Receptionists and Information Clerks	35.1%	$20,650	23.7%	269,000
12. Nursing Aides, Orderlies, and Attendants	26.4%	$19,290	23.5%	268,000
13. Teacher Assistants	46.8%	$18,070	23.9%	256,000
14. Food Preparation Workers	57.4%	$15,910	16.9%	231,000
15. Counter Attendants, Cafeteria, Food Concession, and Coffee Shop	62.9%	$14,760	14.4%	216,000
16. Landscaping and Groundskeeping Workers	28.5%	$19,120	29.0%	193,000
17. Teachers, Postsecondary	32.3%	$52,115	23.5%	184,000
18. Cooks, Restaurant	38.5%	$18,480	21.7%	158,000
19. Counter and Rental Clerks	50.8%	$16,750	19.4%	150,000
20. Farmers and Ranchers	27.7%	$42,170	−25.4%	146,000
21. Registered Nurses	26.3%	$46,670	25.6%	140,000
22. Home Health Aides	26.4%	$17,590	47.3%	120,000
23. Cooks, Institution and Cafeteria	38.5%	$17,750	7.6%	110,000
24. First-Line Supervisors/Managers of Farming, Fishing, and Forestry Workers	25.6%	$33,330	13.0%	89,000
25. Food Servers, Nonrestaurant	58.2%	$15,310	16.4%	85,000

Best Jobs with a High Percentage of Self-Employed Workers

More than 10 percent of the workforce is self-employed. Although you may think of the self-employed as having similar jobs, they actually work in an enormous range of situations, fields, and work environments that you may not have considered.

Among the self-employed are people who own small or large businesses; professionals such as lawyers, psychologists, and medical doctors; part-time workers; people working on a contract basis for one or more employers; people running home consulting or other businesses; and people in many other situations. They may go to the same office every day, like an attorney might; visit multiple employers during the course of a week; or do most of their work from home. Some work part time, others full time, some as a way to have fun, some so they can spend time with their kids or go to school.

The point is that there is an enormous range of situations, and one of them could make sense for you now or in the future.

The 100 Jobs with the Highest Percentage of Self-Employed Workers

Job	Percent Self-Employed Workers	Annual Earnings	Percent Growth	Annual Openings
1. Farmers and Ranchers	99.7%	$42,170	−25.4%	146,000
2. Real Estate Sales Agents	69.7%	$28,570	9.5%	28,000
3. Graphic Designers	60.9%	$36,020	26.7%	28,000
4. Multi-Media Artists and Animators	60.9%	$42,270	22.2%	8,000
5. Real Estate Brokers	59.6%	$51,370	9.6%	8,000
6. First-Line Supervisors/Managers of Landscaping, Lawn Service, and Groundskeeping Workers	58.8%	$32,100	20.1%	10,000
7. Lawn Service Managers	58.8%	$32,100	20.1%	10,000
8. Chiropractors	57.7%	$68,420	23.4%	3,000
9. Child Care Workers	57.5%	$16,030	10.6%	370,000
10. Gaming Managers	49.4%	$53,450	30.0%	fewer than 500
11. General and Operations Managers	49.4%	$65,010	15.2%	235,000
12. Medical and Health Services Managers	49.4%	$59,220	32.3%	27,000
13. Network and Computer Systems Administrators	49.4%	$53,770	81.9%	18,000
14. Social and Community Service Managers	49.4%	$41,260	24.8%	13,000

The 100 Jobs with the Highest Percentage of Self-Employed Workers

Job	Percent Self-Employed Workers	Annual Earnings	Percent Growth	Annual Openings
15. Adult Literacy, Remedial Education, and GED Teachers and Instructors	48.9%	$35,220	19.4%	12,000
16. Self-Enrichment Education Teachers	48.9%	$28,880	18.5%	34,000
17. Management Analysts	46.4%	$57,970	28.9%	50,000
18. Interior Designers	46.3%	$39,580	17.4%	7,000
19. Hairdressers, Hairstylists, and Cosmetologists	46.0%	$18,260	13.0%	78,000
20. Makeup Artists, Theatrical and Performance	46.0%	$30,240	11.4%	27,000
21. Painters, Construction and Maintenance	45.8%	$28,420	19.1%	67,000
22. Paperhangers	45.8%	$31,330	20.2%	3,000
23. Taxi Drivers and Chauffeurs	44.1%	$17,920	24.4%	37,000
24. Tile and Marble Setters	44.0%	$35,390	15.6%	5,000
25. Photographers	43.8%	$23,040	17.0%	13,000
26. Photographers, Scientific	43.8%	$23,040	17.0%	13,000
27. Professional Photographers	43.8%	$23,040	17.0%	13,000
28. Clinical Psychologists	43.7%	$50,420	18.1%	18,000
29. Clinical, Counseling, and School Psychologists	43.7%	$50,420	18.1%	18,000
30. Counseling Psychologists	43.7%	$50,420	18.1%	18,000
31. Educational Psychologists	43.7%	$50,420	18.1%	18,000
32. Industrial-Organizational Psychologists	43.7%	$66,010	18.1%	18,000
33. Property, Real Estate, and Community Association Managers	40.2%	$36,290	22.7%	24,000
34. Veterinarians	39.6%	$62,000	31.8%	2,000
35. Chefs and Head Cooks	37.5%	$26,800	9.0%	35,000
36. First-Line Supervisors/Managers of Food Preparation and Serving Workers	37.5%	$23,600	12.7%	136,000
37. First-Line Supervisors/Managers of Personal Service Workers	37.5%	$28,040	15.1%	8,000
38. Food Service Managers	37.5%	$33,630	15.0%	55,000
39. Optometrists	37.5%	$85,650	18.7%	1,000
40. Manicurists and Pedicurists	37.3%	$16,700	26.5%	5,000
41. First-Line Supervisors/Managers of Non-Retail Sales Workers	36.9%	$51,490	5.8%	41,000

(continued)

(continued)

The 100 Jobs with the Highest Percentage of Self-Employed Workers

Job	Percent Self-Employed Workers	Annual Earnings	Percent Growth	Annual Openings
42. First-Line Supervisors/Managers of Retail Sales Workers	36.9%	$28,590	8.1%	206,000
43. Boat Builders and Shipwrights	36.8%	$33,470	8.2%	161,000
44. Brattice Builders	36.8%	$33,470	8.2%	161,000
45. Carpenter Assemblers and Repairers	36.8%	$33,470	8.2%	161,000
46. Carpenters	36.8%	$33,470	8.2%	161,000
47. Construction Carpenters	36.8%	$33,470	8.2%	161,000
48. Rough Carpenters	36.8%	$33,470	8.2%	161,000
49. Ship Carpenters and Joiners	36.8%	$33,470	8.2%	161,000
50. Lawyers	36.0%	$88,760	18.0%	35,000
51. Art Directors	31.9%	$59,800	21.1%	6,000
52. Commercial and Industrial Designers	31.9%	$49,820	23.8%	7,000
53. Exhibit Designers	31.9%	$33,460	27.0%	2,000
54. Fashion Designers	31.9%	$49,530	20.3%	2,000
55. Floral Designers	31.9%	$19,280	14.9%	15,000
56. Set and Exhibit Designers	31.9%	$33,460	27.0%	2,000
57. Set Designers	31.9%	$33,460	27.0%	2,000
58. Drywall and Ceiling Tile Installers	31.5%	$33,000	9.4%	19,000
59. Drywall Installers	31.5%	$33,000	9.4%	19,000
60. Athletes and Sports Competitors	31.4%	$43,730	22.5%	3,000
61. Coaches and Scouts	31.4%	$29,020	17.6%	19,000
62. Caption Writers	31.2%	$42,450	28.4%	18,000
63. Copy Writers	31.2%	$42,450	28.4%	18,000
64. Creative Writers	31.2%	$42,450	28.4%	18,000
65. Editors	31.2%	$39,960	22.6%	14,000
66. Poets and Lyricists	31.2%	$42,450	28.4%	18,000
67. Technical Writers	31.2%	$49,360	29.6%	5,000
68. Writers and Authors	31.2%	$42,450	28.4%	18,000
69. Roofers	30.9%	$29,460	19.4%	38,000
70. Architects, Except Landscape and Naval	30.8%	$55,470	18.5%	4,000
71. Insurance Sales Agents	30.1%	$38,890	3.3%	43,000
72. Brickmasons and Blockmasons	27.9%	$41,590	12.5%	18,000

The 100 Jobs with the Highest Percentage of Self-Employed Workers

Job	Percent Self-Employed Workers	Annual Earnings	Percent Growth	Annual Openings
73. Landscaping and Groundskeeping Workers	27.9%	$19,120	29.0%	193,000
74. Stonemasons	27.9%	$32,470	20.8%	2,000
75. Composers	25.8%	$33,720	13.1%	9,000
76. Music Arrangers and Orchestrators	25.8%	$33,720	13.1%	9,000
77. Music Directors	25.8%	$33,720	13.1%	9,000
78. Music Directors and Composers	25.8%	$33,720	13.1%	9,000
79. Musicians and Singers	25.8%	$40,320	20.1%	33,000
80. Musicians, Instrumental	25.8%	$40,320	20.1%	33,000
81. Singers	25.8%	$40,320	20.1%	33,000
82. Nonfarm Animal Caretakers	24.0%	$16,570	21.6%	20,000
83. Actors	23.7%	$20,540	26.7%	20,000
84. Directors—Stage, Motion Pictures, Television, and Radio	23.7%	$45,090	27.1%	11,000
85. Film and Video Editors	23.7%	$36,910	25.8%	2,000
86. Producers	23.7%	$45,090	27.1%	11,000
87. Producers and Directors	23.7%	$45,090	27.1%	11,000
88. Program Directors	23.7%	$45,090	27.1%	11,000
89. Talent Directors	23.7%	$45,090	27.1%	11,000
90. Technical Directors/Managers	23.7%	$45,090	27.1%	11,000
91. Sales Agents, Financial Services	22.4%	$59,690	22.3%	55,000
92. Sales Agents, Securities and Commodities	22.4%	$59,690	22.3%	55,000
93. Securities, Commodities, and Financial Services Sales Agents	22.4%	$59,690	22.3%	55,000
94. Automotive Master Mechanics	21.6%	$29,510	18.0%	104,000
95. Automotive Service Technicians and Mechanics	21.6%	$29,510	18.0%	104,000
96. Automotive Specialty Technicians	21.6%	$29,510	18.0%	104,000
97. Landscape Architects	21.6%	$46,710	31.1%	1,000
98. Appraisers and Assessors of Real Estate	21.1%	$38,950	18.0%	6,000
99. Appraisers, Real Estate	21.1%	$38,950	18.0%	6,000
100. Assessors	21.1%	$38,950	18.0%	6,000

Best Jobs Overall for Self-Employed Workers

Job	Percent Self-Employed Workers	Annual Earnings	Percent Growth	Annual Openings
1. Management Analysts	46.4%	$57,970	28.9%	50,000
2. Medical and Health Services Managers	49.4%	$59,220	32.3%	27,000
3. Sales Agents, Financial Services	22.4%	$59,690	22.3%	55,000
4. Sales Agents, Securities and Commodities	22.4%	$59,690	22.3%	55,000
5. Securities, Commodities, and Financial Services Sales Agents	22.4%	$59,690	22.3%	55,000
6. Network and Computer Systems Administrators	49.4%	$53,770	81.9%	18,000
7. General and Operations Managers	49.4%	$65,010	15.2%	235,000
8. Lawyers	36.0%	$88,760	18.0%	35,000
9. Graphic Designers	60.9%	$36,020	26.7%	28,000
10. Caption Writers	31.2%	$42,450	28.4%	18,000
11. Copy Writers	31.2%	$42,450	28.4%	18,000
12. Creative Writers	31.2%	$42,450	28.4%	18,000
13. Poets and Lyricists	31.2%	$42,450	28.4%	18,000
14. Writers and Authors	31.2%	$42,450	28.4%	18,000
15. Musicians and Singers	25.8%	$40,320	20.1%	33,000
16. Musicians, Instrumental	25.8%	$40,320	20.1%	33,000
17. Singers	25.8%	$40,320	20.1%	33,000
18. Landscaping and Groundskeeping Workers	27.9%	$19,120	29.0%	193,000
19. Property, Real Estate, and Community Association Managers	40.2%	$36,290	22.7%	24,000
20. Industrial-Organizational Psychologists	43.7%	$66,010	18.1%	18,000
21. Automotive Master Mechanics	21.6%	$29,510	18.0%	104,000
22. Automotive Service Technicians and Mechanics	21.6%	$29,510	18.0%	104,000
23. Automotive Specialty Technicians	21.6%	$29,510	18.0%	104,000
24. Painters, Construction and Maintenance	45.8%	$28,420	19.1%	67,000
25. Directors—Stage, Motion Pictures, Television, and Radio	23.7%	$45,090	27.1%	11,000

Best-Paying Jobs for Self-Employed Workers

Job	Percent Self-Employed Workers	Annual Earnings	Percent Growth	Annual Openings
1. Lawyers	36.0%	$88,760	18.0%	35,000
2. Optometrists	37.5%	$85,650	18.7%	1,000
3. Chiropractors	57.7%	$68,420	23.4%	3,000
4. Industrial-Organizational Psychologists	43.7%	$66,010	18.1%	18,000
5. General and Operations Managers	49.4%	$65,010	15.2%	235,000
6. Veterinarians	39.6%	$62,000	31.8%	2,000
7. Art Directors	31.9%	$59,800	21.1%	6,000
8. Sales Agents, Financial Services	22.4%	$59,690	22.3%	55,000
9. Sales Agents, Securities and Commodities	22.4%	$59,690	22.3%	55,000
10. Securities, Commodities, and Financial Services Sales Agents	22.4%	$59,690	22.3%	55,000
11. Medical and Health Services Managers	49.4%	$59,220	32.3%	27,000
12. Management Analysts	46.4%	$57,970	28.9%	50,000
13. Architects, Except Landscape and Naval	30.8%	$55,470	18.5%	4,000
14. Network and Computer Systems Administrators	49.4%	$53,770	81.9%	18,000
15. Gaming Managers	49.4%	$53,450	30.0%	fewer than 500
16. First-Line Supervisors/Managers of Non-Retail Sales Workers	36.9%	$51,490	5.8%	41,000
17. Real Estate Brokers	59.6%	$51,370	9.6%	8,000
18. Clinical Psychologists	43.7%	$50,420	18.1%	18,000
19. Clinical, Counseling, and School Psychologists	43.7%	$50,420	18.1%	18,000
20. Counseling Psychologists	43.7%	$50,420	18.1%	18,000
21. Educational Psychologists	43.7%	$50,420	18.1%	18,000
22. Commercial and Industrial Designers	31.9%	$49,820	23.8%	7,000
23. Fashion Designers	31.9%	$49,530	20.3%	2,000
24. Technical Writers	31.2%	$49,360	29.6%	5,000
25. Landscape Architects	21.6%	$46,710	31.1%	1,000

Fastest-Growing Jobs for Self-Employed Workers

Job	Percent Self-Employed Workers	Annual Earnings	Percent Growth	Annual Openings
1. Network and Computer Systems Administrators	49.4%	$53,770	81.9%	18,000
2. Medical and Health Services Managers	49.4%	$59,220	32.3%	27,000
3. Veterinarians	39.6%	$62,000	31.8%	2,000
4. Landscape Architects	21.6%	$46,710	31.1%	1,000
5. Gaming Managers	49.4%	$53,450	30.0%	fewer than 500
6. Technical Writers	31.2%	$49,360	29.6%	5,000
7. Landscaping and Groundskeeping Workers	27.9%	$19,120	29.0%	193,000
8. Management Analysts	46.4%	$57,970	28.9%	50,000
9. Caption Writers	31.2%	$42,450	28.4%	18,000
10. Copy Writers	31.2%	$42,450	28.4%	18,000
11. Creative Writers	31.2%	$42,450	28.4%	18,000
12. Poets and Lyricists	31.2%	$42,450	28.4%	18,000
13. Writers and Authors	31.2%	$42,450	28.4%	18,000
14. Directors—Stage, Motion Pictures, Television, and Radio	23.7%	$45,090	27.1%	11,000
15. Producers	23.7%	$45,090	27.1%	11,000
16. Producers and Directors	23.7%	$45,090	27.1%	11,000
17. Program Directors	23.7%	$45,090	27.1%	11,000
18. Talent Directors	23.7%	$45,090	27.1%	11,000
19. Technical Directors/Managers	23.7%	$45,090	27.1%	11,000
20. Exhibit Designers	31.9%	$33,460	27.0%	2,000
21. Set and Exhibit Designers	31.9%	$33,460	27.0%	2,000
22. Set Designers	31.9%	$33,460	27.0%	2,000
23. Actors	23.7%	$20,540	26.7%	20,000
24. Graphic Designers	60.9%	$36,020	26.7%	28,000
25. Manicurists and Pedicurists	37.3%	$16,700	26.5%	5,000

Jobs with the Most Openings for Self-Employed Workers

Job	Percent Self-Employed Workers	Annual Earnings	Percent Growth	Annual Openings
1. Child Care Workers	57.5%	$16,030	10.6%	370,000
2. General and Operations Managers	49.4%	$65,010	15.2%	235,000
3. First-Line Supervisors/Managers of Retail Sales Workers	36.9%	$28,590	8.1%	206,000
4. Landscaping and Groundskeeping Workers	27.9%	$19,120	29.0%	193,000
5. Boat Builders and Shipwrights	36.8%	$33,470	8.2%	161,000
6. Brattice Builders	36.8%	$33,470	8.2%	161,000
7. Carpenter Assemblers and Repairers	36.8%	$33,470	8.2%	161,000
8. Carpenters	36.8%	$33,470	8.2%	161,000
9. Construction Carpenters	36.8%	$33,470	8.2%	161,000
10. Rough Carpenters	36.8%	$33,470	8.2%	161,000
11. Ship Carpenters and Joiners	36.8%	$33,470	8.2%	161,000
12. Farmers and Ranchers	99.7%	$42,170	−25.4%	146,000
13. First-Line Supervisors/Managers of Food Preparation and Serving Workers	37.5%	$23,600	12.7%	136,000
14. Automotive Master Mechanics	21.6%	$29,510	18.0%	104,000
15. Automotive Service Technicians and Mechanics	21.6%	$29,510	18.0%	104,000
16. Automotive Specialty Technicians	21.6%	$29,510	18.0%	104,000
17. Hairdressers, Hairstylists, and Cosmetologists	46.0%	$18,260	13.0%	78,000
18. Painters, Construction and Maintenance	45.8%	$28,420	19.1%	67,000
19. Food Service Managers	37.5%	$33,630	15.0%	55,000
20. Sales Agents, Financial Services	22.4%	$59,690	22.3%	55,000
21. Sales Agents, Securities and Commodities	22.4%	$59,690	22.3%	55,000
22. Securities, Commodities, and Financial Services Sales Agents	22.4%	$59,690	22.3%	55,000
23. Management Analysts	46.4%	$57,970	28.9%	50,000
24. Insurance Sales Agents	30.1%	$38,890	3.3%	43,000
25. First-Line Supervisors/Managers of Non-Retail Sales Workers	36.9%	$51,490	5.8%	41,000

Best Jobs Employing a High Percentage of Women

These are our most controversial lists, and we knew we would create some controversy when we first included the best jobs lists with high percentages of men and women in earlier editions. But these lists are not meant to restrict women or men from considering job options—our reason for including these lists is exactly the opposite. We hope the lists help people see possibilities that they might not otherwise have considered.

The fact is that jobs with high percentages of women or high percentages of men offer good opportunities for both men and women if they want to do one of these jobs. So we suggest that women browse the lists of jobs that employ high percentages of men and that men browse the lists of jobs with high percentages of women. There are jobs among both lists that pay well, and women or men who are interested in them and who have or can obtain the necessary education and training should consider them.

An interesting and unfortunate tidbit to bring up at your next party is that the average earnings for the 100 jobs with the highest percentage of women is $30,624, compared to average earnings of $35,065 for the 100 jobs with the highest percentage of men.

The 100 Jobs Employing the Highest Percentage of Women

Job	Percent Women	Annual Earnings	Percent Growth	Annual Openings
1. Legal Secretaries	98.8%	$34,610	20.3%	36,000
2. Medical Secretaries	98.8%	$24,670	19.0%	40,000
3. Kindergarten Teachers, Except Special Education	98.0%	$38,740	14.5%	23,000
4. Preschool Teachers, Except Special Education	98.0%	$18,640	20.0%	55,000
5. Dental Assistants	96.6%	$26,720	37.2%	16,000
6. Child Care Workers	95.2%	$16,030	10.6%	370,000
7. Licensed Practical and Licensed Vocational Nurses	94.9%	$30,670	20.3%	58,000
8. Receptionists and Information Clerks	94.2%	$20,650	23.7%	269,000
9. Registered Nurses	93.8%	$46,670	25.6%	140,000
10. Teacher Assistants	92.8%	$18,070	23.9%	256,000
11. Bookkeeping, Accounting, and Auditing Clerks	92.0%	$26,540	2.0%	298,000
12. Dietitians and Nutritionists	91.9%	$40,410	15.2%	5,000
13. Hairdressers, Hairstylists, and Cosmetologists	90.8%	$18,260	13.0%	78,000
14. Makeup Artists, Theatrical and Performance	90.8%	$30,240	11.4%	27,000
15. Manicurists and Pedicurists	90.8%	$16,700	26.5%	5,000

The 100 Jobs Employing the Highest Percentage of Women

Job	Percent Women	Annual Earnings	Percent Growth	Annual Openings
16. Home Health Aides	88.9%	$17,590	47.3%	120,000
17. Nursing Aides, Orderlies, and Attendants	88.9%	$19,290	23.5%	268,000
18. Reservation and Transportation Ticket Agents	88.4%	$24,090	14.5%	39,000
19. Reservation and Transportation Ticket Agents and Travel Clerks	88.4%	$24,090	14.5%	39,000
20. Travel Clerks	88.4%	$24,090	14.5%	39,000
21. Hotel, Motel, and Resort Desk Clerks	87.3%	$16,920	33.4%	73,000
22. Signal and Track Switch Repairers	86.6%	$42,390	11.5%	16,000
23. Cost Estimators	86.5%	$46,960	16.5%	28,000
24. Pharmacists	86.1%	$74,890	24.3%	20,000
25. Physician Assistants	86.1%	$63,970	53.5%	5,000
26. Elementary School Teachers, Except Special Education	85.5%	$41,080	13.2%	144,000
27. Personal and Home Care Aides	85.1%	$16,140	62.5%	84,000
28. Social and Human Service Assistants	85.1%	$23,070	54.2%	45,000
29. Special Education Teachers, Middle School	83.7%	$40,010	24.4%	6,000
30. Special Education Teachers, Preschool, Kindergarten, and Elementary School	83.7%	$42,110	36.8%	15,000
31. Special Education Teachers, Secondary School	83.7%	$42,780	24.6%	8,000
32. Billing, Cost, and Rate Clerks	82.4%	$25,350	8.5%	69,000
33. Flight Attendants	81.6%	$40,600	18.4%	8,000
34. Cardiovascular Technologists and Technicians	81.5%	$35,010	34.9%	3,000
35. Dental Hygienists	81.5%	$54,700	37.1%	5,000
36. Emergency Medical Technicians and Paramedics	81.5%	$23,170	31.3%	19,000
37. Medical Assistants	81.5%	$23,610	57.0%	18,700
38. Medical Records and Health Information Technicians	81.5%	$23,530	49.0%	14,000
39. Medical Transcriptionists	81.5%	$26,460	29.8%	15,000
40. Pharmacy Technicians	81.5%	$21,630	36.4%	22,000
41. Surgical Technologists	81.5%	$30,090	34.7%	8,000
42. Interviewers, Except Eligibility and Loan	81.0%	$21,880	33.4%	53,000
43. Occupational Therapist Assistants	81.0%	$35,840	39.7%	3,000
44. Pharmacy Aides	81.0%	$18,010	19.5%	9,000
45. Office Clerks, General	80.0%	$21,780	15.9%	676,000
46. Cashiers	79.8%	$14,950	14.5%	1,125,000

(continued)

(continued)

The 100 Jobs Employing the Highest Percentage of Women

Job	Percent Women	Annual Earnings	Percent Growth	Annual Openings
47. Gaming Change Persons and Booth Cashiers	79.8%	$18,990	36.1%	13,000
48. Paralegals and Legal Assistants	79.8%	$36,670	33.2%	23,000
49. File Clerks	78.7%	$19,490	9.1%	49,000
50. Ambulance Drivers and Attendants, Except Emergency Medical Technicians	78.5%	$18,890	33.7%	3,000
51. Physical Therapist Aides	78.5%	$20,300	46.3%	7,000
52. Physical Therapist Assistants	78.5%	$35,280	44.8%	9,000
53. Waiters and Waitresses	78.5%	$13,720	18.3%	596,000
54. Human Resources Assistants, Except Payroll and Timekeeping	78.1%	$29,470	19.3%	25,000
55. Diagnostic Medical Sonographers	77.7%	$46,980	26.1%	3,000
56. Dietetic Technicians	77.7%	$21,790	27.6%	3,000
57. Respiratory Therapy Technicians	77.7%	$33,840	34.6%	3,000
58. Library Assistants, Clerical	77.6%	$18,580	19.7%	26,000
59. Statement Clerks	77.1%	$25,350	8.5%	69,000
60. Medical and Clinical Laboratory Technicians	76.8%	$28,810	19.0%	19,000
61. Medical and Clinical Laboratory Technologists	76.8%	$42,240	17.0%	19,000
62. Billing and Posting Clerks and Machine Operators	75.5%	$25,350	8.5%	69,000
63. Billing, Posting, and Calculating Machine Operators	75.5%	$25,350	8.5%	69,000
64. Customer Service Representatives, Utilities	75.5%	$25,430	32.4%	359,000
65. Stock Clerks and Order Fillers	75.5%	$19,060	8.5%	467,000
66. Claims Adjusters, Examiners, and Investigators	74.8%	$42,440	15.1%	25,000
67. Claims Examiners, Property and Casualty Insurance	74.8%	$42,440	15.1%	25,000
68. Court Clerks	74.8%	$27,090	12.0%	14,000
69. Court, Municipal, and License Clerks	74.8%	$27,090	12.0%	14,000
70. Insurance Adjusters, Examiners, and Investigators	74.8%	$42,440	15.1%	25,000
71. License Clerks	74.8%	$27,090	12.0%	14,000
72. Municipal Clerks	74.8%	$27,090	12.0%	14,000
73. Adjustment Clerks	74.6%	$25,430	32.4%	359,000
74. Customer Service Representatives	74.6%	$25,430	32.4%	359,000

The 100 Jobs Employing the Highest Percentage of Women

Job	Percent Women	Annual Earnings	Percent Growth	Annual Openings
75. Combined Food Preparation and Serving Workers, Including Fast Food	74.4%	$14,120	30.5%	737,000
76. Food Preparation Workers	74.4%	$15,910	16.9%	231,000
77. Audiologists	74.2%	$46,900	44.7%	1,000
78. Massage Therapists	74.2%	$28,050	30.4%	7,000
79. Occupational Therapists	74.2%	$51,370	33.9%	4,000
80. Physical Therapists	74.2%	$56,570	33.3%	6,000
81. Respiratory Therapists	74.2%	$39,370	34.8%	4,000
82. Speech-Language Pathologists	74.2%	$48,520	39.2%	4,000
83. Substance Abuse and Behavioral Disorder Counselors	74.2%	$29,870	35.0%	7,000
84. Nuclear Medicine Technologists	74.0%	$47,400	22.4%	1,000
85. Radiation Therapists	74.0%	$49,050	22.8%	1,000
86. Radiologic Technicians	74.0%	$37,680	23.1%	13,000
87. Radiologic Technologists	74.0%	$37,680	23.1%	13,000
88. Radiologic Technologists and Technicians	74.0%	$37,680	23.1%	13,000
89. Counter Attendants, Cafeteria, Food Concession, and Coffee Shop	73.4%	$14,760	14.4%	216,000
90. Child, Family, and School Social Workers	69.3%	$32,950	26.9%	35,000
91. Medical and Public Health Social Workers	69.3%	$36,410	31.6%	13,000
92. Mental Health and Substance Abuse Social Workers	69.3%	$32,080	39.1%	10,000
93. Probation Officers and Correctional Treatment Specialists	69.3%	$38,780	23.8%	14,000
94. Bill and Account Collectors	69.2%	$25,960	25.3%	71,000
95. Educational, Vocational, and School Counselors	67.8%	$43,470	25.3%	22,000
96. Marriage and Family Therapists	67.8%	$32,720	29.9%	2,000
97. Mental Health Counselors	67.8%	$29,050	21.7%	7,000
98. Rehabilitation Counselors	67.8%	$25,610	23.6%	12,000
99. Residential Advisors	67.8%	$19,680	24.0%	9,000
100. Hosts and Hostesses, Restaurant, Lounge, and Coffee Shop	66.9%	$14,920	13.0%	84,000

Best Jobs Overall Employing High Percentages of Women

Job	Percent Women	Annual Earnings	Percent Growth	Annual Openings
1. Registered Nurses	93.8%	$46,670	25.6%	140,000
2. Adjustment Clerks	74.6%	$25,430	32.4%	359,000
3. Customer Service Representatives	74.6%	$25,430	32.4%	359,000
4. Customer Service Representatives, Utilities	75.5%	$25,430	32.4%	359,000
5. Pharmacists	86.1%	$74,890	24.3%	20,000
6. Educational, Vocational, and School Counselors	67.8%	$43,470	25.3%	22,000
7. Child, Family, and School Social Workers	69.3%	$32,950	26.9%	35,000
8. Paralegals and Legal Assistants	79.8%	$36,670	33.2%	23,000
9. Special Education Teachers, Preschool, Kindergarten, and Elementary School	83.7%	$42,110	36.8%	15,000
10. Home Health Aides	88.9%	$17,590	47.3%	120,000
11. Social and Human Service Assistants	85.1%	$23,070	54.2%	45,000
12. Legal Secretaries	98.8%	$34,610	20.3%	36,000
13. Bill and Account Collectors	69.2%	$25,960	25.3%	71,000
14. Combined Food Preparation and Serving Workers, Including Fast Food	74.4%	$14,120	30.5%	737,000
15. Licensed Practical and Licensed Vocational Nurses	94.9%	$30,670	20.3%	58,000
16. Personal and Home Care Aides	85.1%	$16,140	62.5%	84,000
17. Interviewers, Except Eligibility and Loan	81.0%	$21,880	33.4%	53,000
18. Receptionists and Information Clerks	94.2%	$20,650	23.7%	269,000
19. Nursing Aides, Orderlies, and Attendants	88.9%	$19,290	23.5%	268,000
20. Hotel, Motel, and Resort Desk Clerks	87.3%	$16,920	33.4%	73,000
21. Teacher Assistants	92.8%	$18,070	23.9%	256,000
22. Cost Estimators	86.5%	$46,960	16.5%	28,000
23. Medical and Public Health Social Workers	69.3%	$36,410	31.6%	13,000
24. Elementary School Teachers, Except Special Education	85.5%	$41,080	13.2%	144,000
25. Probation Officers and Correctional Treatment Specialists	69.3%	$38,780	23.8%	14,000

Best-Paying Jobs Employing High Percentages of Women

Job	Percent Women	Annual Earnings	Percent Growth	Annual Openings
1. Pharmacists	86.1%	$74,890	24.3%	20,000
2. Physician Assistants	86.1%	$63,970	53.5%	5,000
3. Physical Therapists	74.2%	$56,570	33.3%	6,000
4. Dental Hygienists	81.5%	$54,700	37.1%	5,000
5. Occupational Therapists	74.2%	$51,370	33.9%	4,000
6. Radiation Therapists	74.0%	$49,050	22.8%	1,000
7. Speech-Language Pathologists	74.2%	$48,520	39.2%	4,000
8. Nuclear Medicine Technologists	74.0%	$47,400	22.4%	1,000
9. Diagnostic Medical Sonographers	77.7%	$46,980	26.1%	3,000
10. Cost Estimators	86.5%	$46,960	16.5%	28,000
11. Audiologists	74.2%	$46,900	44.7%	1,000
12. Registered Nurses	93.8%	$46,670	25.6%	140,000
13. Educational, Vocational, and School Counselors	67.8%	$43,470	25.3%	22,000
14. Special Education Teachers, Secondary School	83.7%	$42,780	24.6%	8,000
15. Claims Adjusters, Examiners, and Investigators	74.8%	$42,440	15.1%	25,000
16. Claims Examiners, Property and Casualty Insurance	74.8%	$42,440	15.1%	25,000
17. Insurance Adjusters, Examiners, and Investigators	74.8%	$42,440	15.1%	25,000
18. Signal and Track Switch Repairers	86.6%	$42,390	11.5%	16,000
19. Medical and Clinical Laboratory Technologists	76.8%	$42,240	17.0%	19,000
20. Special Education Teachers, Preschool, Kindergarten, and Elementary School	83.7%	$42,110	36.8%	15,000
21. Elementary School Teachers, Except Special Education	85.5%	$41,080	13.2%	144,000
22. Flight Attendants	81.6%	$40,600	18.4%	8,000
23. Dietitians and Nutritionists	91.9%	$40,410	15.2%	5,000
24. Special Education Teachers, Middle School	83.7%	$40,010	24.4%	6,000
25. Respiratory Therapists	74.2%	$39,370	34.8%	4,000

Fastest-Growing Jobs Employing High Percentages of Women

Job	Percent Women	Annual Earnings	Percent Growth	Annual Openings
1. Personal and Home Care Aides	85.1%	$16,140	62.5%	84,000
2. Medical Assistants	81.5%	$23,610	57.0%	18,700
3. Social and Human Service Assistants	85.1%	$23,070	54.2%	45,000
4. Physician Assistants	86.1%	$63,970	53.5%	5,000
5. Medical Records and Health Information Technicians	81.5%	$23,530	49.0%	14,000
6. Home Health Aides	88.9%	$17,590	47.3%	120,000
7. Physical Therapist Aides	78.5%	$20,300	46.3%	7,000
8. Physical Therapist Assistants	78.5%	$35,280	44.8%	9,000
9. Audiologists	74.2%	$46,900	44.7%	1,000
10. Occupational Therapist Assistants	81.0%	$35,840	39.7%	3,000
11. Speech-Language Pathologists	74.2%	$48,520	39.2%	4,000
12. Mental Health and Substance Abuse Social Workers	69.3%	$32,080	39.1%	10,000
13. Dental Assistants	96.6%	$26,720	37.2%	16,000
14. Dental Hygienists	81.5%	$54,700	37.1%	5,000
15. Special Education Teachers, Preschool, Kindergarten, and Elementary School	83.7%	$42,110	36.8%	15,000
16. Pharmacy Technicians	81.5%	$21,630	36.4%	22,000
17. Gaming Change Persons and Booth Cashiers	79.8%	$18,990	36.1%	13,000
18. Substance Abuse and Behavioral Disorder Counselors	74.2%	$29,870	35.0%	7,000
19. Cardiovascular Technologists and Technicians	81.5%	$35,010	34.9%	3,000
20. Respiratory Therapists	74.2%	$39,370	34.8%	4,000
21. Surgical Technologists	81.5%	$30,090	34.7%	8,000
22. Respiratory Therapy Technicians	77.7%	$33,840	34.6%	3,000
23. Occupational Therapists	74.2%	$51,370	33.9%	4,000
24. Ambulance Drivers and Attendants, Except Emergency Medical Technicians	78.5%	$18,890	33.7%	3,000
25. Hotel, Motel, and Resort Desk Clerks	87.3%	$16,920	33.4%	73,000

Jobs with the Most Openings Employing High Percentages of Women

Job	Percent Women	Annual Earnings	Percent Growth	Annual Openings
1. Cashiers	79.8%	$14,950	14.5%	1,125,000
2. Combined Food Preparation and Serving Workers, Including Fast Food	74.4%	$14,120	30.5%	737,000
3. Office Clerks, General	80.0%	$21,780	15.9%	676,000
4. Waiters and Waitresses	78.5%	$13,720	18.3%	596,000
5. Stock Clerks and Order Fillers	75.5%	$19,060	8.5%	467,000
6. Child Care Workers	95.2%	$16,030	10.6%	370,000
7. Adjustment Clerks	74.6%	$25,430	32.4%	359,000
8. Customer Service Representatives	74.6%	$25,430	32.4%	359,000
9. Customer Service Representatives, Utilities	75.5%	$25,430	32.4%	359,000
10. Bookkeeping, Accounting, and Auditing Clerks	92.0%	$26,540	2.0%	298,000
11. Receptionists and Information Clerks	94.2%	$20,650	23.7%	269,000
12. Nursing Aides, Orderlies, and Attendants	88.9%	$19,290	23.5%	268,000
13. Teacher Assistants	92.8%	$18,070	23.9%	256,000
14. Food Preparation Workers	74.4%	$15,910	16.9%	231,000
15. Counter Attendants, Cafeteria, Food Concession, and Coffee Shop	73.4%	$14,760	14.4%	216,000
16. Elementary School Teachers, Except Special Education	85.5%	$41,080	13.2%	144,000
17. Registered Nurses	93.8%	$46,670	25.6%	140,000
18. Home Health Aides	88.9%	$17,590	47.3%	120,000
19. Hosts and Hostesses, Restaurant, Lounge, and Coffee Shop	66.9%	$14,920	13.0%	84,000
20. Personal and Home Care Aides	85.1%	$16,140	62.5%	84,000
21. Hairdressers, Hairstylists, and Cosmetologists	90.8%	$18,260	13.0%	78,000
22. Hotel, Motel, and Resort Desk Clerks	87.3%	$16,920	33.4%	73,000
23. Bill and Account Collectors	69.2%	$25,960	25.3%	71,000
24. Billing and Posting Clerks and Machine Operators	75.5%	$25,350	8.5%	69,000
25. Billing, Cost, and Rate Clerks	82.4%	$25,350	8.5%	69,000

Best Jobs Employing a High Percentage of Men

If you have not already read the intro to the previous group of lists, jobs with high percentages of women, consider doing so. Much of the content there applies to these lists as well.

We did not include these groups of lists with the assumption that men should consider jobs with high percentages of men or that women should consider jobs with high percentages of women. Instead, these lists are here because we think they are interesting and perhaps helpful in considering nontraditional career options. For example, some men would do very well in and enjoy some of the jobs with high percentages of women but may not have considered them seriously. In a similar way, some women would very much enjoy and do well in some jobs that traditionally have been held by high percentages of men. We hope that these lists help you consider options that you simply did not seriously consider as a result of gender stereotypes.

The 100 Jobs Employing the Highest Percentage of Men

Job	Percent Men	Annual Earnings	Percent Growth	Annual Openings
1. Roofers	99.8%	$29,460	19.4%	38,000
2. Bus and Truck Mechanics and Diesel Engine Specialists	99.6%	$33,570	14.2%	20,000
3. Pipe Fitters	99.3%	$38,710	10.2%	49,000
4. Plumbers	99.3%	$38,710	10.2%	49,000
5. Plumbers, Pipefitters, and Steamfitters	99.3%	$38,710	10.2%	49,000
6. Heating and Air Conditioning Mechanics	99.2%	$34,020	22.3%	21,000
7. Heating, Air Conditioning, and Refrigeration Mechanics and Installers	99.2%	$34,020	22.3%	21,000
8. Refrigeration Mechanics	99.2%	$34,020	22.3%	21,000
9. Boat Builders and Shipwrights	99.0%	$33,470	8.2%	161,000
10. Brattice Builders	99.0%	$33,470	8.2%	161,000
11. Carpenter Assemblers and Repairers	99.0%	$33,470	8.2%	161,000
12. Carpenters	99.0%	$33,470	8.2%	161,000
13. Ceiling Tile Installers	99.0%	$33,000	9.4%	19,000
14. Construction Carpenters	99.0%	$33,470	8.2%	161,000
15. Rough Carpenters	99.0%	$33,470	8.2%	161,000
16. Ship Carpenters and Joiners	99.0%	$33,470	8.2%	161,000
17. Automotive Master Mechanics	98.9%	$29,510	18.0%	104,000
18. Automotive Service Technicians and Mechanics	98.9%	$29,510	18.0%	104,000

The 100 Jobs Employing the Highest Percentage of Men

Job	Percent Men	Annual Earnings	Percent Growth	Annual Openings
19. Automotive Specialty Technicians	98.9%	$29,510	18.0%	104,000
20. Automotive Body and Related Repairers	98.8%	$32,490	10.2%	18,000
21. Brickmasons and Blockmasons	98.7%	$41,590	12.5%	18,000
22. Stonemasons	98.7%	$32,470	20.8%	2,000
23. Reinforcing Iron and Rebar Workers	98.6%	$34,750	17.5%	4,000
24. Structural Iron and Steel Workers	98.6%	$38,950	18.4%	12,000
25. Operating Engineers	98.3%	$34,160	6.9%	25,000
26. Electricians	98.2%	$40,770	17.3%	66,000
27. Mobile Heavy Equipment Mechanics, Except Engines	98.2%	$35,190	14.0%	11,000
28. Drywall and Ceiling Tile Installers	97.9%	$33,000	9.4%	19,000
29. Drywall Installers	97.9%	$33,000	9.4%	19,000
30. Tile and Marble Setters	97.7%	$35,390	15.6%	5,000
31. Grader, Bulldozer, and Scraper Operators	97.3%	$34,160	6.9%	25,000
32. Painters, Construction and Maintenance	97.3%	$28,420	19.1%	67,000
33. Paperhangers	97.3%	$31,330	20.2%	3,000
34. Refuse and Recyclable Material Collectors	97.1%	$23,850	16.6%	34,000
35. Construction Laborers	97.0%	$24,070	17.0%	236,000
36. Segmental Pavers	97.0%	$26,170	26.7%	21,000
37. Commercial Divers	96.9%	$32,770	11.5%	16,000
38. Pipelaying Fitters	96.9%	$38,710	10.2%	49,000
39. Recreational Vehicle Service Technicians	96.9%	$26,410	25.4%	4,000
40. Security and Fire Alarm Systems Installers	96.9%	$30,490	23.4%	4,000
41. Team Assemblers	96.9%	$22,260	5.9%	283,000
42. Commercial Pilots	96.8%	$47,420	26.9%	1,000
43. Refractory Materials Repairers, Except Brickmasons	96.7%	$35,130	11.5%	16,000
44. Helpers—Brickmasons, Blockmasons, Stonemasons, and Tile and Marble Setters	96.6%	$23,620	14.1%	14,000
45. Helpers—Electricians	96.6%	$22,160	13.3%	27,000
46. Helpers—Pipelayers, Plumbers, Pipefitters, and Steamfitters	96.6%	$21,830	11.5%	20,000
47. Machinists	95.5%	$32,090	9.1%	28,000
48. Tractor-Trailer Truck Drivers	95.5%	$32,580	19.8%	240,000
49. Truck Drivers, Heavy	95.5%	$32,580	19.8%	240,000

(continued)

(continued)

The 100 Jobs Employing the Highest Percentage of Men

Job	Percent Men	Annual Earnings	Percent Growth	Annual Openings
50. Truck Drivers, Light or Delivery Services	95.5%	$23,330	19.2%	153,000
51. Welder-Fitters	95.5%	$28,490	19.3%	51,000
52. Welders and Cutters	95.5%	$28,490	19.3%	51,000
53. Welders, Cutters, Solderers, and Brazers	95.5%	$28,490	19.3%	51,000
54. Welders, Production	95.5%	$28,490	19.3%	51,000
55. Welding Machine Operators and Tenders	95.5%	$28,220	15.1%	9,000
56. Welding Machine Setters and Set-Up Operators	95.5%	$28,220	15.1%	9,000
57. Welding, Soldering, and Brazing Machine Setters, Operators, and Tenders	95.5%	$28,220	15.1%	9,000
58. Insulation Workers, Floor, Ceiling, and Wall	95.4%	$28,000	13.6%	12,000
59. Insulation Workers, Mechanical	95.4%	$28,000	13.6%	12,000
60. Aircraft Body and Bonded Structure Repairers	95.2%	$41,990	16.7%	11,000
61. Aircraft Engine Specialists	95.2%	$41,990	16.7%	11,000
62. Aircraft Mechanics and Service Technicians	95.2%	$41,990	16.7%	11,000
63. Airframe-and-Power-Plant Mechanics	95.2%	$41,990	16.7%	11,000
64. Mechanical Engineers	94.8%	$61,440	13.1%	7,000
65. Water and Liquid Waste Treatment Plant and System Operators	94.8%	$32,560	18.1%	6,000
66. Office Machine and Cash Register Servicers	94.3%	$32,890	14.2%	24,000
67. Elevator Installers and Repairers	94.2%	$51,630	17.2%	2,000
68. Landscaping and Groundskeeping Workers	94.1%	$19,120	29.0%	193,000
69. Computer Hardware Engineers	93.5%	$71,560	24.9%	3,000
70. Electrical Engineers	93.5%	$66,890	11.3%	8,000
71. Electronics Engineers, Except Computer	93.5%	$68,350	10.4%	6,000
72. Fitters, Structural Metal—Precision	93.5%	$28,000	19.5%	20,000
73. Industrial Truck and Tractor Operators	93.1%	$25,350	11.3%	91,000
74. Sheet Metal Workers	92.8%	$33,210	23.0%	13,000
75. Maintenance and Repair Workers, General	92.5%	$28,740	4.7%	103,000
76. Mapping Technicians	91.8%	$28,210	25.3%	7,000
77. Surveying and Mapping Technicians	91.8%	$28,210	25.3%	7,000
78. Surveying Technicians	91.8%	$28,210	25.3%	7,000
79. First-Line Supervisors and Manager/Supervisors—Construction Trades Workers	91.0%	$46,570	16.5%	43,000
80. First-Line Supervisors and Manager/Supervisors—Extractive Workers	91.0%	$46,570	16.5%	43,000

The 100 Jobs Employing the Highest Percentage of Men

Job	Percent Men	Annual Earnings	Percent Growth	Annual Openings
81. First-Line Supervisors/Managers of Construction Trades and Extraction Workers	91.0%	$46,570	16.5%	43,000
82. First-Line Supervisors/Managers of Helpers, Laborers, and Material Movers, Hand	91.0%	$36,090	18.9%	14,000
83. First-Line Supervisors/Managers of Mechanics, Installers, and Repairers	91.0%	$46,320	16.0%	38,000
84. First-Line Supervisors/Managers of Production and Operating Workers	91.0%	$42,000	1.0%	71,000
85. First-Line Supervisors/Managers of Transportation and Material-Moving Machine and Vehicle Operators	91.0%	$41,140	19.9%	17,000
86. Hazardous Materials Removal Workers	90.4%	$31,800	32.8%	9,000
87. Irradiated-Fuel Handlers	90.4%	$31,800	32.8%	9,000
88. Operating Engineers and Other Construction Equipment Operators	90.4%	$34,160	6.9%	25,000
89. Taxi Drivers and Chauffeurs	89.8%	$17,920	24.4%	37,000
90. Chemical Equipment Controllers and Operators	89.7%	$36,810	14.9%	9,000
91. Chemical Equipment Operators and Tenders	89.7%	$36,810	14.9%	9,000
92. Chemical Equipment Tenders	89.7%	$36,810	14.9%	9,000
93. Biomedical Engineers	89.6%	$59,790	31.4%	fewer than 500
94. Environmental Engineers	89.6%	$61,250	26.0%	3,000
95. Sales Engineers	89.6%	$59,720	17.7%	4,000
96. Tree Trimmers and Pruners	89.2%	$23,950	16.3%	11,000
97. Parking Lot Attendants	88.9%	$15,690	19.8%	17,000
98. Clergy	88.6%	$33,840	15.0%	12,000
99. Cleaners of Vehicles and Equipment	88.3%	$16,490	18.8%	86,000
100. First-Line Supervisors/Managers of Police and Detectives	88.0%	$59,300	13.1%	9,000

Best Jobs Overall Employing High Percentages of Men

Job	Percent Men	Annual Earnings	Percent Growth	Annual Openings
1. Tractor-Trailer Truck Drivers	95.5%	$32,580	19.8%	240,000
2. Truck Drivers, Heavy	95.5%	$32,580	19.8%	240,000
3. Electricians	98.2%	$40,770	17.3%	66,000
4. Landscaping and Groundskeeping Workers	94.1%	$19,120	29.0%	193,000
5. First-Line Supervisors and Manager/Supervisors —Construction Trades Workers	91.0%	$46,570	16.5%	43,000
6. First-Line Supervisors and Manager/Supervisors —Extractive Workers	91.0%	$46,570	16.5%	43,000
7. First-Line Supervisors/Managers of Construction Trades and Extraction Workers	91.0%	$46,570	16.5%	43,000
8. First-Line Supervisors/Managers of Mechanics, Installers, and Repairers	91.0%	$46,320	16.0%	38,000
9. Automotive Master Mechanics	98.9%	$29,510	18.0%	104,000
10. Automotive Service Technicians and Mechanics	98.9%	$29,510	18.0%	104,000
11. Automotive Specialty Technicians	98.9%	$29,510	18.0%	104,000
12. Painters, Construction and Maintenance	97.3%	$28,420	19.1%	67,000
13. Heating and Air Conditioning Mechanics	99.2%	$34,020	22.3%	21,000
14. Heating, Air Conditioning, and Refrigeration Mechanics and Installers	99.2%	$34,020	22.3%	21,000
15. Refrigeration Mechanics	99.2%	$34,020	22.3%	21,000
16. Welder-Fitters	95.5%	$28,490	19.3%	51,000
17. Welders and Cutters	95.5%	$28,490	19.3%	51,000
18. Welders, Cutters, Solderers, and Brazers	95.5%	$28,490	19.3%	51,000
19. Welders, Production	95.5%	$28,490	19.3%	51,000
20. Roofers	99.8%	$29,460	19.4%	38,000
21. Truck Drivers, Light or Delivery Services	95.5%	$23,330	19.2%	153,000
22. First-Line Supervisors/Managers of Transportation and Material-Moving Machine and Vehicle Operators	91.0%	$41,140	19.9%	17,000
23. Segmental Pavers	97.0%	$26,170	26.7%	21,000
24. Construction Laborers	97.0%	$24,070	17.0%	236,000
25. Taxi Drivers and Chauffeurs	89.8%	$17,920	24.4%	37,000

Best-Paying Jobs Employing High Percentages of Men

Job	Percent Men	Annual Earnings	Percent Growth	Annual Openings
1. Computer Hardware Engineers	93.5%	$71,560	24.9%	3,000
2. Electronics Engineers, Except Computer	93.5%	$68,350	10.4%	6,000
3. Electrical Engineers	93.5%	$66,890	11.3%	8,000
4. Mechanical Engineers	94.8%	$61,440	13.1%	7,000
5. Environmental Engineers	89.6%	$61,250	26.0%	3,000
6. Biomedical Engineers	89.6%	$59,790	31.4%	fewer than 500
7. Sales Engineers	89.6%	$59,720	17.7%	4,000
8. First-Line Supervisors/Managers of Police and Detectives	88.0%	$59,300	13.1%	9,000
9. Elevator Installers and Repairers	94.2%	$51,630	17.2%	2,000
10. Commercial Pilots	96.8%	$47,420	26.9%	1,000
11. First-Line Supervisors and Manager/Supervisors—Construction Trades Workers	91.0%	$46,570	16.5%	43,000
12. First-Line Supervisors and Manager/Supervisors—Extractive Workers	91.0%	$46,570	16.5%	43,000
13. First-Line Supervisors/Managers of Construction Trades and Extraction Workers	91.0%	$46,570	16.5%	43,000
14. First-Line Supervisors/Managers of Mechanics, Installers, and Repairers	91.0%	$46,320	16.0%	38,000
15. First-Line Supervisors/Managers of Production and Operating Workers	91.0%	$42,000	1.0%	71,000
16. Aircraft Body and Bonded Structure Repairers	95.2%	$41,990	16.7%	11,000
17. Aircraft Engine Specialists	95.2%	$41,990	16.7%	11,000
18. Aircraft Mechanics and Service Technicians	95.2%	$41,990	16.7%	11,000
19. Airframe-and-Power-Plant Mechanics	95.2%	$41,990	16.7%	11,000
20. Brickmasons and Blockmasons	98.7%	$41,590	12.5%	18,000
21. First-Line Supervisors/Managers of Transportation and Material-Moving Machine and Vehicle Operators	91.0%	$41,140	19.9%	17,000
22. Electricians	98.2%	$40,770	17.3%	66,000
23. Structural Iron and Steel Workers	98.6%	$38,950	18.4%	12,000
24. Pipe Fitters	99.3%	$38,710	10.2%	49,000
25. Pipelaying Fitters	96.9%	$38,710	10.2%	49,000

Fastest-Growing Jobs Employing High Percentages of Men

Job	Percent Men	Annual Earnings	Percent Growth	Annual Openings
1. Hazardous Materials Removal Workers	90.4%	$31,800	32.8%	9,000
2. Irradiated-Fuel Handlers	90.4%	$31,800	32.8%	9,000
3. Biomedical Engineers	89.6%	$59,790	31.4%	fewer than 500
4. Landscaping and Groundskeeping Workers	94.1%	$19,120	29.0%	193,000
5. Commercial Pilots	96.8%	$47,420	26.9%	1,000
6. Segmental Pavers	97.0%	$26,170	26.7%	21,000
7. Environmental Engineers	89.6%	$61,250	26.0%	3,000
8. Recreational Vehicle Service Technicians	96.9%	$26,410	25.4%	4,000
9. Mapping Technicians	91.8%	$28,210	25.3%	7,000
10. Surveying and Mapping Technicians	91.8%	$28,210	25.3%	7,000
11. Surveying Technicians	91.8%	$28,210	25.3%	7,000
12. Computer Hardware Engineers	93.5%	$71,560	24.9%	3,000
13. Taxi Drivers and Chauffeurs	89.8%	$17,920	24.4%	37,000
14. Security and Fire Alarm Systems Installers	96.9%	$30,490	23.4%	4,000
15. Sheet Metal Workers	92.8%	$33,210	23.0%	13,000
16. Heating and Air Conditioning Mechanics	99.2%	$34,020	22.3%	21,000
17. Heating, Air Conditioning, and Refrigeration Mechanics and Installers	99.2%	$34,020	22.3%	21,000
18. Refrigeration Mechanics	99.2%	$34,020	22.3%	21,000
19. Stonemasons	98.7%	$32,470	20.8%	2,000
20. Paperhangers	97.3%	$31,330	20.2%	3,000
21. First-Line Supervisors/Managers of Transportation and Material-Moving Machine and Vehicle Operators	91.0%	$41,140	19.9%	17,000
22. Parking Lot Attendants	88.9%	$15,690	19.8%	17,000
23. Tractor-Trailer Truck Drivers	95.5%	$32,580	19.8%	240,000
24. Truck Drivers, Heavy	95.5%	$32,580	19.8%	240,000
25. Fitters, Structural Metal—Precision	93.5%	$28,000	19.5%	20,000

Jobs with the Most Openings Employing High Percentages of Men

Job	Percent Men	Annual Earnings	Percent Growth	Annual Openings
1. Team Assemblers	96.9%	$22,260	5.9%	283,000
2. Tractor-Trailer Truck Drivers	95.5%	$32,580	19.8%	240,000
3. Truck Drivers, Heavy	95.5%	$32,580	19.8%	240,000
4. Construction Laborers	97.0%	$24,070	17.0%	236,000
5. Landscaping and Groundskeeping Workers	94.1%	$19,120	29.0%	193,000
6. Boat Builders and Shipwrights	99.0%	$33,470	8.2%	161,000
7. Brattice Builders	99.0%	$33,470	8.2%	161,000
8. Carpenter Assemblers and Repairers	99.0%	$33,470	8.2%	161,000
9. Carpenters	99.0%	$33,470	8.2%	161,000
10. Construction Carpenters	99.0%	$33,470	8.2%	161,000
11. Rough Carpenters	99.0%	$33,470	8.2%	161,000
12. Ship Carpenters and Joiners	99.0%	$33,470	8.2%	161,000
13. Truck Drivers, Light or Delivery Services	95.5%	$23,330	19.2%	153,000
14. Automotive Master Mechanics	98.9%	$29,510	18.0%	104,000
15. Automotive Service Technicians and Mechanics	98.9%	$29,510	18.0%	104,000
16. Automotive Specialty Technicians	98.9%	$29,510	18.0%	104,000
17. Maintenance and Repair Workers, General	92.5%	$28,740	4.7%	103,000
18. Industrial Truck and Tractor Operators	93.1%	$25,350	11.3%	91,000
19. Cleaners of Vehicles and Equipment	88.3%	$16,490	18.8%	86,000
20. First-Line Supervisors/Managers of Production and Operating Workers	91.0%	$42,000	1.0%	71,000
21. Painters, Construction and Maintenance	97.3%	$28,420	19.1%	67,000
22. Electricians	98.2%	$40,770	17.3%	66,000
23. Welder-Fitters	95.5%	$28,490	19.3%	51,000
24. Welders and Cutters	95.5%	$28,490	19.3%	51,000
25. Welders, Cutters, Solderers, and Brazers	95.5%	$28,490	19.3%	51,000

Best Jobs Lists Based on Levels of Education and Experience

The lists in this section organize the 500 best jobs into groups based on the education or training typically required for entry. Unlike many of the previous sections, here we do not include separate lists for highest pay, growth, or number of openings. Instead, we provide one list that includes all the occupations in our database that fit into each of the education levels and ranks them by their total combined score for earnings, growth, and number of openings.

These lists can help you identify a job with higher earnings or upward mobility but with a similar level of education to the job you now hold. For example, you will find jobs within the same level of education that require similar skills, yet one pays significantly better than the other, is projected to grow more rapidly, or has significantly more job openings per year. This information can help you leverage your present skills and experience into jobs that might provide better long-term career opportunities.

You can also use these lists to explore possible job options if you were to get additional training, education, or work experience. For example, you can use these lists to identify occupations that offer high potential and then look into the education or training required to get the jobs that interest you most.

The lists can also help you when you plan your education. For example, you might be thinking about a particular training program or college major because the pay is very good, but the lists may help you identify a job that interests you more and offers even better potential for the same general educational requirements.

The Education Levels

A clear relationship exists between education and earnings—the more education or training you have, the more you are likely to earn. The lists that follow arrange all the jobs that met our criteria for inclusion in this book (see the Introduction) by level of education, training, and work experience. These are the levels typically required for a new entrant to begin work in the occupation.

We included on each list all the occupations in our database that fit into each of the education levels. We then arranged these occupations based on their total scores for earnings, growth, and number of openings.

Once again, our lists use the same categories used by the U.S. Department of Labor for entry into various occupations.

Use the Lists to Locate Better Job Opportunities

Considering jobs with similar requirements can be very helpful because it will tell you how to leverage your present skills and experience into better-paying or more interesting opportunities. As we mentioned in the introduction to the book, doing this could, with just a bit of effort, result in big advances in pay for doing similar work.

You can also use these lists to explore career options if you were to get additional training, education, or work experience. For example, maybe you are a high school graduate interested in the field of medicine. You will find jobs related to medicine at most levels of training and education, and you can consider what jobs you might be qualified for if you were to get, say, a year or so of training. You could then work in that field and, later, get more training for an even better-paying job in the medical area. Or maybe you are enrolled or considering a four-year college degree. Looking over the lists in this section can help you identify a possible area of study or eliminate one you were considering.

The list of jobs by education should also help you when planning your education. For example, a job as restaurant cook requires long-term, on-the-job training, but its pay is quite modest. However, a flight attendant requires the same level of education, but the job pays considerably more. This looks like a good reason to be a flight attendant until you note that there are relatively few job openings per year for flight attendants, while there are many more openings for restaurant cooks. These are also very different types of jobs, and a person who would enjoy and be good at one job would not be likely to enjoy and do well in the other.

The following definitions are used by the federal government to classify jobs based on the minimum level of education or training typically required for entry into a job. We use these definitions to construct the lists in this section. Use the training and education level descriptions as guidelines that can help you understand what is generally required, but understand that you will need to learn more about specific requirements before you make a decision on one career over another.

- ▲ **Short-term on-the-job training:** It is possible to work in these occupations and achieve an average level of performance within a few days or weeks through on-the-job training.
- ▲ **Moderate-term on-the-job training:** Occupations that require this type of training can be performed adequately after a 1- to 12-month period of combined on-the-job and informal training. Typically, untrained workers begin by observing experienced workers performing tasks and are gradually moved into progressively more difficult assignments.

▲ **Long-term on-the-job training:** This type of training requires more than 12 months of on-the-job training or combined work experience and formal classroom instruction. This includes occupations that use formal apprenticeships for training workers that may take up to four years. It also includes intensive occupation-specific, employer-sponsored training like police academies. Furthermore, it includes occupations that require natural talent that must be developed over many years.

▲ **Work experience in a related occupation:** This type of job requires a worker to have experience—usually several years of experience—in a related occupation (such as police detectives, who are selected based on their experience as police patrol officers).

▲ **Postsecondary vocational training:** This training requirement can vary in length; training usually lasts from a few months up to one year. In a few instances, there may be as many as four years of training.

▲ **Associate's degree:** The associate's degree usually requires 60 to 63 semester hours to complete. A normal course load for a full-time student each semester is 15 hours. This means that it typically takes two years to complete an associate's degree.

▲ **Bachelor's degree:** A bachelor's degree usually requires 120 to 130 semester hours to complete. A full-time student usually takes four to five years to complete a bachelor's degree, depending on the complexity of courses. Traditionally, people have thought of the bachelor's degree as a four-year degree. There are some bachelor's degrees—like the Bachelor of Architecture—that are considered a first professional degree and take five or more years to complete.

▲ **Work experience plus degree:** Some jobs require work experience in a related job in addition to a degree. For example, almost all managers have worked in a related job before being promoted into a management position. Most of the jobs in this group require a four-year bachelor's degree, although some require an associate's degree or a master's degree.

▲ **Master's degree:** This degree usually requires 33 to 60 semester hours beyond the bachelor's degree. The academic master's degrees—like a Master of Arts in Political Science—usually require 33 to 36 hours. A first professional degree at the master's level—like a Master of Social Work—requires almost two years of full-time work.

▲ **Doctoral degree:** The doctoral degree prepares students for careers that consist primarily of theory development, research, and/or college teaching. This type of degree is typically the Doctor of Philosophy (Ph.D.) or Doctor of Education (Ed.D.). Normally, a requirement for a doctoral degree is the completion of a master's degree plus an additional two to three years of full-time coursework and a one- to two-semester research project and paper called the dissertation. It usually takes four to five years beyond the bachelor's degree to complete a doctoral degree.

▲ **First professional degree:** Some professional degrees require three or more years of full-time academic study beyond the bachelor's degree. A professional degree prepares students for a specific profession. It uses theory and research to teach practical applications in a professional occupation. Examples of this type of degree are Doctor of Medicine (M.D.) for physicians, Doctor of Ministry (D.Min.) for clergy, and Juris Doctor (J.D.) for attorneys.

Another Warning About the Data

We warned you in the Introduction to use caution in interpreting the data we use, and we want to do it again here. The occupational data we use is the most accurate available anywhere, but it has limitations. For example, a four-year degree in accounting, finance, or a related area is typically required for entry into the accounting profession. But some people working as accountants don't have such a degree, and others have much more education than the "minimum" required for entry.

In a similar way, people with a graduate degree will typically earn considerably more than someone with an associate's or bachelor's degree. However, some people with an associate's degree earn considerably more than the average for those with higher levels of education. In a similar way, new entrants to any job will typically earn less than the average, and some areas of the country have lower wages overall (but may also have lower costs of living).

So as you browse the lists that follow, please use them as a way to be encouraged rather than discouraged. Education and training are very important for success in the labor market, but so are ability, drive, initiative, and, yes, luck.

Having said this, we encourage you to get as much education and training as you can. It used to be that you got your schooling and never went back, but this is not a good attitude to have now. You will probably need to continue learning new things throughout your working life. This can be done by going to school, which is a good thing for many people to do. But there are also many other ways to learn, such as workshops, adult education programs, certification programs, employer training, professional conferences, Internet training, reading related books and magazines, and many others. Upgrading your computer skills—and other technical skills—is particularly important in our rapidly changing workplace, and you avoid doing so at your peril.

Best Jobs Requiring Short-Term On-the-Job Training

Job	Annual Earnings	Percent Growth	Annual Openings
1. Truck Drivers, Heavy	$32,580	19.8%	240,000
2. Security Guards	$18,600	35.4%	242,000
3. Home Health Aides	$17,590	47.3%	120,000
4. Bill and Account Collectors	$25,960	25.3%	71,000
5. Combined Food Preparation and Serving Workers, Including Fast Food	$14,120	30.5%	737,000
6. Landscaping and Groundskeeping Workers	$19,120	29.0%	193,000
7. Personal and Home Care Aides	$16,140	62.5%	84,000
8. Interviewers, Except Eligibility and Loan	$21,880	33.4%	53,000
9. Receptionists and Information Clerks	$20,650	23.7%	269,000
10. Nursing Aides, Orderlies, and Attendants	$19,290	23.5%	268,000
11. Hotel, Motel, and Resort Desk Clerks	$16,920	33.4%	73,000
12. Teacher Assistants	$18,070	23.9%	256,000
13. Brazers	$28,490	19.3%	51,000
14. Solderers	$28,490	19.3%	51,000
15. Welders, Production	$28,490	19.3%	51,000
16. Amusement and Recreation Attendants	$14,600	32.4%	62,000
17. Telemarketers	$19,210	22.2%	145,000
18. Truck Drivers, Light or Delivery Services	$23,330	19.2%	153,000
19. Production, Planning, and Expediting Clerks	$32,420	17.9%	36,000
20. Human Resources Assistants, Except Payroll and Timekeeping	$29,470	19.3%	25,000
21. Packers and Packagers, Hand	$16,280	19.3%	242,000
22. Counter and Rental Clerks	$16,750	19.4%	150,000
23. Taxi Drivers and Chauffeurs	$17,920	24.4%	37,000
24. Waiters and Waitresses	$13,720	18.3%	596,000
25. Office Clerks, General	$21,780	15.9%	676,000
26. Library Technicians	$23,790	19.5%	29,000
27. Cleaners of Vehicles and Equipment	$16,490	18.8%	86,000
28. Food Preparation Workers	$15,910	16.9%	231,000
29. Helpers—Installation, Maintenance, and Repair Workers	$21,210	18.5%	35,000
30. Freight, Stock, and Material Movers, Hand	$19,440	13.9%	519,000
31. Gaming Change Persons and Booth Cashiers	$18,990	36.1%	13,000
32. Grips and Set-Up Workers, Motion Picture Sets, Studios, and Stages	$19,440	13.9%	519,000

Best Jobs Requiring Short-Term On-the-Job Training

Job	Annual Earnings	Percent Growth	Annual Openings
33. Laborers and Freight, Stock, and Material Movers, Hand	$19,440	13.9%	519,000
34. Stevedores, Except Equipment Operators	$19,440	13.9%	519,000
35. Library Assistants, Clerical	$18,580	19.7%	26,000
36. Cashiers	$14,950	14.5%	1,125,000
37. Refuse and Recyclable Material Collectors	$23,850	16.6%	34,000
38. Food Servers, Nonrestaurant	$15,310	16.4%	85,000
39. Janitors and Cleaners, Except Maids and Housekeeping Cleaners	$17,900	13.5%	507,000
40. Counter Attendants, Cafeteria, Food Concession, and Coffee Shop	$14,760	14.4%	216,000
41. Nonfarm Animal Caretakers	$16,570	21.6%	20,000
42. Reservation and Transportation Ticket Agents	$24,090	14.5%	39,000
43. Reservation and Transportation Ticket Agents and Travel Clerks	$24,090	14.5%	39,000
44. Travel Clerks	$24,090	14.5%	39,000
45. Packaging and Filling Machine Operators and Tenders	$20,760	14.4%	56,000
46. Industrial Truck and Tractor Operators	$25,350	11.3%	91,000
47. Retail Salespersons	$17,150	12.4%	1,124,000
48. Helpers—Production Workers	$18,990	11.9%	143,000
49. Production Helpers	$18,990	11.9%	143,000
50. Production Laborers	$18,990	11.9%	143,000
51. Bartenders	$14,610	13.4%	84,000
52. Veterinary Assistants and Laboratory Animal Caretakers	$17,470	39.8%	8,000
53. Parking Lot Attendants	$15,690	19.8%	17,000
54. Bus Drivers, School	$21,990	11.6%	63,000
55. Weighers, Measurers, Checkers, and Samplers, Recordkeeping	$24,690	17.9%	13,000
56. Hosts and Hostesses, Restaurant, Lounge, and Coffee Shop	$14,920	13.0%	84,000
57. Child Care Workers	$16,030	10.6%	370,000
58. Refractory Materials Repairers, Except Brickmasons	$35,130	11.5%	16,000
59. Shipping, Receiving, and Traffic Clerks	$22,710	9.3%	133,000
60. Helpers—Electricians	$22,160	13.3%	27,000
61. Billing, Cost, and Rate Clerks	$25,350	8.5%	69,000

(continued)

(continued)

Best Jobs Requiring Short-Term On-the-Job Training

Job	Annual Earnings	Percent Growth	Annual Openings
62. Billing, Posting, and Calculating Machine Operators	$25,350	8.5%	69,000
63. Statement Clerks	$25,350	8.5%	69,000
64. Marking Clerks	$19,060	8.5%	467,000
65. Stock Clerks and Order Fillers	$19,060	8.5%	467,000
66. Stock Clerks, Sales Floor	$19,060	8.5%	467,000
67. Laundry and Dry-Cleaning Workers	$16,360	11.4%	62,000
68. Spotters, Dry Cleaning	$16,360	11.4%	62,000
69. Metal Molding, Coremaking, and Casting Machine Operators and Tenders	$22,340	9.8%	38,000
70. Plastic Molding and Casting Machine Operators and Tenders	$22,340	9.8%	38,000
71. Soldering and Brazing Machine Operators and Tenders	$28,220	15.1%	9,000
72. File Clerks	$19,490	9.1%	49,000
73. Helpers—Brickmasons, Blockmasons, Stonemasons, and Tile and Marble Setters	$23,620	14.1%	14,000
74. Coating, Painting, and Spraying Machine Setters, Operators, and Tenders	$24,710	11.9%	18,000
75. Tree Trimmers and Pruners	$23,950	16.3%	11,000
76. Court Clerks	$27,090	12.0%	14,000
77. Court, Municipal, and License Clerks	$27,090	12.0%	14,000
78. License Clerks	$27,090	12.0%	14,000
79. Municipal Clerks	$27,090	12.0%	14,000
80. Cooks, Institution and Cafeteria	$17,750	7.6%	110,000
81. Helpers—Pipelayers, Plumbers, Pipefitters, and Steamfitters	$21,830	11.5%	20,000

Best Jobs Requiring Moderate-Term On-the-Job Training

Job	Annual Earnings	Percent Growth	Annual Openings
1. Adjustment Clerks	$25,430	32.4%	359,000
2. Customer Service Representatives	$25,430	32.4%	359,000
3. Customer Service Representatives, Utilities	$25,430	32.4%	359,000
4. Tractor-Trailer Truck Drivers	$32,580	19.8%	240,000
5. Truck Drivers, Heavy and Tractor-Trailer	$32,580	19.8%	240,000
6. Correctional Officers and Jailers	$32,010	32.4%	30,000
7. Caption Writers	$42,450	28.4%	18,000
8. Advertising Sales Agents	$36,560	26.3%	25,000
9. Social and Human Service Assistants	$23,070	54.2%	45,000
10. Painters, Construction and Maintenance	$28,420	19.1%	67,000
11. Roofers	$29,460	19.4%	38,000
12. Dental Assistants	$26,720	37.2%	16,000
13. Medical Assistants	$23,610	57.0%	18,700
14. Pharmacy Technicians	$21,630	36.4%	22,000
15. Segmental Pavers	$26,170	26.7%	21,000
16. Construction Laborers	$24,070	17.0%	236,000
17. Demonstrators and Product Promoters	$20,690	24.9%	34,000
18. Sheet Metal Workers	$33,210	23.0%	13,000
19. Hazardous Materials Removal Workers	$31,800	32.8%	9,000
20. Irradiated-Fuel Handlers	$31,800	32.8%	9,000
21. Executive Secretaries and Administrative Assistants	$32,380	11.5%	185,000
22. Fitters, Structural Metal—Precision	$28,000	19.5%	20,000
23. Metal Fabricators, Structural Metal Products	$28,000	19.5%	20,000
24. Structural Metal Fabricators and Fitters	$28,000	19.5%	20,000
25. Bus Drivers, Transit and Intercity	$28,060	17.4%	24,000
26. Pipelaying Fitters	$38,710	10.2%	49,000
27. Computer-Controlled Machine Tool Operators, Metal and Plastic	$28,390	19.7%	15,000
28. Brattice Builders	$33,470	8.2%	161,000
29. Carpenter Assemblers and Repairers	$33,470	8.2%	161,000
30. Rough Carpenters	$33,470	8.2%	161,000
31. Ship Carpenters and Joiners	$33,470	8.2%	161,000
32. Sales Representatives, Wholesale and Manufacturing, Except Technical and Scientific Products	$41,520	5.7%	86,000

(continued)

(continued)

Best Jobs Requiring Moderate-Term On-the-Job Training

Job	Annual Earnings	Percent Growth	Annual Openings
33. Sales Representatives, Agricultural	$54,360	7.5%	24,000
34. Sales Representatives, Chemical and Pharmaceutical	$54,360	7.5%	24,000
35. Sales Representatives, Electrical/Electronic	$54,360	7.5%	24,000
36. Sales Representatives, Instruments	$54,360	7.5%	24,000
37. Sales Representatives, Mechanical Equipment and Supplies	$54,360	7.5%	24,000
38. Sales Representatives, Medical	$54,360	7.5%	24,000
39. Sales Representatives, Wholesale and Manufacturing, Technical and Scientific Products	$54,360	7.5%	24,000
40. Dispatchers, Except Police, Fire, and Ambulance	$30,070	22.2%	8,000
41. Mapping Technicians	$28,210	25.3%	7,000
42. Surveying and Mapping Technicians	$28,210	25.3%	7,000
43. Combination Machine Tool Operators and Tenders, Metal and Plastic	$27,910	14.7%	21,000
44. Combination Machine Tool Setters and Set-Up Operators, Metal and Plastic	$27,910	14.7%	21,000
45. Residential Advisors	$19,680	24.0%	9,000
46. Chemical Equipment Controllers and Operators	$36,810	14.9%	9,000
47. Chemical Equipment Operators and Tenders	$36,810	14.9%	9,000
48. Chemical Equipment Tenders	$36,810	14.9%	9,000
49. Extruding and Drawing Machine Setters, Operators, and Tenders, Metal and Plastic	$25,170	13.5%	23,000
50. Painters, Transportation Equipment	$32,330	17.5%	8,000
51. Commercial Divers	$32,770	11.5%	16,000
52. Billing and Posting Clerks and Machine Operators	$25,350	8.5%	69,000
53. Order Fillers, Wholesale and Retail Sales	$19,060	8.5%	467,000
54. Stock Clerks—Stockroom, Warehouse, or Storage Yard	$19,060	8.5%	467,000
55. Gaming Cage Workers	$21,540	25.2%	7,000
56. Laundry and Drycleaning Machine Operators and Tenders, Except Pressing	$16,360	11.4%	62,000
57. Ceiling Tile Installers	$33,000	9.4%	19,000
58. Drywall and Ceiling Tile Installers	$33,000	9.4%	19,000
59. Drywall Installers	$33,000	9.4%	19,000
60. Camera Operators, Television, Video, and Motion Picture	$28,980	25.8%	3,000

Best Jobs Requiring Moderate-Term On-the-Job Training

Job	Annual Earnings	Percent Growth	Annual Openings
61. Pest Control Workers	$23,150	22.1%	7,000
62. Grader, Bulldozer, and Scraper Operators	$34,160	6.9%	25,000
63. Operating Engineers	$34,160	6.9%	25,000
64. Operating Engineers and Other Construction Equipment Operators	$34,160	6.9%	25,000
65. Metal Molding, Coremaking, and Casting Machine Setters and Set-Up Operators	$22,340	9.8%	38,000
66. Molding, Coremaking, and Casting Machine Setters, Operators, and Tenders, Metal and Plastic	$22,340	9.8%	38,000
67. Plastic Molding and Casting Machine Setters and Set-Up Operators	$22,340	9.8%	38,000
68. Tax Preparers	$27,680	17.4%	8,000
69. Costume Attendants	$23,570	19.1%	8,000
70. Paperhangers	$31,330	20.2%	3,000
71. Team Assemblers	$22,260	5.9%	283,000
72. Pharmacy Aides	$18,010	19.5%	9,000
73. Soldering and Brazing Machine Setters and Set-Up Operators	$28,220	15.1%	9,000
74. Welding Machine Operators and Tenders	$28,220	15.1%	9,000
75. Welding, Soldering, and Brazing Machine Setters, Operators, and Tenders	$28,220	15.1%	9,000
76. Insulation Workers, Floor, Ceiling, and Wall	$28,000	13.6%	12,000
77. Insulation Workers, Mechanical	$28,000	13.6%	12,000
78. Bookkeeping, Accounting, and Auditing Clerks	$26,540	2.0%	298,000
79. Coating, Painting, and Spraying Machine Operators and Tenders	$24,710	11.9%	18,000
80. Coating, Painting, and Spraying Machine Setters and Set-Up Operators	$24,710	11.9%	18,000
81. Floral Designers	$19,280	14.9%	15,000
82. Dietetic Technicians	$21,790	27.6%	3,000
83. Ambulance Drivers and Attendants, Except Emergency Medical Technicians	$18,890	33.7%	3,000

Best Jobs Requiring Long-Term On-the-Job Training

Job	Annual Earnings	Percent Growth	Annual Openings
1. Musicians and Singers	$40,320	20.1%	33,000
2. Musicians, Instrumental	$40,320	20.1%	33,000
3. Singers	$40,320	20.1%	33,000
4. Electricians	$40,770	17.3%	66,000
5. Highway Patrol Pilots	$40,970	23.2%	21,000
6. Police and Sheriff's Patrol Officers	$40,970	23.2%	21,000
7. Police Patrol Officers	$40,970	23.2%	21,000
8. Sheriffs and Deputy Sheriffs	$40,970	23.2%	21,000
9. Heating and Air Conditioning Mechanics	$34,020	22.3%	21,000
10. Heating, Air Conditioning, and Refrigeration Mechanics and Installers	$34,020	22.3%	21,000
11. Refrigeration Mechanics	$34,020	22.3%	21,000
12. Talent Directors	$45,090	27.1%	11,000
13. Technical Directors/Managers	$45,090	27.1%	11,000
14. Welder-Fitters	$28,490	19.3%	51,000
15. Welders and Cutters	$28,490	19.3%	51,000
16. Welders, Cutters, Solderers, and Brazers	$28,490	19.3%	51,000
17. Cooks, Restaurant	$18,480	21.7%	158,000
18. Claims Adjusters, Examiners, and Investigators	$42,440	15.1%	25,000
19. Claims Examiners, Property and Casualty Insurance	$42,440	15.1%	25,000
20. Insurance Adjusters, Examiners, and Investigators	$42,440	15.1%	25,000
21. Telecommunications Line Installers and Repairers	$39,200	27.6%	9,000
22. Actors	$20,540	26.7%	20,000
23. Structural Iron and Steel Workers	$38,950	18.4%	12,000
24. Pipe Fitters	$38,710	10.2%	49,000
25. Plumbers	$38,710	10.2%	49,000
26. Plumbers, Pipefitters, and Steamfitters	$38,710	10.2%	49,000
27. Numerical Control Machine Tool Operators and Tenders, Metal and Plastic	$28,390	19.7%	15,000
28. Automatic Teller Machine Servicers	$32,890	14.2%	24,000
29. Office Machine and Cash Register Servicers	$32,890	14.2%	24,000
30. Coaches and Scouts	$29,020	17.6%	19,000
31. Boat Builders and Shipwrights	$33,470	8.2%	161,000
32. Carpenters	$33,470	8.2%	161,000
33. Construction Carpenters	$33,470	8.2%	161,000
34. Flight Attendants	$40,600	18.4%	8,000

Best Jobs Requiring Long-Term On-the-Job Training

Job	Annual Earnings	Percent Growth	Annual Openings
35. Brickmasons and Blockmasons	$41,590	12.5%	18,000
36. Bakers	$20,440	16.8%	25,000
37. Bakers, Bread and Pastry	$20,440	16.8%	25,000
38. Bakers, Manufacturing	$20,440	16.8%	25,000
39. Surveying Technicians	$28,210	25.3%	7,000
40. Athletes and Sports Competitors	$43,730	22.5%	3,000
41. Machinists	$32,090	9.1%	28,000
42. Water and Liquid Waste Treatment Plant and System Operators	$32,560	18.1%	6,000
43. Interpreters and Translators	$32,000	23.8%	3,000
44. Photographers	$23,040	17.0%	13,000
45. Photographers, Scientific	$23,040	17.0%	13,000
46. Professional Photographers	$23,040	17.0%	13,000
47. Automotive Body and Related Repairers	$32,490	10.2%	18,000
48. Recreational Vehicle Service Technicians	$26,410	25.4%	4,000
49. Maintenance and Repair Workers, General	$28,740	4.7%	103,000
50. Elevator Installers and Repairers	$51,630	17.2%	2,000
51. Reinforcing Iron and Rebar Workers	$34,750	17.5%	4,000
52. Farmers and Ranchers	$42,170	−25.4%	146,000
53. Tile and Marble Setters	$35,390	15.6%	5,000
54. Stonemasons	$32,470	20.8%	2,000

Best Jobs Requiring Work Experience in a Related Job

Job	Annual Earnings	Percent Growth	Annual Openings
1. First-Line Supervisors and Manager/Supervisors —Construction Trades Workers	$46,570	16.5%	43,000
2. First-Line Supervisors and Manager/Supervisors —Extractive Workers	$46,570	16.5%	43,000
3. First-Line Supervisors/Managers of Construction Trades and Extraction Workers	$46,570	16.5%	43,000
4. First-Line Supervisors/Managers of Mechanics, Installers, and Repairers	$46,320	16.0%	38,000
5. Storage and Distribution Managers	$57,240	20.2%	13,000
6. Transportation Managers	$57,240	20.2%	13,000
7. Transportation, Storage, and Distribution Managers	$57,240	20.2%	13,000
8. First-Line Supervisors/Managers of Transportation and Material-Moving Machine and Vehicle Operators	$41,140	19.9%	17,000
9. Food Service Managers	$33,630	15.0%	55,000
10. Self-Enrichment Education Teachers	$28,880	18.5%	34,000
11. First-Line Supervisors/Managers of Farming, Fishing, and Forestry Workers	$33,330	13.0%	89,000
12. First-Line Supervisors/Managers of Helpers, Laborers, and Material Movers, Hand	$36,090	18.9%	14,000
13. First-Line Supervisors, Administrative Support	$37,990	9.4%	146,000
14. First-Line Supervisors, Customer Service	$37,990	9.4%	146,000
15. First-Line Supervisors/Managers of Office and Administrative Support Workers	$37,990	9.4%	146,000
16. First-Line Supervisors/Managers of Correctional Officers	$44,640	29.6%	3,000
17. First-Line Supervisors and Manager/Supervisors —Landscaping Workers	$32,100	20.1%	10,000
18. First-Line Supervisors/Managers of Landscaping, Lawn Service, and Groundskeeping Workers	$32,100	20.1%	10,000
19. Lawn Service Managers	$32,100	20.1%	10,000
20. Private Detectives and Investigators	$28,380	23.5%	9,000
21. First-Line Supervisors/Managers of Food Preparation and Serving Workers	$23,600	12.7%	136,000
22. First-Line Supervisors/Managers of Non-Retail Sales Workers	$51,490	5.8%	41,000
23. First-Line Supervisors/Managers of Police and Detectives	$59,300	13.1%	9,000

Best Jobs Requiring Work Experience in a Related Job

Job	Annual Earnings	Percent Growth	Annual Openings
24. First-Line Supervisors/Managers of Retail Sales Workers	$28,590	8.1%	206,000
25. Forest Fire Fighting and Prevention Supervisors	$53,420	16.7%	5,000
26. Municipal Fire Fighting and Prevention Supervisors	$53,420	16.7%	5,000
27. First-Line Supervisors/Managers of Housekeeping and Janitorial Workers	$27,200	14.2%	18,000
28. Housekeeping Supervisors	$27,200	14.2%	18,000
29. Janitorial Supervisors	$27,200	14.2%	18,000
30. Child Support, Missing Persons, and Unemployment Insurance Fraud Investigators	$50,960	16.4%	4,000
31. Criminal Investigators and Special Agents	$50,960	16.4%	4,000
32. Detectives and Criminal Investigators	$50,960	16.4%	4,000
33. Immigration and Customs Inspectors	$50,960	16.4%	4,000
34. Police Detectives	$50,960	16.4%	4,000
35. Police Identification and Records Officers	$50,960	16.4%	4,000
36. First-Line Supervisors/Managers of Production and Operating Workers	$42,000	1.0%	71,000
37. Aircraft Cargo Handling Supervisors	$37,330	27.7%	1,000
38. Real Estate Brokers	$51,370	9.6%	8,000
39. First-Line Supervisors/Managers of Personal Service Workers	$28,040	15.1%	8,000

Best Jobs Requiring Postsecondary Vocational Training

Job	Annual Earnings	Percent Growth	Annual Openings
1. Legal Secretaries	$34,610	20.3%	36,000
2. Licensed Practical and Licensed Vocational Nurses	$30,670	20.3%	58,000
3. Automotive Master Mechanics	$29,510	18.0%	104,000
4. Automotive Service Technicians and Mechanics	$29,510	18.0%	104,000
5. Automotive Specialty Technicians	$29,510	18.0%	104,000
6. Fitness Trainers and Aerobics Instructors	$23,340	40.3%	19,000
7. Gaming Dealers	$13,680	32.4%	28,000
8. Emergency Medical Technicians and Paramedics	$23,170	31.3%	19,000
9. Medical Secretaries	$24,670	19.0%	40,000
10. Architectural and Civil Drafters	$37,010	20.8%	12,000
11. Civil Drafters	$37,010	20.8%	12,000
12. Surgical Technologists	$30,090	34.7%	8,000
13. Computer, Automated Teller, and Office Machine Repairers	$32,890	14.2%	24,000
14. Data Processing Equipment Repairers	$32,890	14.2%	24,000
15. Desktop Publishers	$31,200	66.7%	5,000
16. Bus and Truck Mechanics and Diesel Engine Specialists	$33,570	14.2%	20,000
17. Aircraft Body and Bonded Structure Repairers	$41,990	16.7%	11,000
18. Aircraft Engine Specialists	$41,990	16.7%	11,000
19. Aircraft Mechanics and Service Technicians	$41,990	16.7%	11,000
20. Airframe-and-Power-Plant Mechanics	$41,990	16.7%	11,000
21. Electronic Drafters	$40,070	23.3%	5,000
22. Massage Therapists	$28,050	30.4%	7,000
23. Respiratory Therapy Technicians	$33,840	34.6%	3,000
24. Signal and Track Switch Repairers	$42,390	11.5%	16,000
25. Multiple Machine Tool Setters, Operators, and Tenders, Metal and Plastic	$27,910	14.7%	21,000
26. Makeup Artists, Theatrical and Performance	$30,240	11.4%	27,000
27. Appraisers and Assessors of Real Estate	$38,950	18.0%	6,000
28. Appraisers, Real Estate	$38,950	18.0%	6,000
29. Assessors	$38,950	18.0%	6,000
30. Hairdressers, Hairstylists, and Cosmetologists	$18,260	13.0%	78,000
31. Mechanical Drafters	$39,620	15.4%	8,000
32. Commercial Pilots	$47,420	26.9%	1,000

Best Jobs Requiring Postsecondary Vocational Training

Job	Annual Earnings	Percent Growth	Annual Openings
33. Security and Fire Alarm Systems Installers	$30,490	23.4%	4,000
34. Mobile Heavy Equipment Mechanics, Except Engines	$35,190	14.0%	11,000
35. Real Estate Sales Agents	$28,570	9.5%	28,000
36. Precision Dyers	$16,360	11.4%	62,000
37. Chefs and Head Cooks	$26,800	9.0%	35,000
38. Casting Machine Set-Up Operators	$22,340	9.8%	38,000
39. Welding Machine Setters and Set-Up Operators	$28,220	15.1%	9,000
40. Manicurists and Pedicurists	$16,700	26.5%	5,000
41. Gaming Supervisors	$39,240	18.4%	2,000

Best Jobs Requiring an Associate's Degree

Job	Annual Earnings	Percent Growth	Annual Openings
1. Registered Nurses	$46,670	25.6%	140,000
2. Computer Support Specialists	$38,560	97.0%	40,000
3. Paralegals and Legal Assistants	$36,670	33.2%	23,000
4. Nuclear Equipment Operation Technicians	$59,690	20.7%	15,000
5. Nuclear Monitoring Technicians	$59,690	20.7%	15,000
6. Physical Therapist Assistants	$35,280	44.8%	9,000
7. Dental Hygienists	$54,700	37.1%	5,000
8. Radiologic Technicians	$37,680	23.1%	13,000
9. Radiologic Technologists	$37,680	23.1%	13,000
10. Radiologic Technologists and Technicians	$37,680	23.1%	13,000
11. Medical Transcriptionists	$26,460	29.8%	15,000
12. Medical Records and Health Information Technicians	$23,530	49.0%	14,000
13. Architectural Drafters	$37,010	20.8%	12,000
14. Medical and Clinical Laboratory Technicians	$28,810	19.0%	19,000
15. Respiratory Therapists	$39,370	34.8%	4,000
16. Biological Technicians	$32,280	26.4%	7,000
17. Diagnostic Medical Sonographers	$46,980	26.1%	3,000
18. Electrical and Electronics Drafters	$40,070	23.3%	5,000
19. Electrical Drafters	$40,070	23.3%	5,000
20. Occupational Therapist Assistants	$35,840	39.7%	3,000
21. Calibration and Instrumentation Technicians	$42,130	10.8%	22,000
22. Electrical and Electronic Engineering Technicians	$42,130	10.8%	22,000
23. Electrical Engineering Technicians	$42,130	10.8%	22,000
24. Electronics Engineering Technicians	$42,130	10.8%	22,000
25. Cardiovascular Technologists and Technicians	$35,010	34.9%	3,000
26. Semiconductor Processors	$26,480	32.4%	7,000
27. Chemical Technicians	$36,190	15.0%	13,000
28. Physical Therapist Aides	$20,300	46.3%	7,000
29. Veterinary Technologists and Technicians	$22,430	39.3%	6,000
30. Environmental Science and Protection Technicians, Including Health	$34,690	24.5%	3,000
31. Agricultural Technicians	$27,530	15.2%	15,000
32. Food Science Technicians	$27,530	15.2%	15,000
33. Environmental Engineering Technicians	$36,590	29.1%	2,000
34. Radiation Therapists	$49,050	22.8%	1,000

Best Jobs Requiring an Associate's Degree

Job	Annual Earnings	Percent Growth	Annual Openings
35. Nuclear Medicine Technologists	$47,400	22.4%	1,000
36. Civil Engineering Technicians	$37,410	11.9%	9,000
37. Nuclear Technicians	$59,690	20.7%	fewer than 500
38. Mechanical Engineering Technicians	$40,910	13.9%	5,000
39. First-Line Supervisors and Manager/Supervisors —Agricultural Crop Workers	$33,330	13.0%	8,000

Best Jobs Requiring a Bachelor's Degree

Job	Annual Earnings	Percent Growth	Annual Openings
1. Computer Software Engineers, Applications	$70,210	100.0%	28,000
2. Computer Systems Analysts	$61,990	59.7%	34,000
3. Computer Software Engineers, Systems Software	$73,280	89.7%	23,000
4. Sales Agents, Financial Services	$59,690	22.3%	55,000
5. Sales Agents, Securities and Commodities	$59,690	22.3%	55,000
6. Securities, Commodities, and Financial Services Sales Agents	$59,690	22.3%	55,000
7. Computer Security Specialists	$53,770	81.9%	18,000
8. Network and Computer Systems Administrators	$53,770	81.9%	18,000
9. Accountants	$45,380	18.5%	100,000
10. Accountants and Auditors	$45,380	18.5%	100,000
11. Auditors	$45,380	18.5%	100,000
12. Financial Analysts	$55,120	25.5%	20,000
13. Secondary School Teachers, Except Special and Vocational Education	$43,280	18.6%	60,000
14. Personal Financial Advisors	$57,710	34.0%	13,000
15. Public Relations Specialists	$41,010	36.1%	19,000
16. Graphic Designers	$36,020	26.7%	28,000
17. Child, Family, and School Social Workers	$32,950	26.9%	35,000
18. Copy Writers	$42,450	28.4%	18,000
19. Creative Writers	$42,450	28.4%	18,000
20. Poets and Lyricists	$42,450	28.4%	18,000
21. Writers and Authors	$42,450	28.4%	18,000
22. Special Education Teachers, Preschool, Kindergarten, and Elementary School	$42,110	36.8%	15,000
23. Network Systems and Data Communications Analysts	$57,470	77.5%	9,000
24. Computer Programmers	$60,120	16.2%	36,000
25. Market Research Analysts	$53,450	24.4%	13,000
26. Property, Real Estate, and Community Association Managers	$36,290	22.7%	24,000
27. Database Administrators	$54,850	65.9%	8,000
28. Construction Managers	$61,050	16.3%	26,000
29. Cost Estimators	$46,960	16.5%	28,000
30. Medical and Public Health Social Workers	$36,410	31.6%	13,000
31. Training and Development Specialists	$41,780	19.4%	20,000
32. Social and Community Service Managers	$41,260	24.8%	13,000

Best Jobs Requiring a Bachelor's Degree

Job	Annual Earnings	Percent Growth	Annual Openings
33. Elementary School Teachers, Except Special Education	$41,080	13.2%	144,000
34. Probation Officers and Correctional Treatment Specialists	$38,780	23.8%	14,000
35. Physician Assistants	$63,970	53.5%	5,000
36. Editors	$39,960	22.6%	14,000
37. Medical and Clinical Laboratory Technologists	$42,240	17.0%	19,000
38. Commercial and Industrial Designers	$49,820	23.8%	7,000
39. Employment Interviewers, Private or Public Employment Service	$38,010	17.6%	19,000
40. Employment, Recruitment, and Placement Specialists	$38,010	17.6%	19,000
41. Personnel Recruiters	$38,010	17.6%	19,000
42. Technical Writers	$49,360	29.6%	5,000
43. Preschool Teachers, Except Special Education	$18,640	20.0%	55,000
44. Special Education Teachers, Secondary School	$42,780	24.6%	8,000
45. Occupational Therapists	$51,370	33.9%	4,000
46. Multi-Media Artists and Animators	$42,270	22.2%	8,000
47. Kindergarten Teachers, Except Special Education	$38,740	14.5%	23,000
48. Adult Literacy, Remedial Education, and GED Teachers and Instructors	$35,220	19.4%	12,000
49. Middle School Teachers, Except Special and Vocational Education	$41,220	9.6%	54,000
50. Computer Hardware Engineers	$71,560	24.9%	3,000
51. Environmental Engineers	$61,250	26.0%	3,000
52. Recreation Workers	$17,850	20.1%	32,000
53. Purchasing Agents, Except Wholesale, Retail, and Farm Products	$43,230	12.3%	23,000
54. Special Education Teachers, Middle School	$40,010	24.4%	6,000
55. Chemists	$51,860	19.1%	6,000
56. Rehabilitation Counselors	$25,610	23.6%	12,000
57. Environmental Scientists and Specialists, Including Health	$47,330	22.3%	4,000
58. Directors, Religious Activities and Education	$27,420	15.9%	23,000
59. Architects, Except Landscape and Naval	$55,470	18.5%	4,000
60. Economists	$67,050	18.5%	3,000
61. Sales Engineers	$59,720	17.7%	4,000

(continued)

(continued)

Best Jobs Requiring a Bachelor's Degree

Job	Annual Earnings	Percent Growth	Annual Openings
62. Budget Analysts	$50,510	14.6%	8,000
63. Compensation, Benefits, and Job Analysis Specialists	$43,330	15.7%	8,000
64. Industrial Production Managers	$64,510	6.2%	22,000
65. Interior Designers	$39,580	17.4%	7,000
66. Geologists	$58,280	18.1%	3,000
67. Hydrologists	$56,400	25.7%	1,000
68. Landscape Architects	$46,710	31.1%	1,000
69. Meeting and Convention Planners	$36,550	23.3%	3,000
70. Credit Analysts	$41,650	16.0%	7,000
71. Mechanical Engineers	$61,440	13.1%	7,000
72. Fashion Designers	$49,530	20.3%	2,000
73. Biomedical Engineers	$59,790	31.4%	fewer than 500
74. Loan Officers	$43,210	4.9%	28,000
75. Electrical Engineers	$66,890	11.3%	8,000
76. Film and Video Editors	$36,910	25.8%	2,000
77. Geoscientists, Except Hydrologists and Geographers	$58,280	18.1%	2,000
78. Insurance Sales Agents	$38,890	3.3%	43,000
79. Exhibit Designers	$33,460	27.0%	2,000
80. Set and Exhibit Designers	$33,460	27.0%	2,000
81. Set Designers	$33,460	27.0%	2,000
82. Vocational Education Teachers, Secondary School	$43,590	13.4%	7,000
83. Materials Scientists	$62,750	19.8%	1,000
84. Dietitians and Nutritionists	$40,410	15.2%	5,000
85. Survey Researchers	$23,230	34.5%	3,000
86. Music Arrangers and Orchestrators	$33,720	13.1%	9,000
87. Electronics Engineers, Except Computer	$68,350	10.4%	6,000
88. Geographers	$48,410	17.2%	2,000
89. Historians	$42,940	17.2%	2,000

Best Jobs Requiring Work Experience Plus Degree

Job	Annual Earnings	Percent Growth	Annual Openings
1. Computer and Information Systems Managers	$82,480	47.9%	28,000
2. Management Analysts	$57,970	28.9%	50,000
3. Medical and Health Services Managers	$59,220	32.3%	27,000
4. Sales Managers	$71,620	32.8%	21,000
5. Financial Managers	$70,210	18.5%	53,000
6. Financial Managers, Branch or Department	$70,210	18.5%	53,000
7. Treasurers, Controllers, and Chief Financial Officers	$70,210	18.5%	53,000
8. General and Operations Managers	$65,010	15.2%	235,000
9. Chief Executives	$120,450	17.2%	48,000
10. Government Service Executives	$120,450	17.2%	48,000
11. Private Sector Executives	$120,450	17.2%	48,000
12. Administrative Services Managers	$49,810	20.4%	31,000
13. Marketing Managers	$74,370	29.1%	12,000
14. Education Administrators, Elementary and Secondary School	$69,240	13.4%	35,000
15. Public Relations Managers	$57,200	36.3%	7,000
16. Directors—Stage, Motion Pictures, Television, and Radio	$45,090	27.1%	11,000
17. Producers	$45,090	27.1%	11,000
18. Producers and Directors	$45,090	27.1%	11,000
19. Program Directors	$45,090	27.1%	11,000
20. Education Administrators, Postsecondary	$61,700	13.4%	35,000
21. Advertising and Promotions Managers	$55,940	34.3%	7,000
22. Art Directors	$59,800	21.1%	6,000
23. Education Administrators, Preschool and Child Care Center/Program	$31,860	13.4%	35,000
24. Compensation and Benefits Managers	$61,880	12.7%	14,000
25. Human Resources Managers	$61,880	12.7%	14,000
26. Training and Development Managers	$61,880	12.7%	14,000
27. Engineering Managers	$87,490	8.0%	24,000
28. Agents and Business Managers of Artists, Performers, and Athletes	$55,550	27.9%	2,000
29. Gaming Managers	$53,450	30.0%	fewer than 500
30. Arbitrators, Mediators, and Conciliators	$46,660	27.2%	fewer than 500

Best Jobs Requiring a Master's Degree

Job	Annual Earnings	Percent Growth	Annual Openings
1. Teachers, Postsecondary	$52,115	23.5%	184,000
2. Educational, Vocational, and School Counselors	$43,470	25.3%	22,000
3. Instructional Coordinators	$46,600	25.0%	15,000
4. Industrial-Organizational Psychologists	$66,010	18.1%	18,000
5. Clinical Psychologists	$50,420	18.1%	18,000
6. Clinical, Counseling, and School Psychologists	$50,420	18.1%	18,000
7. Counseling Psychologists	$50,420	18.1%	18,000
8. Educational Psychologists	$50,420	18.1%	18,000
9. Physical Therapists	$56,570	33.3%	6,000
10. Mental Health and Substance Abuse Social Workers	$32,080	39.1%	10,000
11. Speech-Language Pathologists	$48,520	39.2%	4,000
12. Substance Abuse and Behavioral Disorder Counselors	$29,870	35.0%	7,000
13. Health Educators	$35,230	23.5%	7,000
14. Audiologists	$46,900	44.7%	1,000
15. Mental Health Counselors	$29,050	21.7%	7,000
16. Marriage and Family Therapists	$32,720	29.9%	2,000
17. Political Scientists	$81,350	17.2%	2,000
18. Urban and Regional Planners	$48,530	16.4%	3,000
19. Sociologists	$54,880	17.2%	2,000
20. Composers	$33,720	13.1%	9,000
21. Music Directors	$33,720	13.1%	9,000
22. Music Directors and Composers	$33,720	13.1%	9,000

Best Jobs Requiring a Doctoral Degree

Job	Annual Earnings	Percent Growth	Annual Openings
1. Computer and Information Scientists, Research	$75,130	40.3%	2,000
2. Biochemists	$57,100	21.0%	5,000
3. Biochemists and Biophysicists	$57,100	21.0%	5,000
4. Biophysicists	$57,100	21.0%	5,000
5. Microbiologists	$49,880	21.0%	5,000
6. Zoologists and Wildlife Biologists	$46,220	21.0%	5,000
7. Biologists	$44,770	21.0%	5,000
8. Medical Scientists, Except Epidemiologists	$55,960	26.5%	2,000
9. Epidemiologists	$52,710	26.5%	2,000

Best Jobs Requiring a First Professional Degree

Job	Annual Earnings	Percent Growth	Annual Openings
1. Pharmacists	$74,890	24.3%	20,000
2. Lawyers	$88,760	18.0%	35,000
3. Anesthesiologists	greater than $146,500	17.9%	27,000
4. Internists, General	greater than $146,500	17.9%	27,000
5. Obstetricians and Gynecologists	greater than $146,500	17.9%	27,000
6. Surgeons	greater than $146,500	17.9%	27,000
7. Psychiatrists	$126,460	17.9%	27,000
8. Pediatricians, General	$126,430	17.9%	27,000
9. Family and General Practitioners	$118,390	17.9%	27,000
10. Chiropractors	$68,420	23.4%	3,000
11. Veterinarians	$62,000	31.8%	2,000
12. Clergy	$33,840	15.0%	12,000
13. Optometrists	$85,650	18.7%	1,000

Best Jobs Lists Based on Interests

This group of lists organizes the 500 best jobs into 14 interest areas. You can use these lists to quickly identify jobs based on your interests.

Find the interest area or areas that interest you most. Then review the jobs in those areas to identify jobs you want to explore in more detail and look up their descriptions in Part II. You can also review interest areas where you have had past experience, education, or training to see if other jobs in those areas would meet your current requirements.

Within each interest area, jobs are listed in order of their total combined scores based on earnings (which is given double the weight), growth, and number of openings.

Note: The 14 interest areas used in these lists are those used in the *Guide for Occupational Exploration*. The *GOE* was developed by the U.S. Department of Labor as an intuitive way to assist in career exploration. The *GOE*'s interest areas are also used in a variety of career assessments and information systems. Our lists use the revised *GOE* interest areas from the *Guide for Occupational Exploration*, Third Edition, published by JIST.

Descriptions for the 14 Interest Areas

Brief descriptions for the 14 interest areas we use in the lists follow. The descriptions are from the *Guide for Occupational Exploration*.

Also note that we put each of the 500 best jobs into only one interest area list, the one it fit into best. However, many jobs could be included in more than one list, so consider reviewing a variety of these interest areas to find jobs that you might otherwise overlook.

▲ **Arts, Entertainment, and Media:** *An interest in creatively expressing feelings or ideas, in communicating news or information, or in performing.* You can satisfy this interest in several creative, verbal, or performing activities. For example, if you enjoy literature, perhaps writing or editing would appeal to you. Do you prefer to work in the performing arts? If so, you could direct or perform in drama, music, or dance. If you especially enjoy the visual arts, you could become a critic in painting, sculpture, or ceramics. You may want to use your hands to create or decorate products. You may prefer to model clothes or develop sets for entertainment. Or you may want to participate in sports professionally as an athlete or coach.

▲ **Science, Math, and Engineering:** *An interest in discovering, collecting, and analyzing information about the natural world; in applying scientific research findings to problems in medicine, the life sciences, and the natural sciences; in imagining and manipulating quantitative data; and in applying technology to manufacturing, transportation, mining, and other economic activities.* You can satisfy this interest by working with the knowledge and processes of the sciences. You may enjoy researching and developing new knowledge in mathematics, or perhaps solving problems in the physical or life sciences would appeal to you. You may wish to study engineering and help create new machines, processes, and structures. If you want to work with scientific equipment and procedures, you could seek a job in a research or testing laboratory.

▲ **Plants and Animals:** *An interest in working with plants and animals, usually outdoors.* You can satisfy this interest by working in farming, forestry, fishing, and related fields. You may like doing physical work outdoors, such as on a farm. You may enjoy animals; perhaps training or taking care of animals would appeal to you. If you have management ability, you could own, operate, or manage a farm or related business.

▲ **Law, Law Enforcement, and Public Safety:** *An interest in upholding people's rights or in protecting people and property by using authority, inspecting, or monitoring.* You can satisfy this interest by working in law, law enforcement, firefighting, and related fields. For example, if you enjoy mental challenge and intrigue, you could investigate crimes or fires for a living. If you enjoy working with verbal skills, you may want to defend citizens in court or research deeds, wills, and other legal documents. You may prefer to fight fires and respond to other emergencies. Or, if you want more routine work, perhaps a job in guarding or patrolling would appeal to you; if you have management ability, you could seek a leadership position in law enforcement and the protective services. Work in the military gives you the chance to use technical and/or leadership skills while serving your country.

▲ **Mechanics, Installers, and Repairers:** *An interest in applying mechanical and electrical/ electronic principles to practical situations by use of machines or hand tools.* You can satisfy this interest working with a variety of tools, technologies, materials, and settings. If you enjoy making machines run efficiently or fixing them when they break down, you could seek a job installing or repairing such devices as copiers, aircraft engines, automobiles, or watches. You may instead prefer to deal directly with certain materials and find work cutting and shaping metal or wood. Or, if electricity and electronics interest you, you could install cables, troubleshoot telephone networks, or repair videocassette recorders. If you prefer routine or physical work in settings other than factories, perhaps work repairing tires or batteries would appeal to you.

▲ **Construction, Mining, and Drilling:** *An interest in assembling components of buildings and other structures or in using mechanical devices to drill or excavate.* If construction interests you, you can find fulfillment in the many building projects that are being undertaken at all times. If you like to organize and plan, you can find careers in management. On the other hand, you can play a more direct role in putting up and finishing buildings by doing jobs such as plumbing, carpentry, masonry, painting, or roofing. You may like working at a mine or oilfield, operating the powerful drilling or digging equipment. There are also several jobs that let you put your hands to the task.

▲ **Transportation:** *An interest in operations that move people or materials.* You can satisfy this interest by managing a transportation service, by helping vehicles keep on their assigned schedules and routes, or by driving or piloting a vehicle. If you enjoy taking responsibility, perhaps managing a rail line would appeal to you. If you work well with details and can take pressure on the job, you might consider being an air traffic controller. Or would you rather get out on the highway, on the water, or up in the air? If so, then you could drive a truck from state to state, sail down the Mississippi on a barge, or fly a crop duster over a cornfield. If you prefer to stay closer to home, you could drive a delivery van, taxi, or school bus. You can use your physical strength to load freight and arrange it so it gets to its destination in one piece.

▲ **Industrial Production:** *An interest in repetitive, concrete, organized activities most often done in a factory setting.* You can satisfy this interest by working in one of many industries that mass-produce goods or for a utility that distributes electric power, gas, telephone service, and related services. You may enjoy manual work, using your hands or hand tools. Perhaps you prefer to operate machines. You may like to inspect, sort, count, or weigh products. Using your training and experience to set up machines or supervise other workers may appeal to you.

▲ **Business Detail:** *An interest in organized, clearly defined activities requiring accuracy and attention to details, primarily in an office setting.* You can satisfy this interest in a variety of jobs in which you attend to the details of a business operation. You may enjoy using your math skills; if so, perhaps a job in billing, computing, or financial record-keeping would satisfy you. If you prefer to deal with people, you may want a job in which you meet the public, talk on the telephone, or supervise other workers. You may like to do word processing on a computer, turn out copies on a duplicating machine, or work out sums on a calculator. Perhaps a job in filing or recording would satisfy you. Or you may wish to use your training and experience to manage an office.

▲ **Sales and Marketing:** *An interest in bringing others to a particular point of view by personal persuasion, using sales and promotional techniques.* You can satisfy this interest in a variety of sales and marketing jobs. If you like using technical knowledge of science or agriculture, you may enjoy selling technical products or services. Or perhaps you are more interested in selling business-related services, such as insurance coverage, advertising space, or investment opportunities. Real estate offers several kinds of sales jobs. Perhaps you'd rather work with something you can pick up and show to people. You may work in stores, sales offices, or customers' homes.

▲ **Recreation, Travel, and Other Personal Services:** *An interest in catering to the personal wishes and needs of others so that they may enjoy cleanliness, good food and drink, comfortable lodging away from home, and enjoyable recreation.* You can satisfy this interest by providing services for the convenience, feeding, and pampering of others in hotels, restaurants, airplanes, and so on. If you enjoy improving the appearance of others, perhaps working in the hair and beauty care field would satisfy you. You may wish to provide personal services such as taking care of small children, tailoring garments, or ushering. Or you may use your knowledge of the field to manage workers who are providing these services.

▲ **Education and Social Service:** *An interest in teaching people or improving their social or spiritual well-being.* You can satisfy this interest by teaching students, who may be preschoolers, retirees, or any age in between. Or, if you are interested in helping people sort out their complicated lives, you may find fulfillment as a counselor, social worker, or religious worker. Working in a museum or library may give you opportunities to expand people's understanding of the world. If you also have an interest in business, you may find satisfaction in managerial work in this field.

▲ **General Management and Support:** *An interest in making an organization run smoothly.* You can satisfy this interest by working in a position of leadership or by specializing in a function that contributes to the overall effort. The organization may be a profit-making business, a non-profit, or a government agency. If you especially enjoy working with people, you may find fulfillment from working in human resources. An interest in numbers may cause you to consider accounting, finance, budgeting, or purchasing. Or perhaps you would enjoy managing the organization's physical resources (such as land, buildings, equipment, and utilities).

▲ **Medical and Health Services:** *An interest in helping people be healthy.* You can satisfy this interest by working in a health-care team as a doctor, therapist, or nurse. You might specialize in one of the many different parts of the body or types of care, or you might be a generalist who deals with the whole patient. If you like technology, you might find satisfaction working with X rays, one of the electronic means of diagnosis, or clinical laboratory testing. You might work with healthy people, helping them stay in condition through exercise and eating right. If you like to organize, analyze, and plan, a managerial role might be right for you.

Best Jobs for People Interested in Arts, Entertainment, and Media

Job	Annual Earnings	Percent Growth	Annual Openings
1. Public Relations Specialists	$41,010	36.1%	19,000
2. Graphic Designers	$36,020	26.7%	28,000
3. Caption Writers	$42,450	28.4%	18,000
4. Copy Writers	$42,450	28.4%	18,000
5. Creative Writers	$42,450	28.4%	18,000
6. Poets and Lyricists	$42,450	28.4%	18,000
7. Writers and Authors	$42,450	28.4%	18,000
8. Musicians and Singers	$40,320	20.1%	33,000
9. Musicians, Instrumental	$40,320	20.1%	33,000
10. Singers	$40,320	20.1%	33,000
11. Directors—Stage, Motion Pictures, Television, and Radio	$45,090	27.1%	11,000
12. Producers	$45,090	27.1%	11,000
13. Producers and Directors	$45,090	27.1%	11,000
14. Program Directors	$45,090	27.1%	11,000
15. Talent Directors	$45,090	27.1%	11,000
16. Technical Directors/Managers	$45,090	27.1%	11,000
17. Editors	$39,960	22.6%	14,000
18. Fitness Trainers and Aerobics Instructors	$23,340	40.3%	19,000
19. Commercial and Industrial Designers	$49,820	23.8%	7,000
20. Technical Writers	$49,360	29.6%	5,000
21. Art Directors	$59,800	21.1%	6,000
22. Actors	$20,540	26.7%	20,000
23. Multi-Media Artists and Animators	$42,270	22.2%	8,000
24. Coaches and Scouts	$29,020	17.6%	19,000
25. Desktop Publishers	$31,200	66.7%	5,000
26. Agents and Business Managers of Artists, Performers, and Athletes	$55,550	27.9%	2,000
27. Athletes and Sports Competitors	$43,730	22.5%	3,000
28. Makeup Artists, Theatrical and Performance	$30,240	11.4%	27,000
29. Interior Designers	$39,580	17.4%	7,000
30. Fashion Designers	$49,530	20.3%	2,000
31. Film and Video Editors	$36,910	25.8%	2,000
32. Interpreters and Translators	$32,000	23.8%	3,000

(continued)

(continued)

Best Jobs for People Interested in Arts, Entertainment, and Media

Job	Annual Earnings	Percent Growth	Annual Openings
33. Exhibit Designers	$33,460	27.0%	2,000
34. Set and Exhibit Designers	$33,460	27.0%	2,000
35. Set Designers	$33,460	27.0%	2,000
36. Photographers	$23,040	17.0%	13,000
37. Professional Photographers	$23,040	17.0%	13,000
38. Camera Operators, Television, Video, and Motion Picture	$28,980	25.8%	3,000
39. Costume Attendants	$23,570	19.1%	8,000
40. Composers	$33,720	13.1%	9,000
41. Music Arrangers and Orchestrators	$33,720	13.1%	9,000
42. Music Directors	$33,720	13.1%	9,000
43. Music Directors and Composers	$33,720	13.1%	9,000
44. Floral Designers	$19,280	14.9%	15,000

Best Jobs for People Interested in Science, Math, and Engineering

Job	Annual Earnings	Percent Growth	Annual Openings
1. Computer Software Engineers, Applications	$70,210	100.0%	28,000
2. Computer Systems Analysts	$61,990	59.7%	34,000
3. Computer and Information Systems Managers	$82,480	47.9%	28,000
4. Computer Software Engineers, Systems Software	$73,280	89.7%	23,000
5. Computer Support Specialists	$38,560	97.0%	40,000
6. Computer Security Specialists	$53,770	81.9%	18,000
7. Network and Computer Systems Administrators	$53,770	81.9%	18,000
8. Network Systems and Data Communications Analysts	$57,470	77.5%	9,000
9. Computer Programmers	$60,120	16.2%	36,000
10. Nuclear Equipment Operation Technicians	$59,690	20.7%	15,000
11. Database Administrators	$54,850	65.9%	8,000
12. Industrial-Organizational Psychologists	$66,010	18.1%	18,000
13. Architectural and Civil Drafters	$37,010	20.8%	12,000
14. Architectural Drafters	$37,010	20.8%	12,000
15. Civil Drafters	$37,010	20.8%	12,000
16. Computer and Information Scientists, Research	$75,130	40.3%	2,000
17. Biochemists	$57,100	21.0%	5,000
18. Biochemists and Biophysicists	$57,100	21.0%	5,000
19. Biophysicists	$57,100	21.0%	5,000
20. Computer Hardware Engineers	$71,560	24.9%	3,000
21. Environmental Engineers	$61,250	26.0%	3,000
22. Microbiologists	$49,880	21.0%	5,000
23. Chemists	$51,860	19.1%	6,000
24. Biological Technicians	$32,280	26.4%	7,000
25. Zoologists and Wildlife Biologists	$46,220	21.0%	5,000
26. Engineering Managers	$87,490	8.0%	24,000
27. Biologists	$44,770	21.0%	5,000
28. Environmental Scientists and Specialists, Including Health	$47,330	22.3%	4,000
29. Electrical and Electronics Drafters	$40,070	23.3%	5,000
30. Electrical Drafters	$40,070	23.3%	5,000
31. Electronic Drafters	$40,070	23.3%	5,000
32. Medical Scientists, Except Epidemiologists	$55,960	26.5%	2,000
33. Calibration and Instrumentation Technicians	$42,130	10.8%	22,000
34. Electrical and Electronic Engineering Technicians	$42,130	10.8%	22,000

(continued)

(continued)

Best Jobs for People Interested in Science, Math, and Engineering

Job	Annual Earnings	Percent Growth	Annual Openings
35. Electrical Engineering Technicians	$42,130	10.8%	22,000
36. Electronics Engineering Technicians	$42,130	10.8%	22,000
37. Epidemiologists	$52,710	26.5%	2,000
38. Architects, Except Landscape and Naval	$55,470	18.5%	4,000
39. Chemical Technicians	$36,190	15.0%	13,000
40. Economists	$67,050	18.5%	3,000
41. Mapping Technicians	$28,210	25.3%	7,000
42. Surveying and Mapping Technicians	$28,210	25.3%	7,000
43. Surveying Technicians	$28,210	25.3%	7,000
44. Sales Engineers	$59,720	17.7%	4,000
45. Geologists	$58,280	18.1%	3,000
46. Environmental Science and Protection Technicians, Including Health	$34,690	24.5%	3,000
47. Hydrologists	$56,400	25.7%	1,000
48. Landscape Architects	$46,710	31.1%	1,000
49. Agricultural Technicians	$27,530	15.2%	15,000
50. Food Science Technicians	$27,530	15.2%	15,000
51. Mechanical Engineers	$61,440	13.1%	7,000
52. Mechanical Drafters	$39,620	15.4%	8,000
53. Environmental Engineering Technicians	$36,590	29.1%	2,000
54. Biomedical Engineers	$59,790	31.4%	fewer than 500
55. Electrical Engineers	$66,890	11.3%	8,000
56. Geoscientists, Except Hydrologists and Geographers	$58,280	18.1%	2,000
57. Photographers, Scientific	$23,040	17.0%	13,000
58. Political Scientists	$81,350	17.2%	2,000
59. Materials Scientists	$62,750	19.8%	1,000
60. Urban and Regional Planners	$48,530	16.4%	3,000
61. Sociologists	$54,880	17.2%	2,000
62. Survey Researchers	$23,230	34.5%	3,000
63. Civil Engineering Technicians	$37,410	11.9%	9,000
64. Electronics Engineers, Except Computer	$68,350	10.4%	6,000
65. Geographers	$48,410	17.2%	2,000
66. Nuclear Technicians	$59,690	20.7%	fewer than 500
67. Mechanical Engineering Technicians	$40,910	13.9%	5,000
68. Historians	$42,940	17.2%	2,000

Best Jobs for People Interested in Plants and Animals

Job	Annual Earnings	Percent Growth	Annual Openings
1. Landscaping and Groundskeeping Workers	$19,120	29.0%	193,000
2. First-Line Supervisors/Managers of Farming, Fishing, and Forestry Workers	$33,330	13.0%	89,000
3. Veterinarians	$62,000	31.8%	2,000
4. First-Line Supervisors and Manager/Supervisors —Landscaping Workers	$32,100	20.1%	10,000
5. First-Line Supervisors/Managers of Landscaping, Lawn Service, and Groundskeeping Workers	$32,100	20.1%	10,000
6. Lawn Service Managers	$32,100	20.1%	10,000
7. Nonfarm Animal Caretakers	$16,570	21.6%	20,000
8. Veterinary Technologists and Technicians	$22,430	39.3%	6,000
9. Veterinary Assistants and Laboratory Animal Caretakers	$17,470	39.8%	8,000
10. Pest Control Workers	$23,150	22.1%	7,000
11. Farmers and Ranchers	$42,170	−25.4%	146,000
12. Tree Trimmers and Pruners	$23,950	16.3%	11,000
13. First-Line Supervisors and Manager/Supervisors —Agricultural Crop Workers	$33,330	13.0%	8,000

Best Jobs for People Interested in Law, Law Enforcement, and Public Safety

Job	Annual Earnings	Percent Growth	Annual Openings
1. Lawyers	$88,760	18.0%	35,000
2. Correctional Officers and Jailers	$32,010	32.4%	30,000
3. Paralegals and Legal Assistants	$36,670	33.2%	23,000
4. Security Guards	$18,600	35.4%	242,000
5. Highway Patrol Pilots	$40,970	23.2%	21,000
6. Police and Sheriff's Patrol Officers	$40,970	23.2%	21,000
7. Police Patrol Officers	$40,970	23.2%	21,000
8. Sheriffs and Deputy Sheriffs	$40,970	23.2%	21,000
9. Nuclear Monitoring Technicians	$59,690	20.7%	15,000
10. Emergency Medical Technicians and Paramedics	$23,170	31.3%	19,000
11. First-Line Supervisors/Managers of Correctional Officers	$44,640	29.6%	3,000
12. Private Detectives and Investigators	$28,380	23.5%	9,000
13. First-Line Supervisors/Managers of Police and Detectives	$59,300	13.1%	9,000
14. Forest Fire Fighting and Prevention Supervisors	$53,420	16.7%	5,000
15. Municipal Fire Fighting and Prevention Supervisors	$53,420	16.7%	5,000
16. Child Support, Missing Persons, and Unemployment Insurance Fraud Investigators	$50,960	16.4%	4,000
17. Criminal Investigators and Special Agents	$50,960	16.4%	4,000
18. Detectives and Criminal Investigators	$50,960	16.4%	4,000
19. Immigration and Customs Inspectors	$50,960	16.4%	4,000
20. Police Detectives	$50,960	16.4%	4,000
21. Police Identification and Records Officers	$50,960	16.4%	4,000
22. Arbitrators, Mediators, and Conciliators	$46,660	27.2%	fewer than 500

Best Jobs for People Interested in Being Mechanics, Installers, and Repairers

Job	Annual Earnings	Percent Growth	Annual Openings
1. First-Line Supervisors/Managers of Mechanics, Installers, and Repairers	$46,320	16.0%	38,000
2. Automotive Master Mechanics	$29,510	18.0%	104,000
3. Automotive Service Technicians and Mechanics	$29,510	18.0%	104,000
4. Automotive Specialty Technicians	$29,510	18.0%	104,000
5. Heating and Air Conditioning Mechanics	$34,020	22.3%	21,000
6. Heating, Air Conditioning, and Refrigeration Mechanics and Installers	$34,020	22.3%	21,000
7. Refrigeration Mechanics	$34,020	22.3%	21,000
8. Telecommunications Line Installers and Repairers	$39,200	27.6%	9,000
9. Helpers—Installation, Maintenance, and Repair Workers	$21,210	18.5%	35,000
10. Computer, Automated Teller, and Office Machine Repairers	$32,890	14.2%	24,000
11. Data Processing Equipment Repairers	$32,890	14.2%	24,000
12. Office Machine and Cash Register Servicers	$32,890	14.2%	24,000
13. Bus and Truck Mechanics and Diesel Engine Specialists	$33,570	14.2%	20,000
14. Aircraft Body and Bonded Structure Repairers	$41,990	16.7%	11,000
15. Aircraft Engine Specialists	$41,990	16.7%	11,000
16. Aircraft Mechanics and Service Technicians	$41,990	16.7%	11,000
17. Airframe-and-Power-Plant Mechanics	$41,990	16.7%	11,000
18. Signal and Track Switch Repairers	$42,390	11.5%	16,000
19. Painters, Transportation Equipment	$32,330	17.5%	8,000
20. Helpers—Electricians	$22,160	13.3%	27,000
21. Mobile Heavy Equipment Mechanics, Except Engines	$35,190	14.0%	11,000
22. Automotive Body and Related Repairers	$32,490	10.2%	18,000
23. Recreational Vehicle Service Technicians	$26,410	25.4%	4,000
24. Maintenance and Repair Workers, General	$28,740	4.7%	103,000
25. Elevator Installers and Repairers	$51,630	17.2%	2,000

Best Jobs for People Interested in Construction, Mining, and Drilling

Job	Annual Earnings	Percent Growth	Annual Openings
1. Electricians	$40,770	17.3%	66,000
2. First-Line Supervisors and Manager/Supervisors —Construction Trades Workers	$46,570	16.5%	43,000
3. First-Line Supervisors and Manager/Supervisors —Extractive Workers	$46,570	16.5%	43,000
4. First-Line Supervisors/Managers of Construction Trades and Extraction Workers	$46,570	16.5%	43,000
5. Construction Managers	$61,050	16.3%	26,000
6. Painters, Construction and Maintenance	$28,420	19.1%	67,000
7. Roofers	$29,460	19.4%	38,000
8. Segmental Pavers	$26,170	26.7%	21,000
9. Construction Laborers	$24,070	17.0%	236,000
10. Sheet Metal Workers	$33,210	23.0%	13,000
11. Hazardous Materials Removal Workers	$31,800	32.8%	9,000
12. Structural Iron and Steel Workers	$38,950	18.4%	12,000
13. Pipe Fitters	$38,710	10.2%	49,000
14. Pipelaying Fitters	$38,710	10.2%	49,000
15. Plumbers	$38,710	10.2%	49,000
16. Plumbers, Pipefitters, and Steamfitters	$38,710	10.2%	49,000
17. Grips and Set-Up Workers, Motion Picture Sets, Studios, and Stages	$19,440	13.9%	519,000
18. Boat Builders and Shipwrights	$33,470	8.2%	161,000
19. Brattice Builders	$33,470	8.2%	161,000
20. Carpenter Assemblers and Repairers	$33,470	8.2%	161,000
21. Carpenters	$33,470	8.2%	161,000
22. Construction Carpenters	$33,470	8.2%	161,000
23. Rough Carpenters	$33,470	8.2%	161,000
24. Ship Carpenters and Joiners	$33,470	8.2%	161,000
25. Brickmasons and Blockmasons	$41,590	12.5%	18,000
26. Refractory Materials Repairers, Except Brickmasons	$35,130	11.5%	16,000
27. Security and Fire Alarm Systems Installers	$30,490	23.4%	4,000
28. Commercial Divers	$32,770	11.5%	16,000
29. Ceiling Tile Installers	$33,000	9.4%	19,000
30. Drywall and Ceiling Tile Installers	$33,000	9.4%	19,000

Best Jobs for People Interested in Construction, Mining, and Drilling

Job	Annual Earnings	Percent Growth	Annual Openings
31. Drywall Installers	$33,000	9.4%	19,000
32. Grader, Bulldozer, and Scraper Operators	$34,160	6.9%	25,000
33. Operating Engineers	$34,160	6.9%	25,000
34. Operating Engineers and Other Construction Equipment Operators	$34,160	6.9%	25,000
35. Paperhangers	$31,330	20.2%	3,000
36. Reinforcing Iron and Rebar Workers	$34,750	17.5%	4,000
37. Insulation Workers, Floor, Ceiling, and Wall	$28,000	13.6%	12,000
38. Insulation Workers, Mechanical	$28,000	13.6%	12,000
39. Helpers—Brickmasons, Blockmasons, Stone-masons, and Tile and Marble Setters	$23,620	14.1%	14,000
40. Tile and Marble Setters	$35,390	15.6%	5,000
41. Stonemasons	$32,470	20.8%	2,000
42. Helpers—Pipelayers, Plumbers, Pipefitters, and Steamfitters	$21,830	11.5%	20,000

Best Jobs for People Interested in Transportation

Job	Annual Earnings	Percent Growth	Annual Openings
1. Tractor-Trailer Truck Drivers	$32,580	19.8%	240,000
2. Truck Drivers, Heavy	$32,580	19.8%	240,000
3. Truck Drivers, Heavy and Tractor-Trailer	$32,580	19.8%	240,000
4. Transportation Managers	$57,240	20.2%	13,000
5. Truck Drivers, Light or Delivery Services	$23,330	19.2%	153,000
6. First-Line Supervisors/Managers of Transportation and Material-Moving Machine and Vehicle Operators	$41,140	19.9%	17,000
7. Taxi Drivers and Chauffeurs	$17,920	24.4%	37,000
8. Bus Drivers, Transit and Intercity	$28,060	17.4%	24,000
9. Stevedores, Except Equipment Operators	$19,440	13.9%	519,000
10. Parking Lot Attendants	$15,690	19.8%	17,000
11. Bus Drivers, School	$21,990	11.6%	63,000
12. Commercial Pilots	$47,420	26.9%	1,000
13. Ambulance Drivers and Attendants, Except Emergency Medical Technicians	$18,890	33.7%	3,000

Best Jobs for People Interested in Industrial Production

Job	Annual Earnings	Percent Growth	Annual Openings
1. Brazers	$28,490	19.3%	51,000
2. Solderers	$28,490	19.3%	51,000
3. Welder-Fitters	$28,490	19.3%	51,000
4. Welders and Cutters	$28,490	19.3%	51,000
5. Welders, Cutters, Solderers, and Brazers	$28,490	19.3%	51,000
6. Welders, Production	$28,490	19.3%	51,000
7. Packers and Packagers, Hand	$16,280	19.3%	242,000
8. Irradiated-Fuel Handlers	$31,800	32.8%	9,000
9. First-Line Supervisors/Managers of Helpers, Laborers, and Material Movers, Hand	$36,090	18.9%	14,000
10. Fitters, Structural Metal—Precision	$28,000	19.5%	20,000
11. Metal Fabricators, Structural Metal Products	$28,000	19.5%	20,000
12. Structural Metal Fabricators and Fitters	$28,000	19.5%	20,000
13. Computer-Controlled Machine Tool Operators, Metal and Plastic	$28,390	19.7%	15,000
14. Numerical Control Machine Tool Operators and Tenders, Metal and Plastic	$28,390	19.7%	15,000
15. Freight, Stock, and Material Movers, Hand	$19,440	13.9%	519,000
16. Laborers and Freight, Stock, and Material Movers, Hand	$19,440	13.9%	519,000
17. Refuse and Recyclable Material Collectors	$23,850	16.6%	34,000
18. Packaging and Filling Machine Operators and Tenders	$20,760	14.4%	56,000
19. Semiconductor Processors	$26,480	32.4%	7,000
20. Industrial Truck and Tractor Operators	$25,350	11.3%	91,000
21. Bakers, Manufacturing	$20,440	16.8%	25,000
22. Combination Machine Tool Operators and Tenders, Metal and Plastic	$27,910	14.7%	21,000
23. Combination Machine Tool Setters and Set-Up Operators, Metal and Plastic	$27,910	14.7%	21,000
24. Multiple Machine Tool Setters, Operators, and Tenders, Metal and Plastic	$27,910	14.7%	21,000
25. Industrial Production Managers	$64,510	6.2%	22,000
26. Helpers—Production Workers	$18,990	11.9%	143,000
27. Production Helpers	$18,990	11.9%	143,000
28. Production Laborers	$18,990	11.9%	143,000
29. Machinists	$32,090	9.1%	28,000

(continued)

(continued)

Best Jobs for People Interested in Industrial Production

Job	Annual Earnings	Percent Growth	Annual Openings
30. Chemical Equipment Controllers and Operators	$36,810	14.9%	9,000
31. Chemical Equipment Operators and Tenders	$36,810	14.9%	9,000
32. Chemical Equipment Tenders	$36,810	14.9%	9,000
33. Extruding and Drawing Machine Setters, Operators, and Tenders, Metal and Plastic	$25,170	13.5%	23,000
34. First-Line Supervisors/Managers of Production and Operating Workers	$42,000	1.0%	71,000
35. Water and Liquid Waste Treatment Plant and System Operators	$32,560	18.1%	6,000
36. Casting Machine Set-Up Operators	$22,340	9.8%	38,000
37. Metal Molding, Coremaking, and Casting Machine Operators and Tenders	$22,340	9.8%	38,000
38. Metal Molding, Coremaking, and Casting Machine Setters and Set-Up Operators	$22,340	9.8%	38,000
39. Molding, Coremaking, and Casting Machine Setters, Operators, and Tenders, Metal and Plastic	$22,340	9.8%	38,000
40. Plastic Molding and Casting Machine Operators and Tenders	$22,340	9.8%	38,000
41. Plastic Molding and Casting Machine Setters and Set-Up Operators	$22,340	9.8%	38,000
42. Team Assemblers	$22,260	5.9%	283,000
43. Soldering and Brazing Machine Operators and Tenders	$28,220	15.1%	9,000
44. Soldering and Brazing Machine Setters and Set-Up Operators	$28,220	15.1%	9,000
45. Welding Machine Operators and Tenders	$28,220	15.1%	9,000
46. Welding Machine Setters and Set-Up Operators	$28,220	15.1%	9,000
47. Welding, Soldering, and Brazing Machine Setters, Operators, and Tenders	$28,220	15.1%	9,000
48. Coating, Painting, and Spraying Machine Operators and Tenders	$24,710	11.9%	18,000
49. Coating, Painting, and Spraying Machine Setters and Set-Up Operators	$24,710	11.9%	18,000
50. Coating, Painting, and Spraying Machine Setters, Operators, and Tenders	$24,710	11.9%	18,000

Best Jobs for People Interested in Business Detail

Job	Annual Earnings	Percent Growth	Annual Openings
1. Adjustment Clerks	$25,430	32.4%	359,000
2. Customer Service Representatives	$25,430	32.4%	359,000
3. Customer Service Representatives, Utilities	$25,430	32.4%	359,000
4. Administrative Services Managers	$49,810	20.4%	31,000
5. Legal Secretaries	$34,610	20.3%	36,000
6. Bill and Account Collectors	$25,960	25.3%	71,000
7. Interviewers, Except Eligibility and Loan	$21,880	33.4%	53,000
8. Receptionists and Information Clerks	$20,650	23.7%	269,000
9. Production, Planning, and Expediting Clerks	$32,420	17.9%	36,000
10. Human Resources Assistants, Except Payroll and Timekeeping	$29,470	19.3%	25,000
11. Counter and Rental Clerks	$16,750	19.4%	150,000
12. Medical Secretaries	$24,670	19.0%	40,000
13. Medical Transcriptionists	$26,460	29.8%	15,000
14. Medical Records and Health Information Technicians	$23,530	49.0%	14,000
15. Office Clerks, General	$21,780	15.9%	676,000
16. Executive Secretaries and Administrative Assistants	$32,380	11.5%	185,000
17. First-Line Supervisors, Administrative Support	$37,990	9.4%	146,000
18. First-Line Supervisors, Customer Service	$37,990	9.4%	146,000
19. First-Line Supervisors/Managers of Office and Administrative Support Workers	$37,990	9.4%	146,000
20. Automatic Teller Machine Servicers	$32,890	14.2%	24,000
21. Gaming Change Persons and Booth Cashiers	$18,990	36.1%	13,000
22. Cashiers	$14,950	14.5%	1,125,000
23. Travel Clerks	$24,090	14.5%	39,000
24. Dispatchers, Except Police, Fire, and Ambulance	$30,070	22.2%	8,000
25. Weighers, Measurers, Checkers, and Samplers, Recordkeeping	$24,690	17.9%	13,000
26. Shipping, Receiving, and Traffic Clerks	$22,710	9.3%	133,000
27. Billing and Posting Clerks and Machine Operators	$25,350	8.5%	69,000
28. Billing, Cost, and Rate Clerks	$25,350	8.5%	69,000
29. Billing, Posting, and Calculating Machine Operators	$25,350	8.5%	69,000
30. Statement Clerks	$25,350	8.5%	69,000
31. Marking Clerks	$19,060	8.5%	467,000
32. Order Fillers, Wholesale and Retail Sales	$19,060	8.5%	467,000

(continued)

(continued)

Best Jobs for People Interested in Business Detail

Job	Annual Earnings	Percent Growth	Annual Openings
33. Stock Clerks and Order Fillers	$19,060	8.5%	467,000
34. Stock Clerks—Stockroom, Warehouse, or Storage Yard	$19,060	8.5%	467,000
35. Gaming Cage Workers	$21,540	25.2%	7,000
36. Tax Preparers	$27,680	17.4%	8,000
37. File Clerks	$19,490	9.1%	49,000
38. Bookkeeping, Accounting, and Auditing Clerks	$26,540	2.0%	298,000
39. Court Clerks	$27,090	12.0%	14,000
40. Court, Municipal, and License Clerks	$27,090	12.0%	14,000
41. License Clerks	$27,090	12.0%	14,000
42. Municipal Clerks	$27,090	12.0%	14,000

Best Jobs for People Interested in Sales and Marketing

Job	Annual Earnings	Percent Growth	Annual Openings
1. Sales Agents, Financial Services	$59,690	22.3%	55,000
2. Sales Agents, Securities and Commodities	$59,690	22.3%	55,000
3. Securities, Commodities, and Financial Services Sales Agents	$59,690	22.3%	55,000
4. Sales Managers	$71,620	32.8%	21,000
5. Marketing Managers	$74,370	29.1%	12,000
6. Advertising Sales Agents	$36,560	26.3%	25,000
7. Advertising and Promotions Managers	$55,940	34.3%	7,000
8. Telemarketers	$19,210	22.2%	145,000
9. Demonstrators and Product Promoters	$20,690	24.9%	34,000
10. First-Line Supervisors/Managers of Non-Retail Sales Workers	$51,490	5.8%	41,000
11. Sales Representatives, Wholesale and Manufacturing, Except Technical and Scientific Products	$41,520	5.7%	86,000
12. Sales Representatives, Agricultural	$54,360	7.5%	24,000
13. Sales Representatives, Chemical and Pharmaceutical	$54,360	7.5%	24,000
14. Sales Representatives, Electrical/Electronic	$54,360	7.5%	24,000
15. Sales Representatives, Instruments	$54,360	7.5%	24,000
16. Sales Representatives, Mechanical Equipment and Supplies	$54,360	7.5%	24,000
17. Sales Representatives, Medical	$54,360	7.5%	24,000
18. Sales Representatives, Wholesale and Manufacturing, Technical and Scientific Products	$54,360	7.5%	24,000
19. Retail Salespersons	$17,150	12.4%	1,124,000
20. First-Line Supervisors/Managers of Retail Sales Workers	$28,590	8.1%	206,000
21. Real Estate Sales Agents	$28,570	9.5%	28,000
22. Insurance Sales Agents	$38,890	3.3%	43,000
23. Stock Clerks, Sales Floor	$19,060	8.5%	467,000
24. Real Estate Brokers	$51,370	9.6%	8,000

Best Jobs for People Interested in Recreation, Travel, and Other Personal Services

Job	Annual Earnings	Percent Growth	Annual Openings
1. Combined Food Preparation and Serving Workers, Including Fast Food	$14,120	30.5%	737,000
2. Personal and Home Care Aides	$16,140	62.5%	84,000
3. Hotel, Motel, and Resort Desk Clerks	$16,920	33.4%	73,000
4. Amusement and Recreation Attendants	$14,600	32.4%	62,000
5. Cooks, Restaurant	$18,480	21.7%	158,000
6. Food Service Managers	$33,630	15.0%	55,000
7. Gaming Dealers	$13,680	32.4%	28,000
8. Waiters and Waitresses	$13,720	18.3%	596,000
9. Cleaners of Vehicles and Equipment	$16,490	18.8%	86,000
10. Food Preparation Workers	$15,910	16.9%	231,000
11. Recreation Workers	$17,850	20.1%	32,000
12. Food Servers, Nonrestaurant	$15,310	16.4%	85,000
13. Janitors and Cleaners, Except Maids and House-keeping Cleaners	$17,900	13.5%	507,000
14. Counter Attendants, Cafeteria, Food Concession, and Coffee Shop	$14,760	14.4%	216,000
15. Reservation and Transportation Ticket Agents	$24,090	14.5%	39,000
16. Reservation and Transportation Ticket Agents and Travel Clerks	$24,090	14.5%	39,000
17. First-Line Supervisors/Managers of Food Preparation and Serving Workers	$23,600	12.7%	136,000
18. Flight Attendants	$40,600	18.4%	8,000
19. Bakers	$20,440	16.8%	25,000
20. Bakers, Bread and Pastry	$20,440	16.8%	25,000
21. Bartenders	$14,610	13.4%	84,000
22. Hairdressers, Hairstylists, and Cosmetologists	$18,260	13.0%	78,000
23. Hosts and Hostesses, Restaurant, Lounge, and Coffee Shop	$14,920	13.0%	84,000
24. Meeting and Convention Planners	$36,550	23.3%	3,000
25. First-Line Supervisors/Managers of Housekeeping and Janitorial Workers	$27,200	14.2%	18,000
26. Housekeeping Supervisors	$27,200	14.2%	18,000
27. Janitorial Supervisors	$27,200	14.2%	18,000
28. Gaming Managers	$53,450	30.0%	fewer than 500
29. Laundry and Dry-Cleaning Workers	$16,360	11.4%	62,000

Best Jobs for People Interested in Recreation, Travel, and Other Personal Services

Job	Annual Earnings	Percent Growth	Annual Openings
30. Laundry and Drycleaning Machine Operators and Tenders, Except Pressing	$16,360	11.4%	62,000
31. Precision Dyers	$16,360	11.4%	62,000
32. Spotters, Dry Cleaning	$16,360	11.4%	62,000
33. Chefs and Head Cooks	$26,800	9.0%	35,000
34. Aircraft Cargo Handling Supervisors	$37,330	27.7%	1,000
35. Manicurists and Pedicurists	$16,700	26.5%	5,000
36. Cooks, Institution and Cafeteria	$17,750	7.6%	110,000
37. Gaming Supervisors	$39,240	18.4%	2,000
38. First-Line Supervisors/Managers of Personal Service Workers	$28,040	15.1%	8,000

Best Jobs for People Interested in Education and Social Service

Job	Annual Earnings	Percent Growth	Annual Openings
1. Teachers, Postsecondary	$52,115	23.5%	184,000
2. Secondary School Teachers, Except Special and Vocational Education	$43,280	18.6%	60,000
3. Personal Financial Advisors	$57,710	34.0%	13,000
4. Educational, Vocational, and School Counselors	$43,470	25.3%	22,000
5. Child, Family, and School Social Workers	$32,950	26.9%	35,000
6. Special Education Teachers, Preschool, Kindergarten, and Elementary School	$42,110	36.8%	15,000
7. Social and Human Service Assistants	$23,070	54.2%	45,000
8. Instructional Coordinators	$46,600	25.0%	15,000
9. Teacher Assistants	$18,070	23.9%	256,000
10. Education Administrators, Elementary and Secondary School	$69,240	13.4%	35,000
11. Education Administrators, Postsecondary	$61,700	13.4%	35,000
12. Medical and Public Health Social Workers	$36,410	31.6%	13,000
13. Clinical Psychologists	$50,420	18.1%	18,000
14. Clinical, Counseling, and School Psychologists	$50,420	18.1%	18,000
15. Counseling Psychologists	$50,420	18.1%	18,000
16. Educational Psychologists	$50,420	18.1%	18,000
17. Social and Community Service Managers	$41,260	24.8%	13,000
18. Elementary School Teachers, Except Special Education	$41,080	13.2%	144,000
19. Probation Officers and Correctional Treatment Specialists	$38,780	23.8%	14,000
20. Self-Enrichment Education Teachers	$28,880	18.5%	34,000
21. Mental Health and Substance Abuse Social Workers	$32,080	39.1%	10,000
22. Preschool Teachers, Except Special Education	$18,640	20.0%	55,000
23. Special Education Teachers, Secondary School	$42,780	24.6%	8,000
24. Library Technicians	$23,790	19.5%	29,000
25. Kindergarten Teachers, Except Special Education	$38,740	14.5%	23,000
26. Adult Literacy, Remedial Education, and GED Teachers and Instructors	$35,220	19.4%	12,000
27. Middle School Teachers, Except Special and Vocational Education	$41,220	9.6%	54,000
28. Education Administrators, Preschool and Child Care Center/Program	$31,860	13.4%	35,000

Best Jobs for People Interested in Education and Social Service

Job	Annual Earnings	Percent Growth	Annual Openings
29. Substance Abuse and Behavioral Disorder Counselors	$29,870	35.0%	7,000
30. Special Education Teachers, Middle School	$40,010	24.4%	6,000
31. Library Assistants, Clerical	$18,580	19.7%	26,000
32. Rehabilitation Counselors	$25,610	23.6%	12,000
33. Directors, Religious Activities and Education	$27,420	15.9%	23,000
34. Clergy	$33,840	15.0%	12,000
35. Mental Health Counselors	$29,050	21.7%	7,000
36. Child Care Workers	$16,030	10.6%	370,000
37. Residential Advisors	$19,680	24.0%	9,000
38. Marriage and Family Therapists	$32,720	29.9%	2,000
39. Vocational Education Teachers, Secondary School	$43,590	13.4%	7,000

Best Jobs for People Interested in General Management and Support

Job	Annual Earnings	Percent Growth	Annual Openings
1. Management Analysts	$57,970	28.9%	50,000
2. Financial Managers	$70,210	18.5%	53,000
3. Financial Managers, Branch or Department	$70,210	18.5%	53,000
4. Treasurers, Controllers, and Chief Financial Officers	$70,210	18.5%	53,000
5. Accountants	$45,380	18.5%	100,000
6. Accountants and Auditors	$45,380	18.5%	100,000
7. Auditors	$45,380	18.5%	100,000
8. General and Operations Managers	$65,010	15.2%	235,000
9. Chief Executives	$120,450	17.2%	48,000
10. Government Service Executives	$120,450	17.2%	48,000
11. Private Sector Executives	$120,450	17.2%	48,000
12. Financial Analysts	$55,120	25.5%	20,000
13. Market Research Analysts	$53,450	24.4%	13,000
14. Property, Real Estate, and Community Association Managers	$36,290	22.7%	24,000
15. Cost Estimators	$46,960	16.5%	28,000
16. Storage and Distribution Managers	$57,240	20.2%	13,000
17. Transportation, Storage, and Distribution Managers	$57,240	20.2%	13,000
18. Public Relations Managers	$57,200	36.3%	7,000
19. Training and Development Specialists	$41,780	19.4%	20,000
20. Claims Adjusters, Examiners, and Investigators	$42,440	15.1%	25,000
21. Claims Examiners, Property and Casualty Insurance	$42,440	15.1%	25,000
22. Insurance Adjusters, Examiners, and Investigators	$42,440	15.1%	25,000
23. Employment Interviewers, Private or Public Employment Service	$38,010	17.6%	19,000
24. Employment, Recruitment, and Placement Specialists	$38,010	17.6%	19,000
25. Personnel Recruiters	$38,010	17.6%	19,000
26. Purchasing Agents, Except Wholesale, Retail, and Farm Products	$43,230	12.3%	23,000
27. Compensation and Benefits Managers	$61,880	12.7%	14,000
28. Human Resources Managers	$61,880	12.7%	14,000
29. Training and Development Managers	$61,880	12.7%	14,000
30. Budget Analysts	$50,510	14.6%	8,000
31. Compensation, Benefits, and Job Analysis Specialists	$43,330	15.7%	8,000
32. Appraisers and Assessors of Real Estate	$38,950	18.0%	6,000
33. Appraisers, Real Estate	$38,950	18.0%	6,000
34. Assessors	$38,950	18.0%	6,000
35. Credit Analysts	$41,650	16.0%	7,000
36. Loan Officers	$43,210	4.9%	28,000

Best Jobs for People Interested in Medical and Health Services

Job	Annual Earnings	Percent Growth	Annual Openings
1. Registered Nurses	$46,670	25.6%	140,000
2. Medical and Health Services Managers	$59,220	32.3%	27,000
3. Pharmacists	$74,890	24.3%	20,000
4. Anesthesiologists	greater than $146,500	17.9%	27,000
5. Internists, General	greater than $146,500	17.9%	27,000
6. Obstetricians and Gynecologists	greater than $146,500	17.9%	27,000
7. Surgeons	greater than $146,500	17.9%	27,000
8. Psychiatrists	$126,460	17.9%	27,000
9. Pediatricians, General	$126,430	17.9%	27,000
10. Family and General Practitioners	$118,390	17.9%	27,000
11. Home Health Aides	$17,590	47.3%	120,000
12. Licensed Practical and Licensed Vocational Nurses	$30,670	20.3%	58,000
13. Nursing Aides, Orderlies, and Attendants	$19,290	23.5%	268,000
14. Physician Assistants	$63,970	53.5%	5,000
15. Physical Therapists	$56,570	33.3%	6,000
16. Physical Therapist Assistants	$35,280	44.8%	9,000
17. Dental Hygienists	$54,700	37.1%	5,000
18. Dental Assistants	$26,720	37.2%	16,000
19. Medical Assistants	$23,610	57.0%	18,700
20. Pharmacy Technicians	$21,630	36.4%	22,000
21. Radiologic Technicians	$37,680	23.1%	13,000
22. Radiologic Technologists	$37,680	23.1%	13,000
23. Radiologic Technologists and Technicians	$37,680	23.1%	13,000
24. Medical and Clinical Laboratory Technologists	$42,240	17.0%	19,000
25. Occupational Therapists	$51,370	33.9%	4,000
26. Speech-Language Pathologists	$48,520	39.2%	4,000
27. Medical and Clinical Laboratory Technicians	$28,810	19.0%	19,000
28. Surgical Technologists	$30,090	34.7%	8,000
29. Respiratory Therapists	$39,370	34.8%	4,000
30. Chiropractors	$68,420	23.4%	3,000
31. Health Educators	$35,230	23.5%	7,000
32. Diagnostic Medical Sonographers	$46,980	26.1%	3,000
33. Occupational Therapist Assistants	$35,840	39.7%	3,000
34. Massage Therapists	$28,050	30.4%	7,000

(continued)

(continued)

Best Jobs for People Interested in Medical and Health Services

Job	Annual Earnings	Percent Growth	Annual Openings
35. Cardiovascular Technologists and Technicians	$35,010	34.9%	3,000
36. Respiratory Therapy Technicians	$33,840	34.6%	3,000
37. Audiologists	$46,900	44.7%	1,000
38. Physical Therapist Aides	$20,300	46.3%	7,000
39. Radiation Therapists	$49,050	22.8%	1,000
40. Nuclear Medicine Technologists	$47,400	22.4%	1,000
41. Optometrists	$85,650	18.7%	1,000
42. Dietitians and Nutritionists	$40,410	15.2%	5,000
43. Pharmacy Aides	$18,010	19.5%	9,000
44. Dietetic Technicians	$21,790	27.6%	3,000

Best Jobs Lists Based on Personality Types

These lists organize the 500 best jobs into groups matching six personality types. The personality types are Realistic, Investigative, Artistic, Social, Enterprising, and Conventional. This system was developed by John Holland and is used in the *Self Directed Search (SDS)* and other career assessment inventories and information systems.

If you have used one of these career inventories or systems, the lists will help you identify jobs that most closely match these personality types. Even if you have not used one of these systems, the concept of personality types and the jobs that are related to them can help you identify jobs that most closely match the type of person you are.

We've ranked the jobs within each personality type based on their total combined scores for earnings (given double the weight), growth, and annual job openings. Like the job lists for education levels, there is only one list for each personality type. Note that each job is listed in the one personality type it most closely matches, even though it might also fit into others. Consider reviewing the jobs for more than one personality type so you don't overlook possible jobs that would interest you. Also, note that we did not have data to crosswalk 84 of the 500 best jobs to their related personality type, so some of the best jobs do not appear on the lists in this section.

Following are brief descriptions for each of the six personality types used in the lists. Select the two or three descriptions that most closely describe you and then use the lists to identify jobs that best fit these personality types.

Descriptions of the Six Personality Types

▲ **Realistic:** These occupations frequently involve work activities that include practical, hands-on problems and solutions. They often deal with plants, animals, and real-world materials like wood, tools, and machinery. Many of the occupations require working outside and do not involve a lot of paperwork or working closely with others.

▲ **Investigative:** These occupations frequently involve working with ideas and require an extensive amount of thinking. These occupations can involve searching for facts and figuring out problems mentally.

▲ **Artistic:** These occupations frequently involve working with forms, designs, and patterns. They often require self-expression, and the work can be done without following a clear set of rules.

▲ **Social:** These occupations frequently involve working with, communicating with, and teaching people. These occupations often involve helping or providing service to others.

▲ **Enterprising:** These occupations frequently involve starting up and carrying out projects. These occupations can involve leading people and making many decisions. They sometimes require risk taking and often deal with business.

▲ **Conventional:** These occupations frequently involve following set procedures and routines. These occupations can include working with data and details more than with ideas. Usually there is a clear line of authority to follow.

Best Jobs for People with a Realistic Personality Type

Job	Annual Earnings	Percent Growth	Annual Openings
1. Tractor-Trailer Truck Drivers	$32,580	19.8%	240,000
2. Truck Drivers, Heavy	$32,580	19.8%	240,000
3. Correctional Officers and Jailers	$32,010	32.4%	30,000
4. Electricians	$40,770	17.3%	66,000
5. Combined Food Preparation and Serving Workers, Including Fast Food	$14,120	30.5%	737,000
6. Landscaping and Groundskeeping Workers	$19,120	29.0%	193,000
7. Highway Patrol Pilots	$40,970	23.2%	21,000
8. Nuclear Equipment Operation Technicians	$59,690	20.7%	15,000
9. Nuclear Monitoring Technicians	$59,690	20.7%	15,000
10. Automotive Master Mechanics	$29,510	18.0%	104,000
11. Automotive Specialty Technicians	$29,510	18.0%	104,000
12. Painters, Construction and Maintenance	$28,420	19.1%	67,000
13. Heating and Air Conditioning Mechanics	$34,020	22.3%	21,000
14. Refrigeration Mechanics	$34,020	22.3%	21,000
15. Technical Directors/Managers	$45,090	27.1%	11,000
16. Brazers	$28,490	19.3%	51,000
17. Solderers	$28,490	19.3%	51,000
18. Welder-Fitters	$28,490	19.3%	51,000
19. Welders and Cutters	$28,490	19.3%	51,000
20. Welders, Production	$28,490	19.3%	51,000
21. Amusement and Recreation Attendants	$14,600	32.4%	62,000
22. Roofers	$29,460	19.4%	38,000
23. Truck Drivers, Light or Delivery Services	$23,330	19.2%	153,000
24. Cooks, Restaurant	$18,480	21.7%	158,000
25. Radiologic Technicians	$37,680	23.1%	13,000
26. Radiologic Technologists	$37,680	23.1%	13,000
27. Packers and Packagers, Hand	$16,280	19.3%	242,000
28. Telecommunications Line Installers and Repairers	$39,200	27.6%	9,000
29. Construction Laborers	$24,070	17.0%	236,000
30. Taxi Drivers and Chauffeurs	$17,920	24.4%	37,000
31. Sheet Metal Workers	$33,210	23.0%	13,000
32. Irradiated-Fuel Handlers	$31,800	32.8%	9,000
33. Architectural Drafters	$37,010	20.8%	12,000
34. Civil Drafters	$37,010	20.8%	12,000
35. Cleaners of Vehicles and Equipment	$16,490	18.8%	86,000

Best Jobs for People with a Realistic Personality Type

Job	Annual Earnings	Percent Growth	Annual Openings
36. Fitters, Structural Metal—Precision	$28,000	19.5%	20,000
37. Metal Fabricators, Structural Metal Products	$28,000	19.5%	20,000
38. Medical and Clinical Laboratory Technicians	$28,810	19.0%	19,000
39. Food Preparation Workers	$15,910	16.9%	231,000
40. Surgical Technologists	$30,090	34.7%	8,000
41. Structural Iron and Steel Workers	$38,950	18.4%	12,000
42. Bus Drivers, Transit and Intercity	$28,060	17.4%	24,000
43. Helpers—Installation, Maintenance, and Repair Workers	$21,210	18.5%	35,000
44. Pipe Fitters	$38,710	10.2%	49,000
45. Pipelaying Fitters	$38,710	10.2%	49,000
46. Plumbers	$38,710	10.2%	49,000
47. Numerical Control Machine Tool Operators and Tenders, Metal and Plastic	$28,390	19.7%	15,000
48. Automatic Teller Machine Servicers	$32,890	14.2%	24,000
49. Data Processing Equipment Repairers	$32,890	14.2%	24,000
50. Office Machine and Cash Register Servicers	$32,890	14.2%	24,000
51. Freight, Stock, and Material Movers, Hand	$19,440	13.9%	519,000
52. Grips and Set-Up Workers, Motion Picture Sets, Studios, and Stages	$19,440	13.9%	519,000
53. Stevedores, Except Equipment Operators	$19,440	13.9%	519,000
54. Desktop Publishers	$31,200	66.7%	5,000
55. Biological Technicians	$32,280	26.4%	7,000
56. Refuse and Recyclable Material Collectors	$23,850	16.6%	34,000
57. First-Line Supervisors and Manager/Supervisors —Landscaping Workers	$32,100	20.1%	10,000
58. Boat Builders and Shipwrights	$33,470	8.2%	161,000
59. Brattice Builders	$33,470	8.2%	161,000
60. Carpenter Assemblers and Repairers	$33,470	8.2%	161,000
61. Construction Carpenters	$33,470	8.2%	161,000
62. Rough Carpenters	$33,470	8.2%	161,000
63. Ship Carpenters and Joiners	$33,470	8.2%	161,000
64. Bus and Truck Mechanics and Diesel Engine Specialists	$33,570	14.2%	20,000
65. Aircraft Body and Bonded Structure Repairers	$41,990	16.7%	11,000
66. Aircraft Engine Specialists	$41,990	16.7%	11,000

(continued)

(continued)

Best Jobs for People with a Realistic Personality Type

Job	Annual Earnings	Percent Growth	Annual Openings
67. Airframe-and-Power-Plant Mechanics	$41,990	16.7%	11,000
68. Janitors and Cleaners, Except Maids and House-keeping Cleaners	$17,900	13.5%	507,000
69. Electronic Drafters	$40,070	23.3%	5,000
70. Nonfarm Animal Caretakers	$16,570	21.6%	20,000
71. Calibration and Instrumentation Technicians	$42,130	10.8%	22,000
72. Electrical Engineering Technicians	$42,130	10.8%	22,000
73. Electronics Engineering Technicians	$42,130	10.8%	22,000
74. Brickmasons and Blockmasons	$41,590	12.5%	18,000
75. Packaging and Filling Machine Operators and Tenders	$20,760	14.4%	56,000
76. Semiconductor Processors	$26,480	32.4%	7,000
77. Industrial Truck and Tractor Operators	$25,350	11.3%	91,000
78. Chemical Technicians	$36,190	15.0%	13,000
79. Bakers, Bread and Pastry	$20,440	16.8%	25,000
80. Bakers, Manufacturing	$20,440	16.8%	25,000
81. Surveying Technicians	$28,210	25.3%	7,000
82. Signal and Track Switch Repairers	$42,390	11.5%	16,000
83. Combination Machine Tool Operators and Tenders, Metal and Plastic	$27,910	14.7%	21,000
84. Combination Machine Tool Setters and Set-Up Operators, Metal and Plastic	$27,910	14.7%	21,000
85. Forest Fire Fighting and Prevention Supervisors	$53,420	16.7%	5,000
86. Municipal Fire Fighting and Prevention Supervisors	$53,420	16.7%	5,000
87. Production Helpers	$18,990	11.9%	143,000
88. Production Laborers	$18,990	11.9%	143,000
89. Veterinary Assistants and Laboratory Animal Caretakers	$17,470	39.8%	8,000
90. Parking Lot Attendants	$15,690	19.8%	17,000
91. Bus Drivers, School	$21,990	11.6%	63,000
92. Agricultural Technicians	$27,530	15.2%	15,000
93. Food Science Technicians	$27,530	15.2%	15,000
94. Machinists	$32,090	9.1%	28,000
95. Mechanical Engineers	$61,440	13.1%	7,000
96. Mechanical Drafters	$39,620	15.4%	8,000
97. Chemical Equipment Controllers and Operators	$36,810	14.9%	9,000
98. Chemical Equipment Tenders	$36,810	14.9%	9,000

Best Jobs for People with a Realistic Personality Type

Job	Annual Earnings	Percent Growth	Annual Openings
99. Refractory Materials Repairers, Except Brickmasons	$35,130	11.5%	16,000
100. Extruding and Drawing Machine Setters, Operators, and Tenders, Metal and Plastic	$25,170	13.5%	23,000
101. Painters, Transportation Equipment	$32,330	17.5%	8,000
102. Commercial Pilots	$47,420	26.9%	1,000
103. Helpers—Electricians	$22,160	13.3%	27,000
104. Mobile Heavy Equipment Mechanics, Except Engines	$35,190	14.0%	11,000
105. Water and Liquid Waste Treatment Plant and System Operators	$32,560	18.1%	6,000
106. Commercial Divers	$32,770	11.5%	16,000
107. Stock Clerks, Sales Floor	$19,060	8.5%	467,000
108. Laundry and Drycleaning Machine Operators and Tenders, Except Pressing	$16,360	11.4%	62,000
109. Precision Dyers	$16,360	11.4%	62,000
110. Spotters, Dry Cleaning	$16,360	11.4%	62,000
111. Automotive Body and Related Repairers	$32,490	10.2%	18,000
112. Ceiling Tile Installers	$33,000	9.4%	19,000
113. Drywall Installers	$33,000	9.4%	19,000
114. Pest Control Workers	$23,150	22.1%	7,000
115. Recreational Vehicle Service Technicians	$26,410	25.4%	4,000
116. Grader, Bulldozer, and Scraper Operators	$34,160	6.9%	25,000
117. Operating Engineers	$34,160	6.9%	25,000
118. Maintenance and Repair Workers, General	$28,740	4.7%	103,000
119. Casting Machine Set-Up Operators	$22,340	9.8%	38,000
120. Metal Molding, Coremaking, and Casting Machine Operators and Tenders	$22,340	9.8%	38,000
121. Metal Molding, Coremaking, and Casting Machine Setters and Set-Up Operators	$22,340	9.8%	38,000
122. Plastic Molding and Casting Machine Operators and Tenders	$22,340	9.8%	38,000
123. Plastic Molding and Casting Machine Setters and Set-Up Operators	$22,340	9.8%	38,000
124. Elevator Installers and Repairers	$51,630	17.2%	2,000
125. Paperhangers	$31,330	20.2%	3,000
126. Soldering and Brazing Machine Operators and Tenders	$28,220	15.1%	9,000

(continued)

(continued)

Best Jobs for People with a Realistic Personality Type

Job	Annual Earnings	Percent Growth	Annual Openings
127. Soldering and Brazing Machine Setters and Set-Up Operators	$28,220	15.1%	9,000
128. Welding Machine Operators and Tenders	$28,220	15.1%	9,000
129. Welding Machine Setters and Set-Up Operators	$28,220	15.1%	9,000
130. Civil Engineering Technicians	$37,410	11.9%	9,000
131. Reinforcing Iron and Rebar Workers	$34,750	17.5%	4,000
132. Farmers and Ranchers	$42,170	−25.4%	146,000
133. Insulation Workers, Floor, Ceiling, and Wall	$28,000	13.6%	12,000
134. Insulation Workers, Mechanical	$28,000	13.6%	12,000
135. Helpers—Brickmasons, Blockmasons, Stone-masons, and Tile and Marble Setters	$23,620	14.1%	14,000
136. Coating, Painting, and Spraying Machine Operators and Tenders	$24,710	11.9%	18,000
137. Coating, Painting, and Spraying Machine Setters and Set-Up Operators	$24,710	11.9%	18,000
138. Tile and Marble Setters	$35,390	15.6%	5,000
139. Tree Trimmers and Pruners	$23,950	16.3%	11,000
140. Mechanical Engineering Technicians	$40,910	13.9%	5,000
141. Cooks, Institution and Cafeteria	$17,750	7.6%	110,000
142. Stonemasons	$32,470	20.8%	2,000
143. Helpers—Pipelayers, Plumbers, Pipefitters, and Steamfitters	$21,830	11.5%	20,000

Best Jobs for People with an Investigative Personality Type

Job	Annual Earnings	Percent Growth	Annual Openings
1. Computer Software Engineers, Applications	$70,210	100.0%	28,000
2. Computer Systems Analysts	$61,990	59.7%	34,000
3. Computer Software Engineers, Systems Software	$73,280	89.7%	23,000
4. Computer Support Specialists	$38,560	97.0%	40,000
5. Computer Security Specialists	$53,770	81.9%	18,000
6. Pharmacists	$74,890	24.3%	20,000
7. Financial Analysts	$55,120	25.5%	20,000
8. Anesthesiologists	greater than $146,500	17.9%	27,000
9. Internists, General	greater than $146,500	17.9%	27,000
10. Obstetricians and Gynecologists	greater than $146,500	17.9%	27,000
11. Surgeons	greater than $146,500	17.9%	27,000
12. Psychiatrists	$126,460	17.9%	27,000
13. Pediatricians, General	$126,430	17.9%	27,000
14. Family and General Practitioners	$118,390	17.9%	27,000
15. Network Systems and Data Communications Analysts	$57,470	77.5%	9,000
16. Computer Programmers	$60,120	16.2%	36,000
17. Market Research Analysts	$53,450	24.4%	13,000
18. Database Administrators	$54,850	65.9%	8,000
19. Industrial-Organizational Psychologists	$66,010	18.1%	18,000
20. Clinical Psychologists	$50,420	18.1%	18,000
21. Educational Psychologists	$50,420	18.1%	18,000
22. Physician Assistants	$63,970	53.5%	5,000
23. Medical and Clinical Laboratory Technologists	$42,240	17.0%	19,000
24. Biochemists	$57,100	21.0%	5,000
25. Biophysicists	$57,100	21.0%	5,000
26. Computer Hardware Engineers	$71,560	24.9%	3,000
27. Respiratory Therapists	$39,370	34.8%	4,000
28. Chiropractors	$68,420	23.4%	3,000
29. Microbiologists	$49,880	21.0%	5,000
30. Veterinarians	$62,000	31.8%	2,000
31. Chemists	$51,860	19.1%	6,000
32. Zoologists and Wildlife Biologists	$46,220	21.0%	5,000
33. Biologists	$44,770	21.0%	5,000

(continued)

(continued)

Best Jobs for People with an Investigative Personality Type

Job	Annual Earnings	Percent Growth	Annual Openings
34. Environmental Scientists and Specialists, Including Health	$47,330	22.3%	4,000
35. Medical Scientists, Except Epidemiologists	$55,960	26.5%	2,000
36. Epidemiologists	$52,710	26.5%	2,000
37. Cardiovascular Technologists and Technicians	$35,010	34.9%	3,000
38. Economists	$67,050	18.5%	3,000
39. Compensation, Benefits, and Job Analysis Specialists	$43,330	15.7%	8,000
40. Geologists	$58,280	18.1%	3,000
41. Environmental Science and Protection Technicians, Including Health	$34,690	24.5%	3,000
42. Hydrologists	$56,400	25.7%	1,000
43. Electrical Engineers	$66,890	11.3%	8,000
44. Political Scientists	$81,350	17.2%	2,000
45. Materials Scientists	$62,750	19.8%	1,000
46. Nuclear Medicine Technologists	$47,400	22.4%	1,000
47. Urban and Regional Planners	$48,530	16.4%	3,000
48. Optometrists	$85,650	18.7%	1,000
49. Sociologists	$54,880	17.2%	2,000
50. Dietitians and Nutritionists	$40,410	15.2%	5,000
51. Electronics Engineers, Except Computer	$68,350	10.4%	6,000
52. Geographers	$48,410	17.2%	2,000
53. Historians	$42,940	17.2%	2,000

Best Jobs for People with an Artistic Personality Type

Job	Annual Earnings	Percent Growth	Annual Openings
1. Graphic Designers	$36,020	26.7%	28,000
2. Caption Writers	$42,450	28.4%	18,000
3. Copy Writers	$42,450	28.4%	18,000
4. Creative Writers	$42,450	28.4%	18,000
5. Poets and Lyricists	$42,450	28.4%	18,000
6. Musicians, Instrumental	$40,320	20.1%	33,000
7. Singers	$40,320	20.1%	33,000
8. Directors—Stage, Motion Pictures, Television, and Radio	$45,090	27.1%	11,000
9. Producers	$45,090	27.1%	11,000
10. Talent Directors	$45,090	27.1%	11,000
11. Advertising and Promotions Managers	$55,940	34.3%	7,000
12. Editors	$39,960	22.6%	14,000
13. Commercial and Industrial Designers	$49,820	23.8%	7,000
14. Technical Writers	$49,360	29.6%	5,000
15. Art Directors	$59,800	21.1%	6,000
16. Actors	$20,540	26.7%	20,000
17. Architects, Except Landscape and Naval	$55,470	18.5%	4,000
18. Makeup Artists, Theatrical and Performance	$30,240	11.4%	27,000
19. Interior Designers	$39,580	17.4%	7,000
20. Landscape Architects	$46,710	31.1%	1,000
21. Fashion Designers	$49,530	20.3%	2,000
22. Film and Video Editors	$36,910	25.8%	2,000
23. Interpreters and Translators	$32,000	23.8%	3,000
24. Exhibit Designers	$33,460	27.0%	2,000
25. Set Designers	$33,460	27.0%	2,000
26. Photographers, Scientific	$23,040	17.0%	13,000
27. Professional Photographers	$23,040	17.0%	13,000
28. Camera Operators, Television, Video, and Motion Picture	$28,980	25.8%	3,000
29. Costume Attendants	$23,570	19.1%	8,000
30. Composers	$33,720	13.1%	9,000
31. Music Arrangers and Orchestrators	$33,720	13.1%	9,000
32. Music Directors	$33,720	13.1%	9,000
33. Floral Designers	$19,280	14.9%	15,000

Best Jobs for People with a Social Personality Type

Job	Annual Earnings	Percent Growth	Annual Openings
1. Registered Nurses	$46,670	25.6%	140,000
2. Secondary School Teachers, Except Special and Vocational Education	$43,280	18.6%	60,000
3. Personal Financial Advisors	$57,710	34.0%	13,000
4. Educational, Vocational, and School Counselors	$43,470	25.3%	22,000
5. Child, Family, and School Social Workers	$32,950	26.9%	35,000
6. Security Guards	$18,600	35.4%	242,000
7. Special Education Teachers, Preschool, Kindergarten, and Elementary School	$42,110	36.8%	15,000
8. Home Health Aides	$17,590	47.3%	120,000
9. Social and Human Service Assistants	$23,070	54.2%	45,000
10. Licensed Practical and Licensed Vocational Nurses	$30,670	20.3%	58,000
11. Police Patrol Officers	$40,970	23.2%	21,000
12. Sheriffs and Deputy Sheriffs	$40,970	23.2%	21,000
13. Instructional Coordinators	$46,600	25.0%	15,000
14. Personal and Home Care Aides	$16,140	62.5%	84,000
15. Nursing Aides, Orderlies, and Attendants	$19,290	23.5%	268,000
16. Teacher Assistants	$18,070	23.9%	256,000
17. Education Administrators, Elementary and Secondary School	$69,240	13.4%	35,000
18. Medical and Public Health Social Workers	$36,410	31.6%	13,000
19. Training and Development Specialists	$41,780	19.4%	20,000
20. Counseling Psychologists	$50,420	18.1%	18,000
21. Social and Community Service Managers	$41,260	24.8%	13,000
22. Elementary School Teachers, Except Special Education	$41,080	13.2%	144,000
23. Probation Officers and Correctional Treatment Specialists	$38,780	23.8%	14,000
24. Physical Therapists	$56,570	33.3%	6,000
25. Physical Therapist Assistants	$35,280	44.8%	9,000
26. Dental Hygienists	$54,700	37.1%	5,000
27. Fitness Trainers and Aerobics Instructors	$23,340	40.3%	19,000
28. Dental Assistants	$26,720	37.2%	16,000
29. Medical Assistants	$23,610	57.0%	18,700
30. Self-Enrichment Education Teachers	$28,880	18.5%	34,000
31. Mental Health and Substance Abuse Social Workers	$32,080	39.1%	10,000
32. Emergency Medical Technicians and Paramedics	$23,170	31.3%	19,000

Best Jobs for People with a Social Personality Type

Job	Annual Earnings	Percent Growth	Annual Openings
33. Waiters and Waitresses	$13,720	18.3%	596,000
34. Employment Interviewers, Private or Public Employment Service	$38,010	17.6%	19,000
35. Preschool Teachers, Except Special Education	$18,640	20.0%	55,000
36. Special Education Teachers, Secondary School	$42,780	24.6%	8,000
37. Occupational Therapists	$51,370	33.9%	4,000
38. Speech-Language Pathologists	$48,520	39.2%	4,000
39. Kindergarten Teachers, Except Special Education	$38,740	14.5%	23,000
40. Adult Literacy, Remedial Education, and GED Teachers and Instructors	$35,220	19.4%	12,000
41. Middle School Teachers, Except Special and Vocational Education	$41,220	9.6%	54,000
42. Recreation Workers	$17,850	20.1%	32,000
43. Education Administrators, Preschool and Child Care Center/Program	$31,860	13.4%	35,000
44. Substance Abuse and Behavioral Disorder Counselors	$29,870	35.0%	7,000
45. Special Education Teachers, Middle School	$40,010	24.4%	6,000
46. Health Educators	$35,230	23.5%	7,000
47. Food Servers, Nonrestaurant	$15,310	16.4%	85,000
48. Counter Attendants, Cafeteria, Food Concession, and Coffee Shop	$14,760	14.4%	216,000
49. Occupational Therapist Assistants	$35,840	39.7%	3,000
50. Directors, Religious Activities and Education	$27,420	15.9%	23,000
51. Audiologists	$46,900	44.7%	1,000
52. Clergy	$33,840	15.0%	12,000
53. Mental Health Counselors	$29,050	21.7%	7,000
54. Physical Therapist Aides	$20,300	46.3%	7,000
55. Child Care Workers	$16,030	10.6%	370,000
56. Residential Advisors	$19,680	24.0%	9,000
57. Vocational Education Teachers, Secondary School	$43,590	13.4%	7,000
58. Radiation Therapists	$49,050	22.8%	1,000
59. Dietetic Technicians	$21,790	27.6%	3,000
60. Ambulance Drivers and Attendants, Except Emergency Medical Technicians	$18,890	33.7%	3,000

Best Jobs for People with an Enterprising Personality Type

Job	Annual Earnings	Percent Growth	Annual Openings
1. Computer and Information Systems Managers	$82,480	47.9%	28,000
2. Management Analysts	$57,970	28.9%	50,000
3. Medical and Health Services Managers	$59,220	32.3%	27,000
4. Sales Agents, Financial Services	$59,690	22.3%	55,000
5. Sales Agents, Securities and Commodities	$59,690	22.3%	55,000
6. Sales Managers	$71,620	32.8%	21,000
7. Financial Managers, Branch or Department	$70,210	18.5%	53,000
8. Treasurers, Controllers, and Chief Financial Officers	$70,210	18.5%	53,000
9. Government Service Executives	$120,450	17.2%	48,000
10. Private Sector Executives	$120,450	17.2%	48,000
11. Lawyers	$88,760	18.0%	35,000
12. Administrative Services Managers	$49,810	20.4%	31,000
13. Public Relations Specialists	$41,010	36.1%	19,000
14. Paralegals and Legal Assistants	$36,670	33.2%	23,000
15. Marketing Managers	$74,370	29.1%	12,000
16. Advertising Sales Agents	$36,560	26.3%	25,000
17. First-Line Supervisors and Manager/Supervisors —Construction Trades Workers	$46,570	16.5%	43,000
18. First-Line Supervisors and Manager/Supervisors —Extractive Workers	$46,570	16.5%	43,000
19. Property, Real Estate, and Community Association Managers	$36,290	22.7%	24,000
20. Construction Managers	$61,050	16.3%	26,000
21. First-Line Supervisors/Managers of Mechanics, Installers, and Repairers	$46,320	16.0%	38,000
22. Storage and Distribution Managers	$57,240	20.2%	13,000
23. Transportation Managers	$57,240	20.2%	13,000
24. Program Directors	$45,090	27.1%	11,000
25. Education Administrators, Postsecondary	$61,700	13.4%	35,000
26. Telemarketers	$19,210	22.2%	145,000
27. First-Line Supervisors/Managers of Transportation and Material-Moving Machine and Vehicle Operators	$41,140	19.9%	17,000
28. Food Service Managers	$33,630	15.0%	55,000
29. Insurance Adjusters, Examiners, and Investigators	$42,440	15.1%	25,000
30. Demonstrators and Product Promoters	$20,690	24.9%	34,000

Best Jobs for People with an Enterprising Personality Type

Job	Annual Earnings	Percent Growth	Annual Openings
31. Gaming Dealers	$13,680	32.4%	28,000
32. Personnel Recruiters	$38,010	17.6%	19,000
33. First-Line Supervisors/Managers of Helpers, Laborers, and Material Movers, Hand	$36,090	18.9%	14,000
34. First-Line Supervisors, Administrative Support	$37,990	9.4%	146,000
35. First-Line Supervisors, Customer Service	$37,990	9.4%	146,000
36. Purchasing Agents, Except Wholesale, Retail, and Farm Products	$43,230	12.3%	23,000
37. Coaches and Scouts	$29,020	17.6%	19,000
38. Compensation and Benefits Managers	$61,880	12.7%	14,000
39. Human Resources Managers	$61,880	12.7%	14,000
40. Training and Development Managers	$61,880	12.7%	14,000
41. Engineering Managers	$87,490	8.0%	24,000
42. Lawn Service Managers	$32,100	20.1%	10,000
43. Agents and Business Managers of Artists, Performers, and Athletes	$55,550	27.9%	2,000
44. Private Detectives and Investigators	$28,380	23.5%	9,000
45. First-Line Supervisors/Managers of Food Preparation and Serving Workers	$23,600	12.7%	136,000
46. Flight Attendants	$40,600	18.4%	8,000
47. First-Line Supervisors/Managers of Non-Retail Sales Workers	$51,490	5.8%	41,000
48. Sales Representatives, Wholesale and Manufacturing, Except Technical and Scientific Products	$41,520	5.7%	86,000
49. Sales Representatives, Agricultural	$54,360	7.5%	24,000
50. Sales Representatives, Chemical and Pharmaceutical	$54,360	7.5%	24,000
51. Sales Representatives, Electrical/Electronic	$54,360	7.5%	24,000
52. Sales Representatives, Instruments	$54,360	7.5%	24,000
53. Sales Representatives, Mechanical Equipment and Supplies	$54,360	7.5%	24,000
54. Sales Representatives, Medical	$54,360	7.5%	24,000
55. Retail Salespersons	$17,150	12.4%	1,124,000
56. Athletes and Sports Competitors	$43,730	22.5%	3,000
57. First-Line Supervisors/Managers of Police and Detectives	$59,300	13.1%	9,000

(continued)

(continued)

Best Jobs for People with an Enterprising Personality Type

Job	Annual Earnings	Percent Growth	Annual Openings
58. Sales Engineers	$59,720	17.7%	4,000
59. First-Line Supervisors/Managers of Retail Sales Workers	$28,590	8.1%	206,000
60. Industrial Production Managers	$64,510	6.2%	22,000
61. Bartenders	$14,610	13.4%	84,000
62. Appraisers, Real Estate	$38,950	18.0%	6,000
63. Hairdressers, Hairstylists, and Cosmetologists	$18,260	13.0%	78,000
64. Hosts and Hostesses, Restaurant, Lounge, and Coffee Shop	$14,920	13.0%	84,000
65. Meeting and Convention Planners	$36,550	23.3%	3,000
66. Housekeeping Supervisors	$27,200	14.2%	18,000
67. Janitorial Supervisors	$27,200	14.2%	18,000
68. Child Support, Missing Persons, and Unemployment Insurance Fraud Investigators	$50,960	16.4%	4,000
69. Criminal Investigators and Special Agents	$50,960	16.4%	4,000
70. Police Detectives	$50,960	16.4%	4,000
71. Loan Officers	$43,210	4.9%	28,000
72. First-Line Supervisors/Managers of Production and Operating Workers	$42,000	1.0%	71,000
73. Real Estate Sales Agents	$28,570	9.5%	28,000
74. Gaming Managers	$53,450	30.0%	fewer than 500
75. Insurance Sales Agents	$38,890	3.3%	43,000
76. Chefs and Head Cooks	$26,800	9.0%	35,000
77. Arbitrators, Mediators, and Conciliators	$46,660	27.2%	fewer than 500
78. Manicurists and Pedicurists	$16,700	26.5%	5,000
79. Gaming Supervisors	$39,240	18.4%	2,000
80. First-Line Supervisors/Managers of Personal Service Workers	$28,040	15.1%	8,000
81. First-Line Supervisors and Manager/Supervisors —Agricultural Crop Workers	$33,330	13.0%	8,000

Best Jobs for People with a Conventional Personality Type

Job	Annual Earnings	Percent Growth	Annual Openings
1. Accountants	$45,380	18.5%	100,000
2. Auditors	$45,380	18.5%	100,000
3. Adjustment Clerks	$25,430	32.4%	359,000
4. Customer Service Representatives, Utilities	$25,430	32.4%	359,000
5. Legal Secretaries	$34,610	20.3%	36,000
6. Bill and Account Collectors	$25,960	25.3%	71,000
7. Interviewers, Except Eligibility and Loan	$21,880	33.4%	53,000
8. Receptionists and Information Clerks	$20,650	23.7%	269,000
9. Hotel, Motel, and Resort Desk Clerks	$16,920	33.4%	73,000
10. Cost Estimators	$46,960	16.5%	28,000
11. Production, Planning, and Expediting Clerks	$32,420	17.9%	36,000
12. Pharmacy Technicians	$21,630	36.4%	22,000
13. Claims Examiners, Property and Casualty Insurance	$42,440	15.1%	25,000
14. Human Resources Assistants, Except Payroll and Timekeeping	$29,470	19.3%	25,000
15. Counter and Rental Clerks	$16,750	19.4%	150,000
16. Medical Secretaries	$24,670	19.0%	40,000
17. Medical Records and Health Information Technicians	$23,530	49.0%	14,000
18. Office Clerks, General	$21,780	15.9%	676,000
19. Executive Secretaries and Administrative Assistants	$32,380	11.5%	185,000
20. Library Technicians	$23,790	19.5%	29,000
21. Library Assistants, Clerical	$18,580	19.7%	26,000
22. Cashiers	$14,950	14.5%	1,125,000
23. Electrical Drafters	$40,070	23.3%	5,000
24. Reservation and Transportation Ticket Agents	$24,090	14.5%	39,000
25. Travel Clerks	$24,090	14.5%	39,000
26. Dispatchers, Except Police, Fire, and Ambulance	$30,070	22.2%	8,000
27. Mapping Technicians	$28,210	25.3%	7,000
28. Budget Analysts	$50,510	14.6%	8,000
29. Assessors	$38,950	18.0%	6,000
30. Weighers, Measurers, Checkers, and Samplers, Recordkeeping	$24,690	17.9%	13,000
31. Credit Analysts	$41,650	16.0%	7,000
32. Shipping, Receiving, and Traffic Clerks	$22,710	9.3%	133,000

(continued)

(continued)

Best Jobs for People with a Conventional Personality Type

Job	Annual Earnings	Percent Growth	Annual Openings
33. Immigration and Customs Inspectors	$50,960	16.4%	4,000
34. Police Identification and Records Officers	$50,960	16.4%	4,000
35. Billing, Cost, and Rate Clerks	$25,350	8.5%	69,000
36. Billing, Posting, and Calculating Machine Operators	$25,350	8.5%	69,000
37. Statement Clerks	$25,350	8.5%	69,000
38. Marking Clerks	$19,060	8.5%	467,000
39. Order Fillers, Wholesale and Retail Sales	$19,060	8.5%	467,000
40. Stock Clerks—Stockroom, Warehouse, or Storage Yard	$19,060	8.5%	467,000
41. Tax Preparers	$27,680	17.4%	8,000
42. File Clerks	$19,490	9.1%	49,000
43. Bookkeeping, Accounting, and Auditing Clerks	$26,540	2.0%	298,000
44. Court Clerks	$27,090	12.0%	14,000
45. License Clerks	$27,090	12.0%	14,000
46. Municipal Clerks	$27,090	12.0%	14,000

Part II

The Job Descriptions

This part of the book provides descriptions for all the jobs included in one or more of the lists in Part I. The Introduction gives more details on how to use and interpret the job descriptions, but here is some additional information:

▲ Job descriptions are arranged in alphabetical order by job title. This approach allows you to quickly find a description if you know its correct title from one of the lists in Part I.

▲ If you are using this section to browse for interesting options, we suggest you begin with the Table of Contents. Part I features many interesting lists that will help you identify job titles to explore in more detail. If you have not browsed Part I's lists, consider spending some time there. The lists are interesting and will help you identify job titles you can find described in the material that follows. The job titles are also listed in the Table of Contents for Part II.

▲ We include descriptions for the many specific jobs that we included under the single job title of Teachers, Postsecondary used in the lists in Part I. Here are the titles of the jobs included in the Teachers, Postsecondary title: Agricultural Sciences Teachers, Postsecondary; Anthropology and Archeology Teachers, Postsecondary; Architecture Teachers, Postsecondary; Area, Ethnic, and Cultural Studies Teachers, Postsecondary; Art, Drama, and Music Teachers, Postsecondary; Atmospheric, Earth, Marine, and Space Sciences Teachers, Postsecondary; Biological Science Teachers, Postsecondary; Business Teachers, Postsecondary; Chemistry Teachers, Postsecondary; Communications Teachers, Postsecondary; Computer Science Teachers, Postsecondary; Criminal Justice and Law Enforcement Teachers, Postsecondary; Economics Teachers, Postsecondary; Education Teachers, Postsecondary; Engineering Teachers,

(continued)

(continued)

Postsecondary; English Language and Literature Teachers, Postsecondary; Environmental Science Teachers, Postsecondary; Foreign Language and Literature Teachers, Postsecondary; Forestry and Conservation Science Teachers, Postsecondary; Geography Teachers, Postsecondary; Graduate Teaching Assistants; Health Specialties Teachers, Postsecondary; History Teachers, Postsecondary; Home Economics Teachers, Postsecondary; Law Teachers, Postsecondary; Library Science Teachers, Postsecondary; Mathematical Science Teachers, Postsecondary; Nursing Instructors and Teachers, Postsecondary; Philosophy and Religion Teachers, Postsecondary; Physics Teachers, Postsecondary; Political Science Teachers, Postsecondary; Postsecondary Teachers, All Other; Psychology Teachers, Postsecondary; Recreation and Fitness Studies Teachers, Postsecondary; Social Sciences Teachers, Postsecondary, All Other; Social Work Teachers, Postsecondary; Sociology Teachers, Postsecondary; and Vocational Education Teachers, Postsecondary.

Accountants

> ▲ Education/Training Required: Bachelor's degree
> ▲ Annual Earnings: $45,380
> ▲ Growth: 18.5%
> ▲ Annual Job Openings: 100,000
> ▲ Self-Employed: 10.6%
> ▲ Part-Time: 7.8%

Analyze financial information and prepare financial reports to determine or maintain record of assets, liabilities, profit and loss, tax liability, or other financial activities within an organization. Analyzes operations, trends, costs, revenues, financial commitments, and obligations incurred to project future revenues and expenses, using computer. Computes taxes owed; ensures compliance with tax payment, reporting, and other tax requirements; and represents establishment before taxing authority. Directs activities of workers performing accounting and bookkeeping tasks. Adapts accounting and record-keeping functions to current technology of computerized accounting systems. Appraises, evaluates, and inventories real property and equipment, and records description, value, location, and other information. Prepares forms and manuals for workers performing accounting and book-keeping tasks. Audits contracts and prepares reports to substantiate transactions prior to settlement. Establishes table of accounts and assigns entries to proper accounts. Surveys establishment operations to ascertain accounting needs. Predicts revenues and expenditures and submits reports to management. Develops, maintains, and analyzes budgets and prepares periodic reports comparing budgeted costs to actual costs. Prepares balance sheet, profit and loss statement, amortization and depreciation schedules, and other financial reports, using calculator or computer. Reports finances of establishment to management and advises management about resource utilization, tax strategies, and assumptions underlying budget forecasts. Develops, implements, modifies, and documents budgeting, cost, general, property, and tax accounting systems. Analyzes records of financial transactions to determine accuracy and completeness of entries, using computer. **SKILLS—Management of Financial Resources:** Determining how money will be spent to get the work done and accounting for these expenditures. **Judgment and Decision Making:** Considering the relative costs and benefits of potential actions to choose the most appropriate one. **Mathematics:** Using mathematics to solve problems. **Systems Evaluation:** Identifying measures or indicators of system performance and the actions needed to improve or correct performance relative to the goals of the system. **Monitoring:** Monitoring/Assessing your performance or that of other individuals or organizations to make improvements or take corrective action.

GOE INFORMATION—Interest Area: 13. General Management and Support. **Work Group:** 13.02. Management Support. **Other Job Titles in This Work Group:** Accountants and Auditors; Appraisers and Assessors of Real Estate; Appraisers, Real Estate; Assessors; Auditors; Budget Analysts; Claims Adjusters, Examiners, and Investigators; Claims Examiners, Property and Casualty Insurance; Compensation, Benefits, and Job Analysis Specialists; Cost Estimators; Credit Analysts; Employment Interviewers, Private or Public Employment Service; Employment, Recruitment, and Placement Specialists; Financial Analysts; Human Resources, Training, and Labor Relations Specialists, All Other; Insurance Adjusters, Examiners, and Investigators; Insurance Appraisers, Auto Damage; Insurance Underwriters; Loan Counselors; Loan Officers; Logisticians; Management Analysts; Market Research Analysts; Personnel Recruiters; Purchasing Agents and Buyers, Farm Products; Purchasing Agents, Except Wholesale, Retail, and Farm Products; Tax Examiners, Collectors, and Revenue Agents; Training and Development Specialists; Wholesale and Retail Buyers, Except Farm Products. **PERSONALITY TYPE—Conventional.** Conventional occupations frequently involve following set procedures and routines. These occupations can include working with data and details more than with ideas. Usually there is a clear line of authority to follow.

EDUCATION/TRAINING PROGRAM(S)—Account-ing; Accounting and Business/Management; Accounting and Computer Science; Accounting and Finance; Auditing; Taxation. **RELATED KNOWLEDGE/COURSES—Economics and Accounting:** Knowledge of economic and accounting principles and practices, the financial markets, banking, and the analysis and reporting of financial data. **Mathematics:** Knowledge of arithmetic, algebra, geometry, calculus, and statistics and their applications. **Administration and Management:** Knowledge of business and management principles involved in strategic planning, resource allocation, human resources modeling, leadership technique, production methods, and coordination of people and resources. **English Language:** Knowledge of the structure and content of the English language, including the meaning and spelling of words, rules of composition, and grammar. **Clerical Studies:** Knowledge of administrative and clerical procedures and systems, such as word processing, managing files and records, stenography and transcription, designing forms, and other office procedures and terminology.

Accountants and Auditors

- ▲ Education/Training Required: Bachelor's degree
- ▲ Annual Earnings: $45,380
- ▲ Growth: 18.5%
- ▲ Annual Job Openings: 100,000
- ▲ Self-Employed: 10.6%
- ▲ Part-Time: 7.8%

Examine, analyze, and interpret accounting records for the purpose of giving advice or preparing statements. Install or advise on systems of recording costs or other financial and budgetary data. **SKILLS**—No data available.

GOE INFORMATION—**Interest Area:** 13. General Management and Support. **Work Group:** 13.02. Management Support. **Other Job Titles in This Work Group:** Accountants; Appraisers and Assessors of Real Estate; Appraisers, Real Estate; Assessors; Auditors; Budget Analysts; Claims Adjusters, Examiners, and Investigators; Claims Examiners, Property and Casualty Insurance; Compensation, Benefits, and Job Analysis Specialists; Cost Estimators; Credit Analysts; Employment Interviewers, Private or Public Employment Service; Employment, Recruitment, and Placement Specialists; Financial Analysts; Human Resources, Training, and Labor Relations Specialists, All Other; Insurance Adjusters, Examiners, and Investigators; Insurance Appraisers, Auto Damage; Insurance Underwriters; Loan Counselors; Loan Officers; Logisticians; Management Analysts; Market Research Analysts; Personnel Recruiters; Purchasing Agents and Buyers, Farm Products; Purchasing Agents, Except Wholesale, Retail, and Farm Products; Tax Examiners, Collectors, and Revenue Agents; Training and Development Specialists; Wholesale and Retail Buyers, Except Farm Products. **PERSONALITY TYPE**—No data available.

EDUCATION/TRAINING PROGRAM(S)—Accounting; Accounting and Business/Management; Accounting and Computer Science; Accounting and Finance; Auditing; Taxation. **RELATED KNOWLEDGE/COURSES**—No data available.

Actors

- ▲ Education/Training Required: Long-term on-the-job training
- ▲ Annual Earnings: $20,540
- ▲ Growth: 26.7%
- ▲ Annual Job Openings: 20,000
- ▲ Self-Employed: 23.7%
- ▲ Part-Time: 25.3%

Play parts in stage, television, radio, video, or motion picture productions for entertainment, information, or instruction. Interpret serious or comic role by speech, gesture, and body movement to entertain or inform audience. May dance and sing. Portrays and interprets role, using speech, gestures, and body movements, to entertain radio, film, television, or live audience. Performs humorous and serious interpretations of emotions, actions, and situations, using only body movements, facial expressions, and gestures. Reads from script or book to narrate action, inform, or entertain audience, utilizing few or no stage props. Prepares for and performs action stunts for motion picture, television, or stage production. Constructs puppets and ventriloquist dummies and sews accessory clothing, using hand tools and machines. Writes original or adapted material for drama, comedy, puppet show, narration, or other performance. Signals start and introduces performers to stimulate excitement and to coordinate smooth transition of acts during circus performance. Manipulates string, wire, rod, or fingers to animate puppet or dummy in synchronization to talking, singing, or recorded program. Sings or dances during dramatic or comedy performance. Dresses in comical clown costume and makeup and performs comedy routines to entertain audience. Reads and rehearses role from script to learn lines, stunts, and cues as directed. Tells jokes, performs comic dances and songs, impersonates mannerisms and voice of others, contorts face, and uses other devices to amuse audience. Performs original and stock tricks of illusion to entertain and mystify audience, occasionally including audience members as participants. **SKILLS—Speaking:** Talking to others to convey information effectively. **Monitoring:** Monitoring/Assessing your performance or that of other individuals or organizations to make improvements or take corrective action. **Reading Comprehension:** Understanding written sentences and paragraphs in work-related documents. **Coordination:** Adjusting actions in relation to others' actions. **Active Learning:** Understanding the implications of new information for both current and future problem-solving and decision-making. **Social Perceptiveness:** Being aware of others' reactions and understanding why they react as they do.

GOE INFORMATION—Interest Area: 01. Arts, Entertainment, and Media. **Work Group:** 01.05. Performing Arts. **Other Job Titles in This Work Group:** Choreographers; Composers; Dancers; Directors—Stage, Motion Pictures, Television, and Radio; Music Arrangers and Orchestrators; Music Directors; Music Directors and Composers; Musicians and Singers; Musicians, Instrumental; Public Address System and Other Announcers; Radio and Television Announcers; Singers; Talent Directors. **PERSONALITY TYPE—Artistic.** Artistic occupations frequently involve working with forms, designs, and patterns. They often require self-expression, and the work can be done without following a clear set of rules.

EDUCATION/TRAINING PROGRAM(S)—Acting; Directing and Theatrical Production; Drama and Dramatics/Theatre Arts, General; Dramatic/Theatre Arts and Stagecraft, Other. **RELATED KNOWLEDGE/COURSES—Fine Arts:** Knowledge of the theory and techniques required to compose, produce, and perform works of music, dance, visual arts, drama, and sculpture. **English Language:** Knowledge of the structure and content of the English language, including the meaning and spelling of words, rules of composition, and grammar. **Communications and Media:** Knowledge of media production, communication, and dissemination techniques and methods. This includes alternative ways to inform and entertain via written, oral, and visual media. **Psychology:** Knowledge of human behavior and performance; individual differences in ability, personality, and interests; learning and motivation; psychological research methods; and the assessment and treatment of behavioral and affective disorders. **Building and Construction:** Knowledge of materials, methods, and tools involved in the construction or repair of houses, buildings, or other structures, such as highways and roads.

Adjustment Clerks

- ▲ Education/Training Required: Moderate-term on-the-job training
- ▲ Annual Earnings: $25,430
- ▲ Growth: 32.4%
- ▲ Annual Job Openings: 359,000
- ▲ Self-Employed: 0%
- ▲ Part-Time: 12.6%

Investigate and resolve customers' inquiries concerning merchandise, service, billing, or credit rating. Examine pertinent information to determine accuracy of customers' complaints and responsibility for errors. Notify customers and appropriate personnel of findings, adjustments, and recommendations, such as exchange of merchandise, refund of money, credit to customers' accounts, or adjustment to customers' bills. Reviews claims adjustments with dealer, examines parts claimed to be defective, and approves or disapproves of dealer's claim. Notifies customer and designated personnel of findings and recommendations, such as exchanging merchandise, refunding money, or adjustment of bill. Examines weather conditions, calculates number of days in billing period, and reviews meter accounts for errors which might explain high utility charges. Writes work order. Prepares reports showing volume, types, and disposition of claims handled. Compares merchandise with original requisition and information on invoice and prepares invoice for returned goods. Orders tests to detect product malfunction and determines if defect resulted from faulty construction. Trains dealers or service personnel in construction of products, service operations, and customer service. **SKILLS—Speaking:** Talking to others to convey information effectively. **Active Listening:** Giving full attention to what other people are saying, taking time to understand the points being made, asking questions as appropriate, and not interrupting at inappropriate times. **Writing:** Communicating effectively in writing as appropriate for the needs of the audience. **Reading Comprehension:** Understanding written sentences and paragraphs in work-related documents. **Instructing:** Teaching others how to do something.

GOE INFORMATION—Interest Area: 09. Business Detail. **Work Group:** 09.05. Customer Service. **Other Job Titles in This Work Group:** Bill and Account Collectors; Cashiers; Counter and Rental Clerks; Customer Service Representatives; Customer Service Representatives, Utilities; Gaming Cage Workers; Gaming Change Persons and Booth Cashiers; New Accounts Clerks; Order Clerks; Receptionists and Information Clerks; Tellers; Travel Clerks. **PERSONALITY TYPE—Conventional.** Conventional occupations frequently involve following set procedures and routines. These occupations can include working with data and details more than with ideas. Usually there is a clear line of authority to follow.

EDUCATION/TRAINING PROGRAM(S)—Customer Service Support/Call Center/Teleservice Operation; Receptionist. **RELATED KNOWLEDGE/COURSES—English Language:** Knowledge of the structure and content of the English language, including the meaning and spelling of words, rules of composition, and grammar. **Mathematics:** Knowledge of arithmetic, algebra, geometry, calculus, and statistics and their applications. **Customer and Personal Service:** Knowledge of principles and processes for providing customer and personal services. This includes customer needs assessment, meeting quality standards for services, and evaluation of customer satisfaction. **Education and Training:** Knowledge of principles and methods for curriculum and training design, teaching and instruction for individuals and groups, and the measurement of training effects. **Economics and Accounting:** Knowledge of economic and accounting principles and practices, the financial markets, banking, and the analysis and reporting of financial data.

Administrative Services Managers

▲ Education/Training Required: Work experience plus degree
▲ Annual Earnings: $49,810
▲ Growth: 20.4%
▲ Annual Job Openings: 31,000
▲ Self-Employed: 0%
▲ Part-Time: 6.1%

Plan, direct, or coordinate supportive services of an organization, such as record-keeping, mail distribution, telephone operator/receptionist, and other office support services. May oversee facilities planning and maintenance and custodial operations. Coordinates activities of clerical and administrative personnel in establishment or organization. Prepares and reviews operational reports and schedules to ensure accuracy and efficiency. Formulates budgetary reports. Hires and terminates clerical and administrative personnel. Conducts classes to teach procedures to staff. Recommends cost-saving methods, such as supply changes and disposal of records, to improve efficiency of department. Analyzes internal processes and plans or implements procedural and policy changes to improve operations. **SKILLS—Reading Comprehension:** Understanding written sentences and paragraphs in work-related documents. **Coordination:** Adjusting actions in relation to others' actions. **Writing:** Communicating effectively in writing as appropriate for the needs of the audience. **Monitoring:** Monitoring/Assessing your performance or that of other individuals or organizations to make improvements or take corrective action. **Speaking:** Talking to others to convey information effectively. **Management of Personnel Resources:** Motivating, developing, and directing people as they work, identifying the best people for the job. **Time Management:** Managing one's own time and the time of others.

GOE INFORMATION—Interest Area: 09. Business Detail. **Work Group:** 09.01. Managerial Work in Business Detail. **Other Job Titles in This Work Group:** First-Line Supervisors, Administrative Support; First-Line Supervisors, Customer Service; First-Line Supervisors/Managers of Office and Administrative Support Workers. **PERSONALITY TYPE—Enterprising.** Enterprising occupations frequently involve starting up and carrying out projects. These occupations can involve leading people and making many decisions. They sometimes require risk taking and often deal with business.

EDUCATION/TRAINING PROGRAM(S)—Business Administration and Management, General; Business/Commerce, General; Medical/Health Management and Clinical Assistant/Specialist; Public Administration; Purchasing, Procurement/Acquisitions, and Contracts Man-

agement. **RELATED KNOWLEDGE/COURSES— Administration and Management:** Knowledge of business and management principles involved in strategic planning, resource allocation, human resources modeling, leadership technique, production methods, and coordination of people and resources. **Personnel and Human Resources:** Knowledge of principles and procedures for personnel recruitment, selection, training, compensation and benefits, labor relations and negotiation, and personnel information systems. **Economics and Accounting:** Knowledge of economic and accounting principles and practices, the financial markets, banking, and the analysis and reporting of financial data. **English Language:** Knowledge of the structure and content of the English language, including the meaning and spelling of words, rules of composition, and grammar. **Clerical Studies:** Knowledge of administrative and clerical procedures and systems, such as word processing, managing files and records, stenography and transcription, designing forms, and other office procedures and terminology.

Adult Literacy, Remedial Education, and GED Teachers and Instructors

- ▲ Education/Training Required: Bachelor's degree
- ▲ Annual Earnings: $35,220
- ▲ Growth: 19.4%
- ▲ Annual Job Openings: 12,000
- ▲ Self-Employed: 48.9%
- ▲ Part-Time: 42.5%

Teach or instruct out-of-school youths and adults in remedial education classes, preparatory classes for the General Educational Development test, literacy, or English as a Second Language. Teaching may or may not take place in a traditional educational institution. Presents lectures and conducts discussions to increase students' knowledge and competence. Observes and evaluates students' work to determine progress and makes suggestions for improvement. Adapts course of study and training methods to meet students' needs and abilities. Conducts classes, workshops, and demonstrations to teach principles, techniques, procedures, or methods of designated subject. Prepares outline of instructional program, plans lessons, and establishes course goals. Observes students to determine and evaluate qualifications, limitations, abilities, interests, aptitudes, temperament, and individual characteristics. Evaluates success of instruction, based on number and enthusiasm of participants, and recommends retaining or eliminating course in future. Confers with leaders of government and other groups to coordinate training or to assist students in

fulfilling required criteria. Writes instructional articles on designated subjects. Orders, stores, and inventories books, materials, and supplies. Maintains records, such as student grades, attendance, and supply inventory. Plans and conducts field trips to enrich instructional programs. Directs and supervises student project activities, performances, tournaments, exhibits, contests, or plays. Selects and assembles books, materials, and supplies for courses or projects. Administers oral, written, and performance tests and issues grades in accordance with performance. Plans course content and method of instruction. **SKILLS—Writing:** Communicating effectively in writing as appropriate for the needs of the audience. **Speaking:** Talking to others to convey information effectively. **Reading Comprehension:** Understanding written sentences and paragraphs in work-related documents. **Instructing:** Teaching others how to do something. **Active Listening:** Giving full attention to what other people are saying, taking time to understand the points being made, asking questions as appropriate, and not interrupting at inappropriate times.

GOE INFORMATION—**Interest Area:** 12. Education and Social Service. **Work Group:** 12.03. Educational Services. **Other Job Titles in This Work Group:** Agricultural Sciences Teachers, Postsecondary; Anthropology and Archeology Teachers, Postsecondary; Architecture Teachers, Postsecondary; Archivists; Area, Ethnic, and Cultural Studies Teachers, Postsecondary; Art, Drama, and Music Teachers, Postsecondary; Atmospheric, Earth, Marine, and Space Sciences Teachers, Postsecondary; Audio-Visual Collections Specialists; Biological Science Teachers, Postsecondary; Business Teachers, Postsecondary; Chemistry Teachers, Postsecondary; Child Care Workers; Communications Teachers, Postsecondary; Computer Science Teachers, Postsecondary; Criminal Justice and Law Enforcement Teachers, Postsecondary; Curators; Economics Teachers, Postsecondary; Education Teachers, Postsecondary; Educational Psychologists; Educational, Vocational, and School Counselors; Elementary School Teachers, Except Special Education; Engineering Teachers, Postsecondary; English Language and Literature Teachers, Postsecondary; Environmental Science Teachers, Postsecondary; Farm and Home Management Advisors; Foreign Language and Literature Teachers, Postsecondary; Forestry and Conservation Science Teachers, Postsecondary; Geography Teachers, Postsecondary; Graduate Teaching Assistants; Health Specialties Teachers, Postsecondary; History Teachers, Postsecondary; Home Economics Teachers, Postsecondary; Kindergarten Teachers, Except Special Education; Law Teachers, Postsecondary; Librarians; Library Assistants, Clerical; Library Science Teachers, Postsecondary; Library Technicians; Mathematical Science Teachers, Postsecondary; Middle School Teachers, Except Special and Vocational Education; Museum Technicians and Conservators; Nursing Instructors and Teachers, Postsecondary; Personal Financial Advisors; Philosophy and Religion Teachers, Postsecondary; Physics Teachers, Postsecondary; Political Science Teachers, Postsecondary; Postsecondary Teachers, All Other; Preschool Teachers, Except Special Education; Psychology Teachers, Postsecondary; others. **PERSONALITY TYPE**—Social. Social occupations frequently involve working with, communicating with, and teaching people. These occupations often involve helping or providing service to others.

EDUCATION/TRAINING PROGRAM(S)—Adult and Continuing Education and Teaching; Adult Literacy Tutor/Instructor; Bilingual and Multilingual Education; Multicultural Education; Teaching English as a Second or Foreign Language/ESL Language Instructor. **RELATED KNOWLEDGE/COURSES**—**Education and Training:** Knowledge of principles and methods for curriculum and training design, teaching and instruction for individuals and groups, and the measurement of training effects. **English Language:** Knowledge of the structure and content of the English language, including the meaning and spelling of words, rules of composition, and grammar. **Administration and Management:** Knowledge of business and management principles involved in strategic planning, resource allocation, human resources modeling, leadership technique, production methods, and coordination of people and resources. **Mathematics:** Knowledge of arithmetic, algebra, geometry, calculus, and statistics and their applications. **Computers and Electronics:** Knowledge of circuit boards, processors, chips, electronic equipment, and computer hardware and software, including applications and programming. **Economics and Accounting:** Knowledge of economic and accounting principles and practices, the financial markets, banking, and the analysis and reporting of financial data. **Clerical Studies:** Knowledge of administrative and clerical procedures and systems, such as word processing, managing files and records, stenography and transcription, designing forms, and other office procedures and terminology.

Advertising and Promotions Managers

- ▲ Education/Training Required: Work experience plus degree
- ▲ Annual Earnings: $55,940
- ▲ Growth: 34.3%
- ▲ Annual Job Openings: 7,000
- ▲ Self-Employed: 2.4%
- ▲ Part-Time: 2.6%

Plan and direct advertising policies and programs or produce collateral materials, such as posters, contests, coupons, or give-aways, to create extra interest in the purchase of a product or service for a department, for an entire organization, or on an account basis. Directs activities of workers engaged in developing and producing advertisements. Plans and executes advertising policies of organization. Plans and prepares advertising and promotional material. Coordinates activities of departments, such as sales, graphic arts, media, finance, and research. Formulates plans to extend business with established accounts and transacts business as agent for advertising accounts. Confers with department heads and/or staff to discuss topics such as contracts, selection of advertising media, or product to be advertised. Confers with clients to provide marketing or technical advice. Inspects layouts and advertising copy and edits scripts, audio and video tapes, and other promotional material for adherence to specifications. Reads trade journals and professional literature to stay informed on trends, innovations, and changes that affect media planning. Inspects premises of assigned stores for adequate security and compliance with safety codes and ordinances. Directs conversion of products from USA to foreign standards. Adjusts broadcasting schedules due to program cancellation. Contacts organizations to explain services and facilities offered or to secure props, audiovisual materials, and sound effects. Directs product research and development. Represents company at trade association meetings to promote products. Consults publications to learn about conventions and social functions and organizes prospect files for promotional purposes. Supervises and trains service representatives. Monitors and analyzes sales promotion results to determine cost-effectiveness of promotion campaign. **SKILLS—Coordination:** Adjusting actions in relation to others' actions. **Reading Comprehension:** Understanding written sentences and paragraphs in work-related documents. **Systems Evaluation:** Identifying measures or indicators of system performance and the actions needed to improve or correct performance relative to the goals of the system. **Judgment and Decision Making:** Considering the relative costs and benefits of potential actions to choose the most appropriate one. **Complex Problem Solving:** Identifying complex problems and reviewing related information to develop and evaluate options and implement solutions.

GOE INFORMATION—Interest Area: 10. Sales and Marketing. **Work Group:** 10.01. Managerial Work in Sales and Marketing. **Other Job Titles in This Work Group:** First-Line Supervisors/Managers of Non-Retail Sales Workers; First-Line Supervisors/Managers of Retail Sales Workers; Marketing Managers; Sales Managers. **PERSONALITY TYPE—Artistic.** Artistic occupations frequently involve working with forms, designs, and patterns. They often require self-expression, and the work can be done without following a clear set of rules.

EDUCATION/TRAINING PROGRAM(S)—Advertising; Marketing/Marketing Management, General; Public Relations/Image Management. RELATED KNOWLEDGE/COURSES—Sales and Marketing: Knowledge of principles and methods for showing, promoting, and selling products or services. This includes marketing strategy and tactics, product demonstration, sales techniques, and sales control systems. **Administration and Management:** Knowledge of business and management principles involved in strategic planning, resource allocation, human resources modeling, leadership technique, production methods, and coordination of people and resources. **Communications and Media:** Knowledge of media production, communication, and dissemination techniques and methods. This includes alternative ways to inform and entertain via written, oral, and visual media. **Customer and Personal Service:** Knowledge of principles and processes for providing customer and personal services. This includes customer needs assessment, meeting quality standards for services, and evaluation of customer satisfaction. **English Language:** Knowledge of the structure and content of the English language, including the meaning and spelling of words, rules of composition, and grammar.

Advertising Sales Agents

- ▲ Education/Training Required: Moderate-term on-the-job training
- ▲ Annual Earnings: $36,560
- ▲ Growth: 26.3%
- ▲ Annual Job Openings: 25,000
- ▲ Self-Employed: 10.7%
- ▲ Part-Time: 22.3%

Sell or solicit advertising, including graphic art, advertising space in publications, custom-made signs, or TV and radio advertising time. May obtain leases for out-door advertising sites or persuade retailer to use sales promotion display items. Advises customer in advantages of various types of programming and methods of composing layouts and designs for signs and displays. Draws up contract covering arrangements for designing, fabricating, erecting, and maintaining sign or display. Sells signs to be made according to customers' specifications, utilizing knowledge of lettering, color harmony, and sign-making processes. Visits advertisers to point out advantages of publication. Exhibits prepared layouts with mats and copy with headings. Calls on prospects and presents outlines of various programs or commercial announcements. Prepares list of prospects for classified and display space for publication from leads in other papers and from old accounts. Arranges for and accompanies prospect to commercial taping sessions. Delivers advertising or illustration proofs to customer for approval. Collects payments due. Writes copy as part of layout. Computes job costs. Plans and sketches layouts to meet customer needs. Prepares promotional plans, sales literature, and sales contracts, using computer. Calls on advertisers and sales promotion people to obtain information concerning prospects for current advertising and sales promotion. Obtains pertinent information concerning prospect's past and current advertising for use in sales presentation. Informs customer of types of artwork available by providing samples. **SKILLS—Speaking:** Talking to others to convey information effectively. **Persuasion:** Persuading others to change their minds or behavior. **Writing:** Communicating effectively in writing as appropriate for the needs of the audience. **Reading Comprehension:** Understanding written sentences and paragraphs in work-related documents. **Active Listening:** Giving full attention to what other people are saying, taking time to understand the points being made, asking questions as appropriate, and not interrupting at inappropriate times. **GOE INFORMATION—Interest Area:** 10. Sales and Marketing. **Work Group:** 10.02. Sales Technology. **Other**

Job Titles in This Work Group: Insurance Sales Agents; Sales Agents, Financial Services; Sales Agents, Securities and Commodities; Sales Representatives, Agricultural; Sales Representatives, Chemical and Pharmaceutical; Sales Representatives, Electrical/Electronic; Sales Representatives, Instruments; Sales Representatives, Mechanical Equipment and Supplies; Sales Representatives, Medical; Sales Representatives, Services, All Other; Sales Representatives, Wholesale and Manufacturing, Technical and Scientific Products; Securities, Commodities, and Financial Services Sales Agents. **PERSONALITY TYPE**—Enterprising. Enterprising occupations frequently involve starting up and carrying out projects. These occupations can involve leading people and making many decisions. They sometimes require risk taking and often deal with business.

EDUCATION/TRAINING PROGRAM(S)—Advertising. **RELATED KNOWLEDGE/COURSES—Sales and Marketing:** Knowledge of principles and methods for showing, promoting, and selling products or services. This includes marketing strategy and tactics, product demonstration, sales techniques, and sales control systems. **English Language:** Knowledge of the structure and content of the English language, including the meaning and spelling of words, rules of composition, and grammar. **Communications and Media:** Knowledge of media production, communication, and dissemination techniques and methods. This includes alternative ways to inform and entertain via written, oral, and visual media. **Fine Arts:** Knowledge of the theory and techniques required to compose, produce, and perform works of music, dance, visual arts, drama, and sculpture. **Mathematics:** Knowledge of arithmetic, algebra, geometry, calculus, and statistics and their applications.

Agents and Business Managers of Artists, Performers, and Athletes

- ▲ Education/Training Required: Work experience plus degree
- ▲ Annual Earnings: $55,550
- ▲ Growth: 27.9%
- ▲ Annual Job Openings: 2,000
- ▲ Self-Employed: 2.4%
- ▲ Part-Time: 2.6%

Represent and promote artists, performers, and athletes to prospective employers. May handle contract negotiation and other business matters for clients. Negotiates with management, promoters, union officials, and other persons to obtain contracts for clients, such as entertain-ers, artists, and athletes. Obtains information and inspects facilities, equipment, and accommodations of potential performance venue. Prepares periodic accounting statements for clients concerning financial affairs. Conducts auditions or interviews new clients. Hires trainer or coach to advise client on performance matters, such as training techniques or presentation of act. Collects fees, commission, or other payment according to contract terms. Manages business affairs for clients, such as obtaining travel and lodging accommodations, selling tickets, marketing and advertising, and paying expenses. Schedules promotional or performance engagements for clients. Advises clients on financial and legal matters, such as investments and taxes. **SKILLS—Negotiation:** Bringing others together and trying to reconcile differences. **Reading Comprehension:** Understanding written sentences and paragraphs in work-related documents. **Speaking:** Talking to others to convey information effectively. **Time Management:** Managing one's own time and the time of others. **Active Listening:** Giving full attention to what other people are saying, taking time to understand the points being made, asking questions as appropriate, and not interrupting at inappropriate times. **Coordination:** Adjusting actions in relation to others' actions. **Critical Thinking:** Using logic and reasoning to identify the strengths and weaknesses of alternative solutions, conclusions, or approaches to problems.

GOE INFORMATION—Interest Area: 01. Arts, Entertainment, and Media. **Work Group:** 01.01. Managerial Work in Arts, Entertainment, and Media. **Other Job Titles in This Work Group:** Art Directors; Producers; Producers and Directors; Program Directors; Technical Directors/

Managers. **PERSONALITY TYPE—Enterprising.** Enterprising occupations frequently involve starting up and carrying out projects. These occupations can involve leading people and making many decisions. They sometimes require risk taking and often deal with business.

EDUCATION/TRAINING PROGRAM(S)—Arts Management; Purchasing, Procurement/Acquisitions, and Contracts Management. **RELATED KNOWLEDGE/ COURSES—Administration and Management:** Knowledge of business and management principles involved in strategic planning, resource allocation, human resources modeling, leadership technique, production methods, and coordination of people and resources. **Economics and Accounting:** Knowledge of economic and accounting principles and practices, the financial markets, banking, and the analysis and reporting of financial data. **Sales and Marketing:** Knowledge of principles and methods for showing, promoting, and selling products or services. This includes marketing strategy and tactics, product demonstration, sales techniques, and sales control systems. **Personnel and Human Resources:** Knowledge of principles and procedures for personnel recruitment, selection, training, compensation and benefits, labor relations and negotiation, and personnel information systems. **Mathematics:** Knowledge of arithmetic, algebra, geometry, calculus, and statistics and their applications.

Agricultural Sciences Teachers, Postsecondary

- ▲ Education/Training Required: Master's degree
- ▲ Annual Earnings: $64,500
- ▲ Growth: 23.5%
- ▲ Annual Job Openings: 184,000
- ▲ Self-Employed: 0%
- ▲ Part-Time: 32.3%

Teach courses in the agricultural sciences. Includes teachers of agronomy, dairy sciences, fisheries management, horticultural sciences, poultry sciences, range management, and agricultural soil conservation. Prepares and delivers lectures to students. Stimulates class discussions. Compiles bibliographies of specialized materials for outside reading assignments. Advises students on academic and vocational curricula. Conducts research in particular field of knowledge and publishes findings in professional journals. Serves on faculty committee providing professional consulting services to government and industry. Acts as adviser to student organizations. Directs research of

other teachers or graduate students working for advanced academic degrees. Compiles, administers, and grades examinations or assigns this work to others. **SKILLS—Reading Comprehension:** Understanding written sentences and paragraphs in work-related documents. **Instructing:** Teaching others how to do something. **Learning Strategies:** Selecting and using training/instructional methods and procedures appropriate for the situation when learning or teaching new things. **Writing:** Communicating effectively in writing as appropriate for the needs of the audience. **Critical Thinking:** Using logic and reasoning to identify the strengths and weaknesses of alternative solutions, conclusions, or approaches to problems. **Active Learning:** Understanding the implications of new information for both current and future problem-solving and decision-making. **Science:** Using scientific rules and methods to solve problems.

GOE INFORMATION—Interest Area: 12. Education and Social Service. **Work Group:** 12.03. Educational Services. **Other Job Titles in This Work Group:** Adult Literacy, Remedial Education, and GED Teachers and Instructors; Anthropology and Archeology Teachers, Postsecondary; Architecture Teachers, Postsecondary; Archivists; Area, Ethnic, and Cultural Studies Teachers, Postsecondary; Art, Drama, and Music Teachers, Postsecondary; Atmospheric, Earth, Marine, and Space Sciences Teachers, Postsecondary; Audio-Visual Collections Specialists; Biological Science Teachers, Postsecondary; Business Teachers, Postsecondary; Chemistry Teachers, Postsecondary; Child Care Workers; Communications Teachers, Postsecondary; Computer Science Teachers, Postsecondary; Criminal Justice and Law Enforcement Teachers, Postsecondary; Curators; Economics Teachers, Postsecondary; Education Teachers, Postsecondary; Educational Psychologists; Educational, Vocational, and School Counselors; Elementary School Teachers, Except Special Education; Engineering Teachers, Postsecondary; English Language and Literature Teachers, Postsecondary; Environmental Science Teachers, Postsecondary; Farm and Home Management Advisors; Foreign Language and Literature Teachers, Postsecondary; Forestry and Conservation Science Teachers, Postsecondary; Geography Teachers, Postsecondary; Graduate Teaching Assistants; Health Specialties Teachers, Postsecondary; History Teachers, Postsecondary; Home Economics Teachers, Postsecondary; Kindergarten Teachers, Except Special Education; Law Teachers, Postsecondary; Librarians; Library Assistants, Clerical; Library Science Teachers, Postsecondary; Library Technicians; Mathematical Science Teachers, Postsecondary; Middle School Teachers, Except Special and Vocational Education; Museum Technicians and Conservators; Nursing Instructors and Teachers, Postsecondary; Personal Financial Advisors; Philosophy and Religion Teachers, Postsecondary; Physics Teachers, Postsecondary; Political Science Teachers, Postsecondary; Postsecondary Teachers, All Other; Preschool Teachers, Except Special Education; Psychology Teachers, Postsecondary; others. **PERSONALITY TYPE—Investigative.** Investigative occupations frequently involve working with ideas and require an extensive amount of thinking. These occupations can involve searching for facts and figuring out problems mentally.

EDUCATION/TRAINING PROGRAM(S)—Agribusiness/Agricultural Business Operations; Agricultural and Domestic Animal Services, Other; Agricultural and Food Products Processing; Agricultural and Horticultural Plant Breeding; Agricultural Animal Breeding; Agricultural Business and Management, General; Agricultural Business and Management, Other; Agricultural Economics; Agricultural Mechanization, General; Agricultural Mechanization, Other; Agricultural Power Machinery Operation; Agricultural Production Operations, General; Agricultural Production Operations, Other; Agricultural Teacher Education; Agricultural/Farm Supplies Retailing and Wholesaling; Agriculture, Agriculture Operations, and Related Sciences, Other; Agriculture, General; Agronomy and Crop Science; Animal Health; Animal Nutrition; Animal Sciences, General; Animal Sciences, Other; Animal Training; Animal/Livestock Husbandry and Production; Applied Horticulture/Horticultural Business Services, Other; Applied Horticulture/Horticultural Operations, General; Aquaculture; Crop Production; Dairy Science; Equestrian/Equine Studies; Farm/Farm and Ranch Management; Food Science; Greenhouse Operations and Management; Horticultural Science; International Agriculture; Landscaping and Groundskeeping; Livestock Management; Ornamental Horticulture; Plant Nursery Operations and Management; Plant Protection and Integrated Pest Management; Plant Sciences, General; Plant Sciences, Other; Poultry Science; Range Science and Management; Soil Science and Agronomy, General; Turf and Turfgrass Management. **RELATED KNOWLEDGE/COURSES—Education and Training:** Knowledge of principles and methods for curriculum and training design, teaching and instruction for individuals and groups, and the measurement of training effects. **Biology:** Knowledge of plant and animal organisms and their tissues, cells, functions, interdependencies, and interactions with each other and the environment. **Psychology:** Knowledge of human behavior and performance; individual differences in ability, personality, and interests; learning and motivation; psychological research methods; and the assessment and treatment of behavioral and affective disorders. **Chemistry:** Knowledge of the chemical composition, structure, and properties of substances and of the chemical processes and transformations that they undergo. This includes uses of chemicals and their interactions, danger signs, production techniques, and disposal methods. **English Language:** Knowledge of the structure and content of the English language, including the meaning and spelling of words, rules of composition, and grammar.

Agricultural Technicians

▲ Education/Training Required: Associate's degree
▲ Annual Earnings: $27,530
▲ Growth: 15.2%
▲ Annual Job Openings: 15,000
▲ Self-Employed: 0.9%
▲ Part-Time: 11.7%

Set up and maintain laboratory and collect and record data to assist scientist in biology or related agricultural science experiments. Sets up laboratory and field equipment to assist research workers. Adjusts testing equipment and prepares culture media, following standard procedures. Measures or weighs ingredients used in testing or as animal feed. Records production and test data for evaluation by personnel. Cleans and maintains laboratory and field equipment and work areas. Examines animals and specimens to determine presence of disease or other problems. Pricks animals and collects blood samples for testing, using hand-held devices. Waters and feeds rations to livestock and laboratory animals. Plants seeds in specified area and counts plants that grow to determine germination rate of seeds. **SKILLS—Mathematics:** Using mathematics to solve problems. **Reading Comprehension:** Understanding written sentences and paragraphs in work-related documents. **Science:** Using scientific rules and methods to solve problems. **Writing:** Communicating effectively in writing as appropriate for the needs of the audience.

GOE INFORMATION—Interest Area: 02. Science, Math, and Engineering. **Work Group:** 02.03. Life Sciences. **Other Job Titles in This Work Group:** Agricultural and Food Science Technicians; Animal Scientists; Biochemists; Biochemists and Biophysicists; Biological Scientists, All Other; Biologists; Biophysicists; Conservation Scientists; Environmental Scientists and Specialists, Including Health; Epidemiologists; Food Science Technicians; Food Scientists and Technologists; Foresters; Life Scientists, All Other; Medical Scientists, Except Epidemiologists; Microbiologists; Plant Scientists; Range Managers; Soil and Plant Scientists; Soil Conservationists; Soil

Scientists; Zoologists and Wildlife Biologists. **PERSONALITY TYPE—Realistic.** Realistic occupations frequently involve work activities that include practical, hands-on problems and solutions. They often deal with plants, animals, and real-world materials like wood, tools, and machinery. Many of the occupations require working outside and do not involve a lot of paperwork or working closely with others.

EDUCATION/TRAINING PROGRAM(S)—Agricultural Animal Breeding; Agronomy and Crop Science; Animal Nutrition; Animal Sciences, General; Animal/Livestock Husbandry and Production; Crop Production; Dairy Science; Food Science. **RELATED KNOWLEDGE/COURSES—Biology:** Knowledge of plant and animal organisms and their tissues, cells, functions, interdependencies, and interactions with each other and the environment. **Mathematics:** Knowledge of arithmetic, algebra, geometry, calculus, and statistics and their applications. **Food Production:** Knowledge of techniques and equipment for planting, growing, and harvesting food products (both plant and animal) for consumption, including storage/handling techniques. **Clerical Studies:** Knowledge of administrative and clerical procedures and systems, such as word processing, managing files and records, stenography and transcription, designing forms, and other office procedures and terminology. **Medicine and Dentistry:** Knowledge of the information and techniques needed to diagnose and treat human injuries, diseases, and deformities. This includes symptoms, treatment alternatives, drug properties and interactions, and preventive health-care measures.

Aircraft Body and Bonded Structure Repairers

▲ Education/Training Required: Postsecondary vocational training
▲ Annual Earnings: $41,990
▲ Growth: 16.7%
▲ Annual Job Openings: 11,000
▲ Self-Employed: 0%
▲ Part-Time: 2.3%

Repair body or structure of aircraft according to specifications. Reinstalls repaired or replacement parts for subsequent riveting or welding, using clamps and wrenches. Repairs or fabricates defective section or part, using metal fabricating machines, saws, brakes, shears, and grinders. Reads work orders, blueprints, and specifications or examines sample or damaged part or structure to determine repair or fabrication procedures and sequence of operations. Communicates with other workers to fit and align heavy parts or expedite processing of repair parts. Removes or cuts out defective part or drills holes to gain access to internal defect or damage, using drill and punch. Locates and marks dimension and reference lines on defective or replacement part, using templates, scribes, compass, and steel rule. Trims and shapes replacement section to specified size and fits and secures section in place, using adhesives, hand tools, and power tools. Cleans, strips, primes, and sands structural surfaces and materials prior to bonding. Spreads plastic film over area to be repaired to prevent damage to surrounding area. Cures bonded structure, using portable or stationary curing equipment. **SKILLS—Equipment Selection:** Determining the kind of tools and equipment needed to do a job. **Mathematics:** Using mathematics to solve problems. **Installation:** Installing equipment, machines, wiring, or programs to meet specifications. **Repairing:** Repairing machines or systems, using the needed tools. **Equipment Maintenance:** Performing routine maintenance on equipment and determining when and what kind of maintenance is needed.

GOE INFORMATION—Interest Area: 05. Mechanics, Installers, and Repairers. **Work Group:** 05.03. Mechanical Work. **Other Job Titles in This Work Group:** Aircraft Engine Specialists; Aircraft Mechanics and Service Technicians; Airframe-and-Power-Plant Mechanics; Automotive Body and Related Repairers; Automotive Glass Installers and Repairers; Automotive Master Mechanics; Automotive Service Technicians and Mechanics; Automotive Specialty Technicians; Bicycle Repairers; Bridge and Lock Tenders; Bus and Truck Mechanics and Diesel Engine Specialists; Camera and Photographic Equipment Repairers; Coin, Vending, and Amusement Machine Servicers and Repairers; Control and Valve Installers and Repairers, Except Mechanical Door; Farm Equipment Mechanics; Gas Appliance Repairers; Hand and Portable Power Tool Repairers; Heating and Air Conditioning Mechanics; Heating, Air Conditioning, and Refrigeration Mechanics and Installers; Helpers—Electricians; Helpers—Installation, Maintenance, and Repair Workers; Industrial Machinery Mechanics; Keyboard Instrument Repairers and Tuners; Locksmiths and Safe Repairers; Maintenance and Repair Workers, General; Maintenance Workers, Machinery; Mechanical Door Repairers; Medical Appliance Technicians; Medical Equipment Repairers; Meter Mechanics; Millwrights; Mobile Heavy Equipment Mechanics, Except Engines; Motorboat Mechanics; Motorcycle Mechanics; Musical Instrument Repairers and Tuners; Ophthalmic Laboratory Technicians; Optical Instrument Assemblers; Outdoor Power Equipment and Other Small Engine Mechanics; Painters, Transportation Equipment; Percussion Instrument Repairers and Tuners; Precision Instrument and Equipment Repairers, All Other; Rail Car Repairers; Railroad Inspectors; Recreational Vehicle Service Technicians; Reed or Wind Instrument Repairers and Tuners; Refrigeration Mechanics; Stringed Instrument Repairers and Tuners; Tire Repairers and Changers; Valve and Regulator Repairers; Watch Repairers. **PERSONALITY TYPE—Realistic.** Realistic occupations frequently involve work activities that include practical, hands-on problems and solutions. They often deal with plants, animals, and real-world materials like wood, tools, and machinery. Many of the occupations require working outside and do not involve a lot of paperwork or working closely with others.

EDUCATION/TRAINING PROGRAM(S)—Agricultural Mechanics and Equipment/Machine Technology; Airframe Mechanics and Aircraft Maintenance Technology/Technician. RELATED KNOWLEDGE/COURSES—Principles of Mechanical Devices: Knowledge of machines and tools, including their designs, uses, repair, and maintenance. **Building and Construction:**

Knowledge of materials, methods, and tools involved in the construction or repair of houses, buildings, or other structures, such as highways and roads. **Design:** Knowledge of design techniques, tools, and principles involved in production of precision technical plans, blueprints, drawings, and models. **Engineering and Technology:**

Knowledge of the practical application of engineering science and technology. This includes applying principles, techniques, procedures, and equipment to the design and production of various goods and services. **Mathematics:** Knowledge of arithmetic, algebra, geometry, calculus, and statistics and their applications.

Aircraft Cargo Handling Supervisors

> ▲ Education/Training Required: Work experience in a related occupation
> ▲ Annual Earnings: $37,330
> ▲ Growth: 27.7%
> ▲ Annual Job Openings: 1,000
> ▲ Self-Employed: No data available.
> ▲ Part-Time: No data available.

Direct ground crew in the loading, unloading, securing, and staging of aircraft cargo or baggage. Determine the quantity and orientation of cargo and compute aircraft center of gravity. May accompany aircraft as member of flight crew, monitor and handle cargo in flight, and assist and brief passengers on safety and emergency procedures. SKILLS—No data available.

GOE INFORMATION—Interest Area: 11. Recreation, Travel, and Other Personal Services. Work Group: 11.01. Managerial Work in Recreation, Travel, and Other Personal Services. Other Job Titles in This Work Group:

First-Line Supervisors/Managers of Food Preparation and Serving Workers; First-Line Supervisors/Managers of Housekeeping and Janitorial Workers; First-Line Supervisors/Managers of Personal Service Workers; Food Service Managers; Gaming Managers; Gaming Supervisors; Housekeeping Supervisors; Janitorial Supervisors; Lodging Managers; Meeting and Convention Planners. **PERSONALITY TYPE**—No data available.

EDUCATION/TRAINING PROGRAM(S)—No data available. **RELATED KNOWLEDGE/COURSES**—No data available.

Aircraft Engine Specialists

> ▲ Education/Training Required: Postsecondary vocational training
> ▲ Annual Earnings: $41,990
> ▲ Growth: 16.7%
> ▲ Annual Job Openings: 11,000
> ▲ Self-Employed: 0%
> ▲ Part-Time: 2.3%

Repair and maintain the operating condition of aircraft engines. Includes helicopter engine mechanics. Replaces or repairs worn, defective, or damaged components, using hand tools, gauges, and testing equipment. Tests engine operation, using test equipment such as ignition analyzer, compression checker, distributor timer, and ammeter, to identify malfunction. Listens to operating engine to detect and diagnose malfunctions, such as sticking or burned valves. Reassembles engine and installs engine in aircraft. Disassembles and inspects engine parts, such as turbine blades and cylinders, for wear, warping, cracks, and leaks. Removes engine from aircraft, using hoist or

forklift truck. Services, repairs, and rebuilds aircraft structures, such as wings, fuselage, rigging, and surface and hydraulic controls, using hand or power tools and equipment. Adjusts, repairs, or replaces electrical wiring system and aircraft accessories. Reads and interprets manufacturers' maintenance manuals, service bulletins, and other specifications to determine feasibility and methods of repair. Services and maintains aircraft and related apparatus by performing activities such as flushing crankcase, cleaning screens, and lubricating moving parts. SKILLS—**Equipment Maintenance:** Performing routine maintenance on equipment and determining when and what kind of maintenance is needed. **Repairing:** Repairing machines or systems, using the needed tools. **Troubleshooting:** Determining causes of operating errors and deciding what to do about them. **Installation:** Installing equipment, machines, wiring, or programs to meet specifications. **Judgment and Decision Making:** Considering the relative costs and benefits of potential actions to choose the most appropriate one.

GOE INFORMATION—Interest Area: 05. Mechanics, Installers, and Repairers. **Work Group:** 05.03. Mechanical Work. **Other Job Titles in This Work Group:** Aircraft Body and Bonded Structure Repairers; Aircraft Mechanics and Service Technicians; Airframe-and-Power-Plant Mechanics; Automotive Body and Related Repairers; Automotive Glass Installers and Repairers; Automotive Master Mechanics; Automotive Service Technicians and Mechanics; Automotive Specialty Technicians; Bicycle Repairers; Bridge and Lock Tenders; Bus and Truck Mechanics and Diesel Engine Specialists; Camera and Photographic Equipment Repairers; Coin, Vending, and Amusement Machine Servicers and Repairers; Control and Valve Installers and Repairers, Except Mechanical Door; Farm Equipment Mechanics; Gas Appliance Repairers; Hand and Portable Power Tool Repairers; Heating and Air Conditioning Mechanics; Heating, Air Conditioning, and Refrigeration Mechanics and Installers; Helpers—Electricians; Helpers—Installation, Maintenance, and Repair Workers; Industrial Machinery Mechanics; Keyboard Instrument Repairers and Tuners; Locksmiths and Safe Repairers; Maintenance and Repair Workers, General; Maintenance Workers, Machinery; Mechanical Door Repairers; Medical Appliance Technicians; Medical Equipment Repairers; Meter Mechanics; Millwrights; Mobile Heavy Equipment Mechanics, Except Engines; Motorboat Mechanics; Motorcycle Mechanics; Musical Instrument Repairers and Tuners; Ophthalmic Laboratory Technicians; Optical Instrument Assemblers; Outdoor Power Equipment and Other Small Engine Mechanics; Painters, Transportation Equipment; Percussion Instrument Repairers and Tuners; Precision Instrument and Equipment Repairers, All Other; Rail Car Repairers; Railroad Inspectors; Recreational Vehicle Service Technicians; Reed or Wind Instrument Repairers and Tuners; Refrigeration Mechanics; Stringed Instrument Repairers and Tuners; Tire Repairers and Changers; Valve and Regulator Repairers; Watch Repairers. **PERSONALITY TYPE—Realistic.** Realistic occupations frequently involve work activities that include practical, hands-on problems and solutions. They often deal with plants, animals, and real-world materials like wood, tools, and machinery. Many of the occupations require working outside and do not involve a lot of paperwork or working closely with others.

EDUCATION/TRAINING PROGRAM(S)—Agricultural Mechanics and Equipment/Machine Technology; Aircraft Powerplant Technology/Technician. RELATED KNOWLEDGE/COURSES—Principles of Mechanical Devices: Knowledge of machines and tools, including their designs, uses, repair, and maintenance. **Engineering and Technology:** Knowledge of the practical application of engineering science and technology. This includes applying principles, techniques, procedures, and equipment to the design and production of various goods and services. **Physics:** Knowledge and prediction of physical principles and laws and their interrelationships and applications to understanding fluid, material, and atmospheric dynamics and mechanical, electrical, atomic, and sub-atomic structures and processes. **Mathematics:** Knowledge of arithmetic, algebra, geometry, calculus, and statistics and their applications. **Building and Construction:** Knowledge of materials, methods, and tools involved in the construction or repair of houses, buildings, or other structures, such as highways and roads. **Public Safety and Security:** Knowledge of relevant equipment, policies, procedures, and strategies to promote effective local, state, or national security operations for the protection of people, data, property, and institutions. **English Language:** Knowledge of the structure and content of the English language, including the meaning and spelling of words, rules of composition, and grammar.

Aircraft Mechanics and Service Technicians

- ▲ Education/Training Required: Postsecondary vocational training
- ▲ Annual Earnings: $41,990
- ▲ Growth: 16.7%
- ▲ Annual Job Openings: 11,000
- ▲ Self-Employed: 0%
- ▲ Part-Time: 2.3%

Diagnose, adjust, repair, or overhaul aircraft engines and assemblies, such as hydraulic and pneumatic systems. **SKILLS**—No data available.

GOE INFORMATION—Interest Area: 05. Mechanics, Installers, and Repairers. **Work Group:** 05.03. Mechanical Work. **Other Job Titles in This Work Group:** Aircraft Body and Bonded Structure Repairers; Aircraft Engine Specialists; Airframe-and-Power-Plant Mechanics; Automotive Body and Related Repairers; Automotive Glass Installers and Repairers; Automotive Master Mechanics; Automotive Service Technicians and Mechanics; Automotive Specialty Technicians; Bicycle Repairers; Bridge and Lock Tenders; Bus and Truck Mechanics and Diesel Engine Specialists; Camera and Photographic Equipment Repairers; Coin, Vending, and Amusement Machine Servicers and Repairers; Control and Valve Installers and Repairers, Except Mechanical Door; Farm Equipment Mechanics; Gas Appliance Repairers; Hand and Portable Power Tool Repairers; Heating and Air Conditioning Mechanics; Heating, Air Conditioning, and Refrigeration Mechanics and Installers; Helpers—Electricians; Helpers—Installation, Maintenance, and Repair Workers; Industrial Machinery Mechanics; Keyboard Instrument Repairers and Tuners; Locksmiths and Safe Repairers; Maintenance and Repair Workers, General; Maintenance Workers, Machinery; Mechanical Door Repairers; Medical Appliance Technicians; Medical Equipment Repairers; Meter Mechanics; Millwrights; Mobile Heavy Equipment Mechanics, Except Engines; Motorboat Mechanics; Motorcycle Mechanics; Musical Instrument Repairers and Tuners; Ophthalmic Laboratory Technicians; Optical Instrument Assemblers; Outdoor Power Equipment and Other Small Engine Mechanics; Painters, Transportation Equipment; Percussion Instrument Repairers and Tuners; Precision Instrument and Equipment Repairers, All Other; Rail Car Repairers; Railroad Inspectors; Recreational Vehicle Service Technicians; Reed or Wind Instrument Repairers and Tuners; Refrigeration Mechanics; Stringed Instrument Repairers and Tuners; Tire Repairers and Changers; Valve and Regulator Repairers; Watch Repairers. **PERSONALITY TYPE**—No data available.

EDUCATION/TRAINING PROGRAM(S)—Agricultural Mechanics and Equipment/Machine Technology; Aircraft Powerplant Technology/Technician; Airframe Mechanics and Aircraft Maintenance Technology/Technician. **RELATED KNOWLEDGE/COURSES**—No data available.

Airframe-and-Power-Plant Mechanics

- ▲ Education/Training Required: Postsecondary vocational training
- ▲ Annual Earnings: $41,990
- ▲ Growth: 16.7%
- ▲ Annual Job Openings: 11,000
- ▲ Self-Employed: 0%
- ▲ Part-Time: 2.3%

Inspect, test, repair, maintain, and service aircraft. Adjusts, aligns, and calibrates aircraft systems, using hand tools, gauges, and test equipment. Examines and inspects engines or other components for cracks, breaks, or leaks. Disassembles and inspects parts for wear, warping, or other defects. Assembles and installs electrical, plumbing, mechanical, hydraulic, and structural components and accessories, using hand tools and power tools. Services and maintains aircraft systems by performing tasks such as flushing crankcase, cleaning screens, greasing moving parts, and checking brakes. Repairs, replaces, and rebuilds aircraft structures, functional components, and parts, such as wings and fuselage, rigging, and hydraulic units. Tests engine and system operations, using testing equipment, and listens to engine sounds to detect and diagnose malfunctions. Removes engine from aircraft or installs engine, using hoist or forklift truck. Modifies aircraft structures, space vehicles, systems, or components, following drawings, engineering orders, and technical publications. Reads and interprets aircraft maintenance manuals and specifications to determine feasibility and method of repairing or replacing malfunctioning or damaged components. **SKILLS—Equipment Maintenance:** Performing routine maintenance on equipment and determining when and what kind of maintenance is needed. **Installation:** Installing equipment, machines, wiring, or programs to meet specifications. **Repairing:** Repairing machines or systems, using the needed tools. **Troubleshooting:** Determining causes of operating errors and deciding what to do about them. **Equipment Selection:** Determining the kind of tools and equipment needed to do a job. **Quality Control Analysis:** Conducting tests and inspections of products, services, or processes to evaluate quality or performance.

GOE INFORMATION—Interest Area: 05. Mechanics, Installers, and Repairers. **Work Group:** 05.03. Mechanical Work. **Other Job Titles in This Work Group:** Aircraft Body and Bonded Structure Repairers; Aircraft Engine Specialists; Aircraft Mechanics and Service Technicians; Automotive Body and Related Repairers; Automotive Glass Installers and Repairers; Automotive Master Mechanics; Automotive Service Technicians and Mechanics; Automotive Specialty Technicians; Bicycle Repairers; Bridge and Lock Tenders; Bus and Truck Mechanics and Diesel Engine Specialists; Camera and Photographic Equipment Repairers; Coin, Vending, and Amusement Machine Servicers and Repairers; Control and Valve Installers and Repairers, Except Mechanical Door; Farm Equipment Mechanics; Gas Appliance Repairers; Hand and Portable Power Tool Repairers; Heating and Air Conditioning Mechanics; Heating, Air Conditioning, and Refrigeration Mechanics and Installers; Helpers—Electricians; Helpers—Installation, Maintenance, and Repair Workers; Industrial Machinery Mechanics; Keyboard Instrument Repairers and Tuners; Locksmiths and Safe Repairers; Maintenance and Repair Workers, General; Maintenance Workers, Machinery; Mechanical Door Repairers; Medical Appliance Technicians; Medical Equipment Repairers;

Meter Mechanics; Millwrights; Mobile Heavy Equipment Mechanics, Except Engines; Motorboat Mechanics; Motorcycle Mechanics; Musical Instrument Repairers and Tuners; Ophthalmic Laboratory Technicians; Optical Instrument Assemblers; Outdoor Power Equipment and Other Small Engine Mechanics; Painters, Transportation Equipment; Percussion Instrument Repairers and Tuners; Precision Instrument and Equipment Repairers, All Other; Rail Car Repairers; Railroad Inspectors; Recreational Vehicle Service Technicians; Reed or Wind Instrument Repairers and Tuners; Refrigeration Mechanics; Stringed Instrument Repairers and Tuners; Tire Repairers and Changers; Valve and Regulator Repairers; Watch Repairers. **PERSONALITY TYPE—Realistic.** Realistic occupations frequently involve work activities that include practical, hands-on problems and solutions. They often deal with plants, animals, and real-world materials like wood, tools, and machinery. Many of the occupations require working outside and do not involve a lot of paperwork or working closely with others.

EDUCATION/TRAINING PROGRAM(S)—Agricultural Mechanics and Equipment/Machine Technology; Aircraft Powerplant Technology/Technician; Airframe Mechanics and Aircraft Maintenance Technology/Technician. **RELATED KNOWLEDGE/COURSES—Principles of Mechanical Devices:** Knowledge of machines and tools, including their designs, uses, repair, and maintenance. **Engineering and Technology:** Knowledge of the practical application of engineering science and technology. This includes applying principles, techniques, procedures, and equipment to the design and production of various goods and services. **Building and Construction:** Knowledge of materials, methods, and tools involved in the construction or repair of houses, buildings, or other structures, such as highways and roads. **Design:** Knowledge of design techniques, tools, and principles involved in production of precision technical plans, blueprints, drawings, and models. **Physics:** Knowledge and prediction of physical principles and laws and their interrelationships and applications to understanding fluid, material, and atmospheric dynamics and mechanical, electrical, atomic, and sub-atomic structures and processes. **Mathematics:** Knowledge of arithmetic, algebra, geometry, calculus, and statistics and their applications.

Ambulance Drivers and Attendants, Except Emergency Medical Technicians

- ▲ Education/Training Required: Moderate-term on-the-job training
- ▲ Annual Earnings: $18,890
- ▲ Growth: 33.7%
- ▲ Annual Job Openings: 3,000
- ▲ Self-Employed: 0%
- ▲ Part-Time: 34.5%

Drive ambulance or assist ambulance driver in transporting sick, injured, or convalescent persons. Assist in lifting patients. Transports sick or injured persons to hospital or convalescents to destination, avoiding sudden motions detrimental to patients. Places patients on stretcher and loads stretcher into ambulance, usually with help of ambulance attendant. Administers first aid as needed. Reports facts concerning accident or emergency to hospital personnel or law enforcement officials. Replaces supplies and disposable items on ambulance. Changes equipment to maintain sanitary conditions. **SKILLS—Service Orientation:** Actively looking for ways to help people. **Active Listening:** Giving full attention to what other people are saying, taking time to understand the points being made, asking questions as appropriate, and not interrupting at inappropriate times. **Speaking:** Talking to others to convey information effectively. **Critical Thinking:** Using logic and reasoning to identify the strengths and weaknesses of alternative solutions, conclusions, or approaches to problems. **Operation and Control:** Controlling operations of equipment or systems. **Coordination:** Adjusting actions in relation to others' actions.

GOE INFORMATION—Interest Area: 07. Transportation. **Work Group:** 07.07. Other Services Requiring Driving. **Other Job Titles in This Work Group:** Bus Drivers, School; Bus Drivers, Transit and Intercity; Driver/Sales Workers; Parking Lot Attendants; Taxi Drivers and Chauffeurs. **PERSONALITY TYPE**—Social. Social occupations frequently involve working with, communicating with, and teaching people. These occupations often involve helping or providing service to others.

EDUCATION/TRAINING PROGRAM(S)—Emergency Medical Technology/Technician (EMT Paramedic). **RELATED KNOWLEDGE/COURSES—Medicine and Dentistry:** Knowledge of the information and techniques needed to diagnose and treat human injuries, diseases, and deformities. This includes symptoms, treatment alternatives, drug properties and interactions, and preventive health-care measures. **Customer and Personal Service:** Knowledge of principles and processes for providing customer and personal services. This includes customer needs assessment, meeting quality standards for services, and evaluation of customer satisfaction. **Geography:** Knowledge of principles and methods for describing the features of land, sea, and air masses, including their physical characteristics, locations, interrelationships, and distribution of plant, animal, and human life. **Transportation:** Knowledge of principles and methods for moving people or goods by air, rail, sea, or road, including the relative costs and benefits. **Therapy and Counseling:** Knowledge of principles, methods, and procedures for diagnosis, treatment, and rehabilitation of physical and mental dysfunctions and for career counseling and guidance.

Amusement and Recreation Attendants

- ▲ Education/Training Required: Short-term on-the-job training
- ▲ Annual Earnings: $14,600
- ▲ Growth: 32.4%
- ▲ Annual Job Openings: 62,000
- ▲ Self-Employed: 0.7%
- ▲ Part-Time: 48.8%

Perform variety of attending duties at amusement or recreation facility. May schedule use of recreation facilities, maintain and provide equipment to participants of sporting events or recreational pursuits, or operate amusement concessions and rides. Schedules use of recreation facilities, such as golf courses, tennis courts, bowling alleys, and softball diamonds. Operates, drives, or explains use of mechanical riding devices or other automatic equipment in amusement parks, carnivals, or recreation areas. Receives, retrieves, replaces, and stores sports equipment and supplies; arranges items in designated areas; and erects or removes equipment. Sells tickets, collects fees from customers, and collects or punches tickets. Rents, sells, and issues sports equipment and supplies, such as bowling shoes, golf balls, swimming suits, and beach chairs. Provides information about facilities, entertainment options, and rules and regulations. Directs patrons of establishment to rides, seats, or attractions or escorts patrons on tours of points of interest. Records details of attendance, sales, receipts, reservations, and repair activities. Inspects, repairs, adjusts, tests, fuels, and oils sporting and recreation equipment, game machines, and amusement rides. Cleans sporting equipment, vehicles, rides, booths, facilities, and grounds. Attends amusement booth in parks, carnivals, or stadiums and awards prizes to winning players. Sells and serves refreshments to customers. Announces and describes amusement park attractions to patrons to entice customers to participate in games and other entertainment. Provides entertainment services, such as guessing patron's weight, conducting games, explaining use of arcade game machines, or photographing patrons. Launches, moors, and demonstrates use of boats, such as rowboats, canoes, and motorboats, or caddies for golfers. Monitors activities to ensure adherence to rules and safety procedures to protect environment and maintain order and ejects unruly patrons. Attends animals, performing such tasks as harnessing, saddling, feeding, watering, and grooming, and drives horse-drawn vehicle for entertainment or advertising purposes. Assists patrons on and off amusement rides, boats, or ski lifts and in mounting and riding animals. Fastens or directs patrons to fasten safety devices. **SKILLS—Active Listening:** Giving full attention to what other people are saying, taking time to understand the points being made, asking questions as appropriate, and not interrupting at inappropriate times. **Operation and Control:** Controlling operations of equipment or systems.

Service Orientation: Actively looking for ways to help people. **Repairing:** Repairing machines or systems, using the needed tools.

GOE INFORMATION—Interest Area: 11. Recreation, Travel, and Other Personal Services. **Work Group:** 11.02. Recreational Services. **Other Job Titles in This Work Group:** Entertainment Attendants and Related Workers, All Other; Gaming and Sports Book Writers and Runners; Gaming Dealers; Gaming Service Workers, All Other; Motion Picture Projectionists; Recreation Workers; Slot Key Persons; Tour Guides and Escorts; Travel Guides; Ushers, Lobby Attendants, and Ticket Takers. **PERSONALITY TYPE—Realistic.** Realistic occupations frequently involve work activities that include practical, hands-on problems and solutions. They often deal with plants, animals, and real-world materials like wood, tools, and machinery. Many of the occupations require working outside and do not involve a lot of paperwork or working closely with others.

EDUCATION/TRAINING PROGRAM(S)—No data available. **RELATED KNOWLEDGE/COURSES— Customer and Personal Service:** Knowledge of principles and processes for providing customer and personal services. This includes customer needs assessment, meeting quality standards for services, and evaluation of customer satisfaction. **Sales and Marketing:** Knowledge of principles and methods for showing, promoting, and selling products or services. This includes marketing strategy and tactics, product demonstration, sales techniques, and sales control systems. **Public Safety and Security:** Knowledge of relevant equipment, policies, procedures, and strategies to promote effective local, state, or national security operations for the protection of people, data, property, and institutions. **Principles of Mechanical Devices:** Knowledge of machines and tools, including their designs, uses, repair, and maintenance. **Mathematics:** Knowledge of arithmetic, algebra, geometry, calculus, and statistics and their applications.

Anesthesiologists

▲ Education/Training Required: First professional degree
▲ Annual Earnings: More than $145,600
▲ Growth: 17.9%
▲ Annual Job Openings: 27,000
▲ Self-Employed: 20.4%
▲ Part-Time: 7.2%

Administer anesthetics during surgery or other medical procedures. Administers anesthetic or sedation during medical procedures, using local, intravenous, spinal, or caudal methods. Monitors patient before, during, and after anesthesia and counteracts adverse reactions or complications. Examines patient to determine risk during surgical, obstetrical, and other medical procedures. Records type and amount of anesthesia and patient condition throughout procedure. Informs students and staff of types and methods of anesthesia administration, signs of complications, and emergency methods to counteract reactions. Positions patient on operating table to maximize patient comfort and surgical accessibility. Confers with medical professional to determine type and method of anesthetic or sedation to render patient insensible to pain. **SKILLS— Reading Comprehension:** Understanding written sentences and paragraphs in work-related documents. **Judgment and Decision Making:** Considering the relative costs and benefits of potential actions to choose the most appropriate one. **Critical Thinking:** Using logic and reasoning to identify the strengths and weaknesses of alternative solutions, conclusions, or approaches to problems. **Active Learning:** Understanding the implications of new information for both current and future problem-solving and decision-making. **Coordination:** Adjusting actions in relation to others' actions. **Monitoring:** Monitoring/Assessing your performance or that of other individuals or organizations to make improvements or take corrective action. **Speaking:** Talking to others to convey information effectively.

GOE INFORMATION—Interest Area: 14. Medical and Health Services. **Work Group:** 14.02. Medicine and Sur-

gery. **Other Job Titles in This Work Group:** Family and General Practitioners; Internists, General; Medical Assistants; Obstetricians and Gynecologists; Pediatricians, General; Pharmacists; Pharmacy Aides; Pharmacy Technicians; Physician Assistants; Physicians and Surgeons, All Other; Psychiatrists; Registered Nurses; Surgeons; Surgical Technologists. **PERSONALITY TYPE**—Investigative. Investigative occupations frequently involve working with ideas and require an extensive amount of thinking. These occupations can involve searching for facts and figuring out problems mentally.

EDUCATION/TRAINING PROGRAM(S)—Anesthesiology; Critical Care Anesthesiology. **RELATED KNOWLEDGE/COURSES—Medicine and Dentistry:** Knowledge of the information and techniques needed to diagnose and treat human injuries, diseases, and deformities. This includes symptoms, treatment alternatives, drug properties and interactions, and preventive health-care measures. **Biology:** Knowledge of plant and animal organisms and their tissues, cells, functions, interdependencies, and interactions with each other and the environment. **Chemistry:** Knowledge of the chemical composition, structure, and properties of substances and of the chemical processes and transformations that they undergo. This includes uses of chemicals and their interactions, danger signs, production techniques, and disposal methods. **Mathematics:** Knowledge of arithmetic, algebra, geometry, calculus, and statistics and their applications. **English Language:** Knowledge of the structure and content of the English language, including the meaning and spelling of words, rules of composition, and grammar.

Anthropology and Archeology Teachers, Postsecondary

- ▲ Education/Training Required: Master's degree
- ▲ Annual Earnings: $59,000
- ▲ Growth: 23.5%
- ▲ Annual Job Openings: 184,000
- ▲ Self-Employed: 0%
- ▲ Part-Time: 32.3%

Teach courses in anthropology or archeology. Prepares and delivers lectures to students. Stimulates class discussions. Compiles bibliographies of specialized materials for outside reading assignments. Directs research of other teachers or graduate students working for advanced academic degrees. Serves on faculty committee providing professional consulting services to government and industry. Acts as adviser to student organizations. Conducts research in particular field of knowledge and publishes findings in professional journals. Advises students on academic and vocational curricula. Compiles, administers, and grades examinations or assigns this work to others. **SKILLS— Reading Comprehension:** Understanding written sentences and paragraphs in work-related documents. **Instructing:** Teaching others how to do something. **Active Learning:** Understanding the implications of new information for both current and future problem-solving and decision-making. **Speaking:** Talking to others to convey information effectively. **Learning Strategies:** Selecting and using training/instructional methods and procedures appropriate for the situation when learning or teaching new things. **Writing:** Communicating effectively in writing as appropriate for the needs of the audience. **Active Listening:** Giving full attention to what other people are saying, taking time to understand the points being made, asking questions as appropriate, and not interrupting at inappropriate times.

GOE INFORMATION—Interest Area: 12. Education and Social Service. **Work Group:** 12.03. Educational Services. **Other Job Titles in This Work Group:** Adult Literacy, Remedial Education, and GED Teachers and Instructors; Agricultural Sciences Teachers, Postsecondary; Architecture Teachers, Postsecondary; Archivists; Area, Ethnic, and Cultural Studies Teachers, Postsecondary; Art, Drama, and Music Teachers, Postsecondary; Atmospheric, Earth, Marine, and Space Sciences Teachers, Postsecondary; Audio-Visual Collections Specialists; Biological Science Teachers, Postsecondary; Business Teachers, Postsecondary; Chemistry Teachers, Postsecondary; Child Care Workers; Communications Teachers, Postsecondary; Computer Sci-

ence Teachers, Postsecondary; Criminal Justice and Law Enforcement Teachers, Postsecondary; Curators; Economics Teachers, Postsecondary; Education Teachers, Postsecondary; Educational Psychologists; Educational, Vocational, and School Counselors; Elementary School Teachers, Except Special Education; Engineering Teachers, Postsecondary; English Language and Literature Teachers, Postsecondary; Environmental Science Teachers, Postsecondary; Farm and Home Management Advisors; Foreign Language and Literature Teachers, Postsecondary; Forestry and Conservation Science Teachers, Postsecondary; Geography Teachers, Postsecondary; Graduate Teaching Assistants; Health Specialties Teachers, Postsecondary; History Teachers, Postsecondary; Home Economics Teachers, Postsecondary; Kindergarten Teachers, Except Special Education; Law Teachers, Postsecondary; Librarians; Library Assistants, Clerical; Library Science Teachers, Postsecondary; Library Technicians; Mathematical Science Teachers, Postsecondary; Middle School Teachers, Except Special and Vocational Education; Museum Technicians and Conservators; Nursing Instructors and Teachers, Postsecondary; Personal Financial Advisors; Philosophy and Religion Teachers, Postsecondary; Physics Teachers, Postsecondary; Political Science Teachers, Postsecondary; Postsecondary Teachers, All Other; Preschool Teachers, Except Special Education; Psychology Teachers, Postsecondary; others. **PERSONALITY TYPE—Social.** Social occupations frequently involve working with, communicating with, and teaching people. These occupations often involve helping or providing service to others.

EDUCATION/TRAINING PROGRAM(S)—Anthropology; Archeology; Physical Anthropology; Social Science Teacher Education. RELATED KNOWLEDGE/ COURSES—Education and Training: Knowledge of principles and methods for curriculum and training design, teaching and instruction for individuals and groups, and the measurement of training effects. **Sociology and Anthropology:** Knowledge of group behavior and dynamics, societal trends and influences, human migrations, ethnicity, and cultures and their history and origins. **Psy-**

chology: Knowledge of human behavior and performance; individual differences in ability, personality, and interests; learning and motivation; psychological research methods; and the assessment and treatment of behavioral and affective disorders. **History and Archeology:** Knowledge of historical events and their causes, indicators, and effects on civilizations and cultures. **English Language:** Knowledge of the structure and content of the English language, including the meaning and spelling of words, rules of composition, and grammar.

Appraisers and Assessors of Real Estate

- ▲ Education/Training Required: Postsecondary vocational training
- ▲ Annual Earnings: $38,950
- ▲ Growth: 18.0%
- ▲ Annual Job Openings: 6,000
- ▲ Self-Employed: 21.1%
- ▲ Part-Time: 16.6%

Appraise real property to determine its fair value. May assess taxes in accordance with prescribed schedules. SKILLS—No data available.

GOE INFORMATION—**Interest Area:** 13. General Management and Support. **Work Group:** 13.02. Management Support. **Other Job Titles in This Work Group:** Accountants; Accountants and Auditors; Appraisers, Real Estate; Assessors; Auditors; Budget Analysts; Claims Adjusters, Examiners, and Investigators; Claims Examiners, Property and Casualty Insurance; Compensation, Benefits, and Job Analysis Specialists; Cost Estimators; Credit Analysts; Employment Interviewers, Private or Public Employment Service; Employment, Recruitment, and Placement Specialists; Financial Analysts; Human Resources, Train-ing, and Labor Relations Specialists, All Other; Insurance Adjusters, Examiners, and Investigators; Insurance Appraisers, Auto Damage; Insurance Underwriters; Loan Counselors; Loan Officers; Logisticians; Management Analysts; Market Research Analysts; Personnel Recruiters; Purchasing Agents and Buyers, Farm Products; Purchasing Agents, Except Wholesale, Retail, and Farm Products; Tax Examiners, Collectors, and Revenue Agents; Training and Development Specialists; Wholesale and Retail Buyers, Except Farm Products. **PERSONALITY TYPE**—No data available.

EDUCATION/TRAINING PROGRAM(S)—Real Estate. **RELATED KNOWLEDGE/COURSES**—No data available.

Appraisers, Real Estate

- ▲ Education/Training Required: Postsecondary vocational training
- ▲ Annual Earnings: $38,950
- ▲ Growth: 18.0%
- ▲ Annual Job Openings: 6,000
- ▲ Self-Employed: 21.1%
- ▲ Part-Time: 16.6%

Appraise real property to determine its value for purchase, sales, investment, mortgage, or loan purposes. Considers such factors as depreciation, value comparison of similar property, and income potential when computing final estimation of property value. Inspects property for construction, condition, and functional design and takes property measurements. Interviews persons familiar with property and immediate surroundings, such as contractors, homeowners, and other realtors, to obtain pertinent information. Considers location and trends or impending changes that could influence future value of property. Prepares written report, utilizing data collected, and submits report to corroborate value established. Photographs interiors and exteriors of property to assist in estimating property value, to substantiate finding, and to complete appraisal report. Searches public records for transactions, such as sales, leases, and assessments. **SKILLS—Writing:** Communicating effectively in writing as appropriate for the needs of the audience. **Reading Comprehension:** Understanding written sentences and paragraphs in work-related documents. **Mathematics:** Using mathematics to solve problems. **Active Listening:** Giving full attention to what other people are saying, taking time to understand the points being made, asking questions as appropriate, and not interrupting at inappropriate times. **Speaking:** Talking to others to convey information effectively.

GOE INFORMATION—Interest Area: 13. General Management and Support. Work Group: 13.02. Management Support. Other Job Titles in This Work Group: Accountants; Accountants and Auditors; Appraisers and Assessors of Real Estate; Assessors; Auditors; Budget Analysts; Claims Adjusters, Examiners, and Investigators; Claims Examiners, Property and Casualty Insurance; Compensation, Benefits, and Job Analysis Specialists; Cost Estimators; Credit Analysts; Employment Interviewers, Private or Public Employment Service; Employment, Recruitment, and Placement Specialists; Financial Analysts; Human Resources, Training, and Labor Relations Specialists, All Other; Insurance Adjusters, Examiners, and Investigators; Insurance Appraisers, Auto Damage; Insurance Underwriters; Loan Counselors; Loan Officers; Logisticians; Management Analysts; Market Research Analysts; Personnel Recruiters; Purchasing Agents and Buyers, Farm Products; Purchasing Agents, Except Wholesale, Retail,

and Farm Products; Tax Examiners, Collectors, and Revenue Agents; Training and Development Specialists; Wholesale and Retail Buyers, Except Farm Products. **PERSONALITY TYPE**—Enterprising. Enterprising occupations frequently involve starting up and carrying out projects. These occupations can involve leading people and making many decisions. They sometimes require risk taking and often deal with business.

EDUCATION/TRAINING PROGRAM(S)—Real Estate. RELATED KNOWLEDGE/COURSES—Mathematics: Knowledge of arithmetic, algebra, geometry, calculus, and statistics and their applications. **Building and Construction:** Knowledge of materials, methods, and tools involved in the construction or repair of houses, buildings, or other structures, such as highways and roads. **Economics and Accounting:** Knowledge of economic and accounting principles and practices, the financial markets, banking, and the analysis and reporting of financial data. **English Language:** Knowledge of the structure and content of the English language, including the meaning and spelling of words, rules of composition, and grammar. **Clerical Studies:** Knowledge of administrative and clerical procedures and systems, such as word processing, managing files and records, stenography and transcription, designing forms, and other office procedures and terminology.

Arbitrators, Mediators, and Conciliators

- ▲ Education/Training Required: Work experience plus degree
- ▲ Annual Earnings: $46,660
- ▲ Growth: 27.2%
- ▲ Annual Job Openings: Fewer than 500
- ▲ Self-Employed: 0.5%
- ▲ Part-Time: 3.6%

Facilitate negotiation and conflict resolution through dialogue. Resolve conflicts outside of the court system by mutual consent of parties involved. Arranges and conducts hearings to obtain information and evidence relative to disposition of claim. Counsels parties and recommends acceptance or rejection of compromise settlement offers. Analyzes evidence and applicable law, regulations, policy, and precedent decisions to determine conclusions. Questions witnesses to obtain information. Rules on exceptions, motions, and admissibility of evidence. Participates in court proceedings. Obtains additional information to clarify evidence. Conducts studies of appeals procedures in field agencies to ensure adherence to legal requirements and to facilitate determination of cases. Notifies claimant of de-

nied claim and appeal rights. Authorizes payment of valid claims. Issues subpoenas and administers oaths to prepare for formal hearing. Researches laws, regulations, policies, and precedent decisions to prepare for hearings. Reviews and evaluates data on documents, such as claim applications, birth or death certificates, and physician or employer records. Interviews or corresponds with claimants or agents to elicit information. Prepares written opinions and decisions. Determines existence and amount of liability according to law, administrative and judicial precedents, and evidence. **SKILLS—Active Listening:** Giving full attention to what other people are saying, taking time to understand the points being made, asking questions as appropriate, and not interrupting at inappropriate times.

Critical Thinking: Using logic and reasoning to identify the strengths and weaknesses of alternative solutions, conclusions, or approaches to problems. **Judgment and Decision Making:** Considering the relative costs and benefits of potential actions to choose the most appropriate one. **Reading Comprehension:** Understanding written sentences and paragraphs in work-related documents. **Writing:** Communicating effectively in writing as appropriate for the needs of the audience.

GOE INFORMATION—Interest Area: 04. Law, Law Enforcement, and Public Safety. **Work Group:** 04.02. Law. **Other Job Titles in This Work Group:** Administrative Law Judges, Adjudicators, and Hearing Officers; Judges, Magistrate Judges, and Magistrates; Law Clerks; Lawyers; Legal Support Workers, All Other; Paralegals and Legal Assistants; Title Examiners and Abstractors; Title Examiners, Abstractors, and Searchers; Title Searchers. **PERSONALITY TYPE**—Enterprising. Enterprising occupations frequently involve starting up and carrying out projects. These occupations can involve leading people and making many decisions. They sometimes require risk taking and often deal with business.

EDUCATION/TRAINING PROGRAM(S)—Law (LL.B., J.D.); Legal Professions and Studies, Other. **RE-LATED KNOWLEDGE/COURSES—Law and Government:** Knowledge of laws, legal codes, court procedures, precedents, government regulations, executive orders, agency rules, and the democratic political process. **Administration and Management:** Knowledge of business and management principles involved in strategic planning, resource allocation, human resources modeling, leadership technique, production methods, and coordination of people and resources. **English Language:** Knowledge of the structure and content of the English language, including the meaning and spelling of words, rules of composition, and grammar. **Psychology:** Knowledge of human behavior and performance; individual differences in ability, personality, and interests; learning and motivation; psychological research methods; and the assessment and treatment of behavioral and affective disorders. **Education and Training:** Knowledge of principles and methods for curriculum and training design, teaching and instruction for individuals and groups, and the measurement of training effects. **Mathematics:** Knowledge of arithmetic, algebra, geometry, calculus, and statistics and their applications. **Computers and Electronics:** Knowledge of circuit boards, processors, chips, electronic equipment, and computer hardware and software, including applications and programming.

Architects, Except Landscape and Naval

- ▲ Education/Training Required: Bachelor's degree
- ▲ Annual Earnings: $55,470
- ▲ Growth: 18.5%
- ▲ Annual Job Openings: 4,000
- ▲ Self-Employed: 30.8%
- ▲ Part-Time: 8.0%

Plan and design structures, such as private residences, office buildings, theaters, factories, and other structural property. Prepares information regarding design, structure specifications, materials, color, equipment, estimated costs, and construction time. Plans layout of project. Integrates engineering element into unified design. Prepares scale drawings. Prepares contract documents for building contractors. Administers construction contracts. Prepares operating and maintenance manuals, studies, and reports. Represents client in obtaining bids and awarding construction contracts. Directs activities of workers engaged in preparing drawings and specification documents. Conducts periodic on-site observation of work during construction to monitor compliance with plans. Consults with client to determine functional and spatial requirements of structure. **SKILLS—Coordination:** Adjusting actions in relation to others' actions. **Reading Comprehension:** Understanding written sentences and paragraphs in work-related documents. **Writing:** Communicating effectively in writing as appropriate for the needs of the audience. **Mathematics:** Using mathematics to solve problems. **Active Listening:** Giving full attention to what other people are saying, taking time to understand the points being made, asking questions as appropriate, and not interrupting at inappropriate times.

GOE INFORMATION—Interest Area: 02. Science, Math, and Engineering. **Work Group:** 02.07. Engineering. **Other Job Titles in This Work Group:** Aerospace Engineers; Agricultural Engineers; Biomedical Engineers;

Chemical Engineers; Civil Engineers; Computer Hardware Engineers; Computer Software Engineers, Applications; Computer Software Engineers, Systems Software; Electrical Engineers; Electronics Engineers, Except Computer; Engineers, All Other; Environmental Engineers; Fire-Prevention and Protection Engineers; Health and Safety Engineers, Except Mining Safety Engineers and Inspectors; Industrial Engineers; Industrial Safety and Health Engineers; Landscape Architects; Marine Architects; Marine Engineers; Marine Engineers and Naval Architects; Materials Engineers; Mechanical Engineers; Mining and Geological Engineers, Including Mining Safety Engineers; Nuclear Engineers; Petroleum Engineers; Product Safety Engineers; Sales Engineers. **PERSONALITY TYPE**—Artistic. Artistic occupations frequently involve working with forms, designs, and patterns. They often require self-expression, and the work can be done without following a clear set of rules.

EDUCATION/TRAINING PROGRAM(S)—Architectural History and Criticism, General; Architecture (BArch, BA/BS, MArch, MA/MS, PhD); Architecture and Related Services, Other; Environmental Design/Architecture. **RELATED KNOWLEDGE/COURSES—Design:** Knowledge of design techniques, tools, and principles involved in production of precision technical plans, blueprints, drawings, and models. **Building and Construction:** Knowledge of materials, methods, and tools involved in the construction or repair of houses, buildings, or other structures, such as highways and roads. **Administration and Management:** Knowledge of business and management principles involved in strategic planning, resource allocation, human resources modeling, leadership technique, production methods, and coordination of people and resources. **Mathematics:** Knowledge of arithmetic, algebra, geometry, calculus, and statistics and their applications. **English Language:** Knowledge of the structure and content of the English language, including the meaning and spelling of words, rules of composition, and grammar.

Architectural and Civil Drafters

▲ Education/Training Required: Postsecondary vocational training
▲ Annual Earnings: $37,010
▲ Growth: 20.8%
▲ Annual Job Openings: 12,000
▲ Self-Employed: 3.0%
▲ Part-Time: 7.9%

Prepare detailed drawings of architectural and structural features of buildings or drawings and topographical relief maps used in civil engineering projects, such as highways, bridges, and public works. Utilize knowledge of building materials, engineering practices, and mathematics to complete drawings. **SKILLS**—No data available.

GOE INFORMATION—Interest Area: 02. Science, Math, and Engineering. **Work Group:** 02.08. Engineering Technology. **Other Job Titles in This Work Group:** Aerospace Engineering and Operations Technicians; Architectural Drafters; Calibration and Instrumentation Technicians; Cartographers and Photogrammetrists; Civil Drafters; Civil Engineering Technicians; Construction and Building Inspectors; Drafters, All Other; Electrical and Electronic Engineering Technicians; Electrical and Electronics Drafters; Electrical Drafters; Electrical Engineering Technicians; Electro-Mechanical Technicians;

Electronic Drafters; Electronics Engineering Technicians; Engineering Technicians, Except Drafters, All Other; Environmental Engineering Technicians; Industrial Engineering Technicians; Mapping Technicians; Mechanical Drafters; Mechanical Engineering Technicians; Numerical Tool and Process Control Programmers; Pressure Vessel Inspectors; Surveying and Mapping Technicians; Surveying Technicians; Surveyors. **PERSONALITY TYPE**—No data available.

EDUCATION/TRAINING PROGRAM(S)—Architectural Drafting and Architectural CAD/CADD; Architectural Technology/Technician; CAD/CADD Drafting and/or Design Technology/Technician; Civil Drafting and Civil Engineering CAD/CADD; Drafting and Design Technology/Technician, General. **RELATED KNOWLEDGE/COURSES**—No data available.

Architectural Drafters

- ▲ Education/Training Required: Associate's degree
- ▲ Annual Earnings: $37,010
- ▲ Growth: 20.8%
- ▲ Annual Job Openings: 12,000
- ▲ Self-Employed: 3.0%
- ▲ Part-Time: 7.9%

Prepare detailed drawings of architectural designs and plans for buildings and structures according to specifications provided by architect. Draws rough and detailed scale plans, to scale, for foundations, buildings, and structures, according to specifications. Prepares colored drawings of landscape and interior designs for presentation to client. Develops diagrams for construction, fabrication, and installation of equipment, structures, components, and systems, using field documents and specifications. Lays out and plans interior room arrangements for commercial buildings and draws charts, forms, and records, using computer-assisted equipment. Lays out schematics and wiring diagrams used to erect, install, and repair establishment cable and electrical systems, using computer equipment. Drafts and corrects topographical maps to represent geological stratigraphy, mineral deposits, and pipeline systems, using survey data and aerial photographs. Builds landscape models, using data provided by landscape architect. Calculates heat loss and gain of buildings and structures to determine required equipment specifications, following standard procedures. Traces copies of plans and drawings, using transparent paper or cloth, ink, pencil, and standard drafting instruments for reproduction purposes. **SKILLS—Mathematics:** Using mathematics to solve problems. **Programming:** Writing computer programs for various purposes. **Reading Comprehension:** Understanding written sentences and paragraphs in work-related documents. **Active Learning:** Understanding the implications of new information for both current and future problem-solving and decision-making. **Operations Analysis:** Analyzing needs and product requirements to create a design.

GOE INFORMATION—**Interest Area:** 02. Science, Math, and Engineering. **Work Group:** 02.08. Engineering Technology. **Other Job Titles in This Work Group:** Aerospace Engineering and Operations Technicians; Architectural and Civil Drafters; Calibration and Instrumentation Technicians; Cartographers and Photogrammetrists; Civil Drafters; Civil Engineering Technicians; Construction and Building Inspectors; Drafters, All Other; Electrical and Electronic Engineering Technicians; Electrical and Electronics Drafters; Electrical Drafters; Electrical Engineering Technicians; Electro-Mechanical Technicians; Electronic Drafters; Electronics Engineering Technicians; Engineering Technicians, Except Drafters, All Other; Environmental Engineering Technicians; Industrial Engineering Technicians; Mapping Technicians; Mechanical Drafters; Mechanical Engineering Technicians; Numerical Tool and Process Control Programmers; Pressure Vessel Inspectors; Surveying and Mapping Technicians; Surveying Technicians; Surveyors. **PERSONALITY TYPE**—Realistic. Realistic occupations frequently involve work activities that include practical, hands-on problems and solutions. They often deal with plants, animals, and real-world materials like wood, tools, and machinery. Many of the occupations require working outside and do not involve a lot of paperwork or working closely with others.

EDUCATION/TRAINING PROGRAM(S)—Architectural Drafting and Architectural CAD/CADD; Architectural Technology/Technician; CAD/CADD Drafting and/or Design Technology/Technician; Civil Drafting and Civil Engineering CAD/CADD; Drafting and Design Technology/Technician, General. **RELATED KNOWLEDGE/COURSES—Design:** Knowledge of design techniques, tools, and principles involved in production of precision technical plans, blueprints, drawings, and models. **Mathematics:** Knowledge of arithmetic, algebra, geometry, calculus, and statistics and their applications. **Engineering and Technology:** Knowledge of the practical application of engineering science and technology. This includes applying principles, techniques, procedures, and equipment to the design and production of various goods and services. **Computers and Electronics:** Knowledge of circuit boards, processors, chips, electronic equipment, and computer hardware and software, including applications and programming. **Physics:** Knowledge and prediction of physical principles and laws and their interrelationships and applications to understanding fluid, material, and atmospheric dynamics and mechanical, electrical, atomic, and sub-atomic structures and processes.

Architecture Teachers, Postsecondary

▲ Education/Training Required: Master's degree
▲ Annual Earnings: $54,480
▲ Growth: 23.5%
▲ Annual Job Openings: 184,000
▲ Self-Employed: 0%
▲ Part-Time: 32.3%

Teach courses in architecture and architectural design, such as architectural environmental design, interior architecture/design, and landscape architecture. **SKILLS**—No data available.

GOE INFORMATION—**Interest Area:** 12. Education and Social Service. **Work Group:** 12.03. Educational Services. **Other Job Titles in This Work Group:** Adult Literacy, Remedial Education, and GED Teachers and Instructors; Agricultural Sciences Teachers, Postsecondary; Anthropology and Archeology Teachers, Postsecondary; Archivists; Area, Ethnic, and Cultural Studies Teachers, Postsecondary; Art, Drama, and Music Teachers, Postsecondary; Atmospheric, Earth, Marine, and Space Sciences Teachers, Postsecondary; Audio-Visual Collections Specialists; Biological Science Teachers, Postsecondary; Business Teachers, Postsecondary; Chemistry Teachers, Postsecondary; Child Care Workers; Communications Teachers, Postsecondary; Computer Science Teachers, Postsecondary; Criminal Justice and Law Enforcement Teachers, Postsecondary; Curators; Economics Teachers, Postsecondary; Education Teachers, Postsecondary; Educational Psychologists; Educational, Vocational, and School Counselors; Elementary School Teachers, Except Special Education; Engineering Teachers, Postsecondary; English Language and Literature Teachers, Postsecondary; Environmental Science Teachers, Postsecondary; Farm and Home Management Advisors; Foreign Language and Literature Teachers, Postsecondary; Forestry and Conservation Science Teachers, Postsecondary; Geography Teachers, Postsecondary; Graduate Teaching Assistants; Health Specialties Teachers, Postsecondary; History Teachers, Postsecondary; Home Economics Teachers, Postsecondary; Kindergarten Teachers, Except Special Education; Law Teachers, Postsecondary; Librarians; Library Assistants, Clerical; Library Science Teachers, Postsecondary; Library Technicians; Mathematical Science Teachers, Postsecondary; Middle School Teachers, Except Special and Vocational Education; Museum Technicians and Conservators; Nursing Instructors and Teachers, Postsecondary; Personal Financial Advisors; Philosophy and Religion Teachers, Postsecondary; Physics Teachers, Postsecondary; Political Science Teachers, Postsecondary; Postsecondary Teachers, All Other; Preschool Teachers, Except Special Education; others. **PERSONALITY TYPE**—No data available.

EDUCATION/TRAINING PROGRAM(S)—Architectural Engineering; Architecture (BArch, BA/BS, MArch, MA/MS, PhD); City/Urban, Community and Regional Planning; Environmental Design/Architecture; Interior Architecture; Landscape Architecture (BS, BSLA, BLA, MSLA, MLA, PhD); Teacher Education and Professional Development, Specific Subject Areas, Other. **RELATED KNOWLEDGE/COURSES**—No data available.

Area, Ethnic, and Cultural Studies Teachers, Postsecondary

▲ Education/Training Required: Master's degree
▲ Annual Earnings: $54,700
▲ Growth: 23.5%
▲ Annual Job Openings: 184,000
▲ Self-Employed: 0%
▲ Part-Time: 32.3%

Teach courses pertaining to the culture and development of an area (e.g., Latin America), an ethnic group, or any other group (e.g., women's studies, urban affairs). Prepares and delivers lectures to students. Compiles, administers, and grades examinations or assigns this work to others. Advises students on academic and vocational curricula.

Conducts research in particular field of knowledge and publishes findings in professional journals. Acts as adviser to student organizations. Serves on faculty committee providing professional consulting services to government and industry. Directs research of other teachers or graduate students working for advanced academic degrees. Compiles bibliographies of specialized materials for outside reading assignments. Stimulates class discussions. **SKILLS—Reading Comprehension:** Understanding written sentences and paragraphs in work-related documents. **Instructing:** Teaching others how to do something. **Speaking:** Talking to others to convey information effectively. **Active Learning:** Understanding the implications of new information for both current and future problem-solving and decision-making. **Learning Strategies:** Selecting and using training/instructional methods and procedures appropriate for the situation when learning or teaching new things. **Writing:** Communicating effectively in writing as appropriate for the needs of the audience. **Active Listening:** Giving full attention to what other people are saying, taking time to understand the points being made, asking questions as appropriate, and not interrupting at inappropriate times.

GOE INFORMATION—Interest Area: 12. Education and Social Service. **Work Group:** 12.03. Educational Services. **Other Job Titles in This Work Group:** Adult Literacy, Remedial Education, and GED Teachers and Instructors; Agricultural Sciences Teachers, Postsecondary; Anthropology and Archeology Teachers, Postsecondary; Architecture Teachers, Postsecondary; Archivists; Art, Drama, and Music Teachers, Postsecondary; Atmospheric, Earth, Marine, and Space Sciences Teachers, Postsecondary; Audio-Visual Collections Specialists; Biological Science Teachers, Postsecondary; Business Teachers, Postsecondary; Chemistry Teachers, Postsecondary; Child Care Workers; Communications Teachers, Postsecondary; Computer Science Teachers, Postsecondary; Criminal Justice and Law Enforcement Teachers, Postsecondary; Curators; Economics Teachers, Postsecondary; Education Teachers, Postsecondary; Educational Psychologists; Educational, Vocational, and School Counselors; Elementary School Teachers, Except Special Education; Engineering Teachers, Postsecondary; English Language and Literature Teachers, Postsecondary; Environmental Science Teachers, Postsecondary; Farm and Home Management Advisors; Foreign Language and Literature Teachers, Postsecondary; Forestry and Conservation Science Teachers, Postsecondary; Geography Teachers, Postsecondary; Graduate Teaching Assistants; Health Specialties Teachers, Postsecondary; History Teachers, Postsecondary; Home Economics Teachers, Postsecondary; Kindergarten Teachers, Except Special Education; Law Teachers, Postsecondary; Librarians; Library Assistants, Clerical; Library Science Teachers, Postsecondary; Library Technicians; Mathematical Science Teachers, Postsecondary; Middle School Teachers, Except Special and Vocational Education; Museum Technicians and Conservators; Nursing Instructors and Teachers, Postsecondary; Personal Financial Advisors; Philosophy and Religion Teachers, Postsecondary; Physics Teachers, Postsecondary; Political Science Teachers, Postsecondary; Postsecondary Teachers, All Other; Preschool Teachers, Except Special Education; Psychology Teachers, Postsecondary; others. **PERSONALITY TYPE—Social.** Social occupations frequently involve working with, communicating with, and teaching people. These occupations often involve helping or providing service to others.

EDUCATION/TRAINING PROGRAM(S)—African Studies; African-American/Black Studies; American Indian/Native American Studies; American/United States Studies/Civilization; Area Studies, Other; Area, Ethnic, Cultural, and Gender Studies, Other; Asian Studies/Civilization; Asian-American Studies; Balkans Studies; Baltic Studies; Canadian Studies; Caribbean Studies; Central/Middle and Eastern European Studies; Chinese Studies; Commonwealth Studies; East Asian Studies; Ethnic, Cultural Minority, and Gender Studies, Other; European Studies/Civilization; French Studies; Gay/Lesbian Studies; German Studies; Hispanic-American, Puerto Rican, and Mexican-American/Chicano Studies; Intercultural/Multicultural and Diversity Studies; Islamic Studies; Italian Studies; Japanese Studies; Jewish/Judaic Studies; Korean Studies; Latin American Studies; Near and Middle Eastern Studies; Pacific Area/Pacific Rim Studies; Polish Studies; Regional Studies (U.S., Canadian, Foreign); Religion/Religious Studies, Other; Russian Studies; Scandinavian Studies; Slavic Studies; Social Studies Teacher Education; South Asian Studies; Southeast Asian Studies; Spanish and Iberian Studies; Tibetan Studies; Ukraine Studies; Ural-Altaic and Central Asian Studies; Western European Studies; Women's Studies. RELATED KNOWLEDGE/COURSES—Education and Training: Knowledge of principles and methods for curriculum and training design, teaching and instruction for individuals and groups, and the measurement of training effects. **Sociology and Anthropology:** Knowledge of group behavior and dynamics, societal trends and influences, human migrations, ethnicity, and cultures and their history and origins. **English Language:** Knowledge of the structure and content of the English language, including the meaning and spelling of words, rules of composition, and grammar. **History and Archeology:** Knowledge of historical events and their causes, indicators, and effects on civilizations and cultures. **Psychology:** Knowledge of human behavior and performance; individual differences in ability, personality, and interests; learning and motivation; psychological research methods; and the assessment and treatment of behavioral and affective disorders.

Art Directors

- ▲ Education/Training Required: Work experience plus degree
- ▲ Annual Earnings: $59,800
- ▲ Growth: 21.1%
- ▲ Annual Job Openings: 6,000
- ▲ Self-Employed: 31.9%
- ▲ Part-Time: 20.0%

Formulate design concepts and presentation approaches. Direct workers engaged in artwork, layout design, and copy writing for visual communications media, such as magazines, books, newspapers, and packaging. Assigns and directs staff members to develop design concepts into art layouts or prepare layouts for printing. Formulates basic layout design or presentation approach and conceives material details, such as style and size of type, photographs, graphics, and arrangement. Reviews and approves art and copy materials developed by staff as well as proofs of printed copy. Reviews illustrative material and confers with client concerning objectives; budget; background information; and presentation approaches, styles, and techniques. Writes typography instructions, such as margin widths and type sizes, and submits for typesetting or printing. Draws custom illustrations for project. Marks up, pastes, and completes layouts to prepare for printing. Prepares detailed storyboard showing sequence and timing of story development for television production. Presents final layouts to client for approval. Confers with creative, art, copy writing, or production department heads to discuss client requirements, outline presentation concepts, and coordinate creative activities. **SKILLS—Coordination:** Adjusting actions in relation to others' actions. **Active Learning:** Understanding the implications of new information for both current and future problem-solving and decision-making. **Speaking:** Talking to others to convey information effectively. **Operations Analysis:** Analyzing needs and product requirements to create a design. **Persuasion:** Persuading others to change their minds or behavior. **Time Management:** Managing one's own time and the time of others.

GOE INFORMATION—Interest Area: 01. Arts, Entertainment, and Media. **Work Group:** 01.01. Managerial Work in Arts, Entertainment, and Media. **Other Job Titles in This Work Group:** Agents and Business Managers of Artists, Performers, and Athletes; Producers; Producers and Directors; Program Directors; Technical Directors/Managers. **PERSONALITY TYPE**—Artistic. Artistic occupations frequently involve working with forms, designs, and patterns. They often require self-expression, and the work can be done without following a clear set of rules.

EDUCATION/TRAINING PROGRAM(S)—Graphic Design; Intermedia/Multimedia. **RELATED KNOWLEDGE/COURSES—Design:** Knowledge of design techniques, tools, and principles involved in production of precision technical plans, blueprints, drawings, and models. **Fine Arts:** Knowledge of the theory and techniques required to compose, produce, and perform works of music, dance, visual arts, drama, and sculpture. **Administration and Management:** Knowledge of business and management principles involved in strategic planning, resource allocation, human resources modeling, leadership technique, production methods, and coordination of people and resources. **Sales and Marketing:** Knowledge of principles and methods for showing, promoting, and selling products or services. This includes marketing strategy and tactics, product demonstration, sales techniques, and sales control systems. **Telecommunications:** Knowledge of transmission, broadcasting, switching, control, and operation of telecommunications systems. **English Language:** Knowledge of the structure and content of the English language, including the meaning and spelling of words, rules of composition, and grammar. **Communications and Media:** Knowledge of media production, communication, and dissemination techniques and methods. This includes alternative ways to inform and entertain via written, oral, and visual media.

Art, Drama, and Music Teachers, Postsecondary

- ▲ Education/Training Required: Master's degree
- ▲ Annual Earnings: $47,080
- ▲ Growth: 23.5%
- ▲ Annual Job Openings: 184,000
- ▲ Self-Employed: 0%
- ▲ Part-Time: 32.3%

Teach courses in drama, music, and the arts, including fine and applied art, such as painting and sculpture, or design and crafts. Prepares and delivers lectures to students. Stimulates class discussions. Compiles bibliographies of specialized materials for outside reading assignments. Compiles, administers, and grades examinations or assigns this work to others. Advises students on academic and vocational curricula. Directs research of other teachers or graduate students working for advanced academic degrees. Conducts research in particular field of knowledge and publishes findings in professional journals. Serves on faculty committee providing professional consulting services to government and industry. Acts as adviser to student organizations. **SKILLS—Reading Comprehension:** Understanding written sentences and paragraphs in work-related documents. **Instructing:** Teaching others how to do something. **Learning Strategies:** Selecting and using training/instructional methods and procedures appropriate for the situation when learning or teaching new things. **Writing:** Communicating effectively in writing as appropriate for the needs of the audience. **Speaking:** Talking to others to convey information effectively.

GOE INFORMATION—Interest Area: 12. Education and Social Service. **Work Group:** 12.03. Educational Services. **Other Job Titles in This Work Group:** Adult Literacy, Remedial Education, and GED Teachers and Instructors; Agricultural Sciences Teachers, Postsecondary; Anthropology and Archeology Teachers, Postsecondary; Architecture Teachers, Postsecondary; Archivists; Area, Ethnic, and Cultural Studies Teachers, Postsecondary; Atmospheric, Earth, Marine, and Space Sciences Teachers, Postsecondary; Audio-Visual Collections Specialists; Biological Science Teachers, Postsecondary; Business Teachers, Postsecondary; Chemistry Teachers, Postsecondary; Child Care Workers; Communications Teachers, Postsecondary; Computer Science Teachers, Postsecondary; Criminal Justice and Law Enforcement Teachers, Postsecondary; Curators; Economics Teachers, Postsecondary; Education Teachers, Postsecondary; Educational Psychologists; Educational, Vocational, and School Counselors; Elementary School Teachers, Except Special Education; Engineering Teachers, Postsecondary; English Language and Literature Teachers, Postsecondary; Environmental Science Teachers, Postsecondary; Farm and Home Management Advisors; Foreign Language and Literature Teachers, Postsecondary; Forestry and Conservation Science Teachers, Postsecondary; Geography Teachers, Postsecondary; Graduate Teaching Assistants; Health Specialties Teachers, Postsecondary; History Teachers, Postsecondary; Home Economics Teachers, Postsecondary; Kindergarten Teachers, Except Special Education; Law Teachers, Postsecondary; Librarians; Library Assistants, Clerical; Library Science Teachers, Postsecondary; Library Technicians; Mathematical Science Teachers, Postsecondary; Middle School Teachers, Except Special and Vocational Education; Museum Technicians and Conservators; Nursing Instructors and Teachers, Postsecondary; Personal Financial Advisors; Philosophy and Religion Teachers, Postsecondary; Physics Teachers, Postsecondary; Political Science Teachers, Postsecondary; Postsecondary Teachers, All Other; Preschool Teachers, Except Special Education; Psychology Teachers, Postsecondary; others. **PERSONALITY TYPE—**Artistic. Artistic occupations frequently involve working with forms, designs, and patterns. They often require self-expression, and the work can be done without following a clear set of rules.

EDUCATION/TRAINING PROGRAM(S)—Art History, Criticism and Conservation; Art/Art Studies, General; Arts Management; Ceramic Arts and Ceramics; Cinematography and Film/Video Production; Commercial Photography; Conducting; Crafts/Craft Design, Folk Art, and Artisanry; Dance, General; Design and Applied Arts, Other; Design and Visual Communications, General; Directing and Theatrical Production; Drama and Dramatics/Theatre Arts, General; Dramatic/Theatre Arts and Stagecraft, Other; Fashion/Apparel Design; Fiber, Textile, and Weaving Arts; Film/Cinema Studies; Film/Video and Photographic Arts, Other; Fine Arts and Art Studies, Other; Fine/Studio Arts, General; Graphic Design; Industrial Design; Interior Design; Intermedia/

Multimedia; Jazz/Jazz Studies; Metal and Jewelry Arts; Music History, Literature, and Theory; Music Management and Merchandising; Music Pedagogy; Music Performance, General; Music Theory and Composition; Music, Other; Musicology and Ethnomusicology; Painting; Photography; Piano and Organ; Playwriting and Screenwriting; Printmaking; Sculpture; Technical Theatre/Theatre Design and Technology; Theatre Literature, History, and Criticism; Theatre/Theatre Arts Management; Violin, Viola, Guitar, and Other Stringed Instruments; Visual and Performing Arts, General; Visual and Performing Arts, Other; Voice and Opera. **RELATED KNOWLEDGE/ COURSES—Fine Arts:** Knowledge of the theory and techniques required to compose, produce, and perform works of music, dance, visual arts, drama, and sculpture. **Educa-**

tion and Training: Knowledge of principles and methods for curriculum and training design, teaching and instruction for individuals and groups, and the measurement of training effects. **English Language:** Knowledge of the structure and content of the English language, including the meaning and spelling of words, rules of composition, and grammar. **Administration and Management:** Knowledge of business and management principles involved in strategic planning, resource allocation, human resources modeling, leadership technique, production methods, and coordination of people and resources. **Communications and Media:** Knowledge of media production, communication, and dissemination techniques and methods. This includes alternative ways to inform and entertain via written, oral, and visual media.

Assessors

- ▲ Education/Training Required: Postsecondary vocational training
- ▲ Annual Earnings: $38,950
- ▲ Growth: 18.0%
- ▲ Annual Job Openings: 6,000
- ▲ Self-Employed: 21.1%
- ▲ Part-Time: 16.6%

Appraise real and personal property to determine its fair value. May assess taxes in accordance with prescribed schedules. Appraises real and personal property, such as aircraft, marine craft, buildings, and land, to determine fair value. Writes and submits appraisal and tax reports for public record. Interprets property laws, formulates operational policies, and directs assessment office activities. Assesses and computes taxes according to prescribed tax tables and schedules. Inspects property, considering factors such as market value, location, and building or replacement costs, to determine appraisal value. **SKILLS—Reading Comprehension:** Understanding written sentences and paragraphs in work-related documents. **Judgment and Decision Making:** Considering the relative costs and benefits of potential actions to choose the most appropriate one. **Writing:** Communicating effectively in writing as appropriate for the needs of the audience. **Mathematics:** Using mathematics to solve problems. **Systems Analysis:** Determining how a system should work and how changes in conditions, operations, and the environment will affect outcomes.

GOE INFORMATION—Interest Area: 13. General Management and Support. **Work Group:** 13.02. Management Support. **Other Job Titles in This Work Group:** Accountants; Accountants and Auditors; Appraisers and

Assessors of Real Estate; Appraisers, Real Estate; Auditors; Budget Analysts; Claims Adjusters, Examiners, and Investigators; Claims Examiners, Property and Casualty Insurance; Compensation, Benefits, and Job Analysis Specialists; Cost Estimators; Credit Analysts; Employment Interviewers, Private or Public Employment Service; Employment, Recruitment, and Placement Specialists; Financial Analysts; Human Resources, Training, and Labor Relations Specialists, All Other; Insurance Adjusters, Examiners, and Investigators; Insurance Appraisers, Auto Damage; Insurance Underwriters; Loan Counselors; Loan Officers; Logisticians; Management Analysts; Market Research Analysts; Personnel Recruiters; Purchasing Agents and Buyers, Farm Products; Purchasing Agents, Except Wholesale, Retail, and Farm Products; Tax Examiners, Collectors, and Revenue Agents; Training and Development Specialists; Wholesale and Retail Buyers, Except Farm Products. **PERSONALITY TYPE—Conventional.** Conventional occupations frequently involve following set procedures and routines. These occupations can include working with data and details more than with ideas. Usually there is a clear line of authority to follow.

EDUCATION/TRAINING PROGRAM(S)—Real Estate. RELATED KNOWLEDGE/COURSES—

Mathematics: Knowledge of arithmetic, algebra, geometry, calculus, and statistics and their applications. **Economics and Accounting:** Knowledge of economic and accounting principles and practices, the financial markets, banking, and the analysis and reporting of financial data. **Law and Government:** Knowledge of laws, legal codes, court procedures, precedents, government regulations, executive orders, agency rules, and the democratic political process. **English Language:** Knowledge of the structure and content of the English language, including the meaning and spelling of words, rules of composition, and grammar. **Building and Construction:** Knowledge of materials, methods, and tools involved in the construction or repair of houses, buildings, or other structures, such as highways and roads.

Athletes and Sports Competitors

- ▲ Education/Training Required: Long-term on-the-job training
- ▲ Annual Earnings: $43,730
- ▲ Growth: 22.5%
- ▲ Annual Job Openings: 3,000
- ▲ Self-Employed: 31.4%
- ▲ Part-Time: 25.3%

Compete in athletic events. Participates in athletic events and competitive sports, according to established rules and regulations. Plays professional sport and is identified according to sport played, such as football, basketball, baseball, hockey, or boxing. Represents team or professional sports club, speaking to groups involved in activities such as sports clinics and fundraisers. Exercises and practices under direction of athletic trainer or professional coach to prepare and train for competitive events. **SKILLS—Monitoring:** Monitoring/Assessing your performance or that of other individuals or organizations to make improvements or take corrective action. **Coordination:** Adjusting actions in relation to others' actions. **Active Learning:** Understanding the implications of new information for both current and future problem-solving and decision-making. **Speaking:** Talking to others to convey information effectively. **Active Listening:** Giving full attention to what other people are saying, taking time to understand the points being made, asking questions as appropriate, and not interrupting at inappropriate times. **Learning Strategies:** Selecting and using training/instructional methods and procedures appropriate for the situation when learning or teaching new things. **Social Perceptiveness:** Being aware of others' reactions and understanding why they react as they do.

GOE INFORMATION—Interest Area: 01. Arts, Entertainment, and Media. **Work Group:** 01.10. Sports: Coaching, Instructing, Officiating, and Performing. **Other Job Titles in This Work Group:** Coaches and Scouts; Fitness Trainers and Aerobics Instructors; Umpires, Referees, and Other Sports Officials. **PERSONALITY TYPE—Enterprising.** Enterprising occupations frequently involve starting up and carrying out projects. These occupations can involve leading people and making many decisions. They sometimes require risk taking and often deal with business.

EDUCATION/TRAINING PROGRAM(S)—Health and Physical Education, General. RELATED KNOWLEDGE/COURSES—Biology: Knowledge of plant and animal organisms and their tissues, cells, functions, interdependencies, and interactions with each other and the environment. **Physics:** Knowledge and prediction of physical principles and laws and their interrelationships and applications to understanding fluid, material, and atmospheric dynamics and mechanical, electrical, atomic, and sub-atomic structures and processes. **Psychology:** Knowledge of human behavior and performance; individual differences in ability, personality, and interests; learning and motivation; psychological research methods; and the assessment and treatment of behavioral and affective disorders. **Communications and Media:** Knowledge of media production, communication, and dissemination techniques and methods. This includes alternative ways to inform and entertain via written, oral, and visual media. **Education and Training:** Knowledge of principles and methods for curriculum and training design, teaching and instruction for individuals and groups, and the measurement of training effects.

Atmospheric, Earth, Marine, and Space Sciences Teachers, Postsecondary

▲ Education/Training Required: Master's degree
▲ Annual Earnings: $60,230
▲ Growth: 23.5%
▲ Annual Job Openings: 184,000
▲ Self-Employed: 0%
▲ Part-Time: 32.3%

Teach courses in the physical sciences, except chemistry and physics. **SKILLS**—No data available.

GOE INFORMATION—**Interest Area:** 12. Education and Social Service. **Work Group:** 12.03. Educational Services. **Other Job Titles in This Work Group:** Adult Literacy, Remedial Education, and GED Teachers and Instructors; Agricultural Sciences Teachers, Postsecondary; Anthropology and Archeology Teachers, Postsecondary; Architecture Teachers, Postsecondary; Archivists; Area, Ethnic, and Cultural Studies Teachers, Postsecondary; Art, Drama, and Music Teachers, Postsecondary; Audio-Visual Collections Specialists; Biological Science Teachers, Postsecondary; Business Teachers, Postsecondary; Chemistry Teachers, Postsecondary; Child Care Workers; Communications Teachers, Postsecondary; Computer Science Teachers, Postsecondary; Criminal Justice and Law Enforcement Teachers, Postsecondary; Curators; Economics Teachers, Postsecondary; Education Teachers, Postsecondary; Educational Psychologists; Educational, Vocational, and School Counselors; Elementary School Teachers, Except Special Education; Engineering Teachers, Postsecondary; English Language and Literature Teachers, Postsecondary; Environmental Science Teachers, Postsecondary; Farm and Home Management Advisors; Foreign Language and Literature Teachers, Postsecondary; Forestry and Conservation Science Teachers, Postsecondary; Geography Teachers, Postsecondary; Graduate Teaching Assistants; Health Specialties Teachers, Postsecondary; History Teachers, Postsecondary; Home Economics Teachers, Postsecondary; Kindergarten Teach-

ers, Except Special Education; Law Teachers, Postsecondary; Librarians; Library Assistants, Clerical; Library Science Teachers, Postsecondary; Library Technicians; Mathematical Science Teachers, Postsecondary; Middle School Teachers, Except Special and Vocational Education; Museum Technicians and Conservators; Nursing Instructors and Teachers, Postsecondary; Personal Financial Advisors; Philosophy and Religion Teachers, Postsecondary; Physics Teachers, Postsecondary; Political Science Teachers, Postsecondary; Postsecondary Teachers, All Other; Preschool Teachers, Except Special Education; Psychology Teachers, Postsecondary; others. **PERSONALITY TYPE**—No data available.

EDUCATION/TRAINING PROGRAM(S)—Acoustics; Astronomy; Astrophysics; Atmospheric Chemistry and Climatology; Atmospheric Physics and Dynamics; Atmospheric Sciences and Meteorology, General; Atmospheric Sciences and Meteorology, Other; Atomic/Molecular Physics; Elementary Particle Physics; Geochemistry; Geochemistry and Petrology; Geological and Earth Sciences/Geosciences, Other; Geology/Earth Science, General; Geophysics and Seismology; Hydrology and Water Resources Science; Meteorology; Nuclear Physics; Oceanography, Chemical and Physical; Optics/Optical Sciences; Paleontology; Physics Teacher Education; Physics, Other; Planetary Astronomy and Science; Plasma and High-Temperature Physics; Science Teacher Education/General Science Teacher Education; Solid State and Low-Temperature Physics; Theoretical and Mathematical Physics. **RELATED KNOWLEDGE/COURSES**—No data available.

Audiologists

- ▲ Education/Training Required: Master's degree
- ▲ Annual Earnings: $46,900
- ▲ Growth: 44.7%
- ▲ Annual Job Openings: 1,000
- ▲ Self-Employed: 10.5%
- ▲ Part-Time: 20.8%

Assess and treat persons with hearing and related disorders. May fit hearing aids and provide auditory training. May perform research related to hearing problems. Refers clients to additional medical or educational services if needed. Advises educators or other medical staff on speech or hearing topics. Counsels and instructs clients in techniques to improve speech or hearing impairment, including sign language or lip-reading. Evaluates hearing and speech/language test results and medical or background information to determine hearing or speech impairment and treatment. Conducts or directs research and reports findings on speech or hearing topics to develop procedures, technology, or treatments. Administers hearing or speech/language evaluations, tests, or examinations to patients to collect information on type and degree of impairment. Participates in conferences or training to update or share knowledge of new hearing or speech disorder treatment methods or technology. Records and maintains reports of speech or hearing research or treatments. Plans and conducts prevention and treatment programs for clients' hearing or speech problems. **SKILLS—Reading Comprehension:** Understanding written sentences and paragraphs in work-related documents. **Writing:** Communicating effectively in writing as appropriate for the needs of the audience. **Instructing:** Teaching others how to do something. **Speaking:** Talking to others to convey information effectively. **Learning Strategies:** Selecting and using training/instructional methods and procedures appropriate for the situation when learning or teaching new things. **Active Learning:** Understanding the implications of new information for both current and future problem-solving and decision-making. **Critical Thinking:** Using logic and reasoning to identify the strengths and weaknesses of alternative solutions, conclusions, or approaches to problems.

GOE INFORMATION—Interest Area: 14. Medical and Health Services. **Work Group:** 14.06. Medical Therapy. **Other Job Titles in This Work Group:** Massage Therapists; Occupational Therapist Aides; Occupational Therapist Assistants; Occupational Therapists; Physical Therapist Aides; Physical Therapist Assistants; Physical Therapists; Radiation Therapists; Recreational Therapists; Respiratory Therapists; Respiratory Therapy Technicians; Speech-Language Pathologists; Therapists, All Other. **PERSONALITY TYPE**—Social. Social occupations frequently involve working with, communicating with, and teaching people. These occupations often involve helping or providing service to others.

EDUCATION/TRAINING PROGRAM(S)—Audiology/Audiologist and Hearing Sciences; Audiology/Audiologist and Speech-Language Pathology/Pathologist; Communication Disorders Sciences and Services, Other; Communication Disorders, General. **RELATED KNOWLEDGE/COURSES—Therapy and Counseling:** Knowledge of principles, methods, and procedures for diagnosis, treatment, and rehabilitation of physical and mental dysfunctions and for career counseling and guidance. **English Language:** Knowledge of the structure and content of the English language, including the meaning and spelling of words, rules of composition, and grammar. **Medicine and Dentistry:** Knowledge of the information and techniques needed to diagnose and treat human injuries, diseases, and deformities. This includes symptoms, treatment alternatives, drug properties and interactions, and preventive health-care measures. **Education and Training:** Knowledge of principles and methods for curriculum and training design, teaching and instruction for individuals and groups, and the measurement of training effects. **Personnel and Human Resources:** Knowledge of principles and procedures for personnel recruitment, selection, training, compensation and benefits, labor relations and negotiation, and personnel information systems. **Administration and Management:** Knowledge of business and management principles involved in strategic planning, resource allocation, human resources modeling, leadership technique, production methods, and coordination of people and resources.

Auditors

> ▲ Education/Training Required: Bachelor's degree
> ▲ Annual Earnings: $45,380
> ▲ Growth: 18.5%
> ▲ Annual Job Openings: 100,000
> ▲ Self-Employed: 10.6%
> ▲ Part-Time: 7.8%

Examine and analyze accounting records to determine financial status of establishment and prepare financial reports concerning operating procedures. Reviews data about material assets, net worth, liabilities, capital stock, surplus, income, and expenditures. Reports to management about asset utilization and audit results and recommends changes in operations and financial activities. Analyzes data for deficient controls; duplicated effort; extravagance; fraud; or non-compliance with laws, regulations, and management policies. Examines payroll and personnel records to determine worker's compensation coverage. Verifies journal and ledger entries by examining inventory. Directs activities of personnel engaged in filing, recording, compiling, and transmitting financial records. Supervises auditing of establishments and determines scope of investigation required. Examines records and interviews workers to ensure recording of transactions and compliance with laws and regulations. Evaluates taxpayer finances to determine tax liability, using knowledge of interest and discount, annuities, valuation of stocks and bonds, and amortization valuation of depletable assets. Confers with company officials about financial and regulatory matters. Examines records, tax returns, and related documents pertaining to settlement of decedent's estate. Audits records to determine unemployment insurance premiums, liabilities, and compliance with tax laws. Reviews taxpayer accounts and conducts audits on-site, by correspondence, or by summoning taxpayer to office. Inspects cash on hand, notes receivable and payable, negotiable securities, and canceled checks. Analyzes annual reports, financial statements, and other records, using accepted accounting and statistical procedures, to determine financial condition. Inspects account books and system for efficiency, effectiveness, and use of accepted accounting procedures to record transactions. **SKILLS—Systems Evaluation:** Identifying measures or indicators of system performance and the actions needed to improve or correct performance relative to the goals of the system. **Critical Thinking:** Using logic and reasoning to identify the strengths and weaknesses of alternative solutions, conclu-

sions, or approaches to problems. **Mathematics:** Using mathematics to solve problems. **Reading Comprehension:** Understanding written sentences and paragraphs in work-related documents. **Complex Problem Solving:** Identifying complex problems and reviewing related information to develop and evaluate options and implement solutions.

GOE INFORMATION—Interest Area: 13. General Management and Support. **Work Group:** 13.02. Management Support. **Other Job Titles in This Work Group:** Accountants; Accountants and Auditors; Appraisers and Assessors of Real Estate; Appraisers, Real Estate; Assessors; Budget Analysts; Claims Adjusters, Examiners, and Investigators; Claims Examiners, Property and Casualty Insurance; Compensation, Benefits, and Job Analysis Specialists; Cost Estimators; Credit Analysts; Employment Interviewers, Private or Public Employment Service; Employment, Recruitment, and Placement Specialists; Financial Analysts; Human Resources, Training, and Labor Relations Specialists, All Other; Insurance Adjusters, Examiners, and Investigators; Insurance Appraisers, Auto Damage; Insurance Underwriters; Loan Counselors; Loan Officers; Logisticians; Management Analysts; Market Research Analysts; Personnel Recruiters; Purchasing Agents and Buyers, Farm Products; Purchasing Agents, Except Wholesale, Retail, and Farm Products; Tax Examiners, Collectors, and Revenue Agents; Training and Development Specialists; Wholesale and Retail Buyers, Except Farm Products. **PERSONALITY TYPE—Conventional.** Conventional occupations frequently involve following set procedures and routines. These occupations can include working with data and details more than with ideas. Usually there is a clear line of authority to follow.

EDUCATION/TRAINING PROGRAM(S)—Accounting; Accounting and Business/Management; Accounting and Computer Science; Accounting and Finance; Auditing; Taxation. **RELATED KNOWLEDGE/COURSES— Economics and Accounting:** Knowledge of economic and accounting principles and practices, the financial markets, banking, and the analysis and reporting of financial data.

Mathematics: Knowledge of arithmetic, algebra, geometry, calculus, and statistics and their applications. **Administration and Management:** Knowledge of business and management principles involved in strategic planning, resource allocation, human resources modeling, leadership technique, production methods, and coordination of people and resources. **Law and Government:** Knowledge of laws, legal codes, court procedures, precedents, government regulations, executive orders, agency rules, and the democratic political process. **English Language:** Knowledge of the structure and content of the English language, including the meaning and spelling of words, rules of composition, and grammar.

Automatic Teller Machine Servicers

▲ Education/Training Required: Long-term on-the-job training
▲ Annual Earnings: $32,890
▲ Growth: 14.2%
▲ Annual Job Openings: 24,000
▲ Self-Employed: 0%
▲ Part-Time: 6.5%

Collect deposits and replenish automatic teller machines with cash and supplies. Removes money canisters from ATM and replenishes machine supplies, such as deposit envelopes, receipt paper, and cash. Counts cash and items deposited by customers and compares to transactions indicated on transaction tape from ATM. Records transaction information on form or log and notifies designated personnel of discrepancies. Tests machine functions and balances machine cash account, using electronic keypad. Corrects malfunctions, such as jammed cash or paper, or calls repair personnel when ATM needs repair. **SKILLS—Mathematics:** Using mathematics to solve problems. **Writing:** Communicating effectively in writing as appropriate for the needs of the audience. **Critical Thinking:** Using logic and reasoning to identify the strengths and weaknesses of alternative solutions, conclusions, or approaches to problems. **Troubleshooting:** Determining causes of operating errors and deciding what to do about them.

GOE INFORMATION—Interest Area: 09. Business Detail. **Work Group:** 09.09. Clerical Machine Operation. **Other Job Titles in This Work Group:** Billing, Posting, and Calculating Machine Operators; Computer Operators; Data Entry Keyers; Duplicating Machine Operators; Mail Clerks and Mail Machine Operators, Except Postal Service; Mail Machine Operators, Preparation and Handling; Office Machine Operators, Except Computer; Postal Service Clerks; Typesetting and Composing Machine Operators and Tenders; Word Processors and Typists. **PERSONALITY TYPE**—Realistic. Realistic occupations frequently involve work activities that include practical, hands-on problems and solutions. They often deal with plants, animals, and real-world materials like wood, tools, and machinery. Many of the occupations require working outside and do not involve a lot of paperwork or working closely with others.

EDUCATION/TRAINING PROGRAM(S)—Business Machine Repair; Computer Installation and Repair Technology/Technician. **RELATED KNOWLEDGE/COURSES—Mathematics:** Knowledge of arithmetic, algebra, geometry, calculus, and statistics and their applications. **Computers and Electronics:** Knowledge of circuit boards, processors, chips, electronic equipment, and computer hardware and software, including applications and programming. **Clerical Studies:** Knowledge of administrative and clerical procedures and systems, such as word processing, managing files and records, stenography and transcription, designing forms, and other office procedures and terminology. **Geography:** Knowledge of principles and methods for describing the features of land, sea, and air masses, including their physical characteristics, locations, interrelationships, and distribution of plant, animal, and human life. **Telecommunications:** Knowledge of transmission, broadcasting, switching, control, and operation of telecommunications systems.

Automotive Body and Related Repairers

▲ Education/Training Required: Long-term on-the-job training
▲ Annual Earnings: $32,490
▲ Growth: 10.2%
▲ Annual Job Openings: 18,000
▲ Self-Employed: 21.1%
▲ Part-Time: 8.6%

Repair and refinish automotive vehicle bodies and straighten vehicle frames. Positions dolly block against surface of dented area and beats opposite surface to remove dents, using hammer. Straightens bent automobile or other vehicle frames, using pneumatic frame-straightening machine. Paints and sands repaired surface, using paint spray gun and motorized sander. Removes damaged fenders and panels, using wrenches and cutting torch, and installs replacement parts, using wrenches or welding equipment. Fits and secures windows, vinyl roof, and metal trim to vehicle body, using caulking gun, adhesive brush, and mallet. Cuts opening in vehicle body for installation of customized windows, using templates and power shears or chisel. Fills depressions with body filler and files, grinds, and sands repaired surfaces, using power tools and hand tools. Measures and marks vinyl material and cuts material to size for roof installation, using rule, straightedge, and hand shears. Adjusts or aligns headlights, wheels, and brake system. Reads specifications or confers with customer to determine custom modifications to alter appearance of vehicle. Removes upholstery, accessories, electrical window and seat operating equipment, and trim to gain access to vehicle body and fenders. Cuts and tapes plastic separating film to outside repair area to avoid damaging surrounding surfaces during repair procedure. Examines vehicle to determine extent and type of damage. Peels separating film from repair area and washes repaired surface with water. Mixes polyester resin and hardener to be used in restoring damaged area. Soaks fiberglass matting in resin mixture and applies layers of matting over repair area to specified thickness. Cuts away damaged fiberglass from automobile body, using air grinder. Cleans work area, using air hose to remove damaged material and to remove discarded fiberglass strips used in repair procedures. **SKILLS—Repairing:** Repairing machines or systems, using the needed tools. **Installation:** Installing equipment, machines, wiring, or programs to meet specifications. **Technology Design:** Generating or adapting equipment and technology to serve user needs. **Quality Control Analysis:** Conducting tests and inspections of products, services, or processes to evaluate quality or performance. **Mathematics:** Using mathematics to solve problems.

GOE INFORMATION—Interest Area: 05. Mechanics, Installers, and Repairers. **Work Group:** 05.03. Mechanical Work. **Other Job Titles in This Work Group:** Aircraft Body and Bonded Structure Repairers; Aircraft Engine Specialists; Aircraft Mechanics and Service Technicians; Airframe-and-Power-Plant Mechanics; Automotive Glass Installers and Repairers; Automotive Master Mechanics; Automotive Service Technicians and Mechanics; Automotive Specialty Technicians; Bicycle Repairers; Bridge and Lock Tenders; Bus and Truck Mechanics and Diesel Engine Specialists; Camera and Photographic Equipment Repairers; Coin, Vending, and Amusement Machine Servicers and Repairers; Control and Valve Installers and Repairers, Except Mechanical Door; Farm Equipment Mechanics; Gas Appliance Repairers; Hand and Portable Power Tool Repairers; Heating and Air Conditioning Mechanics; Heating, Air Conditioning, and Refrigeration Mechanics and Installers; Helpers—Electricians; Helpers—Installation, Maintenance, and Repair Workers; Industrial Machinery Mechanics; Keyboard Instrument Repairers and Tuners; Locksmiths and Safe Repairers; Maintenance and Repair Workers, General; Maintenance Workers, Machinery; Mechanical Door Repairers; Medical Appliance Technicians; Medical Equipment Repairers; Meter Mechanics; Millwrights; Mobile Heavy Equipment Mechanics, Except Engines; Motorboat Mechanics; Motorcycle Mechanics; Musical Instrument Repairers and Tuners; Ophthalmic Laboratory Technicians; Optical Instrument Assemblers; Outdoor Power Equipment and Other Small Engine Mechanics; Painters, Transportation Equipment; Percussion Instrument Repairers and Tuners; Precision Instrument and Equipment Repairers, All Other; Rail Car Repairers; Railroad Inspectors; Recreational Vehicle Service Technicians; Reed or Wind Instrument Repairers and Tuners; Refrigeration Mechanics; Stringed Instrument Repairers and Tuners; Tire Repairers and Changers; Valve and Regulator Repairers; Watch Repairers. **PERSONALITY TYPE—**Realistic. Realistic occupations frequently involve work activities that include practical, hands-on problems and solutions. They often deal with plants, animals, and real-world materials like wood, tools, and machinery. Many of the occupations require working outside and do not involve a lot of paperwork or working closely with others.

EDUCATION/TRAINING PROGRAM(S)—Auto Body/Collision and Repair Technology/Technician. RELATED KNOWLEDGE/COURSES—Principles of Mechanical Devices: Knowledge of machines and tools, including their designs, uses, repair, and maintenance. Engineering and Technology: Knowledge of the practical application of engineering science and technology. This includes applying principles, techniques, procedures, and equipment to the design and production of various goods and services. Building and Construction: Knowledge of materials, methods, and tools involved in the construction or repair of houses, buildings, or other structures, such as highways and roads. Design: Knowledge of design techniques, tools, and principles involved in production of precision technical plans, blueprints, drawings, and models. Customer and Personal Service: Knowledge of principles and processes for providing customer and personal services. This includes customer needs assessment, meeting quality standards for services, and evaluation of customer satisfaction. Physics: Knowledge and prediction of physical principles and laws and their interrelationships and applications to understanding fluid, material, and atmospheric dynamics and mechanical, electrical, atomic, and sub-atomic structures and processes. Mathematics: Knowledge of arithmetic, algebra, geometry, calculus, and statistics and their applications.

Automotive Master Mechanics

- ▲ Education/Training Required: Postsecondary vocational training
- ▲ Annual Earnings: $29,510
- ▲ Growth: 18.0%
- ▲ Annual Job Openings: 104,000
- ▲ Self-Employed: 21.6%
- ▲ Part-Time: 6.8%

Repair automobiles, trucks, buses, and other vehicles. Master mechanics repair virtually any part on the vehicle or specialize in the transmission system. Repairs and overhauls defective automotive units, such as engines, transmissions, or differentials. Installs and repairs accessories, such as radios, heaters, mirrors, and windshield wipers. Repairs damaged automobile bodies. Rebuilds parts such as crankshafts and cylinder blocks. Aligns front end. Examines vehicles and discusses extent of damage or malfunction with customer. Replaces and adjusts headlights. Repairs radiator leaks. Repairs or replaces shock absorbers. Repairs or replaces parts such as pistons, rods, gears, valves, and bearings. Repairs manual and automatic transmissions. Repairs, relines, replaces, and adjusts brakes. Rewires ignition system, lights, and instrument panel. Overhauls or replaces carburetors, blowers, generators, distributors, starts, and pumps. SKILLS—Repairing: Repairing machines or systems, using the needed tools. Troubleshooting: Determining causes of operating errors and deciding what to do about them. Equipment Maintenance: Performing routine maintenance on equipment and determining when and what kind of maintenance is needed. Installation: Installing equipment, machines, wiring, or programs to meet specifications. Critical Thinking: Using logic and reasoning to identify the strengths and weaknesses of alternative solutions, conclusions, or approaches to problems.

GOE INFORMATION—Interest Area: 05. Mechanics, Installers, and Repairers. Work Group: 05.03. Mechanical Work. Other Job Titles in This Work Group: Aircraft Body and Bonded Structure Repairers; Aircraft Engine Specialists; Aircraft Mechanics and Service Technicians; Airframe-and-Power-Plant Mechanics; Automotive Body and Related Repairers; Automotive Glass Installers and Repairers; Automotive Service Technicians and Mechanics; Automotive Specialty Technicians; Bicycle Repairers; Bridge and Lock Tenders; Bus and Truck Mechanics and Diesel Engine Specialists; Camera and Photographic Equipment Repairers; Coin, Vending, and Amusement Machine Servicers and Repairers; Control and Valve Installers and Repairers, Except Mechanical Door; Farm Equipment Mechanics; Gas Appliance Repairers; Hand and Portable Power Tool Repairers; Heating and Air Conditioning Mechanics; Heating, Air Conditioning, and Refrigeration Mechanics and Installers; Helpers—Electricians; Helpers—Installation, Maintenance, and Repair

Workers; Industrial Machinery Mechanics; Keyboard Instrument Repairers and Tuners; Locksmiths and Safe Repairers; Maintenance and Repair Workers, General; Maintenance Workers, Machinery; Mechanical Door Repairers; Medical Appliance Technicians; Medical Equipment Repairers; Meter Mechanics; Millwrights; Mobile Heavy Equipment Mechanics, Except Engines; Motorboat Mechanics; Motorcycle Mechanics; Musical Instrument Repairers and Tuners; Ophthalmic Laboratory Technicians; Optical Instrument Assemblers; Outdoor Power Equipment and Other Small Engine Mechanics; Painters, Transportation Equipment; Percussion Instrument Repairers and Tuners; Precision Instrument and Equipment Repairers, All Other; Rail Car Repairers; Railroad Inspectors; Recreational Vehicle Service Technicians; Reed or Wind Instrument Repairers and Tuners; Refrigeration Mechanics; Stringed Instrument Repairers and Tuners; Tire Repairers and Changers; Valve and Regulator Repairers; Watch Repairers. **PERSONALITY TYPE**—Realistic. Realistic occupations frequently involve work activities that include practical, hands-on problems and solutions. They often deal with plants, animals, and real-world materials like wood, tools, and machinery. Many of the occupations require working outside and do not involve a lot of paperwork or working closely with others.

EDUCATION/TRAINING PROGRAM(S)—Alternative Fuel Vehicle Technology/Technician; Automobile/Automotive Mechanics Technology/Technician; Automotive Engineering Technology/Technician; Medium/Heavy Vehicle and Truck Technology/Technician; Vehicle Emissions Inspection and Maintenance Technology/Technician. **RELATED KNOWLEDGE/COURSES**—**Principles of Mechanical Devices:** Knowledge of machines and tools, including their designs, uses, repair, and maintenance. **Computers and Electronics:** Knowledge of circuit boards, processors, chips, electronic equipment, and computer hardware and software, including applications and programming. **Engineering and Technology:** Knowledge of the practical application of engineering science and technology. This includes applying principles, techniques, procedures, and equipment to the design and production of various goods and services. **Customer and Personal Service:** Knowledge of principles and processes for providing customer and personal services. This includes customer needs assessment, meeting quality standards for services, and evaluation of customer satisfaction. **Physics:** Knowledge and prediction of physical principles and laws and their interrelationships and applications to understanding fluid, material, and atmospheric dynamics and mechanical, electrical, atomic, and sub-atomic structures and processes.

Automotive Service Technicians and Mechanics

▲ Education/Training Required: Postsecondary vocational training
▲ Annual Earnings: $29,510
▲ Growth: 18.0%
▲ Annual Job Openings: 104,000
▲ Self-Employed: 21.6%
▲ Part-Time: 6.8%

Diagnose, adjust, repair, or overhaul automotive vehicles. **SKILLS**—No data available.

GOE INFORMATION—**Interest Area:** 05. Mechanics, Installers, and Repairers. **Work Group:** 05.03. Mechanical Work. **Other Job Titles in This Work Group:** Aircraft Body and Bonded Structure Repairers; Aircraft Engine Specialists; Aircraft Mechanics and Service Technicians; Airframe-and-Power-Plant Mechanics; Automotive Body and Related Repairers; Automotive Glass Installers and Repairers; Automotive Master Mechanics; Automotive Specialty Technicians; Bicycle Repairers; Bridge and Lock Tenders; Bus and Truck Mechanics and Diesel Engine Specialists; Camera and Photographic Equipment Repairers; Coin, Vending, and Amusement Machine Servicers and Repairers; Control and Valve Installers and Repairers, Except Mechanical Door; Farm Equipment Mechanics; Gas Appliance Repairers; Hand and Portable Power Tool Repairers; Heating and Air Conditioning Mechanics; Heating, Air Conditioning, and Refrigeration Mechanics and Installers; Helpers—Electricians; Helpers—Installation, Maintenance, and Repair Workers; Industrial Machinery Mechanics; Keyboard Instrument Repairers and Tuners; Locksmiths and Safe Repairers; Maintenance and Repair Workers, General; Maintenance Workers, Machinery; Mechanical Door Repairers; Medical Appliance Technicians; Medical Equipment Repairers; Meter Mechanics; Millwrights; Mobile Heavy Equipment Mechanics, Except Engines; Motorboat Mechanics; Motorcycle Mechanics; Musical Instrument Repairers and Tuners; Ophthalmic

Laboratory Technicians; Optical Instrument Assemblers; Outdoor Power Equipment and Other Small Engine Mechanics; Painters, Transportation Equipment; Percussion Instrument Repairers and Tuners; Precision Instrument and Equipment Repairers, All Other; Rail Car Repairers; Railroad Inspectors; Recreational Vehicle Service Technicians; Reed or Wind Instrument Repairers and Tuners; Refrigeration Mechanics; Stringed Instrument Repairers and Tuners; Tire Repairers and Changers; Valve and Regulator Repairers; Watch Repairers. **PERSONALITY TYPE**—No data available.

EDUCATION/TRAINING PROGRAM(S)—Alternative Fuel Vehicle Technology/Technician; Automobile/Automotive Mechanics Technology/Technician; Automotive Engineering Technology/Technician; Medium/Heavy Vehicle and Truck Technology/Technician; Vehicle Emissions Inspection and Maintenance Technology/Technician. **RELATED KNOWLEDGE/COURSES**—No data available.

Automotive Specialty Technicians

- ▲ Education/Training Required: Postsecondary vocational training
- ▲ Annual Earnings: $29,510
- ▲ Growth: 18.0%
- ▲ Annual Job Openings: 104,000
- ▲ Self-Employed: 21.6%
- ▲ Part-Time: 6.8%

Repair only one system or component on a vehicle, such as brakes, suspension, or radiator. Repairs, installs, and adjusts hydraulic and electromagnetic automatic lift mechanisms used to raise and lower automobile windows, seats, and tops. Repairs, overhauls, and adjusts automobile brake systems. Rebuilds, repairs, and tests automotive injection units. Aligns and repairs wheels, axles, frames, torsion bars, and steering mechanisms of automobiles. Examines vehicle, compiles estimate of repair costs, and secures customer approval to perform repairs. Tunes automobile engines and tests electronic computer components. Inspects, tests, repairs, and replaces automotive cooling systems and fuel tanks. Inspects and tests new vehicles for damage, records findings, and makes repairs. Repairs and replaces defective ball joint suspension, brake shoes, and wheel bearings. Repairs, replaces, and adjusts defective carburetor parts and gasoline filters. Converts vehicle fuel systems from gasoline to butane gas operations and repairs and services operating butane fuel units. Installs and repairs automotive air-conditioning units. Repairs and rebuilds clutch systems. Repairs and replaces automobile leaf springs. Removes and replaces defective mufflers and tailpipes from automobiles. Repairs and aligns defective wheels of automobiles. **SKILLS—Installation:** Installing equipment, machines, wiring, or programs to meet specifications. **Repairing:** Repairing machines or systems, using the needed tools. **Troubleshooting:** Determining causes of operating errors and deciding what to do about them. **Equipment Maintenance:** Performing routine maintenance on equipment and determining when and what kind of maintenance is needed. **Quality Control Analysis:** Conducting tests and inspections of products, services, or processes to evaluate quality or performance.

GOE INFORMATION—Interest Area: 05. Mechanics, Installers, and Repairers. **Work Group:** 05.03. Mechanical Work. **Other Job Titles in This Work Group:** Aircraft Body and Bonded Structure Repairers; Aircraft Engine Specialists; Aircraft Mechanics and Service Technicians; Airframe-and-Power-Plant Mechanics; Automotive Body and Related Repairers; Automotive Glass Installers and Repairers; Automotive Master Mechanics; Automotive Service Technicians and Mechanics; Bicycle Repairers; Bridge and Lock Tenders; Bus and Truck Mechanics and Diesel Engine Specialists; Camera and Photographic Equipment Repairers; Coin, Vending, and Amusement Machine Servicers and Repairers; Control and Valve Installers and Repairers, Except Mechanical Door; Farm Equipment Mechanics; Gas Appliance Repairers; Hand and Portable Power Tool Repairers; Heating and Air Conditioning Mechanics; Heating, Air Conditioning, and Refrigeration Mechanics and Installers; Helpers—Electricians; Helpers—Installation, Maintenance, and Repair Workers; Industrial Machinery Mechanics; Keyboard Instrument Repairers and Tuners; Locksmiths and Safe Repairers; Maintenance and Repair Workers, General; Maintenance Workers, Machinery; Mechanical Door Repairers; Medical Appliance Technicians; Medical Equipment Repairers; Meter Mechanics; Millwrights; Mobile Heavy Equipment Mechanics, Except Engines; Motorboat Mechanics; Motorcycle Mechanics; Musical Instrument

Repairers and Tuners; Ophthalmic Laboratory Technicians; Optical Instrument Assemblers; Outdoor Power Equipment and Other Small Engine Mechanics; Painters, Transportation Equipment; Percussion Instrument Repairers and Tuners; Precision Instrument and Equipment Repairers, All Other; Rail Car Repairers; Railroad Inspectors; Recreational Vehicle Service Technicians; Reed or Wind Instrument Repairers and Tuners; Refrigeration Mechanics; Stringed Instrument Repairers and Tuners; Tire Repairers and Changers; Valve and Regulator Repairers; Watch Repairers. **PERSONALITY TYPE**—Realistic. Realistic occupations frequently involve work activities that include practical, hands-on problems and solutions. They often deal with plants, animals, and real-world materials like wood, tools, and machinery. Many of the occupations require working outside and do not involve a lot of paperwork or working closely with others.

EDUCATION/TRAINING PROGRAM(S)—Alternative Fuel Vehicle Technology/Technician; Automobile/Automotive Mechanics Technology/Technician; Automotive Engineering Technology/Technician; Medium/Heavy Vehicle and Truck Technology/Technician; Vehicle Emissions Inspection and Maintenance Technology/Technician. **RELATED KNOWLEDGE/COURSES—Principles of Mechanical Devices:** Knowledge of machines and tools, including their designs, uses, repair, and maintenance. **Computers and Electronics:** Knowledge of circuit boards, processors, chips, electronic equipment, and computer hardware and software, including applications and programming. **Engineering and Technology:** Knowledge of the practical application of engineering science and technology. This includes applying principles, techniques, procedures, and equipment to the design and production of various goods and services. **Customer and Personal Service:** Knowledge of principles and processes for providing customer and personal services. This includes customer needs assessment, meeting quality standards for services, and evaluation of customer satisfaction. **Physics:** Knowledge and prediction of physical principles and laws and their interrelationships and applications to understanding fluid, material, and atmospheric dynamics and mechanical, electrical, atomic, and sub-atomic structures and processes.

Bakers

▲ Education/Training Required: Long-term on-the-job training
▲ Annual Earnings: $20,440
▲ Growth: 16.8%
▲ Annual Job Openings: 25,000
▲ Self-Employed: No data available.
▲ Part-Time: No data available.

Mix and bake ingredients according to recipes to produce breads, rolls, cookies, cakes, pies, pastries, or other baked goods. SKILLS—No data available.

GOE INFORMATION—**Interest Area:** 11. Recreation, Travel, and Other Personal Services. **Work Group:** 11.05. Food and Beverage Services. **Other Job Titles in This Work Group:** Bakers, Bread and Pastry; Bartenders; Butchers and Meat Cutters; Chefs and Head Cooks; Combined Food Preparation and Serving Workers, Including Fast Food; Cooks, All Other; Cooks, Fast Food; Cooks, Institution and Cafeteria; Cooks, Restaurant; Cooks, Short Order; Counter Attendants, Cafeteria, Food Concession, and Coffee Shop; Dining Room and Cafeteria Attendants and Bartender Helpers; Dishwashers; Food Preparation and Serving Related Workers, All Other; Food Preparation Workers; Food Servers, Nonrestaurant; Hosts and Hostesses, Restaurant, Lounge, and Coffee Shop; Waiters and Waitresses. **PERSONALITY TYPE**—No data available.

EDUCATION/TRAINING PROGRAM(S)—Baking and Pastry Arts/Baker/Pastry Chef. **RELATED KNOWLEDGE/COURSES**—No data available.

Bakers, Bread and Pastry

▲ Education/Training Required: Long-term on-the-job training
▲ Annual Earnings: $20,440
▲ Growth: 16.8%
▲ Annual Job Openings: 25,000
▲ Self-Employed: 8.2%
▲ Part-Time: 38.5%

Mix and bake ingredients according to recipes to produce small quantities of breads, pastries, and other baked goods for consumption on premises or for sale as specialty baked goods. Weighs and measures ingredients, using measuring cups and spoons. Mixes ingredients to form dough or batter by hand or using electric mixer. Rolls and shapes dough, using rolling pin, and cuts dough in uniform portions with knife, divider, or cookie cutter. Molds dough in desired shapes, places dough in greased or floured pans, and trims overlapping edges with knife. Mixes and cooks pie fillings and pours fillings into pie shells and tops filling with meringue or cream. Checks production schedule to determine variety and quantity of goods to bake. Spreads or sprinkles toppings on loaves or specialties and places dough in oven, using long-handled paddle (peel). Covers filling with top crust, places pies in oven, and adjusts drafts or thermostatic controls to regulate oven temperatures. Mixes ingredients to make icings; decorates cakes and pastries; and blends colors for icings, shaped ornaments, and statuaries. Cuts, peels, and prepares fruit for pie fillings. **SKILLS—Mathematics:** Using mathematics to solve problems. **Monitoring:** Monitoring/Assessing your performance or that of other individuals or organizations to make improvements or take corrective action. **Coordination:** Adjusting actions in relation to others' actions.

GOE INFORMATION—Interest Area: 11. Recreation, Travel, and Other Personal Services. **Work Group:** 11.05. Food and Beverage Services. **Other Job Titles in This Work Group:** Bakers; Bartenders; Butchers and Meat Cutters; Chefs and Head Cooks; Combined Food Preparation and Serving Workers, Including Fast Food; Cooks, All Other; Cooks, Fast Food; Cooks, Institution and Cafeteria; Cooks, Restaurant; Cooks, Short Order; Counter Attendants, Cafeteria, Food Concession, and Coffee Shop; Dining Room and Cafeteria Attendants and Bartender Helpers; Dishwashers; Food Preparation and Serving Related Workers, All Other; Food Preparation Workers; Food Servers, Nonrestaurant; Hosts and Hostesses, Restaurant, Lounge, and Coffee Shop; Waiters and Waitresses. **PERSONALITY TYPE—Realistic.** Realistic occupations frequently involve work activities that include practical, hands-on problems and solutions. They often deal with plants, animals, and real-world materials like wood, tools, and machinery. Many of the occupations require working outside and do not involve a lot of paperwork or working closely with others.

EDUCATION/TRAINING PROGRAM(S)—Baking and Pastry Arts/Baker/Pastry Chef. **RELATED KNOWLEDGE/COURSES—Food Production:** Knowledge of techniques and equipment for planting, growing, and harvesting food products (both plant and animal) for consumption, including storage/handling techniques. **Customer and Personal Service:** Knowledge of principles and processes for providing customer and personal services. This includes customer needs assessment, meeting quality standards for services, and evaluation of customer satisfaction. **Production and Processing:** Knowledge of raw materials, production processes, quality control, costs, and other techniques for maximizing the effective manufacture and distribution of goods. **Mathematics:** Knowledge of arithmetic, algebra, geometry, calculus, and statistics and their applications.

Bakers, Manufacturing

▲ Education/Training Required: Long-term on-the-job training
▲ Annual Earnings: $20,440
▲ Growth: 16.8%
▲ Annual Job Openings: 25,000
▲ Self-Employed: 0%
▲ Part-Time: 22.0%

Mix and bake ingredients according to recipes to produce breads, pastries, and other baked goods. Goods are produced in large quantities for sale through establishments such as grocery stores. Generally, high volume production equipment is used. Measures flour and other ingredients to prepare batters, dough, fillings, and icings, using scale and graduated containers. Places dough in pans, in molds, or on sheets and bakes dough in oven or on grill. Dumps ingredients into mixing-machine bowl or steam kettle to mix or cook ingredients according to specific instructions. Decorates cakes. Applies glace, icing, or other topping to baked goods, using spatula or brush. Rolls, cuts, and shapes dough to form sweet rolls, pie crusts, tarts, cookies, and related products prior to baking. Observes color of products being baked and adjusts oven temperature. Develops new recipes for cakes and icings. **SKILLS—Mathematics:** Using mathematics to solve problems. **Monitoring:** Monitoring/Assessing your performance or that of other individuals or organizations to make improvements or take corrective action. **Equipment Selection:** Determining the kind of tools and equipment needed to do a job.

GOE INFORMATION—Interest Area: 08. Industrial Production. **Work Group:** 08.03. Production Work. **Other Job Titles in This Work Group:** Bindery Machine Operators and Tenders; Brazers; Cementing and Gluing Machine Operators and Tenders; Chemical Equipment Controllers and Operators; Chemical Equipment Operators and Tenders; Chemical Equipment Tenders; Cleaning, Washing, and Metal Pickling Equipment Operators and Tenders; Coating, Painting, and Spraying Machine Operators and Tenders; Coil Winders, Tapers, and Finishers; Combination Machine Tool Operators and Tenders, Metal and Plastic; Computer-Controlled Machine Tool Operators, Metal and Plastic; Cooling and Freezing Equipment Operators and Tenders; Crushing, Grinding, and Polishing Machine Setters, Operators, and Tenders; Cutters and Trimmers, Hand; Cutting and Slicing Machine Operators and Tenders; Cutting and Slicing Machine Setters, Operators, and Tenders; Design Printing Machine Setters and Set-Up Operators; Electrolytic Plating and Coating Machine Operators and Tenders, Metal and Plastic; Electrolytic Plating and Coating Machine Setters and Set-Up Operators, Metal and Plastic; Electrotypers and Stereotypers; Embossing Machine Set-Up Operators; Engraver Set-Up Operators; Extruding and Forming Machine Operators and Tenders, Synthetic or Glass Fibers; Extruding and Forming Machine Setters, Operators, and Tenders, Synthetic and Glass Fibers; Extruding, Forming, Pressing, and Compacting Machine Operators and Tenders; Fabric and Apparel Patternmakers; Fiber Product Cutting Machine Setters and Set-Up Operators; Fiberglass Laminators and Fabricators; Film Laboratory Technicians; Fitters, Structural Metal—Precision; Food and Tobacco Roasting, Baking, and Drying Machine Operators and Tenders; Food Batchmakers; Food Cooking Machine Operators and Tenders; Furnace, Kiln, Oven, Drier, and Kettle Operators and Tenders; Glass Cutting Machine Setters and Set-Up Operators; Graders and Sorters, Agricultural Products; Grinding and Polishing Workers, Hand; Hand Compositors and Typesetters; Heaters, Metal and Plastic; Helpers—Production Workers; others. **PERSONALITY TYPE—Realistic.** Realistic occupations frequently involve work activities that include practical, hands-on problems and solutions. They often deal with plants, animals, and real-world materials like wood, tools, and machinery. Many of the occupations require working outside and do not involve a lot of paperwork or working closely with others.

EDUCATION/TRAINING PROGRAM(S)—Baking and Pastry Arts/Baker/Pastry Chef. RELATED KNOWLEDGE/COURSES—Production and Processing: Knowledge of raw materials, production processes, quality control, costs, and other techniques for maximizing the effective manufacture and distribution of goods. **Food Production:** Knowledge of techniques and equipment for planting, growing, and harvesting food products (both plant and animal) for consumption, including storage/handling techniques. **Mathematics:** Knowledge of arithmetic, algebra, geometry, calculus, and statistics and their applications.

Bartenders

- ▲ Education/Training Required: Short-term on-the-job training
- ▲ Annual Earnings: $14,610
- ▲ Growth: 13.4%
- ▲ Annual Job Openings: 84,000
- ▲ Self-Employed: 3.0%
- ▲ Part-Time: 43.1%

Mix and serve drinks to patrons, directly or through waitstaff. Mixes ingredients, such as liquor, soda, water, sugar, and bitters, to prepare cocktails and other drinks. Arranges bottles and glasses to make attractive display. Slices and pits fruit for garnishing drinks. Orders or requisitions liquors and supplies. Prepares appetizers, such as pickles, cheese, and cold meats. Cleans glasses, utensils, and bar equipment. Collects money for drinks served. Serves wine and draft or bottled beer. **SKILLS—Service Orientation:** Actively looking for ways to help people. **Writing:** Communicating effectively in writing as appropriate for the needs of the audience.

GOE INFORMATION—Interest Area: 11. Recreation, Travel, and Other Personal Services. **Work Group:** 11.05. Food and Beverage Services. **Other Job Titles in This Work Group:** Bakers; Bakers, Bread and Pastry; Butchers and Meat Cutters; Chefs and Head Cooks; Combined Food Preparation and Serving Workers, Including Fast Food; Cooks, All Other; Cooks, Fast Food; Cooks, Institution and Cafeteria; Cooks, Restaurant; Cooks, Short Order; Counter Attendants, Cafeteria, Food Concession, and Coffee Shop; Dining Room and Cafeteria Attendants and Bartender Helpers; Dishwashers; Food Preparation and Serving Related Workers, All Other; Food Preparation Workers; Food Servers, Nonrestaurant; Hosts and Hostesses, Restaurant, Lounge, and Coffee Shop; Waiters and Waitresses. **PERSONALITY TYPE—Enterprising.** Enterprising occupations frequently involve starting up and carrying out projects. These occupations can involve leading people and making many decisions. They sometimes require risk taking and often deal with business.

EDUCATION/TRAINING PROGRAM(S)— Bartending/Bartender. **RELATED KNOWLEDGE/ COURSES—Customer and Personal Service:** Knowledge of principles and processes for providing customer and personal services. This includes customer needs assessment, meeting quality standards for services, and evaluation of customer satisfaction. **Sales and Marketing:** Knowledge of principles and methods for showing, promoting, and selling products or services. This includes marketing strategy and tactics, product demonstration, sales techniques, and sales control systems. **Law and Government:** Knowledge of laws, legal codes, court procedures, precedents, government regulations, executive orders, agency rules, and the democratic political process. **Mathematics:** Knowledge of arithmetic, algebra, geometry, calculus, and statistics and their applications. **English Language:** Knowledge of the structure and content of the English language, including the meaning and spelling of words, rules of composition, and grammar.

Bill and Account Collectors

- ▲ Education/Training Required: Short-term on-the-job training
- ▲ Annual Earnings: $25,960
- ▲ Growth: 25.3%
- ▲ Annual Job Openings: 71,000
- ▲ Self-Employed: 1.2%
- ▲ Part-Time: 12.7%

Locate and notify customers of delinquent accounts by mail, telephone, or personal visit to solicit payment. Duties include receiving payment and posting amount to customer's account; preparing statements to credit department if customer fails to respond; initiating repossession proceedings or service disconnection; keeping records of collection and status of accounts. Mails form letters to customers to encourage payment of delinquent accounts. Receives payments and posts amount paid to customer account, using computer or paper records. Confers with customer by telephone or in person to determine reason for overdue payment and review terms of sales, service, or credit contract. Drives vehicle to visit customer, return merchandise to creditor, or deliver bills. Sorts and files correspondence and performs miscellaneous clerical duties. Traces delinquent customer to new address by inquiring at post office or questioning neighbors. Records information about financial status of customer and status of collection efforts. Notifies credit department, orders merchandise repossession or service disconnection, or turns over account to attorney if customer fails to respond. Persuades customer to pay amount due on credit account, damage claim, or nonpayable check or negotiates extension of credit. **SKILLS—Active Listening:** Giving full attention to what other people are saying, taking time to understand the points being made, asking questions as appropriate, and not interrupting at inappropriate times. **Speaking:** Talking to others to convey information effectively. **Persuasion:** Persuading others to change their minds or behavior. **Writing:** Communicating effectively in writing as appropriate for the needs of the audience. **Reading Comprehension:** Understanding written sentences and paragraphs in work-related documents.

GOE INFORMATION—Interest Area: 09. Business Detail. **Work Group:** 09.05. Customer Service. **Other Job Titles in This Work Group:** Adjustment Clerks; Cashiers; Counter and Rental Clerks; Customer Service Representatives; Customer Service Representatives, Utilities; Gaming Cage Workers; Gaming Change Persons and Booth Cashiers; New Accounts Clerks; Order Clerks; Receptionists and Information Clerks; Tellers; Travel Clerks. **PERSONALITY TYPE—Conventional.** Conventional occupations frequently involve following set procedures and routines. These occupations can include working with data and details more than with ideas. Usually there is a clear line of authority to follow.

EDUCATION/TRAINING PROGRAM(S)—Banking and Financial Support Services. RELATED KNOWLEDGE/COURSES—Clerical Studies: Knowledge of administrative and clerical procedures and systems, such as word processing, managing files and records, stenography and transcription, designing forms, and other office procedures and terminology. **Mathematics:** Knowledge of arithmetic, algebra, geometry, calculus, and statistics and their applications. **Economics and Accounting:** Knowledge of economic and accounting principles and practices, the financial markets, banking, and the analysis and reporting of financial data. **English Language:** Knowledge of the structure and content of the English language, including the meaning and spelling of words, rules of composition, and grammar. **Computers and Electronics:** Knowledge of circuit boards, processors, chips, electronic equipment, and computer hardware and software, including applications and programming.

Billing and Posting Clerks and Machine Operators

- ▲ Education/Training Required: Moderate-term on-the-job training
- ▲ Annual Earnings: $25,350
- ▲ Growth: 8.5%
- ▲ Annual Job Openings: 69,000
- ▲ Self-Employed: 0%
- ▲ Part-Time: 12.8%

Compile, compute, and record billing, accounting, statistical, and other numerical data for billing purposes. Prepare billing invoices for services rendered or for delivery or shipment of goods. SKILLS—No data available.

GOE INFORMATION—Interest Area: 09. Business Detail. **Work Group:** 09.03. Bookkeeping, Auditing, and Accounting. **Other Job Titles in This Work Group:** Billing, Cost, and Rate Clerks; Bookkeeping, Accounting, and Auditing Clerks; Brokerage Clerks; Payroll and Timekeeping Clerks; Statement Clerks; Tax Preparers. **PERSONALITY TYPE—No data available.**

EDUCATION/TRAINING PROGRAM(S)—Accounting Technology/Technician and Bookkeeping. RELATED KNOWLEDGE/COURSES—No data available.

Billing, Cost, and Rate Clerks

- ▲ Education/Training Required: Short-term on-the-job training
- ▲ Annual Earnings: $25,350
- ▲ Growth: 8.5%
- ▲ Annual Job Openings: 69,000
- ▲ Self-Employed: 0%
- ▲ Part-Time: 13.8%

Compile data, compute fees and charges, and prepare invoices for billing purposes. Duties include computing costs and calculating rates for goods, services, and shipment of goods; posting data; and keeping other relevant records. May involve use of computer or typewriter, calculator, and adding and bookkeeping machines. Computes amounts due from such documents as purchase orders, sales tickets, and charge slips. Compiles and computes credit terms, discounts, and purchase prices for billing documents. Keeps records of invoices and support documents. Consults manuals that include rates, rules, regulations, and government tax and tariff information. Verifies compiled data from vendor invoices to ensure accuracy and revises billing data when errors are found. Resolves discrepancies on accounting records. Updates manuals when rates, rules, or regulations are amended. Estimates market value of product or services. Answers mail and telephone inquiries regarding rates, routing, and procedures. Types billing documents, shipping labels, credit memorandums, and credit forms, using typewriter or computer. Compiles cost factor reports, such as labor, production, storage, and equipment. **SKILLS—Mathematics:** Using mathematics to solve problems. **Reading Comprehension:** Understanding written sentences and paragraphs in work-related documents. **Active Listening:** Giving full attention to what other people are saying, taking time to understand the points being made, asking questions as appropriate, and not interrupting at inappropriate times. **Writing:** Communicating effectively in writing as appropriate for the needs of the audience. **Speaking:** Talking to others to convey information effectively.

GOE INFORMATION—Interest Area: 09. Business Detail. **Work Group:** 09.03. Bookkeeping, Auditing, and Accounting. **Other Job Titles in This Work Group:** Billing and Posting Clerks and Machine Operators; Bookkeeping, Accounting, and Auditing Clerks; Brokerage Clerks; Payroll and Timekeeping Clerks; Statement Clerks; Tax Preparers. **PERSONALITY TYPE—Conventional.** Conventional occupations frequently involve following set procedures and routines. These occupations can include working with data and details more than with ideas. Usually there is a clear line of authority to follow.

EDUCATION/TRAINING PROGRAM(S)—Accounting Technology/Technician and Bookkeeping. **RELATED KNOWLEDGE/COURSES—Clerical Studies:** Knowledge of administrative and clerical procedures and systems, such as word processing, managing files and records, stenography and transcription, designing forms, and other office procedures and terminology. **Mathematics:** Knowledge of arithmetic, algebra, geometry, calculus, and statistics and their applications. **Economics and Accounting:** Knowledge of economic and accounting principles and practices, the financial markets, banking, and the analysis and reporting of financial data. **English Language:** Knowledge of the structure and content of the English language, including the meaning and spelling of words, rules of composition, and grammar. **Customer and Personal Service:** Knowledge of principles and processes for providing customer and personal services. This includes customer needs assessment, meeting quality standards for services, and evaluation of customer satisfaction.

B

Billing, Posting, and Calculating Machine Operators

- ▲ Education/Training Required: Short-term on-the-job training
- ▲ Annual Earnings: $25,350
- ▲ Growth: 8.5%
- ▲ Annual Job Openings: 69,000
- ▲ Self-Employed: 0%
- ▲ Part-Time: 12.8%

Operate machines that automatically perform mathematical processes, such as addition, subtraction, multiplication, and division, to calculate and record billing, accounting, statistical, and other numerical data. Duties include operating special billing machines to prepare statements, bills, and invoices and operating bookkeeping machines to copy and post data, make computations, and compile records of transactions. Calculates accounting and other numerical data, such as amounts customers owe, sales totals, and inventory data, using calculating machine. Observes operation of sorter to note document machine cannot read and manually records amount, using keyboard. Manually sorts and lists items for proof or collection. Cleans machines, such as encoding or sorting machines, and replaces ribbons, film, and tape. Bundles sorted documents to prepare those drawn on other banks for collection. Transfers data from machine, such as encoding machine, to computer. Posts totals to records and prepares bill or invoice to be sent to customers, using billing machine. Sorts and microfilms transaction documents, such as checks, using sorting machine. Compares machine totals to records for errors and encodes correct amount or prepares correction record if error is found. Transcribes data from office records, using specified forms, billing machine, and transcribing machine. Encodes and adds amounts of transaction documents, such as checks or money orders, using encoding machine. **SKILLS—Mathematics:** Using mathematics to solve problems. **Operation and Control:** Controlling operations of equipment or systems. **Reading Comprehension:** Understanding written sentences and paragraphs in work-related documents.

GOE INFORMATION—Interest Area: 09. Business Detail. **Work Group:** 09.09. Clerical Machine Operation. **Other Job Titles in This Work Group:** Automatic Teller Machine Servicers; Computer Operators; Data Entry Keyers; Duplicating Machine Operators; Mail Clerks and Mail Machine Operators, Except Postal Service; Mail Machine Operators, Preparation and Handling; Office Machine Operators, Except Computer; Postal Service Clerks; Typesetting and Composing Machine Operators and Tenders; Word Processors and Typists. **PERSONALITY TYPE—**Conventional. Conventional occupations frequently involve following set procedures and routines. These occupations can include working with data and details more than with ideas. Usually there is a clear line of authority to follow.

EDUCATION/TRAINING PROGRAM(S)—Accounting Technology/Technician and Bookkeeping. **RELATED KNOWLEDGE/COURSES—Clerical Studies:** Knowledge of administrative and clerical procedures and systems, such as word processing, managing files and records, stenography and transcription, designing forms, and other office procedures and terminology. **Mathematics:** Knowledge of arithmetic, algebra, geometry, calculus, and statistics and their applications. **Computers and Electronics:** Knowledge of circuit boards, processors, chips, electronic equipment, and computer hardware and software, including applications and programming. **Economics and Accounting:** Knowledge of economic and accounting principles and practices, the financial markets, banking, and the analysis and reporting of financial data. **English Language:** Knowledge of the structure and content of the English language, including the meaning and spelling of words, rules of composition, and grammar.

Biochemists

▲ Education/Training Required: Doctoral degree
▲ Annual Earnings: $57,100
▲ Growth: 21.0%
▲ Annual Job Openings: 5,000
▲ Self-Employed: 4.9%
▲ Part-Time: 6.6%

Research or study chemical composition and processes of living organisms that affect vital processes such as growth and aging to determine chemical actions and effects on organisms, such as the action of foods, drugs, or other substances on body functions and tissues. Studies chemistry of living processes, such as cell development, breathing, and digestion, and living energy changes, such as growth, aging, and death. Researches methods of transferring characteristics, such as resistance to disease, from one organism to another. Examines chemical aspects of formation of antibodies and researches chemistry of cells and blood corpuscles. Develops and executes tests to detect disease, genetic disorders, or other abnormalities. Develops and tests new drugs and medications used for commercial distribution. Designs and builds laboratory equipment needed for special research projects. Analyzes foods to determine nutritional value and effects of cooking, canning, and processing on this value. Cleans, purifies, refines, and otherwise prepares pharmaceutical compounds for commercial distribution. Prepares reports and recommendations based upon research outcomes. Develops methods to process, store, and use food, drugs, and chemical compounds. Isolates, analyzes, and identifies hormones, vitamins, allergens, minerals, and enzymes and determines their effects on body functions. Researches and determines chemical action of substances such as drugs, serums, hormones, and food on tissues and vital processes. **SKILLS—Science:** Using scientific rules and methods to solve problems. **Reading Comprehension:** Understanding written sentences and paragraphs in work-related documents. **Writing:** Communicating effectively in writing as appropriate for the needs of the audience. **Critical Thinking:** Using logic and reasoning to identify the strengths and weaknesses of alternative solutions, conclusions, or approaches to problems. **Active Learning:** Understanding the implications of new information for both current and future problem-solving and decision-making.

GOE INFORMATION—Interest Area: 02. Science, Math, and Engineering. **Work Group:** 02.03. Life Sciences. **Other Job Titles in This Work Group:** Agricultural and Food Science Technicians; Agricultural Technicians; Animal Scientists; Biochemists and Biophysicists; Biological Scientists, All Other; Biologists; Biophysicists; Conservation Scientists; Environmental Scientists and Specialists, Including Health; Epidemiologists; Food Science Technicians; Food Scientists and Technologists; Foresters; Life Scientists, All Other; Medical Scientists, Except Epidemiologists; Microbiologists; Plant Scientists; Range Managers; Soil and Plant Scientists; Soil Conservationists; Soil Scientists; Zoologists and Wildlife Biologists. **PERSONALITY TYPE—Investigative.** Investigative occupations frequently involve working with ideas and require an extensive amount of thinking. These occupations can involve searching for facts and figuring out problems mentally.

EDUCATION/TRAINING PROGRAM(S)—Biochemistry; Biochemistry/Biophysics and Molecular Biology; Biophysics; Cell/Cellular Biology and Anatomical Sciences, Other; Molecular Biochemistry; Molecular Biophysics; Soil Chemistry and Physics; Soil Microbiology. RELATED KNOWLEDGE/COURSES—Chemistry: Knowledge of the chemical composition, structure, and properties of substances and of the chemical processes and transformations that they undergo. This includes uses of chemicals and their interactions, danger signs, production techniques, and disposal methods. **Biology:** Knowledge of plant and animal organisms and their tissues, cells, functions, interdependencies, and interactions with each other and the environment. **Mathematics:** Knowledge of arithmetic, algebra, geometry, calculus, and statistics and their applications. **English Language:** Knowledge of the structure and content of the English language, including the meaning and spelling of words, rules of composition, and grammar. **Building and Construction:** Knowledge of materials, methods, and tools involved in the construction or repair of houses, buildings, or other structures, such as highways and roads.

Biochemists and Biophysicists

- ▲ Education/Training Required: Doctoral degree
- ▲ Annual Earnings: $57,100
- ▲ Growth: 21.0%
- ▲ Annual Job Openings: 5,000
- ▲ Self-Employed: 4.9%
- ▲ Part-Time: 6.6%

Study the chemical composition and physical principles of living cells and organisms, their electrical and mechanical energy, and related phenomena. May conduct research to further understanding of the complex chemical combinations and reactions involved in metabolism, reproduction, growth, and heredity. May determine the effects of foods, drugs, serums, hormones, and other substances on tissues and vital processes of living organisms. SKILLS—No data available.

GOE INFORMATION—Interest Area: 02. Science, Math, and Engineering. Work Group: 02.03. Life Sciences. Other Job Titles in This Work Group: Agricultural and Food Science Technicians; Agricultural Technicians; Animal Scientists; Biochemists; Biological Scientists, All Other; Biologists; Biophysicists; Conservation Scientists; Environmental Scientists and Specialists, Including Health; Epidemiologists; Food Science Technicians; Food Scientists and Technologists; Foresters; Life Scientists, All Other; Medical Scientists, Except Epidemiologists; Microbiologists; Plant Scientists; Range Managers; Soil and Plant Scientists; Soil Conservationists; Soil Scientists; Zoologists and Wildlife Biologists. PERSONALITY TYPE—No data available.

EDUCATION/TRAINING PROGRAM(S)—Biochemistry; Biochemistry/Biophysics and Molecular Biology; Biophysics; Cell/Cellular Biology and Anatomical Sciences, Other; Molecular Biochemistry; Molecular Biophysics; Soil Chemistry and Physics; Soil Microbiology. RELATED KNOWLEDGE/COURSES—No data available.

Biological Science Teachers, Postsecondary

- ▲ Education/Training Required: Master's degree
- ▲ Annual Earnings: $57,240
- ▲ Growth: 23.5%
- ▲ Annual Job Openings: 184,000
- ▲ Self-Employed: 0%
- ▲ Part-Time: 32.3%

Teach courses in biological sciences. Prepares and delivers lectures to students. Stimulates class discussions. Compiles bibliographies of specialized materials for outside reading assignments. Compiles, administers, and grades examinations or assigns this work to others. Acts as adviser to student organizations. Serves on faculty committee providing professional consulting services to government and industry. Conducts research in particular field of knowledge and publishes findings in professional journals. Directs research of other teachers or graduate students working for advanced academic degrees. Advises students on academic and vocational curricula. SKILLS—Reading Comprehension: Understanding written sentences and paragraphs in work-related documents. Instructing: Teaching others how to do something. Learning Strategies: Selecting and using training/instructional methods and procedures appropriate for the situation when learning or teaching new things. Science: Using scientific rules and methods to solve problems. Writing: Communicating effectively in writing as appropriate for the needs of the audience. Active Learning: Understanding the implications of new information for both current and future problem-solving and decision-making. Critical Thinking: Using logic and reasoning to identify the strengths and weaknesses of alternative solutions, conclusions, or approaches to problems.

GOE INFORMATION—Interest Area: 12. Education and Social Service. Work Group: 12.03. Educational Services. Other Job Titles in This Work Group: Adult Literacy, Remedial Education, and GED Teachers and

Instructors; Agricultural Sciences Teachers, Postsecondary; Anthropology and Archeology Teachers, Postsecondary; Architecture Teachers, Postsecondary; Archivists; Area, Ethnic, and Cultural Studies Teachers, Postsecondary; Art, Drama, and Music Teachers, Postsecondary; Atmospheric, Earth, Marine, and Space Sciences Teachers, Postsecondary; Audio-Visual Collections Specialists; Business Teachers, Postsecondary; Chemistry Teachers, Postsecondary; Child Care Workers; Communications Teachers, Postsecondary; Computer Science Teachers, Postsecondary; Criminal Justice and Law Enforcement Teachers, Postsecondary; Curators; Economics Teachers, Postsecondary; Education Teachers, Postsecondary; Educational Psychologists; Educational, Vocational, and School Counselors; Elementary School Teachers, Except Special Education; Engineering Teachers, Postsecondary; English Language and Literature Teachers, Postsecondary; Environmental Science Teachers, Postsecondary; Farm and Home Management Advisors; Foreign Language and Literature Teachers, Postsecondary; Forestry and Conservation Science Teachers, Postsecondary; Geography Teachers, Postsecondary; Graduate Teaching Assistants; Health Specialties Teachers, Postsecondary; History Teachers, Postsecondary; Home Economics Teachers, Postsecondary; Kindergarten Teachers, Except Special Education; Law Teachers, Postsecondary; Librarians; Library Assistants, Clerical; Library Science Teachers, Postsecondary; Library Technicians; Mathematical Science Teachers, Postsecondary; Middle School Teachers, Except Special and Vocational Education; Museum Technicians and Conservators; Nursing Instructors and Teachers, Postsecondary; Personal Financial Advisors; Philosophy and Religion Teachers, Postsecondary; Physics Teachers, Postsecondary; Political Science Teachers, Postsecondary; Postsecondary Teachers, All Other; Preschool Teachers, Except Special Education; others. **PERSONALITY TYPE**—Investigative. Investigative occupations frequently involve working with ideas and require an extensive amount of thinking. These occupations can involve searching for facts and figuring out problems mentally.

EDUCATION/TRAINING PROGRAM(S)—Anatomy; Animal Physiology; Biochemistry; Biological and Biomedical Sciences, Other; Biology/Biological Sciences, General; Biometry/Biometrics; Biophysics; Biotechnology; Botany/Plant Biology; Cell/Cellular Biology and Histology; Ecology; Ecology, Evolution, Systematics and Population Biology, Other; Entomology; Evolutionary Biology; Immunology; Marine Biology and Biological Oceanography; Microbiology, General; Molecular Biology; Neuroscience; Nutrition Sciences; Parasitology; Pathology/Experimental Pathology; Pharmacology; Plant Genetics; Plant Pathology/Phytopathology; Plant Physiology; Radiation Biology/Radiobiology; Toxicology; Virology; Zoology/Animal Biology. **RELATED KNOWLEDGE/COURSES—Education and Training:** Knowledge of principles and methods for curriculum and training design, teaching and instruction for individuals and groups, and the measurement of training effects. **Biology:** Knowledge of plant and animal organisms and their tissues, cells, functions, interdependencies, and interactions with each other and the environment. **Psychology:** Knowledge of human behavior and performance; individual differences in ability, personality, and interests; learning and motivation; psychological research methods; and the assessment and treatment of behavioral and affective disorders. **Chemistry:** Knowledge of the chemical composition, structure, and properties of substances and of the chemical processes and transformations that they undergo. This includes uses of chemicals and their interactions, danger signs, production techniques, and disposal methods. **English Language:** Knowledge of the structure and content of the English language, including the meaning and spelling of words, rules of composition, and grammar.

Biological Technicians

> ▲ Education/Training Required: Associate's degree
> ▲ Annual Earnings: $32,280
> ▲ Growth: 26.4%
> ▲ Annual Job Openings: 7,000
> ▲ Self-Employed: 0.9%
> ▲ Part-Time: 11.7%

Assist biological and medical scientists in laboratories. Set up, operate, and maintain laboratory instruments and equipment, monitor experiments, make observations, and calculate and record results. May analyze organic substances, such as blood, food, and drugs. Sets up laboratory and field equipment to assist research workers.

Cleans and maintains laboratory and field equipment and work areas. Examines animals and specimens to determine presence of disease or other problems. Pricks animals and collects blood samples for testing, using hand-held devices. Plants seeds in specified area and counts plants that grow to determine germination rate of seeds. Waters and feeds rations to livestock and laboratory animals. Adjusts testing equipment and prepares culture media, following standard procedures. Measures or weighs ingredients used in testing or as animal feed. Records production and test data for evaluation by personnel. **SKILLS—Mathematics:** Using mathematics to solve problems. **Reading Comprehension:** Understanding written sentences and paragraphs in work-related documents. **Science:** Using scientific rules and methods to solve problems. **Equipment Selection:** Determining the kind of tools and equipment needed to do a job.

GOE INFORMATION—Interest Area: 02. Science, Math, and Engineering. **Work Group:** 02.05. Laboratory Technology. **Other Job Titles in This Work Group:** Chemical Technicians; Environmental Science and Protection Technicians, Including Health; Geological and Petroleum Technicians; Geological Data Technicians; Geological Sample Test Technicians; Nuclear Equipment Operation Technicians; Nuclear Technicians; Photographers, Scientific. **PERSONALITY TYPE—**Realistic. Realistic occupations frequently involve work activities that include practical, hands-on problems and solutions. They often deal with plants, animals, and real-world materials like wood, tools, and machinery. Many of the occupations require working outside and do not involve a lot of paperwork or working closely with others.

EDUCATION/TRAINING PROGRAM(S)—Biology Technician/Biotechnology Laboratory Technician. **RELATED KNOWLEDGE/COURSES—Biology:** Knowledge of plant and animal organisms and their tissues, cells, functions, interdependencies, and interactions with each other and the environment. **Mathematics:** Knowledge of arithmetic, algebra, geometry, calculus, and statistics and their applications. **Food Production:** Knowledge of techniques and equipment for planting, growing, and harvesting food products (both plant and animal) for consumption, including storage/handling techniques. **Clerical Studies:** Knowledge of administrative and clerical procedures and systems, such as word processing, managing files and records, stenography and transcription, designing forms, and other office procedures and terminology. **Medicine and Dentistry:** Knowledge of the information and techniques needed to diagnose and treat human injuries, diseases, and deformities. This includes symptoms, treatment alternatives, drug properties and interactions, and preventive health-care measures.

Biologists

▲ Education/Training Required: Doctoral degree
▲ Annual Earnings: $44,770
▲ Growth: 21.0%
▲ Annual Job Openings: 5,000
▲ Self-Employed: 4.9%
▲ Part-Time: 6.6%

Research or study basic principles of plant and animal life, such as origin, relationship, development, anatomy, and functions. Studies basic principles of plant and animal life, such as origin, relationship, development, anatomy, and functions. Studies aquatic plants and animals and environmental conditions affecting them, such as radioactivity or pollution. Collects and analyzes biological data about relationship among and between organisms and their environment. Identifies, classifies, and studies structure, behavior, ecology, physiology, nutrition, culture, and distribution of plant and animal species. Develops methods and apparatus for securing representative plant, animal, aquatic, or soil samples. Studies and manages wild animal populations. Measures salinity, acidity, light, oxygen content, and other physical conditions of water to determine their relationship to aquatic life. Studies reactions of plants, animals, and marine species to parasites. Investigates and develops pest management and control measures. Develops methods of extracting drugs from aquatic plants and animals. Researches environmental effects of present and potential uses of land and water areas and determines methods of improving environment or crop yields. Plans and administers biological research programs for government, research firms, medical industries, or manufacturing firms. Cultivates, breeds, and grows aquatic life, such as lobsters, clams, or fish farming.

Prepares environmental impact reports for industry, government, or publication. Communicates test results to state and federal representatives and general public. **SKILLS— Science:** Using scientific rules and methods to solve problems. **Reading Comprehension:** Understanding written sentences and paragraphs in work-related documents. **Writing:** Communicating effectively in writing as appropriate for the needs of the audience. **Mathematics:** Using mathematics to solve problems. **Critical Thinking:** Using logic and reasoning to identify the strengths and weaknesses of alternative solutions, conclusions, or approaches to problems. **Active Learning:** Understanding the implications of new information for both current and future problem-solving and decision-making.

GOE INFORMATION—Interest Area: 02. Science, Math, and Engineering. **Work Group:** 02.03. Life Sciences. **Other Job Titles in This Work Group:** Agricultural and Food Science Technicians; Agricultural Technicians; Animal Scientists; Biochemists; Biochemists and Biophysicists; Biological Scientists, All Other; Biophysicists; Conservation Scientists; Environmental Scientists and Specialists, Including Health; Epidemiologists; Food Science Technicians; Food Scientists and Technologists; Foresters; Life Scientists, All Other; Medical Scientists, Except Epidemiologists; Microbiologists; Plant Scientists; Range Managers; Soil and Plant Scientists; Soil Conservationists; Soil Scientists; Zoologists and Wildlife Biologists. **PERSON-**

ALITY TYPE—Investigative. Investigative occupations frequently involve working with ideas and require an extensive amount of thinking. These occupations can involve searching for facts and figuring out problems mentally.

EDUCATION/TRAINING PROGRAM(S)—Biochemistry; Biochemistry/Biophysics and Molecular Biology; Biology/Biological Sciences, General; Biophysics; Cell/Cellular Biology and Anatomical Sciences, Other; Molecular Biochemistry; Soil Microbiology. **RELATED KNOWLEDGE/COURSES—Biology:** Knowledge of plant and animal organisms and their tissues, cells, functions, interdependencies, and interactions with each other and the environment. **Mathematics:** Knowledge of arithmetic, algebra, geometry, calculus, and statistics and their applications. **Chemistry:** Knowledge of the chemical composition, structure, and properties of substances and of the chemical processes and transformations that they undergo. This includes uses of chemicals and their interactions, danger signs, production techniques, and disposal methods. **English Language:** Knowledge of the structure and content of the English language, including the meaning and spelling of words, rules of composition, and grammar. **Physics:** Knowledge and prediction of physical principles and laws and their interrelationships and applications to understanding fluid, material, and atmospheric dynamics and mechanical, electrical, atomic, and subatomic structures and processes.

Biomedical Engineers

- ▲ Education/Training Required: Bachelor's degree
- ▲ Annual Earnings: $59,790
- ▲ Growth: 31.4%
- ▲ Annual Job Openings: Fewer than 500
- ▲ Self-Employed: 2.7%
- ▲ Part-Time: 4.5%

Apply knowledge of engineering, biology, and biomechanical principles to the design, development, and evaluation of biological and health systems and products, such as artificial organs, prostheses, instrumentation, medical information systems, and health management and care delivery systems. **SKILLS**—No data available.

GOE INFORMATION—Interest Area: 02. Science, Math, and Engineering. **Work Group:** 02.07. Engineering. **Other Job Titles in This Work Group:** Aerospace Engineers; Agricultural Engineers; Architects, Except Landscape and Naval; Chemical Engineers; Civil Engi-

neers; Computer Hardware Engineers; Computer Software Engineers, Applications; Computer Software Engineers, Systems Software; Electrical Engineers; Electronics Engineers, Except Computer; Engineers, All Other; Environmental Engineers; Fire-Prevention and Protection Engineers; Health and Safety Engineers, Except Mining Safety Engineers and Inspectors; Industrial Engineers; Industrial Safety and Health Engineers; Landscape Architects; Marine Architects; Marine Engineers; Marine Engineers and Naval Architects; Materials Engineers; Mechanical Engineers; Mining and Geological Engineers,

Including Mining Safety Engineers; Nuclear Engineers; Petroleum Engineers; Product Safety Engineers; Sales Engineers. **PERSONALITY TYPE**—No data available.

Biophysicists

EDUCATION/TRAINING PROGRAM(S)—Biomedical/Medical Engineering. **RELATED KNOWLEDGE/COURSES**—No data available.

▲ Education/Training Required: Doctoral degree
▲ Annual Earnings: $57,100
▲ Growth: 21.0%
▲ Annual Job Openings: 5,000
▲ Self-Employed: 4.9%
▲ Part-Time: 6.6%

Research or study physical principles of living cells and organisms, their electrical and mechanical energy, and related phenomena. Studies physical principles of living cells and organisms and their electrical and mechanical energy. Investigates transmission of electrical impulses along nerves and muscles. Studies absorption of light by chlorophyll in photosynthesis or by pigments of eye involved in vision. Researches cancer treatment, using radiation and nuclear particles. Analyzes functions of electronic and human brains, such as learning, thinking, and memory. Investigates dynamics of seeing and hearing. Studies spatial configuration of submicroscopic molecules, such as proteins, using X-ray and electron microscope. Researches manner in which characteristics of plants and animals are carried through successive generations. Investigates damage to cells and tissues caused by X rays and nuclear particles. Researches transformation of substances in cells, using atomic isotopes. **SKILLS—Science:** Using scientific rules and methods to solve problems. **Reading Comprehension:** Understanding written sentences and paragraphs in work-related documents. **Writing:** Communicating effectively in writing as appropriate for the needs of the audience. **Active Learning:** Understanding the implications of new information for both current and future problem-solving and decision-making. **Mathematics:** Using mathematics to solve problems.

GOE INFORMATION—Interest Area: 02. Science, Math, and Engineering. **Work Group:** 02.03. Life Sciences. **Other Job Titles in This Work Group:** Agricultural and Food Science Technicians; Agricultural Technicians; Animal Scientists; Biochemists; Biochemists and Biophysicists; Biological Scientists, All Other; Biologists; Conservation Scientists; Environmental Scientists and Specialists, Including Health; Epidemiologists; Food Science Technicians; Food Scientists and Technologists; Foresters; Life Scientists, All Other; Medical Scientists, Except Epidemiologists; Microbiologists; Plant Scientists; Range Managers; Soil and Plant Scientists; Soil Conservationists; Soil Scientists; Zoologists and Wildlife Biologists. **PERSONALITY TYPE**—Investigative. Investigative occupations frequently involve working with ideas and require an extensive amount of thinking. These occupations can involve searching for facts and figuring out problems mentally.

EDUCATION/TRAINING PROGRAM(S)—Biochemistry; Biochemistry/Biophysics and Molecular Biology; Biophysics; Cell/Cellular Biology and Anatomical Sciences, Other; Molecular Biochemistry; Molecular Biophysics; Soil Chemistry and Physics; Soil Microbiology. **RELATED KNOWLEDGE/COURSES—Biology:** Knowledge of plant and animal organisms and their tissues, cells, functions, interdependencies, and interactions with each other and the environment. **Physics:** Knowledge and prediction of physical principles and laws and their interrelationships and applications to understanding fluid, material, and atmospheric dynamics and mechanical, electrical, atomic, and sub-atomic structures and processes. **Mathematics:** Knowledge of arithmetic, algebra, geometry, calculus, and statistics and their applications. **Chemistry:** Knowledge of the chemical composition, structure, and properties of substances and of the chemical processes and transformations that they undergo. This includes uses of chemicals and their interactions, danger signs, production techniques, and disposal methods. **English Language:** Knowledge of the structure and content of the English language, including the meaning and spelling of words, rules of composition, and grammar.

Boat Builders and Shipwrights

▲ Education/Training Required: Long-term on-the-job training
▲ Annual Earnings: $33,470
▲ Growth: 8.2%
▲ Annual Job Openings: 161,000
▲ Self-Employed: 36.8%
▲ Part-Time: 8.1%

Construct and repair ships or boats according to blueprints. Cuts and forms parts, such as keel, ribs, sidings, and support structures and blocks, using woodworking hand tools and power tools. Constructs and shapes wooden frames, structures, and other parts according to blueprint specifications, using hand tools, power tools, and measuring instruments. Attaches metal parts, such as fittings, plates, and bulkheads, to ship, using brace and bits, augers, and wrenches. Establishes dimensional reference points on layout and hull to make template of parts and locate machinery and equipment. Smoothes and finishes ship surfaces, using power sander, broadax, adze, and paint, and waxes and buffs surface to specified finish. Cuts out defect, using power tools and hand tools, and fits and secures replacement part, using caulking gun, adhesive, or hand tools. Assembles and installs hull timbers and other structures in ship, using adhesive, measuring instruments, and hand tools or power tools. Measures and marks dimensional lines on lumber, following template and using scriber. Consults with customer or supervisor and reads blueprint to determine necessary repairs. Attaches hoist to sections of hull and directs hoist operator to align parts over blocks according to layout of boat. Marks outline of boat on building dock, shipway, or mold loft according to blueprint specifications, using measuring instruments and crayon. Inspects boat to determine location and extent of defect. Positions and secures support structures on construction area. **SKILLS—Mathematics:** Using mathematics to solve problems. **Equipment Selection:** Determining the kind of tools and equipment needed to do a job. **Operations Analysis:** Analyzing needs and product requirements to create a design. **Repairing:** Repairing machines or systems, using the needed tools. **Installation:** Installing equipment, machines, wiring, or programs to meet specifications.

GOE INFORMATION—Interest Area: 06. Construction, Mining, and Drilling. **Work Group:** 06.02. Construction. **Other Job Titles in This Work Group:** Boilermakers; Brattice Builders; Brickmasons and Blockmasons; Carpenters; Carpet Installers; Ceiling Tile Installers; Cement Masons and Concrete Finishers; Commercial Divers; Construction Carpenters; Drywall and Ceiling Tile Installers; Drywall Installers; Electricians; Explosives Workers, Ordnance Handling Experts, and Blasters; Fence Erectors; Floor Layers, Except Carpet, Wood, and Hard Tiles; Floor Sanders and Finishers; Glaziers; Grader, Bulldozer, and Scraper Operators; Hazardous Materials Removal Workers; Insulation Workers, Floor, Ceiling, and Wall; Insulation Workers, Mechanical; Manufactured Building and Mobile Home Installers; Operating Engineers; Operating Engineers and Other Construction Equipment Operators; Painters, Construction and Maintenance; Paperhangers; Paving, Surfacing, and Tamping Equipment Operators; Pile-Driver Operators; Pipe Fitters; Pipelayers; Pipelaying Fitters; Plasterers and Stucco Masons; Plumbers; Plumbers, Pipefitters, and Steamfitters; Rail-Track Laying and Maintenance Equipment Operators; Refractory Materials Repairers, Except Brickmasons; Reinforcing Iron and Rebar Workers; Riggers; Roofers; Rough Carpenters; Security and Fire Alarm Systems Installers; Segmental Pavers; Sheet Metal Workers; Ship Carpenters and Joiners; Stone Cutters and Carvers; Stonemasons; Structural Iron and Steel Workers; Tapers; Terrazzo Workers and Finishers; Tile and Marble Setters. **PERSONALITY TYPE—Realistic.** Realistic occupations frequently involve work activities that include practical, hands-on problems and solutions. They often deal with plants, animals, and real-world materials like wood, tools, and machinery. Many of the occupations require working outside and do not involve a lot of paperwork or working closely with others.

EDUCATION/TRAINING PROGRAM(S)—Carpentry/Carpenter. RELATED KNOWLEDGE/COURSES—Building and Construction: Knowledge of materials, methods, and tools involved in the construction or repair of houses, buildings, or other structures, such as highways and roads. **Principles of Mechanical Devices:** Knowledge of machines and tools, including their designs, uses, repair, and maintenance. **Design:** Knowledge of design techniques, tools, and principles involved in production of precision technical plans, blueprints, drawings, and models. **Engineering and Technology:** Knowledge of the practical application of engineering science and technology. This includes applying principles, techniques, procedures, and equipment to the design and production of various goods and services. **Production and Processing:** Knowledge of raw materials, production processes, quality control, costs, and other techniques for maximizing the effective manufacture and distribution of goods.

Bookkeeping, Accounting, and Auditing Clerks

- ▲ Education/Training Required: Moderate-term on-the-job training
- ▲ Annual Earnings: $26,540
- ▲ Growth: 2.0%
- ▲ Annual Job Openings: 298,000
- ▲ Self-Employed: 11.0%
- ▲ Part-Time: 32.8%

Compute, classify, and record numerical data to keep financial records complete. Perform any combination of routine calculating, posting, and verifying duties to obtain primary financial data for use in maintaining accounting records. May also check the accuracy of figures, calculations, and postings pertaining to business transactions recorded by other workers. Records financial transactions and other account information to update and maintain accounting records. Evaluates records for accuracy of balances, postings, calculations, and other records pertaining to business or operating transactions and reconciles or notes discrepancies. Processes negotiable instruments such as checks and vouchers. Compiles reports and tables to show statistics related to cash receipts, expenditures, accounts payable and receivable, and profit and loss. Performs financial calculations such as amounts due, balances, discounts, equity, and principal. Debits or credits accounts. Complies with federal, state, and company policies, procedures, and regulations. Verifies balances and entries, calculations, and postings recorded by other workers. **SKILLS—Reading Comprehension:** Understanding written sentences and paragraphs in work-related documents. **Mathematics:** Using mathematics to solve problems. **Active Listening:** Giving full attention to what other people are saying, taking time to understand the points being made, asking questions as appropriate, and not interrupting at inappropriate times. **Writing:** Communicating effectively in writing as appropriate for the needs of the audience. **Speaking:** Talking to others to convey information effectively. **Management of Financial Resources:** Determining how money will be spent to get the work done and accounting for these expenditures.

GOE INFORMATION—**Interest Area:** 09. Business Detail. **Work Group:** 09.03. Bookkeeping, Auditing, and Accounting. **Other Job Titles in This Work Group:** Billing and Posting Clerks and Machine Operators; Billing, Cost, and Rate Clerks; Brokerage Clerks; Payroll and Timekeeping Clerks; Statement Clerks; Tax Preparers. **PERSONALITY TYPE**—Conventional. Conventional occupations frequently involve following set procedures and routines. These occupations can include working with data and details more than with ideas. Usually there is a clear line of authority to follow.

EDUCATION/TRAINING PROGRAM(S)—Accounting and Related Services, Other; Accounting Technology/Technician and Bookkeeping. RELATED KNOWLEDGE/COURSES—**Economics and Accounting:** Knowledge of economic and accounting principles and practices, the financial markets, banking, and the analysis and reporting of financial data. **Clerical Studies:** Knowledge of administrative and clerical procedures and systems, such as word processing, managing files and records, stenography and transcription, designing forms, and other office procedures and terminology. **Mathematics:** Knowledge of arithmetic, algebra, geometry, calculus, and statistics and their applications. **English Language:** Knowledge of the structure and content of the English language, including the meaning and spelling of words, rules of composition, and grammar. **Computers and Electronics:** Knowledge of circuit boards, processors, chips, electronic equipment, and computer hardware and software, including applications and programming.

Brattice Builders

▲ Education/Training Required: Moderate-term on-the-job training
▲ Annual Earnings: $33,470
▲ Growth: 8.2%
▲ Annual Job Openings: 161,000
▲ Self-Employed: 36.8%
▲ Part-Time: 8.1%

Build doors or brattices (ventilation walls or partitions) in underground passageways to control the proper circulation of air through the passageways and to the working places. Installs rigid and flexible air ducts to transport air to work areas. Drills and blasts obstructing boulders to reopen ventilation shafts. Erects partitions to support roof in areas unsuited to timbering or bolting. **SKILLS—Installation:** Installing equipment, machines, wiring, or programs to meet specifications. **Equipment Selection:** Determining the kind of tools and equipment needed to do a job. **Coordination:** Adjusting actions in relation to others' actions. **Quality Control Analysis:** Conducting tests and inspections of products, services, or processes to evaluate quality or performance. **Technology Design:** Generating or adapting equipment and technology to serve user needs. **Operations Analysis:** Analyzing needs and product requirements to create a design.

GOE INFORMATION—Interest Area: 06. Construction, Mining, and Drilling. **Work Group:** 06.02. Construction. **Other Job Titles in This Work Group:** Boat Builders and Shipwrights; Boilermakers; Brickmasons and Blockmasons; Carpenters; Carpet Installers; Ceiling Tile Installers; Cement Masons and Concrete Finishers; Commercial Divers; Construction Carpenters; Drywall and Ceiling Tile Installers; Drywall Installers; Electricians; Explosives Workers, Ordnance Handling Experts, and Blasters; Fence Erectors; Floor Layers, Except Carpet, Wood, and Hard Tiles; Floor Sanders and Finishers; Glaziers; Grader, Bulldozer, and Scraper Operators; Hazardous Materials Removal Workers; Insulation Workers, Floor, Ceiling, and Wall; Insulation Workers, Mechanical; Manufactured Building and Mobile Home Installers; Operating Engineers; Operating Engineers and Other Construction Equipment Operators; Painters, Construction and Maintenance; Paperhangers; Paving, Surfacing, and Tamping Equipment Operators; Pile-Driver Operators; Pipe Fitters; Pipelayers; Pipelaying Fitters; Plasterers and Stucco Masons; Plumbers; Plumbers, Pipefitters, and Steamfitters; Rail-Track Laying and Maintenance Equipment Operators; Refractory Materials Repairers, Except Brickmasons; Reinforcing Iron and Rebar Workers; Riggers; Roofers; Rough Carpenters; Security and Fire Alarm Systems Installers; Segmental Pavers; Sheet Metal Workers; Ship Carpenters and Joiners; Stone Cutters and Carvers; Stonemasons; Structural Iron and Steel Workers; Tapers; Terrazzo Workers and Finishers; Tile and Marble Setters. **PERSONALITY TYPE—Realistic.** Realistic occupations frequently involve work activities that include practical, hands-on problems and solutions. They often deal with plants, animals, and real-world materials like wood, tools, and machinery. Many of the occupations require working outside and do not involve a lot of paperwork or working closely with others.

EDUCATION/TRAINING PROGRAM(S)— Carpentry/Carpenter. **RELATED KNOWLEDGE/ COURSES—Building and Construction:** Knowledge of materials, methods, and tools involved in the construction or repair of houses, buildings, or other structures, such as highways and roads. **Principles of Mechanical Devices:** Knowledge of machines and tools, including their designs, uses, repair, and maintenance. **Physics:** Knowledge and prediction of physical principles and laws and their interrelationships and applications to understanding fluid, material, and atmospheric dynamics and mechanical, electrical, atomic, and sub-atomic structures and processes. **Engineering and Technology:** Knowledge of the practical application of engineering science and technology. This includes applying principles, techniques, procedures, and equipment to the design and production of various goods and services.

Brazers

▲ Education/Training Required: Short-term on-the-job training
▲ Annual Earnings: $28,490
▲ Growth: 19.3%
▲ Annual Job Openings: 51,000
▲ Self-Employed: 3.7%
▲ Part-Time: 8.6%

Braze together components to assemble fabricated metal parts, using torch or welding machine and flux. Guides torch and rod along joint of workpieces to heat to brazing temperature, melt braze alloy, and bond workpieces together. Cuts carbon electrodes to specified size and shape, using cutoff saw. Removes workpiece from fixture, using tongs, and cools workpiece, using air or water. Cleans joints of workpieces by using wire brush or by dipping them into cleaning solution. Examines seam and rebrazes defective joints or broken parts. Connects hoses from torch to regulator valves and cylinders of oxygen and specified fuel gas, acetylene or natural. Turns valves to start flow of gases, lights flame, and adjusts valves to obtain desired color and size of flame. Brushes flux onto joint of workpiece or dips braze rod into flux to prevent oxidation of metal. Aligns and secures workpieces in fixtures, jigs, or vise, using rule, square, or template. Melts and separates brazed joints to remove and straighten damaged or misaligned components, using hand torch or furnace. Selects torch tip, flux, and brazing alloy from data charts or work order. Adjusts electric current and timing cycle of resistance welding machine to heat metal to bonding temperature. **SKILLS—Operation and Control:** Controlling operations of equipment or systems. **Equipment Selection:** Determining the kind of tools and equipment needed to do a job. **Operation Monitoring:** Watching gauges, dials, or other indicators to make sure a machine is working properly. **Installation:** Installing equipment, machines, wiring, or programs to meet specifications. **Monitoring:** Monitoring/Assessing your performance or that of other individuals or organizations to make improvements or take corrective action.

GOE INFORMATION—Interest Area: 08. Industrial Production. **Work Group:** 08.03. Production Work. **Other Job Titles in This Work Group:** Bakers, Manufacturing; Bindery Machine Operators and Tenders; Cementing and Gluing Machine Operators and Tenders; Chemical Equipment Controllers and Operators; Chemical Equipment Operators and Tenders; Chemical Equipment Tenders; Cleaning, Washing, and Metal Pickling Equipment Operators and Tenders; Coating, Painting, and Spraying Machine Operators and Tenders; Coil Winders, Tapers, and Finishers; Combination Machine Tool Operators and Tenders, Metal and Plastic; Computer-Controlled Machine Tool Operators, Metal and Plastic; Cooling and Freezing Equipment Operators and Tenders; Crushing, Grinding, and Polishing Machine Setters, Operators, and Tenders; Cutters and Trimmers, Hand; Cutting and Slicing Machine Operators and Tenders; Cutting and Slicing Machine Setters, Operators, and Tenders; Design Printing Machine Setters and Set-Up Operators; Electrolytic Plating and Coating Machine Operators and Tenders, Metal and Plastic; Electrolytic Plating and Coating Machine Setters and Set-Up Operators, Metal and Plastic; Electrotypers and Stereotypers; Embossing Machine Set-Up Operators; Engraver Set-Up Operators; Extruding and Forming Machine Operators and Tenders, Synthetic or Glass Fibers; Extruding and Forming Machine Setters, Operators, and Tenders, Synthetic and Glass Fibers; Extruding, Forming, Pressing, and Compacting Machine Operators and Tenders; Fabric and Apparel Patternmakers; Fiber Product Cutting Machine Setters and Set-Up Operators; Fiberglass Laminators and Fabricators; Film Laboratory Technicians; Fitters, Structural Metal—Precision; Food and Tobacco Roasting, Baking, and Drying Machine Operators and Tenders; Food Batchmakers; Food Cooking Machine Operators and Tenders; Furnace, Kiln, Oven, Drier, and Kettle Operators and Tenders; Glass Cutting Machine Setters and Set-Up Operators; Graders and Sorters, Agricultural Products; Grinding and Polishing Workers, Hand; Hand Compositors and Typesetters; Heaters, Metal and Plastic; others. **PERSONALITY TYPE—**Realistic. Realistic occupations frequently involve work activities that include practical, hands-on problems and solutions. They often deal with plants, animals, and real-world materials like wood, tools, and machinery. Many of the occupations require working outside and do not involve a lot of paperwork or working closely with others.

EDUCATION/TRAINING PROGRAM(S)—Welding Technology/Welder. **RELATED KNOWLEDGE/ COURSES—Engineering and Technology:** Knowledge of the practical application of engineering science and technology. This includes applying principles, techniques, procedures, and equipment to the design and production of various goods and services. **Principles of Mechanical Devices:** Knowledge of machines and tools, including their designs, uses, repair, and maintenance. **Production and Processing:** Knowledge of raw materials, production processes, quality control, costs, and other techniques for maximizing the effective manufacture and distribution of goods. **Building and Construction:** Knowledge of materials, methods, and tools involved in the construction or repair of houses, buildings, or other structures, such as highways and roads. **Chemistry:** Knowledge of the chemical composition, structure, and properties of substances and of the chemical processes and transformations that they undergo. This includes uses of chemicals and their interactions, danger signs, production techniques, and disposal methods.

Brickmasons and Blockmasons

▲ Education/Training Required: Bachelor's degree
▲ Annual Earnings: $25,350
▲ Growth: 8.5%
▲ Annual Job Openings: 69,000
▲ Self-Employed: 0%
▲ Part-Time: 12.8%

Lay and bind building materials, such as brick, structural tile, concrete block, cinder block, glass block, and terra-cotta block, with mortar and other substances to construct or repair walls, partitions, arches, sewers, and other structures. Lays and aligns bricks, blocks, or tiles to build or repair structures or high-temperature equipment, such as cupola, kilns, ovens, or furnaces. Applies and smoothes mortar or other mixture over work surface and removes excess, using trowel and hand tools. Examines brickwork or structure to determine need for repair. Measures distance from reference points and marks guidelines to lay out work, using plumb bobs and levels. Breaks or cuts bricks, tiles, or blocks to size, using edge of trowel, hammer, or power saw. Removes burned or damaged brick or mortar, using sledgehammer, crowbar, chipping gun, or chisel. Sprays or spreads refractory material over brickwork to protect against deterioration. Cleans working surface to remove scale, dust, soot, or chips of brick and mortar, using broom, wire brush, or scraper. Fastens or fuses brick or other building material to structure with wire clamps, anchor holes, torch, or cement. Mixes specified amount of sand, clay, dirt, or mortar powder with water to form refractory mixture. Calculates angles and courses and determines vertical and horizontal alignment of courses. **SKILLS—Mathematics:** Using mathematics to solve problems. **Equipment Selection:** Determining the kind of tools and equipment needed to do a job. **Repairing:** Repairing machines or systems, using the needed tools. **Coordination:** Adjusting actions in relation to others' actions.

GOE INFORMATION—Interest Area: 06. Construction, Mining, and Drilling. **Work Group:** 06.02. Construction. **Other Job Titles in This Work Group:** Boat Builders and Shipwrights; Boilermakers; Brattice Builders; Carpenters; Carpet Installers; Ceiling Tile Installers; Cement Masons and Concrete Finishers; Commercial Divers; Construction Carpenters; Drywall and Ceiling Tile Installers; Drywall Installers; Electricians; Explosives Workers, Ordnance Handling Experts, and Blasters; Fence Erectors; Floor Layers, Except Carpet, Wood, and Hard Tiles; Floor Sanders and Finishers; Glaziers; Grader, Bulldozer, and Scraper Operators; Hazardous Materials Removal Workers; Insulation Workers, Floor, Ceiling, and Wall; Insulation Workers, Mechanical; Manufactured Building and Mobile Home Installers; Operating Engineers; Operating Engineers and Other Construction Equipment Operators; Painters, Construction and Maintenance; Paperhangers; Paving, Surfacing, and Tamping Equipment Operators; Pile-Driver Operators; Pipe Fitters; Pipelayers; Pipelaying Fitters; Plasterers and Stucco Masons; Plumbers; Plumbers, Pipefitters, and Steamfitters; Rail-Track Laying and Maintenance Equipment Operators; Refractory Materials Repairers, Except Brickmasons; Reinforcing Iron and Rebar Workers; Riggers; Roofers; Rough Carpenters; Security and Fire Alarm Systems Installers; Segmental Pavers; Sheet Metal Workers; Ship Carpenters and Joiners; Stone Cutters and Carvers; Stonemasons; Structural Iron and Steel Workers; Tapers; Terrazzo Workers and Finishers; Tile and Marble Setters. **PERSONALITY TYPE—**Realistic. Realistic occupations frequently involve work activities that include practical, hands-on problems and solutions. They often deal with plants, animals, and real-world materials like wood, tools, and machinery. Many of the occupations require working outside and do not involve a lot of paperwork or working closely with others.

EDUCATION/TRAINING PROGRAM(S)—Mason/ Masonry. **RELATED KNOWLEDGE/COURSES— Building and Construction:** Knowledge of materials, methods, and tools involved in the construction or repair

of houses, buildings, or other structures, such as highways and roads. **Principles of Mechanical Devices:** Knowledge of machines and tools, including their designs, uses, repair, and maintenance. **Mathematics:** Knowledge of arithmetic, algebra, geometry, calculus, and statistics and their applications. **Physics:** Knowledge and prediction of physical principles and laws and their interrelationships and applications to understanding fluid, material, and atmospheric dynamics and mechanical, electrical, atomic, and sub-atomic structures and processes.

Budget Analysts

▲ Education/Training Required: Bachelor's degree
▲ Annual Earnings: $50,510
▲ Growth: 14.6%
▲ Annual Job Openings: 8,000
▲ Self-Employed: 0%
▲ Part-Time: 7.2%

Examine budget estimates for completeness, accuracy, and conformance with procedures and regulations. Analyze budgeting and accounting reports for the purpose of maintaining expenditure controls. Analyzes accounting records to determine financial resources required to implement program and submits recommendations for budget allocations. Consults with unit heads to ensure adjustments are made in accordance with program changes to facilitate long-term planning. Testifies regarding proposed budgets before examining and fund-granting authorities to clarify reports and gain support for estimated budget needs. Directs compilation of data based on statistical studies and analyses of past and current years to prepare budgets. Directs preparation of regular and special budget reports to interpret budget directives and to establish policies for carrying out directives. Reviews operating budgets periodically to analyze trends affecting budget needs. Recommends approval or disapproval of requests for funds. Advises staff on cost analysis and fiscal allocations. Correlates appropriations for specific programs with appropriations for divisional programs and includes items for emergency funds. Analyzes costs in relation to services performed during previous fiscal years to prepare comparative analyses of operating programs. **SKILLS—Management of Financial Resources:** Determining how money will be spent to get the work done and accounting for these expenditures. **Judgment and Decision Making:** Considering the relative costs and benefits of potential actions to choose the most appropriate one. **Mathematics:** Using mathematics to solve problems. **Systems Analy-**

sis: Determining how a system should work and how changes in conditions, operations, and the environment will affect outcomes. **Critical Thinking:** Using logic and reasoning to identify the strengths and weaknesses of alternative solutions, conclusions, or approaches to problems. **Systems Evaluation:** Identifying measures or indicators of system performance and the actions needed to improve or correct performance relative to the goals of the system.

GOE INFORMATION—Interest Area: 13. General Management and Support. **Work Group:** 13.02. Management Support. **Other Job Titles in This Work Group:** Accountants; Accountants and Auditors; Appraisers and Assessors of Real Estate; Appraisers, Real Estate; Assessors; Auditors; Claims Adjusters, Examiners, and Investigators; Claims Examiners, Property and Casualty Insurance; Compensation, Benefits, and Job Analysis Specialists; Cost Estimators; Credit Analysts; Employment Interviewers, Private or Public Employment Service; Employment, Recruitment, and Placement Specialists; Financial Analysts; Human Resources, Training, and Labor Relations Specialists, All Other; Insurance Adjusters, Examiners, and Investigators; Insurance Appraisers, Auto Damage; Insurance Underwriters; Loan Counselors; Loan Officers; Logisticians; Management Analysts; Market Research Analysts; Personnel Recruiters; Purchasing Agents and Buyers, Farm Products; Purchasing Agents, Except Wholesale, Retail, and Farm Products; Tax Examiners, Collectors, and Revenue Agents; Training and Development

Specialists; Wholesale and Retail Buyers, Except Farm Products. **PERSONALITY TYPE**—Conventional. Conventional occupations frequently involve following set procedures and routines. These occupations can include working with data and details more than with ideas. Usually there is a clear line of authority to follow.

EDUCATION/TRAINING PROGRAM(S)—Accounting; Finance, General. **RELATED KNOWLEDGE/ COURSES**—**Economics and Accounting:** Knowledge of economic and accounting principles and practices, the financial markets, banking, and the analysis and reporting of financial data. **Mathematics:** Knowledge of arithmetic, algebra, geometry, calculus, and statistics and their applications. **Administration and Management:** Knowledge of business and management principles involved in strategic planning, resource allocation, human resources modeling, leadership technique, production methods, and coordination of people and resources. **Computers and Electronics:** Knowledge of circuit boards, processors, chips, electronic equipment, and computer hardware and software, including applications and programming. **English Language:** Knowledge of the structure and content of the English language, including the meaning and spelling of words, rules of composition, and grammar.

Bus and Truck Mechanics and Diesel Engine Specialists

- ▲ Education/Training Required: Postsecondary vocational training
- ▲ Annual Earnings: $33,570
- ▲ Growth: 14.2%
- ▲ Annual Job Openings: 20,000
- ▲ Self-Employed: 4.8%
- ▲ Part-Time: 2.9%

Diagnose, adjust, repair, or overhaul trucks, buses, and all types of diesel engines. Includes mechanics working primarily with automobile diesel engines. Inspects defective equipment and diagnoses malfunctions, using test instruments such as motor analyzers, chassis charts, and pressure gauges. Reads job orders and observes and listens to operating equipment to ensure conformance to specifications or to determine malfunctions. Adjusts brakes, aligns wheels, tightens bolts and screws, and reassembles equipment. Operates valve-grinding machine to grind and reset valves. Examines and adjusts protective guards, loose bolts, and specified safety devices. Changes oil, checks batteries, repairs tires and tubes, and lubricates equipment and machinery. Attaches test instruments to equipment and reads dials and gauges to diagnose malfunctions. Reconditions and replaces parts, pistons, bearings, gears, and valves. Inspects and verifies dimensions and clearances of parts to ensure conformance to factory specifications. Inspects, repairs, and maintains automotive and mechanical equipment and machinery, such as pumps and compressors. Disassembles and overhauls internal combustion engines, pumps, generators, transmissions, clutches, and rear ends. **SKILLS—Repairing:** Repairing machines or systems, using the needed tools. **Troubleshooting:** Determining causes of operating errors and deciding what to do about them. **Equipment Maintenance:** Performing routine maintenance on equipment and determining when and what kind of maintenance is needed. **Installation:** Installing equipment, machines, wiring, or programs to meet specifications. **Quality Control Analysis:** Conducting tests and inspections of products, services, or processes to evaluate quality or performance.

GOE INFORMATION—Interest Area: 05. Mechanics, Installers, and Repairers. **Work Group:** 05.03. Mechanical Work. **Other Job Titles in This Work Group:** Aircraft Body and Bonded Structure Repairers; Aircraft Engine Specialists; Aircraft Mechanics and Service Technicians; Airframe-and-Power-Plant Mechanics; Automotive Body and Related Repairers; Automotive Glass Installers and Repairers; Automotive Master Mechanics; Automotive Service Technicians and Mechanics; Automotive Specialty Technicians; Bicycle Repairers; Bridge and Lock Tenders; Camera and Photographic Equipment Repairers; Coin, Vending, and Amusement Machine Servicers and Repairers; Control and Valve Installers and Repairers, Except Mechanical Door; Farm Equipment Mechanics; Gas Appliance Repairers; Hand and Portable Power Tool Repairers; Heating and Air Conditioning Mechanics; Heating, Air Conditioning, and Refrigeration Mechanics and Installers; Helpers—Electricians; Helpers—Installation, Maintenance, and Repair Workers; Industrial Machinery Mechanics; Keyboard Instrument Repairers and Tuners; Locksmiths and Safe Repairers; Maintenance and Repair Workers, General; Maintenance Workers, Machinery;

Mechanical Door Repairers; Medical Appliance Technicians; Medical Equipment Repairers; Meter Mechanics; Millwrights; Mobile Heavy Equipment Mechanics, Except Engines; Motorboat Mechanics; Motorcycle Mechanics; Musical Instrument Repairers and Tuners; Ophthalmic Laboratory Technicians; Optical Instrument Assemblers; Outdoor Power Equipment and Other Small Engine Mechanics; Painters, Transportation Equipment; Percussion Instrument Repairers and Tuners; Precision Instrument and Equipment Repairers, All Other; Rail Car Repairers; Railroad Inspectors; Recreational Vehicle Service Technicians; Reed or Wind Instrument Repairers and Tuners; Refrigeration Mechanics; Stringed Instrument Repairers and Tuners; Tire Repairers and Changers; Valve and Regulator Repairers; Watch Repairers. **PERSONALITY TYPE**—Realistic. Realistic occupations frequently involve work activities that include practical, hands-on problems and solutions. They often deal with plants, animals, and real-world materials like wood, tools, and machinery. Many of the occupations require working outside and do not involve a lot of paperwork or working closely with others.

EDUCATION/TRAINING PROGRAM(S)—Diesel Mechanics Technology/Technician; Medium/Heavy Vehicle and Truck Technology/Technician. **RELATED KNOWLEDGE/COURSES—Principles of Mechanical Devices:** Knowledge of machines and tools, including their designs, uses, repair, and maintenance. **Engineering and Technology:** Knowledge of the practical application of engineering science and technology. This includes applying principles, techniques, procedures, and equipment to the design and production of various goods and services. **Public Safety and Security:** Knowledge of relevant equipment, policies, procedures, and strategies to promote effective local, state, or national security operations for the protection of people, data, property, and institutions. **Physics:** Knowledge and prediction of physical principles and laws and their interrelationships and applications to understanding fluid, material, and atmospheric dynamics and mechanical, electrical, atomic, and sub-atomic structures and processes.

Bus Drivers, School

▲ Education/Training Required: Short-term on-the-job training
▲ Annual Earnings: $21,990
▲ Growth: 11.6%
▲ Annual Job Openings: 63,000
▲ Self-Employed: 0%
▲ Part-Time: 43.3%

Transport students or special clients, such as the elderly or persons with disabilities. Ensure adherence to safety rules. May assist passengers in boarding or exiting. Drives bus to transport pupils over specified routes. Reports delays or accidents. Regulates heating, lighting, and ventilating systems for passenger comfort. Complies with local traffic regulations. Maintains order among pupils during trip. Inspects bus and checks gas, oil, and water levels. Makes minor repairs to bus. **SKILLS—Operation and Control:** Controlling operations of equipment or systems. **Operation Monitoring:** Watching gauges, dials, or other indicators to make sure a machine is working properly. **Repairing:** Repairing machines or systems, using the needed tools.

GOE INFORMATION—Interest Area: 07. Transportation. **Work Group:** 07.07. Other Services Requiring Driving. **Other Job Titles in This Work Group:** Ambulance Drivers and Attendants, Except Emergency Medical Technicians; Bus Drivers, Transit and Intercity; Driver/Sales Workers; Parking Lot Attendants; Taxi Drivers and Chauffeurs. **PERSONALITY TYPE**—Realistic. Realistic occupations frequently involve work activities that include practical, hands-on problems and solutions. They often deal with plants, animals, and real-world materials like wood, tools, and machinery. Many of the occupations require working outside and do not involve a lot of paperwork or working closely with others.

EDUCATION/TRAINING PROGRAM(S)—Truck and Bus Driver/Commercial Vehicle Operation. **RELATED KNOWLEDGE/COURSES—Transportation:** Knowledge of principles and methods for moving people or goods by air, rail, sea, or road, including the relative costs and benefits. **Public Safety and Security:** Knowledge of relevant equipment, policies, procedures, and strategies to promote effective local, state, or national security operations for the protection of people, data, property, and institutions. **Customer and Personal Service:** Knowledge of principles and processes for providing customer and personal services. This includes customer needs assessment, meeting quality standards for services, and evaluation of customer satisfaction. **Geography:** Knowledge of principles and methods for describing the features of land, sea, and air masses, including their physical characteristics, locations, interrelationships, and distribution of plant, animal, and human life. **Law and Government:** Knowledge of laws, legal codes, court procedures, precedents, government regulations, executive orders, agency rules, and the democratic political process.

Bus Drivers, Transit and Intercity

- ▲ Education/Training Required: Moderate-term on-the-job training
- ▲ Annual Earnings: $28,060
- ▲ Growth: 17.4%
- ▲ Annual Job Openings: 24,000
- ▲ Self-Employed: 6.1%
- ▲ Part-Time: 43.3%

Drive bus or motor coach, including regular route operations, charters, and private carriage. May assist passengers with baggage. May collect fares or tickets. Drives vehicle over specified route or to specified destination according to time schedule to transport passengers, complying with traffic regulations. Assists passengers with baggage and collects tickets or cash fares. Parks vehicle at loading area for passengers to board. Loads and unloads baggage in baggage compartment. Advises passengers to be seated and orderly while on vehicle. Inspects vehicle and checks gas, oil, and water before departure. Makes minor repairs to vehicle and changes tires. Reports delays or accidents. Records cash receipts and ticket fares. Regulates heating, lighting, and ventilating systems for passenger comfort. **SKILLS—Operation and Control:** Controlling operations of equipment or systems. **Repairing:** Repairing machines or systems, using the needed tools. **Operation Monitoring:** Watching gauges, dials, or other indicators to make sure a machine is working properly. **Service Orientation:** Actively looking for ways to help people. **Time Management:** Managing one's own time and the time of others.

GOE INFORMATION—Interest Area: 07. Transportation. **Work Group:** 07.07. Other Services Requiring Driving. **Other Job Titles in This Work Group:** Ambulance Drivers and Attendants, Except Emergency Medical Technicians; Bus Drivers, School; Driver/Sales Workers; Parking Lot Attendants; Taxi Drivers and Chauffeurs.

PERSONALITY TYPE—Realistic. Realistic occupations frequently involve work activities that include practical, hands-on problems and solutions. They often deal with plants, animals, and real-world materials like wood, tools, and machinery. Many of the occupations require working outside and do not involve a lot of paperwork or working closely with others.

EDUCATION/TRAINING PROGRAM(S)—Truck and Bus Driver/Commercial Vehicle Operation. **RELATED KNOWLEDGE/COURSES—Transportation:** Knowledge of principles and methods for moving people or goods by air, rail, sea, or road, including the relative costs and benefits. **Geography:** Knowledge of principles and methods for describing the features of land, sea, and air masses, including their physical characteristics, locations, interrelationships, and distribution of plant, animal, and human life. **Principles of Mechanical Devices:** Knowledge of machines and tools, including their designs, uses, repair, and maintenance. **Public Safety and Security:** Knowledge of relevant equipment, policies, procedures, and strategies to promote effective local, state, or national security operations for the protection of people, data, property, and institutions. **Customer and Personal Service:** Knowledge of principles and processes for providing customer needs assessment, meeting quality standards for services, and evaluation of customer satisfaction.

Business Teachers, Postsecondary

▲ Education/Training Required: Master's degree
▲ Annual Earnings: $54,280
▲ Growth: 23.5%
▲ Annual Job Openings: 184,000
▲ Self-Employed: 0%
▲ Part-Time: 32.3%

Teach courses in business administration and management, such as accounting, finance, human resources, labor relations, marketing, and operations research. **SKILLS**—No data available.

GOE INFORMATION—**Interest Area:** 12. Education and Social Service. **Work Group:** 12.03. Educational Services. **Other Job Titles in This Work Group:** Adult Literacy, Remedial Education, and GED Teachers and Instructors; Agricultural Sciences Teachers, Postsecondary; Anthropology and Archeology Teachers, Postsecondary; Architecture Teachers, Postsecondary; Archivists; Area, Ethnic, and Cultural Studies Teachers, Postsecondary; Art, Drama, and Music Teachers, Postsecondary; Atmospheric, Earth, Marine, and Space Sciences Teachers, Postsecondary; Audio-Visual Collections Specialists; Biological Science Teachers, Postsecondary; Chemistry Teachers, Postsecondary; Child Care Workers; Communications Teachers, Postsecondary; Computer Science Teachers, Postsecondary; Criminal Justice and Law Enforcement Teachers, Postsecondary; Curators; Economics Teachers, Postsecondary; Education Teachers, Postsecondary; Educational Psychologists; Educational, Vocational, and School Counselors; Elementary School Teachers, Except Special Education; Engineering Teachers, Postsecondary; English Language and Literature Teachers, Postsecondary; Environmental Science Teachers, Postsecondary; Farm and Home Management Advisors; Foreign Language and Literature Teachers, Postsecondary; Forestry and Conservation Science Teachers, Postsecondary; Geography Teachers, Postsecondary; Graduate Teaching Assistants; Health Specialties Teachers, Postsecondary; History Teachers, Postsecondary; Home Economics Teachers, Postsecondary; Kindergarten Teachers, Except Special Education; Law Teachers, Postsecondary; Librarians; Library Assistants, Clerical; Library Science Teachers, Postsecondary; Library Technicians; Mathematical Science Teachers, Postsecondary; Middle School Teachers, Except Special and Vocational Education; Museum Technicians and Conservators; Nursing Instructors and Teachers, Postsecondary; Personal Financial Advisors; Philosophy and Religion Teachers, Postsecondary; Physics Teachers, Postsecondary; Political Science Teachers, Postsecondary; Postsecondary Teachers, All Other; Preschool Teachers, Except Special Education; others. **PERSONALITY TYPE**—No data available.

EDUCATION/TRAINING PROGRAM(S)—Accounting; Actuarial Science; Business Administration and Management, General; Business Statistics; Business Teacher Education; Business/Commerce, General; Business/Corporate Communications; Entrepreneurship/Entrepreneurial Studies; Finance, General; Financial Planning and Services; Franchising and Franchise Operations; Human Resources Management/Personnel Administration, General; Insurance; International Business/Trade/Commerce; International Finance; International Marketing; Investments and Securities; Labor and Industrial Relations; Logistics and Materials Management; Management Science, General; Marketing Research; Marketing/Marketing Management, General; Operations Management and Supervision; Organizational Behavior Studies; Public Finance; Purchasing, Procurement/Acquisitions, and Contracts Management. **RELATED KNOWLEDGE/ COURSES**—No data available.

Calibration and Instrumentation Technicians

▲ Education/Training Required: Associate's degree
▲ Annual Earnings: $42,130
▲ Growth: 10.8%
▲ Annual Job Openings: 22,000
▲ Self-Employed: 2.2%
▲ Part-Time: 3.1%

Develop, test, calibrate, operate, and repair electrical, mechanical, electromechanical, electrohydraulic, or electronic measuring and recording instruments, apparatus, and equipment. Plans sequence of testing and calibration program for instruments and equipment according to blueprints, schematics, technical manuals, and other specifications. Performs preventative and corrective maintenance of test apparatus and peripheral equipment. Confers with engineers, supervisor, and other technical workers to assist with equipment installation, maintenance, and repair techniques. Analyzes and converts test data, using mathematical formulas, and reports results and proposed modifications. Sets up test equipment and conducts tests on performance and reliability of mechanical, structural, or electromechanical equipment. Selects sensing, telemetering, and recording instrumentation and circuitry. Disassembles and reassembles instruments and equipment, using hand tools, and inspects instruments and equipment for defects. Sketches plans for developing jigs, fixtures, instruments, and related nonstandard apparatus. Modifies performance and operation of component parts and circuitry to specifications, using test equipment and precision instruments. **SKILLS—Technology Design:** Generating or adapting equipment and technology to serve user needs. **Equipment Selection:** Determining the kind of tools and equipment needed to do a job. **Quality Control Analysis:** Conducting tests and inspections of products, services, or processes to evaluate quality or performance. **Equipment Maintenance:** Performing routine maintenance on equipment and determining when and what kind of maintenance is needed. **Active Listening:** Giving full attention to what other people are saying, taking time to understand the points being made, asking questions as appropriate, and not interrupting at inappropriate times. **Mathematics:** Using mathematics to solve problems.

GOE INFORMATION—Interest Area: 02. Science, Math, and Engineering. **Work Group:** 02.08. Engineering Technology. **Other Job Titles in This Work Group:**

Aerospace Engineering and Operations Technicians; Architectural and Civil Drafters; Architectural Drafters; Cartographers and Photogrammetrists; Civil Drafters; Civil Engineering Technicians; Construction and Building Inspectors; Drafters, All Other; Electrical and Electronic Engineering Technicians; Electrical and Electronics Drafters; Electrical Drafters; Electrical Engineering Technicians; Electro-Mechanical Technicians; Electronic Drafters; Electronics Engineering Technicians; Engineering Technicians, Except Drafters, All Other; Environmental Engineering Technicians; Industrial Engineering Technicians; Mapping Technicians; Mechanical Drafters; Mechanical Engineering Technicians; Numerical Tool and Process Control Programmers; Pressure Vessel Inspectors; Surveying and Mapping Technicians; Surveying Technicians; Surveyors. **PERSONALITY TYPE—**Realistic. Realistic occupations frequently involve work activities that include practical, hands-on problems and solutions. They often deal with plants, animals, and real-world materials like wood, tools, and machinery. Many of the occupations require working outside and do not involve a lot of paperwork or working closely with others.

EDUCATION/TRAINING PROGRAM(S)—Computer Engineering Technology/Technician; Computer Technology/Computer Systems Technology; Electrical and Electronic Engineering Technologies/Technicians, Other; Electrical, Electronic and Communications Engineering Technology/Technician; Telecommunications Technology/Technician. **RELATED KNOWLEDGE/COURSES—Design:** Knowledge of design techniques, tools, and principles involved in production of precision technical plans, blueprints, drawings, and models. **Mathematics:** Knowledge of arithmetic, algebra, geometry, calculus, and statistics and their applications. **Principles of Mechanical Devices:** Knowledge of machines and tools, including their designs, uses, repair, and maintenance. **Engineering and Technology:** Knowledge of the practical application of engineering science and technology. This includes applying principles, techniques, procedures, and equipment to the design and production of various goods and services. **Com-**

puters and Electronics: Knowledge of circuit boards, processors, chips, electronic equipment, and computer hardware and software, including applications and programming.

Camera Operators, Television, Video, and Motion Picture

▲ Education/Training Required: Moderate-term on-the-job training
▲ Annual Earnings: $28,980
▲ Growth: 25.8%
▲ Annual Job Openings: 3,000
▲ Self-Employed: 5.5%
▲ Part-Time: 23.1%

Operate television, video, or motion picture camera to photograph images or scenes for various purposes, such as TV broadcasts, advertising, video production, or motion pictures. Sets up cameras, optical printers, and related equipment to produce photographs and special effects. Adjusts position and controls of camera, printer, and related equipment to produce desired effects, using precision measuring instruments. Selects cameras, accessories, equipment, and film stock to use during filming, using knowledge of filming techniques, requirements, and computations. Reads work order to determine specifications and location of subject material. Views film to resolve problems of exposure control, subject and camera movement, changes in subject distance, and related variables. Observes set or location for potential problems and to determine filming and lighting requirements. Analyzes specifications to determine work procedures, sequence of operations, and machine setup. Reads charts and computes ratios to determine variables, such as lighting, shutter angles, filter factors, and camera distance. Instructs camera operators regarding camera setup, angles, distances, movement, and other variables and cues for starting and stopping filming. Exposes frames of film in sequential order and regulates exposures and aperture to obtain special effects. Confers with director and electrician regarding interpretation of scene, desired effects, and filming and lighting requirements. **SKILLS—Operation and Control:** Controlling operations of equipment or systems. **Technology Design:** Generating or adapting equipment and technology to serve user needs. **Mathematics:** Using mathematics to solve problems. **Equipment Selection:** Determining the kind of tools and equipment needed to do a job. **Reading Comprehension:** Understanding written sentences and paragraphs in work-related documents.

GOE INFORMATION—**Interest Area:** 01. Arts, Entertainment, and Media. **Work Group:** 01.08. Media Technology. **Other Job Titles in This Work Group:** Audio and Video Equipment Technicians; Broadcast Technicians; Film and Video Editors; Media and Communication Equipment Workers, All Other; Photographers; Professional Photographers; Radio Operators; Sound Engineering Technicians. **PERSONALITY TYPE**—Artistic. Artistic occupations frequently involve working with forms, designs, and patterns. They often require self-expression, and the work can be done without following a clear set of rules.

EDUCATION/TRAINING PROGRAM(S)—Audiovisual Communications Technologies/Technicians, Other; Cinematography and Film/Video Production; Radio and Television Broadcasting Technology/Technician. **RELATED KNOWLEDGE/COURSES—Fine Arts:** Knowledge of the theory and techniques required to compose, produce, and perform works of music, dance, visual arts, drama, and sculpture. **Telecommunications:** Knowledge of transmission, broadcasting, switching, control, and operation of telecommunications systems. **Physics:** Knowledge and prediction of physical principles and laws and their interrelationships and applications to understanding fluid, material, and atmospheric dynamics and mechanical, electrical, atomic, and sub-atomic structures and processes. **Mathematics:** Knowledge of arithmetic, algebra, geometry, calculus, and statistics and their applications. **Communications and Media:** Knowledge of media production, communication, and dissemination techniques and methods. This includes alternative ways to inform and entertain via written, oral, and visual media.

Caption Writers

- ▲ Education/Training Required: Moderate-term on-the-job training
- ▲ Annual Earnings: $42,450
- ▲ Growth: 28.4%
- ▲ Annual Job Openings: 18,000
- ▲ Self-Employed: 31.2%
- ▲ Part-Time: 18.5%

Write caption phrases of dialogue for hearing-impaired and foreign language-speaking viewers of movie or television productions. Writes captions to describe music and background noises. Watches production and reviews captions simultaneously to determine which caption phrases require editing. Enters commands to synchronize captions with dialogue and place on the screen. Translates foreign language dialogue into English language captions or English dialogue into foreign language captions. Operates computerized captioning system for movies or television productions for hearing-impaired and foreign language–speaking viewers. Oversees encoding of captions to master tape of television production. Discusses captions with directors or producers of movie and television productions. Edits translations for correctness of grammar, punctuation, and clarity of expression. **SKILLS—Writing:** Communicating effectively in writing as appropriate for the needs of the audience. **Reading Comprehension:** Understanding written sentences and paragraphs in work-related documents. **Active Listening:** Giving full attention to what other people are saying, taking time to understand the points being made, asking questions as appropriate, and not interrupting at inappropriate times. **Monitoring:** Monitoring/Assessing your performance or that of other individuals or organizations to make improvements or take corrective action. **Critical Thinking:** Using logic and reasoning to identify the strengths and weaknesses of alternative solutions, conclusions, or approaches to problems. **Operation and Control:** Controlling operations of equipment or systems. **Speaking:** Talking to others to convey information effectively.

GOE INFORMATION—Interest Area: 01. Arts, Entertainment, and Media. **Work Group:** 01.03. News, Broadcasting, and Public Relations. **Other Job Titles in This**

Work Group: Broadcast News Analysts; Interpreters and Translators; Public Relations Specialists; Reporters and Correspondents. **PERSONALITY TYPE—Artistic.** Artistic occupations frequently involve working with forms, designs, and patterns. They often require self-expression, and the work can be done without following a clear set of rules.

EDUCATION/TRAINING PROGRAM(S)—Broadcast Journalism; Business/Corporate Communications; Communication Studies/Speech Communication and Rhetoric; Communication, Journalism, and Related Programs, Other; Creative Writing; English Composition; Family and Consumer Sciences/Human Sciences Communication; Journalism; Mass Communication/Media Studies; Playwriting and Screenwriting; Technical and Business Writing. **RELATED KNOWLEDGE/COURSES—English Language:** Knowledge of the structure and content of the English language, including the meaning and spelling of words, rules of composition, and grammar. **Foreign Language:** Knowledge of the structure and content of a foreign (non-English) language, including the meaning and spelling of words, rules of composition and grammar, and pronunciation. **Communications and Media:** Knowledge of media production, communication, and dissemination techniques and methods. This includes alternative ways to inform and entertain via written, oral, and visual media. **Computers and Electronics:** Knowledge of circuit boards, processors, chips, electronic equipment, and computer hardware and software, including applications and programming. **Clerical Studies:** Knowledge of administrative and clerical procedures and systems, such as word processing, managing files and records, stenography and transcription, designing forms, and other office procedures and terminology.

Cardiovascular Technologists and Technicians

▲ Education/Training Required: Associate's degree
▲ Annual Earnings: $35,010
▲ Growth: 34.9%
▲ Annual Job Openings: 3,000
▲ Self-Employed: 0%
▲ Part-Time: 22.9%

Conduct tests on pulmonary or cardiovascular systems of patients for diagnostic purposes. May conduct or assist in electrocardiograms, cardiac catheterizations, pulmonary-functions, lung capacity, and similar tests. Operates diagnostic imaging equipment to produce contrast enhanced radiographs of heart and cardiovascular system. Injects contrast medium into blood vessels of patient. Conducts electrocardiogram, phonocardiogram, echocardiogram, stress testing, and other cardiovascular tests, using specialized electronic test equipment, recording devices, and laboratory instruments. Operates monitor to measure and record functions of cardiovascular and pulmonary systems as part of cardiac catheterization team. Observes gauges, recorder, and video screens of data analysis system during imaging of cardiovascular system. Conducts tests of pulmonary system, using spirometer and other respiratory testing equipment. Activates fluoroscope and camera to produce images used to guide catheter through cardiovascular system. Records variations in action of heart muscle, using electrocardiograph. Prepares and positions patients for testing. Records test results and other data into patient s record. Reviews test results with physician. Explains testing procedures to patient to obtain cooperation and reduce anxiety. Adjusts equipment and controls according to physicians' orders or established protocol. Alerts physician to abnormalities or changes in patient responses. Enters factors such as amount and quality of radiation beam and filming sequence into computer. Assesses cardiac physiology and calculates valve areas from blood flow velocity measurements. Compares measurements of heart wall thickness and chamber sizes to standard norms to identify abnormalities. Observes ultrasound display screen and listens to signals to acquire data for measurement of blood flow velocities. Records analyses of heart and related structures, using ultrasound equipment. **SKILLS—Reading Comprehension:** Understanding written sentences and paragraphs in work-related documents. **Mathematics:** Using mathematics to solve problems. **Operation Monitoring:** Watching gauges, dials, or other indicators to make sure a machine is working properly.

Active Listening: Giving full attention to what other people are saying, taking time to understand the points being made, asking questions as appropriate, and not interrupting at inappropriate times. **Operation and Control:** Controlling operations of equipment or systems. **Writing:** Communicating effectively in writing as appropriate for the needs of the audience. **Science:** Using scientific rules and methods to solve problems.

GOE INFORMATION—Interest Area: 14. Medical and Health Services. **Work Group:** 14.05. Medical Technology. **Other Job Titles in This Work Group:** Diagnostic Medical Sonographers; Health Technologists and Technicians, All Other; Medical and Clinical Laboratory Technicians; Medical and Clinical Laboratory Technologists; Medical Equipment Preparers; Nuclear Medicine Technologists; Orthotists and Prosthetists; Radiologic Technicians; Radiologic Technologists; Radiologic Technologists and Technicians. **PERSONALITY TYPE—Investigative.** Investigative occupations frequently involve working with ideas and require an extensive amount of thinking. These occupations can involve searching for facts and figuring out problems mentally.

EDUCATION/TRAINING PROGRAM(S)—Cardiopulmonary Technology/Technologist; Cardiovascular Technology/Technologist; Electrocardiograph Technology/Technician; Perfusion Technology/Perfusionist. **RELATED KNOWLEDGE/COURSES—Medicine and Dentistry:** Knowledge of the information and techniques needed to diagnose and treat human injuries, diseases, and deformities. This includes symptoms, treatment alternatives, drug properties and interactions, and preventive health-care measures. **Computers and Electronics:** Knowledge of circuit boards, processors, chips, electronic equipment, and computer hardware and software, including applications and programming. **Biology:** Knowledge of plant and animal organisms and their tissues, cells, functions, interdependencies, and interactions with each other and the environment. **Mathematics:** Knowledge of arithmetic, algebra, geometry, calculus, and statistics and their applications. **English Language:** Knowledge of the structure and content of the English language, including the meaning and spelling of words, rules of composition, and grammar.

Carpenter Assemblers and Repairers

- ▲ Education/Training Required: Moderate-term on-the-job training
- ▲ Annual Earnings: $33,470
- ▲ Growth: 8.2%
- ▲ Annual Job Openings: 161,000
- ▲ Self-Employed: 36.8%
- ▲ Part-Time: 8.1%

Perform a variety of tasks requiring a limited knowledge of carpentry, such as applying siding and weatherboard to building exteriors or assembling and erecting prefabricated buildings. Measures and marks location of studs, leaders, and receptacle openings, using tape measure, template, and marker. Cuts sidings and moldings, sections of weatherboard, openings in sheetrock, and lumber, using hand tools and power tools. Lays out and aligns materials on worktable or in assembly jig according to specified instructions. Removes surface defects, using knife, scraper, wet sponge, electric iron, and sanding tools. Trims overlapping edges of wood or weatherboard, using portable router or power saw and hand tools. Installs prefabricated windows and doors, insulation, wall, ceiling and floor panels, or siding, using adhesives, hoists, hand tools, and power tools. Aligns and fastens materials together, using hand tools and power tools, to form building or bracing. Repairs or replaces defective locks, hinges, cranks, and pieces of wood, using glue, hand tools, and power tools. Applies stain, paint, or crayons to defects and filter to touch up the repaired area. Directs crane operator in positioning floor, wall, ceiling, and roof panel on house foundation. Moves panel or roof section to other work stations or to storage or shipping area, using electric hoist. Studies blueprints, specification sheets, and drawings to determine style and type of window or wall panel required. Fills cracks, seams, depressions, and nail holes with filler. Examines wood surfaces for defects, such as nicks, cracks, or blisters. Measures cut materials to determine conformance to specifications, using tape measure. Realigns windows and screens to fit casements and oils moving parts. **SKILLS— Repairing:** Repairing machines or systems, using the needed tools. **Installation:** Installing equipment, machines, wiring, or programs to meet specifications. **Operation and Control:** Controlling operations of equipment or systems.

GOE INFORMATION—Interest Area: 06. Construction, Mining, and Drilling. **Work Group:** 06.04. Hands-on Work in Construction, Extraction, and Maintenance. **Other Job Titles in This Work Group:** Construction Laborers; Grips and Set-Up Workers, Motion Picture Sets, Studios, and Stages; Helpers, Construction Trades, All Other; Helpers—Brickmasons, Blockmasons, Stonemasons, and Tile and Marble Setters; Helpers—Carpenters; Helpers—Extraction Workers; Helpers—Painters, Paperhangers, Plasterers, and Stucco Masons; Helpers—Pipelayers, Plumbers, Pipefitters, and Steamfitters; Helpers—Roofers; Highway Maintenance Workers; Septic Tank Servicers and Sewer Pipe Cleaners. **PERSONALITY TYPE**—Realistic. Realistic occupations frequently involve work activities that include practical, hands-on problems and solutions. They often deal with plants, animals, and real-world materials like wood, tools, and machinery. Many of the occupations require working outside and do not involve a lot of paperwork or working closely with others.

EDUCATION/TRAINING PROGRAM(S)— Carpentry/Carpenter. **RELATED KNOWLEDGE/ COURSES—Building and Construction:** Knowledge of materials, methods, and tools involved in the construction or repair of houses, buildings, or other structures, such as highways and roads. **Engineering and Technology:** Knowledge of the practical application of engineering science and technology. This includes applying principles, techniques, procedures, and equipment to the design and production of various goods and services. **Principles of Mechanical Devices:** Knowledge of machines and tools, including their designs, uses, repair, and maintenance. **Design:** Knowledge of design techniques, tools, and principles involved in production of precision technical plans, blueprints, drawings, and models. **Mathematics:** Knowledge of arithmetic, algebra, geometry, calculus, and statistics and their applications.

Carpenters

▲ Education/Training Required: Long-term on-the-job training
▲ Annual Earnings: $33,470
▲ Growth: 8.2%
▲ Annual Job Openings: 161,000
▲ Self-Employed: 36.8%
▲ Part-Time: 8.1%

Construct, erect, install, or repair structures and fixtures made of wood, such as concrete forms; building frameworks, including partitions, joists, studding, and rafters; wood stairways; window and door frames; and hardwood floors. May also install cabinets, siding, drywall, and batt or roll insulation. Includes brattice builders who build doors or brattices (ventilation walls or partitions) in underground passageways to control the proper circulation of air through the passageways and to the working places. **SKILLS**—No data available.

GOE INFORMATION—**Interest Area:** 06. Construction, Mining, and Drilling. **Work Group:** 06.02. Construction. **Other Job Titles in This Work Group:** Boat Builders and Shipwrights; Boilermakers; Brattice Builders; Brickmasons and Blockmasons; Carpet Installers; Ceiling Tile Installers; Cement Masons and Concrete Finishers; Commercial Divers; Construction Carpenters; Drywall and Ceiling Tile Installers; Drywall Installers; Electricians; Explosives Workers, Ordnance Handling Experts, and Blasters; Fence Erectors; Floor Layers, Except Carpet, Wood, and Hard Tiles; Floor Sanders and Finishers; Glaziers; Grader, Bulldozer, and Scraper Operators; Hazard-ous Materials Removal Workers; Insulation Workers, Floor, Ceiling, and Wall; Insulation Workers, Mechanical; Manufactured Building and Mobile Home Installers; Operating Engineers; Operating Engineers and Other Construction Equipment Operators; Painters, Construction and Maintenance; Paperhangers; Paving, Surfacing, and Tamping Equipment Operators; Pile-Driver Operators; Pipe Fitters; Pipelayers; Pipelaying Fitters; Plasterers and Stucco Masons; Plumbers; Plumbers, Pipefitters, and Steamfitters; Rail-Track Laying and Maintenance Equipment Operators; Refractory Materials Repairers, Except Brickmasons; Reinforcing Iron and Rebar Workers; Riggers; Roofers; Rough Carpenters; Security and Fire Alarm Systems Installers; Segmental Pavers; Sheet Metal Workers; Ship Carpenters and Joiners; Stone Cutters and Carvers; Stonemasons; Structural Iron and Steel Workers; Tapers; Terrazzo Workers and Finishers; Tile and Marble Setters. **PERSONALITY TYPE**—No data available.

EDUCATION/TRAINING PROGRAM(S)—Carpentry/Carpenter. **RELATED KNOWLEDGE/COURSES**—No data available.

Cashiers

▲ Education/Training Required: Short-term on-the-job training
▲ Annual Earnings: $14,950
▲ Growth: 14.5%
▲ Annual Job Openings: 1,125,000
▲ Self-Employed: 1.1%
▲ Part-Time: 57.2%

Receive and disburse money in establishments other than financial institutions. Usually involves use of electronic scanners, cash registers, or related equipment. Often involved in processing credit or debit card transactions and validating checks. Receives sales slip, cash, check, voucher, or charge payments and issues receipts, refunds, credits, or change due to customer. Learns prices, stocks shelves, marks prices, weighs items, issues trading stamps, and re-deems food stamps and coupons. Monitors checkout stations, issues and removes cash as needed, and assigns workers to reduce customer delay. Resolves customer complaints. Compiles and maintains non-monetary reports and records. Bags, boxes, or wraps merchandise. Answers questions and provides information to customers. Sorts, counts, and wraps currency and coins. Operates cash register or electronic scanner. Cashes checks.

Keeps periodic balance sheet of amount and number of transactions. Sells tickets and other items to customer. Computes and records totals of transactions. **SKILLS—Active Listening:** Giving full attention to what other people are saying, taking time to understand the points being made, asking questions as appropriate, and not interrupting at inappropriate times. **Mathematics:** Using mathematics to solve problems. **Reading Comprehension:** Understanding written sentences and paragraphs in work-related documents. **Service Orientation:** Actively looking for ways to help people. **Writing:** Communicating effectively in writing as appropriate for the needs of the audience. **Speaking:** Talking to others to convey information effectively.

GOE INFORMATION—Interest Area: 09. Business Detail. **Work Group:** 09.05. Customer Service. **Other Job Titles in This Work Group:** Adjustment Clerks; Bill and Account Collectors; Counter and Rental Clerks; Customer Service Representatives; Customer Service Representatives, Utilities; Gaming Cage Workers; Gaming Change Persons and Booth Cashiers; New Accounts Clerks; Order Clerks; Receptionists and Information Clerks; Tellers; Travel Clerks. **PERSONALITY TYPE—**Conventional. Conventional occupations frequently involve following set procedures and routines. These occupations can include working with data and details more than with ideas. Usually there is a clear line of authority to follow.

EDUCATION/TRAINING PROGRAM(S)—Retailing and Retail Operations. **RELATED KNOWLEDGE/ COURSES—Customer and Personal Service:** Knowledge of principles and processes for providing customer and personal services. This includes customer needs assessment, meeting quality standards for services, and evaluation of customer satisfaction. **Clerical Studies:** Knowledge of administrative and clerical procedures and systems, such as word processing, managing files and records, stenography and transcription, designing forms, and other office procedures and terminology. **Mathematics:** Knowledge of arithmetic, algebra, geometry, calculus, and statistics and their applications. **Computers and Electronics:** Knowledge of circuit boards, processors, chips, electronic equipment, and computer hardware and software, including applications and programming. **English Language:** Knowledge of the structure and content of the English language, including the meaning and spelling of words, rules of composition, and grammar.

Casting Machine Set-Up Operators

- ▲ Education/Training Required: Postsecondary vocational training
- ▲ Annual Earnings: $22,340
- ▲ Growth: 9.8%
- ▲ Annual Job Openings: 38,000
- ▲ Self-Employed: 0%
- ▲ Part-Time: 5.5%

Set up and operate machines to cast and assemble printing type. Sets up matrices in assembly stick by hand according to specifications. Positions composing stick to length of line specified in casting instructions. Places reel of controller paper on holder, threads around reels, and attaches to winding roll. Forwards galley to appropriate personnel for proofing. Removes and stores assembly stick, controller reel, and matrix case. Inserts and locks galley or matrix case into place on machine. Stops machine when galley is full or when strip is completed. Starts machine and monitors operation for proper functioning. **SKILLS— Operation and Control:** Controlling operations of equipment or systems. **Operation Monitoring:** Watching gauges, dials, or other indicators to make sure a machine is working properly.

GOE INFORMATION—Interest Area: 08. Industrial Production. **Work Group:** 08.02. Production Technology. **Other Job Titles in This Work Group:** Aircraft Rigging Assemblers; Aircraft Structure Assemblers, Precision; Aircraft Structure, Surfaces, Rigging, and Systems Assemblers; Aircraft Systems Assemblers, Precision; Bench Workers, Jewelry; Bindery Machine Setters and Set-Up Operators; Bindery Workers; Bookbinders; Buffing and Polishing Set-Up Operators; Coating, Painting, and Spraying Machine Setters and Set-Up Operators; Coating, Painting, and Spraying Machine Setters, Operators, and Tenders; Combination Machine Tool Setters and Set-Up Operators, Metal and Plastic; Cutting, Punching, and Press Machine Setters, Operators, and Tenders, Metal and Plastic; Dental Laboratory Technicians; Drilling and Boring Machine Tool Setters, Operators, and Tenders, Metal and Plastic;

Electrical and Electronic Equipment Assemblers; Electrical and Electronic Inspectors and Testers; Electromechanical Equipment Assemblers; Engine and Other Machine Assemblers; Extruding and Drawing Machine Setters, Operators, and Tenders, Metal and Plastic; Extruding, Forming, Pressing, and Compacting Machine Setters and Set-Up Operators; Extruding, Forming, Pressing, and Compacting Machine Setters, Operators, and Tenders; Forging Machine Setters, Operators, and Tenders, Metal and Plastic; Foundry Mold and Coremakers; Gem and Diamond Workers; Grinding, Honing, Lapping, and Deburring Machine Set-Up Operators; Grinding, Lapping, Polishing, and Buffing Machine Tool Setters, Operators, and Tenders, Metal and Plastic; Heat Treating Equipment Setters, Operators, and Tenders, Metal and Plastic; Heat Treating, Annealing, and Tempering Machine Operators and Tenders, Metal and Plastic; Heating Equipment Setters and Set-Up Operators, Metal and Plastic; Inspectors, Testers, Sorters, Samplers, and Weighers; Jewelers; Jewelers and Precious Stone and Metal Workers; Lathe and Turning Machine Tool Setters, Operators, and Tenders, Metal and Plastic; Log Graders and Scalers; Materials Inspectors; Mechanical Inspectors; others. **PERSONALITY TYPE**—Realistic. Realistic occupations frequently involve work activities that include practical, hands-on problems and solutions. They often deal with plants, animals, and real-world materials like wood, tools, and machinery. Many of the occupations require working outside and do not involve a lot of paperwork or working closely with others.

EDUCATION/TRAINING PROGRAM(S)—No data available. **RELATED KNOWLEDGE/COURSES**— **Principles of Mechanical Devices:** Knowledge of machines and tools, including their designs, uses, repair, and maintenance. **Production and Processing:** Knowledge of raw materials, production processes, quality control, costs, and other techniques for maximizing the effective manufacture and distribution of goods. **Engineering and Technology:** Knowledge of the practical application of engineering science and technology. This includes applying principles, techniques, procedures, and equipment to the design and production of various goods and services. **English Language:** Knowledge of the structure and content of the English language, including the meaning and spelling of words, rules of composition, and grammar.

Ceiling Tile Installers

- ▲ Education/Training Required: Moderate-term on-the-job training
- ▲ Annual Earnings: $33,000
- ▲ Growth: 9.4%
- ▲ Annual Job Openings: 19,000
- ▲ Self-Employed: 0%
- ▲ Part-Time: 8.1%

Apply plasterboard or other wallboard to ceilings or interior walls of buildings. Apply or mount acoustical tiles or blocks, strips, or sheets of shock-absorbing materials to ceilings and walls of buildings to reduce or reflect sound. Materials may be of decorative quality. Includes lathers who fasten wooden, metal, or rockboard lath to walls, ceilings, or partitions of buildings to provide support base for plaster, fire-proofing, or acoustical material. Applies acoustical tiles or shock-absorbing materials to ceilings and walls of buildings to reduce or reflect sound and to decorate rooms. Washes concrete surfaces with washing soda and zinc sulfate solution before mounting tile to increase adhesive qualities of surfaces. Inspects furrings, mechanical mountings, and masonry surface for plumbness and level, using spirit or water level. Hangs dry lines (stretched string) to wall molding to guide positioning of main runners. Nails or screws molding to wall to support and seals joint between ceiling tile and wall. Scribes and cuts edges of tile to fit wall where wall molding is not specified. Nails channels or wood furring strips to surfaces to provide mounting for tile. Measures and marks surface to lay out work according to blueprints and drawings. Cuts tiles for fixture and borders, using keyhole saw, and inserts tiles into supporting framework. Applies cement to back of tile and presses tile into place, aligning with layout marks and joints of previously laid tile. **SKILLS—Mathematics:** Using mathematics to solve problems.

GOE INFORMATION—Interest Area: 06. Construction, Mining, and Drilling. **Work Group:** 06.02. Construction. **Other Job Titles in This Work Group:** Boat Builders and Shipwrights; Boilermakers; Brattice Builders; Brickmasons and Blockmasons; Carpenters; Carpet

Installers; Cement Masons and Concrete Finishers; Commercial Divers; Construction Carpenters; Drywall and Ceiling Tile Installers; Drywall Installers; Electricians; Explosives Workers, Ordnance Handling Experts, and Blasters; Fence Erectors; Floor Layers, Except Carpet, Wood, and Hard Tiles; Floor Sanders and Finishers; Glaziers; Grader, Bulldozer, and Scraper Operators; Hazardous Materials Removal Workers; Insulation Workers, Floor, Ceiling, and Wall; Insulation Workers, Mechanical; Manufactured Building and Mobile Home Installers; Operating Engineers; Operating Engineers and Other Construction Equipment Operators; Painters, Construction and Maintenance; Paperhangers; Paving, Surfacing, and Tamping Equipment Operators; Pile-Driver Operators; Pipe Fitters; Pipelayers; Pipelaying Fitters; Plasterers and Stucco Masons; Plumbers; Plumbers, Pipefitters, and Steamfitters; Rail-Track Laying and Maintenance Equipment Operators; Refractory Materials Repairers, Except Brickmasons; Reinforcing Iron and Rebar Workers; Riggers; Roofers; Rough Carpenters; Security and Fire Alarm Systems Installers; Segmental Pavers; Sheet Metal Workers; Ship Carpenters and Joiners; Stone Cutters and Carvers; Stonemasons; Structural Iron and Steel Workers; Tapers; Terrazzo Workers and Finishers; Tile and Marble Setters. **PERSONALITY TYPE**—Realistic. Realistic oc-cupations frequently involve work activities that include practical, hands-on problems and solutions. They often deal with plants, animals, and real-world materials like wood, tools, and machinery. Many of the occupations require working outside and do not involve a lot of paperwork or working closely with others.

EDUCATION/TRAINING PROGRAM(S)—Drywall Installation/Drywaller. **RELATED KNOWLEDGE/ COURSES—Building and Construction:** Knowledge of materials, methods, and tools involved in the construction or repair of houses, buildings, or other structures, such as highways and roads. **Mathematics:** Knowledge of arithmetic, algebra, geometry, calculus, and statistics and their applications. **Design:** Knowledge of design techniques, tools, and principles involved in production of precision technical plans, blueprints, drawings, and models. **Principles of Mechanical Devices:** Knowledge of machines and tools, including their designs, uses, repair, and maintenance. **Engineering and Technology:** Knowledge of the practical application of engineering science and technology. This includes applying principles, techniques, procedures, and equipment to the design and production of various goods and services.

Chefs and Head Cooks

▲ Education/Training Required: Postsecondary vocational training
▲ Annual Earnings: $26,800
▲ Growth: 9.0%
▲ Annual Job Openings: 35,000
▲ Self-Employed: 37.5%
▲ Part-Time: 8.5%

Direct the preparation, seasoning, and cooking of salads, soups, fish, meats, vegetables, desserts, or other foods. May plan and price menu items, order supplies, and keep records and accounts. May participate in cooking. Supervises and coordinates activities of cooks and workers engaged in food preparation. Observes workers and work procedures to ensure compliance with established standards. Evaluates and solves procedural problems to ensure safe and efficient operations. Records production and operational data on specified forms. Inspects supplies, equipment, and work areas to ensure conformance to established standards. Collaborates with specified personnel and plans and develops recipes and menus. Determines production schedules and worker-time requirements to ensure timely delivery of services. Estimates amounts and costs and requisitions supplies and equipment to ensure efficient operation. Helps cooks and workers cook and prepare food on demand. Trains and otherwise instructs cooks and workers in proper food preparation procedures. **SKILLS—Coordination:** Adjusting actions in relation to others' actions. **Instructing:** Teaching others how to do something. **Management of Financial Resources:** Determining how money will be spent to get the work done and accounting for these expenditures. **Management of Material Resources:** Obtaining and seeing to the appropriate use of equipment, facilities, and materials needed to do certain work. **Management of Personnel Resources:** Motivating, developing, and directing people as they work, identifying the best people for the job.

GOE INFORMATION—**Interest Area:** 11. Recreation, Travel, and Other Personal Services. **Work Group:** 11.05. Food and Beverage Services. **Other Job Titles in This Work Group:** Bakers; Bakers, Bread and Pastry; Bartenders; Butchers and Meat Cutters; Combined Food Preparation and Serving Workers, Including Fast Food; Cooks, All Other; Cooks, Fast Food; Cooks, Institution and Cafeteria; Cooks, Restaurant; Cooks, Short Order; Counter Attendants, Cafeteria, Food Concession, and Coffee Shop; Dining Room and Cafeteria Attendants and Bartender Helpers; Dishwashers; Food Preparation and Serving Related Workers, All Other; Food Preparation Workers; Food Servers, Nonrestaurant; Hosts and Hostesses, Restaurant, Lounge, and Coffee Shop; Waiters and Waitresses. **PERSONALITY TYPE**—Enterprising. Enterprising occupations frequently involve starting up and carrying out projects. These occupations can involve leading people and making many decisions. They sometimes require risk taking and often deal with business.

EDUCATION/TRAINING PROGRAM(S)—Cooking and Related Culinary Arts, General; Culinary Arts/Chef Training. **RELATED KNOWLEDGE/COURSES**—**Administration and Management:** Knowledge of business and management principles involved in strategic planning, resource allocation, human resources modeling, leadership technique, production methods, and coordination of people and resources. **Personnel and Human Resources:** Knowledge of principles and procedures for personnel recruitment, selection, training, compensation and benefits, labor relations and negotiation, and personnel information systems. **Economics and Accounting:** Knowledge of economic and accounting principles and practices, the financial markets, banking, and the analysis and reporting of financial data. **Education and Training:** Knowledge of principles and methods for curriculum and training design, teaching and instruction for individuals and groups, and the measurement of training effects. **Mathematics:** Knowledge of arithmetic, algebra, geometry, calculus, and statistics and their applications.

Chemical Equipment Controllers and Operators

- ▲ Education/Training Required: Moderate-term on-the-job training
- ▲ Annual Earnings: $36,810
- ▲ Growth: 14.9%
- ▲ Annual Job Openings: 9,000
- ▲ Self-Employed: 0%
- ▲ Part-Time: 0.3%

Control or operate equipment to control chemical changes or reactions in the processing of industrial or consumer products. Typical equipment used are reaction kettles, catalytic converters, continuous or batch treating equipment, saturator tanks, electrolytic cells, reactor vessels, recovery units, and fermentation chambers. Sets and adjusts indicating, controlling, or timing devices, such as gauging instruments, thermostat, gas analyzers, or recording calorimeter. Moves controls to adjust feed and flow of liquids and gases through equipment in specified sequence. Adjusts controls to regulate temperature, pressure, and time of prescribed reaction according to knowledge of equipment and process. Opens valves or operates pumps to admit or drain specified amounts of materials, impurities, or treating agents to or from equipment. Starts pumps, agitators, reactors, blowers, or automatic feed of materials. Monitors gauges, recording instruments, flowmeters, or product to regulate or maintain specified conditions. Mixes chemicals according to proportion tables or prescribed formulas. Records operational data such as temperature, pressure, ingredients used, processing time, or test results in operating log. Flushes or cleans equipment, using steam hose or mechanical reamer. Draws samples of product and sends to laboratory for analysis. Tests sample for specific gravity, chemical characteristics, pH level, concentration, or viscosity. Patrols and inspects equipment or unit to detect leaks and malfunctions. Weighs or measures specified amounts of materials. Reads plant specifications to ascertain product, ingredient, and prescribed modifications of plant procedures. Dumps or scoops prescribed solid, granular, or powdered materials into equipment. Adds treating or neutralizing agent to product and pumps product through filter or centrifuge to remove impurities or precipitate product. Directs activities of workers assisting in control or verification of process or in unloading materials. Makes minor repairs and lubricates and maintains equipment, using hand tools. Operates or tends auxiliary equipment, such as heaters, scrubbers, filters, or driers, to prepare or further process materials. **SKILLS—Operation Monitoring:** Watching gauges, dials, or other indicators to make sure a machine is working properly. **Operation and Control:** Controlling operations of equipment or systems. **Science:** Using scientific rules and methods to solve problems. **Reading Comprehension:** Understanding written sentences and paragraphs in work-related documents. **Quality Control Analysis:** Conducting tests and inspections of products, services, or processes to evaluate quality or performance.

GOE INFORMATION—Interest Area: 08. Industrial Production. **Work Group:** 08.03. Production Work. **Other Job Titles in This Work Group:** Bakers, Manufacturing; Bindery Machine Operators and Tenders; Brazers; Cementing and Gluing Machine Operators and Tenders; Chemical Equipment Operators and Tenders; Chemical Equipment Tenders; Cleaning, Washing, and Metal Pickling Equipment Operators and Tenders; Coating, Painting, and Spraying Machine Operators and Tenders; Coil Winders, Tapers, and Finishers; Combination Machine Tool Operators and Tenders, Metal and Plastic; Computer-Controlled Machine Tool Operators, Metal and Plastic; Cooling and Freezing Equipment Operators and Tenders; Crushing, Grinding, and Polishing Machine Setters, Operators, and Tenders; Cutters and Trimmers, Hand; Cutting and Slicing Machine Operators and Tenders; Cutting and Slicing Machine Setters, Operators, and Tenders; Design Printing Machine Setters and Set-Up Operators; Electrolytic Plating and Coating Machine Operators and Tenders, Metal and Plastic; Electrolytic Plating and Coating Machine Setters and Set-Up Operators, Metal and Plastic; Electrotypers and Stereotypers; Embossing Machine Set-Up Operators; Engraver Set-Up Operators; Extruding and Forming Machine Operators and Tenders, Synthetic or Glass Fibers; Extruding and Forming Machine Setters, Operators, and Tenders, Synthetic and Glass Fibers; Extruding, Forming, Pressing, and Compacting Machine Operators and Tenders; Fabric and Apparel Patternmakers; Fiber Product Cutting Machine Setters and Set-Up Operators; Fiberglass Laminators and Fabricators; Film Laboratory Technicians; Fitters, Structural Metal—Precision; Food and Tobacco Roasting, Baking, and Drying Machine Operators and Tenders; Food Batchmakers; Food Cooking Machine Operators and Tenders; Furnace, Kiln, Oven, Drier, and Kettle Operators and Tenders; Glass Cutting Machine Setters and Set-Up Operators; Graders and Sorters, Agricultural Products; Grinding and Polishing Workers, Hand; Hand Compositors and Typesetters; Heaters, Metal and Plastic; Helpers—Production Workers; Job Printers; others. **PERSONALITY TYPE—**Realistic. Realistic occupations frequently involve work activities that include practical, hands-on problems and solutions. They often deal with plants, animals, and real-world materials like wood, tools, and machinery. Many of the occupations require working outside and do not involve a lot of paperwork or working closely with others.

EDUCATION/TRAINING PROGRAM(S)—Chemical Technology/Technician. **RELATED KNOWLEDGE/ COURSES—Chemistry:** Knowledge of the chemical composition, structure, and properties of substances and of the chemical processes and transformations that they undergo. This includes uses of chemicals and their interactions, danger signs, production techniques, and disposal methods. **Principles of Mechanical Devices:** Knowledge of machines and tools, including their designs, uses, repair, and maintenance. **Mathematics:** Knowledge of arithmetic, algebra, geometry, calculus, and statistics and their applications. **Engineering and Technology:** Knowledge of the practical application of engineering science and technology. This includes applying principles, techniques, procedures, and equipment to the design and production of various goods and services. **Public Safety and Security:** Knowledge of relevant equipment, policies, procedures, and strategies to promote effective local, state, or national security operations for the protection of people, data, property, and institutions. **English Language:** Knowledge of the structure and content of the English language, including the meaning and spelling of words, rules of composition, and grammar.

Chemical Equipment Operators and Tenders

- ▲ Education/Training Required: Moderate-term on-the-job training
- ▲ Annual Earnings: $36,810
- ▲ Growth: 14.9%
- ▲ Annual Job Openings: 9,000
- ▲ Self-Employed: 0%
- ▲ Part-Time: 0.3%

Operate or tend equipment to control chemical changes or reactions in the processing of industrial or consumer products. Equipment used includes devulcanizers, steam-jacketed kettles, and reactor vessels. SKILLS—No data available.

GOE INFORMATION—Interest Area: 08. Industrial Production. Work Group: 08.03. Production Work. Other Job Titles in This Work Group: Bakers, Manufacturing; Bindery Machine Operators and Tenders; Brazers; Cementing and Gluing Machine Operators and Tenders; Chemical Equipment Controllers and Operators; Chemical Equipment Tenders; Cleaning, Washing, and Metal Pickling Equipment Operators and Tenders; Coating, Painting, and Spraying Machine Operators and Tenders; Coil Winders, Tapers, and Finishers; Combination Machine Tool Operators and Tenders, Metal and Plastic; Computer-Controlled Machine Tool Operators, Metal and Plastic; Cooling and Freezing Equipment Operators and Tenders; Crushing, Grinding, and Polishing Machine Setters, Operators, and Tenders; Cutters and Trimmers, Hand; Cutting and Slicing Machine Operators and Tenders; Cutting and Slicing Machine Setters, Operators, and Tenders; Design Printing Machine Setters and Set-Up Operators; Electrolytic Plating and Coating Machine Operators and Tenders, Metal and Plastic; Electrolytic Plating and Coat-

ing Machine Setters and Set-Up Operators, Metal and Plastic; Electrotypers and Stereotypers; Embossing Machine Set-Up Operators; Engraver Set-Up Operators; Extruding and Forming Machine Operators and Tenders, Synthetic or Glass Fibers; Extruding and Forming Machine Setters, Operators, and Tenders, Synthetic and Glass Fibers; Extruding, Forming, Pressing, and Compacting Machine Operators and Tenders; Fabric and Apparel Patternmakers; Fiber Product Cutting Machine Setters and Set-Up Operators; Fiberglass Laminators and Fabricators; Film Laboratory Technicians; Fitters, Structural Metal—Precision; Food and Tobacco Roasting, Baking, and Drying Machine Operators and Tenders; Food Batchmakers; Food Cooking Machine Operators and Tenders; Furnace, Kiln, Oven, Drier, and Kettle Operators and Tenders; Glass Cutting Machine Setters and Set-Up Operators; Graders and Sorters, Agricultural Products; Grinding and Polishing Workers, Hand; Hand Compositors and Typesetters; Heaters, Metal and Plastic; Helpers—Production Workers; Job Printers; others. PERSONALITY TYPE—No data available.

EDUCATION/TRAINING PROGRAM(S)—Chemical Technology/Technician. RELATED KNOWLEDGE/COURSES—No data available.

Chemical Equipment Tenders

- ▲ Education/Training Required: Moderate-term on-the-job training
- ▲ Annual Earnings: $36,810
- ▲ Growth: 14.9%
- ▲ Annual Job Openings: 9,000
- ▲ Self-Employed: 0%
- ▲ Part-Time: 0.3%

Tend equipment in which a chemical change or reaction takes place in the processing of industrial or consumer products. Typical equipment used are devulcanizers, batch stills, fermenting tanks, steam-jacketed kettles, and reactor vessels. Starts pumps and agitators, turns valves, or moves controls of processing equipment to admit, transfer, filter, or mix chemicals. Inventories supplies received and consumed. Assists other workers in preparing and maintaining equipment. Observes safety precautions to prevent fires and explosions. Notifies maintenance engineer of equipment malfunction. Records data in log from instruments and gauges concerning temperature, pressure, materials used, treating time, and shift production. Tests samples to determine specific gravity, composition, or acidity, using chemical test equipment such as hydrometer or pH meter. Replaces filtering media or makes minor repairs to equipment, using hand tools. Loads specified amounts of chemicals into processing equipment. Patrols work area to detect leaks and equipment malfunctions and monitor operating conditions. Weighs, measures, or mixes prescribed quantities of materials. Draws sample of products for analysis to aid in process adjustments and maintain production standards. Drains equipment and pumps water or other solution through to flush and clean tanks or equipment. Observes gauges, meters, and panel lights to monitor operating conditions, such as temperature or pressure. Adjusts valves or controls to maintain system within specified operating conditions. **SKILLS—Operation Monitoring:** Watching gauges, dials, or other indicators to make sure a machine is working properly. **Operation and Control:** Controlling operations of equipment or systems. **Science:** Using scientific rules and methods to solve problems. **Quality Control Analysis:** Conducting tests and inspections of products, services, or processes to evaluate quality or performance. **Equipment Maintenance:** Performing routine maintenance on equipment and determining when and what kind of maintenance is needed.

GOE INFORMATION—Interest Area: 08. Industrial Production. **Work Group:** 08.03. Production Work. **Other Job Titles in This Work Group:** Bakers, Manufacturing; Bindery Machine Operators and Tenders; Brazers; Cementing and Gluing Machine Operators and Tenders; Chemical Equipment Controllers and Operators; Chemical Equipment Operators and Tenders; Cleaning, Washing, and Metal Pickling Equipment Operators and Tenders; Coating, Painting, and Spraying Machine Operators and Tenders; Coil Winders, Tapers, and Finishers; Combination Machine Tool Operators and Tenders, Metal and Plastic; Computer-Controlled Machine Tool Operators, Metal and Plastic; Cooling and Freezing Equipment Operators and Tenders; Crushing, Grinding, and Polishing Machine Setters, Operators, and Tenders; Cutters and Trimmers, Hand; Cutting and Slicing Machine Operators and Tenders; Cutting and Slicing Machine Setters, Operators, and Tenders; Design Printing Machine Setters and Set-Up Operators; Electrolytic Plating and Coating Machine Operators and Tenders, Metal and Plastic; Electrolytic Plating and Coating Machine Setters and Set-Up Operators, Metal and Plastic; Electrotypers and Stereotypers; Embossing Machine Set-Up Operators; Engraver Set-Up Operators; Extruding and Forming Machine Operators and Tenders, Synthetic or Glass Fibers; Extruding and Forming Machine Setters, Operators, and Tenders, Synthetic and Glass Fibers; Extruding, Forming, Pressing, and Compacting Machine Operators and Tenders; Fabric and Apparel Patternmakers; Fiber Product Cutting Machine Setters and Set-Up Operators; Fiberglass Laminators and Fabricators; Film Laboratory Technicians; Fitters, Structural Metal—Precision; Food and Tobacco Roasting, Baking, and Drying Machine Operators and Tenders; Food Batchmakers; Food Cooking Machine Operators and Tenders; Furnace, Kiln, Oven, Drier, and Kettle Operators and Tenders; Glass Cutting Machine Setters and Set-Up Operators; Graders and Sorters, Agricultural Products; Grinding and Polishing Workers, Hand; Hand Compositors and Typesetters; Heaters, Metal and Plastic; Helpers—Production Workers; others. **PERSONALITY TYPE—Realistic.** Realistic occupations frequently involve work activities that include practical, hands-on problems and solutions. They often deal with plants, animals, and real-world materials like wood, tools, and machinery. Many of the occupations require working outside and do not involve a lot of paperwork or working closely with others.

EDUCATION/TRAINING PROGRAM(S)—Chemical Technology/Technician. **RELATED KNOWLEDGE/ COURSES—Chemistry:** Knowledge of the chemical composition, structure, and properties of substances and of the chemical processes and transformations that they undergo. This includes uses of chemicals and their interactions, danger signs, production techniques, and disposal methods. **Principles of Mechanical Devices:** Knowledge of machines and tools, including their designs, uses, repair, and maintenance. **Mathematics:** Knowledge of arithmetic, algebra, geometry, calculus, and statistics and their applications. **Public Safety and Security:** Knowledge of relevant equipment, policies, procedures, and strategies to promote effective local, state, or national security operations for the protection of people, data, property, and institutions. **Production and Processing:** Knowledge of raw materials, production processes, quality control, costs, and other techniques for maximizing the effective manufacture and distribution of goods.

Chemical Technicians

▲ Education/Training Required: Associate's degree
▲ Annual Earnings: $36,190
▲ Growth: 15.0%
▲ Annual Job Openings: 13,000
▲ Self-Employed: 0.9%
▲ Part-Time: 11.7%

Conduct chemical and physical laboratory tests to assist scientists in making qualitative and quantitative analyses of solids, liquids, and gaseous materials for purposes such as research and development of new products or processes, quality control, maintenance of environmental standards, and other work involving experimental, theoretical, or practical application of chemistry and related sciences. Tests and analyzes chemical and physical properties of liquids, solids, gases, radioactive and biological materials, and products such as perfumes. Documents results of tests and analyses. Writes technical reports or prepares graphs and charts. Directs other workers in compounding and distilling chemicals. Reviews process paperwork for products to ensure compliance to standards and specifications. Cleans and sterilizes laboratory equipment. Prepares chemical solutions for products and processes, following standardized formulas, or creates experimental formulas. Sets up and calibrates laboratory equipment and instruments used for testing, process control, product development, and research. **SKILLS—Science:** Using scientific rules and methods to solve problems. **Reading Comprehension:** Understanding written sentences and paragraphs in work-related documents. **Mathematics:** Using mathematics to solve problems. **Critical Thinking:** Using logic and reasoning to identify the strengths and weaknesses of alternative solutions, conclusions, or approaches to problems. **Active Listening:** Giving full attention to what other people are saying, taking time to understand the points being made, asking questions as appropriate, and not interrupting at inappropriate times. **Writing:** Communicating effectively in writing as appropriate for the needs of the audience.

GOE INFORMATION—Interest Area: 02. Science, Math, and Engineering. **Work Group:** 02.05. Laboratory Technology. **Other Job Titles in This Work Group:** Biological Technicians; Environmental Science and Protection Technicians, Including Health; Geological and Petroleum Technicians; Geological Data Technicians; Geological Sample Test Technicians; Nuclear Equipment Operation Technicians; Nuclear Technicians; Photographers, Scientific. **PERSONALITY TYPE**—Realistic. Realistic occupations frequently involve work activities that include practical, hands-on problems and solutions. They often deal with plants, animals, and real-world materials like wood, tools, and machinery. Many of the occupations require working outside and do not involve a lot of paperwork or working closely with others.

EDUCATION/TRAINING PROGRAM(S)—Chemical Technology/Technician; Food Science. **RELATED KNOWLEDGE/COURSES—Chemistry:** Knowledge of the chemical composition, structure, and properties of substances and of the chemical processes and transformations that they undergo. This includes uses of chemicals and their interactions, danger signs, production techniques, and disposal methods. **Mathematics:** Knowledge of arithmetic, algebra, geometry, calculus, and statistics and their applications. **English Language:** Knowledge of the structure and content of the English language, including the meaning and spelling of words, rules of composition, and grammar. **Physics:** Knowledge and prediction of physical principles and laws and their interrelationships and applications to understanding fluid, material, and atmospheric dynamics and mechanical, electrical, atomic, and subatomic structures and processes. **Engineering and Technology:** Knowledge of the practical application of engineering science and technology. This includes applying principles, techniques, procedures, and equipment to the design and production of various goods and services.

Chemistry Teachers, Postsecondary

- ▲ Education/Training Required: Master's degree
- ▲ Annual Earnings: $53,750
- ▲ Growth: 23.5%
- ▲ Annual Job Openings: 184,000
- ▲ Self-Employed: 0%
- ▲ Part-Time: 32.3%

Teach courses pertaining to the chemical and physical properties and compositional changes of substances. Work may include instruction in the methods of qualitative and quantitative chemical analysis. Includes both teachers primarily engaged in teaching and those who do a combination of both teaching and research. Prepares and delivers lectures to students. Compiles bibliographies of specialized materials for outside reading assignments. Directs research of other teachers or graduate students working for advanced academic degrees. Compiles, administers, and grades examinations or assigns this work to others. Stimulates class discussions. Advises students on academic and vocational curricula. Acts as adviser to student organizations. Serves on faculty committee providing professional consulting services to government and industry. Conducts research in particular field of knowledge and publishes findings in professional journals. **SKILLS—Writing:** Communicating effectively in writing as appropriate for the needs of the audience. **Reading Comprehension:** Understanding written sentences and paragraphs in work-related documents. **Learning Strategies:** Selecting and using training/instructional methods and procedures appropriate for the situation when learning or teaching new things. **Instructing:** Teaching others how to do something. **Active Learning:** Understanding the implications of new information for both current and future problem-solving and decision-making.

GOE INFORMATION—Interest Area: 12. Education and Social Service. **Work Group:** 12.03. Educational Services. **Other Job Titles in This Work Group:** Adult Literacy, Remedial Education, and GED Teachers and Instructors; Agricultural Sciences Teachers, Postsecondary; Anthropology and Archeology Teachers, Postsecondary; Architecture Teachers, Postsecondary; Archivists; Area, Ethnic, and Cultural Studies Teachers, Postsecondary; Art, Drama, and Music Teachers, Postsecondary; Atmospheric, Earth, Marine, and Space Sciences Teachers, Postsecondary; Audio-Visual Collections Specialists; Biological Science Teachers, Postsecondary; Business Teachers, Postsecondary; Child Care Workers; Communications Teachers, Postsecondary; Computer Science Teachers, Postsecondary; Criminal Justice and Law Enforcement Teachers, Postsecondary; Curators; Economics Teachers, Postsecondary; Education Teachers, Postsecondary; Educational Psychologists; Educational, Vocational, and School Counselors; Elementary School Teachers, Except Special Education; Engineering Teachers, Postsecondary; English Language and Literature Teachers, Postsecondary; Environmental Science Teachers, Postsecondary; Farm and Home Management Advisors; Foreign Language and Literature Teachers, Postsecondary; Forestry and Conservation Science Teachers, Postsecondary; Geography Teachers, Postsecondary; Graduate Teaching Assistants; Health Specialties Teachers, Postsecondary; History Teachers, Postsecondary; Home Economics Teachers, Postsecondary; Kindergarten Teachers, Except Special Education; Law Teachers, Postsecondary; Librarians; Library Assistants, Clerical; Library Science Teachers, Postsecondary; Library Technicians; Mathematical Science Teachers, Postsecondary; Middle School Teachers, Except Special and Vocational Education; Museum Technicians and Conservators; Nursing Instructors and Teachers, Postsecondary; Personal Financial Advisors; Philosophy and Religion Teachers, Postsecondary; Physics Teachers, Postsecondary; Political Science Teachers, Postsecondary; Postsecondary Teachers, All Other; Preschool Teachers, Except Special Education; others. **PERSONALITY TYPE—**Investigative. Investigative occupations frequently involve working with ideas and require an extensive amount of thinking. These occupations can involve searching for facts and figuring out problems mentally.

EDUCATION/TRAINING PROGRAM(S)—Analytical Chemistry; Chemical Physics; Chemistry, General; Chemistry, Other; Geochemistry; Inorganic Chemistry; Organic Chemistry; Physical and Theoretical Chemistry; Polymer Chemistry. **RELATED KNOWLEDGE/ COURSES—Chemistry:** Knowledge of the chemical composition, structure, and properties of substances and of the chemical processes and transformations that they undergo. This includes uses of chemicals and their interactions, danger signs, production techniques, and disposal methods. **Mathematics:** Knowledge of arithmetic, algebra, geometry, calculus, and statistics and their applications. **Education and Training:** Knowledge of principles and methods for curriculum and training design, teaching and instruction for individuals and groups, and the measurement of training effects. **English Language:** Knowledge of the structure and content of the English language, including the meaning and spelling of words, rules of composition, and grammar. **Administration and Management:** Knowledge of business and management principles involved in strategic planning, resource allocation, human resources modeling, leadership technique, production methods, and coordination of people and resources.

Chemists

- ▲ Education/Training Required: Bachelor's degree
- ▲ Annual Earnings: $51,860
- ▲ Growth: 19.1%
- ▲ Annual Job Openings: 6,000
- ▲ Self-Employed: 1.0%
- ▲ Part-Time: 3.3%

Conduct qualitative and quantitative chemical analyses or chemical experiments in laboratories for quality or process control or to develop new products or knowledge. Analyzes organic and inorganic compounds to determine chemical and physical properties, composition, structure, relationships, and reactions, utilizing chromatography, spectroscopy, and spectrophotometry techniques. Develops, improves, and customizes products, equipment, formulas, processes, and analytical methods. Studies effects of various methods of processing, preserving, and packaging on composition and properties of foods. Confers with scientists and engineers to conduct analyses of research projects, interpret test results, or develop nonstandard tests. Directs, coordinates, and advises personnel in test procedures for analyzing components and physical properties of materials. Writes technical papers and reports and prepares standards and specifications for processes, facilities, products, and tests. Prepares test solutions, compounds, and reagents for laboratory personnel to conduct test. Compiles and analyzes test information to determine process or equipment operating efficiency and to diagnose malfunctions. Induces changes in composition of substances by introducing heat, light, energy, and chemical catalysts for quantitative and qualitative analysis. **SKILLS—Science:** Using scientific rules and methods to solve problems. **Active Learning:** Understanding the implications of new information for both current and future problem-solving and decision-making. **Reading Comprehension:** Understanding written sentences and paragraphs in work-related documents. **Writing:** Communicating effectively in writing as appropriate for the needs of the au-

dience. **Judgment and Decision Making:** Considering the relative costs and benefits of potential actions to choose the most appropriate one. **Mathematics:** Using mathematics to solve problems. **Critical Thinking:** Using logic and reasoning to identify the strengths and weaknesses of alternative solutions, conclusions, or approaches to problems.

GOE INFORMATION—Interest Area: 02. Science, Math, and Engineering. **Work Group:** 02.02. Physical Sciences. **Other Job Titles in This Work Group:** Astronomers; Atmospheric and Space Scientists; Geographers; Geologists; Geoscientists, Except Hydrologists and Geographers; Hydrologists; Materials Scientists; Physical Scientists, All Other; Physicists. **PERSONALITY TYPE—**Investigative. Investigative occupations frequently involve working with ideas and require an extensive amount of thinking. These occupations can involve searching for facts and figuring out problems mentally.

EDUCATION/TRAINING PROGRAM(S)—Analytical Chemistry; Chemical Physics; Chemistry, General; Chemistry, Other; Inorganic Chemistry; Organic Chemistry; Physical and Theoretical Chemistry; Polymer Chemistry. **RELATED KNOWLEDGE/COURSES—Chemistry:** Knowledge of the chemical composition, structure, and properties of substances and of the chemical processes and transformations that they undergo. This includes uses of chemicals and their interactions, danger signs, production techniques, and disposal methods. **Mathematics:** Knowledge of arithmetic, algebra, geometry, calculus, and statistics and their applications. **English Language:** Knowledge of the structure and content of the English language, including the meaning and spelling of words, rules of composition, and grammar. **Computers and Electronics:** Knowledge of circuit boards, processors, chips, electronic equipment, and computer hardware and software, including applications and programming. **Physics:** Knowledge and prediction of physical principles and laws and their interrelationships and applications to understanding fluid, material, and atmospheric dynamics and mechanical, electrical, atomic, and sub-atomic structures and processes. **Engineering and Technology:** Knowledge of the practical application of engineering science and technology. This includes applying principles, techniques, procedures, and equipment to the design and production of various goods and services. **Administration and Management:** Knowledge of business and management principles involved in strategic planning, resource allocation, human resources modeling, leadership technique, production methods, and coordination of people and resources.

Chief Executives

- ▲ Education/Training Required: Work experience plus degree
- ▲ Annual Earnings: $120,450
- ▲ Growth: 17.2%
- ▲ Annual Job Openings: 48,000
- ▲ Self-Employed: 0%
- ▲ Part-Time: 6.1%

Determine and formulate policies and provide the overall direction of companies or private and public sector organizations within the guidelines set up by a board of directors or similar governing body. Plan, direct, or coordinate operational activities at the highest level of management with the help of subordinate executives and staff managers. **SKILLS**—No data available.

GOE INFORMATION—**Interest Area:** 13. General Management and Support. **Work Group:** 13.01. General Management Work and Management of Support Functions. **Other Job Titles in This Work Group:** Compensation and Benefits Managers; Farm, Ranch, and Other Agricultural Managers; Financial Managers; Financial Managers, Branch or Department; Funeral Directors; General and Operations Managers; Government Service Executives; Human Resources Managers; Human Resources Managers, All Other; Legislators; Managers, All Other; Postmasters and Mail Superintendents; Private Sector Executives; Property, Real Estate, and Community Association Managers; Public Relations Managers; Purchasing Managers; Storage and Distribution Managers; Training and Development Managers; Transportation, Storage, and Distribution Managers; Treasurers, Controllers, and Chief Financial Officers. **PERSONALITY TYPE**—No data available.

EDUCATION/TRAINING PROGRAM(S)—Business Administration and Management, General; Business/Commerce, General; Entrepreneurship/Entrepreneurial Studies; International Business/Trade/Commerce; Public Administration; Public Administration and Social Service Professions, Other; Public Policy Analysis. **RELATED KNOWLEDGE/COURSES**—No data available.

Child Care Workers

- ▲ Education/Training Required: Short-term on-the-job training
- ▲ Annual Earnings: $16,030
- ▲ Growth: 10.6%
- ▲ Annual Job Openings: 370,000
- ▲ Self-Employed: 57.5%
- ▲ Part-Time: 43.4%

Attend to children at schools, businesses, private households, and child care institutions. Perform a variety of tasks, such as dressing, feeding, bathing, and overseeing play. Cares for children in institutional setting, such as group homes, nursery schools, private businesses, or schools for the handicapped. Monitors children on life-support equipment to detect malfunctioning of equipment and calls for medical assistance when needed. Wheels handicapped children to classes or other areas of facility, secure in equipment such as chairs and slings. Reads to children and teaches them simple painting, drawing, handwork, and songs. Assists in preparing food for children, serves meals and refreshments to children, and regulates rest periods. Instructs children regarding desirable health and personal habits, such as eating, resting, and toilet habits. Organizes and participates in recreational activities, such as games. Places or hoists children into baths or pools. Disciplines children and recommends or initiates other measures to control behavior, such as caring for own clothing and picking up toys and books. **SKILLS—Learning Strategies:** Selecting and using training/instructional methods and procedures appropriate for the situation when learning or teaching new things. **Reading Comprehension:** Understanding written sentences and paragraphs in work-related documents. **Monitoring:** Monitoring/Assessing your performance or that of other individuals or organizations to make improvements or take corrective action. **Service Orientation:** Actively looking for ways to help people. **Social Perceptiveness:** Being aware of others' reactions and understanding why they react as they do. **Active Listening:** Giving full attention to what other people are saying, taking time to understand the points being made, asking questions as appropriate, and not interrupting at inappropriate times.

GOE INFORMATION—Interest Area: 12. Education and Social Service. **Work Group:** 12.03. Educational Services. **Other Job Titles in This Work Group:** Adult Literacy, Remedial Education, and GED Teachers and Instructors; Agricultural Sciences Teachers, Postsecondary; Anthropology and Archeology Teachers, Postsecondary; Architecture Teachers, Postsecondary; Archivists; Area, Ethnic, and Cultural Studies Teachers, Postsecondary; Art, Drama, and Music Teachers, Postsecondary; Atmospheric, Earth, Marine, and Space Sciences Teachers, Postsecondary; Audio-Visual Collections Specialists; Biological Science Teachers, Postsecondary; Business Teachers, Postsecondary; Chemistry Teachers, Postsecondary; Communications Teachers, Postsecondary; Computer Science Teachers, Postsecondary; Criminal Justice and Law Enforcement Teachers, Postsecondary; Curators; Economics Teachers, Postsecondary; Education Teachers, Postsecondary; Educational Psychologists; Educational, Vocational, and School Counselors; Elementary School Teachers, Except Special Education; Engineering Teachers, Postsecondary; English Language and Literature Teachers, Postsecondary; Environmental Science Teachers, Postsecondary; Farm and Home Management Advisors; Foreign Language and Literature Teachers, Postsecondary; Forestry and Conservation Science Teachers, Postsecondary; Geography Teachers, Postsecondary; Graduate Teaching Assistants; Health Specialties Teachers, Postsecondary; History Teachers, Postsecondary; Home Economics Teachers, Postsecondary; Kindergarten Teachers, Except Special Education; Law Teachers, Postsecondary; Librarians; Library Assistants, Clerical; Library Science Teachers, Postsecondary; Library Technicians; Mathematical Science Teachers, Postsecondary; Middle School Teachers, Except Special and Vocational Education; Museum Technicians and Conservators; Nursing Instructors and Teachers, Postsecondary; Personal Financial Advisors; Philosophy and Religion Teachers, Postsecondary; Physics Teachers, Postsecondary; Political Science Teachers, Postsecondary; Postsecondary Teachers, All Other; Preschool Teachers, Except Special Education; others. **PERSONALITY TYPE—**Social. Social occupations frequently involve working with, communicating with, and teaching people. These occupations often involve helping or providing service to others.

EDUCATION/TRAINING PROGRAM(S)—Child Care Provider/Assistant. **RELATED KNOWLEDGE/ COURSES—Customer and Personal Service:** Knowledge of principles and processes for providing customer and personal services. This includes customer needs assessment, meeting quality standards for services, and evaluation of customer satisfaction. **Psychology:** Knowledge of human behavior and performance; individual differences in ability, personality, and interests; learning and motivation; psychological research methods; and the assessment and treatment of behavioral and affective disorders. **Education and Training:** Knowledge of principles and methods for curriculum and training design, teaching and instruction for individuals and groups, and the measurement of training effects. **English Language:** Knowledge of the structure and content of the English language, including the meaning and spelling of words, rules of composition, and grammar. **Administration and Management:** Knowledge of business and management principles involved in strategic planning, resource allocation, human resources modeling, leadership technique, production methods, and coordination of people and resources.

Child Support, Missing Persons, and Unemployment Insurance Fraud Investigators

- ▲ Education/Training Required: Work experience in a related occupation
- ▲ Annual Earnings: $50,960
- ▲ Growth: 16.4%
- ▲ Annual Job Openings: 4,000
- ▲ Self-Employed: 0%
- ▲ Part-Time: 6.5%

Conduct investigations to locate, arrest, and return fugitives and persons wanted for non-payment of support payments and unemployment insurance fraud and to locate missing persons. Serves warrants and makes arrests to return persons sought in connection with crimes or for non-payment of child support. Computes amount of child support payments. Testifies in court to present evidence regarding cases. Examines medical and dental X rays, fingerprints, and other information to identify bodies held in morgue. Examines case file to determine that divorce decree and court-ordered judgment for payment are in order. Completes reports to document information acquired during criminal and child support cases and actions taken. Monitors child support payments awarded by court to ensure compliance and enforcement of child support laws. Determines types of court jurisdiction, according to facts and circumstances surrounding case, and files court action. Confers with prosecuting attorney to prepare court case and with court clerk to obtain arrest warrant and schedule court date. Interviews client to obtain information, such as relocation of absent parent, amount of child support awarded, and names of witnesses. Interviews and discusses case with parent charged with nonpayment of support to resolve issues in lieu of filing court proceedings. Reviews files and criminal records to develop possible leads, such as previous addresses and aliases. Prepares file indicating data such as wage records of accused, witnesses, and blood test results. Obtains extradition papers to bring about return of fugitive. Contacts employers, neighbors, relatives, and law enforcement agencies to locate person sought and verify information gathered about case. **SKILLS—Active Listening:** Giving full attention to what other people are saying, taking time to understand the points being made, asking questions as appropriate, and not interrupting at inappropriate times. **Speaking:** Talking to others to convey information effectively. **Reading Comprehension:** Understanding written sentences and paragraphs in work-related documents. **Critical Thinking:** Using logic and reasoning to identify the strengths and weaknesses of alternative solutions, conclusions, or approaches to problems. **Writing:** Communi-

cating effectively in writing as appropriate for the needs of the audience.

GOE INFORMATION—Interest Area: 04. Law, Law Enforcement, and Public Safety. **Work Group:** 04.03. Law Enforcement. **Other Job Titles in This Work Group:** Animal Control Workers; Bailiffs; Correctional Officers and Jailers; Criminal Investigators and Special Agents; Crossing Guards; Detectives and Criminal Investigators; Fire Investigators; Fish and Game Wardens; Forensic Science Technicians; Gaming Surveillance Officers and Gaming Investigators; Highway Patrol Pilots; Immigration and Customs Inspectors; Lifeguards, Ski Patrol, and Other Recreational Protective Service Workers; Parking Enforcement Workers; Police and Sheriff's Patrol Officers; Police Detectives; Police Identification and Records Officers; Police Patrol Officers; Private Detectives and Investigators; Security Guards; Sheriffs and Deputy Sheriffs; Transit and Railroad Police. **PERSONALITY TYPE—**Enterprising. Enterprising occupations frequently involve starting up and carrying out projects. These occupations can involve leading people and making many decisions. They sometimes require risk taking and often deal with business.

EDUCATION/TRAINING PROGRAM(S)—Criminal Justice/Police Science; Criminalistics and Criminal Science. **RELATED KNOWLEDGE/COURSES—Law and Government:** Knowledge of laws, legal codes, court procedures, precedents, government regulations, executive orders, agency rules, and the democratic political process. **Public Safety and Security:** Knowledge of relevant equipment, policies, procedures, and strategies to promote effective local, state, or national security operations for the protection of people, data, property, and institutions. **Economics and Accounting:** Knowledge of economic and accounting principles and practices, the financial markets, banking, and the analysis and reporting of financial data. **English Language:** Knowledge of the structure and content of the English language, including the meaning and spelling of words, rules of composition, and grammar. **Mathematics:** Knowledge of arithmetic, algebra, geometry, calculus, and statistics and their applications.

Child, Family, and School Social Workers

- ▲ Education/Training Required: Bachelor's degree
- ▲ Annual Earnings: $32,950
- ▲ Growth: 26.9%
- ▲ Annual Job Openings: 35,000
- ▲ Self-Employed: 3.1%
- ▲ Part-Time: 11.9%

Provide social services and assistance to improve the social and psychological functioning of children and their families and to maximize the family well-being and the academic functioning of children. May assist single parents, arrange adoptions, and find foster homes for abandoned or abused children. In schools, they address such problems as teenage pregnancy, misbehavior, and truancy. May also advise teachers on how to deal with problem children. Counsels individuals or family members regarding behavior modifications, rehabilitation, social adjustments, financial assistance, vocational training, child care, or medical care. Refers client to community resources for needed assistance. Leads group counseling sessions to provide support in such areas as grief, stress, or chemical dependency. Arranges for medical, psychiatric, and other tests that may disclose cause of difficulties and indicate remedial measures. Assists travelers, including runaways, migrants, transients, refugees, repatriated Americans, and problem families. Collects supplementary information, such as employment, medical records, or school reports. Maintains case history records and prepares reports. Evaluates personal characteristics of foster home or adoption applicants. Places children in foster or adoptive homes, institutions, or medical treatment centers. Reviews service plan and performs follow-up to determine quantity and quality of service provided to client. Determines client's eligibility for financial assistance. Develops program content, organizes, and leads activities planned to enhance social development of individual members and accomplishment of group goals. Investigates home conditions to determine suitability of foster or adoptive home or to protect children from harmful environment. Serves as liaison between student, home, school, family service agencies, child guidance clinics, courts, protective services, doctors, and clergy members. Consults with parents, teachers, and other school personnel to determine causes of problems and effect solutions. Counsels students whose behavior, school progress, or mental or physical impairment indicates need for assistance. Arranges for day care, homemaker service, prenatal care, and child planning programs for clients in need of such services. Interviews individuals to assess social and emotional capabilities, physical and mental impairments, and financial needs. Counsels parents with child-rearing problems and children and youth with difficulties in social adjustments. **SKILLS—Social Perceptiveness:** Being aware of others' reactions and understanding why they react as they do. **Service Orientation:** Actively looking for ways to help people. **Active Listening:** Giving full attention to what other people are saying, taking time to understand the points being made, asking questions as appropriate, and not interrupting at inappropriate times. **Speaking:** Talking to others to convey information effectively. **Reading Comprehension:** Understanding written sentences and paragraphs in work-related documents.

GOE INFORMATION—Interest Area: 12. Education and Social Service. **Work Group:** 12.02. Social Services. **Other Job Titles in This Work Group:** Clergy; Clinical Psychologists; Clinical, Counseling, and School Psychologists; Community and Social Service Specialists, All Other; Counseling Psychologists; Counselors, All Other; Directors, Religious Activities and Education; Marriage and Family Therapists; Medical and Public Health Social Workers; Mental Health and Substance Abuse Social Workers; Mental Health Counselors; Probation Officers and Correctional Treatment Specialists; Rehabilitation Counselors; Religious Workers, All Other; Residential Advisors; Social and Human Service Assistants; Social Workers, All Other; Substance Abuse and Behavioral Disorder Counselors. **PERSONALITY TYPE—Social.** Social occupations frequently involve working with, communicating with, and teaching people. These occupations often involve helping or providing service to others.

EDUCATION/TRAINING PROGRAM(S)—Juvenile Corrections; Social Work; Youth Services/Administration. RELATED KNOWLEDGE/COURSES—Therapy and Counseling: Knowledge of principles, methods, and procedures for diagnosis, treatment, and rehabilitation of physical and mental dysfunctions and for career counseling and guidance. **Psychology:** Knowledge of human behavior and performance; individual differences in ability, personality, and interests; learning and motivation; psychological research methods; and the assessment and treatment of behavioral and affective disorders. **English Language:** Knowledge of the structure and content of the English language, including the meaning and spelling of words, rules of composition, and grammar. **Sociology and Anthropol-** ogy: Knowledge of group behavior and dynamics, societal trends and influences, human migrations, ethnicity, and cultures and their history and origins. **Administration and Management:** Knowledge of business and management principles involved in strategic planning, resource allocation, human resources modeling, leadership technique, production methods, and coordination of people and resources.

Chiropractors

- ▲ Education/Training Required: First professional degree
- ▲ Annual Earnings: $68,420
- ▲ Growth: 23.4%
- ▲ Annual Job Openings: 3,000
- ▲ Self-Employed: 57.7%
- ▲ Part-Time: 10.5%

Adjust spinal column and other articulations of the body to correct abnormalities of the human body believed to be caused by interference with the nervous system. Examine patient to determine nature and extent of disorder. Manipulate spine or other involved area. May utilize supplementary measures, such as exercise, rest, water, light, heat, and nutritional therapy. Examines patient to determine nature and extent of disorder. Manipulates spinal column and other extremities to adjust, align, or correct abnormalities caused by neurologic and kinetic articular dysfunction. Utilizes supplementary measures, such as exercise, rest, water, light, heat, and nutritional therapy. Performs diagnostic procedures, including physical, neurologic, and orthopedic examinations, and laboratory tests, using instruments and equipment such as X-ray machine and electrocardiograph. **SKILLS—Reading Comprehension:** Understanding written sentences and paragraphs in work-related documents. **Active Listening:** Giving full attention to what other people are saying, taking time to understand the points being made, asking questions as appropriate, and not interrupting at inappropriate times. **Judgment and Decision Making:** Considering the relative costs and benefits of potential actions to choose the most appropriate one. **Active Learning:** Understanding the implications of new information for both current and future problem-solving and decision-making. **Critical Thinking:** Using logic and reasoning to identify the strengths and weaknesses of alternative solutions, conclusions, or approaches to problems.

GOE INFORMATION—Interest Area: 14. Medical and Health Services. **Work Group:** 14.04. Health Specialties. **Other Job Titles in This Work Group:** Opticians, Dispensing; Optometrists; Podiatrists. **PERSONALITY TYPE—**Investigative. Investigative occupations frequently involve working with ideas and require an extensive amount of thinking. These occupations can involve searching for facts and figuring out problems mentally.

EDUCATION/TRAINING PROGRAM(S)—Chiropractic (DC). **RELATED KNOWLEDGE/COURSES— Medicine and Dentistry:** Knowledge of the information and techniques needed to diagnose and treat human injuries, diseases, and deformities. This includes symptoms, treatment alternatives, drug properties and interactions, and preventive health-care measures. **Biology:** Knowledge of plant and animal organisms and their tissues, cells, functions, interdependencies, and interactions with each other and the environment. **English Language:** Knowledge of the structure and content of the English language, including the meaning and spelling of words, rules of composition, and grammar. **Therapy and Counseling:** Knowledge of principles, methods, and procedures for diagnosis, treatment, and rehabilitation of physical and mental dysfunctions and for career counseling and guidance. **Customer and Personal Service:** Knowledge of principles and processes for providing customer and personal services. This includes customer needs assessment, meeting quality standards for services, and evaluation of customer satisfaction.

Civil Drafters

- ▲ Education/Training Required: Postsecondary vocational training
- ▲ Annual Earnings: $37,010
- ▲ Growth: 20.8%
- ▲ Annual Job Openings: 12,000
- ▲ Self-Employed: 3.0%
- ▲ Part-Time: 7.9%

Prepare drawings and topographical and relief maps used in civil engineering projects, such as highways, bridges, pipelines, flood control projects, and water and sewerage control systems. Draws maps, diagrams, and profiles, using cross-sections and surveys, to represent elevations, topographical contours, subsurface formations, and structures. Accompanies field survey crew to locate grading markers or to collect data required to revise construction drawings. Correlates, interprets, and modifies data obtained from topographical surveys, well logs, and geophysical prospecting reports. Finishes and duplicates drawings according to required mediums and specifications for reproduction, using blueprinting, photographing, or other duplicating methods. Identifies symbols located on topographical surveys to denote geological and geophysical formations or oil field installations. Calculates excavation tonnage and prepares graphs and fill-hauling diagrams used in earth-moving operations. Computes and represents characteristics and dimensions of borehole, such as depth, degree, and direction of inclination. Reviews rough sketches, drawings, specifications, and other engineering data received from civil engineer. Plots boreholes for oil and gas wells from photographic subsurface survey recordings and other data, using computer-assisted drafting equipment. Drafts plans and detailed drawings for structures, installations, and construction projects, such as highways, sewage disposal systems, and dikes. **SKILLS—Mathematics:** Using mathematics to solve problems. **Reading Comprehension:** Understanding written sentences and paragraphs in work-related documents. **Operations Analysis:** Analyzing needs and product requirements to create a design. **Active Learning:** Understanding the implications of new information for both current and future problem-solving and decision-making. **Complex Problem Solving:** Identifying complex problems and reviewing related information to develop and evaluate options and implement solutions. **Critical Thinking:** Using logic and reasoning to identify the strengths and weaknesses of alternative solutions, conclusions, or approaches to problems.

GOE INFORMATION—Interest Area: 02. Science, Math, and Engineering. **Work Group:** 02.08. Engineering Technology. **Other Job Titles in This Work Group:** Aerospace Engineering and Operations Technicians; Architectural and Civil Drafters; Architectural Drafters; Calibration and Instrumentation Technicians; Cartographers and Photogrammetrists; Civil Engineering Technicians; Construction and Building Inspectors; Drafters, All Other; Electrical and Electronic Engineering Technicians; Electrical and Electronics Drafters; Electrical Drafters; Electrical Engineering Technicians; Electro-Mechanical Technicians; Electronic Drafters; Electronics Engineering Technicians; Engineering Technicians, Except Drafters, All Other; Environmental Engineering Technicians; Industrial Engineering Technicians; Mapping Technicians; Mechanical Drafters; Mechanical Engineering Technicians; Numerical Tool and Process Control Programmers; Pressure Vessel Inspectors; Surveying and Mapping Technicians; Surveying Technicians; Surveyors. **PERSONALITY TYPE**—Realistic. Realistic occupations frequently involve work activities that include practical, hands-on problems and solutions. They often deal with plants, animals, and real-world materials like wood, tools, and machinery. Many of the occupations require working outside and do not involve a lot of paperwork or working closely with others.

EDUCATION/TRAINING PROGRAM(S)—Architectural Drafting and Architectural CAD/CADD; Architectural Technology/Technician; CAD/CADD Drafting and/or Design Technology/Technician; Civil Drafting and Civil Engineering CAD/CADD; Drafting and Design Technology/Technician, General. **RELATED KNOWLEDGE/ COURSES—Design:** Knowledge of design techniques, tools, and principles involved in production of precision technical plans, blueprints, drawings, and models. **Mathematics:** Knowledge of arithmetic, algebra, geometry, calculus, and statistics and their applications. **Engineering and Technology:** Knowledge of the practical application of engineering science and technology. This includes applying principles, techniques, procedures, and equipment to the design and production of various goods and services. **Computers and Electronics:** Knowledge of circuit boards, processors, chips, electronic equipment, and computer hardware and software, including applications and programming. **Physics:** Knowledge and prediction of physical principles and laws and their interrelationships and applications to understanding fluid, material, and atmospheric dynamics and mechanical, electrical, atomic, and sub-atomic structures and processes.

Civil Engineering Technicians

- ▲ Education/Training Required: Associate's degree
- ▲ Annual Earnings: $37,410
- ▲ Growth: 11.9%
- ▲ Annual Job Openings: 9,000
- ▲ Self-Employed: 1.9%
- ▲ Part-Time: 7.4%

Apply theory and principles of civil engineering in planning, designing, and overseeing construction and maintenance of structures and facilities under the direction of engineering staff or physical scientists. Evaluates facility to determine suitability for occupancy and square footage availability. Responds to public suggestions and complaints. Inspects project site and evaluates contractor work to detect design malfunctions and ensure conformance to design specifications and applicable codes. Analyzes proposed site factors and designs maps, graphs, tracings, and diagrams to illustrate findings. Drafts detailed dimensional drawings and designs layouts for projects and to ensure conformance to specifications. Reads and reviews project blueprints and structural specifications to determine dimensions of structure or system and material requirements. Prepares reports and documents project activities and data. Confers with supervisor to determine project details, such as plan preparation, acceptance testing, and evaluation of field conditions. Conducts materials test and analysis, using tools and equipment and applying engineering knowledge. Reports maintenance problems occurring at project site to supervisor and negotiates changes to resolve system conflicts. Calculates dimensions, square footage, profile and component specifications, and material quantities, using calculator or computer. Develops plans and estimates costs for installation of systems, utilization of facilities, or construction of structures. Plans and conducts field surveys to locate new sites and analyze details of project sites. **SKILLS—Mathematics:** Using mathematics to solve problems. **Operations Analysis:** Analyzing needs and product requirements to create a design. **Reading Comprehension:** Understanding written sentences and paragraphs in work-related documents. **Critical Thinking:** Using logic and reasoning to identify the strengths and weaknesses of alternative solutions, conclusions, or approaches to problems. **Writing:** Communicating effectively in writing as appropriate for the needs of the audience. **Judgment and Decision Making:** Considering the relative costs and benefits of potential actions to choose the most appropriate one. **Active Listening:** Giving full attention to what other people are saying, taking time to understand the points being made, asking questions as appropriate, and not interrupting at inappropriate times.

GOE INFORMATION—Interest Area: 02. Science, Math, and Engineering. **Work Group:** 02.08. Engineering Technology. **Other Job Titles in This Work Group:** Aerospace Engineering and Operations Technicians; Architectural and Civil Drafters; Architectural Drafters; Calibration and Instrumentation Technicians; Cartographers and Photogrammetrists; Civil Drafters; Construction and Building Inspectors; Drafters, All Other; Electrical and Electronic Engineering Technicians; Electrical and Electronics Drafters; Electrical Drafters; Electrical Engineering Technicians; Electro-Mechanical Technicians; Electronic Drafters; Electronics Engineering Technicians; Engineering Technicians, Except Drafters, All Other; Environmental Engineering Technicians; Industrial Engineering Technicians; Mapping Technicians; Mechanical Drafters; Mechanical Engineering Technicians; Numerical Tool and Process Control Programmers; Pressure Vessel Inspectors; Surveying and Mapping Technicians; Surveying Technicians; Surveyors. **PERSONALITY TYPE**—Realistic. Realistic occupations frequently involve work activities that include practical, hands-on problems and solutions. They often deal with plants, animals, and real-world materials like wood, tools, and machinery. Many of the occupations require working outside and do not involve a lot of paperwork or working closely with others.

EDUCATION/TRAINING PROGRAM(S)—Civil Engineering Technology/Technician; Construction Engineering Technology/Technician. **RELATED KNOWLEDGE/ COURSES—Engineering and Technology:** Knowledge of the practical application of engineering science and technology. This includes applying principles, techniques, procedures, and equipment to the design and production of various goods and services. **Design:** Knowledge of design techniques, tools, and principles involved in production of precision technical plans, blueprints, drawings, and models. **Mathematics:** Knowledge of arithmetic, algebra, geometry, calculus, and statistics and their applications. **Building and Construction:** Knowledge of materials, methods, and tools involved in the construction or repair of houses, buildings, or other structures, such as highways and roads. **English Language:** Knowledge of the structure and content of the English language, including the meaning and spelling of words, rules of composition, and grammar.

Claims Adjusters, Examiners, and Investigators

▲ Education/Training Required: Long-term on-the-job training
▲ Annual Earnings: $42,440
▲ Growth: 15.1%
▲ Annual Job Openings: 25,000
▲ Self-Employed: 0%
▲ Part-Time: 7.3%

Review settled claims to determine that payments and settlements have been made in accordance with company practices and procedures, ensuring that proper methods have been followed. Report overpayments, underpayments, and other irregularities. Confer with legal counsel on claims requiring litigation. **SKILLS**—No data available.

GOE INFORMATION—Interest Area: 13. General Management and Support. **Work Group:** 13.02. Management Support. **Other Job Titles in This Work Group:** Accountants; Accountants and Auditors; Appraisers and Assessors of Real Estate; Appraisers, Real Estate; Assessors; Auditors; Budget Analysts; Claims Examiners, Property and Casualty Insurance; Compensation, Benefits, and Job Analysis Specialists; Cost Estimators; Credit Analysts; Employment Interviewers, Private or Public Employment Service; Employment, Recruitment, and Placement Specialists; Financial Analysts; Human Resources, Training, and Labor Relations Specialists, All Other; Insurance Adjusters, Examiners, and Investigators; Insurance Appraisers, Auto Damage; Insurance Underwriters; Loan Counselors; Loan Officers; Logisticians; Management Analysts; Market Research Analysts; Personnel Recruiters; Purchasing Agents and Buyers, Farm Products; Purchasing Agents, Except Wholesale, Retail, and Farm Products; Tax Examiners, Collectors, and Revenue Agents; Training and Development Specialists; Wholesale and Retail Buyers, Except Farm Products. **PERSONALITY TYPE**—No data available.

EDUCATION/TRAINING PROGRAM(S)—Health/ Medical Claims Examiner; Insurance. **RELATED KNOWLEDGE/COURSES**—No data available.

Claims Examiners, Property and Casualty Insurance

▲ Education/Training Required: Long-term on-the-job training
▲ Annual Earnings: $42,440
▲ Growth: 15.1%
▲ Annual Job Openings: 25,000
▲ Self-Employed: 0%
▲ Part-Time: 7.3%

Review settled insurance claims to determine that payments and settlements have been made in accordance with company practices and procedures. Report overpayments, underpayments, and other irregularities. Confer with legal counsel on claims requiring litigation. Analyzes data used in settling claim to determine its validity in payment of claims. Reports overpayments, underpayments, and other irregularities. Confers with legal counsel on claims requiring litigation. **SKILLS—Reading Comprehension:** Understanding written sentences and paragraphs in work-related documents. **Mathematics:** Using mathematics to solve problems. **Writing:** Communicating effectively in writing as appropriate for the needs of the audience. **Critical Thinking:** Using logic and reasoning to identify the strengths and weaknesses of alternative solutions, conclusions, or approaches to problems. **Active Listening:** Giving full attention to what other people are saying, taking time to understand the points being made, asking questions as appropriate, and not interrupting at inappropriate times. **Judgment and Decision Making:** Considering the relative costs and benefits of potential actions to choose the most appropriate one. **Monitoring:** Monitoring/Assessing your performance or that of other individuals or organizations to make improvements or take corrective action.

GOE INFORMATION—Interest Area: 13. General Management and Support. **Work Group:** 13.02. Management Support. **Other Job Titles in This Work Group:** Accountants; Accountants and Auditors; Appraisers and Assessors of Real Estate; Appraisers, Real Estate; Assessors; Auditors; Budget Analysts; Claims Adjusters, Examiners, and Investigators; Compensation, Benefits, and Job Analysis Specialists; Cost Estimators; Credit Analysts; Employment Interviewers, Private or Public Employment Service; Employment, Recruitment, and Placement Specialists; Financial Analysts; Human Resources, Training, and Labor Relations Specialists, All Other; Insurance Adjusters, Examiners, and Investigators; Insurance Appraisers, Auto Damage; Insurance Underwriters; Loan Counselors; Loan Officers; Logisticians; Management Analysts; Market Research Analysts; Personnel Recruiters; Purchasing Agents

and Buyers, Farm Products; Purchasing Agents, Except Wholesale, Retail, and Farm Products; Tax Examiners, Collectors, and Revenue Agents; Training and Development Specialists; Wholesale and Retail Buyers, Except Farm Products. **PERSONALITY TYPE—Conventional.** Conventional occupations frequently involve following set procedures and routines. These occupations can include working with data and details more than with ideas. Usually there is a clear line of authority to follow.

EDUCATION/TRAINING PROGRAM(S)—Health/ Medical Claims Examiner; Insurance. **RELATED KNOWLEDGE/COURSES—Mathematics:** Knowledge of arithmetic, algebra, geometry, calculus, and statistics and their applications. **Law and Government:** Knowledge of laws, legal codes, court procedures, precedents, government regulations, executive orders, agency rules, and the democratic political process. **English Language:** Knowledge of the structure and content of the English language, including the meaning and spelling of words, rules of composition, and grammar. **Computers and Electronics:** Knowledge of circuit boards, processors, chips, electronic equipment, and computer hardware and software, including applications and programming. **Economics and Accounting:** Knowledge of economic and accounting principles and practices, the financial markets, banking, and the analysis and reporting of financial data. **Administration and Management:** Knowledge of business and management principles involved in strategic planning, resource allocation, human resources modeling, leadership technique, production methods, and coordination of people and resources. **Communications and Media:** Knowledge of media production, communication, and dissemination techniques and methods. This includes alternative ways to inform and entertain via written, oral, and visual media.

Cleaners of Vehicles and Equipment

- ▲ Education/Training Required: Short-term on-the-job training
- ▲ Annual Earnings: $16,490
- ▲ Growth: 18.8%
- ▲ Annual Job Openings: 86,000
- ▲ Self-Employed: 6.8%
- ▲ Part-Time: 22.9%

Wash or otherwise clean vehicles, machinery, and other equipment. Use such materials as water, cleaning agents, brushes, cloths, and hoses. Scrubs, scrapes, or sprays machine parts, equipment, or vehicles, using scrapers, brushes, cleaners, disinfectants, insecticides, acid, and abrasives. Monitors operation of cleaning machines and stops machine or notifies supervisor when malfunctions occur. Maintains inventories of supplies. Records production and operational data on specified forms. Collects and tests samples of cleaning solutions and vapors. Transports materials, equipment, or supplies to and from work area, using carts or hoists. Lubricates machinery, vehicles, and equipment and performs minor repairs and adjustments, using hand tools. Applies paints, dyes, polishes, reconditioners, and masking materials to vehicles to preserve, protect, or restore color and condition. Examines and inspects parts, equipment, and vehicles for cleanliness, damage, and compliance with standards or regulations. Places objects on drying racks or dyes surfaces, using cloth, squeegees, or air compressors. Disassembles and reassembles machines or equipment or removes and reattaches vehicle parts and trim, using hand tools. Connects hoses and lines to pumps and other equipment. Mixes cleaning solutions and abrasive compositions and other compounds according to formula. Pre-soaks or rinses machine parts, equipment, or vehicles by immersing objects in cleaning solutions or water manually or using hoists. Turns valves or handles on equipment to regulate pressure and flow of water, air, steam, or abrasives from sprayer nozzles. Turns valves or disconnects hoses to eliminate water, cleaning solutions, or vapors from machinery or tanks. Sweeps, shovels, or vacuums loose debris and salvageable scrap into containers and removes from work area. Presses buttons to activate cleaning equipment or machines. **SKILLS—Operation and Control:** Controlling operations of equipment or systems. **Equipment Selection:** Determining the kind of tools and equipment needed to do a job. **Monitoring:** Monitoring/Assessing your performance or that of other individuals or organizations to make improvements or take corrective action. **Reading Comprehension:** Understanding written sentences and paragraphs in work-related documents.

GOE INFORMATION—Interest Area: 11. Recreation, Travel, and Other Personal Services. **Work Group:** 11.08. Other Personal Services. **Other Job Titles in This Work Group:** Cooks, Private Household; Embalmers; Funeral Attendants; Personal and Home Care Aides; Personal Care and Service Workers, All Other. **PERSONALITY TYPE—Realistic.** Realistic occupations frequently involve work activities that include practical, hands-on problems and solutions. They often deal with plants, animals, and real-world materials like wood, tools, and machinery. Many of the occupations require working outside and do not involve a lot of paperwork or working closely with others.

EDUCATION/TRAINING PROGRAM(S)—No data available. **RELATED KNOWLEDGE/COURSES— Principles of Mechanical Devices:** Knowledge of machines and tools, including their designs, uses, repair, and maintenance. **Chemistry:** Knowledge of the chemical composition, structure, and properties of substances and of the chemical processes and transformations that they undergo. This includes uses of chemicals and their interactions, danger signs, production techniques, and disposal methods. **Mathematics:** Knowledge of arithmetic, algebra, geometry, calculus, and statistics and their applications. **Clerical Studies:** Knowledge of administrative and clerical procedures and systems, such as word processing, managing files and records, stenography and transcription, designing forms, and other office procedures and terminology. **Engineering and Technology:** Knowledge of the practical application of engineering science and technology. This includes applying principles, techniques, procedures, and equipment to the design and production of various goods and services.

Clergy

▲ Education/Training Required: First professional degree
▲ Annual Earnings: $33,840
▲ Growth: 15.0%
▲ Annual Job Openings: 12,000
▲ Self-Employed: 0%
▲ Part-Time: 10.8%

Conduct religious worship and perform other spiritual functions associated with beliefs and practices of religious faith or denomination. Provide spiritual and moral guidance and assistance to members. Leads congregation in worship services. Conducts wedding and funeral services. Administers religious rites or ordinances. Counsels those in spiritual need. Interprets doctrine of religion. Instructs people who seek conversion to faith. Prepares and delivers sermons and other talks. Visits sick and shut-ins and helps poor. Engages in interfaith, community, civic, educational, and recreational activities sponsored by or related to interest of denomination. Writes articles for publication. **SKILLS—Service Orientation:** Actively looking for ways to help people. **Speaking:** Talking to others to convey information effectively. **Social Perceptiveness:** Being aware of others' reactions and understanding why they react as they do. **Reading Comprehension:** Understanding written sentences and paragraphs in work-related documents. **Active Listening:** Giving full attention to what other people are saying, taking time to understand the points being made, asking questions as appropriate, and not interrupting at inappropriate times. **Writing:** Communicating effectively in writing as appropriate for the needs of the audience.

GOE INFORMATION—Interest Area: 12. Education and Social Service. **Work Group:** 12.02. Social Services. **Other Job Titles in This Work Group:** Child, Family, and School Social Workers; Clinical Psychologists; Clinical, Counseling, and School Psychologists; Community and Social Service Specialists, All Other; Counseling Psychologists; Counselors, All Other; Directors, Religious Activities and Education; Marriage and Family Therapists; Medical and Public Health Social Workers; Mental Health and Substance Abuse Social Workers; Mental Health Counselors; Probation Officers and Correctional Treatment Specialists; Rehabilitation Counselors; Religious Workers, All Other; Residential Advisors; Social and Human Service Assistants; Social Workers, All Other; Substance Abuse and Behavioral Disorder Counselors. **PERSONALITY TYPE—**Social. Social occupations frequently involve working with, communicating with, and teaching people. These occupations often involve helping or providing service to others.

EDUCATION/TRAINING PROGRAM(S)—Clinical Pastoral Counseling/Patient Counseling; Divinity/Ministry (BD, MDiv.); Pastoral Counseling and Specialized Ministries, Other; Pastoral Studies/Counseling; Pre-Theology/Pre-Ministerial Studies; Rabbinical Studies; Theological and Ministerial Studies, Other; Theology and Religious Vocations, Other; Theology/Theological Studies; Youth Ministry. **RELATED KNOWLEDGE/COURSES—Philosophy and Theology:** Knowledge of different philosophical systems and religions. This includes their basic principles, values, ethics, ways of thinking, customs, and practices and their impact on human culture. **Education and Training:** Knowledge of principles and methods for curriculum and training design, teaching and instruction for individuals and groups, and the measurement of training effects. **Psychology:** Knowledge of human behavior and performance; individual differences in ability, personality, and interests; learning and motivation; psychological research methods; and the assessment and treatment of behavioral and affective disorders. **Therapy and Counseling:** Knowledge of principles, methods, and procedures for diagnosis, treatment, and rehabilitation of physical and mental dysfunctions and for career counseling and guidance. **English Language:** Knowledge of the structure and content of the English language, including the meaning and spelling of words, rules of composition, and grammar.

Clinical Psychologists

▲ Education/Training Required: Master's degree
▲ Annual Earnings: $50,420
▲ Growth: 18.1%
▲ Annual Job Openings: 18,000
▲ Self-Employed: 43.7%
▲ Part-Time: 23.4%

Diagnose or evaluate mental and emotional disorders of individuals through observation, interview, and psychological tests and formulate and administer programs of treatment. Observes individual at play, in group interactions, or in other situations to detect indications of mental deficiency, abnormal behavior, or maladjustment. Utilizes treatment methods such as psychotherapy, hypnosis, behavior modification, stress reduction therapy, psychodrama, and play therapy. Develops, directs, and participates in staff training programs. Provides psycho-logical services and advice to private firms and community agencies on individual cases or mental health programs. Directs, coordinates, and evaluates activities of psychological staff and student interns engaged in patient evaluation and treatment in psychiatric facility. Plans, supervises, and conducts psychological research in fields such as personality development and diagnosis, treatment, and prevention of mental disorders. Provides occupational, educational, and other information to enable individual to formulate realistic educational and vocational plans.

Assists clients to gain insight, define goals, and plan action to achieve effective personal, social, educational, and vocational development and adjustment. Consults reference material, such as textbooks, manuals, and journals, to identify symptoms, make diagnoses, and develop approach to treatment. Plans and develops accredited psychological service programs in psychiatric center or hospital in collaboration with psychiatrists and other professional staff. Selects, administers, scores, and interprets psychological tests to obtain information on individual's intelligence, achievement, interest, and personality. Develops treatment plan, including type, frequency, intensity, and duration of therapy, in collaboration with psychiatrist and other specialists. Conducts individual and group counseling sessions regarding psychological or emotional problems, such as stress, substance abuse, and family situations. Responds to client reactions, evaluates effectiveness of counseling or treatment, and modifies plan as needed. Interviews individuals, couples, or families and reviews records to obtain information on medical, psychological, emotional, relationship, or other problems. Analyzes information to assess client problems, determine advisability of counseling, and refer client to other specialists, institutions, or support services. **SKILLS—Social Perceptiveness:** Being aware of others' reactions and understanding why they react as they do. **Active Listening:** Giving full attention to what other people are saying, taking time to understand the points being made, asking questions as appropriate, and not interrupting at inappropriate times. **Reading Comprehension:** Understanding written sentences and paragraphs in work-related documents. **Speaking:** Talking to others to convey information effectively. **Critical Thinking:** Using logic and reasoning to identify the strengths and weaknesses of alternative solutions, conclusions, or approaches to problems. **Writing:** Communicating effectively in writing as appropriate for the needs of the audience.

GOE INFORMATION—Interest Area: 12. Education and Social Service. **Work Group:** 12.02. Social Services. **Other Job Titles in This Work Group:** Child, Family, and School Social Workers; Clergy; Clinical, Counseling, and School Psychologists; Community and Social Service Specialists, All Other; Counseling Psychologists; Counselors, All Other; Directors, Religious Activities and Education; Marriage and Family Therapists; Medical and Public Health Social Workers; Mental Health and Substance Abuse Social Workers; Mental Health Counselors; Probation Officers and Correctional Treatment Specialists; Rehabilitation Counselors; Religious Workers, All Other; Residential Advisors; Social and Human Service Assistants; Social Workers, All Other; Substance Abuse and Behavioral Disorder Counselors. **PERSONALITY TYPE—**Investigative. Investigative occupations frequently involve working with ideas and require an extensive amount of thinking. These occupations can involve searching for facts and figuring out problems mentally.

EDUCATION/TRAINING PROGRAM(S)—Clinical Child Psychology; Clinical Psychology; Counseling Psychology; Developmental and Child Psychology; Psychoanalysis and Psychotherapy; Psychology, General; School Psychology. **RELATED KNOWLEDGE/COURSES—Psychology:** Knowledge of human behavior and performance; individual differences in ability, personality, and interests; learning and motivation; psychological research methods; and the assessment and treatment of behavioral and affective disorders. **Therapy and Counseling:** Knowledge of principles, methods, and procedures for diagnosis, treatment, and rehabilitation of physical and mental dysfunctions and for career counseling and guidance. **English Language:** Knowledge of the structure and content of the English language, including the meaning and spelling of words, rules of composition, and grammar. **Customer and Personal Service:** Knowledge of principles and processes for providing customer and personal services. This includes customer needs assessment, meeting quality standards for services, and evaluation of customer satisfaction. **Administration and Management:** Knowledge of business and management principles involved in strategic planning, resource allocation, human resources modeling, leadership technique, production methods, and coordination of people and resources.

Clinical, Counseling, and School Psychologists

▲ Education/Training Required: Master's degree
▲ Annual Earnings: $50,420
▲ Growth: 18.1%
▲ Annual Job Openings: 18,000
▲ Self-Employed: 43.7%
▲ Part-Time: 23.4%

Diagnose and treat mental disorders; learning disabilities; and cognitive, behavioral, and emotional problems using individual, child, family, and group therapies. May design and implement behavior modification programs. SKILLS—No data available.

GOE INFORMATION—Interest Area: 12. Education and Social Service. Work Group: 12.02. Social Services. Other Job Titles in This Work Group: Child, Family, and School Social Workers; Clergy; Clinical Psychologists; Community and Social Service Specialists, All Other; Counseling Psychologists; Counselors, All Other; Directors, Religious Activities and Education; Marriage and Family Therapists; Medical and Public Health Social Workers; Mental Health and Substance Abuse Social Workers; Mental Health Counselors; Probation Officers and Correctional Treatment Specialists; Rehabilitation Counselors; Religious Workers, All Other; Residential Advisors; Social and Human Service Assistants; Social Workers, All Other; Substance Abuse and Behavioral Disorder Counselors. PERSONALITY TYPE—No data available.

EDUCATION/TRAINING PROGRAM(S)—Clinical Child Psychology; Clinical Psychology; Counseling Psychology; Developmental and Child Psychology; Psychoanalysis and Psychotherapy; Psychology, General; School Psychology. RELATED KNOWLEDGE/COURSES—No data available.

Coaches and Scouts

▲ Education/Training Required: Long-term on-the-job training
▲ Annual Earnings: $29,020
▲ Growth: 17.6%
▲ Annual Job Openings: 19,000
▲ Self-Employed: 31.4%
▲ Part-Time: 25.3%

Instruct or coach groups or individuals in the fundamentals of sports. Demonstrate techniques and methods of participation. May evaluate athletes' strengths and weaknesses as possible recruits or to improve the athletes' technique to prepare them for competition. Those required to hold teaching degrees should be reported in the appropriate teaching category. Analyzes athletes' performance and reviews game statistics or records to determine fitness and potential for professional sports. Evaluates team and opposition capabilities to develop and plan game strategy. Evaluates athletes' skills and discusses or recommends acquisition, trade, or position assignment of players. Negotiates with professional athletes or representatives to obtain services and arrange contracts. Prepares scouting reports detailing information such as selection or rejection of athletes and locations identified for future recruitment. Instructs athletes, individually or in groups, demonstrating sport techniques and game strategies. Plans and directs physical conditioning program for athletes to achieve maximum athletic performance. Observes athletes to determine areas of deficiency and need for individual or team improvement. SKILLS—Instructing: Teaching others how to do something. Negotiation: Bringing others together and trying to reconcile differences. Writing: Communicating effectively in writing as appropriate for the needs of the audience. Management of Personnel Resources: Motivating, developing, and directing people as they work, identifying the best people for the job. Judgment and Decision Making: Considering the relative costs and benefits of potential actions to choose the most appropriate one. Reading Comprehension: Understanding written sentences and paragraphs in work-related documents. Time Management: Managing one's own time and the time of others.

GOE INFORMATION—**Interest Area:** 01. Arts, Entertainment, and Media. **Work Group:** 01.10. Sports: Coaching, Instructing, Officiating, and Performing. **Other Job Titles in This Work Group:** Athletes and Sports Competitors; Fitness Trainers and Aerobics Instructors; Umpires, Referees, and Other Sports Officials. **PERSONALITY TYPE**—Enterprising. Enterprising occupations frequently involve starting up and carrying out projects. These occupations can involve leading people and making many decisions. They sometimes require risk taking and often deal with business.

EDUCATION/TRAINING PROGRAM(S)—Health and Physical Education, General; Physical Education Teaching and Coaching; Sport and Fitness Administration/Management. **RELATED KNOWLEDGE/ COURSES**—**Education and Training:** Knowledge of principles and methods for curriculum and training design, teaching and instruction for individuals and groups, and the measurement of training effects. **Psychology:** Knowledge of human behavior and performance; individual differences in ability, personality, and interests; learning and motivation; psychological research methods; and the assessment and treatment of behavioral and affective disorders. **English Language:** Knowledge of the structure and content of the English language, including the meaning and spelling of words, rules of composition, and grammar. **Sales and Marketing:** Knowledge of principles and methods for showing, promoting, and selling products or services. This includes marketing strategy and tactics, product demonstration, sales techniques, and sales control systems. **Administration and Management:** Knowledge of business and management principles involved in strategic planning, resource allocation, human resources modeling, leadership technique, production methods, and coordination of people and resources.

Coating, Painting, and Spraying Machine Operators and Tenders

- ▲ Education/Training Required: Moderate-term on-the-job training
- ▲ Annual Earnings: $24,710
- ▲ Growth: 11.9%
- ▲ Annual Job Openings: 18,000
- ▲ Self-Employed: 0%
- ▲ Part-Time: 5.7%

Coating Machine Operators and Tenders: Operate or tend machines to coat any of a wide variety of items: Coat food products with sugar, chocolate, or butter; coat paper and paper products with chemical solutions, wax, or glazes; or coat fabric with rubber or plastic. Painting and Spraying Machine Operators and Tenders: Operate or tend machines to spray or paint decorative, protective, or other coating or finish, such as adhesive, lacquer, paint, stain, latex, preservative, oil, or other solutions. May apply coating or finish to any of a wide variety of items or materials, such as wood and wood products, ceramics, and glass. Includes workers who apply coating or finish to materials preparatory to further processing or to consumer use. Observes machine operation and gauges to detect defects or deviations from standards. Fills hopper, reservoir, trough, or pan with material used to coat, paint, or spray, using conveyor or pail. Measures and mixes specified quantities of substances to create coatings, paints, or sprays. Threads or feeds item or product through or around machine rollers and dryers. Examines, measures, weighs, or tests sample product to ensure conformance to specifications. Cleans machine, equipment, and work area, using water, solvents, and other cleaning aids. Records production data. Transfers completed item or product from machine to drying or storage area, using handcart, hand truck, or crane. Places item or product on feedrack, spindle, or reel strand to coat, paint, or spray, using hands, hoist, or trucklift. Aligns or fastens machine parts such as rollers, guides, brushes, and blades to secure roll, using hand tools. Attaches specified hose or nozzle to machine, using wrench and pliers. Starts and stops operation of machine, using lever or button. Turns dial, handwheel, valve, or switch to control and adjust temperature, speed, and flow of product or machine. **SKILLS**—**Operation and Control:** Controlling operations of equipment or systems. **Operation Monitoring:** Watching gauges, dials, or other indicators to make sure a machine is working properly. **Mathematics:** Using mathematics to solve problems.

GOE INFORMATION—**Interest Area:** 08. Industrial Production. **Work Group:** 08.03. Production Work. **Other Job Titles in This Work Group:** Bakers, Manufacturing; Bindery Machine Operators and Tenders; Brazers; Cementing and Gluing Machine Operators and Tenders;

Chemical Equipment Controllers and Operators; Chemical Equipment Operators and Tenders; Chemical Equipment Tenders; Cleaning, Washing, and Metal Pickling Equipment Operators and Tenders; Coil Winders, Tapers, and Finishers; Combination Machine Tool Operators and Tenders, Metal and Plastic; Computer-Controlled Machine Tool Operators, Metal and Plastic; Cooling and Freezing Equipment Operators and Tenders; Crushing, Grinding, and Polishing Machine Setters, Operators, and Tenders; Cutters and Trimmers, Hand; Cutting and Slicing Machine Operators and Tenders; Cutting and Slicing Machine Setters, Operators, and Tenders; Design Printing Machine Setters and Set-Up Operators; Electrolytic Plating and Coating Machine Operators and Tenders, Metal and Plastic; Electrolytic Plating and Coating Machine Setters and Set-Up Operators, Metal and Plastic; Electrotypers and Stereotypers; Embossing Machine Set-Up Operators; Engraver Set-Up Operators; Extruding and Forming Machine Operators and Tenders, Synthetic or Glass Fibers; Extruding and Forming Machine Setters, Operators, and Tenders, Synthetic and Glass Fibers; Extruding, Forming, Pressing, and Compacting Machine Operators and Tenders; Fabric and Apparel Patternmakers; Fiber Product Cutting Machine Setters and Set-Up Operators; Fiberglass Laminators and Fabricators; Film Laboratory Technicians; Fitters, Structural Metal—Precision; Food and Tobacco Roasting, Baking, and Drying Machine Operators and Tenders; Food Batchmakers; Food Cooking Machine Operators and Tenders; Furnace, Kiln, Oven, Drier, and Kettle Operators and Tenders; Glass Cutting Machine Setters and Set-Up Operators; Graders and Sort-

ers, Agricultural Products; Grinding and Polishing Workers, Hand; Hand Compositors and Typesetters; Heaters, Metal and Plastic; Helpers—Production Workers; Job Printers; Letterpress Setters and Set-Up Operators; others. **PERSONALITY TYPE**—Realistic. Realistic occupations frequently involve work activities that include practical, hands-on problems and solutions. They often deal with plants, animals, and real-world materials like wood, tools, and machinery. Many of the occupations require working outside and do not involve a lot of paperwork or working closely with others.

EDUCATION/TRAINING PROGRAM(S)—No data available. **RELATED KNOWLEDGE/COURSES—Production and Processing:** Knowledge of raw materials, production processes, quality control, costs, and other techniques for maximizing the effective manufacture and distribution of goods. **Principles of Mechanical Devices:** Knowledge of machines and tools, including their designs, uses, repair, and maintenance. **Engineering and Technology:** Knowledge of the practical application of engineering science and technology. This includes applying principles, techniques, procedures, and equipment to the design and production of various goods and services. **Chemistry:** Knowledge of the chemical composition, structure, and properties of substances and of the chemical processes and transformations that they undergo. This includes uses of chemicals and their interactions, danger signs, production techniques, and disposal methods. **Mathematics:** Knowledge of arithmetic, algebra, geometry, calculus, and statistics and their applications.

Coating, Painting, and Spraying Machine Setters and Set-Up Operators

- ▲ Education/Training Required: Moderate-term on-the-job training
- ▲ Annual Earnings: $24,710
- ▲ Growth: 11.9%
- ▲ Annual Job Openings: 18,000
- ▲ Self-Employed: 0%
- ▲ Part-Time: 5.7%

Set up or set up and operate machines to coat or paint any of a wide variety of products, such as food products, glassware, and cloth, ceramic, metal, plastic, paper, and wood products, with lacquer, silver and copper solution, rubber, paint, varnish, glaze, enamel, oil, or rustproofing materials. Sets up and operates machines to paint or coat products with such materials as silver and copper solution, rubber, paint, glaze, oil, or rustproofing materials. Removes materials, parts, or workpieces from painting or

coating machines, using hand tools. Records operational data on specified forms. Cleans and maintains coating and painting machines, using hand tools. Measures thickness and quality of coating, using micrometer. Examines and tests solutions, paints, products, and workpieces to ensure specifications are met. Observes and adjusts loaded workpiece or machine according to specifications. Selects and loads materials, parts, and workpieces on machine, using hand tools. Starts pumps to mix solutions and to activate coating or painting machines. Operates auxiliary machines or equipment used on the coating or painting process. Weighs or measures chemicals, coatings, or paints and adds to machine. Turns valves and adjusts controls to regulate speed of conveyor, temperature, air pressure and circulation, and flow or spray of coating or paint. **SKILLS—Equipment Selection:** Determining the kind of tools and equipment needed to do a job. **Operation and Control:** Controlling operations of equipment or systems. **Operation Monitoring:** Watching gauges, dials, or other indicators to make sure a machine is working properly. **Quality Control Analysis:** Conducting tests and inspections of products, services, or processes to evaluate quality or performance.

GOE INFORMATION—Interest Area: 08. Industrial Production. **Work Group:** 08.02. Production Technology. **Other Job Titles in This Work Group:** Aircraft Rigging Assemblers; Aircraft Structure Assemblers, Precision; Aircraft Structure, Surfaces, Rigging, and Systems Assemblers; Aircraft Systems Assemblers, Precision; Bench Workers, Jewelry; Bindery Machine Setters and Set-Up Operators; Bindery Workers; Bookbinders; Buffing and Polishing Set-Up Operators; Casting Machine Set-Up Operators; Coating, Painting, and Spraying Machine Setters, Operators, and Tenders; Combination Machine Tool Setters and Set-Up Operators, Metal and Plastic; Cutting, Punching, and Press Machine Setters, Operators, and Tenders, Metal and Plastic; Dental Laboratory Technicians; Drilling and Boring Machine Tool Setters, Operators, and Tenders, Metal and Plastic; Electrical and Electronic Equipment Assemblers; Electrical and Electronic Inspectors and Testers; Electromechanical Equipment Assemblers; Engine and Other Machine Assemblers; Extruding and Drawing Machine Setters, Operators, and Tenders, Metal and Plastic; Extruding, Forming, Pressing, and Compacting Machine Setters and Set-Up Operators; Extruding, Forming, Pressing, and Compacting Machine Setters, Operators, and Tenders; Forging Machine Setters, Operators, and Tenders, Metal and Plastic; Foundry Mold and Coremakers; Gem and Diamond Workers; Grinding, Honing, Lapping,

and Deburring Machine Set-Up Operators; Grinding, Lapping, Polishing, and Buffing Machine Tool Setters, Operators, and Tenders, Metal and Plastic; Heat Treating Equipment Setters, Operators, and Tenders, Metal and Plastic; Heat Treating, Annealing, and Tempering Machine Operators and Tenders, Metal and Plastic; Heating Equipment Setters and Set-Up Operators, Metal and Plastic; Inspectors, Testers, Sorters, Samplers, and Weighers; Jewelers; Jewelers and Precious Stone and Metal Workers; Lathe and Turning Machine Tool Setters, Operators, and Tenders, Metal and Plastic; Log Graders and Scalers; Materials Inspectors; Mechanical Inspectors; Metal Molding, Coremaking, and Casting Machine Operators and Tenders; others. **PERSONALITY TYPE—**Realistic. Realistic occupations frequently involve work activities that include practical, hands-on problems and solutions. They often deal with plants, animals, and real-world materials like wood, tools, and machinery. Many of the occupations require working outside and do not involve a lot of paperwork or working closely with others.

EDUCATION/TRAINING PROGRAM(S)—No data available. **RELATED KNOWLEDGE/COURSES— Principles of Mechanical Devices:** Knowledge of machines and tools, including their designs, uses, repair, and maintenance. **Production and Processing:** Knowledge of raw materials, production processes, quality control, costs, and other techniques for maximizing the effective manufacture and distribution of goods. **Chemistry:** Knowledge of the chemical composition, structure, and properties of substances and of the chemical processes and transformations that they undergo. This includes uses of chemicals and their interactions, danger signs, production techniques, and disposal methods. **Mathematics:** Knowledge of arithmetic, algebra, geometry, calculus, and statistics and their applications. **Clerical Studies:** Knowledge of administrative and clerical procedures and systems, such as word processing, managing files and records, stenography and transcription, designing forms, and other office procedures and terminology.

Coating, Painting, and Spraying Machine Setters, Operators, and Tenders

- ▲ Education/Training Required: Short-term on-the-job training
- ▲ Annual Earnings: $24,710
- ▲ Growth: 11.9%
- ▲ Annual Job Openings: 18,000
- ▲ Self-Employed: 0%
- ▲ Part-Time: 5.7%

Set up, operate, or tend machines to coat or paint any of a wide variety of products, including food, glassware, cloth, ceramics, metal, plastic, paper, or wood, with lacquer, silver, copper, rubber, varnish, glaze, enamel, oil, or rustproofing materials. **SKILLS**—No data available.

GOE INFORMATION—**Interest Area:** 08. Industrial Production. **Work Group:** 08.02. Production Technology. **Other Job Titles in This Work Group:** Aircraft Rigging Assemblers; Aircraft Structure Assemblers, Precision; Aircraft Structure, Surfaces, Rigging, and Systems Assemblers; Aircraft Systems Assemblers, Precision; Bench Workers, Jewelry; Bindery Machine Setters and Set-Up Operators; Bindery Workers; Bookbinders; Buffing and Polishing Set-Up Operators; Casting Machine Set-Up Operators; Coating, Painting, and Spraying Machine Setters and Set-Up Operators; Combination Machine Tool Setters and Set-Up Operators, Metal and Plastic; Cutting, Punching, and Press Machine Setters, Operators, and Tenders, Metal and Plastic; Dental Laboratory Technicians; Drilling and Boring Machine Tool Setters, Operators, and Tenders, Metal and Plastic; Electrical and Electronic Equipment Assemblers; Electrical and Electronic Inspectors and Testers; Electromechanical Equipment Assemblers; Engine and Other Machine Assemblers; Extruding and Drawing Machine Setters, Operators, and Tenders, Metal and Plastic; Extruding, Forming, Pressing, and Compacting Machine Setters and Set-Up Operators; Extruding, Forming, Pressing, and Compacting Machine Setters, Operators, and Tenders; Forging Machine Setters, Operators, and Tenders, Metal and Plastic; Foundry Mold and Coremakers; Gem and Diamond Workers; Grinding, Honing, Lapping, and Deburring Machine Set-Up Operators; Grinding, Lapping, Polishing, and Buffing Machine Tool Setters, Operators, and Tenders, Metal and Plastic; Heat Treating Equipment Setters, Operators, and Tenders, Metal and Plastic; Heat Treating, Annealing, and Tempering Machine Operators and Tenders, Metal and Plastic; Heating Equipment Setters and Set-Up Operators, Metal and Plastic; Inspectors, Testers, Sorters, Samplers, and Weighers; Jewelers; Jewelers and Precious Stone and Metal Workers; Lathe and Turning Machine Tool Setters, Operators, and Tenders, Metal and Plastic; Log Graders and Scalers; Materials Inspectors; Mechanical Inspectors; Metal Molding, Coremaking, and Casting Machine Operators and Tenders; others. **PERSONALITY TYPE**—No data available.

EDUCATION/TRAINING PROGRAM(S)—No data available. **RELATED KNOWLEDGE/COURSES**—No data available.

Combination Machine Tool Operators and Tenders, Metal and Plastic

- ▲ Education/Training Required: Moderate-term on-the-job training
- ▲ Annual Earnings: $27,910
- ▲ Growth: 14.7%
- ▲ Annual Job Openings: 21,000
- ▲ Self-Employed: 0%
- ▲ Part-Time: 2.3%

Operate or tend more than one type of cutting or forming machine tool that has been previously set up. Includes such machine tools as band saws, press brakes, slitting machines, drills, lathes, and boring machines. Activates and tends or operates machines to cut, shape, thread, bore, drill, tap, bend, or mill metal or non-metallic material. Positions, adjusts, and secures workpiece against stops, on arbor, or in chuck, fixture, or automatic feeding mechanism manually or using hoist. Aligns layout marks with die or blade. Inspects workpiece for defects and measures workpiece, using rule, template, or other measuring instruments to determine accuracy of machine operation. Performs minor machine maintenance, such as oiling or cleaning machines, dies, or workpieces or adding coolant to machine reservoir. Removes burrs, sharp edges, rust, or scale from workpiece, using file, hand grinder, wire brush, or power tools. Installs machine components, such as chucks, boring bars, or cutting tools, according to specifications, using hand tools. Sets machine stops or guides to specified length as indicated by scale, rule, or template. Adjusts machine components and changes worn accessories, such as cutting tools and brushes, using hand tools. Extracts or lifts jammed pieces from machine, using fingers, wire hooks, or lift bar. Reads job specifications to determine machine adjustments and material requirements. Observes machine operation to detect workpiece defects or machine malfunction. **SKILLS—Operation and Control:** Controlling operations of equipment or systems. **Operation Monitoring:** Watching gauges, dials, or other indicators to make sure a machine is working properly. **Quality Control Analysis:** Conducting tests and inspections of products, services, or processes to evaluate quality or performance. **Equipment Maintenance:** Performing routine maintenance on equipment and determining when and what kind of maintenance is needed. **Equipment Selection:** Determining the kind of tools and equipment needed to do a job. **Installation:** Installing equipment, machines, wiring, or programs to meet specifications. **Reading Comprehension:** Understanding written sentences and paragraphs in work-related documents.

GOE INFORMATION—Interest Area: 08. Industrial Production. **Work Group:** 08.03. Production Work. **Other Job Titles in This Work Group:** Bakers, Manufacturing; Bindery Machine Operators and Tenders; Brazers; Cementing and Gluing Machine Operators and Tenders; Chemical Equipment Controllers and Operators; Chemical Equipment Operators and Tenders; Chemical Equipment Tenders; Cleaning, Washing, and Metal Pickling Equipment Operators and Tenders; Coating, Painting, and Spraying Machine Operators and Tenders; Coil Winders, Tapers, and Finishers; Computer-Controlled Machine Tool Operators, Metal and Plastic; Cooling and Freezing Equipment Operators and Tenders; Crushing, Grinding, and Polishing Machine Setters, Operators, and Tenders; Cutters and Trimmers, Hand; Cutting and Slicing Machine Operators and Tenders; Cutting and Slicing Machine Setters, Operators, and Tenders; Design Printing Machine Setters and Set-Up Operators; Electrolytic Plating and Coating Machine Operators and Tenders, Metal and Plastic; Electrolytic Plating and Coating Machine Setters and Set-Up Operators, Metal and Plastic; Electrotypers and Stereotypers; Embossing Machine Set-Up Operators; Engraver Set-Up Operators; Extruding and Forming Machine Operators and Tenders, Synthetic or Glass Fibers; Extruding and Forming Machine Setters, Operators, and Tenders, Synthetic and Glass Fibers; Extruding, Forming, Pressing, and Compacting Machine Operators and Tenders; Fabric and Apparel Patternmakers; Fiber Product Cutting Machine Setters and Set-Up Operators; Fiberglass Laminators and Fabricators; Film Laboratory Technicians; Fitters, Structural Metal—Precision; Food and Tobacco Roasting, Baking, and Drying Machine Operators and Tenders; Food Batchmakers; Food Cooking Machine Operators and Tenders; Furnace, Kiln, Oven, Drier, and Kettle Operators and Tenders; Glass Cutting Machine Setters and Set-Up Operators; Graders and Sorters, Agricultural Products; Grinding and Polishing Workers, Hand; Hand Compositors and Typesetters; Heaters, Metal and Plastic; Helpers—Production Workers; Job Printers; Letterpress Setters and Set-Up Operators; others. **PERSONALITY TYPE—**Realistic. Realistic occupations frequently involve work activities that include practical, hands-on problems and solutions. They often deal with plants, animals, and real-world materials like wood, tools, and machinery. Many of the occupations require working outside and do not involve a lot of paperwork or working closely with others.

EDUCATION/TRAINING PROGRAM(S)—Machine Shop Technology/Assistant; Machine Tool Technology/Machinist. **RELATED KNOWLEDGE/COURSES—Production and Processing:** Knowledge of raw materials, production processes, quality control, costs, and other techniques for maximizing the effective manufacture and distribution of goods. **Principles of Mechanical Devices:** Knowledge of machines and tools, including their designs, uses, repair, and maintenance. **Mathematics:** Knowledge of arithmetic, algebra, geometry, calculus, and statistics and their applications. **Engineering and Technology:** Knowledge of the practical application of engineering science and technology. This includes applying principles, techniques, procedures, and equipment to the design and production of various goods and services. **Design:** Knowledge of design techniques, tools, and principles involved in production of precision technical plans, blueprints, drawings, and models. **Building and Construction:** Knowledge of materials, methods, and tools involved in the construction or repair of houses, buildings, or other structures, such as highways and roads.

Combination Machine Tool Setters and Set-Up Operators, Metal and Plastic

▲ Education/Training Required: Moderate-term on-the-job training
▲ Annual Earnings: $27,910
▲ Growth: 14.7%
▲ Annual Job Openings: 21,000
▲ Self-Employed: 0%
▲ Part-Time: 2.3%

Set up or set up and operate more than one type of cutting or forming machine tool, such as gear hobbers, lathes, press brakes, shearing, and boring machines. Sets up and operates lathes, cutters, borers, millers, grinders, presses, drills, and auxiliary machines to make metallic and plastic workpieces. Computes data, such as gear dimensions and machine settings, applying knowledge of shop mathematics. Instructs operators or other workers in machine setup and operation. Records operational data such as pressure readings, length of stroke, feeds, and speeds. Makes minor electrical and mechanical repairs and adjustments to machines and notifies supervisor when major service is required. Lifts, positions, and secures workpieces in holding devices, using hoists and hand tools. Inspects first-run workpieces and verifies conformance to specifications to check accuracy of machine setup. Measures and marks reference points and cutting lines on workpiece, using traced templates, compasses, and rules. Moves controls or mounts gears, cams, or templates in machine to set feed rate and cutting speed, depth, and angle. Selects, installs, and adjusts alignment of drills, cutters, dies, guides, and holding devices, using template, measuring instruments, and hand tools. Starts machine and turns handwheels or valves to engage feeding, cooling, and lubricating mechanisms. Reads blueprint or job order to determine product specifications and tooling instructions and to plan operational sequences. Monitors machine operation and moves controls to align and adjust position of workpieces and action of cutting tools. **SKILLS—Quality Control Analysis:** Conducting tests and inspections of products, services, or processes to evaluate quality or performance. **Operation and Control:** Controlling operations of equipment or systems. **Mathematics:** Using mathematics to solve problems. **Operation Monitoring:** Watching gauges, dials, or other indicators to make sure a machine is working properly. **Equipment Maintenance:** Performing routine maintenance on equipment and determining when and what kind of maintenance is needed. **Instructing:** Teaching others how to do something.

GOE INFORMATION—Interest Area: 08. Industrial Production. **Work Group:** 08.02. Production Technology. **Other Job Titles in This Work Group:** Aircraft Rigging Assemblers; Aircraft Structure Assemblers, Precision; Aircraft Structure, Surfaces, Rigging, and Systems Assemblers; Aircraft Systems Assemblers, Precision; Bench Workers, Jewelry; Bindery Machine Setters and Set-Up Operators; Bindery Workers; Bookbinders; Buffing and Polishing Set-Up Operators; Casting Machine Set-Up Operators; Coating, Painting, and Spraying Machine Setters and Set-Up Operators; Coating, Painting, and Spraying Machine Setters, Operators, and Tenders; Cutting, Punching, and Press Machine Setters, Operators, and Tenders, Metal and Plastic; Dental Laboratory Technicians; Drilling and Boring Machine Tool Setters, Operators, and Tenders, Metal and Plastic; Electrical and Electronic Equipment Assemblers; Electrical and Electronic Inspectors and Testers; Electromechanical Equipment Assemblers; Engine and Other Machine Assemblers; Extruding and Drawing Machine Setters, Operators, and Tenders, Metal and Plastic; Extruding, Forming, Pressing, and Compacting Machine Setters and Set-Up Operators; Extruding, Forming, Pressing, and Compacting Machine Setters, Operators, and Tenders; Forging Machine Setters, Operators, and Tenders, Metal and Plastic; Foundry Mold and Coremakers; Gem and Diamond Workers; Grinding, Honing, Lapping, and Deburring Machine Set-Up Operators; Grinding, Lapping, Polishing, and Buffing Machine Tool Setters, Operators, and Tenders, Metal and Plastic; Heat Treating Equipment Setters, Operators, and Tenders, Metal and Plastic; Heat Treating, Annealing, and Tempering Machine Operators and Tenders, Metal and Plastic; Heating Equipment Setters and Set-Up Operators, Metal and Plastic; Inspectors, Testers, Sorters, Samplers, and Weighers; Jewelers; Jewelers and Precious Stone and Metal Workers; Lathe and Turning Machine Tool Setters, Operators, and Tenders, Metal and Plastic; Log Graders and Scalers; Materials Inspectors; Mechanical Inspectors; Metal Molding, Coremaking, and Casting Machine Operators and Tenders; others. **PERSONALITY TYPE—Realistic.**

Realistic occupations frequently involve work activities that include practical, hands-on problems and solutions. They often deal with plants, animals, and real-world materials like wood, tools, and machinery. Many of the occupations require working outside and do not involve a lot of paperwork or working closely with others.

EDUCATION/TRAINING PROGRAM(S)—Machine Shop Technology/Assistant; Machine Tool Technology/Machinist. **RELATED KNOWLEDGE/COURSES**—**Principles of Mechanical Devices:** Knowledge of machines and tools, including their designs, uses, repair, and maintenance. **Design:** Knowledge of design techniques, tools, and principles involved in production of precision technical plans, blueprints, drawings, and models. **Mathematics:** Knowledge of arithmetic, algebra, geometry, calculus, and statistics and their applications. **Engineering and Technology:** Knowledge of the practical application of engineering science and technology. This includes applying principles, techniques, procedures, and equipment to the design and production of various goods and services. **Production and Processing:** Knowledge of raw materials, production processes, quality control, costs, and other techniques for maximizing the effective manufacture and distribution of goods.

Combined Food Preparation and Serving Workers, Including Fast Food

- ▲ Education/Training Required: Short-term on-the-job training
- ▲ Annual Earnings: $14,120
- ▲ Growth: 30.5%
- ▲ Annual Job Openings: 737,000
- ▲ Self-Employed: 0.3%
- ▲ Part-Time: 57.4%

Perform duties which combine both food preparation and food service. Selects food items from serving or storage areas and places food and beverage items on serving tray or in takeout bag. Notifies kitchen personnel of shortages or special orders. Receives payment. Requests and records customer order and computes bill. Makes and serves hot and cold beverages or desserts. Cooks or reheats food items, such as french fries. **SKILLS**—**Mathematics:** Using mathematics to solve problems. **Speaking:** Talking to others to convey information effectively.

GOE INFORMATION—**Interest Area:** 11. Recreation, Travel, and Other Personal Services. **Work Group:** 11.05. Food and Beverage Services. **Other Job Titles in This Work Group:** Bakers; Bakers, Bread and Pastry; Bartenders; Butchers and Meat Cutters; Chefs and Head Cooks; Cooks, All Other; Cooks, Fast Food; Cooks, Institution and Cafeteria; Cooks, Restaurant; Cooks, Short Order; Counter Attendants, Cafeteria, Food Concession, and Coffee Shop; Dining Room and Cafeteria Attendants and Bartender Helpers; Dishwashers; Food Preparation and Serving Related Workers, All Other; Food Preparation Workers; Food Servers, Nonrestaurant; Hosts and Hostesses, Restaurant, Lounge, and Coffee Shop; Waiters and Waitresses. **PERSONALITY TYPE**—Realistic. Realistic occupations frequently involve work activities that include practical, hands-on problems and solutions. They often deal with plants, animals, and real-world materials like wood, tools, and machinery. Many of the occupations require working outside and do not involve a lot of paperwork or working closely with others.

EDUCATION/TRAINING PROGRAM(S)—Food Preparation/Professional Cooking/Kitchen Assistant; Institutional Food Workers. **RELATED KNOWLEDGE/COURSES**—**Customer and Personal Service:** Knowledge of principles and processes for providing customer and personal services. This includes customer needs assessment, meeting quality standards for services, and evaluation of customer satisfaction. **Mathematics:** Knowledge of arithmetic, algebra, geometry, calculus, and statistics and their applications. **Sales and Marketing:** Knowledge of principles and methods for showing, promoting, and selling products or services. This includes marketing strategy and tactics, product demonstration, sales techniques, and sales control systems. **English Language:** Knowledge of the structure and content of the English language, including the meaning and spelling of words, rules of composition, and grammar. **Clerical Studies:** Knowledge of administrative and clerical procedures and systems, such as word processing, managing files and records, stenography and transcription, designing forms, and other office procedures and terminology.

Commercial and Industrial Designers

- ▲ Education/Training Required: Bachelor's degree
- ▲ Annual Earnings: $49,820
- ▲ Growth: 23.8%
- ▲ Annual Job Openings: 7,000
- ▲ Self-Employed: 31.9%
- ▲ Part-Time: 20.0%

Develop and design manufactured products, such as cars, home appliances, and children's toys. Combine artistic talent with research on product use, marketing, and materials to create the most functional and appealing product design. Confers with engineering, marketing, production, or sales department or customer to establish design concepts for manufactured products. Integrates findings and concepts and sketches design ideas. Designs packaging and containers for products, such as foods, beverages, toiletries, or medicines. Prepares itemized production requirements to produce item. Fabricates model or sample in paper, wood, glass, fabric, plastic, or metal, using hand and power tools. Directs and coordinates preparation of detailed drawings from sketches or fabrication of models or samples. Reads publications, attends showings, and studies traditional, period, and contemporary design styles and motifs to obtain perspective and design concepts. Modifies design to conform with customer specifications, production limitations, or changes in design trends. Presents design to customer or design committee for approval and discusses need for modification. Creates and designs graphic material for use as ornamentation, illustration, or advertising on manufactured materials and packaging. Evaluates design ideas for feasibility based on factors such as appearance, function, serviceability, budget, production costs/methods, and market characteristics. Prepares detailed drawings, illustrations, artwork, or blueprints, using drawing instruments or paints and brushes. **SKILLS—Reading Comprehension:** Understanding written sentences and paragraphs in work-related documents. **Active Learning:** Understanding the implications of new information for both current and future problem-solving and decision-making. **Critical Thinking:** Using logic and reasoning to identify the strengths and weaknesses of alternative solutions, conclusions, or approaches to problems. **Equipment Selection:** Determining the kind of tools and equipment needed to do a job. **Operations Analysis:** Analyzing needs and product requirements to create a design. **Coordination:** Adjusting actions in relation to others' actions. **Monitoring:** Monitoring/Assessing your performance or that of other individuals or organizations to make improvements or take corrective action.

GOE INFORMATION—Interest Area: 01. Arts, Entertainment, and Media. **Work Group:** 01.04. Visual Arts. **Other Job Titles in This Work Group:** Cartoonists; Designers, All Other; Exhibit Designers; Fashion Designers; Fine Artists, Including Painters, Sculptors, and Illustrators; Floral Designers; Graphic Designers; Interior Designers; Merchandise Displayers and Window Trimmers; Multi-Media Artists and Animators; Painters and Illustrators; Sculptors; Set and Exhibit Designers; Set Designers; Sketch Artists. **PERSONALITY TYPE—Artistic.** Artistic occupations frequently involve working with forms, designs, and patterns. They often require self-expression, and the work can be done without following a clear set of rules.

EDUCATION/TRAINING PROGRAM(S)—Commercial and Advertising Art; Design and Applied Arts, Other; Design and Visual Communications, General; Industrial Design. **RELATED KNOWLEDGE/ COURSES—Design:** Knowledge of design techniques, tools, and principles involved in production of precision technical plans, blueprints, drawings, and models. **Sales and Marketing:** Knowledge of principles and methods for showing, promoting, and selling products or services. This includes marketing strategy and tactics, product demonstration, sales techniques, and sales control systems. **Fine Arts:** Knowledge of the theory and techniques required to compose, produce, and perform works of music, dance, visual arts, drama, and sculpture. **Production and Processing:** Knowledge of raw materials, production processes, quality control, costs, and other techniques for maximizing the effective manufacture and distribution of goods. **Principles of Mechanical Devices:** Knowledge of machines and tools, including their designs, uses, repair, and maintenance.

Commercial Divers

- ▲ Education/Training Required: Moderate-term on-the-job training
- ▲ Annual Earnings: $32,770
- ▲ Growth: 11.5%
- ▲ Annual Job Openings: 16,000
- ▲ Self-Employed: 2.2%
- ▲ Part-Time: 5.9%

Work below surface of water, using scuba gear to inspect, repair, remove, or install equipment and structures. May use a variety of power and hand tools, such as drills, sledgehammers, torches, and welding equipment. May conduct tests or experiments, rig explosives, or photograph structures or marine life. Descends into water with aid of diver helper, using scuba gear or diving suit. Communicates with surface while underwater by signal line or telephone. Searches for lost or sunken objects, such as bodies, torpedoes, equipment, and ships. Recovers objects by placing rigging around sunken objects and hooking rigging to crane lines. Inspects docks, hulls and propellers of ships and underwater pipelines, cables, and sewers. Repairs ships and other structures below the water line, using caulk, bolts, and hand tools. Cuts and welds steel, using underwater welding equipment. Removes obstructions from strainers and marine railway or launching ways, using pneumatic and power hand tools. Sets or guides placement of pilings and sandbags to provide support for structures such as docks, bridges, cofferdams, and platforms. Drills holes in rock and rigs explosives for underwater demolitions. Photographs underwater structures or marine life. Levels rails, using wedges and maul or sledgehammer. **SKILLS—Repairing:** Repairing machines or systems, using the needed tools. **Active Listening:** Giving full attention to what other people are saying, taking time to understand the points being made, asking questions as appropriate, and not interrupting at inappropriate times. **Speaking:** Talking to others to convey information effectively. **Coordination:** Adjusting actions in relation to others' actions. **Equipment Selection:** Determining the kind of tools and equipment needed to do a job. **Operation and Control:** Controlling operations of equipment or systems. **Equipment Maintenance:** Performing routine maintenance on equipment and determining when and what kind of maintenance is needed.

GOE INFORMATION—Interest Area: 06. Construction, Mining, and Drilling. **Work Group:** 06.02. Construction. **Other Job Titles in This Work Group:** Boat Builders and Shipwrights; Boilermakers; Brattice Build-

ers; Brickmasons and Blockmasons; Carpenters; Carpet Installers; Ceiling Tile Installers; Cement Masons and Concrete Finishers; Construction Carpenters; Drywall and Ceiling Tile Installers; Drywall Installers; Electricians; Explosives Workers, Ordnance Handling Experts, and Blasters; Fence Erectors; Floor Layers, Except Carpet, Wood, and Hard Tiles; Floor Sanders and Finishers; Glaziers; Grader, Bulldozer, and Scraper Operators; Hazardous Materials Removal Workers; Insulation Workers, Floor, Ceiling, and Wall; Insulation Workers, Mechanical; Manufactured Building and Mobile Home Installers; Operating Engineers; Operating Engineers and Other Construction Equipment Operators; Painters, Construction and Maintenance; Paperhangers; Paving, Surfacing, and Tamping Equipment Operators; Pile-Driver Operators; Pipe Fitters; Pipelayers; Pipelaying Fitters; Plasterers and Stucco Masons; Plumbers; Plumbers, Pipefitters, and Steamfitters; Rail-Track Laying and Maintenance Equipment Operators; Refractory Materials Repairers, Except Brickmasons; Reinforcing Iron and Rebar Workers; Riggers; Roofers; Rough Carpenters; Security and Fire Alarm Systems Installers; Segmental Pavers; Sheet Metal Workers; Ship Carpenters and Joiners; Stone Cutters and Carvers; Stonemasons; Structural Iron and Steel Workers; Tapers; Terrazzo Workers and Finishers; Tile and Marble Setters. **PERSONALITY TYPE—Realistic.** Realistic occupations frequently involve work activities that include practical, hands-on problems and solutions. They often deal with plants, animals, and real-world materials like wood, tools, and machinery. Many of the occupations require working outside and do not involve a lot of paperwork or working closely with others.

EDUCATION/TRAINING PROGRAM(S)—Diver, Professional and Instructor. **RELATED KNOWLEDGE/COURSES—Principles of Mechanical Devices:** Knowledge of machines and tools, including their designs, uses, repair, and maintenance. **Building and Construction:** Knowledge of materials, methods, and tools involved in the construction or repair of houses, buildings, or other structures, such as highways and roads. **Engineering and**

Technology: Knowledge of the practical application of engineering science and technology. This includes applying principles, techniques, procedures, and equipment to the design and production of various goods and services. Physics: Knowledge and prediction of physical principles and laws and their interrelationships and applications to understanding fluid, material, and atmospheric dynamics and mechanical, electrical, atomic, and sub-atomic structures and processes. Telecommunications: Knowledge of transmission, broadcasting, switching, control, and operation of telecommunications systems.

Commercial Pilots

- ▲ Education/Training Required: Postsecondary vocational training
- ▲ Annual Earnings: $47,420
- ▲ Growth: 26.9%
- ▲ Annual Job Openings: 1,000
- ▲ Self-Employed: 2.2%
- ▲ Part-Time: 23.3%

Pilot and navigate the flight of small fixed or rotary winged aircraft, primarily for the transport of cargo and passengers. Requires Commercial Rating. Starts engines, operates controls, and pilots airplane to transport passengers, mail, or freight, adhering to flight plan and regulations and procedures. Obtains and reviews data such as load weight, fuel supply, weather conditions, and flight schedule. Plots flight pattern and files flight plan with appropriate officials. Orders changes in fuel supply, load, route, or schedule to ensure safety of flight. Conducts pre-flight checks and reads gauges to verify that fluids and pressure are at prescribed levels. Operates radio equipment and contacts control tower for takeoff, clearance, arrival instructions, and other information. Coordinates flight activities with ground-crew and air-traffic control and informs crew members of flight and test procedures. Holds commercial pilot's license issued by Federal Aviation Administration. Conducts in-flight tests and evaluations at specified altitudes in all types of weather to determine receptivity and other characteristics of equipment and systems. Logs information such as flight time, altitude flown, and fuel consumption. Plans and formulates flight activities and test schedules and prepares flight evaluation reports. Gives training and instruction in aircraft operations for students and other pilots. SKILLS—Operation and Control: Controlling operations of equipment or systems. Operation Monitoring: Watching gauges, dials, or other indicators to make sure a machine is working properly. Instructing: Teaching others how to do something. Coordination: Adjusting actions in relation to others' actions. Judgment and Decision Making: Considering the relative costs and benefits of potential actions to choose the most appropriate one.

GOE INFORMATION—Interest Area: 07. Transportation. Work Group: 07.03. Air Vehicle Operation. Other Job Titles in This Work Group: Airline Pilots, Copilots, and Flight Engineers. PERSONALITY TYPE—Realistic. Realistic occupations frequently involve work activities that include practical, hands-on problems and solutions. They often deal with plants, animals, and real-world materials like wood, tools, and machinery. Many of the occupations require working outside and do not involve a lot of paperwork or working closely with others.

EDUCATION/TRAINING PROGRAM(S)—Airline/Commercial/Professional Pilot and Flight Crew; Flight Instructor. RELATED KNOWLEDGE/COURSES—Transportation: Knowledge of principles and methods for moving people or goods by air, rail, sea, or road, including the relative costs and benefits. Physics: Knowledge and prediction of physical principles and laws and their interrelationships and applications to understanding fluid, material, and atmospheric dynamics and mechanical, electrical, atomic, and sub-atomic structures and processes. Geography: Knowledge of principles and methods for describing the features of land, sea, and air masses, including their physical characteristics, locations, interrelationships, and distribution of plant, animal, and human life. Public Safety and Security: Knowledge of relevant equipment, policies, procedures, and strategies to promote effective local, state, or national security operations for the protection of people, data, property, and institutions. Mathematics: Knowledge of arithmetic, algebra, geometry, calculus, and statistics and their applications. Telecommunications: Knowledge of transmission, broadcasting, switching, control, and operation of telecommunications systems.

Communications Teachers, Postsecondary

- ▲ Education/Training Required: Master's degree
- ▲ Annual Earnings: $47,110
- ▲ Growth: 23.5%
- ▲ Annual Job Openings: 184,000
- ▲ Self-Employed: 0%
- ▲ Part-Time: 32.3%

Teach courses in communications, such as organizational communications, public relations, radio/television broadcasting, and journalism. SKILLS—No data available.

GOE INFORMATION—Interest Area: 12. Education and Social Service. Work Group: 12.03. Educational Services. Other Job Titles in This Work Group: Adult Literacy, Remedial Education, and GED Teachers and Instructors; Agricultural Sciences Teachers, Postsecondary; Anthropology and Archeology Teachers, Postsecondary; Architecture Teachers, Postsecondary; Archivists; Area, Ethnic, and Cultural Studies Teachers, Postsecondary; Art, Drama, and Music Teachers, Postsecondary; Atmospheric, Earth, Marine, and Space Sciences Teachers, Postsecondary; Audio-Visual Collections Specialists; Biological Science Teachers, Postsecondary; Business Teachers, Postsecondary; Chemistry Teachers, Postsecondary; Child Care Workers; Computer Science Teachers, Postsecondary; Criminal Justice and Law Enforcement Teachers, Postsecondary; Curators; Economics Teachers, Postsecondary; Education Teachers, Postsecondary; Educational Psychologists; Educational, Vocational, and School Counselors; Elementary School Teachers, Except Special Education; Engineering Teachers, Postsecondary; English Language and Literature Teachers, Postsecondary; Environmental Science Teachers, Postsecondary; Farm and Home Management Advisors; Foreign Language and Literature Teachers, Postsecondary; Forestry and Conservation Science Teachers, Postsecondary; Geography Teachers, Postsecondary; Graduate Teaching Assistants; Health Specialties Teachers, Postsecondary; History Teachers, Postsecondary; Home Economics Teachers, Postsecondary; Kindergarten Teachers, Except Special Education; Law Teachers, Postsecondary; Librarians; Library Assistants, Clerical; Library Science Teachers, Postsecondary; Library Technicians; Mathematical Science Teachers, Postsecondary; Middle School Teachers, Except Special and Vocational Education; Museum Technicians and Conservators; Nursing Instructors and Teachers, Postsecondary; Personal Financial Advisors; Philosophy and Religion Teachers, Postsecondary; Physics Teachers, Postsecondary; Political Science Teachers, Postsecondary; Postsecondary Teachers, All Other; Preschool Teachers, Except Special Education; others. PERSONALITY TYPE—No data available.

EDUCATION/TRAINING PROGRAM(S)—Advertising; Broadcast Journalism; Communication Studies/Speech Communication and Rhetoric; Communication, Journalism, and Related Programs, Other; Digital Communication and Media/Multimedia; Health Communication; Journalism; Journalism, Other; Mass Communication/Media Studies; Political Communication; Public Relations/Image Management; Radio and Television. RELATED KNOWLEDGE/COURSES—No data available.

Compensation and Benefits Managers

- ▲ Education/Training Required: Work experience plus degree
- ▲ Annual Earnings: $61,880
- ▲ Growth: 12.7%
- ▲ Annual Job Openings: 14,000
- ▲ Self-Employed: 0.5%
- ▲ Part-Time: 3.6%

Plan, direct, or coordinate compensation and benefits activities and staff of an organization. Formulates policies and procedures for recruitment, testing, placement, classification, orientation, benefits, and labor and industrial relations. Plans, directs, supervises, and coordinates work activities of subordinates and staff relating to employment, compensation, labor relations, and employee relations. Directs preparation and distribution of written and verbal information to inform employees of benefits, compensation, and personnel policies. Evaluates and modifies benefits policies to establish competitive programs and to ensure compliance with legal requirements. Prepares budget for personnel operations. Negotiates bargaining agreements and resolves labor disputes. Conducts exit interviews to identify reasons for employee termination and writes separation notices. Writes directives advising department managers of organization policy in personnel matters such as equal employment opportunity, sexual harassment, and discrimination. Maintains records and compiles statistical reports concerning personnel-related data such as hires, transfers, performance appraisals, and absenteeism rates. Investigates industrial accidents and prepares reports for insurance carrier. Contracts with vendors to provide employee services, such as canteen, transportation, or relocation service. Represents organization at personnel-related hearings and investigations. Analyzes statistical data and reports to identify and determine causes of personnel problems and develop recommendations for improvement of organization's personnel policies and practices. Studies legislation, arbitration decisions, and collective bargaining contracts to assess industry trends. Plans and conducts new employee orientation to foster positive attitude toward organizational objectives. Meets with shop stewards and supervisors to resolve grievances. Prepares and delivers presentations and reports to corporate officers or other management regarding human resource management policies and practices and recommendations for change. Prepares personnel forecast to project employment needs. Develops methods to improve employment policies, processes, and practices and recommends changes to management. Analyzes compensation policies, government regulations, and prevailing wage rates to develop competitive compensation plan. **SKILLS—Management of Personnel Resources:** Motivating, developing, and directing people as they work, identifying the best people for the job. **Systems Analysis:** Determining how a system should work and how changes in conditions, operations, and the environment will affect outcomes. **Systems Evaluation:** Identifying measures or indicators of system performance and the actions needed to improve or correct performance relative to the goals of the system. **Active Learning:** Understanding the implications of new information for both current and future

problem-solving and decision-making. **Reading Comprehension:** Understanding written sentences and paragraphs in work-related documents. **Speaking:** Talking to others to convey information effectively. **Coordination:** Adjusting actions in relation to others' actions.

GOE INFORMATION—Interest Area: 13. General Management and Support. **Work Group:** 13.01. General Management Work and Management of Support Functions. **Other Job Titles in This Work Group:** Chief Executives; Farm, Ranch, and Other Agricultural Managers; Financial Managers; Financial Managers, Branch or Department; Funeral Directors; General and Operations Managers; Government Service Executives; Human Resources Managers; Human Resources Managers, All Other; Legislators; Managers, All Other; Postmasters and Mail Superintendents; Private Sector Executives; Property, Real Estate, and Community Association Managers; Public Relations Managers; Purchasing Managers; Storage and Distribution Managers; Training and Development Managers; Transportation, Storage, and Distribution Managers; Treasurers, Controllers, and Chief Financial Officers. **PERSONALITY TYPE—Enterprising.** Enterprising occupations frequently involve starting up and carrying out projects. These occupations can involve leading people and making many decisions. They sometimes require risk taking and often deal with business.

EDUCATION/TRAINING PROGRAM(S)—Human Resources Management/Personnel Administration, General; Labor and Industrial Relations. RELATED KNOWLEDGE/COURSES—Personnel and Human Resources: Knowledge of principles and procedures for personnel recruitment, selection, training, compensation and benefits, labor relations and negotiation, and personnel information systems. **Administration and Management:** Knowledge of business and management principles involved in strategic planning, resource allocation, human resources modeling, leadership technique, production methods, and coordination of people and resources. **Mathematics:** Knowledge of arithmetic, algebra, geometry, calculus, and statistics and their applications. **English Language:** Knowledge of the structure and content of the English language, including the meaning and spelling of words, rules of composition, and grammar. **Education and Training:** Knowledge of principles and methods for curriculum and training design, teaching and instruction for individuals and groups, and the measurement of training effects.

Compensation, Benefits, and Job Analysis Specialists

▲ Education/Training Required: Bachelor's degree
▲ Annual Earnings: $43,330
▲ Growth: 15.7%
▲ Annual Job Openings: 8,000
▲ Self-Employed: 2.6%
▲ Part-Time: 6.9%

Conduct programs of compensation and benefits and job analysis for employer. May specialize in specific areas, such as position classification and pension programs. Analyzes organizational, occupational, and industrial data to facilitate organizational functions and provide technical information to business, industry, and government. Evaluates and improves methods and techniques for selecting, promoting, evaluating, and training workers. Plans and develops curricula and materials for training programs and conducts training. Determines need for and develops job analysis instruments and materials. Researches job and worker requirements, structural and functional relationships among jobs and occupations, and occupational trends. Prepares reports, such as job descriptions, organization and flow charts, and career path reports, to summarize job analysis information. Consults with business, industry, government, and union officials to arrange for, plan, and design occupational studies and surveys. Prepares research results for publication in form of journals, books, manuals, and film. Observes and interviews employees to collect job, organizational, and occupational information. **SKILLS—Writing:** Communicating effectively in writing as appropriate for the needs of the audience. **Reading Comprehension:** Understanding written sentences and paragraphs in work-related documents. **Systems Evaluation:** Identifying measures or indicators of system performance and the actions needed to improve or correct performance relative to the goals of the system. **Speaking:** Talking to others to convey information effectively. **Learning Strategies:** Selecting and using training/instructional methods and procedures appropriate for the situation when learning or teaching new things. **Active Listening:** Giving full attention to what other people are saying, taking time to understand the points being made, asking questions as appropriate, and not interrupting at inappropriate times. **Coordination:** Adjusting actions in relation to others' actions.

GOE INFORMATION—Interest Area: 13. General Management and Support. **Work Group:** 13.02. Management Support. **Other Job Titles in This Work Group:** Accountants; Accountants and Auditors; Appraisers and Assessors of Real Estate; Appraisers, Real Estate; Assessors; Auditors; Budget Analysts; Claims Adjusters, Examiners, and Investigators; Claims Examiners, Property and Casualty Insurance; Cost Estimators; Credit Analysts; Employment Interviewers, Private or Public Employment Service; Employment, Recruitment, and Placement Specialists; Financial Analysts; Human Resources, Training, and Labor Relations Specialists, All Other; Insurance Adjusters, Examiners, and Investigators; Insurance Appraisers, Auto Damage; Insurance Underwriters; Loan Counselors; Loan Officers; Logisticians; Management Analysts; Market Research Analysts; Personnel Recruiters; Purchasing Agents and Buyers, Farm Products; Purchasing Agents, Except Wholesale, Retail, and Farm Products; Tax Examiners, Collectors, and Revenue Agents; Training and Development Specialists; Wholesale and Retail Buyers, Except Farm Products. **PERSONALITY TYPE—**Investigative. Investigative occupations frequently involve working with ideas and require an extensive amount of thinking. These occupations can involve searching for facts and figuring out problems mentally.

EDUCATION/TRAINING PROGRAM(S)—Human Resources Management/Personnel Administration, General; Labor and Industrial Relations. **RELATED KNOWLEDGE/COURSES—Mathematics:** Knowledge of arithmetic, algebra, geometry, calculus, and statistics and their applications. **English Language:** Knowledge of the structure and content of the English language, including the meaning and spelling of words, rules of composition, and grammar. **Psychology:** Knowledge of human behavior and performance; individual differences in ability, personality, and interests; learning and motivation; psychological research methods; and the assessment and treatment of behavioral and affective disorders. **Personnel and Human Resources:** Knowledge of principles and procedures for personnel recruitment, selection, training, compensation and benefits, labor relations and negotiation, and personnel information systems. **Computers and Electronics:** Knowledge of circuit boards, processors, chips, electronic equipment, and computer hardware and software, including applications and programming.

Composers

- ▲ Education/Training Required: Master's degree
- ▲ Annual Earnings: $33,720
- ▲ Growth: 13.1%
- ▲ Annual Job Openings: 9,000
- ▲ Self-Employed: 25.8%
- ▲ Part-Time: 53.5%

Compose music for orchestra, choral group, or band. Creates original musical form or writes within circumscribed musical form, such as sonata, symphony, or opera. Transcribes or records musical ideas into notes on scored music paper. Develops pattern of harmony, applying knowledge of music theory. Synthesizes ideas for melody of musical scores for choral group or band. Creates musical and tonal structure, applying elements of music theory, such as instrumental and vocal capabilities. Determines basic pattern of melody, applying knowledge of music theory. **SKILLS—Equipment Selection:** Determining the kind of tools and equipment needed to do a job. **Complex Problem Solving:** Identifying complex problems and reviewing related information to develop and evaluate options and implement solutions. **Monitoring:** Monitoring/Assessing your performance or that of other individuals or organizations to make improvements or take corrective action. **Writing:** Communicating effectively in writing as appropriate for the needs of the audience. **Reading Comprehension:** Understanding written sentences and paragraphs in work-related documents.

GOE INFORMATION—Interest Area: 01. Arts, Entertainment, and Media. **Work Group:** 01.05. Performing Arts. **Other Job Titles in This Work Group:** Actors; Choreographers; Dancers; Directors—Stage, Motion Pictures, Television, and Radio; Music Arrangers and Orchestrators; Music Directors; Music Directors and Composers; Musicians and Singers; Musicians, Instrumental; Public Address System and Other Announcers; Radio and Television Announcers; Singers; Talent Directors. **PERSONALITY TYPE—Artistic.** Artistic occupations frequently involve working with forms, designs, and patterns. They often require self-expression, and the work can be done without following a clear set of rules.

EDUCATION/TRAINING PROGRAM(S)—Conducting; Music Management and Merchandising; Music Performance, General; Music Theory and Composition; Music, Other; Musicology and Ethnomusicology; Religious/Sacred Music; Voice and Opera. **RELATED KNOWLEDGE/COURSES—Fine Arts:** Knowledge of the theory and techniques required to compose, produce, and perform works of music, dance, visual arts, drama, and sculpture. **Mathematics:** Knowledge of arithmetic, algebra, geometry, calculus, and statistics and their applications. **English Language:** Knowledge of the structure and content of the English language, including the meaning and spelling of words, rules of composition, and grammar. **Clerical Studies:** Knowledge of administrative and clerical procedures and systems, such as word processing, managing files and records, stenography and transcription, designing forms, and other office procedures and terminology. **Communications and Media:** Knowledge of media production, communication, and dissemination techniques and methods. This includes alternative ways to inform and entertain via written, oral, and visual media.

Computer and Information Scientists, Research

▲ Education/Training Required: Doctoral degree
▲ Annual Earnings: $75,130
▲ Growth: 40.3%
▲ Annual Job Openings: 2,000
▲ Self-Employed: 2.7%
▲ Part-Time: 5.7%

Conduct research into fundamental computer and information science as theorists, designers, or inventors. Solve or develop solutions to problems in the field of computer hardware and software. **SKILLS**—No data available.

GOE INFORMATION—Interest Area: 02. Science, Math, and Engineering. **Work Group:** 02.06. Mathematics and Computers. **Other Job Titles in This Work Group:** Actuaries; Computer Programmers; Computer Security Specialists; Computer Specialists, All Other; Computer Support Specialists; Computer Systems Analysts; Database Administrators; Mathematical Science Occupations, All Other; Mathematical Technicians; Mathematicians; Network and Computer Systems Administrators; Network Systems and Data Communications Analysts; Operations Research Analysts; Statistical Assistants; Statisticians. **PERSONALITY TYPE**—No data available.

EDUCATION/TRAINING PROGRAM(S)—Artificial Intelligence and Robotics; Computer and Information Sciences and Support Services, Other; Computer and Information Sciences, General; Computer Science; Computer Systems Analysis/Analyst; Information Science/Studies; Medical Informatics. **RELATED KNOWLEDGE/COURSES**—No data available.

Computer and Information Systems Managers

▲ Education/Training Required: Work experience plus degree
▲ Annual Earnings: $82,480
▲ Growth: 47.9%
▲ Annual Job Openings: 28,000
▲ Self-Employed: 0%
▲ Part-Time: 6.1%

Plan, direct, or coordinate activities in such fields as electronic data processing, information systems, systems analysis, and computer programming. Evaluates data processing project proposals and assesses project feasibility. Directs daily operations of department and coordinates project activities with other departments. Directs training of subordinates. Participates in staffing decisions. Develops and interprets organizational goals, policies, and procedures and reviews project plans. Develops performance standards and evaluates work in light of established standards. Analyzes workflow and assigns or schedules work to meet priorities and goals. Meets with department heads, managers, supervisors, vendors, and others to solicit cooperation and resolve problems. Approves, prepares, monitors, and adjusts operational budget. Consults with users, management, vendors, and technicians to determine computing needs and system requirements. Prepares and reviews operational reports or project progress reports.

SKILLS—**Management of Material Resources:** Obtaining and seeing to the appropriate use of equipment, facilities, and materials needed to do certain work. **Coordination:** Adjusting actions in relation to others' actions. **Management of Personnel Resources:** Motivating, developing, and directing people as they work, identifying the best people for the job. **Reading Comprehension:** Understanding written sentences and paragraphs in work-related documents. **Systems Evaluation:** Identifying measures or indicators of system performance and the actions needed to improve or correct performance relative to the goals of the system. **Judgment and Decision Making:** Considering the relative costs and benefits of potential actions to choose the most appropriate one.

GOE INFORMATION—Interest Area: 02. Science, Math, and Engineering. **Work Group:** 02.01. Managerial Work in Science, Math, and Engineering. **Other Job Titles in This Work Group:** Engineering Managers; Natural Sciences Managers. **PERSONALITY TYPE**—Enterprising. Enterprising occupations frequently involve starting up and carrying out projects. These occupations can involve leading people and making many decisions. They sometimes require risk taking and often deal with business.

EDUCATION/TRAINING PROGRAM(S)—Computer and Information Sciences, General; Computer Science; Information Resources Management/CIO Training; Information Science/Studies; Knowledge Management; Management Information Systems, General; Operations Management and Supervision; System Administration/Administrator. **RELATED KNOWLEDGE/COURSES**—**Administration and Management:** Knowledge of business and management principles involved in

strategic planning, resource allocation, human resources modeling, leadership technique, production methods, and coordination of people and resources. **Computers and Electronics:** Knowledge of circuit boards, processors, chips, electronic equipment, and computer hardware and software, including applications and programming. **Mathematics:** Knowledge of arithmetic, algebra, geometry, calculus, and statistics and their applications. **English Language:** Knowledge of the structure and content of the English language, including the meaning and spelling of words, rules of composition, and grammar. **Economics and Accounting:** Knowledge of economic and accounting principles and practices, the financial markets, banking, and the analysis and reporting of financial data.

Computer Hardware Engineers

- ▲ Education/Training Required: Bachelor's degree
- ▲ Annual Earnings: $71,560
- ▲ Growth: 24.9%
- ▲ Annual Job Openings: 3,000
- ▲ Self-Employed: 2.9%
- ▲ Part-Time: 2.6%

Research, design, develop, and test computer or computer-related equipment for commercial, industrial, military, or scientific use. May supervise the manufacturing and installation of computer or computer-related equipment and components. Analyzes software requirements to determine feasibility of design within time and cost constraints. Trains users to use new or modified equipment. Recommends purchase of equipment to control dust, temperature, and humidity in area of system installation. Enters data into computer terminal to store, retrieve, and manipulate data for analysis of system capabilities and requirements. Specifies power supply requirements and configuration. Consults with customer concerning maintenance of software system. Monitors functioning of equipment to ensure system operates in conformance with specifications. Evaluates factors such as reporting formats required, cost constraints, and need for security restrictions to determine hardware configuration. Formulates and designs software system, using scientific analysis and mathematical models to predict and measure outcome and consequences of design. Confers with data processing and project managers to obtain information on limitations and capabilities for data processing projects. Coordinates installation of software system. Develops and directs software system testing procedures,

programming, and documentation. Consults with engineering staff to evaluate interface between hardware and software and operational and performance requirements of overall system. Analyzes information to determine, recommend, and plan layout for type of computers and peripheral equipment modifications to existing systems. **SKILLS**—**Troubleshooting:** Determining causes of operating errors and deciding what to do about them. **Programming:** Writing computer programs for various purposes. **Active Learning:** Understanding the implications of new information for both current and future problem-solving and decision-making. **Mathematics:** Using mathematics to solve problems. **Installation:** Installing equipment, machines, wiring, or programs to meet specifications. **Operations Analysis:** Analyzing needs and product requirements to create a design.

GOE INFORMATION—**Interest Area:** 02. Science, Math, and Engineering. **Work Group:** 02.07. Engineering. **Other Job Titles in This Work Group:** Aerospace Engineers; Agricultural Engineers; Architects, Except Landscape and Naval; Biomedical Engineers; Chemical Engineers; Civil Engineers; Computer Software Engineers, Applications; Computer Software Engineers, Systems Software; Electrical Engineers; Electronics Engineers, Except

Computer; Engineers, All Other; Environmental Engineers; Fire-Prevention and Protection Engineers; Health and Safety Engineers, Except Mining Safety Engineers and Inspectors; Industrial Engineers; Industrial Safety and Health Engineers; Landscape Architects; Marine Architects; Marine Engineers; Marine Engineers and Naval Architects; Materials Engineers; Mechanical Engineers; Mining and Geological Engineers, Including Mining Safety Engineers; Nuclear Engineers; Petroleum Engineers; Product Safety Engineers; Sales Engineers. **PERSONALITY TYPE**—Investigative. Investigative occupations frequently involve working with ideas and require an extensive amount of thinking. These occupations can involve searching for facts and figuring out problems mentally.

EDUCATION/TRAINING PROGRAM(S)—Computer Engineering, General; Computer Hardware Engineering. **RELATED KNOWLEDGE/COURSES**—**Computers and Electronics:** Knowledge of circuit boards, processors, chips, electronic equipment, and computer hardware and software, including applications and

programming. **Mathematics:** Knowledge of arithmetic, algebra, geometry, calculus, and statistics and their applications. **Engineering and Technology:** Knowledge of the practical application of engineering science and technology. This includes applying principles, techniques, procedures, and equipment to the design and production of various goods and services. **English Language:** Knowledge of the structure and content of the English language, including the meaning and spelling of words, rules of composition, and grammar. **Education and Training:** Knowledge of principles and methods for curriculum and training design, teaching and instruction for individuals and groups, and the measurement of training effects. **Administration and Management:** Knowledge of business and management principles involved in strategic planning, resource allocation, human resources modeling, leadership technique, production methods, and coordination of people and resources. **Design:** Knowledge of design techniques, tools, and principles involved in production of precision technical plans, blueprints, drawings, and models.

Computer Programmers

- ▲ Education/Training Required: Bachelor's degree
- ▲ Annual Earnings: $60,120
- ▲ Growth: 16.2%
- ▲ Annual Job Openings: 36,000
- ▲ Self-Employed: 4.8%
- ▲ Part-Time: 7.3%

Convert project specifications and statements of problems and procedures to detailed logical flow charts for coding into computer language. Develop and write computer programs to store, locate, and retrieve specific documents, data, and information. May program Web sites. Analyzes, reviews, and rewrites programs, using workflow chart and diagram, applying knowledge of computer capabilities, subject matter, and symbolic logic. Converts detailed logical flow chart to language processible by computer. Resolves symbolic formulations, prepares flow charts and block diagrams, and encodes resultant equations for processing. Develops programs from workflow charts or diagrams, considering computer storage capacity, speed, and intended use of output data. Consults with managerial, engineering, and technical personnel to clarify program intent, identify problems, and suggest changes. Prepares records and reports. Assists computer operators or system analysts to resolve problems in running computer program. Trains subordinates in programming and program coding. Assigns, coor-

dinates, and reviews work and activities of programming personnel. Collaborates with computer manufacturers and other users to develop new programming methods. Writes instructions to guide operating personnel during production runs. Revises or directs revision of existing programs to increase operating efficiency or adapt to new requirements. Compiles and writes documentation of program development and subsequent revisions. Prepares or receives detailed workflow chart and diagram to illustrate sequence of steps to describe input, output, and logical operation. **SKILLS**—**Programming:** Writing computer programs for various purposes. **Reading Comprehension:** Understanding written sentences and paragraphs in work-related documents. **Troubleshooting:** Determining causes of operating errors and deciding what to do about them. **Writing:** Communicating effectively in writing as appropriate for the needs of the audience. **Active Learning:** Understanding the implications of new information for both current and future problem-solving and decision-making.

GOE INFORMATION—**Interest Area:** 02. Science, Math, and Engineering. **Work Group:** 02.06. Mathematics and Computers. **Other Job Titles in This Work Group:** Actuaries; Computer and Information Scientists, Research; Computer Security Specialists; Computer Specialists, All Other; Computer Support Specialists; Computer Systems Analysts; Database Administrators; Mathematical Science Occupations, All Other; Mathematical Technicians; Mathematicians; Network and Computer Systems Administrators; Network Systems and Data Communications Analysts; Operations Research Analysts; Statistical Assistants; Statisticians. PERSONALITY TYPE—Investigative. Investigative occupations frequently involve working with ideas and require an extensive amount of thinking. These occupations can involve searching for facts and figuring out problems mentally.

EDUCATION/TRAINING PROGRAM(S)—Artificial Intelligence and Robotics; Bioinformatics; Computer Graphics; Computer Programming, Specific Applications; Computer Programming, Vendor/Product Certification; Computer Programming/Programmer, General; E-Commerce/Electronic Commerce; Management Information Systems, General; Medical Informatics; Medical Office Computer Specialist/Assistant; Web Page, Digital/Multimedia, and Information Resources Design; Web/Multimedia Management and Webmaster. **RELATED KNOWLEDGE/COURSES—Computers and Electronics:** Knowledge of circuit boards, processors, chips, electronic equipment, and computer hardware and software, including applications and programming. **Mathematics:** Knowledge of arithmetic, algebra, geometry, calculus, and statistics and their applications. **Education and Training:** Knowledge of principles and methods for curriculum and training design, teaching and instruction for individuals and groups, and the measurement of training effects. **English Language:** Knowledge of the structure and content of the English language, including the meaning and spelling of words, rules of composition, and grammar. **Clerical Studies:** Knowledge of administrative and clerical procedures and systems, such as word processing, managing files and records, stenography and transcription, designing forms, and other office procedures and terminology.

Computer Science Teachers, Postsecondary

- ▲ Education/Training Required: Master's degree
- ▲ Annual Earnings: $49,050
- ▲ Growth: 23.5%
- ▲ Annual Job Openings: 184,000
- ▲ Self-Employed: 0%
- ▲ Part-Time: 32.3%

Teach courses in computer science. May specialize in a field of computer science, such as the design and function of computers or operations and research analysis. Prepares and delivers lectures to students. Compiles, administers, and grades examinations or assigns this work to others. Directs research of other teachers or graduate students working for advanced academic degrees. Compiles bibliographies of specialized materials for outside reading assignments. Stimulates class discussions. Conducts research in particular field of knowledge and publishes findings in professional journals. Acts as adviser to student organizations. Serves on faculty committee providing professional consulting services to government and industry. Advises students on academic and vocational curricula. **SKILLS—Reading Comprehension:** Understanding written sentences and paragraphs in work-related documents. **Instructing:** Teaching others how to do something. **Writing:** Communicating effectively in writing as appropriate for the needs of the audience. **Active Learning:** Understanding the implications of new information for both current and future problem-solving and decision-making. **Learning Strategies:** Selecting and using training/instructional methods and procedures appropriate for the situation when learning or teaching new things.

GOE INFORMATION—**Interest Area:** 12. Education and Social Service. **Work Group:** 12.03. Educational Services. **Other Job Titles in This Work Group:** Adult Literacy, Remedial Education, and GED Teachers and Instructors; Agricultural Sciences Teachers, Postsecondary; Anthropology and Archeology Teachers, Postsecondary; Architecture Teachers, Postsecondary; Archivists; Area, Ethnic, and Cultural Studies Teachers, Postsecondary; Art, Drama, and Music Teachers, Postsecondary; Atmospheric, Earth, Marine, and Space Sciences Teachers, Postsecondary; Audio-Visual Collections Specialists; Biological Science

Teachers, Postsecondary; Business Teachers, Postsecondary; Chemistry Teachers, Postsecondary; Child Care Workers; Communications Teachers, Postsecondary; Criminal Justice and Law Enforcement Teachers, Postsecondary; Curators; Economics Teachers, Postsecondary; Education Teachers, Postsecondary; Educational Psychologists; Educational, Vocational, and School Counselors; Elementary School Teachers, Except Special Education; Engineering Teachers, Postsecondary; English Language and Literature Teachers, Postsecondary; Environmental Science Teachers, Postsecondary; Farm and Home Management Advisors; Foreign Language and Literature Teachers, Postsecondary; Forestry and Conservation Science Teachers, Postsecondary; Geography Teachers, Postsecondary; Graduate Teaching Assistants; Health Specialties Teachers, Postsecondary; History Teachers, Postsecondary; Home Economics Teachers, Postsecondary; Kindergarten Teachers, Except Special Education; Law Teachers, Postsecondary; Librarians; Library Assistants, Clerical; Library Science Teachers, Postsecondary; Library Technicians; Mathematical Science Teachers, Postsecondary; Middle School Teachers, Except Special and Vocational Education; Museum Technicians and Conservators; Nursing Instructors and Teachers, Postsecondary; Personal Financial Advisors; Philosophy and Religion Teachers, Postsecondary; Physics Teachers, Postsecondary; Political Science Teachers, Postsecondary; Postsecondary Teachers, All Other; Preschool Teachers, Except Special Education; others. **PERSONALITY TYPE**—Investigative. Investigative occupations frequently involve working with ideas and require an extensive amount of thinking. These occupations can involve searching for facts and figuring out problems mentally.

EDUCATION/TRAINING PROGRAM(S)—Computer and Information Sciences, General; Computer Programming/Programmer, General; Computer Science; Computer Systems Analysis/Analyst; Information Science/Studies. **RELATED KNOWLEDGE/COURSES—Computers and Electronics:** Knowledge of circuit boards, processors, chips, electronic equipment, and computer hardware and software, including applications and programming. **Education and Training:** Knowledge of principles and methods for curriculum and training design, teaching and instruction for individuals and groups, and the measurement of training effects. **Mathematics:** Knowledge of arithmetic, algebra, geometry, calculus, and statistics and their applications. **English Language:** Knowledge of the structure and content of the English language, including the meaning and spelling of words, rules of composition, and grammar. **Administration and Management:** Knowledge of business and management principles involved in strategic planning, resource allocation, human resources modeling, leadership technique, production methods, and coordination of people and resources.

Computer Security Specialists

- ▲ Education/Training Required: Bachelor's degree
- ▲ Annual Earnings: $53,770
- ▲ Growth: 81.9%
- ▲ Annual Job Openings: 18,000
- ▲ Self-Employed: 2.7%
- ▲ Part-Time: 5.7%

Plan, coordinate, and implement security measures for information systems to regulate access to computer data files and prevent unauthorized modification, destruction, or disclosure of information. Develops plans to safeguard computer files against accidental or unauthorized modification, destruction, or disclosure and to meet emergency data processing needs. Writes reports to document computer security and emergency measures policies, procedures, and test results. Tests data processing system to ensure functioning of data processing activities and security measures. Modifies computer security files to incorporate new software, correct errors, or change individual access status. Monitors use of data files and regulates access to safeguard information in computer files. Confers with personnel to discuss issues such as computer data access needs, security violations, and programming changes. Coordinates implementation of computer system plan with establishment personnel and outside vendors. **SKILLS—Programming:** Writing computer programs for various purposes. **Operations Analysis:** Analyzing needs and product requirements to create a design. **Writing:** Communicating effectively in writing as appropriate for the needs of the audience. **Mathematics:** Using mathematics to solve problems. **Technology Design:** Generating or adapting equipment and technology to serve user needs.

GOE INFORMATION—**Interest Area:** 02. Science, Math, and Engineering. **Work Group:** 02.06. Mathematics and Computers. **Other Job Titles in This Work Group:** Actuaries; Computer and Information Scientists, Research; Computer Programmers; Computer Specialists, All Other; Computer Support Specialists; Computer Systems Analysts; Database Administrators; Mathematical Science Occupations, All Other; Mathematical Technicians; Mathematicians; Network and Computer Systems Administrators; Network Systems and Data Communications Analysts; Operations Research Analysts; Statistical Assistants; Statisticians. **PERSONALITY TYPE**—Investigative. Investigative occupations frequently involve working with ideas and require an extensive amount of thinking. These occupations can involve searching for facts and figuring out problems mentally.

EDUCATION/TRAINING PROGRAM(S)—Computer and Information Sciences and Support Services, Other; Computer and Information Sciences, General; Computer and Information Systems Security; Computer Systems Analysis/Analyst; Computer Systems Network-

ing and Telecommunications; Information Science/Studies; System Administration/Administrator; System, Networking, and LAN/WAN Management/Manager. **RELATED KNOWLEDGE/COURSES**—**Computers and Electronics:** Knowledge of circuit boards, processors, chips, electronic equipment, and computer hardware and software, including applications and programming. **English Language:** Knowledge of the structure and content of the English language, including the meaning and spelling of words, rules of composition, and grammar. **Public Safety and Security:** Knowledge of relevant equipment, policies, procedures, and strategies to promote effective local, state, or national security operations for the protection of people, data, property, and institutions. **Administration and Management:** Knowledge of business and management principles involved in strategic planning, resource allocation, human resources modeling, leadership technique, production methods, and coordination of people and resources. **Mathematics:** Knowledge of arithmetic, algebra, geometry, calculus, and statistics and their applications.

Computer Software Engineers, Applications

- ▲ Education/Training Required: Bachelor's degree
- ▲ Annual Earnings: $70,210
- ▲ Growth: 100.0%
- ▲ Annual Job Openings: 28,000
- ▲ Self-Employed: 4.1%
- ▲ Part-Time: 5.7%

Develop, create, and modify general computer applications software or specialized utility programs. Analyze user needs and develop software solutions. Design software or customize software for client use with the aim of optimizing operational efficiency. May analyze and design databases within an application area, working individually or coordinating database development as part of a team. Analyzes software requirements to determine feasibility of design within time and cost constraints. Specifies power supply requirements and configuration. Consults with customer concerning maintenance of software system. Monitors functioning of equipment to ensure system operates in conformance with specifications. Evaluates factors such as reporting formats required, cost constraints, and need for security restrictions to determine hardware configuration. Formulates and designs software system, using scientific analysis and mathematical models to predict and measure outcome and consequences of

design. Confers with data processing and project managers to obtain information on limitations and capabilities for data processing projects. Coordinates installation of software system. Develops and directs software system testing procedures, programming, and documentation. Consults with engineering staff to evaluate interface between hardware and software and operational and performance requirements of overall system. Analyzes information to determine, recommend, and plan layout for type of computers and peripheral equipment modifications to existing systems. Enters data into computer terminal to store, retrieve, and manipulate data for analysis of system capabilities and requirements. Recommends purchase of equipment to control dust, temperature, and humidity in area of system installation. Trains users to use new or modified equipment. **SKILLS—Troubleshooting:** Determining causes of operating errors and deciding what to do about them. **Programming:** Writing computer programs for various purposes. **Active Learning:** Understanding the implications of new information for both current and future problem-solving and decision-making. **Mathematics:** Using mathematics to solve problems. **Installation:** Installing equipment, machines, wiring, or programs to meet specifications. **Operations Analysis:** Analyzing needs and product requirements to create a design.

GOE INFORMATION—Interest Area: 02. Science, Math, and Engineering. **Work Group:** 02.07. Engineering. **Other Job Titles in This Work Group:** Aerospace Engineers; Agricultural Engineers; Architects, Except Landscape and Naval; Biomedical Engineers; Chemical Engineers; Civil Engineers; Computer Hardware Engineers; Computer Software Engineers, Systems Software; Electrical Engineers; Electronics Engineers, Except Computer; Engineers, All Other; Environmental Engineers; Fire-Prevention and Protection Engineers; Health and Safety Engineers, Except Mining Safety Engineers and Inspectors; Industrial Engineers; Industrial Safety and Health Engineers; Landscape Architects; Marine Architects; Marine Engineers; Marine Engineers and Naval Architects; Materials Engineers; Mechanical Engineers; Mining and Geological Engineers, Including Mining Safety Engineers; Nuclear Engineers; Petroleum Engineers; Product Safety Engineers; Sales Engineers. **PERSONALITY TYPE—Investigative.** Investigative occupations frequently involve working with ideas and require an extensive amount of thinking. These occupations can involve searching for facts and figuring out problems mentally.

EDUCATION/TRAINING PROGRAM(S)—Artificial Intelligence and Robotics; Bioinformatics; Computer Engineering Technologies/Technicians, Other; Computer Engineering, General; Computer Science; Computer Software Engineering; Information Technology; Medical Illustration and Informatics, Other; Medical Informatics. **RELATED KNOWLEDGE/COURSES—Computers and Electronics: Knowledge of circuit boards, processors, chips, electronic equipment, and computer hardware and software, including applications and programming. **Mathematics:** Knowledge of arithmetic, algebra, geometry, calculus, and statistics and their applications. **Engineering and Technology:** Knowledge of the practical application of engineering science and technology. This includes applying principles, techniques, procedures, and equipment to the design and production of various goods and services. **English Language:** Knowledge of the structure and content of the English language, including the meaning and spelling of words, rules of composition, and grammar. **Administration and Management:** Knowledge of business and management principles involved in strategic planning, resource allocation, human resources modeling, leadership technique, production methods, and coordination of people and resources. **Education and Training:** Knowledge of principles and methods for curriculum and training design, teaching and instruction for individuals and groups, and the measurement of training effects. **Design:** Knowledge of design techniques, tools, and principles involved in production of precision technical plans, blueprints, drawings, and models.

Computer Software Engineers, Systems Software

- ▲ Education/Training Required: Bachelor's degree
- ▲ Annual Earnings: $73,280
- ▲ Growth: 89.7%
- ▲ Annual Job Openings: 23,000
- ▲ Self-Employed: 4.1%
- ▲ Part-Time: 5.7%

Research, design, develop, and test operating systems–level software, compilers, and network distribution software for medical, industrial, military, communications, aerospace, business, scientific, and general computing applications. Set operational specifications and formulate and analyze software requirements. Apply principles and techniques of computer science, engineering, and mathematical analysis. Analyzes software requirements to determine feasibility of design within time and cost constraints. Coordinates installation of software system. Consults with customer concerning maintenance of software system. Trains users to use new or modified equipment. Recommends purchase of equipment to control dust, temperature, and humidity in area of system installation. Enters data into computer terminal to store, retrieve, and manipulate data for analysis of system capabilities and requirements. Specifies power supply requirements and configuration. Monitors functioning of equipment to ensure that system operates in conformance with specifications. Develops and directs software system testing procedures, programming, and documentation. Consults with engineering staff to evaluate interface between hardware and software and operational and performance requirements of overall system. Evaluates factors such as reporting formats required, cost constraints, and need for security restrictions to determine hardware configuration. Confers with data processing and project managers to obtain information on limitations and capabilities for data processing projects. Formulates and designs software system, using scientific analysis and mathematical models to predict and measure outcome and consequences of design. Analyzes information to determine, recommend, and plan layout for type of computers and peripheral equipment modifications to existing systems. **SKILLS—Troubleshooting:** Determining causes of operating errors and deciding what to do about them. **Programming:** Writing computer programs for various purposes. **Active Learning:** Understanding the implications of new information for both current and future problem-solving and decision-making. **Mathematics:** Using mathematics to solve problems. **Operations Analysis:** Analyzing needs and product requirements to create a design. **Installation:** Installing equipment, machines, wiring, or programs to meet specifications.

GOE INFORMATION—Interest Area: 02. Science, Math, and Engineering. **Work Group:** 02.07. Engineering. **Other Job Titles in This Work Group:** Aerospace Engineers; Agricultural Engineers; Architects, Except Landscape and Naval; Biomedical Engineers; Chemical Engineers; Civil Engineers; Computer Hardware Engineers; Computer Software Engineers, Applications; Electrical Engineers; Electronics Engineers, Except Computer; Engineers, All Other; Environmental Engineers; Fire-Prevention and Protection Engineers; Health and Safety Engineers, Except Mining Safety Engineers and Inspectors; Industrial Engineers; Industrial Safety and Health Engineers; Landscape Architects; Marine Architects; Marine Engineers; Marine Engineers and Naval Architects; Materials Engineers; Mechanical Engineers; Mining and Geological Engineers, Including Mining Safety Engineers; Nuclear Engineers; Petroleum Engineers; Product Safety Engineers; Sales Engineers. **PERSONALITY TYPE—** Investigative. Investigative occupations frequently involve working with ideas and require an extensive amount of thinking. These occupations can involve searching for facts and figuring out problems mentally.

EDUCATION/TRAINING PROGRAM(S)—Artificial Intelligence and Robotics; Computer Engineering Technologies/Technicians, Other; Computer Engineering, General; Computer Science; Information Science/Studies; Information Technology. **RELATED KNOWLEDGE/COURSES—Computers and Electronics:** Knowledge of circuit boards, processors, chips, electronic equipment, and computer hardware and software, including applications and programming. **Engineering and Technology:** Knowledge of the practical application of engineering science and technology. This includes applying principles, techniques, procedures, and equipment to the design and production of various goods and services. **Mathematics:** Knowledge of arithmetic, algebra, geometry, calculus, and statistics and their applications. **English Language:** Knowledge of the structure and content of the English language, including the meaning and spelling of words, rules of composition, and grammar. **Administration and Management:** Knowledge of business and management principles involved in strategic planning, resource allocation, human resources modeling, leadership technique, production methods, and coordination of people and resources. **Design:** Knowledge of design techniques, tools, and principles involved in production of precision technical plans, blueprints, drawings, and models. **Education and Training:** Knowledge of principles and methods for curriculum and training design, teaching and instruction for individuals and groups, and the measurement of training effects.

Computer Support Specialists

- ▲ Education/Training Required: Associate's degree
- ▲ Annual Earnings: $38,560
- ▲ Growth: 97.0%
- ▲ Annual Job Openings: 40,000
- ▲ Self-Employed: No data available.
- ▲ Part-Time: No data available.

Provide technical assistance to computer system users. Answer questions or resolve computer problems for clients in person, via telephone, or from remote location. May provide assistance concerning the use of computer hardware and software, including printing, installation, word processing, electronic mail, and operating systems. Installs and performs minor repairs to hardware, software, and peripheral equipment, following design or installation specifications. Confers with staff, users, and management to determine requirements for new systems or modifications. Reads technical manuals, confers with users, and conducts computer diagnostics to determine nature of problems and provide technical assistance. Develops training materials and procedures; conducts training programs. Refers major hardware or software problems or defective products to vendors or technicians for service. Conducts office automation feasibility studies, including workflow analysis, space design, and cost comparison analysis. Supervises and coordinates workers engaged in problem-solving, monitoring, and installing data communication equipment and software. Inspects equipment and reads order sheets to prepare for delivery to users. Reads trade magazines and technical manuals and attends conferences and seminars to maintain knowledge of hardware and software. Maintains record of daily data communication transactions, problems and remedial action taken, and installation activities. Prepares evaluations of software and hardware and submits recommendations to management for review. Tests and monitors software, hardware, and peripheral equipment to evaluate use, effectiveness, and adequacy of product for user. Enters commands and observes system functioning to verify correct operations and detect errors. **SKILLS—Reading Comprehension:** Understanding written sentences and paragraphs in work-related documents. **Active Learning:** Understanding the implications of new information for both current and future problem-solving and decision-making. **Programming:** Writing computer programs for various purposes. **Troubleshooting:** Determining causes of operating errors and deciding what to do about them. **Writing:** Communicating effectively in writing as appropriate for the needs of the audience. **Judgment and Decision Making:** Considering the relative costs and benefits of potential actions to choose the most appropriate one.

GOE INFORMATION—Interest Area: 02. Science, Math, and Engineering. **Work Group:** 02.06. Mathematics and Computers. **Other Job Titles in This Work Group:** Actuaries; Computer and Information Scientists, Research; Computer Programmers; Computer Security Specialists; Computer Specialists, All Other; Computer Systems Analysts; Database Administrators; Mathematical Science Occupations, All Other; Mathematical Technicians; Mathematicians; Network and Computer Systems Administrators; Network Systems and Data Communications Analysts; Operations Research Analysts; Statistical Assistants; Statisticians. **PERSONALITY TYPE—**Investigative. Investigative occupations frequently involve working with ideas and require an extensive amount of thinking. These occupations can involve searching for facts and figuring out problems mentally.

EDUCATION/TRAINING PROGRAM(S)—Accounting and Computer Science; Agricultural Business Technology; Computer Hardware Technology/Technician; Computer Software Technology/Technician; Data Processing and Data Processing Technology/Technician; Medical Office Computer Specialist/Assistant. **RELATED KNOWLEDGE/COURSES—Computers and Electronics:** Knowledge of circuit boards, processors, chips, electronic equipment, and computer hardware and software, including applications and programming. **Education and Training:** Knowledge of principles and methods for curriculum and training design, teaching and instruction for individuals and groups, and the measurement of training effects. **Mathematics:** Knowledge of arithmetic, algebra, geometry, calculus, and statistics and their applications. **Telecommunications:** Knowledge of transmission, broadcasting, switching, control, and operation of telecommunications systems. **English Language:** Knowledge of the structure and content of the English language, including the meaning and spelling of words, rules of composition, and grammar. **Engineering and Technology:** Knowledge of the practical application of engineering science and technology. This includes applying principles, techniques, procedures, and equipment to the design and production of various goods and services.

Computer Systems Analysts

- ▲ Education/Training Required: Bachelor's degree
- ▲ Annual Earnings: $61,990
- ▲ Growth: 59.7%
- ▲ Annual Job Openings: 34,000
- ▲ Self-Employed: 7.7%
- ▲ Part-Time: 5.7%

Analyze science, engineering, business, and all other data processing problems for application to electronic data processing systems. Analyze user requirements, procedures, and problems to automate or improve existing systems and review computer system capabilities, workflow, and scheduling limitations. May analyze or recommend commercially available software. May supervise computer programmers. Analyzes and tests computer programs or system to identify errors and ensure conformance to standard. Consults with staff and users to identify operating procedure problems. Formulates and reviews plans outlining steps required to develop programs to meet staff and user requirements. Coordinates installation of computer programs and operating systems and tests, maintains, and monitors computer system. Writes documentation to describe and develop installation and operating procedures of programs. Devises flow charts and diagrams to illustrate steps and to describe logical operational steps of program. Reads manuals, periodicals, and technical reports to learn how to develop programs to meet staff and user requirements. Reviews and analyzes computer printouts and performance indications to locate code problems. Assists staff and users in solving computer-related problems, such as malfunctions and program problems. Trains staff and users to use computer system and its programs. Modifies program to correct errors by correcting computer codes. Writes and revises program and system design procedures, test procedures, and quality standards. **SKILLS—Troubleshooting:** Determining causes of operating errors and deciding what to do about them. **Programming:** Writing computer programs for various purposes. **Reading Comprehension:** Understanding written sentences and paragraphs in work-related documents. **Writing:** Communicating effectively in writing as appropriate for the needs of the audience. **Quality Control Analysis:** Conducting tests and inspections of products, services, or processes to evaluate quality or performance.

GOE INFORMATION—Interest Area: 02. Science, Math, and Engineering. **Work Group:** 02.06. Mathematics and Computers. **Other Job Titles in This Work Group:** Actuaries; Computer and Information Scientists, Research; Computer Programmers; Computer Security Specialists; Computer Specialists, All Other; Computer Support Specialists; Database Administrators; Mathematical Science Occupations, All Other; Mathematical Technicians; Mathematicians; Network and Computer Systems Administrators; Network Systems and Data Communications Analysts; Operations Research Analysts; Statistical Assistants; Statisticians. **PERSONALITY TYPE—**Investigative. Investigative occupations frequently involve working with ideas and require an extensive amount of thinking. These occupations can involve searching for facts and figuring out problems mentally.

EDUCATION/TRAINING PROGRAM(S)—Computer and Information Sciences, General; Computer Systems Analysis/Analyst; Information Technology; Web/Multimedia Management and Webmaster. **RELATED KNOWLEDGE/COURSES—Computers and Electronics:** Knowledge of circuit boards, processors, chips, electronic equipment, and computer hardware and software, including applications and programming. **English Language:** Knowledge of the structure and content of the English language, including the meaning and spelling of words, rules of composition, and grammar. **Education and Training:** Knowledge of principles and methods for curriculum and training design, teaching and instruction for individuals and groups, and the measurement of training effects. **Mathematics:** Knowledge of arithmetic, algebra, geometry, calculus, and statistics and their applications. **Customer and Personal Service:** Knowledge of principles and processes for providing customer and personal services. This includes customer needs assessment, meeting quality standards for services, and evaluation of customer satisfaction.

Computer, Automated Teller, and Office Machine Repairers

▲ Education/Training Required: Postsecondary vocational training
▲ Annual Earnings: $32,890
▲ Growth: 14.2%
▲ Annual Job Openings: 24,000
▲ Self-Employed: 10.6%
▲ Part-Time: 6.9%

Repair, maintain, or install computers, word processing systems, automated teller machines, and electronic office machines, such as duplicating and fax machines. SKILLS—No data available.

GOE INFORMATION—Interest Area: 05. Mechanics, Installers, and Repairers. Work Group: 05.02. Electrical and Electronic Systems. Other Job Titles in This Work Group: Avionics Technicians; Battery Repairers; Central Office and PBX Installers and Repairers; Communication Equipment Mechanics, Installers, and Repairers; Data Processing Equipment Repairers; Electric Home Appliance and Power Tool Repairers; Electric Meter Installers and Repairers; Electric Motor and Switch Assemblers and Repairers; Electric Motor, Power Tool, and Related Repairers; Electrical and Electronics Installers and Repairers, Transportation Equipment; Electrical and Electronics Repairers, Commercial and Industrial Equipment; Electrical and Electronics Repairers, Powerhouse, Substation, and Relay; Electrical Parts Reconditioners; Electrical Power-Line Installers and Repairers; Electronic Equipment Installers and Repairers, Motor Vehicles; Electronic Home Entertainment Equipment Installers and Repairers; Elevator Installers and Repairers; Frame Wirers, Central Office; Home Appliance Installers; Home Appliance Repairers; Office Machine and Cash Register Servicers; Radio Mechanics; Signal and Track Switch Repairers; Station Installers and Repairers, Telephone; Telecommunications Equipment Installers and Repairers, Except Line Installers; Telecommunications Facility Examiners; Telecommunications Line Installers and Repairers; Transformer Repairers. PERSONALITY TYPE—No data available.

EDUCATION/TRAINING PROGRAM(S)—Business Machine Repair; Computer Installation and Repair Technology/Technician. RELATED KNOWLEDGE/COURSES—No data available.

Computer-Controlled Machine Tool Operators, Metal and Plastic

▲ Education/Training Required: Moderate-term on-the-job training
▲ Annual Earnings: $28,390
▲ Growth: 19.7%
▲ Annual Job Openings: 15,000
▲ Self-Employed: 0%
▲ Part-Time: 2.3%

Operate computer-controlled machines or robots to perform one or more machine functions on metal or plastic workpieces. SKILLS—No data available.

GOE INFORMATION—Interest Area: 08. Industrial Production. Work Group: 08.03. Production Work. Other Job Titles in This Work Group: Bakers, Manufacturing; Bindery Machine Operators and Tenders; Brazers; Cementing and Gluing Machine Operators and Tenders; Chemical Equipment Controllers and Operators; Chemical Equipment Operators and Tenders; Chemical Equipment Tenders; Cleaning, Washing, and Metal Pickling Equipment Operators and Tenders; Coating, Painting, and Spraying Machine Operators and Tenders; Coil Winders, Tapers, and Finishers; Combination Machine Tool Operators and Tenders, Metal and Plastic; Cooling and Freezing Equipment Operators and Tenders; Crushing, Grinding, and Polishing Machine Setters, Operators, and Tenders; Cutters and Trimmers, Hand; Cutting and Slicing Machine Operators and Tenders; Cutting and Slicing Machine Setters, Operators, and Tenders; Design Printing Machine Setters and Set-Up Operators; Electrolytic Plating and Coating Machine Operators and Tenders, Metal and Plastic; Electrolytic Plating and Coating Machine Setters and Set-Up Operators, Metal and Plastic;

Electrotypers and Stereotypers; Embossing Machine Set-Up Operators; Engraver Set-Up Operators; Extruding and Forming Machine Operators and Tenders, Synthetic or Glass Fibers; Extruding and Forming Machine Setters, Operators, and Tenders, Synthetic and Glass Fibers; Extruding, Forming, Pressing, and Compacting Machine Operators and Tenders; Fabric and Apparel Patternmakers; Fiber Product Cutting Machine Setters and Set-Up Operators; Fiberglass Laminators and Fabricators; Film Laboratory Technicians; Fitters, Structural Metal—Precision; Food and Tobacco Roasting, Baking, and Drying Machine Operators and Tenders; Food Batchmakers; Food Cook-ing Machine Operators and Tenders; Furnace, Kiln, Oven, Drier, and Kettle Operators and Tenders; Glass Cutting Machine Setters and Set-Up Operators; Graders and Sorters, Agricultural Products; Grinding and Polishing Workers, Hand; Hand Compositors and Typesetters; Heaters, Metal and Plastic; Helpers—Production Workers; Job Printers; Letterpress Setters and Set-Up Operators; others. **PERSONALITY TYPE**—No data available.

EDUCATION/TRAINING PROGRAM(S)—Machine Shop Technology/Assistant. **RELATED KNOWLEDGE/COURSES**—No data available.

Construction Carpenters

- ▲ Education/Training Required: Long-term on-the-job training
- ▲ Annual Earnings: $33,470
- ▲ Growth: 8.2%
- ▲ Annual Job Openings: 161,000
- ▲ Self-Employed: 36.8%
- ▲ Part-Time: 8.1%

Construct, erect, install, and repair structures and fixtures of wood, plywood, and wallboard, using carpenter's hand tools and power tools. Shapes or cuts materials to specified measurements, using hand tools, machines, or power saw. Assembles and fastens materials, using hand tools and wood screws, nails, dowel pins, or glue, to make framework or props. Installs structures and fixtures, such as windows, frames, floorings, and trim, or hardware, using carpenter's hand and power tools. Builds or repairs cabinets, doors, frameworks, floors, and other wooden fixtures used in buildings, using woodworking machines, carpenter's hand tools, and power tools. Removes damaged or defective parts or sections of structure and repairs or replaces, using hand tools. Verifies trueness of structure, using plumb bob and level. Prepares layout according to blueprint or oral instructions, using rule, framing square, and calipers. Estimates amount and kind of lumber or other materials required and selects and orders them. Inspects ceiling or floor tile, wall coverings, siding, glass, or woodwork to detect broken or damaged structures. Studies specifications in blueprints, sketches, or building plans to determine materials required and dimensions of structure to be fabricated. Measures and marks cutting lines on materials, using ruler, pencil, chalk, and marking gauge. Finishes surfaces of woodworking or wallboard in houses and buildings, using paint, hand tools, and paneling. Fills cracks and other defects in plaster or plasterboard and sands patch, using patching plaster, trowel, and sanding tool. **SKILLS—Repairing:** Repairing machines or systems, using the needed tools. **Installation:** Installing equipment, machines, wiring, or programs to meet specifications. **Mathematics:** Using mathematics to solve problems. **Management of Material Resources:** Obtaining and seeing to the appropriate use of equipment, facilities, and materials needed to do certain work. **Reading Comprehension:** Understanding written sentences and paragraphs in work-related documents. **Equipment Selection:** Determining the kind of tools and equipment needed to do a job.

GOE INFORMATION—Interest Area: 06. Construction, Mining, and Drilling. **Work Group:** 06.02. Construction. **Other Job Titles in This Work Group:** Boat Builders and Shipwrights; Boilermakers; Brattice Builders; Brickmasons and Blockmasons; Carpenters; Carpet Installers; Ceiling Tile Installers; Cement Masons and Concrete Finishers; Commercial Divers; Drywall and Ceiling Tile Installers; Drywall Installers; Electricians; Explosives Workers, Ordnance Handling Experts, and Blasters; Fence Erectors; Floor Layers, Except Carpet, Wood, and Hard Tiles; Floor Sanders and Finishers; Glaziers; Grader, Bulldozer, and Scraper Operators; Hazardous Materials Removal Workers; Insulation Workers, Floor, Ceiling, and Wall; Insulation Workers, Mechanical; Manufactured Building and Mobile Home Installers; Operating Engineers; Operating Engineers and Other

Construction Equipment Operators; Painters, Construction and Maintenance; Paperhangers; Paving, Surfacing, and Tamping Equipment Operators; Pile-Driver Operators; Pipe Fitters; Pipelayers; Pipelaying Fitters; Plasterers and Stucco Masons; Plumbers; Plumbers, Pipefitters, and Steamfitters; Rail-Track Laying and Maintenance Equipment Operators; Refractory Materials Repairers, Except Brickmasons; Reinforcing Iron and Rebar Workers; Riggers; Roofers; Rough Carpenters; Security and Fire Alarm Systems Installers; Segmental Pavers; Sheet Metal Workers; Ship Carpenters and Joiners; Stone Cutters and Carvers; Stonemasons; Structural Iron and Steel Workers; Tapers; Terrazzo Workers and Finishers; Tile and Marble Setters. **PERSONALITY TYPE**—Realistic. Realistic occupations frequently involve work activities that include practical, hands-on problems and solutions. They often deal with plants, animals, and real-world materials like wood, tools, and machinery. Many of the occupations re-

quire working outside and do not involve a lot of paperwork or working closely with others.

EDUCATION/TRAINING PROGRAM(S)—Carpentry/Carpenter. **RELATED KNOWLEDGE/COURSES**— **Building and Construction:** Knowledge of materials, methods, and tools involved in the construction or repair of houses, buildings, or other structures, such as highways and roads. **Design:** Knowledge of design techniques, tools, and principles involved in production of precision technical plans, blueprints, drawings, and models. **Principles of Mechanical Devices:** Knowledge of machines and tools, including their designs, uses, repair, and maintenance. **Engineering and Technology:** Knowledge of the practical application of engineering science and technology. This includes applying principles, techniques, procedures, and equipment to the design and production of various goods and services. **Mathematics:** Knowledge of arithmetic, algebra, geometry, calculus, and statistics and their applications.

Construction Laborers

- ▲ Education/Training Required: Moderate-term on-the-job training
- ▲ Annual Earnings: $24,070
- ▲ Growth: 17.0%
- ▲ Annual Job Openings: 236,000
- ▲ Self-Employed: 20.7%
- ▲ Part-Time: 8.5%

Perform tasks involving physical labor at building, highway, and heavy construction projects, tunnel and shaft excavations, and demolition sites. May operate hand and power tools of all types: air hammers, earth tampers, cement mixers, small mechanical hoists, surveying and measuring equipment, and a variety of other equipment and instruments. May clean and prepare sites; dig trenches; set braces to support the sides of excavations; erect scaffolding; clean up rubble and debris; and remove asbestos, lead, and other hazardous waste materials. May assist other craft workers. Tends pumps, compressors, and generators to provide power for tools, machinery, and equipment or to heat and move materials such as asphalt. Lubricates, cleans, and repairs machinery, equipment, and tools. Mixes ingredients to create compounds used to cover or clean surfaces. Loads and unloads trucks and hauls and hoists materials. Erects and disassembles scaffolding, shoring, braces, and other temporary structures. Builds and positions forms for pouring concrete and dismantles forms after use, using saws, hammers, nails, or bolts. Measures, marks, and records openings and distances to lay out area to be graded or to

erect building structures. Smooth and finishes freshly poured cement or concrete, using float, trowel, screed, or powered cement-finishing tool. Applies caulking compounds by hand or with caulking gun to seal crevices. Positions, joins, aligns, and seals structural components, such as concrete wall sections and pipes. Digs ditches and levels earth to grade specifications, using pick and shovel. Signals equipment operators to facilitate alignment, movement, and adjustment of machinery, equipment, and materials. Grinds, scrapes, sands, or polishes surfaces, such as concrete, marble, terrazzo, or wood flooring, using abrasive tools or machines. Mixes concrete, using portable mixer. Razes buildings and salvages useful materials. Sprays materials such as water, sand, steam, vinyl, paint, or stucco through hose to clean, coat, or seal surfaces. Tends machine that pumps concrete, grout, cement, sand, plaster, or stucco through spray gun for application to ceilings and walls. Mops, brushes, or spreads paints, cleaning solutions, or other compounds over surfaces to clean or provide protection. Cleans construction site to eliminate possible hazards. **SKILLS—Equipment Maintenance:** Performing routine maintenance on equipment and determining when and what kind of maintenance is needed. **Mathematics:** Using mathematics to solve problems.

GOE INFORMATION—Interest Area: 06. Construction, Mining, and Drilling. **Work Group:** 06.04. Hands-on Work in Construction, Extraction, and Maintenance. **Other Job Titles in This Work Group:** Carpenter Assemblers and Repairers; Grips and Set-Up Workers, Motion Picture Sets, Studios, and Stages; Helpers, Construction Trades, All Other; Helpers—Brickmasons, Blockmasons, Stonemasons, and Tile and Marble Setters; Helpers—Carpenters; Helpers—Extraction Workers; Helpers—Painters, Paperhangers, Plasterers, and Stucco Masons; Helpers—Pipelayers, Plumbers, Pipefitters, and Steamfitters; Helpers—Roofers; Highway Maintenance Workers; Septic Tank Servicers and Sewer Pipe Cleaners. **PERSONALITY TYPE**—Realistic. Realistic occupations frequently involve work activities that include practical, hands-on problems and solutions. They often deal with plants, animals, and real-world materials like wood, tools, and machinery. Many of the occupations require working outside and do not involve a lot of paperwork or working closely with others.

EDUCATION/TRAINING PROGRAM(S)—Construction Trades, Other. **RELATED KNOWLEDGE/ COURSES—Building and Construction:** Knowledge of materials, methods, and tools involved in the construction or repair of houses, buildings, or other structures, such as highways and roads. **Principles of Mechanical Devices:** Knowledge of machines and tools, including their designs, uses, repair, and maintenance. **Engineering and Technology:** Knowledge of the practical application of engineering science and technology. This includes applying principles, techniques, procedures, and equipment to the design and production of various goods and services. **Mathematics:** Knowledge of arithmetic, algebra, geometry, calculus, and statistics and their applications. **Design:** Knowledge of design techniques, tools, and principles involved in production of precision technical plans, blueprints, drawings, and models.

Construction Managers

- ▲ Education/Training Required: Bachelor's degree
- ▲ Annual Earnings: $61,050
- ▲ Growth: 16.3%
- ▲ Annual Job Openings: 26,000
- ▲ Self-Employed: 1.0%
- ▲ Part-Time: 6.1%

Plan, direct, coordinate, or budget, usually through subordinate supervisory personnel, activities concerned with the construction and maintenance of structures, facilities, and systems. Participate in the conceptual development of a construction project and oversee its organization, scheduling, and implementation. Plans, organizes, and directs activities concerned with construction and maintenance of structures, facilities, and systems. Investigates reports of damage at construction sites to ensure that proper procedures are being carried out. Dispatches workers to construction sites to work on specified project. Formulates reports concerning such areas as work progress, costs, and scheduling. Studies job specifications to plan and approve construction of project. Directs and supervises workers on construction site to ensure that project meets specifications. Contracts workers to perform construction work in accordance with specifications. Interprets and explains plans and contract terms to administrative staff, workers, and clients. Requisitions supplies and materials to complete construction project. Inspects and reviews construction work, repair projects, and reports to ensure that work conforms to specifications. Confers with supervisory personnel to discuss such matters as work procedures, complaints, and construction problems. **SKILLS—Coordination:** Adjusting actions in relation to others' actions. **Management of Personnel Resources:** Motivating, developing, and directing people as they work, identifying the best people for the job. **Time Management:** Managing one's own time and the time of others. **Mathematics:** Using mathematics to solve problems. **Management of Financial Resources:** Determining how money will be spent to get the work done and accounting for these expenditures. **Judgment and Decision Making:** Considering the relative costs and benefits of potential actions to choose the most appropriate one. **Reading Comprehension:** Understanding written sentences and paragraphs in work-related documents.

GOE INFORMATION—**Interest Area:** 06. Construction, Mining, and Drilling. **Work Group:** 06.01. Managerial Work in Construction, Mining, and Drilling. **Other Job Titles in This Work Group:** First-Line Supervisors and Manager/Supervisors—Construction Trades Workers; First-Line Supervisors and Manager/Supervisors—Extractive Workers; First-Line Supervisors/Managers of Construction Trades and Extraction Workers. **PERSONALITY TYPE**—Enterprising. Enterprising occupations frequently involve starting up and carrying out projects. These occupations can involve leading people and making many decisions. They sometimes require risk taking and often deal with business.

EDUCATION/TRAINING PROGRAM(S)—Business Administration and Management, General; Business/Commerce, General; Construction Engineering Technology/Technician; Operations Management and Supervision. **RELATED KNOWLEDGE/COURSES**—Administra-

tion and Management: Knowledge of business and management principles involved in strategic planning, resource allocation, human resources modeling, leadership technique, production methods, and coordination of people and resources. **Building and Construction:** Knowledge of materials, methods, and tools involved in the construction or repair of houses, buildings, or other structures, such as highways and roads. **Personnel and Human Resources:** Knowledge of principles and procedures for personnel recruitment, selection, training, compensation and benefits, labor relations and negotiation, and personnel information systems. **Public Safety and Security:** Knowledge of relevant equipment, policies, procedures, and strategies to promote effective local, state, or national security operations for the protection of people, data, property, and institutions. **Principles of Mechanical Devices:** Knowledge of machines and tools, including their designs, uses, repair, and maintenance.

Cooks, Institution and Cafeteria

- ▲ Education/Training Required: Short-term on-the-job training
- ▲ Annual Earnings: $17,750
- ▲ Growth: 7.6%
- ▲ Annual Job Openings: 110,000
- ▲ Self-Employed: 0%
- ▲ Part-Time: 38.5%

Prepare and cook large quantities of food for institutions, such as schools, hospitals, or cafeterias. Cooks foodstuffs according to menu, special dietary or nutritional restrictions, and number of persons to be served. Directs activities of one or more workers who assist in preparing and serving meals. Washes pots, pans, dishes, utensils, and other cooking equipment. Compiles and maintains food cost records and accounts. Apportions and serves food to residents, employees, or patrons. Cleans and inspects galley equipment, kitchen appliances, and work areas for cleanliness and functional operation. Requisitions food supplies, kitchen equipment and appliances, and other supplies and receives deliveries. Plans menus, taking advantage of foods in season and local availability. Bakes breads, rolls, and other pastries. Prepares and cooks vegetables, salads, dressings, and desserts. Cleans, cuts, and cooks meat, fish, and poultry. **SKILLS—Active Learning:** Understanding the implications of new information for both current and future problem-solving and decision-making. **Critical Thinking:** Using logic and reasoning to identify the strengths and weaknesses of alternative solu-

tions, conclusions, or approaches to problems. **Coordination:** Adjusting actions in relation to others' actions. **Management of Personnel Resources:** Motivating, developing, and directing people as they work, identifying the best people for the job. **Mathematics:** Using mathematics to solve problems.

GOE INFORMATION—**Interest Area:** 11. Recreation, Travel, and Other Personal Services. **Work Group:** 11.05. Food and Beverage Services. **Other Job Titles in This Work Group:** Bakers; Bakers, Bread and Pastry; Bartenders; Butchers and Meat Cutters; Chefs and Head Cooks; Combined Food Preparation and Serving Workers, Including Fast Food; Cooks, All Other; Cooks, Fast Food; Cooks, Restaurant; Cooks, Short Order; Counter Attendants, Cafeteria, Food Concession, and Coffee Shop; Dining Room and Cafeteria Attendants and Bartender Helpers; Dishwashers; Food Preparation and Serving Related Workers, All Other; Food Preparation Workers; Food Servers, Nonrestaurant; Hosts and Hostesses, Restaurant, Lounge, and Coffee Shop; Waiters and Waitresses. **PERSONALITY TYPE**—Realistic. Realistic occupations frequently involve work activities that include practical, hands-on problems and solutions. They often deal with plants, animals, and real-world materials like wood, tools, and machinery. Many of the occupations require working outside and do not involve a lot of paperwork or working closely with others.

EDUCATION/TRAINING PROGRAM(S)—Cooking and Related Culinary Arts, General; Culinary Arts and Related Services, Other; Food Preparation/Professional Cooking/Kitchen Assistant; Foodservice Systems Administration/Management; Institutional Food Workers. RELATED KNOWLEDGE/COURSES—Customer and Personal Service: Knowledge of principles and processes for providing customer and personal services. This includes customer needs assessment, meeting quality standards for services, and evaluation of customer satisfaction. Administration and Management: Knowledge of business and management principles involved in strategic planning, re-

source allocation, human resources modeling, leadership technique, production methods, and coordination of people and resources. Mathematics: Knowledge of arithmetic, algebra, geometry, calculus, and statistics and their applications. Food Production: Knowledge of techniques and equipment for planting, growing, and harvesting food products (both plant and animal) for consumption, including storage/handling techniques. Economics and Accounting: Knowledge of economic and accounting principles and practices, the financial markets, banking, and the analysis and reporting of financial data. Personnel and Human Resources: Knowledge of principles and procedures for personnel recruitment, selection, training, compensation and benefits, labor relations and negotiation, and personnel information systems. Production and Processing: Knowledge of raw materials, production processes, quality control, costs, and other techniques for maximizing the effective manufacture and distribution of goods.

Cooks, Restaurant

- ▲ Education/Training Required: Long-term on-the-job training
- ▲ Annual Earnings: $18,480
- ▲ Growth: 21.7%
- ▲ Annual Job Openings: 158,000
- ▲ Self-Employed: 5.7%
- ▲ Part-Time: 38.5%

Prepare, season, and cook soups, meats, vegetables, desserts, or other foodstuffs in restaurants. May order supplies, keep records and accounts, price items on menu, or plan menu. Weighs, measures, and mixes ingredients according to recipe or personal judgment, using various kitchen utensils and equipment. Bakes, roasts, broils, and steams meats, fish, vegetables, and other foods. Observes and tests food to determine that it is cooked, by tasting, smelling, or piercing, and turns or stirs food if necessary. Seasons and cooks food according to recipes or personal judgment and experience. Washes, peels, cuts, and seeds fruits and vegetables to prepare them for use. Plans items on menu. Butchers and dresses animals, fowl, or shellfish or cuts and bones meat prior to cooking. Estimates food consumption and requisitions or purchases supplies or procures food from storage. Carves and trims meats, such as beef, veal, ham, pork, and lamb, for hot or cold service or for sandwiches. Portions, arranges, and garnishes food; serves food to waiter or patron. Inspects food preparation and serving areas to ensure observance of safe, sanitary food-handling practices. Bakes bread, rolls, cakes, and

pastries. Regulates temperature of ovens, broilers, grills, and roasters. SKILLS—Active Learning: Understanding the implications of new information for both current and future problem-solving and decision-making. Speaking: Talking to others to convey information effectively. Coordination: Adjusting actions in relation to others' actions. Monitoring: Monitoring/Assessing your performance or that of other individuals or organizations to make improvements or take corrective action. Learning Strategies: Selecting and using training/instructional methods and procedures appropriate for the situation when learning or teaching new things.

GOE INFORMATION—Interest Area: 11. Recreation, Travel, and Other Personal Services. Work Group: 11.05. Food and Beverage Services. Other Job Titles in This Work Group: Bakers; Bakers, Bread and Pastry; Bartenders; Butchers and Meat Cutters; Chefs and Head Cooks; Combined Food Preparation and Serving Workers, Including Fast Food; Cooks, All Other; Cooks, Fast Food; Cooks, Institution and Cafeteria; Cooks, Short Order; Counter

Attendants, Cafeteria, Food Concession, and Coffee Shop; Dining Room and Cafeteria Attendants and Bartender Helpers; Dishwashers; Food Preparation and Serving Related Workers, All Other; Food Preparation Workers; Food Servers, Nonrestaurant; Hosts and Hostesses, Restaurant, Lounge, and Coffee Shop; Waiters and Waitresses. **PERSONALITY TYPE**—Realistic. Realistic occupations frequently involve work activities that include practical, hands-on problems and solutions. They often deal with plants, animals, and real-world materials like wood, tools, and machinery. Many of the occupations require working outside and do not involve a lot of paperwork or working closely with others.

EDUCATION/TRAINING PROGRAM(S)—Cooking and Related Culinary Arts, General; Culinary Arts/Chef Training. **RELATED KNOWLEDGE/COURSES—Customer and Personal Service:** Knowledge of principles and processes for providing customer and personal services. This includes customer needs assessment, meeting quality standards for services, and evaluation of customer satisfaction.

Mathematics: Knowledge of arithmetic, algebra, geometry, calculus, and statistics and their applications. **Public Safety and Security:** Knowledge of relevant equipment, policies, procedures, and strategies to promote effective local, state, or national security operations for the protection of people, data, property, and institutions. **Education and Training:** Knowledge of principles and methods for curriculum and training design, teaching and instruction for individuals and groups, and the measurement of training effects. **Personnel and Human Resources:** Knowledge of principles and procedures for personnel recruitment, selection, training, compensation and benefits, labor relations and negotiation, and personnel information systems. **Production and Processing:** Knowledge of raw materials, production processes, quality control, costs, and other techniques for maximizing the effective manufacture and distribution of goods. **Food Production:** Knowledge of techniques and equipment for planting, growing, and harvesting food products (both plant and animal) for consumption, including storage/handling techniques.

Copy Writers

- ▲ Education/Training Required: Bachelor's degree
- ▲ Annual Earnings: $42,450
- ▲ Growth: 28.4%
- ▲ Annual Job Openings: 18,000
- ▲ Self-Employed: 31.2%
- ▲ Part-Time: 18.5%

Write advertising copy for use by publication or broadcast media to promote sale of goods and services. Writes advertising copy for use by publication or broadcast media and revises copy according to supervisor's instructions. Writes articles, bulletins, sales letters, speeches, and other related informative and promotional material. Prepares advertising copy, using computer. Consults with sales media and marketing representatives to obtain information on product or service and discuss style and length of advertising copy. Reviews advertising trends, consumer surveys, and other data regarding marketing of goods and services to formulate approach. Obtains additional background and current development information through research and interview. **SKILLS—Writing:** Communicating effectively in writing as appropriate for the needs of the audience. **Reading Comprehension:** Understanding written sentences and paragraphs in work-related documents. **Active Learning:** Understanding the implications of new information for both current and future problem-

solving and decision-making. **Critical Thinking:** Using logic and reasoning to identify the strengths and weaknesses of alternative solutions, conclusions, or approaches to problems. **Active Listening:** Giving full attention to what other people are saying, taking time to understand the points being made, asking questions as appropriate, and not interrupting at inappropriate times.

GOE INFORMATION—Interest Area: 01. Arts, Entertainment, and Media. **Work Group:** 01.02. Writing and Editing. **Other Job Titles in This Work Group:** Creative Writers; Editors; Poets and Lyricists; Technical Writers; Writers and Authors. **PERSONALITY TYPE**—Artistic. Artistic occupations frequently involve working with forms, designs, and patterns. They often require self-expression, and the work can be done without following a clear set of rules.

EDUCATION/TRAINING PROGRAM(S)—Broadcast Journalism; Business/Corporate Communications; Communication Studies/Speech Communication and Rhetoric; Communication, Journalism, and Related Programs, Other; Creative Writing; English Composition; Family and Consumer Sciences/Human Sciences Communication; Journalism; Mass Communication/Media Studies; Playwriting and Screenwriting; Technical and Business Writing. **RELATED KNOWLEDGE/COURSES—Sales and Marketing:** Knowledge of principles and methods for showing, promoting, and selling products or services. This includes marketing strategy and tactics, product demonstration, sales techniques, and sales control systems. **English Language:** Knowledge of the structure and content of the English language, including the meaning and spelling of words, rules of composition, and grammar. **Computers and Electronics:** Knowledge of circuit boards, processors, chips, electronic equipment, and computer hardware and software, including applications and programming. **Communications and Media:** Knowledge of media production, communication, and dissemination techniques and methods. This includes alternative ways to inform and entertain via written, oral, and visual media. **Clerical Studies:** Knowledge of administrative and clerical procedures and systems, such as word processing, managing files and records, stenography and transcription, designing forms, and other office procedures and terminology.

Correctional Officers and Jailers

> ▲ Education/Training Required: Moderate-term on-the-job training
> ▲ Annual Earnings: $32,010
> ▲ Growth: 32.4%
> ▲ Annual Job Openings: 30,000
> ▲ Self-Employed: 0%
> ▲ Part-Time: 1.5%

Guard inmates in penal or rehabilitative institution in accordance with established regulations and procedures. May guard prisoners in transit between jail, courtroom, prison, or other point. Includes deputy sheriffs and police who spend the majority of their time guarding prisoners in correctional institutions. Monitors conduct of prisoners according to established policies, regulations, and procedures to prevent escape or violence. Takes prisoner into custody and escorts to locations within and outside of facility, such as visiting room, courtroom, or airport. Uses weapons, handcuffs, and physical force to maintain discipline and order among prisoners. Records information, such as prisoner identification, charges, and incidences of inmate disturbance. Guards facility entrance to screen visitors. Searches prisoners, cells, and vehicles for weapons, valuables, or drugs. Inspects locks, window bars, grills, doors, and gates at correctional facility to prevent escape. Serves meals and distributes commissary items to prisoners. **SKILLS—Social Perceptiveness:** Being aware of others' reactions and understanding why they react as they do. **Active Listening:** Giving full attention to what other people are saying, taking time to understand the points being made, asking questions as appropriate, and not interrupting at inappropriate times. **Speaking:** Talking to others to convey information effectively. **Reading Comprehension:** Understanding written sentences and paragraphs in work-related documents. **Coordination:** Adjusting actions in relation to others' actions.

GOE INFORMATION—Interest Area: 04. Law, Law Enforcement, and Public Safety. **Work Group:** 04.03. Law Enforcement. **Other Job Titles in This Work Group:** Animal Control Workers; Bailiffs; Child Support, Missing Persons, and Unemployment Insurance Fraud Investigators; Criminal Investigators and Special Agents; Crossing Guards; Detectives and Criminal Investigators; Fire Investigators; Fish and Game Wardens; Forensic Science Technicians; Gaming Surveillance Officers and Gaming Investigators; Highway Patrol Pilots; Immigration and Customs Inspectors; Lifeguards, Ski Patrol, and Other Recreational Protective Service Workers; Parking Enforcement Workers; Police and Sheriff's Patrol Officers; Police Detectives; Police Identification and Records Officers; Police Patrol Officers; Private Detectives and Investigators; Security Guards; Sheriffs and Deputy Sheriffs; Transit and Railroad Police. **PERSONALITY TYPE—Realistic.** Realistic occupations frequently involve work activities that include practical, hands-on problems and solutions. They often deal with plants, animals, and real-world materials like wood, tools, and machinery. Many of the occupations require working outside and do not involve a lot of paperwork or working closely with others.

EDUCATION/TRAINING PROGRAM(S)—Corrections; Corrections and Criminal Justice, Other; Juvenile Corrections. **RELATED KNOWLEDGE/COURSES**—**Public Safety and Security:** Knowledge of relevant equipment, policies, procedures, and strategies to promote effective local, state, or national security operations for the protection of people, data, property, and institutions. **Medicine and Dentistry:** Knowledge of the information and techniques needed to diagnose and treat human injuries, diseases, and deformities. This includes symptoms, treatment alternatives, drug properties and interactions, and preventive health-care measures. **English Language:** Knowledge of the structure and content of the English language, including the meaning and spelling of words, rules of composition, and grammar. **Law and Government:** Knowledge of laws, legal codes, court procedures, precedents, government regulations, executive orders, agency rules, and the democratic political process. **Sociology and Anthropology:** Knowledge of group behavior and dynamics, societal trends and influences, human migrations, ethnicity, and cultures and their history and origins. **Psychology:** Knowledge of human behavior and performance; individual differences in ability, personality, and interests; learning and motivation; psychological research methods; and the assessment and treatment of behavioral and affective disorders.

Cost Estimators

- ▲ Education/Training Required: Bachelor's degree
- ▲ Annual Earnings: $46,960
- ▲ Growth: 16.5%
- ▲ Annual Job Openings: 28,000
- ▲ Self-Employed: 0%
- ▲ Part-Time: 9.4%

Prepare cost estimates for product manufacturing, construction projects, or services to aid management in bidding on or determining price of product or service. May specialize according to particular service performed or type of product manufactured. Analyzes blueprints, specifications, proposals, and other documentation to prepare time, cost, and labor estimates. Prepares estimates for selecting vendors or subcontractors and determining cost-effectiveness. Prepares time, cost, and labor estimates for products, projects, or services, applying specialized methodologies, techniques, or processes. Computes cost factors used for preparing estimates for management and determining cost-effectiveness. Prepares estimates used for management purposes, such as planning, organizing, and scheduling work. Reviews data to determine material and labor requirements and prepares itemized list. Conducts special studies to develop and establish standard hour and related cost data or to effect cost reduction. Consults with clients, vendors, or other individuals to discuss and formulate estimates and resolve issues. **SKILLS**—**Mathematics:** Using mathematics to solve problems. **Reading Comprehension:** Understanding written sentences and paragraphs in work-related documents. **Writing:** Communicating effectively in writing as appropriate for the needs of the audience. **Active Learning:** Understanding the implications of new information for both current and future problem-solving and decision-making. **Complex Problem Solving:** Identifying complex problems and reviewing related information to develop and evaluate options and implement solutions.

GOE INFORMATION—**Interest Area:** 13. General Management and Support. **Work Group:** 13.02. Management Support. **Other Job Titles in This Work Group:** Accountants; Accountants and Auditors; Appraisers and Assessors of Real Estate; Appraisers, Real Estate; Assessors; Auditors; Budget Analysts; Claims Adjusters, Examiners, and Investigators; Claims Examiners, Property and Casualty Insurance; Compensation, Benefits, and Job Analysis Specialists; Credit Analysts; Employment Interviewers, Private or Public Employment Service; Employment, Recruitment, and Placement Specialists; Financial Analysts; Human Resources, Training, and Labor Relations Specialists, All Other; Insurance Adjusters, Examiners, and Investigators; Insurance Appraisers, Auto Damage; Insurance Underwriters; Loan Counselors; Loan Officers; Logisticians; Management Analysts; Market Research Analysts; Personnel Recruiters; Purchasing Agents and Buyers, Farm Products; Purchasing Agents, Except Wholesale, Retail, and Farm Products; Tax Examiners, Collectors, and Revenue Agents; Training and Development Specialists; Wholesale and Retail Buyers, Except Farm Products. **PERSONALITY TYPE**—Conventional. Conventional occupations frequently involve following set procedures and routines. These occupations can include working with data and details more than with ideas. Usually there is a clear line of authority to follow.

EDUCATION/TRAINING PROGRAM(S)—Business Administration and Management, General; Business/Commerce, General; Construction Engineering; Construction Engineering Technology/Technician; Manufacturing Engineering; Materials Engineering; Mechanical Engineering. RELATED KNOWLEDGE/COURSES—Mathematics: Knowledge of arithmetic, algebra, geometry, calculus, and statistics and their applications. Production and Processing: Knowledge of raw materials, production processes, quality control, costs, and other tech-niques for maximizing the effective manufacture and distribution of goods. Economics and Accounting: Knowledge of economic and accounting principles and practices, the financial markets, banking, and the analysis and reporting of financial data. Building and Construction: Knowledge of materials, methods, and tools involved in the construction or repair of houses, buildings, or other structures, such as highways and roads. Administration and Management: Knowledge of business and management principles involved in strategic planning, resource allocation, human resources modeling, leadership technique, production methods, and coordination of people and resources.

Costume Attendants

- ▲ Education/Training Required: Moderate-term on-the-job training
- ▲ Annual Earnings: $23,570
- ▲ Growth: 19.1%
- ▲ Annual Job Openings: 8,000
- ▲ Self-Employed: 8.0%
- ▲ Part-Time: 40.1%

Select, fit, and take care of costumes for cast members and aid entertainers. Inventories stock to determine types and condition of costuming available and selects costumes based on historical analysis and studies. Examines costume fit on cast member and sketches or writes notes for alterations. Repairs, alters, cleans, presses, and refits costume prior to performance and cleans and stores costume following performance. Analyzes or reviews analysis of script to determine locale of story, period, number of characters, and costumes required per character. Studies books, pictures, and examples of period clothing to determine styles worn during specific period in history. Assists cast in donning costumes or assigns cast dresser to assist specific cast members with costume changes. Purchases or rents costumes and other wardrobe accessories from vendor. Arranges or directs cast dresser to arrange costumes on clothing racks in sequence of appearance. Designs and constructs costume or sends it to tailor for construction or major repairs and alterations. SKILLS—Reading Comprehension: Understanding written sentences and paragraphs in work-related documents. Speaking: Talking to others to convey information effectively. Writing: Communicating effectively in writing as appropriate for the needs of the audience. Active Learning: Understanding the implications of new information for both current and future problem-solving and decision-making. Monitor-ing: Monitoring/Assessing your performance or that of other individuals or organizations to make improvements or take corrective action. Active Listening: Giving full attention to what other people are saying, taking time to understand the points being made, asking questions as appropriate, and not interrupting at inappropriate times.

GOE INFORMATION—Interest Area: 01. Arts, Entertainment, and Media. Work Group: 01.09. Modeling and Personal Appearance. Other Job Titles in This Work Group: Makeup Artists, Theatrical and Performance; Models. PERSONALITY TYPE—Artistic. Artistic occupations frequently involve working with forms, designs, and patterns. They often require self-expression, and the work can be done without following a clear set of rules.

EDUCATION/TRAINING PROGRAM(S)—No data available. RELATED KNOWLEDGE/COURSES—Design: Knowledge of design techniques, tools, and principles involved in production of precision technical plans, blueprints, drawings, and models. Fine Arts: Knowledge of the theory and techniques required to compose, produce, and perform works of music, dance, visual arts, drama, and sculpture. English Language: Knowledge of the structure and content of the English language, including the meaning and spelling of words, rules of composition, and grammar. Customer and Personal Service:

Knowledge of principles and processes for providing customer and personal services. This includes customer needs assessment, meeting quality standards for services, and evaluation of customer satisfaction. **History and Archeology:** Knowledge of historical events and their causes, indicators, and effects on civilizations and cultures. **Geography:** Knowledge of principles and methods for de-scribing the features of land, sea, and air masses, including their physical characteristics, locations, interrelationships, and distribution of plant, animal, and human life. **Sociology and Anthropology:** Knowledge of group behavior and dynamics, societal trends and influences, human migrations, ethnicity, and cultures and their history and origins.

Counseling Psychologists

▲ Education/Training Required: Master's degree
▲ Annual Earnings: $50,420
▲ Growth: 18.1%
▲ Annual Job Openings: 18,000
▲ Self-Employed: 43.7%
▲ Part-Time: 23.4%

Assess and evaluate individuals' problems through the use of case history, interview, and observation and provide individual or group counseling services to assist individuals in achieving more effective personal, social, educational, and vocational development and adjustment. Counsels clients to assist them in understanding personal or interactive problems, defining goals, and developing realistic action plans. Collects information about individuals or clients, using interviews, case histories, observational techniques, and other assessment methods. Selects, administers, or interprets psychological tests to assess intelligence, aptitude, ability, or interests. Evaluates results of counseling methods to determine the reliability and validity of treatments. Analyzes data such as interview notes, test results, and reference manuals and texts to identify symptoms and diagnose the nature of client's problems. Advises clients on the potential benefits of counseling or makes referrals to specialists or other institutions for non-counseling problems. Develops therapeutic and treatment plans based on individual interests, abilities, or needs of clients. Consults with other professionals to discuss therapy or treatment and counseling resources or techniques and to share occupational information. Conducts research to develop or improve diagnostic or therapeutic counseling techniques. **SKILLS—Social Perceptiveness:** Being aware of others' reactions and understanding why they react as they do. **Active Listening:** Giving full attention to what other people are saying, taking time to understand the points being made, asking questions as appropriate, and not interrupting at inappropriate times. **Reading Comprehension:** Understanding written sentences and paragraphs in work-related documents. **Critical Thinking:** Using logic and reasoning to identify the strengths and weaknesses of alternative solutions, conclusions, or approaches to problems. **Active Learning:** Understanding the implications of new information for both current and future problem-solving and decision-making. **Learning Strategies:** Selecting and using training/instructional methods and procedures appropriate for the situation when learning or teaching new things.

GOE INFORMATION—Interest Area: 12. Education and Social Service. **Work Group:** 12.02. Social Services. **Other Job Titles in This Work Group:** Child, Family, and School Social Workers; Clergy; Clinical Psychologists; Clinical, Counseling, and School Psychologists; Community and Social Service Specialists, All Other; Counselors, All Other; Directors, Religious Activities and Education; Marriage and Family Therapists; Medical and Public Health Social Workers; Mental Health and Substance Abuse Social Workers; Mental Health Counselors; Probation Officers and Correctional Treatment Specialists; Rehabilitation Counselors; Religious Workers, All Other; Residential Advisors; Social and Human Service Assistants; Social Workers, All Other; Substance Abuse and Behavioral Disorder Counselors. **PERSONALITY TYPE—Social.** Social occupations frequently involve working with, communicating with, and teaching people. These occupations often involve helping or providing service to others.

EDUCATION/TRAINING PROGRAM(S)—Clinical Child Psychology; Clinical Psychology; Counseling Psychology; Developmental and Child Psychology; Psychoanalysis and Psychotherapy; Psychology, General; School Psychology. **RELATED KNOWLEDGE/COURSES—Therapy and Counseling:** Knowledge of principles, methods, and procedures for diagnosis, treatment, and rehabilitation of physical and mental dysfunctions and for career counseling and guidance. **Psychology:** Knowledge of human behavior and performance; individual differences in ability, personality, and interests; learning and motivation; psychological research methods; and the assessment and treatment of behavioral and affective disorders. **Mathematics:** Knowledge of arithmetic, algebra, geometry, calculus, and statistics and their applications.

Communications and Media: Knowledge of media production, communication, and dissemination techniques and methods. This includes alternative ways to inform and entertain via written, oral, and visual media. **English Language:** Knowledge of the structure and content of the English language, including the meaning and spelling of words, rules of composition, and grammar.

Counter and Rental Clerks

▲ Education/Training Required: Short-term on-the-job training
▲ Annual Earnings: $16,750
▲ Growth: 19.4%
▲ Annual Job Openings: 150,000
▲ Self-Employed: 1.2%
▲ Part-Time: 50.8%

Receive orders for repairs, rentals, and services. May describe available options, compute cost, and accept payment. Rents item or arranges for provision of service to customer. Receives, examines, and tags articles to be altered, cleaned, stored, or repaired. Collects deposit or payment or records credit charges. Recommends to customer items offered by rental facility that meet customer needs. Inspects and adjusts rental items to meet needs of customer. Greets customers of agency that rents items such as apparel, tools, and conveyances or that provides services such as rug cleaning. Reserves items for requested time and keeps record of items rented. Answers telephone and receives orders by phone. Explains rental fees and provides information about rented items, such as operation or description. Computes charges based on rental rate. Prepares rental forms, obtaining customer signature and other information, such as required licenses. **SKILLS— Service Orientation:** Actively looking for ways to help people. **Reading Comprehension:** Understanding written sentences and paragraphs in work-related documents. **Active Listening:** Giving full attention to what other people are saying, taking time to understand the points being made, asking questions as appropriate, and not interrupting at inappropriate times. **Mathematics:** Using mathematics to solve problems. **Writing:** Communicating effectively in writing as appropriate for the needs of the audience.

GOE INFORMATION—Interest Area: 09. Business Detail. **Work Group:** 09.05. Customer Service. **Other Job Titles in This Work Group:** Adjustment Clerks; Bill and Account Collectors; Cashiers; Customer Service Representatives; Customer Service Representatives, Utilities; Gaming Cage Workers; Gaming Change Persons and Booth Cashiers; New Accounts Clerks; Order Clerks; Receptionists and Information Clerks; Tellers; Travel Clerks. **PERSONALITY TYPE—Conventional.** Conventional occupations frequently involve following set procedures and routines. These occupations can include working with data and details more than with ideas. Usually there is a clear line of authority to follow.

EDUCATION/TRAINING PROGRAM(S)—Selling Skills and Sales Operations. **RELATED KNOWLEDGE/ COURSES—Customer and Personal Service:** Knowledge of principles and processes for providing customer and personal services. This includes customer needs assessment, meeting quality standards for services, and evaluation of customer satisfaction. **Clerical Studies:** Knowledge of administrative and clerical procedures and systems, such as word processing, managing files and records, stenography and transcription, designing forms, and other office procedures and terminology. **English Language:** Knowledge of the structure and content of the English language, including the meaning and spelling of words, rules of composition, and grammar. **Sales and Marketing:** Knowledge of principles and methods for showing, promoting, and selling products or services. This includes marketing strategy and tactics, product demonstration, sales techniques, and sales control systems. **Mathematics:** Knowledge of arithmetic, algebra, geometry, calculus, and statistics and their applications.

Counter Attendants, Cafeteria, Food Concession, and Coffee Shop

- ▲ Education/Training Required: Short-term on-the-job training
- ▲ Annual Earnings: $14,760
- ▲ Growth: 14.4%
- ▲ Annual Job Openings: 216,000
- ▲ Self-Employed: 0.1%
- ▲ Part-Time: 62.9%

Serve food to diners at counter or from a steam table. Serves food, beverages, or desserts to customers in variety of settings, such as take-out counter of restaurant or lunchroom. Serves salads, vegetables, meat, breads, and cocktails; ladles soups and sauces; portions desserts; and fills beverage cups and glasses. Orders items to replace stocks. Scrubs and polishes counters, steam tables, and other equipment; cleans glasses, dishes, and fountain equipment; and polishes metalwork on fountain. Adds relishes and garnishes according to instructions. Carves meat. Prepares sandwiches, salads, and other short-order items. Accepts payment for food, using cash register or adding machine to total check. Wraps menu items, such as sandwiches, hot entrees, and desserts. Brews coffee and tea and fills containers with requested beverages. Prepares and serves soft drinks and ice cream dishes, such as sundaes, using memorized formulas and methods of following directions. Replenishes foods at serving stations. Serves sandwiches, salads, beverages, desserts, and candies to employees in industrial establishment. Writes items ordered on tickets, totals orders, passes orders to cook, and gives ticket stubs to customers to identify filled orders. Calls order to kitchen and picks up and serves order when it is ready. **SKILLS— Writing:** Communicating effectively in writing as appropriate for the needs of the audience.

GOE INFORMATION—Interest Area: 11. Recreation, Travel, and Other Personal Services. **Work Group:** 11.05. Food and Beverage Services. **Other Job Titles in This Work Group:** Bakers; Bakers, Bread and Pastry; Bartend-

ers; Butchers and Meat Cutters; Chefs and Head Cooks; Combined Food Preparation and Serving Workers, Including Fast Food; Cooks, All Other; Cooks, Fast Food; Cooks, Institution and Cafeteria; Cooks, Restaurant; Cooks, Short Order; Dining Room and Cafeteria Attendants and Bartender Helpers; Dishwashers; Food Preparation and Serving Related Workers, All Other; Food Preparation Workers; Food Servers, Nonrestaurant; Hosts and Hostesses, Restaurant, Lounge, and Coffee Shop; Waiters and Waitresses. **PERSONALITY TYPE**—Social. Social occupations frequently involve working with, communicating with, and teaching people. These occupations often involve helping or providing service to others.

EDUCATION/TRAINING PROGRAM(S)—Food Service, Waiter/Waitress, and Dining Room Management/Manager. **RELATED KNOWLEDGE/COURSES—Customer and Personal Service:** Knowledge of principles and processes for providing customer and personal services. This includes customer needs assessment, meeting quality standards for services, and evaluation of customer satisfaction. **English Language:** Knowledge of the structure and content of the English language, including the meaning and spelling of words, rules of composition, and grammar. **Mathematics:** Knowledge of arithmetic, algebra, geometry, calculus, and statistics and their applications. **Sales and Marketing:** Knowledge of principles and methods for showing, promoting, and selling products or services. This includes marketing strategy and tactics, product demonstration, sales techniques, and sales control systems.

Court Clerks

- ▲ Education/Training Required: Short-term on-the-job training
- ▲ Annual Earnings: $27,090
- ▲ Growth: 12.0%
- ▲ Annual Job Openings: 14,000
- ▲ Self-Employed: 0%
- ▲ Part-Time: 16.0%

Perform clerical duties in court of law; prepare docket of cases to be called; secure information for judges; and con- tact witnesses, attorneys, and litigants to obtain information for court. Prepares docket or calendar of cases to be called, using typewriter or computer. Administers oath to witnesses. Collects court fees or fines and records amounts collected. Records case disposition, court orders, and arrangement for payment of court fees. Records minutes of court proceedings, using stenotype machine or shorthand, and transcribes testimony, using typewriter or computer. Notifies district attorney's office of cases prosecuted by district attorney. Explains procedures or forms to parties in case. Examines legal documents submitted to court for adherence to law or court procedures. Instructs parties when to appear in court. Prepares case folders and posts, files, or routes documents. Secures information for judges and contacts witnesses, attorneys, and litigants to obtain information for court. **SKILLS—Reading Comprehension:** Understanding written sentences and paragraphs in work-related documents. **Active Listening:** Giving full attention to what other people are saying, taking time to understand the points being made, asking questions as appropriate, and not interrupting at inappropriate times. **Writing:** Communicating effectively in writing as appropriate for the needs of the audience. **Speaking:** Talking to others to convey information effectively. **Time Management:** Managing one's own time and the time of others.

GOE INFORMATION—Interest Area: 09. Business Detail. **Work Group:** 09.02. Administrative Detail. **Other Job Titles in This Work Group:** Claims Takers, Unemployment Benefits; Court, Municipal, and License Clerks; Eligibility Interviewers, Government Programs; Executive

Secretaries and Administrative Assistants; Interviewers, Except Eligibility and Loan; Legal Secretaries; License Clerks; Loan Interviewers and Clerks; Medical Secretaries; Municipal Clerks; Secretaries, Except Legal, Medical, and Executive; Welfare Eligibility Workers and Interviewers. **PERSONALITY TYPE**—Conventional. Conventional occupations frequently involve following set procedures and routines. These occupations can include working with data and details more than with ideas. Usually there is a clear line of authority to follow.

EDUCATION/TRAINING PROGRAM(S)—General Office Occupations and Clerical Services. **RELATED KNOWLEDGE/COURSES—Clerical Studies:** Knowledge of administrative and clerical procedures and systems, such as word processing, managing files and records, stenography and transcription, designing forms, and other office procedures and terminology. **Law and Government:** Knowledge of laws, legal codes, court procedures, precedents, government regulations, executive orders, agency rules, and the democratic political process. **English Language:** Knowledge of the structure and content of the English language, including the meaning and spelling of words, rules of composition, and grammar. **Computers and Electronics:** Knowledge of circuit boards, processors, chips, electronic equipment, and computer hardware and software, including applications and programming. **Mathematics:** Knowledge of arithmetic, algebra, geometry, calculus, and statistics and their applications.

Court, Municipal, and License Clerks

- ▲ Education/Training Required: Short-term on-the-job training
- ▲ Annual Earnings: $27,090
- ▲ Growth: 12.0%
- ▲ Annual Job Openings: 14,000
- ▲ Self-Employed: 0%
- ▲ Part-Time: 16.0%

Perform clerical duties in courts of law, municipalities, and governmental licensing agencies and bureaus. May prepare docket of cases to be called, secure information for judges and court, prepare draft agendas or bylaws for town or city council, answer official correspondence, keep fiscal records and accounts, issue licenses or permits, record data, administer tests, or collect fees. **SKILLS—** No data available.

GOE INFORMATION—Interest Area: 09. Business Detail. **Work Group:** 09.02. Administrative Detail. **Other Job Titles in This Work Group:** Claims Takers, Unem-

ployment Benefits; Court Clerks; Eligibility Interviewers, Government Programs; Executive Secretaries and Administrative Assistants; Interviewers, Except Eligibility and Loan; Legal Secretaries; License Clerks; Loan Interviewers and Clerks; Medical Secretaries; Municipal Clerks; Secretaries, Except Legal, Medical, and Executive; Welfare Eligibility Workers and Interviewers. **PERSONALITY TYPE**—No data available.

EDUCATION/TRAINING PROGRAM(S)—General Office Occupations and Clerical Services. **RELATED KNOWLEDGE/COURSES**—No data available.

Creative Writers

▲ Education/Training Required: Bachelor's degree
▲ Annual Earnings: $42,450
▲ Growth: 28.4%
▲ Annual Job Openings: 18,000
▲ Self-Employed: 31.2%
▲ Part-Time: 18.5%

Create original written works, such as plays or prose, for publication or performance. Writes fiction or nonfiction prose work, such as short story, novel, biography, article, descriptive or critical analysis, or essay. Writes play or script for moving pictures or television based on original ideas or adapted from fictional, historical, or narrative sources. Organizes material for project, plans arrangement or outline, and writes synopsis. Collaborates with other writers on specific projects. Confers with client, publisher, or producer to discuss development changes or revisions. Conducts research to obtain factual information and authentic detail, utilizing sources such as newspaper accounts, diaries, and interviews. Reviews, submits for approval, and revises written material to meet personal standards and satisfy needs of client, publisher, director, or producer. Selects subject or theme for writing project based on personal interest and writing specialty or assignment from publisher, client, producer, or director. Develops factors such as theme, plot, characterization, psychological analysis, historical environment, action, and dialogue to create material. Writes humorous material for publication or performance, such as comedy routines, gags, comedy shows, or scripts for entertainers. **SKILLS—Writing:** Communicating effectively in writing as appropriate for the needs of the audience. **Reading Comprehension:** Understanding written sentences and paragraphs in work-related documents. **Coordination:** Adjusting actions in relation to others' actions. **Critical Thinking:** Using logic and reasoning to identify the strengths and weaknesses of alternative solutions, conclusions, or approaches to problems. **Complex Problem Solving:** Identifying complex problems and reviewing related information to develop and evaluate options and implement solutions.

GOE INFORMATION—Interest Area: 01. Arts, Entertainment, and Media. **Work Group:** 01.02. Writing and Editing. **Other Job Titles in This Work Group:** Copy Writers; Editors; Poets and Lyricists; Technical Writers; Writers and Authors. **PERSONALITY TYPE—**Artistic. Artistic occupations frequently involve working with forms, designs, and patterns. They often require self-expression, and the work can be done without following a clear set of rules.

EDUCATION/TRAINING PROGRAM(S)—Broadcast Journalism; Business/Corporate Communications; Communication Studies/Speech Communication and Rhetoric; Communication, Journalism, and Related Programs, Other; Creative Writing; English Composition; Family and Consumer Sciences/Human Sciences Communication; Journalism; Mass Communication/Media Studies; Playwriting and Screenwriting; Technical and Business Writing. **RELATED KNOWLEDGE/COURSES—English Language:** Knowledge of the structure and content of the English language, including the meaning and spelling of words, rules of composition, and grammar. **Communications and Media:** Knowledge of media production, communication, and dissemination techniques and methods. This includes alternative ways to inform and entertain via written, oral, and visual media. **Computers and Electronics:** Knowledge of circuit boards, processors, chips, electronic equipment, and computer hardware and software, including applications and programming. **Fine Arts:** Knowledge of the theory and techniques required to compose, produce, and perform works of music, dance, visual arts, drama, and sculpture. **Psychology:** Knowledge of human behavior and performance; individual differences in ability, personality, and interests; learning and motivation; psychological research methods; and the assessment and treatment of behavioral and affective disorders. **Clerical Studies:** Knowledge of administrative and clerical procedures and systems, such as word processing, managing files and records, stenography and transcription, designing forms, and other office procedures and terminology.

Credit Analysts

- ▲ Education/Training Required: Bachelor's degree
- ▲ Annual Earnings: $41,650
- ▲ Growth: 16.0%
- ▲ Annual Job Openings: 7,000
- ▲ Self-Employed: 0%
- ▲ Part-Time: 7.2%

Analyze current credit data and financial statements of individuals or firms to determine the degree of risk involved in extending credit or lending money. Prepare reports with this credit information for use in decision-making. Analyzes credit data and financial statements to determine degree of risk involved in extending credit or lending money. Compares liquidity, profitability, and credit history with similar establishments of same industry and geographic location. Consults with customers to resolve complaints and verify financial and credit transactions and adjust accounts as needed. Reviews individual or commercial customer files to identify and select delinquent accounts for collection. Confers with credit association and other business representatives to exchange credit information. Completes loan application, including credit analysis and summary of loan request, and submits to loan committee for approval. Evaluates customer records and recommends payment plan based on earnings, savings data, payment history, and purchase activity. Analyzes financial data, such as income growth, quality of management, and market share, to determine profitability of loan. Generates financial ratios, using computer program, to evaluate customer's financial status. **SKILLS—Reading Comprehension:** Understanding written sentences and paragraphs in work-related documents. **Critical Thinking:** Using logic and reasoning to identify the strengths and weaknesses of alternative solutions, conclusions, or approaches to problems. **Active Listening:** Giving full attention to what other people are saying, taking time to understand the points being made, asking questions as appropriate, and not interrupting at inappropriate times. **Judgment and Decision Making:** Considering the relative costs and benefits of potential actions to choose the most appropriate one. **Speaking:** Talking to others to convey information effectively. **Mathematics:** Using mathematics to solve problems.

GOE INFORMATION—Interest Area: 13. General Management and Support. **Work Group:** 13.02. Management Support. **Other Job Titles in This Work Group:** Accountants; Accountants and Auditors; Appraisers and Assessors of Real Estate; Appraisers, Real Estate; Asses-sors; Auditors; Budget Analysts; Claims Adjusters, Examiners, and Investigators; Claims Examiners, Property and Casualty Insurance; Compensation, Benefits, and Job Analysis Specialists; Cost Estimators; Employment Interviewers, Private or Public Employment Service; Employment, Recruitment, and Placement Specialists; Financial Analysts; Human Resources, Training, and Labor Relations Specialists, All Other; Insurance Adjusters, Examiners, and Investigators; Insurance Appraisers, Auto Damage; Insurance Underwriters; Loan Counselors; Loan Officers; Logisticians; Management Analysts; Market Research Analysts; Personnel Recruiters; Purchasing Agents and Buyers, Farm Products; Purchasing Agents, Except Wholesale, Retail, and Farm Products; Tax Examiners, Collectors, and Revenue Agents; Training and Development Specialists; Wholesale and Retail Buyers, Except Farm Products. **PERSONALITY TYPE—**Conventional. Conventional occupations frequently involve following set procedures and routines. These occupations can include working with data and details more than with ideas. Usually there is a clear line of authority to follow.

EDUCATION/TRAINING PROGRAM(S)—Accounting; Credit Management; Finance, General. **RELATED KNOWLEDGE/COURSES—Economics and Accounting:** Knowledge of economic and accounting principles and practices, the financial markets, banking, and the analysis and reporting of financial data. **Mathematics:** Knowledge of arithmetic, algebra, geometry, calculus, and statistics and their applications. **English Language:** Knowledge of the structure and content of the English language, including the meaning and spelling of words, rules of composition, and grammar. **Computers and Electronics:** Knowledge of circuit boards, processors, chips, electronic equipment, and computer hardware and software, including applications and programming. **Law and Government:** Knowledge of laws, legal codes, court procedures, precedents, government regulations, executive orders, agency rules, and the democratic political process. **Customer and Personal Service:** Knowledge of principles and processes for providing customer and personal services. This includes customer needs assessment, meeting quality standards for services, and evaluation of customer satisfaction. **Geography:** Knowledge of principles and methods for describing the features of land, sea, and air masses, including their physical characteristics, locations, interrelationships, and distribution of plant, animal, and human life.

Criminal Investigators and Special Agents

- ▲ Education/Training Required: Work experience in a related occupation
- ▲ Annual Earnings: $50,960
- ▲ Growth: 16.4%
- ▲ Annual Job Openings: 4,000
- ▲ Self-Employed: 0%
- ▲ Part-Time: 1.5%

Investigate alleged or suspected criminal violations of federal, state, or local laws to determine if evidence is sufficient to recommend prosecution. Obtains and verifies evidence or establishes facts by interviewing, observing, and interrogating suspects and witnesses and analyzing records. Analyzes charge, complaint, or allegation of law violation to identify issues involved and types of evidence needed. Assists in determining scope, timing, and direction of investigation. Examines records to detect links in chain of evidence or information. Obtains and uses search and arrest warrants. Develops and uses informants to get leads to information. Testifies before grand juries. Serves subpoenas or other official papers. Photographs, fingerprints, and measures height and weight of arrested suspects, noting physical characteristics, and posts data on record for filing. Reports critical information to and coordinates activities with other offices or agencies when applicable. Presents findings in reports. Maintains surveillance and performs undercover assignments. Compares crime scene fingerprints with those of suspect or fingerprint files to identify perpetrator, using computer. Searches for evidence, dusts surfaces to reveal latent fingerprints, and collects and records evidence and documents, using cameras and investigative equipment. **SKILLS—Speaking:** Talking to others to convey information effectively. **Active Listening:** Giving full attention to what other people are saying, taking time to understand the points being made, asking questions as appropriate, and not interrupting at inappropriate times. **Social Perceptiveness:** Being aware of others' reactions and understanding why they react as they do. **Critical Thinking:** Using logic and reasoning to identify the strengths and weaknesses of alternative solutions, conclusions, or approaches to problems. **Writing:** Communicating effectively in writing as appropriate for the needs of the audience. **Reading Comprehension:** Understanding written sentences and paragraphs in work-related documents.

GOE INFORMATION—Interest Area: 04. Law, Law Enforcement, and Public Safety. **Work Group:** 04.03. Law Enforcement. **Other Job Titles in This Work Group:** Animal Control Workers; Bailiffs; Child Support, Missing Persons, and Unemployment Insurance Fraud Investigators; Correctional Officers and Jailers; Crossing Guards; Detectives and Criminal Investigators; Fire Investigators; Fish and Game Wardens; Forensic Science Technicians; Gaming Surveillance Officers and Gaming Investigators; Highway Patrol Pilots; Immigration and Customs Inspectors; Lifeguards, Ski Patrol, and Other Recreational Protective Service Workers; Parking Enforcement Workers; Police and Sheriff's Patrol Officers; Police Detectives; Police Identification and Records Officers; Police Patrol Officers; Private Detectives and Investigators; Security Guards; Sheriffs and Deputy Sheriffs; Transit and Railroad Police. **PERSONALITY TYPE—Enterprising.** Enterprising occupations frequently involve starting up and carrying out projects. These occupations can involve leading people and making many decisions. They sometimes require risk taking and often deal with business.

EDUCATION/TRAINING PROGRAM(S)—Criminal Justice/Police Science; Criminalistics and Criminal Science. RELATED KNOWLEDGE/COURSES—Public Safety and Security: Knowledge of relevant equipment, policies, procedures, and strategies to promote effective local, state, or national security operations for the protection of people, data, property, and institutions. **Law and Government:** Knowledge of laws, legal codes, court procedures, precedents, government regulations, executive orders, agency rules, and the democratic political process. **Sociology and Anthropology:** Knowledge of group behavior and dynamics, societal trends and influences, human migrations, ethnicity, and cultures and their history and origins. **Telecommunications:** Knowledge of transmission, broadcasting, switching, control, and operation of telecommunications systems. **English Language:** Knowledge of the structure and content of the English language, including the meaning and spelling of words, rules of composition, and grammar. **Psychology:** Knowledge of human behavior and performance; individual differences in ability, personality, and interests; learning and motivation; psychological research methods; and the assessment and treatment of behavioral and affective disorders.

Criminal Justice and Law Enforcement Teachers, Postsecondary

▲ Education/Training Required: Master's degree
▲ Annual Earnings: $43,770
▲ Growth: 23.5%
▲ Annual Job Openings: 184,000
▲ Self-Employed: 0%
▲ Part-Time: 32.3%

Teach courses in criminal justice, corrections, and law enforcement administration. **SKILLS**—No data available.

GOE INFORMATION—Interest Area: 12. Education and Social Service. **Work Group:** 12.03. Educational Services. **Other Job Titles in This Work Group:** Adult Literacy, Remedial Education, and GED Teachers and Instructors; Agricultural Sciences Teachers, Postsecondary; Anthropology and Archeology Teachers, Postsecondary; Architecture Teachers, Postsecondary; Archivists; Area, Ethnic, and Cultural Studies Teachers, Postsecondary; Art, Drama, and Music Teachers, Postsecondary; Atmospheric, Earth, Marine, and Space Sciences Teachers, Postsecondary; Audio-Visual Collections Specialists; Biological Science Teachers, Postsecondary; Business Teachers, Postsecondary; Chemistry Teachers, Postsecondary; Child Care Workers; Communications Teachers, Postsecondary; Computer Science Teachers, Postsecondary; Curators; Economics Teachers, Postsecondary; Education Teachers, Postsecondary; Educational Psychologists; Educational, Vocational, and School Counselors; Elementary School Teachers, Except Special Education; Engineering Teachers, Postsecondary; English Language and Literature Teachers, Postsecondary; Environmental Science Teachers, Postsecondary; Farm and Home Management Advisors; Foreign Language and Literature Teachers, Postsecondary; Forestry and Conservation Science Teachers, Postsecondary; Geography Teachers, Postsecondary; Graduate Teaching Assistants; Health Specialties Teachers, Postsecondary; History Teachers, Postsecondary; Home Economics Teachers, Postsecondary; Kindergarten Teachers, Except Special Education; Law Teachers, Postsecondary; Librarians; Library Assistants, Clerical; Library Science Teachers, Postsecondary; Library Technicians; Mathematical Science Teachers, Postsecondary; Middle School Teachers, Except Special and Vocational Education; Museum Technicians and Conservators; Nursing Instructors and Teachers, Postsecondary; Personal Financial Advisors; Philosophy and Religion Teachers, Postsecondary; Physics Teachers, Postsecondary; Political Science Teachers, Postsecondary; Postsecondary Teachers, All Other; Preschool Teachers, Except Special Education; Psychology Teachers, Postsecondary; others. **PERSONALITY TYPE**—No data available.

EDUCATION/TRAINING PROGRAM(S)—Corrections; Corrections Administration; Corrections and Criminal Justice, Other; Criminal Justice/Law Enforcement Administration; Criminal Justice/Police Science; Criminal Justice/Safety Studies; Criminalistics and Criminal Science; Forensic Science and Technology; Juvenile Corrections; Security and Loss Prevention Services; Teacher Education and Professional Development, Specific Subject Areas, Other. **RELATED KNOWLEDGE/ COURSES**—No data available.

Customer Service Representatives

- ▲ Education/Training Required: Moderate-term on-the-job training
- ▲ Annual Earnings: $25,430
- ▲ Growth: 32.4%
- ▲ Annual Job Openings: 359,000
- ▲ Self-Employed: 0%
- ▲ Part-Time: 12.6%

Interact with customers to provide information in response to inquiries about products and services and to handle and resolve complaints. **SKILLS**—No data available.

GOE INFORMATION—Interest Area: 09. Business Detail. **Work Group:** 09.05. Customer Service. **Other Job Titles in This Work Group:** Adjustment Clerks; Bill and Account Collectors; Cashiers; Counter and Rental Clerks; Customer Service Representatives, Utilities; Gaming Cage Workers; Gaming Change Persons and Booth Cashiers; New Accounts Clerks; Order Clerks; Receptionists and Information Clerks; Tellers; Travel Clerks. **PERSONALITY TYPE**—No data available.

EDUCATION/TRAINING PROGRAM(S)—Customer Service Support/Call Center/Teleservice Operation; Receptionist. **RELATED KNOWLEDGE/COURSES**—No data available.

Customer Service Representatives, Utilities

- ▲ Education/Training Required: Moderate-term on-the-job training
- ▲ Annual Earnings: $25,430
- ▲ Growth: 32.4%
- ▲ Annual Job Openings: 359,000
- ▲ Self-Employed: 0%
- ▲ Part-Time: 12.8%

Interview applicants for water, gas, electric, or telephone service. Talk with customer by phone or in person and receive orders for installation, turn-on, discontinuance, or change in services. Confers with customer by phone or in person to receive orders for installation, turn-on, discontinuance, or change in service. Completes contract forms, prepares change of address records, and issues discontinuance orders, using computer. Determines charges for service requested and collects deposits. Solicits sale of new or additional utility services. Resolves billing or service complaints and refers grievances to designated departments for investigation. **SKILLS—Active Listening:** Giving full attention to what other people are saying, taking time to understand the points being made, asking questions as appropriate, and not interrupting at inappropriate times. **Speaking:** Talking to others to convey information effectively. **Service Orientation:** Actively looking for ways to help people. **Writing:** Communicating effectively in writing as appropriate for the needs of the audience. **Mathematics:** Using mathematics to solve problems. **Reading Comprehension:** Understanding written sentences and paragraphs in work-related documents.

GOE INFORMATION—Interest Area: 09. Business Detail. **Work Group:** 09.05. Customer Service. **Other Job Titles in This Work Group:** Adjustment Clerks; Bill and Account Collectors; Cashiers; Counter and Rental Clerks; Customer Service Representatives; Gaming Cage Workers; Gaming Change Persons and Booth Cashiers; New Accounts Clerks; Order Clerks; Receptionists and Information Clerks; Tellers; Travel Clerks. **PERSONALITY TYPE**—Conventional. Conventional occupations frequently involve following set procedures and routines. These occupations can include working with data and details more than with ideas. Usually there is a clear line of authority to follow.

EDUCATION/TRAINING PROGRAM(S)—Customer Service Support/Call Center/Teleservice Operation; Receptionist. **RELATED KNOWLEDGE/COURSES—Customer and Personal Service:** Knowledge of principles and processes for providing customer and personal services. This includes customer needs assessment, meeting quality standards for services, and evaluation of customer satisfaction. **English Language:** Knowledge of the structure and content of the English language, including the meaning and spelling of words, rules of composition, and grammar. **Sales and Marketing:** Knowledge of principles and methods for showing, promoting, and selling products or services. This includes marketing strategy and tactics, product demonstration, sales techniques, and sales control systems. **Mathematics:** Knowledge of arithmetic, algebra, geometry, calculus, and statistics and their applications. **Telecommunications:** Knowledge of transmission, broadcasting, switching, control, and operation of telecommunications systems.

Data Processing Equipment Repairers

- ▲ Education/Training Required: Postsecondary vocational training
- ▲ Annual Earnings: $32,890
- ▲ Growth: 14.2%
- ▲ Annual Job Openings: 24,000
- ▲ Self-Employed: 10.6%
- ▲ Part-Time: 6.9%

Repair, maintain, and install computer hardware such as peripheral equipment and word-processing systems. Replaces defective components and wiring. Tests faulty equipment and applies knowledge of functional operation of electronic units and systems to diagnose cause of malfunction. Aligns, adjusts, and calibrates equipment according to specifications. Calibrates testing instruments. Adjusts mechanical parts, using hand tools and soldering iron. Converses with equipment operators to ascertain problems with equipment before breakdown or cause of breakdown. Tests electronic components and circuits to locate defects, using oscilloscopes, signal generators, ammeters, and voltmeters. Maintains records of repairs, calibrations, and tests. Enters information into computer to copy program from one electronic component to another or to draw, modify, or store schematics. **SKILLS—Installation:** Installing equipment, machines, wiring, or programs to meet specifications. **Repairing:** Repairing machines or systems, using the needed tools. **Troubleshooting:** Determining causes of operating errors and deciding what to do about them. **Reading Comprehension:** Understanding written sentences and paragraphs in work-related documents. **Quality Control Analysis:** Conducting tests and inspections of products, services, or processes to evaluate quality or performance. **Science:** Using scientific rules and methods to solve problems. **Equipment Maintenance:** Performing routine maintenance on equipment and determining when and what kind of maintenance is needed.

GOE INFORMATION—Interest Area: 05. Mechanics, Installers, and Repairers. **Work Group:** 05.02. Electrical and Electronic Systems. **Other Job Titles in This Work Group:** Avionics Technicians; Battery Repairers; Central Office and PBX Installers and Repairers; Communication Equipment Mechanics, Installers, and Repairers; Computer, Automated Teller, and Office Machine Repairers; Electric Home Appliance and Power Tool Repairers; Electric Meter Installers and Repairers; Electric Motor and Switch Assemblers and Repairers; Electric Motor, Power Tool, and Related Repairers; Electrical and Electronics Installers and Repairers, Transportation Equipment; Electrical and Electronics Repairers, Commercial and Industrial Equipment; Electrical and Electronics Repairers, Powerhouse, Substation, and Relay; Electrical Parts Reconditioners; Electrical Power-Line Installers and Repairers; Electronic Equipment Installers and Repairers, Motor Vehicles; Electronic Home Entertainment Equipment Installers and Repairers; Elevator Installers and Repairers; Frame Wirers, Central Office; Home Appliance Installers; Home Appliance Repairers; Office Machine and Cash Register Servicers; Radio Mechanics; Signal and Track Switch Repairers; Station Installers and Repairers, Telephone; Telecommunications Equipment Installers and Repairers, Except Line Installers; Telecommunications Facility Examiners; Telecommunications Line Installers and Repairers; Transformer Repairers. **PERSONALITY TYPE—Realistic.** Realistic occupations frequently involve work activities that include practical, hands-on problems and solutions. They often deal with plants, animals, and real-world materials like wood, tools, and machinery. Many of the occupations require working outside and do not involve a lot of paperwork or working closely with others.

EDUCATION/TRAINING PROGRAM(S)—Business Machine Repair; Computer Installation and Repair Technology/Technician. **RELATED KNOWLEDGE/ COURSES—Computers and Electronics:** Knowledge of circuit boards, processors, chips, electronic equipment, and computer hardware and software, including applications and programming. **Principles of Mechanical Devices:** Knowledge of machines and tools, including their designs, uses, repair, and maintenance. **Telecommunications:** Knowledge of transmission, broadcasting, switching, control, and operation of telecommunications systems. **Math-** ematics: Knowledge of arithmetic, algebra, geometry, calculus, and statistics and their applications. **Design:** Knowledge of design techniques, tools, and principles involved in production of precision technical plans, blueprints, drawings, and models.

Database Administrators

▲ Education/Training Required: Bachelor's degree
▲ Annual Earnings: $54,850
▲ Growth: 65.9%
▲ Annual Job Openings: 8,000
▲ Self-Employed: 2.7%
▲ Part-Time: 5.7%

Coordinate changes to computer databases. Test and implement the database, applying knowledge of database management systems. May plan, coordinate, and implement security measures to safeguard computer databases. Writes logical and physical database descriptions, including location, space, access method, and security. Trains users and answers questions. Specifies user and user access levels for each segment of database. Revises company definition of data as defined in data dictionary. Confers with coworkers to determine scope and limitations of project. Reviews procedures in database management system manuals for making changes to database. Reviews workflow charts developed by programmer analyst to understand tasks computer will perform, such as updating records. Codes database descriptions and specifies identifiers of database to management system or directs others in coding descriptions. Tests, corrects errors, and modifies changes to programs or to database. Reviews project request describing database user needs, estimating time and cost required to accomplish project. Directs programmers and analysts to make changes to database management system. Selects and enters codes to monitor database performance and to create production database. Develops data model describing data elements and how they are used, following procedures using pen, template, or computer software. Establishes and calculates optimum values for database parameters, using manuals and calculator. **SKILLS—Programming:** Writing computer programs for various purposes. **Mathematics:** Using mathematics to solve problems. **Operations Analysis:** Analyzing needs and product requirements to create a design. **Reading Comprehension:** Understanding written sentences and paragraphs in work-related documents. **Critical Thinking:** Using logic and reasoning to identify the strengths and weaknesses of alternative solutions, conclusions, or approaches to problems.

GOE INFORMATION—Interest Area: 02. Science, Math, and Engineering. **Work Group:** 02.06. Mathematics and Computers. **Other Job Titles in This Work Group:** Actuaries; Computer and Information Scientists, Research; Computer Programmers; Computer Security Specialists; Computer Specialists, All Other; Computer Support Specialists; Computer Systems Analysts; Mathematical Science Occupations, All Other; Mathematical Technicians; Mathematicians; Network and Computer Systems Administrators; Network Systems and Data Communications Analysts; Operations Research Analysts; Statistical Assistants; Statisticians. **PERSONALITY TYPE—**Investigative. Investigative occupations frequently involve working with ideas and require an extensive amount of thinking. These occupations can involve searching for facts and figuring out problems mentally.

EDUCATION/TRAINING PROGRAM(S)—Computer and Information Sciences, General; Computer and Information Systems Security; Computer Systems Analysis/Analyst; Data Modeling/Warehousing and Database Administration; Management Information Systems, General. **RELATED KNOWLEDGE/COURSES—Computers and Electronics:** Knowledge of circuit boards, processors, chips, electronic equipment, and computer hardware and software, including applications and programming. **Administration and Management:** Knowledge of business and management principles involved in strategic planning, resource allocation, human resources modeling, leadership technique, production methods, and coordination of people and resources. **Mathematics:** Knowledge of arithmetic, algebra, geometry, calculus, and statistics and their applications. **English Language:** Knowledge of the structure and content of the English language, including the meaning and spelling of words, rules of composition, and grammar. **Education and Training:** Knowledge of principles and methods for curriculum and train-

ing design, teaching and instruction for individuals and groups, and the measurement of training effects.

Demonstrators and Product Promoters

- ▲ Education/Training Required: Moderate-term on-the-job training
- ▲ Annual Earnings: $20,690
- ▲ Growth: 24.9%
- ▲ Annual Job Openings: 34,000
- ▲ Self-Employed: 4.0%
- ▲ Part-Time: 40.2%

Demonstrate merchandise and answer questions for the purpose of creating public interest in buying the product. May sell demonstrated merchandise. Demonstrates and explains products, methods, or services to persuade customers to purchase products or utilize services available and answers questions. Visits homes, community organizations, stores, and schools to demonstrate products or services. Attends trade, traveling, promotional, educational, or amusement exhibit to answer visitors' questions and to protect exhibit against theft or damage. Sets up and arranges display to attract attention of prospective customers. Suggests product improvements to employer and product to purchase to customer. Gives product samples or token gifts to customers and distributes handbills, brochures, or gift certificates to passers-by. Answers telephone and written requests from customers for information about product use and writes articles and pamphlets on product. Lectures and shows slides to users of company product. Advises customers on homemaking problems related to products or services offered by company. Wears costume or signboards and walks in public to attract attention to advertise merchandise, services, or belief. Contacts businesses and civic establishments and arranges to exhibit and sell merchandise made by disadvantaged persons. Instructs customers in alteration of products. Develops list of prospective clients from sources such as newspaper items, company records, local merchants, and customers. Solicits new organization membership. Trains demonstrators to present company's products or services. Conducts guided tours of plant where product is made. Prepares reports of services rendered and visits made. Drives truck and trailer to transport exhibit. Collects fees or accepts donations. **SKILLS—Speaking:** Talking to others to convey information effectively. **Persuasion:** Persuading others to change their minds or behavior. **Social Perceptiveness:** Being aware of others' reactions and understanding why they react as they do.

Learning Strategies: Selecting and using training/instructional methods and procedures appropriate for the situation when learning or teaching new things. **Active Learning:** Understanding the implications of new information for both current and future problem-solving and decision-making. **Writing:** Communicating effectively in writing as appropriate for the needs of the audience.

GOE INFORMATION—Interest Area: 10. Sales and Marketing. **Work Group:** 10.04. Personal Soliciting. **Other Job Titles in This Work Group:** Door-To-Door Sales Workers, News and Street Vendors, and Related Workers; Telemarketers. **PERSONALITY TYPE—**Enterprising. Enterprising occupations frequently involve starting up and carrying out projects. These occupations can involve leading people and making many decisions. They sometimes require risk taking and often deal with business.

EDUCATION/TRAINING PROGRAM(S)—Retailing and Retail Operations. **RELATED KNOWLEDGE/ COURSES—Sales and Marketing:** Knowledge of principles and methods for showing, promoting, and selling products or services. This includes marketing strategy and tactics, product demonstration, sales techniques, and sales control systems. **Communications and Media:** Knowledge of media production, communication, and dissemination techniques and methods. This includes alternative ways to inform and entertain via written, oral, and visual media. **English Language:** Knowledge of the structure and content of the English language, including the meaning and spelling of words, rules of composition, and grammar. **Education and Training:** Knowledge of principles and methods for curriculum and training design, teaching and instruction for individuals and groups, and the measurement of training effects. **Customer and Personal Service:** Knowledge of principles and processes for providing customer and personal services. This includes customer needs assessment, meeting quality standards for services, and evaluation of customer satisfaction.

Dental Assistants

- ▲ Education/Training Required: Moderate-term on-the-job training
- ▲ Annual Earnings: $26,720
- ▲ Growth: 37.2%
- ▲ Annual Job Openings: 16,000
- ▲ Self-Employed: 0%
- ▲ Part-Time: 39.7%

Assist dentist, set up patient and equipment, and keep records. Prepares patient, sterilizes and disinfects instruments, sets up instrument trays, prepares materials, and assists dentist during dental procedures. Takes and records medical and dental histories and vital signs of patients. Assists dentist in management of medical and dental emergencies. Provides postoperative instructions prescribed by dentist. Applies protective coating of fluoride to teeth. Exposes dental diagnostic X rays. Records treatment information in patient records. Makes preliminary impressions for study casts and occlusal registrations for mounting study casts. Fabricates temporary restorations and custom impressions from preliminary impressions. Cleans teeth, using dental instruments. Schedules appointments, prepares bills and receives payment for dental services, completes insurance forms, and maintains records manually or using computer. Instructs patients in oral hygiene and plaque control programs. Cleans and polishes removable appliances. Pours, trims, and polishes study casts. **SKILLS—Reading Comprehension:** Understanding written sentences and paragraphs in work-related documents. **Active Listening:** Giving full attention to what other people are saying, taking time to understand the points being made, asking questions as appropriate, and not interrupting at inappropriate times. **Speaking:** Talking to others to convey information effectively. **Writing:** Communicating effectively in writing as appropriate for the needs of the audience. **Service Orientation:** Actively looking for ways to help people. **Mathematics:** Using mathematics to solve problems.

GOE INFORMATION—Interest Area: 14. Medical and Health Services. **Work Group:** 14.03. Dentistry. **Other Job Titles in This Work Group:** Dental Hygienists; Dentists, All Other Specialists; Dentists, General; Oral and Maxillofacial Surgeons; Orthodontists; Prosthodontists. **PERSONALITY TYPE—Social.** Social occupations frequently involve working with, communicating with, and teaching people. These occupations often involve helping or providing service to others.

EDUCATION/TRAINING PROGRAM(S)—Dental Assisting/Assistant. RELATED KNOWLEDGE/ COURSES—Medicine and Dentistry: Knowledge of the information and techniques needed to diagnose and treat human injuries, diseases, and deformities. This includes symptoms, treatment alternatives, drug properties and interactions, and preventive health-care measures. **Clerical Studies:** Knowledge of administrative and clerical procedures and systems, such as word processing, managing files and records, stenography and transcription, designing forms, and other office procedures and terminology. **English Language:** Knowledge of the structure and content of the English language, including the meaning and spelling of words, rules of composition, and grammar. **Customer and Personal Service:** Knowledge of principles and processes for providing customer and personal services. This includes customer needs assessment, meeting quality standards for services, and evaluation of customer satisfaction. **Mathematics:** Knowledge of arithmetic, algebra, geometry, calculus, and statistics and their applications.

Dental Hygienists

- ▲ Education/Training Required: Associate's degree
- ▲ Annual Earnings: $54,700
- ▲ Growth: 37.1%
- ▲ Annual Job Openings: 5,000
- ▲ Self-Employed: 1.6%
- ▲ Part-Time: 22.9%

Clean teeth and examine oral areas, head, and neck for signs of oral disease. May educate patients on oral hygiene, take and develop X rays, or apply fluoride or sealants. Cleans calcareous deposits, accretions, and stains from teeth and beneath margins of gums, using dental instruments. Conducts dental health clinics for community groups to augment services of dentist. Charts conditions of decay and disease for diagnosis and treatment by dentist. Examines gums, using probes, to locate periodontal recessed gums and signs of gum disease. Administers local anesthetic agents. Exposes and develops X-ray film. Removes sutures and dressings. Makes impressions for study casts. Places, carves, and finishes amalgam restorations. Feels and visually examines gums for sores and signs of disease. Feels lymph nodes under patient's chin to detect swelling or tenderness that could indicate presence of oral cancer. Places and removes rubber dams, matrices, and temporary restorations. Removes excess cement from coronal surfaces of teeth. Provides clinical services and health education to improve and maintain oral health of school children. Applies fluorides and other cavity-preventing agents to arrest dental decay. **SKILLS—Reading Comprehension:** Understanding written sentences and paragraphs in work-related documents. **Active Learning:** Understanding the implications of new information for both current and future problem-solving and decision-making. **Speaking:** Talking to others to convey information effectively. **Critical Thinking:** Using logic and reasoning to identify the strengths and weaknesses of alternative solutions, conclusions, or approaches to problems. **Service Orientation:** Actively looking for ways to help people. **Science:** Using scientific rules and methods to solve problems.

GOE INFORMATION—Interest Area: 14. Medical and Health Services. **Work Group:** 14.03. Dentistry. **Other Job Titles in This Work Group:** Dental Assistants; Dentists, All Other Specialists; Dentists, General; Oral and Maxillofacial Surgeons; Orthodontists; Prosthodontists. **PERSONALITY TYPE—Social.** Social occupations frequently involve working with, communicating with, and teaching people. These occupations often involve helping or providing service to others.

EDUCATION/TRAINING PROGRAM(S)—Dental Hygiene/Hygienist. **RELATED KNOWLEDGE/ COURSES—Medicine and Dentistry:** Knowledge of the information and techniques needed to diagnose and treat human injuries, diseases, and deformities. This includes symptoms, treatment alternatives, drug properties and interactions, and preventive health-care measures. **Biology:** Knowledge of plant and animal organisms and their tissues, cells, functions, interdependencies, and interactions with each other and the environment. **Education and Training:** Knowledge of principles and methods for curriculum and training design, teaching and instruction for individuals and groups, and the measurement of training effects. **English Language:** Knowledge of the structure and content of the English language, including the meaning and spelling of words, rules of composition, and grammar. **Customer and Personal Service:** Knowledge of principles and processes for providing customer and personal services. This includes customer needs assessment, meeting quality standards for services, and evaluation of customer satisfaction.

Desktop Publishers

▲ Education/Training Required: Postsecondary vocational training
▲ Annual Earnings: $31,200
▲ Growth: 66.7%
▲ Annual Job Openings: 5,000
▲ Self-Employed: 0%
▲ Part-Time: 19.4%

Format typescript and graphic elements using computer software to produce publication-ready material. Views monitors for visual representation of work in progress and for instructions and feedback throughout process. Activates options such as masking, pixel (picture element) editing, airbrushing, or image retouching. Saves completed work on floppy disks or magnetic tape. Studies layout or other instructions to determine work to be done and sequence of operations. Creates special effects, such as vignettes, mosaics, and image combining. Loads floppy disks or tapes containing information into system. Enters digitized data into electronic prepress system computer memory, using scanner, camera, keyboard, or mouse. Enters data, such as coordinates of images and color specifications, into system to retouch and make color corrections. Enters data such as background color, shapes, and coordinates of images; retrieves data from system memory. Activates options such as masking or text processing. **SKILLS—Equipment Selection:** Determining the kind of tools and equipment needed to do a job. **Operation and Control:** Controlling operations of equipment or systems. **Reading Comprehension:** Understanding written sentences and paragraphs in work-related documents. **Operations Analysis:** Analyzing needs and product requirements to create a design. **Monitoring:** Monitoring/Assessing your performance or that of other individuals or organizations to make improvements or take corrective action.

GOE INFORMATION—**Interest Area:** 01. Arts, Entertainment, and Media. **Work Group:** 01.07. Graphic Arts. **Other Job Titles in This Work Group:** Camera Operators; Dot Etchers; Electronic Masking System Operators; Engravers, Hand; Engravers/Carvers; Etchers; Etchers and Engravers; Etchers, Hand; Pantograph Engravers; Paste-Up Workers; Photoengravers; Precision Etchers and Engravers, Hand or Machine. **PERSONALITY TYPE**—Realistic. Realistic occupations frequently involve work activities that include practical, hands-on problems and solutions. They often deal with plants, animals, and real-world materials like wood, tools, and machinery. Many of the occupations require working outside and do not involve a lot of paperwork or working closely with others.

EDUCATION/TRAINING PROGRAM(S)—Prepress/ Desktop Publishing and Digital Imaging Design. **RELATED KNOWLEDGE/COURSES—Computers and Electronics:** Knowledge of circuit boards, processors, chips, electronic equipment, and computer hardware and software, including applications and programming. **Clerical Studies:** Knowledge of administrative and clerical procedures and systems, such as word processing, managing files and records, stenography and transcription, designing forms, and other office procedures and terminology. **Communications and Media:** Knowledge of media production, communication, and dissemination techniques and methods. This includes alternative ways to inform and entertain via written, oral, and visual media. **English Language:** Knowledge of the structure and content of the English language, including the meaning and spelling of words, rules of composition, and grammar. **Production and Processing:** Knowledge of raw materials, production processes, quality control, costs, and other techniques for maximizing the effective manufacture and distribution of goods. **Design:** Knowledge of design techniques, tools, and principles involved in production of precision technical plans, blueprints, drawings, and models.

Detectives and Criminal Investigators

- Education/Training Required: Work experience in a related occupation
- Annual Earnings: $50,960
- Growth: 16.4%
- Annual Job Openings: 4,000
- Self-Employed: 0%
- Part-Time: 1.5%

Conduct investigations related to suspected violations of federal, state, or local laws to prevent or solve crimes. **SKILLS**—No data available.

GOE INFORMATION—**Interest Area:** 04. Law, Law Enforcement, and Public Safety. **Work Group:** 04.03. Law Enforcement. **Other Job Titles in This Work Group:** Animal Control Workers; Bailiffs; Child Support, Missing Persons, and Unemployment Insurance Fraud Investigators; Correctional Officers and Jailers; Criminal Investigators and Special Agents; Crossing Guards; Fire Investigators; Fish and Game Wardens; Forensic Science Technicians; Gaming Surveillance Officers and Gaming Investigators; High-

way Patrol Pilots; Immigration and Customs Inspectors; Lifeguards, Ski Patrol, and Other Recreational Protective Service Workers; Parking Enforcement Workers; Police and Sheriff's Patrol Officers; Police Detectives; Police Identification and Records Officers; Police Patrol Officers; Private Detectives and Investigators; Security Guards; Sheriffs and Deputy Sheriffs; Transit and Railroad Police. **PERSONALITY TYPE**—No data available.

EDUCATION/TRAINING PROGRAM(S)—Criminal Justice/Police Science; Criminalistics and Criminal Science. **RELATED KNOWLEDGE/COURSES**—No data available.

Diagnostic Medical Sonographers

- Education/Training Required: Associate's degree
- Annual Earnings: $46,980
- Growth: 26.1%
- Annual Job Openings: 3,000
- Self-Employed: 4.0%
- Part-Time: 22.3%

Produce ultrasonic recordings of internal organs for use by physicians. **SKILLS**—No data available.

GOE INFORMATION—**Interest Area:** 14. Medical and Health Services. **Work Group:** 14.05. Medical Technology. **Other Job Titles in This Work Group:** Cardiovascular Technologists and Technicians; Health Technologists and Technicians, All Other; Medical and Clinical Laboratory Technicians; Medical and Clinical Laboratory Technologists; Medical Equipment Preparers; Nuclear Medicine

Technologists; Orthotists and Prosthetists; Radiologic Technicians; Radiologic Technologists; Radiologic Technologists and Technicians. **PERSONALITY TYPE**—No data available.

EDUCATION/TRAINING PROGRAM(S)—Allied Health Diagnostic, Intervention, and Treatment Professions, Other; Diagnostic Medical Sonography/Sonographer and Ultrasound Technician. **RELATED KNOWLEDGE/COURSES**—No data available.

Dietetic Technicians

▲ Education/Training Required: Moderate-term on-the-job training
▲ Annual Earnings: $21,790
▲ Growth: 27.6%
▲ Annual Job Openings: 3,000
▲ Self-Employed: 4.0%
▲ Part-Time: 22.3%

Assist dietitians in the provision of food service and nutritional programs. Under the supervision of dietitians, may plan and produce meals based on established guidelines, teach principles of food and nutrition, or counsel individuals. Guides individuals and families in food selection, preparation, and menu planning based upon nutritional needs. Standardizes recipes and tests new products for use in facility. Assists in referrals for continuity of patient care. Develops job specifications, job descriptions, and work schedules. Assists in implementing established cost control procedures. Supervises food production and service. Selects, schedules, and conducts orientation and in-service education programs. Obtains and evaluates dietary histories of individuals to plan nutritional programs. Plans menus based on established guidelines. **SKILLS— Reading Comprehension:** Understanding written sentences and paragraphs in work-related documents. **Writing:** Communicating effectively in writing as appropriate for the needs of the audience. **Speaking:** Talking to others to convey information effectively. **Learning Strategies:** Selecting and using training/instructional methods and procedures appropriate for the situation when learning or teaching new things. **Active Listening:** Giving full attention to what other people are saying, taking time to understand the points being made, asking questions as appropriate, and not interrupting at inappropriate times.

GOE INFORMATION—Interest Area: 14. Medical and Health Services. **Work Group:** 14.08. Health Protection and Promotion. **Other Job Titles in This Work Group:** Athletic Trainers; Dietitians and Nutritionists; Health Educators. **PERSONALITY TYPE**—Social. Social occupations frequently involve working with, communicating with, and teaching people. These occupations often involve helping or providing service to others.

EDUCATION/TRAINING PROGRAM(S)—Dietetic Technician (DTR); Dietetics/Dietitian (RD); Dietitian Assistant; Foods, Nutrition, and Wellness Studies, General; Nutrition Sciences. **RELATED KNOWLEDGE/ COURSES—Customer and Personal Service:** Knowledge of principles and processes for providing customer and personal services. This includes customer needs assessment, meeting quality standards for services, and evaluation of customer satisfaction. **Education and Training:** Knowledge of principles and methods for curriculum and training design, teaching and instruction for individuals and groups, and the measurement of training effects. **Biology:** Knowledge of plant and animal organisms and their tissues, cells, functions, interdependencies, and interactions with each other and the environment. **English Language:** Knowledge of the structure and content of the English language, including the meaning and spelling of words, rules of composition, and grammar. **Administration and Management:** Knowledge of business and management principles involved in strategic planning, resource allocation, human resources modeling, leadership technique, production methods, and coordination of people and resources.

Dietitians and Nutritionists

- ▲ Education/Training Required: Bachelor's degree
- ▲ Annual Earnings: $40,410
- ▲ Growth: 15.2%
- ▲ Annual Job Openings: 5,000
- ▲ Self-Employed: 13.2%
- ▲ Part-Time: 29.1%

Plan and conduct food service or nutritional programs to assist in the promotion of health and control of disease. May supervise activities of a department providing quantity food services, counsel individuals, or conduct nutritional research. Develops and implements dietary-care plans based on assessments of nutritional needs, diet restrictions, and other current health plans. Instructs patients and their families in nutritional principles, dietary plans, and food selection and preparation. Confers with design, building, and equipment personnel to plan for construction and remodeling of food service units. Plans and prepares grant proposals to request program funding. Writes research reports and other publications to document and communicate research findings. Develops curriculum and prepares manuals, visual aids, course outlines, and other materials used in teaching. Inspects meals served for conformance to prescribed diets and standards of palatability and appearance. Plans, conducts, and evaluates dietary, nutritional, and epidemiological research and analyzes findings for practical applications. Evaluates nutritional care plans and provides follow-up on continuity of care. Supervises activities of workers engaged in planning, preparing, and serving meals. Plans, organizes, and conducts training programs in dietetics, nutrition, and institutional management and administration for medical students and hospital personnel. Monitors food service operations and ensures conformance to nutritional and quality standards. Consults with physicians and health care personnel to determine nutritional needs and diet restrictions of patient or client. **SKILLS—Writing:** Communicating effectively in writing as appropriate for the needs of the audience. **Reading Comprehension:** Understanding written sentences and paragraphs in work-related documents. **Management of Financial Resources:** Determining how money will be spent to get the work done and accounting for these expenditures. **Critical Thinking:** Using logic and reasoning to identify the strengths and weaknesses of alternative solutions, conclusions, or approaches to problems. **Active Learning:** Understanding the implications of new information for both current and future problem-solving and decision-making.

GOE INFORMATION—Interest Area: 14. Medical and Health Services. **Work Group:** 14.08. Health Protection and Promotion. **Other Job Titles in This Work Group:** Athletic Trainers; Dietetic Technicians; Health Educators. **PERSONALITY TYPE—**Investigative. Investigative occupations frequently involve working with ideas and require an extensive amount of thinking. These occupations can involve searching for facts and figuring out problems mentally.

EDUCATION/TRAINING PROGRAM(S)—Clinical Nutrition/Nutritionist; Dietetics and Clinical Nutrition Services, Other; Dietetics/Dietitian (RD); Foods, Nutrition, and Related Services, Other; Foods, Nutrition, and Wellness Studies, General; Foodservice Systems Administration/Management; Human Nutrition; Nutrition Sciences. **RELATED KNOWLEDGE/COURSES—English Language:** Knowledge of the structure and content of the English language, including the meaning and spelling of words, rules of composition, and grammar. **Education and Training:** Knowledge of principles and methods for curriculum and training design, teaching and instruction for individuals and groups, and the measurement of training effects. **Biology:** Knowledge of plant and animal organisms and their tissues, cells, functions, interdependencies, and interactions with each other and the environment. **Administration and Management:** Knowledge of business and management principles involved in strategic planning, resource allocation, human resources modeling, leadership technique, production methods, and coordination of people and resources. **Food Production:** Knowledge of techniques and equipment for planting, growing, and harvesting food products (both plant and animal) for consumption, including storage/handling techniques.

Directors, Religious Activities and Education

- ▲ Education/Training Required: Bachelor's degree
- ▲ Annual Earnings: $27,420
- ▲ Growth: 15.9%
- ▲ Annual Job Openings: 23,000
- ▲ Self-Employed: 1.2%
- ▲ Part-Time: 14.0%

Direct and coordinate activities of a denominational group to meet religious needs of students. Plan, direct, or coordinate church school programs designed to promote religious education among church membership. May provide counseling and guidance relative to marital, health, financial, and religious problems. Coordinates activities with religious advisers, councils, and university officials to meet religious needs of students. Assists and advises groups in promoting interfaith understanding. Solicits support, participation, and interest in religious education programs from congregation members, organizations, officials, and clergy. Orders and distributes school supplies. Analyzes revenue and program cost data to determine budget priorities. Interprets religious education to public through speaking, leading discussions, and writing articles for local and national publications. Interprets policies of university to community religious workers. Analyzes member participation and changes in congregation emphasis to determine needs for religious education. Plans and conducts conferences dealing with interpretation of religious ideas and convictions. Promotes student participation in extracurricular congregational activities. Counsels individuals regarding marital, health, financial, and religious problems. Plans congregational activities and projects to encourage participation in religious education programs. Supervises instructional staff in religious education program. Develops, organizes, and directs study courses and religious education programs within congregation. **SKILLS—Social Perceptiveness:** Being aware of others' reactions and understanding why they react as they do. **Reading Comprehension:** Understanding written sentences and paragraphs in work-related documents. **Writing:** Communicating effectively in writing as appropriate for the needs of the audience. **Active Listening:** Giving full attention to what other people are saying, taking time to understand the points being made, asking questions as appropriate, and not interrupting at inappropriate times. **Service Orientation:** Actively looking for ways to help people. **Speaking:** Talking to others to convey information effectively.

GOE INFORMATION—Interest Area: 12. Education and Social Service. **Work Group:** 12.02. Social Services. **Other Job Titles in This Work Group:** Child, Family, and School Social Workers; Clergy; Clinical Psychologists; Clinical, Counseling, and School Psychologists; Community and Social Service Specialists, All Other; Counseling Psychologists; Counselors, All Other; Marriage and Family Therapists; Medical and Public Health Social Workers; Mental Health and Substance Abuse Social Workers; Mental Health Counselors; Probation Officers and Correctional Treatment Specialists; Rehabilitation Counselors; Religious Workers, All Other; Residential Advisors; Social and Human Service Assistants; Social Workers, All Other; Substance Abuse and Behavioral Disorder Counselors. **PERSONALITY TYPE—Social.** Social occupations frequently involve working with, communicating with, and teaching people. These occupations often involve helping or providing service to others.

EDUCATION/TRAINING PROGRAM(S)—Bible/ Biblical Studies; Missions/Missionary Studies and Missiology; Religious Education; Youth Ministry. RELATED KNOWLEDGE/COURSES—Administration and Management: Knowledge of business and management principles involved in strategic planning, resource allocation, human resources modeling, leadership technique, production methods, and coordination of people and resources. **Therapy and Counseling:** Knowledge of principles, methods, and procedures for diagnosis, treatment, and rehabilitation of physical and mental dysfunctions and for career counseling and guidance. **Psychology:** Knowledge of human behavior and performance; individual differences in ability, personality, and interests; learning and motivation; psychological research methods; and the assessment and treatment of behavioral and affective disorders. **Education and Training:** Knowledge of principles and methods for curriculum and training design, teaching and instruction for individuals and groups, and the measurement of training effects. **Sociology and Anthropology:** Knowledge of group behavior and dynamics, societal trends and influences, human migrations, ethnicity, and cultures and their history and origins. **Philosophy and Theology:** Knowledge of different philosophical systems and religions. This includes their basic principles, values, ethics, ways of thinking, customs, and practices and their

impact on human culture. **English Language:** Knowledge of the structure and content of the English language, including the meaning and spelling of words, rules of composition, and grammar.

Directors—Stage, Motion Pictures, Television, and Radio

- ▲ Education/Training Required: Work experience plus degree
- ▲ Annual Earnings: $45,090
- ▲ Growth: 27.1%
- ▲ Annual Job Openings: 11,000
- ▲ Self-Employed: 23.7%
- ▲ Part-Time: 25.3%

Interpret script, conduct rehearsals, and direct activities of cast and technical crew for stage, motion pictures, television, or radio programs. Reads and rehearses cast to develop performance based on script interpretations. Directs cast, crew, and technicians during production or recording and filming in studio or on location. Directs live broadcasts, films and recordings, or non-broadcast programming for public entertainment or education. Establishes pace of program and sequences of scenes according to time requirements and cast and set accessibility. Approves equipment and elements required for production, such as scenery, lights, props, costumes, choreography, and music. Auditions and selects cast and technical staff. Cuts and edits film or tape to integrate component parts of film into desired sequence. Reviews educational material to gather information for scripts. Writes and compiles letters, memos, notes, scripts, and other program material, using computer. Compiles cue words and phrases and cues announcers, cast members, and technicians during performances. Interprets stage-set diagrams to determine stage layout and supervises placement of equipment and scenery. Coaches performers in acting techniques to develop and improve performance and image. Confers with technical directors, managers, and writers to discuss details of production, such as photography, script, music, sets, and costumes. **SKILLS—Coordination:** Adjusting actions in relation to others' actions. **Reading Comprehension:** Understanding written sentences and paragraphs in work-related documents. **Instructing:** Teaching others how to do something. **Speaking:** Talking to others to convey information effectively. **Management of Personnel Resources:** Motivating, developing, and directing people as they work, identifying the best people for the job. **Critical Thinking:** Using logic and reasoning to identify the strengths and weaknesses of alternative solutions, conclusions, or approaches to problems.

GOE INFORMATION—Interest Area: 01. Arts, Entertainment, and Media. **Work Group:** 01.05. Performing Arts. **Other Job Titles in This Work Group:** Actors; Choreographers; Composers; Dancers; Music Arrangers and Orchestrators; Music Directors; Music Directors and Composers; Musicians and Singers; Musicians, Instrumental; Public Address System and Other Announcers; Radio and Television Announcers; Singers; Talent Directors. **PERSONALITY TYPE—Artistic.** Artistic occupations frequently involve working with forms, designs, and patterns. They often require self-expression, and the work can be done without following a clear set of rules.

EDUCATION/TRAINING PROGRAM(S)—Cinematography and Film/Video Production; Directing and Theatrical Production; Drama and Dramatics/Theatre Arts, General; Dramatic/Theatre Arts and Stagecraft, Other; Film/Cinema Studies; Radio and Television; Theatre/Theatre Arts Management. RELATED KNOWLEDGE/ COURSES—Fine Arts: Knowledge of the theory and techniques required to compose, produce, and perform works of music, dance, visual arts, drama, and sculpture. **Administration and Management:** Knowledge of business and management principles involved in strategic planning, resource allocation, human resources modeling, leadership technique, production methods, and coordination of people and resources. **Communications and Media:** Knowledge of media production, communication, and dissemination techniques and methods. This includes alternative ways to inform and entertain via written, oral, and visual media. **English Language:** Knowledge of the structure and content of the English language, including the meaning and spelling of words, rules of composition, and grammar. **Computers and Electronics:** Knowledge of circuit boards, processors, chips, electronic equipment, and computer hardware and software, including applica-

D

tions and programming. **Clerical Studies:** Knowledge of administrative and clerical procedures and systems, such as word processing, managing files and records, stenogra-phy and transcription, designing forms, and other office procedures and terminology.

Dispatchers, Except Police, Fire, and Ambulance

▲ Education/Training Required: Moderate-term on-the-job training
▲ Annual Earnings: $30,070
▲ Growth: 22.2%
▲ Annual Job Openings: 8,000
▲ Self-Employed: 2.1%
▲ Part-Time: 8.6%

Schedule and dispatch workers, work crews, equipment, or service vehicles for conveyance of materials, freight, or passengers or for normal installation, service, or emergency repairs rendered outside the place of business. Duties may include using radio, telephone, or computer to transmit assignments and compiling statistics and reports on work progress. Routes or assigns workers or equipment to appropriate location, according to customer request, specifications, or needs. Confers with customer or supervising personnel regarding questions, problems, and requests for service or equipment. Orders supplies and equipment; issues to personnel. Records and maintains files and records regarding customer requests, work or services performed, charges, expenses, inventory, and other dispatch information. Determines types or amount of equipment, vehicles, materials, or personnel required, according to work order or specifications. Receives or prepares work orders according to customer request or specifications. Relays work orders, messages, and information to or from work crews, supervisors, and field inspectors, using telephone or two-way radio. **SKILLS—Active Listening:** Giving full attention to what other people are saying, taking time to understand the points being made, asking questions as appropriate, and not interrupting at inappropriate times. **Time Management:** Managing one's own time and the time of others. **Equipment Selection:** Determining the kind of tools and equipment needed to do a job. **Coordination:** Adjusting actions in relation to others' actions. **Speaking:** Talking to others to convey information effectively.

GOE INFORMATION—Interest Area: 09. Business Detail. **Work Group:** 09.06. Communications. **Other Job Titles in This Work Group:** Central Office Operators; Communications Equipment Operators, All Other; Directory Assistance Operators; Police, Fire, and Ambulance Dispatchers; Switchboard Operators, Including Answering Service; Telephone Operators. **PERSONALITY TYPE—**Conventional. Conventional occupations frequently involve following set procedures and routines. These occupations can include working with data and details more than with ideas. Usually there is a clear line of authority to follow.

EDUCATION/TRAINING PROGRAM(S)—No data available. **RELATED KNOWLEDGE/COURSES—Telecommunications:** Knowledge of transmission, broadcasting, switching, control, and operation of telecommunications systems. **Transportation:** Knowledge of principles and methods for moving people or goods by air, rail, sea, or road, including the relative costs and benefits. **Customer and Personal Service:** Knowledge of principles and processes for providing customer and personal services. This includes customer needs assessment, meeting quality standards for services, and evaluation of customer satisfaction. **Clerical Studies:** Knowledge of administrative and clerical procedures and systems, such as word processing, managing files and records, stenography and transcription, designing forms, and other office procedures and terminology. **English Language:** Knowledge of the structure and content of the English language, including the meaning and spelling of words, rules of composition, and grammar.

Drywall and Ceiling Tile Installers

- ▲ Education/Training Required: Moderate-term on-the-job training
- ▲ Annual Earnings: $33,000
- ▲ Growth: 9.4%
- ▲ Annual Job Openings: 19,000
- ▲ Self-Employed: 31.5%
- ▲ Part-Time: 8.4%

Apply plasterboard or other wallboard to ceilings or interior walls of buildings. Apply or mount acoustical tiles or blocks, strips, or sheets of shock-absorbing materials to ceilings and walls of buildings to reduce or reflect sound. Materials may be of decorative quality. Includes lathers who fasten wooden, metal, or rockboard lath to walls, ceilings, or partitions of buildings to provide support base for plaster, fire-proofing, or acoustical material. SKILLS—No data available.

GOE INFORMATION—**Interest Area:** 06. Construction, Mining, and Drilling. **Work Group:** 06.02. Construction. **Other Job Titles in This Work Group:** Boat Builders and Shipwrights; Boilermakers; Brattice Builders; Brickmasons and Blockmasons; Carpenters; Carpet Installers; Ceiling Tile Installers; Cement Masons and Concrete Finishers; Commercial Divers; Construction Carpenters; Drywall Installers; Electricians; Explosives Workers, Ordnance Handling Experts, and Blasters; Fence Erectors; Floor Layers, Except Carpet, Wood, and Hard Tiles; Floor Sanders and Finishers; Glaziers; Grader, Bulldozer, and Scraper Operators; Hazardous Materials Removal Workers; Insulation Workers, Floor, Ceiling, and Wall; Insulation Workers, Mechanical; Manufactured Building and Mobile Home Installers; Operating Engineers; Operating Engineers and Other Construction Equipment Operators; Painters, Construction and Maintenance; Paperhangers; Paving, Surfacing, and Tamping Equipment Operators; Pile-Driver Operators; Pipe Fitters; Pipelayers; Pipelaying Fitters; Plasterers and Stucco Masons; Plumbers; Plumbers, Pipefitters, and Steamfitters; Rail-Track Laying and Maintenance Equipment Operators; Refractory Materials Repairers, Except Brickmasons; Reinforcing Iron and Rebar Workers; Riggers; Roofers; Rough Carpenters; Security and Fire Alarm Systems Installers; Segmental Pavers; Sheet Metal Workers; Ship Carpenters and Joiners; Stone Cutters and Carvers; Stonemasons; Structural Iron and Steel Workers; Tapers; Terrazzo Workers and Finishers; Tile and Marble Setters. **PERSONALITY TYPE**—No data available.

EDUCATION/TRAINING PROGRAM(S)—Drywall Installation/Drywaller. **RELATED KNOWLEDGE/ COURSES**—No data available.

Drywall Installers

- ▲ Education/Training Required: Moderate-term on-the-job training
- ▲ Annual Earnings: $33,000
- ▲ Growth: 9.4%
- ▲ Annual Job Openings: 19,000
- ▲ Self-Employed: 31.5%
- ▲ Part-Time: 8.4%

Apply plasterboard or other wallboard to ceilings and interior walls of buildings. Trims rough edges from wallboard to maintain even joints, using knife. Fits and fastens wallboard or sheetrock into specified position, using hand tools, portable power tools, or adhesive. Measures and marks cutting lines on framing, drywall, and trim, using tape measure, straightedge, or square and marking devices. Installs blanket insulation between studs and tacks plastic moisture barrier over insulation. Removes plaster, drywall, or paneling, using crowbar and hammer. Assembles and installs metal framing and decorative trim for windows, doorways, and bents. Reads blueprints and other specifications to determine method of installation, work procedures, and material and tool requirements. Lays out reference lines and points, computes position of framing and furring channels, and marks position, using chalkline. Suspends angle iron grid and channel iron from ceiling, using wire. Installs horizontal and vertical metal or wooden studs for attachment of wallboard on interior walls, using hand tools. Cuts metal or wood framing, angle and channel iron, and trim to size, using cutting tools. Cuts openings into board for electrical outlets, windows, vents, or fixtures, using keyhole saw or other cutting tools. **SKILLS—Installation:** Installing equipment, machines, wiring, or programs to meet specifications. **Equipment Selection:** Determining the kind of tools and equipment needed to do a job. **Mathematics:** Using mathematics to solve problems. **Judgment and Decision Making:** Considering the relative costs and benefits of potential actions to choose the most appropriate one.

GOE INFORMATION—Interest Area: 06. Construction, Mining, and Drilling. **Work Group:** 06.02. Construction. **Other Job Titles in This Work Group:** Boat Builders and Shipwrights; Boilermakers; Brattice Builders; Brickmasons and Blockmasons; Carpenters; Carpet Installers; Ceiling Tile Installers; Cement Masons and Concrete Finishers; Commercial Divers; Construction Carpenters; Drywall and Ceiling Tile Installers; Electricians; Explosives Workers, Ordnance Handling Experts, and Blasters; Fence Erectors; Floor Layers, Except Carpet, Wood, and Hard Tiles; Floor Sanders and Finishers; Glaziers; Grader, Bulldozer, and Scraper Operators; Hazardous Materials Removal Workers; Insulation Workers, Floor, Ceiling, and Wall; Insulation Workers, Mechanical; Manufactured Building and Mobile Home Installers; Operating Engineers; Operating Engineers and Other Construction Equipment Operators; Painters, Construction and Maintenance; Paperhangers; Paving, Surfacing, and Tamping Equipment Operators; Pile-Driver Operators; Pipe Fitters; Pipelayers; Pipelaying Fitters; Plasterers and Stucco Masons; Plumb-ers; Plumbers, Pipefitters, and Steamfitters; Rail-Track Laying and Maintenance Equipment Operators; Refractory Materials Repairers, Except Brickmasons; Reinforcing Iron and Rebar Workers; Riggers; Roofers; Rough Carpenters; Security and Fire Alarm Systems Installers; Segmental Pavers; Sheet Metal Workers; Ship Carpenters and Joiners; Stone Cutters and Carvers; Stonemasons; Structural Iron and Steel Workers; Tapers; Terrazzo Workers and Finishers; Tile and Marble Setters. **PERSONALITY TYPE—**Realistic. Realistic occupations frequently involve work activities that include practical, hands-on problems and solutions. They often deal with plants, animals, and real-world materials like wood, tools, and machinery. Many of the occupations require working outside and do not involve a lot of paperwork or working closely with others.

EDUCATION/TRAINING PROGRAM(S)—Drywall Installation/Drywaller. **RELATED KNOWLEDGE/COURSES—Building and Construction:** Knowledge of materials, methods, and tools involved in the construction or repair of houses, buildings, or other structures, such as highways and roads. **Design:** Knowledge of design techniques, tools, and principles involved in production of precision technical plans, blueprints, drawings, and models. **Principles of Mechanical Devices:** Knowledge of machines and tools, including their designs, uses, repair, and maintenance. **Engineering and Technology:** Knowledge of the practical application of engineering science and technology. This includes applying principles, techniques, procedures, and equipment to the design and production of various goods and services. **Mathematics:** Knowledge of arithmetic, algebra, geometry, calculus, and statistics and their applications.

Economics Teachers, Postsecondary

- ▲ Education/Training Required: Master's degree
- ▲ Annual Earnings: $62,820
- ▲ Growth: 23.5%
- ▲ Annual Job Openings: 184,000
- ▲ Self-Employed: 0%
- ▲ Part-Time: 32.3%

Teach courses in economics. Prepares and delivers lectures to students. Compiles bibliographies of specialized materials for outside reading assignments. Directs research of other teachers or graduate students working for advanced academic degrees. Serves on faculty committee providing professional consulting services to government and industry. Acts as adviser to student organizations. Conducts research in particular field of knowledge and publishes findings in professional journals. Advises students on academic and vocational curricula. Stimulates class discussions. Compiles, administers, and grades examinations or assigns this work to others. **SKILLS—Read-**

ing Comprehension: Understanding written sentences and paragraphs in work-related documents. **Instructing:** Teaching others how to do something. **Active Learning:** Understanding the implications of new information for both current and future problem-solving and decision-making. **Speaking:** Talking to others to convey information effectively. **Learning Strategies:** Selecting and using training/instructional methods and procedures appropriate for the situation when learning or teaching new things. **Active Listening:** Giving full attention to what other people are saying, taking time to understand the points being made, asking questions as appropriate, and not interrupting at inappropriate times. **Writing:** Communicating effectively in writing as appropriate for the needs of the audience.

GOE INFORMATION—Interest Area: 12. Education and Social Service. **Work Group:** 12.03. Educational Services. **Other Job Titles in This Work Group:** Adult Literacy, Remedial Education, and GED Teachers and Instructors; Agricultural Sciences Teachers, Postsecondary; Anthropology and Archeology Teachers, Postsecondary; Architecture Teachers, Postsecondary; Archivists; Area, Ethnic, and Cultural Studies Teachers, Postsecondary; Art, Drama, and Music Teachers, Postsecondary; Atmospheric, Earth, Marine, and Space Sciences Teachers, Postsecondary; Audio-Visual Collections Specialists; Biological Science Teachers, Postsecondary; Business Teachers, Postsecondary; Chemistry Teachers, Postsecondary; Child Care Workers; Communications Teachers, Postsecondary; Computer Science Teachers, Postsecondary; Criminal Justice and Law Enforcement Teachers, Postsecondary; Curators; Education Teachers, Postsecondary; Educational Psychologists; Educational, Vocational, and School Counselors; Elementary School Teachers, Except Special Education; Engineering Teachers, Postsecondary; English Language and Literature Teachers, Postsecondary; Environmental Science Teachers, Postsecondary; Farm and Home Management Advisors; Foreign Language and Literature Teachers, Postsecondary; Forestry and Conservation Science Teachers, Postsecondary; Geography Teachers, Postsecondary; Graduate Teaching Assistants; Health Specialties Teach-

ers, Postsecondary; History Teachers, Postsecondary; Home Economics Teachers, Postsecondary; Kindergarten Teachers, Except Special Education; Law Teachers, Postsecondary; Librarians; Library Assistants, Clerical; Library Science Teachers, Postsecondary; Library Technicians; Mathematical Science Teachers, Postsecondary; Middle School Teachers, Except Special and Vocational Education; Museum Technicians and Conservators; Nursing Instructors and Teachers, Postsecondary; Personal Financial Advisors; Philosophy and Religion Teachers, Postsecondary; Physics Teachers, Postsecondary; Political Science Teachers, Postsecondary; Postsecondary Teachers, All Other; Preschool Teachers, Except Special Education; others. **PERSONALITY TYPE**—Social. Social occupations frequently involve working with, communicating with, and teaching people. These occupations often involve helping or providing service to others.

EDUCATION/TRAINING PROGRAM(S)—Applied Economics; Business/Managerial Economics; Development Economics and International Development; Econometrics and Quantitative Economics; Economics, General; Economics, Other; International Economics; Social Science Teacher Education. **RELATED KNOWLEDGE/ COURSES—Education and Training:** Knowledge of principles and methods for curriculum and training design, teaching and instruction for individuals and groups, and the measurement of training effects. **Sociology and Anthropology:** Knowledge of group behavior and dynamics, societal trends and influences, human migrations, ethnicity, and cultures and their history and origins. **Psychology:** Knowledge of human behavior and performance; individual differences in ability, personality, and interests; learning and motivation; psychological research methods; and the assessment and treatment of behavioral and affective disorders. **History and Archeology:** Knowledge of historical events and their causes, indicators, and effects on civilizations and cultures. **English Language:** Knowledge of the structure and content of the English language, including the meaning and spelling of words, rules of composition, and grammar.

E

Economists

▲ Education/Training Required: Bachelor's degree
▲ Annual Earnings: $67,050
▲ Growth: 18.5%
▲ Annual Job Openings: 3,000
▲ Self-Employed: 18.9%
▲ Part-Time: 8.8%

Conduct research, prepare reports, or formulate plans to aid in solution of economic problems arising from production and distribution of goods and services. May collect and process economic and statistical data using econometric and sampling techniques. Studies economic and statistical data in area of specialization, such as finance, labor, or agriculture. Supervises research projects and students' study projects. Assigns work to staff. Teaches theories, principles, and methods of economics. Testifies at regulatory or legislative hearings to present recommendations. Provides advice and consultation to business and public and private agencies. Develops economic guidelines and standards and preparing points of view used in forecasting trends and formulating economic policy. Reviews and analyzes data to prepare reports, to forecast future marketing trends, and to stay abreast of economic changes. Compiles data relating to research area, such as employment, productivity, and wages and hours. Formulates recommendations, policies, or plans to interpret markets or solve economic problems. Devises methods and procedures for collecting and processing data, using various econometric and sampling techniques. Organizes research data into report format, including graphic illustrations of research findings. **SKILLS—Systems Evaluation:** Identifying measures or indicators of system performance and the actions needed to improve or correct performance relative to the goals of the system. **Systems Analysis:** Determining how a system should work and how changes in conditions, operations, and the environment will affect outcomes. **Judgment and Decision Making:** Considering the relative costs and benefits of potential actions to choose the most appropriate one. **Writing:** Communicating effectively in writing as appropriate for the needs of the audience. **Complex Problem Solving:** Identifying complex problems and reviewing related information to develop and evaluate options and implement solutions.

GOE INFORMATION—Interest Area: 02. Science, Math, and Engineering. **Work Group:** 02.04. Social Sciences. **Other Job Titles in This Work Group:** Anthropologists; Anthropologists and Archeologists; Archeologists; City Planning Aides; Historians; Industrial-Organizational Psychologists; Political Scientists; Psychologists, All Other; Social Science Research Assistants; Social Scientists and Related Workers, All Other; Sociologists; Survey Researchers; Urban and Regional Planners. **PERSONALITY TYPE—Investigative.** Investigative occupations frequently involve working with ideas and require an extensive amount of thinking. These occupations can involve searching for facts and figuring out problems mentally.

EDUCATION/TRAINING PROGRAM(S)—Agricultural Economics; Applied Economics; Business/Managerial Economics; Development Economics and International Development; Econometrics and Quantitative Economics; Economics, General; Economics, Other; International Economics. RELATED KNOWLEDGE/COURSES—Mathematics: Knowledge of arithmetic, algebra, geometry, calculus, and statistics and their applications. **Economics and Accounting:** Knowledge of economic and accounting principles and practices, the financial markets, banking, and the analysis and reporting of financial data. **English Language:** Knowledge of the structure and content of the English language, including the meaning and spelling of words, rules of composition, and grammar. **Education and Training:** Knowledge of principles and methods for curriculum and training design, teaching and instruction for individuals and groups, and the measurement of training effects. **Computers and Electronics:** Knowledge of circuit boards, processors, chips, electronic equipment, and computer hardware and software, including applications and programming. **Administration and Management:** Knowledge of business and management principles involved in strategic planning, resource allocation, human resources modeling, leadership technique, production methods, and coordination of people and resources. **Production and Processing:** Knowledge of raw materials, production processes, quality control, costs, and other techniques for maximizing the effective manufacture and distribution of goods.

Editors

▲ Education/Training Required: Bachelor's degree
▲ Annual Earnings: $39,960
▲ Growth: 22.6%
▲ Annual Job Openings: 14,000
▲ Self-Employed: 31.2%
▲ Part-Time: 18.5%

Perform variety of editorial duties, such as laying out, indexing, and revising content of written materials, in preparation for final publication. Plans and prepares page layouts to position and space articles and photographs or illustrations. Determines placement of stories based on relative significance, available space, and knowledge of layout principles. Confers with management and editorial staff members regarding placement of developing news stories. Writes and rewrites headlines, captions, columns, articles, and stories to conform to publication's style, editorial policy, and publishing requirements. Reads and evaluates manuscripts or other materials submitted for publication and confers with authors regarding changes or publication. Reads copy or proof to detect and correct errors in spelling, punctuation, and syntax and indicates corrections, using standard proofreading and typesetting symbols. Reviews and approves proofs submitted by composing room. Selects local, state, national, and international news items received by wire from press associations. Compiles index cross-references and related items, such as glossaries, bibliographies, and footnotes. Verifies facts, dates, and statistics, using standard reference sources. Arranges topical or alphabetical list of index items according to page or chapter, indicating location of item in text. Reads material to determine items to be included in index of book or other publication. Selects and crops photographs and illustrative materials to conform to space and subject matter requirements. **SKILLS—Writing:** Communicating effectively in writing as appropriate for the needs of the audience. **Reading Comprehension:** Understanding written sentences and paragraphs in work-related documents. **Critical Thinking:** Using logic and reasoning to identify the strengths and weaknesses of alternative solutions, conclusions, or approaches to problems. **Coordination:** Adjusting actions in relation to others' actions. **Active Learning:** Understanding the implications of new information for both current and future problem-solving and decision-making.

GOE INFORMATION—Interest Area: 01. Arts, Entertainment, and Media. **Work Group:** 01.02. Writing and Editing. **Other Job Titles in This Work Group:** Copy Writers; Creative Writers; Poets and Lyricists; Technical Writers; Writers and Authors. **PERSONALITY TYPE—** Artistic. Artistic occupations frequently involve working with forms, designs, and patterns. They often require self-expression, and the work can be done without following a clear set of rules.

EDUCATION/TRAINING PROGRAM(S)—Broadcast Journalism; Business/Corporate Communications; Communication, Journalism, and Related Programs, Other; Creative Writing; Journalism; Mass Communication/Media Studies; Publishing; Technical and Business Writing. **RELATED KNOWLEDGE/COURSES—English Language:** Knowledge of the structure and content of the English language, including the meaning and spelling of words, rules of composition, and grammar. **Communications and Media:** Knowledge of media production, communication, and dissemination techniques and methods. This includes alternative ways to inform and entertain via written, oral, and visual media. **Administration and Management:** Knowledge of business and management principles involved in strategic planning, resource allocation, human resources modeling, leadership technique, production methods, and coordination of people and resources. **Computers and Electronics:** Knowledge of circuit boards, processors, chips, electronic equipment, and computer hardware and software, including applications and programming. **Clerical Studies:** Knowledge of administrative and clerical procedures and systems, such as word processing, managing files and records, stenography and transcription, designing forms, and other office procedures and terminology.

Education Administrators, Elementary and Secondary School

▲ Education/Training Required: Work experience plus degree
▲ Annual Earnings: $69,240
▲ Growth: 13.4%
▲ Annual Job Openings: 35,000
▲ Self-Employed: 13.8%
▲ Part-Time: 9.8%

Plan, direct, or coordinate the academic, clerical, or auxiliary activities of public or private elementary or secondary-level schools. Establishes program philosophy plans, policies, and academic codes of ethics to maintain educational standards for student screening, placement, and training. Teaches classes or courses to students. Completes, maintains, or assigns preparation of attendance, activity, planning, or personnel reports and records for officials and agencies. Reviews and interprets government codes and develops programs to ensure facility safety, security, and maintenance. Counsels and provides guidance to students regarding personal, academic, or behavioral problems. Confers with parents and staff to discuss educational activities, policies, and student behavioral or learning problems. Writes articles, manuals, and other publications and assists in the distribution of promotional literature. Contacts and addresses commercial, community, or political groups to promote educational programs and services or lobby for legislative changes. Recruits, hires, trains, and evaluates primary and supplemental staff and recommends personnel actions for programs and services. Plans and coordinates consumer research and educational services to assist organizations in product development and marketing. Organizes and directs committees of specialists, volunteers, and staff to provide technical and advisory assistance for programs. Determines allocations of funds for staff, supplies, materials, and equipment and authorizes purchases. Directs and coordinates activities of teachers or administrators at daycare centers, schools, public agencies, and institutions. Evaluates programs to determine effectiveness, efficiency, and utilization and to ensure activities comply with federal, state, and local regulations. Prepares and submits budget requests or grant proposals to solicit program funding. Determines scope of educational program offerings and prepares drafts of course schedules and descriptions to estimate staffing and facility requirements. Collects and analyzes survey data, regulatory information, and demographic and employment trends to forecast enrollment patterns and curriculum changes. Coordinates outreach activities with businesses, communities, and other institutions or organizations to identify educational needs and establish and coordinate programs. Reviews and approves new programs or recommends modifications to existing programs. Plans, directs, and monitors instructional methods and content for educational, vocational, or student activity programs. **SKILLS—Coordination:** Adjusting actions in relation to others' actions. **Writing:** Communicating effectively in writing as appropriate for the needs of the audience. **Reading Comprehension:** Understanding written sentences and paragraphs in work-related documents. **Learning Strategies:** Selecting and using training/instructional methods and procedures appropriate for the situation when learning or teaching new things. **Management of Personnel Resources:** Motivating, developing, and directing people as they work, identifying the best people for the job.

GOE INFORMATION—Interest Area: 12. Education and Social Service. **Work Group:** 12.01. Managerial Work in Education and Social Service. **Other Job Titles in This Work Group:** Education Administrators, All Other; Education Administrators, Postsecondary; Education Administrators, Preschool and Child Care Center/Program; Instructional Coordinators; Park Naturalists; Social and Community Service Managers. **PERSONALITY TYPE—Social.** Social occupations frequently involve working with, communicating with, and teaching people. These occupations often involve helping or providing service to others.

EDUCATION/TRAINING PROGRAM(S)—Educational Administration and Supervision, Other; Educational Leadership and Administration, General; Educational, Instructional, and Curriculum Supervision; Elementary and Middle School Administration/Principalship; Secondary School Administration/Principalship. **RELATED KNOWLEDGE/COURSES—Education and Training:** Knowledge of principles and methods for curriculum and training design, teaching and instruction for individuals and groups, and the measurement of training effects. **Administration and Management:** Knowledge of business and management principles involved in strategic planning, resource allocation, human resources modeling, leadership technique, production methods, and coordination of people and resources. **English Language:** Knowledge of the structure and content of the English language, including the meaning and spelling of words, rules of composition, and grammar. **Personnel and Human Resources:** Knowledge of principles and procedures for personnel recruitment, selection, training, compensation and benefits, labor relations and negotiation, and personnel information systems. **Sales and Marketing:** Knowledge of principles and methods for showing, promoting, and selling products or services. This includes marketing strategy and tactics, product demonstration, sales techniques, and sales control systems.

Education Administrators, Postsecondary

- ▲ Education/Training Required: Work experience plus degree
- ▲ Annual Earnings: $61,700
- ▲ Growth: 13.4%
- ▲ Annual Job Openings: 35,000
- ▲ Self-Employed: 13.8%
- ▲ Part-Time: 9.8%

Plan, direct, or coordinate research, instructional, student administration and services, and other educational activities at postsecondary institutions, including universities, colleges, and junior and community colleges. Establishes operational policies and procedures and develops academic objectives. Selects and counsels candidates for financial aid and coordinates issuing and collecting student aid payments. Advises student organizations, sponsors faculty activities, and arranges for caterers, entertainers, and decorators at scheduled events. Audits financial status of student organization and facility accounts and certifies income reports from event ticket sales. Assists faculty and staff to conduct orientation programs, teach classes, issue student transcripts, and prepare commencement lists. Plans and promotes athletic policies, sports events, ticket sales, and student participation in social, cultural, and recreational activities. Coordinates alumni functions and encourages alumni endorsement of recruiting and fundraising activities. Reviews student misconduct reports requiring disciplinary action and counsels students to ensure conformance to university policies. Recruits, employs, trains, and terminates department personnel. Negotiates with foundation and industry representatives to secure loans for university and identify costs and materials for building construction. Confers with other academic staff to explain admission requirements and transfer credit policies and compares course equivalencies to university/college curriculum. Determines course schedules and correlates room assignments to ensure optimum use of buildings and equipment. Represents college/university as liaison officer with accrediting agencies and to exchange information between academic institutions and in community. Evaluates personnel and physical plant operations, student programs, and statistical and research data to implement procedures or modifications to administrative policies. Advises staff and students on problems relating to policies, program administration, and financial and personal matters and recommends solutions. Estimates and allocates department funding based on financial success of previous courses and other pertinent factors. Consults with staff, students, alumni, and subject experts to determine needs/feasibility and to formulate admission policies and educational programs. Completes and submits operating budget for approval, controls expenditures, and maintains financial reports and records. Meets with academic and administrative personnel to disseminate information, identify problems, monitor progress reports, and ensure adherence to goals/objectives. Directs work activities of personnel engaged in administration of academic institutions, departments, and alumni organizations. **SKILLS—Coordination:** Adjusting actions in relation to others' actions. **Management of Financial Resources:** Determining how money will be spent to get the work done and accounting for these expenditures. **Systems Evaluation:** Identifying measures or indicators of system performance and the actions needed to improve or correct performance relative to the goals of the system. **Reading Comprehension:** Understanding written sentences and paragraphs in work-related documents. **Monitoring:** Monitoring/Assessing your performance or that of other individuals or organizations to make improvements or take corrective action. **Judgment and Decision Making:** Considering the relative costs and benefits of potential actions to choose the most appropriate one.

GOE INFORMATION—Interest Area: 12. Education and Social Service. **Work Group:** 12.01. Managerial Work in Education and Social Service. **Other Job Titles in This Work Group:** Education Administrators, All Other; Education Administrators, Elementary and Secondary School; Education Administrators, Preschool and Child Care Center/Program; Instructional Coordinators; Park Naturalists; Social and Community Service Managers. **PERSONALITY TYPE—Enterprising.** Enterprising occupations frequently involve starting up and carrying out projects. These occupations can involve leading people and making many decisions. They sometimes require risk taking and often deal with business.

EDUCATION/TRAINING PROGRAM(S)—Community College Education; Educational Administration and Supervision, Other; Educational Leadership and Administration, General; Educational, Instructional, and Curriculum Supervision; Higher Education/Higher Education Administration. **RELATED KNOWLEDGE/**

COURSES—Administration and Management: Knowledge of business and management principles involved in strategic planning, resource allocation, human resources modeling, leadership technique, production methods, and coordination of people and resources. **Education and Training:** Knowledge of principles and methods for curriculum and training design, teaching and instruction for individuals and groups, and the measurement of training effects. **Economics and Accounting:** Knowledge of economic and accounting principles and practices, the financial markets, banking, and the analysis and reporting of financial data. **Personnel and Human Resources:** Knowledge of principles and procedures for personnel recruitment, selection, training, compensation and benefits, labor relations and negotiation, and personnel information systems. **English Language:** Knowledge of the structure and content of the English language, including the meaning and spelling of words, rules of composition, and grammar.

Education Administrators, Preschool and Child Care Center/Program

- ▲ Education/Training Required: Work experience plus degree
- ▲ Annual Earnings: $31,860
- ▲ Growth: 13.4%
- ▲ Annual Job Openings: 35,000
- ▲ Self-Employed: 13.8%
- ▲ Part-Time: 9.8%

Plan, direct, or coordinate the academic and nonacademic activities of preschool and child care centers or programs. Establishes program philosophy plans, policies, and academic codes of ethics to maintain educational standards for student screening, placement, and training. Determines scope of educational program offerings and prepares drafts of course schedules and descriptions to estimate staffing and facility requirements. Collects and analyzes survey data, regulatory information, and demographic and employment trends to forecast enrollment patterns and curriculum changes. Determines allocations of funds for staff, supplies, materials, and equipment and authorizes purchases. Plans and coordinates consumer research and educational services to assist organizations in product development and marketing. Teaches classes or courses to students. Completes, maintains, or assigns preparation of attendance, activity, planning, or personnel reports and records for officials and agencies. Reviews and interprets government codes and develops programs to ensure facility safety, security, and maintenance. Counsels and provides guidance to students regarding personal, academic, or behavioral problems. Confers with parents and staff to discuss educational activities, policies, and student behavioral or learning problems. Writes articles, manuals, and other publications and assists in the distribution of promotional literature. Contacts and addresses commercial, community, or political groups to promote educational programs and services or lobby for legislative changes. Recruits, hires, trains, and evaluates primary and supplemental staff and recommends personnel actions for programs and services. Organizes and directs committees of specialists, volunteers, and staff to provide technical and advisory assistance for programs. Directs and coordinates activities of teachers or administrators at daycare centers, schools, public agencies, and institutions. Coordinates outreach activities with businesses, communities, and other institutions or organizations to identify educational needs and establish and coordinate programs. Prepares and submits budget requests or grant proposals to solicit program funding. Plans, directs, and monitors instructional methods and content for educational, vocational, or student activity programs. Evaluates programs to determine effectiveness, efficiency, and utilization and to ensure that activities comply with federal, state, and local regulations.

Reviews and approves new programs or recommends modifications to existing programs. **SKILLS—Writing:** Communicating effectively in writing as appropriate for the needs of the audience. **Coordination:** Adjusting actions in relation to others' actions. **Reading Comprehension:** Understanding written sentences and paragraphs in work-related documents. **Learning Strategies:** Selecting and using training/instructional methods and procedures appropriate for the situation when learning or teaching new things. **Management of Personnel Resources:** Motivating, developing, and directing people as they work, identifying the best people for the job.

GOE INFORMATION—Interest Area: 12. Education and Social Service. **Work Group:** 12.01. Managerial Work in Education and Social Service. **Other Job Titles in This Work Group:** Education Administrators, All Other; Education Administrators, Elementary and Secondary School; Education Administrators, Postsecondary; Instructional Coordinators; Park Naturalists; Social and Community Service Managers. **PERSONALITY TYPE—Social.** Social occupations frequently involve working with, communicating with, and teaching people. These occupations often involve helping or providing service to others.

Education Teachers, Postsecondary

EDUCATION/TRAINING PROGRAM(S)—Educational Administration and Supervision, Other; Educational Leadership and Administration, General; Educational, Instructional, and Curriculum Supervision. **RELATED KNOWLEDGE/COURSES—Education and Training:** Knowledge of principles and methods for curriculum and training design, teaching and instruction for individuals and groups, and the measurement of training effects. **Administration and Management:** Knowledge of business and management principles involved in strategic planning, resource allocation, human resources modeling, leadership technique, production methods, and coordination of people and resources. **English Language:** Knowledge of the structure and content of the English language, including the meaning and spelling of words, rules of composition, and grammar. **Personnel and Human Resources:** Knowledge of principles and procedures for personnel recruitment, selection, training, compensation and benefits, labor relations and negotiation, and personnel information systems. **Sales and Marketing:** Knowledge of principles and methods for showing, promoting, and selling products or services. This includes marketing strategy and tactics, product demonstration, sales techniques, and sales control systems.

- Education/Training Required: Master's degree
- Annual Earnings: $47,060
- Growth: 23.5%
- Annual Job Openings: 184,000
- Self-Employed: 0%
- Part-Time: 32.3%

Teach courses pertaining to education, such as counseling, curriculum, guidance, instruction, teacher education, and teaching English as a second language. **SKILLS—**No data available.

GOE INFORMATION—Interest Area: 12. Education and Social Service. **Work Group:** 12.03. Educational Services. **Other Job Titles in This Work Group:** Adult Literacy, Remedial Education, and GED Teachers and Instructors; Agricultural Sciences Teachers, Postsecondary; Anthropology and Archeology Teachers, Postsecondary; Architecture Teachers, Postsecondary; Archivists; Area, Ethnic, and Cultural Studies Teachers, Postsecondary; Art, Drama, and Music Teachers, Postsecondary; Atmospheric, Earth, Marine, and Space Sciences Teachers, Postsecondary; Audio-Visual Collections Specialists; Biological Science Teachers, Postsecondary; Business Teachers, Postsecondary; Chemistry Teachers, Postsecondary; Child Care Workers; Communications Teachers, Postsecondary; Computer Science Teachers, Postsecondary; Criminal Justice and Law Enforcement Teachers, Postsecondary; Curators; Economics Teachers, Postsecondary; Educational Psychologists; Educational, Vocational, and School Counselors; Elementary School Teachers, Except Special Education; Engineering Teachers, Postsecondary; English Language and Literature Teachers, Postsecondary; Environmental Science Teachers, Postsecondary; Farm and Home Management Advisors; Foreign Language and Literature Teachers, Postsecondary; Forestry and Conservation Science Teachers, Postsecondary; Geography Teachers, Postsecondary; Graduate Teaching Assistants; Health Specialties Teachers, Postsecondary; History Teachers, Postsecondary; Home

Economics Teachers, Postsecondary; Kindergarten Teachers, Except Special Education; Law Teachers, Postsecondary; Librarians; Library Assistants, Clerical; Library Science Teachers, Postsecondary; Library Technicians; Mathematical Science Teachers, Postsecondary; Middle School Teachers, Except Special and Vocational Education; Museum Technicians and Conservators; Nursing Instructors and Teachers, Postsecondary; Personal Financial Advisors; Philosophy and Religion Teachers, Postsecondary; Physics Teachers, Postsecondary; Political Science Teachers, Postsecondary; Postsecondary Teachers, All Other; Preschool Teachers, Except Special Education; others. **PERSONALITY TYPE**—No data available.

EDUCATION/TRAINING PROGRAM(S)—Agricultural Teacher Education; Art Teacher Education; Biology Teacher Education; Business Teacher Education; Chemistry Teacher Education; Computer Teacher Education; Drama and Dance Teacher Education; Driver and Safety Teacher Education; Education, General; English/Language Arts Teacher Education; Family and Consumer Sciences/Home Economics Teacher Education; Foreign Language Teacher Education; French Language Teacher Education; Geography Teacher Education; German Language Teacher Education; Health Occupations Teacher Education; Health Teacher Education; History Teacher Education; Mathematics Teacher Education; Music Teacher Education; Physical Education Teaching and Coaching; Physics Teacher Education; Reading Teacher Education; Sales and Marketing Operations/Marketing and Distribution Teacher Education; Science Teacher Education/General Science Teacher Education; Social Science Teacher Education; Social Studies Teacher Education; Spanish Language Teacher Education; Speech Teacher Education; Teacher Education and Professional Development, Specific Subject Areas, Other; Technical Teacher Education; Technology Teacher Education/Industrial Arts Teacher Education; Trade and Industrial Teacher Education. **RELATED KNOWLEDGE/COURSES**—No data available.

Educational Psychologists

- ▲ Education/Training Required: Master's degree
- ▲ Annual Earnings: $50,420
- ▲ Growth: 18.1%
- ▲ Annual Job Openings: 18,000
- ▲ Self-Employed: 43.7%
- ▲ Part-Time: 23.4%

Investigate processes of learning and teaching and develop psychological principles and techniques applicable to educational problems. Conducts experiments to study educational problems, such as motivation, adjustment, teacher training, and individual differences in mental abilities. Formulates achievement, diagnostic, and predictive tests to aid teachers in planning methods and content of instruction. Plans remedial classes and testing programs designed to meet needs of special students. Analyzes characteristics and adjustment needs of students having various mental abilities and recommends educational program to promote maximum adjustment. Administers standardized tests to evaluate intelligence, achievement, and personality and to diagnose disabilities and difficulties among students. Recommends placement of students in classes and treatment programs based on individual needs. Refers individuals to community agencies to obtain medical, vocational, or social services for child or family. Advises school board, superintendent, administrative committees, and parent-teacher groups regarding provision of psychological services within educational system or school. Counsels pupils individually and in groups to assist pupils in achieving personal, social, and emotional adjustment. Collaborates with education specialists in developing curriculum content and methods of organizing and conducting classroom work. Evaluates needs, limitations, and potentials of child through observation, review of school records, and consultation with parents and school personnel. Advises teachers and other school personnel on methods to enhance school and classroom atmosphere to maximize student learning and motivation. Interprets and explains test results in terms of norms, reliability, and validity to teachers, counselors, students, and other entitled parties. Investigates traits, attitudes, and feelings of teachers to predict conditions that affect teachers' mental health and success with students. Conducts research to aid introduction of programs in schools to meet current psychological, educational, and sociological needs of children.

SKILLS—Social Perceptiveness: Being aware of others' reactions and understanding why they react as they do. **Writing:** Communicating effectively in writing as appropriate for the needs of the audience. **Learning Strategies:** Selecting and using training/instructional methods and procedures appropriate for the situation when learning or teaching new things. **Reading Comprehension:** Understanding written sentences and paragraphs in work-related documents. **Systems Evaluation:** Identifying measures or indicators of system performance and the actions needed to improve or correct performance relative to the goals of the system.

GOE INFORMATION—Interest Area: 12. Education and Social Service. **Work Group:** 12.03. Educational Services. **Other Job Titles in This Work Group:** Adult Literacy, Remedial Education, and GED Teachers and Instructors; Agricultural Sciences Teachers, Postsecondary; Anthropology and Archeology Teachers, Postsecondary; Architecture Teachers, Postsecondary; Archivists; Area, Ethnic, and Cultural Studies Teachers, Postsecondary; Art, Drama, and Music Teachers, Postsecondary; Atmospheric, Earth, Marine, and Space Sciences Teachers, Postsecondary; Audio-Visual Collections Specialists; Biological Science Teachers, Postsecondary; Business Teachers, Postsecondary; Chemistry Teachers, Postsecondary; Child Care Workers; Communications Teachers, Postsecondary; Computer Science Teachers, Postsecondary; Criminal Justice and Law Enforcement Teachers, Postsecondary; Curators; Economics Teachers, Postsecondary; Education Teachers, Postsecondary; Educational, Vocational, and School Counselors; Elementary School Teachers, Except Special Education; Engineering Teachers, Postsecondary; English Language and Literature Teachers, Postsecondary; Environmental Science Teachers, Postsecondary; Farm and Home Management Advisors; Foreign Language and Literature Teachers, Postsecondary; Forestry and Conservation Science Teachers, Postsecondary; Geography Teachers, Postsecondary; Graduate Teaching Assistants; Health Specialties Teachers, Postsecondary; History Teachers, Postsecondary; Home Economics Teachers, Postsecondary; Kindergarten Teachers, Except Special Education; Law Teachers, Postsecondary; Librarians; Library Assistants, Clerical; Library Science Teachers, Postsecondary; Library Technicians; Mathematical Science Teachers, Postsecondary; Middle School Teachers, Except Special and Vocational Education; Museum Technicians and Conservators; Nursing Instructors and Teachers, Postsecondary; Personal Financial Advisors; Philosophy and Religion Teachers, Postsecondary; Physics Teachers, Postsecondary; Political Science Teachers, Postsecondary; Postsecondary Teachers, All Other; Preschool Teachers, Except Special Education; others. **PERSONALITY TYPE—**Investigative. Investigative occupations frequently involve working with ideas and require an extensive amount of thinking. These occupations can involve searching for facts and figuring out problems mentally.

EDUCATION/TRAINING PROGRAM(S)—Clinical Child Psychology; Clinical Psychology; Counseling Psychology; Developmental and Child Psychology; Psychoanalysis and Psychotherapy; Psychology, General; School Psychology. **RELATED KNOWLEDGE/COURSES— Psychology:** Knowledge of human behavior and performance; individual differences in ability, personality, and interests; learning and motivation; psychological research methods; and the assessment and treatment of behavioral and affective disorders. **Education and Training:** Knowledge of principles and methods for curriculum and training design, teaching and instruction for individuals and groups, and the measurement of training effects. **English Language:** Knowledge of the structure and content of the English language, including the meaning and spelling of words, rules of composition, and grammar. **Therapy and Counseling:** Knowledge of principles, methods, and procedures for diagnosis, treatment, and rehabilitation of physical and mental dysfunctions and for career counseling and guidance. **Mathematics:** Knowledge of arithmetic, algebra, geometry, calculus, and statistics and their applications.

Educational, Vocational, and School Counselors

- ▲ Education/Training Required: Master's degree
- ▲ Annual Earnings: $43,470
- ▲ Growth: 25.3%
- ▲ Annual Job Openings: 22,000
- ▲ Self-Employed: 0.6%
- ▲ Part-Time: 18.0%

Counsel individuals and provide group educational and vocational guidance services. Advises counselees to assist them in developing their educational and vocational objectives. Advises counselees to assist them in understanding and overcoming personal and social problems. Collects and evaluates information about counselees' abilities, interests, and personality characteristics, using records, tests, and interviews. Compiles and studies occupational, educational, and economic information to assist counselees in making and carrying out vocational and educational objectives. Interprets program regulations or benefit requirements and assists counselees in obtaining needed supportive services. Refers qualified counselees to employer or employment service for placement. Conducts follow-up interviews with counselees and maintains case records. Establishes and maintains relationships with employers and personnel from supportive service agencies to develop opportunities for counselees. Plans and conducts orientation programs and group conferences to promote adjustment of individuals to new life experiences. Teaches vocational and educational guidance classes. Addresses community groups and faculty members to explain counseling services. **SKILLS—Active Listening:** Giving full attention to what other people are saying, taking time to understand the points being made, asking questions as appropriate, and not interrupting at inappropriate times. **Reading Comprehension:** Understanding written sentences and paragraphs in work-related documents. **Social Perceptiveness:** Being aware of others' reactions and understanding why they react as they do. **Speaking:** Talking to others to convey information effectively. **Service Orientation:** Actively looking for ways to help people.

GOE INFORMATION—Interest Area: 12. Education and Social Service. **Work Group:** 12.03. Educational Services. **Other Job Titles in This Work Group:** Adult Literacy, Remedial Education, and GED Teachers and Instructors; Agricultural Sciences Teachers, Postsecondary; Anthropology and Archeology Teachers, Postsecondary; Architecture Teachers, Postsecondary; Archivists; Area, Ethnic, and Cultural Studies Teachers, Postsecondary; Art, Drama, and Music Teachers, Postsecondary; Atmospheric, Earth, Marine, and Space Sciences Teachers, Postsecondary; Audio-Visual Collections Specialists; Biological Science Teachers, Postsecondary; Business Teachers, Postsecondary; Chemistry Teachers, Postsecondary; Child Care Workers; Communications Teachers, Postsecondary; Computer Science Teachers, Postsecondary; Criminal Justice and Law Enforcement Teachers, Postsecondary; Curators; Economics Teachers, Postsecondary; Education Teachers, Postsecondary; Educational Psychologists; Elementary School Teachers, Except Special Education; Engineering Teachers, Postsecondary; English Language and Literature Teachers, Postsecondary; Environmental Science Teachers, Postsecondary; Farm and Home Management Advisors; Foreign Language and Literature Teachers, Postsecondary; Forestry and Conservation Science Teachers, Postsecondary; Geography Teachers, Postsecondary; Graduate Teaching Assistants; Health Specialties Teachers, Postsecondary; History Teachers, Postsecondary; Home Economics Teachers, Postsecondary; Kindergarten Teachers, Except Special Education; Law Teachers, Postsecondary; Librarians; Library Assistants, Clerical; Library Science Teachers, Postsecondary; Library Technicians; Mathematical Science Teachers, Postsecondary; Middle School Teachers, Except Special and Vocational Education; Museum Technicians and Conservators; Nursing Instructors and Teachers, Postsecondary; Personal Financial Advisors; Philosophy and Religion Teachers, Postsecondary; Physics Teachers, Postsecondary; Political Science Teachers, Postsecondary; Postsecondary Teachers, All Other; Preschool Teachers, Except Special Education; Psychology Teachers, Postsecondary; others. **PERSONALITY TYPE—Social.** Social occupations frequently involve working with, communicating with, and teaching people. These occupations often involve helping or providing service to others.

EDUCATION/TRAINING PROGRAM(S)—College Student Counseling and Personnel Services; Counselor Education/School Counseling and Guidance Services. **RELATED KNOWLEDGE/COURSES—Therapy and Counseling:** Knowledge of principles, methods, and procedures for diagnosis, treatment, and rehabilitation of physical and mental dysfunctions and for career counseling and guidance. **Education and Training:** Knowledge of principles and methods for curriculum and training design, teaching and instruction for individuals and groups, and the measurement of training effects. **Psychology:** Knowledge of human behavior and performance; individual differences in ability, personality, and interests; learning and motivation; psychological research methods; and the assessment and treatment of behavioral and affective disorders. **English Language:** Knowledge of the structure and content of the English language, including the meaning and spelling of words, rules of composition, and grammar. **Personnel and Human Resources:** Knowledge of principles and procedures for personnel recruitment, selection, training, compensation and benefits, labor relations and negotiation, and personnel information systems.

Electrical and Electronic Engineering Technicians

▲ Education/Training Required: Associate's degree
▲ Annual Earnings: $42,130
▲ Growth: 10.8%
▲ Annual Job Openings: 22,000
▲ Self-Employed: 1.9%
▲ Part-Time: 7.4%

Apply electrical and electronic theory and related knowledge, usually under the direction of engineering staff, to design, build, repair, calibrate, and modify electrical components, circuitry, controls, and machinery for subsequent evaluation and use by engineering staff in making engineering design decisions. SKILLS—No data available.

GOE INFORMATION—**Interest Area:** 02. Science, Math, and Engineering. **Work Group:** 02.08. Engineering Technology. **Other Job Titles in This Work Group:** Aerospace Engineering and Operations Technicians; Architectural and Civil Drafters; Architectural Drafters; Calibration and Instrumentation Technicians; Cartographers and Photogrammetrists; Civil Drafters; Civil Engineering Technicians; Construction and Building Inspectors; Drafters, All Other; Electrical and Electronics Drafters; Electrical Drafters; Electrical Engineering Technicians; Electro-Mechanical Technicians; Electronic Drafters; Electronics Engineering Technicians; Engineering Technicians, Except Drafters, All Other; Environmental Engineering Technicians; Industrial Engineering Technicians; Mapping Technicians; Mechanical Drafters; Mechanical Engineering Technicians; Numerical Tool and Process Control Programmers; Pressure Vessel Inspectors; Surveying and Mapping Technicians; Surveying Technicians; Surveyors. **PERSONALITY TYPE**—No data available.

EDUCATION/TRAINING PROGRAM(S)—Computer Engineering Technology/Technician; Computer Technology/Computer Systems Technology; Electrical and Electronic Engineering Technologies/Technicians, Other; Electrical, Electronic and Communications Engineering Technology/Technician; Telecommunications Technology/Technician. **RELATED KNOWLEDGE/COURSES**—No data available.

Electrical and Electronics Drafters

▲ Education/Training Required: Associate's degree
▲ Annual Earnings: $40,070
▲ Growth: 23.3%
▲ Annual Job Openings: 5,000
▲ Self-Employed: 3.0%
▲ Part-Time: 7.9%

Prepare wiring diagrams, circuit board assembly diagrams, and layout drawings used for manufacture, installation, and repair of electrical equipment in factories, power plants, and buildings. SKILLS—No data available.

GOE INFORMATION—**Interest Area:** 02. Science, Math, and Engineering. **Work Group:** 02.08. Engineering Technology. **Other Job Titles in This Work Group:** Aerospace Engineering and Operations Technicians; Architectural and Civil Drafters; Architectural Drafters; Calibration and Instrumentation Technicians; Cartographers and Photogrammetrists; Civil Drafters; Civil Engineering Technicians; Construction and Building Inspectors; Drafters, All Other; Electrical and Electronic Engineering Technicians; Electrical Drafters; Electrical Engineering Technicians; Electro-Mechanical Technicians; Electronic Drafters; Electronics Engineering Technicians; Engineering Technicians, Except Drafters, All Other; Environmental Engineering Technicians; Industrial Engineering Technicians; Mapping Technicians; Mechanical Drafters; Mechanical Engineering Technicians; Numerical Tool and Process Control Programmers; Pressure Vessel Inspectors; Surveying and Mapping Technicians; Surveying Technicians; Surveyors. **PERSONALITY TYPE**—No data available.

EDUCATION/TRAINING PROGRAM(S)—Electrical/Electronics Drafting and Electrical/Electronics CAD/CADD. **RELATED KNOWLEDGE/COURSES**—No data available.

Electrical Drafters

- ▲ Education/Training Required: Associate's degree
- ▲ Annual Earnings: $40,070
- ▲ Growth: 23.3%
- ▲ Annual Job Openings: 5,000
- ▲ Self-Employed: 3.0%
- ▲ Part-Time: 7.9%

Develop specifications and instructions for installation of voltage transformers, overhead or underground cables, and related electrical equipment used to conduct electrical energy from transmission lines or high-voltage distribution lines to consumers. Drafts working drawing, wiring diagrams, wiring connections, or cross section of underground cables as required for instructions to installation crew. Takes measurements, such as distances to be spanned by wire and cable, that affect installation and arrangement of equipment. Reviews completed construction drawings and cost estimates for accuracy and conformity to standards and regulations. Draws master sketch showing relation of proposed installation to existing facilities. Drafts sketches to scale. Studies work order request to determine type of service, such as lighting or power, demanded by installation. Estimates labor and material costs for installation of electrical equipment and distribution systems. Confers with engineering staff and other personnel to resolve problems. Visits site of proposed installation and draws rough sketch of location. **SKILLS— Operations Analysis:** Analyzing needs and product requirements to create a design. **Judgment and Decision Making:** Considering the relative costs and benefits of potential actions to choose the most appropriate one. **Mathematics:** Using mathematics to solve problems. **Equipment Selection:** Determining the kind of tools and equipment needed to do a job. **Management of Personnel Resources:** Motivating, developing, and directing people as they work, identifying the best people for the job. **Reading Compre-**

hension: Understanding written sentences and paragraphs in work-related documents.

GOE INFORMATION—Interest Area: 02. Science, Math, and Engineering. **Work Group:** 02.08. Engineering Technology. **Other Job Titles in This Work Group:** Aerospace Engineering and Operations Technicians; Architectural and Civil Drafters; Architectural Drafters; Calibration and Instrumentation Technicians; Cartographers and Photogrammetrists; Civil Drafters; Civil Engineering Technicians; Construction and Building Inspectors; Drafters, All Other; Electrical and Electronic Engineering Technicians; Electrical and Electronics Drafters; Electrical Engineering Technicians; Electro-Mechanical Technicians; Electronic Drafters; Electronics Engineering Technicians; Engineering Technicians, Except Drafters, All Other; Environmental Engineering Technicians; Industrial Engineering Technicians; Mapping Technicians; Mechanical Drafters; Mechanical Engineering Technicians; Numerical Tool and Process Control Programmers; Pressure Vessel Inspectors; Surveying and Mapping Technicians; Surveying Technicians; Surveyors. **PERSONALITY TYPE**—Conventional. Conventional occupations frequently involve following set procedures and routines. These occupations can include working with data and details more than with ideas. Usually there is a clear line of authority to follow.

EDUCATION/TRAINING PROGRAM(S)—Electrical/Electronics Drafting and Electrical/Electronics CAD/

CADD. **RELATED KNOWLEDGE/COURSES—Design:** Knowledge of design techniques, tools, and principles involved in production of precision technical plans, blueprints, drawings, and models. **Engineering and Technology:** Knowledge of the practical application of engineering science and technology. This includes applying principles, techniques, procedures, and equipment to the design and production of various goods and services. **Mathematics:** Knowledge of arithmetic, algebra, geometry, calculus, and statistics and their applications. **Administration and Management:** Knowledge of business and management principles involved in strategic planning, resource allocation, human resources modeling, leadership technique, production methods, and coordination of people and resources. **Building and Construction:** Knowledge of materials, methods, and tools involved in the construction or repair of houses, buildings, or other structures, such as highways and roads.

Electrical Engineering Technicians

- ▲ Education/Training Required: Associate's degree
- ▲ Annual Earnings: $42,130
- ▲ Growth: 10.8%
- ▲ Annual Job Openings: 22,000
- ▲ Self-Employed: 2.2%
- ▲ Part-Time: 3.1%

Apply electrical theory and related knowledge to test and modify developmental or operational electrical machinery and electrical control equipment and circuitry in industrial or commercial plants and laboratories. Usually work under direction of engineering staff. Sets up and operates test equipment to evaluate performance of developmental parts, assemblies, or systems under simulated operating conditions. Maintains and repairs testing equipment. Plans method and sequence of operations for testing and developing experimental electronic and electrical equipment. Assembles electrical and electronic systems and prototypes according to engineering data and knowledge of electrical principles, using hand tools and measuring instruments. Analyzes and interprets test information. Collaborates with electrical engineer and other personnel to solve developmental problems. Draws diagrams and writes engineering specifications to clarify design details and functional criteria of experimental electronics units. Modifies electrical prototypes, parts, assemblies, and systems to correct functional deviations. **SKILLS—Technology Design:** Generating or adapting equipment and technology to serve user needs. **Active Learning:** Understanding the implications of new information for both current and future problem-solving and decision-making. **Troubleshooting:** Determining causes of operating errors and deciding what to do about them. **Operations Analysis:** Analyzing needs and product requirements to create a design. **Reading Comprehension:** Understanding written sentences and paragraphs in work-related documents. **Equipment Selection:** Determining the kind of tools and equipment needed to do a job.

GOE INFORMATION—Interest Area: 02. Science, Math, and Engineering. **Work Group:** 02.08. Engineering Technology. **Other Job Titles in This Work Group:** Aerospace Engineering and Operations Technicians; Architectural and Civil Drafters; Architectural Drafters; Calibration and Instrumentation Technicians; Cartographers and Photogrammetrists; Civil Drafters; Civil Engineering Technicians; Construction and Building Inspectors; Drafters, All Other; Electrical and Electronic Engineering Technicians; Electrical and Electronics Drafters; Electrical Drafters; Electro-Mechanical Technicians; Electronic Drafters; Electronics Engineering Technicians; Engineering Technicians, Except Drafters, All Other; Environmental Engineering Technicians; Industrial Engineering Technicians; Mapping Technicians; Mechanical Drafters; Mechanical Engineering Technicians; Numerical Tool and Process Control Programmers; Pressure Vessel Inspectors; Surveying and Mapping Technicians; Surveying Technicians; Surveyors. **PERSONALITY TYPE—Realistic.** Realistic occupations frequently involve work activities that include practical, hands-on problems and solutions. They often deal with plants, animals, and real-world materials like wood, tools, and machinery. Many of the occupations require working outside and do not involve a lot of paperwork or working closely with others.

EDUCATION/TRAINING PROGRAM(S)—Computer Engineering Technology/Technician; Computer Technology/Computer Systems Technology; Electrical and Electronic Engineering Technologies/Technicians, Other; Electrical, Electronic and Communications Engineering

Technology/Technician; Telecommunications Technology/ Technician. **RELATED KNOWLEDGE/COURSES— Engineering and Technology:** Knowledge of the practical application of engineering science and technology. This includes applying principles, techniques, procedures, and equipment to the design and production of various goods and services. **Mathematics:** Knowledge of arithmetic, algebra, geometry, calculus, and statistics and their applications. **Design:** Knowledge of design techniques, tools, and principles involved in production of precision technical plans, blueprints, drawings, and models. **Computers and Electronics:** Knowledge of circuit boards, processors, chips, electronic equipment, and computer hardware and software, including applications and programming. **Physics:** Knowledge and prediction of physical principles and laws and their interrelationships and applications to understanding fluid, material, and atmospheric dynamics and mechanical, electrical, atomic, and sub-atomic structures and processes.

Electrical Engineers

- ▲ Education/Training Required: Bachelor's degree
- ▲ Annual Earnings: $66,890
- ▲ Growth: 11.3%
- ▲ Annual Job Openings: 8,000
- ▲ Self-Employed: 2.9%
- ▲ Part-Time: 2.6%

Design, develop, test, or supervise the manufacturing and installation of electrical equipment, components, or systems for commercial, industrial, military, or scientific use. Designs electrical instruments, equipment, facilities, components, products, and systems for commercial, industrial, and domestic purposes. Plans and implements research methodology and procedures to apply principles of electrical theory to engineering projects. Prepares and studies technical drawings, specifications of electrical systems, and topographical maps to ensure installation and operations conform to standards and customer requirements. Develops applications of controls, instruments, and systems for new commercial, domestic, and industrial uses. Plans layout of electric power generating plants and distribution lines and stations. Operates computer-assisted engineering and design software and equipment to perform engineering tasks. Compiles data and writes reports regarding existing and potential engineering studies and projects. Collects data relating to commercial and residential development, population, and power system interconnection to determine operating efficiency of electrical systems. Estimates labor, material, and construction costs and prepares specifications for purchase of materials and equipment. Evaluates and analyzes data regarding electric power systems and stations and recommends changes to improve operating efficiency. Inspects completed installations and observes operations for conformance to design and equipment specifications and operational and safety standards. Confers with engineers, customers, and others to discuss existing or potential engineering projects and products. Performs detailed calculations to compute and establish manufacturing, construction, and installation standards and specifications. Conducts field surveys and studies maps, graphs, diagrams, and other data to identify and correct power system problems. Investigates customer or public complaints, determines nature and extent of problem, and recommends remedial measures. Directs operations and coordinates manufacturing, construction, installation, maintenance, and testing activities to ensure compliance with specifications, codes, and customer requirements. **SKILLS—Mathematics:** Using mathematics to solve problems. **Critical Thinking:** Using logic and reasoning to identify the strengths and weaknesses of alternative solutions, conclusions, or approaches to problems. **Reading Comprehension:** Understanding written sentences and paragraphs in work-related documents. **Active Learning:** Understanding the implications of new information for both current and future problem-solving and decision-making. **Writing:** Communicating effectively in writing as appropriate for the needs of the audience.

GOE INFORMATION—Interest Area: 02. Science, Math, and Engineering. **Work Group:** 02.07. Engineering. **Other Job Titles in This Work Group:** Aerospace Engineers; Agricultural Engineers; Architects, Except Landscape and Naval; Biomedical Engineers; Chemical Engineers; Civil Engineers; Computer Hardware Engineers; Computer Software Engineers, Applications; Computer Software Engineers, Systems Software; Electronics Engineers, Except Computer; Engineers, All Other; Environmental Engineers; Fire-Prevention and Protection Engineers; Health and Safety Engineers, Except Mining

Safety Engineers and Inspectors; Industrial Engineers; Industrial Safety and Health Engineers; Landscape Architects; Marine Architects; Marine Engineers; Marine Engineers and Naval Architects; Materials Engineers; Mechanical Engineers; Mining and Geological Engineers, Including Mining Safety Engineers; Nuclear Engineers; Petroleum Engineers; Product Safety Engineers; Sales Engineers. **PERSONALITY TYPE**—Investigative. Investigative occupations frequently involve working with ideas and require an extensive amount of thinking. These occupations can involve searching for facts and figuring out problems mentally.

EDUCATION/TRAINING PROGRAM(S)—Electrical, Electronics, and Communications Engineering. **RELATED KNOWLEDGE/COURSES**—**Engineering and Technology:** Knowledge of the practical application of engineering science and technology. This includes apply-

ing principles, techniques, procedures, and equipment to the design and production of various goods and services. **Mathematics:** Knowledge of arithmetic, algebra, geometry, calculus, and statistics and their applications. **Computers and Electronics:** Knowledge of circuit boards, processors, chips, electronic equipment, and computer hardware and software, including applications and programming. **Design:** Knowledge of design techniques, tools, and principles involved in production of precision technical plans, blueprints, drawings, and models. **Building and Construction:** Knowledge of materials, methods, and tools involved in the construction or repair of houses, buildings, or other structures, such as highways and roads. **Production and Processing:** Knowledge of raw materials, production processes, quality control, costs, and other techniques for maximizing the effective manufacture and distribution of goods.

Electricians

▲ Education/Training Required: Long-term on-the-job training
▲ Annual Earnings: $40,770
▲ Growth: 17.3%
▲ Annual Job Openings: 66,000
▲ Self-Employed: 9.8%
▲ Part-Time: 4.4%

Install, maintain, and repair electrical wiring, equipment, and fixtures. Ensure that work is in accordance with relevant codes. May install or service street lights, intercom systems, or electrical control systems. Installs electrical wiring, equipment, apparatus, and fixtures, using hand tools and power tools. Tests electrical systems and continuity of circuits in electrical wiring, equipment, and fixtures, using testing devices, such as ohmmeter, voltmeter, and oscilloscope. Readies and assembles electrical wiring, equipment and fixtures, using specifications and hand tools. Climbs ladder to install, maintain, or repair electrical wiring, equipment, and fixtures. Possesses electrician's license or identification card to meet governmental regulations. Drives vehicle, operates floodlights, and places flares during power failure or emergency. Directs and trains workers to install, maintain, or repair electrical wiring, equipment, and fixtures. Constructs and fabricates parts, using hand tools and specifications. Prepares sketches of location of wiring and equipment or follows blueprints to determine location of equipment and conformance to safety codes. Diagnoses malfunctioning systems, apparatus, and components, using test equipment and hand tools.

Inspects systems and electrical parts to detect hazards, defects, and need for adjustments or repair. Maintains and repairs or replaces wiring, equipment, and fixtures, using hand tools. Plans layout and installation of electrical wiring, equipment, and fixtures consistent with specifications and local codes. **SKILLS**—**Installation:** Installing equipment, machines, wiring, or programs to meet specifications. **Repairing:** Repairing machines or systems, using the needed tools. **Equipment Selection:** Determining the kind of tools and equipment needed to do a job. **Troubleshooting:** Determining causes of operating errors and deciding what to do about them. **Mathematics:** Using mathematics to solve problems.

GOE INFORMATION—**Interest Area:** 06. Construction, Mining, and Drilling. **Work Group:** 06.02. Construction. **Other Job Titles in This Work Group:** Boat Builders and Shipwrights; Boilermakers; Brattice Builders; Brickmasons and Blockmasons; Carpenters; Carpet Installers; Ceiling Tile Installers; Cement Masons and Concrete Finishers; Commercial Divers; Construction Carpenters; Drywall and Ceiling Tile Installers; Drywall Installers; Explosives Workers, Ordnance Handling

Experts, and Blasters; Fence Erectors; Floor Layers, Except Carpet, Wood, and Hard Tiles; Floor Sanders and Finishers; Glaziers; Grader, Bulldozer, and Scraper Operators; Hazardous Materials Removal Workers; Insulation Workers, Floor, Ceiling, and Wall; Insulation Workers, Mechanical; Manufactured Building and Mobile Home Installers; Operating Engineers; Operating Engineers and Other Construction Equipment Operators; Painters, Construction and Maintenance; Paperhangers; Paving, Surfacing, and Tamping Equipment Operators; Pile-Driver Operators; Pipe Fitters; Pipelayers; Pipelaying Fitters; Plasterers and Stucco Masons; Plumbers; Plumbers, Pipefitters, and Steamfitters; Rail-Track Laying and Maintenance Equipment Operators; Refractory Materials Repairers, Except Brickmasons; Reinforcing Iron and Rebar Workers; Riggers; Roofers; Rough Carpenters; Security and Fire Alarm Systems Installers; Segmental Pavers; Sheet Metal Workers; Ship Carpenters and Joiners; Stone Cutters and Carvers; Stonemasons; Structural Iron and Steel Workers; Tapers; Terrazzo Workers and Finishers; Tile and Marble Setters. **PERSONALITY TYPE**—Realistic. Realistic occupations frequently involve work activities that include practical, hands-on problems and solutions. They often deal with plants, animals, and real-world materials like wood, tools, and machinery. Many of the occupations require working outside and do not involve a lot of paperwork or working closely with others.

EDUCATION/TRAINING PROGRAM(S)—Electrician. **RELATED KNOWLEDGE/COURSES—Design:** Knowledge of design techniques, tools, and principles involved in production of precision technical plans, blueprints, drawings, and models. **Engineering and Technology:** Knowledge of the practical application of engineering science and technology. This includes applying principles, techniques, procedures, and equipment to the design and production of various goods and services. **Computers and Electronics:** Knowledge of circuit boards, processors, chips, electronic equipment, and computer hardware and software, including applications and programming. **Building and Construction:** Knowledge of materials, methods, and tools involved in the construction or repair of houses, buildings, or other structures, such as highways and roads. **Principles of Mechanical Devices:** Knowledge of machines and tools, including their designs, uses, repair, and maintenance. **Physics:** Knowledge and prediction of physical principles and laws and their interrelationships and applications to understanding fluid, material, and atmospheric dynamics and mechanical, electrical, atomic, and sub-atomic structures and processes. **Education and Training:** Knowledge of principles and methods for curriculum and training design, teaching and instruction for individuals and groups, and the measurement of training effects.

Electronic Drafters

▲ Education/Training Required: Postsecondary vocational training
▲ Annual Earnings: $40,070
▲ Growth: 23.3%
▲ Annual Job Openings: 5,000
▲ Self-Employed: 3.0%
▲ Part-Time: 7.9%

Draw wiring diagrams, circuit board assembly diagrams, schematics, and layout drawings used for manufacture, installation, and repair of electronic equipment. Drafts detail and assembly drawings and designs of electromechanical equipment and related data processing systems. Plots electrical test points on layout sheet, using pencil, and draws schematics to wire test fixture heads to frame. Creates master layout of design components and circuitry and printed circuit boards according to specifications and utilizing computer-assisted equipment. Consults with engineers to discuss and interpret design concepts and determine requirements of detailed working drawings.

Compares logic element configuration on display screen with engineering schematics and calculates figures to convert, redesign, and modify element. Copies drawings of printed circuit board fabrication, using print machine or blueprinting procedure. Generates computer tapes of final layout design to produce layered photo masks and photo plotting design onto film. Examines and verifies master layout for electrical and mechanical accuracy. Supervises and coordinates work activities of workers engaged in drafting, designing layouts, and assembling and testing printed circuit boards. Locates files relating to specified design projection database library, loads program into computer, and records completed job data. Reviews work orders and procedural manuals and confers with vendors and design staff to resolve problems and modify design. Keys and programs specified commands and engineering specifications into computer system to change functions and test final layout. Compiles data, computes quantities, and prepares cost estimates to determine equipment needs; requisitions materials as required. Selects drill size to drill test head, according to test design and specifications, and submits guide layout to designated department. Reviews blueprints to determine customer requirements and consults with assembler regarding schematics, wiring procedures, and conductor paths. Examines electronic schematics and analyzes logic diagrams and design documents to plan layout of printed circuit board components and circuitry. **SKILLS—Mathematics:** Using mathematics to solve problems. **Operations Analysis:** Analyzing needs and product requirements to create a design. **Reading Comprehension:** Understanding written sentences and paragraphs in work-related documents. **Technology Design:** Generating or adapting equipment and technology to serve user needs. **Programming:** Writing computer programs for various purposes.

GOE INFORMATION—**Interest Area:** 02. Science, Math, and Engineering. **Work Group:** 02.08. Engineering Technology. **Other Job Titles in This Work Group:** Aerospace Engineering and Operations Technicians; Architectural and Civil Drafters; Architectural Drafters; Calibration and Instrumentation Technicians; Cartographers and Photogrammetrists; Civil Drafters; Civil Engineering Technicians; Construction and Building Inspectors; Drafters, All Other; Electrical and Electronic Engineering Technicians; Electrical and Electronics Drafters; Electrical Drafters; Electrical Engineering Technicians; Electro-Mechanical Technicians; Electronics Engineering Technicians; Engineering Technicians, Except Drafters, All Other; En-

vironmental Engineering Technicians; Industrial Engineering Technicians; Mapping Technicians; Mechanical Drafters; Mechanical Engineering Technicians; Numerical Tool and Process Control Programmers; Pressure Vessel Inspectors; Surveying and Mapping Technicians; Surveying Technicians; Surveyors. **PERSONALITY TYPE—**Realistic. Realistic occupations frequently involve work activities that include practical, hands-on problems and solutions. They often deal with plants, animals, and real-world materials like wood, tools, and machinery. Many of the occupations require working outside and do not involve a lot of paperwork or working closely with others.

EDUCATION/TRAINING PROGRAM(S)—Electrical/Electronics Drafting and Electrical/Electronics CAD/CADD. **RELATED KNOWLEDGE/COURSES—Design:** Knowledge of design techniques, tools, and principles involved in production of precision technical plans, blueprints, drawings, and models. **Computers and Electronics:** Knowledge of circuit boards, processors, chips, electronic equipment, and computer hardware and software, including applications and programming. **Mathematics:** Knowledge of arithmetic, algebra, geometry, calculus, and statistics and their applications. **Engineering and Technology:** Knowledge of the practical application of engineering science and technology. This includes applying principles, techniques, procedures, and equipment to the design and production of various goods and services. **English Language:** Knowledge of the structure and content of the English language, including the meaning and spelling of words, rules of composition, and grammar. **Administration and Management:** Knowledge of business and management principles involved in strategic planning, resource allocation, human resources modeling, leadership technique, production methods, and coordination of people and resources.

Electronics Engineering Technicians

- ▲ Education/Training Required: Associate's degree
- ▲ Annual Earnings: $42,130
- ▲ Growth: 10.8%
- ▲ Annual Job Openings: 22,000
- ▲ Self-Employed: 2.2%
- ▲ Part-Time: 3.1%

Lay out, build, test, troubleshoot, repair, and modify developmental and production electronic components, parts, equipment, and systems, such as computer equipment, missile control instrumentation, electron tubes, test equipment, and machine tool numerical controls, applying principles and theories of electronics, electrical circuitry, engineering mathematics, electronic and electrical testing, and physics. Usually work under direction of engineering staff. Reads blueprints, wiring diagrams, schematic drawings, and engineering instructions for assembling electronics units, applying knowledge of electronic theory and components. Assembles circuitry or electronic components according to engineering instructions, technical manuals, and knowledge of electronics, using hand tools and power tools. Tests electronics unit, using standard test equipment, to evaluate performance and determine needs for adjustments. Adjusts and replaces defective or improperly functioning circuitry and electronics components, using hand tools and soldering iron. Assists engineers in development of testing techniques, laboratory equipment, and circuitry or installation specifications by writing reports and recording data. Designs basic circuitry and sketches for design documentation as directed by engineers, using drafting instruments and computer-aided design equipment. Fabricates parts, such as coils, terminal boards, and chassis, using bench lathes, drills, or other machine tools. **SKILLS—Mathematics:** Using mathematics to solve problems. **Active Learning:** Understanding the implications of new information for both current and future problem-solving and decision-making. **Operations Analysis:** Analyzing needs and product requirements to create a design. **Troubleshooting:** Determining causes of operating errors and deciding what to do about them. **Technology Design:** Generating or adapting equipment and technology to serve user needs. **Critical Thinking:** Using logic and reasoning to identify the strengths and weaknesses of alternative solutions, conclusions, or approaches to problems. **Installation:** Installing equipment, machines, wiring, or programs to meet specifications.

GOE INFORMATION—Interest Area: 02. Science, Math, and Engineering. **Work Group:** 02.08. Engineering Technology. **Other Job Titles in This Work Group:** Aerospace Engineering and Operations Technicians; Architectural and Civil Drafters; Architectural Drafters; Calibration and Instrumentation Technicians; Cartographers and Photogrammetrists; Civil Drafters; Civil Engineering Technicians; Construction and Building Inspectors; Drafters, All Other; Electrical and Electronic Engineering Technicians; Electrical and Electronics Drafters; Electrical Drafters; Electrical Engineering Technicians; Electro-Mechanical Technicians; Electronic Drafters; Engineering Technicians, Except Drafters, All Other; Environmental Engineering Technicians; Industrial Engineering Technicians; Mapping Technicians; Mechanical Drafters; Mechanical Engineering Technicians; Numerical Tool and Process Control Programmers; Pressure Vessel Inspectors; Surveying and Mapping Technicians; Surveying Technicians; Surveyors. **PERSONALITY TYPE—Realistic.** Realistic occupations frequently involve work activities that include practical, hands-on problems and solutions. They often deal with plants, animals, and real-world materials like wood, tools, and machinery. Many of the occupations require working outside and do not involve a lot of paperwork or working closely with others.

EDUCATION/TRAINING PROGRAM(S)—Computer Engineering Technology/Technician; Computer Technology/Computer Systems Technology; Electrical and Electronic Engineering Technologies/Technicians, Other; Electrical, Electronic, and Communications Engineering Technology/Technician; Telecommunications Technology/Technician. RELATED KNOWLEDGE/COURSES—Computers and Electronics: Knowledge of circuit boards, processors, chips, electronic equipment, and computer hardware and software, including applications and programming. **Engineering and Technology:** Knowledge of the practical application of engineering science and technology. This includes applying principles, techniques, procedures, and equipment to the design and production of various goods and services. **Design:** Knowledge of design techniques, tools, and principles involved in production of precision technical plans, blueprints, drawings, and models. **Mathematics:** Knowledge of arithmetic, algebra, geometry, calculus, and statistics and their applications. **English Language:** Knowledge of the structure and content of the English language, including the meaning and spelling of words, rules of composition, and grammar.

Electronics Engineers, Except Computer

- ▲ Education/Training Required: Bachelor's degree
- ▲ Annual Earnings: $68,350
- ▲ Growth: 10.4%
- ▲ Annual Job Openings: 6,000
- ▲ Self-Employed: 2.9%
- ▲ Part-Time: 2.6%

Research, design, develop, and test electronic components and systems for commercial, industrial, military, or scientific use, utilizing knowledge of electronic theory and materials properties. Design electronic circuits and components for use in fields such as telecommunications, aerospace guidance and propulsion control, acoustics, or instruments and controls. Designs electronic components, products, and systems for commercial, industrial, medical, military, and scientific applications. Investigates causes of personal injury resulting from contact with high-voltage communications equipment. Determines material and equipment needs and orders supplies. Reviews or prepares budget and cost estimates for equipment, construction, and installation projects and controls expenditures. Prepares, reviews, and maintains maintenance schedules and operational reports and charts. Provides technical assistance to field and laboratory staff regarding equipment standards and problems and applications of transmitting and receiving methods. Operates computer-assisted engineering and design software and equipment to perform engineering tasks. Confers with engineers, customers, and others to discuss existing and potential engineering projects or products. Prepares engineering sketches and specifications for construction, relocation, and installation of transmitting and receiving equipment, facilities, products, and systems. Inspects electronic equipment, instruments, products, and systems to ensure conformance to specifications, safety standards, and applicable codes and regulations. Plans and implements research, methodology, and procedures to apply principles of electronic theory to engineering projects. Directs and coordinates activities concerned with manufacture, construction, installation, maintenance, operation, and modification of electronic equipment, products, and systems. Evaluates operational systems and recommends repair or design modifications based on factors such as environment, service, cost, and system capabilities. Conducts studies to gather information regarding current services, equipment capacities, traffic data, and acquisition and installation costs. Analyzes system requirements, capacity, cost, and customer needs to determine feasibility of project and develop system plan. Plans and develops applications and modifications for electronic properties used in components, products, and systems to improve technical performance. Develops operational, maintenance, and testing procedures for electronic products, components, equipment, and systems. **SKILLS—Mathematics:** Using mathematics to solve problems. **Reading Comprehension:** Understanding written sentences and paragraphs in work-related documents. **Writing:** Communicating effectively in writing as appropriate for the needs of the audience. **Science:** Using scientific rules and methods to solve problems. **Judgment and Decision Making:** Considering the relative costs and benefits of potential actions to choose the most appropriate one.

GOE INFORMATION—Interest Area: 02. Science, Math, and Engineering. **Work Group:** 02.07. Engineering. **Other Job Titles in This Work Group:** Aerospace Engineers; Agricultural Engineers; Architects, Except Landscape and Naval; Biomedical Engineers; Chemical Engineers; Civil Engineers; Computer Hardware Engineers; Computer Software Engineers, Applications; Computer Software Engineers, Systems Software; Electrical Engineers; Engineers, All Other; Environmental Engineers; Fire-Prevention and Protection Engineers; Health and Safety Engineers, Except Mining Safety Engineers and Inspectors; Industrial Engineers; Industrial Safety and Health Engineers; Landscape Architects; Marine Architects; Marine Engineers; Marine Engineers and Naval Architects; Materials Engineers; Mechanical Engineers; Mining and Geological Engineers, Including Mining Safety Engineers; Nuclear Engineers; Petroleum Engineers; Product Safety Engineers; Sales Engineers. **PERSONALITY TYPE—**Investigative. Investigative occupations frequently involve working with ideas and require an extensive amount of thinking. These occupations can involve searching for facts and figuring out problems mentally.

EDUCATION/TRAINING PROGRAM(S)—Electrical, Electronics, and Communications Engineering. **RELATED KNOWLEDGE/COURSES—Engineering and Technology:** Knowledge of the practical application of engineering science and technology. This includes applying principles, techniques, procedures, and equipment to the design and production of various goods and services. **Mathematics:** Knowledge of arithmetic, algebra, geometry, calculus, and statistics and their applications. **Design:** Knowledge of design techniques, tools, and principles involved in production of precision technical plans, blueprints, drawings, and models. **Computers and Electronics:** Knowledge of circuit boards, processors, chips,

electronic equipment, and computer hardware and software, including applications and programming. **Production and Processing:** Knowledge of raw materials, production processes, quality control, costs, and other techniques for maximizing the effective manufacture and distribution of goods. **Telecommunications:** Knowledge of transmission, broadcasting, switching, control, and operation of telecommunications systems.

Elementary School Teachers, Except Special Education

- ▲ Education/Training Required: Bachelor's degree
- ▲ Annual Earnings: $41,080
- ▲ Growth: 13.2%
- ▲ Annual Job Openings: 144,000
- ▲ Self-Employed: 0%
- ▲ Part-Time: 11.7%

Teach pupils in public or private schools at the elementary level basic academic, social, and other formative skills. Lectures, demonstrates, and uses audiovisual aids and computers to present academic, social, and motor skill subject matter to class. Teaches subjects such as math, science, or social studies. Prepares course objectives and outline for course of study, following curriculum guidelines or requirements of state and school. Prepares, administers, and corrects tests and records results. Assigns lessons, corrects papers, and hears oral presentations. Teaches rules of conduct and maintains discipline and suitable learning environment in classroom and on playground. Evaluates student performance and discusses pupil academic and behavioral attitudes and achievements with parents. Keeps attendance and grade records and prepares reports as required by school. Counsels pupils when adjustment and academic problems arise. Supervises outdoor and indoor play activities. Teaches combined grade classes. Attends staff meetings, serves on committees, and attends workshops or in-service training activities. Coordinates class field trips. Prepares bulletin boards. **SKILLS—Learning Strategies:** Selecting and using training/instructional methods and procedures appropriate for the situation when learning or teaching new things. **Social Perceptiveness:** Being aware of others' reactions and understanding why they react as they do. **Instructing:** Teaching others how to do something. **Reading Comprehension:** Understanding written sentences and paragraphs in work-related documents. **Speaking:** Talking to others to convey information effectively.

GOE INFORMATION—Interest Area: 12. Education and Social Service. **Work Group:** 12.03. Educational Services. **Other Job Titles in This Work Group:** Adult Literacy, Remedial Education, and GED Teachers and Instructors; Agricultural Sciences Teachers, Postsecondary; Anthropology and Archeology Teachers, Postsecondary; Architecture Teachers, Postsecondary; Archivists; Area, Ethnic, and Cultural Studies Teachers, Postsecondary; Art, Drama, and Music Teachers, Postsecondary; Atmospheric, Earth, Marine, and Space Sciences Teachers, Postsecondary; Audio-Visual Collections Specialists; Biological Science Teachers, Postsecondary; Business Teachers, Postsecondary; Chemistry Teachers, Postsecondary; Child Care Workers; Communications Teachers, Postsecondary; Computer Science Teachers, Postsecondary; Criminal Justice and Law Enforcement Teachers, Postsecondary; Curators; Economics Teachers, Postsecondary; Education Teachers, Postsecondary; Educational Psychologists; Educational, Vocational, and School Counselors; Engineering Teachers, Postsecondary; English Language and Literature Teachers, Postsecondary; Environmental Science Teachers, Postsecondary; Farm and Home Management Advisors; Foreign Language and Literature Teachers, Postsecondary; Forestry and Conservation Science Teachers, Postsecondary; Geography Teachers, Postsecondary; Graduate Teaching Assistants; Health Specialties Teachers, Postsecondary; History Teachers, Postsecondary; Home Economics Teachers, Postsecondary; Kindergarten Teachers, Except Special Education; Law

Teachers, Postsecondary; Librarians; Library Assistants, Clerical; Library Science Teachers, Postsecondary; Library Technicians; Mathematical Science Teachers, Postsecondary; Middle School Teachers, Except Special and Vocational Education; Museum Technicians and Conservators; Nursing Instructors and Teachers, Postsecondary; Personal Financial Advisors; Philosophy and Religion Teachers, Postsecondary; Physics Teachers, Postsecondary; Political Science Teachers, Postsecondary; Postsecondary Teachers, All Other; Preschool Teachers, Except Special Education; Psychology Teachers, Postsecondary; others. **PERSONALITY TYPE**—Social. Social occupations frequently involve working with, communicating with, and teaching people. These occupations often involve helping or providing service to others.

EDUCATION/TRAINING PROGRAM(S)—Elementary Education and Teaching; Teacher Education, Multiple Levels. **RELATED KNOWLEDGE/ COURSES—Education and Training:** Knowledge of

principles and methods for curriculum and training design, teaching and instruction for individuals and groups, and the measurement of training effects. **English Language:** Knowledge of the structure and content of the English language, including the meaning and spelling of words, rules of composition, and grammar. **Psychology:** Knowledge of human behavior and performance; individual differences in ability, personality, and interests; learning and motivation; psychological research methods; and the assessment and treatment of behavioral and affective disorders. **Mathematics:** Knowledge of arithmetic, algebra, geometry, calculus, and statistics and their applications. **History and Archeology:** Knowledge of historical events and their causes, indicators, and effects on civilizations and cultures. **Customer and Personal Service:** Knowledge of principles and processes for providing customer and personal services. This includes customer needs assessment, meeting quality standards for services, and evaluation of customer satisfaction.

Elevator Installers and Repairers

- ▲ Education/Training Required: Long-term on-the-job training
- ▲ Annual Earnings: $51,630
- ▲ Growth: 17.2%
- ▲ Annual Job Openings: 2,000
- ▲ Self-Employed: 0%
- ▲ Part-Time: 7.5%

Assemble, install, repair, or maintain electric or hydraulic freight or passenger elevators, escalators, or dumbwaiters. Studies blueprints to determine layout of framework and foundations. Cuts prefabricated sections of framework, rails, and other components to specified dimensions. Locates malfunction in brakes, motor, switches, and signal and control systems, using test equipment. Connects electrical wiring to control panels and electric motors. Installs safety and control devices, cables, drives, rails, motors, and elevator cars. Disassembles defective unit and repairs or replaces parts, such as locks, gears, cables, and electric wiring. Completes service reports to verify conformance to prescribed standards. Inspects wiring connections, control panel hookups, door installation, and alignment and clearance of car hoistway. Lubricates bearings and other parts to minimize friction. Operates elevator to determine power demand and tests power consumption to detect overload factors. Adjusts safety controls, counterweights, and mechanism of doors.

SKILLS—**Installation:** Installing equipment, machines, wiring, or programs to meet specifications. **Repairing:** Repairing machines or systems, using the needed tools. **Troubleshooting:** Determining causes of operating errors and deciding what to do about them. **Equipment Maintenance:** Performing routine maintenance on equipment and determining when and what kind of maintenance is needed. **Quality Control Analysis:** Conducting tests and inspections of products, services, or processes to evaluate quality or performance.

GOE INFORMATION—**Interest Area:** 05. Mechanics, Installers, and Repairers. **Work Group:** 05.02. Electrical and Electronic Systems. **Other Job Titles in This Work Group:** Avionics Technicians; Battery Repairers; Central Office and PBX Installers and Repairers; Communication Equipment Mechanics, Installers, and Repairers; Computer, Automated Teller, and Office Machine Repairers; Data Processing Equipment Repairers; Electric Home

Appliance and Power Tool Repairers; Electric Meter Installers and Repairers; Electric Motor and Switch Assemblers and Repairers; Electric Motor, Power Tool, and Related Repairers; Electrical and Electronics Installers and Repairers, Transportation Equipment; Electrical and Electronics Repairers, Commercial and Industrial Equipment; Electrical and Electronics Repairers, Powerhouse, Substation, and Relay; Electrical Parts Reconditioners; Electrical Power-Line Installers and Repairers; Electronic Equipment Installers and Repairers, Motor Vehicles; Electronic Home Entertainment Equipment Installers and Repairers; Frame Wirers, Central Office; Home Appliance Installers; Home Appliance Repairers; Office Machine and Cash Register Servicers; Radio Mechanics; Signal and Track Switch Repairers; Station Installers and Repairers, Telephone; Telecommunications Equipment Installers and Repairers, Except Line Installers; Telecommunications Facility Examiners; Telecommunications Line Installers and Repairers; Transformer Repairers. **PERSONALITY TYPE—** Realistic. Realistic occupations frequently involve work activities that include practical, hands-on problems and solutions. They often deal with plants, animals, and real-world materials like wood, tools, and machinery. Many of the occupations require working outside and do not involve a lot of paperwork or working closely with others.

EDUCATION/TRAINING PROGRAM(S)—Industrial Mechanics and Maintenance Technology. **RELATED KNOWLEDGE/COURSES—Principles of Mechanical Devices:** Knowledge of machines and tools, including their designs, uses, repair, and maintenance. **Building and Construction:** Knowledge of materials, methods, and tools involved in the construction or repair of houses, buildings, or other structures, such as highways and roads. **Engineering and Technology:** Knowledge of the practical application of engineering science and technology. This includes applying principles, techniques, procedures, and equipment to the design and production of various goods and services. **Public Safety and Security:** Knowledge of relevant equipment, policies, procedures, and strategies to promote effective local, state, or national security operations for the protection of people, data, property, and institutions. **Mathematics:** Knowledge of arithmetic, algebra, geometry, calculus, and statistics and their applications.

Emergency Medical Technicians and Paramedics

▲ Education/Training Required: Postsecondary vocational training
▲ Annual Earnings: $23,170
▲ Growth: 31.3%
▲ Annual Job Openings: 19,000
▲ Self-Employed: 0%
▲ Part-Time: 22.9%

Assess injuries, administer emergency medical care, and extricate trapped individuals. Transport injured or sick persons to medical facilities. Administers first-aid treatment and life support care to sick or injured persons in prehospital setting. Assesses nature and extent of illness or injury to establish and prioritize medical procedures. Observes, records, and reports patient's condition and reactions to drugs and treatment to physician. Communicates with treatment center personnel to arrange reception of victims and to receive instructions for further treatment. Assists treatment center personnel to obtain information relating to circumstances of emergency. Maintains vehicles and medical and communication equipment and replenishes first-aid equipment and supplies. Drives mobile intensive care unit to specified location, following instructions from emergency medical dispatcher. Assists treatment center personnel to obtain and record victim's vital statistics and to administer emergency treatment. Monitors patient's condition, using electrocardiograph. Assists in removal and transport of victims to treatment center. **SKILLS—Coordination:** Adjusting actions in relation to others' actions. **Service Orientation:** Actively looking for ways to help people. **Active Listening:** Giving full attention to what other people are saying, taking time to understand the points being made, asking questions as appropriate, and not interrupting at inappropriate times. **Judgment and Decision Making:** Considering the relative costs and benefits of potential actions to choose the most appropriate one. **Social Perceptiveness:** Being aware of others' reactions and understanding why they react as they do.

GOE INFORMATION—Interest Area: 04. Law, Law Enforcement, and Public Safety. **Work Group:** 04.04. Public Safety. **Other Job Titles in This Work Group:**

Agricultural Inspectors; Aviation Inspectors; Compliance Officers, Except Agriculture, Construction, Health and Safety, and Transportation; Environmental Compliance Inspectors; Equal Opportunity Representatives and Officers; Financial Examiners; Fire Fighters; Fire Inspectors; Fire Inspectors and Investigators; Forest Fire Fighters; Forest Fire Inspectors and Prevention Specialists; Government Property Inspectors and Investigators; Licensing Examiners and Inspectors; Marine Cargo Inspectors; Municipal Fire Fighters; Nuclear Monitoring Technicians; Occupational Health and Safety Specialists; Occupational Health and Safety Technicians; Public Transportation Inspectors. **PERSONALITY TYPE**—Social. Social occupations frequently involve working with, communicating with, and teaching people. These occupations often involve helping or providing service to others.

EDUCATION/TRAINING PROGRAM(S)—Emergency Care Attendant (EMT Ambulance); Emergency Medical Technology/Technician (EMT Paramedic). **RELATED KNOWLEDGE/COURSES—Medicine and Dentistry:** Knowledge of the information and techniques needed to diagnose and treat human injuries, diseases, and deformities. This includes symptoms, treatment alternatives, drug properties and interactions, and preventive health-care measures. **Therapy and Counseling:** Knowledge of principles, methods, and procedures for diagnosis, treatment, and rehabilitation of physical and mental dysfunctions and for career counseling and guidance. **Biology:** Knowledge of plant and animal organisms and their tissues, cells, functions, interdependencies, and interactions with each other and the environment. **Transportation:** Knowledge of principles and methods for moving people or goods by air, rail, sea, or road, including the relative costs and benefits. **Telecommunications:** Knowledge of transmission, broadcasting, switching, control, and operation of telecommunications systems.

Employment Interviewers, Private or Public Employment Service

- ▲ Education/Training Required: Bachelor's degree
- ▲ Annual Earnings: $38,010
- ▲ Growth: 17.6%
- ▲ Annual Job Openings: 19,000
- ▲ Self-Employed: 0%
- ▲ Part-Time: 6.9%

Interview job applicants in employment office and refer them to prospective employers for consideration. Search application files, notify selected applicants of job openings, and refer qualified applicants to prospective employers. Contact employers to verify referral results. Record and evaluate various pertinent data. Interviews job applicants to select people meeting employer qualifications. Reviews employment applications and evaluates work history, education and training, job skills, compensation needs, and other qualifications of applicants. Records additional knowledge, skills, abilities, interests, test results, and other data pertinent to selection and referral of applicants. Informs applicants of job duties and responsibilities, compensation and benefits, work schedules, working conditions, promotional opportunities, and other related information. Searches for and recruits applicants for open positions. Performs reference and background checks on applicants. Contacts employers to solicit orders for job vacancies and records information on forms to describe duties, hiring requirements, and related data. Refers applicants to vocational counseling services. Evaluates selection and testing techniques by conducting research or follow-up activities and conferring with management and supervisory personnel. Conducts or arranges for skills, intelligence, or psychological testing of applicants. Keeps records of applicants not selected for employment. Reviews job orders and matches applicants with job requirements, utilizing manual or computerized file search. Refers selected applicants to person placing job order according to policy of organization. **SKILLS—Reading Comprehension:** Understanding written sentences and paragraphs in work-related documents. **Active Listening:** Giving full attention to what other people are saying, taking time to understand the points being made, asking questions as appropriate, and not interrupting at inappropriate times. **Speaking:** Talking to others to convey information effectively. **Writing:** Communicating effectively in writing as appropriate for the needs of the audience. **Judgment and Decision Making:** Considering the relative costs and benefits of potential actions to choose the most appropriate one.

GOE INFORMATION—**Interest Area:** 13. General Management and Support. **Work Group:** 13.02. Management Support. **Other Job Titles in This Work Group:** Accountants; Accountants and Auditors; Appraisers and Assessors of Real Estate; Appraisers, Real Estate; Assessors; Auditors; Budget Analysts; Claims Adjusters, Examiners, and Investigators; Claims Examiners, Property and Casualty Insurance; Compensation, Benefits, and Job Analysis Specialists; Cost Estimators; Credit Analysts; Employment, Recruitment, and Placement Specialists; Financial Analysts; Human Resources, Training, and Labor Relations Specialists, All Other; Insurance Adjusters, Examiners, and Investigators; Insurance Appraisers, Auto Damage; Insurance Underwriters; Loan Counselors; Loan Officers; Logisticians; Management Analysts; Market Research Analysts; Personnel Recruiters; Purchasing Agents and Buyers, Farm Products; Purchasing Agents, Except Wholesale, Retail, and Farm Products; Tax Examiners, Collectors, and Revenue Agents; Training and Development Specialists; Wholesale and Retail Buyers, Except Farm Products. **PERSONALITY TYPE**—Social. Social occupations frequently involve working with, communicating with, and teaching people. These occupations often involve helping or providing service to others.

Employment, Recruitment, and Placement Specialists

- ▲ Education/Training Required: Bachelor's degree
- ▲ Annual Earnings: $38,010
- ▲ Growth: 17.6%
- ▲ Annual Job Openings: 19,000
- ▲ Self-Employed: 2.6%
- ▲ Part-Time: 6.9%

EDUCATION/TRAINING PROGRAM(S)—Human Resources Management/Personnel Administration, General; Labor and Industrial Relations. **RELATED KNOWLEDGE/COURSES—Personnel and Human Resources:** Knowledge of principles and procedures for personnel recruitment, selection, training, compensation and benefits, labor relations and negotiation, and personnel information systems. **Therapy and Counseling:** Knowledge of principles, methods, and procedures for diagnosis, treatment, and rehabilitation of physical and mental dysfunctions and for career counseling and guidance. **English Language:** Knowledge of the structure and content of the English language, including the meaning and spelling of words, rules of composition, and grammar. **Administration and Management:** Knowledge of business and management principles involved in strategic planning, resource allocation, human resources modeling, leadership technique, production methods, and coordination of people and resources. **Clerical Studies:** Knowledge of administrative and clerical procedures and systems, such as word processing, managing files and records, stenography and transcription, designing forms, and other office procedures and terminology.

Recruit and place workers. SKILLS—No data available.

GOE INFORMATION—**Interest Area:** 13. General Management and Support. **Work Group:** 13.02. Management Support. **Other Job Titles in This Work Group:** Accountants; Accountants and Auditors; Appraisers and Assessors of Real Estate; Appraisers, Real Estate; Assessors; Auditors; Budget Analysts; Claims Adjusters, Examiners, and Investigators; Claims Examiners, Property and Casualty Insurance; Compensation, Benefits, and Job Analysis Specialists; Cost Estimators; Credit Analysts; Employment Interviewers, Private or Public Employment Service; Financial Analysts; Human Resources, Training, and Labor Relations Specialists, All Other; Insurance Adjusters, Examiners, and Investigators; Insurance Apprais-ers, Auto Damage; Insurance Underwriters; Loan Counselors; Loan Officers; Logisticians; Management Analysts; Market Research Analysts; Personnel Recruiters; Purchasing Agents and Buyers, Farm Products; Purchasing Agents, Except Wholesale, Retail, and Farm Products; Tax Examiners, Collectors, and Revenue Agents; Training and Development Specialists; Wholesale and Retail Buyers, Except Farm Products. **PERSONALITY TYPE**—No data available.

EDUCATION/TRAINING PROGRAM(S)—Human Resources Management/Personnel Administration, General; Labor and Industrial Relations. **RELATED KNOWLEDGE/COURSES**—No data available.

Engineering Managers

▲ Education/Training Required: Work experience plus degree
▲ Annual Earnings: $87,490
▲ Growth: 8.0%
▲ Annual Job Openings: 24,000
▲ Self-Employed: 0%
▲ Part-Time: 6.1%

Plan, direct, or coordinate activities in such fields as architecture and engineering or research and development in these fields. Establishes procedures and directs testing, operation, maintenance, and repair of transmitter equipment. Plans and directs oil field development, gas and oil production, and geothermal drilling. Plans, directs, and coordinates survey work with activities of other staff, certifies survey work, and writes land legal descriptions. Analyzes technology, resource needs, and market demand and confers with management, production, and marketing staff to plan and assess feasibility of project. Plans, coordinates, and directs engineering project; organizes and assigns staff; and directs integration of technical activities with products. Evaluates contract proposals, directs negotiation of research contracts, and prepares bids and contracts. Directs, reviews, and approves product design and changes; directs testing. Plans and directs installation, maintenance, testing, and repair of facilities and equipment. Administers highway planning, construction, and maintenance and reviews and recommends or approves contracts and cost estimates. Directs engineering of water control, treatment, and distribution projects. Confers with and prepares reports for officials and speaks to public to solicit support. **SKILLS—Coordination:** Adjusting actions in relation to others' actions. **Operations Analysis:** Analyzing needs and product requirements to create a design. **Science:** Using scientific rules and methods to solve problems. **Troubleshooting:** Determining causes of operating errors and deciding what to do about them. **Reading Comprehension:** Understanding written sentences and paragraphs in work-related documents.

GOE INFORMATION—Interest Area: 02. Science, Math, and Engineering. **Work Group:** 02.01. Managerial Work in Science, Math, and Engineering. **Other Job Titles in This Work Group:** Computer and Information Systems Managers; Natural Sciences Managers. **PERSONALITY TYPE—**Enterprising. Enterprising occupations frequently involve starting up and carrying out projects. These occupations can involve leading people and mak-

ing many decisions. They sometimes require risk taking and often deal with business.

EDUCATION/TRAINING PROGRAM(S)—Aerospace, Aeronautical, and Astronautical Engineering; Agricultural/Biological Engineering and Bioengineering; Architectural Engineering; Architecture (BArch, BA/BS, MArch, MA/MS, PhD); Biomedical/Medical Engineering; Ceramic Sciences and Engineering; Chemical Engineering; City/Urban, Community, and Regional Planning; Civil Engineering, General; Civil Engineering, Other; Computer Engineering, General; Computer Engineering, Other; Computer Hardware Engineering; Computer Software Engineering; Construction Engineering; Electrical, Electronics, and Communications Engineering; Engineering Mechanics; Engineering Physics; Engineering Science; Engineering, General; Engineering, Other; Environmental Design/Architecture; Environmental/Environmental Health Engineering; Forest Engineering; Geological/Geophysical Engineering; Geotechnical Engineering; Industrial Engineering; Interior Architecture; Landscape Architecture (BS, BSLA, BLA, MSLA, MLA, PhD); Manufacturing Engineering; Materials Engineering; Materials Science; Mechanical Engineering; Metallurgical Engineering; Mining and Mineral Engineering; Naval Architecture and Marine Engineering; Nuclear Engineering; Ocean Engineering; Petroleum Engineering; Polymer/Plastics Engineering; Structural Engineering; Surveying Engineering; Systems Engineering; Textile Sciences and Engineering; Transportation and Highway Engineering; Water Resources Engineering. **RELATED KNOWLEDGE/COURSES—Engineering and Technology:** Knowledge of the practical application of engineering science and technology. This includes applying principles, techniques, procedures, and equipment to the design and production of various goods and services. **Administration and Management:** Knowledge of business and management principles involved in strategic planning, resource allocation, human resources modeling, leadership technique, production methods, and coordination of people and resources. **Design:** Knowledge of design techniques, tools, and principles involved in production of precision technical plans, blueprints, drawings, and models. **Physics:** Knowledge and prediction of physical principles and laws and their interrelationships and applications to understanding fluid, material, and atmospheric dynamics and mechanical, electrical, atomic, and sub-atomic structures and processes. **Mathematics:** Knowledge of arithmetic, algebra, geometry, calculus, and statistics and their applications.

Engineering Teachers, Postsecondary

- ▲ Education/Training Required: Master's degree
- ▲ Annual Earnings: $67,310
- ▲ Growth: 23.5%
- ▲ Annual Job Openings: 184,000
- ▲ Self-Employed: 0%
- ▲ Part-Time: 32.3%

Teach courses pertaining to the application of physical laws and principles of engineering for the development of machines, materials, instruments, processes, and services. Includes teachers of subjects such as chemical, civil, electrical, industrial, mechanical, mineral, and petroleum engineering. Includes both teachers primarily engaged in teaching and those who do a combination of both teaching and research. Prepares and delivers lectures to students. Serves on faculty committee providing professional consulting services to government and industry. Acts as adviser to student organizations. Conducts research in particular field of knowledge and publishes findings in professional journals. Stimulates class discussions. Compiles, administers, and grades examinations or assigns this work to others. Advises students on academic and vocational curricula. Directs research of other teachers or graduate students working for advanced academic degrees. Compiles bibliographies of specialized materials for outside reading assignments. **SKILLS—Mathematics:** Using mathematics to solve problems. **Active Learning:** Understanding the implications of new information for both current and future problem-solving and decision-making. **Reading Comprehension:** Understanding written sentences and paragraphs in work-related documents. **Critical Thinking:** Using logic and reasoning to identify the strengths and weaknesses of alternative solutions, conclusions, or approaches to problems. **Science:** Using scientific rules and methods to solve problems.

GOE INFORMATION—Interest Area: 12. Education and Social Service. **Work Group:** 12.03. Educational Services. **Other Job Titles in This Work Group:** Adult Literacy, Remedial Education, and GED Teachers and Instructors; Agricultural Sciences Teachers, Postsecondary; Anthropology and Archeology Teachers, Postsecondary; Architecture Teachers, Postsecondary; Archivists; Area, Ethnic, and Cultural Studies Teachers, Postsecondary; Art, Drama, and Music Teachers, Postsecondary; Atmospheric, Earth, Marine, and Space Sciences Teachers, Postsecondary; Audio-Visual Collections Specialists; Biological Science Teachers, Postsecondary; Business Teachers, Postsecondary; Chemistry Teachers, Postsecondary; Child Care Workers; Communications Teachers, Postsecondary; Computer Science Teachers, Postsecondary; Criminal Justice and Law Enforcement Teachers, Postsecondary; Curators; Economics Teachers, Postsecondary; Education Teachers, Postsecondary; Educational Psychologists; Educational, Vocational, and School Counselors; Elementary School Teachers, Except Special Education; English Language and Literature Teachers, Postsecondary; Environmental Science Teachers, Postsecondary; Farm and Home Management Advisors; Foreign Language and Literature Teachers, Postsecondary; Forestry and Conservation Science Teachers, Postsecondary; Geography Teachers, Postsecondary; Graduate Teaching Assistants; Health Specialties Teachers, Postsecondary; History Teachers, Postsecondary; Home Economics Teachers, Postsecondary; Kindergarten Teachers, Except Special Education; Law Teachers, Postsecondary; Librarians; Library Assistants, Clerical; Library Science Teachers, Postsecondary; Library Technicians; Mathematical Science Teachers, Postsecondary; Middle School Teachers, Except Special and Vocational Education; Museum Technicians and Conservators; Nursing Instructors and Teachers, Postsecondary; Personal Financial Advisors; Philosophy and Religion Teachers, Postsecondary; Physics Teachers, Postsecondary; Political Science Teachers, Postsecondary; Postsecondary Teachers, All Other; Preschool Teachers, Except Special Education;

others. **PERSONALITY TYPE**—Investigative. Investigative occupations frequently involve working with ideas and require an extensive amount of thinking. These occupations can involve searching for facts and figuring out problems mentally.

EDUCATION/TRAINING PROGRAM(S)—Aerospace, Aeronautical, and Astronautical Engineering; Agricultural/Biological Engineering and Bioengineering; Architectural Engineering; Biomedical/Medical Engineering; Ceramic Sciences and Engineering; Chemical Engineering; Civil Engineering, General; Civil Engineering, Other; Computer Engineering, General; Computer Engineering, Other; Computer Hardware Engineering; Computer Software Engineering; Construction Engineering; Electrical, Electronics and Communications Engineering; Engineering Mechanics; Engineering Physics; Engineering Science; Engineering, General; Engineering, Other; Environmental/Environmental Health Engineering; Forest Engineering; Geological/Geophysical Engineering; Geotechnical Engineering; Industrial Engineering; Manufacturing Engineering; Materials Engineering; Materials Science; Mechanical Engineering; Metallurgical Engineering; Mining and Mineral Engineering; Naval Architecture and Marine Engineering; Nuclear Engineering; Ocean Engineering; Petroleum Engineering; Polymer/Plastics

Engineering; Structural Engineering; Surveying Engineering; Systems Engineering; Teacher Education and Professional Development, Specific Subject Areas, Other; Textile Sciences and Engineering; Transportation and Highway Engineering; Water Resources Engineering. **RELATED KNOWLEDGE/COURSES—Engineering and Technology:** Knowledge of the practical application of engineering science and technology. This includes applying principles, techniques, procedures, and equipment to the design and production of various goods and services. **Education and Training:** Knowledge of principles and methods for curriculum and training design, teaching and instruction for individuals and groups, and the measurement of training effects. **Mathematics:** Knowledge of arithmetic, algebra, geometry, calculus, and statistics and their applications. **Physics:** Knowledge and prediction of physical principles and laws and their interrelationships and applications to understanding fluid, material, and atmospheric dynamics and mechanical, electrical, atomic, and sub-atomic structures and processes. **English Language:** Knowledge of the structure and content of the English language, including the meaning and spelling of words, rules of composition, and grammar. **Design:** Knowledge of design techniques, tools, and principles involved in production of precision technical plans, blueprints, drawings, and models.

English Language and Literature Teachers, Postsecondary

- ▲ Education/Training Required: Master's degree
- ▲ Annual Earnings: $45,590
- ▲ Growth: 23.5%
- ▲ Annual Job Openings: 184,000
- ▲ Self-Employed: 0%
- ▲ Part-Time: 32.3%

Teach courses in English language and literature, including linguistics and comparative literature. Prepares and delivers lectures to students. Stimulates class discussions. Advises students on academic and vocational curricula. Conducts research in particular field of knowledge and publishes findings in professional journals. Serves on faculty committee providing professional consulting services to government and industry. Acts as adviser to student organizations. Directs research of other teachers or graduate students working for advanced academic degrees. Compiles, administers, and grades examinations or assigns this work to others. Compiles bibliographies of specialized materials for outside reading assignments. **SKILLS—Reading Comprehension:** Understanding written sentences and

paragraphs in work-related documents. **Instructing:** Teaching others how to do something. **Speaking:** Talking to others to convey information effectively. **Learning Strategies:** Selecting and using training/instructional methods and procedures appropriate for the situation when learning or teaching new things. **Writing:** Communicating effectively in writing as appropriate for the needs of the audience.

GOE INFORMATION—Interest Area: 12. Education and Social Service. **Work Group:** 12.03. Educational Services. **Other Job Titles in This Work Group:** Adult Literacy, Remedial Education, and GED Teachers and Instructors; Agricultural Sciences Teachers, Postsecondary;

Anthropology and Archeology Teachers, Postsecondary; Architecture Teachers, Postsecondary; Archivists; Area, Ethnic, and Cultural Studies Teachers, Postsecondary; Art, Drama, and Music Teachers, Postsecondary; Atmospheric, Earth, Marine, and Space Sciences Teachers, Postsecondary; Audio-Visual Collections Specialists; Biological Science Teachers, Postsecondary; Business Teachers, Postsecondary; Chemistry Teachers, Postsecondary; Child Care Workers; Communications Teachers, Postsecondary; Computer Science Teachers, Postsecondary; Criminal Justice and Law Enforcement Teachers, Postsecondary; Curators; Economics Teachers, Postsecondary; Education Teachers, Postsecondary; Educational Psychologists; Educational, Vocational, and School Counselors; Elementary School Teachers, Except Special Education; Engineering Teachers, Postsecondary; Environmental Science Teachers, Postsecondary; Farm and Home Management Advisors; Foreign Language and Literature Teachers, Postsecondary; Forestry and Conservation Science Teachers, Postsecondary; Geography Teachers, Postsecondary; Graduate Teaching Assistants; Health Specialties Teachers, Postsecondary; History Teachers, Postsecondary; Home Economics Teachers, Postsecondary; Kindergarten Teachers, Except Special Education; Law Teachers, Postsecondary; Librarians; Library Assistants, Clerical; Library Science Teachers, Postsecondary; Library Technicians; Mathematical Science Teachers, Postsecondary; Middle School Teachers, Except Special and Vocational Education; Museum Technicians and Conservators; Nursing Instructors and Teachers, Postsecondary; Personal Financial Advisors; Philosophy and Religion Teachers, Postsecondary; Physics Teachers, Postsecondary; Political Science Teachers, Postsecondary; Postsecondary Teachers, All Other; Preschool Teachers, Except Special Education; Psychology Teachers, Postsecondary; others. **PERSONALITY TYPE**—Artistic. Artistic occupations frequently involve working with forms, designs, and patterns. They often require self-expression, and the work can be done without following a clear set of rules.

EDUCATION/TRAINING PROGRAM(S)—American Literature (Canadian); American Literature (United States); Comparative Literature; Creative Writing; English Composition; English Language and Literature, General; English Language and Literature/Letters, Other; English Literature (British and Commonwealth); Technical and Business Writing. **RELATED KNOWLEDGE/COURSES**—**Education and Training:** Knowledge of principles and methods for curriculum and training design, teaching and instruction for individuals and groups, and the measurement of training effects. **English Language:** Knowledge of the structure and content of the English language, including the meaning and spelling of words, rules of composition, and grammar. **Foreign Language:** Knowledge of the structure and content of a foreign (non-English) language, including the meaning and spelling of words, rules of composition and grammar, and pronunciation. **Communications and Media:** Knowledge of media production, communication, and dissemination techniques and methods. This includes alternative ways to inform and entertain via written, oral, and visual media. **Computers and Electronics:** Knowledge of circuit boards, processors, chips, electronic equipment, and computer hardware and software, including applications and programming. **Clerical Studies:** Knowledge of administrative and clerical procedures and systems, such as word processing, managing files and records, stenography and transcription, designing forms, and other office procedures and terminology.

Environmental Engineering Technicians

- ▲ Education/Training Required: Associate's degree
- ▲ Annual Earnings: $36,590
- ▲ Growth: 29.1%
- ▲ Annual Job Openings: 2,000
- ▲ Self-Employed: 1.9%
- ▲ Part-Time: 7.4%

Apply theory and principles of environmental engineering to modify, test, and operate equipment and devices used in the prevention, control, and remediation of environmental pollution, including waste treatment and site remediation. May assist in the development of environmental pollution remediation devices under direction of engineer. **SKILLS**—No data available.

GOE INFORMATION—**Interest Area:** 02. Science, Math, and Engineering. **Work Group:** 02.08. Engineering Technology. **Other Job Titles in This Work Group:** Aerospace Engineering and Operations Technicians; Architectural and Civil Drafters; Architectural Drafters; Calibration and Instrumentation Technicians; Cartographers and Photogrammetrists; Civil Drafters; Civil Engineering Technicians; Construction and Building Inspectors; Drafters, All Other; Electrical and Electronic Engineering Technicians; Electrical and Electronics Drafters; Electrical Drafters; Electrical Engineering Technicians; Electro-Mechanical Technicians; Electronic Drafters; Electronics Engineering Technicians; Engineering Technicians, Except Drafters, All Other; Industrial Engineering Technicians; Mapping Technicians; Mechanical Drafters; Mechanical Engineering Technicians; Numerical Tool and Process Control Programmers; Pressure Vessel Inspectors; Surveying and Mapping Technicians; Surveying Technicians; Surveyors. **PERSONALITY TYPE**—No data available.

EDUCATION/TRAINING PROGRAM(S)—Environmental Engineering Technology/Environmental Technology; Hazardous Materials Information Systems Technology/Technician. **RELATED KNOWLEDGE/COURSES**—No data available.

Environmental Engineers

- ▲ Education/Training Required: Bachelor's degree
- ▲ Annual Earnings: $61,250
- ▲ Growth: 26.0%
- ▲ Annual Job Openings: 3,000
- ▲ Self-Employed: 2.7%
- ▲ Part-Time: 4.5%

Design, plan, or perform engineering duties in the prevention, control, and remediation of environmental health hazards, utilizing various engineering disciplines. Work may include waste treatment, site remediation, or pollution control technology. SKILLS—No data available.

GOE INFORMATION—**Interest Area:** 02. Science, Math, and Engineering. **Work Group:** 02.07. Engineering. **Other Job Titles in This Work Group:** Aerospace Engineers; Agricultural Engineers; Architects, Except Landscape and Naval; Biomedical Engineers; Chemical Engineers; Civil Engineers; Computer Hardware Engineers; Computer Software Engineers, Applications; Computer Software Engineers, Systems Software; Electrical Engineers; Electronics Engineers, Except Computer; Engineers, All Other; Fire-Prevention and Protection Engineers; Health and Safety Engineers, Except Mining Safety Engineers and Inspectors; Industrial Engineers; Industrial Safety and Health Engineers; Landscape Architects; Marine Architects; Marine Engineers; Marine Engineers and Naval Architects; Materials Engineers; Mechanical Engineers; Mining and Geological Engineers, Including Mining Safety Engineers; Nuclear Engineers; Petroleum Engineers; Product Safety Engineers; Sales Engineers. **PERSONALITY TYPE**—No data available.

EDUCATION/TRAINING PROGRAM(S)—Environmental/Environmental Health Engineering. **RELATED KNOWLEDGE/COURSES**—No data available.

Environmental Science and Protection Technicians, Including Health

- ▲ Education/Training Required: Associate's degree
- ▲ Annual Earnings: $34,690
- ▲ Growth: 24.5%
- ▲ Annual Job Openings: 3,000
- ▲ Self-Employed: 0.9%
- ▲ Part-Time: 11.7%

Performs laboratory and field tests to monitor the environment and investigate sources of pollution, including those that affect health. Under direction of an environmental scientist or specialist, may collect samples of gases, soil, water, and other materials for testing and take corrective actions as assigned. Collects samples of gases, soils, water, industrial wastewater, and asbestos products to conduct tests on pollutant levels. Discusses test results and analyses with customers. Calibrates microscopes and test instruments. Develops procedures and directs activities of workers in laboratory. Records test data and prepares reports, summaries, and charts that interpret test results and recommend changes. Sets up equipment or station to monitor and collect pollutants from sites such as smoke stacks, manufacturing plants, or mechanical equipment. Determines amounts and kinds of chemicals to use in destroying harmful organisms and removing impurities from purification systems. Conducts standardized tests to ensure that materials and supplies used throughout power supply system meet processing and safety specifications. Examines and analyzes material for presence and concentration of contaminants such as asbestos in environment, using variety of microscopes. Weighs, analyzes, and measures collected sample particles, such as lead, coal dust, or rock, to determine concentration of pollutants. Prepares samples or photomicrographs for testing and analysis. Calculates amount of pollutant in samples or computes air pollution or gas flow in industrial processes, using chemical and mathematical formulas. Performs chemical and physical laboratory and field tests on collected samples to assess compliance with pollution standards, using test instruments. **SKILLS—Science:** Using scientific rules and methods to solve problems. **Mathematics:** Using mathematics to solve problems. **Reading Comprehension:** Understanding written sentences and paragraphs in work-related documents. **Writing:** Communicating effectively in writing as appropriate for the needs of the audience. **Critical Thinking:** Using logic and reasoning to identify the strengths and weaknesses of alternative solutions, conclusions, or approaches to problems.

GOE INFORMATION—Interest Area: 02. Science, Math, and Engineering. **Work Group:** 02.05. Laboratory Technology. **Other Job Titles in This Work Group:** Biological Technicians; Chemical Technicians; Geological and Petroleum Technicians; Geological Data Technicians; Geological Sample Test Technicians; Nuclear Equipment Operation Technicians; Nuclear Technicians; Photographers, Scientific. **PERSONALITY TYPE—**Investigative. Investigative occupations frequently involve working with ideas and require an extensive amount of thinking. These occupations can involve searching for facts and figuring out problems mentally.

EDUCATION/TRAINING PROGRAM(S)—Environmental Science; Environmental Studies; Physical Science Technologies/Technicians, Other; Science Technologies/Technicians, Other. **RELATED KNOWLEDGE/COURSES—Chemistry:** Knowledge of the chemical composition, structure, and properties of substances and of the chemical processes and transformations that they undergo. This includes uses of chemicals and their interactions, danger signs, production techniques, and disposal methods. **Mathematics:** Knowledge of arithmetic, algebra, geometry, calculus, and statistics and their applications. **Public Safety and Security:** Knowledge of relevant equipment, policies, procedures, and strategies to promote effective local, state, or national security operations for the protection of people, data, property, and institutions. **English Language:** Knowledge of the structure and content of the English language, including the meaning and spelling of words, rules of composition, and grammar. **Computers and Electronics:** Knowledge of circuit boards, processors, chips, electronic equipment, and computer hardware and software, including applications and programming.

Environmental Science Teachers, Postsecondary

- ▲ Education/Training Required: Master's degree
- ▲ Annual Earnings: $57,160
- ▲ Growth: 23.5%
- ▲ Annual Job Openings: 184,000
- ▲ Self-Employed: 0%
- ▲ Part-Time: 32.3%

Teach courses in environmental science. **SKILLS—**No data available.

GOE INFORMATION—Interest Area: 12. Education and Social Service. **Work Group:** 12.03. Educational Services. **Other Job Titles in This Work Group:** Adult Literacy, Remedial Education, and GED Teachers and

Instructors; Agricultural Sciences Teachers, Postsecondary; Anthropology and Archeology Teachers, Postsecondary; Architecture Teachers, Postsecondary; Archivists; Area, Ethnic, and Cultural Studies Teachers, Postsecondary; Art, Drama, and Music Teachers, Postsecondary; Atmospheric, Earth, Marine, and Space Sciences Teachers,

Postsecondary; Audio-Visual Collections Specialists; Biological Science Teachers, Postsecondary; Business Teachers, Postsecondary; Chemistry Teachers, Postsecondary; Child Care Workers; Communications Teachers, Postsecondary; Computer Science Teachers, Postsecondary; Criminal Justice and Law Enforcement Teachers, Postsecondary; Curators; Economics Teachers, Postsecondary; Education Teachers, Postsecondary; Educational Psychologists; Educational, Vocational, and School Counselors; Elementary School Teachers, Except Special Education; Engineering Teachers, Postsecondary; English Language and Literature Teachers, Postsecondary; Farm and Home Management Advisors; Foreign Language and Literature Teachers, Postsecondary; Forestry and Conservation Science Teachers, Postsecondary; Geography Teachers, Postsecondary; Graduate Teaching Assistants; Health Specialties Teachers, Postsecondary; History Teachers, Postsecondary; Home Economics Teachers, Postsecondary; Kindergarten Teachers, Except Special Education; Law Teachers, Postsecondary; Librarians; Library Assistants, Clerical; Library Science Teachers, Postsecondary; Library Technicians; Mathematical Science Teachers, Postsecondary; Middle School Teachers, Except Special and Vocational Education; Museum Technicians and Conservators; Nursing Instructors and Teachers, Postsecondary; Personal Financial Advisors; Philosophy and Religion Teachers, Postsecondary; Physics Teachers, Postsecondary; Political Science Teachers, Postsecondary; Postsecondary Teachers, All Other; Preschool Teachers, Except Special Education; Psychology Teachers, Postsecondary; others. **PERSONALITY TYPE**—No data available.

EDUCATION/TRAINING PROGRAM(S)—Environmental Science; Environmental Studies; Science Teacher Education/General Science Teacher Education. **RELATED KNOWLEDGE/COURSES**—No data available.

Environmental Scientists and Specialists, Including Health

- ▲ Education/Training Required: Bachelor's degree
- ▲ Annual Earnings: $47,330
- ▲ Growth: 22.3%
- ▲ Annual Job Openings: 4,000
- ▲ Self-Employed: 7.6%
- ▲ Part-Time: 6.6%

Conduct research or perform investigation for the purpose of identifying, abating, or eliminating sources of pollutants or hazards that affect either the environment or the health of the population. Utilizing knowledge of various scientific disciplines, may collect, synthesize, study, report, and take action based on data derived from measurements or observations of air, food, soil, water, and other sources. Plans and develops research models using knowledge of mathematical and statistical concepts. Collects, identifies, and analyzes data to assess sources of pollution, determine their effects, and establish standards. Prepares graphs or charts from data samples and advises enforcement personnel on proper standards and regulations. Determines data collection methods to be employed in research projects and surveys. **SKILLS—Active Learning:** Understanding the implications of new information for both current and future problem-solving and decision-making. **Mathematics:** Using mathematics to solve problems. **Science:** Using scientific rules and methods to solve problems. **Reading Comprehension:** Understanding written sentences and paragraphs in work-related documents.

Complex Problem Solving: Identifying complex problems and reviewing related information to develop and evaluate options and implement solutions.

GOE INFORMATION—Interest Area: 02. Science, Math, and Engineering. **Work Group:** 02.03. Life Sciences. **Other Job Titles in This Work Group:** Agricultural and Food Science Technicians; Agricultural Technicians; Animal Scientists; Biochemists; Biochemists and Biophysicists; Biological Scientists, All Other; Biologists; Biophysicists; Conservation Scientists; Epidemiologists; Food Science Technicians; Food Scientists and Technologists; Foresters; Life Scientists, All Other; Medical Scientists, Except Epidemiologists; Microbiologists; Plant Scientists; Range Managers; Soil and Plant Scientists; Soil Conservationists; Soil Scientists; Zoologists and Wildlife Biologists. **PERSONALITY TYPE**—Investigative. Investigative occupations frequently involve working with ideas and require an extensive amount of thinking. These occupations can involve searching for facts and figuring out problems mentally.

E

EDUCATION/TRAINING PROGRAM(S)—Environmental Science; Environmental Studies. **RELATED KNOWLEDGE/COURSES—Mathematics:** Knowledge of arithmetic, algebra, geometry, calculus, and statistics and their applications. **Biology:** Knowledge of plant and animal organisms and their tissues, cells, functions, interdependencies, and interactions with each other and the environment. **Chemistry:** Knowledge of the chemical composition, structure, and properties of substances and of the chemical processes and transformations that they undergo. This includes uses of chemicals and their interactions, danger signs, production techniques, and disposal methods. **English Language:** Knowledge of the structure and content of the English language, including the meaning and spelling of words, rules of composition, and grammar. **Physics:** Knowledge and prediction of physical principles and laws and their interrelationships and applications to understanding fluid, material, and atmospheric dynamics and mechanical, electrical, atomic, and subatomic structures and processes.

Epidemiologists

▲ Education/Training Required: Doctoral degree
▲ Annual Earnings: $52,710
▲ Growth: 26.5%
▲ Annual Job Openings: 2,000
▲ Self-Employed: 2.8%
▲ Part-Time: 6.6%

Investigate and describe the determinants and distribution of disease, disability, and other health outcomes and develop the means for prevention and control. Plans and directs studies to investigate human or animal disease, preventive methods, and treatments for disease. Studies effects of drugs, gases, pesticides, parasites, or microorganisms or health and physiological processes of animals and humans. Plans methodological design of research study and arranges for data collection. Consults with and advises physicians, educators, researchers, and others regarding medical applications of sciences such as physics, biology, and chemistry. Confers with health department, industry personnel, physicians, and others to develop health safety standards and programs to improve public health. Teaches principles of medicine and medical and laboratory procedures to physicians, residents, students, and technicians. Supervises activities of clerical and statistical or laboratory personnel. Standardizes drug dosages, methods of immunization, and procedures for manufacture of drugs and medicinal compounds. Prepares and analyzes samples for toxicity, bacteria, or microorganisms or to study cell structure and properties. Examines organs, tissues, cell structures, or microorganisms by systematic observation or using microscope. Conducts research to develop methodologies; instrumentation; or identification, diagnosing, and treatment procedures for medical application. Investigates cause, progress, life cycle, or mode of transmission of diseases or parasites. Analyzes data, applying statistical techniques and scientific knowledge; prepares reports; and presents findings. **SKILLS—** **Instructing:** Teaching others how to do something. **Active Learning:** Understanding the implications of new information for both current and future problem-solving and decision-making. **Reading Comprehension:** Understanding written sentences and paragraphs in work-related documents. **Writing:** Communicating effectively in writing as appropriate for the needs of the audience. **Science:** Using scientific rules and methods to solve problems.

GOE INFORMATION—Interest Area: 02. Science, Math, and Engineering. **Work Group:** 02.03. Life Sciences. **Other Job Titles in This Work Group:** Agricultural and Food Science Technicians; Agricultural Technicians; Animal Scientists; Biochemists; Biochemists and Biophysicists; Biological Scientists, All Other; Biologists; Biophysicists; Conservation Scientists; Environmental Scientists and Specialists, Including Health; Food Science Technicians; Food Scientists and Technologists; Foresters; Life Scientists, All Other; Medical Scientists, Except Epidemiologists; Microbiologists; Plant Scientists; Range Managers; Soil and Plant Scientists; Soil Conservationists; Soil Scientists; Zoologists and Wildlife Biologists. **PERSONALITY TYPE—**Investigative. Investigative occupations frequently involve working with ideas and require an extensive amount of thinking. These occupations can involve searching for facts and figuring out problems mentally.

EDUCATION/TRAINING PROGRAM(S)—Cell/Cellular Biology and Histology; Epidemiology; Medical Scientist (MS, PhD). **RELATED KNOWLEDGE/ COURSES—Mathematics:** Knowledge of arithmetic, algebra, geometry, calculus, and statistics and their applications. **Biology:** Knowledge of plant and animal organisms and their tissues, cells, functions, interdependencies, and interactions with each other and the environment. **Chemistry:** Knowledge of the chemical composition, structure, and properties of substances and of the chemical processes and transformations that they undergo. This includes uses of chemicals and their interactions, danger signs, production techniques, and disposal methods. **Computers and Electronics:** Knowledge of circuit boards, processors, chips, electronic equipment, and computer hardware and software, including applications and programming. **Medicine and Dentistry:** Knowledge of the information and techniques needed to diagnose and treat human injuries, diseases, and deformities. This includes symptoms, treatment alternatives, drug properties and interactions, and preventive health-care measures. **English Language:** Knowledge of the structure and content of the English language, including the meaning and spelling of words, rules of composition, and grammar.

Executive Secretaries and Administrative Assistants

- ▲ Education/Training Required: Moderate-term on-the-job training
- ▲ Annual Earnings: $32,380
- ▲ Growth: 11.5%
- ▲ Annual Job Openings: 185,000
- ▲ Self-Employed: 5.4%
- ▲ Part-Time: 7.7%

Provide high-level administrative support by conducting research, preparing statistical reports, handling information requests, and performing clerical functions such as preparing correspondence, receiving visitors, arranging conference calls, and scheduling meetings. May also train and supervise lower-level clerical staff. Coordinates and directs office services, such as records and budget preparation, personnel, and housekeeping, to aid executives. Prepares records and reports, such as recommendations for solutions of administrative problems and annual reports. Files and retrieves corporation documents, records, and reports. Analyzes operating practices and procedures to create new or revise existing methods. Studies management methods to improve workflow, simplify reporting procedures, or implement cost reductions. Reads and answers correspondence. Plans conferences. Interprets administrative and operating policies and procedures for employees. **SKILLS—Reading Comprehension:** Understanding written sentences and paragraphs in work-related documents. **Coordination:** Adjusting actions in relation to others' actions. **Writing:** Communicating effectively in writing as appropriate for the needs of the audience. **Active Listening:** Giving full attention to what other people are saying, taking time to understand the points being made, asking questions as appropriate, and not interrupting at inappropriate times. **Speaking:** Talking to others to convey information effectively. **Mathematics:** Using mathematics to solve problems. **Monitoring:** Monitoring/Assessing your performance or that of other individuals or organizations to make improvements or take corrective action.

GOE INFORMATION—Interest Area: 09. Business Detail. **Work Group:** 09.02. Administrative Detail. **Other Job Titles in This Work Group:** Claims Takers, Unemployment Benefits; Court Clerks; Court, Municipal, and License Clerks; Eligibility Interviewers, Government Programs; Interviewers, Except Eligibility and Loan; Legal Secretaries; License Clerks; Loan Interviewers and Clerks; Medical Secretaries; Municipal Clerks; Secretaries, Except Legal, Medical, and Executive; Welfare Eligibility Workers and Interviewers. **PERSONALITY TYPE—**Conventional. Conventional occupations frequently involve following set procedures and routines. These occupations can include working with data and details more than with ideas. Usually there is a clear line of authority to follow.

EDUCATION/TRAINING PROGRAM(S)—Administrative Assistant and Secretarial Science, General; Executive Assistant/Executive Secretary; Medical Administrative/Executive Assistant and Medical Secretary. **RELATED KNOWLEDGE/COURSES—Clerical Studies:** Knowledge of administrative and clerical procedures and systems, such as word processing, managing files and records, stenography and transcription, designing forms, and other office procedures and terminology. **Administration and Management:** Knowledge of business and management principles involved in strategic planning, resource allocation, human resources modeling, leadership technique, production methods, and coordination of people and resources. **Computers and Electronics:** Knowledge of circuit boards, processors, chips, electronic equipment, and computer hardware and software, including applications and programming. **English Language:** Knowledge of the structure and content of the English language, including the meaning and spelling of words, rules of composition, and grammar. **Mathematics:** Knowledge of arithmetic, algebra, geometry, calculus, and statistics and their applications. **Economics and Accounting:** Knowledge of economic and accounting principles and practices, the financial markets, banking, and the analysis and reporting of financial data.

Exhibit Designers

- ▲ Education/Training Required: Bachelor's degree
- ▲ Annual Earnings: $33,460
- ▲ Growth: 27.0%
- ▲ Annual Job Openings: 2,000
- ▲ Self-Employed: 31.9%
- ▲ Part-Time: 20.0%

Plan, design, and oversee construction and installation of permanent and temporary exhibits and displays. Prepares preliminary drawings of proposed exhibit, including detailed construction, layout, material specifications, or special-effects diagrams. Arranges for acquisition of specimens or graphics or building of exhibit structures by outside contractors to complete exhibit. Inspects installed exhibit for conformance to specifications and satisfactory operation of special effects components. Submits plans for approval and adapts plan to serve intended purpose or to conform to budget or fabrication restrictions. Designs, draws, paints, or sketches backgrounds and fixtures for use in windows or interior displays. Oversees preparation of artwork, construction of exhibit components, and placement of collection to ensure intended interpretation of concepts and conformance to specifications. Confers with client or staff regarding theme, interpretive or informational purpose, planned location, budget, materials, or promotion. Designs display to decorate streets, fairgrounds, building, or other places for celebrations, using paper, cloth, plastic, or other materials. **SKILLS—Writing:** Communicating effectively in writing as appropriate for the needs of the audience. **Coordination:** Adjusting actions in relation to others' actions. **Time Management:** Managing one's own time and the time of others. **Reading Comprehension:** Understanding written sentences and paragraphs in work-related documents. **Management of Material Resources:** Obtaining and seeing to the appropriate use of equipment, facilities, and materials needed to do certain work. **Mathematics:** Using mathematics to solve problems. **Active Learning:** Understanding the implications of new information for both current and future problem-solving and decision-making.

GOE INFORMATION—Interest Area: 01. Arts, Entertainment, and Media. **Work Group:** 01.04. Visual Arts. **Other Job Titles in This Work Group:** Cartoonists; Commercial and Industrial Designers; Designers, All Other; Fashion Designers; Fine Artists, Including Painters, Sculptors, and Illustrators; Floral Designers; Graphic Designers; Interior Designers; Merchandise Displayers and Window Trimmers; Multi-Media Artists and Animators; Painters and Illustrators; Sculptors; Set and Exhibit Designers; Set Designers; Sketch Artists. **PERSONALITY TYPE—Artistic.** Artistic occupations frequently involve working with forms, designs, and patterns. They often require self-expression, and the work can be done without following a clear set of rules.

EDUCATION/TRAINING PROGRAM(S)—Design and Applied Arts, Other; Design and Visual Communications, General; Illustration; Technical Theatre/Theatre Design and Technology. **RELATED KNOWLEDGE/ COURSES—Design:** Knowledge of design techniques, tools, and principles involved in production of precision technical plans, blueprints, drawings, and models. **Fine Arts:** Knowledge of the theory and techniques required to compose, produce, and perform works of music, dance, visual arts, drama, and sculpture. **Building and Construction:** Knowledge of materials, methods, and tools involved in the construction or repair of houses, buildings, or other structures, such as highways and roads. **Psychology:** Knowledge of human behavior and performance; individual differences in ability, personality, and interests; learning and motivation; psychological research methods; and the assessment and treatment of behavioral and affective disorders. **Mathematics:** Knowledge of arithmetic, algebra, geometry, calculus, and statistics and their applications. **Principles of Mechanical Devices:** Knowledge of machines and tools, including their designs, uses, repair, and maintenance. **English Language:** Knowledge of the structure and content of the English language, including the meaning and spelling of words, rules of composition, and grammar.

Extruding and Drawing Machine Setters, Operators, and Tenders, Metal and Plastic

- ▲ Education/Training Required: Moderate-term on-the-job training
- ▲ Annual Earnings: $25,170
- ▲ Growth: 13.5%
- ▲ Annual Job Openings: 23,000
- ▲ Self-Employed: 0.5%
- ▲ Part-Time: 2.7%

Set up, operate, or tend machines to extrude or draw thermoplastic or metal materials into tubes, rods, hoses, wire, bars, or structural shapes. Installs dies, machine screws, and sizing rings on machine extruding thermoplastic or metal materials. Starts machine and sets controls to regulate vacuum, air pressure, sizing rings, and temperature and synchronizes speed of extrusion. Loads machine hopper with mixed materials, using auger, or stuffs rolls of plastic dough into machine cylinders. Operates shearing mechanism to cut rods to specified length. Studies specifications, determines setup procedures, and selects machine dies and parts. Adjusts controls to draw or press metal into specified shape and diameter. Selects nozzles, spacers, and wire guides, according to diameter and length of rod. Weighs and mixes pelletized, granular, or powdered thermoplastic materials and coloring pigments. Reels extruded product into rolls of specified length and weight. Tests physical properties of product with testing devices such as acid-bath tester, burst tester, and impact tester. Measures extruded articles for conformance to specifications and adjusts controls to obtain product of specified dimensions. Examines extruded product for defects, such as wrinkles, bubbles, and splits. Replaces worn dies when products vary from specifications. **SKILLS—Quality Control Analysis:** Conducting tests and inspections of products, services, or processes to evaluate quality or performance. **Operation and Control:** Controlling operations of equipment or systems. **Operation Monitoring:** Watching gauges, dials, or other indicators to make sure a machine is working properly. **Equipment Maintenance:** Performing routine maintenance on equipment and determining when and what kind of maintenance is needed. **Equipment Selection:** Determining the kind of tools and equipment needed to do a job.

GOE INFORMATION—Interest Area: 08. Industrial Production. **Work Group:** 08.02. Production Technology.

Other Job Titles in This Work Group: Aircraft Rigging Assemblers; Aircraft Structure Assemblers, Precision; Aircraft Structure, Surfaces, Rigging, and Systems Assemblers; Aircraft Systems Assemblers, Precision; Bench Workers, Jewelry; Bindery Machine Setters and Set-Up Operators; Bindery Workers; Bookbinders; Buffing and Polishing Set-Up Operators; Casting Machine Set-Up Operators; Coating, Painting, and Spraying Machine Setters and Set-Up Operators; Coating, Painting, and Spraying Machine Setters, Operators, and Tenders; Combination Machine Tool Setters and Set-Up Operators, Metal and Plastic; Cutting, Punching, and Press Machine Setters, Operators, and Tenders, Metal and Plastic; Dental Laboratory Technicians; Drilling and Boring Machine Tool Setters, Operators, and Tenders, Metal and Plastic; Electrical and Electronic Equipment Assemblers; Electrical and Electronic Inspectors and Testers; Electromechanical Equipment Assemblers; Engine and Other Machine Assemblers; Extruding, Forming, Pressing, and Compacting Machine Setters and Set-Up Operators; Extruding, Forming, Pressing, and Compacting Machine Setters, Operators, and Tenders; Forging Machine Setters, Operators, and Tenders, Metal and Plastic; Foundry Mold and Coremakers; Gem and Diamond Workers; Grinding, Honing, Lapping, and Deburring Machine Set-Up Operators; Grinding, Lapping, Polishing, and Buffing Machine Tool Setters, Operators, and Tenders, Metal and Plastic; Heat Treating Equipment Setters, Operators, and Tenders, Metal and Plastic; Heat Treating, Annealing, and Tempering Machine Operators and Tenders, Metal and Plastic; Heating Equipment Setters and Set-Up Operators, Metal and Plastic; Inspectors, Testers, Sorters, Samplers, and Weighers; Jewelers; Jewelers and Precious Stone and Metal Workers; Lathe and Turning Machine Tool Setters, Operators, and Tenders, Metal and Plastic; Log Graders and Scalers; Materials Inspectors; Mechanical Inspectors; Metal Molding, Coremaking, and Casting Machine

Operators and Tenders; others. **PERSONALITY TYPE—** Realistic. Realistic occupations frequently involve work activities that include practical, hands-on problems and solutions. They often deal with plants, animals, and real-world materials like wood, tools, and machinery. Many of the occupations require working outside and do not involve a lot of paperwork or working closely with others.

EDUCATION/TRAINING PROGRAM(S)—Machine Tool Technology/Machinist. **RELATED KNOWLEDGE/ COURSES—Production and Processing:** Knowledge of raw materials, production processes, quality control, costs, and other techniques for maximizing the effective manufacture and distribution of goods. **Principles of Mechanical Devices:** Knowledge of machines and tools, including their designs, uses, repair, and maintenance. **Engineering and Technology:** Knowledge of the practical application of engineering science and technology. This includes applying principles, techniques, procedures, and equipment to the design and production of various goods and services. **Mathematics:** Knowledge of arithmetic, algebra, geometry, calculus, and statistics and their applications.

Family and General Practitioners

- ▲ Education/Training Required: First professional degree
- ▲ Annual Earnings: $118,390
- ▲ Growth: 17.9%
- ▲ Annual Job Openings: 27,000
- ▲ Self-Employed: 20.4%
- ▲ Part-Time: 7.2%

Diagnose, treat, and help prevent diseases and injuries that commonly occur in the general population. Examines or conducts tests on patient to provide information on medical condition. Analyzes records, reports, test results, or examination information to diagnose medical condition of patient. Prescribes or administers treatment, therapy, medication, vaccination, and other specialized medical care to treat or prevent illness, disease, or injury. Explains procedures and discusses test results or prescribed treatments with patents. Advises patients and community concerning diet, activity, hygiene, and disease prevention. Directs and coordinates activities of nurses, students, assistants, specialists, therapists, and other medical staff. Conducts research to study anatomy and develop or test medications, treatments, or procedures to prevent or control disease or injury. Prepares reports for government or management of birth, death, and disease statistics, workforce evaluations, or medical status of individuals. Plans, implements, or administers health programs or standards in hospital, business, or community for information, prevention, or treatment of injury or illness. Refers patient to medical specialist or other practitioner when necessary. Collects, records, and maintains patient information, such as medical history, reports, and examination results. Operates on patients to remove, repair, or improve functioning of diseased or injured body parts and systems and delivers babies. **SKILLS—Reading Comprehension:** Understanding written sentences and paragraphs in work-related documents. **Active Learning:** Understanding the implications of new information for both current and future problem-solving and decision-making. **Science:** Using scientific rules and methods to solve problems. **Judgment and Decision Making:** Considering the relative costs and benefits of potential actions to choose the most appropriate one. **Critical Thinking:** Using logic and reasoning to identify the strengths and weaknesses of alternative solutions, conclusions, or approaches to problems. **Speaking:** Talking to others to convey information effectively. **Writing:** Communicating effectively in writing as appropriate for the needs of the audience.

GOE INFORMATION—Interest Area: 14. Medical and Health Services. **Work Group:** 14.02. Medicine and Surgery. **Other Job Titles in This Work Group:** Anesthesiologists; Internists, General; Medical Assistants; Obstetricians and Gynecologists; Pediatricians, General; Pharmacists; Pharmacy Aides; Pharmacy Technicians; Physician Assistants; Physicians and Surgeons, All Other; Psychiatrists; Registered Nurses; Surgeons; Surgical Technologists. **PERSONALITY TYPE—**Investigative. Investigative occupations frequently involve working with ideas and require an extensive amount of thinking. These occupations can involve searching for facts and figuring out problems mentally.

EDUCATION/TRAINING PROGRAM(S)—Family Medicine; Medicine (MD); Osteopathic Medicine/Osteopathy (DO). **RELATED KNOWLEDGE/COURSES—Medicine and Dentistry:** Knowledge of the information and techniques needed to diagnose and treat human injuries, diseases, and deformities. This includes symptoms, treatment alternatives, drug properties and interactions, and preventive health-care measures. **Biology:** Knowledge of plant and animal organisms and their tissues, cells, functions, interdependencies, and interactions with each other and the environment. **English Language:** Knowledge of the structure and content of the English language, including the meaning and spelling of words, rules of composition, and grammar. **Therapy and Counseling:** Knowledge of principles, methods, and procedures for diagnosis, treatment, and rehabilitation of physical and mental dysfunctions and for career counseling and guidance. **Administration and Management:** Knowledge of business and management principles involved in strategic planning, resource allocation, human resources modeling, leadership technique, production methods, and coordination of people and resources.

Farmers and Ranchers

▲ Education/Training Required: Long-term on-the-job training
▲ Annual Earnings: $42,170
▲ Growth: -25.4%
▲ Annual Job Openings: 146,000
▲ Self-Employed: 99.7%
▲ Part-Time: 27.7%

On an ownership or rental basis, operate farms, ranches, greenhouses, nurseries, timber tracts, or other agricultural production establishments that produce crops, horticultural specialties, livestock, poultry, finfish, shellfish, or animal specialties. May plant, cultivate, harvest, perform post-harvest activities, and market crops and livestock; may hire, train, and supervise farm workers or supervise a farm labor contractor; may prepare cost, production, and other records. May maintain and operate machinery and perform physical work. Harvests crops and collects specialty products, such as royal jelly from queen bee cells and honey from honeycombs. Sets up and operates farm machinery to till soil, plant, prune, fertilize, apply herbicides and pesticides, and haul harvested crops. Inspects growing environment to maintain optimum growing or breeding conditions. Plans harvesting, considering ripeness and maturity of crop and weather conditions. Breeds and raises stock, such as animals, poultry, honeybees, or earthworms. Arranges with buyers for sale and shipment of crops. Hires and directs workers engaged in planting, cultivating, irrigating, harvesting, and marketing crops and raising livestock. Assembles, positions, and secures structures such as trellises or beehives, using hand tools. Lubricates, adjusts, and makes minor repairs on farm equipment, using oilcan, grease gun, and hand tools. Maintains employee and financial records. Grades and packages crop for marketing. Demonstrates and explains farm work techniques and safety regulations to workers. Installs irrigation systems and irrigates fields. Grows out-of-season crops in greenhouse or early crops in cold-frame bed or buds and grafts plant stock.

Selects and purchases supplies and equipment, such as seed, tree stock, fertilizers, farm machinery, implements, livestock, and feed. Destroys diseased or superfluous crops, such as queen bee cells, bee colonies, parasites, and vermin. Determines kind and quantity of crops or livestock to be raised, according to market conditions, weather, and farm size. **SKILLS—Equipment Selection:** Determining the kind of tools and equipment needed to do a job. **Management of Financial Resources:** Determining how money will be spent to get the work done and accounting for these expenditures. **Operation and Control:** Controlling operations of equipment or systems. **Coordination:** Adjusting actions in relation to others' actions. **Critical Thinking:** Using logic and reasoning to identify the strengths and weaknesses of alternative solutions, conclusions, or approaches to problems.

GOE INFORMATION—Interest Area: 03. Plants and Animals. **Work Group:** 03.01. Managerial Work in Plants and Animals. **Other Job Titles in This Work Group:** Agricultural Crop Farm Managers; Farm Labor Contractors; First-Line Supervisors and Manager/Supervisors—Agricultural Crop Workers; First-Line Supervisors and Manager/Supervisors—Animal Care Workers, Except Livestock; First-Line Supervisors and Manager/Supervisors—Animal Husbandry Workers; First-Line Supervisors and Manager/Supervisors—Fishery Workers; First-Line Supervisors and Manager/Supervisors—Horticultural Workers; First-Line Supervisors and Manager/Supervisors—Landscaping Workers; First-Line Supervisors and Manager/Supervisors—

Logging Workers; First-Line Supervisors/Managers of Farming, Fishing, and Forestry Workers; First-Line Supervisors/Managers of Landscaping, Lawn Service, and Groundskeeping Workers; Fish Hatchery Managers; Lawn Service Managers; Nursery and Greenhouse Managers. **PERSONALITY TYPE**—Realistic. Realistic occupations frequently involve work activities that include practical, hands-on problems and solutions. They often deal with plants, animals, and real-world materials like wood, tools, and machinery. Many of the occupations require working outside and do not involve a lot of paperwork or working closely with others.

EDUCATION/TRAINING PROGRAM(S)— Agribusiness/Agricultural Business Operations; Agricultural Animal Breeding; Agricultural Business and Management, General; Agricultural Production Operations, General; Agricultural Production Operations, Other; Agronomy and Crop Science; Animal Nutrition; Animal Sciences, General; Animal/Livestock Husbandry and Production; Aquaculture; Crop Production; Dairy Husbandry and Production; Dairy Science; Farm/Farm and Ranch Management; Greenhouse Operations and Management; Horticultural Science; Livestock Management; Ornamen-

tal Horticulture; Plant Nursery Operations and Management; Plant Protection and Integrated Pest Management; Plant Sciences, General; Poultry Science; Range Science and Management. **RELATED KNOWLEDGE/ COURSES**—**Food Production:** Knowledge of techniques and equipment for planting, growing, and harvesting food products (both plant and animal) for consumption, including storage/handling techniques. **Personnel and Human Resources:** Knowledge of principles and procedures for personnel recruitment, selection, training, compensation and benefits, labor relations and negotiation, and personnel information systems. **Production and Processing:** Knowledge of raw materials, production processes, quality control, costs, and other techniques for maximizing the effective manufacture and distribution of goods. **Sales and Marketing:** Knowledge of principles and methods for showing, promoting, and selling products or services. This includes marketing strategy and tactics, product demonstration, sales techniques, and sales control systems. **Biology:** Knowledge of plant and animal organisms and their tissues, cells, functions, interdependencies, and interactions with each other and the environment.

Fashion Designers

> ▲ Education/Training Required: Bachelor's degree
> ▲ Annual Earnings: $49,530
> ▲ Growth: 20.3%
> ▲ Annual Job Openings: 2,000
> ▲ Self-Employed: 31.9%
> ▲ Part-Time: 20.0%

Design clothing and accessories. Create original garments or design garments that follow well-established fashion trends. May develop the line of color and kinds of materials. Designs custom garments for clients. Attends fashion shows and reviews garment magazines and manuals to analyze fashion trends, predictions, and consumer preferences. Sews together sections to form mockup or sample of garment or article, using sewing equipment. Directs and coordinates workers who draw and cut patterns and construct sample or finished garment. Arranges for showing of sample garments at sales meetings or fashion shows. Confers with sales and management executives or clients regarding design ideas. Examines sample garment on and off model and modifies design to achieve desired effect. Integrates findings of analysis and discussion, personal tastes, and knowledge of design to originate design ideas.

Sketches rough and detailed drawings of apparel or accessories and writes specifications, such as color scheme, construction, or material type. Draws pattern for article designed, cuts pattern, and cuts material according to pattern, using measuring and drawing instruments and scissors. **SKILLS**—**Coordination:** Adjusting actions in relation to others' actions. **Operations Analysis:** Analyzing needs and product requirements to create a design. **Persuasion:** Persuading others to change their minds or behavior. **Active Learning:** Understanding the implications of new information for both current and future problem-solving and decision-making. **Judgment and Decision Making:** Considering the relative costs and benefits of potential actions to choose the most appropriate one.

GOE INFORMATION—**Interest Area:** 01. Arts, Entertainment, and Media. **Work Group:** 01.04. Visual Arts.

Other Job Titles in This Work Group: Cartoonists; Commercial and Industrial Designers; Designers, All Other; Exhibit Designers; Fine Artists, Including Painters, Sculptors, and Illustrators; Floral Designers; Graphic Designers; Interior Designers; Merchandise Displayers and Window Trimmers; Multi-Media Artists and Animators; Painters and Illustrators; Sculptors; Set and Exhibit Designers; Set Designers; Sketch Artists. **PERSONALITY TYPE**—Artistic. Artistic occupations frequently involve working with forms, designs, and patterns. They often require self-expression, and the work can be done without following a clear set of rules.

EDUCATION/TRAINING PROGRAM(S)—Apparel and Textile Manufacture; Fashion and Fabric Consultant; Fashion/Apparel Design; Textile Science. **RELATED KNOWLEDGE/COURSES—Design:** Knowledge of design techniques, tools, and principles involved in production of precision technical plans, blueprints, drawings, and models. **Fine Arts:** Knowledge of the theory and techniques required to compose, produce, and perform works of music, dance, visual arts, drama, and sculpture. **Sales and Marketing:** Knowledge of principles and methods for showing, promoting, and selling products or services. This includes marketing strategy and tactics, product demonstration, sales techniques, and sales control systems. **Psychology:** Knowledge of human behavior and performance; individual differences in ability, personality, and interests; learning and motivation; psychological research methods; and the assessment and treatment of behavioral and affective disorders. **Sociology and Anthropology:** Knowledge of group behavior and dynamics, societal trends and influences, human migrations, ethnicity, and cultures and their history and origins. **Customer and Personal Service:** Knowledge of principles and processes for providing customer and personal services. This includes customer needs assessment, meeting quality standards for services, and evaluation of customer satisfaction.

File Clerks

- ▲ Education/Training Required: Short-term on-the-job training
- ▲ Annual Earnings: $19,490
- ▲ Growth: 9.1%
- ▲ Annual Job Openings: 49,000
- ▲ Self-Employed: 0.7%
- ▲ Part-Time: 36.1%

File correspondence, cards, invoices, receipts, and other records in alphabetical or numerical order or according to the filing system used. Locate and remove material from file when requested. Sorts or classifies information according to content; purpose; user criteria; or chronological, alphabetical, or numerical order. Locates and retrieves files upon request from authorized users. Removes or destroys outdated materials in accordance with file maintenance schedules or legal requirements. Inspects or examines materials or files for accuracy, legibility, or damage. Assigns and records or stamps identification numbers or codes to index materials for filing. Scans or reads incoming materials to determine filing order or location. Places materials into storage receptacles, such as file cabinets, boxes, bins, or drawers, according to classification and identification information. Inserts additional data on file records. Photographs or makes copies of data and records, using photocopying or microfilming equipment. Authorizes or documents materials movement, using logbook or computer, and traces missing files. **SKILLS**—Reading Comprehension: Understanding written sentences and paragraphs in work-related documents. **Writing:** Communicating effectively in writing as appropriate for the needs of the audience.

GOE INFORMATION—Interest Area: 09. Business Detail. **Work Group:** 09.07. Records Processing. **Other Job Titles in This Work Group:** Correspondence Clerks; Court Reporters; Credit Authorizers; Credit Authorizers, Checkers, and Clerks; Credit Checkers; Human Resources Assistants, Except Payroll and Timekeeping; Information and Record Clerks, All Other; Insurance Claims and Policy Processing Clerks; Insurance Claims Clerks; Insurance Policy Processing Clerks; Medical Records and Health Information Technicians; Medical Transcriptionists; Office Clerks, General; Procurement Clerks; Proofreaders and Copy Markers. **PERSONALITY TYPE**—Conventional. Conventional occupations frequently involve following set procedures and routines. These occupations can include working with data and details more than with ideas. Usually there is a clear line of authority to follow.

EDUCATION/TRAINING PROGRAM(S)—General Office Occupations and Clerical Services. **RELATED KNOWLEDGE/COURSES—Clerical Studies:** Knowledge of administrative and clerical procedures and systems, such as word processing, managing files and records, stenography and transcription, designing forms, and other office procedures and terminology. **Computers and Electronics:** Knowledge of circuit boards, processors, chips, electronic equipment, and computer hardware and software, including applications and programming. **English Language:** Knowledge of the structure and content of the English language, including the meaning and spelling of words, rules of composition, and grammar.

Film and Video Editors

- ▲ Education/Training Required: Bachelor's degree
- ▲ Annual Earnings: $36,910
- ▲ Growth: 25.8%
- ▲ Annual Job Openings: 2,000
- ▲ Self-Employed: 23.7%
- ▲ Part-Time: 25.3%

Edit motion picture soundtracks, film, and video. Edits film and video tape to insert music, dialogue, and sound effects and to correct errors, using editing equipment. Reviews assembled film or edited video tape on screen or monitor and makes corrections. Trims film segments to specified lengths and reassembles segments in sequence that presents story with maximum effect. Evaluates and selects scenes in terms of dramatic and entertainment value and story continuity. Supervises and coordinates activities of workers engaged in editing and assembling filmed scenes photographed by others. Studies script and confers with producers and directors concerning layout or editing to increase dramatic or entertainment value of production. **SKILLS—Monitoring:** Monitoring/Assessing your performance or that of other individuals or organizations to make improvements or take corrective action. **Critical Thinking:** Using logic and reasoning to identify the strengths and weaknesses of alternative solutions, conclusions, or approaches to problems. **Reading Comprehension:** Understanding written sentences and paragraphs in work-related documents. **Active Listening:** Giving full attention to what other people are saying, taking time to understand the points being made, asking questions as appropriate, and not interrupting at inappropriate times. **Coordination:** Adjusting actions in relation to others' actions. **Active Learning:** Understanding the implications of new information for both current and future problem-solving and decision-making.

GOE INFORMATION—Interest Area: 01. Arts, Entertainment, and Media. **Work Group:** 01.08. Media Technology. **Other Job Titles in This Work Group:** Audio and Video Equipment Technicians; Broadcast Technicians; Camera Operators, Television, Video, and Motion Picture; Media and Communication Equipment Workers, All Other; Photographers; Professional Photographers; Radio Operators; Sound Engineering Technicians. **PERSONALITY TYPE—Artistic.** Artistic occupations frequently involve working with forms, designs, and patterns. They often require self-expression, and the work can be done without following a clear set of rules.

EDUCATION/TRAINING PROGRAM(S)—Audiovisual Communications Technologies/Technicians, Other; Cinematography and Film/Video Production; Communications Technology/Technician; Photojournalism; Radio and Television; Radio and Television Broadcasting Technology/Technician. **RELATED KNOWLEDGE/COURSES—Communications and Media:** Knowledge of media production, communication, and dissemination techniques and methods. This includes alternative ways to inform and entertain via written, oral, and visual media. **Fine Arts:** Knowledge of the theory and techniques required to compose, produce, and perform works of music, dance, visual arts, drama, and sculpture. **Computers and Electronics:** Knowledge of circuit boards, processors, chips, electronic equipment, and computer hardware and software, including applications and programming. **English Language:** Knowledge of the structure and content of the English language, including the meaning and spelling of words, rules of composition, and grammar. **Telecommunications:** Knowledge of transmission, broadcasting, switching, control, and operation of telecommunications systems.

Financial Analysts

- ▲ Education/Training Required: Bachelor's degree
- ▲ Annual Earnings: $55,120
- ▲ Growth: 25.5%
- ▲ Annual Job Openings: 20,000
- ▲ Self-Employed: 0%
- ▲ Part-Time: 5.2%

Conduct quantitative analyses of information affecting investment programs of public or private institutions. Analyzes financial information to forecast business, industry, and economic conditions for use in making investment decisions. Interprets data concerning price, yield, stability, and future trends in investment risks and economic influences pertinent to investments. Gathers information such as industry, regulatory, and economic information, company financial statements, financial periodicals, and newspapers. Calls brokers and purchases investments for company according to company policy. Draws charts and graphs to illustrate reports, using computer. Recommends investment timing and buy-and-sell orders to company or to staff of investment establishment. **SKILLS—Judgment and Decision Making:** Considering the relative costs and benefits of potential actions to choose the most appropriate one. **Reading Comprehension:** Understanding written sentences and paragraphs in work-related documents. **Critical Thinking:** Using logic and reasoning to identify the strengths and weaknesses of alternative solutions, conclusions, or approaches to problems. **Active Learning:** Understanding the implications of new information for both current and future problem-solving and decision-making. **Mathematics:** Using mathematics to solve problems.

GOE INFORMATION—Interest Area: 13. General Management and Support. **Work Group:** 13.02. Management Support. **Other Job Titles in This Work Group:** Accountants; Accountants and Auditors; Appraisers and Assessors of Real Estate; Appraisers, Real Estate; Assessors; Auditors; Budget Analysts; Claims Adjusters, Examiners, and Investigators; Claims Examiners, Property and Casualty Insurance; Compensation, Benefits, and Job Analysis Specialists; Cost Estimators; Credit Analysts; Employment Interviewers, Private or Public Employment Service; Employment, Recruitment, and Placement Specialists; Human Resources, Training, and Labor Relations Specialists, All Other; Insurance Adjusters, Examiners, and Investigators; Insurance Appraisers, Auto Damage; Insurance Underwriters; Loan Counselors; Loan Officers; Logisticians; Management Analysts; Market Research Analysts; Personnel Recruiters; Purchasing Agents and Buyers, Farm Products; Purchasing Agents, Except Wholesale, Retail, and Farm Products; Tax Examiners, Collectors, and Revenue Agents; Training and Development Specialists; Wholesale and Retail Buyers, Except Farm Products. **PERSONALITY TYPE**—Investigative. Investigative occupations frequently involve working with ideas and require an extensive amount of thinking. These occupations can involve searching for facts and figuring out problems mentally.

EDUCATION/TRAINING PROGRAM(S)—Accounting and Business/Management; Accounting and Finance; Finance, General. **RELATED KNOWLEDGE/COURSES—Economics and Accounting:** Knowledge of economic and accounting principles and practices, the financial markets, banking, and the analysis and reporting of financial data. **Mathematics:** Knowledge of arithmetic, algebra, geometry, calculus, and statistics and their applications. **Computers and Electronics:** Knowledge of circuit boards, processors, chips, electronic equipment, and computer hardware and software, including applications and programming. **English Language:** Knowledge of the structure and content of the English language, including the meaning and spelling of words, rules of composition, and grammar. **Law and Government:** Knowledge of laws, legal codes, court procedures, precedents, government regulations, executive orders, agency rules, and the democratic political process.

Financial Managers

▲ Education/Training Required: Work experience plus degree
▲ Annual Earnings: $70,210
▲ Growth: 18.5%
▲ Annual Job Openings: 53,000
▲ Self-Employed: 1.4%
▲ Part-Time: 2.6%

Plan, direct, and coordinate accounting, investing, banking, insurance, securities, and other financial activities of a branch, office, or department of an establishment. **SKILLS**—No data available.

GOE INFORMATION—Interest Area: 13. General Management and Support. **Work Group:** 13.01. General Management Work and Management of Support Functions. **Other Job Titles in This Work Group:** Chief Executives; Compensation and Benefits Managers; Farm, Ranch, and Other Agricultural Managers; Financial Managers, Branch or Department; Funeral Directors; General and Operations Managers; Government Service Executives; Human Resources Managers; Human Resources Managers, All Other; Legislators; Managers, All Other; Postmasters and Mail Superintendents; Private Sector Executives; Property, Real Estate, and Community Association Managers; Public Relations Managers; Purchasing Managers; Storage and Distribution Managers; Training and Development Managers; Transportation, Storage, and Distribution Managers; Treasurers, Controllers, and Chief Financial Officers. **PERSONALITY TYPE**—No data available.

EDUCATION/TRAINING PROGRAM(S)—Accounting and Business/Management; Accounting and Finance; Credit Management; Finance and Financial Management Services, Other; Finance, General; International Finance; Public Finance. **RELATED KNOWLEDGE/COURSES**—No data available.

Financial Managers, Branch or Department

▲ Education/Training Required: Work experience plus degree
▲ Annual Earnings: $70,210
▲ Growth: 18.5%
▲ Annual Job Openings: 53,000
▲ Self-Employed: 1.4%
▲ Part-Time: 2.6%

Direct and coordinate financial activities of workers in a branch, office, or department of an establishment, such as branch bank, brokerage firm, risk and insurance department, or credit department. Directs and coordinates activities of workers engaged in conducting credit investigations and collecting delinquent accounts of customers. Directs and coordinates activities to implement institution policies, procedures, and practices concerning granting or extending lines of credit and loans. Prepares financial and regulatory reports required by law, regulations, and board of directors. Selects appropriate technique to minimize loss, such as avoidance and loss prevention and reduction. Directs floor operations of brokerage firm engaged in buying and selling securities at exchange. Evaluates effectiveness of current collection policies and procedures.

Evaluates data pertaining to costs to plan budget. Monitors order flow and transactions that brokerage firm executes on floor of exchange. Submits delinquent accounts to attorney or outside agency for collection. Examines, evaluates, and processes loan applications. Establishes credit limitations on customer account. Reviews reports of securities transactions and price lists to analyze market conditions. Reviews collection reports to ascertain status of collections and balances outstanding. Directs insurance negotiations, selects insurance brokers and carriers, and places insurance. Establishes procedures for custody and control of assets, records, loan collateral, and securities to ensure safekeeping. Prepares operational and risk reports for management analysis. Analyzes and classifies risks as to frequency and financial impact of risk on company.

Plans, directs, and coordinates risk and insurance programs of establishment to control risks and losses. Manages branch or office of financial institution. **SKILLS—Writing:** Communicating effectively in writing as appropriate for the needs of the audience. **Monitoring:** Monitoring/Assessing your performance or that of other individuals or organizations to make improvements or take corrective action. **Management of Financial Resources:** Determining how money will be spent to get the work done and accounting for these expenditures. **Critical Thinking:** Using logic and reasoning to identify the strengths and weaknesses of alternative solutions, conclusions, or approaches to problems. **Judgment and Decision Making:** Considering the relative costs and benefits of potential actions to choose the most appropriate one.

GOE INFORMATION—Interest Area: 13. General Management and Support. **Work Group:** 13.01. General Management Work and Management of Support Functions. **Other Job Titles in This Work Group:** Chief Executives; Compensation and Benefits Managers; Farm, Ranch, and Other Agricultural Managers; Financial Managers; Funeral Directors; General and Operations Managers; Government Service Executives; Human Resources Managers; Human Resources Managers, All Other; Legislators; Managers, All Other; Postmasters and Mail Superintendents; Private Sector Executives; Property, Real Estate, and Community Association Managers; Public Relations Managers; Purchasing Managers; Storage and Distribution Managers; Training and Development Managers; Transportation, Storage, and Distribution Managers; Treasurers, Controllers, and Chief Financial Officers. **PERSONALITY TYPE—**Enterprising. Enterprising occupations frequently involve starting up and carrying out projects. These occupations can involve leading people and making many decisions. They sometimes require risk taking and often deal with business.

EDUCATION/TRAINING PROGRAM(S)—Accounting and Business/Management; Accounting and Finance; Credit Management; Finance and Financial Management Services, Other; Finance, General; International Finance; Public Finance. **RELATED KNOWLEDGE/COURSES—Economics and Accounting:** Knowledge of economic and accounting principles and practices, the financial markets, banking, and the analysis and reporting of financial data. **Administration and Management:** Knowledge of business and management principles involved in strategic planning, resource allocation, human resources modeling, leadership technique, production methods, and coordination of people and resources. **Mathematics:** Knowledge of arithmetic, algebra, geometry, calculus, and statistics and their applications. **English Language:** Knowledge of the structure and content of the English language, including the meaning and spelling of words, rules of composition, and grammar. **Law and Government:** Knowledge of laws, legal codes, court procedures, precedents, government regulations, executive orders, agency rules, and the democratic political process.

First-Line Supervisors and Manager/Supervisors— Agricultural Crop Workers

- ▲ Education/Training Required: Associate's degree
- ▲ Annual Earnings: $33,330
- ▲ Growth: 13.0%
- ▲ Annual Job Openings: 8,000
- ▲ Self-Employed: 10.6%
- ▲ Part-Time: 25.6%

Directly supervise and coordinate activities of agricultural crop workers. Manager/Supervisors are generally found in smaller establishments, where they perform both supervisory and management functions, such as accounting, marketing, and personnel work and may also engage in the same agricultural work as the workers they supervise. Assigns duties, such as tilling soil, planting, irrigating, storing crops, and maintaining machines, and assigns fields or rows to workers. Determines number and kind of workers needed to perform required work and schedules activities. Observes workers to detect inefficient and unsafe work procedures or identify problems and initiates actions to correct improper procedure or solve problem. Issues farm implements and machinery, ladders, or containers to workers and collects them at end of workday. Investigates grievances and settles disputes to maintain harmony among workers. Opens gate to permit entry of water into ditches or pipes and signals worker to start flow of water to irrigate fields. Drives and operates farm machinery, such as trucks, tractors, or self-propelled harvesters, to transport workers or cultivate and harvest fields. Requisitions and purchases farm supplies, such as insecticides, machine parts or lubricants, and tools. Confers with manager to evaluate weather and soil conditions and to develop and revise plans and procedures. Prepares time, payroll, and production reports, such as farm conditions, amount of yield, machinery breakdowns, and labor problems. Directs or assists in adjustment, repair, and maintenance of farm machinery and equipment. Trains workers in methods of field work and safety regulations and briefs them on identifying characteristics of insects and diseases. Contracts with seasonal workers and farmers to provide employment and arranges for transportation, equipment, and living quarters. Recruits, hires, and discharges workers. Inspects crops and fields to determine maturity, yield, infestation, or work requirements, such as cultivating, spraying, weeding, or harvesting. **SKILLS—Coordination:** Adjusting actions in relation to others' actions. **Management of Personnel Resources:** Motivating, developing, and directing people as they work, identifying the best people for the job. **Speaking:** Talking to others to convey information effectively. **Time Management:** Managing one's own time and the time of others. **Management of Material Resources:** Obtaining and seeing to the appropriate use of equipment, facilities, and materials needed to do certain work. **Equipment Selection:** Determining the kind of tools and equipment needed to do a job. **Instructing:** Teaching others how to do something.

GOE INFORMATION—Interest Area: 03. Plants and Animals. **Work Group:** 03.01. Managerial Work in Plants and Animals. **Other Job Titles in This Work Group:** Agricultural Crop Farm Managers; Farm Labor Contractors; Farmers and Ranchers; First-Line Supervisors and Manager/Supervisors—Agricultural Crop Workers; First-Line Supervisors and Manager/Supervisors—Animal Husbandry Workers; First-Line Supervisors and Manager/Supervisors—Fishery Workers; First-Line Supervisors and Manager/Supervisors—Horticultural Workers; First-Line Supervisors and Manager/Supervisors—Landscaping Workers; First-Line Supervisors and Manager/Supervisors—Logging Workers; First-Line Supervisors/Managers of Farming, Fishing, and Forestry Workers; First-Line Supervisors/Managers of Landscaping, Lawn Service, and Groundskeeping Workers; Fish Hatchery Managers; Lawn Service Managers; Nursery and Greenhouse Managers. **PERSONALITY TYPE—**Enterprising. Enterprising occupations frequently involve starting up and carrying out projects. These occupations can involve leading people and making many decisions. They sometimes require risk taking and often deal with business.

EDUCATION/TRAINING PROGRAM(S)—Agricultural Business and Management, Other; Agricultural Production Operations, General; Agricultural Production Operations, Other; Agriculture, Agriculture Operations, and Related Sciences, Other; Agronomy and Crop Science; Aquaculture; Crop Production; Farm/Farm and Ranch Management; Fishing and Fisheries Sciences and Management; Plant Sciences, General; Range Science and Management. **RELATED KNOWLEDGE/ COURSES—Food Production:** Knowledge of techniques and equipment for planting, growing, and harvesting food products (both plant and animal) for consumption, including storage/handling techniques. **Administration and Management:** Knowledge of business and management principles involved in strategic planning, resource allocation, human resources modeling, leadership technique, production methods, and coordination of people and resources. **Personnel and Human Resources:** Knowledge of principles and procedures for personnel recruitment, selection, training, compensation and benefits, labor relations and negotiation, and personnel information systems. **Biology:** Knowledge of plant and animal organisms and their tissues, cells, functions, interdependencies, and interactions with each other and the environment. **Principles of Mechanical Devices:** Knowledge of machines and tools, including their designs, uses, repair, and maintenance. **English Language:** Knowledge of the structure and content of the English language, including the meaning and spelling of words, rules of composition, and grammar.

First-Line Supervisors and Manager/Supervisors— Construction Trades Workers

- ▲ Education/Training Required: Work experience in a related occupation
- ▲ Annual Earnings: $46,570
- ▲ Growth: 16.5%
- ▲ Annual Job Openings: 43,000
- ▲ Self-Employed: 10.4%
- ▲ Part-Time: 2.3%

Directly supervise and coordinate activities of construction trades workers and their helpers. Manager/Supervisors are generally found in smaller establishments, where they perform both supervisory and management functions, such as accounting, marketing, and personnel work, and may also engage in the same construction trades work as the workers they supervise. Supervises and coordinates activities of construction trades workers. Directs and leads workers engaged in construction activities. Assigns work to employees, using material and worker requirements data. Confers with staff and worker to ensure production and personnel problems are resolved. Suggests and initiates personnel actions, such as promotions, transfers, and hires. Analyzes and resolves worker problems and recommends motivational plans. Examines and inspects work progress, equipment, and construction sites to verify safety and ensure that specifications are met. Estimates material and worker requirements to complete job. Reads specifications, such as blueprints and data, to determine construction requirements. Analyzes and plans installation and construction of equipment and structures. Locates, measures, and marks location and placement of structures and equipment. Records information, such as personnel, production, and operational data, on specified forms and reports. Trains workers in construction methods and operation of equipment. Recommends measures to improve production methods and equipment performance to increase efficiency and safety. Assists workers engaged in construction activities, using hand tools and equipment. **SKILLS—Management of Personnel Resources:** Motivating, developing, and directing people as they work, identifying the best people for the job. **Coordination:** Adjusting actions in relation to others' actions. **Time Management:** Managing one's own time and the time of others. **Equipment Selection:** Determining the kind of tools and equipment needed to do a job. **Instructing:** Teaching others how to do something.

GOE INFORMATION—Interest Area: 06. Construction, Mining, and Drilling. **Work Group:** 06.01. Managerial Work in Construction, Mining, and Drilling. **Other**

Job Titles in This Work Group: Construction Managers; First-Line Supervisors and Manager/Supervisors—Extractive Workers; First-Line Supervisors/Managers of Construction Trades and Extraction Workers. **PERSONALITY TYPE**—Enterprising. Enterprising occupations frequently involve starting up and carrying out projects. These occupations can involve leading people and making many decisions. They sometimes require risk taking and often deal with business.

EDUCATION/TRAINING PROGRAM(S)—Building/Construction Finishing, Management, and Inspection, Other; Building/Construction Site Management/Manager; Building/Home/Construction Inspection/Inspector; Building/Property Maintenance and Management; Carpentry/Carpenter; Concrete Finishing/Concrete Finisher; Construction Trades, Other; Drywall Installation/Drywaller; Electrical and Power Transmission Installation/Installer, General; Electrical and Power Transmission Installers, Other; Electrician; Glazier; Lineworker; Mason/Masonry; Painting/Painter and Wall Coverer; Plumbing Technology/Plumber; Roofer; Well Drilling/Driller. **RELATED KNOWLEDGE/COURSES—Building and Construction:** Knowledge of materials, methods, and tools involved in the construction or repair of houses, buildings, or other structures, such as highways and roads. **Administration and Management:** Knowledge of business and management principles involved in strategic planning, resource allocation, human resources modeling, leadership technique, production methods, and coordination of people and resources. **Personnel and Human Resources:** Knowledge of principles and procedures for personnel recruitment, selection, training, compensation and benefits, labor relations and negotiation, and personnel information systems. **Design:** Knowledge of design techniques, tools, and principles involved in production of precision technical plans, blueprints, drawings, and models. **English Language:** Knowledge of the structure and content of the English language, including the meaning and spelling of words, rules of composition, and grammar. **Engineering and Technology:** Knowledge of the practical application of engineering science and technology. This includes applying principles, techniques, procedures, and equipment

to the design and production of various goods and services.

First-Line Supervisors and Manager/Supervisors— Extractive Workers

- ▲ Education/Training Required: Work experience in a related occupation
- ▲ Annual Earnings: $46,570
- ▲ Growth: 16.5%
- ▲ Annual Job Openings: 43,000
- ▲ Self-Employed: 10.4%
- ▲ Part-Time: 2.3%

Directly supervise and coordinate activities of extractive workers and their helpers. Manager/Supervisors are generally found in smaller establishments, where they perform both supervisory and management functions, such as accounting, marketing, and personnel work, and may also engage in the same extractive work as the workers they supervise. Supervises and coordinates activities of workers engaged in the extraction of geological materials. Directs and leads workers engaged in extraction of geological materials. Assigns work to employees, using material and worker requirements data. Confers with staff and workers to ensure that production personnel problems are resolved. Analyzes and resolves worker problems and recommends motivational plans. Analyzes and plans extraction process of geological materials. Trains workers in construction methods and operation of equipment. Examines and inspects equipment, site, and materials to verify that specifications are met. Recommends measures to improve production methods and equipment performance to increase efficiency and safety. Suggests and initiates personnel actions, such as promotions, transfers, and hires. Records information such as personnel, production, and operational data on specified forms. Assists workers engaged in extraction activities, using hand tools and equipment. Locates, measures, and marks materials and site location, using measuring and marking equipment. Orders materials, supplies, and repair of equipment and machinery. **SKILLS—Management of Personnel Resources:** Motivating, developing, and directing people as they work, identifying the best people for the job. **Coordination:** Adjusting actions in relation to others' actions. **Instructing:** Teaching others how to do something. **Monitoring:** Monitoring/Assessing your performance or that of other individuals or organizations to make improvements or take corrective action. **Speaking:** Talking to others to convey information effectively. **Time Management:** Managing one's own time and the time of others. **Judgment and Decision Making:** Considering the relative costs and

benefits of potential actions to choose the most appropriate one.

GOE INFORMATION—Interest Area: 06. Construction, Mining, and Drilling. **Work Group:** 06.01. Managerial Work in Construction, Mining, and Drilling. **Other Job Titles in This Work Group:** Construction Managers; First-Line Supervisors and Manager/Supervisors—Construction Trades Workers; First-Line Supervisors/Managers of Construction Trades and Extraction Workers. **PERSONALITY TYPE—Enterprising.** Enterprising occupations frequently involve starting up and carrying out projects. These occupations can involve leading people and making many decisions. They sometimes require risk taking and often deal with business.

EDUCATION/TRAINING PROGRAM(S)—Blasting/ Blaster; Well Drilling/Driller. RELATED KNOWLEDGE/COURSES—Administration and Management: Knowledge of business and management principles involved in strategic planning, resource allocation, human resources modeling, leadership technique, production methods, and coordination of people and resources. **Personnel and Human Resources:** Knowledge of principles and procedures for personnel recruitment, selection, training, compensation and benefits, labor relations and negotiation, and personnel information systems. **English Language:** Knowledge of the structure and content of the English language, including the meaning and spelling of words, rules of composition, and grammar. **Engineering and Technology:** Knowledge of the practical application of engineering science and technology. This includes applying principles, techniques, procedures, and equipment to the design and production of various goods and services. **Education and Training:** Knowledge of principles and methods for curriculum and training design, teaching and instruction for individuals and groups, and the measurement of training effects.

First-Line Supervisors and Manager/Supervisors— Landscaping Workers

- ▲ Education/Training Required: Work experience in a related occupation
- ▲ Annual Earnings: $32,100
- ▲ Growth: 20.1%
- ▲ Annual Job Openings: 10,000
- ▲ Self-Employed: 10.6%
- ▲ Part-Time: 25.6%

Directly supervise and coordinate activities of landscaping workers. Manager/Supervisors are generally found in smaller establishments, where they perform both supervisory and management functions, such as accounting, marketing, and personnel work, and may also engage in the same landscaping work as the workers they supervise. Directs workers in maintenance and repair of driveways, walkways, benches, graves, and mausoleums. Observes ongoing work to ascertain if work is being performed according to instructions and will be completed on time. Determines work priority and crew and equipment requirements; assigns workers tasks such as planting, fertilizing, irrigating, and mowing. Directs and assists workers engaged in maintenance and repair of equipment such as power mower and backhoe, using hand tools and power tools. Confers with manager to develop plans and schedules for maintenance and improvement of grounds. Keeps employee time records; records daily work performed. Interviews, hires, and discharges workers. Assists workers in performing work when completion is critical. Tours grounds, such as park, botanical garden, cemetery, or golf course, to inspect conditions. Trains workers in tasks such as transplanting and pruning trees and shrubs, finishing cement, using equipment, and caring for turf. Mixes and prepares spray and dust solutions and directs application of fertilizer, insecticide, and fungicide. **SKILLS—Coordination:** Adjusting actions in relation to others' actions. **Management of Personnel Resources:** Motivating, developing, and directing people as they work, identifying the best people for the job. **Speaking:** Talking to others to convey information effectively. **Instructing:** Teaching others how to do something. **Time Management:** Managing one's own time and the time of others.

GOE INFORMATION—Interest Area: 03. Plants and Animals. **Work Group:** 03.01. Managerial Work in Plants and Animals. **Other Job Titles in This Work Group:** Agricultural Crop Farm Managers; Farm Labor Contractors; Farmers and Ranchers; First-Line Supervisors and Manager/Supervisors—Animal Care Workers, Except Livestock; First-Line Supervisors and Manager/Supervi-

sors—Animal Husbandry Workers; First-Line Supervisors and Manager/Supervisors—Fishery Workers; First-Line Supervisors and Manager/Supervisors—Horticultural Workers; First-Line Supervisors and Manager/Supervisors—Landscaping Workers; First-Line Supervisors and Manager/Supervisors—Logging Workers; First-Line Supervisors/Managers of Farming, Fishing, and Forestry Workers; First-Line Supervisors/Managers of Landscaping, Lawn Service, and Groundskeeping Workers; Fish Hatchery Managers; Lawn Service Managers; Nursery and Greenhouse Managers. **PERSONALITY TYPE—**Realistic. Realistic occupations frequently involve work activities that include practical, hands-on problems and solutions. They often deal with plants, animals, and real-world materials like wood, tools, and machinery. Many of the occupations require working outside and do not involve a lot of paperwork or working closely with others.

EDUCATION/TRAINING PROGRAM(S)—Landscaping and Groundskeeping; Ornamental Horticulture; Turf and Turfgrass Management. **RELATED KNOWLEDGE/COURSES—Administration and Management:** Knowledge of business and management principles involved in strategic planning, resource allocation, human resources modeling, leadership technique, production methods, and coordination of people and resources. **Personnel and Human Resources:** Knowledge of principles and procedures for personnel recruitment, selection, training, compensation and benefits, labor relations and negotiation, and personnel information systems. **Chemistry:** Knowledge of the chemical composition, structure, and properties of substances and of the chemical processes and transformations that they undergo. This includes uses of chemicals and their interactions, danger signs, production techniques, and disposal methods. **Biology:** Knowledge of plant and animal organisms and their tissues, cells, functions, interdependencies, and interactions with each other and the environment. **Principles of Mechanical Devices:** Knowledge of machines and tools, including their designs, uses, repair, and maintenance.

First-Line Supervisors, Administrative Support

▲ Education/Training Required: Work experience in a related occupation
▲ Annual Earnings: $37,990
▲ Growth: 9.4%
▲ Annual Job Openings: 146,000
▲ Self-Employed: 0.1%
▲ Part-Time: 3.3%

Supervise and coordinate activities of workers involved in providing administrative support. Supervises and coordinates activities of workers engaged in clerical or administrative support activities. Plans, prepares, and revises work schedules and duty assignments according to budget allotments, customer needs, problems, workloads, and statistical forecasts. Verifies completeness and accuracy of subordinates' work, computations, and records. Interviews, selects, and discharges employees. Oversees, coordinates, or performs activities associated with shipping, receiving, distribution, and transportation. Evaluates subordinate job performance and conformance to regulations and recommends appropriate personnel action. Consults with supervisor and other personnel to resolve problems such as equipment performance, output quality, and work schedules. Trains employees in work and safety procedures and company policies. Computes figures such as balances, totals, and commissions. Analyzes financial activities of establishment or department and assists in planning budget. Inspects equipment for defects and notifies maintenance personnel or outside service contractors for repairs. Plans layout of stockroom, warehouse, or other storage areas, considering turnover, size, weight, and related factors pertaining to items stored. Compiles reports and information required by management or governmental agencies. Identifies and resolves discrepancies or errors. Maintains records of such matters as inventory, personnel, orders, supplies, and machine maintenance. Examines procedures and recommends changes to save time, labor, and other costs and to improve quality control and operating efficiency. Participates in work of subordinates to facilitate productivity or overcome difficult aspects of work. Requisitions supplies. Reviews records and reports pertaining to such activities as production, operation, payroll, customer accounts, and shipping. **SKILLS—Monitoring:** Monitoring/Assessing your performance or that of other individuals or organizations to make improvements or take corrective action. **Active Listening:** Giving full attention to what other people are saying, taking time to understand the points being made, asking questions as appro-

priate, and not interrupting at inappropriate times. **Time Management:** Managing one's own time and the time of others. **Management of Personnel Resources:** Motivating, developing, and directing people as they work, identifying the best people for the job. **Coordination:** Adjusting actions in relation to others' actions. **Reading Comprehension:** Understanding written sentences and paragraphs in work-related documents. **Speaking:** Talking to others to convey information effectively.

GOE INFORMATION—Interest Area: 09. Business Detail. **Work Group:** 09.01. Managerial Work in Business Detail. **Other Job Titles in This Work Group:** Administrative Services Managers; First-Line Supervisors, Customer Service; First-Line Supervisors/Managers of Office and Administrative Support Workers. **PERSONALITY TYPE—Enterprising.** Enterprising occupations frequently involve starting up and carrying out projects. These occupations can involve leading people and making many decisions. They sometimes require risk taking and often deal with business.

EDUCATION/TRAINING PROGRAM(S)—Agricultural Business Technology; Customer Service Management; Medical/Health Management and Clinical Assistant/Specialist; Office Management and Supervision. **RELATED KNOWLEDGE/COURSES—Administration and Management:** Knowledge of business and management principles involved in strategic planning, resource allocation, human resources modeling, leadership technique, production methods, and coordination of people and resources. **Clerical Studies:** Knowledge of administrative and clerical procedures and systems, such as word processing, managing files and records, stenography and transcription, designing forms, and other office procedures and terminology. **English Language:** Knowledge of the structure and content of the English language, including the meaning and spelling of words, rules of composition, and grammar. **Personnel and Human Resources:** Knowledge of principles and procedures for personnel recruitment, selection, training, compensation and benefits, labor relations and negotiation, and personnel information systems. **Education and Training:** Knowledge of principles and methods for curriculum and training design, teaching and instruction for individuals and groups, and the

measurement of training effects. **Mathematics:** Knowledge of arithmetic, algebra, geometry, calculus, and statistics and their applications.

First-Line Supervisors, Customer Service

- ▲ Education/Training Required: Work experience in a related occupation
- ▲ Annual Earnings: $37,990
- ▲ Growth: 9.4%
- ▲ Annual Job Openings: 146,000
- ▲ Self-Employed: 0.1%
- ▲ Part-Time: 3.3%

Supervise and coordinate activities of workers involved in providing customer service. Supervises and coordinates activities of workers engaged in customer service activities. Plans, prepares, and devises work schedules according to budgets and workloads. Observes and evaluates workers' performance. Issues instructions and assigns duties to workers. Trains and instructs employees. Hires and discharges workers. Communicates with other departments and management to resolve problems and expedite work. Interprets and communicates work procedures and company policies to staff. Helps workers in resolving problems and completing work. Resolves complaints and answers customer questions regarding services and procedures. Reviews and checks work of subordinates, such as reports, records, and applications for accuracy and content, and corrects errors. Prepares, maintains, and submits reports and records, such as budgets and operational and personnel reports. Makes recommendations to management concerning staff and improvement of procedures. Plans and develops improved procedures. Requisitions or purchases supplies. **SKILLS—Management of Personnel Resources:** Motivating, developing, and directing people as they work, identifying the best people for the job. **Coordination:** Adjusting actions in relation to others' actions. **Monitoring:** Monitoring/Assessing your performance or that of other individuals or organizations to make improvements or take corrective action. **Critical Thinking:** Using logic and reasoning to identify the strengths and weaknesses of alternative solutions, conclusions, or approaches to problems. **Speaking:** Talking to others to convey information effectively.

GOE INFORMATION—Interest Area: 09. Business Detail. **Work Group:** 09.01. Managerial Work in Business Detail. **Other Job Titles in This Work Group:** Administrative Services Managers; First-Line Supervisors,

Administrative Support; First-Line Supervisors/Managers of Office and Administrative Support Workers. **PERSONALITY TYPE—Enterprising.** Enterprising occupations frequently involve starting up and carrying out projects. These occupations can involve leading people and making many decisions. They sometimes require risk taking and often deal with business.

EDUCATION/TRAINING PROGRAM(S)—Agricultural Business Technology; Customer Service Management; Medical/Health Management and Clinical Assistant/Specialist; Office Management and Supervision. **RELATED KNOWLEDGE/COURSES—Administration and Management: Knowledge of business and management principles involved in strategic planning, resource allocation, human resources modeling, leadership technique, production methods, and coordination of people and resources. **Customer and Personal Service:** Knowledge of principles and processes for providing customer and personal services. This includes customer needs assessment, meeting quality standards for services, and evaluation of customer satisfaction. **Personnel and Human Resources:** Knowledge of principles and procedures for personnel recruitment, selection, training, compensation and benefits, labor relations and negotiation, and personnel information systems. **Clerical Studies:** Knowledge of administrative and clerical procedures and systems, such as word processing, managing files and records, stenography and transcription, designing forms, and other office procedures and terminology. **Education and Training:** Knowledge of principles and methods for curriculum and training design, teaching and instruction for individuals and groups, and the measurement of training effects. **English Language:** Knowledge of the structure and content of the English language, including the meaning and spelling of words, rules of composition, and grammar.

First-Line Supervisors/Managers of Construction Trades and Extraction Workers

▲ Education/Training Required: Work experience in a related occupation
▲ Annual Earnings: $46,570
▲ Growth: 16.5%
▲ Annual Job Openings: 43,000
▲ Self-Employed: 10.4%
▲ Part-Time: 2.3%

Directly supervise and coordinate activities of construction or extraction workers. SKILLS—No data available.

GOE INFORMATION—Interest Area: 06. Construction, Mining, and Drilling. Work Group: 06.01. Managerial Work in Construction, Mining, and Drilling. Other Job Titles in This Work Group: Construction Managers; First-Line Supervisors and Manager/Supervisors—Construction Trades Workers; First-Line Supervisors and Manager/Supervisors—Extractive Workers. PERSONALITY TYPE—No data available.

EDUCATION/TRAINING PROGRAM(S)—Blasting/Blaster; Building/Construction Finishing, Management, and Inspection, Other; Building/Construction Site Management/Manager; Building/Home/Construction Inspection/Inspector; Building/Property Maintenance and Management; Carpentry/Carpenter; Concrete Finishing/Concrete Finisher; Construction Trades, Other; Drywall Installation/Drywaller; Electrical and Power Transmission Installation/Installer, General; Electrical and Power Transmission Installers, Other; Electrician; Glazier; Lineworker; Mason/Masonry; Painting/Painter and Wall Coverer; Plumbing Technology/Plumber; Roofer; Well Drilling/Driller. RELATED KNOWLEDGE/COURSES—No data available.

First-Line Supervisors/Managers of Correctional Officers

▲ Education/Training Required: Work experience in a related occupation
▲ Annual Earnings: $44,640
▲ Growth: 29.6%
▲ Annual Job Openings: 3,000
▲ Self-Employed: No data available.
▲ Part-Time: No data available.

Supervise and coordinate activities of correctional officers and jailers. SKILLS—No data available.

GOE INFORMATION—Interest Area: 04. Law, Law Enforcement, and Public Safety. Work Group: 04.01. Managerial Work in Law, Law Enforcement, and Public Safety. Other Job Titles in This Work Group: Emergency Management Specialists; First-Line Supervisors/Managers of Fire Fighting and Prevention Workers; First-Line Supervisors/Managers of Police and Detectives; First-Line Supervisors/Managers, Protective Service Workers, All Other; Forest Fire Fighting and Prevention Supervisors; Municipal Fire Fighting and Prevention Supervisors. PERSONALITY TYPE—No data available.

EDUCATION/TRAINING PROGRAM(S)—Corrections; Corrections Administration. RELATED KNOWLEDGE/COURSES—No data available.

First-Line Supervisors/Managers of Farming, Fishing, and Forestry Workers

- ▲ Education/Training Required: Work experience in a related occupation
- ▲ Annual Earnings: $33,330
- ▲ Growth: 13.0%
- ▲ Annual Job Openings: 89,000
- ▲ Self-Employed: 10.6%
- ▲ Part-Time: 25.6%

Directly supervise and coordinate the activities of agricultural, forestry, aquacultural, and related workers. SKILLS—No data available.

GOE INFORMATION—**Interest Area:** 03. Plants and Animals. **Work Group:** 03.01. Managerial Work in Plants and Animals. **Other Job Titles in This Work Group:** Agricultural Crop Farm Managers; Farm Labor Contractors; Farmers and Ranchers; First-Line Supervisors and Manager/Supervisors—Agricultural Crop Workers; First-Line Supervisors and Manager/Supervisors—Animal Care Workers, Except Livestock; First-Line Supervisors and Manager/Supervisors—Animal Husbandry Workers; First-Line Supervisors and Manager/Supervisors—Fishery Workers; First-Line Supervisors and Manager/Supervisors—Horticultural Workers; First-Line Supervisors and Manager/Supervisors—Landscaping Workers; First-Line Supervisors and Manager/Supervisors—Logging Workers; First-Line Supervisors/Managers of Landscaping, Lawn Service, and Groundskeeping Workers; Fish Hatchery Managers; Lawn Service Managers; Nursery and Greenhouse Managers. **PERSONALITY TYPE**—No data available.

EDUCATION/TRAINING PROGRAM(S)—Agricultural Animal Breeding; Agricultural Business and Management, Other; Agricultural Production Operations, General; Agricultural Production Operations, Other; Agriculture, Agriculture Operations, and Related Sciences, Other; Agronomy and Crop Science; Animal Nutrition; Animal Sciences, General; Animal/Livestock Husbandry and Production; Aquaculture; Crop Production; Dairy Husbandry and Production; Dairy Science; Farm/Farm and Ranch Management; Fishing and Fisheries Sciences and Management; Horse Husbandry/Equine Science and Management; Livestock Management; Plant Sciences, General; Poultry Science; Range Science and Management. **RELATED KNOWLEDGE/COURSES**—No data available.

First-Line Supervisors/Managers of Food Preparation and Serving Workers

- ▲ Education/Training Required: Work experience in a related occupation
- ▲ Annual Earnings: $23,600
- ▲ Growth: 12.7%
- ▲ Annual Job Openings: 136,000
- ▲ Self-Employed: 37.5%
- ▲ Part-Time: 8.5%

Supervise workers engaged in preparing and serving food. Supervises and coordinates activities of workers engaged in preparing and serving food and other related duties. Observes and evaluates workers and work procedures to ensure quality standards and service. Assigns duties, responsibilities, and work stations to employees, following work requirements. Collaborates with specified personnel to plan menus, serving arrangements, and other related details. Recommends measures to improve work procedures and worker performance to increase quality of services and job safety. Purchases or requisitions supplies and equipment to ensure quality and timely delivery of services. Initiates personnel actions, such as hires and discharges, to ensure proper staffing. Analyzes operational problems, such as theft and wastage, and establishes controls. Schedules parties and reservations; greets and escorts guests to seating arrangements. Receives, issues, and takes inventory of supplies and equipment; reports shortages to designated personnel. Resolves customer complaints regarding food service. Records production and operational data on specified forms. Trains workers in proper food preparation and service procedures. Inspects supplies, equipment, and work areas to ensure efficient service and conformance to standards. Specifies food portions and courses, production and time sequences, and work station and equipment arrangements. **SKILLS— Management of Personnel Resources:** Motivating, developing, and directing people as they work, identifying the best people for the job. **Coordination:** Adjusting actions in relation to others' actions. **Speaking:** Talking to others to convey information effectively. **Time Management:** Managing one's own time and the time of others. **Active Listening:** Giving full attention to what other people are saying, taking time to understand the points being made, asking questions as appropriate, and not interrupting at inappropriate times.

GOE INFORMATION—Interest Area: 11. Recreation, Travel, and Other Personal Services. **Work Group:** 11.01. Managerial Work in Recreation, Travel, and Other Personal Services. **Other Job Titles in This Work Group:** Aircraft Cargo Handling Supervisors; First-Line Supervisors/Managers of Housekeeping and Janitorial Workers; First-Line Supervisors/Managers of Personal Service Workers; Food Service Managers; Gaming Managers; Gaming Supervisors; Housekeeping Supervisors; Janitorial Supervisors; Lodging Managers; Meeting and Convention Planners. **PERSONALITY TYPE—**Enterprising. Enterprising occupations frequently involve starting up and carrying out projects. These occupations can involve leading people and making many decisions. They sometimes require risk taking and often deal with business.

EDUCATION/TRAINING PROGRAM(S)—Cooking and Related Culinary Arts, General; Foodservice Systems

Administration/Management; Restaurant, Culinary, and Catering Management/Manager. **RELATED KNOWLEDGE/COURSES—Administration and Management:** Knowledge of business and management principles involved in strategic planning, resource allocation, human resources modeling, leadership technique, production methods, and coordination of people and resources. **Customer and Personal Service:** Knowledge of principles and processes for providing customer and personal services. This includes customer needs assessment, meeting quality standards for services, and evaluation of customer satisfaction. **Personnel and Human Resources:** Knowledge of principles and procedures for personnel recruitment, selection, training, compensation and benefits, labor relations and negotiation, and personnel information systems. **English Language:** Knowledge of the structure and content of the English language, including the meaning and spelling of words, rules of composition, and grammar. **Clerical Studies:** Knowledge of administrative and clerical procedures and systems, such as word processing, managing files and records, stenography and transcription, designing forms, and other office procedures and terminology. **Education and Training:** Knowledge of principles and methods for curriculum and training design, teaching and instruction for individuals and groups, and the measurement of training effects. **Production and Processing:** Knowledge of raw materials, production processes, quality control, costs, and other techniques for maximizing the effective manufacture and distribution of goods.

First-Line Supervisors/Managers of Helpers, Laborers, and Material Movers, Hand

- ▲ Education/Training Required: Work experience in a related occupation
- ▲ Annual Earnings: $36,090
- ▲ Growth: 18.9%
- ▲ Annual Job Openings: 14,000
- ▲ Self-Employed: 10.4%
- ▲ Part-Time: 2.3%

Supervise and coordinate the activities of helpers, laborers, or material movers. Supervises and coordinates activities of workers performing assigned tasks. Verifies materials loaded or unloaded against work order and schedules times of shipment and mode of transportation. Inspects equipment for wear and completed work for conformance to standards. Informs designated employee or department of items loaded or reports loading deficiencies. Resolves customer complaints. Quotes prices to customers. Inventories and orders supplies. Examines freight to determine sequence of loading and examines equipment to determine compliance with specifications. Records information such as daily receipts, employee time and wage data, description of freight, and inspection results. Determines work sequence and equipment needed according to work order, shipping records, and experience. Observes work procedures to ensure quality of work. Trains and instructs workers. Assigns duties and work schedules.

SKILLS—**Instructing:** Teaching others how to do something. **Social Perceptiveness:** Being aware of others' reactions and understanding why they react as they do. **Critical Thinking:** Using logic and reasoning to identify the strengths and weaknesses of alternative solutions, conclusions, or approaches to problems. **Speaking:** Talking to others to convey information effectively. **Management of Personnel Resources:** Motivating, developing, and directing people as they work, identifying the best people for the job. **Coordination:** Adjusting actions in relation to others' actions. **Learning Strategies:** Selecting and using training/instructional methods and procedures appropriate for the situation when learning or teaching new things.

GOE INFORMATION—**Interest Area:** 08. Industrial Production. **Work Group:** 08.01. Managerial Work in Industrial Production. **Other Job Titles in This Work Group:** First-Line Supervisors/Managers of Production and Operating Workers; Industrial Production Managers. PERSONALITY TYPE—Enterprising. Enterprising occupations frequently involve starting up and carrying out projects. These occupations can involve leading people and making many decisions. They sometimes require risk taking and often deal with business.

EDUCATION/TRAINING PROGRAM(S)—No data available. **RELATED KNOWLEDGE/COURSES—Production and Processing:** Knowledge of raw materials, production processes, quality control, costs, and other techniques for maximizing the effective manufacture and distribution of goods. **Administration and Management:** Knowledge of business and management principles involved in strategic planning, resource allocation, human resources modeling, leadership technique, production methods, and coordination of people and resources. **Personnel and Human Resources:** Knowledge of principles and procedures for personnel recruitment, selection, training, compensation and benefits, labor relations and negotiation, and personnel information systems. **Mathematics:** Knowledge of arithmetic, algebra, geometry, calculus, and statistics and their applications. **Economics and Accounting:** Knowledge of economic and accounting principles and practices, the financial markets, banking, and the analysis and reporting of financial data.

First-Line Supervisors/Managers of Housekeeping and Janitorial Workers

- ▲ Education/Training Required: Work experience in a related occupation
- ▲ Annual Earnings: $27,200
- ▲ Growth: 14.2%
- ▲ Annual Job Openings: 18,000
- ▲ Self-Employed: 1.6%
- ▲ Part-Time: 6.4%

Supervise work activities of cleaning personnel in hotels, hospitals, offices, and other establishments. SKILLS—No data available.

GOE INFORMATION—**Interest Area:** 11. Recreation, Travel, and Other Personal Services. **Work Group:** 11.01. Managerial Work in Recreation, Travel, and Other Personal Services. **Other Job Titles in This Work Group:** Aircraft Cargo Handling Supervisors; First-Line Supervisors/Managers of Food Preparation and Serving Workers; First-Line Supervisors/Managers of Personal Service Workers; Food Service Managers; Gaming Managers; Gaming Supervisors; Housekeeping Supervisors; Janitorial Supervisors; Lodging Managers; Meeting and Convention Planners. PERSONALITY TYPE—No data available.

EDUCATION/TRAINING PROGRAM(S)—No data available. **RELATED KNOWLEDGE/COURSES—**No data available.

First-Line Supervisors/Managers of Landscaping, Lawn Service, and Groundskeeping Workers

- ▲ Education/Training Required: Work experience in a related occupation
- ▲ Annual Earnings: $32,100
- ▲ Growth: 20.1%
- ▲ Annual Job Openings: 10,000
- ▲ Self-Employed: 58.8%
- ▲ Part-Time: 24.5%

Plan, organize, direct, or coordinate activities of workers engaged in landscaping or groundskeeping activities, such as planting and maintaining ornamental trees, shrubs, flowers, and lawns and applying fertilizers, pesticides, and other chemicals, according to contract specifications. May also coordinate activities of workers engaged in terracing hillsides, building retaining walls, constructing pathways, installing patios, and similar activities in following a landscape design plan. Work may involve reviewing contracts to ascertain service, machine, and work force requirements; answering inquiries from potential customers regarding methods, material, and price ranges; and preparing estimates according to labor, material, and machine costs. SKILLS—No data available.

GOE INFORMATION—Interest Area: 03. Plants and Animals. Work Group: 03.01. Managerial Work in Plants and Animals. Other Job Titles in This Work Group: Agricultural Crop Farm Managers; Farm Labor Contractors; Farmers and Ranchers; First-Line Supervisors and Manager/Supervisors—Agricultural Crop Workers; First-Line Supervisors and Manager/Supervisors—Animal Care Workers, Except Livestock; First-Line Supervisors and Manager/Supervisors—Animal Husbandry Workers; First-Line Supervisors and Manager/Supervisors—Fishery Workers; First-Line Supervisors and Manager/Supervisors—Horticultural Workers; First-Line Supervisors and Manager/Supervisors—Landscaping Workers; First-Line Supervisors and Manager/Supervisors—Logging Workers; First-Line Supervisors/Managers of Farming, Fishing, and Forestry Workers; Fish Hatchery Managers; Lawn Service Managers; Nursery and Greenhouse Managers. PERSONALITY TYPE—No data available.

EDUCATION/TRAINING PROGRAM(S)—Landscaping and Groundskeeping; Ornamental Horticulture; Turf and Turfgrass Management. RELATED KNOWLEDGE/COURSES—No data available.

First-Line Supervisors/Managers of Mechanics, Installers, and Repairers

- ▲ Education/Training Required: Work experience in a related occupation
- ▲ Annual Earnings: $46,320
- ▲ Growth: 16.0%
- ▲ Annual Job Openings: 38,000
- ▲ Self-Employed: 10.4%
- ▲ Part-Time: 2.3%

Supervise and coordinate the activities of mechanics, installers, and repairers. Assigns workers to perform activities such as servicing appliances, repairing and maintaining vehicles, and installing machinery and equipment. Confers with personnel, such as management, engineering, quality control, customers, and workers' representatives, to coordinate work activities and resolve problems. Recommends or initiates personnel actions, such as employment, performance evaluations, promotions, transfers, discharges, and disciplinary measures. Directs, coordinates, and assists in performance of workers' activities, such as engine tune-up, hydroelectric turbine repair, or circuit breaker installation. Examines object, system, or facilities, such as telephone, air conditioning, or industrial plant, and analyzes information to determine installation, service, or repair needed. Monitors operations and inspects, tests, and measures completed work, using devices such as hand tools, gauges, and specifications to verify conformance to standards. Computes estimates and actual costs of factors such as materials, labor, and outside contractors; prepares budgets. Patrols work area and examines tools and equipment to detect unsafe conditions or violations of safety rules. Recommends measures such as procedural changes, service manuals revisions, and equipment purchases to improve work performance and minimize operating costs. Trains workers in methods, procedures, and use of equipment and work aids such as blueprints, hand tools, and test equipment. Completes and maintains reports, such as time and production records, inventories, and test results. Requisitions materials and supplies, such as tools, equipment, and replacement parts for work activities. Establishes or adjusts work methods and procedures to meet production schedules, using knowledge of capacities of machines, equipment, and personnel. Interprets specifications, blueprints, and job orders; constructs templates and lays out reference points for workers. SKILLS—Coordination: Adjusting actions in relation to others' actions. Management of Personnel Resources: Motivating, developing, and directing people as they work, identifying the best people for the job. Reading Comprehension: Understanding written sentences and paragraphs in work-related documents. Active Listening: Giving full attention to what other people are saying, taking time to understand the points being made, asking questions as appropriate, and not interrupting at inappropriate times. Management of Material Resources: Obtaining and seeing to the appropriate use of equipment, facilities, and materials needed to do certain work. Management of Financial Resources: Determining how money will be spent to get the work done and accounting for these expenditures. Time Management: Managing one's own time and the time of others.

GOE INFORMATION—Interest Area: 05. Mechanics, Installers, and Repairers. Work Group: 05.01. Manage-

rial Work in Mechanics, Installers, and Repairers. Other Job Titles in This Work Group: No other jobs are in this work group. PERSONALITY TYPE—Enterprising. Enterprising occupations frequently involve starting up and carrying out projects. These occupations can involve leading people and making many decisions. They sometimes require risk taking and often deal with business.

EDUCATION/TRAINING PROGRAM(S)—Operations Management and Supervision. RELATED KNOWLEDGE/COURSES—Principles of Mechanical Devices: Knowledge of machines and tools, including their designs, uses, repair, and maintenance. Administration and Management: Knowledge of business and management principles involved in strategic planning, resource allocation, human resources modeling, leadership technique, production methods, and coordination of people and resources. Personnel and Human Resources: Knowledge of principles and procedures for personnel recruitment, selection, training, compensation and benefits, labor relations and negotiation, and personnel information systems. English Language: Knowledge of the structure and content of the English language, including the meaning and spelling of words, rules of composition, and grammar. Engineering and Technology: Knowledge of the practical application of engineering science and technology. This includes applying principles, techniques, procedures, and equipment to the design and production of various goods and services.

First-Line Supervisors/Managers of Non-Retail Sales Workers

- ▲ Education/Training Required: Work experience in a related occupation
- ▲ Annual Earnings: $51,490
- ▲ Growth: 5.8%
- ▲ Annual Job Openings: 41,000
- ▲ Self-Employed: 36.9%
- ▲ Part-Time: 8.2%

Directly supervise and coordinate activities of sales workers other than retail sales workers. May perform duties such as budgeting, accounting, and personnel work in addition to supervisory duties. Directs and supervises employees engaged in sales, inventory-taking, reconciling cash receipts, or performing specific service such as pumping gasoline for customers. Plans and prepares work schedules and assigns employees to specific duties. Hires, trains, and evaluates personnel in sales or marketing establishment. Coordinates sales promotion activities and prepares

merchandise displays and advertising copy. Listens to and resolves customer complaints regarding service, product, or personnel. Examines merchandise to ensure that it is correctly priced or displayed or functions as advertised. Inventories stock and reorders when inventories drop to specified level. Examines products purchased for resale or received for storage to determine condition of product or item. Prepares rental or lease agreement specifying charges and payment procedures for use of machinery, tools, or other such items. Formulates pricing policies on merchandise according to requirements for profitability of store operations. Keeps records pertaining to purchases, sales, and requisitions. Assists sales staff in completing complicated and difficult sales. Prepares sales and inventory reports for management and budget departments. Confers with company officials to develop methods and procedures to increase sales, expand markets, and promote business. **SKILLS—Active Listening:** Giving full attention to what other people are saying, taking time to understand the points being made, asking questions as appropriate, and not interrupting at inappropriate times. **Coordination:** Adjusting actions in relation to others' actions. **Speaking:** Talking to others to convey information effectively. **Management of Personnel Resources:** Motivating, developing, and directing people as they work, identifying the best people for the job. **Mathematics:** Using mathematics to solve problems. **Reading Comprehension:** Understanding written sentences and paragraphs in work-related documents.

GOE INFORMATION—Interest Area: 10. Sales and Marketing. **Work Group:** 10.01. Managerial Work in Sales and Marketing. **Other Job Titles in This Work Group:** Advertising and Promotions Managers; First-Line Supervisors/Managers of Retail Sales Workers; Marketing Managers; Sales Managers. **PERSONALITY TYPE—**Enterprising. Enterprising occupations frequently involve starting up and carrying out projects. These occupations can involve leading people and making many decisions. They sometimes require risk taking and often deal with business.

EDUCATION/TRAINING PROGRAM(S)—Business, Management, Marketing, and Related Support Services, Other; General Merchandising, Sales, and Related Marketing Operations, Other; Special Products Marketing Operations; Specialized Merchandising, Sales, and Related Marketing Operations, Other. **RELATED KNOWLEDGE/COURSES—Administration and Management:** Knowledge of business and management principles involved in strategic planning, resource allocation, human resources modeling, leadership technique, production methods, and coordination of people and resources. **Personnel and Human Resources:** Knowledge of principles and procedures for personnel recruitment, selection, training, compensation and benefits, labor relations and negotiation, and personnel information systems. **Mathematics:** Knowledge of arithmetic, algebra, geometry, calculus, and statistics and their applications. **Sales and Marketing:** Knowledge of principles and methods for showing, promoting, and selling products or services. This includes marketing strategy and tactics, product demonstration, sales techniques, and sales control systems. **Economics and Accounting:** Knowledge of economic and accounting principles and practices, the financial markets, banking, and the analysis and reporting of financial data.

First-Line Supervisors/Managers of Office and Administrative Support Workers

- ▲ Education/Training Required: Work experience in a related occupation
- ▲ Annual Earnings: $37,990
- ▲ Growth: 9.4%
- ▲ Annual Job Openings: 146,000
- ▲ Self-Employed: 0.1%
- ▲ Part-Time: 3.3%

Supervise and coordinate the activities of clerical and administrative support workers. SKILLS—No data available.

GOE INFORMATION—Interest Area: 09. Business Detail. **Work Group:** 09.01. Managerial Work in Business Detail. **Other Job Titles in This Work Group:** Administrative Services Managers; First-Line Supervisors, Administrative Support; First-Line Supervisors, Customer Service. **PERSONALITY TYPE—**No data available.

EDUCATION/TRAINING PROGRAM(S)—Agricultural Business Technology; Customer Service Management; Medical/Health Management and Clinical Assistant/Specialist; Office Management and Supervision. **RELATED KNOWLEDGE/COURSES—**No data available.

First-Line Supervisors/Managers of Personal Service Workers

- ▲ Education/Training Required: Work experience in a related occupation
- ▲ Annual Earnings: $28,040
- ▲ Growth: 15.1%
- ▲ Annual Job Openings: 8,000
- ▲ Self-Employed: 37.5%
- ▲ Part-Time: 8.5%

Supervise and coordinate activities of personal service workers, such as flight attendants, hairdressers, or caddies. Supervises and coordinates activities of workers engaged in lodging and personal services. Observes and evaluates workers' appearance and performance to ensure quality service and compliance with specifications. Trains workers in proper operational procedures and functions; explains company policy. Analyzes and records personnel and operational data and writes activity reports. Collaborates with personnel to plan and develop programs of events, schedules of activities, and menus. Resolves customer complaints regarding worker performance and services rendered. Assigns work schedules, following work requirements to ensure quality and timely delivery of services. Inspects work areas and operating equipment to ensure conformance to established standards. Furnishes customers with information on events and activities. Informs workers about interests of specific groups. Requisitions supplies, equipment, and designated services to ensure quality and timely service and efficient operations. **SKILLS—Coordination:** Adjusting actions in relation to others' actions. **Service Orientation:** Actively looking for ways to help people. **Active Listening:** Giving full attention to what other people are saying, taking time to understand the points being made, asking questions as appropriate, and not interrupting at inappropriate times. **Speaking:** Talking to others to convey information effectively. **Time Management:** Managing one's own time and the time of others.

GOE INFORMATION—Interest Area: 11. Recreation, Travel, and Other Personal Services. **Work Group:** 11.01. Managerial Work in Recreation, Travel, and Other Personal Services. **Other Job Titles in This Work Group:** Aircraft Cargo Handling Supervisors; First-Line Supervisors/Managers of Food Preparation and Serving Workers; First-Line Supervisors/Managers of Housekeeping and Janitorial Workers; Food Service Managers; Gaming Managers; Gaming Supervisors; Housekeeping Supervisors; Janitorial Supervisors; Lodging Managers; Meeting and Convention Planners. **PERSONALITY TYPE—**Enterprising. Enterprising occupations frequently involve starting up and carrying out projects. These occupations can involve leading people and making many decisions. They sometimes require risk taking and often deal with business.

EDUCATION/TRAINING PROGRAM(S)—No data available. **RELATED KNOWLEDGE/COURSES—Administration and Management:** Knowledge of business and management principles involved in strategic planning, resource allocation, human resources modeling, leadership technique, production methods, and coordination of people and resources. **Customer and Personal Service:** Knowledge of principles and processes for providing customer and personal services. This includes customer needs assessment, meeting quality standards for services, and evaluation of customer satisfaction. **Personnel and Human Resources:** Knowledge of principles and procedures for personnel recruitment, selection, training, compensation and benefits, labor relations and negotiation, and personnel information systems. **English Language:** Knowledge of the structure and content of the English language, including the meaning and spelling of words, rules of composition, and grammar. **Education and Training:** Knowledge of principles and methods for curriculum and training design, teaching and instruction for individuals and groups, and the measurement of training effects.

First-Line Supervisors/Managers of Police and Detectives

- ▲ Education/Training Required: Work experience in a related occupation
- ▲ Annual Earnings: $59,300
- ▲ Growth: 13.1%
- ▲ Annual Job Openings: 9,000
- ▲ Self-Employed: 0%
- ▲ Part-Time: 0%

Supervise and coordinate activities of members of police force. Prepares work schedules, assigns duties, and develops and revises departmental procedures. Supervises and coordinates investigation of criminal cases. Disciplines staff for violation of department rules and regulations. Investigates and resolves personnel problems within organization. Assists subordinates in performing job duties. Directs collection, preparation, and handling of evidence and personal property of prisoners. Monitors and evaluates job performance of subordinates. Investigates charges of misconduct against staff. Cooperates with court personnel and officials from other law enforcement agencies and testifies in court. Prepares news releases and responds to police correspondence. Reviews contents of written orders to ensure adherence to legal requirements. Directs release or transfer of prisoners. Requisitions and issues department equipment and supplies. Inspects facilities, supplies, vehicles, and equipment to ensure conformance to standards. Prepares budgets and manages expenditures of department funds. Trains staff. Prepares reports and directs preparation, handling, and maintenance of departmental records. Meets with civic, educational, and community groups to develop community programs and events and addresses groups concerning law enforcement subjects. Conducts raids and orders detention of witnesses and suspects for questioning. **SKILLS—Management of Personnel Resources:** Motivating, developing, and directing people as they work, identifying the best people for the job. **Judgment and Decision Making:** Considering the relative costs and benefits of potential actions to choose the most appropriate one. **Coordination:** Adjusting actions in relation to others' actions. **Time Management:** Managing one's own time and the time of others. **Management of Financial Resources:** Determining how money will be spent to get the work done and accounting for these expenditures. **Social Perceptiveness:** Being aware of others' reactions and understanding why they react as they do.

GOE INFORMATION—Interest Area: 04. Law, Law Enforcement, and Public Safety. **Work Group:** 04.01. Managerial Work in Law, Law Enforcement, and Public Safety. **Other Job Titles in This Work Group:** Emergency Management Specialists; First-Line Supervisors/Managers of Correctional Officers; First-Line Supervisors/Managers of Fire Fighting and Prevention Workers; First-Line Supervisors/Managers, Protective Service Workers, All Other; Forest Fire Fighting and Prevention Supervisors; Municipal Fire Fighting and Prevention Supervisors. **PERSONALITY TYPE—**Enterprising. Enterprising occupations frequently involve starting up and carrying out projects. These occupations can involve leading people and making many decisions. They sometimes require risk taking and often deal with business.

EDUCATION/TRAINING PROGRAM(S)—Corrections; Criminal Justice/Law Enforcement Administration; Criminal Justice/Safety Studies. **RELATED KNOWLEDGE/COURSES—Public Safety and Security:** Knowledge of relevant equipment, policies, procedures, and strategies to promote effective local, state, or national security operations for the protection of people, data, property, and institutions. **Administration and Management:** Knowledge of business and management principles involved in strategic planning, resource allocation, human resources modeling, leadership technique, production methods, and coordination of people and resources. **Law and Government:** Knowledge of laws, legal codes, court procedures, precedents, government regulations, executive orders, agency rules, and the democratic political process. **Personnel and Human Resources:** Knowledge of principles and procedures for personnel recruitment, selection, training, compensation and benefits, labor relations and negotiation, and personnel information systems. **English Language:** Knowledge of the structure and content of the English language, including the meaning and spelling of words, rules of composition, and grammar.

First-Line Supervisors/Managers of Production and Operating Workers

- ▲ Education/Training Required: Work experience in a related occupation
- ▲ Annual Earnings: $42,000
- ▲ Growth: 1.0%
- ▲ Annual Job Openings: 71,000
- ▲ Self-Employed: 10.4%
- ▲ Part-Time: 2.3%

Supervise and coordinate the activities of production and operating workers, such as inspectors, precision workers, machine setters and operators, assemblers, fabricators, and plant and system operators. Direct and coordinate the activities of employees engaged in production or processing of goods. Plans and establishes work schedules, assignments, and production sequences to meet production goals. Calculates labor and equipment requirements and production specifications, using standard formulas. Determines standards, production, and rates based on company policy, equipment and labor availability, and workload. Reviews operations and accounting records or reports to determine the feasibility of production estimates and evaluate current production. Confers with management or subordinates to resolve worker problems, complaints, or grievances. Confers with other supervisors to coordinate operations and activities within departments or between departments. Reads and analyzes charts, work orders, or production schedules to determine production requirements. Maintains operations data, such as time, production, and cost records, and prepares management reports. Recommends or implements measures to motivate employees and improve production methods, equipment performance, product quality, or efficiency. Requisitions materials, supplies, equipment parts, or repair services. Interprets specifications, blueprints, job orders, and company policies and procedures for workers. Inspects materials, products, or equipment to detect defects or malfunctions. Demonstrates equipment operations or work procedures to new employees or assigns employees to experienced workers for training. Monitors or patrols work area and enforces safety or sanitation regulations. Monitors gauges, dials, and other indicators to ensure operators conform to production or processing standards. Sets up and adjusts machines and equipment. **SKILLS— Coordination:** Adjusting actions in relation to others' actions. **Management of Personnel Resources:** Motivating, developing, and directing people as they work, identifying the best people for the job. **Mathematics:** Using mathematics to solve problems. **Management of Material Resources:** Obtaining and seeing to the appropriate use of equipment, facilities, and materials needed to do certain work. **Writing:** Communicating effectively in writing as appropriate for the needs of the audience. **Reading Comprehension:** Understanding written sentences and paragraphs in work-related documents.

GOE INFORMATION—Interest Area: 08. Industrial Production. **Work Group:** 08.01. Managerial Work in Industrial Production. **Other Job Titles in This Work Group:** First-Line Supervisors/Managers of Helpers, Laborers, and Material Movers, Hand; Industrial Production Managers. **PERSONALITY TYPE—**Enterprising. Enterprising occupations frequently involve starting up and carrying out projects. These occupations can involve leading people and making many decisions. They sometimes require risk taking and often deal with business.

EDUCATION/TRAINING PROGRAM(S)—Operations Management and Supervision. **RELATED KNOWLEDGE/COURSES—Production and Processing:** Knowledge of raw materials, production processes, quality control, costs, and other techniques for maximizing the effective manufacture and distribution of goods. **Administration and Management:** Knowledge of business and management principles involved in strategic planning, resource allocation, human resources modeling, leadership technique, production methods, and coordination of people and resources. **Personnel and Human Resources:** Knowledge of principles and procedures for personnel recruitment, selection, training, compensation and benefits, labor relations and negotiation, and personnel information systems. **Education and Training:** Knowledge of principles and methods for curriculum and training design, teaching and instruction for individuals and groups, and the measurement of training effects. **Mathematics:** Knowledge of arithmetic, algebra, geometry, calculus, and statistics and their applications.

First-Line Supervisors/Managers of Retail Sales Workers

▲ Education/Training Required: Work experience in a related occupation
▲ Annual Earnings: $28,590
▲ Growth: 8.1%
▲ Annual Job Openings: 206,000
▲ Self-Employed: 36.9%
▲ Part-Time: 8.2%

Directly supervise sales workers in a retail establishment or department. Duties may include management functions, such as purchasing, budgeting, accounting, and personnel work, in addition to supervisory duties. Directs and supervises employees engaged in sales, inventory-taking, reconciling cash receipts, or performing specific service such as pumping gasoline for customers. Plans and prepares work schedules and assigns employees to specific duties. Hires, trains, and evaluates personnel in sales or marketing establishment. Prepares sales and inventory reports for management and budget departments. Confers with company officials to develop methods and procedures to increase sales, expand markets, and promote business. Coordinates sales promotion activities and prepares merchandise displays and advertising copy. Assists sales staff in completing complicated and difficult sales. Keeps records pertaining to purchases, sales, and requisitions. Formulates pricing policies on merchandise according to requirements for profitability of store operations. Examines products purchased for resale or received for storage to determine condition of product or item. Prepares rental or lease agreement specifying charges and payment procedures for use of machinery, tools, or other such items. Inventories stock and reorders when inventories drop to specified level. Examines merchandise to ensure that it is correctly priced or displayed or functions as advertised. Listens to and resolves customer complaints regarding service, product, or personnel. Keeps records of employees' work schedules and time cards. **SKILLS—Speaking:** Talking to others to convey information effectively. **Coordination:** Adjusting actions in relation to others' actions. **Active Listening:** Giving full attention to what other people are saying, taking time to understand the points being made, asking questions as appropriate, and not interrupting at inappropriate times. **Mathematics:** Using mathematics to solve problems. **Management of Personnel Resources:** Motivating, developing, and directing people as they work, identifying the best people for the job. **Reading Comprehension:** Understanding written sentences and paragraphs in work-related documents.

GOE INFORMATION—Interest Area: 10. Sales and Marketing. **Work Group:** 10.01. Managerial Work in Sales and Marketing. **Other Job Titles in This Work Group:** Advertising and Promotions Managers; First-Line Supervisors/Managers of Non-Retail Sales Workers; Marketing Managers; Sales Managers. **PERSONALITY TYPE—** Enterprising. Enterprising occupations frequently involve starting up and carrying out projects. These occupations can involve leading people and making many decisions. They sometimes require risk taking and often deal with business.

EDUCATION/TRAINING PROGRAM(S)—Business, Management, Marketing, and Related Support Services, Other; Consumer Merchandising/Retailing Management; E-Commerce/Electronic Commerce; Floriculture/Floristry Operations and Management; Retailing and Retail Operations; Selling Skills and Sales Operations; Special Products Marketing Operations; Specialized Merchandising, Sales, and Related Marketing Operations, Other. **RELATED KNOWLEDGE/COURSES—Administration and Management:** Knowledge of business and management principles involved in strategic planning, resource allocation, human resources modeling, leadership technique, production methods, and coordination of people and resources. **Personnel and Human Resources:** Knowledge of principles and procedures for personnel recruitment, selection, training, compensation and benefits, labor relations and negotiation, and personnel information systems. **Mathematics:** Knowledge of arithmetic, algebra, geometry, calculus, and statistics and their applications. **Sales and Marketing:** Knowledge of principles and methods for showing, promoting, and selling products or services. This includes marketing strategy and tactics, product demonstration, sales techniques, and sales control systems. **Economics and Accounting:** Knowledge of economic and accounting principles and practices, the financial markets, banking, and the analysis and reporting of financial data.

First-Line Supervisors/ Managers of Transportation and Material-Moving Machine and Vehicle Operators

- ▲ Education/Training Required: Work experience in a related occupation
- ▲ Annual Earnings: $41,140
- ▲ Growth: 19.9%
- ▲ Annual Job Openings: 17,000
- ▲ Self-Employed: 10.4%
- ▲ Part-Time: 2.3%

Directly supervise and coordinate activities of transportation and material-moving machine and vehicle operators and helpers. Reviews orders, production schedules, and shipping/receiving notices to determine work sequence and material shipping dates, type, volume, and destinations. Plans and establishes transportation routes, work schedules, and assignments and allocates equipment to meet transportation, operations, or production goals. Directs workers in transportation or related services, such as pumping, moving, storing, and loading/unloading of materials or people. Maintains or verifies time, transportation, financial, inventory, and personnel records. Explains and demonstrates work tasks to new workers or assigns workers to experienced workers for further training. Resolves worker problems or assists workers in solving problems. Computes and estimates cash, payroll, transportation, personnel, and storage requirements, using calculator. Requisitions needed personnel, supplies, equipment, parts, or repair services. Recommends and implements measures to improve worker motivation, equipment performance, work methods, and customer services. Prepares, compiles, and submits reports on work activities, operations, production, and work-related accidents. Inspects or tests materials, stock, vehicles, equipment, and facilities to locate defects, meet maintenance or production specifications, and verify safety standards. Interprets transportation and tariff regulations, shipping orders, safety regulations, and company policies and procedures for workers. Recommends or implements personnel actions, such as hiring, firing, and performance evaluations. Receives telephone or radio reports of emergencies and dispatches personnel and vehicle in response to request. Confers with customers, supervisors, contractors, and other personnel to exchange information and resolve problems. Assists workers in performing tasks such as coupling railroad cars or loading vehicles. Repairs or schedules repair and preventive maintenance of vehicles and other equipment. Examines, measures, and weighs cargo or materials to determine specific handling requirements. Drives vehicles or operates machines or equipment. **SKILLS—Reading Comprehension:** Understanding written sentences and paragraphs in work-related documents. **Coordination:** Adjusting actions in relation to others' actions. **Management of Financial Resources:** Determining how money will be spent to get the work done and accounting for these expenditures. **Management of Personnel Resources:** Motivating, developing, and directing people as they work, identifying the best people for the job. **Active Listening:** Giving full attention to what other people are saying, taking time to understand the points being made, asking questions as appropriate, and not interrupting at inappropriate times. **Speaking:** Talking to others to convey information effectively.

GOE INFORMATION—Interest Area: 07. Transportation. **Work Group:** 07.01. Managerial Work in Transportation. **Other Job Titles in This Work Group:** Railroad Conductors and Yardmasters; Transportation Managers. **PERSONALITY TYPE—**Enterprising. Enterprising occupations frequently involve starting up and carrying out projects. These occupations can involve leading people and making many decisions. They sometimes require risk taking and often deal with business.

EDUCATION/TRAINING PROGRAM(S)—No data available. **RELATED KNOWLEDGE/COURSES— Transportation:** Knowledge of principles and methods for moving people or goods by air, rail, sea, or road, including the relative costs and benefits. **Administration and Management:** Knowledge of business and management principles involved in strategic planning, resource allocation, human resources modeling, leadership technique, production methods, and coordination of people and resources. **Personnel and Human Resources:** Knowledge of principles and procedures for personnel recruitment, selection, training, compensation and benefits, labor relations and negotiation, and personnel information systems. **Mathematics:** Knowledge of arithmetic, algebra, geometry, calculus, and statistics and their applications. **Economics and Accounting:** Knowledge of economic and accounting principles and practices, the financial markets, banking, and the analysis and reporting of financial data.

Fitness Trainers and Aerobics Instructors

▲ Education/Training Required: Postsecondary vocational training
▲ Annual Earnings: $23,340
▲ Growth: 40.3%
▲ Annual Job Openings: 19,000
▲ Self-Employed: 0%
▲ Part-Time: 42.5%

Instruct or coach groups or individuals in exercise activities and the fundamentals of sports. Demonstrate techniques and methods of participation. Observe participants and inform them of corrective measures necessary to improve their skills. Those required to hold teaching degrees should be reported in the appropriate teaching category. Organizes and conducts competition and tournaments. Selects, stores, orders, issues, and inventories equipment, materials, and supplies. Advises participants in use of heat or ultraviolet treatments and hot baths. Teaches individual and team sports to participants, utilizing knowledge of sports techniques and of physical capabilities of participants. Explains and enforces safety rules and regulations. Teaches and demonstrates use of gymnastic and training apparatus, such as trampolines and weights. Plans physical education program to promote development of participant physical attributes and social skills. Organizes, leads, instructs, and referees indoor and outdoor games, such as volleyball, baseball, and basketball. **SKILLS—Instructing:** Teaching others how to do something. **Coordination:** Adjusting actions in relation to others' actions. **Learning Strategies:** Selecting and using training/instructional methods and procedures appropriate for the situation when learning or teaching new things. **Speaking:** Talking to others to convey information effectively. **Monitoring:** Monitoring/Assessing your performance or that of other individuals or organizations to make improvements or take corrective action.

GOE INFORMATION—Interest Area: 01. Arts, Entertainment, and Media. **Work Group:** 01.10. Sports: Coaching, Instructing, Officiating, and Performing. **Other Job Titles in This Work Group:** Athletes and Sports Competitors; Coaches and Scouts; Umpires, Referees, and Other Sports Officials. **PERSONALITY TYPE**—Social. Social occupations frequently involve working with, communicating with, and teaching people. These occupations often involve helping or providing service to others.

EDUCATION/TRAINING PROGRAM(S)—Health and Physical Education, General; Physical Education Teaching and Coaching; Sport and Fitness Administration/Management. **RELATED KNOWLEDGE/ COURSES—Education and Training:** Knowledge of principles and methods for curriculum and training design, teaching and instruction for individuals and groups, and the measurement of training effects. **Psychology:** Knowledge of human behavior and performance; individual differences in ability, personality, and interests; learning and motivation; psychological research methods; and the assessment and treatment of behavioral and affective disorders. **Customer and Personal Service:** Knowledge of principles and processes for providing customer and personal services. This includes customer needs assessment, meeting quality standards for services, and evaluation of customer satisfaction. **Biology:** Knowledge of plant and animal organisms and their tissues, cells, functions, interdependencies, and interactions with each other and the environment. **English Language:** Knowledge of the structure and content of the English language, including the meaning and spelling of words, rules of composition, and grammar.

Fitters, Structural Metal— Precision

▲ Education/Training Required: Moderate-term on-the-job training
▲ Annual Earnings: $28,000
▲ Growth: 19.5%
▲ Annual Job Openings: 20,000
▲ Self-Employed: 0%
▲ Part-Time: 3.4%

Lay out, position, align, and fit together fabricated parts of structural metal products preparatory to welding or riveting. Aligns parts, using jack, turnbuckles, wedges, drift pins, pry bars, and hammer. Moves parts into position manually or by hoist or crane. Marks reference points onto floor or face block and transposes them to workpiece, using measuring devices, squares, chalk, and soapstone. Gives directions to welder to build up low spots or short pieces with weld. Heat-treats parts with acetylene torch. Straightens warped or bent parts, using sledge, hand torch, straightening press, or bulldozer. Locates reference points, using transit, and erects ladders and scaffolding to fit together large assemblies. Removes high spots and cuts bevels, using hand files, portable grinders, and cutting torch. Sets up face block, jigs, and fixtures. Examines blueprints and plans sequence of operation, applying knowledge of geometry, effects of heat, weld shrinkage, machining, and metal thickness. Tack welds fitted parts together. Positions or tightens braces, jacks, clamps, ropes, or bolt straps or bolts parts in positions for welding or riveting. **SKILLS— Mathematics:** Using mathematics to solve problems. **Equipment Selection:** Determining the kind of tools and equipment needed to do a job. **Reading Comprehension:** Understanding written sentences and paragraphs in work-related documents. **Critical Thinking:** Using logic and reasoning to identify the strengths and weaknesses of alternative solutions, conclusions, or approaches to problems. **Coordination:** Adjusting actions in relation to others' actions. **Judgment and Decision Making:** Considering the relative costs and benefits of potential actions to choose the most appropriate one.

GOE INFORMATION—Interest Area: 08. Industrial Production. **Work Group:** 08.03. Production Work. **Other Job Titles in This Work Group:** Bakers, Manufacturing; Bindery Machine Operators and Tenders; Brazers; Cementing and Gluing Machine Operators and Tenders; Chemical Equipment Controllers and Operators; Chemical Equipment Operators and Tenders; Chemical Equipment Tenders; Cleaning, Washing, and Metal Pickling Equipment Operators and Tenders; Coating, Painting, and Spraying Machine Operators and Tenders; Coil Winders, Tapers, and Finishers; Combination Machine Tool Operators and Tenders, Metal and Plastic; Computer-Controlled Machine Tool Operators, Metal and Plastic; Cooling and Freezing Equipment Operators and Tenders; Crushing, Grinding, and Polishing Machine Setters, Operators, and Tenders; Cutters and Trimmers, Hand; Cutting and Slicing Machine Operators and Tenders; Cutting and Slicing Machine Setters, Operators, and Tenders; Design Printing Machine Setters and Set-Up Operators; Electrolytic Plating and Coating Machine Operators and Tenders, Metal and Plastic; Electrolytic Plating and Coating Machine Setters and Set-Up Operators, Metal and Plastic; Electrotypers and Stereotypers; Embossing Machine Set-Up Operators; Engraver Set-Up Operators; Extruding and Forming Machine Operators and Tenders, Synthetic or Glass Fibers; Extruding and Forming Machine Setters, Operators, and Tenders, Synthetic and Glass Fibers; Extruding, Forming, Pressing, and Compacting Machine Operators and Tenders; Fabric and Apparel Patternmakers; Fiber Product Cutting Machine Setters and Set-Up Operators; Fiberglass Laminators and Fabricators; Film Laboratory Technicians; Food and Tobacco Roasting, Baking, and Drying Machine Operators and Tenders; Food Batchmakers; Food Cooking Machine Operators and Tenders; Furnace, Kiln, Oven, Drier, and Kettle Operators and Tenders; Glass Cutting Machine Setters and Set-Up Operators; Graders and Sorters, Agricultural Products; Grinding and Polishing Workers, Hand; Hand Compositors and Typesetters; Heaters, Metal and Plastic; Helpers— Production Workers; Job Printers; others. **PERSONALITY TYPE—**Realistic. Realistic occupations frequently involve work activities that include practical, hands-on problems and solutions. They often deal with plants, animals, and real-world materials like wood, tools, and machinery. Many of the occupations require working outside and do not involve a lot of paperwork or working closely with others.

EDUCATION/TRAINING PROGRAM(S)—Machine Shop Technology/Assistant. **RELATED KNOWLEDGE/**

COURSES—**Building and Construction:** Knowledge of materials, methods, and tools involved in the construction or repair of houses, buildings, or other structures, such as highways and roads. **Principles of Mechanical Devices:** Knowledge of machines and tools, including their designs, uses, repair, and maintenance. **Mathematics:** Knowledge of arithmetic, algebra, geometry, calculus, and statistics and their applications. **Engineering and Technology:** Knowl-edge of the practical application of engineering science and technology. This includes applying principles, techniques, procedures, and equipment to the design and production of various goods and services. **Physics:** Knowledge and pre-diction of physical principles and laws and their interrela-tionships and applications to understanding fluid, material, and atmospheric dynamics and mechanical, electrical, atomic, and sub-atomic structures and processes.

Flight Attendants

- ▲ Education/Training Required: Long-term on-the-job training
- ▲ Annual Earnings: $40,600
- ▲ Growth: 18.4%
- ▲ Annual Job Openings: 8,000
- ▲ Self-Employed: 1.0%
- ▲ Part-Time: 45.7%

Provide personal services to ensure the safety and com-fort of airline passengers during flight. Greet passengers, verify tickets, explain use of safety equipment, and serve food or beverages. Greets passengers, verifies tickets, records destinations, and directs passengers to assigned seats. Explains use of safety equipment to passengers. Serves prepared meals and beverages. Walks aisle of plane to verify that passengers have complied with federal regulations prior to takeoff. Collects money for meals and beverages. Pre-pares reports showing place of departure and destination, passenger ticket numbers, meal and beverage inventories, and lost and found articles. Administers first aid to pas-sengers in distress when needed. Assists passengers in stor-ing carry-on luggage in overhead, garment, or under-seat storage. SKILLS—**Service Orientation:** Actively looking for ways to help people. **Social Perceptiveness:** Being aware of others' reactions and understanding why they react as they do. **Reading Comprehension:** Understanding writ-ten sentences and paragraphs in work-related documents. **Active Listening:** Giving full attention to what other people are saying, taking time to understand the points being made, asking questions as appropriate, and not in-terrupting at inappropriate times. **Coordination:** Adjust-ing actions in relation to others' actions.

GOE INFORMATION—**Interest Area:** 11. Recreation, Travel, and Other Personal Services. **Work Group:** 11.03. Transportation and Lodging Services. **Other Job Titles in This Work Group:** Baggage Porters and Bellhops; Con-cierges; Hotel, Motel, and Resort Desk Clerks; Reserva-tion and Transportation Ticket Agents; Reservation and Transportation Ticket Agents and Travel Clerks; Transpor-tation Attendants, Except Flight Attendants and Baggage Porters. **PERSONALITY TYPE**—Enterprising. Enter-prising occupations frequently involve starting up and carrying out projects. These occupations can involve lead-ing people and making many decisions. They sometimes require risk taking and often deal with business.

EDUCATION/TRAINING PROGRAM(S)—Airline Flight Attendant. **RELATED KNOWLEDGE/ COURSES—Customer and Personal Service:** Knowledge of principles and processes for providing customer and personal services. This includes customer needs assessment, meeting quality standards for services, and evaluation of customer satisfaction. **Public Safety and Security:** Knowl-edge of relevant equipment, policies, procedures, and strat-egies to promote effective local, state, or national security operations for the protection of people, data, property, and institutions. **Medicine and Dentistry:** Knowledge of the information and techniques needed to diagnose and treat human injuries, diseases, and deformities. This in-cludes symptoms, treatment alternatives, drug properties and interactions, and preventive health-care measures. **English Language:** Knowledge of the structure and con-tent of the English language, including the meaning and spelling of words, rules of composition, and grammar. **Transportation:** Knowledge of principles and methods for moving people or goods by air, rail, sea, or road, including the relative costs and benefits. **Law and Government:** Knowledge of laws, legal codes, court procedures, prece-dents, government regulations, executive orders, agency rules, and the democratic political process.

Floral Designers

▲ Education/Training Required: Moderate-term on-the-job training
▲ Annual Earnings: $19,280
▲ Growth: 14.9%
▲ Annual Job Openings: 15,000
▲ Self-Employed: 31.9%
▲ Part-Time: 20.0%

Design, cut, and arrange live, dried, or artificial flowers and foliage. Plans arrangement according to client's requirements, utilizing knowledge of design and properties of materials, or selects appropriate standard design pattern. Confers with client regarding price and type of arrangement desired. Decorates buildings, halls, churches, or other facilities where events are planned. Trims material and arranges bouquets, wreaths, terrariums, and other items, using trimmers, shapers, wire, pin, floral tape, foam, and other materials. Selects flora and foliage for arrangement. Packs and wraps completed arrangements. Conducts classes or demonstrations; trains other workers. Estimates costs and prices arrangements. **SKILLS—Learning Strategies:** Selecting and using training/instructional methods and procedures appropriate for the situation when learning or teaching new things. **Service Orientation:** Actively looking for ways to help people. **Writing:** Communicating effectively in writing as appropriate for the needs of the audience. **Time Management:** Managing one's own time and the time of others. **Instructing:** Teaching others how to do something. **Negotiation:** Bringing others together and trying to reconcile differences. **Monitoring:** Monitoring/Assessing your performance or that of other individuals or organizations to make improvements or take corrective action.

GOE INFORMATION—Interest Area: 01. Arts, Entertainment, and Media. **Work Group:** 01.04. Visual Arts. **Other Job Titles in This Work Group:** Cartoonists; Commercial and Industrial Designers; Designers, All Other; Exhibit Designers; Fashion Designers; Fine Artists, Including Painters, Sculptors, and Illustrators; Graphic Designers; Interior Designers; Merchandise Displayers and Window Trimmers; Multi-Media Artists and Animators; Painters and Illustrators; Sculptors; Set and Exhibit Designers; Set Designers; Sketch Artists. **PERSONALITY TYPE—Artistic.** Artistic occupations frequently involve working with forms, designs, and patterns. They often require self-expression, and the work can be done without following a clear set of rules.

EDUCATION/TRAINING PROGRAM(S)—Floriculture/Floristry Operations and Management. **RELATED KNOWLEDGE/COURSES—Fine Arts:** Knowledge of the theory and techniques required to compose, produce, and perform works of music, dance, visual arts, drama, and sculpture. **Customer and Personal Service:** Knowledge of principles and processes for providing customer and personal services. This includes customer needs assessment, meeting quality standards for services, and evaluation of customer satisfaction. **Design:** Knowledge of design techniques, tools, and principles involved in production of precision technical plans, blueprints, drawings, and models. **Education and Training:** Knowledge of principles and methods for curriculum and training design, teaching and instruction for individuals and groups, and the measurement of training effects. **Biology:** Knowledge of plant and animal organisms and their tissues, cells, functions, interdependencies, and interactions with each other and the environment.

Food Preparation Workers

▲ Education/Training Required: Short-term on-the-job training
▲ Annual Earnings: $15,910
▲ Growth: 16.9%
▲ Annual Job Openings: 231,000
▲ Self-Employed: 0.3%
▲ Part-Time: 57.4%

Perform a variety of food preparation duties other than cooking, such as preparing cold foods and shellfish, slicing meat, and brewing coffee or tea. Cleans, portions, and cuts or peels various foods to prepare for cooking or serving. Stores food in designated containers and storage areas to prevent spoilage. Cleans and maintains work areas, equipment, and utensils. Butchers and cleans fowl, fish, poultry, and shellfish to prepare for cooking or serving. Requisitions, stores, and distributes food supplies, equipment, and utensils. Distributes food to waiters and waitresses to serve to customers. Carries food supplies, equipment, and utensils to and from storage and work areas. Portions and arranges food on serving dishes, trays, carts, or conveyor belts. Cleans, cuts, slices, or disjoints meats and poultry to prepare for cooking. Prepares and serves variety of beverages, such as coffee, tea, and soft drinks. Prepares variety of foods according to customers' orders or instructions of superior, following approved procedures. **SKILLS—Service Orientation:** Actively looking for ways to help people.

GOE INFORMATION—Interest Area: 11. Recreation, Travel, and Other Personal Services. **Work Group:** 11.05. Food and Beverage Services. **Other Job Titles in This Work Group:** Bakers; Bakers, Bread and Pastry; Bartenders; Butchers and Meat Cutters; Chefs and Head Cooks; Combined Food Preparation and Serving Workers, Including Fast Food; Cooks, All Other; Cooks, Fast Food; Cooks, Institution and Cafeteria; Cooks, Restaurant; Cooks, Short Order; Counter Attendants, Cafeteria, Food Concession, and Coffee Shop; Dining Room and Cafeteria Attendants and Bartender Helpers; Dishwashers; Food Preparation and Serving Related Workers, All Other; Food Servers,

Nonrestaurant; Hosts and Hostesses, Restaurant, Lounge, and Coffee Shop; Waiters and Waitresses. **PERSONALITY TYPE—Realistic.** Realistic occupations frequently involve work activities that include practical, hands-on problems and solutions. They often deal with plants, animals, and real-world materials like wood, tools, and machinery. Many of the occupations require working outside and do not involve a lot of paperwork or working closely with others.

EDUCATION/TRAINING PROGRAM(S)—Cooking and Related Culinary Arts, General; Food Preparation/Professional Cooking/Kitchen Assistant; Institutional Food Workers. **RELATED KNOWLEDGE/COURSES—Customer and Personal Service:** Knowledge of principles and processes for providing customer and personal services. This includes customer needs assessment, meeting quality standards for services, and evaluation of customer satisfaction. **Food Production:** Knowledge of techniques and equipment for planting, growing, and harvesting food products (both plant and animal) for consumption, including storage/handling techniques. **Public Safety and Security:** Knowledge of relevant equipment, policies, procedures, and strategies to promote effective local, state, or national security operations for the protection of people, data, property, and institutions. **Principles of Mechanical Devices:** Knowledge of machines and tools, including their designs, uses, repair, and maintenance. **Chemistry:** Knowledge of the chemical composition, structure, and properties of substances and of the chemical processes and transformations that they undergo. This includes uses of chemicals and their interactions, danger signs, production techniques, and disposal methods.

Food Science Technicians

- ▲ Education/Training Required: Associate's degree
- ▲ Annual Earnings: $27,530
- ▲ Growth: 15.2%
- ▲ Annual Job Openings: 15,000
- ▲ Self-Employed: 0.9%
- ▲ Part-Time: 11.7%

Perform standardized qualitative and quantitative tests to determine physical or chemical properties of food or beverage products. Conducts standardized tests on food, beverages, additives, and preservatives to ensure compliance to standards for factors such as color, texture, nutrients, and coloring. Prepares slides and incubates slides with cell cultures. Cleans and sterilizes laboratory equipment. Orders supplies to maintain inventory in laboratory or in storage facility of food or beverage processing plant. Measures, tests, and weighs bottles, cans, and other containers to ensure that hardness, strength, and dimensions meet specifications. Records and compiles test results and prepares graphs, charts, and reports. Tastes or smells food or beverages to ensure that flavor meets specifications or to select samples with specific characteristics. Computes moisture or salt content, percentage of ingredients, formulas, or other product factors, using mathematical and chemical procedures. Examines chemical and biological samples to identify cell structure, bacteria, or extraneous material, using microscope. Mixes, blends, or cultivates ingredients to make reagents or to manufacture food or beverage products. Analyzes test results to classify product or compares results with standard tables. **SKILLS—Mathematics:** Using mathematics to solve problems. **Reading Comprehension:** Understanding written sentences and paragraphs in work-related documents. **Writing:** Communicating effectively in writing as appropriate for the needs of the audience. **Active Learning:** Understanding the implications of new information for both current and future problem-solving and decision-making. **Science:** Using scientific rules and methods to solve problems.

GOE INFORMATION—Interest Area: 02. Science, Math, and Engineering. **Work Group:** 02.03. Life Sciences. **Other Job Titles in This Work Group:** Agricultural and Food Science Technicians; Agricultural Technicians; Animal Scientists; Biochemists; Biochemists and Biophysicists; Biological Scientists, All Other; Biologists; Biophysicists; Conservation Scientists; Environmental Scientists and Specialists, Including Health; Epidemiologists; Food Scientists and Technologists; Foresters; Life Scientists, All Other; Medical Scientists, Except Epidemiologists; Microbiologists; Plant Scientists; Range Managers; Soil and Plant Scientists; Soil Conservationists; Soil Scientists; Zoologists and Wildlife Biologists. **PERSONALITY TYPE—Realistic.** Realistic occupations frequently involve work activities that include practical, hands-on problems and solutions. They often deal with plants, animals, and real-world materials like wood, tools, and machinery. Many of the occupations require working outside and do not involve a lot of paperwork or working closely with others.

EDUCATION/TRAINING PROGRAM(S)—Food Science. RELATED KNOWLEDGE/COURSES—Chemistry: Knowledge of the chemical composition, structure, and properties of substances and of the chemical processes and transformations that they undergo. This includes uses of chemicals and their interactions, danger signs, production techniques, and disposal methods. **Biology:** Knowledge of plant and animal organisms and their tissues, cells, functions, interdependencies, and interactions with each other and the environment. **Mathematics:** Knowledge of arithmetic, algebra, geometry, calculus, and statistics and their applications. **English Language:** Knowledge of the structure and content of the English language, including the meaning and spelling of words, rules of composition, and grammar. **Food Production:** Knowledge of techniques and equipment for planting, growing, and harvesting food products (both plant and animal) for consumption, including storage/handling techniques.

Food Servers, Nonrestaurant

- ▲ Education/Training Required: Short-term on-the-job training
- ▲ Annual Earnings: $15,310
- ▲ Growth: 16.4%
- ▲ Annual Job Openings: 85,000
- ▲ Self-Employed: 0.5%
- ▲ Part-Time: 58.2%

Serve food to patrons outside of a restaurant environment, such as in hotels, hospital rooms, or cars. Prepares and delivers food trays. Washes dishes and cleans work area, tables, cabinets, and ovens; sweeps service area with broom. Restocks service counter with items such as ice, napkins, and straws. Totals and presents check to customer and accepts payment for service. Records amount and types of special food items served to customers. Prepares fountain drinks, such as sodas, milkshakes, and malted milks. Prepares food items, such as sandwiches, salads, soups, and beverages, and places items such as eating utensils, napkins, and condiments on trays. Reads orders to determine items to place on food tray. Examines filled tray for completeness. Takes order and relays order to kitchen or serving counter to be filled. Carries silverware, linen, and food on tray or uses cart. Removes tray and stacks dishes for return to kitchen. Pushes carts to rooms and serves trays to patients or guests. Apportions and places food servings on plates and trays according to order or instructions. **SKILLS—Service Orientation:** Actively looking for ways to help people. **Speaking:** Talking to others to convey information effectively.

GOE INFORMATION—Interest Area: 11. Recreation, Travel, and Other Personal Services. **Work Group:** 11.05. Food and Beverage Services. **Other Job Titles in This Work Group:** Bakers; Bakers, Bread and Pastry; Bartenders; Butchers and Meat Cutters; Chefs and Head Cooks; Combined Food Preparation and Serving Workers, Includ-

ing Fast Food; Cooks, All Other; Cooks, Fast Food; Cooks, Institution and Cafeteria; Cooks, Restaurant; Cooks, Short Order; Counter Attendants, Cafeteria, Food Concession, and Coffee Shop; Dining Room and Cafeteria Attendants and Bartender Helpers; Dishwashers; Food Preparation and Serving Related Workers, All Other; Food Preparation Workers; Hosts and Hostesses, Restaurant, Lounge, and Coffee Shop; Waiters and Waitresses. **PERSONALITY TYPE—Social.** Social occupations frequently involve working with, communicating with, and teaching people. These occupations often involve helping or providing service to others.

EDUCATION/TRAINING PROGRAM(S)—Food Service, Waiter/Waitress, and Dining Room Management/Manager. RELATED KNOWLEDGE/COURSES—Customer and Personal Service: Knowledge of principles and processes for providing customer and personal services. This includes customer needs assessment, meeting quality standards for services, and evaluation of customer satisfaction. **Mathematics:** Knowledge of arithmetic, algebra, geometry, calculus, and statistics and their applications. **English Language:** Knowledge of the structure and content of the English language, including the meaning and spelling of words, rules of composition, and grammar. **Sales and Marketing:** Knowledge of principles and methods for showing, promoting, and selling products or services. This includes marketing strategy and tactics, product demonstration, sales techniques, and sales control systems.

Food Service Managers

- ▲ Education/Training Required: Work experience in a related occupation
- ▲ Annual Earnings: $33,630
- ▲ Growth: 15.0%
- ▲ Annual Job Openings: 55,000
- ▲ Self-Employed: 37.5%
- ▲ Part-Time: 8.5%

Plan, direct, or coordinate activities of an organization or department that serves food and beverages. Monitors compliance with health and fire regulations regarding food

preparation, serving, and building maintenance in lodging and dining facility. Coordinates assignments of cooking personnel to ensure economical use of food and timely preparation. Estimates food, liquor, wine, and other beverage consumption to anticipate amount to be purchased or requisitioned. Organizes and directs worker training programs, resolves personnel problems, hires new staff, and evaluates employee performance in dining and lodging facilities. Plans menus and food utilization based on anticipated number of guests, nutritional value, palatability, popularity, and costs. Monitors food preparation and methods, size of portions, and garnishing and presentation of food to ensure that food is prepared and presented in accepted manner. Investigates and resolves complaints regarding food quality, service, or accommodations. Creates specialty dishes and develops recipes to be used in dining facility. Tests cooked food by tasting and smelling to ensure palatability and flavor conformity. Keeps records required by government agencies regarding sanitation and regarding food subsidies where indicated. Establishes and enforces nutrition standards for dining establishment based on accepted industry standards. Reviews menus and analyzes recipes to determine labor and overhead costs and assigns prices to menu items. Monitors budget and payroll records and reviews financial transactions to ensure expenditures are authorized and budgeted. **SKILLS—Coordination:** Adjusting actions in relation to others' actions. **Management of Personnel Resources:** Motivating, developing, and directing people as they work, identifying the best people for the job. **Speaking:** Talking to others to convey information effectively. **Monitoring:** Monitoring/Assessing your performance or that of other individuals or organizations to make improvements or take corrective action. **Time Management:** Managing one's own time and the time of others.

GOE INFORMATION—Interest Area: 11. Recreation, Travel, and Other Personal Services. **Work Group:** 11.01. Managerial Work in Recreation, Travel, and Other Personal Services. **Other Job Titles in This Work Group:** Aircraft Cargo Handling Supervisors; First-Line Supervisors/Managers of Food Preparation and Serving Workers; First-Line Supervisors/Managers of Housekeeping and Janitorial Workers; First-Line Supervisors/Managers of Personal Service Workers; Gaming Managers; Gaming Supervisors; Housekeeping Supervisors; Janitorial Supervisors; Lodging Managers; Meeting and Convention Planners. **PERSONALITY TYPE**—Enterprising. Enterprising occupations frequently involve starting up and carrying out projects. These occupations can involve leading people and making many decisions. They sometimes require risk taking and often deal with business.

EDUCATION/TRAINING PROGRAM(S)—Hospitality Administration/Management, General; Hotel/Motel Administration/Management; Restaurant, Culinary, and Catering Management/Manager; Restaurant/Food Services Management. **RELATED KNOWLEDGE/ COURSES—Administration and Management:** Knowledge of business and management principles involved in strategic planning, resource allocation, human resources modeling, leadership technique, production methods, and coordination of people and resources. **Customer and Personal Service:** Knowledge of principles and processes for providing customer and personal services. This includes customer needs assessment, meeting quality standards for services, and evaluation of customer satisfaction. **Economics and Accounting:** Knowledge of economic and accounting principles and practices, the financial markets, banking, and the analysis and reporting of financial data. **Education and Training:** Knowledge of principles and methods for curriculum and training design, teaching and instruction for individuals and groups, and the measurement of training effects. **Mathematics:** Knowledge of arithmetic, algebra, geometry, calculus, and statistics and their applications. **Personnel and Human Resources:** Knowledge of principles and procedures for personnel recruitment, selection, training, compensation and benefits, labor relations and negotiation, and personnel information systems. **Public Safety and Security:** Knowledge of relevant equipment, policies, procedures, and strategies to promote effective local, state, or national security operations for the protection of people, data, property, and institutions.

Foreign Language and Literature Teachers, Postsecondary

▲ Education/Training Required: Master's degree
▲ Annual Earnings: $45,030
▲ Growth: 23.5%
▲ Annual Job Openings: 184,000
▲ Self-Employed: 0%
▲ Part-Time: 32.3%

Teach courses in foreign (i.e., other than English) languages and literature. Prepares and delivers lectures to students. Compiles, administers, and grades examinations or assigns this work to others. Compiles bibliographies of specialized materials for outside reading assignments. Stimulates class discussions. Advises students on academic and vocational curricula. Directs research of other teachers or graduate students working for advanced academic degrees. Conducts research in particular field of knowledge and publishes findings in professional journals. Acts as adviser to student organizations. Serves on faculty committee providing professional consulting services to government and industry. **SKILLS—Reading Comprehension:** Understanding written sentences and paragraphs in work-related documents. **Speaking:** Talking to others to convey information effectively. **Instructing:** Teaching others how to do something. **Writing:** Communicating effectively in writing as appropriate for the needs of the audience. **Learning Strategies:** Selecting and using training/instructional methods and procedures appropriate for the situation when learning or teaching new things.

GOE INFORMATION—Interest Area: 12. Education and Social Service. **Work Group:** 12.03. Educational Services. **Other Job Titles in This Work Group:** Adult Literacy, Remedial Education, and GED Teachers and Instructors; Agricultural Sciences Teachers, Postsecondary; Anthropology and Archeology Teachers, Postsecondary; Architecture Teachers, Postsecondary; Archivists; Area, Ethnic, and Cultural Studies Teachers, Postsecondary; Art, Drama, and Music Teachers, Postsecondary; Atmospheric, Earth, Marine, and Space Sciences Teachers, Postsecondary; Audio-Visual Collections Specialists; Biological Science Teachers, Postsecondary; Business Teachers, Postsecondary; Chemistry Teachers, Postsecondary; Child Care Workers; Communications Teachers, Postsecondary; Computer Science Teachers, Postsecondary; Criminal Justice and Law Enforcement Teachers, Postsecondary; Curators; Economics Teachers, Postsecondary; Education Teachers, Postsecondary; Edu-

cational Psychologists; Educational, Vocational, and School Counselors; Elementary School Teachers, Except Special Education; Engineering Teachers, Postsecondary; English Language and Literature Teachers, Postsecondary; Environmental Science Teachers, Postsecondary; Farm and Home Management Advisors; Forestry and Conservation Science Teachers, Postsecondary; Geography Teachers, Postsecondary; Graduate Teaching Assistants; Health Specialties Teachers, Postsecondary; History Teachers, Postsecondary; Home Economics Teachers, Postsecondary; Kindergarten Teachers, Except Special Education; Law Teachers, Postsecondary; Librarians; Library Assistants, Clerical; Library Science Teachers, Postsecondary; Library Technicians; Mathematical Science Teachers, Postsecondary; Middle School Teachers, Except Special and Vocational Education; Museum Technicians and Conservators; Nursing Instructors and Teachers, Postsecondary; Personal Financial Advisors; Philosophy and Religion Teachers, Postsecondary; Physics Teachers, Postsecondary; Political Science Teachers, Postsecondary; Postsecondary Teachers, All Other; Preschool Teachers, Except Special Education; Psychology Teachers, Postsecondary; others. **PERSONALITY TYPE—Artistic.** Artistic occupations frequently involve working with forms, designs, and patterns. They often require self-expression, and the work can be done without following a clear set of rules.

EDUCATION/TRAINING PROGRAM(S)—African Languages, Literatures, and Linguistics; Albanian Language and Literature; American Indian/Native American Languages, Literatures, and Linguistics; Ancient Near Eastern and Biblical Languages, Literatures, and Linguistics; Ancient/Classical Greek Language and Literature; Arabic Language and Literature; Australian/Oceanic/Pacific Languages, Literatures, and Linguistics; Bahasa Indonesian/Bahasa Malay Languages and Literatures; Baltic Languages, Literatures, and Linguistics; Bengali Language and Literature; Bulgarian Language and Literature; Burmese Language and Literature; Catalan Language and Literature; Celtic Languages, Literatures, and Linguistics; Chinese Language and Literature; Classics and Classical Languages,

Literatures, and Linguistics, General; Classics and Classical Languages, Literatures, and Linguistics, Other; Czech Language and Literature; Danish Language and Literature; Dutch/Flemish Language and Literature; East Asian Languages, Literatures, and Linguistics, General; East Asian Languages, Literatures, and Linguistics, Other; Filipino/Tagalog Language and Literature; Finnish and Related Languages, Literatures, and Linguistics; Foreign Languages and Literatures, General; Foreign Languages, Literatures, and Linguistics, Other; French Language and Literature; German Language and Literature; Germanic Languages, Literatures, and Linguistics, General; Germanic Languages, Literatures, and Linguistics, Other; Hebrew Language and Literature; Hindi Language and Literature; Hungarian/Magyar Language and Literature; Iranian/Persian Languages, Literatures, and Linguistics; Italian Language and Literature; Japanese Language and Literature; Khmer/Cambodian Language and Literature; Korean Language and Literature; Language Interpretation and Translation; Lao/Laotian Language and Literature; Latin Language and Literature; Latin Teacher Education; Linguistics; Middle/Near Eastern and Semitic Languages, Literatures, and Linguistics, Other; others. **RELATED KNOWLEDGE/**

COURSES—English Language: Knowledge of the structure and content of the English language, including the meaning and spelling of words, rules of composition, and grammar. **Education and Training:** Knowledge of principles and methods for curriculum and training design, teaching and instruction for individuals and groups, and the measurement of training effects. **Foreign Language:** Knowledge of the structure and content of a foreign (non-English) language, including the meaning and spelling of words, rules of composition and grammar, and pronunciation. **Communications and Media:** Knowledge of media production, communication, and dissemination techniques and methods. This includes alternative ways to inform and entertain via written, oral, and visual media. **Clerical Studies:** Knowledge of administrative and clerical procedures and systems, such as word processing, managing files and records, stenography and transcription, designing forms, and other office procedures and terminology. **Computers and Electronics:** Knowledge of circuit boards, processors, chips, electronic equipment, and computer hardware and software, including applications and programming.

Forest Fire Fighting and Prevention Supervisors

- ▲ Education/Training Required: Work experience in a related occupation
- ▲ Annual Earnings: $53,420
- ▲ Growth: 16.7%
- ▲ Annual Job Openings: 5,000
- ▲ Self-Employed: 0%
- ▲ Part-Time: 2.1%

Supervise fire fighters who control and suppress fires in forests or vacant public land. Dispatches crews according to reported size, location, and condition of forest fires. Trains workers in parachute jumping, fire suppression, aerial observation, and radio communication. Parachutes to major fire locations and directs fire containment and suppression activities. Maintains radio communication with crews at fire scene to inform crew and base of changing conditions and learn of casualties. Observes fire and crews from air to determine force requirements and note changing conditions. Directs loading of fire suppression equipment into aircraft and parachuting of equipment to crews on ground. **SKILLS—Coordination:** Adjusting actions in relation to others' actions. **Management of Personnel Resources:** Motivating, developing, and directing people as they work, identifying the best people for the job. **Judgment and De-**

cision Making: Considering the relative costs and benefits of potential actions to choose the most appropriate one. **Monitoring:** Monitoring/Assessing your performance or that of other individuals or organizations to make improvements or take corrective action. **Service Orientation:** Actively looking for ways to help people. **Instructing:** Teaching others how to do something.

GOE INFORMATION—Interest Area: 04. Law, Law Enforcement, and Public Safety. **Work Group:** 04.01. Managerial Work in Law, Law Enforcement, and Public Safety. **Other Job Titles in This Work Group:** Emergency Management Specialists; First-Line Supervisors/Managers of Correctional Officers; First-Line Supervisors/Managers of Fire Fighting and Prevention Workers; First-Line Supervisors/Managers of Police and Detectives; First-Line Supervisors/Managers, Protective Service Workers, All

Other; Municipal Fire Fighting and Prevention Supervisors. **PERSONALITY TYPE**—Realistic. Realistic occupations frequently involve work activities that include practical, hands-on problems and solutions. They often deal with plants, animals, and real-world materials like wood, tools, and machinery. Many of the occupations require working outside and do not involve a lot of paperwork or working closely with others.

EDUCATION/TRAINING PROGRAM(S)—Fire Protection and Safety Technology/Technician; Fire Services Administration. **RELATED KNOWLEDGE/ COURSES**—**Public Safety and Security:** Knowledge of relevant equipment, policies, procedures, and strategies to promote effective local, state, or national security opera-tions for the protection of people, data, property, and institutions. **Transportation:** Knowledge of principles and methods for moving people or goods by air, rail, sea, or road, including the relative costs and benefits. **Administration and Management:** Knowledge of business and management principles involved in strategic planning, resource allocation, human resources modeling, leadership technique, production methods, and coordination of people and resources. **Education and Training:** Knowledge of principles and methods for curriculum and training design, teaching and instruction for individuals and groups, and the measurement of training effects. **Telecommunications:** Knowledge of transmission, broadcasting, switching, control, and operation of telecommunications systems.

Forestry and Conservation Science Teachers, Postsecondary

▲ Education/Training Required: Master's degree
▲ Annual Earnings: $63,460
▲ Growth: 23.5%
▲ Annual Job Openings: 184,000
▲ Self-Employed: 0%
▲ Part-Time: 32.3%

Teach courses in environmental and conservation science. Prepares and delivers lectures to students. Compiles, administers, and grades examinations or assigns this work to others. Advises students on academic and vocational curricula. Conducts research in particular field of knowledge and publishes findings in professional journals. Serves on faculty committee providing professional consulting services to government and industry. Acts as adviser to student organizations. Directs research of other teachers or graduate students working for advanced academic degrees. Stimulates class discussions. Compiles bibliographies of specialized materials for outside reading assignments. **SKILLS—Reading Comprehension:** Understanding written sentences and paragraphs in work-related documents. **Instructing:** Teaching others how to do something. **Learning Strategies:** Selecting and using training/instructional methods and procedures appropriate for the situation when learning or teaching new things. **Writing:** Communicating effectively in writing as appropriate for the needs of the audience. **Science:** Using scientific rules and methods to solve problems. **Critical Thinking:** Using logic and reasoning to identify the strengths and weaknesses of alternative solutions, conclusions, or approaches to problems. **Active Learning:** Understanding the implications of new information for both current and future problem-solving and decision-making.

GOE INFORMATION—Interest Area: 12. Education and Social Service. **Work Group:** 12.03. Educational Services. **Other Job Titles in This Work Group:** Adult Literacy, Remedial Education, and GED Teachers and Instructors; Agricultural Sciences Teachers, Postsecondary; Anthropology and Archeology Teachers, Postsecondary; Architecture Teachers, Postsecondary; Archivists; Area, Ethnic, and Cultural Studies Teachers, Postsecondary; Art, Drama, and Music Teachers, Postsecondary; Atmospheric, Earth, Marine, and Space Sciences Teachers, Postsecondary; Audio-Visual Collections Specialists; Biological Science Teachers, Postsecondary; Business Teachers, Postsecondary; Chemistry Teachers, Postsecondary; Child Care Workers; Communications Teachers, Postsecondary; Computer Science Teachers, Postsecondary; Criminal Justice and Law Enforcement Teachers, Postsecondary; Curators; Economics Teachers, Postsecondary; Education Teachers, Postsecondary; Educational Psychologists; Educational, Vocational, and School Counselors; Elementary School Teachers, Except Special Education; Engineering Teachers, Postsecondary; English Language and Literature Teachers, Postsecondary; Environmental Science Teachers,

Postsecondary; Farm and Home Management Advisors; Foreign Language and Literature Teachers, Postsecondary; Geography Teachers, Postsecondary; Graduate Teaching Assistants; Health Specialties Teachers, Postsecondary; History Teachers, Postsecondary; Home Economics Teachers, Postsecondary; Kindergarten Teachers, Except Special Education; Law Teachers, Postsecondary; Librarians; Library Assistants, Clerical; Library Science Teachers, Postsecondary; Library Technicians; Mathematical Science Teachers, Postsecondary; Middle School Teachers, Except Special and Vocational Education; Museum Technicians and Conservators; Nursing Instructors and Teachers, Postsecondary; Personal Financial Advisors; Philosophy and Religion Teachers, Postsecondary; Physics Teachers, Postsecondary; Political Science Teachers, Postsecondary; Postsecondary Teachers, All Other; Preschool Teachers, Except Special Education; Psychology Teachers, Postsecondary; others. **PERSONALITY TYPE**—Investigative. Investigative occupations frequently involve working with ideas and require an extensive amount of thinking. These occupations can involve searching for facts and figuring out problems mentally.

EDUCATION/TRAINING PROGRAM(S)—Science Teacher Education/General Science Teacher Education. **RELATED KNOWLEDGE/COURSES**—**Education and Training:** Knowledge of principles and methods for curriculum and training design, teaching and instruction for individuals and groups, and the measurement of training effects. **Biology:** Knowledge of plant and animal organisms and their tissues, cells, functions, interdependencies, and interactions with each other and the environment. **Psychology:** Knowledge of human behavior and performance; individual differences in ability, personality, and interests; learning and motivation; psychological research methods; and the assessment and treatment of behavioral and affective disorders. **Chemistry:** Knowledge of the chemical composition, structure, and properties of substances and of the chemical processes and transformations that they undergo. This includes uses of chemicals and their interactions, danger signs, production techniques, and disposal methods. **English Language:** Knowledge of the structure and content of the English language, including the meaning and spelling of words, rules of composition, and grammar.

Freight, Stock, and Material Movers, Hand

▲ Education/Training Required: Short-term on-the-job training
▲ Annual Earnings: $19,440
▲ Growth: 13.9%
▲ Annual Job Openings: 519,000
▲ Self-Employed: 2.1%
▲ Part-Time: 38.4%

Load, unload and move materials at plant, yard, or other work site. Loads and unloads materials to and from designated storage areas, such as racks and shelves, or vehicles, such as trucks. Stacks or piles materials, such as lumber, boards, or pallets. Bundles and bands material, such as fodder and tobacco leaves, using banding machines. Sorts and stores items according to specifications. Assembles product containers and crates, using hand tools and precut lumber. Adjusts or replaces equipment parts, such as rollers, belts, plugs and caps, using hand tools. Records number of units handled and moved, using daily production sheet or work tickets. Attaches identifying tags or marks information on containers. Cleans work area, using brooms, rags, and cleaning compounds. Installs protective devices, such as bracing, padding or strapping, to prevent shifting or damage to items being transported. Reads work orders or receives and listens to oral instructions to determine work assignment. Shovels materials, such as gravel, ice, or spilled concrete, into containers or bins or onto conveyors. Directs spouts and positions receptacles, such as bins, carts, and containers, to receive loads. Transports receptacles to and from designated areas, by hand or using dollies, hand trucks, and wheelbarrows. Secures lifting attachments to materials and conveys load to destination, using crane or hoist. **SKILLS**—**Equipment Selection:** Determining the kind of tools and equipment needed to do a job. **Active Listening:** Giving full attention to what other people are saying, taking time to understand the points being made, asking questions as appropriate, and not interrupting at inappropriate times. **Installation:** Installing equipment, machines, wiring, or programs to meet specifications.

GOE INFORMATION—**Interest Area:** 08. Industrial Production. **Work Group:** 08.07. Hands-on Work: Loading, Moving, Hoisting, and Conveying. **Other Job Titles in This Work Group:** Conveyor Operators and Tenders; Crane and Tower Operators; Dragline Operators; Excavating and Loading Machine and Dragline Operators; Hoist and Winch Operators; Industrial Truck and Tractor Operators; Irradiated-Fuel Handlers; Laborers and Freight, Stock, and Material Movers, Hand; Machine Feeders and Offbearers; Material Moving Workers, All Other; Packers and Packagers, Hand; Pump Operators, Except Wellhead Pumpers; Refuse and Recyclable Material Collectors; Tank Car, Truck, and Ship Loaders. **PERSONALITY TYPE—** Realistic. Realistic occupations frequently involve work activities that include practical, hands-on problems and solutions. They often deal with plants, animals, and real-world materials like wood, tools, and machinery. Many of the occupations require working outside and do not involve a lot of paperwork or working closely with others.

EDUCATION/TRAINING PROGRAM(S)—No data available. **RELATED KNOWLEDGE/COURSES—Pro-**

duction and Processing: Knowledge of raw materials, production processes, quality control, costs, and other techniques for maximizing the effective manufacture and distribution of goods. **Principles of Mechanical Devices:** Knowledge of machines and tools, including their designs, uses, repair, and maintenance. **Engineering and Technology:** Knowledge of the practical application of engineering science and technology. This includes applying principles, techniques, procedures, and equipment to the design and production of various goods and services. **Clerical Studies:** Knowledge of administrative and clerical procedures and systems, such as word processing, managing files and records, stenography and transcription, designing forms, and other office procedures and terminology. **Physics:** Knowledge and prediction of physical principles and laws and their interrelationships and applications to understanding fluid, material, and atmospheric dynamics and mechanical, electrical, atomic, and sub-atomic structures and processes.

Gaming Cage Workers

- ▲ Education/Training Required: Moderate-term on-the-job training
- ▲ Annual Earnings: $21,540
- ▲ Growth: 25.2%
- ▲ Annual Job Openings: 7,000
- ▲ Self-Employed: No data available.
- ▲ Part-Time: No data available

In a gaming establishment, conduct financial transactions for patrons. May reconcile daily summaries of transactions to balance books. Accept patron's credit application and verify credit references to provide check-cashing authorization or to establish house credit accounts. May sell gambling chips, tokens, or tickets to patrons or to other workers for resale to patrons. May convert gaming chips, tokens, or tickets to currency upon patron's request. May use a cash register or computer to record transaction. **SKILLS**—No data available.

GOE INFORMATION—**Interest Area:** 09. Business Detail. **Work Group:** 09.05. Customer Service. **Other Job Titles in This Work Group:** Adjustment Clerks; Bill and Account Collectors; Cashiers; Counter and Rental Clerks; Customer Service Representatives; Customer Service Representatives, Utilities; Gaming Change Persons and Booth Cashiers; New Accounts Clerks; Order Clerks; Receptionists and Information Clerks; Tellers; Travel Clerks. **PERSONALITY TYPE**—No data available.

EDUCATION/TRAINING PROGRAM(S)—Accounting Technology/Technician and Bookkeeping. **RELATED KNOWLEDGE/COURSES**—No data available.

Gaming Change Persons and Booth Cashiers

▲ Education/Training Required: Short-term on-the-job training
▲ Annual Earnings: $18,990
▲ Growth: 36.1%
▲ Annual Job Openings: 13,000
▲ Self-Employed: 1.1%
▲ Part-Time: 57.2%

Exchange coins and tokens for patrons' money. May issue payoffs and obtain customer's signature on receipt when winnings exceed the amount held in the slot machine. May operate a booth in the slot machine area and furnish change persons with money bank at the start of the shift or count and audit money in drawers. SKILLS—No data available.

GOE INFORMATION—Interest Area: 09. Business Detail. Work Group: 09.05. Customer Service. Other Job Titles in This Work Group: Adjustment Clerks; Bill and Account Collectors; Cashiers; Counter and Rental Clerks; Customer Service Representatives; Customer Service Representatives, Utilities; Gaming Cage Workers; New Accounts Clerks; Order Clerks; Receptionists and Information Clerks; Tellers; Travel Clerks. PERSONALITY TYPE—No data available.

EDUCATION/TRAINING PROGRAM(S)—Retailing and Retail Operations. RELATED KNOWLEDGE/COURSES—No data available.

Gaming Dealers

▲ Education/Training Required: Postsecondary vocational training
▲ Annual Earnings: $13,680
▲ Growth: 32.4%
▲ Annual Job Openings: 28,000
▲ Self-Employed: 0.7%
▲ Part-Time: 48.8%

Operate table games. Stand or sit behind table and operate games of chance by dispensing the appropriate number of cards or blocks to players or operating other gaming equipment. Compare the house's hand against players' hands and pay off or collect players' money or chips. Conducts gambling table or game, such as dice, roulette, cards, or keno, and ensures that game rules are followed. Exchanges paper currency for playing chips or coin money and collects game fees or wagers. Verifies, computes, and pays out winnings. Participates in game for gambling establishment to provide minimum complement of players at table. Prepares collection report for submission to supervisor. Seats patrons at gaming tables. Sells food, beverages, and tobacco to players. SKILLS—Service Orientation: Actively looking for ways to help people. Monitoring: Monitoring/Assessing your performance or that of other individuals or organizations to make improvements or take corrective action.

GOE INFORMATION—Interest Area: 11. Recreation, Travel, and Other Personal Services. Work Group: 11.02. Recreational Services. Other Job Titles in This Work Group: Amusement and Recreation Attendants; Entertainment Attendants and Related Workers, All Other; Gaming and Sports Book Writers and Runners; Gaming Service Workers, All Other; Motion Picture Projectionists; Recreation Workers; Slot Key Persons; Tour Guides and Escorts; Travel Guides; Ushers, Lobby Attendants, and Ticket Takers. PERSONALITY TYPE—Enterprising. Enterprising occupations frequently involve starting up and carrying out projects. These occupations can involve leading people and making many decisions. They sometimes require risk taking and often deal with business.

EDUCATION/TRAINING PROGRAM(S)—No data available. RELATED KNOWLEDGE/COURSES—Customer and Personal Service: Knowledge of principles and processes for providing customer and personal services. This includes customer needs assessment, meeting quality standards for services, and evaluation of customer satisfaction. Mathematics: Knowledge of arithmetic, algebra, geometry, calculus, and statistics and their applications. **Sales and Marketing:** Knowledge of principles and methods for showing, promoting, and selling products or services. This includes marketing strategy and tactics, product demonstration, sales techniques, and sales control systems. **English Language:** Knowledge of the structure and content of the English language, including the meaning and spelling of words, rules of composition, and grammar. **Law and Government:** Knowledge of laws, legal codes, court procedures, precedents, government regulations, executive orders, agency rules, and the democratic political process. **Education and Training:** Knowledge of principles and methods for curriculum and training design, teaching and instruction for individuals and groups, and the measurement of training effects.

Gaming Managers

- ▲ Education/Training Required: Work experience plus degree
- ▲ Annual Earnings: $53,450
- ▲ Growth: 30.0%
- ▲ Annual Job Openings: Fewer than 500
- ▲ Self-Employed: 49.4%
- ▲ Part-Time: 7.2%

Plan, organize, direct, control, or coordinate gaming operations in a casino. Formulate gaming policies for their area of responsibility. Reviews operational expenses, budget estimates, betting accounts, and collection reports for accuracy. Observes and supervises operation to ensure that employees render prompt and courteous service to patrons. Establishes policies on types of gambling offered, odds, extension of credit, and serving of food and beverages. Directs workers compiling summary sheets for each race or event to show amount wagered and amount to be paid to winners. Trains new workers and evaluates their performance. Records, issues receipts for, and pays off bets. Explains and interprets house rules, such as game rules and betting limits, to patrons. Interviews and hires workers. Resolves customer complaints regarding service. Prepares work schedules, assigns work stations, and keeps attendance records. **SKILLS—Management of Personnel Resources:** Motivating, developing, and directing people as they work, identifying the best people for the job. **Management of Financial Resources:** Determining how money will be spent to get the work done and accounting for these expenditures. **Critical Thinking:** Using logic and reasoning to identify the strengths and weaknesses of alternative solutions, conclusions, or approaches to problems. **Speaking:** Talking to others to convey information effectively. **Reading Comprehension:** Understanding written sentences and paragraphs in work-related documents. **Mathematics:** Using mathematics to solve problems. **Time Management:** Managing one's own time and the time of others.

GOE INFORMATION—Interest Area: 11. Recreation, Travel, and Other Personal Services. **Work Group:** 11.01. Managerial Work in Recreation, Travel, and Other Personal Services. **Other Job Titles in This Work Group:** Aircraft Cargo Handling Supervisors; First-Line Supervisors/Managers of Food Preparation and Serving Workers; First-Line Supervisors/Managers of Housekeeping and Janitorial Workers; First-Line Supervisors/Managers of Personal Service Workers; Food Service Managers; Gaming Supervisors; Housekeeping Supervisors; Janitorial Supervisors; Lodging Managers; Meeting and Convention Planners. **PERSONALITY TYPE—Enterprising.** Enterprising occupations frequently involve starting up and carrying out projects. These occupations can involve leading people and making many decisions. They sometimes require risk taking and often deal with business.

EDUCATION/TRAINING PROGRAM(S)—Personal and Culinary Services, Other. RELATED KNOWLEDGE/COURSES—Administration and Management: Knowledge of business and management principles involved in strategic planning, resource allocation, human resources modeling, leadership technique, production methods, and coordination of people and resources. **Economics and Accounting:** Knowledge of economic and accounting principles and practices, the financial markets, banking, and the analysis and reporting of financial data. **Personnel and Human Resources:** Knowledge of principles and procedures for personnel recruitment, selection, training, compensation and benefits, labor relations and negotiation, and personnel information systems. **Math-**

ematics: Knowledge of arithmetic, algebra, geometry, calculus, and statistics and their applications. **Customer and Personal Service:** Knowledge of principles and processes for providing customer and personal services. This includes customer needs assessment, meeting quality standards for services, and evaluation of customer satisfaction.

Gaming Supervisors

- ▲ Education/Training Required: Postsecondary vocational training
- ▲ Annual Earnings: $39,240
- ▲ Growth: 18.4%
- ▲ Annual Job Openings: 2,000
- ▲ Self-Employed: 0.7%
- ▲ Part-Time: 48.8%

Supervise gaming operations and personnel in an assigned area. Circulate among tables and observe operations. Ensure that stations and games are covered for each shift. May explain and interpret operating rules of house to patrons. May plan and organize activities and create friendly atmosphere for guests in hotels/casinos. May adjust service complaints. Reviews operational expenses, budget estimates, betting accounts, and collection reports for accuracy. Observes and supervises operation to ensure that employees render prompt and courteous service to patrons. Establishes policies on types of gambling offered, odds, extension of credit, and serving food and beverages. Directs workers compiling summary sheets for each race or event to show amount wagered and amount to be paid to winners. Prepares work schedules, assigns work stations, and keeps attendance records. Resolves customer complaints regarding service. Interviews and hires workers. Trains new workers and evaluates their performance. Explains and interprets house rules, such as game rules and betting limits, to patrons. Records, issues receipts for, and pays off bets. **SKILLS—Management of Financial Resources:** Determining how money will be spent to get the work done and accounting for these expenditures. **Management of Personnel Resources:** Motivating, developing, and directing people as they work, identifying the best people for the job. **Critical Thinking:** Using logic and reasoning to identify the strengths and weaknesses of alternative solutions, conclusions, or approaches to problems. **Speaking:** Talking to others to convey information effectively. **Time Management:** Managing one's own time and the time of others. **Monitoring:** Monitoring/Assessing your performance or that of other individuals or organizations to make improvements or take corrective action. **Mathematics:** Using mathematics to solve problems.

GOE INFORMATION—Interest Area: 11. Recreation, Travel, and Other Personal Services. **Work Group:** 11.01.

Managerial Work in Recreation, Travel, and Other Personal Services. **Other Job Titles in This Work Group:** Aircraft Cargo Handling Supervisors; First-Line Supervisors/Managers of Food Preparation and Serving Workers; First-Line Supervisors/Managers of Housekeeping and Janitorial Workers; First-Line Supervisors/Managers of Personal Service Workers; Food Service Managers; Gaming Managers; Housekeeping Supervisors; Janitorial Supervisors; Lodging Managers; Meeting and Convention Planners. **PERSONALITY TYPE**—Enterprising. Enterprising occupations frequently involve starting up and carrying out projects. These occupations can involve leading people and making many decisions. They sometimes require risk taking and often deal with business.

EDUCATION/TRAINING PROGRAM(S)—No data available. **RELATED KNOWLEDGE/COURSES—Administration and Management:** Knowledge of business and management principles involved in strategic planning, resource allocation, human resources modeling, leadership technique, production methods, and coordination of people and resources. **Economics and Accounting:** Knowledge of economic and accounting principles and practices, the financial markets, banking, and the analysis and reporting of financial data. **Personnel and Human Resources:** Knowledge of principles and procedures for personnel recruitment, selection, training, compensation and benefits, labor relations and negotiation, and personnel information systems. **Customer and Personal Service:** Knowledge of principles and processes for providing customer and personal services. This includes customer needs assessment, meeting quality standards for services, and evaluation of customer satisfaction. **Mathematics:** Knowledge of arithmetic, algebra, geometry, calculus, and statistics and their applications.

General and Operations Managers

> ▲ Education/Training Required: Work experience plus degree
> ▲ Annual Earnings: $65,010
> ▲ Growth: 15.2%
> ▲ Annual Job Openings: 235,000
> ▲ Self-Employed: 49.4%
> ▲ Part-Time: 7.2%

Plan, direct, or coordinate the operations of companies or public and private sector organizations. Duties and responsibilities include formulating policies, managing daily operations, and planning the use of materials and human resources, but are too diverse and general in nature to be classified in any one functional area of management or administration, such as personnel, purchasing, or administrative services. Includes owners and managers who head small business establishments whose duties are primarily managerial. SKILLS—No data available.

GOE INFORMATION—Interest Area: 13. General Management and Support. Work Group: 13.01. General Management Work and Management of Support Functions. Other Job Titles in This Work Group: Chief Executives; Compensation and Benefits Managers; Farm, Ranch, and Other Agricultural Managers; Financial Man-

agers; Financial Managers, Branch or Department; Funeral Directors; Government Service Executives; Human Resources Managers; Human Resources Managers, All Other; Legislators; Managers, All Other; Postmasters and Mail Superintendents; Private Sector Executives; Property, Real Estate, and Community Association Managers; Public Relations Managers; Purchasing Managers; Storage and Distribution Managers; Training and Development Managers; Transportation, Storage, and Distribution Managers; Treasurers, Controllers, and Chief Financial Officers. PERSONALITY TYPE—No data available.

EDUCATION/TRAINING PROGRAM(S)—Business Administration and Management, General; Business/Commerce, General; Entrepreneurship/Entrepreneurial Studies; International Business/Trade/Commerce; Public Administration. RELATED KNOWLEDGE/COURSES—No data available.

Geographers

> ▲ Education/Training Required: Bachelor's degree
> ▲ Annual Earnings: $48,410
> ▲ Growth: 17.2%
> ▲ Annual Job Openings: 2,000
> ▲ Self-Employed: 7.6%
> ▲ Part-Time: 6.6%

Study nature and use of areas of earth's surface, relating and interpreting interactions of physical and cultural phenomena. Conduct research on physical aspects of a region, including land forms, climates, soils, plants and animals, and conduct research on the spatial implications of human activities within a given area, including social characteristics, economic activities, and political organization, as well as researching interdependence between regions at scales ranging from local to global. Collects data on physical characteristics of specified area, such as geological formation, climate, and vegetation, using surveying or meteorological equipment. Advises gov-

ernments and organizations on ethnic and natural boundaries between nation or administrative areas. Studies population characteristics within area, such as ethnic distribution and economic activity. Constructs and interprets maps, graphs, and diagrams. Prepares environmental impact reports based on results of study. Uses surveying equipment to assess geology, physics, and biology within given area. SKILLS—Writing: Communicating effectively in writing as appropriate for the needs of the audience. Reading Comprehension: Understanding written sentences and paragraphs in work-related documents. Mathematics: Using mathematics to solve problems. Critical

Thinking: Using logic and reasoning to identify the strengths and weaknesses of alternative solutions, conclusions, or approaches to problems. **Speaking:** Talking to others to convey information effectively. **Active Learning:** Understanding the implications of new information for both current and future problem-solving and decision-making.

GOE INFORMATION—Interest Area: 02. Science, Math, and Engineering. **Work Group:** 02.02. Physical Sciences. **Other Job Titles in This Work Group:** Astronomers; Atmospheric and Space Scientists; Chemists; Geologists; Geoscientists, Except Hydrologists and Geographers; Hydrologists; Materials Scientists; Physical Scientists, All Other; Physicists. **PERSONALITY TYPE**—Investigative. Investigative occupations frequently involve working with ideas and require an extensive amount of thinking. These occupations can involve searching for facts and figuring out problems mentally.

Geography Teachers, Postsecondary

Teach courses in geography. **SKILLS**—No data available.

GOE INFORMATION—Interest Area: 12. Education and Social Service. **Work Group:** 12.03. Educational Services. **Other Job Titles in This Work Group:** Adult Literacy, Remedial Education, and GED Teachers and Instructors; Agricultural Sciences Teachers, Postsecondary; Anthropology and Archeology Teachers, Postsecondary; Architecture Teachers, Postsecondary; Archivists; Area, Ethnic, and Cultural Studies Teachers, Postsecondary; Art, Drama, and Music Teachers, Postsecondary; Atmospheric, Earth, Marine, and Space Sciences Teachers, Postsecondary; Audio-Visual Collections Specialists; Biological Science Teachers, Postsecondary; Business Teachers, Postsecondary; Chemistry Teachers, Postsecondary; Child Care Workers; Communications Teachers, Postsecondary; Computer Science Teachers, Postsecondary; Criminal Justice and Law Enforcement Teachers, Postsecondary; Curators; Economics Teachers, Postsecondary; Education Teachers, Postsecondary; Edu-

EDUCATION/TRAINING PROGRAM(S)—Geography. **RELATED KNOWLEDGE/COURSES—Geography:** Knowledge of principles and methods for describing the features of land, sea, and air masses, including their physical characteristics, locations, interrelationships, and distribution of plant, animal, and human life. **Sociology and Anthropology:** Knowledge of group behavior and dynamics, societal trends and influences, human migrations, ethnicity, and cultures and their history and origins. **Biology:** Knowledge of plant and animal organisms and their tissues, cells, functions, interdependencies, and interactions with each other and the environment. **Physics:** Knowledge and prediction of physical principles and laws and their interrelationships and applications to understanding fluid, material, and atmospheric dynamics and mechanical, electrical, atomic, and sub-atomic structures and processes. **Mathematics:** Knowledge of arithmetic, algebra, geometry, calculus, and statistics and their applications.

- ▲ Education/Training Required: Master's degree
- ▲ Annual Earnings: $55,250
- ▲ Growth: 23.5%
- ▲ Annual Job Openings: 184,000
- ▲ Self-Employed: 0%
- ▲ Part-Time: 32.3%

cational Psychologists; Educational, Vocational, and School Counselors; Elementary School Teachers, Except Special Education; Engineering Teachers, Postsecondary; English Language and Literature Teachers, Postsecondary; Environmental Science Teachers, Postsecondary; Farm and Home Management Advisors; Foreign Language and Literature Teachers, Postsecondary; Forestry and Conservation Science Teachers, Postsecondary; Graduate Teaching Assistants; Health Specialties Teachers, Postsecondary; History Teachers, Postsecondary; Home Economics Teachers, Postsecondary; Kindergarten Teachers, Except Special Education; Law Teachers, Postsecondary; Librarians; Library Assistants, Clerical; Library Science Teachers, Postsecondary; Library Technicians; Mathematical Science Teachers, Postsecondary; Middle School Teachers, Except Special and Vocational Education; Museum Technicians and Conservators; Nursing Instructors and Teachers, Postsecondary; Personal Financial Advisors; Philosophy and Religion Teachers, Postsecondary; Physics Teachers, Postsecondary; Political Science Teachers, Postsecondary;

Postsecondary Teachers, All Other; Preschool Teachers, Except Special Education; others. **PERSONALITY TYPE**—No data available.

EDUCATION/TRAINING PROGRAM(S)—Geography; Geography Teacher Education. **RELATED KNOWLEDGE/COURSES**—No data available.

Geologists

- ▲ Education/Training Required: Bachelor's degree
- ▲ Annual Earnings: $58,280
- ▲ Growth: 18.1%
- ▲ Annual Job Openings: 3,000
- ▲ Self-Employed: 15.1%
- ▲ Part-Time: 6.3%

Study composition, structure, and history of the earth's crust; examine rocks, minerals, and fossil remains to identify and determine the sequence of processes affecting the development of the earth; apply knowledge of chemistry, physics, biology, and mathematics to explain these phenomena and to help locate mineral and petroleum deposits and underground water resources; prepare geologic reports and maps; and interpret research data to recommend further action for study. Studies, examines, measures, and classifies composition, structure, and history of earth's crust, including rocks, minerals, fossils, soil, and ocean floor. Prepares geological reports, maps, charts, and diagrams. Analyzes engineering problems at construction projects, such as dams, tunnels, and large buildings, applying geological knowledge. Inspects proposed construction site and sets up test equipment and drilling machinery. Recommends and prepares reports on foundation design, acquisition, retention, or release of property leases or areas of further research. Develops instruments for geological work, such as diamond tool and dies, jeweled bearings, and grinding laps and wheels. Measures characteristics of earth, using seismograph, gravimeter, torsion balance, magnetometer, pendulum devices, and electrical resistivity apparatus. Tests industrial diamonds and abrasives, soil, or rocks to determine geological characteristics, using optical, X-ray, heat, acid, and precision instruments. Interprets research data and recommends further study or action. Locates and estimates probable gas and oil deposits, using aerial photographs, charts, and research and survey results. Identifies and determines sequence of processes affecting development of earth. **SKILLS—Mathematics:** Using mathematics to solve problems. **Technology Design:** Generating or adapting equipment and technology to serve user needs. **Reading Comprehension:** Understanding written sentences and paragraphs in work-related documents. **Writing:** Communicating effectively in writing as appropriate for the needs of the audience. **Active Learning:** Understanding the implications of new information for both current and future problem-solving and decision-making.

GOE INFORMATION—Interest Area: 02. Science, Math, and Engineering. **Work Group:** 02.02. Physical Sciences. **Other Job Titles in This Work Group:** Astronomers; Atmospheric and Space Scientists; Chemists; Geographers; Geoscientists, Except Hydrologists and Geographers; Hydrologists; Materials Scientists; Physical Scientists, All Other; Physicists. **PERSONALITY TYPE**—Investigative. Investigative occupations frequently involve working with ideas and require an extensive amount of thinking. These occupations can involve searching for facts and figuring out problems mentally.

EDUCATION/TRAINING PROGRAM(S)—Geochemistry; Geochemistry and Petrology; Geological and Earth Sciences/Geosciences, Other; Geology/Earth Science, General; Geophysics and Seismology; Oceanography, Chemical and Physical; Paleontology. **RELATED KNOWLEDGE/COURSES—Physics:** Knowledge and prediction of physical principles and laws and their interrelationships and applications to understanding fluid, material, and atmospheric dynamics and mechanical, electrical, atomic, and sub-atomic structures and processes. **Mathematics:** Knowledge of arithmetic, algebra, geometry, calculus, and statistics and their applications. **Engineering and Technology:** Knowledge of the practical application of engineering science and technology. This includes applying principles, techniques, procedures, and equipment to the design and production of various goods and services. **Chemistry:** Knowledge of the chemical composition, structure, and properties of substances and of the chemical processes and transformations that they undergo. This includes uses of chemicals and their interactions, danger signs, production techniques, and disposal methods. **English Language:** Knowledge of the structure and content of the En-

glish language, including the meaning and spelling of words, rules of composition, and grammar.

Geoscientists, Except Hydrologists and Geographers

▲ Education/Training Required: Bachelor's degree
▲ Annual Earnings: $58,280
▲ Growth: 18.1%
▲ Annual Job Openings: 2,000
▲ Self-Employed: 15.1%
▲ Part-Time: 6.3%

Study the composition, structure, and other physical aspects of the earth. May use geological, physics, and mathematics knowledge in exploration for oil, gas, minerals, or underground water or in waste disposal, land reclamation, or other environmental problems. May study the earth's internal composition, atmospheres, and oceans and its magnetic, electrical, and gravitational forces. Includes mineralogists, crystallographers, paleontologists, stratigraphers, geodesists, and seismologists. **SKILLS—** No data available.

GOE INFORMATION—Interest Area: 02. Science, Math, and Engineering. **Work Group:** 02.02. Physical

Sciences. **Other Job Titles in This Work Group:** Astronomers; Atmospheric and Space Scientists; Chemists; Geographers; Geologists; Hydrologists; Materials Scientists; Physical Scientists, All Other; Physicists. **PERSONALITY TYPE—**No data available.

EDUCATION/TRAINING PROGRAM(S)— Geochemistry; Geochemistry and Petrology; Geological and Earth Sciences/Geosciences, Other; Geology/Earth Science, General; Geophysics and Seismology; Oceanography, Chemical and Physical; Paleontology. **RELATED KNOWLEDGE/COURSES—**No data available.

Government Service Executives

▲ Education/Training Required: Work experience plus degree
▲ Annual Earnings: $120,450
▲ Growth: 17.2%
▲ Annual Job Openings: 48,000
▲ Self-Employed: 0%
▲ Part-Time: 5.8%

Determine and formulate policies and provide overall direction of federal, state, local, or international government activities. Plan, direct, and coordinate operational activities at the highest level of management with the help of subordinate managers. Directs organization charged with administering and monitoring regulated activities to interpret and clarify laws and ensure compliance with laws. Administers, interprets, and explains policies, rules, regulations, and laws to organizations and individuals under authority of commission or applicable legislation. Develops, plans, organizes, and administers policies and procedures for organization to ensure administrative and operational objectives are met. Directs and coordinates activities of workers in public organization to ensure continuing operations, maximize returns on invest-

ments, and increase productivity. Negotiates contracts and agreements with federal and state agencies and other organizations and prepares budget for funding and implementation of programs. Implements corrective action plan to solve problems. Reviews and analyzes legislation, laws, and public policy and recommends changes to promote and support interests of general population as well as special groups. Develops, directs, and coordinates testing, hiring, training, and evaluation of staff personnel. Establishes and maintains comprehensive and current recordkeeping system of activities and operational procedures in business office. Testifies in court, before control or review board, or at legislature. Participates in activities to promote business and expand services and provides technical assistance in conducting of conferences, seminars, and workshops. Delivers speeches, writes articles, and presents information for organization at meetings or conventions to promote services, exchange ideas, and accomplish objectives. Plans, promotes, organizes, and coordinates public community service program and maintains cooperative working relationships among public and agency participants. Conducts or directs investigations or hearings to resolve complaints and violations of laws. Prepares, reviews, and submits reports concerning activities, expenses, budget, government statutes and rulings, and other items affecting business or program services. Directs, coordinates, and conducts activities between United States government and foreign entities to provide information to promote international interest and harmony. Evaluates findings of investigations, surveys, and studies to formulate policies and techniques and recommend improvements for personnel actions, programs, or business services. Consults with staff and others in government, business, and private organizations to discuss issues, coordinate activities, and resolve problems. Directs and conducts studies and research; prepares reports and other publications relating to operational trends and program objectives and accomplishments. Prepares budget and directs and monitors expenditures of department funds. **SKILLS—Coordination:** Adjusting actions in relation to others' actions. **Judgment and Decision Making:** Considering the relative costs and benefits of potential actions to choose the most appropriate one. **Monitoring:** Monitoring/Assessing your performance or that of other individuals or organizations to make improvements or take corrective action. **Critical Thinking:** Using logic and reasoning to identify the strengths and weaknesses of alternative solutions, conclusions, or approaches to problems. **Systems Evaluation:** Identifying measures or indicators of system performance and the actions needed to improve or correct performance relative to the goals of the system.

GOE INFORMATION—Interest Area: 13. General Management and Support. **Work Group:** 13.01. General Management Work and Management of Support Functions. **Other Job Titles in This Work Group:** Chief Executives; Compensation and Benefits Managers; Farm, Ranch, and Other Agricultural Managers; Financial Managers; Financial Managers, Branch or Department; Funeral Directors; General and Operations Managers; Human Resources Managers; Human Resources Managers, All Other; Legislators; Managers, All Other; Postmasters and Mail Superintendents; Private Sector Executives; Property, Real Estate, and Community Association Managers; Public Relations Managers; Purchasing Managers; Storage and Distribution Managers; Training and Development Managers; Transportation, Storage, and Distribution Managers; Treasurers, Controllers, and Chief Financial Officers. **PERSONALITY TYPE—**Enterprising. Enterprising occupations frequently involve starting up and carrying out projects. These occupations can involve leading people and making many decisions. They sometimes require risk taking and often deal with business.

EDUCATION/TRAINING PROGRAM(S)—Business Administration and Management, General; Business/Commerce, General; Entrepreneurship/Entrepreneurial Studies; International Business/Trade/Commerce; Public Administration; Public Administration and Social Service Professions, Other; Public Policy Analysis. **RELATED KNOWLEDGE/COURSES—Administration and Management:** Knowledge of business and management principles involved in strategic planning, resource allocation, human resources modeling, leadership technique, production methods, and coordination of people and resources. **Law and Government:** Knowledge of laws, legal codes, court procedures, precedents, government regulations, executive orders, agency rules, and the democratic political process. **English Language:** Knowledge of the structure and content of the English language, including the meaning and spelling of words, rules of composition, and grammar. **Education and Training:** Knowledge of principles and methods for curriculum and training design, teaching and instruction for individuals and groups, and the measurement of training effects. **Economics and Accounting:** Knowledge of economic and accounting principles and practices, the financial markets, banking, and the analysis and reporting of financial data. **Personnel and Human Resources:** Knowledge of principles and procedures for personnel recruitment, selection, training, compensation and benefits, labor relations and negotiation, and personnel information systems.

Grader, Bulldozer, and Scraper Operators

- ▲ Education/Training Required: Moderate-term on-the-job training
- ▲ Annual Earnings: $34,160
- ▲ Growth: 6.9%
- ▲ Annual Job Openings: 25,000
- ▲ Self-Employed: 8.4%
- ▲ Part-Time: 5.0%

Operate machines or vehicles equipped with blades to remove, distribute, level, or grade earth. Starts engine; moves throttle, switches, and levers; and depresses pedals to operate machines, equipment, and attachments. Drives equipment in successive passes over working area to achieve specified result, such as grading terrain or removing, dumping, or spreading earth and rock. Aligns machine, cutterhead, or depth gauge marker with reference stakes and guidelines on ground or positions equipment following hand signals of assistant. Fastens bulldozer blade or other attachment to tractor, using hitches. Greases, oils, and performs minor repairs on tractor, using grease gun, oilcans, and hand tools. Signals operator to guide movement of tractor-drawn machine. Connects hydraulic hoses, belts, mechanical linkage, or power takeoff shaft to tractor. **SKILLS—Operation and Control:** Controlling operations of equipment or systems. **Equipment Selection:** Determining the kind of tools and equipment needed to do a job. **Operation Monitoring:** Watching gauges, dials, or other indicators to make sure a machine is working properly.

GOE INFORMATION—Interest Area: 06. Construction, Mining, and Drilling. **Work Group:** 06.02. Construction. **Other Job Titles in This Work Group:** Boat Builders and Shipwrights; Boilermakers; Brattice Builders; Brickmasons and Blockmasons; Carpenters; Carpet Installers; Ceiling Tile Installers; Cement Masons and Concrete Finishers; Commercial Divers; Construction Carpenters; Drywall and Ceiling Tile Installers; Drywall Installers; Electricians; Explosives Workers, Ordnance Handling Experts, and Blasters; Fence Erectors; Floor Layers, Except Carpet, Wood, and Hard Tiles; Floor Sanders and Finishers; Glaziers; Hazardous Materials Removal Workers; Insulation Workers, Floor, Ceiling, and Wall; Insulation Workers, Mechanical; Manufactured Building and Mobile Home Installers; Operating Engineers; Operating Engineers and Other Construction Equipment Operators; Painters, Construction and Maintenance; Paperhangers; Paving, Surfacing, and Tamping Equipment Operators; Pile-Driver Operators; Pipe Fitters; Pipelayers; Pipelaying Fitters; Plasterers and Stucco Masons; Plumbers; Plumbers, Pipefitters, and Steamfitters; Rail-Track Laying and Maintenance Equipment Operators; Refractory Materials Repairers, Except Brickmasons; Reinforcing Iron and Rebar Workers; Riggers; Roofers; Rough Carpenters; Security and Fire Alarm Systems Installers; Segmental Pavers; Sheet Metal Workers; Ship Carpenters and Joiners; Stone Cutters and Carvers; Stonemasons; Structural Iron and Steel Workers; Tapers; Terrazzo Workers and Finishers; Tile and Marble Setters. **PERSONALITY TYPE—Realistic.** Realistic occupations frequently involve work activities that include practical, hands-on problems and solutions. They often deal with plants, animals, and real-world materials like wood, tools, and machinery. Many of the occupations require working outside and do not involve a lot of paperwork or working closely with others.

EDUCATION/TRAINING PROGRAM(S)—Construction/Heavy Equipment/Earthmoving Equipment Operation; Mobile Crane Operation/Operator. **RELATED KNOWLEDGE/COURSES—Principles of Mechanical Devices:** Knowledge of machines and tools, including their designs, uses, repair, and maintenance. **Transportation:** Knowledge of principles and methods for moving people or goods by air, rail, sea, or road, including the relative costs and benefits. **Physics:** Knowledge and prediction of physical principles and laws and their interrelationships and applications to understanding fluid, material, and atmospheric dynamics and mechanical, electrical, atomic, and sub-atomic structures and processes. **Engineering and Technology:** Knowledge of the practical application of engineering science and technology. This includes applying principles, techniques, procedures, and equipment to the design and production of various goods and services. **Building and Construction:** Knowledge of materials, methods, and tools involved in the construction or repair of houses, buildings, or other structures, such as highways and roads.

Graduate Teaching Assistants

▲ Education/Training Required: Master's degree
▲ Annual Earnings: $22,150
▲ Growth: 23.5%
▲ Annual Job Openings: 184,000
▲ Self-Employed: 0%
▲ Part-Time: 32.3%

Assist department chairperson, faculty members, or other professional staff members in college or university by performing teaching or teaching-related duties, such as teaching lower-level courses, developing teaching materials, preparing and giving examinations, and grading examinations or papers. Graduate assistants must be enrolled in a graduate school program. Graduate assistants who primarily perform non-teaching duties, such as laboratory research, should be reported in the occupational category related to the work performed. Develops teaching materials, such as syllabi and visual aids. Assists faculty member or staff with student conferences. Assists library staff in maintaining library collection. Assists faculty member or staff with laboratory or field research. Teaches lower-level courses. Prepares and gives examinations. Grades examinations and papers. **SKILLS—Reading Comprehension:** Understanding written sentences and paragraphs in work-related documents. **Instructing:** Teaching others how to do something. **Speaking:** Talking to others to convey information effectively. **Writing:** Communicating effectively in writing as appropriate for the needs of the audience. **Learning Strategies:** Selecting and using training/instructional methods and procedures appropriate for the situation when learning or teaching new things.

GOE INFORMATION—Interest Area: 12. Education and Social Service. **Work Group:** 12.03. Educational Services. **Other Job Titles in This Work Group:** Adult Literacy, Remedial Education, and GED Teachers and Instructors; Agricultural Sciences Teachers, Postsecondary; Anthropology and Archeology Teachers, Postsecondary; Architecture Teachers, Postsecondary; Archivists; Area, Ethnic, and Cultural Studies Teachers, Postsecondary; Art, Drama, and Music Teachers, Postsecondary; Atmospheric, Earth, Marine, and Space Sciences Teachers, Postsecondary; Audio-Visual Collections Specialists; Biological Science Teachers, Postsecondary; Business Teachers, Postsecondary; Chemistry Teachers, Postsecondary; Child Care Workers; Communications Teachers, Postsecondary; Computer Science Teachers, Postsecondary; Criminal Justice and Law Enforcement Teachers, Postsecondary; Curators; Economics Teachers, Postsecondary; Education Teachers, Postsecondary; Educational Psychologists; Educational, Vocational, and School Counselors; Elementary School Teachers, Except Special Education; Engineering Teachers, Postsecondary; English Language and Literature Teachers, Postsecondary; Environmental Science Teachers, Postsecondary; Farm and Home Management Advisors; Foreign Language and Literature Teachers, Postsecondary; Forestry and Conservation Science Teachers, Postsecondary; Geography Teachers, Postsecondary; Health Specialties Teachers, Postsecondary; History Teachers, Postsecondary; Home Economics Teachers, Postsecondary; Kindergarten Teachers, Except Special Education; Law Teachers, Postsecondary; Librarians; Library Assistants, Clerical; Library Science Teachers, Postsecondary; Library Technicians; Mathematical Science Teachers, Postsecondary; Middle School Teachers, Except Special and Vocational Education; Museum Technicians and Conservators; Nursing Instructors and Teachers, Postsecondary; Personal Financial Advisors; Philosophy and Religion Teachers, Postsecondary; Physics Teachers, Postsecondary; Political Science Teachers, Postsecondary; Postsecondary Teachers, All Other; Preschool Teachers, Except Special Education; others. **PERSONALITY TYPE**—Social. Social occupations frequently involve working with, communicating with, and teaching people. These occupations often involve helping or providing service to others.

EDUCATION/TRAINING PROGRAM(S)—No data available. **RELATED KNOWLEDGE/COURSES—Education and Training:** Knowledge of principles and methods for curriculum and training design, teaching and instruction for individuals and groups, and the measurement of training effects. **English Language:** Knowledge of the structure and content of the English language, including the meaning and spelling of words, rules of composition, and grammar. **Mathematics:** Knowledge of arithmetic, algebra, geometry, calculus, and statistics and their applications. **Clerical Studies:** Knowledge of administrative and clerical procedures and systems, such as word processing, managing files and records, stenography and transcription, designing forms, and other office procedures and terminology. **Computers and Electronics:** Knowledge of circuit boards, processors, chips, electronic equipment, and computer hardware and software, including applications and programming.

Graphic Designers

- ▲ Education/Training Required: Bachelor's degree
- ▲ Annual Earnings: $36,020
- ▲ Growth: 26.7%
- ▲ Annual Job Openings: 28,000
- ▲ Self-Employed: 60.9%
- ▲ Part-Time: 24.0%

Design or create graphics to meet specific commercial or promotional needs, such as packaging, displays, or logos. May use a variety of mediums to achieve artistic or decorative effects. Draws sample of finished layout and presents sample to art director for approval. Produces still and animated graphic formats for on-air and taped portions of television news broadcasts, using electronic video equipment. Reviews final layout and suggests improvements as needed. Develops negatives and prints, using negative and print developing equipment and tools and work aids to produce layout photographs. Prepares notes and instructions for workers who assemble and prepare final layouts for printing. Photographs layouts, using camera, to make layout prints for supervisor or client. Confers with client regarding layout design. Prepares series of drawings to illustrate sequence and timing of story development for television production. Studies illustrations and photographs to plan presentation of material, product, or service. Prepares illustrations or rough sketches of material according to instructions of client or supervisor. Arranges layout based upon available space, knowledge of layout principles, and aesthetic design concepts. Marks up, pastes, and assembles final layouts to prepare layouts for printer. Determines size and arrangement of illustrative material and copy and selects style and size of type. Keys information into computer equipment to create layouts for client or supervisor. Draws and prints charts, graphs, illustrations, and other artwork, using computer. **SKILLS—Reading Comprehension:** Understanding written sentences and paragraphs in work-related documents. **Active Listening:** Giving full attention to what other people are saying, taking time to understand the points being made, asking questions as appropriate, and not interrupting at inappropriate times. **Speaking:** Talking to others to convey information effectively. **Equipment Selection:** Determining the kind of tools and equipment needed to do a job. **Writing:** Communicating effectively in writing as appropriate for the needs of the audience.

GOE INFORMATION—Interest Area: 01. Arts, Entertainment, and Media. **Work Group:** 01.04. Visual Arts. **Other Job Titles in This Work Group:** Cartoonists; Commercial and Industrial Designers; Designers, All Other; Exhibit Designers; Fashion Designers; Fine Artists, Including Painters, Sculptors, and Illustrators; Floral Designers; Interior Designers; Merchandise Displayers and Window Trimmers; Multi-Media Artists and Animators; Painters and Illustrators; Sculptors; Set and Exhibit Designers; Set Designers; Sketch Artists. **PERSONALITY TYPE—**Artistic. Artistic occupations frequently involve working with forms, designs, and patterns. They often require self-expression, and the work can be done without following a clear set of rules.

EDUCATION/TRAINING PROGRAM(S)—Agricultural Communication/Journalism; Commercial and Advertising Art; Computer Graphics; Design and Visual Communications, General; Graphic Design; Industrial Design; Web Page, Digital/Multimedia, and Information Resources Design. **RELATED KNOWLEDGE/ COURSES—Fine Arts:** Knowledge of the theory and techniques required to compose, produce, and perform works of music, dance, visual arts, drama, and sculpture. **Communications and Media:** Knowledge of media production, communication, and dissemination techniques and methods. This includes alternative ways to inform and entertain via written, oral, and visual media. **Design:** Knowledge of design techniques, tools, and principles involved in production of precision technical plans, blueprints, drawings, and models. **Computers and Electronics:** Knowledge of circuit boards, processors, chips, electronic equipment, and computer hardware and software, including applications and programming. **English Language:** Knowledge of the structure and content of the English language, including the meaning and spelling of words, rules of composition, and grammar.

Grips and Set-Up Workers, Motion Picture Sets, Studios, and Stages

▲ Education/Training Required: Short-term on-the-job training
▲ Annual Earnings: $19,440
▲ Growth: 13.9%
▲ Annual Job Openings: 519,000
▲ Self-Employed: 1.6%
▲ Part-Time: 16.2%

Arrange equipment; raise and lower scenery; move dollies, cranes, and booms; and perform other duties for motion-picture, recording, or television industry. Arranges equipment preparatory to sessions and performances, following work order specifications, and handles props during performances. Rigs and dismantles stage or set equipment, such as frames, scaffolding, platforms, or backdrops, using carpenter's hand tools. Adjusts controls to raise and lower scenery and stage curtain during performance, following cues. Adjusts controls to guide, position, and move equipment, such as cranes, booms, and cameras. Erects canvas covers to protect equipment from weather. Reads work orders and follows oral instructions to determine specified material and equipment to be moved and its relocation. Connects electrical equipment to power source and tests equipment before performance. Orders equipment and maintains equipment storage areas. Sews and repairs items, using materials and hand tools such as canvas and sewing machines. Produces special lighting and sound effects during performances, using various machines and devices. **SKILLS—Monitoring:** Monitoring/Assessing your performance or that of other individuals or organizations to make improvements or take corrective action. **Operation and Control:** Controlling operations of equipment or systems. **Coordination:** Adjusting actions in relation to others' actions. **Active Listening:** Giving full attention to what other people are saying, taking time to understand the points being made, asking questions as appropriate, and not interrupting at inappropriate times. **Reading Comprehension:** Understanding written sentences and paragraphs in work-related documents.

GOE INFORMATION—Interest Area: 06. Construction, Mining, and Drilling. **Work Group:** 06.04. Hands-on Work in Construction, Extraction, and Maintenance. **Other Job Titles in This Work Group:** Carpenter Assemblers and Repairers; Construction Laborers; Helpers, Construction Trades, All Other; Helpers—Brickmasons, Blockmasons, Stonemasons, and Tile and Marble Setters; Helpers—Carpenters; Helpers—Extraction Workers; Helpers—Painters, Paperhangers, Plasterers, and Stucco Masons; Helpers—Pipelayers, Plumbers, Pipefitters, and Steamfitters; Helpers—Roofers; Highway Maintenance Workers; Septic Tank Servicers and Sewer Pipe Cleaners. **PERSONALITY TYPE—**Realistic. Realistic occupations frequently involve work activities that include practical, hands-on problems and solutions. They often deal with plants, animals, and real-world materials like wood, tools, and machinery. Many of the occupations require working outside and do not involve a lot of paperwork or working closely with others.

EDUCATION/TRAINING PROGRAM(S)—No data available. **RELATED KNOWLEDGE/COURSES— Building and Construction:** Knowledge of materials, methods, and tools involved in the construction or repair of houses, buildings, or other structures, such as highways and roads. **Engineering and Technology:** Knowledge of the practical application of engineering science and technology. This includes applying principles, techniques, procedures, and equipment to the design and production of various goods and services. **Principles of Mechanical Devices:** Knowledge of machines and tools, including their designs, uses, repair, and maintenance. **Fine Arts:** Knowledge of the theory and techniques required to compose, produce, and perform works of music, dance, visual arts, drama, and sculpture. **Design:** Knowledge of design techniques, tools, and principles involved in production of precision technical plans, blueprints, drawings, and models. **English Language:** Knowledge of the structure and content of the English language, including the meaning and spelling of words, rules of composition, and grammar.

Hairdressers, Hairstylists, and Cosmetologists

▲ Education/Training Required: Postsecondary vocational training
▲ Annual Earnings: $18,260
▲ Growth: 13.0%
▲ Annual Job Openings: 78,000
▲ Self-Employed: 46.0%
▲ Part-Time: 36.5%

Provide beauty services, such as shampooing, cutting, coloring, and styling hair and massaging and treating scalp. May also apply makeup, dress wigs, perform hair removal, and provide nail and skin care services. Cuts, trims, and shapes hair or hairpieces, using clippers, scissors, trimmers, and razors. Bleaches, dyes, or tints hair, using applicator or brush. Combs, brushes, and sprays hair or wigs to set style. Analyzes patron's hair and other physical features or reads makeup instructions to determine and recommend beauty treatment. Administers therapeutic medication and advises patron to seek medical treatment for chronic or contagious scalp conditions. Shapes and colors eyebrows or eyelashes and removes facial hair, using depilatory cream and tweezers. Updates and maintains customer information records, such as beauty services provided. Cleans, shapes, and polishes fingernails and toenails, using files and nail polish. Recommends and applies cosmetics, lotions, and creams to patron to soften and lubricate skin and enhance and restore natural appearance. Massages and treats scalp for hygienic and remedial purposes, using hands, fingers, or vibrating equipment. Attaches wig or hairpiece to model head and dresses wigs and hairpieces according to instructions, samples, sketches, or photographs. Applies water, setting, or waving solutions to hair and winds hair on curlers or rollers. Shampoos, rinses, and dries hair and scalp or hairpieces with water, liquid soap, or other solutions. **SKILLS—Service Orientation:** Actively looking for ways to help people. **Active Listening:** Giving full attention to what other people are saying, taking time to understand the points being made, asking questions as appropriate, and not interrupting at inappropriate times.

GOE INFORMATION—Interest Area: 11. Recreation, Travel, and Other Personal Services. **Work Group:** 11.04. Barber and Beauty Services. **Other Job Titles in This Work Group:** Barbers; Manicurists and Pedicurists; Shampooers;

Skin Care Specialists. **PERSONALITY TYPE—**Enterprising. Enterprising occupations frequently involve starting up and carrying out projects. These occupations can involve leading people and making many decisions. They sometimes require risk taking and often deal with business.

EDUCATION/TRAINING PROGRAM(S)—Cosmetology and Related Personal Grooming Arts, Other; Cosmetology, Barber/Styling, and Nail Instructor; Cosmetology/Cosmetologist, General; Electrolysis/Electrology and Electrolysis Technician; Hair Styling/Stylist and Hair Design; Make-Up Artist/Specialist; Permanent Cosmetics/Makeup and Tattooing; Salon/Beauty Salon Management/Manager. **RELATED KNOWLEDGE/ COURSES—Customer and Personal Service:** Knowledge of principles and processes for providing customer and personal services. This includes customer needs assessment, meeting quality standards for services, and evaluation of customer satisfaction. **Clerical Studies:** Knowledge of administrative and clerical procedures and systems, such as word processing, managing files and records, stenography and transcription, designing forms, and other office procedures and terminology. **Sales and Marketing:** Knowledge of principles and methods for showing, promoting, and selling products or services. This includes marketing strategy and tactics, product demonstration, sales techniques, and sales control systems. **English Language:** Knowledge of the structure and content of the English language, including the meaning and spelling of words, rules of composition, and grammar. **Medicine and Dentistry:** Knowledge of the information and techniques needed to diagnose and treat human injuries, diseases, and deformities. This includes symptoms, treatment alternatives, drug properties and interactions, and preventive health-care measures. **Mathematics:** Knowledge of arithmetic, algebra, geometry, calculus, and statistics and their applications.

H

Hazardous Materials Removal Workers

- ▲ Education/Training Required: Moderate-term on-the-job training
- ▲ Annual Earnings: $31,800
- ▲ Growth: 32.8%
- ▲ Annual Job Openings: 9,000
- ▲ Self-Employed: 1.5%
- ▲ Part-Time: 5.2%

Identify, remove, pack, transport, or dispose of hazardous materials, including asbestos, lead-based paint, waste oil, fuel, transmission fluid, radioactive materials, contaminated soil, etc. Specialized training and certification in hazardous materials handling or a confined entry permit are generally required. May operate earth-moving equipment or trucks. **SKILLS**—No data available.

GOE INFORMATION—**Interest Area:** 06. Construction, Mining, and Drilling. **Work Group:** 06.02. Construction. **Other Job Titles in This Work Group:** Boat Builders and Shipwrights; Boilermakers; Brattice Builders; Brickmasons and Blockmasons; Carpenters; Carpet Installers; Ceiling Tile Installers; Cement Masons and Concrete Finishers; Commercial Divers; Construction Carpenters; Drywall and Ceiling Tile Installers; Drywall Installers; Electricians; Explosives Workers, Ordnance Handling Experts, and Blasters; Fence Erectors; Floor Layers, Except Carpet, Wood, and Hard Tiles; Floor Sanders and Finishers; Glaziers; Grader, Bulldozer, and Scraper Operators; Insulation Workers, Floor, Ceiling, and Wall; Insulation Workers, Mechanical; Manufactured Building and Mobile Home Installers; Operating Engineers; Operating Engineers and Other Construction Equipment Operators; Painters, Construction and Maintenance; Paperhangers; Paving, Surfacing, and Tamping Equipment Operators; Pile-Driver Operators; Pipe Fitters; Pipelayers; Pipelaying Fitters; Plasterers and Stucco Masons; Plumbers; Plumbers, Pipefitters, and Steamfitters; Rail-Track Laying and Maintenance Equipment Operators; Refractory Materials Repairers, Except Brickmasons; Reinforcing Iron and Rebar Workers; Riggers; Roofers; Rough Carpenters; Security and Fire Alarm Systems Installers; Segmental Pavers; Sheet Metal Workers; Ship Carpenters and Joiners; Stone Cutters and Carvers; Stonemasons; Structural Iron and Steel Workers; Tapers; Terrazzo Workers and Finishers; Tile and Marble Setters. **PERSONALITY TYPE**—No data available.

EDUCATION/TRAINING PROGRAM(S)—Construction Trades, Other; Hazardous Materials Management and Waste Technology/Technician; Mechanic and Repair Technologies/Technicians, Other. **RELATED KNOWLEDGE/COURSES**—No data available.

Health Educators

- ▲ Education/Training Required: Master's degree
- ▲ Annual Earnings: $35,230
- ▲ Growth: 23.5%
- ▲ Annual Job Openings: 7,000
- ▲ Self-Employed: 3.9%
- ▲ Part-Time: 39.7%

Promote, maintain, and improve individual and community health by assisting individuals and communities to adopt healthy behaviors. Collect and analyze data to identify community needs prior to planning, implementing, monitoring, and evaluating programs designed to encourage healthy lifestyles, policies, and environments. May also serve as a resource to assist individuals, other professionals, or the community and may administer fiscal resources for health education programs. Plans and provides educational opportunities for health personnel. Collaborates with health specialists and civic groups to ascertain community health needs, determine availability of services, and develop goals. Promotes health discussions in schools, industry, and community agencies. Conducts community surveys to ascertain health needs, develop desirable health goals, and determine availability of professional health services. Prepares and disseminates educational and informational materials. Develops and maintains cooperation between public, civic, professional, and voluntary agencies. **SKILLS—Speaking:** Talking to others to convey information effectively. **Writing:** Communicating effectively in writing as appropriate for the needs of the audience. **Coordination:** Adjusting actions in relation to others' actions. **Active Listening:** Giving full attention to what other people are saying, taking time to understand the points being made, asking questions as appropriate, and not interrupting at inappropriate times. **Active Learning:** Understanding the implications of new information for both current and future problem-solving and decision-making. **Reading Comprehension:** Understanding written sentences and paragraphs in work-related documents.

GOE INFORMATION—Interest Area: 14. Medical and Health Services. **Work Group:** 14.08. Health Protection and Promotion. **Other Job Titles in This Work Group:** Athletic Trainers; Dietetic Technicians; Dietitians and Nutritionists. **PERSONALITY TYPE—**Social. Social occupations frequently involve working with, communicating with, and teaching people. These occupations often involve helping or providing service to others.

EDUCATION/TRAINING PROGRAM(S)—Community Health Services/Liaison/Counseling; Health Communication; International Public Health/International Health;

Maternal and Child Health; Public Health Education and Promotion. **RELATED KNOWLEDGE/COURSES— Education and Training:** Knowledge of principles and methods for curriculum and training design, teaching and instruction for individuals and groups, and the measurement of training effects. **English Language:** Knowledge of the structure and content of the English language, including the meaning and spelling of words, rules of composition, and grammar. **Communications and Media:** Knowledge of media production, communication, and dissemination techniques and methods. This includes alternative ways to inform and entertain via written, oral, and visual media. **Customer and Personal Service:** Knowledge of principles and processes for providing customer and personal services. This includes customer needs assessment, meeting quality standards for services, and evaluation of customer satisfaction. **Medicine and Dentistry:** Knowledge of the information and techniques needed to diagnose and treat human injuries, diseases, and deformities. This includes symptoms, treatment alternatives, drug properties and interactions, and preventive health-care measures. **Therapy and Counseling:** Knowledge of principles, methods, and procedures for diagnosis, treatment, and rehabilitation of physical and mental dysfunctions and for career counseling and guidance.

Health Specialties Teachers, Postsecondary

- ▲ Education/Training Required: Master's degree
- ▲ Annual Earnings: $59,100
- ▲ Growth: 23.5%
- ▲ Annual Job Openings: 184,000
- ▲ Self-Employed: 0%
- ▲ Part-Time: 32.3%

Teach courses in health specialties, such as veterinary medicine, dentistry, pharmacy, therapy, laboratory technology, and public health. Prepares and delivers lectures to students. Compiles bibliographies of specialized materials for outside reading assignments. Stimulates class discussions. Compiles, administers, and grades examinations or assigns this work to others. Directs research of other teachers or graduate students working for advanced academic degrees. Serves on faculty committee providing professional consulting services to government and industry. Acts as adviser to student organizations. Conducts research in particular field of knowledge and publishes findings in professional journals. Advises students on academic and vocational curricula. **SKILLS—Reading Comprehension:**

Understanding written sentences and paragraphs in work-related documents. **Science:** Using scientific rules and methods to solve problems. **Writing:** Communicating effectively in writing as appropriate for the needs of the audience. **Instructing:** Teaching others how to do something. **Critical Thinking:** Using logic and reasoning to identify the strengths and weaknesses of alternative solutions, conclusions, or approaches to problems. **Active Listening:** Giving full attention to what other people are saying, taking time to understand the points being made, asking questions as appropriate, and not interrupting at inappropriate times. **Active Learning:** Understanding the implications of new information for both current and future problem-solving and decision-making.

GOE INFORMATION—Interest Area: 12. Education and Social Service. **Work Group:** 12.03. Educational Services. **Other Job Titles in This Work Group:** Adult Literacy, Remedial Education, and GED Teachers and Instructors; Agricultural Sciences Teachers, Postsecondary; Anthropology and Archeology Teachers, Postsecondary; Architecture Teachers, Postsecondary; Archivists; Area, Ethnic, and Cultural Studies Teachers, Postsecondary; Art, Drama, and Music Teachers, Postsecondary; Atmospheric, Earth, Marine, and Space Sciences Teachers, Postsecondary; Audio-Visual Collections Specialists; Biological Science Teachers, Postsecondary; Business Teachers, Postsecondary; Chemistry Teachers, Postsecondary; Child Care Workers; Communications Teachers, Postsecondary; Computer Science Teachers, Postsecondary; Criminal Justice and Law Enforcement Teachers, Postsecondary; Curators; Economics Teachers, Postsecondary; Education Teachers, Postsecondary; Educational Psychologists; Educational, Vocational, and School Counselors; Elementary School Teachers, Except Special Education; Engineering Teachers, Postsecondary; English Language and Literature Teachers, Postsecondary; Environmental Science Teachers, Postsecondary; Farm and Home Management Advisors; Foreign Language and Literature Teachers, Postsecondary; Forestry and Conservation Science Teachers, Postsecondary; Geography Teachers, Postsecondary; Graduate Teaching Assistants; History Teachers, Postsecondary; Home Economics Teachers, Postsecondary; Kindergarten Teachers, Except Special Education; Law Teachers, Postsecondary; Librarians; Library Assistants, Clerical; Library Science Teachers, Postsecondary; Library Technicians; Mathematical Science Teachers, Postsecondary; Middle School Teachers, Except Special and Vocational Education; Museum Technicians and Conservators; Nursing Instructors and Teachers, Postsecondary; Personal Financial Advisors; Philosophy and Religion Teachers, Postsecondary; Physics Teachers, Postsecondary; Political Science Teachers, Postsecondary; Postsecondary Teachers, All Other; Preschool Teachers, Except Special Education; others. **PERSONALITY TYPE**—Investigative. Investigative occupations frequently involve working with ideas and require an extensive amount of thinking. These occupations can involve searching for facts and figuring out problems mentally.

EDUCATION/TRAINING PROGRAM(S)—Allied Health and Medical Assisting Services, Other; Allied Health Diagnostic, Intervention, and Treatment Professions, Other; Art Therapy/Therapist; Asian Bodywork Therapy; Audiology/Audiologist and Hearing Sciences; Audiology/Audiologist and Speech-Language Pathology/Pathologist; Biostatistics; Blood Bank Technology Specialist; Cardiovascular Technology/Technologist; Chiropractic (DC); Clinical Laboratory Science/Medical Technology/Technologist; Clinical/Medical Laboratory Assistant; Clinical/Medical Laboratory Technician; Communication Disorders, General; Cytotechnology/Cytotechnologist; Dance Therapy/Therapist; Dental Assisting/Assistant; Dental Clinical Sciences, General (MS, PhD); Dental Hygiene/Hygienist; Dental Laboratory Technology/Technician; Dental Services and Allied Professions, Other; Dentistry (DDS, DMD); Diagnostic Medical Sonography/Sonographer and Ultrasound Technician; Electrocardiograph Technology/Technician; Electroneurodiagnostic/Electroencephalographic Technology/Technologist; Emergency Medical Technology/Technician (EMT Paramedic); Environmental Health; Epidemiology; Health Occupations Teacher Education; Health/Medical Physics; Health/Medical Preparatory Programs, Other; Hematology Technology/Technician; Hypnotherapy/Hypnotherapist; Massage Therapy/Therapeutic Massage; Medical Radiologic Technology/Science—Radiation Therapist; Music Therapy/Therapist; Nuclear Medical Technology/Technologist; Occupational Health and Industrial Hygiene; Occupational Therapist Assistant; Occupational Therapy/Therapist; Orthotist/Prosthetist; Perfusion Technology/Perfusionist; Pharmacy (PharmD [USA] PharmD, BS/BPharm [Canada]); Pharmacy Administration and Pharmacy Policy and Regulatory Affairs (MS, PhD); Pharmacy Technician/Assistant; Pharmacy, Pharmaceutical Sciences, and Administration, Other; Physical Therapist Assistant; Physical Therapy/Therapist; Physician Assistant; Pre-Dentistry Studies; Pre-Medicine/Pre-Medical Studies; Pre-Nursing Studies; others. **RELATED KNOWLEDGE/COURSES—Education and Training:** Knowledge of principles and methods for curriculum and training design, teaching and instruction for individuals and groups, and the measurement of training effects. **Biology:** Knowledge of plant and animal organisms and their tissues, cells, functions, interdependencies, and interactions with each other and the environment. **Medicine and Dentistry:** Knowledge of the information and techniques needed to diagnose and treat human injuries, diseases, and deformities. This includes symptoms, treatment alternatives, drug properties and interactions, and preventive health-care measures. **English Language:** Knowledge of the structure and content of the English language, including the meaning and spelling of words, rules of composition, and grammar.

Therapy and Counseling: Knowledge of principles, methods, and procedures for diagnosis, treatment, and rehabilitation of physical and mental dysfunctions and for career counseling and guidance.

Heating and Air Conditioning Mechanics

▲ Education/Training Required: Long-term on-the-job training
▲ Annual Earnings: $34,020
▲ Growth: 22.3%
▲ Annual Job Openings: 21,000
▲ Self-Employed: 12.9%
▲ Part-Time: 4.9%

Install, service, and repair heating and air conditioning systems in residences and commercial establishments. Installs, connects, and adjusts thermostats, humidistats, and timers, using hand tools. Repairs or replaces defective equipment, components, or wiring. Joins pipes or tubing to equipment and to fuel, water, or refrigerant source to form complete circuit. Fabricates, assembles, and installs duct work and chassis parts, using portable metal-working tools and welding equipment. Tests electrical circuits and components for continuity, using electrical test equipment. Disassembles system and cleans and oils parts. Assembles, positions, and mounts heating or cooling equipment, following blueprints. Tests pipe or tubing joints and connections for leaks, using pressure gauge or soap-and-water solution. Installs auxiliary components to heating-cooling equipment, such as expansion and discharge valves, air ducts, pipes, blowers, dampers, flues, and stokers, following blueprints. Adjusts system controls to setting recommended by manufacturer to balance system, using hand tools. Inspects and tests system to verify system compliance with plans and specifications and to detect malfunctions. Discusses heating-cooling system malfunctions with users to isolate problems or to verify that malfunctions have been corrected. Inspects inoperative equipment to locate source of trouble. Studies blueprints to determine configuration of heating or cooling equipment components. Wraps pipes in insulation and secures in place with cement or wire bands. Lays out and connects electrical wiring between controls and equipment according to wiring diagram, using electrician's hand tools. Reassembles equipment and starts unit to test operation. Measures, cuts, threads, and bends pipe or tubing, using pipefitter's tools. Cuts and drills holes in floors, walls, and roof to install equipment, using power saws and drills. **SKILLS—Installation:** Installing equipment, machines, wiring, or programs to meet specifications. **Troubleshooting:** Determining causes of operating errors and deciding what to do about them. **Repairing:** Repairing machines or systems, using the needed tools. **Equipment Maintenance:** Performing routine maintenance on equipment and determining when and what kind of maintenance is needed. **Quality Control Analysis:** Conducting tests and inspections of products, services, or processes to evaluate quality or performance.

GOE INFORMATION—Interest Area: 05. Mechanics, Installers, and Repairers. **Work Group:** 05.03. Mechanical Work. **Other Job Titles in This Work Group:** Aircraft Body and Bonded Structure Repairers; Aircraft Engine Specialists; Aircraft Mechanics and Service Technicians; Airframe-and-Power-Plant Mechanics; Automotive Body and Related Repairers; Automotive Glass Installers and Repairers; Automotive Master Mechanics; Automotive Service Technicians and Mechanics; Automotive Specialty Technicians; Bicycle Repairers; Bridge and Lock Tenders; Bus and Truck Mechanics and Diesel Engine Specialists; Camera and Photographic Equipment Repairers; Coin, Vending, and Amusement Machine Servicers and Repairers; Control and Valve Installers and Repairers, Except Mechanical Door; Farm Equipment Mechanics; Gas Appliance Repairers; Hand and Portable Power Tool Repairers; Heating, Air Conditioning, and Refrigeration Mechanics and Installers; Helpers—Electricians; Helpers—Installation, Maintenance, and Repair Workers; Industrial Machinery Mechanics; Keyboard Instrument Repairers and Tuners; Locksmiths and Safe Repairers; Maintenance and Repair Workers, General; Maintenance Workers, Machinery; Mechanical Door Repairers; Medical Appliance Technicians; Medical Equipment Repairers; Meter Mechanics; Millwrights; Mobile Heavy Equipment Mechanics, Except Engines; Motorboat Mechanics; Motorcycle Mechanics; Musical Instrument Repairers and Tuners; Ophthalmic Laboratory Technicians; Optical Instrument Assemblers; Outdoor Power Equipment and Other Small Engine Mechanics; Painters, Transportation

Equipment; Percussion Instrument Repairers and Tuners; Precision Instrument and Equipment Repairers, All Other; Rail Car Repairers; Railroad Inspectors; Recreational Vehicle Service Technicians; Reed or Wind Instrument Repairers and Tuners; Refrigeration Mechanics; Stringed Instrument Repairers and Tuners; Tire Repairers and Changers; Valve and Regulator Repairers; Watch Repairers. **PERSONALITY TYPE**—Realistic. Realistic occupations frequently involve work activities that include practical, hands-on problems and solutions. They often deal with plants, animals, and real-world materials like wood, tools, and machinery. Many of the occupations require working outside and do not involve a lot of paperwork or working closely with others.

EDUCATION/TRAINING PROGRAM(S)—Heating, Air Conditioning and Refrigeration Technology/Technician (ACH/ACR/ACHR/HRAC/HVAC/AC Technology); Heating, Air Conditioning, Ventilation, and Refrigeration Maintenance Technology/Technician (HAC, HACR, HVAC, HVACR). **RELATED KNOWLEDGE/**

COURSES—**Principles of Mechanical Devices:** Knowledge of machines and tools, including their designs, uses, repair, and maintenance. **Design:** Knowledge of design techniques, tools, and principles involved in production of precision technical plans, blueprints, drawings, and models. **Building and Construction:** Knowledge of materials, methods, and tools involved in the construction or repair of houses, buildings, or other structures, such as highways and roads. **Engineering and Technology:** Knowledge of the practical application of engineering science and technology. This includes applying principles, techniques, procedures, and equipment to the design and production of various goods and services. **Customer and Personal Service:** Knowledge of principles and processes for providing customer and personal services. This includes customer needs assessment, meeting quality standards for services, and evaluation of customer satisfaction. **English Language:** Knowledge of the structure and content of the English language, including the meaning and spelling of words, rules of composition, and grammar.

Heating, Air Conditioning, and Refrigeration Mechanics and Installers

- ▲ Education/Training Required: Long-term on-the-job training
- ▲ Annual Earnings: $34,020
- ▲ Growth: 22.3%
- ▲ Annual Job Openings: 21,000
- ▲ Self-Employed: 12.9%
- ▲ Part-Time: 4.9%

Install or repair heating, central air conditioning, or refrigeration systems, including oil burners, hot-air furnaces, and heating stoves. SKILLS—No data available.

GOE INFORMATION—**Interest Area:** 05. Mechanics, Installers, and Repairers. **Work Group:** 05.03. Mechanical Work. **Other Job Titles in This Work Group:** Aircraft Body and Bonded Structure Repairers; Aircraft Engine Specialists; Aircraft Mechanics and Service Technicians; Airframe-and-Power-Plant Mechanics; Automotive Body and Related Repairers; Automotive Glass Installers and Repairers; Automotive Master Mechanics; Automotive Service Technicians and Mechanics; Automotive Specialty Technicians; Bicycle Repairers; Bridge and Lock Tenders; Bus and Truck Mechanics and Diesel Engine Specialists; Camera and Photographic Equipment Repairers; Coin, Vending, and Amusement Machine Servicers and Repairers; Control and Valve Installers and Repairers, Except Mechanical Door; Farm Equipment Mechanics; Gas Appliance Repairers; Hand and Portable Power Tool Repairers; Heating and Air Conditioning Mechanics; Helpers—Electricians; Helpers—Installation, Maintenance, and Repair Workers; Industrial Machinery Mechanics; Keyboard Instrument Repairers and Tuners; Locksmiths and Safe Repairers; Maintenance and Repair Workers, General; Maintenance Workers, Machinery; Mechanical Door Repairers; Medical Appliance Technicians; Medical Equipment Repairers; Meter Mechanics; Millwrights; Mobile Heavy Equipment Mechanics, Except Engines; Motorboat Mechanics; Motorcycle Mechanics; Musical Instrument Repairers and Tuners; Ophthalmic Laboratory Technicians; Optical Instrument Assemblers; Outdoor Power Equipment and Other Small Engine Mechanics; Painters, Transportation Equipment; Percussion Instrument Repairers and Tuners; Precision Instrument and Equipment Repairers, All Other; Rail Car Repairers; Railroad Inspectors; Recreational Vehicle Service Technicians; Reed or Wind Instrument Repairers and Tuners; Refrigeration Mechanics;

Stringed Instrument Repairers and Tuners; Tire Repairers and Changers; Valve and Regulator Repairers; Watch Repairers. **PERSONALITY TYPE**—No data available.

EDUCATION/TRAINING PROGRAM(S)—Heating, Air Conditioning and Refrigeration Technology/Techni-cian (ACH/ACR/ACHR/HRAC/HVAC/AC Technology); Heating, Air Conditioning, Ventilation and Refrigeration Maintenance Technology/Technician (HAC, HACR, HVAC, HVACR). **RELATED KNOWLEDGE/ COURSES**—No data available.

Helpers—Brickmasons, Blockmasons, Stonemasons, and Tile and Marble Setters

▲ Education/Training Required: Short-term on-the-job training
▲ Annual Earnings: $23,620
▲ Growth: 14.1%
▲ Annual Job Openings: 14,000
▲ Self-Employed: 0.8%
▲ Part-Time: 16.0%

Help brickmasons, blockmasons, stonemasons, or tile and marble setters by performing duties of lesser skill. Duties include using, supplying, or holding materials or tools and cleaning work area and equipment. Assists in the preparation, installation, repair, or rebuilding of tile, brick or stone surfaces. Applies caulk, sealants, or other agents to installed surface. Removes excess grout and residue from tile or brick joints with wet sponge or trowel. Applies grout between joints of bricks or tiles, using grouting trowel. Removes damaged tile, brick, or mortar and prepares installation surfaces, using pliers, chipping hammers, chisels, drills, and metal wire anchors. Cleans installation surfaces, equipment, tools, work site, and storage areas, using water, chemical solutions, oxygen lance, or polishing machines. Corrects surface imperfections or fills chipped, cracked, or broken bricks or tiles, using fillers, adhesives, and grouting materials. Modifies material moving, mixing, grouting, grinding, polishing, or cleaning procedures according to the type of installation or materials required. Manually or machine-mixes mortar, plaster, and grout according to standard formulae. Cuts materials to specified size for installation, using power saw or tile cutter. Arranges and stores materials, machines, tools, and equipment. Erects scaffolding or other installation structures. Moves or positions marble slabs and ingot covers, using crane, hoist, or dolly. Selects materials for installation, following numbered sequence or drawings. Transports materials, tools, and machines to installation site manually or using conveyance equipment. **SKILLS—Installation:** Installing equipment, machines, wiring, or programs to meet specifications.

GOE INFORMATION—Interest Area: 06. Construction, Mining, and Drilling. **Work Group:** 06.04. Hands-on Work in Construction, Extraction, and Maintenance. **Other Job Titles in This Work Group:** Carpenter Assemblers and Repairers; Construction Laborers; Grips and Set-Up Workers, Motion Picture Sets, Studios, and Stages; Helpers, Construction Trades, All Other; Helpers—Carpenters; Helpers—Extraction Workers; Helpers—Painters, Paperhangers, Plasterers, and Stucco Masons; Helpers—Pipelayers, Plumbers, Pipefitters, and Steamfitters; Helpers—Roofers; Highway Maintenance Workers; Septic Tank Servicers and Sewer Pipe Cleaners. **PERSONALITY TYPE**—Realistic. Realistic occupations frequently involve work activities that include practical, hands-on problems and solutions. They often deal with plants, animals, and real-world materials like wood, tools, and machinery. Many of the occupations require working outside and do not involve a lot of paperwork or working closely with others.

EDUCATION/TRAINING PROGRAM(S)—Mason/ Masonry. **RELATED KNOWLEDGE/COURSES**— **Building and Construction:** Knowledge of materials, methods, and tools involved in the construction or repair of houses, buildings, or other structures, such as highways and roads. **Principles of Mechanical Devices:** Knowledge of machines and tools, including their designs, uses, repair, and maintenance. **Design:** Knowledge of design techniques, tools, and principles involved in production of precision technical plans, blueprints, drawings, and models. **Mathematics:** Knowledge of arithmetic, algebra, geometry, calculus, and statistics and their applications. **English Language:** Knowledge of the structure and content of the English language, including the meaning and spelling of words, rules of composition, and grammar. **Physics:** Knowledge and prediction of physical principles

H

and laws and their interrelationships and applications to understanding fluid, material, and atmospheric dynamics

and mechanical, electrical, atomic, and sub-atomic structures and processes.

Helpers—Electricians

- ▲ Education/Training Required: Short-term on-the-job training
- ▲ Annual Earnings: $22,160
- ▲ Growth: 13.3%
- ▲ Annual Job Openings: 27,000
- ▲ Self-Employed: 0.8%
- ▲ Part-Time: 16.0%

Help electricians by performing duties of lesser skill. Duties include using, supplying, or holding materials or tools and cleaning work area and equipment. Maintains tools and equipment, washes parts, and keeps supplies and parts in order. Threads conduit ends, connects couplings, and fabricates and secures conduit support brackets, using hand tools. Disassembles defective electrical equipment, replaces defective or worn parts, and reassembles equipment, using hand tools. Strings transmission lines or cables through ducts or conduits, underground, through equipment, or to towers. Examines electrical units for loose connections and broken insulation and tightens connections, using hand tools. Traces out short circuits in wiring, using test meter. Rigs scaffolds, hoists, and shoring; erects barricades; and digs trenches. Solders electrical connections, using soldering iron. Bolts component parts together to form tower assemblies, using hand tools. Drills holes for wiring, using power drill, and pulls or pushes wiring through opening. Raises, lowers, or positions equipment, tools, and materials for installation or use, using hoist, handline, or block and tackle. Breaks up concrete to facilitate installation or repair of equipment, using airhammer. Trims trees and clears undergrowth along right-of-way. Measures, cuts, and bends wire and conduit, using measuring instruments and hand tools. Strips insulation from wire ends, using wire-stripping pliers, and attaches wires to terminals for subsequent soldering. Transports tools, materials, equipment, and supplies to work site manually or using hand truck or by driving truck. **SKILLS—Equipment Maintenance:** Performing routine maintenance on equipment and determining when and what kind of maintenance is needed.

GOE INFORMATION—Interest Area: 05. Mechanics, Installers, and Repairers. **Work Group:** 05.03. Mechanical Work. **Other Job Titles in This Work Group:** Aircraft Body and Bonded Structure Repairers; Aircraft Engine Specialists; Aircraft Mechanics and Service Technicians; Airframe-

and-Power-Plant Mechanics; Automotive Body and Related Repairers; Automotive Glass Installers and Repairers; Automotive Master Mechanics; Automotive Service Technicians and Mechanics; Automotive Specialty Technicians; Bicycle Repairers; Bridge and Lock Tenders; Bus and Truck Mechanics and Diesel Engine Specialists; Camera and Photographic Equipment Repairers; Coin, Vending, and Amusement Machine Servicers and Repairers; Control and Valve Installers and Repairers, Except Mechanical Door; Farm Equipment Mechanics; Gas Appliance Repairers; Hand and Portable Power Tool Repairers; Heating and Air Conditioning Mechanics; Heating, Air Conditioning, and Refrigeration Mechanics and Installers; Helpers—Installation, Maintenance, and Repair Workers; Industrial Machinery Mechanics; Keyboard Instrument Repairers and Tuners; Locksmiths and Safe Repairers; Maintenance and Repair Workers, General; Maintenance Workers, Machinery; Mechanical Door Repairers; Medical Appliance Technicians; Medical Equipment Repairers; Meter Mechanics; Millwrights; Mobile Heavy Equipment Mechanics, Except Engines; Motorboat Mechanics; Motorcycle Mechanics; Musical Instrument Repairers and Tuners; Ophthalmic Laboratory Technicians; Optical Instrument Assemblers; Outdoor Power Equipment and Other Small Engine Mechanics; Painters, Transportation Equipment; Percussion Instrument Repairers and Tuners; Precision Instrument and Equipment Repairers, All Other; Rail Car Repairers; Railroad Inspectors; Recreational Vehicle Service Technicians; Reed or Wind Instrument Repairers and Tuners; Refrigeration Mechanics; Stringed Instrument Repairers and Tuners; Tire Repairers and Changers; Valve and Regulator Repairers; Watch Repairers. **PERSONALITY TYPE—** Realistic. Realistic occupations frequently involve work activities that include practical, hands-on problems and solutions. They often deal with plants, animals, and real-world materials like wood, tools, and machinery. Many of the occupations require working outside and do not involve a lot of paperwork or working closely with others.

EDUCATION/TRAINING PROGRAM(S)—Electrician. RELATED KNOWLEDGE/COURSES—Engineering and Technology: Knowledge of the practical application of engineering science and technology. This includes applying principles, techniques, procedures, and equipment to the design and production of various goods and services. Principles of Mechanical Devices: Knowledge of machines and tools, including their designs, uses, repair, and maintenance. Computers and Electronics: Knowledge of circuit boards, processors, chips, electronic equipment, and computer hardware and software, including applications and programming. Public Safety and Security: Knowledge of relevant equipment, policies, procedures, and strategies to promote effective local, state, or national security operations for the protection of people, data, property, and institutions. Building and Construction: Knowledge of materials, methods, and tools involved in the construction or repair of houses, buildings, or other structures, such as highways and roads.

Helpers—Installation, Maintenance, and Repair Workers

- ▲ Education/Training Required: Short-term on-the-job training
- ▲ Annual Earnings: $21,210
- ▲ Growth: 18.5%
- ▲ Annual Job Openings: 35,000
- ▲ Self-Employed: 1.6%
- ▲ Part-Time: 16.2%

Help installation, maintenance, and repair workers in maintenance, parts replacement, and repair of vehicles, industrial machinery, and electrical and electronic equipment. Perform duties such as furnishing tools, materials, and supplies to other workers; cleaning work area, machines, and tools; and holding materials or tools for other workers. Helps mechanics and repairers maintain and repair vehicles, industrial machinery, and electrical and electronic equipment. Tends and observes equipment and machinery to verify efficient and safe operation. Builds or erects and maintains physical structures, using hand tools or power tools. Examines and tests machinery, equipment, components, and parts for defects and to ensure proper functioning. Positions vehicles, machinery, equipment, physical structures, and other objects for assembly or installation, using hand tools, power tools, and moving equipment. Applies protective materials to equipment, components, and parts to prevent defects and corrosion. Cleans or lubricates vehicles, machinery, equipment, instruments, tools, work areas, and other objects, using hand tools, power tools, and cleaning equipment. Assembles and disassembles machinery, equipment, components, and other parts, using hand tools and power tools. Installs or replaces machinery, equipment, and new or replacement parts and instruments, using hand tools or power tools. Adjusts and connects or disconnects wiring, piping, tubing, and other parts, using hand tools or power tools. Transfers equipment, tools, parts, and other objects to and from work stations and other areas, using hand tools, power tools, and moving equipment. Furnishes tools, parts, equipment, and supplies to other workers. SKILLS—Equipment Maintenance: Performing routine maintenance on equipment and determining when and what kind of maintenance is needed. Repairing: Repairing machines or systems, using the needed tools. Installation: Installing equipment, machines, wiring, or programs to meet specifications. Operation and Control: Controlling operations of equipment or systems. Quality Control Analysis: Conducting tests and inspections of products, services, or processes to evaluate quality or performance.

GOE INFORMATION—Interest Area: 05. Mechanics, Installers, and Repairers. Work Group: 05.03. Mechanical Work. Other Job Titles in This Work Group: Aircraft Body and Bonded Structure Repairers; Aircraft Engine Specialists; Aircraft Mechanics and Service Technicians; Airframe-and-Power-Plant Mechanics; Automotive Body and Related Repairers; Automotive Glass Installers and Repairers; Automotive Master Mechanics; Automotive Service Technicians and Mechanics; Automotive Specialty Technicians; Bicycle Repairers; Bridge and Lock Tenders; Bus and Truck Mechanics and Diesel Engine Specialists; Camera and Photographic Equipment Repairers; Coin, Vending, and Amusement Machine Servicers and Repairers; Control and Valve Installers and Repairers, Except Mechanical Door; Farm Equipment Mechanics; Gas Appliance Repairers; Hand and Portable Power Tool Repairers; Heating and Air Conditioning Mechanics; Heating, Air Conditioning, and Refrigeration Mechanics and Installers; Helpers—Electricians; Industrial Machinery Mechanics; Keyboard Instrument Repairers and Tuners;

Locksmiths and Safe Repairers; Maintenance and Repair Workers, General; Maintenance Workers, Machinery; Mechanical Door Repairers; Medical Appliance Technicians; Medical Equipment Repairers; Meter Mechanics; Millwrights; Mobile Heavy Equipment Mechanics, Except Engines; Motorboat Mechanics; Motorcycle Mechanics; Musical Instrument Repairers and Tuners; Ophthalmic Laboratory Technicians; Optical Instrument Assemblers; Outdoor Power Equipment and Other Small Engine Mechanics; Painters, Transportation Equipment; Percussion Instrument Repairers and Tuners; Precision Instrument and Equipment Repairers, All Other; Rail Car Repairers; Railroad Inspectors; Recreational Vehicle Service Technicians; Reed or Wind Instrument Repairers and Tuners; Refrigeration Mechanics; Stringed Instrument Repairers and Tuners; Tire Repairers and Changers; Valve and Regulator Repairers; Watch Repairers. **PERSONALITY TYPE**—Realistic. Realistic occupations frequently involve work activities that include practical, hands-on problems and solutions. They often deal with plants, animals, and real-world materials like wood, tools, and machinery. Many of the occupations require working outside and do not involve a lot of paperwork or working closely with others.

EDUCATION/TRAINING PROGRAM(S)—Industrial Mechanics and Maintenance Technology. **RELATED KNOWLEDGE/COURSES—Principles of Mechanical Devices:** Knowledge of machines and tools, including their designs, uses, repair, and maintenance. **Engineering and Technology:** Knowledge of the practical application of engineering science and technology. This includes applying principles, techniques, procedures, and equipment to the design and production of various goods and services. **Building and Construction:** Knowledge of materials, methods, and tools involved in the construction or repair of houses, buildings, or other structures, such as highways and roads. **Computers and Electronics:** Knowledge of circuit boards, processors, chips, electronic equipment, and computer hardware and software, including applications and programming. **English Language:** Knowledge of the structure and content of the English language, including the meaning and spelling of words, rules of composition, and grammar. **Production and Processing:** Knowledge of raw materials, production processes, quality control, costs, and other techniques for maximizing the effective manufacture and distribution of goods.

Helpers—Pipelayers, Plumbers, Pipefitters, and Steamfitters

- ▲ Education/Training Required: Short-term on-the-job training
- ▲ Annual Earnings: $21,830
- ▲ Growth: 11.5%
- ▲ Annual Job Openings: 20,000
- ▲ Self-Employed: 0.8%
- ▲ Part-Time: 16.0%

Help plumbers, pipefitters, steamfitters, or pipelayers by performing duties of lesser skill. Duties include using, supplying, or holding materials or tools and cleaning work area and equipment. Fits or assists in fitting valves, couplings, or assemblies to tanks, pumps, or systems, using hand tools. Mounts brackets and hangers on walls and ceilings to hold pipes. Cuts or drills holes in walls to accommodate passage of pipes, using pneumatic drill. Cleans shop, work area, and machines, using solvent and rags. Disassembles and removes damaged or worn pipe. Requisitions tools and equipment and selects type and size of pipe. Fills pipe with sand or resin to prevent distortion and holds pipes during bending and installation. Immerses pipe in chemical solution to remove dirt, oil, and scale. Assists in installing gas burner to convert furnaces from wood, coal, or oil. **SKILLS—Equipment Selection:** De-termining the kind of tools and equipment needed to do a job. **Equipment Maintenance:** Performing routine maintenance on equipment and determining when and what kind of maintenance is needed.

GOE INFORMATION—Interest Area: 06. Construction, Mining, and Drilling. **Work Group:** 06.04. Hands-on Work in Construction, Extraction, and Maintenance. **Other Job Titles in This Work Group:** Carpenter Assemblers and Repairers; Construction Laborers; Grips and Set-Up Workers, Motion Picture Sets, Studios, and Stages; Helpers, Construction Trades, All Other; Helpers—Brickmasons, Blockmasons, Stonemasons, and Tile and Marble Setters; Helpers—Carpenters; Helpers—Extraction Workers; Helpers—Painters, Paperhangers, Plasterers, and Stucco Masons; Helpers—Roofers; Highway

Maintenance Workers; Septic Tank Servicers and Sewer Pipe Cleaners. **PERSONALITY TYPE**—Realistic. Realistic occupations frequently involve work activities that include practical, hands-on problems and solutions. They often deal with plants, animals, and real-world materials like wood, tools, and machinery. Many of the occupations require working outside and do not involve a lot of paperwork or working closely with others.

EDUCATION/TRAINING PROGRAM(S)—Plumbing Technology/Plumber. **RELATED KNOWLEDGE/ COURSES**—**Principles of Mechanical Devices:** Knowledge of machines and tools, including their designs, uses, repair, and maintenance. **Building and Construction:** Knowledge of materials, methods, and tools involved in the construction or repair of houses, buildings, or other structures, such as highways and roads. **Engineering and**

Technology: Knowledge of the practical application of engineering science and technology. This includes applying principles, techniques, procedures, and equipment to the design and production of various goods and services. **Production and Processing:** Knowledge of raw materials, production processes, quality control, costs, and other techniques for maximizing the effective manufacture and distribution of goods. **Chemistry:** Knowledge of the chemical composition, structure, and properties of substances and of the chemical processes and transformations that they undergo. This includes uses of chemicals and their interactions, danger signs, production techniques, and disposal methods. **Physics:** Knowledge and prediction of physical principles and laws and their interrelationships and applications to understanding fluid, material, and atmospheric dynamics and mechanical, electrical, atomic, and subatomic structures and processes.

Helpers—Production Workers

- ▲ Education/Training Required: Short-term on-the-job training
- ▲ Annual Earnings: $18,990
- ▲ Growth: 11.9%
- ▲ Annual Job Openings: 143,000
- ▲ Self-Employed: 1.6%
- ▲ Part-Time: 16.2%

Help production workers by performing duties of lesser skill. Duties include supplying or holding materials or tools and cleaning work area and equipment. SKILLS— No data available.

GOE INFORMATION—**Interest Area:** 08. Industrial Production. **Work Group:** 08.03. Production Work. **Other Job Titles in This Work Group:** Bakers, Manufacturing; Bindery Machine Operators and Tenders; Brazers; Cementing and Gluing Machine Operators and Tenders; Chemical Equipment Controllers and Operators; Chemical Equipment Operators and Tenders; Chemical Equipment Tenders; Cleaning, Washing, and Metal Pickling Equipment Operators and Tenders; Coating, Painting, and Spraying Machine Operators and Tenders; Coil Winders, Tapers, and Finishers; Combination Machine Tool Operators and Tenders, Metal and Plastic; Computer-Controlled Machine Tool Operators, Metal and Plastic; Cooling and Freezing Equipment Operators and Tenders; Crushing, Grinding, and Polishing Machine Setters, Operators, and Tenders; Cutters and Trimmers, Hand; Cutting and Slicing Machine Operators and Tenders; Cutting

and Slicing Machine Setters, Operators, and Tenders; Design Printing Machine Setters and Set-Up Operators; Electrolytic Plating and Coating Machine Operators and Tenders, Metal and Plastic; Electrolytic Plating and Coating Machine Setters and Set-Up Operators, Metal and Plastic; Electrotypers and Stereotypers; Embossing Machine Set-Up Operators; Engraver Set-Up Operators; Extruding and Forming Machine Operators and Tenders, Synthetic or Glass Fibers; Extruding and Forming Machine Setters, Operators, and Tenders, Synthetic and Glass Fibers; Extruding, Forming, Pressing, and Compacting Machine Operators and Tenders; Fabric and Apparel Patternmakers; Fiber Product Cutting Machine Setters and Set-Up Operators; Fiberglass Laminators and Fabricators; Film Laboratory Technicians; Fitters, Structural Metal— Precision; Food and Tobacco Roasting, Baking, and Drying Machine Operators and Tenders; Food Batchmakers; Food Cooking Machine Operators and Tenders; Furnace, Kiln, Oven, Drier, and Kettle Operators and Tenders; Glass Cutting Machine Setters and Set-Up Operators; Graders and Sorters, Agricultural Products; Grinding and Polishing Workers, Hand; Hand Compositors and Typesetters; Heaters, Metal and Plastic; others. **PERSONALITY TYPE**—No data available.

Highway Patrol Pilots

EDUCATION/TRAINING PROGRAM(S)—No data available. **RELATED KNOWLEDGE/COURSES**—No data available.

> ▲ Education/Training Required: Long-term on-the-job training
> ▲ Annual Earnings: $40,970
> ▲ Growth: 23.2%
> ▲ Annual Job Openings: 21,000
> ▲ Self-Employed: 0%
> ▲ Part-Time: 1.5%

Pilot aircraft to patrol highway and enforce traffic laws. Pilots airplane to maintain order, respond to emergencies, enforce traffic and criminal laws, and apprehend criminals. Investigates traffic accidents and other accidents to determine causes and to determine if crime was committed. Arrests perpetrator of criminal act or submits citation or warning to violator of motor vehicle ordinance. Informs ground personnel where to re-route traffic in case of emergencies. Informs ground personnel of traffic congestion or unsafe driving conditions to ensure traffic flow and reduce incidence of accidents. Reviews facts to determine if criminal act or statute violation was involved. Expedites processing of prisoners, prepares and maintains records of prisoner bookings, and maintains record of prisoner status during booking and pre-trial process. Prepares reports to document activities. Relays complaint and emergency request information to appropriate agency dispatcher. Evaluates complaint and emergency request information to determine response requirements. Renders aid to accident victims and other persons requiring first aid for physical injuries. Testifies in court to present evidence or act as witness in traffic and criminal cases. Records facts, photographs and diagrams crime or accident scene, and interviews witnesses to gather information for possible use in legal action or safety programs. **SKILLS—Operation and Control:** Controlling operations of equipment or systems. **Social Perceptiveness:** Being aware of others' reactions and understanding why they react as they do. **Active Listening:** Giving full attention to what other people are saying, taking time to understand the points being made, asking questions as appropriate, and not interrupting at inappropriate times. **Reading Comprehension:** Understanding written sentences and paragraphs in work-related documents. **Judgment and Decision Making:** Considering the relative costs and benefits of potential actions to choose the most appropriate one. **Critical Thinking:** Using logic

and reasoning to identify the strengths and weaknesses of alternative solutions, conclusions, or approaches to problems.

GOE INFORMATION—Interest Area: 04. Law, Law Enforcement, and Public Safety. **Work Group:** 04.03. Law Enforcement. **Other Job Titles in This Work Group:** Animal Control Workers; Bailiffs; Child Support, Missing Persons, and Unemployment Insurance Fraud Investigators; Correctional Officers and Jailers; Criminal Investigators and Special Agents; Crossing Guards; Detectives and Criminal Investigators; Fire Investigators; Fish and Game Wardens; Forensic Science Technicians; Gaming Surveillance Officers and Gaming Investigators; Immigration and Customs Inspectors; Lifeguards, Ski Patrol, and Other Recreational Protective Service Workers; Parking Enforcement Workers; Police and Sheriff's Patrol Officers; Police Detectives; Police Identification and Records Officers; Police Patrol Officers; Private Detectives and Investigators; Security Guards; Sheriffs and Deputy Sheriffs; Transit and Railroad Police. **PERSONALITY TYPE**—Realistic. Realistic occupations frequently involve work activities that include practical, hands-on problems and solutions. They often deal with plants, animals, and real-world materials like wood, tools, and machinery. Many of the occupations require working outside and do not involve a lot of paperwork or working closely with others.

EDUCATION/TRAINING PROGRAM(S)—Criminal Justice/Police Science; Criminalistics and Criminal Science. **RELATED KNOWLEDGE/COURSES—Transportation:** Knowledge of principles and methods for moving people or goods by air, rail, sea, or road, including the relative costs and benefits. **Public Safety and Security:** Knowledge of relevant equipment, policies, procedures, and strategies to promote effective local, state, or national security operations for the protection of people, data, property, and institutions. **Law and Government:** Knowledge of laws, legal codes, court procedures, precedents, government regulations, executive orders, agency rules, and the democratic political process. **Telecommunications:** Knowledge of transmission, broadcasting, switching, control, and operation of telecommunications systems. **Geography:** Knowledge of principles and methods for describing the features of land, sea, and air masses, including their physical characteristics, locations, interrelationships, and distribution of plant, animal, and human life.

Historians

- ▲ Education/Training Required: Bachelor's degree
- ▲ Annual Earnings: $42,940
- ▲ Growth: 17.2%
- ▲ Annual Job Openings: 2,000
- ▲ Self-Employed: 5.2%
- ▲ Part-Time: 18.1%

Research, analyze, record, and interpret the past as recorded in sources such as government and institutional records; newspapers and other periodicals; photographs; interviews; films; and unpublished manuscripts, such as personal diaries and letters. Conducts historical research on subjects of import to society and presents finding and theories in textbooks, journals, and other publications. Assembles historical data by consulting sources such as archives, court records, diaries, news files, and miscellaneous published and unpublished materials. Organizes and evaluates data on basis of authenticity and relative significance. Consults with or advises other individuals on historical authenticity of various materials. Consults experts or witnesses of historical events. Reviews and collects data, such as books, pamphlets, periodicals, and rare newspapers, to provide source material for research. Traces historical development in fields such as economics, sociology, or philosophy. Reviews publications and exhibits prepared by others prior to public release in order to ensure historical accuracy of presentations. Coordinates activities of workers engaged in cataloging and filing materials. Edits society publications. Speaks before various groups, organizations, and clubs to promote societal aims and activities. Translates or requests translation of reference materials. Advises or consults with individuals, institutions, and commercial organizations on technological evolution or customs peculiar to certain historical period. **SKILLS—Writing:** Communicating effectively in writing as appropriate for the needs of the audience. **Reading Comprehension:** Understanding written sentences and paragraphs in work-related documents. **Speaking:** Talking to others to convey information effectively. **Critical Thinking:** Using logic and reasoning to identify the strengths and weaknesses of alternative solutions, conclusions, or approaches to problems. **Active Learning:** Understanding the implications of new information for both current and future problem-solving and decision-making.

GOE INFORMATION—Interest Area: 02. Science, Math, and Engineering. **Work Group:** 02.04. Social Sciences. **Other Job Titles in This Work Group:** Anthropologists; Anthropologists and Archeologists; Archeologists; City Planning Aides; Economists; Industrial-Organizational Psychologists; Political Scientists; Psychologists, All Other; Social Science Research Assistants; Social Scientists and Related Workers, All Other; Sociologists; Survey Researchers; Urban and Regional Planners. **PERSONALITY TYPE—**Investigative. Investigative occupations frequently involve working with ideas and require an extensive amount of thinking. These occupations can involve searching for facts and figuring out problems mentally.

EDUCATION/TRAINING PROGRAM(S)—American History (United States); Ancient Studies/Civilization; Architectural History and Criticism, General; Asian History; Canadian History; Classical, Ancient Mediterranean, and Near Eastern Studies and Archaeology; Cultural Resource Management and Policy Analysis; European History; Historic Preservation and Conservation; Historic Preservation and Conservation, Other; History and Philosophy of Science and Technology; History, General; History, Other; Holocaust and Related Studies; Medieval and Renaissance Studies. **RELATED KNOWLEDGE/COURSES— History and Archeology:** Knowledge of historical events and their causes, indicators, and effects on civilizations and cultures. **English Language:** Knowledge of the structure and content of the English language, including the meaning and spelling of words, rules of composition, and grammar. **Administration and Management:** Knowledge of business and management principles involved in strategic planning, resource allocation, human resources modeling, leadership technique, production methods, and coordination of people and resources. **Sociology and Anthropology:** Knowledge of group behavior and dynamics, societal trends and influences, human migrations, ethnicity, and cultures and their history and origins. **Communications and Media:** Knowledge of media production, communication, and dissemination techniques and methods. This includes alternative ways to inform and entertain via written, oral, and visual media.

History Teachers, Postsecondary

- ▲ Education/Training Required: Master's degree
- ▲ Annual Earnings: $50,400
- ▲ Growth: 23.5%
- ▲ Annual Job Openings: 184,000
- ▲ Self-Employed: 0%
- ▲ Part-Time: 32.3%

Teach courses in human history and historiography. Prepares and delivers lectures to students. Compiles bibliographies of specialized materials for outside reading assignments. Advises students on academic and vocational curricula. Compiles, administers, and grades examinations or assigns this work to others. Stimulates class discussions. Directs research of other teachers or graduate students working for advanced academic degrees. Serves on faculty committee providing professional consulting services to government and industry. Acts as adviser to student organizations. Conducts research in particular field of knowledge and publishes findings in professional journals. **SKILLS—Reading Comprehension:** Understanding written sentences and paragraphs in work-related documents. **Instructing:** Teaching others how to do something. **Speaking:** Talking to others to convey information effectively. **Active Learning:** Understanding the implications of new information for both current and future problem-solving and decision-making. **Active Listening:** Giving full attention to what other people are saying, taking time to understand the points being made, asking questions as appropriate, and not interrupting at inappropriate times. **Writing:** Communicating effectively in writing as appropriate for the needs of the audience. **Learning Strategies:** Selecting and using training/instructional methods and procedures appropriate for the situation when learning or teaching new things.

GOE INFORMATION—Interest Area: 12. Education and Social Service. **Work Group:** 12.03. Educational Services. **Other Job Titles in This Work Group:** Adult Literacy, Remedial Education, and GED Teachers and Instructors; Agricultural Sciences Teachers, Postsecondary; Anthropology and Archeology Teachers, Postsecondary; Architecture Teachers, Postsecondary; Archivists; Area, Ethnic, and Cultural Studies Teachers, Postsecondary; Art, Drama, and Music Teachers, Postsecondary; Atmospheric, Earth, Marine, and Space Sciences Teachers, Postsecondary; Audio-Visual Collections Specialists; Biological Science Teachers, Postsecondary; Business Teachers, Postsecondary; Chemistry Teachers, Postsecondary; Child Care Workers; Communications Teachers, Postsecondary; Computer Science Teachers, Postsecondary; Criminal Justice and Law Enforcement Teachers, Postsecondary; Curators; Economics Teachers, Postsecondary; Education Teachers, Postsecondary; Educational Psychologists; Educational, Vocational, and School Counselors; Elementary School Teachers, Except Special Education; Engineering Teachers, Postsecondary; English Language and Literature Teachers, Postsecondary; Environmental Science Teachers, Postsecondary; Farm and Home Management Advisors; Foreign Language and Literature Teachers, Postsecondary; Forestry and Conservation Science Teachers, Postsecondary; Geography Teachers, Postsecondary; Graduate Teaching Assistants; Health Specialties Teachers, Postsecondary; Home Economics Teachers, Postsecondary; Kindergarten Teachers, Except Special Education; Law Teachers, Postsecondary; Librarians; Library Assistants, Clerical; Library Science Teachers, Postsecondary; Library Technicians; Mathematical Science Teachers, Postsecondary; Middle School Teachers, Except Special and Vocational Education; Museum Technicians and Conservators; Nursing Instructors and Teachers, Postsecondary; Personal Financial Advisors; Philosophy and Religion Teachers, Postsecondary; Physics Teachers, Postsecondary; Political Science Teachers, Postsecondary; Postsecondary Teachers, All Other; Preschool Teachers, Except Special Education; others. **PERSONALITY**

TYPE—Social. Social occupations frequently involve working with, communicating with, and teaching people. These occupations often involve helping or providing service to others.

EDUCATION/TRAINING PROGRAM(S)—American History (United States); Asian History; Canadian History; European History; History and Philosophy of Science and Technology; History, General; History, Other; Public/Applied History and Archival Administration. **RELATED KNOWLEDGE/COURSES—Education and Training:** Knowledge of principles and methods for curriculum and training design, teaching and instruction for individuals and groups, and the measurement of training effects. **So-** ciology and Anthropology: Knowledge of group behavior and dynamics, societal trends and influences, human migrations, ethnicity, and cultures and their history and origins. **English Language:** Knowledge of the structure and content of the English language, including the meaning and spelling of words, rules of composition, and grammar. **History and Archeology:** Knowledge of historical events and their causes, indicators, and effects on civilizations and cultures. **Psychology:** Knowledge of human behavior and performance; individual differences in ability, personality, and interests; learning and motivation; psychological research methods; and the assessment and treatment of behavioral and affective disorders.

Home Economics Teachers, Postsecondary

- ▲ Education/Training Required: Master's degree
- ▲ Annual Earnings: $48,040
- ▲ Growth: 23.5%
- ▲ Annual Job Openings: 184,000
- ▲ Self-Employed: 0%
- ▲ Part-Time: 32.3%

Teach courses in child care, family relations, finance, nutrition, and related subjects as pertaining to home management. SKILLS—No data available.

GOE INFORMATION—Interest Area: 12. Education and Social Service. **Work Group:** 12.03. Educational Services. **Other Job Titles in This Work Group:** Adult Literacy, Remedial Education, and GED Teachers and Instructors; Agricultural Sciences Teachers, Postsecondary; Anthropology and Archeology Teachers, Postsecondary; Architecture Teachers, Postsecondary; Archivists; Area, Ethnic, and Cultural Studies Teachers, Postsecondary; Art, Drama, and Music Teachers, Postsecondary; Atmospheric, Earth, Marine, and Space Sciences Teachers, Postsecondary; Audio-Visual Collections Specialists; Biological Science Teachers, Postsecondary; Business Teachers, Postsecondary; Chemistry Teachers, Postsecondary; Child Care Workers; Communications Teachers, Postsecondary; Computer Science Teachers, Postsecondary; Criminal Justice and Law Enforcement Teachers, Postsecondary; Curators; Economics Teachers, Postsecondary; Education Teachers, Postsecondary; Educational Psychologists; Educational, Vocational, and School Counselors; Elementary School Teachers, Except Special Education; Engineering Teachers, Postsecondary; English Language and Literature Teachers, Postsecondary; Environmental Science Teachers, Postsecondary; Farm and Home Management Advisors; Foreign Language and Literature Teachers, Postsecondary; Forestry and Conservation Science Teachers, Postsecondary; Geography Teachers, Postsecondary; Graduate Teaching Assistants; Health Specialties Teachers, Postsecondary; History Teachers, Postsecondary; Kindergarten Teachers, Except Special Education; Law Teachers, Postsecondary; Librarians; Library Assistants, Clerical; Library Science Teachers, Postsecondary; Library Technicians; Mathematical Science Teachers, Postsecondary; Middle School Teachers, Except Special and Vocational Education; Museum Technicians and Conservators; Nursing Instructors and Teachers, Postsecondary; Personal Financial Advisors; Philosophy and Religion Teachers, Postsecondary; Physics Teachers, Postsecondary; Political Science Teachers, Postsecondary; Postsecondary Teachers, All Other; Preschool Teachers, Except Special Education; others. **PERSONALITY TYPE**—No data available.

EDUCATION/TRAINING PROGRAM(S)—Business Family and Consumer Sciences/Human Sciences; Child Care and Support Services Management; Family and Consumer Sciences/Human Sciences, General; Foodservice Systems Administration/Management; Human Development and Family Studies, General. **RELATED KNOWLEDGE/COURSES**—No data available.

Home Health Aides

▲ Education/Training Required: Short-term on-the-job training
▲ Annual Earnings: $17,590
▲ Growth: 47.3%
▲ Annual Job Openings: 120,000
▲ Self-Employed: 3.3%
▲ Part-Time: 26.4%

Provide routine, personal health care, such as bathing, dressing, or grooming, to elderly, convalescent, or disabled persons in the home of patients or in a residential care facility. Changes bed linens, washes and irons patient's laundry, and cleans patient's quarters. Assists patients into and out of bed, automobiles, or wheelchair; to lavatory; and up and down stairs. Administers prescribed oral medication under written direction of physician or as directed by home care nurse and aide. Massages patient and applies preparations and treatment, such as liniment or alcohol rubs and heat-lamp stimulation. Performs variety of miscellaneous duties as requested, such as obtaining household supplies and running errands. Entertains patient, reads aloud, and plays cards and other games with patient. Maintains records of services performed and of apparent condition of patient. Purchases, prepares, and serves food for patient and other members of family, following special prescribed diets. **SKILLS—Service Orientation:** Actively looking for ways to help people. **Reading Comprehension:** Understanding written sentences and paragraphs in work-related documents. **Social Perceptiveness:** Being aware of others' reactions and understanding why they react as they do. **Critical Thinking:** Using logic and reasoning to identify the strengths and weaknesses of alternative solutions, conclusions, or approaches to problems. **Monitoring:** Monitoring/Assessing your performance or that of other individuals or organizations to make improvements or take corrective action. **Speaking:** Talking to others to convey information effectively. **Active Listening:** Giving full attention to what other people are saying, taking time to understand the points being made, asking questions as appropriate, and not interrupting at inappropriate times.

GOE INFORMATION—Interest Area: 14. Medical and Health Services. **Work Group:** 14.07. Patient Care and Assistance. **Other Job Titles in This Work Group:** Licensed Practical and Licensed Vocational Nurses; Nursing Aides, Orderlies, and Attendants; Psychiatric Aides; Psychiatric Technicians. **PERSONALITY TYPE—Social.** Social occupations frequently involve working with, communicating with, and teaching people. These occupations often involve helping or providing service to others.

EDUCATION/TRAINING PROGRAM(S)—Home Health Aide/Home Attendant. RELATED KNOWLEDGE/COURSES—Customer and Personal Service: Knowledge of principles and processes for providing customer and personal services. This includes customer needs assessment, meeting quality standards for services, and evaluation of customer satisfaction. **Medicine and Dentistry:** Knowledge of the information and techniques needed to diagnose and treat human injuries, diseases, and deformities. This includes symptoms, treatment alternatives, drug properties and interactions, and preventive health-care measures. **Psychology:** Knowledge of human behavior and performance; individual differences in ability, personality, and interests; learning and motivation; psychological research methods; and the assessment and treatment of behavioral and affective disorders. **Therapy and Counseling:** Knowledge of principles, methods, and procedures for diagnosis, treatment, and rehabilitation of physical and mental dysfunctions and for career counseling and guidance. **Clerical Studies:** Knowledge of administrative and clerical procedures and systems, such as word processing, managing files and records, stenography and transcription, designing forms, and other office procedures and terminology.

Hosts and Hostesses, Restaurant, Lounge, and Coffee Shop

- ▲ Education/Training Required: Short-term on-the-job training
- ▲ Annual Earnings: $14,920
- ▲ Growth: 13.0%
- ▲ Annual Job Openings: 84,000
- ▲ Self-Employed: 2.0%
- ▲ Part-Time: 38.3%

Welcome patrons, seat them at tables or in lounge, and help ensure quality of facilities and service. Greets and escorts guests to tables and provides menus. Adjusts complaints of patrons. Inspects dining room serving stations for neatness and cleanliness. Requisitions table linens and other supplies for tables and serving stations. Assigns work tasks and coordinates activities of dining room personnel to ensure prompt and courteous service to patrons. Schedules dining reservations and arranges parties or special service for diners. **SKILLS—Time Management:** Managing one's own time and the time of others. **Management of Personnel Resources:** Motivating, developing, and directing people as they work, identifying the best people for the job. **Speaking:** Talking to others to convey information effectively. **Coordination:** Adjusting actions in relation to others' actions. **Learning Strategies:** Selecting and using training/instructional methods and procedures appropriate for the situation when learning or teaching new things.

GOE INFORMATION—Interest Area: 11. Recreation, Travel, and Other Personal Services. **Work Group:** 11.05. Food and Beverage Services. **Other Job Titles in This Work Group:** Bakers; Bakers, Bread and Pastry; Bartenders; Butchers and Meat Cutters; Chefs and Head Cooks; Combined Food Preparation and Serving Workers, Including Fast Food; Cooks, All Other; Cooks, Fast Food; Cooks, Institution and Cafeteria; Cooks, Restaurant; Cooks, Short Order; Counter Attendants, Cafeteria, Food Concession, and Coffee Shop; Dining Room and Cafeteria Attendants and Bartender Helpers; Dishwashers; Food Preparation and Serving Related Workers, All Other; Food Preparation Workers; Food Servers, Nonrestaurant; Waiters and Waitresses. **PERSONALITY TYPE—**Enterprising. Enterprising occupations frequently involve starting up and carrying out projects. These occupations can involve leading people and making many decisions. They sometimes require risk taking and often deal with business.

EDUCATION/TRAINING PROGRAM(S)—Food Service, Waiter/Waitress, and Dining Room Management/Manager. **RELATED KNOWLEDGE/COURSES—Customer and Personal Service:** Knowledge of principles and processes for providing customer and personal services. This includes customer needs assessment, meeting quality standards for services, and evaluation of customer satisfaction. **Administration and Management:** Knowledge of business and management principles involved in strategic planning, resource allocation, human resources modeling, leadership technique, production methods, and coordination of people and resources. **Personnel and Human Resources:** Knowledge of principles and procedures for personnel recruitment, selection, training, compensation and benefits, labor relations and negotiation, and personnel information systems. **Mathematics:** Knowledge of arithmetic, algebra, geometry, calculus, and statistics and their applications. **English Language:** Knowledge of the structure and content of the English language, including the meaning and spelling of words, rules of composition, and grammar.

Hotel, Motel, and Resort Desk Clerks

- ▲ Education/Training Required: Short-term on-the-job training
- ▲ Annual Earnings: $16,920
- ▲ Growth: 33.4%
- ▲ Annual Job Openings: 73,000
- ▲ Self-Employed: 1.5%
- ▲ Part-Time: 25.8%

Accommodate hotel, motel, and resort patrons by registering and assigning rooms to guests, issuing room keys, transmitting and receiving messages, keeping records of occupied rooms and guests' accounts, making and confirming reservations, and presenting statements to and collecting payments from departing guests. Greets, registers, and assigns rooms to guests of hotel or motel. Makes and confirms reservations. Transmits and receives messages, using telephone or telephone switchboard. Date-stamps, sorts, and racks incoming mail and messages. Deposits guests' valuables in hotel safe or safe-deposit box. Answers inquiries pertaining to hotel services; registration of guests; and shopping, dining, entertainment, and travel directions. Issues room key and escort instructions to bellhop. Posts charges, such as room, food, liquor, or telephone, to ledger, manually or using computer. Computes bill, collects payment, and makes change for guests. Keeps records of room availability and guests' accounts manually or using computer. **SKILLS—Service Orientation:** Actively looking for ways to help people. **Active Listening:** Giving full attention to what other people are saying, taking time to understand the points being made, asking questions as appropriate, and not interrupting at inappropriate times. **Reading Comprehension:** Understanding written sentences and paragraphs in work-related documents. **Coordination:** Adjusting actions in relation to others' actions. **Speaking:** Talking to others to convey information effectively.

GOE INFORMATION—Interest Area: 11. Recreation, Travel, and Other Personal Services. **Work Group:** 11.03. Transportation and Lodging Services. **Other Job Titles in This Work Group:** Baggage Porters and Bellhops; Con-

cierges; Flight Attendants; Reservation and Transportation Ticket Agents; Reservation and Transportation Ticket Agents and Travel Clerks; Transportation Attendants, Except Flight Attendants and Baggage Porters. **PERSONALITY TYPE**—Conventional. Conventional occupations frequently involve following set procedures and routines. These occupations can include working with data and details more than with ideas. Usually there is a clear line of authority to follow.

EDUCATION/TRAINING PROGRAM(S)—Selling Skills and Sales Operations. **RELATED KNOWLEDGE/COURSES—Customer and Personal Service:** Knowledge of principles and processes for providing customer and personal services. This includes customer needs assessment, meeting quality standards for services, and evaluation of customer satisfaction. **Clerical Studies:** Knowledge of administrative and clerical procedures and systems, such as word processing, managing files and records, stenography and transcription, designing forms, and other office procedures and terminology. **English Language:** Knowledge of the structure and content of the English language, including the meaning and spelling of words, rules of composition, and grammar. **Mathematics:** Knowledge of arithmetic, algebra, geometry, calculus, and statistics and their applications. **Computers and Electronics:** Knowledge of circuit boards, processors, chips, electronic equipment, and computer hardware and software, including applications and programming.

Housekeeping Supervisors

▲ Education/Training Required: Work experience in a related occupation
▲ Annual Earnings: $27,200
▲ Growth: 14.2%
▲ Annual Job Openings: 18,000
▲ Self-Employed: 1.6%
▲ Part-Time: 6.4%

Supervise work activities of cleaning personnel to ensure clean, orderly, and attractive rooms in hotels, hospitals, educational institutions, and similar establishments. Assign duties, inspect work, and investigate complaints regarding housekeeping service and equipment and take corrective action. May purchase housekeeping supplies and equipment, take periodic inventories, screen applicants, train new employees, and recommend dismissals. Assigns workers their duties and inspects work for conformance to prescribed standards of cleanliness. Investigates complaints regarding housekeeping service and

equipment and takes corrective action. Obtains list of rooms to be cleaned immediately and list of prospective checkouts or discharges to prepare work assignments. Coordinates work activities among departments. Conducts orientation training and in-service training to explain policies and work procedures and to demonstrate use and maintenance of equipment. Inventories stock to ensure adequate supplies. Evaluates records to forecast department personnel requirements. Makes recommendations to improve service and ensure more efficient operation. Prepares reports concerning room occupancy, payroll, and department expenses. Selects and purchases new furnishings. Performs cleaning duties in cases of emergency or staff shortage. Examines building to determine need for repairs or replacement of furniture or equipment and makes recommendations to management. Attends staff meetings to discuss company policies and patrons' complaints. Issues supplies and equipment to workers. Establishes standards and procedures for work of housekeeping staff. Advises manager, desk clerk, or admitting personnel of rooms ready for occupancy. Records data regarding work assignments, personnel actions, and time cards and prepares periodic reports. Screens job applicants, hires new employees, and recommends promotions, transfers, and dismissals. **SKILLS—Time Management:** Managing one's own time and the time of others. **Speaking:** Talking to others to convey information effectively. **Management of Personnel Resources:** Motivating, developing, and directing people as they work, identifying the best people for the job. **Coordination:** Adjusting actions in relation to others' actions. **Reading Comprehension:** Understanding written sentences and paragraphs in work-related documents.

GOE INFORMATION—Interest Area: 11. Recreation, Travel, and Other Personal Services. **Work Group:** 11.01. Managerial Work in Recreation, Travel, and Other Personal Services. **Other Job Titles in This Work Group:** Aircraft Cargo Handling Supervisors; First-Line Supervisors/Managers of Food Preparation and Serving Workers; First-Line Supervisors/Managers of Housekeeping and Janitorial Workers; First-Line Supervisors/Managers of

Personal Service Workers; Food Service Managers; Gaming Managers; Gaming Supervisors; Janitorial Supervisors; Lodging Managers; Meeting and Convention Planners. **PERSONALITY TYPE—**Enterprising. Enterprising occupations frequently involve starting up and carrying out projects. These occupations can involve leading people and making many decisions. They sometimes require risk taking and often deal with business.

EDUCATION/TRAINING PROGRAM(S)—No data available. **RELATED KNOWLEDGE/COURSES—Customer and Personal Service:** Knowledge of principles and processes for providing customer and personal services. This includes customer needs assessment, meeting quality standards for services, and evaluation of customer satisfaction. **Personnel and Human Resources:** Knowledge of principles and procedures for personnel recruitment, selection, training, compensation and benefits, labor relations and negotiation, and personnel information systems. **Administration and Management:** Knowledge of business and management principles involved in strategic planning, resource allocation, human resources modeling, leadership technique, production methods, and coordination of people and resources. **Education and Training:** Knowledge of principles and methods for curriculum and training design, teaching and instruction for individuals and groups, and the measurement of training effects. **English Language:** Knowledge of the structure and content of the English language, including the meaning and spelling of words, rules of composition, and grammar.

Human Resources Assistants, Except Payroll and Timekeeping

- ▲ Education/Training Required: Short-term on-the-job training
- ▲ Annual Earnings: $29,470
- ▲ Growth: 19.3%
- ▲ Annual Job Openings: 25,000
- ▲ Self-Employed: 0%
- ▲ Part-Time: 6.3%

Compile and keep personnel records. Record data for each employee, such as address, weekly earnings, absences, amount of sales or production, supervisory reports on ability, and date of and reason for termination. Compile and type reports from employment records. File employment records. Search employee files and furnish information to authorized persons. Examines employee files to answer inquiries and provide information for personnel actions. Prepares listing of vacancies and notifies eligible workers of position availability. Requests informa-

tion from law enforcement officials, previous employers, and other references to determine applicant's employment acceptability. Selects applicants having specified job requirements and refers to employing official. Explains company insurance policies and options to employees and files claim and cancellation forms. Communicates with employees or applicants to explain company personnel policies and procedures. Administers and scores employee aptitude, skills, personality, and interests tests. Answers questions regarding examinations, eligibility, salaries, benefits, and other pertinent information. Records employee data, such as address, rate of pay, absences, and benefits, using personal computer. Maintains and updates employee records to document personnel actions and changes in employee status. Processes and reviews employment application to evaluate qualifications or eligibility of applicant. Interviews applicants to obtain and verify information. Compiles and types reports from employment records. **SKILLS—Reading Comprehension:** Understanding written sentences and paragraphs in work-related documents. **Speaking:** Talking to others to convey information effectively. **Active Listening:** Giving full attention to what other people are saying, taking time to understand the points being made, asking questions as appropriate, and not interrupting at inappropriate times. **Equipment Selection:** Determining the kind of tools and equipment needed to do a job. **Writing:** Communicating effectively in writing as appropriate for the needs of the audience.

GOE INFORMATION—Interest Area: 09. Business Detail. **Work Group:** 09.07. Records Processing. **Other Job Titles in This Work Group:** Correspondence Clerks; Court Reporters; Credit Authorizers; Credit Authorizers, Checkers, and Clerks; Credit Checkers; File Clerks; Information and Record Clerks, All Other; Insurance Claims and Policy Processing Clerks; Insurance Claims Clerks; Insurance Policy Processing Clerks; Medical Records and

Health Information Technicians; Medical Transcriptionists; Office Clerks, General; Procurement Clerks; Proofreaders and Copy Markers. **PERSONALITY TYPE**—Conventional. Conventional occupations frequently involve following set procedures and routines. These occupations can include working with data and details more than with ideas. Usually there is a clear line of authority to follow.

EDUCATION/TRAINING PROGRAM(S)—General Office Occupations and Clerical Services. **RELATED KNOWLEDGE/COURSES—Clerical Studies:** Knowledge of administrative and clerical procedures and systems, such as word processing, managing files and records, stenography and transcription, designing forms, and other office procedures and terminology. **Personnel and Human Resources:** Knowledge of principles and procedures for personnel recruitment, selection, training, compensation and benefits, labor relations and negotiation, and personnel information systems. **English Language:** Knowledge of the structure and content of the English language, including the meaning and spelling of words, rules of composition, and grammar. **Mathematics:** Knowledge of arithmetic, algebra, geometry, calculus, and statistics and their applications. **Computers and Electronics:** Knowledge of circuit boards, processors, chips, electronic equipment, and computer hardware and software, including applications and programming.

Human Resources Managers

▲ Education/Training Required: Work experience plus degree
▲ Annual Earnings: $61,880
▲ Growth: 12.7%
▲ Annual Job Openings: 14,000
▲ Self-Employed: 0.5%
▲ Part Time: 3.6%

Plan, direct, and coordinate human resource management activities of an organization to maximize the strategic use of human resources and maintain functions such as employee compensation, recruitment, personnel policies, and regulatory compliance. Formulates policies and procedures for recruitment, testing, placement, classification, orientation, benefits, and labor and industrial relations. Plans, directs, supervises, and coordinates work activities of subordinates and staff relating to employment, compensation, labor relations, and employee relations. Analyzes compensation policies, government regulations, and prevailing wage rates to develop competitive compen-

sation plan. Develops methods to improve employment policies, processes, and practices and recommends changes to management. Prepares personnel forecast to project employment needs. Prepares budget for personnel operations. Prepares and delivers presentations and reports to corporate officers or other management regarding human resource management policies and practices and recommendations for change. Negotiates bargaining agreements and resolves labor disputes. Meets with shop stewards and supervisors to resolve grievances. Conducts exit interviews to identify reasons for employee termination and writes separation notices. Plans and conducts new employee orientation to foster positive attitude toward organizational objectives. Writes directives advising department managers of organization policy in personnel matters such as equal employment opportunity, sexual harassment, and discrimination. Studies legislation, arbitration decisions, and collective bargaining contracts to assess industry trends. Maintains records and compiles statistical reports concerning personnel-related data such as hires, transfers, performance appraisals, and absenteeism rates. Analyzes statistical data and reports to identify and determine causes of personnel problems and develop recommendations for improvement of organization's personnel policies and practices. Represents organization at personnel-related hearings and investigations. Contracts with vendors to provide employee services, such as canteen, transportation, or relocation service. Investigates industrial accidents and prepares reports for insurance carrier. **SKILLS—Management of Personnel Resources:** Motivating, developing, and directing people as they work, identifying the best people for the job. **Systems Analysis:** Determining how a system should work and how changes in conditions, operations, and the environment will affect outcomes. **Systems Evaluation:** Identifying measures or indicators of system performance and the actions needed to improve or correct performance relative to the goals of the system. **Active Learning:** Understanding the implications of new information for both current and future problem-solving and decision-making. **Coordination:** Adjusting actions in relation to others' actions. **Speaking:** Talking to others to convey information effectively. **Reading Comprehension:** Understanding written sentences and paragraphs in work-related documents.

GOE INFORMATION—Interest Area: 13. General Management and Support. **Work Group:** 13.01. General Management Work and Management of Support Functions. **Other Job Titles in This Work Group:** Chief Executives; Compensation and Benefits Managers; Farm, Ranch, and Other Agricultural Managers; Financial Managers; Financial Managers, Branch or Department; Funeral Directors; General and Operations Managers; Government Service Executives; Human Resources Managers, All Other; Legislators; Managers, All Other; Postmasters and Mail Superintendents; Private Sector Executives; Property, Real Estate, and Community Association Managers; Public Relations Managers; Purchasing Managers; Storage and Distribution Managers; Training and Development Managers; Transportation, Storage, and Distribution Managers; Treasurers, Controllers, and Chief Financial Officers. **PERSONALITY TYPE**—Enterprising. Enterprising occupations frequently involve starting up and carrying out projects. These occupations can involve leading people and making many decisions. They sometimes require risk taking and often deal with business.

EDUCATION/TRAINING PROGRAM(S)—Human Resources Development; Human Resources Management/Personnel Administration, General; Labor and Industrial Relations; Labor Studies. **RELATED KNOWLEDGE/COURSES—Personnel and Human Resources:** Knowledge of principles and procedures for personnel recruitment, selection, training, compensation and benefits, labor relations and negotiation, and personnel information systems. **Administration and Management:** Knowledge of business and management principles involved in strategic planning, resource allocation, human resources modeling, leadership technique, production methods, and coordination of people and resources. **Mathematics:** Knowledge of arithmetic, algebra, geometry, calculus, and statistics and their applications. **English Language:** Knowledge of the structure and content of the English language, including the meaning and spelling of words, rules of composition, and grammar. **Education and Training:** Knowledge of principles and methods for curriculum and training design, teaching and instruction for individuals and groups, and the measurement of training effects.

Hydrologists

- ▲ Education/Training Required: Bachelor's degree
- ▲ Annual Earnings: $56,400
- ▲ Growth: 25.7%
- ▲ Annual Job Openings: 1,000
- ▲ Self-Employed: 15.1%
- ▲ Part-Time: 6.3%

Research the distribution, circulation, and physical properties of underground and surface waters; study the form and intensity of precipitation, its rate of infiltration into the soil, movement through the earth, and its return to the ocean and atmosphere. Studies and analyzes physical aspects of earth, including atmosphere and hydrosphere, and interior structure. Studies waters of land areas to determine modes of return to ocean and atmosphere. Compiles and evaluates data to prepare navigational charts and maps, predict atmospheric conditions, and prepare environmental reports. Prepares and issues maps and reports indicating areas of seismic risk to existing or proposed construction or development. Evaluates data in reference to project planning, such as flood and drought control, water power and supply, drainage, irrigation, and inland navigation. Investigates origin and activity of glaciers, volcanoes, and earthquakes. Studies, maps, and charts distribution, disposition, and development of waters of land areas, including form and intensity of precipitation. Studies, measures, and interprets seismic, gravitational, electrical, thermal, and magnetic forces and data affecting the earth. **SKILLS—Mathematics:** Using mathematics to solve problems. **Science:** Using scientific rules and methods to solve problems. **Writing:** Communicating effectively in writing as appropriate for the needs of the audience. **Active Learning:** Understanding the implications of new information for both current and future problem-solving and decision-making. **Critical Thinking:** Using logic and reasoning to identify the strengths and weaknesses of alternative solutions, conclusions, or approaches to problems.

GOE INFORMATION—Interest Area: 02. Science, Math, and Engineering. **Work Group:** 02.02. Physical Sciences. **Other Job Titles in This Work Group:** Astronomers; Atmospheric and Space Scientists; Chemists; Geog-

raphers; Geologists; Geoscientists, Except Hydrologists and Geographers; Materials Scientists; Physical Scientists, All Other; Physicists. **PERSONALITY TYPE**—Investigative. Investigative occupations frequently involve working with ideas and require an extensive amount of thinking. These occupations can involve searching for facts and figuring out problems mentally.

EDUCATION/TRAINING PROGRAM(S)—Geology/ Earth Science, General; Hydrology and Water Resources Science; Oceanography, Chemical and Physical. **RELATED KNOWLEDGE/COURSES—Physics:** Knowledge and prediction of physical principles and laws and their interrelationships and applications to understanding fluid, material, and atmospheric dynamics and mechanical, electrical, atomic, and sub-atomic structures and processes. **Mathematics:** Knowledge of arithmetic, algebra, geometry, calculus, and statistics and their applications. **Geography:** Knowledge of principles and methods for describing the features of land, sea, and air masses, including their physical characteristics, locations, interrelationships, and distribution of plant, animal, and human life. **Chemistry:** Knowledge of the chemical composition, structure, and properties of substances and of the chemical processes and transformations that they undergo. This includes uses of chemicals and their interactions, danger signs, production techniques, and disposal methods. **English Language:** Knowledge of the structure and content of the English language, including the meaning and spelling of words, rules of composition, and grammar.

Immigration and Customs Inspectors

- ▲ Education/Training Required: Work experience in a related occupation
- ▲ Annual Earnings: $50,960
- ▲ Growth: 16.4%
- ▲ Annual Job Openings: 4,000
- ▲ Self-Employed: 1.3%
- ▲ Part-Time: 2.9%

Investigate and inspect persons, common carriers, goods, and merchandise arriving in or departing from the United States or between states to detect violations of immigration and customs laws and regulations. Inspects cargo, baggage, personal articles, and common carriers entering or leaving U.S. for compliance with revenue laws and U.S. Customs Service regulations. Testifies in administrative and judicial proceedings. Collects samples of merchandise for examination, appraising, or testing and requests laboratory analyses. Institutes civil and criminal prosecutions and

assists other governmental agencies with regulation violation issues. Issues or denies permits. Interprets and explains laws and regulations to others. Determines duty and taxes to be paid, investigates applications for duty refunds, or petitions for remission or mitigation of penalties. Examines, classifies, weighs, measures, and appraises merchandise to enforce regulations of U.S. Customs Service and prevent illegal importing and exporting. Determines investigative and seizure techniques to be used and seizes contraband, undeclared merchandise, vehicles, and air or sea craft carrying smuggled merchandise. Arrests, detains, paroles, or arranges for deportation of persons in violation of customs or immigration laws. Reviews private and public records and documents to establish, assemble, and verify facts and secure legal evidence. Keeps records and writes reports of activities, findings, transactions, violations, discrepancies, and decisions. Examines visas and passports and interviews persons to determine eligibility for admission, residence, and travel in U.S. **SKILLS—Writing:** Communicating effectively in writing as appropriate for the needs of the audience. **Speaking:** Talking to others to convey information effectively. **Reading Comprehension:** Understanding written sentences and paragraphs in work-related documents. **Judgment and Decision Making:** Considering the relative costs and benefits of potential actions to choose the most appropriate one. **Active Listening:** Giving full attention to what other people are saying, taking time to understand the points being made, asking questions as appropriate, and not interrupting at inappropriate times.

GOE INFORMATION—Interest Area: 04. Law, Law Enforcement, and Public Safety. **Work Group:** 04.03. Law Enforcement. **Other Job Titles in This Work Group:** Animal Control Workers; Bailiffs; Child Support, Missing Persons, and Unemployment Insurance Fraud Investigators; Correctional Officers and Jailers; Criminal Investigators and Special Agents; Crossing Guards; Detectives and Criminal Investigators; Fire Investigators; Fish and Game Wardens; Forensic Science Technicians; Gaming Surveillance Officers and Gaming Investigators; Highway Patrol Pilots; Lifeguards, Ski Patrol, and Other Recreational Protective Service Workers; Parking Enforcement Workers; Police and Sheriff's Patrol Officers; Police Detectives; Police Identification and Records Officers; Police Patrol Officers; Private Detectives and Investigators; Security Guards; Sheriffs and Deputy Sheriffs; Transit and Railroad Police. **PERSONALITY TYPE—Conventional.** Conventional occupations frequently involve following set procedures and routines. These occupations can include working with data and details more than with ideas. Usually there is a clear line of authority to follow.

EDUCATION/TRAINING PROGRAM(S)—Criminal Justice/Police Science; Criminalistics and Criminal Science. RELATED KNOWLEDGE/COURSES—Law and Government: Knowledge of laws, legal codes, court procedures, precedents, government regulations, executive orders, agency rules, and the democratic political process. **English Language:** Knowledge of the structure and content of the English language, including the meaning and spelling of words, rules of composition, and grammar. **Public Safety and Security:** Knowledge of relevant equipment, policies, procedures, and strategies to promote effective local, state, or national security operations for the protection of people, data, property, and institutions. **Communications and Media:** Knowledge of media production, communication, and dissemination techniques and methods. This includes alternative ways to inform and entertain via written, oral, and visual media. **Mathematics:** Knowledge of arithmetic, algebra, geometry, calculus, and statistics and their applications.

Industrial Production Managers

- ▲ Education/Training Required: Bachelor's degree
- ▲ Annual Earnings: $64,510
- ▲ Growth: 6.2%
- ▲ Annual Job Openings: 22,000
- ▲ Self-Employed: 0%
- ▲ Part-Time: 6.1%

Plan, direct, or coordinate the work activities and resources necessary for manufacturing products in accordance with cost, quality, and quantity specifications. Directs and coordinates production, processing, distribution, and marketing activities of industrial organization. Reviews processing schedules and production orders to determine staffing requirements, work procedures, and duty assignments. Reviews plans and confers with research and support staff to develop new products and processes or the quality of existing products. Initiates and coordinates inventory and cost-control programs. Develops budgets and approves expenditures for supplies, materials, and human resources. Examines samples of raw products or directs testing during processing to ensure that finished products conform to prescribed quality standards. Hires, trains, evaluates, and discharges staff. Resolves personnel grievances. Prepares and maintains production reports and personnel records. Coordinates and recommends procedures for facility and equipment maintenance or modification. Negotiates materials prices with suppliers. Reviews operations and confers with technical or administrative staff to resolve production or processing problems. Analyzes production, quality control, maintenance, and other operational reports to detect production problems. **SKILLS—Coordination:** Adjusting actions in relation to others' actions. **Judgment and Decision Making:** Considering the relative costs and benefits of potential actions to choose the most appropriate one. **Management of Personnel Resources:** Motivating, developing, and directing people as they work, identifying the best people for the job. **Systems Evaluation:** Identifying measures or indicators of system performance and the actions needed to improve or correct performance relative to the goals of the system. **Management of Material Resources:** Obtaining and seeing to the appropriate use of equipment, facilities, and materials needed to do certain work. **Monitoring:** Monitoring/Assessing your performance or that of other individuals or organizations to make improvements or take corrective action.

GOE INFORMATION—Interest Area: 08. Industrial Production. **Work Group:** 08.01. Managerial Work in Industrial Production. **Other Job Titles in This Work Group:** First-Line Supervisors/Managers of Helpers, Laborers, and Material Movers, Hand; First-Line Supervisors/Managers of Production and Operating Workers.

PERSONALITY TYPE—Enterprising. Enterprising occupations frequently involve starting up and carrying out projects. These occupations can involve leading people and making many decisions. They sometimes require risk taking and often deal with business.

EDUCATION/TRAINING PROGRAM(S)—Business Administration and Management, General; Business/Commerce, General; Operations Management and Supervision. **RELATED KNOWLEDGE/COURSES—Production and Processing:** Knowledge of raw materials, production processes, quality control, costs, and other techniques for maximizing the effective manufacture and distribution of goods. **Administration and Management:** Knowledge of business and management principles involved in strategic planning, resource allocation, human resources modeling, leadership technique, production methods, and coordination of people and resources. **Personnel and Human Resources:** Knowledge of principles and procedures for personnel recruitment, selection, training, compensation and benefits, labor relations and negotiation, and personnel information systems. **English Language:** Knowledge of the structure and content of the English language, including the meaning and spelling of words, rules of composition, and grammar. **Food Production:** Knowledge of techniques and equipment for planting, growing, and harvesting food products (both plant and animal) for consumption, including storage/handling techniques.

Industrial Truck and Tractor Operators

- ▲ Education/Training Required: Short-term on-the-job training
- ▲ Annual Earnings: $25,350
- ▲ Growth: 11.3%
- ▲ Annual Job Openings: 91,000
- ▲ Self-Employed: 0.2%
- ▲ Part-Time: 3.0%

Operate industrial trucks or tractors equipped to move materials around a warehouse, storage yard, factory, construction site, or similar location. Moves controls to drive gasoline- or electric-powered trucks, cars, or tractors and transport materials between loading, processing, and storage areas. Moves levers and controls to operate lifting devices, such as forklifts, lift beams and swivel-hooks, hoists, and elevating platforms, to load, unload, transport, and stack material. Positions lifting device under, over, or around loaded pallets, skids, and boxes; secures material or products for transport to designated areas. Hooks tow trucks to trailer hitches and fastens attachments, such as graders, plows, rollers, and winch cables, to tractor, using hitchpins. Turns valves and opens chutes to dump, spray, or release materials from dump cars or storage bins into hoppers. Performs routine maintenance on vehicles and auxiliary equipment, such as cleaning, lubricating, recharging batteries, fueling, or replacing liquefied-gas tank. Manually loads or unloads materials onto or off pallets, skids, platforms, cars, or lifting devices. Operates or tends automatic stacking, loading, packaging, or cutting machines. Weighs materials or products and records weight and other production data on tags or labels. Signals workers to discharge, dump, or level materials. **SKILLS—Op-**

eration and Control: Controlling operations of equipment or systems. **Equipment Selection:** Determining the kind of tools and equipment needed to do a job. **Operation Monitoring:** Watching gauges, dials, or other indicators to make sure a machine is working properly. **Troubleshooting:** Determining causes of operating errors and deciding what to do about them. **Coordination:** Adjusting actions in relation to others' actions. **Repairing:** Repairing machines or systems, using the needed tools.

GOE INFORMATION—Interest Area: 08. Industrial Production. **Work Group:** 08.07. Hands-on Work: Loading, Moving, Hoisting, and Conveying. **Other Job Titles in This Work Group:** Conveyor Operators and Tenders; Crane and Tower Operators; Dragline Operators; Excavating and Loading Machine and Dragline Operators; Freight, Stock, and Material Movers, Hand; Hoist and Winch Operators; Irradiated-Fuel Handlers; Laborers and Freight, Stock, and Material Movers, Hand; Machine Feeders and Offbearers; Material Moving Workers, All Other; Packers and Packagers, Hand; Pump Operators, Except Wellhead Pumpers; Refuse and Recyclable Material Collectors; Tank Car, Truck, and Ship Loaders. **PERSONALITY TYPE—**Realistic. Realistic occupations frequently involve work activities that include practical, hands-on problems and solutions. They often deal with plants, animals, and real-world materials like wood, tools, and machinery. Many of the occupations require working outside and do not involve a lot of paperwork or working closely with others.

EDUCATION/TRAINING PROGRAM(S)—Ground Transportation, Other. **RELATED KNOWLEDGE/COURSES—Transportation:** Knowledge of principles and methods for moving people or goods by air, rail, sea, or road, including the relative costs and benefits. **Principles of Mechanical Devices:** Knowledge of machines and tools, including their designs, uses, repair, and maintenance. **Mathematics:** Knowledge of arithmetic, algebra, geometry, calculus, and statistics and their applications. **Production and Processing:** Knowledge of raw materials, production processes, quality control, costs, and other techniques for maximizing the effective manufacture and distribution of goods. **Physics:** Knowledge and prediction of physical principles and laws and their interrelationships and applications to understanding fluid, material, and atmospheric dynamics and mechanical, electrical, atomic, and sub-atomic structures and processes. **Clerical Studies:** Knowledge of administrative and clerical procedures and systems, such as word processing, managing files and records, stenography and transcription, designing forms, and other office procedures and terminology.

Industrial-Organizational Psychologists

▲ Education/Training Required: Master's degree
▲ Annual Earnings: $66,010
▲ Growth: 18.1%
▲ Annual Job Openings: 18,000
▲ Self-Employed: 43.7%
▲ Part-Time: 23.4%

Apply principles of psychology to personnel, administration, management, sales, and marketing problems. Activities may include policy planning; employee screening, training, and development; and organizational development and analysis. May work with management to reorganize the work setting to improve worker productivity. Develops interview techniques, rating scales, and psychological tests to assess skills, abilities, and interests as aids in selection, placement, and promotion. Analyzes data, using statistical methods and applications, to evaluate and measure the effectiveness of program implementation or training. Plans, develops, and organizes training programs, applying principles of learning and individual differences. Studies consumer reaction to new products and package designs, using surveys and tests, and measures the effectiveness of advertising media. Advises management in strategic changes to personnel, managerial, and marketing policies and practices to improve organizational effectiveness and efficiency. Conducts research studies of physical work environments, organizational structure, communication systems, group interaction, morale, and motivation to assess organizational functioning. Analyzes job requirements to establish criteria for classification, selection, training, and other related personnel functions. Observes and interviews workers to identify the physical, mental, and educational requirements of job. **SKILLS—Systems Evaluation:** Identifying measures or indicators of system performance and the actions needed to improve or correct performance relative to the goals of the system. **Reading Comprehension:** Understanding written sentences and paragraphs in work-related documents. **Active Learning:** Understanding the implications of new information for both current and future problem-solving and decision-making. **Mathematics:** Using mathematics to solve problems. **Writing:** Communicating effectively in writing as appropriate for the needs of the audience.

GOE INFORMATION—Interest Area: 02. Science, Math, and Engineering. **Work Group:** 02.04. Social Sciences. **Other Job Titles in This Work Group:** Anthropologists; Anthropologists and Archeologists; Archeologists; City Planning Aides; Economists; Historians; Political Scientists; Psychologists, All Other; Social Science Research Assistants; Social Scientists and Related Workers, All Other; Sociologists; Survey Researchers; Urban and Regional Planners. **PERSONALITY TYPE—**Investigative. Investigative occupations frequently involve working with ideas and require an extensive amount of thinking. These occupations can involve searching for facts and figuring out problems mentally.

EDUCATION/TRAINING PROGRAM(S)—Industrial and Organizational Psychology; Psychology, General. **RELATED KNOWLEDGE/COURSES—Psychology:** Knowledge of human behavior and performance; individual differences in ability, personality, and interests; learning and motivation; psychological research methods; and the assessment and treatment of behavioral and affective disorders. **Personnel and Human Resources:** Knowledge of principles and procedures for personnel recruitment, selection, training, compensation and benefits, labor relations and negotiation, and personnel information systems. **Education and Training:** Knowledge of principles and methods for curriculum and training design, teaching and instruction for individuals and groups, and the measurement of training effects. **Mathematics:** Knowledge of arithmetic, algebra, geometry, calculus, and statistics and their applications. **Administration and Management:** Knowledge of business and management principles involved in strategic planning, resource allocation, human resources modeling, leadership technique, production methods, and coordination of people and resources.

Instructional Coordinators

▲ Education/Training Required: Master's degree
▲ Annual Earnings: $46,600
▲ Growth: 25.0%
▲ Annual Job Openings: 15,000
▲ Self-Employed: 13.8%
▲ Part-Time: 9.8%

Develop instructional material, coordinate educational content, and incorporate current technology in specialized fields that provide guidelines to educators and instructors for developing curricula and conducting courses. Researches, evaluates, and prepares recommendations on curricula, instructional methods, and materials for school system. Develops tests, questionnaires, and procedures to measure effectiveness of curriculum and to determine if program objectives are being met. Prepares or approves manuals, guidelines, and reports on state educational policies and practices for distribution to school districts. Orders or authorizes purchase of instructional materials, supplies, equipment, and visual aids designed to meet educational needs of students. Confers with school officials, teachers, and administrative staff to plan and develop curricula and establish guidelines for educational programs. Confers with educational committees and advisory groups to gather information on instructional methods and materials related to specific academic subjects. Advises teaching and administrative staff in assessment, curriculum development, management of student behavior, and use of materials and equipment. Observes, evaluates, and recommends changes in work of teaching staff to strengthen teaching skills in classroom. Plans, conducts, and evaluates training programs and conferences for teachers to study new classroom procedures, instructional materials, and teaching aids. Advises school officials on implementation of state and federal programs and procedures. Conducts or participates in workshops, committees, and conferences designed to promote intellectual, social, and physical welfare of students. Coordinates activities of workers engaged in cataloging, distributing, and maintaining educational materials and equipment in curriculum library and laboratory. Interprets and enforces provisions of state education codes and rules and regulations of State Board of Education. Prepares or assists in preparation of grant proposals, budgets, and program policies and goals. Addresses public audiences to explain and elicit support for program objectives. Reviews student files and confers with educators, parents, and other concerned parties to decide student placement and provision of services. Inspects and authorizes repair of instructional equipment, such as musical instruments. **SKILLS—Learning Strategies:** Selecting and using training/instructional methods and procedures appropriate for the situation when learning or teaching new things. **Speaking:** Talking to others to convey information effectively. **Instructing:** Teaching others how to do something. **Reading Comprehension:** Understanding written sentences and paragraphs in work-related documents. **Writing:** Communicating effectively in writing as appropriate for the needs of the audience.

GOE INFORMATION—Interest Area: 12. Education and Social Service. **Work Group:** 12.01. Managerial Work in Education and Social Service. **Other Job Titles in This Work Group:** Education Administrators, All Other; Education Administrators, Elementary and Secondary School; Education Administrators, Postsecondary; Education Administrators, Preschool and Child Care Center/Program; Park Naturalists; Social and Community Service Managers. **PERSONALITY TYPE—Social.** Social occupations frequently involve working with, communicating with, and teaching people. These occupations often involve helping or providing service to others.

EDUCATION/TRAINING PROGRAM(S)—Curriculum and Instruction; Educational/Instructional Media Design. **RELATED KNOWLEDGE/COURSES—Education and Training:** Knowledge of principles and methods for curriculum and training design, teaching and instruction for individuals and groups, and the measurement of training effects. **English Language:** Knowledge of the structure and content of the English language, including the meaning and spelling of words, rules of composition, and grammar. **Administration and Management:** Knowledge of business and management principles involved in strategic planning, resource allocation, human resources modeling, leadership technique, production methods, and coordination of people and resources. **Psychology:** Knowledge of human behavior and performance; individual differences in ability, personality, and interests; learning and motivation; psychological research methods; and the assessment and treatment of behavioral and affective disorders. **Personnel and Human Resources:** Knowledge of principles and procedures for personnel recruitment, selection, training, compensation and benefits, labor relations and negotiation, and personnel information systems.

Insulation Workers, Floor, Ceiling, and Wall

- ▲ Education/Training Required: Moderate-term on-the-job training
- ▲ Annual Earnings: $28,000
- ▲ Growth: 13.6%
- ▲ Annual Job Openings: 12,000
- ▲ Self-Employed: 3.1%
- ▲ Part-Time: 4.7%

Line and cover structures with insulating materials. May work with batt, roll, or blown insulation materials. Fits, wraps, or attaches insulating materials to structures of surfaces, using hand tools or wires, following blueprint specifications. Fills blower hopper with insulating materials. Covers, seals, or finishes insulated surfaces or access holes with plastic covers, canvas ships, sealant, tape, cement, or asphalt mastic. Reads blueprints and selects appropriate insulation, based on the heat-retaining or -excluding characteristics of the material. Measures and cuts insulation for covering surfaces, using tape measure, handsaw, knife, or scissors. Moves controls, buttons, or levers to start blower and regulate flow of materials through nozzle. Prepares surfaces for insulation application by brushing or spreading on adhesives, cement, or asphalt or attaching metal pins to surfaces. Evenly distributes insulating materials into small spaces within floors, ceilings, or walls, using blower and hose attachments or cement mortar. **SKILLS—Equipment Selection:** Determining the kind of tools and equipment needed to do a job.

GOE INFORMATION—Interest Area: 06. Construction, Mining, and Drilling. **Work Group:** 06.02. Construction. **Other Job Titles in This Work Group:** Boat Builders and Shipwrights; Boilermakers; Brattice Builders; Brickmasons and Blockmasons; Carpenters; Carpet Installers; Ceiling Tile Installers; Cement Masons and Concrete Finishers; Commercial Divers; Construction

Carpenters; Drywall and Ceiling Tile Installers; Drywall Installers; Electricians; Explosives Workers, Ordnance Handling Experts, and Blasters; Fence Erectors; Floor Layers, Except Carpet, Wood, and Hard Tiles; Floor Sanders and Finishers; Glaziers; Grader, Bulldozer, and Scraper Operators; Hazardous Materials Removal Workers; Insulation Workers, Mechanical; Manufactured Building and Mobile Home Installers; Operating Engineers; Operating Engineers and Other Construction Equipment Operators; Painters, Construction and Maintenance; Paperhangers; Paving, Surfacing, and Tamping Equipment Operators; Pile-Driver Operators; Pipe Fitters; Pipelayers; Pipelaying Fitters; Plasterers and Stucco Masons; Plumbers; Plumbers, Pipefitters, and Steamfitters; Rail-Track Laying and Maintenance Equipment Operators; Refractory Materials Repairers, Except Brickmasons; Reinforcing Iron and Rebar Workers; Riggers; Roofers; Rough Carpenters; Security and Fire Alarm Systems Installers; Segmental Pavers; Sheet Metal Workers; Ship Carpenters and Joiners; Stone Cutters and Carvers; Stonemasons; Structural Iron and Steel Workers; Tapers; Terrazzo Workers and Finishers; Tile and Marble Setters. **PERSONALITY TYPE—** Realistic. Realistic occupations frequently involve work activities that include practical, hands-on problems and solutions. They often deal with plants, animals, and real-world materials like wood, tools, and machinery. Many of the occupations require working outside and do not involve a lot of paperwork or working closely with others.

EDUCATION/TRAINING PROGRAM(S)—Construction Trades, Other. **RELATED KNOWLEDGE/ COURSES—Building and Construction:** Knowledge of materials, methods, and tools involved in the construction or repair of houses, buildings, or other structures, such as highways and roads. **Principles of Mechanical Devices:** Knowledge of machines and tools, including their designs, uses, repair, and maintenance. **Design:** Knowledge of design techniques, tools, and principles involved in production of precision technical plans, blueprints, drawings, and models.

Insulation Workers, Mechanical

- ▲ Education/Training Required: Moderate-term on-the-job training
- ▲ Annual Earnings: $28,000
- ▲ Growth: 13.6%
- ▲ Annual Job Openings: 12,000
- ▲ Self-Employed: 3.1%
- ▲ Part-Time: 4.7%

Apply insulating materials to pipes, ductwork, or other mechanical systems in order to help control and maintain temperature. Fits, wraps, or attaches insulating materials to structures of surfaces, using hand tools or wires, following blueprint specifications. Fills blower hopper with insulating materials. Covers, seals, or finishes insulated surfaces or access holes with plastic covers, canvas ships, sealant, tape, cement, or asphalt mastic. Reads blueprints and selects appropriate insulation, based on the heat-retaining or -excluding characteristics of the material. Measures and cuts insulation for covering surfaces, using tape measure, handsaw, knife, or scissors. Moves controls, buttons, or levers to start blower and regulate flow of materials through nozzle. Prepare surfaces for insulation application by brushing or spreading on adhesives, cement, or asphalt or attaching metal pins to surfaces. Evenly distributes insulating materials into small spaces within floors, ceilings, or walls, using blower and hose attachments or cement mortar. **SKILLS— Equipment Selection:** Determining the kind of tools and equipment needed to do a job.

GOE INFORMATION—Interest Area: 06. Construction, Mining, and Drilling. **Work Group:** 06.02. Construction. **Other Job Titles in This Work Group:** Boat Builders and Shipwrights; Boilermakers; Brattice Builders; Brickmasons and Blockmasons; Carpenters; Carpet Installers; Ceiling Tile Installers; Cement Masons and Concrete Finishers; Commercial Divers; Construction Carpenters; Drywall and Ceiling Tile Installers; Drywall Installers; Electricians; Explosives Workers, Ordnance Handling Experts, and Blasters; Fence Erectors; Floor Layers, Except Carpet, Wood, and Hard Tiles; Floor Sanders and Finishers; Glaziers; Grader, Bulldozer, and Scraper Operators; Hazardous Materials Removal Workers; Insulation Workers, Floor, Ceiling, and Wall; Manufactured Building and Mobile Home Installers; Operating Engineers; Operating Engineers and Other Construction Equipment Operators; Painters, Construction and Maintenance; Paperhangers; Paving, Surfacing, and Tamping Equipment Operators; Pile-Driver Operators; Pipe Fitters; Pipelayers; Pipelaying Fitters; Plasterers and Stucco Masons; Plumbers; Plumbers, Pipefitters, and Steamfitters; Rail-Track Laying and Maintenance Equipment Operators; Refractory Materials Repairers, Except Brickmasons; Reinforcing Iron and Rebar Workers; Riggers; Roofers; Rough Carpenters; Security and Fire Alarm Systems Installers; Segmental Pavers; Sheet Metal Workers; Ship Carpenters and Joiners; Stone Cutters and Carvers; Stonemasons; Structural Iron and Steel Workers; Tapers; Terrazzo Workers and Finishers; Tile and Marble Setters. **PERSONALITY TYPE**—Realistic. Realistic occupations frequently involve work activities that include practical, hands-on problems and solutions. They often deal with plants, animals, and real-world materials like wood, tools, and machinery. Many of the occupations require working outside and do not involve a lot of paperwork or working closely with others.

EDUCATION/TRAINING PROGRAM(S)—Construction Trades, Other. **RELATED KNOWLEDGE/ COURSES—Building and Construction:** Knowledge of materials, methods, and tools involved in the construction or repair of houses, buildings, or other structures, such as highways and roads. **Principles of Mechanical Devices:** Knowledge of machines and tools, including their designs, uses, repair, and maintenance. **Design:** Knowledge of design techniques, tools, and principles involved in production of precision technical plans, blueprints, drawings, and models.

Insurance Adjusters, Examiners, and Investigators

- ▲ Education/Training Required: Long-term on-the-job training
- ▲ Annual Earnings: $42,440
- ▲ Growth: 15.1%
- ▲ Annual Job Openings: 25,000
- ▲ Self-Employed: 3.7%
- ▲ Part-Time: 7.3%

Investigate, analyze, and determine the extent of insurance company's liability concerning personal, casualty, or property loss or damages; attempt to effect settlement with claimants. Correspond with or interview medical specialists, agents, witnesses, or claimants to compile information. Calculate benefit payments and approve payment of claims within a certain monetary limit. Investigates and assesses damage to property. Interviews or corresponds with claimant and witnesses, consults police and hospital records, and inspects property damage to determine extent of liability. Interviews or corresponds with agents and claimants to correct errors or omissions and to investigate questionable entries. Analyzes information gathered by investigation and reports findings and recommendations. Collects evidence to support contested claims in court. Communicates with former associates to verify employment record and to obtain background information regarding persons or businesses applying for credit. Obtains credit information from banks and other credit services. Refers questionable claims to investigator or claims adjuster for investigation or settlement. Prepares report of findings of investigation. Examines claims form and other records to determine insurance coverage. Examines titles to property to determine validity and acts as company agent in transactions with property owners. Negotiates claim settlements and recommends litigation when settlement cannot be negotiated. **SKILLS—Active Listening:** Giving full attention to what other people are saying, taking time to understand the points being made, asking questions as appropriate, and not interrupting at inappropriate times. **Writing:** Communicating effectively in writing as appropriate for the needs of the audience. **Reading Comprehension:** Understanding written sentences and paragraphs in work-related documents. **Critical Thinking:** Using logic and reasoning to identify the strengths and weaknesses of alternative solutions, conclusions, or approaches to problems. **Speaking:** Talking to others to convey information effectively.

GOE INFORMATION—Interest Area: 13. General Management and Support. **Work Group:** 13.02. Management Support. **Other Job Titles in This Work Group:** Accountants; Accountants and Auditors; Appraisers and Assessors of Real Estate; Appraisers, Real Estate; Assessors; Auditors; Budget Analysts; Claims Adjusters, Examiners, and Investigators; Claims Examiners, Property and Casualty Insurance; Compensation, Benefits, and Job Analysis Specialists; Cost Estimators; Credit Analysts; Employment Interviewers, Private or Public Employment Service; Employment, Recruitment, and Placement Specialists; Financial Analysts; Human Resources, Training, and Labor Relations Specialists, All Other; Insurance

Appraisers, Auto Damage; Insurance Underwriters; Loan Counselors; Loan Officers; Logisticians; Management Analysts; Market Research Analysts; Personnel Recruiters; Purchasing Agents and Buyers, Farm Products; Purchasing Agents, Except Wholesale, Retail, and Farm Products; Tax Examiners, Collectors, and Revenue Agents; Training and Development Specialists; Wholesale and Retail Buyers, Except Farm Products. **PERSONALITY TYPE—** Enterprising. Enterprising occupations frequently involve starting up and carrying out projects. These occupations can involve leading people and making many decisions. They sometimes require risk taking and often deal with business.

EDUCATION/TRAINING PROGRAM(S)—Health/ Medical Claims Examiner; Insurance. **RELATED**

KNOWLEDGE/COURSES—Mathematics: Knowledge of arithmetic, algebra, geometry, calculus, and statistics and their applications. **Law and Government:** Knowledge of laws, legal codes, court procedures, precedents, government regulations, executive orders, agency rules, and the democratic political process. **Economics and Accounting:** Knowledge of economic and accounting principles and practices, the financial markets, banking, and the analysis and reporting of financial data. **Public Safety and Security:** Knowledge of relevant equipment, policies, procedures, and strategies to promote effective local, state, or national security operations for the protection of people, data, property, and institutions. **English Language:** Knowledge of the structure and content of the English language, including the meaning and spelling of words, rules of composition, and grammar.

Insurance Sales Agents

▲ Education/Training Required: Bachelor's degree
▲ Annual Earnings: $38,890
▲ Growth: 3.3%
▲ Annual Job Openings: 43,000
▲ Self-Employed: 30.1%
▲ Part-Time: 9.3%

Sell life, property, casualty, health, automotive, or other types of insurance. May refer clients to independent brokers, work as independent broker, or be employed by an insurance company. Advises clients of broker (independent agent) in selecting casualty, life, or property insurance. Explains group insurance programs to promote sale of insurance plan. Selects company that offers type of coverage requested by client to underwrite policy. Discusses advantages and disadvantages of various policies. Calls on policyholders to deliver and explain policy, to suggest additions or changes in insurance program, or to change beneficiaries. Explains necessary bookkeeping requirements for customer to implement and provide group insurance program. Establishes client's method of payment. Installs bookkeeping systems and resolves system problems. Plans and oversees incorporation of insurance program into bookkeeping system of company. Contacts underwriter and submits forms to obtain binder coverage. **SKILLS— Speaking:** Talking to others to convey information effectively. **Reading Comprehension:** Understanding written sentences and paragraphs in work-related documents. **Persuasion:** Persuading others to change their minds or behavior. **Critical Thinking:** Using logic and reasoning to identify the strengths and weaknesses of alternative solutions, conclusions, or approaches to problems. **Active Listening:** Giving full attention to what other people are saying, taking time to understand the points being made, asking questions as appropriate, and not interrupting at inappropriate times.

GOE INFORMATION—Interest Area: 10. Sales and Marketing. **Work Group:** 10.02. Sales Technology. **Other Job Titles in This Work Group:** Advertising Sales Agents; Sales Agents, Financial Services; Sales Agents, Securities and Commodities; Sales Representatives, Agricultural; Sales Representatives, Chemical and Pharmaceutical; Sales Representatives, Electrical/Electronic; Sales Representatives, Instruments; Sales Representatives, Mechanical Equipment and Supplies; Sales Representatives, Medical; Sales Representatives, Services, All Other; Sales Representatives, Wholesale and Manufacturing, Technical and Scientific Products; Securities, Commodities, and Financial Services Sales Agents. **PERSONALITY TYPE—**Enterprising. Enterprising occupations frequently involve starting up and carrying out projects. These occupations can involve leading people and making many decisions. They sometimes require risk taking and often deal with business.

EDUCATION/TRAINING PROGRAM(S)—Insurance. **RELATED KNOWLEDGE/COURSES—Sales and Marketing:** Knowledge of principles and methods for showing, promoting, and selling products or services. This includes marketing strategy and tactics, product demonstration, sales techniques, and sales control systems. **Clerical Studies:** Knowledge of administrative and clerical procedures and systems, such as word processing, managing files and records, stenography and transcription, designing forms, and other office procedures and terminology. **English Language:** Knowledge of the structure and content of the English language, including the meaning and spelling of words, rules of composition, and grammar. **Mathematics:** Knowledge of arithmetic, algebra, geometry, calculus, and statistics and their applications. **Administration and Management:** Knowledge of business and management principles involved in strategic planning, resource allocation, human resources modeling, leadership technique, production methods, and coordination of people and resources.

Interior Designers

- ▲ Education/Training Required: Bachelor's degree
- ▲ Annual Earnings: $39,580
- ▲ Growth: 17.4%
- ▲ Annual Job Openings: 7,000
- ▲ Self-Employed: 46.3%
- ▲ Part-Time: 20.0%

Plan, design, and furnish interiors of residential, commercial, or industrial buildings. Formulate design that is practical, aesthetic, and conducive to intended purposes, such as raising productivity, selling merchandise, or improving lifestyle. May specialize in a particular field, style, or phase of interior design. Formulates environmental plan to be practical, aesthetic, and conducive to intended purposes, such as raising productivity or selling merchandise. Estimates material requirements and costs; presents design to client for approval. Subcontracts fabrication, installation, and arrangement of carpeting, fixtures, accessories, draperies, paint and wall coverings, artwork, furniture, and related items. Renders design ideas in form of pasteups or drawings. Confers with client to determine factors affecting planning interior environments, such as budget, architectural preferences, and purpose and function. Plans and designs interior environments for boats, planes, buses, trains, and other enclosed spaces. Advises client on interior design factors, such as space planning, layout and utilization of furnishings and equipment, and color coordination. Selects or designs and purchases furnishings, artwork, and accessories. **SKILLS—Coordination:** Adjusting actions in relation to others' actions. **Active Listening:** Giving full attention to what other people are saying, taking time to understand the points being made, asking questions as appropriate, and not interrupting at inappropriate times. **Operations Analysis:** Analyzing needs and product requirements to create a design. **Management of Financial Resources:** Determining how money will be spent to get the work done and accounting for these expenditures. **Speaking:** Talking to others to convey information effectively. **Mathematics:** Using mathematics to solve problems.

GOE INFORMATION—Interest Area: 01. Arts, Entertainment, and Media. **Work Group:** 01.04. Visual Arts. **Other Job Titles in This Work Group:** Cartoonists; Commercial and Industrial Designers; Designers, All Other; Exhibit Designers; Fashion Designers; Fine Artists, Including Painters, Sculptors, and Illustrators; Floral Designers; Graphic Designers; Merchandise Displayers and Window Trimmers; Multi-Media Artists and Animators; Painters and Illustrators; Sculptors; Set and Exhibit Designers; Set Designers; Sketch Artists. **PERSONALITY TYPE—Artistic.** Artistic occupations frequently involve working with forms, designs, and patterns. They often require self-expression, and the work can be done without following a clear set of rules.

EDUCATION/TRAINING PROGRAM(S)—Facilities Planning and Management; Interior Architecture; Interior Design; Textile Science. RELATED KNOWLEDGE/COURSES—Design: Knowledge of design techniques, tools, and principles involved in production of precision technical plans, blueprints, drawings, and models. **Administration and Management:** Knowledge of business and management principles involved in strategic planning, resource allocation, human resources modeling, leadership technique, production methods, and coordination of people and resources. **Sales and Marketing:** Knowledge of principles and methods for showing, promoting, and selling products or services. This includes marketing strategy and tactics, product demonstration, sales techniques, and sales control systems. **Mathematics:** Knowledge of arithmetic, algebra, geometry, calculus, and statistics and their applications. **Fine Arts:** Knowledge of the theory and techniques required to compose, produce, and perform works of music, dance, visual arts, drama, and sculpture.

Internists, General

- ▲ Education/Training Required: First professional degree
- ▲ Annual Earnings: More than $145,600
- ▲ Growth: 17.9%
- ▲ Annual Job Openings: 27,000
- ▲ Self-Employed: 20.4%
- ▲ Part-Time: 7.2%

Diagnose and provide non-surgical treatment of diseases and injuries of internal organ systems. Provide care mainly for adults who have a wide range of problems associated with the internal organs. Examines or conducts tests on patient to provide information on medical condition. Analyzes records, reports, test results, or examination information to diagnose medical condition of patient. Explains procedures and discusses test results on prescribed treatments with patents. Prescribes or administers treatment, therapy, medication, vaccination, and other specialized medical care to treat or prevent illness, disease, or injury. Refers patient to medical specialist or other practitioner when necessary. Plans, implements, or administers health programs or standards in hospital, business, or community for information, prevention, or treatment of injury or illness. Prepares reports for government or management of birth, death, and disease statistics, workforce evaluations, or medical status of individuals. Conducts research to study anatomy and develop or test medications, treatments, or procedures to prevent or control disease or injury. Directs and coordinates activities of nurses, students, assistants, specialists, therapists, and other medical staff. Advises patients and community concerning diet, activity, hygiene, and disease prevention. Collects, records, and maintains patient information, such as medical history, reports, and examination results. Operates on patients to remove, repair, or improve functioning of diseased or injured body parts and systems and delivers babies. Monitors patients' condition and progress and re-evaluates treatments as necessary. **SKILLS—Reading Comprehension:** Understanding written sentences and paragraphs in work-related documents. **Science:** Using scientific rules and methods to solve problems. **Active Learning:** Understanding the implications of new information for both current and future problem-solving and decision-making. **Judgment and Decision Making:** Considering the relative costs and benefits of potential actions to choose the most appropriate one. **Mathematics:** Using mathematics to solve problems. **Writing:** Communicating effectively in writing as appropriate for the needs of the audience. **Active Listening:** Giving full attention to what other people are saying, taking time to understand the points being made, asking questions as appropriate, and not interrupting at inappropriate times.

GOE INFORMATION—Interest Area: 14. Medical and Health Services. **Work Group:** 14.02. Medicine and Surgery. **Other Job Titles in This Work Group:** Anesthesiologists; Family and General Practitioners; Medical Assistants; Obstetricians and Gynecologists; Pediatricians, General; Pharmacists; Pharmacy Aides; Pharmacy Technicians; Physician Assistants; Physicians and Surgeons, All Other; Psychiatrists; Registered Nurses; Surgeons; Surgical Technologists. **PERSONALITY TYPE—Investigative.** Investigative occupations frequently involve working with ideas and require an extensive amount of thinking. These occupations can involve searching for facts and figuring out problems mentally.

EDUCATION/TRAINING PROGRAM(S)—Cardiology; Critical Care Medicine; Endocrinology and Metabolism; Gastroenterology; Geriatric Medicine; Hematology; Infectious Disease; Internal Medicine; Nephrology; Neurology; Nuclear Medicine; Oncology; Pulmonary Disease; Rheumatology. **RELATED KNOWLEDGE/ COURSES—Medicine and Dentistry:** Knowledge of the information and techniques needed to diagnose and treat human injuries, diseases, and deformities. This includes symptoms, treatment alternatives, drug properties and interactions, and preventive health-care measures. **Biology:** Knowledge of plant and animal organisms and their tissues, cells, functions, interdependencies, and interactions with each other and the environment. **English Language:** Knowledge of the structure and content of the English language, including the meaning and spelling of words, rules of composition, and grammar. **Therapy and Counseling:** Knowledge of principles, methods, and procedures for diagnosis, treatment, and rehabilitation of physical and mental dysfunctions and for career counseling and guidance. **Administration and Management:** Knowledge of business and management principles involved in strategic planning, resource allocation, human resources modeling, leadership technique, production methods, and coordination of people and resources.

Interpreters and Translators

- ▲ Education/Training Required: Long-term on-the-job training
- ▲ Annual Earnings: $32,000
- ▲ Growth: 23.8%
- ▲ Annual Job Openings: 3,000
- ▲ Self-Employed: 2.4%
- ▲ Part-Time: 20.6%

Translate or interpret written, oral, or sign language text into another language for others. Translates approximate or exact message of speaker into specified language orally or by using hand signs for hearing impaired. Listens to statements of speaker to ascertain meaning and to remember what is said, using electronic audio system. Translates responses from second language to first. Reads written material, such as legal documents, scientific works, or news reports, and rewrites material into specified language according to established rules of grammar. Receives information on subject to be discussed prior to interpreting session. **SKILLS—Active Listening:** Giving full attention to what other people are saying, taking time to understand the points being made, asking questions as appropriate, and not interrupting at inappropriate times. **Writing:** Communicating effectively in writing as appropriate for the needs of the audience. **Reading Comprehension:** Understanding written sentences and paragraphs in work-related documents. **Speaking:** Talking to others to convey information effectively. **Service Orientation:** Actively looking for ways to help people.

GOE INFORMATION—Interest Area: 01. Arts, Entertainment, and Media. **Work Group:** 01.03. News, Broadcasting, and Public Relations. **Other Job Titles in This Work Group:** Broadcast News Analysts; Caption Writers; Public Relations Specialists; Reporters and Correspondents. **PERSONALITY TYPE—Artistic.** Artistic occupations frequently involve working with forms, designs, and patterns. They often require self-expression, and the work can be done without following a clear set of rules.

EDUCATION/TRAINING PROGRAM(S)—African Languages, Literatures, and Linguistics; Albanian Language and Literature; American Indian/Native American Languages, Literatures, and Linguistics; Ancient Near Eastern and Biblical Languages, Literatures, and Linguistics; Ancient/Classical Greek Language and Literature; Arabic Language and Literature; Australian/Oceanic/Pacific Languages, Literatures, and Linguistics; Bahasa Indonesian/Bahasa Malay Languages and Literatures; Baltic Languages, Literatures, and Linguistics; Bengali Language and Literature; Bulgarian Language and Literature; Burmese Language and Literature; Catalan Language and Literature; Celtic Languages, Literatures, and Linguistics; Chinese Language and Literature; Classics and Classical Languages, Literatures, and Linguistics, General; Classics and Classical Languages, Literatures, and Linguistics, Other; Czech Language and Literature; Danish Language and Literature; Dutch/Flemish Language and Literature; East Asian Languages, Literatures, and Linguistics, General; East Asian Languages, Literatures, and Linguistics, Other; Filipino/Tagalog Language and Literature; Finnish and Related Languages, Literatures, and Linguistics; Foreign Languages and Literatures, General; Foreign Languages, Literatures, and Linguistics, Other; French Language and Literature; German Language and Literature; Germanic Languages, Literatures, and Linguistics, General; Germanic Languages, Literatures, and Linguistics, Other; Hebrew Language and Literature; Hindi Language and Literature; Hungarian/Magyar Language and Literature; Iranian/Persian Languages, Literatures, and Linguistics; Italian Language and Literature; Japanese Language and Literature; Khmer/Cambodian Language and Literature; Korean Language and Literature; Language Interpretation and Translation; Lao/Laotian Language and Literature; Latin Language and Literature; Latin Teacher Education; Linguistics; Middle/

Near Eastern and Semitic Languages, Literatures, and Linguistics, Other; others. **RELATED KNOWLEDGE/ COURSES—Foreign Language:** Knowledge of the structure and content of a foreign (non-English) language, including the meaning and spelling of words, rules of composition and grammar, and pronunciation. **English Language:** Knowledge of the structure and content of the English language, including the meaning and spelling of words, rules of composition, and grammar. **Communications and Media:** Knowledge of media production, com-

munication, and dissemination techniques and methods. This includes alternative ways to inform and entertain via written, oral, and visual media. **Sociology and Anthropology:** Knowledge of group behavior and dynamics, societal trends and influences, human migrations, ethnicity, and cultures and their history and origins. **Customer and Personal Service:** Knowledge of principles and processes for providing customer and personal services. This includes customer needs assessment, meeting quality standards for services, and evaluation of customer satisfaction.

Interviewers, Except Eligibility and Loan

- ▲ Education/Training Required: Short-term on-the-job training
- ▲ Annual Earnings: $21,880
- ▲ Growth: 33.4%
- ▲ Annual Job Openings: 53,000
- ▲ Self-Employed: 0%
- ▲ Part-Time: 32.5%

Interview persons by telephone, by mail, in person, or by other means for the purpose of completing forms, applications, or questionnaires. Ask specific questions, record answers, and assist persons with completing form. May sort, classify, and file forms. Contacts persons at home, place of business, or field location by telephone, by mail, or in person. Explains reason for questioning and other specified information. Compiles and sorts data from interview and reviews to correct errors. Asks questions to obtain various specified information, such as person's name, address, age, religion, and state of residency. Assists person in filling out application or questionnaire. Records results and data from interview or survey, using computer or specified form. **SKILLS—Speaking:** Talking to others to convey information effectively. **Active Listening:** Giving full attention to what other people are saying, taking time to understand the points being made, asking questions as appropriate, and not interrupting at inappropriate times. **Reading Comprehension:** Understanding written sentences and paragraphs in work-related documents. **Social Perceptiveness:** Being aware of others' reactions and understanding why they react as they do.

GOE INFORMATION—Interest Area: 09. Business Detail. **Work Group:** 09.02. Administrative Detail. **Other Job Titles in This Work Group:** Claims Takers, Unemployment Benefits; Court Clerks; Court, Municipal, and License Clerks; Eligibility Interviewers, Government Programs; Executive Secretaries and Administrative Assistants; Legal Secretaries; License Clerks; Loan Interviewers and

Clerks; Medical Secretaries; Municipal Clerks; Secretaries, Except Legal, Medical, and Executive; Welfare Eligibility Workers and Interviewers. **PERSONALITY TYPE—Conventional.** Conventional occupations frequently involve following set procedures and routines. These occupations can include working with data and details more than with ideas. Usually there is a clear line of authority to follow.

EDUCATION/TRAINING PROGRAM(S)—Receptionist. RELATED KNOWLEDGE/COURSES—Clerical Studies: Knowledge of administrative and clerical procedures and systems, such as word processing, managing files and records, stenography and transcription, designing forms, and other office procedures and terminology. **Computers and Electronics:** Knowledge of circuit boards, processors, chips, electronic equipment, and computer hardware and software, including applications and programming. **English Language:** Knowledge of the structure and content of the English language, including the meaning and spelling of words, rules of composition, and grammar. **Telecommunications:** Knowledge of transmission, broadcasting, switching, control, and operation of telecommunications systems. **Mathematics:** Knowledge of arithmetic, algebra, geometry, calculus, and statistics and their applications. **Personnel and Human Resources:** Knowledge of principles and procedures for personnel recruitment, selection, training, compensation and benefits, labor relations and negotiation, and personnel information systems.

Irradiated-Fuel Handlers

▲ Education/Training Required: Moderate-term on-the-job training
▲ Annual Earnings: $31,800
▲ Growth: 32.8%
▲ Annual Job Openings: 9,000
▲ Self-Employed: 1.5%
▲ Part-Time: 5.2%

Package, store, and convey irradiated fuels and wastes, using hoists, mechanical arms, shovels, and industrial truck. Operates machines and equipment to package, store, or transport loads of waste materials. Follows prescribed safety procedures and complies with federal laws regulating waste disposal methods. Cleans contaminated equipment for reuse, using detergents and solvents, sandblasters, filter pumps, and steam cleaners. Records number of containers stored at disposal site and specifies amount and type of equipment and waste disposed. Mixes and pours concrete into forms to encase waste material for disposal. Drives truck to convey contaminated waste to designated sea or ground location. Loads and unloads materials into containers and onto trucks, using hoists or forklift. **SKILLS—Reading Comprehension:** Understanding written sentences and paragraphs in work-related documents. **Operation and Control:** Controlling operations of equipment or systems.

GOE INFORMATION—Interest Area: 08. Industrial Production. **Work Group:** 08.07. Hands-on Work: Loading, Moving, Hoisting, and Conveying. **Other Job Titles in This Work Group:** Conveyor Operators and Tenders; Crane and Tower Operators; Dragline Operators; Excavating and Loading Machine and Dragline Operators; Freight, Stock, and Material Movers, Hand; Hoist and Winch Operators; Industrial Truck and Tractor Operators; Laborers and Freight, Stock, and Material Movers, Hand; Machine Feeders and Offbearers; Material Moving Workers, All Other; Packers and Packagers, Hand; Pump Operators, Except Wellhead Pumpers; Refuse and Recyclable Material Collectors; Tank Car, Truck, and Ship Loaders. **PERSONALITY TYPE—Realistic.** Realistic occupations frequently involve work activities that include practical, hands-on problems and solutions. They often deal with plants, animals, and real-world materials like wood, tools, and machinery. Many of the occupations require working outside and do not involve a lot of paperwork or working closely with others.

EDUCATION/TRAINING PROGRAM(S)—Hazardous Materials Management and Waste Technology/Technician. **RELATED KNOWLEDGE/COURSES—Production and Processing:** Knowledge of raw materials, production processes, quality control, costs, and other techniques for maximizing the effective manufacture and distribution of goods. **Transportation:** Knowledge of principles and methods for moving people or goods by air, rail, sea, or road, including the relative costs and benefits. **Chemistry:** Knowledge of the chemical composition, structure, and properties of substances and of the chemical processes and transformations that they undergo. This includes uses of chemicals and their interactions, danger signs, production techniques, and disposal methods. **Public Safety and Security:** Knowledge of relevant equipment, policies, procedures, and strategies to promote effective local, state, or national security operations for the protection of people, data, property, and institutions. **Law and Government:** Knowledge of laws, legal codes, court procedures, precedents, government regulations, executive orders, agency rules, and the democratic political process.

Janitorial Supervisors

▲ Education/Training Required: Work experience in a related occupation
▲ Annual Earnings: $27,200
▲ Growth: 14.2%
▲ Annual Job Openings: 18,000
▲ Self-Employed: 1.6%
▲ Part-Time: 6.4%

Supervise work activities of janitorial personnel in commercial and industrial establishments. Assign duties, inspect work, and investigate complaints regarding janitorial services and take corrective action. May purchase janitorial supplies and equipment, take periodic inventories, screen applicants, train new employees, and recommend dismissals. Supervises and coordinates activities of workers engaged in janitorial services. Assigns janitorial work to employees, following material and work requirements. Inspects work performed to ensure conformance to specifications and established standards. Records personnel data on specified forms. Recommends personnel actions, such as hires and discharges, to ensure proper staffing. Confers with staff to resolve production and personnel problems. Trains workers in janitorial methods and procedures and proper operation of equipment. Issues janitorial supplies and equipment to workers to ensure quality and timely delivery of services. **SKILLS—Coordination:** Adjusting actions in relation to others' actions. **Time Management:** Managing one's own time and the time of others. **Management of Personnel Resources:** Motivating, developing, and directing people as they work, identifying the best people for the job. **Speaking:** Talking to others to convey information effectively. **Social Perceptiveness:** Being aware of others' reactions and understanding why they react as they do. **Writing:** Communicating effectively in writing as appropriate for the needs of the audience.

GOE INFORMATION—Interest Area: 11. Recreation, Travel, and Other Personal Services. **Work Group:** 11.01. Managerial Work in Recreation, Travel, and Other Personal Services. **Other Job Titles in This Work Group:** Aircraft Cargo Handling Supervisors; First-Line Supervisors/Managers of Food Preparation and Serving Workers; First-Line Supervisors/Managers of Housekeeping and Janitorial Workers; First-Line Supervisors/Managers of Personal Service Workers; Food Service Managers; Gaming Managers; Gaming Supervisors; Housekeeping Supervisors; Lodging Managers; Meeting and Convention Planners. **PERSONALITY TYPE**—Enterprising. Enterprising occupations frequently involve starting up and carrying out projects. These occupations can involve leading people and making many decisions. They sometimes require risk taking and often deal with business.

EDUCATION/TRAINING PROGRAM(S)—No data available. **RELATED KNOWLEDGE/COURSES—Administration and Management:** Knowledge of business and management principles involved in strategic planning, resource allocation, human resources modeling, leadership technique, production methods, and coordination of people and resources. **Personnel and Human Resources:** Knowledge of principles and procedures for personnel recruitment, selection, training, compensation and benefits, labor relations and negotiation, and personnel information systems. **Education and Training:** Knowledge of principles and methods for curriculum and training design, teaching and instruction for individuals and groups, and the measurement of training effects. **Customer and Personal Service:** Knowledge of principles and processes for providing customer and personal services. This includes customer needs assessment, meeting quality standards for services, and evaluation of customer satisfaction. **Chemistry:** Knowledge of the chemical composition, structure, and properties of substances and of the chemical processes and transformations that they undergo. This includes uses of chemicals and their interactions, danger signs, production techniques, and disposal methods. **English Language:** Knowledge of the structure and content of the English language, including the meaning and spelling of words, rules of composition, and grammar. **Principles of Mechanical Devices:** Knowledge of machines and tools, including their designs, uses, repair, and maintenance.

Janitors and Cleaners, Except Maids and Housekeeping Cleaners

- ▲ Education/Training Required: Short-term on-the-job training
- ▲ Annual Earnings: $17,900
- ▲ Growth: 13.5%
- ▲ Annual Job Openings: 507,000
- ▲ Self-Employed: 5.6%
- ▲ Part-Time: 32.3%

Keep buildings in clean and orderly condition. Perform heavy cleaning duties, such as cleaning floors, shampooing rugs, washing walls and glass, and removing rubbish. Duties may include tending furnace and boiler, performing routine maintenance activities, notifying management of need for repairs, and cleaning snow or debris from sidewalk. Sweeps, mops, scrubs, and vacuums floors of buildings, using cleaning solutions, tools, and equipment. Cleans or polishes walls, ceilings, windows, plant equipment, and building fixtures, using steam cleaning equipment, scrapers, brooms, and variety of hand and power tools. Gathers and empties trash. Notifies management personnel concerning need for major repairs or additions to building operating systems. Dusts furniture, walls, machines, and equipment. Moves items between departments manually or using hand truck. Sets up, arranges, and removes decorations, tables, chairs, ladders, and scaffolding for events such as banquets and social functions. Requisitions supplies and equipment used in cleaning and maintenance duties. Sprays insecticides and fumigants to prevent insect and rodent infestation. Cleans laboratory equipment, such as glassware and metal instruments, using solvents, brushes, rags, and power cleaning equipment. Mows and trims lawns and shrubbery, using mowers and hand and power trimmers, and clears debris from grounds. Mixes water and detergents or acids in container to prepare cleaning solutions according to specifications. Drives vehicles, such as van, industrial truck, or industrial vacuum cleaner. Cleans chimneys, flues, and connecting pipes, using power and hand tools. Cleans and restores building interiors damaged by fire, smoke, or water, using commercial cleaning equipment. Services and repairs cleaning and maintenance equipment and machinery and performs minor routine painting, plumbing, electrical, and related activities. Removes snow from sidewalks, driveways, and parking areas, using snowplow, snowblower, and snow shovel, and spreads snow-melting chemicals. Tends, cleans, adjusts, and services furnaces, air conditioners, boilers, and other building heating and cooling systems. Applies waxes or sealers to wood or concrete floors. **SKILLS—Equipment Maintenance:** Perform-

ing routine maintenance on equipment and determining when and what kind of maintenance is needed. **Repairing:** Repairing machines or systems, using the needed tools. **Equipment Selection:** Determining the kind of tools and equipment needed to do a job. **Troubleshooting:** Determining causes of operating errors and deciding what to do about them. **Operation and Control:** Controlling operations of equipment or systems.

GOE INFORMATION—Interest Area: 11. Recreation, Travel, and Other Personal Services. **Work Group:** 11.07. Cleaning and Building Services. **Other Job Titles in This Work Group:** Building Cleaning Workers, All Other; Locker Room, Coatroom, and Dressing Room Attendants; Maids and Housekeeping Cleaners. **PERSONALITY TYPE—Realistic.** Realistic occupations frequently involve work activities that include practical, hands-on problems and solutions. They often deal with plants, animals, and real-world materials like wood, tools, and machinery. Many of the occupations require working outside and do not involve a lot of paperwork or working closely with others.

EDUCATION/TRAINING PROGRAM(S)—No data available. **RELATED KNOWLEDGE/COURSES— Principles of Mechanical Devices:** Knowledge of machines and tools, including their designs, uses, repair, and maintenance. **Chemistry:** Knowledge of the chemical composition, structure, and properties of substances and of the chemical processes and transformations that they undergo. This includes uses of chemicals and their interactions, danger signs, production techniques, and disposal methods. **Customer and Personal Service:** Knowledge of principles and processes for providing customer and personal services. This includes customer needs assessment, meeting quality standards for services, and evaluation of customer satisfaction. **Building and Construction:** Knowledge of materials, methods, and tools involved in the construction or repair of houses, buildings, or other structures, such as highways and roads. **Mathematics:** Knowledge of arithmetic, algebra, geometry, calculus, and statistics and their applications.

Kindergarten Teachers, Except Special Education

▲ Education/Training Required: Bachelor's degree
▲ Annual Earnings: $38,740
▲ Growth: 14.5%
▲ Annual Job Openings: 23,000
▲ Self-Employed: 1.5%
▲ Part-Time: 32.4%

Teach elemental natural and social science, personal hygiene, music, art, and literature to children from 4 to 6 years old. Promote physical, mental, and social development. May be required to hold state certification. Teaches elemental science, personal hygiene, and humanities to children to promote physical, mental, and social development. Supervises student activities, such as field visits, to stimulate student interest and broaden understanding of physical and social environment. Organizes and conducts games and group projects to develop cooperative behavior and assist children in forming satisfying relationships. Encourages students in activities, such as singing, dancing, and rhythmic activities, to promote self-expression and appreciation of aesthetic experience. Instructs children in practices of personal cleanliness and self-care. Observes children to detect signs of ill health or emotional disturbance and to evaluate progress. Discusses student problems and progress with parents. Alternates periods of strenuous activity with periods of rest or light activity to avoid overstimulation and fatigue. **SKILLS—Learning Strategies:** Selecting and using training/instructional methods and procedures appropriate for the situation when learning or teaching new things. **Monitoring:** Monitoring/Assessing your performance or that of other individuals or organizations to make improvements or take corrective action. **Speaking:** Talking to others to convey information effectively. **Reading Comprehension:** Understanding written sentences and paragraphs in work-related documents. **Active Listening:** Giving full attention to what other people are saying, taking time to understand the points being made, asking questions as appropriate, and not interrupting at inappropriate times.

GOE INFORMATION—Interest Area: 12. Education and Social Service. **Work Group:** 12.03. Educational Services. **Other Job Titles in This Work Group:** Adult Literacy, Remedial Education, and GED Teachers and Instructors; Agricultural Sciences Teachers, Postsecondary; Anthropology and Archeology Teachers, Postsecondary; Architecture Teachers, Postsecondary; Archivists; Area, Ethnic, and Cultural Studies Teachers, Postsecondary; Art, Drama, and Music Teachers, Postsecondary; Atmospheric, Earth, Marine, and Space Sciences Teachers, Postsecondary; Audio-Visual Collections Specialists; Biological Science Teachers, Postsecondary; Business Teachers, Postsecondary; Chemistry Teachers, Postsecondary; Child Care Workers; Communications Teachers, Postsecondary; Computer Science Teachers, Postsecondary; Criminal Justice and Law Enforcement Teachers, Postsecondary; Curators; Economics Teachers, Postsecondary; Education Teachers, Postsecondary; Educational Psychologists; Educational, Vocational, and School Counselors; Elementary School Teachers, Except Special Education; Engineering Teachers, Postsecondary; English Language and Literature Teachers, Postsecondary; Environmental Science Teachers, Postsecondary; Farm and Home Management Advisors; Foreign Language and Literature Teachers, Postsecondary; Forestry and Conservation Science Teachers, Postsecondary; Geography Teachers, Postsecondary; Graduate Teaching Assistants; Health Specialties Teachers, Postsecondary; History Teachers, Postsecondary; Home Economics Teachers, Postsecondary; Law Teachers, Postsecondary; Librarians; Library Assistants, Clerical; Library Science Teachers, Postsecondary; Library Technicians; Mathematical Science Teachers, Postsecondary; Middle School Teachers, Except Special and Vocational Education; Museum Technicians and Conservators; Nursing Instructors and Teachers, Postsecondary; Personal Financial Advisors; Philosophy and Religion Teachers, Postsecondary; Physics Teachers, Postsecondary; Political Science Teachers, Postsecondary; Postsecondary Teachers, All Other; Preschool Teachers, Except Special Education; Psychology Teachers, Postsecondary; others. **PERSONALITY TYPE—Social.** Social occupations frequently involve working with, communicating with, and teaching people. These occupations often involve helping or providing service to others.

EDUCATION/TRAINING PROGRAM(S)—Early Childhood Education and Teaching; Kindergarten/Preschool Education and Teaching. RELATED KNOWLEDGE/COURSES—Education and Training: Knowledge of principles and methods for curriculum and training design, teaching and instruction for individuals and groups, and the measurement of training effects. **Customer and Personal Service:** Knowledge of principles and processes for providing customer and personal services. This includes customer needs assessment, meeting quality standards for services, and evaluation of customer satisfaction. **English Language:** Knowledge of the structure and content of the English language, including the meaning and spelling of words, rules of composition, and grammar. **Psychology:** Knowledge of human behavior and performance; individual differences in ability, personality, and interests; learning and motivation; psychological research methods; and the assessment and treatment of behavioral and affective disorders. **Fine Arts:** Knowledge of the theory and techniques required to compose, produce, and perform works of music, dance, visual arts, drama, and sculpture.

Laborers and Freight, Stock, and Material Movers, Hand

- ▲ Education/Training Required: Short-term on-the-job training
- ▲ Annual Earnings: $19,440
- ▲ Growth: 13.9%
- ▲ Annual Job Openings: 519,000
- ▲ Self-Employed: 2.1%
- ▲ Part-Time: 38.4%

Manually move freight, stock, or other materials or perform other unskilled general labor. Includes all unskilled manual laborers not elsewhere classified. SKILLS—No data available.

GOE INFORMATION—Interest Area: 08. Industrial Production. **Work Group:** 08.07. Hands-on Work: Loading, Moving, Hoisting, and Conveying. **Other Job Titles in This Work Group:** Conveyor Operators and Tenders; Crane and Tower Operators; Dragline Operators; Excavating and Loading Machine and Dragline Operators; Freight, Stock, and Material Movers, Hand; Hoist and Winch Operators; Industrial Truck and Tractor Operators; Irradiated-Fuel Handlers; Machine Feeders and Offbearers; Material Moving Workers, All Other; Packers and Packagers, Hand; Pump Operators, Except Wellhead Pumpers; Refuse and Recyclable Material Collectors; Tank Car, Truck, and Ship Loaders. **PERSONALITY TYPE**—No data available.

EDUCATION/TRAINING PROGRAM(S)—No data available. **RELATED KNOWLEDGE/COURSES**—No data available.

Landscape Architects

- ▲ Education/Training Required: Bachelor's degree
- ▲ Annual Earnings: $46,710
- ▲ Growth: 31.1%
- ▲ Annual Job Openings: 1,000
- ▲ Self-Employed: 21.6%
- ▲ Part-Time: 8.0%

Plan and design land areas for such projects as parks and other recreational facilities; airports; highways; hospitals; schools; land subdivisions; and commercial, industrial, and residential sites. Prepares site plans, specifications, and cost estimates for land development, coordinating arrangement of existing and proposed land features and structures. Compiles and analyzes data on conditions such as location, drainage, and location of structures for environmental reports and landscaping plans. Confers with clients, engineering personnel, and architects on overall program. Inspects landscape work to ensure compliance with specifications, approve quality of materials and work, and advise client and construction personnel. **SKILLS— Judgment and Decision Making:** Considering the relative costs and benefits of potential actions to choose the most appropriate one. **Critical Thinking:** Using logic and reasoning to identify the strengths and weaknesses of alternative solutions, conclusions, or approaches to problems. **Active Listening:** Giving full attention to what other people are saying, taking time to understand the points being made, asking questions as appropriate, and not interrupting at inappropriate times. **Active Learning:** Understanding the implications of new information for both current and future problem-solving and decision-making. **Complex Problem Solving:** Identifying complex problems and reviewing related information to develop and evaluate options and implement solutions.

GOE INFORMATION—Interest Area: 02. Science, Math, and Engineering. **Work Group:** 02.07. Engineering. **Other Job Titles in This Work Group:** Aerospace Engineers; Agricultural Engineers; Architects, Except Landscape and Naval; Biomedical Engineers; Chemical Engineers; Civil Engineers; Computer Hardware Engineers; Computer Software Engineers, Applications; Computer Software Engineers, Systems Software; Electrical Engineers; Electronics Engineers, Except Computer; Engineers, All Other; Environmental Engineers; Fire-Prevention and Protection Engineers; Health and Safety Engineers, Except Mining Safety Engineers and Inspectors; Industrial Engineers; Industrial Safety and Health Engineers; Marine Architects; Marine Engineers; Marine Engineers and Naval Architects; Materials Engineers; Mechanical Engineers; Mining and Geological Engineers, Including Mining Safety Engineers; Nuclear Engineers; Petroleum Engineers; Product Safety Engineers; Sales En-

gineers. **PERSONALITY TYPE—Artistic.** Artistic occupations frequently involve working with forms, designs, and patterns. They often require self-expression, and the work can be done without following a clear set of rules.

EDUCATION/TRAINING PROGRAM(S)—Environmental Design/Architecture; Landscape Architecture (BS, BSLA, BLA, MSLA, MLA, PhD). **RELATED KNOWLEDGE/COURSES—Design:** Knowledge of design techniques, tools, and principles involved in production of precision technical plans, blueprints, drawings, and models. **Mathematics:** Knowledge of arithmetic, algebra, geometry, calculus, and statistics and their applications. **Engineering and Technology:** Knowledge of the practical application of engineering science and technology. This includes applying principles, techniques, procedures, and equipment to the design and production of various goods and services. **Administration and Management:** Knowledge of business and management principles involved in strategic planning, resource allocation, human resources modeling, leadership technique, production methods, and coordination of people and resources. **Biology:** Knowledge of plant and animal organisms and their tissues, cells, functions, interdependencies, and interactions with each other and the environment.

Landscaping and Groundskeeping Workers

▲ Education/Training Required: Short-term on-the-job training
▲ Annual Earnings: $19,120
▲ Growth: 29.0%
▲ Annual Job Openings: 193,000
▲ Self-Employed: 27.9%
▲ Part-Time: 28.5%

Landscape or maintain grounds of property using hand or power tools or equipment. Workers typically perform a variety of tasks, which may include any combination of the following: sod laying, mowing, trimming, planting, watering, fertilizing, digging, raking, sprinkler installation, and installation of mortarless segmental concrete masonry wall units. Mows lawns, using power mower. Trims and picks flowers and cleans flower beds. Hauls or spreads topsoil; spreads straw over seeded soil to hold soil in place. Applies herbicides, fungicides, fertilizers, and pesticides, using spreaders or spray equipment. Decorates garden with stones and plants. Waters lawns, trees, and plants, using portable sprinkler system, hose, or watering can. Digs holes for plants, mixes fertilizer or lime

with dirt in holes, inserts plants, and fills holes with dirt. Attaches wires from planted trees to support stakes. Shovels snow from walks and driveways. Builds forms and mixes and pours cement to form garden borders. Maintains tools and equipment. Seeds and fertilizes lawns. **SKILLS—Operation and Control:** Controlling operations of equipment or systems. **Installation:** Installing equipment, machines, wiring, or programs to meet specifications. **Mathematics:** Using mathematics to solve problems.

GOE INFORMATION—Interest Area: 03. Plants and Animals. **Work Group:** 03.03. Hands-on Work in Plants and Animals. **Other Job Titles in This Work Group:** Agricultural Equipment Operators; Fallers; Farmworkers and Laborers, Crop, Nursery, and Greenhouse; Farmworkers, Farm and Ranch Animals; Fishers and Related Fishing Workers; Forest and Conservation Technicians; Forest and Conservation Workers; General Farmworkers; Grounds Maintenance Workers, All Other; Hunters and Trappers; Logging Equipment Operators; Logging Tractor Operators; Logging Workers, All Other; Nursery Workers; Pest Control Workers; Pesticide Handlers, Sprayers, and Applicators, Vegetation; Tree Trimmers and Pruners. **PERSONALITY TYPE**—Realistic. Realistic occupations frequently involve work activities that include practical, hands-on problems and solutions. They often deal with plants, animals, and real-world materials like wood, tools, and machinery. Many of the occupations require working outside and do not involve a lot of paperwork or working closely with others.

EDUCATION/TRAINING PROGRAM(S)—Landscaping and Groundskeeping; Turf and Turfgrass Management. **RELATED KNOWLEDGE/COURSES**—**Chemistry:** Knowledge of the chemical composition, structure, and properties of substances and of the chemical processes and transformations that they undergo. This includes uses of chemicals and their interactions, danger signs, production techniques, and disposal methods. **Principles of Mechanical Devices:** Knowledge of machines and tools, including their designs, uses, repair, and maintenance. **Building and Construction:** Knowledge of materials, methods, and tools involved in the construction or repair of houses, buildings, or other structures, such as highways and roads. **Biology:** Knowledge of plant and animal organisms and their tissues, cells, functions, interdependencies, and interactions with each other and the environment.

Laundry and Dry-Cleaning Workers

- ▲ Education/Training Required: Short-term on-the-job training
- ▲ Annual Earnings: $16,360
- ▲ Growth: 11.4%
- ▲ Annual Job Openings: 62,000
- ▲ Self-Employed: 11.4%
- ▲ Part-Time: 26.3%

Operate or tend washing or dry-cleaning machines to wash or dry-clean industrial or household articles, such as cloth garments, suede, leather, furs, blankets, draperies, fine linens, rugs, and carpets. SKILLS—No data available.

GOE INFORMATION—**Interest Area:** 11. Recreation, Travel, and Other Personal Services. **Work Group:** 11.06. Apparel, Shoes, Leather, and Fabric Care. **Other Job Titles in This Work Group:** Custom Tailors; Fabric Menders, Except Garment; Laundry and Drycleaning Machine Op-

erators and Tenders, Except Pressing; Precision Dyers; Pressers, Delicate Fabrics; Pressers, Hand; Pressers, Textile, Garment, and Related Materials; Shoe and Leather Workers and Repairers; Shop and Alteration Tailors; Spotters, Dry Cleaning; Tailors, Dressmakers, and Custom Sewers; Textile, Apparel, and Furnishings Workers, All Other; Upholsterers. **PERSONALITY TYPE**—No data available.

EDUCATION/TRAINING PROGRAM(S)—No data available. **RELATED KNOWLEDGE/COURSES**—No data available.

Laundry and Drycleaning Machine Operators and Tenders, Except Pressing

- ▲ Education/Training Required: Moderate-term on-the-job training
- ▲ Annual Earnings: $16,360
- ▲ Growth: 11.4%
- ▲ Annual Job Openings: 62,000
- ▲ Self-Employed: 11.4%
- ▲ Part-Time: 26.3%

Operate or tend washing or dry-cleaning machines to wash or dry-clean commercial, industrial, or household articles, such as cloth garments, suede, leather, furs, blan-

kets, draperies, fine linens, rugs, and carpets. Starts washer, dry-cleaner, drier, or extractor and turns valves or levers to regulate and monitor cleaning or drying operations. Loads or directs other workers to load articles into washer or dry-cleaning machine. Starts pumps to operate distilling system that drains and reclaims dry-cleaning solvents. Adjusts switches to tend and regulate equipment that fumigates and removes foreign matter from furs. Cleans machine filters and lubricates equipment. Mends and sews articles, using hand stitching, adhesive patch, or power sewing machine. Hangs curtains, drapes, blankets, pants, and other garments on stretch frames to dry and transports items between specified locations. Irons or presses articles, fabrics, and furs, using hand iron or pressing machine. Receives and marks articles for laundry or dry cleaning with identifying code number or name, using hand or machine marker. Sorts and counts articles removed from dryer and folds, wraps, or hangs items for airing out, pickup, or delivery. Examines and sorts articles to be cleaned into lots, according to color, fabric, dirt content, and cleaning technique required. Pre-soaks, sterilizes, scrubs, spot-cleans, and dries contaminated or stained articles, using neutralizer solutions and portable machines. Washes, dry-cleans, or glazes delicate articles or fur garment linings by hand, using mild detergent or dry-cleaning solutions. Removes or directs other workers to remove items from washer or dry-cleaning machine and move them into extractor or tumbler. Tends variety of automatic machines that comb and polish furs; clean, sterilize, and fluff feathers and blankets; and roll and package towels. Mixes and adds detergents, dyes, bleach, starch, and other solutions and chemicals to clean, color, dry, or stiffen articles. **SKILLS—Operation and Control:** Controlling operations of equipment or systems. **Operation Monitoring:** Watching gauges, dials, or other indicators to make sure a machine is working properly.

GOE INFORMATION—Interest Area: 11. Recreation, Travel, and Other Personal Services. **Work Group:** 11.06. Apparel, Shoes, Leather, and Fabric Care. **Other Job Titles in This Work Group:** Custom Tailors; Fabric Menders,

Except Garment; Laundry and Dry-Cleaning Workers; Precision Dyers; Pressers, Delicate Fabrics; Pressers, Hand; Pressers, Textile, Garment, and Related Materials; Shoe and Leather Workers and Repairers; Shop and Alteration Tailors; Spotters, Dry Cleaning; Tailors, Dressmakers, and Custom Sewers; Textile, Apparel, and Furnishings Workers, All Other; Upholsterers. **PERSONALITY TYPE—** Realistic. Realistic occupations frequently involve work activities that include practical, hands-on problems and solutions. They often deal with plants, animals, and real-world materials like wood, tools, and machinery. Many of the occupations require working outside and do not involve a lot of paperwork or working closely with others.

EDUCATION/TRAINING PROGRAM(S)—No data available. **RELATED KNOWLEDGE/COURSES— Customer and Personal Service:** Knowledge of principles and processes for providing customer and personal services. This includes customer needs assessment, meeting quality standards for services, and evaluation of customer satisfaction. **Principles of Mechanical Devices:** Knowledge of machines and tools, including their designs, uses, repair, and maintenance. **Chemistry:** Knowledge of the chemical composition, structure, and properties of substances and of the chemical processes and transformations that they undergo. This includes uses of chemicals and their interactions, danger signs, production techniques, and disposal methods. **Clerical Studies:** Knowledge of administrative and clerical procedures and systems, such as word processing, managing files and records, stenography and transcription, designing forms, and other office procedures and terminology. **Production and Processing:** Knowledge of raw materials, production processes, quality control, costs, and other techniques for maximizing the effective manufacture and distribution of goods. **Mathematics:** Knowledge of arithmetic, algebra, geometry, calculus, and statistics and their applications.

Law Teachers, Postsecondary

- ▲ Education/Training Required: First professional degree
- ▲ Annual Earnings: $77,920
- ▲ Growth: 23.5%
- ▲ Annual Job Openings: 184,000
- ▲ Self-Employed: 0%
- ▲ Part-Time: 32.3%

Teach courses in law. **SKILLS—**No data available.

GOE INFORMATION—Interest Area: 12. Education

and Social Service. **Work Group:** 12.03. Educational Services. **Other Job Titles in This Work Group:** Adult Literacy, Remedial Education, and GED Teachers and Instructors; Agricultural Sciences Teachers, Postsecondary; Anthropology and Archeology Teachers, Postsecondary; Architecture Teachers, Postsecondary; Archivists; Area, Ethnic, and Cultural Studies Teachers, Postsecondary; Art, Drama, and Music Teachers, Postsecondary; Atmospheric, Earth, Marine, and Space Sciences Teachers, Postsecondary; Audio-Visual Collections Specialists; Biological Science Teachers, Postsecondary; Business Teachers, Postsecondary; Chemistry Teachers, Postsecondary; Child Care Workers; Communications Teachers, Postsecondary; Computer Science Teachers, Postsecondary; Criminal Justice and Law Enforcement Teachers, Postsecondary; Curators; Economics Teachers, Postsecondary; Education Teachers, Postsecondary; Educational Psychologists; Educational, Vocational, and School Counselors; Elementary School Teachers, Except Special Education; Engineering Teachers, Postsecondary; English Language and Literature Teachers, Postsecondary; Environmental Science Teachers, Postsecondary; Farm and Home Management Advisors; Foreign Language and Literature Teachers, Postsecondary; Forestry and Conservation Science Teachers, Postsecondary; Geography Teachers, Postsecondary; Graduate Teaching Assistants; Health Specialties Teachers, Postsecondary; History Teachers, Postsecondary; Home Economics Teachers, Postsecondary; Kindergarten Teachers, Except Special Education; Librarians; Library Assistants, Clerical; Library Science Teachers, Postsecondary; Library Technicians; Mathematical Science Teachers, Postsecondary; Middle School Teachers, Except Special and Vocational Education; Museum Technicians and Conservators; Nursing Instructors and Teachers, Postsecondary; Personal Financial Advisors; Philosophy and Religion Teachers, Postsecondary; Physics Teachers, Postsecondary; Political Science Teachers, Postsecondary; Postsecondary Teachers, All Other; Preschool Teachers, Except Special Education; others. **PERSONALITY TYPE**—No data available.

EDUCATION/TRAINING PROGRAM(S)—Law (LL.B., J.D.); Legal Studies, General. **RELATED KNOWLEDGE/COURSES**—No data available.

Lawn Service Managers

- ▲ Education/Training Required: Work experience in a related occupation
- ▲ Annual Earnings: $32,100
- ▲ Growth: 20.1%
- ▲ Annual Job Openings: 10,000
- ▲ Self-Employed: 58.8%
- ▲ Part-Time: 24.5%

Plan, direct, and coordinate activities of workers engaged in pruning trees and shrubs, cultivating lawns, and applying pesticides and other chemicals according to service contract specifications. Supervises workers who provide groundskeeping services on a contract basis. Investigates customer complaints. Prepares work activity and personnel reports. Suggests changes in work procedures and orders corrective work done. Spot-checks completed work to improve quality of service and to ensure contract compliance. Schedules work for crew according to weather conditions, availability of equipment, and seasonal limitations. Reviews contracts to ascertain service, machine, and work force requirements for job. Prepares service cost estimates for customers. Answers customers' questions about groundskeeping care requirements. **SKILLS—Time Management:** Managing one's own time and the time of others. **Management of Personnel Resources:** Motivating, developing, and directing people as they work, identifying the best people for the job. **Coordination:** Adjusting actions in relation to others' actions. **Speaking:** Talking to others to convey information effectively. **Mathematics:** Using mathematics to solve problems.

GOE INFORMATION—Interest Area: 03. Plants and Animals. **Work Group:** 03.01. Managerial Work in Plants and Animals. **Other Job Titles in This Work Group:** Agricultural Crop Farm Managers; Farm Labor Contractors; Farmers and Ranchers; First-Line Supervisors and Manager/Supervisors—Agricultural Crop Workers; First-Line Supervisors and Manager/Supervisors—Animal Care Workers, Except Livestock; First-Line Supervisors and Manager/Supervisors—Animal Husbandry Workers; First-Line Supervisors and Manager/Supervisors—Fishery Workers; First-Line Supervisors and Manager/Supervisors—Horticultural Workers; First-Line Supervisors and Manager/Supervisors—Landscaping Workers; First-Line Supervisors and Manager/Supervisors—Logging Workers;

First-Line Supervisors/Managers of Farming, Fishing, and Forestry Workers; First-Line Supervisors/Managers of Landscaping, Lawn Service, and Groundskeeping Workers; Fish Hatchery Managers; Nursery and Greenhouse Managers. **PERSONALITY TYPE**—Enterprising. Enterprising occupations frequently involve starting up and carrying out projects. These occupations can involve leading people and making many decisions. They sometimes require risk taking and often deal with business.

EDUCATION/TRAINING PROGRAM(S)—Landscaping and Groundskeeping; Ornamental Horticulture; Turf and Turfgrass Management. **RELATED KNOWLEDGE/COURSES—Administration and Management:** Knowledge of business and management principles involved in strategic planning, resource allocation, human resources modeling, leadership technique, production methods, and coordination of people and resources. **Customer and Personal Service:** Knowledge of principles and processes for providing customer and personal services. This includes customer needs assessment, meeting quality standards for services, and evaluation of customer satisfaction. **Personnel and Human Resources:** Knowledge of principles and procedures for personnel recruitment, selection, training, compensation and benefits, labor relations and negotiation, and personnel information systems. **Economics and Accounting:** Knowledge of economic and accounting principles and practices, the financial markets, banking, and the analysis and reporting of financial data. **English Language:** Knowledge of the structure and content of the English language, including the meaning and spelling of words, rules of composition, and grammar.

Lawyers

- ▲ Education/Training Required: First professional degree
- ▲ Annual Earnings: $88,760
- ▲ Growth: 18.0%
- ▲ Annual Job Openings: 35,000
- ▲ Self-Employed: 36.0%
- ▲ Part-Time: 7.0%

Represent clients in criminal and civil litigation and other legal proceedings, draw up legal documents, and manage or advise clients on legal transactions. May specialize in a single area or may practice broadly in many areas of law. Conducts case, examining and cross-examining witnesses, and summarizes case to judge or jury. Examines legal data to determine advisability of defending or prosecuting lawsuit. Studies Constitution, statutes, decisions, regulations, and ordinances of quasi-judicial bodies. Interprets laws, rulings, and regulations for individuals and business. Presents evidence to defend client in civil or criminal litigation. Presents evidence to prosecute defendant in civil or criminal litigation. Represents client in court or before government agency. Searches for and examines public and other legal records to write opinions or establish ownership. Acts as agent, trustee, guardian, or executor for business or individuals. Probates wills and represents and advises executors and administrators of estates. Prepares opinions on legal issues. Prepares and drafts legal documents, such as wills, deeds, patent applications, mortgages, leases, and contracts. Prepares and files legal briefs. Confers with colleagues with specialty in area of legal issue to establish and verify basis for legal proceeding. Evaluates findings and develops strategy and arguments in preparation for presentation of case. Gathers evidence to formulate defense or to initiate legal actions. Advises clients concerning business transactions, claim liability, advisability of prosecuting or defending lawsuits, or legal rights and obligations. Interviews clients and witnesses to ascertain facts of case. **SKILLS—Reading Comprehension:** Understanding written sentences and paragraphs in work-related documents. **Persuasion:** Persuading others to change their minds or behavior. **Speaking:** Talking to others to convey information effectively. **Critical Thinking:** Using logic and reasoning to identify the strengths and weaknesses of alternative solutions, conclusions, or approaches to problems. **Writing:** Communicating effectively in writing as appropriate for the needs of the audience.

GOE INFORMATION—Interest Area: 04. Law, Law Enforcement, and Public Safety. **Work Group:** 04.02. Law. **Other Job Titles in This Work Group:** Administrative Law Judges, Adjudicators, and Hearing Officers; Arbitrators, Mediators, and Conciliators; Judges, Magistrate Judges, and Magistrates; Law Clerks; Legal Support Workers, All Other; Paralegals and Legal Assistants; Title Examiners and Abstractors; Title Examiners, Abstractors, and Searchers; Title

Searchers. **PERSONALITY TYPE**—Enterprising. Enterprising occupations frequently involve starting up and carrying out projects. These occupations can involve leading people and making many decisions. They sometimes require risk taking and often deal with business.

EDUCATION/TRAINING PROGRAM(S)—Advanced Legal Research/Studies, General (LL.M., M.C.L., M.L.I., M.S.L., J.S.D./S.J.D.); American/U.S. Law/Legal Studies/Jurisprudence (LL.M., M.C.J., J.S.D./S.J.D.); Banking, Corporate, Finance, and Securities Law (LL.M., J.S.D./S.J.D.); Canadian Law/Legal Studies/Jurisprudence (LL.M., M.C.J., J.S.D./S.J.D.); Comparative Law (LL.M., M.C.L., J.S.D./S.J.D.); Energy, Environment, and Natural Resources Law (LL.M., M.S., J.S.D./S.J.D.); Health Law (LL.M., M.J., J.S.D./S.J.D.); International Business, Trade, and Tax Law (LL.M., J.S.D./S.J.D.); International Law and Legal Studies (LL.M., J.S.D./S.J.D.); Law (LL.B., J.D.); Legal Professions and Studies, Other; Legal Research and Advanced Professional Studies, Other; Programs for Foreign Lawyers (LL.M., M.C.L.); Tax Law/Taxation (LL.M, J.S.D./S.J.D.). **RELATED KNOWLEDGE/ COURSES**—**Law and Government:** Knowledge of laws, legal codes, court procedures, precedents, government regulations, executive orders, agency rules, and the democratic political process. **English Language:** Knowledge of the structure and content of the English language, including the meaning and spelling of words, rules of composition, and grammar. **Administration and Management:** Knowledge of business and management principles involved in strategic planning, resource allocation, human resources modeling, leadership technique, production methods, and coordination of people and resources. **Education and Training:** Knowledge of principles and methods for curriculum and training design, teaching and instruction for individuals and groups, and the measurement of training effects. **Clerical Studies:** Knowledge of administrative and clerical procedures and systems, such as word processing, managing files and records, stenography and transcription, designing forms, and other office procedures and terminology.

Legal Secretaries

- ▲ Education/Training Required: Postsecondary vocational training
- ▲ Annual Earnings: $34,610
- ▲ Growth: 20.3%
- ▲ Annual Job Openings: 36,000
- ▲ Self-Employed: 0%
- ▲ Part-Time: 19.8%

Perform secretarial duties utilizing legal terminology, procedures, and documents. Prepare legal papers and correspondence, such as summonses, complaints, motions, and subpoenas. May also assist with legal research. Prepares and processes legal documents and papers, such as summonses, subpoenas, complaints, appeals, motions, and pretrial agreements. Reviews legal publications and performs database searches to identify laws and court decisions relevant to pending cases. Submits articles and information from searches to attorneys for review and approval for use. Assists attorneys in collecting information such as employment, medical, and other records. Organizes and maintains law libraries and document and case files. Completes various forms, such as accident reports, trial and courtroom requests, and applications for clients. Mails, faxes, or arranges for delivery of legal correspondence to clients, witnesses, and court officials. Attends legal meetings, such as client interviews, hearings, or depositions, and takes notes. Drafts and types office memos. Receives and places telephone calls. Schedules and makes appointments. Makes photocopies of correspondence, document, and other printed matter. **SKILLS**— **Reading Comprehension:** Understanding written sentences and paragraphs in work-related documents. **Writing:** Communicating effectively in writing as appropriate for the needs of the audience. **Active Listening:** Giving full attention to what other people are saying, taking time to understand the points being made, asking questions as appropriate, and not interrupting at inappropriate times. **Critical Thinking:** Using logic and reasoning to identify the strengths and weaknesses of alternative solutions, conclusions, or approaches to problems. **Active Learning:** Understanding the implications of new information for both current and future problem-solving and decision-making.

GOE INFORMATION—**Interest Area:** 09. Business Detail. **Work Group:** 09.02. Administrative Detail. **Other**

Job Titles in This Work Group: Claims Takers, Unemployment Benefits; Court Clerks; Court, Municipal, and License Clerks; Eligibility Interviewers, Government Programs; Executive Secretaries and Administrative Assistants; Interviewers, Except Eligibility and Loan; License Clerks; Loan Interviewers and Clerks; Medical Secretaries; Municipal Clerks; Secretaries, Except Legal, Medical, and Executive; Welfare Eligibility Workers and Interviewers. **PERSONALITY TYPE**—Conventional. Conventional occupations frequently involve following set procedures and routines. These occupations can include working with data and details more than with ideas. Usually there is a clear line of authority to follow.

EDUCATION/TRAINING PROGRAM(S)—Legal Administrative Assistant/Secretary. **RELATED KNOWLEDGE/COURSES**—**Clerical Studies:** Knowledge of administrative and clerical procedures and systems, such as word processing, managing files and records, stenography and transcription, designing forms, and other office procedures and terminology. **Law and Government:** Knowledge of laws, legal codes, court procedures, precedents, government regulations, executive orders, agency rules, and the democratic political process. **English Language:** Knowledge of the structure and content of the English language, including the meaning and spelling of words, rules of composition, and grammar. **Computers and Electronics:** Knowledge of circuit boards, processors, chips, electronic equipment, and computer hardware and software, including applications and programming. **Telecommunications:** Knowledge of transmission, broadcasting, switching, control, and operation of telecommunications systems. **Communications and Media:** Knowledge of media production, communication, and dissemination techniques and methods. This includes alternative ways to inform and entertain via written, oral, and visual media.

Library Assistants, Clerical

- ▲ Education/Training Required: Short-term on-the-job training
- ▲ Annual Earnings: $18,580
- ▲ Growth: 19.7%
- ▲ Annual Job Openings: 26,000
- ▲ Self-Employed: 0%
- ▲ Part-Time: 61.7%

Compile records, sort and shelve books, and issue and receive library materials, such as pictures, cards, slides and microfilm. Locate library materials for loan and replace material in shelving area, stacks, or files according to identification number and title. Register patrons to permit them to borrow books, periodicals, and other library materials. Issues borrower's identification card according to established procedures. Drives bookmobile to specified locations following library services schedule and to garage for preventive maintenance and repairs. Locates library materials for patrons, such as books, periodicals, tape cassettes, Braille volumes, and pictures. Classifies and catalogs items according to contents and purpose. Sorts books, publications, and other items according to procedure and returns them to shelves, files, or other designated storage area. Issues books to patrons and records or scans information on borrower's card. Maintains records of items received, stored, issued, and returned and files catalog cards according to system used. Delivers and retrieves items to and from departments by hand or push cart. Repairs books, using mending tape and paste and brush, and places plastic covers on new books. Prepares address labels for books to be mailed, overdue notices, and duty schedules, using computer or typewriter. Operates and maintains audio-visual equipment and explains use of reference equipment to patrons. Places books in mailing container, affixes address label, and secures container with straps for mailing to blind library patrons. Selects substitute titles, following criteria such as age, education, and interest, when requested materials are unavailable. Inspects returned books for damage, verifies due date, and computes and receives overdue fines. Reviews records, such as microfilm and issue cards, to determine title of overdue materials and to identify borrower. Prepares, stores, and retrieves classification and catalog information, lecture notes, or other documents related to document stored, using computer. Answers routine inquiries and refers patrons who need professional assistance to librarian. **SKILLS**—**Reading Comprehension:** Understanding written sentences and paragraphs in work-related documents. **Active Listening:** Giving full attention to what other people are saying, taking time to understand the points being made, asking questions as appropriate, and not interrupting at inappropriate times. **Service Orientation:** Actively looking for ways to help people. **Writing:** Communicating effectively in writing as appropriate for the needs of the audience. **Speaking:** Talking to others to convey information effectively.

GOE INFORMATION—Interest Area: 12. Education and Social Service. **Work Group:** 12.03. Educational Services. **Other Job Titles in This Work Group:** Adult Literacy, Remedial Education, and GED Teachers and Instructors; Agricultural Sciences Teachers, Postsecondary; Anthropology and Archeology Teachers, Postsecondary; Architecture Teachers, Postsecondary; Archivists; Area, Ethnic, and Cultural Studies Teachers, Postsecondary; Art, Drama, and Music Teachers, Postsecondary; Atmospheric, Earth, Marine, and Space Sciences Teachers, Postsecondary; Audio-Visual Collections Specialists; Biological Science Teachers, Postsecondary; Business Teachers, Postsecondary; Chemistry Teachers, Postsecondary; Child Care Workers; Communications Teachers, Postsecondary; Computer Science Teachers, Postsecondary; Criminal Justice and Law Enforcement Teachers, Postsecondary; Curators; Economics Teachers, Postsecondary; Education Teachers, Postsecondary; Educational Psychologists; Educational, Vocational, and School Counselors; Elementary School Teachers, Except Special Education; Engineering Teachers, Postsecondary; English Language and Literature Teachers, Postsecondary; Environmental Science Teachers, Postsecondary; Farm and Home Management Advisors; Foreign Language and Literature Teachers, Postsecondary; Forestry and Conservation Science Teachers, Postsecondary; Geography Teachers, Postsecondary; Graduate Teaching Assistants; Health Specialties Teachers, Postsecondary; History Teachers, Postsecondary; Home Economics Teachers, Postsecondary; Kindergarten Teachers, Except Special Education; Law Teachers, Postsecondary; Librarians; Library Science Teachers, Postsecondary; Library Technicians; Mathematical Science Teachers, Postsecondary; Middle School Teachers, Except Special and Vocational Education; Museum Technicians and Conservators; Nursing Instructors and Teachers, Postsecondary; Personal Financial Advisors; Philosophy and Religion Teachers, Postsecondary; Physics Teachers, Postsecondary; Political Science Teachers, Postsecondary; Postsecondary Teachers, All Other; Preschool Teachers, Except Special Education; others. **PERSONALITY TYPE**—Conventional. Conventional occupations frequently involve following set procedures and routines. These occupations can include working with data and details more than with ideas. Usually there is a clear line of authority to follow.

EDUCATION/TRAINING PROGRAM(S)—Library Assistant/Technician. **RELATED KNOWLEDGE/COURSES**—Clerical Studies: Knowledge of administrative and clerical procedures and systems, such as word processing, managing files and records, stenography and transcription, designing forms, and other office procedures and terminology. **English Language:** Knowledge of the structure and content of the English language, including the meaning and spelling of words, rules of composition, and grammar. **Customer and Personal Service:** Knowledge of principles and processes for providing customer and personal services. This includes customer needs assessment, meeting quality standards for services, and evaluation of customer satisfaction. **Computers and Electronics:** Knowledge of circuit boards, processors, chips, electronic equipment, and computer hardware and software, including applications and programming. **Communications and Media:** Knowledge of media production, communication, and dissemination techniques and methods. This includes alternative ways to inform and entertain via written, oral, and visual media.

Library Science Teachers, Postsecondary

- ▲ Education/Training Required: Master's degree
- ▲ Annual Earnings: $51,050
- ▲ Growth: 23.5%
- ▲ Annual Job Openings: 184,000
- ▲ Self-Employed: 0%
- ▲ Part-Time: 32.3%

Teach courses in library science. **SKILLS**—No data available.

GOE INFORMATION—Interest Area: 12. Education and Social Service. **Work Group:** 12.03. Educational

Services. **Other Job Titles in This Work Group:** Adult Literacy, Remedial Education, and GED Teachers and Instructors; Agricultural Sciences Teachers, Postsecondary; Anthropology and Archeology Teachers, Postsecondary; Architecture Teachers, Postsecondary; Archivists; Area, Ethnic, and Cultural Studies Teachers, Postsecondary; Art, Drama, and Music Teachers, Postsecondary; Atmospheric, Earth, Marine, and Space Sciences Teachers, Postsecondary; Audio-Visual Collections Specialists; Biological Science Teachers, Postsecondary; Business Teachers, Postsecondary; Chemistry Teachers, Postsecondary; Child Care Workers; Communications Teachers, Postsecondary; Computer Science Teachers, Postsecondary; Criminal Justice and Law Enforcement Teachers, Postsecondary; Curators; Economics Teachers, Postsecondary; Education Teachers, Postsecondary; Educational Psychologists; Educational, Vocational, and School Counselors; Elementary School Teachers, Except Special Education; Engineering Teachers, Postsecondary; English Language and Literature Teachers, Postsecondary; Environmental Science Teachers, Postsecondary; Farm and Home Management Advisors; Foreign Language and Literature Teachers, Postsecondary; Forestry and Conservation Science Teachers, Postsecondary; Geography Teachers, Postsecondary; Graduate Teaching Assistants; Health Specialties Teachers, Postsecondary; History Teachers, Postsecondary; Home Economics Teachers, Postsecondary; Kindergarten Teachers, Except Special Education; Law Teachers, Postsecondary; Librarians; Library Assistants, Clerical; Library Technicians; Mathematical Science Teachers, Postsecondary; Middle School Teachers, Except Special and Vocational Education; Museum Technicians and Conservators; Nursing Instructors and Teachers, Postsecondary; Personal Financial Advisors; Philosophy and Religion Teachers, Postsecondary; Physics Teachers, Postsecondary; Political Science Teachers, Postsecondary; Postsecondary Teachers, All Other; Preschool Teachers, Except Special Education; others. **PERSONALITY TYPE**—No data available.

EDUCATION/TRAINING PROGRAM(S)—Library Science/Librarianship; Teacher Education and Professional Development, Specific Subject Areas, Other. **RELATED KNOWLEDGE/COURSES**—No data available.

Library Technicians

- ▲ Education/Training Required: Short-term on-the-job training
- ▲ Annual Earnings: $23,790
- ▲ Growth: 19.5%
- ▲ Annual Job Openings: 29,000
- ▲ Self-Employed: 0%
- ▲ Part-Time: 11.7%

Assist librarians by helping readers in the use of library catalogs, databases, and indexes to locate books and other materials and by answering questions that require only brief consultation of standard reference. Compile records; sort and shelve books; remove or repair damaged books; register patrons; check materials in and out of the circulation process. Replace materials in shelving area (stacks) or files. Includes bookmobile drivers who operate bookmobiles or light trucks that pull trailers to specific locations on a predetermined schedule and assist with providing services in mobile libraries. Assists patrons in operating equipment and obtaining library materials and services; explains use of reference tools. Reviews subject matter of materials to be classified and selects classification numbers and headings according to classification system. Files catalog cards according to system used. Verifies bibliographical data, including author, title, publisher, publication date, and edition, on computer terminal. Processes print and non-print library materials; classifies and catalogs materials. Issues identification card to borrowers and checks materials in and out. Compiles and maintains records relating to circulation, materials, and equipment. Composes explanatory summaries of contents of books or other reference materials. Designs posters and special displays to promote use of library facilities or specific reading program at library. Prepares order slips for materials, follows up on orders, and compiles lists of materials acquired or withdrawn. Directs activities of library clerks and aides. **SKILLS—Reading Comprehension:** Understanding written sentences and paragraphs in work-related documents. **Active Listening:** Giving full attention to what other people are saying, taking time to understand the points being made, asking questions as appropriate, and not interrupting at inappropriate times. **Writing:** Communicating effectively in writing as appropriate for the needs of the audience. **Service Orientation:** Actively looking for ways to help people. **Speaking:** Talking to others to convey information effectively.

GOE INFORMATION—Interest Area: 12. Education and Social Service. **Work Group:** 12.03. Educational Services. **Other Job Titles in This Work Group:** Adult Literacy, Remedial Education, and GED Teachers and Instructors; Agricultural Sciences Teachers, Postsecondary; Anthropology and Archeology Teachers, Postsecondary; Architecture Teachers, Postsecondary; Archivists; Area, Ethnic, and Cultural Studies Teachers, Postsecondary; Art, Drama, and Music Teachers, Postsecondary; Atmospheric, Earth, Marine, and Space Sciences Teachers, Postsecondary; Audio-Visual Collections Specialists; Biological Science Teachers, Postsecondary; Business Teachers, Postsecondary; Chemistry Teachers, Postsecondary; Child Care Workers; Communications Teachers, Postsecondary; Computer Science Teachers, Postsecondary; Criminal Justice and Law Enforcement Teachers, Postsecondary; Curators; Economics Teachers, Postsecondary; Education Teachers, Postsecondary; Educational Psychologists; Educational, Vocational, and School Counselors; Elementary School Teachers, Except Special Education; Engineering Teachers, Postsecondary; English Language and Literature Teachers, Postsecondary; Environmental Science Teachers, Postsecondary; Farm and Home Management Advisors; Foreign Language and Literature Teachers, Postsecondary; Forestry and Conservation Science Teachers, Postsecondary; Geography Teachers, Postsecondary; Graduate Teaching Assistants; Health Specialties Teachers, Postsecondary; History Teachers, Postsecondary; Home Economics Teachers, Postsecondary; Kindergarten Teachers, Except Special Education; Law Teachers, Postsecondary; Librarians; Library Assistants, Clerical; Library Science Teachers, Postsecondary; Mathematical Science Teachers, Postsecondary; Middle School Teachers, Except Special and Vocational Education; Museum Technicians and Conservators; Nursing Instructors and Teachers, Postsecondary; Personal Financial Advisors; Philosophy and Religion Teachers, Postsecondary; Physics Teachers, Postsecondary; Political Science Teachers, Postsecondary; Postsecondary Teachers, All Other; Preschool Teachers, Except Special Education; others. **PERSONALITY TYPE**—Conventional. Conventional occupations frequently involve following set procedures and routines. These occupations can include working with data and details more than with ideas. Usually there is a clear line of authority to follow.

EDUCATION/TRAINING PROGRAM(S)—Library Assistant/Technician. **RELATED KNOWLEDGE/ COURSES—Clerical Studies:** Knowledge of administrative and clerical procedures and systems, such as word processing, managing files and records, stenography and transcription, designing forms, and other office procedures and terminology. **Customer and Personal Service:** Knowledge of principles and processes for providing customer and personal services. This includes customer needs assessment, meeting quality standards for services, and evaluation of customer satisfaction. **English Language:** Knowledge of the structure and content of the English language, including the meaning and spelling of words, rules of composition, and grammar. **Computers and Electronics:** Knowledge of circuit boards, processors, chips, electronic equipment, and computer hardware and software, including applications and programming. **Mathematics:** Knowledge of arithmetic, algebra, geometry, calculus, and statistics and their applications. **Communications and Media:** Knowledge of media production, communication, and dissemination techniques and methods. This includes alternative ways to inform and entertain via written, oral, and visual media.

License Clerks

- ▲ Education/Training Required: Short-term on-the-job training
- ▲ Annual Earnings: $27,090
- ▲ Growth: 12.0%
- ▲ Annual Job Openings: 14,000
- ▲ Self-Employed: 0%
- ▲ Part-Time: 16.0%

Issue licenses or permits to qualified applicants. Obtain necessary information, record data, advise applicants on requirements, collect fees, and issue licenses. May conduct oral, written, visual, or performance testing. Questions applicant to obtain information, such as name, address, and age, and records data on prescribed forms. Collects prescribed fee. Conducts oral, visual, written, or performance test to determine applicant qualifications.

Evaluates information obtained to determine applicant qualification for licensure. Issues driver, automobile, marriage, dog, or other license. Counts collected fees and applications. Submits fees and reports to government for record. **SKILLS—Speaking:** Talking to others to convey information effectively. **Active Listening:** Giving full attention to what other people are saying, taking time to understand the points being made, asking questions as appropriate, and not interrupting at inappropriate times. **Reading Comprehension:** Understanding written sentences and paragraphs in work-related documents. **Writing:** Communicating effectively in writing as appropriate for the needs of the audience. **Monitoring:** Monitoring/Assessing your performance or that of other individuals or organizations to make improvements or take corrective action.

GOE INFORMATION—Interest Area: 09. Business Detail. **Work Group:** 09.02. Administrative Detail. **Other Job Titles in This Work Group:** Claims Takers, Unemployment Benefits; Court Clerks; Court, Municipal, and License Clerks; Eligibility Interviewers, Government Programs; Executive Secretaries and Administrative Assistants; Interviewers, Except Eligibility and Loan; Legal Secretaries; Loan Interviewers and Clerks; Medical Secretaries; Municipal Clerks; Secretaries, Except Legal, Medical, and

Executive; Welfare Eligibility Workers and Interviewers. **PERSONALITY TYPE—Conventional.** Conventional occupations frequently involve following set procedures and routines. These occupations can include working with data and details more than with ideas. Usually there is a clear line of authority to follow.

EDUCATION/TRAINING PROGRAM(S)—General Office Occupations and Clerical Services. **RELATED KNOWLEDGE/COURSES—Clerical Studies:** Knowledge of administrative and clerical procedures and systems, such as word processing, managing files and records, stenography and transcription, designing forms, and other office procedures and terminology. **Mathematics:** Knowledge of arithmetic, algebra, geometry, calculus, and statistics and their applications. **Law and Government:** Knowledge of laws, legal codes, court procedures, precedents, government regulations, executive orders, agency rules, and the democratic political process. **Customer and Personal Service:** Knowledge of principles and processes for providing customer and personal services. This includes customer needs assessment, meeting quality standards for services, and evaluation of customer satisfaction. **English Language:** Knowledge of the structure and content of the English language, including the meaning and spelling of words, rules of composition, and grammar.

Licensed Practical and Licensed Vocational Nurses

▲ Education/Training Required: Postsecondary vocational training
▲ Annual Earnings: $30,670
▲ Growth: 20.3%
▲ Annual Job Openings: 58,000
▲ Self-Employed: 0.6%
▲ Part-Time: 22.1%

Care for ill, injured, convalescent, or disabled persons in hospitals, nursing homes, clinics, private homes, group homes, and similar institutions. May work under the supervision of a registered nurse. Licensing required. Administers specified medication, orally or by subcutaneous or intramuscular injection, and notes time and amount on patients' charts. Provides medical treatment and personal care to patients in private home settings. Takes and records patients' vital signs. Dresses wounds and gives enemas, douches, alcohol rubs, and massages. Applies compresses, ice bags, and hot water bottles. Observes patients and reports adverse reactions to medication or treatment to medical personnel in charge. Bathes, dresses, and assists patients in walking and turning. Assembles and uses

such equipment as catheters, tracheotomy tubes, and oxygen suppliers. Collects samples, such as urine, blood, and sputum, from patients for testing and performs routine laboratory tests on samples. Sterilizes equipment and supplies, using germicides, sterilizer, or autoclave. Records food and fluid intake and output. Prepares or examines food trays for prescribed diet and feeds patients. Assists in delivery, care, and feeding of infants. Cleans rooms, makes beds, and answers patients' calls. Washes and dresses bodies of deceased persons. Inventories and requisitions supplies. **SKILLS—Service Orientation:** Actively looking for ways to help people. **Reading Comprehension:** Understanding written sentences and paragraphs in work-related documents. **Social Perceptiveness:** Being aware of others' reactions and understanding why they react as they do. **Critical Thinking:** Using logic and reasoning to identify the strengths and weaknesses of alternative solutions, conclusions, or approaches to problems. **Active Listening:** Giving full attention to what other people are saying, taking time to understand the points being made, asking questions as appropriate, and not interrupting at inappropriate times.

GOE INFORMATION—Interest Area: 14. Medical and Health Services. **Work Group:** 14.07. Patient Care and Assistance. **Other Job Titles in This Work Group:** Home Health Aides; Nursing Aides, Orderlies, and Attendants; Psychiatric Aides; Psychiatric Technicians. **PERSONALITY TYPE—**Social. Social occupations frequently involve working with, communicating with, and teaching people. These occupations often involve helping or providing service to others.

EDUCATION/TRAINING PROGRAM(S)—Licensed Practical/Vocational Nurse Training (LPN, LVN, Cert, Dipl, AAS). **RELATED KNOWLEDGE/COURSES— Medicine and Dentistry:** Knowledge of the information and techniques needed to diagnose and treat human injuries, diseases, and deformities. This includes symptoms, treatment alternatives, drug properties and interactions, and preventive health-care measures. **Customer and Personal Service:** Knowledge of principles and processes for providing customer and personal services. This includes customer needs assessment, meeting quality standards for services, and evaluation of customer satisfaction. **Biology:** Knowledge of plant and animal organisms and their tissues, cells, functions, interdependencies, and interactions with each other and the environment. **Psychology:** Knowledge of human behavior and performance; individual differences in ability, personality, and interests; learning and motivation; psychological research methods; and the assessment and treatment of behavioral and affective disorders. **Clerical Studies:** Knowledge of administrative and clerical procedures and systems, such as word processing, managing files and records, stenography and transcription, designing forms, and other office procedures and terminology. **Chemistry:** Knowledge of the chemical composition, structure, and properties of substances and of the chemical processes and transformations that they undergo. This includes uses of chemicals and their interactions, danger signs, production techniques, and disposal methods.

Loan Officers

- ▲ Education/Training Required: Bachelor's degree
- ▲ Annual Earnings: $43,210
- ▲ Growth: 4.9%
- ▲ Annual Job Openings: 28,000
- ▲ Self-Employed: 0%
- ▲ Part-Time: 7.2%

Evaluate, authorize, or recommend approval of commercial, real estate, or credit loans. Advise borrowers on financial status and methods of payments. Includes mortgage loan officers and agents, collection analysts, loan servicing officers, and loan underwriters. Analyzes applicant's financial status, credit, and property evaluation to determine feasibility of granting loan. Approves loan within specified limits. Refers loan to loan committee for approval. Interviews applicant and requests specified information for loan application. Submits application to credit analyst for verification and recommendation. Confers with underwriters to aid in resolving mortgage application problems. Arranges for maintenance and liquidation of delinquent property. Supervises loan personnel. Negotiates payment arrangements with customers for delinquent loan balance. Analyzes potential loan markets to develop prospects for loans. Petitions court to transfer title and deeds of collateral to bank. Computes payment schedule. Ensures that loan agreements are complete and accurate according to policy. Contacts applicant or creditors to resolve questions regarding application information. **SKILLS—Reading Comprehension:** Understanding written sentences and paragraphs in work-related documents. **Speaking:** Talking to others to convey information effectively. **Active Listening:** Giving full attention to what other people are saying, taking time to understand the points being made, asking questions as appropriate, and not interrupting at inappropriate times. **Writing:** Communicating effectively in writing as appropriate for the needs of the audience. **Mathematics:** Using mathematics to solve problems. **Judgment and Decision Making:** Considering the relative costs and benefits of potential actions to choose the most appropriate one.

GOE INFORMATION—**Interest Area:** 13. General Management and Support. **Work Group:** 13.02. Management Support. **Other Job Titles in This Work Group:** Accountants; Accountants and Auditors; Appraisers and Assessors of Real Estate; Appraisers, Real Estate; Assessors; Auditors; Budget Analysts; Claims Adjusters, Examiners, and Investigators; Claims Examiners, Property and Casualty Insurance; Compensation, Benefits, and Job Analysis Specialists; Cost Estimators; Credit Analysts; Employment Interviewers, Private or Public Employment Service; Employment, Recruitment, and Placement Specialists; Financial Analysts; Human Resources, Training, and Labor Relations Specialists, All Other; Insurance Adjusters, Examiners, and Investigators; Insurance Appraisers, Auto Damage; Insurance Underwriters; Loan Counselors; Logisticians; Management Analysts; Market Research Analysts; Personnel Recruiters; Purchasing Agents and Buyers, Farm Products; Purchasing Agents, Except Wholesale, Retail, and Farm Products; Tax Examiners, Collectors, and Revenue Agents; Training and Development Specialists; Wholesale and Retail Buyers, Except Farm Products. **PERSONALITY TYPE**—Enterprising. Enterprising occupations frequently involve starting up and carrying out projects. These occupations can involve leading people and making many decisions. They sometimes require risk taking and often deal with business.

EDUCATION/TRAINING PROGRAM(S)—Credit Management; Finance, General. **RELATED KNOWLEDGE/COURSES**—**Economics and Accounting:** Knowledge of economic and accounting principles and practices, the financial markets, banking, and the analysis and reporting of financial data. **Mathematics:** Knowledge of arithmetic, algebra, geometry, calculus, and statistics and their applications. **English Language:** Knowledge of the structure and content of the English language, including the meaning and spelling of words, rules of composition, and grammar. **Clerical Studies:** Knowledge of administrative and clerical procedures and systems, such as word processing, managing files and records, stenography and transcription, designing forms, and other office procedures and terminology. **Law and Government:** Knowledge of laws, legal codes, court procedures, precedents, government regulations, executive orders, agency rules, and the democratic political process. **Customer and Personal Service:** Knowledge of principles and processes for providing customer and personal services. This includes customer needs assessment, meeting quality standards for services, and evaluation of customer satisfaction.

Machinists

- ▲ Education/Training Required: Long-term on-the-job training
- ▲ Annual Earnings: $32,090
- ▲ Growth: 9.1%
- ▲ Annual Job Openings: 28,000
- ▲ Self-Employed: 2.7%
- ▲ Part-Time: 2.1%

Set up and operate a variety of machine tools to produce precision parts and instruments. Includes precision instrument makers who fabricate, modify, or repair mechanical instruments. May also fabricate and modify parts to make or repair machine tools or maintain industrial machines, applying knowledge of mechanics, shop mathematics, metal properties, layout, and machining procedures. Studies sample parts, blueprints, drawings, and engineering information to determine methods and sequence of operations to fabricate product. Operates metalworking machine tools, such as lathe, milling machine, shaper, or grinder, to machine parts to specifications. Assembles parts into completed units, using jigs, fixtures, hand tools, and power tools. Fabricates, assembles, and modifies tooling, such as jigs, fixtures, templates, and molds or dies, to produce parts and assemblies. Lays out and verifies dimensions of parts, using precision measuring and marking instruments and knowledge of trigonometry. Calculates and sets controls to regulate machining or enters commands to retrieve, input, or edit computerized machine control media. Selects, aligns, and secures holding fixtures, cutting tools, attachments, accessories, and materials onto machines. Measures, examines, and tests completed units to detect defects and ensure conformance to specifications. Installs repaired part into equipment and operates equipment to verify operational efficiency. Operates brazing, heat-treating, and welding equipment to cut, solder, and braze metal. Dismantles machine or equipment, using hand tools and power tools, to examine parts for defect or to remove defective parts. Cleans, lubricates, and maintains machines, tools, and equipment to remove grease, rust, stains, and foreign matter. Observes and listens to operating machines or equipment to diagnose machine malfunction and determine need for adjustment or repair. Cuts and shapes sheet metal and heats and bends metal to specified shape. Installs experimental parts and assemblies, such as hydraulic systems, electrical wiring, lubricants, and batteries, into machines and mechanisms. Establishes work procedures for fabricating new structural products, using variety of metalworking machines. Confers with engineering, supervisory, and manufacturing personnel to exchange technical information. Designs fixtures, tooling, and experimental parts to meet special engineering needs. Tests experimental models under simulated operating conditions for such purposes as development, standardization, and evaluating feasibility of design. Evaluates experimental procedures and recommends changes or modifications for efficiency and adaptability to setup and production processes. **SKILLS—Installation:** Installing equipment, machines, wiring, or programs to meet specifications. **Mathematics:** Using mathematics to solve problems. **Equipment Selection:** Determining the kind of tools and equipment needed to do a job. **Quality Control Analysis:** Conducting tests and inspections of products, services, or processes to evaluate quality or performance. **Critical Thinking:** Using logic and reasoning to identify the strengths and weaknesses of alternative solutions, conclusions, or approaches to problems. **Operations Analysis:** Analyzing needs and product requirements to create a design.

GOE INFORMATION—Interest Area: 08. Industrial Production. **Work Group:** 08.04. Metal and Plastics Machining Technology. **Other Job Titles in This Work Group:** Lay-Out Workers, Metal and Plastic; Metal Workers and Plastic Workers, All Other; Model Makers, Metal and Plastic; Patternmakers, Metal and Plastic; Tool and Die Makers; Tool Grinders, Filers, and Sharpeners. **PERSONALITY TYPE—**Realistic. Realistic occupations frequently involve work activities that include practical, hands-on problems and solutions. They often deal with plants, animals, and real-world materials like wood, tools, and machinery. Many of the occupations require working outside and do not involve a lot of paperwork or working closely with others.

EDUCATION/TRAINING PROGRAM(S)—Machine Shop Technology/Assistant; Machine Tool Technology/Machinist. **RELATED KNOWLEDGE/COURSES— Principles of Mechanical Devices:** Knowledge of machines and tools, including their designs, uses, repair, and maintenance. **Design:** Knowledge of design techniques, tools, and principles involved in production of precision technical plans, blueprints, drawings, and models. **Engineering and Technology:** Knowledge of the practical application of engineering science and technology. This includes applying principles, techniques, procedures, and equipment to the design and production of various goods and services. **Mathematics:** Knowledge of arithmetic, algebra, geometry, calculus, and statistics and their applications. **Production and Processing:** Knowledge of raw materials, production processes, quality control, costs, and other techniques for maximizing the effective manufacture and distribution of goods.

Maintenance and Repair Workers, General

- ▲ Education/Training Required: Long-term on-the-job training
- ▲ Annual Earnings: $28,740
- ▲ Growth: 4.7%
- ▲ Annual Job Openings: 103,000
- ▲ Self-Employed: 2.2%
- ▲ Part-Time: 9.3%

Perform work involving the skills of two or more maintenance or craft occupations to keep machines, mechanical equipment, or the structure of an establishment in repair. Duties may involve pipe fitting; boiler making; insulating; welding; machining; carpentry; repairing electrical or mechanical equipment; installing, aligning, and balancing new equipment; and repairing buildings, floors, or stairs. Inspects and tests machinery and equipment to diagnose machine malfunctions. Paints and repairs woodwork and plaster. Estimates costs of repairs. Records repairs made and costs. Fabricates and repairs counters, benches, partitions, and other wooden structures, such as sheds and outbuildings. Operates cutting torch or welding equipment to cut or join metal parts. Sets up and operates machine tools to repair or fabricate machine parts, jigs and fixtures, and tools. Lays brick to repair and maintain physical structure of establishment. Assembles, installs, and/or repairs plumbing. Installs new or repaired parts. Installs and/or repairs wiring and electrical and electronic components. Assembles, installs, and/or repairs pipe systems and hydraulic and pneumatic equipment. Installs machinery and equipment. Cleans and lubricates shafts, bearings, gears, and other parts of machinery. Dismantles and reassembles defective machines and equipment. **SKILLS—Repairing:** Repairing machines or systems, using the needed tools. **Installation:** Installing equipment, machines, wiring, or programs to meet specifications. **Equipment Maintenance:** Performing routine maintenance on equipment and determining when and what kind of maintenance is needed. **Troubleshooting:** Determining causes of operating errors and deciding what to do about them. **Equipment Selection:** Determining the kind of tools and equipment needed to do a job.

GOE INFORMATION—Interest Area: 05. Mechanics, Installers, and Repairers. **Work Group:** 05.03. Mechanical Work. **Other Job Titles in This Work Group:** Aircraft Body and Bonded Structure Repairers; Aircraft Engine Specialists; Aircraft Mechanics and Service Technicians; Airframe-and-Power-Plant Mechanics; Automotive Body and Related Repairers; Automotive Glass Installers and Repairers; Automotive Master Mechanics; Automotive Service Technicians and Mechanics; Automotive Specialty Technicians; Bicycle Repairers; Bridge and Lock Tenders; Bus and Truck Mechanics and Diesel Engine Specialists; Camera and Photographic Equipment Repairers; Coin, Vending, and Amusement Machine Servicers and Repairers; Control and Valve Installers and Repairers, Except Mechanical Door; Farm Equipment Mechanics; Gas Appliance Repairers; Hand and Portable Power Tool Repairers; Heating and Air Conditioning Mechanics; Heating, Air Conditioning, and Refrigeration Mechanics and Installers; Helpers—Electricians; Helpers—Installation, Maintenance, and Repair Workers; Industrial Machinery Mechanics; Keyboard Instrument Repairers and Tuners; Locksmiths and Safe Repairers; Maintenance Workers, Machinery; Mechanical Door Repairers; Medical Appliance Technicians; Medical Equipment Repairers; Meter Mechanics; Millwrights; Mobile Heavy Equipment Mechanics, Except Engines;

Motorboat Mechanics; Motorcycle Mechanics; Musical Instrument Repairers and Tuners; Ophthalmic Laboratory Technicians; Optical Instrument Assemblers; Outdoor Power Equipment and Other Small Engine Mechanics; Painters, Transportation Equipment; Percussion Instrument Repairers and Tuners; Precision Instrument and Equipment Repairers, All Other; Rail Car Repairers; Railroad Inspectors; Recreational Vehicle Service Technicians; Reed or Wind Instrument Repairers and Tuners; Refrigeration Mechanics; Stringed Instrument Repairers and Tuners; Tire Repairers and Changers; Valve and Regulator Repairers; Watch Repairers. **PERSONALITY TYPE—Realistic.** Realistic occupations frequently involve work activities that include practical, hands-on problems and solutions. They often deal with plants, animals, and real-world materials like wood, tools, and machinery. Many of the occupations require working outside and do not involve a lot of paperwork or working closely with others.

EDUCATION/TRAINING PROGRAM(S)—Building/Construction Site Management/Manager. **RELATED KNOWLEDGE/COURSES—Building and Construction:** Knowledge of materials, methods, and tools involved in the construction or repair of houses, buildings, or other structures, such as highways and roads. **Principles of Mechanical Devices:** Knowledge of machines and tools, including their designs, uses, repair, and maintenance. **Engineering and Technology:** Knowledge of the practical application of engineering science and technology. This includes applying principles, techniques, procedures, and equipment to the design and production of various goods and services. **Public Safety and Security:** Knowledge of relevant equipment, policies, procedures, and strategies to promote effective local, state, or national security operations for the protection of people, data, property, and institutions. **Computers and Electronics:** Knowledge of circuit boards, processors, chips, electronic equipment, and computer hardware and software, including applications and programming. **Physics:** Knowledge and prediction of physical principles and laws and their interrelationships and applications to understanding fluid, material, and atmospheric dynamics and mechanical, electrical, atomic, and sub-atomic structures and processes. **Mathematics:** Knowledge of arithmetic, algebra, geometry, calculus, and statistics and their applications.

Makeup Artists, Theatrical and Performance

- ▲ Education/Training Required: Postsecondary vocational training
- ▲ Annual Earnings: $30,240
- ▲ Growth: 11.4%
- ▲ Annual Job Openings: 27,000
- ▲ Self-Employed: 46.0%
- ▲ Part-Time: 36.5%

Apply makeup to performers to reflect period, setting, and situation of their role. Applies makeup to performers to alter their appearance to accord with their roles. Attaches prostheses to performer and applies makeup to change physical features and depict desired character. Selects desired makeup shades from stock or mixes oil, grease, and coloring to achieve special color effects. Designs rubber or plastic prostheses; requisitions materials such as wigs, beards, and special cosmetics. Confers with stage or motion picture officials and performers to determine dress or makeup alterations. Creates character drawings or models based upon independent research to augment period production files. Examines sketches, photographs, and plaster models to obtain desired character image depiction. Studies production information, such as character, period settings, and situations to determine makeup requirements. **SKILLS—Reading Comprehension:** Understanding written sentences and paragraphs in work-related documents. **Active Listening:** Giving full attention to what other people are saying, taking time to understand the points being made, asking questions as appropriate, and not interrupting at inappropriate times. **Coordination:** Adjusting actions in relation to others' actions. **Equipment Selection:** Determining the kind of tools and equipment needed to do a job. **Active Learning:** Understanding the implications of new information for both current and future problem-solving and decision-making.

GOE INFORMATION—**Interest Area:** 01. Arts, Entertainment, and Media. **Work Group:** 01.09. Modeling and Personal Appearance. **Other Job Titles in This Work Group:** Costume Attendants; Models. **PERSONALITY TYPE**—Artistic. Artistic occupations frequently involve working with forms, designs, and patterns. They often require self-expression, and the work can be done without following a clear set of rules.

EDUCATION/TRAINING PROGRAM(S)—Cosmetology/Cosmetologist, General; Make-Up Artist/Specialist; Permanent Cosmetics/Makeup and Tattooing. **RELATED KNOWLEDGE/COURSES**—**Fine Arts:** Knowledge of the theory and techniques required to compose, produce, and perform works of music, dance, visual arts, drama, and sculpture. **Customer and Personal Service:** Knowledge of principles and processes for providing customer and personal services. This includes customer needs assessment, meeting quality standards for services, and evaluation of customer satisfaction. **Design:** Knowledge of design techniques, tools, and principles involved in production of precision technical plans, blueprints, drawings, and models. **Sociology and Anthropology:** Knowledge of group behavior and dynamics, societal trends and influences, human migrations, ethnicity, and cultures and their history and origins. **Communications and Media:** Knowledge of media production, communication, and dissemination techniques and methods. This includes alternative ways to inform and entertain via written, oral, and visual media. **English Language:** Knowledge of the structure and content of the English language, including the meaning and spelling of words, rules of composition, and grammar.

Management Analysts

- ▲ Education/Training Required: Work experience plus degree
- ▲ Annual Earnings: $57,970
- ▲ Growth: 28.9%
- ▲ Annual Job Openings: 50,000
- ▲ Self-Employed: 46.4%
- ▲ Part-Time: 19.5%

Conduct organizational studies and evaluations, design systems and procedures, conduct work simplifications and measurement studies, and prepare operations and procedures manuals to assist management in operating more efficiently and effectively. **Includes program analysts and management consultants.** Reviews forms and reports; confers with management and users about format, distribution, and purpose and to identify problems and improvements. Gathers and organizes information on problems or procedures. Confers with personnel concerned to ensure successful functioning of newly implemented systems or procedures. Documents findings of study and prepares recommendations for implementation of new systems, procedures, or organizational changes. Analyzes data gathered and develops solutions or alternative methods of proceeding. Plans study of work problems and procedures, such as organizational change, communications, information flow, integrated production methods, inventory control, or cost analysis. Develops and implements records management program for filing, protection, and retrieval of records; assures compliance with program. Prepares manuals and trains workers in use of new forms, reports, procedures, or equipment according to organizational policy. Designs, evaluates, recommends, and approves changes of forms and reports. Recommends purchase of storage equipment and designs area layout to locate equipment in space available. Interviews personnel and conducts on-site observation to ascertain unit functions; work performed; and methods, equipment, and personnel used. **SKILLS—Systems Evaluation:** Identifying measures or indicators of system performance and the actions needed to improve or correct performance relative to the goals of the system. **Writing:** Communicating effectively in writing as appropriate for the needs of the audience. **Monitoring:** Monitoring/Assessing your performance or that of other individuals or organizations to make improvements or take corrective action. **Judgment and Decision Making:** Considering the relative costs and benefits of potential actions to choose the most appropriate one. **Reading Comprehension:** Understanding written sentences and paragraphs in work-related documents.

GOE INFORMATION—Interest Area: 13. General Management and Support. **Work Group:** 13.02. Management Support. **Other Job Titles in This Work Group:** Accountants; Accountants and Auditors; Appraisers and Assessors of Real Estate; Appraisers, Real Estate; Assessors; Auditors; Budget Analysts; Claims Adjusters, Examiners, and Investigators; Claims Examiners, Property and Casualty Insurance; Compensation, Benefits, and Job Analysis Specialists; Cost Estimators; Credit Analysts; Employment Interviewers, Private or Public Employment Service; Employment, Recruitment, and Placement Specialists; Financial Analysts; Human Resources, Training, and Labor Relations Specialists, All Other; Insurance Adjusters, Examiners, and Investigators; Insurance Appraisers, Auto Damage; Insurance Underwriters; Loan Counselors; Loan Officers; Logisticians; Market Research Analysts; Personnel Recruiters; Purchasing Agents and Buyers, Farm Products; Purchasing Agents, Except Wholesale, Retail, and Farm Products; Tax Examiners, Collectors, and Revenue Agents; Training and Development Specialists; Wholesale and Retail Buyers, Except Farm Products. **PERSONALITY TYPE—Enterprising.** Enterprising occupations frequently involve starting up and carrying out projects. These occupations can involve leading people and making many decisions. They sometimes require risk taking and often deal with business.

EDUCATION/TRAINING PROGRAM(S)—Business Administration and Management, General; Business/Commerce, General. **RELATED KNOWLEDGE/COURSES—Administration and Management:** Knowledge of business and management principles involved in strategic planning, resource allocation, human resources modeling, leadership technique, production methods, and coordination of people and resources. **English Language:** Knowledge of the structure and content of the English language, including the meaning and spelling of words, rules of composition, and grammar. **Education and Training:** Knowledge of principles and methods for curriculum and training design, teaching and instruction for individuals and groups, and the measurement of training effects. **Mathematics:** Knowledge of arithmetic, algebra, geometry, calculus, and statistics and their applications. **Personnel and Human Resources:** Knowledge of principles and procedures for personnel recruitment, selection, training, compensation and benefits, labor relations and negotiation, and personnel information systems.

Manicurists and Pedicurists

- ▲ Education/Training Required: Postsecondary vocational training
- ▲ Annual Earnings: $16,700
- ▲ Growth: 26.5%
- ▲ Annual Job Openings: 5,000
- ▲ Self-Employed: 37.3%
- ▲ Part-Time: 36.5%

Clean and shape customers' fingernails and toenails. May polish or decorate nails. Removes previously applied nail polish, using liquid remover and swabs. Cleans customers' nails in soapy water, using swabs, files, and orange sticks. Shapes and smoothes ends of nails, using scissors, files, and emery boards. Applies clear or colored liquid polish onto nails with brush. Roughens surfaces of fingernails, using abrasive wheel. Attaches paper forms to tips of customer's fingers to support and shape artificial nails. Softens nail cuticles with water and oil; pushes back cuticles, using cuticle knife; and trims cuticles, using scissors or nippers. Whitens underside of nails with white paste or pencil. Removes paper forms and shapes and smoothes edges of nails, using rotary abrasive wheel. Brushes coats of powder and solvent onto nails and paper forms with handbrush to maintain nail appearance and to extend nails to desired length. Polishes nails, using powdered polish and buffer. Forms artificial fingernails on customer's fingers. **SKILLS—Monitoring:** Monitoring/Assessing your performance or that of other individuals or organizations to make improvements or take corrective action. **Service Orientation:** Actively looking for ways to help people. **Active Listening:** Giving full attention to what other people are saying, taking time to understand the points being made, asking questions as appropriate, and not interrupting at inappropriate times.

GOE INFORMATION—Interest Area: 11. Recreation, Travel, and Other Personal Services. **Work Group:** 11.04. Barber and Beauty Services. **Other Job Titles in This Work Group:** Barbers; Hairdressers, Hairstylists, and Cosmetologists; Shampooers; Skin Care Specialists. **PERSONALITY TYPE—**Enterprising. Enterprising occupations frequently involve starting up and carrying out projects. These occupations can involve leading people and making many decisions. They sometimes require risk taking and often deal with business.

EDUCATION/TRAINING PROGRAM(S)—Cosmetology/Cosmetologist, General; Nail Technician/Specialist and Manicurist. **RELATED KNOWLEDGE/ COURSES—Customer and Personal Service:** Knowledge of principles and processes for providing customer and personal services. This includes customer needs assessment, meeting quality standards for services, and evaluation of customer satisfaction. **Chemistry:** Knowledge of the chemical composition, structure, and properties of substances and of the chemical processes and transformations that they undergo. This includes uses of chemicals and their interactions, danger signs, production techniques, and disposal methods.

Mapping Technicians

- ▲ Education/Training Required: Moderate-term on-the-job training
- ▲ Annual Earnings: $28,210
- ▲ Growth: 25.3%
- ▲ Annual Job Openings: 7,000
- ▲ Self-Employed: 7.3%
- ▲ Part-Time: 4.5%

Calculate mapmaking information from field notes; draw and verify accuracy of topographical maps. Computes and measures scaled distances between reference points to establish exact relative position of adjoining points. Calculates latitude, longitude, angles, areas, and other information for mapmaking from survey field notes, using reference tables and computer. Forms three-dimensional image of aerial photographs taken from different locations, using mathematical aides and plotting instruments. Marks errors and makes corrections, such as numbering grid lines or lettering names of rivers or towns. Analyzes aerial photographs to detect and interpret significant military, industrial, resource, or topographical data. Supervises and coordinates activities of workers engaged in drafting maps or in production of blueprints, photostats, and photographs. Stores, retrieves, and compares map information, using computers and data banks. Trims, aligns, and joins prints to form photographic mosaic, maintaining scaled distances between reference points. Lays out and matches aerial photographs in sequence taken, looking for missing areas. Verifies identification of topographical features and accuracy of contour lines by comparison with aerial photographs, old maps, and other reference materials. Traces contours and topographical details to produce map. **SKILLS—Mathematics:** Using mathematics to solve problems. **Active Learning:** Understanding the implications of new information for both current and future problem-solving and decision-making. **Monitoring:** Monitoring/ Assessing your performance or that of other individuals or organizations to make improvements or take corrective action. **Critical Thinking:** Using logic and reasoning to identify the strengths and weaknesses of alternative solutions, conclusions, or approaches to problems. **Reading Comprehension:** Understanding written sentences and paragraphs in work-related documents.

GOE INFORMATION—Interest Area: 02. Science, Math, and Engineering. **Work Group:** 02.08. Engineering Technology. **Other Job Titles in This Work Group:** Aerospace Engineering and Operations Technicians; Architectural and Civil Drafters; Architectural Drafters; Calibration and Instrumentation Technicians; Cartographers and Photogrammetrists; Civil Drafters; Civil Engineering Technicians; Construction and Building Inspectors; Drafters, All Other; Electrical and Electronic Engineering Technicians; Electrical and Electronics Drafters; Electrical Drafters; Electrical Engineering Technicians; Electro-Mechanical Technicians; Electronic Drafters; Electronics Engineering Technicians; Engineering Technicians, Except Drafters, All Other; Environmental Engineering Technicians; Industrial Engineering Technicians; Mechanical Drafters; Mechanical Engineering Technicians; Numerical Tool and Process Control Programmers; Pressure Vessel Inspectors; Surveying and Mapping Technicians; Surveying Technicians; Surveyors. **PERSONALITY TYPE**—Conventional. Conventional occupations frequently involve following set procedures and routines. These occupations can include working with data and details more than with ideas. Usually there is a clear line of authority to follow.

EDUCATION/TRAINING PROGRAM(S)—Cartography; Surveying Technology/Surveying. **RELATED KNOWLEDGE/COURSES—Geography:** Knowledge of principles and methods for describing the features of land, sea, and air masses, including their physical characteristics, locations, interrelationships, and distribution of plant, animal, and human life. **Mathematics:** Knowledge of arithmetic, algebra, geometry, calculus, and statistics and their applications. **Design:** Knowledge of design techniques, tools, and principles involved in production of precision technical plans, blueprints, drawings, and models. **Computers and Electronics:** Knowledge of circuit boards, processors, chips, electronic equipment, and computer hardware and software, including applications and programming. **Engineering and Technology:** Knowledge of the practical application of engineering science and technology. This includes applying principles, techniques, procedures, and equipment to the design and production of various goods and services.

Market Research Analysts

▲ Education/Training Required: Bachelor's degree
▲ Annual Earnings: $53,450
▲ Growth: 24.4%
▲ Annual Job Openings: 13,000
▲ Self-Employed: 18.9%
▲ Part-Time: 8.8%

Research market conditions in local, regional, or national areas to determine potential sales of a product or service. May gather information on competitors, prices, sales, and methods of marketing and distribution. May use survey results to create a marketing campaign based on regional preferences and buying habits. Examines and analyzes statistical data to forecast future marketing trends and to identify potential markets. Collects data on customer preferences and buying habits. Prepares reports and graphic illustrations of findings. Translates complex numerical data into nontechnical written text. Attends staff conferences to submit findings and proposals to management for consideration. Checks consumer reaction to new or improved products or services. Establishes research methodology and designs format for data gathering, such as surveys, opinion polls, or questionnaires. Gathers data on competitors and analyzes prices, sales, and method of marketing and distribution. **SKILLS—Writing:** Communicating effectively in writing as appropriate for the needs of the audience. **Mathematics:** Using mathematics to solve problems. **Reading Comprehension:** Understanding written sentences and paragraphs in work-related documents. **Monitoring:** Monitoring/Assessing your performance or that of other individuals or organizations to make improvements or take corrective action. **Active Listening:** Giving full attention to what other people are saying, taking time to understand the points being made, asking questions as appropriate, and not interrupting at inappropriate times.

GOE INFORMATION—Interest Area: 13. General Management and Support. **Work Group:** 13.02. Management Support. **Other Job Titles in This Work Group:** Accountants; Accountants and Auditors; Appraisers and Assessors of Real Estate; Appraisers, Real Estate; Assessors; Auditors; Budget Analysts; Claims Adjusters, Examiners, and Investigators; Claims Examiners, Property and Casualty Insurance; Compensation, Benefits, and Job Analysis Specialists; Cost Estimators; Credit Analysts; Employment Interviewers, Private or Public Employment Service; Employment, Recruitment, and Placement Specialists; Financial Analysts; Human Resources, Training, and Labor Relations Specialists, All Other; Insurance Adjusters, Examiners, and Investigators; Insurance Appraisers, Auto Damage; Insurance Underwriters; Loan Counselors; Loan Officers; Logisticians; Management Analysts; Personnel Recruiters; Purchasing Agents and

Buyers, Farm Products; Purchasing Agents, Except Wholesale, Retail, and Farm Products; Tax Examiners, Collectors, and Revenue Agents; Training and Development Specialists; Wholesale and Retail Buyers, Except Farm Products. **PERSONALITY TYPE**—Investigative. Investigative occupations frequently involve working with ideas and require an extensive amount of thinking. These occupations can involve searching for facts and figuring out problems mentally.

EDUCATION/TRAINING PROGRAM(S)—Applied Economics; Business/Managerial Economics; Econometrics and Quantitative Economics; Economics, General; International Economics; Marketing Research. **RELATED KNOWLEDGE/COURSES—Mathematics:** Knowledge of arithmetic, algebra, geometry, calculus, and statistics and their applications. **Sales and Marketing:** Knowledge of principles and methods for showing, promoting, and selling products or services. This includes marketing strategy and tactics, product demonstration, sales techniques, and sales control systems. **English Language:** Knowledge of the structure and content of the English language, including the meaning and spelling of words, rules of composition, and grammar. **Computers and Electronics:** Knowledge of circuit boards, processors, chips, electronic equipment, and computer hardware and software, including applications and programming. **Geography:** Knowledge of principles and methods for describing the features of land, sea, and air masses, including their physical characteristics, locations, interrelationships, and distribution of plant, animal, and human life. **Economics and Accounting:** Knowledge of economic and accounting principles and practices, the financial markets, banking, and the analysis and reporting of financial data.

Marketing Managers

▲ Education/Training Required: Work experience plus degree
▲ Annual Earnings: $74,370
▲ Growth: 29.1%
▲ Annual Job Openings: 12,000
▲ Self-Employed: 2.4%
▲ Part-Time: 2.6%

Determine the demand for products and services offered by a firm and its competitors and identify potential customers. Develop pricing strategies with the goal of maximizing the firm's profits or share of the market while ensuring that the firm's customers are satisfied. Oversee product development or monitor trends that indicate the

need for new products and services. Develops marketing strategy, based on knowledge of establishment policy, nature or market, and cost and markup factors. Coordinates and publicizes marketing activities to promote products and services. Conducts economic and commercial surveys to identify potential markets for products and services.

Analyzes business developments and consults trade journals to monitor market trends and determine market opportunities for products. Advises business and other groups on local, national, and international factors affecting the buying and selling of products and services. Selects products and accessories to be displayed at trade or special production shows. Compiles list describing product or service offerings and sets prices or fees. Prepares report of marketing activities. Confers with legal staff to resolve problems, such as copyright infringement and royalty sharing with outside producers and distributors. Consults with buying personnel to gain advice regarding the types of products or services that are expected to be in demand. Coordinates promotional activities and shows to market products and services. **SKILLS—Systems Analysis:** Determining how a system should work and how changes in conditions, operations, and the environment will affect outcomes. **Judgment and Decision Making:** Considering the relative costs and benefits of potential actions to choose the most appropriate one. **Coordination:** Adjusting actions in relation to others' actions. **Speaking:** Talking to others to convey information effectively. **Complex Problem Solving:** Identifying complex problems and reviewing related information to develop and evaluate options and implement solutions.

GOE INFORMATION—Interest Area: 10. Sales and Marketing. **Work Group:** 10.01. Managerial Work in Sales and Marketing. **Other Job Titles in This Work Group:** Advertising and Promotions Managers; First-Line Supervisors/Managers of Non-Retail Sales Workers; First-Line

Supervisors/Managers of Retail Sales Workers; Sales Managers. **PERSONALITY TYPE—**Enterprising. Enterprising occupations frequently involve starting up and carrying out projects. These occupations can involve leading people and making many decisions. They sometimes require risk taking and often deal with business.

EDUCATION/TRAINING PROGRAM(S)—Apparel and Textile Marketing Management; Consumer Merchandising/Retailing Management; International Marketing; Marketing Research; Marketing, Other; Marketing/Marketing Management, General. **RELATED KNOWLEDGE/COURSES—Sales and Marketing:** Knowledge of principles and methods for showing, promoting, and selling products or services. This includes marketing strategy and tactics, product demonstration, sales techniques, and sales control systems. **Administration and Management:** Knowledge of business and management principles involved in strategic planning, resource allocation, human resources modeling, leadership technique, production methods, and coordination of people and resources. **Mathematics:** Knowledge of arithmetic, algebra, geometry, calculus, and statistics and their applications. **Communications and Media:** Knowledge of media production, communication, and dissemination techniques and methods. This includes alternative ways to inform and entertain via written, oral, and visual media. **English Language:** Knowledge of the structure and content of the English language, including the meaning and spelling of words, rules of composition, and grammar.

Marking Clerks

- ▲ Education/Training Required: Short-term on-the-job training
- ▲ Annual Earnings: $19,060
- ▲ Growth: 8.5%
- ▲ Annual Job Openings: 467,000
- ▲ Self-Employed: 0%
- ▲ Part-Time: 16.8%

Print and attach price tickets to articles of merchandise using one or several methods, such as marking price on tickets by hand or using ticket-printing machine. Marks selling price by hand on boxes containing merchandise or on price tickets. Performs other clerical tasks during periods between auction sales. Keeps records of production, returned goods, and related transactions. Records number and types of articles marked and packs articles in boxes. Pins, pastes, sews, ties, or staples tickets, tags, or labels to

article, using tagging mechanism. Records price, buyer, and grade of product on tickets attached to products auctioned. Indicates price, size, style, color, and inspection results on tags, tickets, and labels, using rubber stamp or writing instrument. Compares printed price tickets with entries on purchase order to verify accuracy and notifies supervisor of discrepancies. Prints information on tickets, using ticket-printing machine. **SKILLS—Mathematics:** Using mathematics to solve problems.

GOE INFORMATION—**Interest Area:** 09. Business Detail. **Work Group:** 09.08. Records and Materials Processing. **Other Job Titles in This Work Group:** Cargo and Freight Agents; Couriers and Messengers; Mail Clerks, Except Mail Machine Operators and Postal Service; Order Fillers, Wholesale and Retail Sales; Postal Service Mail Carriers; Postal Service Mail Sorters, Processors, and Processing Machine Operators; Shipping, Receiving, and Traffic Clerks; Stock Clerks and Order Fillers; Stock Clerks—Stockroom, Warehouse, or Storage Yard; Weighers, Measurers, Checkers, and Samplers, Recordkeeping. **PERSONALITY TYPE**—Conventional. Conventional occupations frequently involve following set procedures and routines. These occupations can include working with data and details more than with ideas. Usually there is a clear line of authority to follow.

EDUCATION/TRAINING PROGRAM(S)—Retailing and Retail Operations. **RELATED KNOWLEDGE/COURSES—Clerical Studies:** Knowledge of administrative and clerical procedures and systems, such as word processing, managing files and records, stenography and transcription, designing forms, and other office procedures and terminology. **Mathematics:** Knowledge of arithmetic, algebra, geometry, calculus, and statistics and their applications. **Production and Processing:** Knowledge of raw materials, production processes, quality control, costs, and other techniques for maximizing the effective manufacture and distribution of goods.

Marriage and Family Therapists

- ▲ Education/Training Required: Master's degree
- ▲ Annual Earnings: $32,720
- ▲ Growth: 29.9%
- ▲ Annual Job Openings: 2,000
- ▲ Self-Employed: 0.6%
- ▲ Part-Time: 18.0%

Diagnose and treat mental and emotional disorders, whether cognitive, affective, or behavioral, within the context of marriage and family systems. Apply psychotherapeutic and family systems theories and techniques in the delivery of professional services to individuals, couples, and families for the purpose of treating such diagnosed nervous and mental disorders. SKILLS—No data available.

GOE INFORMATION—**Interest Area:** 12. Education and Social Service. **Work Group:** 12.02. Social Services. **Other Job Titles in This Work Group:** Child, Family, and School Social Workers; Clergy; Clinical Psychologists; Clinical, Counseling, and School Psychologists; Community and Social Service Specialists, All Other; Counseling Psychologists; Counselors, All Other; Directors, Religious Activities and Education; Medical and Public Health Social Workers; Mental Health and Substance Abuse Social Workers; Mental Health Counselors; Probation Officers and Correctional Treatment Specialists; Rehabilitation Counselors; Religious Workers, All Other; Residential Advisors; Social and Human Service Assistants; Social Workers, All Other; Substance Abuse and Behavioral Disorder Counselors. **PERSONALITY TYPE**—No data available.

EDUCATION/TRAINING PROGRAM(S)—Clinical Pastoral Counseling/Patient Counseling; Marriage and Family Therapy/Counseling; Social Work. **RELATED KNOWLEDGE/COURSES**—No data available.

Massage Therapists

- ▲ Education/Training Required: Postsecondary vocational training
- ▲ Annual Earnings: $28,050
- ▲ Growth: 30.4%
- ▲ Annual Job Openings: 7,000
- ▲ Self-Employed: 8.4%
- ▲ Part-Time: 20.8%

Massage customers for hygienic or remedial purposes. **SKILLS**—No data available.

GOE INFORMATION—Interest Area: 14. Medical and Health Services. **Work Group:** 14.06. Medical Therapy. **Other Job Titles in This Work Group:** Audiologists; Occupational Therapist Aides; Occupational Therapist Assistants; Occupational Therapists; Physical Therapist Aides; Physical Therapist Assistants; Physical Therapists; Radiation Therapists; Recreational Therapists; Respiratory Therapists; Respiratory Therapy Technicians; Speech-Language Pathologists; Therapists, All Other. **PERSONALITY TYPE**—No data available.

EDUCATION/TRAINING PROGRAM(S)—Asian Bodywork Therapy; Massage Therapy/Therapeutic Massage; Somatic Bodywork; Somatic Bodywork and Related Therapeutic Services, Other. **RELATED KNOWLEDGE/COURSES**—No data available.

Materials Scientists

- ▲ Education/Training Required: Bachelor's degree
- ▲ Annual Earnings: $62,750
- ▲ Growth: 19.8%
- ▲ Annual Job Openings: 1,000
- ▲ Self-Employed: 7.6%
- ▲ Part-Time: 6.6%

Research and study the structures and chemical properties of various natural and manmade materials, including metals, alloys, rubber, ceramics, semiconductors, polymers, and glass. Determine ways to strengthen or combine materials or develop new materials with new or specific properties for use in a variety of products and applications. Plans laboratory experiments to confirm feasibility of processes and techniques to produce materials having special characteristics. Guides technical staff engaged in developing materials for specific use in projected product or device. Reports materials study findings for other scientists and requesters. Studies structures and properties of materials, such as metals, alloys, polymers, and ceramics, to obtain research data. **SKILLS—Science:** Using scientific rules and methods to solve problems. **Active Learning:** Understanding the implications of new information for both current and future problem-solving and decision-making. **Writing:** Communicating effectively in writing as appropriate for the needs of the audience. **Reading Comprehension:** Understanding written sentences and paragraphs in work-related documents. **Mathematics:** Using mathematics to solve problems.

GOE INFORMATION—Interest Area: 02. Science, Math, and Engineering. **Work Group:** 02.02. Physical Sciences. **Other Job Titles in This Work Group:** Astronomers; Atmospheric and Space Scientists; Chemists; Geographers; Geologists; Geoscientists, Except Hydrologists and Geographers; Hydrologists; Physical Scientists, All Other; Physicists. **PERSONALITY TYPE**—Investigative. Investigative occupations frequently involve working with ideas and require an extensive amount of thinking. These occupations can involve searching for facts and figuring out problems mentally.

EDUCATION/TRAINING PROGRAM(S)—Materials Science. **RELATED KNOWLEDGE/COURSES—Engineering and Technology:** Knowledge of the practical application of engineering science and technology. This includes applying principles, techniques, procedures, and equipment to the design and production of various goods and services. **Mathematics:** Knowledge of arithmetic, algebra, geometry, calculus, and statistics and their applications. **Chemistry:** Knowledge of the chemical composition, structure, and properties of substances and of the chemical processes and transformations that they undergo. This includes uses of chemicals and their interactions, danger signs, production techniques, and disposal methods. **English Lan-** guage: Knowledge of the structure and content of the English language, including the meaning and spelling of words, rules of composition, and grammar. **Physics:** Knowledge and prediction of physical principles and laws and their interrelationships and applications to understanding fluid, material, and atmospheric dynamics and mechanical, electrical, atomic, and sub-atomic structures and processes.

Mathematical Science Teachers, Postsecondary

▲ Education/Training Required: Master's degree
▲ Annual Earnings: $49,420
▲ Growth: 23.5%
▲ Annual Job Openings: 184,000
▲ Self-Employed: 0%
▲ Part-Time: 32.3%

Teach courses pertaining to mathematical concepts, statistics, and actuarial science and to the application of original and standardized mathematical techniques in solving specific problems and situations. Prepares and delivers lectures to students. Acts as adviser to student organizations. Serves on faculty committee providing professional consulting services to government and industry. Advises students on academic and vocational curricula. Compiles, administers, and grades examinations or assigns this work to others. Directs research of other teachers or graduate students working for advanced academic degrees. Compiles bibliographies of specialized materials for outside reading assignments. Conducts research in particular field of knowledge and publishes findings in professional journals. Stimulates class discussions. **SKILLS—Mathematics:** Using mathematics to solve problems. **Reading Comprehension:** Understanding written sentences and paragraphs in work-related documents. **Instructing:** Teaching others how to do something. **Learning Strategies:** Selecting and using training/instructional methods and procedures appropriate for the situation when learning or teaching new things. **Writing:** Communicating effectively in writing as appropriate for the needs of the audience. **Active Learning:** Understanding the implications of new information for both current and future problem-solving and decision-making.

GOE INFORMATION—Interest Area: 12. Education and Social Service. **Work Group:** 12.03. Educational Services. **Other Job Titles in This Work Group:** Adult Literacy, Remedial Education, and GED Teachers and Instructors; Agricultural Sciences Teachers, Postsecondary; Anthropology and Archeology Teachers, Postsecondary; Architecture Teachers, Postsecondary; Archivists; Area, Ethnic, and Cultural Studies Teachers, Postsecondary; Art, Drama, and Music Teachers, Postsecondary; Atmospheric, Earth, Marine, and Space Sciences Teachers, Postsecondary; Audio-Visual Collections Specialists; Biological Science Teachers, Postsecondary; Business Teachers, Postsecondary; Chemistry Teachers, Postsecondary; Child Care Workers; Communications Teachers, Postsecondary; Computer Science Teachers, Postsecondary; Criminal Justice and Law Enforcement Teachers, Postsecondary; Curators; Economics Teachers, Postsecondary; Education Teachers, Postsecondary; Educational Psychologists; Educational, Vocational, and School Counselors; Elementary School Teachers, Except Special Education; Engineering Teachers, Postsecondary; English Language and Literature Teachers, Postsecondary; Environmental Science Teachers, Postsecondary; Farm and Home Management Advisors; Foreign Language and Literature Teachers, Postsecondary; Forestry and Conservation Science Teachers, Postsecondary; Geography Teachers, Postsecondary; Graduate Teaching Assistants; Health Specialties Teachers, Postsecondary; History Teachers, Postsecondary; Home Economics Teachers, Postsecondary; Kindergarten Teachers, Except Special Education; Law Teachers, Postsecondary; Librarians; Library Assistants, Clerical; Library Science Teachers, Postsecondary; Library Technicians; Middle School Teachers, Except Special and Vocational Education; Museum Technicians and Conservators; Nursing Instructors and Teachers, Postsecondary; Personal Financial Advisors; Philosophy and Religion Teachers, Postsecondary; Physics Teachers, Postsecondary; Political Science Teachers, Postsecondary; Postsecondary Teachers, All Other; Preschool Teachers, Except Special

Education; others. **PERSONALITY TYPE**—Investigative. Investigative occupations frequently involve working with ideas and require an extensive amount of thinking. These occupations can involve searching for facts and figuring out problems mentally.

EDUCATION/TRAINING PROGRAM(S)—Algebra and Number Theory; Analysis and Functional Analysis; Applied Mathematics; Business Statistics; Geometry/Geometric Analysis; Logic; Mathematical Statistics and Probability; Mathematics and Statistics, Other; Mathematics, General; Mathematics, Other; Statistics, General; Topology and Foundations. **RELATED KNOWLEDGE/COURSES**—**Mathematics:** Knowledge of arithmetic, algebra, geometry, calculus, and statistics and their applications. **Education and Training:** Knowledge of principles and methods for curriculum and training design, teaching and instruction for individuals and groups, and the measurement of training effects. **English Language:** Knowledge of the structure and content of the English language, including the meaning and spelling of words, rules of composition, and grammar. **Computers and Electronics:** Knowledge of circuit boards, processors, chips, electronic equipment, and computer hardware and software, including applications and programming. **Administration and Management:** Knowledge of business and management principles involved in strategic planning, resource allocation, human resources modeling, leadership technique, production methods, and coordination of people and resources. **Clerical Studies:** Knowledge of administrative and clerical procedures and systems, such as word processing, managing files and records, stenography and transcription, designing forms, and other office procedures and terminology.

Mechanical Drafters

- ▲ Education/Training Required: Postsecondary vocational training
- ▲ Annual Earnings: $39,620
- ▲ Growth: 15.4%
- ▲ Annual Job Openings: 8,000
- ▲ Self-Employed: 3.0%
- ▲ Part-Time: 7.9%

Prepare detailed working diagrams of machinery and mechanical devices, including dimensions, fastening methods, and other engineering information. Develops detailed design drawings and specifications for mechanical equipment, dies/tools, and controls, according to engineering sketches and design proposals. Designs scale or full-size blueprints of specialty items, such as furniture and automobile body or chassis components. Lays out and draws schematic, orthographic, or angle views to depict functional relationships of components, assemblies, systems, and machines. Draws freehand sketches of designs and traces finished drawings onto designated paper for reproduction of blueprints. Shades or colors drawings to clarify and emphasize details and dimensions and eliminate background, using ink, crayon, airbrush, and overlays. Reviews and analyzes specifications, sketches, engineering drawings, ideas, and related design data to determine factors affecting component designs. Modifies and revises designs to correct operating deficiencies or to reduce production problems. Measures machine setup and parts during production to ensure compliance with design specifications, using precision measuring instruments. Directs work activities of detailer and confers with staff and supervisors to resolve design or other problems. Coordinates and works in conjunction with other workers to design, lay out, or detail components and systems. Confers with customer representatives to review schematics and answer questions pertaining to installation of systems. Compiles and analyzes test data to determine effect of machine design on various factors, such as temperature and pressure. Observes setup and gauges during programmed machine or equipment trial run to verify conformance of signals and systems to specifications. Computes mathematical formulas to develop and design detailed specifications for components or machinery, using computer-assisted equipment. Positions instructions and comments onto drawings and illustrates and describes installation and maintenance details. Lays out, draws, and reproduces illustrations for reference manuals and technical publications to describe operation and maintenance of mechanical systems. **SKILLS**—**Mathematics:** Using mathematics to solve problems. **Operations Analysis:** Analyzing needs and product requirements to create a design. **Critical Thinking:** Using logic and reasoning to identify the strengths and weaknesses of alternative solutions, conclusions, or approaches to problems. **Technology Design:** Generating or adapting equipment and technology to serve user needs. **Quality Control Analysis:** Conducting tests and inspections of products, services, or processes to evaluate quality or performance.

GOE INFORMATION—**Interest Area:** 02. Science, Math, and Engineering. **Work Group:** 02.08. Engineering Technology. **Other Job Titles in This Work Group:** Aerospace Engineering and Operations Technicians; Architectural and Civil Drafters; Architectural Drafters; Calibration and Instrumentation Technicians; Cartographers and Photogrammetrists; Civil Drafters; Civil Engineering Technicians; Construction and Building Inspectors; Drafters, All Other; Electrical and Electronic Engineering Technicians; Electrical and Electronics Drafters; Electrical Drafters; Electrical Engineering Technicians; Electro-Mechanical Technicians; Electronic Drafters; Electronics Engineering Technicians; Engineering Technicians, Except Drafters, All Other; Environmental Engineering Technicians; Industrial Engineering Technicians; Mapping Technicians; Mechanical Engineering Technicians; Numerical Tool and Process Control Programmers; Pressure Vessel Inspectors; Surveying and Mapping Technicians; Surveying Technicians; Surveyors. **PERSONALITY TYPE—** Realistic. Realistic occupations frequently involve work activities that include practical, hands-on problems and solutions. They often deal with plants, animals, and real-world materials like wood, tools, and machinery. Many of the occupations require working outside and do not involve a lot of paperwork or working closely with others.

EDUCATION/TRAINING PROGRAM(S)—Mechanical Drafting and Mechanical Drafting CAD/CADD. RELATED KNOWLEDGE/COURSES—**Design:** Knowledge of design techniques, tools, and principles involved in production of precision technical plans, blueprints, drawings, and models. **Engineering and Technology:** Knowledge of the practical application of engineering science and technology. This includes applying principles, techniques, procedures, and equipment to the design and production of various goods and services. **Mathematics:** Knowledge of arithmetic, algebra, geometry, calculus, and statistics and their applications. **English Language:** Knowledge of the structure and content of the English language, including the meaning and spelling of words, rules of composition, and grammar. **Computers and Electronics:** Knowledge of circuit boards, processors, chips, electronic equipment, and computer hardware and software, including applications and programming.

Mechanical Engineering Technicians

- ▲ Education/Training Required: Associate's degree
- ▲ Annual Earnings: $40,910
- ▲ Growth: 13.9%
- ▲ Annual Job Openings: 5,000
- ▲ Self-Employed: 1.9%
- ▲ Part-Time: 7.4%

Apply theory and principles of mechanical engineering to modify, develop, and test machinery and equipment under direction of engineering staff or physical scientists. Reviews project instructions and blueprints to ascertain test specifications, procedures, objectives, and nature of technical problems, such as redesign. Estimates cost factors, including labor and material for purchased and fabricated parts and costs for assembly, testing, and installing. Inspects lines and figures for clarity and returns erroneous drawings to designer for correction. Prepares parts sketches and writes work orders and purchase requests to be furnished by outside contractors. Reads dials and meters to determine amperage, voltage, and electrical out- and input at specific operating temperature to analyze parts performance. Operates drill press, grinders, engine lathe, or other machines to modify parts tested or to fabricate experimental parts for testing. Evaluates tool drawing designs by measuring drawing dimensions and comparing with original specifications for form and function, using engineering skills. Confers with technicians, submits reports of test results to engineering department, and recommends design or material changes. Records test procedures and results, numerical and graphical data, and recommendations for changes in product or test methods. Drafts detail drawing or sketch for drafting room completion or to request parts fabrication by machine, sheet, or wood shops. Calculates required capacities for equipment of proposed system to obtain specified performance and submits data to engineering personnel for approval. Discusses changes in design, method of manufacture and assembly, and drafting techniques and procedures with staff and coordinates corrections. Devises, fabricates, and assembles new or modified mechanical components for products such as industrial machinery or equipment and measuring instruments. Analyzes tests results in relation to design or rated specifications and test objectives and modifies or adjusts equipment to meet specifications. Tests equipment, using test devices attached to generator, voltage regulator, or other electrical parts, such as generators or spark plugs. Reviews project instructions and specifications to identify, modify, and plan requirements fabrication, assembly and testing. Sets up prototype and test apparatus and operates test controlling equipment to observe and record prototype test results. Sets up and conducts tests of complete units and components under operational conditions to investigate proposals for improving equipment performance. **SKILLS—Mathematics:** Using mathematics to solve problems. **Technology Design:** Generating or adapting equipment and technology to serve user needs. **Reading Comprehension:** Understanding written sentences and paragraphs in work-related documents. **Operation and Control:** Controlling operations of equipment or systems. **Active Learning:** Understanding the implications of new information for both current and future problem-solving and decision-making. **Active Listening:** Giving full attention to what other people are saying, taking time to understand the points being made, asking questions as appropriate, and not interrupting at inappropriate times.

GOE INFORMATION—Interest Area: 02. Science, Math, and Engineering. **Work Group:** 02.08. Engineering Technology. **Other Job Titles in This Work Group:** Aerospace Engineering and Operations Technicians; Architectural and Civil Drafters; Architectural Drafters; Calibration and Instrumentation Technicians; Cartographers and Photogrammetrists; Civil Drafters; Civil Engineering Technicians; Construction and Building Inspectors; Drafters, All Other; Electrical and Electronic Engineering Technicians; Electrical and Electronics Drafters; Electrical Drafters; Electrical Engineering Technicians; Electro-Mechanical Technicians; Electronic Drafters; Electronics Engineering Technicians; Engineering Technicians, Except Drafters, All Other; Environmental Engineering Technicians; Industrial Engineering Technicians; Mapping Technicians; Mechanical Drafters; Numerical Tool and Process Control Programmers; Pressure Vessel Inspectors; Surveying and Mapping Technicians; Surveying Technicians; Surveyors. **PERSONALITY TYPE—Realistic.** Realistic occupations frequently involve work activities that include practical, hands-on problems and solutions. They often deal with plants, animals, and real-world materials like wood, tools, and machinery. Many of the occupations require working outside and do not involve a lot of paperwork or working closely with others.

EDUCATION/TRAINING PROGRAM(S)—Mechanical Engineering Related Technologies/Technicians, Other; Mechanical Engineering/Mechanical Technology/Technician. **RELATED KNOWLEDGE/COURSES—Engineering and Technology:** Knowledge of the practical application of engineering science and technology. This includes applying principles, techniques, procedures, and equipment to the design and production of various goods and services. **Principles of Mechanical Devices:** Knowledge of machines and tools, including their designs, uses, repair, and maintenance. **Design:** Knowledge of design techniques, tools, and principles involved in production of precision technical plans, blueprints, drawings, and models. **Mathematics:** Knowledge of arithmetic, algebra, geometry, calculus, and statistics and their applications. **Physics:** Knowledge and prediction of physical principles and laws and their interrelationships and applications to understanding fluid, material, and atmospheric dynamics and mechanical, electrical, atomic, and sub-atomic structures and processes.

Mechanical Engineers

- ▲ Education/Training Required: Bachelor's degree
- ▲ Annual Earnings: $61,440
- ▲ Growth: 13.1%
- ▲ Annual Job Openings: 7,000
- ▲ Self-Employed: 3.5%
- ▲ Part-Time: 2.1%

Perform engineering duties in planning and designing tools, engines, machines, and other mechanically functioning equipment. Oversee installation, operation, maintenance, and repair of such equipment as centralized heat, gas, water, and steam systems. Designs products and systems to meet process requirements, applying knowledge of engineering principles. Oversees installation to ensure that machines and equipment are installed and functioning according to specifications. Specifies system components or directs modification of products to ensure conformance with engineering design and performance specifications. Alters or modifies design to obtain specified functional and operational performance. Assists drafter in developing structural design of product, using drafting tools or computer-assisted design/drafting equipment and software. Selects or designs tools to meet specifications, using manuals, drafting tools, computer, and specialized software programs. Tests ability of machines to perform tasks. Develops models of alternate processing methods to test feasibility or new applications of system components and recommends implementation of procedures. Confers with establishment personnel and engineers to implement operating procedures and resolve system malfunctions and to provide technical information. Plans and directs engineering personnel in fabrication of test control apparatus and equipment and develops procedures for testing products. Researches and analyzes data, such as customer design proposal, specifications, and manuals, to determine feasibility of design or application. Studies industrial processes to determine where and how application of equipment can be made. Investigates equipment failures and difficulties, diagnoses faulty operation, and makes recommendations to maintenance crew. Determines parts supply, maintenance tasks, safety procedures, and service schedule required to maintain machines and equipment in prescribed condition. Conducts experiments to test and analyze existing designs and equipment to obtain data on performance of product and prepares reports. Inspects, evaluates, and arranges field installations and recommends design modifications to eliminate machine or system malfunctions. Coordinates building, fabrication, and installation of product design and operation, maintenance, and repair activities to utilize machines and equipment. **SKILLS—Mathematics:** Using mathematics to solve problems. **Active Learning:** Understanding the implications of new information for both current and future problem-solving and decision-making. **Reading Comprehension:** Understanding written sentences and paragraphs in work-related documents. **Science:** Using scientific rules and methods to solve problems. **Technology Design:** Generating or adapting equipment and technology to serve user needs.

GOE INFORMATION—Interest Area: 02. Science, Math, and Engineering. **Work Group:** 02.07. Engineering. **Other Job Titles in This Work Group:** Aerospace Engineers; Agricultural Engineers; Architects, Except Landscape and Naval; Biomedical Engineers; Chemical Engineers; Civil Engineers; Computer Hardware Engineers; Computer Software Engineers, Applications; Computer Software Engineers, Systems Software; Electrical Engineers; Electronics Engineers, Except Computer; Engineers, All Other; Environmental Engineers; Fire-Prevention and Protection Engineers; Health and Safety Engineers, Except Mining Safety Engineers and Inspectors; Industrial Engineers; Industrial Safety and Health Engineers; Landscape Architects; Marine Architects; Marine Engineers; Marine Engineers and Naval Architects; Materials Engineers; Mining and Geological Engineers, Including Mining Safety Engineers; Nuclear Engineers; Petroleum Engineers; Product Safety Engineers; Sales Engineers. **PERSONALITY TYPE—**Realistic. Realistic occupations frequently involve work activities that include practical, hands-on problems and solutions. They often deal with plants, animals, and real-world materials like wood, tools, and machinery. Many of the occupations require working outside and do not involve a lot of paperwork or working closely with others.

EDUCATION/TRAINING PROGRAM(S)—Mechanical Engineering. **RELATED KNOWLEDGE/COURSES—Engineering and Technology:** Knowledge of the practical application of engineering science and technology. This includes applying principles, techniques, procedures, and equipment to the design and production of various goods and services. **Design:** Knowledge of design techniques, tools, and principles involved in production of precision technical plans, blueprints, drawings, and models. **Mathematics:** Knowledge of arithmetic, algebra, geometry, calculus, and statistics and their applications. **Computers and Electronics:** Knowledge of circuit boards, processors, chips, electronic equipment, and computer hardware and software, including applications and programming. **Physics:** Knowledge and prediction of physical principles and laws and their interrelationships and applications to understanding fluid, material, and atmospheric dynamics and mechanical, electrical, atomic, and sub-atomic structures and processes.

Medical and Clinical Laboratory Technicians

- ▲ Education/Training Required: Associate's degree
- ▲ Annual Earnings: $28,810
- ▲ Growth: 19.0%
- ▲ Annual Job Openings: 19,000
- ▲ Self-Employed: 0.7%
- ▲ Part-Time: 19.5%

Perform routine medical laboratory tests for the diagnosis, treatment, and prevention of disease. May work under the supervision of a medical technologist. Conducts quantitative and qualitative chemical analyses of body fluids, such as blood, urine, and spinal fluid. Conducts blood tests for transfusion purposes. Tests vaccines for sterility and virus inactivity. Draws blood from patient, observing principles of asepsis to obtain blood sample. Prepares standard volumetric solutions and reagents used in testing. Inoculates fertilized eggs, broths, or other bacteriological media with organisms. Incubates bacteria for specified period and prepares vaccines and serums by standard laboratory methods. Performs blood counts, using microscope. **SKILLS—Science:** Using scientific rules and methods to solve problems. **Reading Comprehension:** Understanding written sentences and paragraphs in work-related documents. **Quality Control Analysis:** Conducting tests and inspections of products, services, or processes to evaluate quality or performance. **Mathematics:** Using mathematics to solve problems. **Equipment Selection:** Determining the kind of tools and equipment needed to do a job.

GOE INFORMATION—Interest Area: 14. Medical and Health Services. **Work Group:** 14.05. Medical Technology. **Other Job Titles in This Work Group:** Cardiovascular Technologists and Technicians; Diagnostic Medical Sonographers; Health Technologists and Technicians, All Other; Medical and Clinical Laboratory Technologists; Medical Equipment Preparers; Nuclear Medicine Technologists; Orthotists and Prosthetists; Radiologic Technicians; Radiologic Technologists; Radiologic Technologists

and Technicians. **PERSONALITY TYPE—Realistic.** Realistic occupations frequently involve work activities that include practical, hands-on problems and solutions. They often deal with plants, animals, and real-world materials like wood, tools, and machinery. Many of the occupations require working outside and do not involve a lot of paperwork or working closely with others.

EDUCATION/TRAINING PROGRAM(S)—Blood Bank Technology Specialist; Clinical/Medical Laboratory Assistant; Clinical/Medical Laboratory Technician; Hematology Technology/Technician; Histologic Technician. RELATED KNOWLEDGE/COURSES—Chemistry: Knowledge of the chemical composition, structure, and properties of substances and of the chemical processes and transformations that they undergo. This includes uses of chemicals and their interactions, danger signs, production techniques, and disposal methods. **Biology:** Knowledge of plant and animal organisms and their tissues, cells, functions, interdependencies, and interactions with each other and the environment. **Medicine and Dentistry:** Knowledge of the information and techniques needed to diagnose and treat human injuries, diseases, and deformities. This includes symptoms, treatment alternatives, drug properties and interactions, and preventive health-care measures. **Mathematics:** Knowledge of arithmetic, algebra, geometry, calculus, and statistics and their applications. **Public Safety and Security:** Knowledge of relevant equipment, policies, procedures, and strategies to promote effective local, state, or national security operations for the protection of people, data, property, and institutions.

Medical and Clinical Laboratory Technologists

▲ Education/Training Required: Bachelor's degree
▲ Annual Earnings: $42,240
▲ Growth: 17.0%
▲ Annual Job Openings: 19,000
▲ Self-Employed: 0.7%
▲ Part-Time: 19.5%

Perform complex medical laboratory tests for diagnosis, treatment, and prevention of disease. May train or supervise staff. Cuts, stains, and mounts biological material on slides for microscopic study and diagnosis, following standard laboratory procedures. Analyzes samples of biological material for chemical content or reaction. Harvests cell culture at optimum time sequence based on knowledge of cell cycle differences and culture conditions. Cultivates, isolates, and assists in identifying microbial organisms and performs various tests on these microorganisms. Conducts chemical analysis of body fluids, including blood, urine, and spinal fluid, to determine presence of normal and abnormal components. Sets up, cleans, and maintains laboratory equipment. Enters analysis of medical tests and clinical results into computer for storage. Calibrates and maintains equipment used in quantitative and qualitative analysis, such as spectrophotometers, calorimeters, flame photometers, and computer-controlled analyzers. Communicates with physicians, family members, and researchers requesting technical information regarding test results. Conducts research under direction of microbiologist or biochemist. Cuts images of chromosomes from photograph and identifies and arranges them in numbered pairs on karyotype chart, using standard practices. Studies blood cells, number of blood cells, and morphology, using microscopic technique. Performs tests to determine blood group, type, and compatibility for transfusion purposes. Examines and tests human, animal, or other materials for microbial organisms. Prepares slide of cell culture to identify chromosomes, views and photographs slide under photo-microscope, and prints picture. Selects and prepares specimen and media for cell culture, using aseptic technique and knowledge of medium components and cell requirements. Examines slides under microscope to detect deviations from norm and to report abnormalities for further study. **SKILLS—Reading Comprehension:** Understanding written sentences and paragraphs in work-related documents. **Science:** Using scientific rules and methods to solve problems. **Writing:** Communicating effectively in writing as appropriate for the needs of the audience. **Ac-** tive **Learning:** Understanding the implications of new information for both current and future problem-solving and decision-making. **Speaking:** Talking to others to convey information effectively.

GOE INFORMATION—Interest Area: 14. Medical and Health Services. **Work Group:** 14.05. Medical Technology. **Other Job Titles in This Work Group:** Cardiovascular Technologists and Technicians; Diagnostic Medical Sonographers; Health Technologists and Technicians, All Other; Medical and Clinical Laboratory Technicians; Medical Equipment Preparers; Nuclear Medicine Technologists; Orthotists and Prosthetists; Radiologic Technicians; Radiologic Technologists; Radiologic Technologists and Technicians. **PERSONALITY TYPE—**Investigative. Investigative occupations frequently involve working with ideas and require an extensive amount of thinking. These occupations can involve searching for facts and figuring out problems mentally.

EDUCATION/TRAINING PROGRAM(S)—Clinical Laboratory Science/Medical Technology/Technologist; Clinical/Medical Laboratory Science and Allied Professions, Other; Cytogenetics/Genetics/Clinical Genetics Technology/Technologist; Cytotechnology/Cytotechnologist; Histologic Technology/Histotechnologist; Renal/Dialysis Technologist/Technician. **RELATED KNOWLEDGE/COURSES—Biology:** Knowledge of plant and animal organisms and their tissues, cells, functions, interdependencies, and interactions with each other and the environment. **Chemistry:** Knowledge of the chemical composition, structure, and properties of substances and of the chemical processes and transformations that they undergo. This includes uses of chemicals and their interactions, danger signs, production techniques, and disposal methods. **English Language:** Knowledge of the structure and content of the English language, including the meaning and spelling of words, rules of composition, and grammar. **Medicine and Dentistry:** Knowledge of the information and techniques needed to diagnose and treat human injuries, diseases, and deformities. This includes symptoms, treatment alternatives, drug properties and interactions, and preventive health-care measures. **Education and Training:** Knowledge of principles and methods for curriculum and training design, teaching and instruction for individuals and groups, and the measurement of training effects.

Medical and Health Services Managers

- ▲ Education/Training Required: Work experience plus degree
- ▲ Annual Earnings: $59,220
- ▲ Growth: 32.3%
- ▲ Annual Job Openings: 27,000
- ▲ Self-Employed: 49.4%
- ▲ Part-Time: 7.2%

Plan, direct, or coordinate medicine and health services in hospitals, clinics, managed care organizations, public health agencies, or similar organizations. Administers fiscal operations, such as planning budgets, authorizing expenditures, and coordinating financial reporting. Develops organizational policies and procedures and establishes evaluative or operational criteria for facility or medical unit. Develops or expands medical programs or health services for research, rehabilitation, and community health promotion. Directs and coordinates activities of medical, nursing, technical, clerical, service, and maintenance personnel of health care facility or mobile unit. Implements and administers programs and services for health care or medical facility. Prepares activity reports to inform management of the status and implementation plans of programs, services, and quality initiatives. Reviews and analyzes facility activities and data to aid planning and cash and risk management and to improve service utilization. Develops and maintains computerized records management system to store or process personnel, activity, or personnel data. Inspects facilities for emergency readiness and compliance of access, safety, and sanitation regulations and recommends building or equipment modifications. Develops instructional materials and conducts in-service and community-based educational programs. Consults with medical, business, and community groups to discuss service problems, coordinate activities and plans, and promote health programs. Recruits, hires, and evaluates the performance of medical staff and auxiliary personnel. Establishes work schedules and assignments for staff according to workload, space, and equipment availability. **SKILLS—Systems Evaluation:** Identifying measures or indicators of system performance and the actions needed to improve or correct performance relative to the goals of the system. **Management of Financial Resources:** Determining how money will be spent to get the work done and accounting for these expenditures. **Reading Comprehension:** Understanding written sentences and paragraphs in work-related documents. **Coordination:** Adjusting actions in relation to others' actions. **Management of Personnel Resources:** Motivating, developing, and directing people as they work, identifying the best people for the job. **Writing:** Communicating effectively in writing as appropriate for the needs of the audience. **Systems Analysis:** Determining how a system should work and how changes in conditions, operations, and the environment will affect outcomes.

GOE INFORMATION—Interest Area: 14. Medical and Health Services. **Work Group:** 14.01. Managerial Work in Medical and Health Services. **Other Job Titles in This Work Group:** Coroners. **PERSONALITY TYPE—**Enterprising. Enterprising occupations frequently involve starting up and carrying out projects. These occupations can involve leading people and making many decisions. They sometimes require risk taking and often deal with business.

EDUCATION/TRAINING PROGRAM(S)—Community Health and Preventive Medicine; Health and Medical Administrative Services, Other; Health Information/Medical Records Administration/Administrator; Health Services Administration; Health Unit Manager/Ward Supervisor; Health/Health Care Administration/Management; Hospital and Health Care Facilities Administration/Management; Medical Staff Services Technology/Technician; Nursing Administration (MSN, MS, PhD); Public Health, General (MPH, DPH). **RELATED KNOWLEDGE/ COURSES—Administration and Management:** Knowledge of business and management principles involved in strategic planning, resource allocation, human resources modeling, leadership technique, production methods, and coordination of people and resources. **Personnel and Hu-**

man **Resources:** Knowledge of principles and procedures for personnel recruitment, selection, training, compensation and benefits, labor relations and negotiation, and personnel information systems. **Education and Training:** Knowledge of principles and methods for curriculum and training design, teaching and instruction for individuals and groups, and the measurement of training effects. **Economics and Accounting:** Knowledge of economic and accounting principles and practices, the financial markets, banking, and the analysis and reporting of financial data. **Mathematics:** Knowledge of arithmetic, algebra, geometry, calculus, and statistics and their applications.

Medical and Public Health Social Workers

- ▲ Education/Training Required: Bachelor's degree
- ▲ Annual Earnings: $36,410
- ▲ Growth: 31.6%
- ▲ Annual Job Openings: 13,000
- ▲ Self-Employed: 3.1%
- ▲ Part-Time: 11.9%

Provide persons, families, or vulnerable populations with the psychosocial support needed to cope with chronic, acute, or terminal illnesses, such as Alzheimer's, cancer, or AIDS. Services include advising family caregivers, providing patient education and counseling, and making necessary referrals for other social services. Counsels clients and patients, individually and in group sessions, to assist in overcoming dependencies, adjusting to life, and making changes. Monitors, evaluates, and records client progress according to measurable goals described in treatment and care plan. Refers patient, client, or family to community resources to assist in recovery from mental or physical illness. Plans and conducts programs to prevent substance abuse or improve health and counseling services in community. Supervises and directs other workers providing services to client or patient. Intervenes as advocate for client or patient to resolve emergency problems in crisis situation. Modifies treatment plan to comply with changes in client's status. Formulates or coordinates program plan for treatment, care, and rehabilitation of client or patient, based on social work experience and knowledge. Counsels family members to assist in understanding, dealing with, and supporting client or patient. Interviews clients, reviews records, and confers with other professionals to evaluate mental or physical condition of client or patient. **SKILLS—Social Perceptiveness:** Being aware of others' reactions and understanding why they react as they do. **Critical Thinking:** Using logic and reasoning to identify the strengths and weaknesses of alternative solutions, conclusions, or approaches to problems. **Management of Financial Resources:** Determining how money will be spent to get the work done and accounting for these expenditures. **Reading Comprehension:** Under-

standing written sentences and paragraphs in work-related documents. **Active Listening:** Giving full attention to what other people are saying, taking time to understand the points being made, asking questions as appropriate, and not interrupting at inappropriate times. **Service Orientation:** Actively looking for ways to help people.

GOE INFORMATION—Interest Area: 12. Education and Social Service. **Work Group:** 12.02. Social Services. **Other Job Titles in This Work Group:** Child, Family, and School Social Workers; Clergy; Clinical Psychologists; Clinical, Counseling, and School Psychologists; Community and Social Service Specialists, All Other; Counseling Psychologists; Counselors, All Other; Directors, Religious Activities and Education; Marriage and Family Therapists; Mental Health and Substance Abuse Social Workers; Mental Health Counselors; Probation Officers and Correctional Treatment Specialists; Rehabilitation Counselors; Religious Workers, All Other; Residential Advisors; Social and Human Service Assistants; Social Workers, All Other; Substance Abuse and Behavioral Disorder Counselors. **PERSONALITY TYPE**—Social. Social occupations frequently involve working with, communicating with, and teaching people. These occupations often involve helping or providing service to others.

EDUCATION/TRAINING PROGRAM(S)—Clinical/ Medical Social Work. **RELATED KNOWLEDGE/ COURSES—Therapy and Counseling:** Knowledge of principles, methods, and procedures for diagnosis, treatment, and rehabilitation of physical and mental dysfunctions and for career counseling and guidance. **Customer and Personal Service:** Knowledge of principles and processes for providing customer and personal services. This includes customer needs assessment, meeting quality standards for services, and evaluation of customer satisfaction. **Psychology:** Knowledge of human behavior and performance; individual differences in ability, personality, and interests; learning and motivation; psychological research methods; and the assessment and treatment of behavioral and affective disorders. **Education and Training:** Knowledge of principles and methods for curriculum and training design, teaching and instruction for individuals and groups, and the measurement of training effects. **English Language:** Knowledge of the structure and content of the English language, including the meaning and spelling of words, rules of composition, and grammar.

Medical Assistants

▲ Education/Training Required: Moderate-term on-the-job training
▲ Annual Earnings: $23,610
▲ Growth: 57.0%
▲ Annual Job Openings: 18,700
▲ Self-Employed: 0%
▲ Part-Time: 22.9%

Perform administrative and certain clinical duties under the direction of physician. Administrative duties may include scheduling appointments, maintaining medical records, billing, and coding for insurance purposes. Clinical duties may include taking and recording vital signs and medical histories, preparing patients for examination, drawing blood, and administering medications as directed by physician. Prepares treatment rooms for examination of patients. Hands instruments and materials to physician. Schedules appointments. Maintains medical records. Contacts medical facility or department to schedule patients for tests. Lifts and turns patients. Gives physiotherapy treatments, such as diathermy, galvanics, and hydrotherapy. Receives payment for bills. Performs routine laboratory tests. Gives injections or treatments to patients. Operates X-ray, electrocardiograph (EKG), and other equipment to administer routine diagnostic tests. Completes insurance forms. Computes and mails monthly statements to patients and records transactions. Cleans and sterilizes instruments. Inventories and orders medical supplies and materials. Interviews patients; measures vital signs, weight, and height; and records information. **SKILLS—Reading Comprehension:** Understanding written sentences and paragraphs in work-related documents. **Active Listening:** Giving full attention to what other people are saying, taking time to understand the points being made, asking questions as appropriate, and not interrupting at inappropriate times. **Service Orientation:** Actively looking for ways to help people. **Speaking:** Talking to others to convey information effectively. **Writing:** Communicating effectively in writing as appropriate for the needs of the audience.

GOE INFORMATION—Interest Area: 14. Medical and Health Services. **Work Group:** 14.02. Medicine and Surgery. **Other Job Titles in This Work Group:** Anesthesiologists; Family and General Practitioners; Internists, General; Obstetricians and Gynecologists; Pediatricians, General; Pharmacists; Pharmacy Aides; Pharmacy Technicians; Physician Assistants; Physicians and Surgeons, All Other; Psychiatrists; Registered Nurses; Surgeons; Surgical Technologists. **PERSONALITY TYPE—Social.** Social occupations frequently involve working with, communicating with, and teaching people. These occupations often involve helping or providing service to others.

EDUCATION/TRAINING PROGRAM(S)—Allied Health and Medical Assisting Services, Other; Anesthesiologist Assistant; Chiropractic Assistant/Technician; Medical Administrative/Executive Assistant and Medical Secretary; Medical Insurance Coding Specialist/Coder; Medical Office Assistant/Specialist; Medical Office Management/Administration; Medical Reception/Receptionist; Medical/Clinical Assistant; Opthalmic Technician/Technologist; Optomeric Technician/Assistant; Orthoptics/Orthoptist. **RELATED KNOWLEDGE/ COURSES—Medicine and Dentistry:** Knowledge of the information and techniques needed to diagnose and treat human injuries, diseases, and deformities. This includes symptoms, treatment alternatives, drug properties and interactions, and preventive health-care measures. **Clerical Studies:** Knowledge of administrative and clerical procedures and systems, such as word processing, managing files and records, stenography and transcription, designing forms, and other office procedures and terminology.

Biology: Knowledge of plant and animal organisms and their tissues, cells, functions, interdependencies, and interactions with each other and the environment. **English Language:** Knowledge of the structure and content of the English language, including the meaning and spelling of words, rules of composition, and grammar. **Therapy and Counseling:** Knowledge of principles, methods, and procedures for diagnosis, treatment, and rehabilitation of physical and mental dysfunctions and for career counseling and guidance.

Medical Records and Health Information Technicians

- ▲ Education/Training Required: Associate's degree
- ▲ Annual Earnings: $23,530
- ▲ Growth: 49.0%
- ▲ Annual Job Openings: 14,000
- ▲ Self-Employed: 0%
- ▲ Part-Time: 22.9%

Compile, process, and maintain medical records of hospital and clinic patients in a manner consistent with medical, administrative, ethical, legal, and regulatory requirements of the health care system. Process, maintain, compile, and report patient information for health requirements and standards. Compiles and maintains medical records of patients to document condition and treatment and to provide data for research studies. Maintains variety of health record indexes and storage and retrieval systems. Enters data such as demographic characteristics, history and extent of disease, diagnostic procedures, and treatment into computer. Prepares statistical reports, narrative reports, and graphic presentations of tumor registry data for use by hospital staff, researchers, and other users. Assists in special studies or research as needed. Contacts discharged patients, their families, and physicians to maintain registry with follow-up information, such as quality of life and length of survival of cancer patients. Reviews records for completeness and to abstract and code data, using standard classification systems, and to identify and compile patient data. Compiles medical care and census data for statistical reports on diseases treated, surgery performed, and use of hospital beds. **SKILLS—Reading Comprehension:** Understanding written sentences and paragraphs in work-related documents. **Writing:** Communicating effectively in writing as appropriate for the needs of the audience. **Speaking:** Talking to others to convey information effectively. **Active Listening:** Giving full attention to what other people are saying, taking time to understand the points being made, asking questions as appropriate, and not interrupting at inappropriate times. **Mathematics:** Using mathematics to solve problems.

GOE INFORMATION—Interest Area: 09. Business Detail. **Work Group:** 09.07. Records Processing. **Other Job Titles in This Work Group:** Correspondence Clerks; Court Reporters; Credit Authorizers; Credit Authorizers, Checkers, and Clerks; Credit Checkers; File Clerks; Human Resources Assistants, Except Payroll and Timekeeping; Information and Record Clerks, All Other; Insurance Claims and Policy Processing Clerks; Insurance Claims Clerks; Insurance Policy Processing Clerks; Medical Transcriptionists; Office Clerks, General; Procurement Clerks; Proofreaders and Copy Markers. **PERSONALITY TYPE—Conventional.** Conventional occupations frequently involve following set procedures and routines. These occupations can include working with data and details more than with ideas. Usually there is a clear line of authority to follow.

EDUCATION/TRAINING PROGRAM(S)—Health Information/Medical Records Technology/Technician; Medical Insurance Coding Specialist/Coder. RELATED KNOWLEDGE/COURSES—Clerical Studies: Knowledge of administrative and clerical procedures and systems, such as word processing, managing files and records, stenography and transcription, designing forms, and other office procedures and terminology. **Computers and Electronics:** Knowledge of circuit boards, processors, chips, electronic equipment, and computer hardware and software, including applications and programming. **Mathematics:** Knowledge of arithmetic, algebra, geometry, calculus, and statistics and their applications. **English Language:** Knowledge of the structure and content of the English language, including the meaning and spelling of words, rules of composition, and grammar. **Medicine and Dentistry:** Knowledge of the information and techniques needed to diagnose and treat human injuries, diseases, and deformities. This includes symptoms, treatment alternatives, drug properties and interactions, and preventive health-care measures.

Medical Scientists, Except Epidemiologists

- ▲ Education/Training Required: Doctoral degree
- ▲ Annual Earnings: $55,960
- ▲ Growth: 26.5%
- ▲ Annual Job Openings: 2,000
- ▲ Self-Employed: 2.8%
- ▲ Part-Time: 6.6%

Conduct research dealing with the understanding of human diseases and the improvement of human health. Engage in clinical investigation or other research, production, technical writing, or related activities. Plans and directs studies to investigate human or animal disease, preventive methods, and treatments for disease. Consults with and advises physicians, educators, researchers, and others regarding medical applications of sciences such as physics, biology, and chemistry. Confers with health department, industry personnel, physicians, and others to develop health safety standards and programs to improve public health. Supervises activities of clerical and statistical or laboratory personnel. Teaches principles of medicine and medical and laboratory procedures to physicians, residents, students, and technicians. Standardizes drug dosages, methods of immunization, and procedures for manufacture of drugs and medicinal compounds. Prepares and analyzes samples for toxicity, bacteria, or microorganisms or to study cell structure and properties. Examines organs, tissues, cell structures, or microorganisms by systematic observation or using microscope. Investigates cause, progress, life cycle, or mode of transmission of diseases or parasites. Studies effects of drugs, gases, pesticides, parasites, or microorganisms or health and physiological processes of animals and humans. Plans methodological design of research study and arranges for data collection. Conducts research to develop methodologies; instrumentation; or identification, diagnosing, and treatment procedures for medical application. Analyzes data, applying statistical techniques and scientific knowledge; prepares reports; and presents findings. **SKILLS—Instructing:** Teaching others how to do something. **Active Learning:** Understanding the implications of new information for both current and future problem-solving and decision-making. **Reading Comprehension:** Understanding written sentences and paragraphs in work-related documents. **Writing:** Communicating effectively in writing as appro-

priate for the needs of the audience. **Science:** Using scientific rules and methods to solve problems.

GOE INFORMATION—Interest Area: 02. Science, Math, and Engineering. **Work Group:** 02.03. Life Sciences. **Other Job Titles in This Work Group:** Agricultural and Food Science Technicians; Agricultural Technicians; Animal Scientists; Biochemists; Biochemists and Biophysicists; Biological Scientists, All Other; Biologists; Biophysicists; Conservation Scientists; Environmental Scientists and Specialists, Including Health; Epidemiologists; Food Science Technicians; Food Scientists and Technologists; Foresters; Life Scientists, All Other; Microbiologists; Plant Scientists; Range Managers; Soil and Plant Scientists; Soil Conservationists; Soil Scientists; Zoologists and Wildlife Biologists. **PERSONALITY TYPE—**Investigative. Investigative occupations frequently involve working with ideas and require an extensive amount of thinking. These occupations can involve searching for facts and figuring out problems mentally.

EDUCATION/TRAINING PROGRAM(S)— Anatomy; Biochemistry; Biomedical Sciences, General; Biophysics; Biostatistics; Cardiovascular Science; Cell Physiology; Cell/Cellular Biology and Histology; Endocrinology; Environmental Toxicology; Epidemiology; Exercise Physiology; Human/Medical Genetics; Immunology; Medical Microbiology and Bacteriology; Medical Scientist (MS, PhD); Molecular Biology; Molecular Pharmacology; Molecular Physiology; Molecular Toxicology; Neurobiology and Neurophysiology; Neuropharmacology; Oncology and Cancer Biology; Pathology/Experimental Pathology; Pharmacology; Pharmacology and Toxicology; Pharmacology and Toxicology, Other; Physiology, General; Physiology, Pathology, and Related Sciences, Other; Reproductive Biology; Toxicology; Vision Science/Physiological Optics. **RELATED KNOWLEDGE/COURSES—Mathematics:** Knowledge of arithmetic, algebra, geometry, calculus, and statistics and their applications. **Biology:** Knowledge of plant and animal organisms and their tissues, cells, functions, interdependencies, and interactions with each other and the environment. **Chemistry:** Knowledge of the chemical composition, structure, and properties of substances and of the chemical processes and transformations that they undergo. This includes uses of chemicals and their interactions, danger signs, production techniques, and disposal methods. **Computers and Electronics:** Knowledge of circuit boards, processors, chips, electronic equipment, and computer hardware and software, including applications and programming. **English Language:** Knowledge of the structure and content of the English language, including the meaning and spelling of words, rules of composition, and grammar. **Medicine and Dentistry:** Knowledge of the information and techniques needed to diagnose and treat human injuries, diseases, and deformities. This includes symptoms, treatment alternatives, drug properties and interactions, and preventive health-care measures.

Medical Secretaries

- ▲ Education/Training Required: Postsecondary vocational training
- ▲ Annual Earnings: $24,670
- ▲ Growth: 19.0%
- ▲ Annual Job Openings: 40,000
- ▲ Self-Employed: 0%
- ▲ Part-Time: 19.8%

Perform secretarial duties utilizing specific knowledge of medical terminology and hospital, clinic, or laboratory procedures. Duties include scheduling appointments; billing patients; and compiling and recording medical charts, reports, and correspondence. Compiles and records medical charts, reports, and correspondence, using typewriter or personal computer. Transcribes recorded messages and practitioner's diagnosis and recommendations into patient's medical record. Transmits correspondence and medical records by mail, e-mail, or fax. Greets visitors, ascertains purpose of visits, and directs to appropriate staff. Routes messages and documents such as laboratory results to appropriate staff. Prepares and transmits patients' bills. Maintains medical records and correspondence files. Answers telephone and directs call to appropriate staff. Schedules patient diagnostic appointments and medical consultations. Takes dictation in shorthand. **SKILLS—Active Listening:** Giving full attention to what other people are saying, taking time to understand the points being made, asking questions as appropriate, and not interrupting at inappropriate times. **Reading Comprehension:** Understanding written sentences and paragraphs in work-related documents. **Writing:** Communicating effectively in writing as appropriate for the needs of the audience. **Speaking:** Talking to others to convey information effectively. **Coordination:** Adjusting actions in relation to others' actions.

GOE INFORMATION—Interest Area: 09. Business Detail. **Work Group:** 09.02. Administrative Detail. **Other Job Titles in This Work Group:** Claims Takers, Unemployment Benefits; Court Clerks; Court, Municipal, and License Clerks; Eligibility Interviewers, Government Programs; Executive Secretaries and Administrative Assistants; Interviewers, Except Eligibility and Loan; Legal Secretaries; License Clerks; Loan Interviewers and Clerks; Municipal Clerks; Secretaries, Except Legal, Medical, and Executive; Welfare Eligibility Workers and Interviewers. **PERSONALITY TYPE—Conventional.** Conventional occupations frequently involve following set procedures and routines. These occupations can include working with data and details more than with ideas. Usually there is a clear line of authority to follow.

EDUCATION/TRAINING PROGRAM(S)—Medical Administrative/Executive Assistant and Medical Secretary; Medical Insurance Specialist/Medical Biller; Medical Office Assistant/Specialist. RELATED KNOWLEDGE/COURSES—Clerical Studies: Knowledge of administrative and clerical procedures and systems, such as word processing, managing files and records, stenography and transcription, designing forms, and other office procedures and terminology. **Computers and Electronics:** Knowledge of circuit boards, processors, chips, electronic equipment, and computer hardware and software, including applications and programming. **English Language:** Knowledge of the structure and content of the English language, including the meaning and spelling of words, rules of composition, and grammar. **Mathematics:** Knowledge of arithmetic, algebra, geometry, calculus, and statistics and their applications. **Customer and Personal Service:** Knowledge of principles and processes for providing customer and personal services. This includes customer needs assessment, meeting quality standards for services, and evaluation of customer satisfaction.

Medical Transcriptionists

- ▲ Education/Training Required: Associate's degree
- ▲ Annual Earnings: $26,460
- ▲ Growth: 29.8%
- ▲ Annual Job Openings: 15,000
- ▲ Self-Employed: 0%
- ▲ Part-Time: 22.9%

Use transcribing machines with headset and foot pedal to listen to recordings by physicians and other health care professionals dictating a variety of medical reports, such as emergency room visits, diagnostic imaging studies, operations, chart reviews, and final summaries. Transcribe dictated reports and translate medical jargon and abbreviations into their expanded forms. Edit as necessary and return reports in either printed or electronic form to the dictator for review and signature or correction. **SKILLS**—No data available.

GOE INFORMATION—**Interest Area:** 09. Business Detail. **Work Group:** 09.07. Records Processing. **Other Job Titles in This Work Group:** Correspondence Clerks; Court Reporters; Credit Authorizers; Credit Authorizers, Checkers, and Clerks; Credit Checkers; File Clerks; Human Resources Assistants, Except Payroll and Timekeeping; Information and Record Clerks, All Other; Insurance Claims and Policy Processing Clerks; Insurance Claims Clerks; Insurance Policy Processing Clerks; Medical Records and Health Information Technicians; Office Clerks, General; Procurement Clerks; Proofreaders and Copy Markers. **PERSONALITY TYPE**—No data available.

EDUCATION/TRAINING PROGRAM(S)—Medical Transcription/Transcriptionist. **RELATED KNOWLEDGE/COURSES**—No data available.

Meeting and Convention Planners

- ▲ Education/Training Required: Bachelor's degree
- ▲ Annual Earnings: $36,550
- ▲ Growth: 23.3%
- ▲ Annual Job Openings: 3,000
- ▲ Self-Employed: 5.4%
- ▲ Part-Time: 7.7%

Coordinate activities of staff and convention personnel to make arrangements for group meetings and conventions. Directs and coordinates activities of staff and convention personnel to make arrangements, prepare facilities, and provide services for events. Reads trade publications, attends seminars, and consults with other meeting professionals to keep abreast of meeting management standards and trends. Maintains records of events. Reviews bills for accuracy and approves payment. Obtains permits from fire and health departments to erect displays and exhibits and serve food at events. Speaks with attendees and resolves complaints to maintain goodwill. Inspects rooms and displays for conformance to customer requirements and conducts post-meeting evaluations to improve future events. Negotiates contracts with such providers as hotels, convention centers, and speakers. Evaluates and selects providers of services such as meeting facilities, speakers, and transportation according to customer requirements. Consults with customer to determine objectives and requirements for events such as meetings, conferences, and conventions. Plans and develops programs; budgets; and services such as lodging, catering, and entertainment according to customer requirements. **SKILLS—Coordination:** Adjusting actions in relation to others' actions.

Management of Personnel Resources: Motivating, developing, and directing people as they work, identifying the best people for the job. **Service Orientation:** Actively looking for ways to help people. **Speaking:** Talking to others to convey information effectively. **Writing:** Communicating effectively in writing as appropriate for the needs of the audience. **Active Listening:** Giving full attention to what other people are saying, taking time to understand the points being made, asking questions as appropriate, and not interrupting at inappropriate times.

GOE INFORMATION—Interest Area: 11. Recreation, Travel, and Other Personal Services. **Work Group:** 11.01. Managerial Work in Recreation, Travel, and Other Personal Services. **Other Job Titles in This Work Group:** Aircraft Cargo Handling Supervisors; First-Line Supervisors/Managers of Food Preparation and Serving Workers; First-Line Supervisors/Managers of Housekeeping and Janitorial Workers; First-Line Supervisors/Managers of Personal Service Workers; Food Service Managers; Gaming Managers; Gaming Supervisors; Housekeeping Supervisors; Janitorial Supervisors; Lodging Managers. **PERSONALITY TYPE—Enterprising.** Enterprising occupations frequently involve starting up and carrying out projects. These occupations can involve leading people and making many decisions. They sometimes require risk taking and often deal with business.

EDUCATION/TRAINING PROGRAM(S)—Selling Skills and Sales Operations. **RELATED KNOWLEDGE/COURSES—Administration and Management:** Knowledge of business and management principles involved in strategic planning, resource allocation, human resources modeling, leadership technique, production methods, and coordination of people and resources. **Customer and Personal Service:** Knowledge of principles and processes for providing customer and personal services. This includes customer needs assessment, meeting quality standards for services, and evaluation of customer satisfaction. **English Language:** Knowledge of the structure and content of the English language, including the meaning and spelling of words, rules of composition, and grammar. **Sales and Marketing:** Knowledge of principles and methods for showing, promoting, and selling products or services. This includes marketing strategy and tactics, product demonstration, sales techniques, and sales control systems. **Communications and Media:** Knowledge of media production, communication, and dissemination techniques and methods. This includes alternative ways to inform and entertain via written, oral, and visual media.

Mental Health and Substance Abuse Social Workers

- ▲ Education/Training Required: Master's degree
- ▲ Annual Earnings: $32,080
- ▲ Growth: 39.1%
- ▲ Annual Job Openings: 10,000
- ▲ Self-Employed: 3.1%
- ▲ Part-Time: 11.9%

Assess and treat individuals with mental, emotional, or substance abuse problems, including abuse of alcohol, tobacco, and/or other drugs. Activities may include individual and group therapy, crisis intervention, case management, client advocacy, prevention, and education. Counsels clients and patients, individually and in group sessions, to assist in overcoming dependencies, adjusting to life, and making changes. Refers patient, client, or family to community resources to assist in recovery from mental or physical illness. Plans and conducts programs to prevent substance abuse or improve health and counseling services in community. Supervises and directs other workers providing services to client or patient. Intervenes as advocate for client or patient to resolve emergency problems in crisis situation. Modifies treatment plan to comply with changes in client's status. Interviews clients, reviews records, and confers with other professionals to evaluate mental or physical condition of client or patient. Formulates or coordinates program plan for treatment, care, and rehabilitation of client or patient based on social work experience and knowledge. Monitors, evaluates, and records client progress according to measurable goals described in treatment and care plan. Counsels family members to assist in understanding, dealing with, and supporting client or patient. **SKILLS—Social Perceptiveness:** Being aware of others' reactions and understanding why they react as they do. **Service Orientation:** Actively looking for ways to help people. **Critical Thinking:** Using logic and reasoning to identify the strengths and weaknesses of alternative solutions, conclusions, or approaches to problems. **Management of Financial Resources:** Determining how money will be spent to get the work done and accounting for these expenditures. **Active Listening:** Giving full attention to what other people are saying, taking time to understand the points being made, asking questions as appropriate, and not interrupting at inappropriate times. **Reading Comprehension:** Understanding written sentences and paragraphs in work-related documents.

GOE INFORMATION—Interest Area: 12. Education and Social Service. **Work Group:** 12.02. Social Services. **Other Job Titles in This Work Group:** Child, Family, and School Social Workers; Clergy; Clinical Psychologists; Clinical, Counseling, and School Psychologists; Community and Social Service Specialists, All Other; Counseling Psychologists; Counselors, All Other; Directors, Religious Activities and Education; Marriage and Family Therapists; Medical and Public Health Social Workers; Mental Health Counselors; Probation Officers and Correctional Treatment Specialists; Rehabilitation Counselors; Religious Workers, All Other; Residential Advisors; Social and Human Service Assistants; Social Workers, All Other; Substance Abuse and Behavioral Disorder Counselors. **PERSONALITY TYPE—**Social. Social occupations frequently involve working with, communicating with, and teaching people. These occupations often involve helping or providing service to others.

EDUCATION/TRAINING PROGRAM(S)—Clinical/Medical Social Work. **RELATED KNOWLEDGE/COURSES—Therapy and Counseling:** Knowledge of principles, methods, and procedures for diagnosis, treatment, and rehabilitation of physical and mental dysfunctions and for career counseling and guidance. **Psychology:** Knowledge of human behavior and performance; individual differences in ability, personality, and interests; learning and motivation; psychological research methods; and the assessment and treatment of behavioral and affective disorders. **Customer and Personal Service:** Knowledge of principles and processes for providing customer and personal services. This includes customer needs assessment, meeting quality standards for services, and evaluation of customer satisfaction. **Education and Training:** Knowledge of principles and methods for curriculum and training design, teaching and instruction for individuals and groups, and the measurement of training effects. **English Language:** Knowledge of the structure and content of the English language, including the meaning and spelling of words, rules of composition, and grammar.

Mental Health Counselors

- ▲ Education/Training Required: Master's degree
- ▲ Annual Earnings: $29,050
- ▲ Growth: 21.7%
- ▲ Annual Job Openings: 7,000
- ▲ Self-Employed: 0.6%
- ▲ Part-Time: 18.0%

Counsel with emphasis on prevention. Work with individuals and groups to promote optimum mental health. May help individuals deal with addictions and substance abuse; family, parenting, and marital problems; suicide; stress management; problems with self-esteem; and issues associated with aging and mental and emotional health. Counsels clients and patients, individually and in group sessions, to assist in overcoming dependencies, adjusting to life, and making changes. Modifies treatment plan to comply with changes in client's status. Intervenes as advocate for client or patient to resolve emergency problems in crisis situation. Supervises and directs other workers providing services to client or patient. Plans and conducts programs to prevent substance abuse or improve health and counseling services in community. Refers patient, client, or family to community resources to assist in recovery from mental or physical illness. Monitors, evaluates, and records client progress according to measurable goals described in treatment and care plan. Counsels family members to assist in understanding, dealing with, and supporting client or patient. Formulates or coordinates program plan for treatment, care, and rehabilitation of client or patient, based on social work experience and knowledge. Interviews clients, reviews records, and confers with other professionals to evaluate mental or physical condition of client or patient. **SKILLS—Social Perceptiveness:** Being aware of others' reactions and understanding why they react as they do. **Service Orientation:** Actively looking for ways to help people. **Management of Financial Resources:** Determining how money will be spent to get the work done and accounting for these expenditures. **Critical Thinking:** Using logic and reasoning to identify the strengths and weaknesses of alternative solutions, conclusions, or approaches to problems. **Active Listening:** Giving full attention to what other people are saying, taking time to understand the points being made, asking questions as appropriate, and not interrupting at inappropriate times. **Reading Comprehension:** Understanding written sentences and paragraphs in work-related documents.

GOE INFORMATION—Interest Area: 12. Education and Social Service. **Work Group:** 12.02. Social Services. **Other Job Titles in This Work Group:** Child, Family, and School Social Workers; Clergy; Clinical Psychologists; Clinical, Counseling, and School Psychologists; Community and Social Service Specialists, All Other; Counseling Psychologists; Counselors, All Other; Directors, Religious Activities and Education; Marriage and Family Therapists; Medical and Public Health Social Workers; Mental Health and Substance Abuse Social Workers; Probation Officers and Correctional Treatment Specialists; Rehabilitation Counselors; Religious Workers, All Other; Residential Advisors; Social and Human Service Assistants; Social Workers, All Other; Substance Abuse and Behavioral Disorder Counselors. **PERSONALITY TYPE—Social.** Social occupations frequently involve working with,

communicating with, and teaching people. These occupations often involve helping or providing service to others.

EDUCATION/TRAINING PROGRAM(S)—Clinical/Medical Social Work; Mental and Social Health Services and Allied Professions, Other; Mental Health Counseling/Counselor; Substance Abuse/Addiction Counseling. **RELATED KNOWLEDGE/COURSES—Therapy and Counseling:** Knowledge of principles, methods, and procedures for diagnosis, treatment, and rehabilitation of physical and mental dysfunctions and for career counseling and guidance. **Customer and Personal Service:** Knowledge of principles and processes for providing customer and personal services. This includes customer needs assessment, meeting quality standards for services, and evaluation of customer satisfaction. **Psychology:** Knowledge of human behavior and performance; individual differences in ability, personality, and interests; learning and motivation; psychological research methods; and the assessment and treatment of behavioral and affective disorders. **Education and Training:** Knowledge of principles and methods for curriculum and training design, teaching and instruction for individuals and groups, and the measurement of training effects. **English Language:** Knowledge of the structure and content of the English language, including the meaning and spelling of words, rules of composition, and grammar.

Metal Fabricators, Structural Metal Products

- ▲ Education/Training Required: Moderate-term on-the-job training
- ▲ Annual Earnings: $28,000
- ▲ Growth: 19.5%
- ▲ Annual Job Openings: 20,000
- ▲ Self-Employed: 0%
- ▲ Part-Time: 2.3%

Fabricate and assemble structural metal products, such as frameworks or shells for machinery, ovens, tanks, and stacks and metal parts for buildings and bridges according to job order or blueprints. Develops layout and plans sequence of operations for fabricating and assembling structural metal products, applying trigonometry and knowledge of metal. Locates and marks bending and cutting lines onto workpiece, allowing for stock thickness and machine and welding shrinkage. Hammers, chips, and grinds workpiece to cut, bend, and straighten metal. Verifies conformance of workpiece to specifications, using square, ruler, and measuring tape. Preheats workpieces to render them malleable, using hand torch or furnace. Posi-

tions, aligns, fits, and welds together parts, using jigs, welding torch, and hand tools. Sets up and operates fabricating machines, such as brakes, rolls, shears, flame cutters, and drill presses. Sets up and operates machine tools associated with fabricating shops, such as radial drill, end mill, and edge planer. Designs and constructs templates and fixtures, using hand tools. **SKILLS—Mathematics:** Using mathematics to solve problems. **Operation and Control:** Controlling operations of equipment or systems. **Equipment Selection:** Determining the kind of tools and equipment needed to do a job. **Quality Control Analysis:** Conducting tests and inspections of products, services, or processes to evaluate quality or performance. **Operations**

Analysis: Analyzing needs and product requirements to create a design.

GOE INFORMATION—Interest Area: 08. Industrial Production. **Work Group:** 08.03. Production Work. **Other Job Titles in This Work Group:** Bakers, Manufacturing; Bindery Machine Operators and Tenders; Brazers; Cementing and Gluing Machine Operators and Tenders; Chemical Equipment Controllers and Operators; Chemical Equipment Operators and Tenders; Chemical Equipment Tenders; Cleaning, Washing, and Metal Pickling Equipment Operators and Tenders; Coating, Painting, and Spraying Machine Operators and Tenders; Coil Winders, Tapers, and Finishers; Combination Machine Tool Operators and Tenders, Metal and Plastic; Computer-Controlled Machine Tool Operators, Metal and Plastic; Cooling and Freezing Equipment Operators and Tenders; Crushing, Grinding, and Polishing Machine Setters, Operators, and Tenders; Cutters and Trimmers, Hand; Cutting and Slicing Machine Operators and Tenders; Cutting and Slicing Machine Setters, Operators, and Tenders; Design Printing Machine Setters and Set-Up Operators; Electrolytic Plating and Coating Machine Operators and Tenders, Metal and Plastic; Electrolytic Plating and Coating Machine Setters and Set-Up Operators, Metal and Plastic; Electrotypers and Stereotypers; Embossing Machine Set-Up Operators; Engraver Set-Up Operators; Extruding and Forming Machine Operators and Tenders, Synthetic or Glass Fibers; Extruding and Forming Machine Setters, Operators, and Tenders, Synthetic and Glass Fibers; Extruding, Forming, Pressing, and Compacting Machine Operators and Tenders; Fabric and Apparel Patternmakers; Fiber Product Cutting Machine Setters and Set-Up Operators; Fiberglass Laminators and Fabricators; Film Laboratory Technicians; Fitters, Structural Metal—Precision; Food and Tobacco Roasting, Baking, and Drying Machine Operators and Tenders; Food Batchmakers; Food Cooking Machine Operators and Tenders; Furnace, Kiln, Oven, Drier, and Kettle Operators and Tenders; Glass Cutting Machine Setters and Set-Up Operators; Graders and Sorters, Agricultural Products; Grinding and Polishing Workers, Hand; Hand Compositors and Typesetters; Heaters, Metal and Plastic; others. **PERSONALITY TYPE**—Realistic. Realistic occupations frequently involve work activities that include practical, hands-on problems and solutions. They often deal with plants, animals, and real-world materials like wood, tools, and machinery. Many of the occupations require working outside and do not involve a lot of paperwork or working closely with others.

EDUCATION/TRAINING PROGRAM(S)—Machine Shop Technology/Assistant. **RELATED KNOWLEDGE/ COURSES—Principles of Mechanical Devices:** Knowledge of machines and tools, including their designs, uses, repair, and maintenance. **Building and Construction:** Knowledge of materials, methods, and tools involved in the construction or repair of houses, buildings, or other structures, such as highways and roads. **Design:** Knowledge of design techniques, tools, and principles involved in production of precision technical plans, blueprints, drawings, and models. **Production and Processing:** Knowledge of raw materials, production processes, quality control, costs, and other techniques for maximizing the effective manufacture and distribution of goods. **Engineering and Technology:** Knowledge of the practical application of engineering science and technology. This includes applying principles, techniques, procedures, and equipment to the design and production of various goods and services.

Metal Molding, Coremaking, and Casting Machine Operators and Tenders

- ▲ Education/Training Required: Short-term on-the-job training
- ▲ Annual Earnings: $22,340
- ▲ Growth: 9.8%
- ▲ Annual Job Openings: 38,000
- ▲ Self-Employed: 0%
- ▲ Part-Time: 2.6%

Operate or tend metal molding, casting, or coremaking machines to mold or cast metal products, such as pipes, brake drums, and rods, and metal parts, such as automobile trim, carburetor housings, and motor parts. Machines include centrifugal casting machines, vacuum casting machines, turnover draw-type coremaking machines, conveyor-screw coremaking machines, and die casting machines. Starts and operates furnace, oven, diecasting, coremaking, metal molding, or rotating machines to pour metal or create molds and casts. Removes casting from mold, mold from press, or core from core box, using tongs, pliers, or hydraulic ram or by inversion.

Pours or loads metal or sand into melting pot, furnace, mold, core box, or hopper, using shovel, ladle, or machine. Inspects metal casts and molds for cracks, bubbles, or other defects and measures castings to ensure that specifications are met. Cleans, glues, and racks cores, ingots, or finished products for storage. Cuts spouts and pouring holes in molds and sizes hardened cores, using saws. Signals or directs other workers to load conveyor, spray molds, or remove ingots. Requisitions molds and supplies; inventories and records finished products. Weighs metals and powders and computes amounts of materials necessary to produce mixture of specified content. Smoothes and cleans inner surface of mold, using brush, scraper, air hose, or grinding wheel, and fills imperfections with refractory material. Sprays, smokes, or coats molds with compounds to lubricate or insulate mold, using acetylene torches or sprayers. Skims or pours dross, slag, or impurities from molten metal, using ladle, rake, hoe, spatula, or spoon. Assembles shell halves, patterns, and foundry flasks and reinforces core boxes, using glue, clamps, wire, bolts, rams, or machines. Repairs or replaces damaged molds, pipes, belts, chains, or other equipment, using hand tools, hand-powered press, or jib crane. Fills core boxes and mold patterns with sand or powders, using ramming tools or pneumatic hammers, and removes excess. Observes and records data from pyrometers, lights, and gauges to monitor molding process and adjust furnace temperature. Positions, aligns, and secures molds or core boxes in holding devices or under pouring spouts and tubes, using hand tools. Positions ladles or pourers and adjusts controls to regulate the flow of metal, sand, or coolant into mold. **SKILLS—Operation and Control:** Controlling operations of equipment or systems. **Operation Monitoring:** Watching gauges, dials, or other indicators to make sure a machine is working properly. **Quality Control Analysis:** Conducting tests and inspections of products, services, or processes to evaluate quality or performance. **Equipment Maintenance:** Performing routine maintenance on equipment and determining when and what kind of maintenance is needed. **Repairing:** Repairing machines or systems, using the needed tools.

GOE INFORMATION—Interest Area: 08. Industrial Production. **Work Group:** 08.02. Production Technology. **Other Job Titles in This Work Group:** Aircraft Rigging Assemblers; Aircraft Structure Assemblers, Precision; Aircraft Structure, Surfaces, Rigging, and Systems Assemblers; Aircraft Systems Assemblers, Precision; Bench Workers, Jewelry; Bindery Machine Setters and Set-Up Operators;

Bindery Workers; Bookbinders; Buffing and Polishing Set-Up Operators; Casting Machine Set-Up Operators; Coating, Painting, and Spraying Machine Setters and Set-Up Operators; Coating, Painting, and Spraying Machine Setters, Operators, and Tenders; Combination Machine Tool Setters and Set-Up Operators, Metal and Plastic; Cutting, Punching, and Press Machine Setters, Operators, and Tenders, Metal and Plastic; Dental Laboratory Technicians; Drilling and Boring Machine Tool Setters, Operators, and Tenders, Metal and Plastic; Electrical and Electronic Equipment Assemblers; Electrical and Electronic Inspectors and Testers; Electromechanical Equipment Assemblers; Engine and Other Machine Assemblers; Extruding and Drawing Machine Setters, Operators, and Tenders, Metal and Plastic; Extruding, Forming, Pressing, and Compacting Machine Setters and Set-Up Operators; Extruding, Forming, Pressing, and Compacting Machine Setters, Operators, and Tenders; Forging Machine Setters, Operators, and Tenders, Metal and Plastic; Foundry Mold and Coremakers; Gem and Diamond Workers; Grinding, Honing, Lapping, and Deburring Machine Set-Up Operators; Grinding, Lapping, Polishing, and Buffing Machine Tool Setters, Operators, and Tenders, Metal and Plastic; Heat Treating Equipment Setters, Operators, and Tenders, Metal and Plastic; Heat Treating, Annealing, and Tempering Machine Operators and Tenders, Metal and Plastic; Heating Equipment Setters and Set-Up Operators, Metal and Plastic; Inspectors, Testers, Sorters, Samplers, and Weighers; Jewelers; Jewelers and Precious Stone and Metal Workers; Lathe and Turning Machine Tool Setters, Operators, and Tenders, Metal and Plastic; Log Graders and Scalers; Materials Inspectors; Mechanical Inspectors; others. **PERSONALITY TYPE—**Realistic. Realistic occupations frequently involve work activities that include practical, hands-on problems and solutions. They often deal with plants, animals, and real-world materials like wood, tools, and machinery. Many of the occupations require working outside and do not involve a lot of paperwork or working closely with others.

EDUCATION/TRAINING PROGRAM(S)—No data available. **RELATED KNOWLEDGE/COURSES—Principles of Mechanical Devices:** Knowledge of machines and tools, including their designs, uses, repair, and maintenance. **Production and Processing:** Knowledge of raw materials, production processes, quality control, costs, and other techniques for maximizing the effective manufacture and distribution of goods. **Building and Construction:** Knowledge of materials, methods, and tools involved in the construction or repair of houses, buildings, or other structures, such as highways and roads. **Mathematics:** Knowledge of arithmetic, algebra, geometry, calculus, and statistics and their applications. **Engineering and Tech-** **nology:** Knowledge of the practical application of engineering science and technology. This includes applying principles, techniques, procedures, and equipment to the design and production of various goods and services.

Metal Molding, Coremaking, and Casting Machine Setters and Set-Up Operators

- ▲ Education/Training Required: Moderate-term on-the-job training
- ▲ Annual Earnings: $22,340
- ▲ Growth: 9.8%
- ▲ Annual Job Openings: 38,000
- ▲ Self-Employed: 0%
- ▲ Part-Time: 2.6%

Set up or set up and operate metal casting, molding, and coremaking machines to mold or cast metal parts and products, such as tubes, rods, automobile trim, carburetor housings, and motor parts. **Machines include die casting and continuous casting machines and roll-over, squeeze, and shell molding machines.** Moves controls to start, set, or adjust casting, molding, or pressing machines. Cleans and lubricates casting machine and dies, using air hose and brushes. Inspects castings and core slots for defects, using fixed gauges. Repairs or replaces worn or defective machine parts and dies. Obtains and moves specified pattern to work station manually or using hoist and secures pattern to machine, using wrenches. Removes castings from dies and dips castings in water to cool, using pliers or tongs. Preheats die sections with torch or electric heater. Pours molten metal into cold-chamber machine or cylinders, using hand ladle. Connects water hose to cooling system of die, using hand tools. Loads metal ingots or aluminum bars into melting furnace and transfers molten metal to reservoir of die casting machine. Stacks and mounts rotor core laminations over keyed mandrel of casting machine and removes and stamps rotor with identifying data. Lines cylinder pot with asbestos strips and disk to prevent chilling. Loads die sections into machine, using equipment such as chain fall or hoist, and secures in position, using hand tools. **SKILLS—Equipment Selection:** Determining the kind of tools and equipment needed to do a job. **Operation Monitoring:** Watching gauges, dials, or other indicators to make sure a machine is working properly. **Operation and Control:** Controlling operations of equipment or systems. **Equipment Maintenance:** Performing routine maintenance on equipment and determining when and what kind of maintenance is needed. **Quality Control Analysis:** Conducting tests and inspections of products, services, or processes to evaluate quality or performance.

GOE INFORMATION—Interest Area: 08. Industrial Production. **Work Group:** 08.02. Production Technology. **Other Job Titles in This Work Group:** Aircraft Rigging Assemblers; Aircraft Structure Assemblers, Precision; Aircraft Structure, Surfaces, Rigging, and Systems Assemblers; Aircraft Systems Assemblers, Precision; Bench Workers, Jewelry; Bindery Machine Setters and Set-Up Operators; Bindery Workers; Bookbinders; Buffing and Polishing Set-Up Operators; Casting Machine Set-Up Operators; Coating, Painting, and Spraying Machine Setters and Set-Up Operators; Coating, Painting, and Spraying Machine Setters, Operators, and Tenders; Combination Machine Tool Setters and Set-Up Operators, Metal and Plastic; Cutting, Punching, and Press Machine Setters, Operators, and Tenders, Metal and Plastic; Dental Laboratory Technicians; Drilling and Boring Machine Tool Setters, Operators, and Tenders, Metal and Plastic; Electrical and Electronic Equipment Assemblers; Electrical and Electronic Inspectors and Testers; Electromechanical Equipment Assemblers; Engine and Other Machine Assemblers; Extruding and Drawing Machine Setters, Operators, and Tenders, Metal and Plastic; Extruding, Forming, Pressing, and Compacting Machine Setters and Set-Up Operators; Extruding, Forming, Pressing, and Compacting Machine Setters, Operators, and Tenders; Forging Machine Setters, Operators, and Tenders, Metal and Plastic; Foundry Mold and Coremakers; Gem and Diamond Workers; Grinding, Honing, Lapping, and Deburring Machine Set-Up Operators; Grinding, Lapping, Polishing, and Buffing Machine Tool Setters, Operators, and Tenders, Metal and Plastic; Heat Treating Equipment Setters, Operators, and Tenders, Metal and Plastic; Heat Treating, Annealing, and Tempering Machine Operators and Tenders, Metal and Plastic; Heating Equipment Setters and Set-Up Operators, Metal and Plastic; Inspectors, Testers, Sorters, Samplers, and Weighers; Jewelers; Jewelers and Precious Stone and Metal Workers;

Lathe and Turning Machine Tool Setters, Operators, and Tenders, Metal and Plastic; Log Graders and Scalers; Materials Inspectors; Mechanical Inspectors; others. **PERSONALITY TYPE—Realistic.** Realistic occupations frequently involve work activities that include practical, hands-on problems and solutions. They often deal with plants, animals, and real-world materials like wood, tools, and machinery. Many of the occupations require working outside and do not involve a lot of paperwork or working closely with others.

EDUCATION/TRAINING PROGRAM(S)—No data available. **RELATED KNOWLEDGE/COURSES**—**Production and Processing:** Knowledge of raw materials, production processes, quality control, costs, and other techniques for maximizing the effective manufacture and distribution of goods. **Principles of Mechanical Devices:** Knowledge of machines and tools, including their designs, uses, repair, and maintenance. **Engineering and Technology:** Knowledge of the practical application of engineering science and technology. This includes applying principles, techniques, procedures, and equipment to the design and production of various goods and services. **Physics:** Knowledge and prediction of physical principles and laws and their interrelationships and applications to understanding fluid, material, and atmospheric dynamics and mechanical, electrical, atomic, and sub-atomic structures and processes.

Microbiologists

- ▲ Education/Training Required: Doctoral degree
- ▲ Annual Earnings: $49,880
- ▲ Growth: 21.0%
- ▲ Annual Job Openings: 5,000
- ▲ Self-Employed: 4.9%
- ▲ Part-Time: 6.6%

Investigate the growth, structure, development, and other characteristics of microscopic organisms, such as bacteria, algae, or fungi. Includes medical microbiologists who study the relationship between organisms and disease or the effects of antibiotics on microorganisms. Studies growth, structure, development, and general characteristics of bacteria and other microorganisms. Studies growth structure and development of viruses and rickettsiae. Examines physiological, morphological, and cultural characteristics, using microscope, to identify microorganisms. Observes action of microorganisms upon living tissues of plants, higher animals, and other microorganisms and on dead organic matter. Conducts chemical analyses of substances such as acids, alcohols, and enzymes. Prepares technical reports and recommendations based upon research outcomes. Researches use of bacteria and microorganisms to develop vitamins, antibiotics, amino acids, grain alcohol, sugars, and polymers. Isolates and makes cultures of bacteria or other microorganisms in prescribed media, controlling moisture, aeration, temperature, and nutrition. **SKILLS—Science:** Using scientific rules and methods to solve problems. **Reading Comprehension:** Understanding written sentences and paragraphs in work-related documents. **Writing:** Communicating effectively in writing as appropriate for the needs of the audience. **Active Learning:** Understanding the implications of new information for both current and future problem-solving and decision-making. **Mathematics:** Using mathematics to solve problems.

GOE INFORMATION—Interest Area: 02. Science, Math, and Engineering. **Work Group:** 02.03. Life Sciences. **Other Job Titles in This Work Group:** Agricultural and Food Science Technicians; Agricultural Technicians; Animal Scientists; Biochemists; Biochemists and Biophysicists; Biological Scientists, All Other; Biologists; Biophysicists; Conservation Scientists; Environmental Scientists and Specialists, Including Health; Epidemiologists; Food Science Technicians; Food Scientists and Technologists; Foresters; Life Scientists, All Other; Medical Scientists, Except Epidemiologists; Plant Scientists; Range Managers; Soil and Plant Scientists; Soil Conservationists; Soil Scientists; Zoologists and Wildlife Biologists. **PERSONALITY TYPE—Investigative.** Investigative occupations frequently involve working with ideas and require an extensive amount of thinking. These occupations can involve searching for facts and figuring out problems mentally.

EDUCATION/TRAINING PROGRAM(S)—Biochemistry/Biophysics and Molecular Biology; Cell/Cellular

Biology and Anatomical Sciences, Other; Microbiology, General; Neuroanatomy; Soil Microbiology; Structural Biology. **RELATED KNOWLEDGE/COURSES—Biology:** Knowledge of plant and animal organisms and their tissues, cells, functions, interdependencies, and interactions with each other and the environment. **Mathematics:** Knowledge of arithmetic, algebra, geometry, calculus, and statistics and their applications. **Chemistry:** Knowledge of the chemical composition, structure, and properties of substances and of the chemical processes and transformations

that they undergo. This includes uses of chemicals and their interactions, danger signs, production techniques, and disposal methods. **Administration and Management:** Knowledge of business and management principles involved in strategic planning, resource allocation, human resources modeling, leadership technique, production methods, and coordination of people and resources. **English Language:** Knowledge of the structure and content of the English language, including the meaning and spelling of words, rules of composition, and grammar.

Middle School Teachers, Except Special and Vocational Education

▲ Education/Training Required: Bachelor's degree
▲ Annual Earnings: $41,220
▲ Growth: 9.6%
▲ Annual Job Openings: 54,000
▲ Self-Employed: 0%
▲ Part-Time: 10.6%

Teach students in public or private schools in one or more subjects at the middle, intermediate, or junior high level, which falls between elementary and senior high school as defined by applicable state laws and regulations. Instructs students by using various teaching methods, such as lecture and demonstration. Prepares course outlines and objectives according to curriculum guidelines or state and local requirements. Evaluates, records, and reports student progress. Maintains discipline in classroom. Selects, stores, orders, issues, and inventories classroom equipment, materials, and supplies. Performs advisory duties, such as sponsoring student organizations or clubs, helping students select courses, and counseling students with problems. Keeps attendance records. Participates in faculty and professional meetings, educational conferences, and teacher training workshops. Confers with students, parents, and school counselors to resolve behavioral and academic problems. Uses audiovisual aids and other materials to supplement presentations. Assigns lessons and corrects homework. Develops and administers tests. **SKILLS—Learning Strategies:** Selecting and using training/instructional methods and procedures appropriate for the situation when learning or teaching new things. **Speaking:** Talking to others to convey information effectively. **Reading Comprehension:** Understanding written sentences and paragraphs in work-related documents. **Mathematics:** Using mathematics to solve problems. **Instructing:** Teaching others how to do something.

GOE INFORMATION—Interest Area: 12. Education and Social Service. **Work Group:** 12.03. Educational Services. **Other Job Titles in This Work Group:** Adult Literacy, Remedial Education, and GED Teachers and Instructors; Agricultural Sciences Teachers, Postsecondary; Anthropology and Archeology Teachers, Postsecondary; Architecture Teachers, Postsecondary; Archivists; Area, Ethnic, and Cultural Studies Teachers, Postsecondary; Art, Drama, and Music Teachers, Postsecondary; Atmospheric, Earth, Marine, and Space Sciences Teachers, Postsecondary; Audio-Visual Collections Specialists; Biological Science Teachers, Postsecondary; Business Teachers, Postsecondary; Chemistry Teachers, Postsecondary; Child Care Workers; Communications Teachers, Postsecondary; Computer Science Teachers, Postsecondary; Criminal Justice and Law Enforcement Teachers, Postsecondary; Curators; Economics Teachers, Postsecondary; Education Teachers, Postsecondary; Educational Psychologists; Educational, Vocational, and School Counselors; Elementary School Teachers, Except Special Education; Engineering Teachers, Postsecondary; English Language and Literature Teachers, Postsecondary; Environmental Science Teachers, Postsecondary; Farm and Home Management Advisors; Foreign Language and Literature Teachers, Postsecondary; Forestry and Conservation Science Teachers, Postsecondary; Geography Teachers, Postsecondary; Graduate Teaching Assistants; Health Specialties Teachers, Postsecondary; History Teachers, Postsecondary; Home Economics Teachers, Postsecondary; Kindergarten Teachers, Except Special Education; Law Teachers, Postsecondary; Librarians; Library Assistants, Clerical; Library Science Teachers, Postsecondary; Library Technicians; Mathematical Science Teachers, Postsecondary; Museum Technicians and Conservators; Nursing Instructors and Teachers, Postsecondary; Personal Financial Advisors; Philosophy and Religion Teachers, Postsecondary; Physics Teachers, Postsecondary; Political Science Teachers, Postsecondary; Postsecondary Teachers, All Other; Preschool Teachers, Except Special Education; Psychology Teachers, Postsecondary; others. **PERSONALITY TYPE**—Social. Social occupations frequently involve working with, communicating with, and teaching people. These occupations often involve helping or providing service to others.

EDUCATION/TRAINING PROGRAM(S)—Art Teacher Education; Computer Teacher Education; English/Language Arts Teacher Education; Family and Consumer Sciences/Home Economics Teacher Education; Foreign Language Teacher Education; Health Occupations Teacher Education; Health Teacher Education; History Teacher Education; Junior High/Intermediate/Middle School Education and Teaching; Mathematics Teacher Education; Music Teacher Education; Physical Education Teaching and Coaching; Reading Teacher Education; Science Teacher Education/General Science Teacher Education; Social Science Teacher Education; Social Studies Teacher Education; Teacher Education and Professional Development, Specific Subject Areas, Other; Technology Teacher Education/Industrial Arts Teacher Education. **RELATED KNOWLEDGE/COURSES**—**Education and Training:** Knowledge of principles and methods for curriculum and training design, teaching and instruction for individuals and groups, and the measurement of training effects. **English Language:** Knowledge of the structure and content of the English language, including the meaning and spelling of words, rules of composition, and grammar. **Mathematics:** Knowledge of arithmetic, algebra, geometry, calculus, and statistics and their applications. **Therapy and Counseling:** Knowledge of principles, methods, and procedures for diagnosis, treatment, and rehabilitation of physical and mental dysfunctions and for career counseling and guidance. **Clerical Studies:** Knowledge of administrative and clerical procedures and systems, such as word processing, managing files and records, stenography and transcription, designing forms, and other office procedures and terminology. **Psychology:** Knowledge of human behavior and performance; individual differences in ability, personality, and interests; learning and motivation; psychological research methods; and the assessment and treatment of behavioral and affective disorders.

Mobile Heavy Equipment Mechanics, Except Engines

- ▲ Education/Training Required: Postsecondary vocational training
- ▲ Annual Earnings: $35,190
- ▲ Growth: 14.0%
- ▲ Annual Job Openings: 11,000
- ▲ Self-Employed: 4.9%
- ▲ Part-Time: 2.4%

Diagnose, adjust, repair, or overhaul mobile mechanical, hydraulic, and pneumatic equipment, such as cranes, bulldozers, graders, and conveyors, used in construction, logging, and surface mining. Repairs and replaces damaged or worn parts. Adjusts, maintains, and repairs or replaces engines and subassemblies, including transmissions and crawler heads, using hand tools, jacks, and cranes. Dismantles and reassembles heavy equipment, using hoists and hand tools. Overhauls and tests machines or equipment to ensure operating efficiency. Examines parts for damage or excessive wear, using micrometers and gauges. Operates and inspects machines or heavy equipment to diagnose defects. Welds or cuts metal and welds broken parts and structural members, using electric or gas welder.

Immerses parts in tanks of solvent or sprays parts with grease solvent to clean parts. Directs workers engaged in cleaning parts and assisting with assembly or disassembly of equipment. **SKILLS**—**Repairing:** Repairing machines or systems, using the needed tools. **Equipment Maintenance:** Performing routine maintenance on equipment and determining when and what kind of maintenance is needed. **Troubleshooting:** Determining causes of operating errors and deciding what to do about them. **Quality Control Analysis:** Conducting tests and inspections of products, services, or processes to evaluate quality or performance. **Operation and Control:** Controlling operations of equipment or systems.

GOE INFORMATION—**Interest Area:** 05. Mechanics, Installers, and Repairers. **Work Group:** 05.03. Mechanical Work. **Other Job Titles in This Work Group:** Aircraft Body and Bonded Structure Repairers; Aircraft Engine Specialists; Aircraft Mechanics and Service Technicians; Airframe-and-Power-Plant Mechanics; Automotive Body and Related Repairers; Automotive Glass Installers and Repairers; Automotive Master Mechanics; Automotive Service Technicians and Mechanics; Automotive Specialty Technicians; Bicycle Repairers; Bridge and Lock Tenders; Bus and Truck Mechanics and Diesel Engine Specialists; Camera and Photographic Equipment Repairers; Coin, Vending, and Amusement Machine Servicers and Repairers; Control and Valve Installers and Repairers, Except Mechanical Door; Farm Equipment Mechanics; Gas Appliance Repairers; Hand and Portable Power Tool Repairers; Heating and Air Conditioning Mechanics; Heating, Air Conditioning, and Refrigeration Mechanics and Installers; Helpers—Electricians; Helpers—Installation, Maintenance, and Repair Workers; Industrial Machinery Mechanics; Keyboard Instrument Repairers and Tuners; Locksmiths and Safe Repairers; Maintenance and Repair Workers, General; Maintenance Workers, Machinery; Mechanical Door Repairers; Medical Appliance Technicians; Medical Equipment Repairers; Meter Mechanics; Millwrights; Motorboat Mechanics; Motorcycle Mechanics; Musical Instrument Repairers and Tuners; Ophthalmic Laboratory Technicians; Optical Instrument Assemblers; Outdoor Power Equipment and Other Small Engine Mechanics; Painters, Transportation Equipment; Percussion Instrument Repairers and Tuners; Precision Instrument and Equipment Repairers, All Other; Rail Car Repairers; Railroad Inspectors; Recreational Vehicle Service Technicians; Reed or Wind Instrument Repairers and Tuners; Refrigeration Mechanics; Stringed Instrument Repairers and Tuners; Tire Repairers and Changers; Valve and Regulator Repairers; Watch Repairers. **PERSONALITY TYPE**—Realistic. Realistic occupations frequently involve work activities that include practical, hands-on problems and solutions. They often deal with plants, animals, and real-world materials like wood, tools, and machinery. Many of the occupations require working outside and do not involve a lot of paperwork or working closely with others.

EDUCATION/TRAINING PROGRAM(S)—Agricultural Mechanics and Equipment/Machine Technology; Heavy Equipment Maintenance Technology/Technician. **RELATED KNOWLEDGE/COURSES—Principles of Mechanical Devices:** Knowledge of machines and tools, including their designs, uses, repair, and maintenance. **Engineering and Technology:** Knowledge of the practical application of engineering science and technology. This includes applying principles, techniques, procedures, and equipment to the design and production of various goods and services. **English Language:** Knowledge of the structure and content of the English language, including the meaning and spelling of words, rules of composition, and grammar. **Production and Processing:** Knowledge of raw materials, production processes, quality control, costs, and other techniques for maximizing the effective manufacture and distribution of goods. **Physics:** Knowledge and prediction of physical principles and laws and their interrelationships and applications to understanding fluid, material, and atmospheric dynamics and mechanical, electrical, atomic, and sub-atomic structures and processes.

Molding, Coremaking, and Casting Machine Setters, Operators, and Tenders, Metal and Plastic

- ▲ Education/Training Required: Moderate-term on-the-job training
- ▲ Annual Earnings: $22,340
- ▲ Growth: 9.8%
- ▲ Annual Job Openings: 38,000
- ▲ Self-Employed: 0%
- ▲ Part-Time: 2.6%

Set up, operate, or tend metal or plastic molding, casting, or coremaking machines to mold or cast metal or thermoplastic parts or products. SKILLS—No data available.

GOE INFORMATION—**Interest Area:** 08. Industrial Production. **Work Group:** 08.02. Production Technology.

Other Job Titles in This Work Group: Aircraft Rigging Assemblers; Aircraft Structure Assemblers, Precision; Aircraft Structure, Surfaces, Rigging, and Systems Assemblers; Aircraft Systems Assemblers, Precision; Bench Workers, Jewelry; Bindery Machine Setters and Set-Up Operators; Bindery Workers; Bookbinders; Buffing and Polishing Set-

Up Operators; Casting Machine Set-Up Operators; Coating, Painting, and Spraying Machine Setters and Set-Up Operators; Coating, Painting, and Spraying Machine Setters, Operators, and Tenders; Combination Machine Tool Setters and Set-Up Operators, Metal and Plastic; Cutting, Punching, and Press Machine Setters, Operators, and Tenders, Metal and Plastic; Dental Laboratory Technicians; Drilling and Boring Machine Tool Setters, Operators, and Tenders, Metal and Plastic; Electrical and Electronic Equipment Assemblers; Electrical and Electronic Inspectors and Testers; Electromechanical Equipment Assemblers; Engine and Other Machine Assemblers; Extruding and Drawing Machine Setters, Operators, and Tenders, Metal and Plastic; Extruding, Forming, Pressing, and Compacting Machine Setters and Set-Up Operators; Extruding, Forming, Pressing, and Compacting Machine Setters, Operators, and Tenders; Forging Machine Setters, Operators, and Tenders, Metal and Plastic; Foundry Mold and Coremakers; Gem and Diamond Workers; Grinding, Honing, Lapping, and Deburring Machine Set-Up Operators; Grinding, Lapping, Polishing, and Buffing Machine Tool Setters, Operators, and Tenders, Metal and Plastic; Heat Treating Equipment Setters, Operators, and Tenders, Metal and Plastic; Heat Treating, Annealing, and Tempering Machine Operators and Tenders, Metal and Plastic; Heating Equipment Setters and Set-Up Operators, Metal and Plastic; Inspectors, Testers, Sorters, Samplers, and Weighers; Jewelers; Jewelers and Precious Stone and Metal Workers; Lathe and Turning Machine Tool Setters, Operators, and Tenders, Metal and Plastic; Log Graders and Scalers; Materials Inspectors; Mechanical Inspectors; others. **PERSONALITY TYPE**—No data available.

EDUCATION/TRAINING PROGRAM(S)—No data available. **RELATED KNOWLEDGE/COURSES**—No data available.

Multi-Media Artists and Animators

- ▲ Education/Training Required: Bachelor's degree
- ▲ Annual Earnings: $42,270
- ▲ Growth: 22.2%
- ▲ Annual Job Openings: 8,000
- ▲ Self-Employed: 60.9%
- ▲ Part-Time: 24.0%

Create special effects, animation, or other visual images, using film, video, computers, or other electronic tools and media for use in products or creations, such as computer games, movies, music videos, and commercials. **SKILLS**—No data available.

GOE INFORMATION—**Interest Area:** 01. Arts, Entertainment, and Media. **Work Group:** 01.04. Visual Arts. **Other Job Titles in This Work Group:** Cartoonists; Commercial and Industrial Designers; Designers, All Other; Exhibit Designers; Fashion Designers; Fine Artists, Including Painters, Sculptors, and Illustrators; Floral Designers; Graphic Designers; Interior Designers; Merchandise Displayers and Window Trimmers; Painters and Illustrators; Sculptors; Set and Exhibit Designers; Set Designers; Sketch Artists. **PERSONALITY TYPE**—No data available.

EDUCATION/TRAINING PROGRAM(S)—Animation, Interactive Technology, Video Graphics and Special Effects; Drawing; Graphic Design; Intermedia/Multimedia; Painting; Printmaking; Web Page, Digital/Multimedia and Information Resources Design. **RELATED KNOWLEDGE/COURSES**—No data available.

Multiple Machine Tool Setters, Operators, and Tenders, Metal and Plastic

▲ Education/Training Required: Postsecondary vocational training
▲ Annual Earnings: $27,910
▲ Growth: 14.7%
▲ Annual Job Openings: 21,000
▲ Self-Employed: 0%
▲ Part-Time: 2.3%

Set up, operate, or tend more than one type of cutting or forming machine tool or robot. **SKILLS**—No data available.

GOE INFORMATION—**Interest Area:** 08. Industrial Production. **Work Group:** 08.02. Production Technology. **Other Job Titles in This Work Group:** Aircraft Rigging Assemblers; Aircraft Structure Assemblers, Precision; Aircraft Structure, Surfaces, Rigging, and Systems Assemblers; Aircraft Systems Assemblers, Precision; Bench Workers, Jewelry; Bindery Machine Setters and Set-Up Operators; Bindery Workers; Bookbinders; Buffing and Polishing Set-Up Operators; Casting Machine Set-Up Operators; Coating, Painting, and Spraying Machine Setters and Set-Up Operators; Coating, Painting, and Spraying Machine Setters, Operators, and Tenders; Combination Machine Tool Setters and Set-Up Operators, Metal and Plastic; Cutting, Punching, and Press Machine Setters, Operators, and Tenders, Metal and Plastic; Dental Laboratory Technicians; Drilling and Boring Machine Tool Setters, Operators, and Tenders, Metal and Plastic; Electrical and Electronic Equipment Assemblers; Electrical and Electronic Inspectors and Testers; Electromechanical Equipment Assemblers; Engine and Other Machine Assemblers; Extruding and Drawing Machine Setters, Operators, and Tenders, Metal and Plastic; Extruding, Forming, Pressing, and Compacting Machine Setters and Set-Up Operators; Extruding, Forming, Pressing, and Compacting Machine Setters, Operators, and Tenders; Forging Machine Setters, Operators, and Tenders, Metal and Plastic; Foundry Mold and Coremakers; Gem and Diamond Workers; Grinding, Honing, Lapping, and Deburring Machine Set-Up Operators; Grinding, Lapping, Polishing, and Buffing Machine Tool Setters, Operators, and Tenders, Metal and Plastic; Heat Treating Equipment Setters, Operators, and Tenders, Metal and Plastic; Heat Treating, Annealing, and Tempering Machine Operators and Tenders, Metal and Plastic; Heating Equipment Setters and Set-Up Operators, Metal and Plastic; Inspectors, Testers, Sorters, Samplers, and Weighers; Jewelers; Jewelers and Precious Stone and Metal Workers; Lathe and Turning Machine Tool Setters, Operators, and Tenders, Metal and Plastic; Log Graders and Scalers; Materials Inspectors; Mechanical Inspectors; others. **PERSONALITY TYPE**—No data available.

EDUCATION/TRAINING PROGRAM(S)—Machine Shop Technology/Assistant; Machine Tool Technology/Machinist. **RELATED KNOWLEDGE/COURSES**—No data available.

Municipal Clerks

▲ Education/Training Required: Short-term on-the-job training
▲ Annual Earnings: $27,090
▲ Growth: 12.0%
▲ Annual Job Openings: 14,000
▲ Self-Employed: 0%
▲ Part-Time: 16.0%

Draft agendas and bylaws for town or city council, record minutes of council meetings, answer official correspondence, keep fiscal records and accounts, and prepare reports on civic needs. Prepares agendas and bylaws for town council. Prepares reports on civic needs. Keeps fiscal records and accounts. Records minutes of council meetings. Answers official correspondence. **SKILLS—Writing:** Communicating effectively in writing as appropriate for the needs of the audience. **Active Listening:** Giving full attention to what other people are saying, taking time to understand the points being made, asking questions as appropriate, and not interrupting at inappropriate times.

Reading Comprehension: Understanding written sentences and paragraphs in work-related documents. **Critical Thinking:** Using logic and reasoning to identify the strengths and weaknesses of alternative solutions, conclusions, or approaches to problems. **Mathematics:** Using mathematics to solve problems.

GOE INFORMATION—Interest Area: 09. Business Detail. **Work Group:** 09.02. Administrative Detail. **Other Job Titles in This Work Group:** Claims Takers, Unemployment Benefits; Court Clerks; Court, Municipal, and License Clerks; Eligibility Interviewers, Government Programs; Executive Secretaries and Administrative Assistants; Interviewers, Except Eligibility and Loan; Legal Secretaries; License Clerks; Loan Interviewers and Clerks; Medical Secretaries; Secretaries, Except Legal, Medical, and Executive; Welfare Eligibility Workers and Interviewers. **PERSONALITY TYPE**—Conventional. Conventional occupations frequently involve following set procedures and routines. These occupations can include working with data and details more than with ideas. Usually there is a clear line of authority to follow.

EDUCATION/TRAINING PROGRAM(S)—General Office Occupations and Clerical Services. **RELATED KNOWLEDGE/COURSES—Clerical Studies:** Knowledge of administrative and clerical procedures and systems, such as word processing, managing files and records, stenography and transcription, designing forms, and other office procedures and terminology. **Economics and Accounting:** Knowledge of economic and accounting principles and practices, the financial markets, banking, and the analysis and reporting of financial data. **English Language:** Knowledge of the structure and content of the English language, including the meaning and spelling of words, rules of composition, and grammar. **Mathematics:** Knowledge of arithmetic, algebra, geometry, calculus, and statistics and their applications. **Administration and Management:** Knowledge of business and management principles involved in strategic planning, resource allocation, human resources modeling, leadership technique, production methods, and coordination of people and resources.

Municipal Fire Fighting and Prevention Supervisors

- ▲ Education/Training Required: Work experience in a related occupation
- ▲ Annual Earnings: $53,420
- ▲ Growth: 16.7%
- ▲ Annual Job Openings: 5,000
- ▲ Self-Employed: 0%
- ▲ Part-Time: 2.1%

Supervise fire fighters who control and extinguish municipal fires, protect life and property, and conduct rescue efforts. Coordinates and supervises fire fighting and rescue activities and reports events to supervisor, using two-way radio. Assesses nature and extent of fire, condition of building, danger to adjacent buildings, and water supply to determine crew or company requirements. Directs investigation of cases of suspected arson, hazards, and false alarms. Inspects fire stations, equipment, and records to ensure efficiency and enforcement of departmental regulations. Directs building inspections to ensure compliance with fire and safety regulations. Trains subordinates in use of equipment, methods of extinguishing fires, and rescue operations. Evaluates efficiency and performance of employees and recommends awards for service. Keeps equipment and personnel records. Compiles report of fire call, listing location, type, probable cause, estimated damage, and disposition. Studies and interprets fire safety codes to establish procedures for issuing permits regulating storage or use of hazardous or flammable substances. Writes and submits proposal for new equipment or modification of existing equipment. Orders and directs fire drills for occupants of buildings. Oversees review of new building plans to ensure compliance with laws, ordinances, and administrative rules for public fire safety. Confers with civic representatives and plans talks and demonstrations of fire safety to direct fire prevention information program. **SKILLS—Coordination:** Adjusting actions in relation to others' actions. **Active Listening:** Giving full attention to what other people are saying, taking time to understand the points being made, asking questions as appropriate, and not interrupting at inappropriate times. **Service Orientation:** Actively looking for ways to help people. **Reading Comprehension:** Understanding written sentences and paragraphs in work-related documents. **Management of Personnel Resources:** Motivating, developing, and directing people as they work, identifying the best people for the job. **Critical Thinking:** Using logic and reasoning to identify the strengths and weaknesses of alternative solutions, conclusions, or approaches to problems. **Judgment and Decision Making:** Considering the relative costs and benefits of potential actions to choose the most appropriate one.

GOE INFORMATION—Interest Area: 04. Law, Law Enforcement, and Public Safety. **Work Group:** 04.01. Managerial Work in Law, Law Enforcement, and Public Safety. **Other Job Titles in This Work Group:** Emergency Management Specialists; First-Line Supervisors/Managers of Correctional Officers; First-Line Supervisors/Managers of Fire Fighting and Prevention Workers; First-Line Supervisors/Managers of Police and Detectives; First-Line Supervisors/Managers, Protective Service Workers, All Other; Forest Fire Fighting and Prevention Supervisors. **PERSONALITY TYPE—**Realistic. Realistic occupations frequently involve work activities that include practical, hands-on problems and solutions. They often deal with plants, animals, and real-world materials like wood, tools, and machinery. Many of the occupations require working outside and do not involve a lot of paperwork or working closely with others.

EDUCATION/TRAINING PROGRAM(S)—Fire Protection and Safety Technology/Technician; Fire Services Administration. **RELATED KNOWLEDGE/ COURSES—Public Safety and Security:** Knowledge of relevant equipment, policies, procedures, and strategies to promote effective local, state, or national security operations for the protection of people, data, property, and institutions. **Education and Training:** Knowledge of principles and methods for curriculum and training design, teaching and instruction for individuals and groups, and the measurement of training effects. **Principles of Mechanical Devices:** Knowledge of machines and tools, including their designs, uses, repair, and maintenance. **Personnel and Human Resources:** Knowledge of principles and procedures for personnel recruitment, selection, training, compensation and benefits, labor relations and negotiation, and personnel information systems. **Administration and Management:** Knowledge of business and management principles involved in strategic planning, resource allocation, human resources modeling, leadership technique, production methods, and coordination of people and resources. **Transportation:** Knowledge of principles and methods for moving people or goods by air, rail, sea, or road, including the relative costs and benefits.

Music Arrangers and Orchestrators

- ▲ Education/Training Required: Bachelor's degree
- ▲ Annual Earnings: $33,720
- ▲ Growth: 13.1%
- ▲ Annual Job Openings: 9,000
- ▲ Self-Employed: 25.8%
- ▲ Part-Time: 53.5%

Write and transcribe musical scores. Composes musical scores for orchestra, band, choral group, or individual instrumentalist or vocalist, using knowledge of music theory and instrumental and vocal capabilities. Transposes music from one voice or instrument to another to accommodate particular musician in musical group. Adapts musical composition for orchestra, band, choral group, or individual to style for which it was not originally written. Copies parts from score for individual performers. Determines voice, instrument, harmonic structure, rhythm, tempo, and tone balance to achieve desired effect. Transcribes musical parts from score written by arranger or orchestrator for each instrument or voice, using knowledge of music composition. **SKILLS—Coordination:** Adjusting

actions in relation to others' actions. **Writing:** Communicating effectively in writing as appropriate for the needs of the audience. **Active Listening:** Giving full attention to what other people are saying, taking time to understand the points being made, asking questions as appropriate, and not interrupting at inappropriate times. **Complex Problem Solving:** Identifying complex problems and reviewing related information to develop and evaluate options and implement solutions. **Reading Comprehension:** Understanding written sentences and paragraphs in work-related documents.

GOE INFORMATION—Interest Area: 01. Arts, Entertainment, and Media. **Work Group:** 01.05. Performing Arts. **Other Job Titles in This Work Group:** Actors; Choreographers; Composers; Dancers; Directors—Stage, Motion Pictures, Television, and Radio; Music Directors; Music Directors and Composers; Musicians and Singers; Musicians, Instrumental; Public Address System and Other Announcers; Radio and Television Announcers; Singers; Talent Directors. **PERSONALITY TYPE**—Artistic. Artistic occupations frequently involve working with forms, designs, and patterns. They often require self-expression, and the work can be done without following a clear set of rules.

Music Directors

Direct and conduct instrumental or vocal performances by musical groups, such as orchestras or choirs. Directs group at rehearsals and live or recorded performances to achieve desired effects, such as tonal and harmonic balance dynamics, rhythm, and tempo. Positions members within group to obtain balance among instrumental sections. Auditions and selects vocal and instrumental groups for musical presentations. Transcribes musical compositions and melodic lines to adapt them to or create particular style for group. Engages services of composer to write score. Issues assignments and reviews work of staff in such areas as scoring, arranging, and copying music and lyric and vocal coaching. Selects vocal, instrumental, and recorded music suitable to type of performance requirements to accommodate ability of group. **SKILLS—Coordination:** Adjusting actions in relation to others' actions. **Time Management:** Managing one's own time and the time of others. **Management of Personnel Resources:** Motivating, developing, and directing people as they work, identifying the best people for the job. **Monitoring:** Monitoring/Assessing your performance or that of other individuals or organizations to make improvements or take corrective action. **Instructing:** Teaching others how to do something.

GOE INFORMATION—Interest Area: 01. Arts, Entertainment, and Media. **Work Group:** 01.05. Performing Arts. **Other Job Titles in This Work Group:** Actors; Choreographers; Composers; Dancers; Directors—Stage,

EDUCATION/TRAINING PROGRAM(S)—Conducting; Music Management and Merchandising; Music Performance, General; Music Theory and Composition; Music, Other; Musicology and Ethnomusicology; Religious/Sacred Music; Voice and Opera. **RELATED KNOWLEDGE/ COURSES—Fine Arts:** Knowledge of the theory and techniques required to compose, produce, and perform works of music, dance, visual arts, drama, and sculpture. **English Language:** Knowledge of the structure and content of the English language, including the meaning and spelling of words, rules of composition, and grammar.

- ▲ Education/Training Required: Master's degree
- ▲ Annual Earnings: $33,720
- ▲ Growth: 13.1%
- ▲ Annual Job Openings: 9,000
- ▲ Self-Employed: 25.8%
- ▲ Part-Time: 53.5%

Motion Pictures, Television, and Radio; Music Arrangers and Orchestrators; Music Directors and Composers; Musicians and Singers; Musicians, Instrumental; Public Address System and Other Announcers; Radio and Television Announcers; Singers; Talent Directors. **PERSONALITY TYPE**—Artistic. Artistic occupations frequently involve working with forms, designs, and patterns. They often require self-expression, and the work can be done without following a clear set of rules.

EDUCATION/TRAINING PROGRAM(S)—Conducting; Music Management and Merchandising; Music Performance, General; Music Theory and Composition; Music, Other; Musicology and Ethnomusicology; Religious/Sacred Music; Voice and Opera. **RELATED KNOWLEDGE/COURSES—Fine Arts:** Knowledge of the theory and techniques required to compose, produce, and perform works of music, dance, visual arts, drama, and sculpture. **Administration and Management:** Knowledge of business and management principles involved in strategic planning, resource allocation, human resources modeling, leadership technique, production methods, and coordination of people and resources. **Personnel and Human Resources:** Knowledge of principles and procedures for personnel recruitment, selection, training, compensation and benefits, labor relations and negotiation, and personnel information systems. **English Language:** Knowledge of the structure and content of the English language, including the meaning and spelling of words, rules of composition, and grammar. **Transportation:** Knowledge of principles and methods for moving people or goods by air, rail, sea, or road, including the relative costs and benefits. **Psychology:** Knowledge of human behavior and performance; individual differences in ability, personality, and interests; learning and motivation; psy-chological research methods; and the assessment and treatment of behavioral and affective disorders. **Education and Training:** Knowledge of principles and methods for curriculum and training design, teaching and instruction for individuals and groups, and the measurement of training effects.

Music Directors and Composers

- ▲ Education/Training Required: Master's degree
- ▲ Annual Earnings: $33,720
- ▲ Growth: 13.1%
- ▲ Annual Job Openings: 9,000
- ▲ Self-Employed: 25.8%
- ▲ Part-Time: 53.5%

Conduct, direct, plan, and lead instrumental or vocal performances by musical groups, such as orchestras, choirs, and glee clubs. Includes arrangers, composers, choral directors, and orchestrators. **SKILLS**—No data available.

GOE INFORMATION—**Interest Area:** 01. Arts, Entertainment, and Media. **Work Group:** 01.05. Performing Arts. **Other Job Titles in This Work Group:** Actors; Choreographers; Composers; Dancers; Directors—Stage, Motion Pictures, Television, and Radio; Music Arrangers and Orchestrators; Music Directors; Musicians and Singers; Musicians, Instrumental; Public Address System and Other Announcers; Radio and Television Announcers; Singers; Talent Directors. **PERSONALITY TYPE**—No data available.

EDUCATION/TRAINING PROGRAM(S)—Conducting; Music Management and Merchandising; Music Performance, General; Music Theory and Composition; Music, Other; Musicology and Ethnomusicology; Religious/Sacred Music; Voice and Opera. **RELATED KNOWLEDGE/COURSES**—No data available.

Musicians and Singers

- ▲ Education/Training Required: Long-term on-the-job training
- ▲ Annual Earnings: $40,320
- ▲ Growth: 20.1%
- ▲ Annual Job Openings: 33,000
- ▲ Self-Employed: 25.8%
- ▲ Part-Time: 53.5%

Play one or more musical instruments or entertain by singing songs in recital, in accompaniment, or as a member of an orchestra, band, or other musical group. Musical performers may entertain on-stage, radio, TV, film, video, or record in studios. **SKILLS**—No data available.

GOE INFORMATION—**Interest Area:** 01. Arts, Entertainment, and Media. **Work Group:** 01.05. Performing Arts. **Other Job Titles in This Work Group:** Actors; Choreographers; Composers; Dancers; Directors—Stage, Motion Pictures, Television, and Radio; Music Arrangers and Orchestrators; Music Directors; Music Directors and Composers; Musicians, Instrumental; Public Address System and Other Announcers; Radio and Television Announcers; Singers; Talent Directors. **PERSONALITY TYPE**—No data available.

EDUCATION/TRAINING PROGRAM(S)—Jazz/Jazz Studies; Music Pedagogy; Music Performance, General; Music, General; Music, Other; Piano and Organ; Violin, Viola, Guitar and Other Stringed Instruments; Voice and Opera. **RELATED KNOWLEDGE/COURSES**—No data available.

Musicians, Instrumental

▲ Education/Training Required: Long-term on-the-job training
▲ Annual Earnings: $40,320
▲ Growth: 20.1%
▲ Annual Job Openings: 33,000
▲ Self-Employed: 25.8%
▲ Part-Time: 53.5%

Play one or more musical instruments in recital, in accompaniment, or as member of an orchestra, band, or other musical group. Plays musical instrument as soloist or as member of musical group, such as orchestra or band, to entertain audience. Practices performance on musical instrument to maintain and improve skills. Transposes music to play in alternate key or to fit individual style or purposes. Directs band/orchestra. Teaches music for specific instruments. Composes new musical scores. Memorizes musical scores. Improvises music during performance. Plays from memory or by following score. Studies and rehearses music to learn and interpret score. **SKILLS—Coordination:** Adjusting actions in relation to others' actions. **Active Learning:** Understanding the implications of new information for both current and future problem-solving and decision-making. **Instructing:** Teaching others how to do something. **Monitoring:** Monitoring/Assessing your performance or that of other individuals or organizations to make improvements or take corrective action. **Learning Strategies:** Selecting and using training/instructional methods and procedures appropriate for the situation when learning or teaching new things.

GOE INFORMATION—Interest Area: 01. Arts, Entertainment, and Media. **Work Group:** 01.05. Performing Arts. **Other Job Titles in This Work Group:** Actors; Choreographers; Composers; Dancers; Directors—Stage, Motion Pictures, Television, and Radio; Music Arrangers and Orchestrators; Music Directors; Music Directors and

Composers; Musicians and Singers; Public Address System and Other Announcers; Radio and Television Announcers; Singers; Talent Directors. **PERSONALITY TYPE—Artistic.** Artistic occupations frequently involve working with forms, designs, and patterns. They often require self-expression, and the work can be done without following a clear set of rules.

EDUCATION/TRAINING PROGRAM(S)—Jazz/Jazz Studies; Music Pedagogy; Music Performance, General; Music, General; Music, Other; Piano and Organ; Violin, Viola, Guitar and Other Stringed Instruments. **RELATED KNOWLEDGE/COURSES—Fine Arts:** Knowledge of the theory and techniques required to compose, produce, and perform works of music, dance, visual arts, drama, and sculpture. **Education and Training:** Knowledge of principles and methods for curriculum and training design, teaching and instruction for individuals and groups, and the measurement of training effects. **Mathematics:** Knowledge of arithmetic, algebra, geometry, calculus, and statistics and their applications. **English Language:** Knowledge of the structure and content of the English language, including the meaning and spelling of words, rules of composition, and grammar. **Psychology:** Knowledge of human behavior and performance; individual differences in ability, personality, and interests; learning and motivation; psychological research methods; and the assessment and treatment of behavioral and affective disorders.

Network and Computer Systems Administrators

▲ Education/Training Required: Bachelor's degree
▲ Annual Earnings: $53,770
▲ Growth: 81.9%
▲ Annual Job Openings: 18,000
▲ Self-Employed: 49.4%
▲ Part-Time: 7.2%

Install, configure, and support an organization's local area network (LAN), wide area network (WAN), and Internet system or a segment of a network system. Maintain network hardware and software. Monitor network to ensure network availability to all system users and perform necessary maintenance to support network availability. May supervise other network support and client server specialists and plan, coordinate, and implement network security measures. **SKILLS**—No data available.

GOE INFORMATION—**Interest Area:** 02. Science, Math, and Engineering. **Work Group:** 02.06. Mathematics and Computers. **Other Job Titles in This Work Group:** Actuaries; Computer and Information Scientists, Research; Computer Programmers; Computer Security Specialists; Computer Specialists, All Other; Computer Support Specialists; Computer Systems Analysts; Database Administrators; Mathematical Science Occupations, All Other;

Mathematical Technicians; Mathematicians; Network Systems and Data Communications Analysts; Operations Research Analysts; Statistical Assistants; Statisticians. **PERSONALITY TYPE**—No data available.

EDUCATION/TRAINING PROGRAM(S)—Computer and Information Sciences and Support Services, Other; Computer and Information Sciences, General; Computer and Information Systems Security; Computer Systems Analysis/Analyst; Computer Systems Networking and Telecommunications; Information Science/Studies; System Administration/Administrator; System, Networking, and LAN/WAN Management/Manager. **RELATED KNOWLEDGE/COURSES**—No data available.

Network Systems and Data Communications Analysts

- ▲ Education/Training Required: Bachelor's degree
- ▲ Annual Earnings: $57,470
- ▲ Growth: 77.5%
- ▲ Annual Job Openings: 9,000
- ▲ Self-Employed: No data available.
- ▲ Part-Time: No data available.

Analyze, design, test, and evaluate network systems, such as local area networks (LAN), wide area networks (WAN), Internet, intranet, and other data communications systems. Perform network modeling, analysis, and planning. Research and recommend network and data communications hardware and software. Includes telecommunications specialists who deal with the interfacing of computer and communications equipment. May supervise computer programmers. Analyzes test data and recommends hardware or software for purchase. Develops and writes procedures for installation, use, and solving problems of communications hardware and software. Assists users to identify and solve data communication problems. Trains users in use of equipment. Visits vendors to learn about available products or services. Conducts surveys to determine user needs. Tests and evaluates hardware and software to determine efficiency, reliability, and compatibility with existing system. Reads technical manuals and brochures to determine which equipment meets establishment requirements. Monitors system performance. Identifies areas of operation that need upgraded equipment, such as modems, fiber-optic cables, and telephone wires. **SKILLS**—**Reading Comprehension:** Understanding written sentences and paragraphs in work-related documents. **Troubleshooting:** Determining causes of op-

erating errors and deciding what to do about them. **Management of Material Resources:** Obtaining and seeing to the appropriate use of equipment, facilities, and materials needed to do certain work. **Writing:** Communicating effectively in writing as appropriate for the needs of the audience. **Active Learning:** Understanding the implications of new information for both current and future problem-solving and decision-making. **Operations Analysis:** Analyzing needs and product requirements to create a design. **Active Listening:** Giving full attention to what other people are saying, taking time to understand the points being made, asking questions as appropriate, and not interrupting at inappropriate times.

GOE INFORMATION—**Interest Area:** 02. Science, Math, and Engineering. **Work Group:** 02.06. Mathematics and Computers. **Other Job Titles in This Work Group:** Actuaries; Computer and Information Scientists, Research; Computer Programmers; Computer Security Specialists; Computer Specialists, All Other; Computer Support Specialists; Computer Systems Analysts; Database Administrators; Mathematical Science Occupations, All Other; Mathematical Technicians; Mathematicians; Network and Computer Systems Administrators; Operations Research Analysts; Statistical Assistants; Statisticians. **PERSONALITY TYPE**—Investigative. Investigative occupations frequently involve working with ideas and require an extensive amount of thinking. These occupations can involve searching for facts and figuring out problems mentally.

EDUCATION/TRAINING PROGRAM(S)—Computer and Information Sciences, General; Computer and Information Systems Security; Computer Systems Analysis/Analyst; Computer Systems Networking and Telecommunications; Information Technology. **RELATED KNOWLEDGE/COURSES**—**Telecommunications:** Knowledge of transmission, broadcasting, switching, control, and operation of telecommunications systems. **Computers and Electronics:** Knowledge of circuit boards, processors, chips, electronic equipment, and computer hardware and software, including applications and programming. **Mathematics:** Knowledge of arithmetic, algebra, geometry, calculus, and statistics and their applications. **Education and Training:** Knowledge of principles and methods for curriculum and training design, teaching and instruction for individuals and groups, and the measurement of training effects. **Public Safety and Security:** Knowledge of relevant equipment, policies, procedures, and strategies to promote effective local, state, or national security operations for the protection of people, data, property, and institutions.

Nonfarm Animal Caretakers

▲ Education/Training Required: Short-term on-the-job training
▲ Annual Earnings: $16,570
▲ Growth: 21.6%
▲ Annual Job Openings: 20,000
▲ Self-Employed: 24.0%
▲ Part-Time: 38.1%

Feed, water, groom, bathe, exercise, or otherwise care for pets and other nonfarm animals, such as dogs, cats, ornamental fish or birds, zoo animals, and mice. Work in settings such as kennels, animal shelters, zoos, circuses, and aquariums. May keep records of feedings, treatments, and animals received or discharged. May clean, disinfect, and repair cages, pens, or fish tanks. Feeds and waters animals according to schedules and feeding instructions. Mixes food, liquid formulas, medications, or food supplements according to instructions, prescriptions, and knowledge of animal species. Adjusts controls to regulate specified temperature and humidity of animal quarters, nursery, or exhibit area. Cleans and disinfects animal quarters, such as pens, stables, cages, and yards, and surgical or other equipment, such as saddles and bridles. Washes, brushes, clips, trims, and grooms animals. Examines and observes animals for signs of illness, disease, or injury and provides treatment or informs veterinarian. Exercises animals to maintain their fitness and health or trains animals to perform certain tasks. Anesthetizes and inoculates animals according to instructions. Repairs fences, cages, or pens. Installs equipment in animal care facility, such as infrared lights, feeding devices, or cribs. Observes and cautions children petting and feeding animals in designated area. Responds to questions from patrons and provides information about animals, such as behavior, habitat, breeding habits, or facility activities. Saddles and shoes animals. Orders, unloads, and stores feed and supplies. Records information about animals, such as weight, size, physical condition, diet, medications, and food intake. Transfers animals between enclosures for breeding, birthing, shipping, or rearranging exhibits. **SKILLS**—**Service Orientation:** Actively looking for ways to help people. **Mathematics:** Using mathematics to solve problems. **Active Listening:** Giving full attention to what other people are saying, taking time to understand the points being made, asking questions as appropriate, and not interrupting at inappropriate times. **Speaking:** Talking to others to convey information effectively. **Equipment Maintenance:** Performing routine maintenance on equipment and determining when and what kind of maintenance is needed. **Equipment Selection:** Determining the kind of tools and equipment needed to do a job.

GOE INFORMATION—**Interest Area:** 03. Plants and Animals. **Work Group:** 03.02. Animal Care and Training. **Other Job Titles in This Work Group:** Animal Breeders; Animal Trainers; Veterinarians; Veterinary Assistants and Laboratory Animal Caretakers; Veterinary Technologists and Technicians. **PERSONALITY TYPE**—Realistic. Realistic occupations frequently involve work activities that include practical, hands-on problems and solutions. They often deal with plants, animals, and real-world materials like wood, tools, and machinery. Many of the occupations require working outside and do not involve a lot of paperwork or working closely with others.

EDUCATION/TRAINING PROGRAM(S)—Agricultural/Farm Supplies Retailing and Wholesaling; Dog/Pet/Animal Grooming. RELATED KNOWLEDGE/COURSES—Biology: Knowledge of plant and animal organisms and their tissues, cells, functions, interdependencies, and interactions with each other and the environment. Medicine and Dentistry: Knowledge of the information and techniques needed to diagnose and treat human injuries, diseases, and deformities. This includes symptoms, treatment alternatives, drug properties and interactions, and preventive health-care measures. Building and Construction: Knowledge of materials, methods, and tools involved in the construction or repair of houses, buildings, or other structures, such as highways and roads. Principles of Mechanical Devices: Knowledge of machines and tools, including their designs, uses, repair, and maintenance. English Language: Knowledge of the structure and content of the English language, including the meaning and spelling of words, rules of composition, and grammar.

Nuclear Equipment Operation Technicians

- ▲ Education/Training Required: Associate's degree
- ▲ Annual Earnings: $59,690
- ▲ Growth: 20.7%
- ▲ Annual Job Openings: 15,000
- ▲ Self-Employed: 0.9%
- ▲ Part-Time: 11.7%

Operate equipment used for the release, control, and utilization of nuclear energy to assist scientists in laboratory and production activities. Sets control panel switches and activates equipment, such as nuclear reactor, particle accelerator, or gamma radiation equipment, according to specifications. Adjusts controls of equipment to control particle beam, chain reaction, or radiation according to specifications. Installs instrumentation leads in reactor core to measure operating temperature and pressure according to mockups, blueprints, and diagrams. Controls laboratory compounding equipment enclosed in protective hot cell to prepare radioisotopes and other radioactive materials. Sets up and operates machines to saw fuel elements to size or to cut and polish test pieces, following blueprints and other specifications. Tests physical, chemical, or metallurgical properties of experimental materials according to standardized procedures, using test equipment and measuring instruments. Modifies, devises, and maintains equipment used in operations. Disassembles, cleans, and decontaminates hot cells and reactor parts during maintenance shutdown, using slave manipulators, crane, and hand tools. Writes summary of activities or records experiment data in log for further analysis by engineers, scientists, or customers or for future reference. Communicates with maintenance personnel to ensure readiness of support systems and to warn of radiation hazards. Withdraws radioactive sample for analysis, fills container with prescribed quantity of material for shipment, or removes spent fuel elements. Transfers experimental materials to and from specified containers and to tube, chamber or tunnel, using slave manipulators or extension tools. Positions fuel elements in reactor or environmental chamber according to specified configuration, using slave manipulators or extension tools. Reviews experiment schedule to determine specifications such as subatomic particle parameters, radiation time, dosage, and gamma intensity. Monitors instruments, gauges, and recording devices in control room during operation of equipment under direction of nuclear experimenter. Calculates equipment operating factors, such as radiation time, dosage, temperature, and pressure, using standard formulas and conversion tables. SKILLS—Mathematics: Using mathematics to solve problems. Science: Using scientific rules and methods to solve problems. Installation: Installing equipment, machines, wiring, or programs to meet specifications. Operation and Control: Controlling operations of equipment or systems. Reading Comprehension: Understanding written sentences and paragraphs in work-related documents.

GOE INFORMATION—Interest Area: 02. Science, Math, and Engineering. Work Group: 02.05. Laboratory Technology. Other Job Titles in This Work Group: Biological Technicians; Chemical Technicians; Environmental Science and Protection Technicians, Including Health;

Geological and Petroleum Technicians; Geological Data Technicians; Geological Sample Test Technicians; Nuclear Technicians; Photographers, Scientific. **PERSONALITY TYPE**—Realistic. Realistic occupations frequently involve work activities that include practical, hands-on problems and solutions. They often deal with plants, animals, and real-world materials like wood, tools, and machinery. Many of the occupations require working outside and do not involve a lot of paperwork or working closely with others.

EDUCATION/TRAINING PROGRAM(S)—Industrial Radiologic Technology/Technician; Nuclear and Industrial Radiologic Technologies/Technicians, Other; Nuclear Engineering Technology/Technician; Nuclear/Nuclear Power Technology/Technician; Radiation Protection/Health Physics Technician. **RELATED KNOWLEDGE/COURSES—Engineering and Technology:** Knowledge of the practical application of engineering science and tech-

nology. This includes applying principles, techniques, procedures, and equipment to the design and production of various goods and services. **Physics:** Knowledge and prediction of physical principles and laws and their interrelationships and applications to understanding fluid, material, and atmospheric dynamics and mechanical, electrical, atomic, and sub-atomic structures and processes. **Public Safety and Security:** Knowledge of relevant equipment, policies, procedures, and strategies to promote effective local, state, or national security operations for the protection of people, data, property, and institutions. **Mathematics:** Knowledge of arithmetic, algebra, geometry, calculus, and statistics and their applications. **Chemistry:** Knowledge of the chemical composition, structure, and properties of substances and of the chemical processes and transformations that they undergo. This includes uses of chemicals and their interactions, danger signs, production techniques, and disposal methods.

Nuclear Medicine Technologists

- ▲ Education/Training Required: Associate's degree
- ▲ Annual Earnings: $47,400
- ▲ Growth: 22.4%
- ▲ Annual Job Openings: 1,000
- ▲ Self-Employed: 0%
- ▲ Part-Time: 17.5%

Prepare, administer, and measure radioactive isotopes in therapeutic, diagnostic, and tracer studies, utilizing a variety of radioisotope equipment. Prepare stock solutions of radioactive materials and calculate doses to be administered by radiologists. Subject patients to radiation. Execute blood volume, red cell survival, and fat absorption studies following standard laboratory techniques. Administers radiopharmaceuticals or radiation to patient to detect or treat diseases under direction of physician, using radioisotope equipment. Measures glandular activity, blood volume, red cell survival, and radioactivity of patient, using scanners, Geiger counters, scintillometers, and other laboratory equipment. Maintains and calibrates radioisotope and laboratory equipment. Disposes of radioactive materials and stores radiopharmaceuticals, following radiation safety procedures. Develops treatment procedures for nuclear medicine treatment programs. Positions radiation fields, radiation beams, and patient to develop most effective treatment of patient's disease, using computer. Calculates, measures, prepares, and records radiation dosage or radiopharmaceuticals, using computer

and following physician's prescription and X rays. **SKILLS—Reading Comprehension:** Understanding written sentences and paragraphs in work-related documents. **Mathematics:** Using mathematics to solve problems. **Instructing:** Teaching others how to do something. **Science:** Using scientific rules and methods to solve problems. **Speaking:** Talking to others to convey information effectively. **Active Listening:** Giving full attention to what other people are saying, taking time to understand the points being made, asking questions as appropriate, and not interrupting at inappropriate times.

GOE INFORMATION—Interest Area: 14. Medical and Health Services. **Work Group:** 14.05. Medical Technology. **Other Job Titles in This Work Group:** Cardiovascular Technologists and Technicians; Diagnostic Medical Sonographers; Health Technologists and Technicians, All Other; Medical and Clinical Laboratory Technicians; Medical and Clinical Laboratory Technologists; Medical Equipment Preparers; Orthotists and Prosthetists; Radiologic Technicians; Radiologic Technologists; Radiologic Technologists and Technicians. **PERSONALITY TYPE—**

Investigative. Investigative occupations frequently involve working with ideas and require an extensive amount of thinking. These occupations can involve searching for facts and figuring out problems mentally.

EDUCATION/TRAINING PROGRAM(S)—Nuclear Medical Technology/Technologist; Radiation Protection/ Health Physics Technician. RELATED KNOWLEDGE/ COURSES—Medicine and Dentistry: Knowledge of the information and techniques needed to diagnose and treat human injuries, diseases, and deformities. This includes symptoms, treatment alternatives, drug properties and interactions, and preventive health-care measures. Biology: Knowledge of plant and animal organisms and their tissues, cells, functions, interdependencies, and interactions with each other and the environment. Computers and Electronics: Knowledge of circuit boards, processors, chips, electronic equipment, and computer hardware and software, including applications and programming. Mathematics: Knowledge of arithmetic, algebra, geometry, calculus, and statistics and their applications. Chemistry: Knowledge of the chemical composition, structure, and properties of substances and of the chemical processes and transformations that they undergo. This includes uses of chemicals and their interactions, danger signs, production techniques, and disposal methods.

Nuclear Monitoring Technicians

- ▲ Education/Training Required: Associate's degree
- ▲ Annual Earnings: $59,690
- ▲ Growth: 20.7%
- ▲ Annual Job Openings: 15,000
- ▲ Self-Employed: 0.9%
- ▲ Part-Time: 11.7%

Collect and test samples to monitor results of nuclear experiments and contamination of humans, facilities, and environment. Measures intensity and identifies type of radiation in work areas, equipment, and materials, using radiation detectors and other instruments. Calculates safe radiation exposure time for personnel, using plant contamination readings and prescribed safe levels of radiation. Scans photographic emulsions exposed to direct radiation to compute track properties from standard formulas, using microscope with scales and protractors. Calibrates and maintains chemical instrumentation sensing elements and sampling system equipment, using calibration instruments and hand tools. Prepares reports on contamination tests, material and equipment decontaminated, and methods used in decontamination process. Instructs personnel in radiation safety procedures and demonstrates use of protective clothing and equipment. Places radioactive waste, such as sweepings and broken sample bottles, into containers for disposal. Decontaminates objects by cleaning with soap or solvents or by abrading, using wire brush, buffing wheel, or sandblasting machine. Enters data into computer to record characteristics of nuclear events and locating coordinates of particles. Weighs and mixes decontamination chemical solutions in tank and immerses objects in solution for specified time, using hoist. Determines or recommends radioactive decontamination procedures according to size and nature of equipment and degree of contamination. Confers with scientist directing project to determine significant events to watch for during test. Informs supervisors of need to take action when individual exposures or area radiation levels approach maximum permissible limits. Monitors personnel for length and intensity of exposure to radiation for health and safety purposes. Observes projected photographs to locate particle tracks and events and compiles lists of events from particle detectors. Assists in setting up equipment that automatically detects area radiation deviations and tests detection equipment to ensure accuracy. Collects samples of air, water, gases, and solids to determine radioactivity levels of contamination. **SKILLS—Science:** Using scientific rules and methods to solve problems. **Mathematics:** Using mathematics to solve problems. **Reading Comprehension:** Understanding written sentences and paragraphs in work-related documents. **Speaking:** Talking to others to convey information effectively. **Operation Monitoring:** Watching gauges, dials, or other indicators to make sure a machine is working properly. **Critical Thinking:** Using logic and reasoning to identify the strengths and weaknesses of alternative solutions, conclusions, or approaches to problems. **Writing:** Communicating effectively in writing as appropriate for the needs of the audience.

GOE INFORMATION—**Interest Area:** 04. Law, Law Enforcement, and Public Safety. **Work Group:** 04.04. Public Safety. **Other Job Titles in This Work Group:** Agricultural Inspectors; Aviation Inspectors; Compliance Officers, Except Agriculture, Construction, Health and Safety, and Transportation; Emergency Medical Technicians and Paramedics; Environmental Compliance Inspectors; Equal Opportunity Representatives and Officers; Financial Examiners; Fire Fighters; Fire Inspectors; Fire Inspectors and Investigators; Forest Fire Fighters; Forest Fire Inspectors and Prevention Specialists; Government Property Inspectors and Investigators; Licensing Examiners and Inspectors; Marine Cargo Inspectors; Municipal Fire Fighters; Occupational Health and Safety Specialists; Occupational Health and Safety Technicians; Public Transportation Inspectors. **PERSONALITY TYPE**—Realistic. Realistic occupations frequently involve work activities that include practical, hands-on problems and solutions. They often deal with plants, animals, and real-world materials like wood, tools, and machinery. Many of the occupations require working outside and do not involve a lot of paperwork or working closely with others.

EDUCATION/TRAINING PROGRAM(S)—Industrial Radiologic Technology/Technician; Nuclear and Industrial Radiologic Technologies/Technicians, Other; Nuclear Engineering Technology/Technician; Nuclear/Nuclear Power Technology/Technician; Radiation Protection/ Health Physics Technician. **RELATED KNOWLEDGE/ COURSES**—**Physics:** Knowledge and prediction of physical principles and laws and their interrelationships and applications to understanding fluid, material, and atmospheric dynamics and mechanical, electrical, atomic, and sub-atomic structures and processes. **Mathematics:** Knowledge of arithmetic, algebra, geometry, calculus, and statistics and their applications. **Public Safety and Security:** Knowledge of relevant equipment, policies, procedures, and strategies to promote effective local, state, or national security operations for the protection of people, data, property, and institutions. **Chemistry:** Knowledge of the chemical composition, structure, and properties of substances and of the chemical processes and transformations that they undergo. This includes uses of chemicals and their interactions, danger signs, production techniques, and disposal methods. **Education and Training:** Knowledge of principles and methods for curriculum and training design, teaching and instruction for individuals and groups, and the measurement of training effects.

Nuclear Technicians

- ▲ Education/Training Required: Associate's degree
- ▲ Annual Earnings: $59,690
- ▲ Growth: 20.7%
- ▲ Annual Job Openings: Fewer than 500
- ▲ Self-Employed: 0.9%
- ▲ Part-Time: 11.7%

Assist scientists in both laboratory and production activities by performing technical tasks involving nuclear physics, primarily in operation, maintenance, production, and quality control support activities. **SKILLS**— No data available.

GOE INFORMATION—**Interest Area:** 02. Science, Math, and Engineering. **Work Group:** 02.05. Laboratory Technology. **Other Job Titles in This Work Group:** Biological Technicians; Chemical Technicians; Environmental Science and Protection Technicians, Including Health; Geological and Petroleum Technicians; Geological Data Technicians; Geological Sample Test Technicians; Nuclear Equipment Operation Technicians; Photographers, Scientific. **PERSONALITY TYPE**—No data available.

EDUCATION/TRAINING PROGRAM(S)—Industrial Radiologic Technology/Technician; Nuclear and Industrial Radiologic Technologies/Technicians, Other; Nuclear Engineering Technology/Technician; Nuclear/Nuclear Power Technology/Technician; Radiation Protection/ Health Physics Technician. **RELATED KNOWLEDGE/ COURSES**—No data available.

Numerical Control Machine Tool Operators and Tenders, Metal and Plastic

▲ Education/Training Required: Long-term on-the-job training
▲ Annual Earnings: $28,390
▲ Growth: 19.7%
▲ Annual Job Openings: 15,000
▲ Self-Employed: 0%
▲ Part-Time: 2.3%

Set up and operate numerical control (magnetic- or punched-tape-controlled) machine tools that automatically mill, drill, broach, and ream metal and plastic parts. May adjust machine feed and speed, change cutting tools, or adjust machine controls when automatic programming is faulty or if machine malfunctions. Selects, measures, assembles, and sets machine tools, such as drill bits and milling or cutting tools, using precision gauges and instruments. Mounts, installs, aligns, and secures tools, attachments, fixtures, and workpiece on machine, using hand tools and precision measuring instruments. Determines specifications or procedures for tooling setup, machine operation, workpiece dimensions, or numerical control sequences, using blueprints, instructions, and machine knowledge. Calculates and sets machine controls to position tools, synchronize tape and tool, or regulate cutting depth, speed, feed, or coolant flow. Lays out and marks areas of part to be shot-peened and fills hopper with shot. Positions and secures workpiece on machine bed, indexing table, fixture, or dispensing or holding device. Loads control media, such as tape, card, or disk, in machine controller or enters commands to retrieve programmed instructions. Starts automatic operation of numerical control machine to machine parts or test setup, workpiece dimensions, or programming. Confers with supervisor or programmer to resolve machine malfunctions and production errors and obtains approval to continue production. Maintains machines and removes and replaces broken or worn machine tools, using hand tools. Examines electronic components for defects and completeness of laser-beam trimming, using microscope. Operates lathe, drill press, jig-boring machine, or other machines manually or semiautomatically. Measures dimensions of finished workpiece to ensure conformance to specifications, using precision measuring instruments, templates, and fixtures. Lifts workpiece to machine manually, with hoist or crane, or with tweezers. Enters commands or manually adjusts machine controls to correct malfunctions or tolerances. Stops machine to remove finished workpiece or change tooling, setup, or workpiece placement, according to required machining sequence. Monitors machine operation and control panel displays to detect malfunctions and compare readings to specifications. Cleans machine, tooling, and parts, using solvent or solution and rag. SKILLS— Operation and Control: Controlling operations of equipment or systems. Mathematics: Using mathematics to solve problems. Operation Monitoring: Watching gauges, dials, or other indicators to make sure a machine is working properly. Equipment Maintenance: Performing routine maintenance on equipment and determining when and what kind of maintenance is needed. Equipment Selection: Determining the kind of tools and equipment needed to do a job.

GOE INFORMATION—Interest Area: 08. Industrial Production. Work Group: 08.03. Production Work. Other Job Titles in This Work Group: Bakers, Manufacturing; Bindery Machine Operators and Tenders; Brazers; Cementing and Gluing Machine Operators and Tenders; Chemical Equipment Controllers and Operators; Chemical Equipment Operators and Tenders; Chemical Equipment Tenders; Cleaning, Washing, and Metal Pickling Equipment Operators and Tenders; Coating, Painting, and Spraying Machine Operators and Tenders; Coil Winders, Tapers, and Finishers; Combination Machine Tool Operators and Tenders, Metal and Plastic; Computer-Controlled Machine Tool Operators, Metal and Plastic; Cooling and Freezing Equipment Operators and Tenders; Crushing, Grinding, and Polishing Machine Setters, Operators, and Tenders; Cutters and Trimmers, Hand; Cutting and Slicing Machine Operators and Tenders; Cutting and Slicing Machine Setters, Operators, and Tenders; Design Printing Machine Setters and Set-Up Operators; Electrolytic Plating and Coating Machine Operators and Tenders, Metal and Plastic; Electrolytic Plating and Coating Machine Setters and Set-Up Operators, Metal and Plastic; Electrotypers and Stereotypers; Embossing Machine Set-Up Operators; Engraver Set-Up Operators; Extruding and Forming Machine Operators and Tenders, Synthetic or Glass Fibers; Extruding and Forming Machine Setters, Operators, and Tenders, Synthetic and Glass Fibers; Extruding, Forming, Pressing, and Compacting Machine Operators and Tenders; Fabric and Apparel

Patternmakers; Fiber Product Cutting Machine Setters and Set-Up Operators; Fiberglass Laminators and Fabricators; Film Laboratory Technicians; Fitters, Structural Metal—Precision; Food and Tobacco Roasting, Baking, and Drying Machine Operators and Tenders; Food Batchmakers; Food Cooking Machine Operators and Tenders; Furnace, Kiln, Oven, Drier, and Kettle Operators and Tenders; Glass Cutting Machine Setters and Set-Up Operators; Graders and Sorters, Agricultural Products; Grinding and Polishing Workers, Hand; Hand Compositors and Typesetters; Heaters, Metal and Plastic; others. **PERSONALITY TYPE—** Realistic. Realistic occupations frequently involve work activities that include practical, hands-on problems and solutions. They often deal with plants, animals, and real-world materials like wood, tools, and machinery. Many of the occupations require working outside and do not involve a lot of paperwork or working closely with others.

EDUCATION/TRAINING PROGRAM(S)—Machine Shop Technology/Assistant. **RELATED KNOWLEDGE/ COURSES—Principles of Mechanical Devices:** Knowledge of machines and tools, including their designs, uses, repair, and maintenance. **Production and Processing:** Knowledge of raw materials, production processes, quality control, costs, and other techniques for maximizing the effective manufacture and distribution of goods. **Engineering and Technology:** Knowledge of the practical application of engineering science and technology. This includes applying principles, techniques, procedures, and equipment to the design and production of various goods and services. **Mathematics:** Knowledge of arithmetic, algebra, geometry, calculus, and statistics and their applications. **Computers and Electronics:** Knowledge of circuit boards, processors, chips, electronic equipment, and computer hardware and software, including applications and programming.

Nursing Aides, Orderlies, and Attendants

- ▲ Education/Training Required: Short-term on-the-job training
- ▲ Annual Earnings: $19,290
- ▲ Growth: 23.5%
- ▲ Annual Job Openings: 268,000
- ▲ Self-Employed: 1.7%
- ▲ Part-Time: 26.4%

Provide basic patient care under direction of nursing staff. Perform duties such as feeding, bathinge, dressing, grooming, or moving patients or changing linens. Feeds patients unable to feed themselves. Sets up equipment, such as oxygen tents, portable X-ray machines, and overhead irrigation bottles. Prepares food trays. Bathes, grooms, and dresses patients. Measures and records food and liquid intake and output. Measures and records vital signs. Administers medication as directed by physician or nurse. Cleans room and changes linen. Stores, prepares, and issues dressing packs, treatment trays, and other supplies. Administers catheterizations, bladder irrigations, enemas, and douches. Sterilizes equipment and supplies. Administers massages and alcohol rubs. Transports patient to areas such as operating and X-ray rooms. Turns and re-positions bedfast patients, alone or with assistance, to prevent bedsores. Assists patient in walking. **SKILLS—Social Perceptiveness:** Being aware of others' reactions and understanding why they react as they do. **Active Listening:** Giving full attention to what other people are saying, taking time to understand the points being made, asking questions as appropriate, and not interrupting at inappropriate

times. **Reading Comprehension:** Understanding written sentences and paragraphs in work-related documents. **Speaking:** Talking to others to convey information effectively. **Service Orientation:** Actively looking for ways to help people.

GOE INFORMATION—Interest Area: 14. Medical and Health Services. **Work Group:** 14.07. Patient Care and Assistance. **Other Job Titles in This Work Group:** Home Health Aides; Licensed Practical and Licensed Vocational Nurses; Psychiatric Aides; Psychiatric Technicians. **PERSONALITY TYPE—**Social. Social occupations frequently involve working with, communicating with, and teaching people. These occupations often involve helping or providing service to others.

EDUCATION/TRAINING PROGRAM(S)—Health Aide; Nurse/Nursing Assistant/Aide and Patient Care Assistant. **RELATED KNOWLEDGE/COURSES—Customer and Personal Service:** Knowledge of principles and processes for providing customer and personal services. This includes customer needs assessment, meeting quality standards for services, and evaluation of customer satisfaction. **Medicine and Dentistry:** Knowledge of the information and techniques needed to diagnose and treat human injuries, diseases, and deformities. This includes symptoms, treatment alternatives, drug properties and interactions, and preventive health-care measures. **Chemistry:** Knowledge of the chemical composition, structure, and properties of substances and of the chemical processes and transformations that they undergo. This includes uses of chemicals and their interactions, danger signs, produc-

tion techniques, and disposal methods. **Therapy and Counseling:** Knowledge of principles, methods, and procedures for diagnosis, treatment, and rehabilitation of physical and mental dysfunctions and for career counseling and guidance. **Public Safety and Security:** Knowledge of relevant equipment, policies, procedures, and strategies to promote effective local, state, or national security operations for the protection of people, data, property, and institutions.

Nursing Instructors and Teachers, Postsecondary

▲ Education/Training Required: Master's degree
▲ Annual Earnings: $49,470
▲ Growth: 23.5%
▲ Annual Job Openings: 184,000
▲ Self-Employed: 0%
▲ Part-Time: 32.3%

Demonstrate and teach patient care in classroom and clinical units to nursing students. Includes both teachers primarily engaged in teaching and those who do a combination of both teaching and research. Instructs and lectures nursing students in principles and application of physical, biological, and psychological subjects related to nursing. Conducts and supervises laboratory work. Issues assignments to students. Participates in planning curriculum, teaching schedule, and course outline with medical and nursing personnel. Directs seminars and panels. Supervises student nurses and demonstrates patient care in clinical units of hospital. Cooperates with medical and nursing personnel in evaluating and improving teaching and nursing practices. Prepares and administers examinations to nursing students. Evaluates student progress and maintains records of student classroom and clinical experience. Conducts classes for patients in health practices and procedures. **SKILLS—Learning Strategies:** Selecting and using training/instructional methods and procedures appropriate for the situation when learning or teaching new things. **Instructing:** Teaching others how to do something. **Reading Comprehension:** Understanding written sentences and paragraphs in work-related documents. **Speaking:** Talking to others to convey information effectively. **Science:** Using scientific rules and methods to solve problems.

GOE INFORMATION—Interest Area: 12. Education and Social Service. **Work Group:** 12.03. Educational Services. **Other Job Titles in This Work Group:** Adult Literacy, Remedial Education, and GED Teachers and

Instructors; Agricultural Sciences Teachers, Postsecondary; Anthropology and Archeology Teachers, Postsecondary; Architecture Teachers, Postsecondary; Archivists; Area, Ethnic, and Cultural Studies Teachers, Postsecondary; Art, Drama, and Music Teachers, Postsecondary; Atmospheric, Earth, Marine, and Space Sciences Teachers, Postsecondary; Audio-Visual Collections Specialists; Biological Science Teachers, Postsecondary; Business Teachers, Postsecondary; Chemistry Teachers, Postsecondary; Child Care Workers; Communications Teachers, Postsecondary; Computer Science Teachers, Postsecondary; Criminal Justice and Law Enforcement Teachers, Postsecondary; Curators; Economics Teachers, Postsecondary; Education Teachers, Postsecondary; Educational Psychologists; Educational, Vocational, and School Counselors; Elementary School Teachers, Except Special Education; Engineering Teachers, Postsecondary; English Language and Literature Teachers, Postsecondary; Environmental Science Teachers, Postsecondary; Farm and Home Management Advisors; Foreign Language and Literature Teachers, Postsecondary; Forestry and Conservation Science Teachers, Postsecondary; Geography Teachers, Postsecondary; Graduate Teaching Assistants; Health Specialties Teachers, Postsecondary; History Teachers, Postsecondary; Home Economics Teachers, Postsecondary; Kindergarten Teachers, Except Special Education; Law Teachers, Postsecondary; Librarians; Library Assistants, Clerical; Library Science Teachers, Postsecondary; Library Technicians; Mathematical Science Teachers, Postsecondary; Middle School Teachers, Except Special and

Vocational Education; Museum Technicians and Conservators; Personal Financial Advisors; Philosophy and Religion Teachers, Postsecondary; Physics Teachers, Postsecondary; Political Science Teachers, Postsecondary; Postsecondary Teachers, All Other; Preschool Teachers, Except Special Education; Psychology Teachers, Postsecondary; others. **PERSONALITY TYPE**—Social. Social occupations frequently involve working with, communicating with, and teaching people. These occupations often involve helping or providing service to others.

EDUCATION/TRAINING PROGRAM(S)—Adult Health Nurse/Nursing; Clinical Nurse Specialist; Family Practice Nurse/Nurse Practitioner; Maternal/Child Health and Neonatal Nurse/Nursing; Nurse Anesthetist; Nurse Midwife/Nursing Midwifery; Nursing—Registered Nurse Training (RN, ASN, BSN, MSN); Nursing Science (MS, PhD); Nursing, Other; Pediatric Nurse/Nursing; Perioperative/Operating Room and Surgical Nurse/Nursing; Pre-Nursing Studies; Psychiatric/Mental Health Nurse/Nursing; Public Health/Community Nurse/Nurs-

ing. **RELATED KNOWLEDGE/COURSES**—**Education and Training:** Knowledge of principles and methods for curriculum and training design, teaching and instruction for individuals and groups, and the measurement of training effects. **Medicine and Dentistry:** Knowledge of the information and techniques needed to diagnose and treat human injuries, diseases, and deformities. This includes symptoms, treatment alternatives, drug properties and interactions, and preventive health-care measures. **Biology:** Knowledge of plant and animal organisms and their tissues, cells, functions, interdependencies, and interactions with each other and the environment. **English Language:** Knowledge of the structure and content of the English language, including the meaning and spelling of words, rules of composition, and grammar. **Psychology:** Knowledge of human behavior and performance; individual differences in ability, personality, and interests; learning and motivation; psychological research methods; and the assessment and treatment of behavioral and affective disorders.

Obstetricians and Gynecologists

- ▲ Education/Training Required: First professional degree
- ▲ Annual Earnings: More than $145,600
- ▲ Growth: 17.9%
- ▲ Annual Job Openings: 27,000
- ▲ Self-Employed: 20.4%
- ▲ Part-Time: 7.2%

Diagnose, treat, and help prevent diseases of women, especially those affecting the reproductive system and the process of childbirth. Monitors patients' condition and progress and re-evaluates treatments as necessary. Examines or conducts tests on patient to provide information on medical condition. Collects, records, and maintains patient information, such as medical history, reports, and examination results. Advises patients and community concerning diet, activity, hygiene, and disease prevention. Directs and coordinates activities of nurses, students, assistants, specialists, therapists, and other medical staff. Conducts research to study anatomy and develop or test medications, treatments, or procedures to prevent or control disease or injury. Prepares reports for government or management of birth, death, and disease statistics, workforce evaluations, or medical status of individuals. Plans, implements, or administers health programs or standards in hospital, business, or community for information, prevention, or treatment of injury or illness. Refers

patient to medical specialist or other practitioner when necessary. Operates on patients to remove, repair, or improve functioning of diseased or injured body parts and systems and delivers babies. Analyzes records, reports, test results, or examination information to diagnose medical condition of patient. Explains procedures and discusses test results on prescribed treatments with patents. Prescribes or administers treatment, therapy, medication, vaccination, and other specialized medical care to treat or prevent illness, disease, or injury. **SKILLS**—**Reading Comprehension:** Understanding written sentences and paragraphs in work-related documents. **Science:** Using scientific rules and methods to solve problems. **Active Learning:** Understanding the implications of new information for both current and future problem-solving and decision-making. **Judgment and Decision Making:** Considering the relative costs and benefits of potential actions to choose the most appropriate one. **Active Listening:** Giving full attention to what other people are saying, taking time to understand the points being made, asking questions as appropriate, and not interrupting at inappropriate times. **Critical Thinking:** Using logic and reasoning to identify the strengths and weaknesses of alternative solutions, conclusions, or approaches to problems. **Writing:** Communicating effectively in writing as appropriate for the needs of the audience.

GOE INFORMATION—Interest Area: 14. Medical and Health Services. **Work Group:** 14.02. Medicine and Surgery. **Other Job Titles in This Work Group:** Anesthesiologists; Family and General Practitioners; Internists, General; Medical Assistants; Pediatricians, General; Pharmacists; Pharmacy Aides; Pharmacy Technicians; Physician Assistants; Physicians and Surgeons, All Other; Psychiatrists; Registered Nurses; Surgeons; Surgical Technologists. **PERSONALITY TYPE—**Investigative. Investigative occupations frequently involve working with ideas and require an extensive amount of thinking. These occupations can involve searching for facts and figuring out problems mentally.

EDUCATION/TRAINING PROGRAM(S)—Neonatal-Perinatal Medicine; Obstetrics and Gynecology. **RELATED KNOWLEDGE/COURSES—Medicine and Dentistry:** Knowledge of the information and techniques needed to diagnose and treat human injuries, diseases, and deformities. This includes symptoms, treatment alternatives, drug properties and interactions, and preventive health-care measures. **Biology:** Knowledge of plant and animal organisms and their tissues, cells, functions, interdependencies, and interactions with each other and the environment. **English Language:** Knowledge of the structure and content of the English language, including the meaning and spelling of words, rules of composition, and grammar. **Therapy and Counseling:** Knowledge of principles, methods, and procedures for diagnosis, treatment, and rehabilitation of physical and mental dysfunctions and for career counseling and guidance. **Administration and Management:** Knowledge of business and management principles involved in strategic planning, resource allocation, human resources modeling, leadership technique, production methods, and coordination of people and resources.

Occupational Therapist Assistants

- ▲ Education/Training Required: Associate's degree
- ▲ Annual Earnings: $35,840
- ▲ Growth: 39.7%
- ▲ Annual Job Openings: 3,000
- ▲ Self-Employed: 0%
- ▲ Part-Time: 24.9%

Assist occupational therapists in providing occupational therapy treatments and procedures. May, in accordance with state laws, assist in development of treatment plans, carry out routine functions, direct activity programs, and document the progress of treatments. Generally requires formal training. Assists occupational therapist to plan, implement, and administer educational, vocational, and recreational activities to restore, reinforce, and enhance task performances. Reports information and observations to supervisor verbally. Transports patient to and from occupational therapy work area. Maintains observed information in client records and prepares written reports. Prepares work material, assembles and maintains equipment, and orders supplies. Fabricates splints and other assistant devices. Assists educational specialist or clinical psychologist in administering situational or diagnostic tests to measure client's abilities or progress. Designs and adapts equipment and working-living environment. Helps professional staff demonstrate therapy techniques, such as

manual and creative arts and games. Instructs or assists in instructing patient and family in home programs and basic living skills as well as care and use of adaptive equipment. Assists in evaluation of physically disabled, developmentally disabled, mentally retarded, or emotionally disabled client's daily living skills and capacities. **SKILLS—Social Perceptiveness:** Being aware of others' reactions and understanding why they react as they do. **Reading Comprehension:** Understanding written sentences and paragraphs in work-related documents. **Active Listening:** Giving full attention to what other people are saying, taking time to understand the points being made, asking questions as appropriate, and not interrupting at inappropriate times. **Speaking:** Talking to others to convey information effectively. **Service Orientation:** Actively looking for ways to help people.

GOE INFORMATION—Interest Area: 14. Medical and Health Services. **Work Group:** 14.06. Medical Therapy.

Other Job Titles in This Work Group: Audiologists; Massage Therapists; Occupational Therapist Aides; Occupational Therapists; Physical Therapist Aides; Physical Therapist Assistants; Physical Therapists; Radiation Therapists; Recreational Therapists; Respiratory Therapists; Respiratory Therapy Technicians; Speech-Language Pathologists; Therapists, All Other. **PERSONALITY TYPE**—Social. Social occupations frequently involve working with, communicating with, and teaching people. These occupations often involve helping or providing service to others.

EDUCATION/TRAINING PROGRAM(S)—Occupational Therapist Assistant. **RELATED KNOWLEDGE/ COURSES**—**Therapy and Counseling:** Knowledge of principles, methods, and procedures for diagnosis, treatment, and rehabilitation of physical and mental dysfunctions and for career counseling and guidance. **Education and Training:** Knowledge of principles and methods for curriculum and training design, teaching and instruction for individuals and groups, and the measurement of training effects. **Medicine and Dentistry:** Knowledge of the information and techniques needed to diagnose and treat human injuries, diseases, and deformities. This includes symptoms, treatment alternatives, drug properties and interactions, and preventive health-care measures. **Psychology:** Knowledge of human behavior and performance; individual differences in ability, personality, and interests; learning and motivation; psychological research methods; and the assessment and treatment of behavioral and affective disorders. **English Language:** Knowledge of the structure and content of the English language, including the meaning and spelling of words, rules of composition, and grammar. **Customer and Personal Service:** Knowledge of principles and processes for providing customer and personal services. This includes customer needs assessment, meeting quality standards for services, and evaluation of customer satisfaction.

Occupational Therapists

▲ Education/Training Required: Bachelor's degree
▲ Annual Earnings: $51,370
▲ Growth: 33.9%
▲ Annual Job Openings: 4,000
▲ Self-Employed: 5.6%
▲ Part-Time: 20.8%

Assess, plan, organize, and participate in rehabilitative programs that help restore vocational, homemaking, and daily living skills, as well as general independence, to disabled persons. Plans, organizes, and conducts occupational therapy program in hospital, institutional, or community setting. Plans programs and social activities to help patients learn work skills and adjust to handicaps. Teaches individuals skills and techniques required for participation in activities and evaluates individual's progress. Consults with rehabilitation team to select activity programs and coordinate occupational therapy with other therapeutic activities. Requisitions supplies and equipment. Completes and maintains necessary records. Trains nurses and other medical staff in therapy techniques and objectives. Designs and constructs special equipment, such as splints and braces. Lays out materials for individual's use and cleans and repairs tools after therapy sessions. Recommends changes in individual's work or living environment consistent with needs and capabilities. Selects activities that will help individual learn work skills within limits of individual's mental and physical capabilities. **SKILLS**—**Instructing:** Teaching others how to do something. **Active Listening:** Giving full attention to what other people are saying, taking time to understand the points being made, asking questions as appropriate, and not interrupting at inappropriate times. **Social Perceptiveness:** Being aware of others' reactions and understanding why they react as they do. **Speaking:** Talking to others to convey information effectively. **Reading Comprehension:** Understanding written sentences and paragraphs in work-related documents.

GOE INFORMATION—**Interest Area:** 14. Medical and Health Services. **Work Group:** 14.06. Medical Therapy. **Other Job Titles in This Work Group:** Audiologists; Massage Therapists; Occupational Therapist Aides; Occupational Therapist Assistants; Physical Therapist Aides; Physical Therapist Assistants; Physical Therapists; Radiation Therapists; Recreational Therapists; Respiratory Therapists; Respiratory Therapy Technicians; Speech-Language Pathologists; Therapists, All Other. **PERSONALITY TYPE**—Social. Social occupations frequently involve working with, communicating with, and teaching people. These occupations often involve helping or providing service to others.

EDUCATION/TRAINING PROGRAM(S)—Occupational Therapy/Therapist. RELATED KNOWLEDGE/ COURSES—Therapy and Counseling: Knowledge of principles, methods, and procedures for diagnosis, treatment, and rehabilitation of physical and mental dysfunctions and for career counseling and guidance. Education and Training: Knowledge of principles and methods for curriculum and training design, teaching and instruction for individuals and groups, and the measurement of training effects. Administration and Management: Knowledge of business and management principles involved in strategic planning, resource allocation, human resources modeling, leadership technique, production methods, and coordination of people and resources. Psychology: Knowl-

edge of human behavior and performance; individual differences in ability, personality, and interests; learning and motivation; psychological research methods; and the assessment and treatment of behavioral and affective disorders. Clerical Studies: Knowledge of administrative and clerical procedures and systems, such as word processing, managing files and records, stenography and transcription, designing forms, and other office procedures and terminology. Customer and Personal Service: Knowledge of principles and processes for providing customer and personal services. This includes customer needs assessment, meeting quality standards for services, and evaluation of customer satisfaction. Medicine and Dentistry: Knowledge of the information and techniques needed to diagnose and treat human injuries, diseases, and deformities. This includes symptoms, treatment alternatives, drug properties and interactions, and preventive health-care measures.

Office Clerks, General

▲ Education/Training Required: Short-term on-the-job training
▲ Annual Earnings: $21,780
▲ Growth: 15.9%
▲ Annual Job Openings: 676,000
▲ Self-Employed: 0.5%
▲ Part-Time: 30.7%

Perform duties too varied and diverse to be classified in any specific office clerical occupation that require limited knowledge of office management systems and procedures. Clerical duties may be assigned in accordance with the office procedures of individual establishments and may include a combination of answering telephones, bookkeeping, typing or word processing, stenography, office machine operation, and filing. Compiles, copies, sorts, and files records of office activities, business transactions, and other activities. Communicates with customers, employees, and other individuals to disseminate or explain information. Collects, counts, and disburses money, completes banking transactions, and processes payroll. Completes work schedules and arranges appointments for staff and students. Reviews files, records, and other documents to obtain information to respond to requests. Answers telephone, responds to requests, delivers messages, and runs errands. Orders materials, supplies, and services and completes records and reports. Transcribes dictation and composes and types letters and other correspondence, using typewriter or computer. Stuffs envelopes and addresses, stamps, sorts, and distributes mail, pack-

ages, and other materials. Completes and mails bills, contracts, policies, invoices, or checks. Operates office machines, such as photocopier, telecopier, and personal computer. Computes, records, and proofreads data and other information, such as records or reports. SKILLS— Reading Comprehension: Understanding written sentences and paragraphs in work-related documents. Active Listening: Giving full attention to what other people are saying, taking time to understand the points being made, asking questions as appropriate, and not interrupting at inappropriate times. Mathematics: Using mathematics to solve problems. Writing: Communicating effectively in writing as appropriate for the needs of the audience. Speaking: Talking to others to convey information effectively.

GOE INFORMATION—Interest Area: 09. Business Detail. Work Group: 09.07. Records Processing. Other Job Titles in This Work Group: Correspondence Clerks; Court Reporters; Credit Authorizers; Credit Authorizers, Checkers, and Clerks; Credit Checkers; File Clerks; Human Resources Assistants, Except Payroll and Timekeeping; Information and Record Clerks, All Other; Insurance

Claims and Policy Processing Clerks; Insurance Claims Clerks; Insurance Policy Processing Clerks; Medical Records and Health Information Technicians; Medical Transcriptionists; Procurement Clerks; Proofreaders and Copy Markers. **PERSONALITY TYPE**—Conventional. Conventional occupations frequently involve following set procedures and routines. These occupations can include working with data and details more than with ideas. Usually there is a clear line of authority to follow.

EDUCATION/TRAINING PROGRAM(S)—General Office Occupations and Clerical Services. **RELATED KNOWLEDGE/COURSES**—**Clerical Studies:** Knowledge of administrative and clerical procedures and systems, such as word processing, managing files and records, stenography and transcription, designing forms, and other office procedures and terminology. **Customer and Personal Service:** Knowledge of principles and processes for providing customer and personal services. This includes customer needs assessment, meeting quality standards for services, and evaluation of customer satisfaction. **English Language:** Knowledge of the structure and content of the English language, including the meaning and spelling of words, rules of composition, and grammar. **Mathematics:** Knowledge of arithmetic, algebra, geometry, calculus, and statistics and their applications. **Computers and Electronics:** Knowledge of circuit boards, processors, chips, electronic equipment, and computer hardware and software, including applications and programming. **Economics and Accounting:** Knowledge of economic and accounting principles and practices, the financial markets, banking, and the analysis and reporting of financial data.

Office Machine and Cash Register Servicers

- ▲ Education/Training Required: Long-term on-the-job training
- ▲ Annual Earnings: $32,890
- ▲ Growth: 14.2%
- ▲ Annual Job Openings: 24,000
- ▲ Self-Employed: 6.8%
- ▲ Part-Time: 1.8%

Repair and service office machines, such as adding, accounting, calculating, duplicating, and typewriting machines. Includes the repair of manual, electrical, and electronic office machines. Tests machine to locate cause of electrical problems, using testing devices such as voltmeter, ohmmeter, and circuit test equipment. Disassembles machine and examines parts such as wires, gears, and bearings for wear and defects, using hand tools, power tools, and measuring devices. Operates machine such as typewriter, cash register, or adding machine to test functioning of parts and mechanisms. Assembles and installs machine according to specifications, using hand tools, power tools, and measuring devices. Cleans and oils mechanical parts to maintain machine. Reads specifications, such as blueprints, charts, and schematics, to determine machine settings and adjustments. Repairs, adjusts, or replaces electrical and mechanical components and parts, using hand tools, power tools, and soldering or welding equipment. Instructs operators and servicers in operation, maintenance, and repair of machine. **SKILLS**—**Instructing:** Teaching others how to do something. **Reading Comprehension:** Understanding written sentences and paragraphs in work-related documents. **Equipment Maintenance:** Performing routine maintenance on equipment and determining when and what kind of maintenance is needed. **Repairing:** Repairing machines or systems, using the needed tools. **Installation:** Installing equipment, machines, wiring, or programs to meet specifications. **Troubleshooting:** Determining causes of operating errors and deciding what to do about them. **Learning Strategies:** Selecting and using training/instructional methods and procedures appropriate for the situation when learning or teaching new things.

GOE INFORMATION—**Interest Area:** 05. Mechanics, Installers, and Repairers. **Work Group:** 05.02. Electrical and Electronic Systems. **Other Job Titles in This Work Group:** Avionics Technicians; Battery Repairers; Central Office and PBX Installers and Repairers; Communication Equipment Mechanics, Installers, and Repairers; Computer, Automated Teller, and Office Machine Repairers; Data Processing Equipment Repairers; Electric Home Appliance and Power Tool Repairers; Electric Meter Installers and Repairers; Electric Motor and Switch Assemblers and Repairers; Electric Motor, Power Tool, and Related Repairers; Electrical and Electronics Installers and Repairers, Transportation Equipment; Electrical and Electronics Repairers, Commercial and Industrial Equipment;

Electrical and Electronics Repairers, Powerhouse, Substation, and Relay; Electrical Parts Reconditioners; Electrical Power-Line Installers and Repairers; Electronic Equipment Installers and Repairers, Motor Vehicles; Electronic Home Entertainment Equipment Installers and Repairers; Elevator Installers and Repairers; Frame Wirers, Central Office; Home Appliance Installers; Home Appliance Repairers; Radio Mechanics; Signal and Track Switch Repairers; Station Installers and Repairers, Telephone; Telecommunications Equipment Installers and Repairers, Except Line Installers; Telecommunications Facility Examiners; Telecommunications Line Installers and Repairers; Transformer Repairers. **PERSONALITY TYPE—** Realistic. Realistic occupations frequently involve work activities that include practical, hands-on problems and solutions. They often deal with plants, animals, and real-world materials like wood, tools, and machinery. Many of the occupations require working outside and do not involve a lot of paperwork or working closely with others.

EDUCATION/TRAINING PROGRAM(S)—Business Machine Repair; Computer Installation and Repair Technology/Technician. **RELATED KNOWLEDGE/ COURSES—Principles of Mechanical Devices:** Knowledge of machines and tools, including their designs, uses, repair, and maintenance. **Computers and Electronics:** Knowledge of circuit boards, processors, chips, electronic equipment, and computer hardware and software, including applications and programming. **Engineering and Technology:** Knowledge of the practical application of engineering science and technology. This includes applying principles, techniques, procedures, and equipment to the design and production of various goods and services. **Education and Training:** Knowledge of principles and methods for curriculum and training design, teaching and instruction for individuals and groups, and the measurement of training effects. **Design:** Knowledge of design techniques, tools, and principles involved in production of precision technical plans, blueprints, drawings, and models.

Operating Engineers

- ▲ Education/Training Required: Moderate-term on-the-job training
- ▲ Annual Earnings: $34,160
- ▲ Growth: 6.9%
- ▲ Annual Job Openings: 25,000
- ▲ Self-Employed: 6.8%
- ▲ Part-Time: 2.0%

Operate several types of power construction equipment, such as compressors, pumps, hoists, derricks, cranes, shovels, tractors, scrapers, or motor graders, to excavate, move and grade earth, erect structures, or pour concrete or other hard-surface pavement. May repair and maintain equipment in addition to other duties. Adjusts handwheels and depresses pedals to drive machines and control attachments, such as blades, buckets, scrapers, and swing booms. Turns valves to control air and water output of compressors and pumps. Repairs and maintains equipment. **SKILLS—Operation and Control:** Controlling operations of equipment or systems. **Equipment Maintenance:** Performing routine maintenance on equipment and determining when and what kind of maintenance is needed. **Repairing:** Repairing machines or systems, using the needed tools. **Troubleshooting:** Determining causes of operating errors and deciding what to do about them. **Operation Monitoring:** Watching gauges, dials, or other indicators to make sure a machine is working properly.

GOE INFORMATION—Interest Area: 06. Construction, Mining, and Drilling. **Work Group:** 06.02. Construction. **Other Job Titles in This Work Group:** Boat Builders and Shipwrights; Boilermakers; Brattice Builders; Brickmasons and Blockmasons; Carpenters; Carpet Installers; Ceiling Tile Installers; Cement Masons and Concrete Finishers; Commercial Divers; Construction Carpenters; Drywall and Ceiling Tile Installers; Drywall Installers; Electricians; Explosives Workers, Ordnance Handling Experts, and Blasters; Fence Erectors; Floor Layers, Except Carpet, Wood, and Hard Tiles; Floor Sanders and Finishers; Glaziers; Grader, Bulldozer, and Scraper Operators; Hazardous Materials Removal Workers; Insulation Workers, Floor, Ceiling, and Wall; Insulation Workers, Mechanical; Manufactured Building and Mobile Home Installers; Operating Engineers and Other Construction Equipment Operators; Painters, Construction and Maintenance; Paperhangers; Paving, Surfacing, and Tamping Equipment Operators; Pile-Driver Operators; Pipe Fitters; Pipelayers; Pipelaying Fitters; Plasterers and

Stucco Masons; Plumbers; Plumbers, Pipefitters, and Steamfitters; Rail-Track Laying and Maintenance Equipment Operators; Refractory Materials Repairers, Except Brickmasons; Reinforcing Iron and Rebar Workers; Riggers; Roofers; Rough Carpenters; Security and Fire Alarm Systems Installers; Segmental Pavers; Sheet Metal Workers; Ship Carpenters and Joiners; Stone Cutters and Carvers; Stonemasons; Structural Iron and Steel Workers; Tapers; Terrazzo Workers and Finishers; Tile and Marble Setters. **PERSONALITY TYPE**—Realistic. Realistic occupations frequently involve work activities that include practical, hands-on problems and solutions. They often deal with plants, animals, and real-world materials like wood, tools, and machinery. Many of the occupations require working outside and do not involve a lot of paperwork or working closely with others.

EDUCATION/TRAINING PROGRAM(S)—Construction/Heavy Equipment/Earthmoving Equipment Operation; Mobile Crane Operation/Operator. **RELATED KNOWLEDGE/COURSES**—**Principles of Mechanical Devices:** Knowledge of machines and tools, including their designs, uses, repair, and maintenance. **Building and Construction:** Knowledge of materials, methods, and tools involved in the construction or repair of houses, buildings, or other structures, such as highways and roads. **Engineering and Technology:** Knowledge of the practical application of engineering science and technology. This includes applying principles, techniques, procedures, and equipment to the design and production of various goods and services. **Physics:** Knowledge and prediction of physical principles and laws and their interrelationships and applications to understanding fluid, material, and atmospheric dynamics and mechanical, electrical, atomic, and sub-atomic structures and processes. **Sales and Marketing:** Knowledge of principles and methods for showing, promoting, and selling products or services. This includes marketing strategy and tactics, product demonstration, sales techniques, and sales control systems.

Operating Engineers and Other Construction Equipment Operators

- ▲ Education/Training Required: Moderate-term on-the-job training
- ▲ Annual Earnings: $34,160
- ▲ Growth: 6.9%
- ▲ Annual Job Openings: 25,000
- ▲ Self-Employed: 1.5%
- ▲ Part-Time: 5.2%

Operate one or several types of power construction equipment, such as motor graders, bulldozers, scrapers, compressors, pumps, derricks, shovels, tractors, or front-end loaders, to excavate, move, and grade earth, erect structures, or pour concrete or other hard-surface pavement. May repair and maintain equipment in addition to other duties. **SKILLS**—No data available.

GOE INFORMATION—**Interest Area:** 06. Construction, Mining, and Drilling. **Work Group:** 06.02. Construction. **Other Job Titles in This Work Group:** Boat Builders and Shipwrights; Boilermakers; Brattice Builders; Brickmasons and Blockmasons; Carpenters; Carpet Installers; Ceiling Tile Installers; Cement Masons and Concrete Finishers; Commercial Divers; Construction Carpenters; Drywall and Ceiling Tile Installers; Drywall Installers; Electricians; Explosives Workers, Ordnance Handling Experts, and Blasters; Fence Erectors; Floor Layers, Except Carpet, Wood, and Hard Tiles; Floor Sanders and Finishers; Glaziers; Grader, Bulldozer, and Scraper Operators; Hazardous Materials Removal Workers; Insulation Workers, Floor, Ceiling, and Wall; Insulation Workers, Mechanical; Manufactured Building and Mobile Home Installers; Operating Engineers; Painters, Construction and Maintenance; Paperhangers; Paving, Surfacing, and Tamping Equipment Operators; Pile-Driver Operators; Pipe Fitters; Pipelayers; Pipelaying Fitters; Plasterers and Stucco Masons; Plumbers; Plumbers, Pipefitters, and Steamfitters; Rail-Track Laying and Maintenance Equipment Operators; Refractory Materials Repairers, Except Brickmasons; Reinforcing Iron and Rebar Workers; Riggers; Roofers; Rough Carpenters; Security and Fire Alarm Systems Installers; Segmental Pavers; Sheet Metal Workers; Ship Carpenters and Joiners; Stone Cutters and Carvers; Stonemasons; Structural Iron and Steel Workers; Tapers; Terrazzo Workers and Finishers; Tile and Marble Setters. **PERSONALITY TYPE**—No data available.

EDUCATION/TRAINING PROGRAM(S)—Construction/Heavy Equipment/Earthmoving Equipment Operation; Mobile Crane Operation/Operator. **RELATED KNOWLEDGE/COURSES**—No data available.

Optometrists

- ▲ Education/Training Required: First professional degree
- ▲ Annual Earnings: $85,650
- ▲ Growth: 18.7%
- ▲ Annual Job Openings: 1,000
- ▲ Self-Employed: 37.5%
- ▲ Part-Time: 10.5%

Diagnose, manage, and treat conditions and diseases of the human eye and visual system. Examine eyes and visual system, diagnose problems or impairments, prescribe corrective lenses, and provide treatment. May prescribe therapeutic drugs to treat specific eye conditions. Prescribes eyeglasses, contact lenses, and other vision aids or therapeutic procedures to correct or conserve vision. Consults with and refers patients to ophthalmologist or other health care practitioner if additional medical treatment is determined necessary. Examines eyes to determine visual acuity and perception and to diagnose diseases and other abnormalities, such as glaucoma and color blindness. Prescribes medications to treat eye diseases if state laws permit. **SKILLS—Reading Comprehension:** Understanding written sentences and paragraphs in work-related documents. **Active Listening:** Giving full attention to what other people are saying, taking time to understand the points being made, asking questions as appropriate, and not interrupting at inappropriate times. **Mathematics:** Using mathematics to solve problems. **Science:** Using scientific rules and methods to solve problems. **Instructing:** Teaching others how to do something. **Writing:** Communicating effectively in writing as appropriate for the needs of the audience.

GOE INFORMATION—**Interest Area:** 14. Medical and Health Services. **Work Group:** 14.04. Health Specialties. **Other Job Titles in This Work Group:** Chiropractors; Opticians, Dispensing; Podiatrists. **PERSONALITY**

TYPE—Investigative. Investigative occupations frequently involve working with ideas and require an extensive amount of thinking. These occupations can involve searching for facts and figuring out problems mentally.

EDUCATION/TRAINING PROGRAM(S)—Optometry (OD). **RELATED KNOWLEDGE/COURSES— Medicine and Dentistry:** Knowledge of the information and techniques needed to diagnose and treat human injuries, diseases, and deformities. This includes symptoms, treatment alternatives, drug properties and interactions, and preventive health-care measures. **Biology:** Knowledge of plant and animal organisms and their tissues, cells, functions, interdependencies, and interactions with each other and the environment. **English Language:** Knowledge of the structure and content of the English language, including the meaning and spelling of words, rules of composition, and grammar. **Customer and Personal Service:** Knowledge of principles and processes for providing customer and personal services. This includes customer needs assessment, meeting quality standards for services, and evaluation of customer satisfaction. **Mathematics:** Knowledge of arithmetic, algebra, geometry, calculus, and statistics and their applications. **Chemistry:** Knowledge of the chemical composition, structure, and properties of substances and of the chemical processes and transformations that they undergo. This includes uses of chemicals and their interactions, danger signs, production techniques, and disposal methods.

Order Fillers, Wholesale and Retail Sales

- ▲ Education/Training Required: Moderate-term on-the-job training
- ▲ Annual Earnings: $19,060
- ▲ Growth: 8.5%
- ▲ Annual Job Openings: 467,000
- ▲ Self-Employed: 0.1%
- ▲ Part-Time: 13.7%

Fill customers' mail and telephone orders from stored merchandise in accordance with specifications on sales slips or order forms. Duties include computing prices of items; completing order receipts; keeping records of outgoing orders; and requisitioning additional materials, supplies, and equipment. Computes price of each group of items. Obtains merchandise from bins or shelves. Places merchandise on conveyor leading to wrapping area. Reads order to ascertain catalog number, size, color, and quantity of merchandise. **SKILLS—Mathematics:** Using mathematics to solve problems. **Operation and Control:** Controlling operations of equipment or systems. **Coordination:** Adjusting actions in relation to others' actions.

GOE INFORMATION—Interest Area: 09. Business Detail. **Work Group:** 09.08. Records and Materials Processing. **Other Job Titles in This Work Group:** Cargo and Freight Agents; Couriers and Messengers; Mail Clerks, Except Mail Machine Operators and Postal Service; Marking Clerks; Postal Service Mail Carriers; Postal Service Mail Sorters, Processors, and Processing Machine Operators; Shipping, Receiving, and Traffic Clerks; Stock Clerks and Order Fillers; Stock Clerks—Stockroom, Warehouse, or Storage Yard; Weighers, Measurers, Checkers, and Samplers, Recordkeeping. **PERSONALITY TYPE—**Conventional. Conventional occupations frequently involve following set procedures and routines. These occupations can include working with data and details more than with ideas. Usually there is a clear line of authority to follow.

EDUCATION/TRAINING PROGRAM(S)—Retailing and Retail Operations. **RELATED KNOWLEDGE/ COURSES—Clerical Studies:** Knowledge of administrative and clerical procedures and systems, such as word processing, managing files and records, stenography and transcription, designing forms, and other office procedures and terminology. **English Language:** Knowledge of the structure and content of the English language, including the meaning and spelling of words, rules of composition, and grammar. **Mathematics:** Knowledge of arithmetic, algebra, geometry, calculus, and statistics and their applications. **Production and Processing:** Knowledge of raw materials, production processes, quality control, costs, and other techniques for maximizing the effective manufacture and distribution of goods.

Packaging and Filling Machine Operators and Tenders

- Education/Training Required: Short-term on-the-job training
- Annual Earnings: $20,760
- Growth: 14.4%
- Annual Job Openings: 56,000
- Self-Employed: 0%
- Part-Time: 7.1%

Operate or tend machines to prepare industrial or consumer products for storage or shipment. Includes cannery workers who pack food products. Tends or operates machine that packages product. Starts machine by engaging controls. Adjusts machine tension and pressure and machine components according to size or processing angle of product. Removes finished packaged items from machine and separates rejected items. Stocks product for packaging or filling machine operation. Tests and evaluates product and verifies product weight or measurement to ensure quality standards. Attaches identification labels to finished packaged items. Stacks finished packaged items or packs items in cartons or containers. Counts and records finished and rejected packaged items. Cleans, oils, and makes minor repairs to machinery and equipment. Secures finished packaged items by hand tying, sewing, or attaching fastener. Stocks packaging material for machine processing. Inspects and removes defective product and packaging material. Observes machine operations to ensure quality and conformity of filled or packaged products to standards. Stops or resets machine when malfunction occurs and clears machine jams. Regulates machine flow, speed, or temperature. Operates mechanism to cut filler product or packaging material. **SKILLS—Equipment Maintenance:** Performing routine maintenance on equipment and determining when and what kind of maintenance is needed. **Operation and Control:** Controlling operations of equipment or systems. **Operation Monitoring:** Watching gauges, dials, or other indicators to make sure a machine is working properly. **Repairing:** Repairing machines or systems, using the needed tools. **Quality Control Analysis:** Conducting tests and inspections of products, services, or processes to evaluate quality or performance.

GOE INFORMATION—Interest Area: 08. Industrial Production. **Work Group:** 08.03. Production Work. **Other Job Titles in This Work Group:** Bakers, Manufacturing; Bindery Machine Operators and Tenders; Brazers; Cementing and Gluing Machine Operators and Tenders;

Chemical Equipment Controllers and Operators; Chemical Equipment Operators and Tenders; Chemical Equipment Tenders; Cleaning, Washing, and Metal Pickling Equipment Operators and Tenders; Coating, Painting, and Spraying Machine Operators and Tenders; Coil Winders, Tapers, and Finishers; Combination Machine Tool Operators and Tenders, Metal and Plastic; Computer-Controlled Machine Tool Operators, Metal and Plastic; Cooling and Freezing Equipment Operators and Tenders; Crushing, Grinding, and Polishing Machine Setters, Operators, and Tenders; Cutters and Trimmers, Hand; Cutting and Slicing Machine Operators and Tenders; Cutting and Slicing Machine Setters, Operators, and Tenders; Design Printing Machine Setters and Set-Up Operators; Electrolytic Plating and Coating Machine Operators and Tenders, Metal and Plastic; Electrolytic Plating and Coating Machine Setters and Set-Up Operators, Metal and Plastic; Electrotypers and Stereotypers; Embossing Machine Set-Up Operators; Engraver Set-Up Operators; Extruding and Forming Machine Operators and Tenders, Synthetic or Glass Fibers; Extruding and Forming Machine Setters, Operators, and Tenders, Synthetic and Glass Fibers; Extruding, Forming, Pressing, and Compacting Machine Operators and Tenders; Fabric and Apparel Patternmakers; Fiber Product Cutting Machine Setters and Set-Up Operators; Fiberglass Laminators and Fabricators; Film Laboratory Technicians; Fitters, Structural Metal—Precision; Food and Tobacco Roasting, Baking, and Drying Machine Operators and Tenders; Food Batchmakers; Food Cooking Machine Operators and Tenders; Furnace, Kiln, Oven, Drier, and Kettle Operators and Tenders; Glass Cutting Machine Setters and Set-Up Operators; Graders and Sorters, Agricultural Products; Grinding and Polishing Workers, Hand; Hand Compositors and Typesetters; Heaters, Metal and Plastic; others. **PERSONALITY TYPE**—Realistic. Realistic occupations frequently involve work activities that include practical, hands-on problems and solutions. They often deal with plants, animals, and real-world materials like wood, tools, and machinery. Many of the occupations require working outside and do not involve a lot of paperwork or working closely with others.

EDUCATION/TRAINING PROGRAM(S)—No data available. **RELATED KNOWLEDGE/COURSES**—**Production and Processing:** Knowledge of raw materials, production processes, quality control, costs, and other techniques for maximizing the effective manufacture and distribution of goods. **Principles of Mechanical Devices:** Knowledge of machines and tools, including their designs, uses, repair, and maintenance. **Mathematics:** Knowledge of arithmetic, algebra, geometry, calculus, and statistics and their applications. **Physics:** Knowledge and prediction of physical principles and laws and their interrelationships and applications to understanding fluid, material, and atmospheric dynamics and mechanical, electrical, atomic, and sub-atomic structures and processes. **Public Safety and Security:** Knowledge of relevant equipment, policies, procedures, and strategies to promote effective local, state, or national security operations for the protection of people, data, property, and institutions. **Engineering and Technology:** Knowledge of the practical application of engineering science and technology. This includes applying principles, techniques, procedures, and equipment to the design and production of various goods and services.

Packers and Packagers, Hand

- ▲ Education/Training Required: Short-term on-the-job training
- ▲ Annual Earnings: $16,280
- ▲ Growth: 19.3%
- ▲ Annual Job Openings: 242,000
- ▲ Self-Employed: 0.1%
- ▲ Part-Time: 16.1%

Pack or package by hand a wide variety of products and materials. Fastens and wraps products and materials, using hand tools. Seals containers or materials, using glues, fasteners, and hand tools. Assembles and lines cartons, crates, and containers, using hand tools. Places or pours products or materials into containers, using hand tools and equipment. Marks and labels containers or products, using marking instruments. Loads materials and products into package processing equipment. Cleans containers, materials, or work area, using cleaning solutions and hand tools. Tends packing machines and equipment that prepare and package materials and products. Removes and places completed or defective product or materials on moving equipment or in specified area. Measures, weighs, and counts products and materials, using equipment. Records product and packaging information on specified forms and records. Examines and inspects containers, materials, and products to ensure packaging process meets specifications. Obtains and sorts products, materials, and orders, using hand tools. **SKILLS—Operation and Control:** Controlling operations of equipment or systems.

GOE INFORMATION—Interest Area: 08. Industrial Production. **Work Group:** 08.07. Hands-on Work: Loading, Moving, Hoisting, and Conveying. **Other Job Titles in This Work Group:** Conveyor Operators and Tenders; Crane and Tower Operators; Dragline Operators; Excavating and Loading Machine and Dragline Operators; Freight, Stock, and Material Movers, Hand; Hoist and Winch Operators; Industrial Truck and Tractor Operators; Irradiated-Fuel Handlers; Laborers and Freight, Stock, and Material Movers, Hand; Machine Feeders and Offbearers; Material Moving Workers, All Other; Pump Operators, Except Wellhead Pumpers; Refuse and Recyclable Material Collectors; Tank Car, Truck, and Ship Loaders. **PERSONALITY TYPE—**Realistic. Realistic occupations frequently involve work activities that include

practical, hands-on problems and solutions. They often deal with plants, animals, and real-world materials like wood, tools, and machinery. Many of the occupations require working outside and do not involve a lot of paperwork or working closely with others.

EDUCATION/TRAINING PROGRAM(S)—No data available. **RELATED KNOWLEDGE/COURSES—Production and Processing:** Knowledge of raw materials, production processes, quality control, costs, and other techniques for maximizing the effective manufacture and distribution of goods. **Clerical Studies:** Knowledge of administrative and clerical procedures and systems, such as word processing, managing files and records, stenography and transcription, designing forms, and other office procedures and terminology. **Mathematics:** Knowledge of arithmetic, algebra, geometry, calculus, and statistics and their applications. **English Language:** Knowledge of the structure and content of the English language, including the meaning and spelling of words, rules of composition, and grammar.

Painters, Construction and Maintenance

- ▲ Education/Training Required: Moderate-term on-the-job training
- ▲ Annual Earnings: $28,420
- ▲ Growth: 19.1%
- ▲ Annual Job Openings: 67,000
- ▲ Self-Employed: 45.8%
- ▲ Part-Time: 9.2%

Paint walls, equipment, buildings, bridges, and other structural surfaces, using brushes, rollers, and spray guns. May remove old paint to prepare surface prior to painting. May mix colors or oils to obtain desired color or consistency. Paints surfaces, using brushes, spray gun, or rollers. Applies paint to simulate wood grain, marble, brick, or stonework. Cuts stencils; brushes and sprays lettering and decorations on surfaces. Sands surfaces between coats and polishes final coat to specified finish. Bakes finish on painted and enameled articles in baking oven. Washes and treats surfaces with oil, turpentine, mildew remover, or other preparations. Mixes and matches colors of paint, stain, or varnish. Fills cracks, holes, and joints with caulk putty, plaster, or other filler, using caulking gun or putty knife. Reads work order or receives instructions from supervisor or homeowner. Erects scaffolding or sets up ladders to work above ground level. Covers surfaces with dropcloths or masking tape and paper to protect surface during painting. Burns off old paint, using blowtorch.

Removes fixtures, such as pictures and electric switchcovers, from walls prior to painting. Sprays or brushes hot plastics or pitch onto surfaces. Smoothes surfaces, using sandpaper, scrapers, brushes, steel wool, or sanding machine. **SKILLS—Mathematics:** Using mathematics to solve problems. **Reading Comprehension:** Understanding written sentences and paragraphs in work-related documents.

GOE INFORMATION—Interest Area: 06. Construction, Mining, and Drilling. **Work Group:** 06.02. Construction. **Other Job Titles in This Work Group:** Boat Builders and Shipwrights; Boilermakers; Brattice Builders; Brickmasons and Blockmasons; Carpenters; Carpet Installers; Ceiling Tile Installers; Cement Masons and Concrete Finishers; Commercial Divers; Construction Carpenters; Drywall and Ceiling Tile Installers; Drywall Installers; Electricians; Explosives Workers, Ordnance Handling Experts, and Blasters; Fence Erectors; Floor Layers, Except Carpet, Wood, and Hard Tiles; Floor Sanders and Finishers; Glaziers; Grader, Bulldozer, and Scraper Operators; Hazardous Materials Removal Workers; Insulation Workers, Floor, Ceiling, and Wall; Insulation Workers, Mechanical; Manufactured Building and Mobile Home Installers; Operating Engineers; Operating Engineers and Other Construction Equipment Operators; Paperhangers; Paving, Surfacing, and Tamping Equipment Operators; Pile-Driver Operators; Pipe Fitters; Pipelayers; Pipelaying Fitters; Plasterers and Stucco Masons; Plumbers; Plumbers, Pipefitters, and Steamfitters; Rail-Track Laying and Maintenance Equipment Operators; Refractory Materials Repairers, Except Brickmasons; Reinforcing Iron and Rebar Workers; Riggers; Roofers; Rough Carpenters; Security and Fire Alarm Systems Installers; Segmental Pavers; Sheet Metal Workers; Ship Carpenters and Joiners; Stone Cutters and Carvers; Stonemasons; Structural Iron and Steel Workers; Tapers; Terrazzo Workers and Finishers; Tile and Marble Setters. **PERSONALITY TYPE**—Realistic. Realistic occupations frequently involve work activities that include practical, hands-on problems and solutions. They often deal with plants, animals, and real-world materials like wood, tools, and machinery. Many of the occupations require working outside and do not involve a lot of paperwork or working closely with others.

EDUCATION/TRAINING PROGRAM(S)—Painting/Painter and Wall Coverer. **RELATED KNOWLEDGE/COURSES—Building and Construction:** Knowledge of materials, methods, and tools involved in the construction or repair of houses, buildings, or other structures, such as highways and roads. **Customer and Personal Service:** Knowledge of principles and processes for providing customer and personal services. This includes customer needs assessment, meeting quality standards for services, and evaluation of customer satisfaction. **Chemistry:** Knowledge of the chemical composition, structure, and properties of substances and of the chemical processes and transformations that they undergo. This includes uses of chemicals and their interactions, danger signs, production techniques, and disposal methods. **Principles of Mechanical Devices:** Knowledge of machines and tools, including their designs, uses, repair, and maintenance. **Fine Arts:** Knowledge of the theory and techniques required to compose, produce, and perform works of music, dance, visual arts, drama, and sculpture.

Painters, Transportation Equipment

- ▲ Education/Training Required: Moderate-term on-the-job training
- ▲ Annual Earnings: $32,330
- ▲ Growth: 17.5%
- ▲ Annual Job Openings: 8,000
- ▲ Self-Employed: 18.0%
- ▲ Part-Time: 5.7%

Operate or tend painting machines to paint surfaces of transportation equipment, such as automobiles, buses, trucks, trains, boats, and airplanes. Pours paint into spray gun and sprays specified amount of primer, decorative, or finish coatings onto prepared surfaces. Paints designs, lettering, or other identifying information on vehicles, using paint brush or paint sprayer. Operates lifting and moving devices to move equipment or materials to access areas to be painted. Removes accessories from vehicles, such as chrome or mirrors, and masks other surfaces with tape or paper. Sets up portable ventilators, exhaust units, ladders, and scaffolding. Strips grease, dirt, paint, and rust from vehicle surface, using abrasives, solvents, brushes, blowtorch, or sandblaster. Lays out logos, symbols, or designs on painted surfaces according to blueprint specifications, using measuring instruments, stencils, and patterns. Regulates controls on portable ventilators and exhaust units to cure and dry paint or other coatings. Disassembles sprayer and power equipment, such as sandblaster, and cleans equipment and hand tools, using solvents, wire brushes, and cloths. Selects paint according to company requirements and matches colors of paint following specified color charts. Mixes, stirs, and thins paint or other coatings, using spatula or power mixing equipment. Paints areas inaccessible to spray gun or retouches painted surface, using brush. **SKILLS—Operation and Control:** Controlling operations of equipment or systems.

GOE INFORMATION—Interest Area: 05. Mechanics, Installers, and Repairers. **Work Group:** 05.03. Mechanical Work. **Other Job Titles in This Work Group:** Aircraft Body and Bonded Structure Repairers; Aircraft Engine Specialists; Aircraft Mechanics and Service Technicians; Airframe-and-Power-Plant Mechanics; Automotive Body and Related Repairers; Automotive Glass Installers and Repairers; Automotive Master Mechanics; Automotive Service Technicians and Mechanics; Automotive Specialty Technicians; Bicycle Repairers; Bridge and Lock Tenders; Bus and Truck Mechanics and Diesel Engine Specialists; Camera and Photographic Equipment Repairers; Coin, Vending, and Amusement Machine Servicers and Repairers; Control and Valve Installers and Repairers, Except Mechanical Door; Farm Equipment Mechanics; Gas Appliance Repairers; Hand and Portable Power Tool Repairers; Heating and Air Conditioning Mechanics; Heating, Air Conditioning, and Refrigeration Mechanics and Installers; Helpers—Electricians; Helpers—Installation, Maintenance, and Repair Workers; Industrial Machinery Mechanics; Keyboard Instrument Repairers and Tuners; Locksmiths and Safe Repairers; Maintenance and Repair Workers, General; Maintenance Workers, Machinery; Mechanical Door Repairers; Medical Appliance Technicians; Medical Equipment Repairers; Meter Mechanics; Millwrights; Mobile Heavy Equipment Mechanics, Except Engines; Motorboat Mechanics; Motorcycle Mechanics; Musical Instrument Repairers and Tuners; Ophthalmic Laboratory Technicians; Optical Instrument Assemblers; Outdoor Power Equipment and Other Small Engine Mechanics; Percussion Instrument Repairers and Tuners; Precision Instrument and Equipment Repairers, All Other; Rail Car Repairers; Railroad Inspectors; Recreational Vehicle Service Technicians; Reed or Wind Instrument Repairers and Tuners; Refrigeration Mechanics; Stringed Instrument Repairers and Tuners; Tire Repairers and Changers; Valve and Regulator Repairers; Watch Repairers. **PERSONALITY TYPE**—Realistic. Realistic occupations frequently involve work activities that include practical, hands-on problems and solutions. They often deal with plants, animals, and real-world materials like wood, tools, and machinery. Many of the occupations require working outside and do not involve a lot of paperwork or working closely with others.

EDUCATION/TRAINING PROGRAM(S)—Auto body/Collision and Repair Technology/Technician. **RELATED KNOWLEDGE/COURSES—Principles of Mechanical Devices:** Knowledge of machines and tools, including their designs, uses, repair, and maintenance. **Mathematics:** Knowledge of arithmetic, algebra, geometry, calculus, and statistics and their applications. **Design:** Knowledge of design techniques, tools, and principles involved in production of precision technical plans, blueprints, drawings, and models. **Fine Arts:** Knowledge of the theory and techniques required to compose, produce, and perform works of music, dance, visual arts, drama, and sculpture. **Chemistry:** Knowledge of the chemical composition, structure, and properties of substances and of the chemical processes and transformations that they undergo. This includes uses of chemicals and their interactions, danger signs, production techniques, and disposal methods.

Paperhangers

- ▲ Education/Training Required: Moderate-term on-the-job training
- ▲ Annual Earnings: $31,330
- ▲ Growth: 20.2%
- ▲ Annual Job Openings: 3,000
- ▲ Self-Employed: 45.8%
- ▲ Part-Time: 9.2%

Cover interior walls and ceilings of rooms with decorative wallpaper or fabric or attach advertising posters on surfaces, such as walls and billboards. Duties include removing old materials from surface to be papered. Applies thinned glue to waterproof porous surfaces, using brush, roller, or pasting machine. Measures and cuts strips from roll of wallpaper or fabric, using shears or razor. Trims rough edges from strips, using straightedge and trimming knife. Trims excess material at ceiling or baseboard, using knife. Smoothes strips or poster sections with brush or roller to remove wrinkles and bubbles and to smooth joints. Aligns and places strips or poster sections of billboard on surface to match adjacent edges. Mixes paste, using paste powder and water, and brushes paste onto surface. Marks vertical guideline on wall to align first strip, using plumb bob and chalkline. Applies acetic acid to damp plaster to prevent lime from bleeding through paper. Staples or tacks advertising posters onto fences, walls, or poles. Measures walls and ceiling to compute number and length of strips required to cover surface. Fills holes and cracks with plaster, using trowel. Removes paint, varnish, and grease from surfaces, using paint remover and water soda solution. Erects and works from scaffold. Removes old paper, using water, steam machine, or chemical remover and scraper.

Smoothes rough spots on walls and ceilings, using sandpaper. **SKILLS—Mathematics:** Using mathematics to solve problems. **Reading Comprehension:** Understanding written sentences and paragraphs in work-related documents. **Critical Thinking:** Using logic and reasoning to identify the strengths and weaknesses of alternative solutions, conclusions, or approaches to problems.

GOE INFORMATION—Interest Area: 06. Construction, Mining, and Drilling. **Work Group:** 06.02. Construction. **Other Job Titles in This Work Group:** Boat Builders and Shipwrights; Boilermakers; Brattice Builders; Brickmasons and Blockmasons; Carpenters; Carpet Installers; Ceiling Tile Installers; Cement Masons and Concrete Finishers; Commercial Divers; Construction Carpenters; Drywall and Ceiling Tile Installers; Drywall Installers; Electricians; Explosives Workers, Ordnance Handling Experts, and Blasters; Fence Erectors; Floor Layers, Except Carpet, Wood, and Hard Tiles; Floor Sanders and Finishers; Glaziers; Grader, Bulldozer, and Scraper Operators; Hazardous Materials Removal Workers; Insulation Workers, Floor, Ceiling, and Wall; Insulation Workers, Mechanical; Manufactured Building and Mobile Home Installers; Operating Engineers; Operating Engineers and Other Construction Equipment Operators; Painters, Construction and Maintenance; Paving, Surfacing, and Tamping Equipment Operators; Pile-Driver Operators; Pipe Fitters; Pipelayers; Pipelaying Fitters; Plasterers and Stucco Masons; Plumbers; Plumbers, Pipefitters, and Steamfitters; Rail-Track Laying and Maintenance Equipment Operators; Refractory Materials Repairers, Except Brickmasons; Reinforcing Iron and Rebar Workers; Riggers; Roofers; Rough Carpenters; Security and Fire Alarm Systems Installers; Segmental Pavers; Sheet Metal Workers; Ship Carpenters and Joiners; Stone Cutters and Carvers; Stonemasons; Structural Iron and Steel Workers; Tapers; Terrazzo Workers and Finishers; Tile and Marble Setters. **PERSONALITY TYPE—**Realistic. Realistic occupations frequently involve work activities that include practical, hands-on problems and solutions. They often deal with plants, animals, and real-world materials like wood, tools, and machinery. Many of the occupations require working outside and do not involve a lot of paperwork or working closely with others.

EDUCATION/TRAINING PROGRAM(S)—Painting/Painter and Wall Coverer. **RELATED KNOWLEDGE/COURSES—Building and Construction:** Knowledge of materials, methods, and tools involved in the construction or repair of houses, buildings, or other structures, such as highways and roads. **Design:** Knowledge of design techniques, tools, and principles involved in production of precision technical plans, blueprints, drawings, and models. **Mathematics:** Knowledge of arithmetic, algebra, geometry, calculus, and statistics and their applications. **Chemistry:** Knowledge of the chemical composition, structure, and properties of substances and of the chemical processes and transformations that they undergo. This includes uses of chemicals and their interactions, danger signs, production techniques, and disposal methods. **Principles of Mechanical Devices:** Knowledge of machines and tools, including their designs, uses, repair, and maintenance.

Paralegals and Legal Assistants

▲ Education/Training Required: Associate's degree
▲ Annual Earnings: $36,670
▲ Growth: 33.2%
▲ Annual Job Openings: 23,000
▲ Self-Employed: 0.9%
▲ Part-Time: 12.5%

Assist lawyers by researching legal precedent, investigating facts, or preparing legal documents. Conduct research to support a legal proceeding, to formulate a defense, or to initiate legal action. Gathers and analyzes research data, such as statutes; decisions; and legal articles, codes, and documents. Prepares legal documents, including briefs, pleadings, appeals, wills, contracts, and real estate closing statements. Prepares affidavits or other documents, maintains document file, and files pleadings with court clerk. Arbitrates disputes between parties and assists in real estate closing process. Answers questions regarding legal issues pertaining to civil service hearings. Presents arguments and evidence to support appeal at appeal hearing. Keeps and monitors legal volumes to ensure that law library is up-to-date. Directs and coordinates law office activity, including delivery of subpoenas. Calls upon witnesses to testify at hearing. Appraises and inventories real and personal property for estate planning. Investigates facts and law of cases to determine causes of action and to prepare cases. **SKILLS—Reading Comprehension:** Understanding written sentences and paragraphs in work-related documents. **Critical Thinking:** Using logic and reasoning to identify the strengths and weaknesses of alternative solutions, conclusions, or approaches to problems. **Speaking:** Talking to others to convey information effectively. **Writing:** Communicating effectively in writing as appropriate for the needs of the audience. **Negotiation:** Bringing others together and trying to reconcile differences. **Persuasion:** Persuading others to change their minds or behavior. **Active Listening:** Giving full attention to what other people are saying, taking time to understand the points being made, asking questions as appropriate, and not interrupting at inappropriate times.

GOE INFORMATION—Interest Area: 04. Law, Law Enforcement, and Public Safety. **Work Group:** 04.02. Law. **Other Job Titles in This Work Group:** Administrative Law Judges, Adjudicators, and Hearing Officers; Arbitrators, Mediators, and Conciliators; Judges, Magistrate Judges, and Magistrates; Law Clerks; Lawyers; Legal Support Workers, All Other; Title Examiners and Abstractors; Title Examiners, Abstractors, and Searchers; Title Searchers. **PERSONALITY TYPE—Enterprising.** Enterprising occupations frequently involve starting up and carrying out projects. These occupations can involve leading people and making many decisions. They sometimes require risk taking and often deal with business.

EDUCATION/TRAINING PROGRAM(S)—Legal Assistant/Paralegal. RELATED KNOWLEDGE/ COURSES—Law and Government: Knowledge of laws, legal codes, court procedures, precedents, government regulations, executive orders, agency rules, and the democratic political process. **Clerical Studies:** Knowledge of administrative and clerical procedures and systems, such as word processing, managing files and records, stenography and transcription, designing forms, and other office procedures and terminology. **English Language:** Knowledge of the structure and content of the English language, including the meaning and spelling of words, rules of composition, and grammar. **Computers and Electronics:** Knowledge of circuit boards, processors, chips, electronic equipment, and computer hardware and software, including applications and programming. **Administration and Management:** Knowledge of business and management principles involved in strategic planning, resource allocation, human resources modeling, leadership technique, production methods, and coordination of people and resources.

Parking Lot Attendants

- ▲ Education/Training Required: Short-term on-the-job training
- ▲ Annual Earnings: $15,690
- ▲ Growth: 19.8%
- ▲ Annual Job Openings: 17,000
- ▲ Self-Employed: 0%
- ▲ Part-Time: 15.4%

Park automobiles or issue tickets for customers in a parking lot or garage. May collect fee. Parks automobiles in parking lot, storage garage, or new car lot. Takes numbered tag from customer, locates car, and delivers it to customer or directs customer to parked car. Patrols area to prevent thefts of parked automobiles or items in automobiles. Collects parking fee from customer, based on charges for time automobile is parked. Places numbered tag on windshield of automobile to be parked and hands customer similar tag to be used in locating parked automobile. Signals or directs vehicle drivers with hands or flashlight to parking area. Lifts, positions, and removes barricades to open or close parking areas. Services cars in storage to protect tires, battery, and finish against deterioration. Services vehicles with gas, oil, and water. Inspects vehicles to detect damage. Keeps new car lot in order and maximizes use of space. **SKILLS—Writing:** Communicating effectively in writing as appropriate for the needs of the audience.

GOE INFORMATION—Interest Area: 07. Transportation. **Work Group:** 07.07. Other Services Requiring Driving. **Other Job Titles in This Work Group:** Ambulance Drivers and Attendants, Except Emergency Medical Technicians; Bus Drivers, School; Bus Drivers, Transit and Intercity; Driver/Sales Workers; Taxi Drivers and Chauffeurs. **PERSONALITY TYPE—Realistic.** Realistic occupations frequently involve work activities that include practical, hands-on problems and solutions. They often deal with plants, animals, and real-world materials like wood, tools, and machinery. Many of the occupations require working outside and do not involve a lot of paperwork or working closely with others.

EDUCATION/TRAINING PROGRAM(S)—No data available. RELATED KNOWLEDGE/COURSES— **Customer and Personal Service:** Knowledge of principles and processes for providing customer and personal services. This includes customer needs assessment, meeting quality standards for services, and evaluation of customer satisfaction. **Mathematics:** Knowledge of arithmetic, algebra, geometry, calculus, and statistics and their applica-tions. **Public Safety and Security:** Knowledge of relevant equipment, policies, procedures, and strategies to promote effective local, state, or national security operations for the protection of people, data, property, and institutions. **Principles of Mechanical Devices:** Knowledge of machines and tools, including their designs, uses, repair, and main-tenance. **Clerical Studies:** Knowledge of administrative and clerical procedures and systems, such as word pro-cessing, managing files and records, stenography and tran-scription, designing forms, and other office procedures and terminology.

Pediatricians, General

- ▲ Education/Training Required: First professional degree
- ▲ Annual Earnings: $126,430
- ▲ Growth: 17.9%
- ▲ Annual Job Openings: 27,000
- ▲ Self-Employed: 20.4%
- ▲ Part-Time: 7.2%

Diagnose, treat, and help prevent children's diseases and injuries. Examines or conducts tests on patient to provide information on medical condition. Conducts research to study anatomy and develop or test medications, treat-ments, or procedures to prevent or control disease or in-jury. Prepares reports for government or management of birth, death, and disease statistics, workforce evaluations, or medical status of individuals. Directs and coordinates activities of nurses, students, assistants, specialists, thera-pists, and other medical staff. Plans, implements, or ad-ministers health programs or standards in hospital, business, or community for information, prevention, or treatment of injury or illness. Explains procedures and discusses test results on prescribed treatments with pat-ents. Operates on patients to remove, repair, or improve functioning of diseased or injured body parts and systems and delivers babies. Collects, records, and maintains pa-tient information, such as medical history, reports, and examination results. Advises patients and community con-cerning diet, activity, hygiene, and disease prevention. Refers patient to medical specialist or other practitioner when necessary. Prescribes or administers treatment, therapy, medication, vaccination, and other specialized medical care to treat or prevent illness, disease, or injury. Analyzes records, reports, test results, or examination in-formation to diagnose medical condition of patient. Moni-tors patients' condition and progress and re-evaluates treatments as necessary. **SKILLS—Reading Comprehen-sion:** Understanding written sentences and paragraphs in work-related documents. **Active Learning:** Understand-ing the implications of new information for both current and future problem-solving and decision-making. **Science:** Using scientific rules and methods to solve problems. **Judg-ment and Decision Making:** Considering the relative costs and benefits of potential actions to choose the most ap-propriate one. **Mathematics:** Using mathematics to solve problems. **Active Listening:** Giving full attention to what other people are saying, taking time to understand the points being made, asking questions as appropriate, and not interrupting at inappropriate times. **Writing:** Com-municating effectively in writing as appropriate for the needs of the audience.

GOE INFORMATION—**Interest Area:** 14. Medical and Health Services. **Work Group:** 14.02. Medicine and Sur-gery. **Other Job Titles in This Work Group:** Anesthesi-ologists; Family and General Practitioners; Internists, General; Medical Assistants; Obstetricians and Gynecolo-gists; Pharmacists; Pharmacy Aides; Pharmacy Technicians; Physician Assistants; Physicians and Surgeons, All Other; Psychiatrists; Registered Nurses; Surgeons; Surgical Tech-nologists. **PERSONALITY TYPE**—Investigative. Inves-tigative occupations frequently involve working with ideas and require an extensive amount of thinking. These occu-pations can involve searching for facts and figuring out problems mentally.

EDUCATION/TRAINING PROGRAM(S)—Child/Pediatric Neurology; Family Medicine; Neonatal-Perinatal Medicine; Pediatric Cardiology; Pediatric Endocrinology; Pediatric Hemato-Oncology; Pediatric Nephrology; Pediatric Orthopedics; Pediatric Surgery; Pediatrics. **RELATED KNOWLEDGE/COURSES—Medicine and Dentistry:** Knowledge of the information and techniques needed to diagnose and treat human injuries, diseases, and deformities. This includes symptoms, treatment alternatives, drug properties and interactions, and preventive health-care measures. **Biology:** Knowledge of plant and animal organisms and their tissues, cells, functions, interdependencies, and interactions with each other and the environment. **English Language:** Knowledge of the structure and content of the English language, including the meaning and spelling of words, rules of composition, and grammar. **Therapy and Counseling:** Knowledge of principles, methods, and procedures for diagnosis, treatment, and rehabilitation of physical and mental dysfunctions and for career counseling and guidance. **Administration and Management:** Knowledge of business and management principles involved in strategic planning, resource allocation, human resources modeling, leadership technique, production methods, and coordination of people and resources.

Personal and Home Care Aides

- ▲ Education/Training Required: Short-term on-the-job training
- ▲ Annual Earnings: $16,140
- ▲ Growth: 62.5%
- ▲ Annual Job Openings: 84,000
- ▲ Self-Employed: 0%
- ▲ Part-Time: 42.4%

Assist elderly or disabled adults with daily living activities at the person's home or in a daytime non-residential facility. Duties performed at a place of residence may include keeping house (making beds, doing laundry, washing dishes) and preparing meals. May provide meals and supervised activities at non-residential care facilities. May advise families, the elderly, and disabled on such things as nutrition, cleanliness, and household utilities. Advises and assists family members in planning nutritious meals, purchasing and preparing foods, and utilizing commodities from surplus food programs. Evaluates needs of individuals served and plans for continuing services. Prepares and maintains records of assistance rendered. Assists client with dressing, undressing, and toilet activities. Assists parents in establishing good study habits for children. Drives motor vehicle to transport client to specified locations. Types correspondence and reports. Obtains information for client for personal and business purposes. Assigns housekeeping duties according to children's capabilities. Gives bedside care to incapacitated individuals and trains family members to provide bedside care. Assists in training children. Explains fundamental hygiene principles. **SKILLS—Service Orientation:** Actively looking for ways to help people. **Speaking:** Talking to others to convey information effectively. **Social Perceptiveness:** Being aware of others' reactions and understanding why they react as they do. **Learning Strategies:** Selecting and using training/instructional methods and procedures appropriate for the situation when learning or teaching new things. **Active Listening:** Giving full attention to what other people are saying, taking time to understand the points being made, asking questions as appropriate, and not interrupting at inappropriate times.

GOE INFORMATION—Interest Area: 11. Recreation, Travel, and Other Personal Services. **Work Group:** 11.08. Other Personal Services. **Other Job Titles in This Work Group:** Cleaners of Vehicles and Equipment; Cooks, Private Household; Embalmers; Funeral Attendants; Personal Care and Service Workers, All Other. **PERSONALITY TYPE—Social.** Social occupations frequently involve working with, communicating with, and teaching people. These occupations often involve helping or providing service to others.

EDUCATION/TRAINING PROGRAM(S)—No data available. RELATED KNOWLEDGE/COURSES—Customer and Personal Service: Knowledge of principles and processes for providing customer and personal services. This includes customer needs assessment, meeting quality standards for services, and evaluation of customer satisfaction. **Medicine and Dentistry:** Knowledge of the information and techniques needed to diagnose and treat human injuries, diseases, and deformities. This includes symptoms, treatment alternatives, drug properties and interactions, and preventive health-care measures. **Education and Training:** Knowledge of principles and methods for curriculum and training design, teaching and instruction for individuals and groups, and the measurement of training effects. **Clerical Studies:** Knowledge of administrative and clerical procedures and systems, such as word processing, managing files and records, stenography and

transcription, designing forms, and other office procedures and terminology. **Administration and Management:** Knowledge of business and management principles involved in strategic planning, resource allocation, human resources modeling, leadership technique, production methods, and coordination of people and resources.

Personal Financial Advisors

▲ Education/Training Required: Bachelor's degree
▲ Annual Earnings: $57,710
▲ Growth: 34.0%
▲ Annual Job Openings: 13,000
▲ Self-Employed: 5.4%
▲ Part-Time: 7.7%

Advise clients on financial plans, utilizing knowledge of tax and investment strategies, securities, insurance, pension plans, and real estate. Duties include assessing clients' assets, liabilities, cash flow, insurance coverage, tax status, and financial objectives to establish investment strategies. Interviews client with debt problems to determine available monthly income after living expenses to meet credit obligations. Establishes payment priorities to plan payoff method and estimate time for debt liquidation. Explains to individuals and groups financial assistance available to college and university students, such as loans, grants, and scholarships. Interviews students to obtain information and compares data on students' applications with eligibility requirements to determine eligibility for assistance program. Contacts creditors to arrange for payment adjustments so that payments are feasible for client and agreeable to creditors. Prepares required records and reports. Assists in selection of candidates for specific financial awards or aid. Authorizes release of funds to students. Opens account for client and disburses funds from account to creditors as agent for client. Determines amount of aid to be granted, considering such factors as funds available, extent of demand, and needs of students. Calculates amount of debt and funds available. Counsels client on financial problems, such as excessive spending and borrowing of funds. **SKILLS—Active Listening:** Giving full attention to what other people are saying, taking time to understand the points being made, asking questions as appropriate, and not interrupting at inappropriate times. **Speaking:** Talking to others to convey information effectively. **Reading Comprehension:** Understanding written sentences and paragraphs in work-related documents. **Mathematics:** Using mathematics to solve problems. **Criti-**

cal **Thinking:** Using logic and reasoning to identify the strengths and weaknesses of alternative solutions, conclusions, or approaches to problems. **Judgment and Decision Making:** Considering the relative costs and benefits of potential actions to choose the most appropriate one. **Service Orientation:** Actively looking for ways to help people.

GOE INFORMATION—Interest Area: 12. Education and Social Service. **Work Group:** 12.03. Educational Services. **Other Job Titles in This Work Group:** Adult Literacy, Remedial Education, and GED Teachers and Instructors; Agricultural Sciences Teachers, Postsecondary; Anthropology and Archeology Teachers, Postsecondary; Architecture Teachers, Postsecondary; Archivists; Area, Ethnic, and Cultural Studies Teachers, Postsecondary; Art, Drama, and Music Teachers, Postsecondary; Atmospheric, Earth, Marine, and Space Sciences Teachers, Postsecondary; Audio-Visual Collections Specialists; Biological Science Teachers, Postsecondary; Business Teachers, Postsecondary; Chemistry Teachers, Postsecondary; Child Care Workers; Communications Teachers, Postsecondary; Computer Science Teachers, Postsecondary; Criminal Justice and Law Enforcement Teachers, Postsecondary; Curators; Economics Teachers, Postsecondary; Education Teachers, Postsecondary; Educational Psychologists; Educational, Vocational, and School Counselors; Elementary School Teachers, Except Special Education; Engineering Teachers, Postsecondary; English Language and Literature Teachers, Postsecondary; Environmental Science Teachers, Postsecondary; Farm and Home Management Advisors; Foreign Language and Literature Teachers, Postsecondary; Forestry and Conservation Science Teachers, Postsecondary; Geography Teachers, Postsecondary; Graduate Teaching Assistants; Health Specialties Teachers, Postsecondary; History Teachers, Postsecondary; Home Economics Teachers, Postsecondary; Kindergarten Teachers, Except Special Education; Law Teachers, Postsecondary; Librarians; Library Assistants, Clerical; Library Science Teachers, Postsecondary; Library Technicians; Mathematical Science Teachers, Postsecondary; Middle School Teachers, Except Special and Vocational Education; Museum Technicians and Conservators; Nursing Instructors and Teachers, Postsecondary; Philosophy and Religion Teachers, Postsecondary; Physics Teachers, Postsecondary; Political Science Teachers, Postsecondary; Postsecondary Teachers, All Other; Preschool Teachers, Except Special Education; others. **PERSONALITY TYPE**—Social. Social occupations frequently involve working with, communicating with, and teaching people. These occupations often involve helping or providing service to others.

EDUCATION/TRAINING PROGRAM(S)—Finance, General; Financial Planning and Services. **RELATED KNOWLEDGE/COURSES**—**Economics and Accounting:** Knowledge of economic and accounting principles and practices, the financial markets, banking, and the analysis and reporting of financial data. **Mathematics:** Knowledge of arithmetic, algebra, geometry, calculus, and statistics and their applications. **Administration and Management:** Knowledge of business and management principles involved in strategic planning, resource allocation, human resources modeling, leadership technique, production methods, and coordination of people and resources. **Customer and Personal Service:** Knowledge of principles and processes for providing customer and personal services. This includes customer needs assessment, meeting quality standards for services, and evaluation of customer satisfaction. **English Language:** Knowledge of the structure and content of the English language, including the meaning and spelling of words, rules of composition, and grammar.

Personnel Recruiters

▲ Education/Training Required: Bachelor's degree
▲ Annual Earnings: $38,010
▲ Growth: 17.6%
▲ Annual Job Openings: 19,000
▲ Self-Employed: 2.6%
▲ Part-Time: 6.9%

Seek out, interview, and screen applicants to fill existing and future job openings and promote career opportunities within an organization. Interviews applicants to obtain work history, training, education, job skills, and other background information. Arranges for interviews and travel and lodging for selected applicants at company expense. Projects yearly recruitment expenditures for budgetary consideration and control. Corrects and scores portions of examinations used to screen and select applicants. Prepares and maintains employment records and authorizes paperwork assigning applicant to positions. Speaks to civic, social, and other groups to provide information concerning job possibilities and career opportunities. Assists and advises establishment management in organizing, preparing, and implementing recruiting and retention programs. Evaluates recruitment and selection criteria to ensure conformance to professional, statistical, and testing standards and recommends revision as needed. Hires or refers applicant to other hiring personnel in organization. Provides potential applicants with information regarding facilities, operations, benefits, and job or career opportunities in organization. Contacts college representatives to arrange for and schedule on-campus interviews with students. Reviews and evaluates applicant qualifications or eligibility for specified licensing, according to established guidelines and designated licensing codes. Notifies applicants by mail or telephone to inform them of employment possibilities, consideration, and selection. Conducts reference and background checks on applicants. **SKILLS**—**Active Listening:** Giving full attention to what other people are saying, taking time to understand the points being made, asking questions as appropriate, and not interrupting at inappropriate times. **Reading Comprehension:** Understanding written sentences and paragraphs in work-related documents. **Writing:** Communicating effectively in writing as appropriate for the needs of the audience. **Speaking:** Talking to others to convey information effectively. **Management of Personnel Resources:** Motivating, developing, and directing people as they work, identifying the best people for the job. **Judgment and Decision Making:** Considering the relative costs and benefits of potential actions to choose the most appropriate one.

GOE INFORMATION—Interest Area: 13. General Management and Support. **Work Group:** 13.02. Management Support. **Other Job Titles in This Work Group:** Accountants; Accountants and Auditors; Appraisers and Assessors of Real Estate; Appraisers, Real Estate; Assessors; Auditors; Budget Analysts; Claims Adjusters, Examiners, and Investigators; Claims Examiners, Property and Casualty Insurance; Compensation, Benefits, and Job Analysis Specialists; Cost Estimators; Credit Analysts; Employment Interviewers, Private or Public Employment Service; Employment, Recruitment, and Placement Specialists; Financial Analysts; Human Resources, Training, and Labor Relations Specialists, All Other; Insurance Adjusters, Examiners, and Investigators; Insurance Appraisers, Auto Damage; Insurance Underwriters; Loan Counselors; Loan Officers; Logisticians; Management Analysts; Market Research Analysts; Purchasing Agents and Buyers, Farm Products; Purchasing Agents, Except Wholesale, Retail, and Farm Products; Tax Examiners, Collectors, and Revenue Agents; Training and Development Specialists; Wholesale and Retail Buyers, Except Farm Products. **PERSONALITY TYPE**—Enterprising. Enterprising occupations frequently involve starting up and carrying out projects. These occupations can involve leading people and making many decisions. They sometimes require risk taking and often deal with business.

EDUCATION/TRAINING PROGRAM(S)—Human Resources Management/Personnel Administration, General; Labor and Industrial Relations. **RELATED KNOWLEDGE/COURSES—Personnel and Human Resources:** Knowledge of principles and procedures for personnel recruitment, selection, training, compensation and benefits, labor relations and negotiation, and personnel information systems. **Psychology:** Knowledge of human behavior and performance; individual differences in ability, personality, and interests; learning and motivation; psychological research methods; and the assessment and treatment of behavioral and affective disorders. **English Language:** Knowledge of the structure and content of the English language, including the meaning and spelling of words, rules of composition, and grammar. **Administration and Management:** Knowledge of business and management principles involved in strategic planning, resource allocation, human resources modeling, leadership technique, production methods, and coordination of people and resources. **Sales and Marketing:** Knowledge of principles and methods for showing, promoting, and selling products or services. This includes marketing strategy and tactics, product demonstration, sales techniques, and sales control systems. **Mathematics:** Knowledge of arithmetic, algebra, geometry, calculus, and statistics and their applications.

Pest Control Workers

- ▲ Education/Training Required: Moderate-term on-the-job training
- ▲ Annual Earnings: $23,150
- ▲ Growth: 22.1%
- ▲ Annual Job Openings: 7,000
- ▲ Self-Employed: 7.1%
- ▲ Part-Time: 30.4%

Spray or release chemical solutions or toxic gases and set traps to kill pests and vermin, such as mice, termites, and roaches, that infest buildings and surrounding areas. Sprays or dusts chemical solutions, powders, or gases into rooms; onto clothing, furnishings or wood; and over marshlands, ditches, or catch-basins. Sets mechanical traps and places poisonous paste or bait in sewers, burrows, and ditches. Cuts or bores openings in building or surrounding concrete, accesses infested areas, inserts nozzle, and injects pesticide to impregnate ground. Directs and/or assists other workers in treatment and extermination processes to eliminate and control rodents, insects, and weeds.

Cleans and removes blockages from infested areas to facilitate spraying procedure and provide drainage, using broom, mop, shovel, and rake. Digs up and burns or sprays weeds with herbicides. Cleans work site after completion of job. Records work activities performed. Drives truck equipped with power spraying equipment. Posts warning signs and locks building doors to secure area to be fumigated. Positions and fastens edges of tarpaulins over building and tapes vents to ensure airtight environment and checks for leaks. Measures area dimensions requiring treatment, using rule; calculates fumigant requirements; and estimates cost for service. Studies preliminary reports and diagrams of infested area and determines treatment type required to eliminate and prevent recurrence of infestation. Inspects premises to identify infestation source and extent of damage to property, wall, and roof porosity and access to infested locations. **SKILLS—Mathematics:** Using mathematics to solve problems. **Reading Comprehension:** Understanding written sentences and paragraphs in work-related documents. **Judgment and Decision Making:** Considering the relative costs and benefits of potential actions to choose the most appropriate one. **Operation and Control:** Controlling operations of equipment or systems. **Equipment Selection:** Determining the kind of tools and equipment needed to do a job.

GOE INFORMATION—Interest Area: 03. Plants and Animals. **Work Group:** 03.03. Hands-on Work in Plants and Animals. **Other Job Titles in This Work Group:** Agricultural Equipment Operators; Fallers; Farmworkers and Laborers, Crop, Nursery, and Greenhouse; Farmworkers, Farm and Ranch Animals; Fishers and Related Fishing Workers; Forest and Conservation Technicians; Forest and Conservation Workers; General Farmworkers; Grounds Maintenance Workers, All Other; Hunters and Trappers; Landscaping and Groundskeeping Workers; Logging Equipment Operators; Logging Tractor Operators; Logging Workers, All Other; Nursery Workers; Pesticide Handlers, Sprayers, and Applicators,

Vegetation; Tree Trimmers and Pruners. **PERSONALITY TYPE—Realistic.** Realistic occupations frequently involve work activities that include practical, hands-on problems and solutions. They often deal with plants, animals, and real-world materials like wood, tools, and machinery. Many of the occupations require working outside and do not involve a lot of paperwork or working closely with others.

EDUCATION/TRAINING PROGRAM(S)—Agricultural/Farm Supplies Retailing and Wholesaling. **RELATED KNOWLEDGE/COURSES—Chemistry:** Knowledge of the chemical composition, structure, and properties of substances and of the chemical processes and transformations that they undergo. This includes uses of chemicals and their interactions, danger signs, production techniques, and disposal methods. **Principles of Mechanical Devices:** Knowledge of machines and tools, including their designs, uses, repair, and maintenance. **Mathematics:** Knowledge of arithmetic, algebra, geometry, calculus, and statistics and their applications. **Customer and Personal Service:** Knowledge of principles and processes for providing customer and personal services. This includes customer needs assessment, meeting quality standards for services, and evaluation of customer satisfaction. **Biology:** Knowledge of plant and animal organisms and their tissues, cells, functions, interdependencies, and interactions with each other and the environment.

Pharmacists

- ▲ Education/Training Required: First professional degree
- ▲ Annual Earnings: $74,890
- ▲ Growth: 24.3%
- ▲ Annual Job Openings: 20,000
- ▲ Self-Employed: 4.2%
- ▲ Part-Time: 24.6%

Compound and dispense medications following prescriptions issued by physicians, dentists, or other authorized medical practitioners. Compounds medications, using standard formulas and processes, such as weighing, measuring, and mixing ingredients. Compounds radioactive substances and reagents to prepare radiopharmaceutical, following radiopharmacy laboratory procedures. Plans and implements procedures in pharmacy, such as mixing, packaging, and labeling pharmaceuticals according to policies and legal requirements. Reviews prescription to assure accuracy and determine ingredients needed and suitability of radiopharmaceutical prescriptions. Consults medical staff to advise on drug applications and characteristics and

to review and evaluate quality and effectiveness of radiopharmaceuticals. Maintains records, such as pharmacy files, charge system, inventory, and control records for radioactive nuclei. Verifies that specified radioactive substance and reagent will give desired results in examination or treatment procedures. Analyzes records to indicate prescribing trends and excessive usage. Oversees preparation and dispensation of experimental drugs. Maintains established procedures concerning quality assurance, security of controlled substances, and disposal of hazardous waste. Calculates volume of radioactive pharmaceutical required to provide patient desired level of radioactivity at prescribed time. Assays prepared radiopharmaceutical, using instruments and equipment to verify rate of drug disintegration and ensure patient receives required dose. Answers questions and provides information to pharmacy customers on drug interactions, side effects, dosage, and storage of pharmaceuticals. **SKILLS—Reading Comprehension:** Understanding written sentences and paragraphs in work-related documents. **Writing:** Communicating effectively in writing as appropriate for the needs of the audience. **Mathematics:** Using mathematics to solve problems. **Science:** Using scientific rules and methods to solve problems. **Instructing:** Teaching others how to do something. **Active Learning:** Understanding the implications of new information for both current and future problem-solving and decision-making.

GOE INFORMATION—Interest Area: 14. Medical and Health Services. **Work Group:** 14.02. Medicine and Surgery. **Other Job Titles in This Work Group:** Anesthesiologists; Family and General Practitioners; Internists, General; Medical Assistants; Obstetricians and Gynecologists; Pediatricians, General; Pharmacy Aides; Pharmacy Technicians; Physician Assistants; Physicians and Surgeons, All Other; Psychiatrists; Registered Nurses; Surgeons; Surgical Technologists. **PERSONALITY TYPE—**Investigative. Investigative occupations frequently involve working with ideas and require an extensive amount of thinking. These occupations can involve searching for facts and figuring out problems mentally.

EDUCATION/TRAINING PROGRAM(S)—Clinical and Industrial Drug Development (MS, PhD); Clinical, Hospital, and Managed Care Pharmacy (MS, PhD); Industrial and Physical Pharmacy and Cosmetic Sciences (MS, PhD); Medicinal and Pharmaceutical Chemistry (MS, PhD); Natural Products Chemistry and Pharmacognosy (MS, PhD); Pharmaceutics and Drug Design (MS, PhD); Pharmacoeconomics/Pharmaceutical Economics (MS, PhD); Pharmacy (PharmD [USA] PharmD, BS/BPharm [Canada]); Pharmacy Administration and Pharmacy Policy and Regulatory Affairs (MS, PhD); Pharmacy, Pharmaceutical Sciences, and Administration, Other. **RELATED KNOWLEDGE/COURSES—Chemistry:** Knowledge of the chemical composition, structure, and properties of substances and of the chemical processes and transformations that they undergo. This includes uses of chemicals and their interactions, danger signs, production techniques, and disposal methods. **Medicine and Dentistry:** Knowledge of the information and techniques needed to diagnose and treat human injuries, diseases, and deformities. This includes symptoms, treatment alternatives, drug properties and interactions, and preventive health-care measures. **Administration and Management:** Knowledge of business and management principles involved in strategic planning, resource allocation, human resources modeling, leadership technique, production methods, and coordination of people and resources. **Biology:** Knowledge of plant and animal organisms and their tissues, cells, functions, interdependencies, and interactions with each other and the environment. **Computers and Electronics:** Knowledge of circuit boards, processors, chips, electronic equipment, and computer hardware and software, including applications and programming. **English Language:** Knowledge of the structure and content of the English language, including the meaning and spelling of words, rules of composition, and grammar.

Pharmacy Aides

- ▲ Education/Training Required: Moderate-term on-the-job training
- ▲ Annual Earnings: $18,010
- ▲ Growth: 19.5%
- ▲ Annual Job Openings: 9,000
- ▲ Self-Employed: 0%
- ▲ Part-Time: 24.9%

Record drugs delivered to the pharmacy, store incoming merchandise, and inform the supervisor of stock needs. May operate cash register and accept prescriptions for filling. **SKILLS—**No data available.

GOE INFORMATION—Interest Area: 14. Medical and Health Services. **Work Group:** 14.02. Medicine and Surgery. **Other Job Titles in This Work Group:** Anesthesiologists; Family and General Practitioners; Internists, General; Medical Assistants; Obstetricians and Gynecologists; Pediatricians, General; Pharmacists; Pharmacy Technicians; Physician Assistants; Physicians and Surgeons, All Other; Psychiatrists; Registered Nurses; Surgeons; Surgical Technologists. **PERSONALITY TYPE**—No data available.

EDUCATION/TRAINING PROGRAM(S)—Pharmacy Technician/Assistant. **RELATED KNOWLEDGE/ COURSES**—No data available.

Pharmacy Technicians

- ▲ Education/Training Required: Moderate-term on-the-job training
- ▲ Annual Earnings: $21,630
- ▲ Growth: 36.4%
- ▲ Annual Job Openings: 22,000
- ▲ Self-Employed: 0%
- ▲ Part-Time: 22.9%

Prepare medications under the direction of a pharmacist. May measure, mix, count out, label, and record amounts and dosages of medications. Assists pharmacist to prepare and dispense medication. Receives and stores incoming supplies. Prepares intravenous (IV) packs, using sterile technique, under supervision of hospital pharmacist. Cleans equipment and sterilizes glassware according to prescribed methods. Counts stock and enters data in computer to maintain inventory records. Processes records of medication and equipment dispensed to hospital patient, computes charges, and enters data in computer. Mixes pharmaceutical preparations, fills bottles with prescribed tablets and capsules, and types labels for bottles. **SKILLS— Reading Comprehension:** Understanding written sentences and paragraphs in work-related documents. **Mathematics:** Using mathematics to solve problems. **Active Listening:** Giving full attention to what other people are saying, taking time to understand the points being made, asking questions as appropriate, and not interrupting at inappropriate times. **Science:** Using scientific rules and methods to solve problems. **Writing:** Communicating effectively in writing as appropriate for the needs of the audience.

GOE INFORMATION—Interest Area: 14. Medical and Health Services. **Work Group:** 14.02. Medicine and Surgery. **Other Job Titles in This Work Group:** Anesthesiologists; Family and General Practitioners; Internists, General; Medical Assistants; Obstetricians and Gynecologists; Pediatricians, General; Pharmacists; Pharmacy Aides;

Physician Assistants; Physicians and Surgeons, All Other; Psychiatrists; Registered Nurses; Surgeons; Surgical Technologists. **PERSONALITY TYPE**—Conventional. Conventional occupations frequently involve following set procedures and routines. These occupations can include working with data and details more than with ideas. Usually there is a clear line of authority to follow.

EDUCATION/TRAINING PROGRAM(S)—Pharmacy Technician/Assistant. **RELATED KNOWLEDGE/ COURSES—Clerical Studies:** Knowledge of administrative and clerical procedures and systems, such as word processing, managing files and records, stenography and transcription, designing forms, and other office procedures and terminology. **Medicine and Dentistry:** Knowledge of the information and techniques needed to diagnose and treat human injuries, diseases, and deformities. This includes symptoms, treatment alternatives, drug properties and interactions, and preventive health-care measures. **Computers and Electronics:** Knowledge of circuit boards, processors, chips, electronic equipment, and computer hardware and software, including applications and programming. **Mathematics:** Knowledge of arithmetic, algebra, geometry, calculus, and statistics and their applications. **Chemistry:** Knowledge of the chemical composition, structure, and properties of substances and of the chemical processes and transformations that they undergo. This includes uses of chemicals and their interactions, danger signs, production techniques, and disposal methods.

P

Philosophy and Religion Teachers, Postsecondary

▲ Education/Training Required: Bachelor's degree
▲ Annual Earnings: $25,350
▲ Growth: 8.5%
▲ Annual Job Openings: 69,000
▲ Self-Employed: 0%
▲ Part-Time: 12.8%

Teach courses in philosophy, religion, and theology. **SKILLS**—No data available.

GOE INFORMATION—Interest Area: 12. Education and Social Service. **Work Group:** 12.03. Educational Services. **Other Job Titles in This Work Group:** Adult Literacy, Remedial Education, and GED Teachers and Instructors; Agricultural Sciences Teachers, Postsecondary; Anthropology and Archeology Teachers, Postsecondary; Architecture Teachers, Postsecondary; Archivists; Area, Ethnic, and Cultural Studies Teachers, Postsecondary; Art, Drama, and Music Teachers, Postsecondary; Atmospheric, Earth, Marine, and Space Sciences Teachers, Postsecondary; Audio-Visual Collections Specialists; Biological Science Teachers, Postsecondary; Business Teachers, Postsecondary; Chemistry Teachers, Postsecondary; Child Care Workers; Communications Teachers, Postsecondary; Computer Science Teachers, Postsecondary; Criminal Justice and Law Enforcement Teachers, Postsecondary; Curators; Economics Teachers, Postsecondary; Education Teachers, Postsecondary; Educational Psychologists; Educational, Vocational, and School Counselors; Elementary School Teachers, Except Special Education; Engineering Teachers, Postsecondary; English Language and Literature Teachers, Postsecondary; Environmental Science Teachers, Postsecondary; Farm and Home Management Advisors; Foreign Language and Literature Teachers, Postsecondary; Forestry and Conservation Science Teachers, Postsecondary; Geography Teachers, Postsecondary; Graduate Teaching Assistants; Health Specialties Teachers, Postsecondary; History Teachers, Postsecondary; Home Economics Teachers, Postsecondary; Kindergarten Teachers, Except Special Education; Law Teachers, Postsecondary; Librarians; Library Assistants, Clerical; Library Science Teachers, Postsecondary; Library Technicians; Mathematical Science Teachers, Postsecondary; Middle School Teachers, Except Special and Vocational Education; Museum Technicians and Conservators; Nursing Instructors and Teachers, Postsecondary; Personal Financial Advisors; Physics Teachers, Postsecondary; Political Science Teachers, Postsecondary; Postsecondary Teachers, All Other; Preschool Teachers, Except Special Education; Psychology Teachers, Postsecondary; others. **PERSONALITY TYPE**—No data available.

EDUCATION/TRAINING PROGRAM(S)—Bible/Biblical Studies; Buddhist Studies; Christian Studies; Divinity/Ministry (BD, MDiv.); Ethics; Hindu Studies; Missions/Missionary Studies and Missiology; Pastoral Counseling and Specialized Ministries, Other; Pastoral Studies/Counseling; Philosophy; Philosophy and Religious Studies, Other; Philosophy, Other; Pre-Theology/Pre-Ministerial Studies; Rabbinical Studies; Religion/Religious Studies; Religious Education; Religious/Sacred Music; Talmudic Studies; Theological and Ministerial Studies, Other; Theology and Religious Vocations, Other; Theology/Theological Studies. **RELATED KNOWLEDGE/COURSES**—No data available.

Photographers

▲ Education/Training Required: Long-term on-the-job training
▲ Annual Earnings: $23,040
▲ Growth: 17.0%
▲ Annual Job Openings: 13,000
▲ Self-Employed: 43.8%
▲ Part-Time: 23.1%

Photograph persons, subjects, merchandise, or other commercial products. May develop negatives and produce finished prints. **SKILLS**—No data available.

GOE INFORMATION—Interest Area: 01. Arts, Entertainment, and Media. **Work Group:** 01.08. Media Technology. **Other Job Titles in This Work Group:** Audio and Video Equipment Technicians; Broadcast Technicians; Camera Operators, Television, Video, and Motion Picture; Film and Video Editors; Media and Communication Equipment Workers, All Other; Professional Photographers; Radio Operators; Sound Engineering Technicians. **PERSONALITY TYPE**—No data available.

Photographers, Scientific

EDUCATION/TRAINING PROGRAM(S)—Art/Art Studies, General; Commercial Photography; Film/Video and Photographic Arts, Other; Photography; Photojournalism; Visual and Performing Arts, General. **RELATED KNOWLEDGE/COURSES**—No data available.

- ▲ Education/Training Required: Long-term on-the-job training
- ▲ Annual Earnings: $23,040
- ▲ Growth: 17.0%
- ▲ Annual Job Openings: 13,000
- ▲ Self-Employed: 43.8%
- ▲ Part-Time: 23.1%

Photograph variety of subject material to illustrate or record scientific/medical data or phenomena, utilizing knowledge of scientific procedures and photographic technology and techniques. Photographs variety of subject material to illustrate or record scientific or medical data or phenomena related to an area of interest. Sights and focuses camera to take picture of subject material to illustrate or record scientific or medical data or phenomena. Plans methods and procedures for photographing subject material and setup of required equipment. Observes and arranges subject material to desired position. Engages in research to develop new photographic procedure, materials, and scientific data. Sets up, mounts, or installs photographic equipment and cameras. Removes exposed film and develops film, using chemicals, touch up tools, and equipment. **SKILLS—Reading Comprehension:** Understanding written sentences and paragraphs in work-related documents. **Equipment Selection:** Determining the kind of tools and equipment needed to do a job. **Active Learning:** Understanding the implications of new information for both current and future problem-solving and decision-making. **Science:** Using scientific rules and methods to solve problems. **Writing:** Communicating effectively in writing as appropriate for the needs of the audience.

GOE INFORMATION—Interest Area: 02. Science, Math, and Engineering. **Work Group:** 02.05. Laboratory Technology. **Other Job Titles in This Work Group:** Biological Technicians; Chemical Technicians; Environmental Science and Protection Technicians, Including Health; Geological and Petroleum Technicians; Geological Data Technicians; Geological Sample Test Technicians; Nuclear Equipment Operation Technicians; Nuclear Technicians.

PERSONALITY TYPE—Artistic. Artistic occupations frequently involve working with forms, designs, and patterns. They often require self-expression, and the work can be done without following a clear set of rules.

EDUCATION/TRAINING PROGRAM(S)—Art/Art Studies, General; Commercial Photography; Film/Video and Photographic Arts, Other; Photography; Photojournalism; Visual and Performing Arts, General. **RELATED KNOWLEDGE/COURSES—Fine Arts:** Knowledge of the theory and techniques required to compose, produce, and perform works of music, dance, visual arts, drama, and sculpture. **Chemistry:** Knowledge of the chemical composition, structure, and properties of substances and of the chemical processes and transformations that they undergo. This includes uses of chemicals and their interactions, danger signs, production techniques, and disposal methods. **Physics:** Knowledge and prediction of physical principles and laws and their interrelationships and applications to understanding fluid, material, and atmospheric dynamics and mechanical, electrical, atomic, and subatomic structures and processes. **Biology:** Knowledge of plant and animal organisms and their tissues, cells, functions, interdependencies, and interactions with each other and the environment. **Medicine and Dentistry:** Knowledge of the information and techniques needed to diagnose and treat human injuries, diseases, and deformities. This includes symptoms, treatment alternatives, drug properties and interactions, and preventive health-care measures. **Communications and Media:** Knowledge of media production, communication, and dissemination techniques and methods. This includes alternative ways to inform and entertain via written, oral, and visual media.

Physical Therapist Aides

▲ Education/Training Required: Associate's degree
▲ Annual Earnings: $20,300
▲ Growth: 46.3%
▲ Annual Job Openings: 7,000
▲ Self-Employed: 0%
▲ Part-Time: 34.5%

Under close supervision of a physical therapist or physical therapy assistant, perform only delegated, selected, or routine tasks in specific situations. These duties include preparing the patient and the treatment area. Observes patients during treatment, compiles and evaluates data on patients' responses to treatments and progress, and reports to physical therapist. Administers active and passive manual therapeutic exercises; therapeutic massage; and heat, light, sound, water, and electrical modality treatments, such as ultrasound. Administers traction to relieve neck and back pain, using intermittent and static traction equipment. Provides routine treatments, such as hydrotherapy, hot and cold packs, and paraffin bath. Secures patients into or onto therapy equipment. Measures patient's range-of-joint motion, body parts, and vital signs to determine effects of treatments or for patient evaluations. Records treatment given and equipment used. Performs clerical duties, such as taking inventory, ordering supplies, answering telephone, taking messages, and filling out forms. Cleans work area and equipment after treatment. Transports patients to and from treatment area. Fits patients for orthopedic braces, prostheses, and supportive devices, such as crutches. Assists patients in dressing, undressing, and putting on and removing supportive devices, such as braces, splints, and slings. Confers with physical therapy staff and others to discuss and evaluate patient information for planning, modifying, and coordinating treatment. Adjusts fit of supportive devices for patients as instructed. Trains patients in use and care of orthopedic braces, prostheses, and supportive devices, such as crutches. Safeguards, motivates, and assists patients practicing exercises and functional activities under direction of professional staff. Instructs, motivates, and assists patients with learning and improving functional activities, such as perambulation, transfer, ambulation, and daily-living activities. SKILLS—Reading Comprehension: Understanding written sentences and paragraphs in work-related documents. Learning Strategies: Selecting and using training/instructional methods and procedures appropriate for the situation when learning or teaching new things. Service Orientation: Actively looking for ways to help people. Active Listening: Giving full attention to what other people are saying, taking time to understand the points being made, asking questions as appropriate, and not interrupting at inappropriate times. Instructing: Teaching others how to do something.

GOE INFORMATION—Interest Area: 14. Medical and Health Services. Work Group: 14.06. Medical Therapy. Other Job Titles in This Work Group: Audiologists; Massage Therapists; Occupational Therapist Aides; Occupational Therapist Assistants; Occupational Therapists; Physical Therapist Assistants; Physical Therapists; Radiation Therapists; Recreational Therapists; Respiratory Therapists; Respiratory Therapy Technicians; Speech-Language Pathologists; Therapists, All Other. PERSONALITY TYPE—Social. Social occupations frequently involve working with, communicating with, and teaching people. These occupations often involve helping or providing service to others.

EDUCATION/TRAINING PROGRAM(S)—Physical Therapist Assistant. RELATED KNOWLEDGE/ COURSES—Therapy and Counseling: Knowledge of principles, methods, and procedures for diagnosis, treatment, and rehabilitation of physical and mental dysfunctions and for career counseling and guidance. Customer and Personal Service: Knowledge of principles and processes for providing customer and personal services. This includes customer needs assessment, meeting quality standards for services, and evaluation of customer satisfaction. Education and Training: Knowledge of principles and methods for curriculum and training design, teaching and instruction for individuals and groups, and the measurement of training effects. Clerical Studies: Knowledge of administrative and clerical procedures and systems, such as word processing, managing files and records, stenography and transcription, designing forms, and other office procedures and terminology. Psychology: Knowledge of human behavior and performance; individual differences in ability, personality, and interests; learning and motivation; psychological research methods; and the assessment and treatment of behavioral and affective disorders. **Biology:** Knowledge of plant and animal organisms and their

tissues, cells, functions, interdependencies, and interactions with each other and the environment.

Physical Therapist Assistants

▲ Education/Training Required: Associate's degree
▲ Annual Earnings: $35,280
▲ Growth: 44.8%
▲ Annual Job Openings: 9,000
▲ Self-Employed: 0%
▲ Part-Time: 34.5%

Assist physical therapists in providing physical therapy treatments and procedures. May, in accordance with state laws, assist in the development of treatment plans, carry out routine functions, document the progress of treatment, and modify specific treatments in accordance with patient status and within the scope of treatment plans established by a physical therapist. Generally requires formal training. Records treatment given and equipment used. Fits patients for orthopedic braces, prostheses, and supportive devices, such as crutches. Transports patients to and from treatment area. Cleans work area and equipment after treatment. Performs clerical duties, such as taking inventory, ordering supplies, answering telephone, taking messages, and filling out forms. Administers active and passive manual therapeutic exercises; therapeutic massage; and heat, light, sound, water, and electrical modality treatments, such as ultrasound. Instructs, motivates, and assists patients to learn and improve functional activities, such as perambulation, transfer, ambulation, and daily-living activities. Safeguards, motivates, and assists patients practicing exercises and functional activities under direction of professional staff. Administers traction to relieve neck and back pain, using intermittent and static traction equipment. Secures patients into or onto therapy equipment. Measures patient's range-of-joint motion, body parts, and vital signs to determine effects of treatments or for patient evaluations. Assists patients in dressing, undressing, and putting on and removing supportive devices, such as braces, splints, and slings. Confers with physical therapy staff and others to discuss and evaluate patient information for planning, modifying, and coordinating treatment. Adjusts fit of supportive devices for patients as instructed. Provides routine treatments, such as hydrotherapy, hot and cold packs, and paraffin bath. Trains patients in use and care of orthopedic braces, prostheses, and supportive devices, such as crutches. Observes patients during treatments, compiles and evaluates data on patients'

responses to treatments and progress, and reports to physical therapist. **SKILLS—Reading Comprehension:** Understanding written sentences and paragraphs in work-related documents. **Learning Strategies:** Selecting and using training/instructional methods and procedures appropriate for the situation when learning or teaching new things. **Service Orientation:** Actively looking for ways to help people. **Instructing:** Teaching others how to do something. **Active Listening:** Giving full attention to what other people are saying, taking time to understand the points being made, asking questions as appropriate, and not interrupting at inappropriate times.

GOE INFORMATION—Interest Area: 14. Medical and Health Services. **Work Group:** 14.06. Medical Therapy. **Other Job Titles in This Work Group:** Audiologists; Massage Therapists; Occupational Therapist Aides; Occupational Therapist Assistants; Occupational Therapists; Physical Therapist Aides; Physical Therapists; Radiation Therapists; Recreational Therapists; Respiratory Therapists; Respiratory Therapy Technicians; Speech-Language Pathologists; Therapists, All Other. **PERSONALITY TYPE—**Social. Social occupations frequently involve working with, communicating with, and teaching people. These occupations often involve helping or providing service to others.

EDUCATION/TRAINING PROGRAM(S)—Physical Therapist Assistant. **RELATED KNOWLEDGE/ COURSES—Therapy and Counseling:** Knowledge of principles, methods, and procedures for diagnosis, treatment, and rehabilitation of physical and mental dysfunctions and for career counseling and guidance. **Customer and Personal Service:** Knowledge of principles and processes for providing customer and personal services. This includes customer needs assessment, meeting quality standards for services, and evaluation of customer satisfaction. **Education and Training:** Knowledge of principles and methods for curriculum and training design, teaching and instruction for individuals and groups, and the measurement of training effects. **Clerical Studies:** Knowledge of administrative and clerical procedures and systems, such as word processing, managing files and records, stenography and transcription, designing forms, and other office procedures and terminology. **Psychology:** Knowledge of

human behavior and performance; individual differences in ability, personality, and interests; learning and motivation; psychological research methods; and the assessment and treatment of behavioral and affective disorders. **Biology:** Knowledge of plant and animal organisms and their tissues, cells, functions, interdependencies, and interactions with each other and the environment.

Physical Therapists

- ▲ Education/Training Required: Master's degree
- ▲ Annual Earnings: $56,570
- ▲ Growth: 33.3%
- ▲ Annual Job Openings: 6,000
- ▲ Self-Employed: 5.9%
- ▲ Part-Time: 20.8%

Assess, plan, organize, and participate in rehabilitative programs that improve mobility, relieve pain, increase strength, and decrease or prevent deformity of patients suffering from disease or injury. Administers manual exercises to improve and maintain function. Administers treatment involving application of physical agents, using equipment, moist packs, ultraviolet and infrared lamps, and ultrasound machines. Administers traction to relieve pain, using traction equipment. Evaluates effects of treatment at various stages and adjusts treatments to achieve maximum benefit. Instructs, motivates, and assists patient to perform various physical activities and use supportive devices, such as crutches, canes, and prostheses. Administers massage, applying knowledge of massage techniques and body physiology. Tests and measures patient's strength, motor development, sensory perception, functional capacity, and respiratory and circulatory efficiency and records data. Reviews physician's referral and patient's condition and medical records to determine physical therapy treatment required. Plans and prepares written treatment program based on evaluation of patient data. Evaluates, fits, and adjusts prosthetic and orthotic devices and recommends modification to orthotist. Records treatment, response, and progress in patient's chart or enters information into computer. Confers with medical practitioners to obtain additional information, suggest revisions in treatment, and integrate physical therapy into patient's care. Instructs patient and family in treatment procedures to be continued at home. **SKILLS—Reading Comprehension:** Understanding written sentences and paragraphs in work-related documents. **Writing:** Communicating effectively in writing as appropriate for the needs of the audi-

ence. **Judgment and Decision Making:** Considering the relative costs and benefits of potential actions to choose the most appropriate one. **Active Listening:** Giving full attention to what other people are saying, taking time to understand the points being made, asking questions as appropriate, and not interrupting at inappropriate times. **Critical Thinking:** Using logic and reasoning to identify the strengths and weaknesses of alternative solutions, conclusions, or approaches to problems. **Speaking:** Talking to others to convey information effectively. **Instructing:** Teaching others how to do something.

GOE INFORMATION—Interest Area: 14. Medical and Health Services. **Work Group:** 14.06. Medical Therapy. **Other Job Titles in This Work Group:** Audiologists; Massage Therapists; Occupational Therapist Aides; Occupational Therapist Assistants; Occupational Therapists; Physical Therapist Aides; Physical Therapist Assistants; Radiation Therapists; Recreational Therapists; Respiratory Therapists; Respiratory Therapy Technicians; Speech-Language Pathologists; Therapists, All Other. **PERSONALITY TYPE—**Social. Social occupations frequently involve working with, communicating with, and teaching people. These occupations often involve helping or providing service to others.

EDUCATION/TRAINING PROGRAM(S)— Kinesiotherapy/Kinesiotherapist; Physical Therapy/Therapist. **RELATED KNOWLEDGE/COURSES—Therapy and Counseling:** Knowledge of principles, methods, and procedures for diagnosis, treatment, and rehabilitation of physical and mental dysfunctions and for career counseling and guidance. **Medicine and Dentistry:** Knowledge of the information and techniques needed to diagnose and treat human injuries, diseases, and deformities. This includes symptoms, treatment alternatives, drug properties and interactions, and preventive health-care measures. **English Language:** Knowledge of the structure and content of the English language, including the meaning and spelling of words, rules of composition, and grammar. **Psychology:** Knowledge of human behavior and perfor-mance; individual differences in ability, personality, and interests; learning and motivation; psychological research methods; and the assessment and treatment of behavioral and affective disorders. **Administration and Management:** Knowledge of business and management principles involved in strategic planning, resource allocation, human resources modeling, leadership technique, production methods, and coordination of people and resources.

Physician Assistants

- ▲ Education/Training Required: Bachelor's degree
- ▲ Annual Earnings: $63,970
- ▲ Growth: 53.5%
- ▲ Annual Job Openings: 5,000
- ▲ Self-Employed: 0%
- ▲ Part-Time: 24.6%

Provide health care services typically performed by a physician under the supervision of a physician. Conduct complete physicals, provide treatment, and counsel patients. May, in some cases, prescribe medication. Must graduate from an accredited educational program for physician assistants. Examines patient. Interprets diagnostic test results for deviations from normal. Counsels patients regarding prescribed therapeutic regimens, normal growth and development, family planning, emotional problems of daily living, and health maintenance. Develops and implements patient management plans, records progress notes, and assists in provision of continuity of care. Performs therapeutic procedures, such as injections, immunizations, suturing and wound care, and managing infection. Compiles patient medical data, including health history and results of physical examination. Administers or orders diagnostic tests, such as X-ray, electrocardiogram, and laboratory tests. **SKILLS—Reading Comprehension:** Understanding written sentences and paragraphs in work-related documents. **Active Learning:** Understanding the implications of new information for both current and future problem-solving and decision-making. **Active Listening:** Giving full attention to what other people are saying, taking time to understand the points being made, asking questions as appropriate, and not interrupting at inappropriate times. **Speaking:** Talking to others to convey information effectively. **Science:** Using scientific rules and methods to solve problems. **Critical Thinking:** Using logic and reasoning to identify the strengths and weaknesses of alternative solutions, conclusions, or approaches to problems. **Service Orientation:** Actively looking for ways to help people.

GOE INFORMATION—Interest Area: 14. Medical and Health Services. **Work Group:** 14.02. Medicine and Surgery. **Other Job Titles in This Work Group:** Anesthesiologists; Family and General Practitioners; Internists, General; Medical Assistants; Obstetricians and Gynecologists; Pediatricians, General; Pharmacists; Pharmacy Aides; Pharmacy Technicians; Physicians and Surgeons, All Other; Psychiatrists; Registered Nurses; Surgeons; Surgical Technologists. **PERSONALITY TYPE—**Investigative. Investigative occupations frequently involve working with ideas and require an extensive amount of thinking. These occupations can involve searching for facts and figuring out problems mentally.

EDUCATION/TRAINING PROGRAM(S)—Physician Assistant. **RELATED KNOWLEDGE/COURSES—Medicine and Dentistry:** Knowledge of the information and techniques needed to diagnose and treat human injuries, diseases, and deformities. This includes symptoms, treatment alternatives, drug properties and interactions, and preventive health-care measures. **Biology:** Knowledge of plant and animal organisms and their tissues, cells, functions, interdependencies, and interactions with each other and the environment. **Chemistry:** Knowledge of the chemical composition, structure, and properties of substances and of the chemical processes and transformations that they undergo. This includes uses of chemicals and their interactions, danger signs, production techniques, and disposal methods. **Therapy and Counseling:** Knowledge of principles, methods, and procedures for diagnosis, treatment, and rehabilitation of physical and mental dysfunctions and for career counseling and guidance. **Psychology:** Knowledge of human behavior and performance; individual differences in ability, personality, and interests; learning and motivation; psychological research methods; and the assessment and treatment of behavioral and affective disorders.

Physics Teachers, Postsecondary

- ▲ Education/Training Required: Master's degree
- ▲ Annual Earnings: $61,300
- ▲ Growth: 23.5%
- ▲ Annual Job Openings: 184,000
- ▲ Self-Employed: 0%
- ▲ Part-Time: 32.3%

Teach courses pertaining to the laws of matter and energy. Includes both teachers primarily engaged in teaching and those who do a combination of both teaching and research. Prepares and delivers lectures to students. Compiles bibliographies of specialized materials for outside reading assignments. Stimulates class discussions. Compiles, administers, and grades examinations or assigns this work to others. Advises students on academic and vocational curricula. Conducts research in particular field of knowledge and publishes findings in professional journals. Acts as adviser to student organizations. Serves on faculty committee providing professional consulting services to government and industry. Directs research of other teachers or graduate students working for advanced academic degrees. **SKILLS—Reading Comprehension:** Understanding written sentences and paragraphs in work-related documents. **Writing:** Communicating effectively in writing as appropriate for the needs of the audience. **Instructing:** Teaching others how to do something. **Science:** Using scientific rules and methods to solve problems. **Learning Strategies:** Selecting and using training/instructional methods and procedures appropriate for the situation when learning or teaching new things.

GOE INFORMATION—Interest Area: 12. Education and Social Service. **Work Group:** 12.03. Educational Services. **Other Job Titles in This Work Group:** Adult Literacy, Remedial Education, and GED Teachers and Instructors; Agricultural Sciences Teachers, Postsecondary; Anthropology and Archeology Teachers, Postsecondary; Architecture Teachers, Postsecondary; Archivists; Area, Ethnic, and Cultural Studies Teachers, Postsecondary; Art, Drama, and Music Teachers, Postsecondary; Atmospheric, Earth, Marine, and Space Sciences Teachers, Postsecondary; Audio-Visual Collections Specialists; Biological Science Teachers, Postsecondary; Business Teachers, Postsecondary; Chemistry Teachers, Postsecondary; Child Care Workers; Communications Teachers, Postsecondary; Computer Science Teachers, Postsecondary; Criminal Justice and Law Enforcement Teachers, Postsecondary; Curators; Economics Teachers, Postsecondary; Education Teachers, Postsecondary; Educational Psychologists; Educational, Vocational, and School Counselors; Elementary School Teachers, Except Special Education; Engineering Teachers, Postsecondary; English Language and Literature Teachers, Postsecondary; Environmental Science Teachers, Postsecondary; Farm and Home Management Advisors; Foreign Language and Literature Teachers, Postsecondary; Forestry and Conservation Science Teachers, Postsecondary; Geography Teachers, Postsecondary; Graduate Teaching Assistants; Health Specialties Teachers, Postsecondary; History Teachers, Postsecondary; Home Economics Teachers, Postsecondary; Kindergarten Teachers, Except Special Education; Law Teachers, Postsecondary; Librarians; Library Assistants, Clerical; Library Science Teachers, Postsecondary; Library Technicians; Mathematical Science Teachers, Postsecondary; Middle School Teachers, Except Special and Vocational Education; Museum Technicians and Conservators; Nursing Instructors and Teachers, Postsecondary; Personal Financial Advisors; Philosophy and Religion Teachers, Postsecondary; Political Science Teachers, Postsecondary; Postsecondary Teachers, All Other; Preschool Teachers, Except Special Education; others. **PERSONALITY TYPE—Investigative.** Investigative occupations frequently involve working with ideas and require an extensive amount of thinking. These occupations can involve searching for facts and figuring out problems mentally.

EDUCATION/TRAINING PROGRAM(S)—Acoustics; Atomic/Molecular Physics; Elementary Particle Physics; Nuclear Physics; Optics/Optical Sciences; Physics, General; Physics, Other; Plasma and High-Temperature

Physics; Solid State and Low-Temperature Physics; Theoretical and Mathematical Physics. **RELATED KNOWLEDGE/COURSES—Physics:** Knowledge and prediction of physical principles and laws and their interrelationships and applications to understanding fluid, material, and atmospheric dynamics and mechanical, electrical, atomic, and sub-atomic structures and processes. **Education and Training:** Knowledge of principles and methods for curriculum and training design, teaching and instruction for individuals and groups, and the measurement of training

effects. **Mathematics:** Knowledge of arithmetic, algebra, geometry, calculus, and statistics and their applications. **English Language:** Knowledge of the structure and content of the English language, including the meaning and spelling of words, rules of composition, and grammar. **Administration and Management:** Knowledge of business and management principles involved in strategic planning, resource allocation, human resources modeling, leadership technique, production methods, and coordination of people and resources.

Pipe Fitters

▲ Education/Training Required: Long-term on-the-job training
▲ Annual Earnings: $38,710
▲ Growth: 10.2%
▲ Annual Job Openings: 49,000
▲ Self-Employed: 19.7%
▲ Part-Time: 5.5%

Lay out, assemble, install, and maintain pipe systems, pipe supports, and related hydraulic and pneumatic equipment for steam, hot water, heating, cooling, lubricating, sprinkling, and industrial production and processing systems. Plans pipe system layout, installation, or repair according to specifications. Operates motorized pump to remove water from flooded manholes, basements, or facility floors. Turns valve to shut off steam, water, or other gases or liquids from pipe section, using valve key or wrenches. Cuts and bores holes in structures, such as bulkheads, decks, walls, and mains, using hand and power tools, prior to pipe installation. Coats nonferrous piping materials by dipping in mixture of molten tin and lead to prevent erosion or galvanic and electrolytic action. Inspects work site to determine presence of obstruction and ensure that holes will not cause structure weakness. Lays out full-scale drawings of pipe systems, supports, and related equipment, following blueprints. Inspects, examines, and tests installed systems and pipe lines, using pressure gauge, hydrostatic testing, observation, or other methods. Attaches pipes to walls, structures, and fixtures, such as radiators or tanks, using brackets, clamps, tools, or welding equipment. Modifies and maintains pipe systems and related machines and equipment components following specifications, using hand tools and power tools. Selects pipe sizes and types and related materials, such as supports, hangers, and hydraulic cylinders, according to specifications. Assembles pipes, tubes, and fittings according to specifications. Measures and marks pipes for cutting and threading. Cuts, threads, and hammers pipe to speci-

fications, using tools such as saws, cutting torches, and pipe threaders and benders. **SKILLS—Installation:** Installing equipment, machines, wiring, or programs to meet specifications. **Quality Control Analysis:** Conducting tests and inspections of products, services, or processes to evaluate quality or performance. **Equipment Selection:** Determining the kind of tools and equipment needed to do a job. **Operation and Control:** Controlling operations of equipment or systems. **Equipment Maintenance:** Performing routine maintenance on equipment and determining when and what kind of maintenance is needed. **Mathematics:** Using mathematics to solve problems.

GOE INFORMATION—Interest Area: 06. Construction, Mining, and Drilling. **Work Group:** 06.02. Construction. **Other Job Titles in This Work Group:** Boat Builders and Shipwrights; Boilermakers; Brattice Builders; Brickmasons and Blockmasons; Carpenters; Carpet Installers; Ceiling Tile Installers; Cement Masons and Concrete Finishers; Commercial Divers; Construction Carpenters; Drywall and Ceiling Tile Installers; Drywall Installers; Electricians; Explosives Workers, Ordnance Handling Experts, and Blasters; Fence Erectors; Floor Layers, Except Carpet, Wood, and Hard Tiles; Floor Sanders and Finishers; Glaziers; Grader, Bulldozer, and Scraper Operators; Hazardous Materials Removal Workers; Insulation Workers, Floor, Ceiling, and Wall; Insulation Workers, Mechanical; Manufactured Building and Mobile Home Installers; Operating Engineers; Operating Engineers and Other Construction Equipment Operators;

Painters, Construction and Maintenance; Paperhangers; Paving, Surfacing, and Tamping Equipment Operators; Pile-Driver Operators; Pipelayers; Pipelaying Fitters; Plasterers and Stucco Masons; Plumbers; Plumbers, Pipefitters, and Steamfitters; Rail-Track Laying and Maintenance Equipment Operators; Refractory Materials Repairers, Except Brickmasons; Reinforcing Iron and Rebar Workers; Riggers; Roofers; Rough Carpenters; Security and Fire Alarm Systems Installers; Segmental Pavers; Sheet Metal Workers; Ship Carpenters and Joiners; Stone Cutters and Carvers; Stonemasons; Structural Iron and Steel Workers; Tapers; Terrazzo Workers and Finishers; Tile and Marble Setters. **PERSONALITY TYPE**—Realistic. Realistic occupations frequently involve work activities that include practical, hands-on problems and solutions. They often deal with plants, animals, and real-world materials like wood, tools, and machinery. Many of the occupations require working outside and do not involve a lot of paperwork or working closely with others.

EDUCATION/TRAINING PROGRAM(S)—Pipefitting/Pipefitter and Sprinkler Fitter; Plumbing and Related Water Supply Services, Other; Plumbing Technology/Plumber. **RELATED KNOWLEDGE/COURSES—Building and Construction:** Knowledge of materials, methods, and tools involved in the construction or repair of houses, buildings, or other structures, such as highways and roads. **Principles of Mechanical Devices:** Knowledge of machines and tools, including their designs, uses, repair, and maintenance. **Design:** Knowledge of design techniques, tools, and principles involved in production of precision technical plans, blueprints, drawings, and models. **Engineering and Technology:** Knowledge of the practical application of engineering science and technology. This includes applying principles, techniques, procedures, and equipment to the design and production of various goods and services. **Mathematics:** Knowledge of arithmetic, algebra, geometry, calculus, and statistics and their applications.

Pipelaying Fitters

- ▲ Education/Training Required: Moderate-term on-the-job training
- ▲ Annual Earnings: $38,710
- ▲ Growth: 10.2%
- ▲ Annual Job Openings: 49,000
- ▲ Self-Employed: 5.3%
- ▲ Part-Time: 8.5%

Align pipeline section in preparation for welding. Signal tractor driver for placement of pipeline sections in proper alignment. Insert steel spacer. Guides pipe into trench and signals hoist operator to move pipe until specified alignment with other pipes is achieved. Corrects misalignment of pipe, using sledgehammer. Inserts spacers between pipe ends. Inspects joint to verify uniformity of spacing and alignment of pipe surfaces. **SKILLS—Equipment Selection:** Determining the kind of tools and equipment needed to do a job.

GOE INFORMATION—Interest Area: 06. Construction, Mining, and Drilling. **Work Group:** 06.02. Construction. **Other Job Titles in This Work Group:** Boat Builders and Shipwrights; Boilermakers; Brattice Builders; Brickmasons and Blockmasons; Carpenters; Carpet Installers; Ceiling Tile Installers; Cement Masons and Concrete Finishers; Commercial Divers; Construction Carpenters; Drywall and Ceiling Tile Installers; Drywall Installers; Electricians; Explosives Workers, Ordnance Handling Experts, and Blasters; Fence Erectors; Floor Lay-ers, Except Carpet, Wood, and Hard Tiles; Floor Sanders and Finishers; Glaziers; Grader, Bulldozer, and Scraper Operators; Hazardous Materials Removal Workers; Insulation Workers, Floor, Ceiling, and Wall; Insulation Workers, Mechanical; Manufactured Building and Mobile Home Installers; Operating Engineers; Operating Engineers and Other Construction Equipment Operators; Painters, Construction and Maintenance; Paperhangers; Paving, Surfacing, and Tamping Equipment Operators; Pile-Driver Operators; Pipe Fitters; Pipelayers; Plasterers and Stucco Masons; Plumbers; Plumbers, Pipefitters, and Steamfitters; Rail-Track Laying and Maintenance Equipment Operators; Refractory Materials Repairers, Except Brickmasons; Reinforcing Iron and Rebar Workers; Riggers; Roofers; Rough Carpenters; Security and Fire Alarm Systems Installers; Segmental Pavers; Sheet Metal Workers; Ship Carpenters and Joiners; Stone Cutters and Carvers; Stonemasons; Structural Iron and Steel Workers; Tapers; Terrazzo Workers and Finishers; Tile and Marble Setters. **PERSONALITY TYPE**—Realistic. Realistic occupations frequently involve work activities that include practical, hands-on problems and solutions. They often deal with plants, animals, and real-world materials like wood, tools, and machinery. Many of the occupations require working outside and do not involve a lot of paperwork or working closely with others.

EDUCATION/TRAINING PROGRAM(S)—Pipefitting/Pipefitter and Sprinkler Fitter; Plumbing and Related Water Supply Services, Other; Plumbing Technology/Plumber. **RELATED KNOWLEDGE/COURSES—Principles of Mechanical Devices:** Knowledge of machines and tools, including their designs, uses,

repair, and maintenance. **Building and Construction:** Knowledge of materials, methods, and tools involved in the construction or repair of houses, buildings, or other structures, such as highways and roads. **Food Production:** Knowledge of techniques and equipment for planting, growing, and harvesting food products (both plant and animal) for consumption, including storage/handling techniques. **Production and Processing:** Knowledge of raw materials, production processes, quality control, costs, and other techniques for maximizing the effective manufacture and distribution of goods.

Plastic Molding and Casting Machine Operators and Tenders

- ▲ Education/Training Required: Short-term on-the-job training
- ▲ Annual Earnings: $22,340
- ▲ Growth: 9.8%
- ▲ Annual Job Openings: 38,000
- ▲ Self-Employed: 0%
- ▲ Part-Time: 2.6%

Operate or tend plastic molding machines, such as compression or injection molding machines, to mold, form, or cast thermoplastic materials to specified shape. Starts machine that automatically liquefies plastic material in heating chamber, injects liquefied material into mold, and ejects molded product. Observes meters and gauges to verify specified temperatures, pressures, and press-cycle times. Turns valves and dials of machines to regulate pressure and temperature, to set press-cycle time, and to close press. Observes continuous operation of automatic machine and width and alignment of plastic sheeting to ensure side flanges. Weighs prescribed amounts of material for molded part and finished product to ensure specifications are maintained. Removes product from mold or conveyor and cleans and reloads mold. Positions mold frame to correct alignment and tubs containing mixture on top of mold to facilitate loading of molds. Examines molded product for surface defects, such as dents, bubbles, thin areas, and cracks. Fills tubs, molds, or cavities of machine with plastic material in solid or liquid form prior to activating machine. Mixes and pours liquid plastic into rotating drum of machine that spreads, hardens, and shapes mixture. Pulls level and toggle latches to fill mold and regulate tension on sheeting and to release mold covers. Dumps plastic powder, preformed plastic pellets, or preformed rubber slugs into hopper of molding machine. Heats plastic material prior to forming product or cools product after processing to prevent distortion. Breaks seals

that hold plastic product in molds, using hand tool, and removes product from mold. Feels stiffness and consistency of molded sheeting to detect machinery malfunction. Reports defect in molds to supervisor. Signals coworker to synchronize feed of materials into molding process. Trims flashing from product. Throws flash and rejected parts into grinder machine to be recycled. Stacks molded parts in boxes or on conveyor for subsequent processing or leaves parts in mold to cool. **SKILLS—Operation and Control:** Controlling operations of equipment or systems. **Operation Monitoring:** Watching gauges, dials, or other indicators to make sure a machine is working properly. **Quality Control Analysis:** Conducting tests and inspections of products, services, or processes to evaluate quality or performance. **Mathematics:** Using mathematics to solve problems. **Equipment Selection:** Determining the kind of tools and equipment needed to do a job.

GOE INFORMATION—Interest Area: 08. Industrial Production. **Work Group:** 08.02. Production Technology. **Other Job Titles in This Work Group:** Aircraft Rigging Assemblers; Aircraft Structure Assemblers, Precision; Aircraft Structure, Surfaces, Rigging, and Systems Assemblers; Aircraft Systems Assemblers, Precision; Bench Workers, Jewelry; Bindery Machine Setters and Set-Up Operators; Bindery Workers; Bookbinders; Buffing and Polishing Set-Up Operators; Casting Machine Set-Up Operators; Coating, Painting, and Spraying Machine Setters and Set-Up

Operators; Coating, Painting, and Spraying Machine Setters, Operators, and Tenders; Combination Machine Tool Setters and Set-Up Operators, Metal and Plastic; Cutting, Punching, and Press Machine Setters, Operators, and Tenders, Metal and Plastic; Dental Laboratory Technicians; Drilling and Boring Machine Tool Setters, Operators, and Tenders, Metal and Plastic; Electrical and Electronic Equipment Assemblers; Electrical and Electronic Inspectors and Testers; Electromechanical Equipment Assemblers; Engine and Other Machine Assemblers; Extruding and Drawing Machine Setters, Operators, and Tenders, Metal and Plastic; Extruding, Forming, Pressing, and Compacting Machine Setters and Set-Up Operators; Extruding, Forming, Pressing, and Compacting Machine Setters, Operators, and Tenders; Forging Machine Setters, Operators, and Tenders, Metal and Plastic; Foundry Mold and Coremakers; Gem and Diamond Workers; Grinding, Honing, Lapping, and Deburring Machine Set-Up Operators; Grinding, Lapping, Polishing, and Buffing Machine Tool Setters, Operators, and Tenders, Metal and Plastic; Heat Treating Equipment Setters, Operators, and Tenders, Metal and Plastic; Heat Treating, Annealing, and Tempering Machine Operators and Tenders, Metal and Plastic; Heating Equipment Setters and Set-Up Operators, Metal and Plastic; Inspectors, Testers, Sorters, Samplers, and Weighers; Jewelers; Jewelers and Precious Stone and Metal Workers; Lathe and Turning Machine Tool Setters, Operators, and Tenders, Metal and Plastic; Log Graders and Scalers; Materials Inspectors; Mechanical Inspectors; others. **PER-**

SONALITY TYPE—Realistic. Realistic occupations frequently involve work activities that include practical, hands-on problems and solutions. They often deal with plants, animals, and real-world materials like wood, tools, and machinery. Many of the occupations require working outside and do not involve a lot of paperwork or working closely with others.

EDUCATION/TRAINING PROGRAM(S)—No data available. **RELATED KNOWLEDGE/COURSES**—**Production and Processing:** Knowledge of raw materials, production processes, quality control, costs, and other techniques for maximizing the effective manufacture and distribution of goods. **Principles of Mechanical Devices:** Knowledge of machines and tools, including their designs, uses, repair, and maintenance. **Mathematics:** Knowledge of arithmetic, algebra, geometry, calculus, and statistics and their applications. **Physics:** Knowledge and prediction of physical principles and laws and their interrelationships and applications to understanding fluid, material, and atmospheric dynamics and mechanical, electrical, atomic, and sub-atomic structures and processes. **English Language:** Knowledge of the structure and content of the English language, including the meaning and spelling of words, rules of composition, and grammar. **Engineering and Technology:** Knowledge of the practical application of engineering science and technology. This includes applying principles, techniques, procedures, and equipment to the design and production of various goods and services.

Plastic Molding and Casting Machine Setters and Set-Up Operators

▲ Education/Training Required: Moderate-term on-the-job training
▲ Annual Earnings: $22,340
▲ Growth: 9.8%
▲ Annual Job Openings: 38,000
▲ Self-Employed: 0%
▲ Part-Time: 2.6%

Set up or set up and operate plastic molding machines, such as compression or injection molding machines, to mold, form, or cast thermoplastic materials to specified shape. Positions, aligns, and secures assembled mold, mold components, and machine accessories onto machine press bed and attaches connecting lines. Installs dies onto machine or press and coats dies with parting agent according to work order specifications. Presses button or pulls lever to activate machine to inject dies and compress compounds to form and cure specified products. Observes and adjusts

machine setup and operations to eliminate production of defective parts and products. Weighs premixed compounds and dumps compound into die well or fills hoppers of machines that automatically supply compound to die. Reads specifications to determine setup and prescribed temperature and time settings to mold, form, or cast plastic materials. Sets machine controls to regulate molding temperature, volume, pressure, and time, according to knowledge of plastics and molding procedures. Mixes catalysts, thermoplastic materials, and coloring pigments according to formula, using paddle and mixing machine. Repairs and maintains machines and auxiliary equipment, using hand tools and power tools. Trims excess material from part, using knife, and grinds scrap plastic into powder for reuse. Removes finished or cured product from dies or mold, using hand tools and air hose. Measures and visually inspects products for surface and dimension defects, using precision measuring instruments, to ensure conformance to specifications. **SKILLS—Operation Monitoring:** Watching gauges, dials, or other indicators to make sure a machine is working properly. **Operation and Control:** Controlling operations of equipment or systems. **Equipment Maintenance:** Performing routine maintenance on equipment and determining when and what kind of maintenance is needed. **Repairing:** Repairing machines or systems, using the needed tools. **Troubleshooting:** Determining causes of operating errors and deciding what to do about them. **Reading Comprehension:** Understanding written sentences and paragraphs in work-related documents. **Quality Control Analysis:** Conducting tests and inspections of products, services, or processes to evaluate quality or performance.

GOE INFORMATION—**Interest Area:** 08. Industrial Production. **Work Group:** 08.02. Production Technology. **Other Job Titles in This Work Group:** Aircraft Rigging Assemblers; Aircraft Structure Assemblers, Precision; Aircraft Structure, Surfaces, Rigging, and Systems Assemblers; Aircraft Systems Assemblers, Precision; Bench Workers, Jewelry; Bindery Machine Setters and Set-Up Operators; Bindery Workers; Bookbinders; Buffing and Polishing Set-Up Operators; Casting Machine Set-Up Operators; Coating, Painting, and Spraying Machine Setters and Set-Up Operators; Coating, Painting, and Spraying Machine Setters, Operators, and Tenders; Combination Machine Tool Setters and Set-Up Operators, Metal and Plastic; Cutting, Punching, and Press Machine Setters, Operators, and Tenders, Metal and Plastic; Dental Laboratory Technicians; Drilling and Boring Machine Tool Setters, Operators, and Tenders, Metal and Plastic; Electrical and Electronic Equipment Assemblers; Electrical and Electronic Inspectors and Testers; Electromechanical Equipment Assemblers; Engine and Other Machine Assemblers; Extruding and Drawing Machine Setters, Operators, and Tenders, Metal and Plastic; Extruding, Forming, Pressing, and Compacting Machine Setters and Set-Up Operators; Extruding, Forming, Pressing, and Compacting Machine Setters, Operators, and Tenders; Forging Machine Setters, Operators, and Tenders, Metal and Plastic; Foundry Mold and Coremakers; Gem and Diamond Workers; Grinding, Honing, Lapping, and Deburring Machine Set-Up Operators; Grinding, Lapping, Polishing, and Buffing Machine Tool Setters, Operators, and Tenders, Metal and Plastic; Heat Treating Equipment Setters, Operators, and Tenders, Metal and Plastic; Heat Treating, Annealing, and Tempering Machine Operators and Tenders, Metal and Plastic; Heating Equipment Setters and Set-Up Operators, Metal and Plastic; Inspectors, Testers, Sorters, Samplers, and Weighers; Jewelers; Jewelers and Precious Stone and Metal Workers; Lathe and Turning Machine Tool Setters, Operators, and Tenders, Metal and Plastic; Log Graders and Scalers; Materials Inspectors; Mechanical Inspectors; others. **PERSONALITY TYPE**—Realistic. Realistic occupations frequently involve work activities that include practical, hands-on problems and solutions. They often deal with plants, animals, and real-world materials like wood, tools, and machinery. Many of the occupations require working outside and do not involve a lot of paperwork or working closely with others.

EDUCATION/TRAINING PROGRAM(S)—No data available. **RELATED KNOWLEDGE/COURSES**— **Principles of Mechanical Devices:** Knowledge of machines and tools, including their designs, uses, repair, and maintenance. **Production and Processing:** Knowledge of raw materials, production processes, quality control, costs, and other techniques for maximizing the effective manufacture and distribution of goods. **Chemistry:** Knowledge of the chemical composition, structure, and properties of substances and of the chemical processes and transformations that they undergo. This includes uses of chemicals and their interactions, danger signs, production techniques, and disposal methods. **Mathematics:** Knowledge of arithmetic, algebra, geometry, calculus, and statistics and their applications. **Computers and Electronics:** Knowledge of circuit boards, processors, chips, electronic equipment, and computer hardware and software, including applications and programming.

Plumbers

> ▲ Education/Training Required: Long-term on-the-job training
> ▲ Annual Earnings: $38,710
> ▲ Growth: 10.2%
> ▲ Annual Job Openings: 49,000
> ▲ Self-Employed: 19.7%
> ▲ Part-Time: 5.5%

Assemble, install, and repair pipes, fittings, and fixtures of heating, water, and drainage systems, according to specifications and plumbing codes. Repairs and maintains plumbing by replacing defective washers, replacing or mending broken pipes, and opening clogged drains. Assembles pipe sections, tubing, and fittings, using screws, bolts, solder, plastic solvent, and caulking. Installs pipe assemblies, fittings, valves, and fixtures, such as sinks, toilets and tubs, using hand and power tools. Cuts, threads, and bends pipe to required angle, using pipe cutters, pipe-threading machine, and pipe bending machine. Directs workers engaged in pipe cutting and preassembly and installation of plumbing systems and components. Fills pipes or plumbing fixtures with water or air and observes pressure gauges to detect and locate leaks. Locates and marks position of pipe installations and passage holes in structures, using measuring instruments such as ruler and level. Cuts opening in structures to accommodate pipe and pipe fittings, using hand and power tools. Studies building plans and inspects structure to determine required materials and equipment and sequence of pipe installations. **SKILLS— Installation:** Installing equipment, machines, wiring, or programs to meet specifications. **Coordination:** Adjusting actions in relation to others' actions. **Repairing:** Repairing machines or systems, using the needed tools. **Equipment Selection:** Determining the kind of tools and equipment needed to do a job. **Operation and Control:** Controlling operations of equipment or systems. **Equipment Maintenance:** Performing routine maintenance on equipment and determining when and what kind of maintenance is needed. **Active Listening:** Giving full attention to what other people are saying, taking time to understand the points being made, asking questions as appropriate, and not interrupting at inappropriate times.

GOE INFORMATION—Interest Area: 06. Construction, Mining, and Drilling. **Work Group:** 06.02. Construction. **Other Job Titles in This Work Group:** Boat Builders and Shipwrights; Boilermakers; Brattice Builders; Brickmasons and Blockmasons; Carpenters; Carpet Installers; Ceiling Tile Installers; Cement Masons and Concrete Finishers; Commercial Divers; Construction Carpenters; Drywall and Ceiling Tile Installers; Drywall Installers; Electricians; Explosives Workers, Ordnance Handling Experts, and Blasters; Fence Erectors; Floor Layers, Except Carpet, Wood, and Hard Tiles; Floor Sanders and Finishers; Glaziers; Grader, Bulldozer, and Scraper Operators; Hazardous Materials Removal Workers; Insulation Workers, Floor, Ceiling, and Wall; Insulation Workers, Mechanical; Manufactured Building and Mobile Home Installers; Operating Engineers; Operating Engineers and Other Construction Equipment Operators; Painters, Construction and Maintenance; Paperhangers; Paving, Surfacing, and Tamping Equipment Operators; Pile-Driver Operators; Pipe Fitters; Pipelayers; Pipelaying Fitters; Plasterers and Stucco Masons; Plumbers, Pipefitters, and Steamfitters; Rail-Track Laying and Maintenance Equipment Operators; Refractory Materials Repairers, Except Brickmasons; Reinforcing Iron and Rebar Workers; Riggers; Roofers; Rough Carpenters; Security and Fire Alarm Systems Installers; Segmental Pavers; Sheet Metal Workers; Ship Carpenters and Joiners; Stone Cutters and Carvers; Stonemasons; Structural Iron and Steel Workers; Tapers; Terrazzo Workers and Finishers; Tile and Marble Setters. **PERSONALITY TYPE—**Realistic. Realistic occupations frequently involve work activities that include practical, hands-on problems and solutions. They often deal with plants, animals, and real-world materials like wood, tools, and machinery. Many of the occupations require working outside and do not involve a lot of paperwork or working closely with others.

EDUCATION/TRAINING PROGRAM(S)— Pipefitting/Pipefitter and Sprinkler Fitter; Plumbing and Related Water Supply Services, Other; Plumbing Technology/Plumber. **RELATED KNOWLEDGE/ COURSES—Principles of Mechanical Devices:** Knowledge of machines and tools, including their designs, uses, repair, and maintenance. **Building and Construction:** Knowledge of materials, methods, and tools involved in the construction or repair of houses, buildings, or other structures, such as highways and roads. **Engineering and Technology:** Knowledge of the practical application of engineering science and technology. This includes applying principles, techniques, procedures, and equipment to the design and production of various goods and services.

Mathematics: Knowledge of arithmetic, algebra, geometry, calculus, and statistics and their applications. **Design:** Knowledge of design techniques, tools, and principles involved in production of precision technical plans, blueprints, drawings, and models.

Plumbers, Pipefitters, and Steamfitters

- ▲ Education/Training Required: Long-term on-the-job training
- ▲ Annual Earnings: $38,710
- ▲ Growth: 10.2%
- ▲ Annual Job Openings: 49,000
- ▲ Self-Employed: 19.7%
- ▲ Part-Time: 5.5%

Assemble, install, alter, and repair pipelines or pipe systems that carry water, steam, air, or other liquids or gases. May install heating and cooling equipment and mechanical control systems. SKILLS—No data available.

GOE INFORMATION—Interest Area: 06. Construction, Mining, and Drilling. **Work Group:** 06.02. Construction. **Other Job Titles in This Work Group:** Boat Builders and Shipwrights; Boilermakers; Brattice Builders; Brickmasons and Blockmasons; Carpenters; Carpet Installers; Ceiling Tile Installers; Cement Masons and Concrete Finishers; Commercial Divers; Construction Carpenters; Drywall and Ceiling Tile Installers; Drywall Installers; Electricians; Explosives Workers, Ordnance Handling Experts, and Blasters; Fence Erectors; Floor Layers, Except Carpet, Wood, and Hard Tiles; Floor Sanders and Finishers; Glaziers; Grader, Bulldozer, and Scraper Operators; Hazardous Materials Removal Workers; Insulation Workers, Floor, Ceiling, and Wall; Insulation Workers, Mechanical; Manufactured Building and Mobile Home Installers; Operating Engineers; Operating Engineers and Other Construction Equipment Operators; Painters, Construction and Maintenance; Paperhangers; Paving, Surfacing, and Tamping Equipment Operators; Pile-Driver Operators; Pipe Fitters; Pipelayers; Pipelaying Fitters; Plasterers and Stucco Masons; Plumbers; Rail-Track Laying and Maintenance Equipment Operators; Refractory Materials Repairers, Except Brickmasons; Reinforcing Iron and Rebar Workers; Riggers; Roofers; Rough Carpenters; Security and Fire Alarm Systems Installers; Segmental Pavers; Sheet Metal Workers; Ship Carpenters and Joiners; Stone Cutters and Carvers; Stonemasons; Structural Iron and Steel Workers; Tapers; Terrazzo Workers and Finishers; Tile and Marble Setters. **PERSONALITY TYPE**—No data available.

EDUCATION/TRAINING PROGRAM(S)—Pipefitting/Pipefitter and Sprinkler Fitter; Plumbing and Related Water Supply Services, Other; Plumbing Technology/Plumber. **RELATED KNOWLEDGE/COURSES**—No data available.

Poets and Lyricists

- ▲ Education/Training Required: Bachelor's degree
- ▲ Annual Earnings: $42,450
- ▲ Growth: 28.4%
- ▲ Annual Job Openings: 18,000
- ▲ Self-Employed: 31.2%
- ▲ Part-Time: 18.5%

Write poetry or song lyrics for publication or performance. Writes words to fit musical compositions, including lyrics for operas, musical plays, and choral works. Chooses subject matter and suitable form to express personal feeling and experience or ideas or to narrate story or event. Adapts text to accommodate musical requirements of composer and singer. Writes narrative, dramatic, lyric, or other types of poetry for publication. **SKILLS—Writing:** Communicating effectively in writing as appropriate for the needs of the audience. **Reading Comprehension:**

Understanding written sentences and paragraphs in work-related documents. **Learning Strategies:** Selecting and using training/instructional methods and procedures appropriate for the situation when learning or teaching new things. **Monitoring:** Monitoring/Assessing your performance or that of other individuals or organizations to make improvements or take corrective action.

GOE INFORMATION—Interest Area: 01. Arts, Entertainment, and Media. **Work Group:** 01.02. Writing and Editing. **Other Job Titles in This Work Group:** Copy Writers; Creative Writers; Editors; Technical Writers; Writers and Authors. **PERSONALITY TYPE—**Artistic. Artistic occupations frequently involve working with forms, designs, and patterns. They often require self-expression, and the work can be done without following a clear set of rules.

EDUCATION/TRAINING PROGRAM(S)—Broadcast Journalism; Business/Corporate Communications; Communication Studies/Speech Communication and Rhetoric; Communication, Journalism, and Related Programs, Other; Creative Writing; English Composition; Family and Consumer Sciences/Human Sciences Communication; Journalism; Mass Communication/Media Studies; Playwriting and Screenwriting; Technical and Business Writing. **RELATED KNOWLEDGE/COURSES—Fine Arts:** Knowledge of the theory and techniques required to compose, produce, and perform works of music, dance, visual arts, drama, and sculpture. **English Language:** Knowledge of the structure and content of the English language, including the meaning and spelling of words, rules of composition, and grammar. **Communications and Media:** Knowledge of media production, communication, and dissemination techniques and methods. This includes alternative ways to inform and entertain via written, oral, and visual media. **Customer and Personal Service:** Knowledge of principles and processes for providing customer and personal services. This includes customer needs assessment, meeting quality standards for services, and evaluation of customer satisfaction.

Police and Sheriff's Patrol Officers

- ▲ Education/Training Required: Long-term on-the-job training
- ▲ Annual Earnings: $40,970
- ▲ Growth: 23.2%
- ▲ Annual Job Openings: 21,000
- ▲ Self-Employed: 0%
- ▲ Part-Time: 6.5%

Maintain order, enforce laws and ordinances, and protect life and property in an assigned patrol district. Perform combination of following duties: Patrol a specific area on foot or in a vehicle, direct traffic, issue traffic summonses, investigate accidents, apprehend and arrest suspects, or serve legal processes of courts. **SKILLS—**No data available.

GOE INFORMATION—Interest Area: 04. Law, Law Enforcement, and Public Safety. **Work Group:** 04.03. Law Enforcement. **Other Job Titles in This Work Group:** Animal Control Workers; Bailiffs; Child Support, Missing Persons, and Unemployment Insurance Fraud Investigators; Correctional Officers and Jailers; Criminal Investigators and Special Agents; Crossing Guards; Detectives and Criminal Investigators; Fire Investigators; Fish and Game Wardens; Forensic Science Technicians; Gaming Surveillance Officers and Gaming Investigators; Highway Patrol Pilots; Immigration and Customs Inspectors; Lifeguards, Ski Patrol, and Other Recreational Protective Service Workers; Parking Enforcement Workers; Police Detectives; Police Identification and Records Officers; Police Patrol Officers; Private Detectives and Investigators; Security Guards; Sheriffs and Deputy Sheriffs; Transit and Railroad Police. **PERSONALITY TYPE—**No data available.

EDUCATION/TRAINING PROGRAM(S)—Criminal Justice/Police Science; Criminalistics and Criminal Science. **RELATED KNOWLEDGE/COURSES—**No data available.

Police Detectives

- ▲ Education/Training Required: Work experience in a related occupation
- ▲ Annual Earnings: $50,960
- ▲ Growth: 16.4%
- ▲ Annual Job Openings: 4,000
- ▲ Self-Employed: 0%
- ▲ Part-Time: 1.5%

Conduct investigations to prevent crimes or solve criminal cases. Examines scene of crime to obtain clues and gather evidence. Records progress of investigation, maintains informational files on suspects, and submits reports to commanding officer or magistrate to authorize warrants. Reviews governmental agency files to obtain identifying data pertaining to suspects or establishments suspected of violating laws. Testifies before court and grand jury and appears in court as witness. Schedules polygraph test for consenting parties and records results of test interpretations for presentation with findings. Prepares assigned cases for court and charges or responses to charges according to formalized procedures. Observes and photographs narcotic purchase transaction to compile evidence and protect undercover investigators. Arrests or assists in arrest of criminals or suspects. Interviews complainant, witnesses, and accused persons to obtain facts or statements; records interviews, using recording device. Investigates establishments or persons to establish facts supporting complainant or accused, using supportive information from witnesses or tangible evidence. Maintains surveillance of establishments to attain identifying information on suspects. **SKILLS—Critical Thinking:** Using logic and reasoning to identify the strengths and weaknesses of alternative solutions, conclusions, or approaches to problems. **Active Listening:** Giving full attention to what other people are saying, taking time to understand the points being made, asking questions as appropriate, and not interrupting at inappropriate times. **Social Perceptiveness:** Being aware of others' reactions and understanding why they react as they do. **Active Learning:** Understanding the implications of new information for both current and future problem-solving and decision-making. **Speaking:** Talking to others to convey information effectively.

GOE INFORMATION—Interest Area: 04. Law, Law Enforcement, and Public Safety. **Work Group:** 04.03. Law Enforcement. **Other Job Titles in This Work Group:** Animal Control Workers; Bailiffs; Child Support, Missing Persons, and Unemployment Insurance Fraud Investigators; Correctional Officers and Jailers; Criminal Investigators and Special Agents; Crossing Guards; Detectives and Criminal Investigators; Fire Investigators; Fish and Game Wardens; Forensic Science Technicians; Gaming Surveillance Officers and Gaming Investigators; Highway Patrol Pilots; Immigration and Customs Inspectors; Lifeguards, Ski Patrol, and Other Recreational Protective Service Workers; Parking Enforcement Workers; Police and Sheriff's Patrol Officers; Police Identification and Records Officers; Police Patrol Officers; Private Detectives and Investigators; Security Guards; Sheriffs and Deputy Sheriffs; Transit and Railroad Police. **PERSONALITY TYPE—Enterprising.** Enterprising occupations frequently involve starting up and carrying out projects. These occupations can involve leading people and making many decisions. They sometimes require risk taking and often deal with business.

EDUCATION/TRAINING PROGRAM(S)—Criminal Justice/Police Science; Criminalistics and Criminal Science. RELATED KNOWLEDGE/COURSES—Public Safety and Security: Knowledge of relevant equipment, policies, procedures, and strategies to promote effective local, state, or national security operations for the protection of people, data, property, and institutions. **Law and Government:** Knowledge of laws, legal codes, court procedures, precedents, government regulations, executive orders, agency rules, and the democratic political process. **Psychology:** Knowledge of human behavior and performance; individual differences in ability, personality, and interests; learning and motivation; psychological research methods; and the assessment and treatment of behavioral and affective disorders. **English Language:** Knowledge of the structure and content of the English language, including the meaning and spelling of words, rules of composition, and grammar. **Clerical Studies:** Knowledge of administrative and clerical procedures and systems, such as word processing, managing files and records, stenography and transcription, designing forms, and other office procedures and terminology.

Police Identification and Records Officers

▲ Education/Training Required: Work experience in a related occupation
▲ Annual Earnings: $50,960
▲ Growth: 16.4%
▲ Annual Job Openings: 4,000
▲ Self-Employed: 0%
▲ Part-Time: 1.5%

Collect evidence at crime scene, classify and identify fingerprints, and photograph evidence for use in criminal and civil cases. Dusts selected areas of crime scene to locate and reveal latent fingerprints. Lifts prints from crime site, using special tape. Photographs, records physical description, and fingerprints homicide victims and suspects for identification. Submits evidence to supervisor. Develops film and prints, using photographic developing equipment. Classifies and files fingerprints. Photographs crime or accident scene to obtain record of evidence. **SKILLS—Active Listening:** Giving full attention to what other people are saying, taking time to understand the points being made, asking questions as appropriate, and not interrupting at inappropriate times. **Operation and Control:** Controlling operations of equipment or systems. **Equipment Selection:** Determining the kind of tools and equipment needed to do a job. **Science:** Using scientific rules and methods to solve problems. **Reading Comprehension:** Understanding written sentences and paragraphs in work-related documents. **Writing:** Communicating effectively in writing as appropriate for the needs of the audience.

GOE INFORMATION—Interest Area: 04. Law, Law Enforcement, and Public Safety. **Work Group:** 04.03. Law Enforcement. **Other Job Titles in This Work Group:** Animal Control Workers; Bailiffs; Child Support, Missing Persons, and Unemployment Insurance Fraud Investigators; Correctional Officers and Jailers; Criminal Investigators and Special Agents; Crossing Guards; Detectives and Criminal Investigators; Fire Investigators; Fish and Game Wardens; Forensic Science Technicians; Gaming Surveillance Officers and Gaming Investigators; Highway Patrol Pilots; Immigration and Customs Inspectors; Lifeguards, Ski Patrol, and Other Recreational Protective Service Workers; Parking Enforcement Workers; Police and Sheriff's Patrol Officers; Police Detectives; Police Patrol Officers; Private Detectives and Investigators; Security Guards; Sheriffs and Deputy Sheriffs; Transit and Railroad Police. **PERSONALITY TYPE—Conventional.** Conventional occupations frequently involve following set procedures and routines. These occupations can include working with data and details more than with ideas. Usually there is a clear line of authority to follow.

EDUCATION/TRAINING PROGRAM(S)—Criminal Justice/Police Science; Criminalistics and Criminal Science. RELATED KNOWLEDGE/COURSES—Public Safety and Security: Knowledge of relevant equipment, policies, procedures, and strategies to promote effective local, state, or national security operations for the protection of people, data, property, and institutions. **Clerical Studies:** Knowledge of administrative and clerical procedures and systems, such as word processing, managing files and records, stenography and transcription, designing forms, and other office procedures and terminology. **Law and Government:** Knowledge of laws, legal codes, court procedures, precedents, government regulations, executive orders, agency rules, and the democratic political process. **English Language:** Knowledge of the structure and content of the English language, including the meaning and spelling of words, rules of composition, and grammar. **Chemistry:** Knowledge of the chemical composition, structure, and properties of substances and of the chemical processes and transformations that they undergo. This includes uses of chemicals and their interactions, danger signs, production techniques, and disposal methods.

Police Patrol Officers

▲ Education/Training Required: Long-term on-the-job training
▲ Annual Earnings: $40,970
▲ Growth: 23.2%
▲ Annual Job Openings: 21,000
▲ Self-Employed: 0%
▲ Part-Time: 1.5%

Patrol assigned area to enforce laws and ordinances, regulate traffic, control crowds, prevent crime, and arrest violators. Patrols specific area on foot, horseback, or motorized conveyance. Draws diagram of crime or accident scene. Photographs crime or accident scene. Interviews principal witnesses and eyewitnesses. Renders aid to accident victims and other persons requiring first aid for physical injuries. Records facts and prepares reports to document activities. Testifies in court to present evidence or act as witness in traffic and criminal cases. Expedites processing of prisoners and prepares and maintains records of prisoner bookings and prisoner status during booking and pretrial process. Relays complaint and emergency-request information to appropriate agency dispatcher. Provides road information to assist motorists. Investigates traffic accidents and other accidents to determine causes and to determine if crime has been committed. Evaluates complaint and emergency-request information to determine response requirements. Reviews facts to determine if criminal act or statute violation is involved. Directs traffic flow and reroutes traffic in case of emergencies. Monitors traffic to ensure that motorists observe traffic regulations and exhibit safe driving procedures. Arrests perpetrator of criminal act or submits citation or warning to violator of motor vehicle ordinance. Maintains order, responds to emergencies, protects people and property, and enforces motor vehicle and criminal law. **SKILLS—Active Listening:** Giving full attention to what other people are saying, taking time to understand the points being made, asking questions as appropriate, and not interrupting at inappropriate times. **Critical Thinking:** Using logic and reasoning to identify the strengths and weaknesses of alternative solutions, conclusions, or approaches to problems. **Service Orientation:** Actively looking for ways to help people. **Social Perceptiveness:** Being aware of others' reactions and understanding why they react as they do. **Speaking:** Talking to others to convey information effectively. **Judgment and Decision Making:** Considering the relative costs and benefits of potential actions to choose the most appropriate one.

GOE INFORMATION—Interest Area: 04. Law, Law Enforcement, and Public Safety. **Work Group:** 04.03. Law

Enforcement. **Other Job Titles in This Work Group:** Animal Control Workers; Bailiffs; Child Support, Missing Persons, and Unemployment Insurance Fraud Investigators; Correctional Officers and Jailers; Criminal Investigators and Special Agents; Crossing Guards; Detectives and Criminal Investigators; Fire Investigators; Fish and Game Wardens; Forensic Science Technicians; Gaming Surveillance Officers and Gaming Investigators; Highway Patrol Pilots; Immigration and Customs Inspectors; Lifeguards, Ski Patrol, and Other Recreational Protective Service Workers; Parking Enforcement Workers; Police and Sheriff's Patrol Officers; Police Detectives; Police Identification and Records Officers; Private Detectives and Investigators; Security Guards; Sheriffs and Deputy Sheriffs; Transit and Railroad Police. **PERSONALITY TYPE—Social.** Social occupations frequently involve working with, communicating with, and teaching people. These occupations often involve helping or providing service to others.

EDUCATION/TRAINING PROGRAM(S)—Criminal Justice/Police Science; Criminalistics and Criminal Science. RELATED KNOWLEDGE/COURSES—Public Safety and Security: Knowledge of relevant equipment, policies, procedures, and strategies to promote effective local, state, or national security operations for the protection of people, data, property, and institutions. **Law and Government:** Knowledge of laws, legal codes, court procedures, precedents, government regulations, executive orders, agency rules, and the democratic political process. **English Language:** Knowledge of the structure and content of the English language, including the meaning and spelling of words, rules of composition, and grammar. **Medicine and Dentistry:** Knowledge of the information and techniques needed to diagnose and treat human injuries, diseases, and deformities. This includes symptoms, treatment alternatives, drug properties and interactions, and preventive health-care measures. **Psychology:** Knowledge of human behavior and performance; individual differences in ability, personality, and interests; learning and motivation; psychological research methods; and the assessment and treatment of behavioral and affective disorders.

P

Political Science Teachers, Postsecondary

▲ Education/Training Required: Master's degree
▲ Annual Earnings: $54,930
▲ Growth: 23.5%
▲ Annual Job Openings: 184,000
▲ Self-Employed: 0%
▲ Part-Time: 32.3%

Teach courses in political science, international affairs, and international relations. Acts as adviser to student organizations. Compiles bibliographies of specialized materials for outside reading assignments. Directs research of other teachers or graduate students working for advanced academic degrees. Serves on faculty committee providing professional consulting services to government and industry. Conducts research in particular field of knowledge and publishes findings in professional journals. Advises students on academic and vocational curricula. Compiles, administers, and grades examinations or assigns this work to others. Prepares and delivers lectures to students. Stimulates class discussions. **SKILLS—Reading Comprehension:** Understanding written sentences and paragraphs in work-related documents. **Instructing:** Teaching others how to do something. **Speaking:** Talking to others to convey information effectively. **Active Learning:** Understanding the implications of new information for both current and future problem-solving and decision-making. **Active Listening:** Giving full attention to what other people are saying, taking time to understand the points being made, asking questions as appropriate, and not interrupting at inappropriate times. **Writing:** Communicating effectively in writing as appropriate for the needs of the audience. **Learning Strategies:** Selecting and using training/instructional methods and procedures appropriate for the situation when learning or teaching new things.

GOE INFORMATION—Interest Area: 12. Education and Social Service. **Work Group:** 12.03. Educational Services. **Other Job Titles in This Work Group:** Adult Literacy, Remedial Education, and GED Teachers and Instructors; Agricultural Sciences Teachers, Postsecondary; Anthropology and Archeology Teachers, Postsecondary; Architecture Teachers, Postsecondary; Archivists; Area, Ethnic, and Cultural Studies Teachers, Postsecondary; Art, Drama, and Music Teachers, Postsecondary; Atmospheric, Earth, Marine, and Space Sciences Teachers, Postsecondary; Audio-Visual Collections Specialists; Biological Science Teachers, Postsecondary; Business Teachers, Postsecondary; Chemistry Teachers, Postsecondary; Child Care Workers; Communications Teachers, Postsecondary; Computer Science Teachers, Postsecondary; Criminal Justice and Law Enforcement Teachers, Postsecondary; Curators; Economics Teachers, Postsecondary; Education Teachers, Postsecondary; Educational Psychologists; Educational, Vocational, and School Counselors; Elementary School Teachers, Except Special Education; Engineering Teachers, Postsecondary; English Language and Literature Teachers, Postsecondary; Environmental Science Teachers, Postsecondary; Farm and Home Management Advisors; Foreign Language and Literature Teachers, Postsecondary; Forestry and Conservation Science Teachers, Postsecondary; Geography Teachers, Postsecondary; Graduate Teaching Assistants; Health Specialties Teachers, Postsecondary; History Teachers, Postsecondary; Home Economics Teachers, Postsecondary; Kindergarten Teachers, Except Special Education; Law Teachers, Postsecondary; Librarians; Library Assistants, Clerical; Library Science Teachers, Postsecondary; Library Technicians; Mathematical Science Teachers, Postsecondary; Middle School Teachers, Except Special and Vocational Education; Museum Technicians and Conservators; Nursing Instructors and Teachers, Postsecondary; Personal Financial Advisors; Philosophy and Religion Teachers, Postsecondary; Physics Teachers, Postsecondary; Postsecondary Teachers, All Other; Preschool Teachers, Except Special Education; others. **PERSONALITY TYPE—Social.** Social occupations frequently involve working with, communicating with, and teaching people. These occupations often involve helping or providing service to others.

EDUCATION/TRAINING PROGRAM(S)—American Government and Politics (United States); Political Science and Government, General; Political Science and Government, Other; Social Science Teacher Education. RELATED KNOWLEDGE/COURSES—Education and Training: Knowledge of principles and methods for curriculum and training design, teaching and instruction for individuals and groups, and the measurement of training effects. **Sociology and Anthropology:** Knowledge of group behavior and dynamics, societal trends and influences, human migrations, ethnicity, and cultures and their history and origins. **History and Archeology:** Knowledge of historical events and their causes, indicators, and effects on civilizations and cultures. **Psychology:** Knowledge of human behavior and performance; individual differences in ability, personality, and interests; learning and motivation; psychological research methods; and the assessment and treatment of behavioral and affective disorders. **English Language:** Knowledge of the structure and content of the English language, including the meaning and spelling of words, rules of composition, and grammar.

Political Scientists

- ▲ Education/Training Required: Master's degree
- ▲ Annual Earnings: $81,350
- ▲ Growth: 17.2%
- ▲ Annual Job Openings: 2,000
- ▲ Self-Employed: 5.2%
- ▲ Part-Time: 18.1%

Study the origin, development, and operation of political systems. Research a wide range of subjects, such as relations between the United States and foreign countries, the beliefs and institutions of foreign nations, or the politics of small towns or a major metropolis. May study topics such as public opinion, political decision making, and ideology. May analyze the structure and operation of governments as well as various political entities. May conduct public opinion surveys, analyze election results, or analyze public documents. Conducts research into political philosophy and theories of political systems, such as governmental institutions, public laws, and international law. Analyzes and interprets results of studies and prepares reports detailing findings, recommendations, or conclusions. Organizes and conducts public opinion surveys and interprets results. Recommends programs and policies to institutions and organizations. Prepares reports detailing findings and conclusions. Consults with government officials, civic bodies, research agencies, and political parties. **SKILLS—Writing:** Communicating effectively in writing as appropriate for the needs of the audience. **Reading Comprehension:** Understanding written sentences and paragraphs in work-related documents. **Mathematics:** Using mathematics to solve problems. **Active Learning:** Understanding the implications of new information for both current and future problem-solving and decision-making. **Speaking:** Talking to others to convey information effectively. **Active Listening:** Giving full attention to what other people are saying, taking time to understand the points being made, asking questions as appropriate, and not interrupting at inappropriate times.

GOE INFORMATION—Interest Area: 02. Science, Math, and Engineering. **Work Group:** 02.04. Social Sci-

ences. **Other Job Titles in This Work Group:** Anthropologists; Anthropologists and Archeologists; Archeologists; City Planning Aides; Economists; Historians; Industrial-Organizational Psychologists; Psychologists, All Other; Social Science Research Assistants; Social Scientists and Related Workers, All Other; Sociologists; Survey Researchers; Urban and Regional Planners. **PERSONALITY TYPE—**Investigative. Investigative occupations frequently involve working with ideas and require an extensive amount of thinking. These occupations can involve searching for facts and figuring out problems mentally.

EDUCATION/TRAINING PROGRAM(S)—American Government and Politics (United States); Canadian Government and Politics; International/Global Studies; Political Science and Government, General; Political Science and Government, Other. **RELATED KNOWLEDGE/COURSES—Law and Government:** Knowledge of laws, legal codes, court procedures, precedents, government regulations, executive orders, agency rules, and the democratic political process. **English Language:** Knowledge of the structure and content of the English language, including the meaning and spelling of words, rules of composition, and grammar. **Communications and Media:** Knowledge of media production, communication, and dissemination techniques and methods. This includes alternative ways to inform and entertain via written, oral, and visual media. **Mathematics:** Knowledge of arithmetic, algebra, geometry, calculus, and statistics and their applications. **Philosophy and Theology:** Knowledge of different philosophical systems and religions. This includes their basic principles, values, ethics, ways of thinking, customs, and practices and their impact on human culture.

Postsecondary Teachers, All Other

▲ Education/Training Required: Master's degree
▲ Annual Earnings: No data available
▲ Growth: 23.5%
▲ Annual Job Openings: 184,000
▲ Self-Employed: 0%
▲ Part-Time: 32.3%

All postsecondary teachers not listed separately. **SKILLS**—No data available.

GOE INFORMATION—**Interest Area:** 12. Education and Social Service. **Work Group:** 12.03. Educational Services. **Other Job Titles in This Work Group:** Adult Literacy, Remedial Education, and GED Teachers and Instructors; Agricultural Sciences Teachers, Postsecondary; Anthropology and Archeology Teachers, Postsecondary; Architecture Teachers, Postsecondary; Archivists; Area, Ethnic, and Cultural Studies Teachers, Postsecondary; Art, Drama, and Music Teachers, Postsecondary; Atmospheric, Earth, Marine, and Space Sciences Teachers, Postsecondary; Audio-Visual Collections Specialists; Biological Science Teachers, Postsecondary; Business Teachers, Postsecondary; Chemistry Teachers, Postsecondary; Child Care Workers; Communications Teachers, Postsecondary; Computer Science Teachers, Postsecondary; Criminal Justice and Law Enforcement Teachers, Postsecondary; Curators; Economics Teachers, Postsecondary; Education Teachers, Postsecondary; Educational Psychologists; Educational, Vocational, and School Counselors; Elementary School Teachers, Except Special Education; Engineering Teachers, Postsecondary; English Language and Literature Teachers, Postsecondary; Environmental Science Teachers, Postsecondary; Farm and Home Management Advisors; Foreign Language and Literature Teachers, Postsecondary; Forestry and Conservation Science Teachers, Postsecondary; Geography Teachers, Postsecondary; Graduate Teaching Assistants; Health Specialties Teachers, Postsecondary; History Teachers, Postsecondary; Home Economics Teachers, Postsecondary; Kindergarten Teachers, Except Special Education; Law Teachers, Postsecondary; Librarians; Library Assistants, Clerical; Library Science Teachers, Postsecondary; Library Technicians; Mathematical Science Teachers, Postsecondary; Middle School Teachers, Except Special and Vocational Education; Museum Technicians and Conservators; Nursing Instructors and Teachers, Postsecondary; Personal Financial Advisors; Philosophy and Religion Teachers, Postsecondary; Physics Teachers, Postsecondary; Political Science Teachers, Postsecondary; Preschool Teachers, Except Special Education; others. **PERSONALITY TYPE**—No data available.

EDUCATION/TRAINING PROGRAM(S)—Creative Writing; General Studies; Humanities/Humanistic Studies; Liberal Arts and Sciences, General Studies and Humanities, Other; Liberal Arts and Sciences/Liberal Studies; Speech and Rhetorical Studies. **RELATED KNOWLEDGE/COURSES**—No data available.

Precision Dyers

▲ Education/Training Required: Postsecondary vocational training
▲ Annual Earnings: $16,360
▲ Growth: 11.4%
▲ Annual Job Openings: 62,000
▲ Self-Employed: 5.9%
▲ Part-Time: 22.7%

Change or restore the color of articles, such as garments, drapes, and slipcovers, by means of dyes. Work requires knowledge of the composition of the textiles being dyed or restored, the chemical properties of bleaches and dyes, and their effects upon such textiles. Matches sample color, applying knowledge of bleaching agent and dye properties and type, construction, condition, and color of article. Immerses article in bleaching bath to strip colors. Immerses article in dye solution and stirs with stick or dyes article in rotary-drum or paddle dyeing machine.

Rinses article in water and acetic acid solution to remove excess dye and to fix colors. Dissolves dye or bleaching chemicals in water. Operates or directs operation of extractor and drier. Sprays or brushes article with prepared solution to remove stains. Measures and mixes amounts of bleaches, dyes, oils, and acids, following formulas. Applies dye to article, using spray gun, electrically rotated brush, or handbrush. Examines article to identify fabric and original dye by sight, by touch, or by testing sample with fire or chemical reagent. Tests dye on swatch of fabric to ensure color match. **SKILLS—Science:** Using scientific rules and methods to solve problems. **Equipment Selection:** Determining the kind of tools and equipment needed to do a job. **Reading Comprehension:** Understanding written sentences and paragraphs in work-related documents. **Critical Thinking:** Using logic and reasoning to identify the strengths and weaknesses of alternative solutions, conclusions, or approaches to problems.

GOE INFORMATION—Interest Area: 11. Recreation, Travel, and Other Personal Services. **Work Group:** 11.06. Apparel, Shoes, Leather, and Fabric Care. **Other Job Titles in This Work Group:** Custom Tailors; Fabric Menders, Except Garment; Laundry and Drycleaning Machine Operators and Tenders, Except Pressing; Laundry and Dry-Cleaning Workers; Pressers, Delicate Fabrics; Pressers, Hand; Pressers, Textile, Garment, and Related Materials; Shoe and Leather Workers and Repairers; Shop and Alteration Tailors; Spotters, Dry Cleaning; Tailors, Dressmakers, and Custom Sewers; Textile, Apparel, and Furnishings Workers, All Other; Upholsterers. **PERSONALITY TYPE—Realistic.** Realistic occupations frequently involve work activities that include practical, hands-on problems and solutions. They often deal with plants, animals, and real-world materials like wood, tools, and machinery. Many of the occupations require working outside and do not involve a lot of paperwork or working closely with others.

EDUCATION/TRAINING PROGRAM(S)—No data available. **RELATED KNOWLEDGE/COURSES— Chemistry:** Knowledge of the chemical composition, structure, and properties of substances and of the chemical processes and transformations that they undergo. This includes uses of chemicals and their interactions, danger signs, production techniques, and disposal methods. **Production and Processing:** Knowledge of raw materials, production processes, quality control, costs, and other techniques for maximizing the effective manufacture and distribution of goods. **English Language:** Knowledge of the structure and content of the English language, including the meaning and spelling of words, rules of composition, and grammar.

Preschool Teachers, Except Special Education

- ▲ Education/Training Required: Bachelor's degree
- ▲ Annual Earnings: $18,640
- ▲ Growth: 20.0%
- ▲ Annual Job Openings: 55,000
- ▲ Self-Employed: 1.5%
- ▲ Part-Time: 32.4%

Instruct children (normally up to 5 years of age) in activities designed to promote social, physical, and intellectual growth needed for primary school in preschool, day care center, or other child development facility. May be required to hold state certification. Instructs children in activities designed to promote social, physical, and intellectual growth in facility such as preschool or day care center. Plans individual and group activities for children, such as learning to listen to instructions, playing with others, and using play equipment. Demonstrates activity. Structures play activities to instill concepts of respect and concern for others. Monitors individual and/or group activities to prevent accidents and promote social skills. Reads books to entire class or to small groups. Confers with parents to explain preschool program and to discuss ways they can develop their child's interest. Plans instructional activities for teacher aide. Administers tests to determine each child's level of development according to design of test. Attends staff meetings. **SKILLS—Learning Strategies:** Selecting and using training/instructional methods and procedures appropriate for the situation when learning or teaching new things. **Monitoring:** Monitoring/Assessing your performance or that of other individuals or organizations to make improvements or take corrective action. **Social Perceptiveness:** Being aware of others' reactions and understanding why they react as they do. **Active Listening:** Giving full attention to what other people are saying, taking time to understand the points being made, asking questions as appropriate, and not interrupting at inappropriate times. **Reading Comprehension:** Understanding written sentences and paragraphs in work-related documents. **Speaking:** Talking to others to convey information effectively.

GOE INFORMATION—Interest Area: 12. Education and Social Service. **Work Group:** 12.03. Educational Services. **Other Job Titles in This Work Group:** Adult Literacy, Remedial Education, and GED Teachers and Instructors; Agricultural Sciences Teachers, Postsecondary; Anthropology and Archeology Teachers, Postsecondary; Architecture Teachers, Postsecondary; Archivists; Area, Ethnic, and Cultural Studies Teachers, Postsecondary; Art, Drama, and Music Teachers, Postsecondary; Atmospheric, Earth, Marine, and Space Sciences Teachers, Postsecondary; Audio-Visual Collections Specialists; Biological Science Teachers, Postsecondary; Business Teachers, Postsecondary; Chemistry Teachers, Postsecondary; Child Care Workers; Communications Teachers, Postsecondary; Computer Science Teachers, Postsecondary; Criminal Justice and Law Enforcement Teachers, Postsecondary; Curators; Economics Teachers, Postsecondary; Education Teachers, Postsecondary; Educational Psychologists; Educational, Vocational, and School Counselors; Elementary School Teachers, Except Special Education; Engineering Teachers, Postsecondary; English Language and Literature Teachers, Postsecondary; Environmental Science Teachers, Postsecondary; Farm and Home Management Advisors; Foreign Language and Literature Teachers, Postsecondary; Forestry and Conservation Science Teachers, Postsecondary; Geography Teachers, Postsecondary; Graduate Teaching Assistants; Health Specialties Teachers, Postsecondary; History Teachers, Postsecondary; Home Economics Teachers, Postsecondary; Kindergarten Teachers, Except Special Education; Law Teachers, Postsecondary; Librarians; Library Assistants, Clerical; Library Science Teachers, Postsecondary; Library Technicians; Mathematical Science Teachers, Postsecondary; Middle School Teachers, Except Special and Vocational Education; Museum Technicians and Conservators; Nursing Instructors and Teachers, Postsecondary; Personal Financial Advisors; Philosophy and Religion Teachers, Postsecondary; Physics Teachers, Postsecondary; Political Science Teachers, Postsecondary; Postsecondary Teachers, All Other; Psychology Teachers, Postsecondary; others. **PERSONALITY TYPE**—Social. Social occupations frequently involve working with, communicating with, and teaching people. These occupations often involve helping or providing service to others.

EDUCATION/TRAINING PROGRAM(S)—Child Care and Support Services Management; Early Childhood Education and Teaching; Kindergarten/Preschool Education and Teaching. **RELATED KNOWLEDGE/ COURSES—Education and Training:** Knowledge of principles and methods for curriculum and training design, teaching and instruction for individuals and groups, and the measurement of training effects. **Customer and Personal Service:** Knowledge of principles and processes for providing customer and personal services. This includes customer needs assessment, meeting quality standards for services, and evaluation of customer satisfaction. **English Language:** Knowledge of the structure and content of the English language, including the meaning and spelling of words, rules of composition, and grammar. **Psychology:** Knowledge of human behavior and performance; individual differences in ability, personality, and interests; learning and motivation; psychological research methods; and the assessment and treatment of behavioral and affective disorders. **Fine Arts:** Knowledge of the theory and techniques required to compose, produce, and perform works of music, dance, visual arts, drama, and sculpture.

Private Detectives and Investigators

- ▲ Education/Training Required: Work experience in a related occupation
- ▲ Annual Earnings: $28,380
- ▲ Growth: 23.5%
- ▲ Annual Job Openings: 9,000
- ▲ Self-Employed: 20.1%
- ▲ Part-Time: 19.8%

Detect occurrences of unlawful acts or infractions of rules in private establishment or seek, examine, and compile information for client. Confers with establishment officials, security department, police, or postal officials to identify problems, provide information, and receive instructions. Alerts staff and superiors of presence of suspect in establishment. Writes reports and case summaries to document investigations or inform supervisors. Testifies at hearings and court trials to present evidence. Locates persons, using phone or mail directories, to collect money owed or to serve legal papers. Evaluates performance and honesty of employees by posing as customer or employee and comparing employee to standards. Assists victims, police, fire department, and others during emergencies. Enforces conformance to establishment rules and protects persons or property. Counts cash and reviews transactions, sales checks, and register tapes to verify amount of cash and shortages. Obtains and analyzes information on suspects, crimes, and disturbances to solve cases, identify criminal activity, and maintain public peace and order. Warns and ejects troublemakers from premises and apprehends and releases suspects to authorities or security personnel. Examines crime scene for clues or fingerprints and submits evidence to laboratory for analysis. Questions persons to obtain evidence for cases of divorce, child custody, or missing persons or individual's character or financial status. Observes employees or customers and patrols premises to detect violations and obtain evidence, using binoculars, cameras, and television. **SKILLS—Active Listening:** Giving full attention to what other people are saying, taking time to understand the points being made, asking questions as appropriate, and not interrupting at inappropriate times. **Critical Thinking:** Using logic and reasoning to identify the strengths and weaknesses of alternative solutions, conclusions, or approaches to problems. **Speaking:** Talking to others to convey information effectively. **Writing:** Communicating effectively in writing as appropriate for the needs of the audience. **Judgment and Decision Making:** Considering the relative costs and benefits of potential actions to choose the most appropriate one.

GOE INFORMATION—Interest Area: 04. Law, Law Enforcement, and Public Safety. **Work Group:** 04.03. Law Enforcement. **Other Job Titles in This Work Group:** Animal Control Workers; Bailiffs; Child Support, Missing Persons, and Unemployment Insurance Fraud Investigators; Correctional Officers and Jailers; Criminal Investigators and Special Agents; Crossing Guards; Detectives and Criminal Investigators; Fire Investigators; Fish and Game Wardens; Forensic Science Technicians; Gaming Surveillance Officers and Gaming Investigators; Highway Patrol Pilots; Immigration and Customs Inspectors; Lifeguards, Ski Patrol, and Other Recreational Protective Service Workers; Parking Enforcement Workers; Police and Sheriff's Patrol Officers; Police Detectives; Police Identification and Records Officers; Police Patrol Officers; Security Guards; Sheriffs and Deputy Sheriffs; Transit and Railroad Police. **PERSONALITY TYPE—**Enterprising. Enterprising occupations frequently involve starting up and carrying out projects. These occupations can involve leading people and making many decisions. They sometimes require risk taking and often deal with business.

EDUCATION/TRAINING PROGRAM(S)—Criminal Justice/Police Science. **RELATED KNOWLEDGE/ COURSES—Public Safety and Security:** Knowledge of relevant equipment, policies, procedures, and strategies to promote effective local, state, or national security operations for the protection of people, data, property, and institutions. **English Language:** Knowledge of the structure and content of the English language, including the meaning and spelling of words, rules of composition, and grammar. **Law and Government:** Knowledge of laws, legal codes, court procedures, precedents, government regulations, executive orders, agency rules, and the democratic political process. **Telecommunications:** Knowledge of transmission, broadcasting, switching, control, and operation of telecommunications systems. **Customer and Personal Service:** Knowledge of principles and processes for providing customer and personal services. This includes customer needs assessment, meeting quality standards for services, and evaluation of customer satisfaction. **Communications and Media:** Knowledge of media production, communication, and dissemination techniques and methods. This includes alternative ways to inform and entertain via written, oral, and visual media.

Private Sector Executives

▲ Education/Training Required: Work experience plus degree
▲ Annual Earnings: $120,450
▲ Growth: 17.2%
▲ Annual Job Openings: 48,000
▲ Self-Employed: 0%
▲ Part-Time: 6.1%

Determine and formulate policies and business strategies and provide overall direction of private sector organizations. Plan, direct, and coordinate operational activities at the highest level of management with the help of subordinate managers. Directs, plans, and implements policies and objectives of organization or business in accordance with charter and board of directors. Directs activities of organization to plan procedures, establish responsibilities, and coordinate functions among departments and sites. Analyzes operations to evaluate performance of company and staff and to determine areas of cost reduction and program improvement. Confers with board members, organization officials, and staff members to establish policies and formulate plans. Reviews financial statements and sales and activity reports to ensure that organization's objectives are achieved. Assigns or delegates responsibilities to subordinates. Directs and coordinates activities of business involved with buying and selling investment products and financial services. Establishes internal control procedures. Presides over or serves on board of directors, management committees, or other governing boards. Directs inservice training of staff. Administers program for selection of sites, construction of buildings, and provision of equipment and supplies. Screens, selects, hires, transfers, and discharges employees. Promotes objectives of institution or business before associations, public, government agencies, or community groups. Negotiates or approves contracts with suppliers and distributors and with maintenance, janitorial, and security providers. Prepares reports and budgets. Directs non-merchandising departments of business, such as advertising, purchasing, credit, and accounting. Directs and coordinates activities of business or department concerned with production, pricing, sales, and/or distribution of products. Directs and coordinates organization's financial and budget activities to fund operations, maximize investments, and increase efficiency. **SKILLS—Judgment and Decision Making:** Considering the relative costs and benefits of potential actions to choose the most appropriate one. **Coordination:** Adjusting actions in relation to others' actions. **Systems Evaluation:** Identifying measures or indicators of system performance and the actions needed to improve or correct performance relative to the goals of the system. **Systems Analysis:** Determining how a system should work and how changes in conditions, operations, and the environment will affect outcomes. **Management of Financial Resources:** Determining how money will be spent to get the work done and accounting for these expenditures.

GOE INFORMATION—Interest Area: 13. General Management and Support. **Work Group:** 13.01. General Management Work and Management of Support Functions. **Other Job Titles in This Work Group:** Chief Executives; Compensation and Benefits Managers; Farm, Ranch, and Other Agricultural Managers; Financial Managers; Financial Managers, Branch or Department; Funeral Directors; General and Operations Managers; Government Service Executives; Human Resources Managers; Human Resources Managers, All Other; Legislators; Managers, All Other; Postmasters and Mail Superintendents; Property, Real Estate, and Community Association Managers; Public Relations Managers; Purchasing Managers; Storage and Distribution Managers; Training and Development Managers; Transportation, Storage, and Distribution Managers; Treasurers, Controllers, and Chief Financial Officers. **PERSONALITY TYPE—**Enterprising. Enterprising occupations frequently involve starting up and carrying out projects. These occupations can involve leading people and making many decisions. They sometimes require risk taking and often deal with business.

EDUCATION/TRAINING PROGRAM(S)—Business Administration and Management, General; Business/Commerce, General; Entrepreneurship/Entrepreneurial Studies; International Business/Trade/Commerce; Public Administration; Public Administration and Social Service Professions, Other; Public Policy Analysis. **RELATED KNOWLEDGE/COURSES—Administration and Management:** Knowledge of business and management principles involved in strategic planning, resource allocation, human resources modeling, leadership technique, production methods, and coordination of people and resources.

English Language: Knowledge of the structure and content of the English language, including the meaning and spelling of words, rules of composition, and grammar. Economics and Accounting: Knowledge of economic and accounting principles and practices, the financial markets, banking, and the analysis and reporting of financial data. Mathematics: Knowledge of arithmetic, algebra, geometry, calculus, and statistics and their applications. Sales and Marketing: Knowledge of principles and methods for showing, promoting, and selling products or services. This includes marketing strategy and tactics, product demonstration, sales techniques, and sales control systems. Production and Processing: Knowledge of raw materials, production processes, quality control, costs, and other techniques for maximizing the effective manufacture and distribution of goods.

Probation Officers and Correctional Treatment Specialists

- ▲ Education/Training Required: Bachelor's degree
- ▲ Annual Earnings: $38,780
- ▲ Growth: 23.8%
- ▲ Annual Job Openings: 14,000
- ▲ Self-Employed: 3.1%
- ▲ Part-Time: 11.9%

Provide social services to assist in rehabilitation of law offenders in custody or on probation or parole. Make recommendations for actions involving formulation of rehabilitation plan and treatment of offender, including conditional release and education and employment stipulations. Counsels offender and refers offender to social resources of community for assistance. Interviews offender or inmate to determine social progress, individual problems, needs, interests, and attitude. Conducts follow-up interview with offender or inmate to ascertain progress made. Reviews and evaluates legal and social history and progress of offender or inmate. Conducts prehearing or presentencing investigations and testifies in court. Prepares and maintains case folder for each assigned inmate or offender. Develops and prepares informational packets of social agencies and assistance organizations and programs for inmate or offender. Assists offender or inmate with matters concerning detainers, sentences in other jurisdictions, writs, and applications for social assistance. Makes recommendations concerning conditional release or institutionalization of offender or inmate. Confers with inmate's or offender's family to identify needs and problems and to ensure that family and business are attended to. Informs offender or inmate of requirements of conditional release, such as office visits, restitution payments, or educational and employment stipulations. Determines nature and extent of inmate's or offender's criminal record and current and prospective social problems. Consults with attorneys, judges, and institution personnel to evaluate inmate's social progress. Formulates rehabilitation plan for each assigned offender or inmate. Provides guidance to inmates or offenders, such as development of vocational and educational plans and available social services. **SKILLS—Active Listening:** Giving full attention to what other people are saying, taking time to understand the points being made, asking questions as appropriate, and not interrupting at inappropriate times. **Speaking:** Talking to others to convey information effectively. **Judgment and Decision Making:** Considering the relative costs and benefits of potential actions to choose the most appropriate one. **Reading Comprehension:** Understanding written sentences and paragraphs in work-related documents. **Service Orientation:** Actively looking for ways to help people.

GOE INFORMATION—Interest Area: 12. Education and Social Service. **Work Group:** 12.02. Social Services. **Other Job Titles in This Work Group:** Child, Family, and School Social Workers; Clergy; Clinical Psychologists; Clinical, Counseling, and School Psychologists; Community and Social Service Specialists, All Other; Counseling Psychologists; Counselors, All Other; Directors, Religious Activities and Education; Marriage and Family Therapists; Medical and Public Health Social Workers; Mental Health and Substance Abuse Social Workers; Mental Health Counselors; Rehabilitation Counselors; Religious Workers, All Other; Residential Advisors; Social and Human Service Assistants; Social Workers, All Other; Substance Abuse and Behavioral Disorder Counselors. **PERSONALITY TYPE—Social.** Social occupations frequently involve working with, communicating with, and teaching people. These occupations often involve helping or providing service to others.

P

EDUCATION/TRAINING PROGRAM(S)—Social Work. **RELATED KNOWLEDGE/COURSES—Therapy and Counseling:** Knowledge of principles, methods, and procedures for diagnosis, treatment, and rehabilitation of physical and mental dysfunctions and for career counseling and guidance. **Psychology:** Knowledge of human behavior and performance; individual differences in ability, personality, and interests; learning and motivation; psychological research methods; and the assessment and treatment of behavioral and affective disorders. **Law and Government:** Knowledge of laws, legal codes, court procedures, precedents, government regulations, executive orders, agency rules, and the democratic political process. **Public Safety and Security:** Knowledge of relevant equipment, policies, procedures, and strategies to promote effective local, state, or national security operations for the protection of people, data, property, and institutions. **English Language:** Knowledge of the structure and content of the English language, including the meaning and spelling of words, rules of composition, and grammar.

Producers

- ▲ Education/Training Required: Work experience plus degree
- ▲ Annual Earnings: $45,090
- ▲ Growth: 27.1%
- ▲ Annual Job Openings: 11,000
- ▲ Self-Employed: 23.7%
- ▲ Part-Time: 25.3%

Plan and coordinate various aspects of radio, television, stage, or motion picture production, such as selecting script; coordinating writing, directing and editing; and arranging financing. Coordinates various aspects of production, such as audio and camera work, music, timing, writing, and staging. Represents network or company in negotiations with independent producers. Selects scenes from taped program to be used for promotional purposes. Reads manuscript and selects play for stage performance. Times scene and calculates program timing. Distributes rehearsal call sheets and copies of script, arranges for rehearsal quarters, and contacts cast members to verify readiness for rehearsal. Establishes management policies, production schedules, and operating budgets for production. Directs activities of one or more departments of motion picture studio and prepares rehearsal call sheets and reports of activities and operating costs. Reviews film, recordings, or rehearsals to ensure conformance to production and broadcast standards. Produces shows for special occasions, such as holiday or testimonial. Obtains and distributes costumes, props, music, and studio equipment to complete production. Composes and edits script or outlines story for screenwriter to write script. Selects and hires cast and staff members and arbitrates personnel disputes. Conducts meetings with staff to discuss production progress and to ensure production objectives are attained. **SKILLS—Coordination:** Adjusting actions in relation to others' actions. **Reading Comprehension:** Understanding written sentences and paragraphs in work-related documents. **Management of Personnel Resources:** Motivating, developing, and directing people as they work, identifying the best people for the job. **Speaking:** Talking to others to convey information effectively. **Writing:** Communicating effectively in writing as appropriate for the needs of the audience.

GOE INFORMATION—Interest Area: 01. Arts, Entertainment, and Media. **Work Group:** 01.01. Managerial Work in Arts, Entertainment, and Media. **Other Job Titles in This Work Group:** Agents and Business Managers of Artists, Performers, and Athletes; Art Directors; Producers and Directors; Program Directors; Technical Directors/Managers. **PERSONALITY TYPE—**Artistic. Artistic occupations frequently involve working with forms, designs, and patterns. They often require self-expression, and the work can be done without following a clear set of rules.

EDUCATION/TRAINING PROGRAM(S)—Cinematography and Film/Video Production; Directing and Theatrical Production; Drama and Dramatics/Theatre Arts, General; Dramatic/Theatre Arts and Stagecraft, Other; Film/Cinema Studies; Radio and Television; Theatre/Theatre Arts Management. **RELATED KNOWLEDGE/COURSES—Communications and Media:** Knowledge of media production, communication, and dissemination techniques and methods. This includes alternative ways to inform and entertain via written, oral, and visual media. **Administration and Management:** Knowledge of business and management principles involved in strategic planning, resource allocation, human resources modeling, leadership technique, production methods, and coordination of people and resources. **Personnel and Human Resources:** Knowledge of principles and procedures for personnel recruitment, selection, training, compensation and benefits, labor relations and negotiation, and personnel information systems. **English**

Language: Knowledge of the structure and content of the English language, including the meaning and spelling of words, rules of composition, and grammar. **Fine Arts:** Knowledge of the theory and techniques required to compose, produce, and perform works of music, dance, visual arts, drama, and sculpture.

Producers and Directors

- ▲ Education/Training Required: Work experience plus degree
- ▲ Annual Earnings: $45,090
- ▲ Growth: 27.1%
- ▲ Annual Job Openings: 11,000
- ▲ Self-Employed: 23.7%
- ▲ Part-Time: 25.3%

Produce or direct stage, television, radio, video, or motion picture productions for entertainment, information, or instruction. Responsible for creative decisions, such as interpretation of script, choice of guests, set design, sound, special effects, and choreography. **SKILLS**—No data available.

GOE INFORMATION—**Interest Area:** 01. Arts, Entertainment, and Media. **Work Group:** 01.01. Managerial Work in Arts, Entertainment, and Media. **Other Job Titles in This Work Group:** Agents and Business Managers of

Artists, Performers, and Athletes; Art Directors; Producers; Program Directors; Technical Directors/Managers. **PERSONALITY TYPE**—No data available.

EDUCATION/TRAINING PROGRAM(S)—Cinematography and Film/Video Production; Directing and Theatrical Production; Drama and Dramatics/Theatre Arts, General; Dramatic/Theatre Arts and Stagecraft, Other; Film/Cinema Studies; Radio and Television; Theatre/Theatre Arts Management. **RELATED KNOWLEDGE/COURSES**—No data available.

Production Helpers

- ▲ Education/Training Required: Short-term on-the-job training
- ▲ Annual Earnings: $18,990
- ▲ Growth: 11.9%
- ▲ Annual Job Openings: 143,000
- ▲ Self-Employed: 1.6%
- ▲ Part-Time: 16.2%

Perform variety of tasks requiring limited knowledge of production processes in support of skilled production workers. Cleans and lubricates equipment. Signals coworkers to facilitate moving product during processing. Measures amount of ingredients, length of extruded article, or work to ensure conformance to specifications. Replaces damaged or worm equipment parts. Tends equipment to facilitate process. Mixes ingredients according to procedure. Turns valves to regulate flow of liquids or air, to reverse machine, to start pump, and to regulate equipment. Starts machines or equipment to begin process. Marks or tags identification on parts. Observes operation and notifies equipment operator of malfunctions. Places or posi-

tions equipment or partially assembled product for further processing, manually or using hoist. Removes product, machine attachments, and waste material from machine. Reads gauges and charts and records data. Loads and unloads processing equipment or conveyance used to receive raw materials or to ship finished products. Dumps materials into machine hopper prior to mixing. **SKILLS**— **Equipment Maintenance:** Performing routine maintenance on equipment and determining when and what kind of maintenance is needed. **Operation and Control:** Controlling operations of equipment or systems. **Operation Monitoring:** Watching gauges, dials, or other indicators to make sure a machine is working properly. **Repairing:**

Repairing machines or systems, using the needed tools. **Equipment Selection:** Determining the kind of tools and equipment needed to do a job.

GOE INFORMATION—Interest Area: 08. Industrial Production. **Work Group:** 08.03. Production Work. **Other Job Titles in This Work Group:** Bakers, Manufacturing; Bindery Machine Operators and Tenders; Brazers; Cementing and Gluing Machine Operators and Tenders; Chemical Equipment Controllers and Operators; Chemical Equipment Operators and Tenders; Chemical Equipment Tenders; Cleaning, Washing, and Metal Pickling Equipment Operators and Tenders; Coating, Painting, and Spraying Machine Operators and Tenders; Coil Winders, Tapers, and Finishers; Combination Machine Tool Operators and Tenders, Metal and Plastic; Computer-Controlled Machine Tool Operators, Metal and Plastic; Cooling and Freezing Equipment Operators and Tenders; Crushing, Grinding, and Polishing Machine Setters, Operators, and Tenders; Cutters and Trimmers, Hand; Cutting and Slicing Machine Operators and Tenders; Cutting and Slicing Machine Setters, Operators, and Tenders; Design Printing Machine Setters and Set-Up Operators; Electrolytic Plating and Coating Machine Operators and Tenders, Metal and Plastic; Electrolytic Plating and Coating Machine Setters and Set-Up Operators, Metal and Plastic; Electrotypers and Stereotypers; Embossing Machine Set-Up Operators; Engraver Set-Up Operators; Extruding and Forming Machine Operators and Tenders, Synthetic or Glass Fibers; Extruding and Forming Machine Setters, Operators, and Tenders, Synthetic and Glass Fibers; Extruding, Forming, Pressing, and Compacting Machine Operators and Tenders; Fabric and Apparel Patternmakers; Fiber Product Cutting Machine Setters and Set-Up Operators; Fiberglass Laminators and Fabricators; Film Laboratory Technicians; Fitters, Structural Metal—Precision; Food and Tobacco Roasting, Baking, and Drying Machine Operators and Tenders; Food Batchmakers; Food Cooking Machine Operators and Tenders; Furnace, Kiln, Oven, Drier, and Kettle Operators and Tenders; Glass Cutting Machine Setters and Set-Up Operators; Graders and Sorters, Agricultural Products; Grinding and Polishing Workers, Hand; Hand Compositors and Typesetters; Heaters, Metal and Plastic; others. **PERSONALITY TYPE**—Realistic. Realistic occupations frequently involve work activities that include practical, hands-on problems and solutions. They often deal with plants, animals, and real-world materials like wood, tools, and machinery. Many of the occupations require working outside and do not involve a lot of paperwork or working closely with others.

EDUCATION/TRAINING PROGRAM(S)—No data available. **RELATED KNOWLEDGE/COURSES—Production and Processing:** Knowledge of raw materials, production processes, quality control, costs, and other techniques for maximizing the effective manufacture and distribution of goods. **Principles of Mechanical Devices:** Knowledge of machines and tools, including their designs, uses, repair, and maintenance. **Engineering and Technology:** Knowledge of the practical application of engineering science and technology. This includes applying principles, techniques, procedures, and equipment to the design and production of various goods and services. **Mathematics:** Knowledge of arithmetic, algebra, geometry, calculus, and statistics and their applications. **English Language:** Knowledge of the structure and content of the English language, including the meaning and spelling of words, rules of composition, and grammar.

Production Laborers

▲ Education/Training Required: Short-term on-the-job training
▲ Annual Earnings: $18,990
▲ Growth: 11.9%
▲ Annual Job Openings: 143,000
▲ Self-Employed: 1.6%
▲ Part-Time: 16.2%

Perform variety of routine tasks to assist in production activities. Carries or handtrucks supplies to work stations. Records information such as number of product tested, meter readings, and date and time product placed in oven. Examines product to verify conformance to company standards. Mixes ingredients according to formula. Feeds item into processing machine. Inserts parts into partial assembly during various stages of assembly to complete product. Counts finished product to determine completion of production order. Washes machines, equipment, vehicles, and products such as prints, rugs, and table linens. Folds parts of product and final product during processing. Separates product according to weight, grade, size, and composition of material used to produced product. Cuts or breaks flashing from materials or products. Places product in equipment or on worksurface for further processing, inspecting, or wrapping. Positions spout or chute of storage bin to fill containers during processing. Breaks up defective products for reprocessing. Attaches slings, ropes, cables, or identification tags to objects such as pipes, hoses, and bundles. Weighs raw materials for distribution. Threads ends of items such as thread, cloth, and lace through needles and rollers and around takeup tube. Ties product in bundles for further processing or shipment, following prescribed procedure. Lifts raw materials, final products, and items packed for shipment manually or using hoist. Loads and unloads items from machines, conveyors, and conveyance. **SKILLS—Equipment Selection:** Determining the kind of tools and equipment needed to do a job.

GOE INFORMATION—Interest Area: 08. Industrial Production. **Work Group:** 08.03. Production Work. **Other Job Titles in This Work Group:** Bakers, Manufacturing; Bindery Machine Operators and Tenders; Brazers; Cementing and Gluing Machine Operators and Tenders; Chemical Equipment Controllers and Operators; Chemical Equipment Operators and Tenders; Chemical Equipment Tenders; Cleaning, Washing, and Metal Pickling Equipment Operators and Tenders; Coating, Painting, and Spraying Machine Operators and Tenders; Coil Winders, Tapers, and Finishers; Combination Machine Tool Operators and Tenders, Metal and Plastic; Computer-Controlled Machine Tool Operators, Metal and Plastic; Cooling and Freezing Equipment Operators and Tenders; Crushing, Grinding, and Polishing Machine Setters, Operators, and Tenders; Cutters and Trimmers, Hand; Cutting and Slicing Machine Operators and Tenders; Cutting and Slicing Machine Setters, Operators, and Tenders; Design Printing Machine Setters and Set-Up Operators; Electrolytic Plating and Coating Machine Operators and Tenders, Metal and Plastic; Electrolytic Plating and Coating Machine Setters and Set-Up Operators, Metal and Plastic; Electrotypers and Stereotypers; Embossing Machine Set-Up Operators; Engraver Set-Up Operators; Extruding and Forming Machine Operators and Tenders, Synthetic or Glass Fibers; Extruding and Forming Machine Setters, Operators, and Tenders, Synthetic and Glass Fibers; Extruding, Forming, Pressing, and Compacting Machine Operators and Tenders; Fabric and Apparel Patternmakers; Fiber Product Cutting Machine Setters and Set-Up Operators; Fiberglass Laminators and Fabricators; Film Laboratory Technicians; Fitters, Structural Metal—Precision; Food and Tobacco Roasting, Baking, and Drying Machine Operators and Tenders; Food Batchmakers; Food Cooking Machine Operators and Tenders; Furnace, Kiln, Oven, Drier, and Kettle Operators and Tenders; Glass Cutting Machine Setters and Set-Up Operators; Graders and Sorters, Agricultural Products; Grinding and Polishing Workers, Hand; Hand Compositors and Typesetters; Heaters, Metal and Plastic; others. **PERSONALITY TYPE—Realistic.** Realistic occupations frequently involve work activities that include practical, hands-on problems and solutions. They often deal with plants, animals, and real-world materials like wood, tools, and machinery. Many of the occupations require working outside and do not involve a lot of paperwork or working closely with others.

EDUCATION/TRAINING PROGRAM(S)—No data available. **RELATED KNOWLEDGE/COURSES—Production and Processing:** Knowledge of raw materials, production processes, quality control, costs, and other techniques for maximizing the effective manufacture and distribution of goods. **Clerical Studies:** Knowledge of administrative and clerical procedures and systems, such as word processing, managing files and records, stenography and transcription, designing forms, and other office procedures and terminology. **Mathematics:** Knowledge of arithmetic, algebra, geometry, calculus, and statistics and their applications.

Production, Planning, and Expediting Clerks

- ▲ Education/Training Required: Short-term on-the-job training
- ▲ Annual Earnings: $32,420
- ▲ Growth: 17.9%
- ▲ Annual Job Openings: 36,000
- ▲ Self-Employed: 1.7%
- ▲ Part-Time: 18.8%

Coordinate and expedite the flow of work and materials within or between departments of an establishment according to production schedule. Duties include reviewing and distributing production, work, and shipment schedules; conferring with department supervisors to determine progress of work and completion dates; and compiling reports on progress of work, inventory levels, costs, and production problems. Reviews documents such as production schedules, staffing tables, and specifications to obtain information such as materials, priorities, and personnel requirements. Compiles schedules and orders, such as personnel assignments, production, work flow, transportation, and maintenance and repair. Monitors work progress; provides services, such as furnishing permits, tickets, and union information; and directs workers to expedite work flow. Requisitions and maintains inventory of materials and supplies to meet production demands. Calculates figures such as labor and materials amounts, manufacturing costs, and wages, using pricing schedules, adding machine, or calculator. Maintains files, such as maintenance records, bills of lading, and cost reports. Arranges for delivery and distributes supplies and parts to expedite flow of materials to meet production schedules. Examines documents, materials, and products; monitors work processes for completeness, accuracy, and conformance to standards and specifications. Completes status reports, such as production progress, customer information, and materials inventory. Confers with establishment personnel, vendors, and customers to coordinate processing and shipping and to resolve complaints. **SKILLS—Active Listening:** Giving full attention to what other people are saying, taking time to understand the points being made, asking questions as appropriate, and not interrupting at inappropriate times. **Writing:** Communicating effectively in writing as appropriate for the needs of the audience. **Reading Comprehension:** Understanding written sentences and paragraphs in work-related documents. **Monitoring:** Monitoring/Assessing your performance or that of other individuals or organizations to make improvements or take corrective action. **Time Management:** Managing one's own time and the time of others. **Management of Material Resources:** Obtaining and seeing to the appropriate use of equipment, facilities, and materials needed to do certain work.

GOE INFORMATION—Interest Area: 09. Business Detail. **Work Group:** 09.04. Material Control. **Other Job Titles in This Work Group:** Meter Readers, Utilities. **PERSONALITY TYPE—Conventional.** Conventional occupations frequently involve following set procedures and routines. These occupations can include working with data and details more than with ideas. Usually there is a clear line of authority to follow.

EDUCATION/TRAINING PROGRAM(S)—Parts, Warehousing, and Inventory Management Operations. **RELATED KNOWLEDGE/COURSES—Clerical Studies:** Knowledge of administrative and clerical procedures and systems, such as word processing, managing files and records, stenography and transcription, designing forms, and other office procedures and terminology. **Production and Processing:** Knowledge of raw materials, production processes, quality control, costs, and other techniques for maximizing the effective manufacture and distribution of goods. **Mathematics:** Knowledge of arithmetic, algebra, geometry, calculus, and statistics and their applications. **Economics and Accounting:** Knowledge of economic and accounting principles and practices, the financial markets, banking, and the analysis and reporting of financial data. **Transportation:** Knowledge of principles and methods for moving people or goods by air, rail, sea, or road, including the relative costs and benefits.

Professional Photographers

- ▲ Education/Training Required: Long-term on-the-job training
- ▲ Annual Earnings: $23,040
- ▲ Growth: 17.0%
- ▲ Annual Job Openings: 13,000
- ▲ Self-Employed: 43.8%
- ▲ Part-Time: 23.1%

Photograph subjects or newsworthy events, using still cameras, color or black-and-white film, and variety of photographic accessories. Frames subject matter and background in lens to capture desired image. Focuses camera and adjusts settings based on lighting, subject material, distance, and film speed. Selects and assembles equipment and required background properties according to subject, materials, and conditions. Directs activities of workers assisting in setting up photographic equipment. Arranges subject material in desired position. Estimates or measures light level, distance, and number of exposures needed, using measuring devices and formulas. **SKILLS—Equipment Selection:** Determining the kind of tools and equipment needed to do a job. **Monitoring:** Monitoring/Assessing your performance or that of other individuals or organizations to make improvements or take corrective action. **Coordination:** Adjusting actions in relation to others' actions. **Mathematics:** Using mathematics to solve problems. **Operation and Control:** Controlling operations of equipment or systems.

GOE INFORMATION—Interest Area: 01. Arts, Entertainment, and Media. **Work Group:** 01.08. Media Technology. **Other Job Titles in This Work Group:** Audio and Video Equipment Technicians; Broadcast Technicians; Camera Operators, Television, Video, and Motion Picture; Film and Video Editors; Media and Communication Equipment Workers, All Other; Photographers; Radio Operators; Sound Engineering Technicians. **PERSONALITY TYPE—Artistic.** Artistic occupations frequently involve working with forms, designs, and patterns. They often require self-expression, and the work can be done without following a clear set of rules.

EDUCATION/TRAINING PROGRAM(S)—Art/Art Studies, General; Commercial Photography; Film/Video and Photographic Arts, Other; Photography; Photojournalism; Visual and Performing Arts, General. RELATED KNOWLEDGE/COURSES—Fine Arts: Knowledge of the theory and techniques required to compose, produce, and perform works of music, dance, visual arts, drama, and sculpture. **Chemistry:** Knowledge of the chemical composition, structure, and properties of substances and of the chemical processes and transformations that they undergo. This includes uses of chemicals and their interactions, danger signs, production techniques, and disposal methods. **Geography:** Knowledge of principles and methods for describing the features of land, sea, and air masses, including their physical characteristics, locations, interrelationships, and distribution of plant, animal, and human life. **Communications and Media:** Knowledge of media production, communication, and dissemination techniques and methods. This includes alternative ways to inform and entertain via written, oral, and visual media. **Mathematics:** Knowledge of arithmetic, algebra, geometry, calculus, and statistics and their applications. **English Language:** Knowledge of the structure and content of the English language, including the meaning and spelling of words, rules of composition, and grammar.

Program Directors

- ▲ Education/Training Required: Work experience plus degree
- ▲ Annual Earnings: $45,090
- ▲ Growth: 27.1%
- ▲ Annual Job Openings: 11,000
- ▲ Self-Employed: 23.7%
- ▲ Part-Time: 25.3%

Direct and coordinate activities of personnel engaged in preparation of radio or television station program sched- ules and programs, such as sports or news. Directs and coordinates activities of personnel engaged in broadcast news, sports, or programming. Establishes work schedules and hires, assigns, and evaluates staff. Originates feature ideas and researches program topics for implementation. Writes news copy, notes, letters, and memos, using computer. Examines expenditures to ensure that programming and broadcasting activities are within budget. Monitors and reviews news and programming copy and film, using audio or video equipment. Directs setup of remote facilities and installs or cancels programs at remote stations. Evaluates length, content, and suitability of programs for broadcast. Reviews, corrects, and advises member stations concerning programs and schedules. Confers with directors and production staff to discuss issues, such as production and casting problems, budget, policy, and news coverage. Coordinates activities between departments, such as news and programming. Plans and schedules programming and event coverage based on length of broadcast and available station or network time. **SKILLS—Coordination:** Adjusting actions in relation to others' actions. **Writing:** Communicating effectively in writing as appropriate for the needs of the audience. **Management of Personnel Resources:** Motivating, developing, and directing people as they work, identifying the best people for the job. **Reading Comprehension:** Understanding written sentences and paragraphs in work-related documents. **Time Management:** Managing one's own time and the time of others. **Active Learning:** Understanding the implications of new information for both current and future problem-solving and decision-making.

GOE INFORMATION—Interest Area: 01. Arts, Entertainment, and Media. **Work Group:** 01.01. Managerial Work in Arts, Entertainment, and Media. **Other Job Titles**

in This Work Group: Agents and Business Managers of Artists, Performers, and Athletes; Art Directors; Producers; Producers and Directors; Technical Directors/Managers. **PERSONALITY TYPE**—Enterprising. Enterprising occupations frequently involve starting up and carrying out projects. These occupations can involve leading people and making many decisions. They sometimes require risk taking and often deal with business.

EDUCATION/TRAINING PROGRAM(S)—Cinematography and Film/Video Production; Directing and Theatrical Production; Drama and Dramatics/Theatre Arts, General; Dramatic/Theatre Arts and Stagecraft, Other; Film/Cinema Studies; Radio and Television; Theatre/Theatre Arts Management. **RELATED KNOWLEDGE/COURSES—Communications and Media:** Knowledge of media production, communication, and dissemination techniques and methods. This includes alternative ways to inform and entertain via written, oral, and visual media. **Administration and Management:** Knowledge of business and management principles involved in strategic planning, resource allocation, human resources modeling, leadership technique, production methods, and coordination of people and resources. **Personnel and Human Resources:** Knowledge of principles and procedures for personnel recruitment, selection, training, compensation and benefits, labor relations and negotiation, and personnel information systems. **English Language:** Knowledge of the structure and content of the English language, including the meaning and spelling of words, rules of composition, and grammar. **Economics and Accounting:** Knowledge of economic and accounting principles and practices, the financial markets, banking, and the analysis and reporting of financial data.

Property, Real Estate, and Community Association Managers

▲ Education/Training Required: Bachelor's degree
▲ Annual Earnings: $36,290
▲ Growth: 22.7%
▲ Annual Job Openings: 24,000
▲ Self-Employed: 40.2%
▲ Part-Time: 21.9%

Plan, direct, or coordinate selling, buying, leasing, or governance activities of commercial, industrial, or residential real estate properties. Manages and oversees operations, maintenance, and administrative functions for commercial, industrial, or residential properties. Plans, schedules, and coordinates general maintenance, major repairs, and remodeling or construction projects for commercial or residential property. Recruits, hires, and trains managerial, clerical, and maintenance staff or contracts with vendors for security, maintenance, extermination, or groundskeeping personnel. Maintains records of sales, rental or usage activity, special permits issued, maintenance and operating costs, or property availability. Develops and administers annual operating budget. Inspects facilities and equipment and inventories building contents to document damage and determine repair needs. Meets with prospective leasers to show property, explain terms of occupancy, and provide information about local area. Prepares reports summarizing financial and operational status of property or facility. Maintains contact with insurance carrier, fire and police departments, and other agencies to ensure protection and compliance with codes and regulations. Confers with legal authority to ensure that transactions and terminations of contracts and agreements are in accordance with court orders, laws, and regulations. Assembles and analyzes construction and vendor service contract bids. Negotiates for sale, lease, or development of property and completes or reviews appropriate documents and forms. Purchases building and maintenance supplies, equipment, or furniture. Directs and coordinates the activities of staff and contract personnel and evaluates performance. Investigates complaints, disturbances, and violations and resolves problems following management rules and regulations. Meets with clients to negotiate management and service contracts, determine priorities, and discuss financial and operational status of property. Directs collection of monthly assessments, rental fees, and deposits and payment of insurance premiums, mortgage, taxes, and incurred operating expenses. **SKILLS—Management of Financial Resources:** Determining how money will be spent to get the work done and accounting for these expenditures. **Coordination:** Adjusting actions in relation to others' actions. **Active Listening:** Giving full attention to what other people are saying, taking time to understand the points being made, asking questions as appropriate, and not interrupting at inappropriate times. **Management of Personnel Resources:** Motivating, developing, and directing people as they work, identifying the best people for the job. **Writing:** Communicating effectively in writing as appropriate for the needs of the audience. **Reading Comprehension:** Understanding written sentences and paragraphs in work-related documents. **Judgment and Decision Making:** Considering the relative costs and benefits of potential actions to choose the most appropriate one.

GOE INFORMATION—Interest Area: 13. General Management and Support. **Work Group:** 13.01. General Management Work and Management of Support Functions. **Other Job Titles in This Work Group:** Chief Executives; Compensation and Benefits Managers; Farm, Ranch, and Other Agricultural Managers; Financial Managers; Financial Managers, Branch or Department; Funeral Directors; General and Operations Managers; Government Service Executives; Human Resources Managers; Human Resources Managers, All Other; Legislators; Managers, All Other; Postmasters and Mail Superintendents; Private Sector Executives; Public Relations Managers; Purchasing Managers; Storage and Distribution Managers; Training and Development Managers; Transportation, Storage, and Distribution Managers; Treasurers, Controllers, and Chief Financial Officers. **PERSONALITY TYPE—**Enterprising. Enterprising occupations frequently involve starting up and carrying out projects. These occupations can involve leading people and making many decisions. They sometimes require risk taking and often deal with business.

EDUCATION/TRAINING PROGRAM(S)—Real Estate. **RELATED KNOWLEDGE/COURSES—Administration and Management:** Knowledge of business and management principles involved in strategic planning, resource allocation, human resources modeling, leadership technique, production methods, and coordination of people and resources. **English Language:** Knowledge of the structure and content of the English language, including the meaning and spelling of words, rules of composition, and grammar. **Law and Government:** Knowledge of laws, legal codes, court procedures, precedents, government regulations, executive orders, agency rules, and the democratic political process. **Personnel and Human Resources:** Knowledge of principles and procedures for personnel recruitment, selection, training, compensation and benefits, labor relations and negotiation, and personnel information systems. **Mathematics:** Knowledge of arithmetic, algebra, geometry, calculus, and statistics and their applications.

P

Psychiatrists

▲ Education/Training Required: First professional degree
▲ Annual Earnings: $126,460
▲ Growth: 17.9%
▲ Annual Job Openings: 27,000
▲ Self-Employed: 20.4%
▲ Part-Time: 7.2%

Diagnose, treat, and help prevent disorders of the mind. Analyzes and evaluates patient data and test or examination findings to diagnose nature and extent of mental disorder. Prescribes, directs, and administers psychotherapeutic treatments or medications to treat mental, emotional, or behavioral disorders. Examines or conducts laboratory or diagnostic tests on patient to provide information on general physical condition and mental disorder. Reviews and evaluates treatment procedures and outcomes of other psychiatrists and medical professionals. Prepares case reports and summaries for government agencies. Teaches, conducts research, and publishes findings to increase understanding of mental, emotional, and behavioral states and disorders. Advises and informs guardians, relatives, and significant others of patient's condition and treatment. Gathers and maintains patient information and records, including social and medical history obtained from patient, relatives, and other professionals. **SKILLS—Social Perceptiveness:** Being aware of others' reactions and understanding why they react as they do. **Reading Comprehension:** Understanding written sentences and paragraphs in work-related documents. **Judgment and Decision Making:** Considering the relative costs and benefits of potential actions to choose the most appropriate one. **Writing:** Communicating effectively in writing as appropriate for the needs of the audience. **Active Listening:** Giving full attention to what other people are saying, taking time to understand the points being made, asking questions as appropriate, and not interrupting at inappropriate times. **Service Orientation:** Actively looking for ways to help people.

GOE INFORMATION—Interest Area: 14. Medical and Health Services. **Work Group:** 14.02. Medicine and Surgery. **Other Job Titles in This Work Group:** Anthropologists; Anthropologists and Archeologists; Archeologists; City Planning Aides; Economists; Historians; Industrial-Organizational Psychologists; Political Scientists; Social Science Research Assistants; Social Scientists and Related Workers, All Other; Sociologists; Survey Researchers; Urban and Regional Planners. **PERSONALITY TYPE—** Investigative. Investigative occupations frequently involve working with ideas and require an extensive amount of thinking. These occupations can involve searching for facts and figuring out problems mentally.

EDUCATION/TRAINING PROGRAM(S)—Child Psychiatry; Physical Medical and Rehabilitation/Psychiatry; Psychiatry. **RELATED KNOWLEDGE/ COURSES—Psychology:** Knowledge of human behavior and performance; individual differences in ability, personality, and interests; learning and motivation; psychological research methods; and the assessment and treatment of behavioral and affective disorders. **Therapy and Counseling:** Knowledge of principles, methods, and procedures for diagnosis, treatment, and rehabilitation of physical and mental dysfunctions and for career counseling and guidance. **Medicine and Dentistry:** Knowledge of the information and techniques needed to diagnose and treat human injuries, diseases, and deformities. This includes symptoms, treatment alternatives, drug properties and interactions, and preventive health-care measures. **English Language:** Knowledge of the structure and content of the English language, including the meaning and spelling of words, rules of composition, and grammar. **Education and Training:** Knowledge of principles and methods for curriculum and training design, teaching and instruction for individuals and groups, and the measurement of training effects.

Psychology Teachers, Postsecondary

▲ Education/Training Required: Master's degree
▲ Annual Earnings: $53,120
▲ Growth: 23.5%
▲ Annual Job Openings: 184,000
▲ Self-Employed: 0%
▲ Part-Time: 32.3%

Teach courses in psychology, such as child, clinical, and developmental psychology and psychological counseling. Prepares and delivers lectures to students. Stimulates class discussions. Compiles, administers, and grades examinations or assigns this work to others. Compiles bibliographies of specialized materials for outside reading assignments. Directs research of other teachers or graduate students working for advanced academic degrees. Advises students on academic and vocational curricula. Conducts research in particular field of knowledge and publishes findings in professional journals. Serves on faculty committee providing professional consulting services to government and industry. Acts as adviser to student organizations. **SKILLS—Reading Comprehension:** Understanding written sentences and paragraphs in work-related documents. **Instructing:** Teaching others how to do something. **Speaking:** Talking to others to convey information effectively. **Active Learning:** Understanding the implications of new information for both current and future problem-solving and decision-making. **Learning Strategies:** Selecting and using training/instructional methods and procedures appropriate for the situation when learning or teaching new things. **Active Listening:** Giving full attention to what other people are saying, taking time to understand the points being made, asking questions as appropriate, and not interrupting at inappropriate times. **Writing:** Communicating effectively in writing as appropriate for the needs of the audience.

GOE INFORMATION—Interest Area: 12. Education and Social Service. **Work Group:** 12.03. Educational Services. **Other Job Titles in This Work Group:** Adult Literacy, Remedial Education, and GED Teachers and Instructors; Agricultural Sciences Teachers, Postsecondary; Anthropology and Archeology Teachers, Postsecondary; Architecture Teachers, Postsecondary; Archivists; Area, Ethnic, and Cultural Studies Teachers, Postsecondary; Art, Drama, and Music Teachers, Postsecondary; Atmospheric, Earth, Marine, and Space Sciences Teachers, Postsecondary; Audio-Visual Collections Specialists; Biological Science Teachers, Postsecondary; Business Teachers, Postsecondary; Chemistry Teachers, Postsecondary; Child Care Workers; Communications Teachers, Postsecondary; Computer Science Teachers, Postsecondary; Criminal Justice and Law Enforcement Teachers, Postsecondary; Curators; Economics Teachers, Postsecondary; Education Teachers, Postsecondary; Educational Psychologists; Educational, Vocational, and School Counselors; Elementary School Teachers, Except Special Education; Engineering Teachers, Postsecondary; English Language and Literature Teachers, Postsecondary; Environmental Science Teachers, Postsecondary; Farm and Home Management Advisors; Foreign Language and Literature Teachers, Postsecondary; Forestry and Conservation Science Teachers, Postsecondary; Geography Teachers, Postsecondary; Graduate Teaching Assistants; Health Specialties Teachers, Postsecondary; History Teachers, Postsecondary; Home Economics Teachers, Postsecondary; Kindergarten Teachers, Except Special Education; Law Teachers, Postsecondary; Librarians; Library Assistants, Clerical; Library Science Teachers, Postsecondary; Library Technicians; Mathematical Science Teachers, Postsecondary; Middle School Teachers, Except Special and Vocational Education; Museum Technicians and Conservators; Nursing Instructors and Teachers, Postsecondary; Personal Financial Advisors; Philosophy and Religion Teachers, Postsecondary; Physics Teachers, Postsecondary; Political Science Teachers, Postsecondary; Postsecondary Teachers, All Other; others. **PERSONALITY TYPE—Social.** Social occupations frequently involve working with, communicating with, and teaching people. These occupations often involve helping or providing service to others.

EDUCATION/TRAINING PROGRAM(S)—Clinical Psychology; Cognitive Psychology and Psycholinguistics; Community Psychology; Comparative Psychology; Counseling Psychology; Developmental and Child Psychology; Educational Psychology; Experimental Psychology; Industrial and Organizational Psychology; Marriage and Family Therapy/Counseling; Personality Psychology; Physiological Psychology/Psychobiology; Psychology Teacher Education; Psychology, General; Psychology,

Other; Psychometrics and Quantitative Psychology; School Psychology; Social Psychology; Social Science Teacher Education. **RELATED KNOWLEDGE/COURSES— Education and Training:** Knowledge of principles and methods for curriculum and training design, teaching and instruction for individuals and groups, and the measurement of training effects. **Sociology and Anthropology:** Knowledge of group behavior and dynamics, societal trends and influences, human migrations, ethnicity, and cultures and their history and origins. **History and Archeology:**

Knowledge of historical events and their causes, indicators, and effects on civilizations and cultures. **English Language:** Knowledge of the structure and content of the English language, including the meaning and spelling of words, rules of composition, and grammar. **Psychology:** Knowledge of human behavior and performance; individual differences in ability, personality, and interests; learning and motivation; psychological research methods; and the assessment and treatment of behavioral and affective disorders.

Public Relations Managers

- ▲ Education/Training Required: Work experience plus degree
- ▲ Annual Earnings: $57,200
- ▲ Growth: 36.3%
- ▲ Annual Job Openings: 7,000
- ▲ Self-Employed: 2.4%
- ▲ Part-Time: 2.6%

Plan and direct public relations programs designed to create and maintain a favorable public image for employer or client, or if engaged in fundraising, plan and direct activities to solicit and maintain funds for special projects and nonprofit organizations. **SKILLS**—No data available.

GOE INFORMATION—Interest Area: 13. General Management and Support. **Work Group:** 13.01. General Management Work and Management of Support Functions. **Other Job Titles in This Work Group:** Chief Executives; Compensation and Benefits Managers; Farm, Ranch, and Other Agricultural Managers; Financial Managers; Financial Managers, Branch or Department; Funeral

Directors; General and Operations Managers; Government Service Executives; Human Resources Managers; Human Resources Managers, All Other; Legislators; Managers, All Other; Postmasters and Mail Superintendents; Private Sector Executives; Property, Real Estate, and Community Association Managers; Purchasing Managers; Storage and Distribution Managers; Training and Development Managers; Transportation, Storage, and Distribution Managers; Treasurers, Controllers, and Chief Financial Officers. **PERSONALITY TYPE**—No data available.

EDUCATION/TRAINING PROGRAM(S)—Public Relations/Image Management. **RELATED KNOWLEDGE/COURSES**—No data available.

Public Relations Specialists

- ▲ Education/Training Required: Bachelor's degree
- ▲ Annual Earnings: $41,010
- ▲ Growth: 36.1%
- ▲ Annual Job Openings: 19,000
- ▲ Self-Employed: 5.6%
- ▲ Part-Time: 25.3%

Engage in promoting or creating good will for individuals, groups, or organizations by writing or selecting favorable publicity material and releasing it through various communications media. May prepare and arrange displays and make speeches. Plans and directs development

and communication of informational programs designed to keep public informed of client's products, accomplishments, or agenda. Prepares and distributes fact sheets, news releases, photographs, scripts, motion pictures, or tape recordings to media representatives and others. Promotes sales and/or creates goodwill for client's products, services, or persona by coordinating exhibits, lectures, contests, or public appearances. Prepares or edits organizational publications, such as newsletters to employees or public or stockholders' reports, to favorably present client's viewpoint. Consults with advertising agencies or staff to arrange promotional campaigns in all types of media for products, organizations, or individuals. Arranges for and conducts public-contact programs designed to meet client's objectives. Represents client during community projects and at public, social, and business gatherings. Confers with production and support personnel to coordinate production of advertisements and promotions. Purchases advertising space and time as required to promote client's product or agenda. Counsels clients in effective ways of communicating with public. Conducts market and public opinion research to introduce or test specific products or measure public opinion. Studies needs, objectives, and policies of organization or individual seeking to influence public opinion or promote specific products. **SKILLS— Speaking:** Talking to others to convey information effectively. **Writing:** Communicating effectively in writing as appropriate for the needs of the audience. **Reading Comprehension:** Understanding written sentences and paragraphs in work-related documents. **Persuasion:** Persuading others to change their minds or behavior. **Active Listening:** Giving full attention to what other people are saying, taking time to understand the points being made, asking questions as appropriate, and not interrupting at inappropriate times. **Critical Thinking:** Using logic and reasoning to identify the strengths and weaknesses of alternative solutions, conclusions, or approaches to problems.

GOE INFORMATION—Interest Area: 01. Arts, Entertainment, and Media. **Work Group:** 01.03. News, Broadcasting, and Public Relations. **Other Job Titles in This Work Group:** Broadcast News Analysts; Caption Writers; Interpreters and Translators; Reporters and Correspondents. **PERSONALITY TYPE—**Enterprising. Enterprising occupations frequently involve starting up and carrying out projects. These occupations can involve leading people and making many decisions. They sometimes require risk taking and often deal with business.

EDUCATION/TRAINING PROGRAM(S)—Communication Studies/Speech Communication and Rhetoric; Family and Consumer Sciences/Human Sciences Communication; Health Communication; Political Communication; Public Relations/Image Management. **RELATED KNOWLEDGE/COURSES—Sales and Marketing:** Knowledge of principles and methods for showing, promoting, and selling products or services. This includes marketing strategy and tactics, product demonstration, sales techniques, and sales control systems. **Communications and Media:** Knowledge of media production, communication, and dissemination techniques and methods. This includes alternative ways to inform and entertain via written, oral, and visual media. **Mathematics:** Knowledge of arithmetic, algebra, geometry, calculus, and statistics and their applications. **Telecommunications:** Knowledge of transmission, broadcasting, switching, control, and operation of telecommunications systems. **Psychology:** Knowledge of human behavior and performance; individual differences in ability, personality, and interests; learning and motivation; psychological research methods; and the assessment and treatment of behavioral and affective disorders.

Purchasing Agents, Except Wholesale, Retail, and Farm Products

- ▲ Education/Training Required: Bachelor's degree
- ▲ Annual Earnings: $43,230
- ▲ Growth: 12.3%
- ▲ Annual Job Openings: 23,000
- ▲ Self-Employed: 0%
- ▲ Part-Time: 2.3%

Purchase machinery, equipment, tools, parts, supplies, or services necessary for the operation of an establishment. Purchase raw or semi-finished materials for manufacturing. Negotiates or renegotiates and administers contracts with suppliers, vendors, and other representatives. Arbitrates claims and resolves complaints generated during performance of contract. Confers with personnel, users, and vendors to discuss defective or unacceptable goods or services and determines corrective action. Maintains and reviews computerized or manual records of items purchased, costs, delivery, product performance, and inventories. Evaluates and monitors contract performance to determine need for changes and to ensure compliance with contractual obligations. Locates and arranges for purchase of goods and services necessary for efficient operation of organization. Analyzes price proposals, financial reports, and other data and information to determine reasonable prices. Prepares purchase orders or bid proposals and reviews requisitions for goods and services. Directs and coordinates workers' activities involving bid proposals and procurement of goods and services. Formulates policies and procedures for bid proposals and procurement of goods and services. **SKILLS—Judgment and Decision Making:** Considering the relative costs and benefits of potential actions to choose the most appropriate one. **Reading Comprehension:** Understanding written sentences and paragraphs in work-related documents. **Writing:** Communicating effectively in writing as appropriate for the needs of the audience. **Management of Financial Resources:** Determining how money will be spent to get the work done and accounting for these expenditures. **Mathematics:** Using mathematics to solve problems. **Negotiation:** Bringing others together and trying to reconcile differences. **Active Listening:** Giving full attention to what other people are saying, taking time to understand the points being made, asking questions as appropriate, and not interrupting at inappropriate times.

GOE INFORMATION—**Interest Area:** 13. General Management and Support. **Work Group:** 13.02. Management Support. **Other Job Titles in This Work Group:** Accountants; Accountants and Auditors; Appraisers and Assessors of Real Estate; Appraisers, Real Estate; Assessors; Auditors; Budget Analysts; Claims Adjusters, Examiners, and Investigators; Claims Examiners, Property and Casualty Insurance; Compensation, Benefits, and Job Analysis Specialists; Cost Estimators; Credit Analysts; Employment Interviewers, Private or Public Employment Service; Employment, Recruitment, and Placement Specialists; Financial Analysts; Human Resources, Training, and Labor Relations Specialists, All Other; Insurance Ad-

justers, Examiners, and Investigators; Insurance Appraisers, Auto Damage; Insurance Underwriters; Loan Counselors; Loan Officers; Logisticians; Management Analysts; Market Research Analysts; Personnel Recruiters; Purchasing Agents and Buyers, Farm Products; Tax Examiners, Collectors, and Revenue Agents; Training and Development Specialists; Wholesale and Retail Buyers, Except Farm Products. **PERSONALITY TYPE**—Enterprising. Enterprising occupations frequently involve starting up and carrying out projects. These occupations can involve leading people and making many decisions. They sometimes require risk taking and often deal with business.

EDUCATION/TRAINING PROGRAM(S)—Sales, Distribution, and Marketing Operations, General. **RELATED KNOWLEDGE/COURSES—Administration and Management:** Knowledge of business and management principles involved in strategic planning, resource allocation, human resources modeling, leadership technique, production methods, and coordination of people and resources. **Mathematics:** Knowledge of arithmetic, algebra, geometry, calculus, and statistics and their applications. **Economics and Accounting:** Knowledge of economic and accounting principles and practices, the financial markets, banking, and the analysis and reporting of financial data. **English Language:** Knowledge of the structure and content of the English language, including the meaning and spelling of words, rules of composition, and grammar. **Computers and Electronics:** Knowledge of circuit boards, processors, chips, electronic equipment, and computer hardware and software, including applications and programming. **Clerical Studies:** Knowledge of administrative and clerical procedures and systems, such as word processing, managing files and records, stenography and transcription, designing forms, and other office procedures and terminology.

Radiation Therapists

- ▲ Education/Training Required: Associate's degree
- ▲ Annual Earnings: $49,050
- ▲ Growth: 22.8%
- ▲ Annual Job Openings: 1,000
- ▲ Self-Employed: 0%
- ▲ Part-Time: 17.5%

Provide radiation therapy to patients as prescribed by a radiologist according to established practices and standards. Duties may include reviewing prescription and

diagnosis; acting as liaison with physician and supportive care personnel; preparing equipment, such as immobilization, treatment, and protection devices; and maintaining records, reports, and files. **May assist in do-simetry procedures and tumor localization.** Reviews prescription, diagnosis, patient chart, and identification. Enters data into computer and sets controls to operate and adjust equipment and regulate dosage. Photographs treated area of patient and processes film. Observes and reassures patient during treatment and reports unusual reactions to physician. Follows principles of radiation protection for patient, self, and others. Prepares equipment, such as immobilization, treatment, and protection devices, and positions patient according to prescription. Acts as liaison with physicist and supportive care personnel. Maintains records, reports, and files as required. **SKILLS—Reading Comprehension:** Understanding written sentences and paragraphs in work-related documents. **Operation and Control:** Controlling operations of equipment or systems. **Science:** Using scientific rules and methods to solve problems. **Active Listening:** Giving full attention to what other people are saying, taking time to understand the points being made, asking questions as appropriate, and not interrupting at inappropriate times. **Coordination:** Adjusting actions in relation to others' actions. **Critical Thinking:** Using logic and reasoning to identify the strengths and weaknesses of alternative solutions, conclusions, or approaches to problems. **Writing:** Communicating effectively in writing as appropriate for the needs of the audience.

GOE INFORMATION—Interest Area: 14. Medical and Health Services. **Work Group:** 14.06. Medical Therapy. **Other Job Titles in This Work Group:** Audiologists; Massage Therapists; Occupational Therapist Aides; Occupational Therapist Assistants; Occupational Therapists; Physical Therapist Aides; Physical Therapist Assistants; Physical Therapists; Recreational Therapists; Respiratory Therapists; Respiratory Therapy Technicians; Speech-Language Pathologists; Therapists, All Other. **PERSONALITY TYPE**—Social. Social occupations frequently involve working with, communicating with, and teaching people. These occupations often involve helping or providing service to others.

EDUCATION/TRAINING PROGRAM(S)—Medical Radiologic Technology/Science—Radiation Therapist. **RELATED KNOWLEDGE/COURSES—Medicine and Dentistry:** Knowledge of the information and techniques needed to diagnose and treat human injuries, diseases, and deformities. This includes symptoms, treatment alternatives, drug properties and interactions, and preventive health-care measures. **Computers and Electronics:** Knowledge of circuit boards, processors, chips, electronic equipment, and computer hardware and software, including applications and programming. **English Language:** Knowledge of the structure and content of the English language, including the meaning and spelling of words, rules of composition, and grammar. **Therapy and Counseling:** Knowledge of principles, methods, and procedures for diagnosis, treatment, and rehabilitation of physical and mental dysfunctions and for career counseling and guidance. **Clerical Studies:** Knowledge of administrative and clerical procedures and systems, such as word processing, managing files and records, stenography and transcription, designing forms, and other office procedures and terminology.

Radiologic Technicians

- ▲ Education/Training Required: Associate's degree
- ▲ Annual Earnings: $37,680
- ▲ Growth: 23.1%
- ▲ Annual Job Openings: 13,000
- ▲ Self-Employed: 0%
- ▲ Part-Time: 17.5%

Maintain and use equipment and supplies necessary to demonstrate portions of the human body on X-ray film or fluoroscopic screen for diagnostic purposes. Uses beam-restrictive devices and patient-shielding skills to minimize radiation exposure to patient and staff. Moves X-ray equipment into position and adjusts controls to set exposure factors, such as time and distance. Operates mobile X-ray equipment in operating room, in emergency room, or at patient's bedside. Explains procedures to patient to reduce anxieties and obtain patient cooperation. Positions patient on examining table and adjusts equipment to obtain optimum view of specific body area requested by physician. **SKILLS—Reading Comprehension:** Understanding written sentences and paragraphs in work-related documents. **Active Listening:** Giving full attention to what other people are saying, taking time to understand the points being made, asking questions as appropriate, and not interrupting at inappropriate times. **Operation and Control:** Controlling operations of equipment or systems. **Social Perceptiveness:** Being aware of others' reactions and understanding why they react as they do. **Speaking:** Talking to others to convey information effectively.

GOE INFORMATION—Interest Area: 14. Medical and Health Services. **Work Group:** 14.05. Medical Technology. **Other Job Titles in This Work Group:** Cardiovascular Technologists and Technicians; Diagnostic Medical Sonographers; Health Technologists and Technicians, All Other; Medical and Clinical Laboratory Technicians; Medical and Clinical Laboratory Technologists; Medical Equipment Preparers; Nuclear Medicine Technologists; Orthotists and Prosthetists; Radiologic Technologists; Radiologic Technologists and Technicians. **PERSONALITY TYPE—Realistic.** Realistic occupations frequently involve work activities that include practical, hands-on problems and solutions. They often deal with plants, animals, and real-world materials like wood, tools, and machinery. Many of the occupations require working outside and do not involve a lot of paperwork or working closely with others.

EDUCATION/TRAINING PROGRAM(S)—Allied Health Diagnostic, Intervention, and Treatment Professions, Other; Medical Radiologic Technology/Science— Radiation Therapist; Radiologic Technology/ Science—Radiographer. **RELATED KNOWLEDGE/ COURSES—Medicine and Dentistry:** Knowledge of the information and techniques needed to diagnose and treat human injuries, diseases, and deformities. This includes symptoms, treatment alternatives, drug properties and interactions, and preventive health-care measures. **English Language:** Knowledge of the structure and content of the English language, including the meaning and spelling of words, rules of composition, and grammar. **Biology:** Knowledge of plant and animal organisms and their tissues, cells, functions, interdependencies, and interactions with each other and the environment. **Customer and Personal Service:** Knowledge of principles and processes for providing customer and personal services. This includes customer needs assessment, meeting quality standards for services, and evaluation of customer satisfaction. **Computers and Electronics:** Knowledge of circuit boards, processors, chips, electronic equipment, and computer hardware and software, including applications and programming.

Radiologic Technologists

- ▲ Education/Training Required: Associate's degree
- ▲ Annual Earnings: $37,680
- ▲ Growth: 23.1%
- ▲ Annual Job Openings: 13,000
- ▲ Self-Employed: 0%
- ▲ Part-Time: 17.5%

Take X rays and CAT scans or administer nonradioactive materials into patient's bloodstream for diagnostic purposes. Includes technologists who specialize in other modalities, such as computed tomography, ultrasound, and magnetic resonance. Operates or oversees operation of radiologic and magnetic imaging equipment to produce photographs of the body for diagnostic purposes. Administers oral or injected contrast media to patients. Positions imaging equipment and adjusts controls to set exposure time and distance according to specification of examination. Monitors use of radiation safety measures to comply with government regulations and to ensure safety of patients and staff. Monitors video display of area being scanned and adjusts density or contrast to improve picture quality. Keys commands and data into computer to document and specify scan sequences, adjust transmit-

ters and receivers, or photograph certain images. Operates fluoroscope to aid physician to view and guide wire or catheter through blood vessels to area of interest. Positions and immobilizes patient on examining table. Develops departmental operating budget and coordinates purchase of supplies and equipment. Assigns duties to radiologic staff to maintain patient flows and achieve production goals. Demonstrates new equipment, procedures, and techniques and provides technical assistance to staff. Explains procedures and observes patients to ensure safety and comfort during scan. Reviews and evaluates developed X rays, video tape, or computer-generated information for technical quality. **SKILLS—Reading Comprehension:** Understanding written sentences and paragraphs in work-related documents. **Operation and Control:** Controlling operations of equipment or systems.

Operation Monitoring: Watching gauges, dials, or other indicators to make sure a machine is working properly. **Mathematics:** Using mathematics to solve problems. **Equipment Selection:** Determining the kind of tools and equipment needed to do a job. **Critical Thinking:** Using logic and reasoning to identify the strengths and weaknesses of alternative solutions, conclusions, or approaches to problems. **Active Listening:** Giving full attention to what other people are saying, taking time to understand the points being made, asking questions as appropriate, and not interrupting at inappropriate times.

GOE INFORMATION—Interest Area: 14. Medical and Health Services. **Work Group:** 14.05. Medical Technology. **Other Job Titles in This Work Group:** Cardiovascular Technologists and Technicians; Diagnostic Medical Sonographers; Health Technologists and Technicians, All Other; Medical and Clinical Laboratory Technicians; Medical and Clinical Laboratory Technologists; Medical Equipment Preparers; Nuclear Medicine Technologists; Orthotists and Prosthetists; Radiologic Technicians; Radiologic Technologists and Technicians. **PERSONALITY TYPE—**Realistic. Realistic occupations frequently involve work activities that include practical, hands-on problems and solutions. They often deal with plants, animals, and real-world materials like wood, tools, and machinery. Many of the occupations require working outside and do not involve a lot of paperwork or working closely with others.

Radiologic Technologists and Technicians

▲ Education/Training Required: Associate's degree
▲ Annual Earnings: $37,680
▲ Growth: 23.1%
▲ Annual Job Openings: 13,000
▲ Self-Employed: 0%
▲ Part-Time: 17.5%

EDUCATION/TRAINING PROGRAM(S)—Allied Health Diagnostic, Intervention, and Treatment Professions, Other; Medical Radiologic Technology/Science—Radiation Therapist; Radiologic Technology/Science—Radiographer. **RELATED KNOWLEDGE/COURSES—Medicine and Dentistry:** Knowledge of the information and techniques needed to diagnose and treat human injuries, diseases, and deformities. This includes symptoms, treatment alternatives, drug properties and interactions, and preventive health-care measures. **Computers and Electronics:** Knowledge of circuit boards, processors, chips, electronic equipment, and computer hardware and software, including applications and programming. **Biology:** Knowledge of plant and animal organisms and their tissues, cells, functions, interdependencies, and interactions with each other and the environment. **Chemistry:** Knowledge of the chemical composition, structure, and properties of substances and of the chemical processes and transformations that they undergo. This includes uses of chemicals and their interactions, danger signs, production techniques, and disposal methods. **Public Safety and Security:** Knowledge of relevant equipment, policies, procedures, and strategies to promote effective local, state, or national security operations for the protection of people, data, property, and institutions.

Take X rays and CAT scans or administer nonradioactive materials into patient's blood stream for diagnostic purposes. Includes technologists who specialize in other modalities, such as computed tomography and magnetic resonance. Includes workers whose primary duties are to demonstrate portions of the human body on X-ray film or fluoroscopic screen. **SKILLS—**No data available.

GOE INFORMATION—Interest Area: 14. Medical and Health Services. **Work Group:** 14.05. Medical Technology. **Other Job Titles in This Work Group:** Cardiovascular Technologists and Technicians; Diagnostic Medical Sonographers; Health Technologists and Technicians, All Other; Medical and Clinical Laboratory Technicians; Medical and Clinical Laboratory Technologists; Medical Equipment Preparers; Nuclear Medicine Technologists; Orthotists and Prosthetists; Radiologic Technicians; Radiologic Technologists. **PERSONALITY TYPE—**No data available.

EDUCATION/TRAINING PROGRAM(S)—Allied Health Diagnostic, Intervention, and Treatment Professions, Other; Medical Radiologic Technology/Science—Radiation Therapist; Radiologic Technology/Science—Radiographer. **RELATED KNOWLEDGE/COURSES—**No data available.

Real Estate Brokers

> ▲ Education/Training Required: Work experience in a related occupation
> ▲ Annual Earnings: $51,370
> ▲ Growth: 9.6%
> ▲ Annual Job Openings: 8,000
> ▲ Self-Employed: 59.6%
> ▲ Part-Time: 16.6%

Operate real estate office or work for commercial real estate firm, overseeing real estate transactions. Other duties usually include selling real estate or renting properties and arranging loans. **SKILLS**—No data available.

GOE INFORMATION—**Interest Area:** 10. Sales and Marketing. **Work Group:** 10.03. General Sales. **Other Job Titles in This Work Group:** Parts Salespersons; Real Estate Sales Agents; Retail Salespersons; Sales Representa-tives, Wholesale and Manufacturing, Except Technical and Scientific Products; Service Station Attendants; Stock Clerks, Sales Floor; Travel Agents. **PERSONALITY TYPE**—No data available.

EDUCATION/TRAINING PROGRAM(S)—Real Estate. **RELATED KNOWLEDGE/COURSES**—No data available.

Real Estate Sales Agents

> ▲ Education/Training Required: Postsecondary vocational training
> ▲ Annual Earnings: $28,570
> ▲ Growth: 9.5%
> ▲ Annual Job Openings: 28,000
> ▲ Self-Employed: 69.7%
> ▲ Part-Time: 16.6%

Rent, buy, or sell property for clients. Perform duties such as studying property listings, interviewing prospective clients, accompanying clients to property site, discussing conditions of sale, and drawing up real estate contracts. Includes agents who represent buyer. Displays and explains features of property to client and discusses conditions of sale or terms of lease. Prepares real estate contracts, such as closing statements, deeds, leases, and mortgages, and ne-gotiates loans on property. Oversees signing of real estate documents, disburses funds, and coordinates closing ac-tivities. Secures construction financing with own firm or mortgage company. Inspects condition of premises and arranges for or notifies owner of necessary maintenance. Reviews trade journals and relevant literature and attends staff and association meetings to remain knowledgeable about real estate market. Searches public records to ascer-tain that client has clear title to property. Investigates client's financial and credit status to determine eligibility for fi-nancing. Plans and organizes sales promotion programs and materials, including newspaper advertisements and real estate promotional booklets. Appraises client's unimproved property to determine loan value. Locates and appraises undeveloped areas for building sites, based on evaluation of area market conditions. Collects rental deposit. Reviews plans, recommends construction features to client, and enumerates options on new home sales. Solicits and com-piles listings of available rental property. Answers client's questions regarding work under construction, financing, maintenance, repairs, and appraisals. Interviews prospec-tive tenants and records information to ascertain needs and qualifications. Contacts utility companies for service hookup to client's property. Conducts seminars and train-ing sessions for sales agents to improve sales techniques. **SKILLS**—**Active Listening:** Giving full attention to what other people are saying, taking time to understand the points being made, asking questions as appropriate, and not interrupting at inappropriate times. **Persuasion:** Per-suading others to change their minds or behavior. **Speak-ing:** Talking to others to convey information effectively. **Reading Comprehension:** Understanding written sentences and paragraphs in work-related documents. **Mathematics:** Using mathematics to solve problems. **Judgment and De-cision Making:** Considering the relative costs and benefits of potential actions to choose the most appropriate one.

GOE INFORMATION—**Interest Area:** 10. Sales and Marketing. **Work Group:** 10.03. General Sales. **Other Job Titles in This Work Group:** Parts Salespersons; Real Estate Brokers; Retail Salespersons; Sales Representatives, Wholesale and Manufacturing, Except Technical and Scientific Products; Service Station Attendants; Stock Clerks, Sales Floor; Travel Agents. **PERSONALITY TYPE**—Enterprising. Enterprising occupations frequently involve starting up and carrying out projects. These occupations can involve leading people and making many decisions. They sometimes require risk taking and often deal with business.

EDUCATION/TRAINING PROGRAM(S)—Real Estate. **RELATED KNOWLEDGE/COURSES**—**Sales and Marketing:** Knowledge of principles and methods for showing, promoting, and selling products or services. This includes marketing strategy and tactics, product demon-stration, sales techniques, and sales control systems. **Law and Government:** Knowledge of laws, legal codes, court procedures, precedents, government regulations, executive orders, agency rules, and the democratic political process. **Mathematics:** Knowledge of arithmetic, algebra, geometry, calculus, and statistics and their applications. **Economics and Accounting:** Knowledge of economic and accounting principles and practices, the financial markets, banking, and the analysis and reporting of financial data. **Administration and Management:** Knowledge of business and management principles involved in strategic planning, resource allocation, human resources modeling, leadership technique, production methods, and coordination of people and resources. **English Language:** Knowledge of the structure and content of the English language, including the meaning and spelling of words, rules of composition, and grammar.

Receptionists and Information Clerks

> ▲ Education/Training Required: Short-term on-the-job training
> ▲ Annual Earnings: $20,650
> ▲ Growth: 23.7%
> ▲ Annual Job Openings: 269,000
> ▲ Self-Employed: 3.1%
> ▲ Part-Time: 35.1%

Answer inquiries and obtain information for general public, customers, visitors, and other interested parties. Provide information regarding activities conducted at establishment and location of departments, offices, and employees within organization. Greets persons entering establishment, determines nature and purpose of visit, and directs visitor to specific destination or answers questions and provides information. Provides information to public concerning available land leases, land classification, or mineral resources. Registers visitors of public facility, such as national park or military base; collects fees; explains regulations; and assigns sites. Answers telephone to schedule future appointments, provide information, or forward call. Provides information to public regarding tours, classes, workshops, and other programs. Transmits information or documents to customer, using computer, mail, or facsimile. Records, compiles, enters, and retrieves information by hand or using computer. Operates telephone switchboard to receive incoming calls. Performs duties such as taking care of plants and straightening magazines to maintain lobby or reception area. Monitors facility to ensure compliance with regulations. Receives payment and records receipts for services. Conducts tours or delivers talks describing features of public facility, such as historic site or national park. Hears and resolves complaints from customers and public. Files and maintains records. Enrolls individuals to participate in programs, prepares lists, notifies individuals of acceptance in programs, and arranges and schedules space and equipment for participants. Types memos, correspondence, travel vouchers, or other documents. Calculates and quotes rates for tours, stocks, insurance policies, and other products and services. Collects and distributes messages for employees of organization. Analyzes data to determine answer to customer or public inquiry. **SKILLS—Reading Comprehension:** Understanding written sentences and paragraphs in work-related documents. **Active Listening:** Giving full attention to what other people are saying, taking time to understand the points being made, asking questions as appropriate, and not interrupting at inappropriate times. **Service Orientation:** Actively looking for ways to help people. **Speaking:** Talking to others to convey information effectively. **Writing:** Communicating effectively in writing as appropriate for the needs of the audience.

GOE INFORMATION—**Interest Area:** 09. Business Detail. **Work Group:** 09.05. Customer Service. **Other Job Titles in This Work Group:** Adjustment Clerks; Bill and Account Collectors; Cashiers; Counter and Rental Clerks; Customer Service Representatives; Customer Service Representatives, Utilities; Gaming Cage Workers; Gaming Change Persons and Booth Cashiers; New Accounts Clerks; Order Clerks; Tellers; Travel Clerks. **PERSONALITY TYPE**—Conventional. Conventional occupations frequently involve following set procedures and routines. These occupations can include working with data and details more than with ideas. Usually there is a clear line of authority to follow.

EDUCATION/TRAINING PROGRAM(S)—General Office Occupations and Clerical Services; Health Unit Coordinator/Ward Clerk; Medical Reception/Reception-ist; Receptionist. **RELATED KNOWLEDGE/ COURSES**—**Clerical Studies:** Knowledge of administrative and clerical procedures and systems, such as word processing, managing files and records, stenography and transcription, designing forms, and other office procedures and terminology. **Customer and Personal Service:** Knowledge of principles and processes for providing customer and personal services. This includes customer needs assessment, meeting quality standards for services, and evaluation of customer satisfaction. **English Language:** Knowledge of the structure and content of the English language, including the meaning and spelling of words, rules of composition, and grammar. **Telecommunications:** Knowledge of transmission, broadcasting, switching, control, and operation of telecommunications systems. **Mathematics:** Knowledge of arithmetic, algebra, geometry, calculus, and statistics and their applications.

Recreation and Fitness Studies Teachers, Postsecondary

- ▲ Education/Training Required: Master's degree
- ▲ Annual Earnings: $42,140
- ▲ Growth: 23.5%
- ▲ Annual Job Openings: 184,000
- ▲ Self-Employed: 0%
- ▲ Part-Time: 32.3%

Teach courses pertaining to recreation, leisure, and fitness studies, including exercise physiology and facilities management. SKILLS—No data available.

GOE INFORMATION—**Interest Area:** 12. Education and Social Service. **Work Group:** 12.03. Educational Services. **Other Job Titles in This Work Group:** Adult Literacy, Remedial Education, and GED Teachers and Instructors; Agricultural Sciences Teachers, Postsecondary; Anthropology and Archeology Teachers, Postsecondary; Architecture Teachers, Postsecondary; Archivists; Area, Ethnic, and Cultural Studies Teachers, Postsecondary; Art, Drama, and Music Teachers, Postsecondary; Atmospheric, Earth, Marine, and Space Sciences Teachers, Postsecondary; Audio-Visual Collections Specialists; Biological Science Teachers, Postsecondary; Business Teachers, Postsecondary; Chemistry Teachers, Postsecondary; Child Care Workers; Communications Teachers, Postsecondary; Computer Science Teachers, Postsecondary; Criminal Justice and Law Enforcement Teachers, Postsecondary; Curators; Economics Teachers, Postsecondary; Education Teachers, Postsecondary; Educational Psychologists; Educational, Vocational, and School Counselors; Elementary School Teachers, Except Special Education; Engineering Teachers, Postsecondary; English Language and Literature Teachers, Postsecondary; Environmental Science Teachers, Postsecondary; Farm and Home Management Advisors; Foreign Language and Literature Teachers, Postsecondary; Forestry and Conservation Science Teachers, Postsecondary; Geography Teachers, Postsecondary; Graduate Teaching Assistants; Health Specialties Teachers, Postsecondary; History Teachers, Postsecondary; Home Economics Teachers, Postsecondary; Kindergarten Teachers, Except Special Education; Law Teachers, Postsecondary; Librarians; Library Assistants, Clerical; Library Science Teachers, Postsecondary; Library Technicians; Mathematical Science Teachers, Postsecondary; Middle School Teachers, Except Special and Vocational Education; Museum Technicians and Conservators; Nursing Instructors and Teachers, Postsecondary; Personal Financial Advisors; Philosophy and Religion Teachers, Postsecondary; Physics Teachers, Postsecondary; Political Science Teachers, Postsecondary; Postsecondary Teachers, All Other; others. **PERSONALITY TYPE**—No data available.

EDUCATION/TRAINING PROGRAM(S)—Health and Physical Education, General; Parks, Recreation and Leisure Studies; Sport and Fitness Administration/Man-

Recreation Workers

agement. **RELATED KNOWLEDGE/COURSES**—No data available.

- ▲ Education/Training Required: Bachelor's degree
- ▲ Annual Earnings: $17,850
- ▲ Growth: 20.1%
- ▲ Annual Job Openings: 32,000
- ▲ Self-Employed: 0%
- ▲ Part-Time: 14.0%

Conduct recreation activities with groups in public, private, or volunteer agencies or recreation facilities. Organize and promote activities such as arts and crafts, sports, games, music, dramatics, social recreation, camping, and hobbies, taking into account the needs and interests of individual members. Organizes, leads, and promotes interest in facility activities, such as arts, crafts, sports, games, camping, and hobbies. Conducts recreational activities and instructs participants to develop skills in provided activities. Arranges for activity requirements, such as entertainment and setup of equipment and decorations. Schedules facility activities and maintains record of programs. Explains principles, techniques, and safety procedures of facility activities to participants and demonstrates use of material and equipment. Ascertains and interprets group interests, evaluates equipment and facilities, and adapts activities to meet participant needs. Meets and collaborates with agency personnel, community organizations, and other professional personnel to plan balanced recreational programs for participants. Enforces rules and regulations of facility, maintains discipline, and ensures safety. Greets and introduces new arrivals to other guests, acquaints arrivals with facilities, and encourages group participation. Tests and documents content of swimming pool water and schedules maintenance and use of facilities. Supervises and coordinates work activities of personnel, trains staff, and assigns duties. Schedules maintenance and use of facilities. Evaluates staff performance and records reflective information on performance evaluation forms. Completes and maintains time and attendance forms and inventory lists. Meets with staff to discuss rules, regulations, and work-related problems. Administers first aid according to prescribed procedures or notifies emergency medical personnel when necessary. Assists management to resolve complaints. **SKILLS—Coordination:** Adjusting actions in relation to others' actions. **Speaking:** Talking to others to convey information effectively. **Service**

Orientation: Actively looking for ways to help people. **Social Perceptiveness:** Being aware of others' reactions and understanding why they react as they do. **Time Management:** Managing one's own time and the time of others.

GOE INFORMATION—Interest Area: 11. Recreation, Travel, and Other Personal Services. **Work Group:** 11.02. Recreational Services. **Other Job Titles in This Work Group:** Amusement and Recreation Attendants; Entertainment Attendants and Related Workers, All Other; Gaming and Sports Book Writers and Runners; Gaming Dealers; Gaming Service Workers, All Other; Motion Picture Projectionists; Slot Key Persons; Tour Guides and Escorts; Travel Guides; Ushers, Lobby Attendants, and Ticket Takers. **PERSONALITY TYPE—**Social. Social occupations frequently involve working with, communicating with, and teaching people. These occupations often involve helping or providing service to others.

EDUCATION/TRAINING PROGRAM(S)—Health and Physical Education/Fitness, Other; Parks, Recreation, and Leisure Facilities Management; Parks, Recreation, and Leisure Studies; Parks, Recreation, Leisure, and Fitness Studies, Other; Sport and Fitness Administration/Management. **RELATED KNOWLEDGE/COURSES—Customer and Personal Service:** Knowledge of principles and processes for providing customer and personal services. This includes customer needs assessment, meeting quality standards for services, and evaluation of customer satisfaction. **Administration and Management:** Knowledge of business and management principles involved in strategic planning, resource allocation, human resources modeling, leadership technique, production methods, and coordination of people and resources. **Education and Training:** Knowledge of principles and methods for curriculum and training design, teaching and instruction for individuals and groups, and the measurement of training effects. **English Language:** Knowledge of the structure and content of the English language, including the meaning and spelling of words, rules of composition, and grammar. **Psychology:** Knowledge of human behavior and performance; individual differences in ability, personality, and interests; learning and motivation; psychological research methods; and the assessment and treatment of behavioral and affective disorders.

Recreational Vehicle Service Technicians

- ▲ Education/Training Required: Long-term on-the-job training
- ▲ Annual Earnings: $26,410
- ▲ Growth: 25.4%
- ▲ Annual Job Openings: 4,000
- ▲ Self-Employed: 2.2%
- ▲ Part-Time: 5.9%

Diagnose, inspect, adjust, repair, or overhaul recreational vehicles, including travel trailers. May specialize in maintaining gas, electrical, hydraulic, plumbing, or chassis/towing systems as well as repairing generators, appliances, and interior components. Locates and repairs frayed wiring, broken connections, or incorrect wiring, using ohmmeter, soldering iron, tape, and hand tools. Repairs plumbing and propane gas lines, using caulking compounds and plastic or copper pipe. Removes damaged exterior panels, repairs and replaces structural frame members, and seals leaks, using hand tools. Connects electrical system to outside power source and activates switches to test operation of appliances and light fixtures. Confers with customer or reads work order to determine nature and extent of damage to unit. Seals open side of modular units to prepare them for shipment, using polyethylene sheets, nails, and hammer. Resets hardware, using chisel, mallet, and screwdriver. Refinishes wood surfaces on cabinets, doors, moldings, and floors, using power sander, putty, spray equipment, brush, paints, or varnishes. Opens and closes doors, windows, and drawers to test their operation and trims edges to fit, using jack-plane or drawknife. Lists parts needed, estimates costs, and plans work procedure, using parts list, technical manuals, and diagrams. Connects water hose to inlet pipe of plumbing system and tests operation of toilets and sinks. Repairs leaks with caulking compound or replaces pipes, using pipe wrench. Inspects, examines, and tests operation of parts or systems to be repaired and to verify completeness of work performed. **SKILLS—Installation:** Installing equipment, machines, wiring, or programs to meet specifications. **Repairing:** Repairing machines or systems, using the needed tools. **Troubleshooting:** Determining causes of operating errors and deciding what to do about them. **Mathematics:** Using mathematics to solve problems. **Reading Comprehension:** Understanding written sentences and paragraphs in work-related documents. **Active Listening:** Giving full attention to what other people are saying, taking time to understand the points being made, asking questions as appropriate, and not interrupting at inappropriate times. **Equipment Selection:** Determining the kind of tools and equipment needed to do a job.

GOE INFORMATION—Interest Area: 05. Mechanics, Installers, and Repairers. **Work Group:** 05.03. Mechanical Work. **Other Job Titles in This Work Group:** Aircraft Body and Bonded Structure Repairers; Aircraft Engine Specialists; Aircraft Mechanics and Service Technicians; Airframe-and-Power-Plant Mechanics; Automotive Body and Related Repairers; Automotive Glass Installers and Repairers; Automotive Master Mechanics; Automotive Service Technicians and Mechanics; Automotive Specialty Technicians; Bicycle Repairers; Bridge and Lock Tenders; Bus and Truck Mechanics and Diesel Engine Specialists; Camera and Photographic Equipment Repairers; Coin, Vending, and Amusement Machine Servicers and Repairers; Control and Valve Installers and Repairers, Except Mechanical Door; Farm Equipment Mechanics; Gas Appliance Repairers; Hand and Portable Power Tool Repairers; Heating and Air Conditioning Mechanics; Heating, Air Conditioning, and Refrigeration Mechanics and Installers; Helpers—Electricians; Helpers—Installation, Maintenance, and Repair Workers; Industrial Machinery Mechanics; Keyboard Instrument Repairers and Tuners; Locksmiths and Safe Repairers; Maintenance and Repair Workers, General; Maintenance Workers, Machinery; Mechanical Door Repairers; Medical Appliance Technicians; Medical Equipment Repairers; Meter Mechanics; Millwrights; Mobile Heavy Equipment Mechanics, Except Engines; Motorboat Mechanics; Motorcycle Mechanics; Musical Instrument Repairers and Tuners; Ophthalmic Laboratory Technicians; Optical Instrument Assemblers;

Outdoor Power Equipment and Other Small Engine Mechanics; Painters, Transportation Equipment; Percussion Instrument Repairers and Tuners; Precision Instrument and Equipment Repairers, All Other; Rail Car Repairers; Railroad Inspectors; Reed or Wind Instrument Repairers and Tuners; Refrigeration Mechanics; Stringed Instrument Repairers and Tuners; Tire Repairers and Changers; Valve and Regulator Repairers; Watch Repairers. **PERSONALITY TYPE**—Realistic. Realistic occupations frequently involve work activities that include practical, hands-on problems and solutions. They often deal with plants, animals, and real-world materials like wood, tools, and machinery. Many of the occupations require working outside and do not involve a lot of paperwork or working closely with others.

EDUCATION/TRAINING PROGRAM(S)—Vehicle Maintenance and Repair Technologies, Other. **RELATED**

KNOWLEDGE/COURSES—Building and Construction: Knowledge of materials, methods, and tools involved in the construction or repair of houses, buildings, or other structures, such as highways and roads. **Principles of Mechanical Devices:** Knowledge of machines and tools, including their designs, uses, repair, and maintenance. **Engineering and Technology:** Knowledge of the practical application of engineering science and technology. This includes applying principles, techniques, procedures, and equipment to the design and production of various goods and services. **Design:** Knowledge of design techniques, tools, and principles involved in production of precision technical plans, blueprints, drawings, and models. **Customer and Personal Service:** Knowledge of principles and processes for providing customer and personal services. This includes customer needs assessment, meeting quality standards for services, and evaluation of customer satisfaction.

Refractory Materials Repairers, Except Brickmasons

▲ Education/Training Required: Short-term on-the-job training
▲ Annual Earnings: $35,130
▲ Growth: 11.5%
▲ Annual Job Openings: 16,000
▲ Self-Employed: 3.0%
▲ Part-Time: 2.1%

Build or repair furnaces, kilns, cupolas, boilers, converters, ladles, soaking pits, ovens, etc., using refractory materials. Relines or repairs ladle and pouring spout with refractory clay, using trowel. Dries and bakes new lining by placing inverted lining over burner, building fire in ladle, or using blowtorch. Fastens stopper head to rod with metal pin to assemble refractory stopper used to plug pouring nozzles of steel ladles. Drills holes in furnace wall, bolts overlapping layers of plastic to walls, and hammers surface to compress layers into solid sheets. Spreads mortar on stopper head and rod, using trowel, and slides brick sleeves over rod to form refractory jacket. Installs clay structures in melting tanks and drawing kilns to control flow and temperature of molten glass, using hoists and hand tools. Measures furnace wall and cuts required number of sheets from plastic block, using saw. Bolts sections of wooden mold together, using wrench, and lines mold with paper to prevent adherence of clay to mold. Removes worn or damaged plastic block refractory lining of furnace, using hand tools. Disassembles mold and cuts, chips, and smoothes clay structures, such as floaters, drawbars, and L-blocks, using square rule and hand tools. Dumps and tamps clay in mold, using tamping tool. Mixes specified amounts of sand, clay, mortar powder, and water to form refractory clay or mortar, using shovel or mixing machine. Tightens locknuts holding assembly together, spreads mortar on jacket to seal sleeve joints, and dries mortar in oven. Climbs scaffolding with hose and sprays surfaces of cupola with refractory mixture, using spray equipment. Transfers clay structures to curing ovens, melting tanks, and drawing kilns, using electric forklift truck. Chips slag from lining of ladle or removes entire lining when beyond repair, using hammer and chisel. Installs preformed metal scaffolding in interior of cupola, using hand tools. **SKILLS—Repairing:** Repairing machines or systems, using the needed tools. **Equipment Selection:** Determining the kind of tools and equipment needed to do a job. **Operation and Control:** Controlling operations of equipment or systems. **Mathematics:** Using mathematics to solve problems. **Installation:** Installing equipment, machines, wiring, or programs to meet specifications.

GOE INFORMATION—Interest Area: 06. Construction, Mining, and Drilling. **Work Group:** 06.02. Construction. **Other Job Titles in This Work Group:** Boat

Builders and Shipwrights; Boilermakers; Brattice Builders; Brickmasons and Blockmasons; Carpenters; Carpet Installers; Ceiling Tile Installers; Cement Masons and Concrete Finishers; Commercial Divers; Construction Carpenters; Drywall and Ceiling Tile Installers; Drywall Installers; Electricians; Explosives Workers, Ordnance Handling Experts, and Blasters; Fence Erectors; Floor Layers, Except Carpet, Wood, and Hard Tiles; Floor Sanders and Finishers; Glaziers; Grader, Bulldozer, and Scraper Operators; Hazardous Materials Removal Workers; Insulation Workers, Floor, Ceiling, and Wall; Insulation Workers, Mechanical; Manufactured Building and Mobile Home Installers; Operating Engineers; Operating Engineers and Other Construction Equipment Operators; Painters, Construction and Maintenance; Paperhangers; Paving, Surfacing, and Tamping Equipment Operators; Pile-Driver Operators; Pipe Fitters; Pipelayers; Pipelaying Fitters; Plasterers and Stucco Masons; Plumbers; Plumbers, Pipefitters, and Steamfitters; Rail-Track Laying and Maintenance Equipment Operators; Reinforcing Iron and Rebar Workers; Riggers; Roofers; Rough Carpenters; Security and Fire Alarm Systems Installers; Segmental Pavers; Sheet Metal Workers; Ship Carpenters and Joiners; Stone Cutters and Carvers; Stonemasons; Structural Iron and Steel Workers; Tapers; Terrazzo Workers and Finishers; Tile and Marble Setters. **PERSONALITY TYPE—** Realistic. Realistic occupations frequently involve work activities that include practical, hands-on problems and solutions. They often deal with plants, animals, and real-world materials like wood, tools, and machinery. Many of the occupations require working outside and do not involve a lot of paperwork or working closely with others.

EDUCATION/TRAINING PROGRAM(S)—Industrial Mechanics and Maintenance Technology. **RELATED KNOWLEDGE/COURSES—Building and Construction:** Knowledge of materials, methods, and tools involved in the construction or repair of houses, buildings, or other structures, such as highways and roads. **Principles of Mechanical Devices:** Knowledge of machines and tools, including their designs, uses, repair, and maintenance. **Engineering and Technology:** Knowledge of the practical application of engineering science and technology. This includes applying principles, techniques, procedures, and equipment to the design and production of various goods and services. **Production and Processing:** Knowledge of raw materials, production processes, quality control, costs, and other techniques for maximizing the effective manufacture and distribution of goods. **Physics:** Knowledge and prediction of physical principles and laws and their interrelationships and applications to understanding fluid, material, and atmospheric dynamics and mechanical, electrical, atomic, and sub-atomic structures and processes. **Chemistry:** Knowledge of the chemical composition, structure, and properties of substances and of the chemical processes and transformations that they undergo. This includes uses of chemicals and their interactions, danger signs, production techniques, and disposal methods.

Refrigeration Mechanics

- ▲ Education/Training Required: Long-term on-the-job training
- ▲ Annual Earnings: $34,020
- ▲ Growth: 22.3%
- ▲ Annual Job Openings: 21,000
- ▲ Self-Employed: 12.9%
- ▲ Part-Time: 4.9%

Install and repair industrial and commercial refrigerating systems. Mounts compressor, condenser, and other components in specified location on frame, using hand tools and acetylene welding equipment. Assembles structural and functional components, such as controls, switches, gauges, wiring harnesses, valves, pumps, compressors, condensers, cores, and pipes. Replaces or adjusts defective or worn parts to repair system and reassembles system. Installs expansion and control valves, using acetylene torch and wrenches. Cuts, bends, threads, and connects pipe to functional components and water, power, or refrigeration system. Keeps records of repairs and replacements made and causes of malfunctions. Reads blueprints to determine location, size, capacity, and type of components needed to build refrigeration system. Tests lines, components, and connections for leaks. Lays out reference points for installation of structural and functional components, using measuring instruments. Dismantles malfunctioning systems and tests components, using electrical, mechanical, and pneumatic testing equipment.

Observes system operation, using gauges and instruments, and adjusts or replaces mechanisms and parts according to specifications. Adjusts valves according to specifications and charges system with specified type of refrigerant. Lifts and aligns components into position, using hoist or block and tackle. Drills holes and installs mounting brackets and hangers into floor and walls of building. Fabricates and assembles components and structural portions of refrigeration system, using hand tools, powered tools, and welding equipment. Brazes or solders parts to repair defective joints and leaks. **SKILLS—Installation:** Installing equipment, machines, wiring, or programs to meet specifications. **Repairing:** Repairing machines or systems, using the needed tools. **Troubleshooting:** Determining causes of operating errors and deciding what to do about them. **Quality Control Analysis:** Conducting tests and inspections of products, services, or processes to evaluate quality or performance. **Equipment Maintenance:** Performing routine maintenance on equipment and determining when and what kind of maintenance is needed.

GOE INFORMATION—Interest Area: 05. Mechanics, Installers, and Repairers. **Work Group:** 05.03. Mechanical Work. **Other Job Titles in This Work Group:** Aircraft Body and Bonded Structure Repairers; Aircraft Engine Specialists; Aircraft Mechanics and Service Technicians; Airframe-and-Power-Plant Mechanics; Automotive Body and Related Repairers; Automotive Glass Installers and Repairers; Automotive Master Mechanics; Automotive Service Technicians and Mechanics; Automotive Specialty Technicians; Bicycle Repairers; Bridge and Lock Tenders; Bus and Truck Mechanics and Diesel Engine Specialists; Camera and Photographic Equipment Repairers; Coin, Vending, and Amusement Machine Servicers and Repairers; Control and Valve Installers and Repairers, Except Mechanical Door; Farm Equipment Mechanics; Gas Appliance Repairers; Hand and Portable Power Tool Repairers; Heating and Air Conditioning Mechanics; Heating, Air Conditioning, and Refrigeration Mechanics and Installers; Helpers—Electricians; Helpers—Installation, Maintenance, and Repair Workers; Industrial Machinery Mechanics; Keyboard Instrument Repairers and Tuners; Locksmiths and Safe Repairers; Maintenance and Repair Workers, General; Maintenance Workers, Machinery; Mechanical Door Repairers; Medical Appliance Technicians; Medical Equipment Repairers; Meter Mechanics; Millwrights; Mobile Heavy Equipment Mechanics, Except Engines; Motorboat Mechanics; Motorcycle Mechanics; Musical Instrument Repairers and Tuners; Ophthalmic Laboratory Technicians; Optical Instrument Assemblers; Outdoor Power Equipment and Other Small Engine Mechanics; Painters, Transportation Equipment; Percussion Instrument Repairers and Tuners; Precision Instrument and Equipment Repairers, All Other; Rail Car Repairers; Railroad Inspectors; Recreational Vehicle Service Technicians; Reed or Wind Instrument Repairers and Tuners; Stringed Instrument Repairers and Tuners; Tire Repairers and Changers; Valve and Regulator Repairers; Watch Repairers. **PERSONALITY TYPE—Realistic.** Realistic occupations frequently involve work activities that include practical, hands-on problems and solutions. They often deal with plants, animals, and real-world materials like wood, tools, and machinery. Many of the occupations require working outside and do not involve a lot of paperwork or working closely with others.

EDUCATION/TRAINING PROGRAM(S)—Heating, Air Conditioning, and Refrigeration Technology/Technician (ACH/ACR/ACHR/HRAC/HVAC/AC Technology); Heating, Air Conditioning, Ventilation, and Refrigeration Maintenance Technology/Technician (HAC, HACR, HVAC, HVACR) . **RELATED KNOWLEDGE/ COURSES—Principles of Mechanical Devices:** Knowledge of machines and tools, including their designs, uses, repair, and maintenance. **Engineering and Technology:** Knowledge of the practical application of engineering science and technology. This includes applying principles, techniques, procedures, and equipment to the design and production of various goods and services. **Design:** Knowledge of design techniques, tools, and principles involved in production of precision technical plans, blueprints, drawings, and models. **Clerical Studies:** Knowledge of administrative and clerical procedures and systems, such as word processing, managing files and records, stenography and transcription, designing forms, and other office procedures and terminology. **Building and Construction:** Knowledge of materials, methods, and tools involved in the construction or repair of houses, buildings, or other structures, such as highways and roads.

Refuse and Recyclable Material Collectors

- ▲ Education/Training Required: Short-term on-the-job training
- ▲ Annual Earnings: $23,850
- ▲ Growth: 16.6%
- ▲ Annual Job Openings: 34,000
- ▲ Self-Employed: 0.9%
- ▲ Part-Time: 11.0%

Collect and dump refuse or recyclable materials from containers into truck. May drive truck. Drives truck. Starts hoisting device that raises refuse bin attached to rear of truck and dumps contents into opening in enclosed truck body. **SKILLS—Operation and Control:** Controlling operations of equipment or systems. **Operation Monitoring:** Watching gauges, dials, or other indicators to make sure a machine is working properly. **Troubleshooting:** Determining causes of operating errors and deciding what to do about them.

GOE INFORMATION—Interest Area: 08. Industrial Production. **Work Group:** 08.07. Hands-on Work: Loading, Moving, Hoisting, and Conveying. **Other Job Titles in This Work Group:** Conveyor Operators and Tenders; Crane and Tower Operators; Dragline Operators; Excavating and Loading Machine and Dragline Operators; Freight, Stock, and Material Movers, Hand; Hoist and Winch Operators; Industrial Truck and Tractor Operators; Irradiated-Fuel Handlers; Laborers and Freight, Stock, and Material Movers, Hand; Machine Feeders and Offbearers; Material Moving Workers, All Other; Packers and Packagers, Hand; Pump Operators, Except Wellhead Pumpers; Tank Car, Truck, and Ship Loaders. **PERSONALITY TYPE—**Realistic. Realistic occupations frequently involve work activities that include practical, hands-on problems and solutions. They often deal with plants, animals, and real-world materials like wood, tools, and machinery. Many of the occupations require working outside and do not involve a lot of paperwork or working closely with others.

EDUCATION/TRAINING PROGRAM(S)—No data available. **RELATED KNOWLEDGE/COURSES—Transportation:** Knowledge of principles and methods for moving people or goods by air, rail, sea, or road, including the relative costs and benefits. **Principles of Mechanical Devices:** Knowledge of machines and tools, including their designs, uses, repair, and maintenance. **Geography:** Knowledge of principles and methods for describing the features of land, sea, and air masses, including their physical characteristics, locations, interrelationships, and distribution of plant, animal, and human life.

Registered Nurses

- ▲ Education/Training Required: Associate's degree
- ▲ Annual Earnings: $46,670
- ▲ Growth: 25.6%
- ▲ Annual Job Openings: 140,000
- ▲ Self-Employed: 0.9%
- ▲ Part-Time: 26.3%

Assess patient health problems and needs, develop and implement nursing care plans, and maintain medical records. Administer nursing care to ill, injured, convalescent, or disabled patients. May advise patients on health maintenance and disease prevention or provide case management. Licensing or registration required. Includes advance practice nurses such as nurse practitioners, clinical nurse specialists, certified nurse midwives, and certified registered nurse anesthetists. Advanced practice nursing is practiced by RNs who have specialized formal, post-basic education and who function in highly autonomous and specialized roles. Provides health care, first aid, and immunization in facilities such as schools, hospitals, and industry. Observes patient's skin color, dilation of pupils, and computerized equipment to monitor vital signs. Administers local, inhalation, intravenous, and other anesthetics. Orders, interprets, and evaluates diagnostic tests to identify and assess patient's condition. Prescribes or recommends drugs or other forms of treatment, such as physical therapy, inhalation therapy, or related therapeutic procedures. Refers students or patients to community agencies furnishing assistance and cooperates with agencies. Delivers infants and performs postpartum examinations and treatment. Instructs on topics such as health education, disease prevention, childbirth, and home nursing and develops health improvement programs. Advises and consults with specified personnel concerning necessary precautions to be taken to prevent possible contamination or infection. Administers stipulated emergency measures and contacts obstetrician when deviations from standard are encountered during pregnancy or delivery. Informs physician of patient's condition during anesthesia. Discusses cases with physician or obstetrician. Provides prenatal and postnatal care to obstetrical patients under supervision of obstetrician. Contracts independently to render nursing care, usually to one patient, in hospital or private home. Directs and coordinates infection control program in hospital. Maintains stock of supplies. Conducts specified laboratory tests. Prepares rooms, sterile instruments, equipment, and supplies; hands items to surgeon. Prepares patients for and assists with examinations. Records patient's medical information and vital signs. **SKILLS—Reading Comprehension:** Understanding written sentences and paragraphs in work-related documents. **Active Listening:** Giving full attention to what other people are saying, taking time to understand the points being made, asking questions as appropriate, and not interrupting at inappropriate times. **Speaking:** Talking to others to convey information effectively. **Service Orientation:** Actively looking for ways to help people. **Instructing:** Teaching others how to do something.

GOE INFORMATION—Interest Area: 14. Medical and Health Services. **Work Group:** 14.02. Medicine and Surgery. **Other Job Titles in This Work Group:** Anesthesiologists; Family and General Practitioners; Internists, General; Medical Assistants; Obstetricians and Gynecologists; Pediatricians, General; Pharmacists; Pharmacy Aides; Pharmacy Technicians; Physician Assistants; Physicians and Surgeons, All Other; Psychiatrists; Surgeons; Surgical Technologists. **PERSONALITY TYPE—Social.** Social occupations frequently involve working with, communicating with, and teaching people. These occupations often involve helping or providing service to others.

EDUCATION/TRAINING PROGRAM(S)—Adult Health Nurse/Nursing; Clinical Nurse Specialist; Critical Care Nursing; Family Practice Nurse/Nurse Practitioner; Maternal/Child Health and Neonatal Nurse/Nursing; Nurse Anesthetist; Nurse Midwife/Nursing Midwifery; Nursing—Registered Nurse Training (RN, ASN, BSN, MSN); Nursing Science (MS, PhD); Nursing, Other; Occupational and Environmental Health Nursing; Pediatric Nurse/Nursing; Perioperative/Operating Room and Surgical Nurse/Nursing; Psychiatric/Mental Health Nurse/ Nursing; Public Health/Community Nurse/Nursing. **RELATED KNOWLEDGE/COURSES—Medicine and Dentistry:** Knowledge of the information and techniques needed to diagnose and treat human injuries, diseases, and deformities. This includes symptoms, treatment alternatives, drug properties and interactions, and preventive health-care measures. **Biology:** Knowledge of plant and animal organisms and their tissues, cells, functions, interdependencies, and interactions with each other and the environment. **Customer and Personal Service:** Knowledge of principles and processes for providing customer and personal services. This includes customer needs assessment, meeting quality standards for services, and evaluation of customer satisfaction. **Chemistry:** Knowledge of the chemical composition, structure, and properties of substances and of the chemical processes and transformations that they undergo. This includes uses of chemicals and their interactions, danger signs, production techniques, and disposal methods. **Therapy and Counseling:** Knowledge of principles, methods, and procedures for diagnosis, treatment, and rehabilitation of physical and mental dysfunctions and for career counseling and guidance.

Rehabilitation Counselors

▲ Education/Training Required: Bachelor's degree
▲ Annual Earnings: $25,610
▲ Growth: 23.6%
▲ Annual Job Openings: 12,000
▲ Self-Employed: 0.6%
▲ Part-Time: 18.0%

Counsel individuals to maximize the independence and employability of persons coping with personal, social, and vocational difficulties that result from birth defects, illness, disease, accidents, or the stress of daily life. Coordinate activities for residents of care and treatment facilities. Assess client needs and design and implement rehabilitation programs that may include personal and vocational counseling, training, and job placement. SKILLS—No data available.

GOE INFORMATION—Interest Area: 12. Education and Social Service. Work Group: 12.02. Social Services. Other Job Titles in This Work Group: Child, Family, and School Social Workers; Clergy; Clinical Psychologists; Clinical, Counseling, and School Psychologists; Community and Social Service Specialists, All Other; Counseling Psychologists; Counselors, All Other; Directors, Religious Activities and Education; Marriage and Family Therapists; Medical and Public Health Social Workers; Mental Health and Substance Abuse Social Workers; Mental Health Counselors; Probation Officers and Correctional Treatment Specialists; Religious Workers, All Other; Residential Advisors; Social and Human Service Assistants; Social Workers, All Other; Substance Abuse and Behavioral Disorder Counselors. PERSONALITY TYPE—No data available.

EDUCATION/TRAINING PROGRAM(S)—Assistive/Augmentative Technology and Rehabilitation Engineering; Vocational Rehabilitation Counseling/Counselor. RELATED KNOWLEDGE/COURSES—No data available.

Reinforcing Iron and Rebar Workers

▲ Education/Training Required: Long-term on-the-job training
▲ Annual Earnings: $34,750
▲ Growth: 17.5%
▲ Annual Job Openings: 4,000
▲ Self-Employed: 0%
▲ Part-Time: 4.9%

Position and secure steel bars or mesh in concrete forms in order to reinforce concrete. Use a variety of fasteners, rod-bending machines, blowtorches, and hand tools. Determines number, sizes, shapes, and locations of reinforcing rods from blueprints, sketches, or oral instructions. Selects and places rods in forms, spacing and fastening them together, using wire and pliers. Bends steel rods with hand tools and rod-bending machine. Cuts rods to required lengths, using hacksaw, bar cutters, or acetylene torch. Reinforces concrete with wire mesh. Welds reinforcing bars together, using arch-welding equipment. SKILLS—Active Listening: Giving full attention to what other people are saying, taking time to understand the points being made, asking questions as appropriate, and not interrupting at inappropriate times.

GOE INFORMATION—Interest Area: 06. Construction, Mining, and Drilling. Work Group: 06.02. Construction. Other Job Titles in This Work Group: Boat Builders and Shipwrights; Boilermakers; Brattice Builders; Brickmasons and Blockmasons; Carpenters; Carpet Installers; Ceiling Tile Installers; Cement Masons and Concrete Finishers; Commercial Divers; Construction Carpenters; Drywall and Ceiling Tile Installers; Drywall Installers; Electricians; Explosives Workers, Ordnance Handling Experts, and Blasters; Fence Erectors; Floor Layers, Except Carpet, Wood, and Hard Tiles; Floor Sanders and Finishers; Glaziers; Grader, Bulldozer, and Scraper Operators; Hazardous Materials Removal Workers; Insulation Workers, Floor, Ceiling, and Wall; Insulation Workers, Mechanical; Manufactured Building and Mobile

Home Installers; Operating Engineers; Operating Engineers and Other Construction Equipment Operators; Painters, Construction and Maintenance; Paperhangers; Paving, Surfacing, and Tamping Equipment Operators; Pile-Driver Operators; Pipe Fitters; Pipelayers; Pipelaying Fitters; Plasterers and Stucco Masons; Plumbers; Plumbers, Pipefitters, and Steamfitters; Rail-Track Laying and Maintenance Equipment Operators; Refractory Materials Repairers, Except Brickmasons; Riggers; Roofers; Rough Carpenters; Security and Fire Alarm Systems Installers; Segmental Pavers; Sheet Metal Workers; Ship Carpenters and Joiners; Stone Cutters and Carvers; Stonemasons; Structural Iron and Steel Workers; Tapers; Terrazzo Workers and Finishers; Tile and Marble Setters. **PERSONALITY TYPE**—Realistic. Realistic occupations frequently involve work activities that include practical, hands-on problems and solutions. They often deal with plants, animals, and real-world materials like wood, tools, and machinery. Many of the occupations require working outside and do not involve a lot of paperwork or working closely with others.

EDUCATION/TRAINING PROGRAM(S)—Construction Trades, Other. **RELATED KNOWLEDGE/ COURSES—Building and Construction:** Knowledge of materials, methods, and tools involved in the construction or repair of houses, buildings, or other structures, such as highways and roads. **Design:** Knowledge of design techniques, tools, and principles involved in production of precision technical plans, blueprints, drawings, and models. **Engineering and Technology:** Knowledge of the practical application of engineering science and technology. This includes applying principles, techniques, procedures, and equipment to the design and production of various goods and services. **Physics:** Knowledge and prediction of physical principles and laws and their interrelationships and applications to understanding fluid, material, and atmospheric dynamics and mechanical, electrical, atomic, and sub-atomic structures and processes. **Mathematics:** Knowledge of arithmetic, algebra, geometry, calculus, and statistics and their applications.

Reservation and Transportation Ticket Agents

▲ Education/Training Required: Short-term on-the-job training
▲ Annual Earnings: $24,090
▲ Growth: 14.5%
▲ Annual Job Openings: 39,000
▲ Self-Employed: 0%
▲ Part-Time: 31.7%

Make and confirm reservations for passengers and sell tickets for transportation agencies such as airlines, bus companies, railroads, and steamship lines. May check baggage and direct passengers to designated concourse, pier, or track. Arranges reservations and routing for passengers at request of Ticket Agent. Examines passenger ticket or pass to direct passenger to specified area for loading. Plans route and computes ticket cost, using schedules, rate books, and computer. Reads coded data on tickets to ascertain destination, marks tickets, and assigns boarding pass. Assists passengers requiring special assistance to board or depart conveyance. Informs travel agents in other locations of space reserved or available. Sells travel insurance. Announces arrival and departure information, using public-address system. Telephones customer or ticket agent to advise of changes with travel conveyance or to confirm reservation. Sells and assembles tickets for transmittal or mailing to customers. Answers inquiries made to travel agencies or transportation firms, such as airlines,

bus companies, railroad companies, and steamship lines. Checks baggage and directs passenger to designated location for loading. Assigns specified space to customers and maintains computerized inventory of passenger space available. Determines whether space is available on travel dates requested by customer. **SKILLS—Service Orientation:** Actively looking for ways to help people. **Active Listening:** Giving full attention to what other people are saying, taking time to understand the points being made, asking questions as appropriate, and not interrupting at inappropriate times. **Speaking:** Talking to others to convey information effectively. **Reading Comprehension:** Understanding written sentences and paragraphs in work-related documents. **Coordination:** Adjusting actions in relation to others' actions.

GOE INFORMATION—Interest Area: 11. Recreation, Travel, and Other Personal Services. **Work Group:** 11.03. Transportation and Lodging Services. **Other Job Titles in This Work Group:** Baggage Porters and Bellhops; Concierges; Flight Attendants; Hotel, Motel, and Resort Desk Clerks; Reservation and Transportation Ticket Agents and Travel Clerks; Transportation Attendants, Except Flight Attendants and Baggage Porters. **PERSONALITY TYPE**—Conventional. Conventional occupations frequently involve following set procedures and routines. These occupations can include working with data and details more than with ideas. Usually there is a clear line of authority to follow.

EDUCATION/TRAINING PROGRAM(S)—Selling Skills and Sales Operations; Tourism and Travel Services Marketing Operations; Tourism Promotion Operations. **RELATED KNOWLEDGE/COURSES—Customer and Personal Service:** Knowledge of principles and processes for providing customer and personal services. This includes customer needs assessment, meeting quality standards for services, and evaluation of customer satisfaction. **Transportation:** Knowledge of principles and methods for moving people or goods by air, rail, sea, or road, including the relative costs and benefits. **Geography:** Knowledge of principles and methods for describing the features of land, sea, and air masses, including their physical characteristics, locations, interrelationships, and distribution of plant, animal, and human life. **Clerical Studies:** Knowledge of administrative and clerical procedures and systems, such as word processing, managing files and records, stenography and transcription, designing forms, and other office procedures and terminology. **Computers and Electronics:** Knowledge of circuit boards, processors, chips, electronic equipment, and computer hardware and software, including applications and programming. **English Language:** Knowledge of the structure and content of the English language, including the meaning and spelling of words, rules of composition, and grammar. **Mathematics:** Knowledge of arithmetic, algebra, geometry, calculus, and statistics and their applications.

Reservation and Transportation Ticket Agents and Travel Clerks

- ▲ Education/Training Required: Short-term on-the-job training
- ▲ Annual Earnings: $24,090
- ▲ Growth: 14.5%
- ▲ Annual Job Openings: 39,000
- ▲ Self-Employed: 0%
- ▲ Part-Time: 31.7%

Make and confirm reservations and sell tickets to passengers for large hotel or motel chains. May check baggage and direct passengers to designated concourse, pier, or track; make reservations; deliver tickets; arrange for visas; contact individuals and groups to inform them of package tours; or provide tourists with travel information, such as points of interest, restaurants, rates, and emergency service. **SKILLS**—No data available.

GOE INFORMATION—**Interest Area:** 11. Recreation, Travel, and Other Personal Services. **Work Group:** 11.03. Transportation and Lodging Services. **Other Job Titles in** This Work Group: Baggage Porters and Bellhops; Concierges; Flight Attendants; Hotel, Motel, and Resort Desk Clerks; Reservation and Transportation Ticket Agents; Transportation Attendants, Except Flight Attendants and Baggage Porters. **PERSONALITY TYPE**—No data available.

EDUCATION/TRAINING PROGRAM(S)—Selling Skills and Sales Operations; Tourism and Travel Services Marketing Operations; Tourism Promotion Operations. **RELATED KNOWLEDGE/COURSES**—No data available.

Residential Advisors

- ▲ Education/Training Required: Moderate-term on-the-job training
- ▲ Annual Earnings: $19,680
- ▲ Growth: 24.0%
- ▲ Annual Job Openings: 9,000
- ▲ Self-Employed: 0%
- ▲ Part-Time: 18.0%

Coordinate activities for residents of boarding schools, college fraternities or sororities, college dormitories, or similar establishments. Order supplies and determine need for maintenance, repairs, and furnishings. May maintain household records and assign rooms. May refer residents to counseling resources if needed. Assigns room, assists in planning recreational activities, and supervises work and study programs. Orders supplies and determines need for maintenance, repairs, and furnishings. Ascertains need for and secures service of physician. Chaperons group-sponsored trips and social functions. Plans menus of meals for residents of establishment. Sorts and distributes mail. Answers telephone. Hires and supervises activities of housekeeping personnel. Escorts individuals on trips outside establishment for shopping or to obtain medical or dental services. Compiles records of daily activities of residents. Counsels residents in identifying and resolving social and other problems. **SKILLS—Social Perceptiveness:** Being aware of others' reactions and understanding why they react as they do. **Active Listening:** Giving full attention to what other people are saying, taking time to understand the points being made, asking questions as appropriate, and not interrupting at inappropriate times. **Coordination:** Adjusting actions in relation to others' actions. **Speaking:** Talking to others to convey information effectively. **Critical Thinking:** Using logic and reasoning to identify the strengths and weaknesses of alternative solutions, conclusions, or approaches to problems.

GOE INFORMATION—Interest Area: 12. Education and Social Service. **Work Group:** 12.02. Social Services. **Other Job Titles in This Work Group:** Child, Family, and School Social Workers; Clergy; Clinical Psychologists; Clinical, Counseling, and School Psychologists; Community and Social Service Specialists, All Other; Counseling Psychologists; Counselors, All Other; Directors, Religious Activities and Education; Marriage and Family Therapists; Medical and Public Health Social Workers; Mental Health and Substance Abuse Social Workers; Mental Health Counselors; Probation Officers and Correctional Treatment Specialists; Rehabilitation Counselors; Religious Workers, All Other; Social and Human Service Assistants; Social Workers, All Other; Substance Abuse and Behavioral Disorder Counselors. **PERSONALITY TYPE**—Social. Social occupations frequently involve working with, communicating with, and teaching people. These occupations often involve helping or providing service to others.

EDUCATION/TRAINING PROGRAM(S)—Hotel/Motel Administration/Management. **RELATED KNOWLEDGE/COURSES—Customer and Personal Service:** Knowledge of principles and processes for providing customer and personal services. This includes customer needs assessment, meeting quality standards for services, and evaluation of customer satisfaction. **Psychology:** Knowledge of human behavior and performance; individual differences in ability, personality, and interests; learning and motivation; psychological research methods; and the assessment and treatment of behavioral and affective disorders. **Therapy and Counseling:** Knowledge of principles, methods, and procedures for diagnosis, treatment, and rehabilitation of physical and mental dysfunctions and for career counseling and guidance. **Administration and Management:** Knowledge of business and management principles involved in strategic planning, resource allocation, human resources modeling, leadership technique, production methods, and coordination of people and resources. **Personnel and Human Resources:** Knowledge of principles and procedures for personnel recruitment, selection, training, compensation and benefits, labor relations and negotiation, and personnel information systems.

Respiratory Therapists

▲ Education/Training Required: Associate's degree
▲ Annual Earnings: $39,370
▲ Growth: 34.8%
▲ Annual Job Openings: 4,000
▲ Self-Employed: 0%
▲ Part-Time: 20.8%

Assess, treat, and care for patients with breathing disorders. Assume primary responsibility for all respiratory care modalities, including the supervision of respiratory therapy technicians. Initiate and conduct therapeutic procedures; maintain patient records; and select, assemble, check, and operate equipment. Sets up and operates devices such as mechanical ventilators, therapeutic gas administration apparatus, environmental control systems, and aerosol generators. Operates equipment to administer medicinal gases and aerosol drugs to patients following specified parameters of treatment. Reads prescription, measures arterial blood gases, and reviews patient information to assess patient condition. Monitors patient's physiological responses to therapy, such as vital signs, arterial blood gases, and blood chemistry changes. Performs pulmonary function and adjusts equipment to obtain optimum results to therapy. Inspects and tests respiratory therapy equipment to ensure equipment is functioning safely and efficiently. Determines requirements for treatment, such as type and duration of therapy and medication and dosages. Determines most suitable method of administering inhalants, precautions to be observed, and potential modifications needed, compatible with physician's orders. Performs bronchopulmonary drainage and assists patient in performing breathing exercises. Consults with physician in event of adverse reactions. Maintains patient's chart, which contains pertinent identification and therapy information. Orders repairs when necessary. Demonstrates respiratory care procedures to trainees and other health care personnel. **SKILLS—Reading Comprehension:** Understanding written sentences and paragraphs in work-related documents. **Service Orientation:** Actively looking for ways to help people. **Active Listening:** Giving full attention to what other people are saying, taking time to understand the points being made, asking questions as appropriate, and not interrupting at inappropriate times. **Monitoring:** Monitoring/Assessing your performance or that of other individuals or organizations to make improvements or take corrective action. **Critical Thinking:** Using logic and reasoning to identify the strengths and weaknesses of alternative solutions,

conclusions, or approaches to problems. **Active Learning:** Understanding the implications of new information for both current and future problem-solving and decision-making.

GOE INFORMATION—Interest Area: 14. Medical and Health Services. **Work Group:** 14.06. Medical Therapy. **Other Job Titles in This Work Group:** Audiologists; Massage Therapists; Occupational Therapist Aides; Occupational Therapist Assistants; Occupational Therapists; Physical Therapist Aides; Physical Therapist Assistants; Physical Therapists; Radiation Therapists; Recreational Therapists; Respiratory Therapy Technicians; Speech-Language Pathologists; Therapists, All Other. **PERSONALITY TYPE**—Investigative. Investigative occupations frequently involve working with ideas and require an extensive amount of thinking. These occupations can involve searching for facts and figuring out problems mentally.

EDUCATION/TRAINING PROGRAM(S)—Respiratory Care Therapy/Therapist. **RELATED KNOWLEDGE/COURSES—Medicine and Dentistry:** Knowledge of the information and techniques needed to diagnose and treat human injuries, diseases, and deformities. This includes symptoms, treatment alternatives, drug properties and interactions, and preventive health-care measures. **Biology:** Knowledge of plant and animal organisms and their tissues, cells, functions, interdependencies, and interactions with each other and the environment. **Therapy and Counseling:** Knowledge of principles, methods, and procedures for diagnosis, treatment, and rehabilitation of physical and mental dysfunctions and for career counseling and guidance. **Chemistry:** Knowledge of the chemical composition, structure, and properties of substances and of the chemical processes and transformations that they undergo. This includes uses of chemicals and their interactions, danger signs, production techniques, and disposal methods. **Psychology:** Knowledge of human behavior and performance; individual differences in ability, personality, and interests; learning and motivation; psychological research methods; and the assessment and treatment of behavioral and affective disorders.

Respiratory Therapy Technicians

▲ Education/Training Required: Postsecondary vocational training
▲ Annual Earnings: $33,840
▲ Growth: 34.6%
▲ Annual Job Openings: 3,000
▲ Self-Employed: 4.0%
▲ Part-Time: 22.3%

Provide specific, well-defined respiratory care procedures under the direction of respiratory therapists and physicians. SKILLS—No data available.

GOE INFORMATION—**Interest Area:** 14. Medical and Health Services. **Work Group:** 14.06. Medical Therapy. **Other Job Titles in This Work Group:** Audiologists; Massage Therapists; Occupational Therapist Aides; Occupational Therapist Assistants; Occupational Therapists; Physical Therapist Aides; Physical Therapist Assistants;

Physical Therapists; Radiation Therapists; Recreational Therapists; Respiratory Therapists; Speech-Language Pathologists; Therapists, All Other. **PERSONALITY TYPE**—No data available.

EDUCATION/TRAINING PROGRAM(S)—Respiratory Care Therapy/Therapist; Respiratory Therapy Technician/Assistant. **RELATED KNOWLEDGE/ COURSES**—No data available.

Retail Salespersons

▲ Education/Training Required: Short-term on-the-job training
▲ Annual Earnings: $17,150
▲ Growth: 12.4%
▲ Annual Job Openings: 1,124,000
▲ Self-Employed: 4.0%
▲ Part-Time: 40.2%

Sell merchandise such as furniture, motor vehicles, appliances, or apparel in a retail establishment. Prepares sales slip or sales contract. Sells or arranges for delivery, insurance, financing, or service contracts for merchandise. Recommends, selects, and obtains merchandise based on customer needs and desires. Greets customer. Inventories stock. Rents merchandise to customers. Wraps merchandise. Estimates cost of repair or alteration of merchandise. Estimates and quotes trade-in allowances. Maintains records related to sales. Tickets, arranges, and displays merchandise to promote sales. Estimates quantity and cost of merchandise required, such as paint or floor covering. Fits or assists customers in trying on merchandise. Cleans shelves, counters, and tables. Requisitions new stock. Demonstrates use or operation of merchandise. Totals purchases, receives payment, makes change, or processes credit transaction. Describes merchandise and explains use, operation, and care of merchandise to customers. Computes sales price of merchandise. **SKILLS—Active Listening:** Giving full attention to what other people are saying, taking time to understand the points being made, asking

questions as appropriate, and not interrupting at inappropriate times. **Service Orientation:** Actively looking for ways to help people. **Speaking:** Talking to others to convey information effectively. **Mathematics:** Using mathematics to solve problems. **Writing:** Communicating effectively in writing as appropriate for the needs of the audience.

GOE INFORMATION—**Interest Area:** 10. Sales and Marketing. **Work Group:** 10.03. General Sales. **Other Job Titles in This Work Group:** Parts Salespersons; Real Estate Brokers; Real Estate Sales Agents; Sales Representatives, Wholesale and Manufacturing, Except Technical and Scientific Products; Service Station Attendants; Stock Clerks, Sales Floor; Travel Agents. **PERSONALITY TYPE**—Enterprising. Enterprising occupations frequently involve starting up and carrying out projects. These occupations can involve leading people and making many decisions. They sometimes require risk taking and often deal with business.

EDUCATION/TRAINING PROGRAM(S)—Floriculture/Floristry Operations and Management; Retailing and

Retail Operations; Sales, Distribution, and Marketing Operations, General; Selling Skills and Sales Operations. **RELATED KNOWLEDGE/COURSES—Sales and Marketing:** Knowledge of principles and methods for showing, promoting, and selling products or services. This includes marketing strategy and tactics, product demonstration, sales techniques, and sales control systems. **Customer and Personal Service:** Knowledge of principles and processes for providing customer and personal services. This includes customer needs assessment, meeting quality stan-dards for services, and evaluation of customer satisfaction. **Mathematics:** Knowledge of arithmetic, algebra, geometry, calculus, and statistics and their applications. **English Language:** Knowledge of the structure and content of the English language, including the meaning and spelling of words, rules of composition, and grammar. **Clerical Studies:** Knowledge of administrative and clerical procedures and systems, such as word processing, managing files and records, stenography and transcription, designing forms, and other office procedures and terminology.

Roofers

- ▲ Education/Training Required: Moderate-term on-the-job training
- ▲ Annual Earnings: $29,460
- ▲ Growth: 19.4%
- ▲ Annual Job Openings: 38,000
- ▲ Self-Employed: 30.9%
- ▲ Part-Time: 13.8%

Cover roofs of structures with shingles, slate, asphalt, aluminum, wood, and related materials. May spray roofs, sidings, and walls with material to bind, seal, insulate, or soundproof sections of structures. Fastens composition shingles or sheets to roof with asphalt, cement, or nails. Cuts roofing paper to size and nails or staples paper to roof in overlapping strips to form base for roofing materials. Cleans and maintains equipment. Removes snow, water, or debris from roofs prior to applying roofing materials. Insulates, soundproofs, and seals buildings with foam, using spray gun, air compressor, and heater. Punches holes in slate, tile, terra cotta, or wooden shingles, using punch and hammer. Applies gravel or pebbles over top layer, using rake or stiff-bristled broom. Applies alternate layers of hot asphalt or tar and roofing paper until roof covering is completed as specified. Overlaps successive layers of roofing material, determining distance of overlap, using chalkline, gauge on shingling hatchet, or lines on shingles. Cuts strips of flashing and fits them into angles formed by walls, vents, and intersecting roof surfaces. Mops or pours hot asphalt or tar onto roof base when applying asphalt or tar and gravel to roof. Aligns roofing material with edge of roof. **SKILLS—Coordination:** Adjusting actions in relation to others' actions. **Equipment Selection:** Determining the kind of tools and equipment needed to do a job. **Operation and Control:** Controlling operations of equipment or systems. **Repairing:** Repairing machines or systems, using the needed tools.

GOE INFORMATION—Interest Area: 06. Construction, Mining, and Drilling. **Work Group:** 06.02. Construction. **Other Job Titles in This Work Group:** Boat Builders and Shipwrights; Boilermakers; Brattice Builders; Brickmasons and Blockmasons; Carpenters; Carpet Installers; Ceiling Tile Installers; Cement Masons and Concrete Finishers; Commercial Divers; Construction Carpenters; Drywall and Ceiling Tile Installers; Drywall Installers; Electricians; Explosives Workers, Ordnance Handling Experts, and Blasters; Fence Erectors; Floor Layers, Except Carpet, Wood, and Hard Tiles; Floor Sanders and Finishers; Glaziers; Grader, Bulldozer, and Scraper Operators; Hazardous Materials Removal Workers; Insulation Workers, Floor, Ceiling, and Wall; Insulation Workers, Mechanical; Manufactured Building and Mobile Home Installers; Operating Engineers; Operating Engineers and Other Construction Equipment Operators; Painters, Construction and Maintenance; Paperhangers; Paving, Surfacing, and Tamping Equipment Operators; Pile-Driver Operators; Pipe Fitters; Pipelayers; Pipelaying Fitters; Plasterers and Stucco Masons; Plumbers; Plumbers, Pipefitters, and Steamfitters; Rail-Track Laying and Maintenance Equipment Operators; Refractory Materials Repairers, Except Brickmasons; Reinforcing Iron and Rebar Workers; Riggers; Rough Carpenters; Security and Fire Alarm Systems Installers; Segmental Pavers; Sheet Metal Workers; Ship Carpenters and Joiners; Stone Cutters and Carvers; Stonemasons; Structural Iron and Steel

Workers; Tapers; Terrazzo Workers and Finishers; Tile and Marble Setters. **PERSONALITY TYPE**—Realistic. Realistic occupations frequently involve work activities that include practical, hands-on problems and solutions. They often deal with plants, animals, and real-world materials like wood, tools, and machinery. Many of the occupations require working outside and do not involve a lot of paperwork or working closely with others.

EDUCATION/TRAINING PROGRAM(S)—Roofer. **RELATED KNOWLEDGE/COURSES**—Building and

Construction: Knowledge of materials, methods, and tools involved in the construction or repair of houses, buildings, or other structures, such as highways and roads. **Principles of Mechanical Devices:** Knowledge of machines and tools, including their designs, uses, repair, and maintenance. **Engineering and Technology:** Knowledge of the practical application of engineering science and technology. This includes applying principles, techniques, procedures, and equipment to the design and production of various goods and services.

Rough Carpenters

- ▲ Education/Training Required: Moderate-term on-the-job training
- ▲ Annual Earnings: $33,470
- ▲ Growth: 8.2%
- ▲ Annual Job Openings: 161,000
- ▲ Self-Employed: 36.8%
- ▲ Part-Time: 8.1%

Build rough wooden structures, such as concrete forms, scaffolds, tunnel, bridge, or sewer supports; billboard signs; and temporary frame shelters according to sketches, blueprints, or oral instructions. Assembles and fastens material together to construct wood or metal framework of structure, using bolts, nails, or screws. Erects forms of prefabricated forms, framework, scaffolds, hoists, roof supports, or chutes, using hand tools, plumb rule, and level. Anchors and braces forms and other structures in place, using nails, bolts, anchor rods, steel cables, planks, wedges, and timbers. Fabricates parts, using woodworking and metalworking machines. Digs or directs digging of post holes and sets pole to support structure. Examines structural timbers and supports to detect decay and replaces timber, using hand tools, nuts, and bolts. Installs rough door and window frames, subflooring, fixtures, or temporary supports in structures undergoing construction or repair. Bores boltholes in timber with masonry or concrete walls, using power drill. Studies blueprints and diagrams to determine dimensions of structure or form to be constructed or erected. Measures materials or distances, using square, measuring tape, or rule to lay out work. Cuts or saws boards, timbers, or plywood to required size, using handsaw, power saw, or woodworking machine. **SKILLS—Installation:** Installing equipment, machines, wiring, or programs to meet specifications. **Operation and Control:** Controlling operations of equipment or systems. **Mathematics:** Using mathematics to solve problems.

GOE INFORMATION—Interest Area: 06. Construction, Mining, and Drilling. **Work Group:** 06.02. Construction. **Other Job Titles in This Work Group:** Boat Builders and Shipwrights; Boilermakers; Brattice Builders; Brickmasons and Blockmasons; Carpenters; Carpet Installers; Ceiling Tile Installers; Cement Masons and Concrete Finishers; Commercial Divers; Construction Carpenters; Drywall and Ceiling Tile Installers; Drywall Installers; Electricians; Explosives Workers, Ordnance Handling Experts, and Blasters; Fence Erectors; Floor Layers, Except Carpet, Wood, and Hard Tiles; Floor Sanders and Finishers; Glaziers; Grader, Bulldozer, and Scraper Operators; Hazardous Materials Removal Workers; Insulation Workers, Floor, Ceiling, and Wall; Insulation Workers, Mechanical; Manufactured Building and Mobile Home Installers; Operating Engineers; Operating Engineers and Other Construction Equipment Operators; Painters, Construction and Maintenance; Paperhangers; Paving, Surfacing, and Tamping Equipment Operators; Pile-Driver Operators; Pipe Fitters; Pipelayers; Pipelaying Fitters; Plasterers and Stucco Masons; Plumbers; Plumbers, Pipefitters, and Steamfitters; Rail-Track Laying and Maintenance Equipment Operators; Refractory Materials Repairers, Except Brickmasons; Reinforcing Iron and Rebar Workers; Riggers; Roofers; Security and Fire Alarm Systems Installers; Segmental Pavers; Sheet Metal Workers; Ship Carpenters and Joiners; Stone Cutters and Carvers; Stonemasons; Structural Iron and Steel Workers; Tapers; Terrazzo Workers and Finishers; Tile and Marble

Setters. **PERSONALITY TYPE**—Realistic. Realistic occupations frequently involve work activities that include practical, hands-on problems and solutions. They often deal with plants, animals, and real-world materials like wood, tools, and machinery. Many of the occupations require working outside and do not involve a lot of paperwork or working closely with others.

EDUCATION/TRAINING PROGRAM(S)—Carpentry/Carpenter. **RELATED KNOWLEDGE/ COURSES**—**Building and Construction:** Knowledge of materials, methods, and tools involved in the construction or repair of houses, buildings, or other structures,

such as highways and roads. **Engineering and Technology:** Knowledge of the practical application of engineering science and technology. This includes applying principles, techniques, procedures, and equipment to the design and production of various goods and services. **Design:** Knowledge of design techniques, tools, and principles involved in production of precision technical plans, blueprints, drawings, and models. **Principles of Mechanical Devices:** Knowledge of machines and tools, including their designs, uses, repair, and maintenance. **Mathematics:** Knowledge of arithmetic, algebra, geometry, calculus, and statistics and their applications.

Sales Agents, Financial Services

- ▲ Education/Training Required: Bachelor's degree
- ▲ Annual Earnings: $59,690
- ▲ Growth: 22.3%
- ▲ Annual Job Openings: 55,000
- ▲ Self-Employed: 22.4%
- ▲ Part-Time: 8.6%

Sell financial services, such as loan, tax, and securities counseling to customers of financial institutions and business establishments. Sells services and equipment, such as trust, investment, and check processing services. Develops prospects from current commercial customers, referral leads, and sales and trade meetings. Reviews business trends and advises customers regarding expected fluctuations. Makes presentations on financial services to groups to attract new clients. Determines customers' financial services needs and prepares proposals to sell services. Contacts prospective customers to present information and explain available services. Prepares forms or agreement to complete sale. Evaluates costs and revenue of agreements to determine continued profitability. **SKILLS—Persuasion:** Persuading others to change their minds or behavior. **Active Learning:** Understanding the implications of new information for both current and future problem-solving and decision-making. **Monitoring:** Monitoring/Assessing your performance or that of other individuals or organizations to make improvements or take corrective action. **Systems Analysis:** Determining how a system should work and how changes in conditions, operations, and the environment will affect outcomes. **Critical Thinking:** Using logic and reasoning to identify the strengths and weaknesses of alternative solutions, conclusions, or approaches to problems. **Reading Comprehension:** Understanding written sentences and paragraphs in work-related documents.

GOE INFORMATION—Interest Area: 10. Sales and Marketing. **Work Group:** 10.02. Sales Technology. **Other Job Titles in This Work Group:** Advertising Sales Agents; Insurance Sales Agents; Sales Agents, Securities and Commodities; Sales Representatives, Agricultural; Sales Representatives, Chemical and Pharmaceutical; Sales Representatives, Electrical/Electronic; Sales Representatives, Instruments; Sales Representatives, Mechanical Equipment and Supplies; Sales Representatives, Medical; Sales Representatives, Services, All Other; Sales Representatives, Wholesale and Manufacturing, Technical and Scientific Products; Securities, Commodities, and Financial Services Sales Agents. **PERSONALITY TYPE**—Enterprising. Enterprising occupations frequently involve starting up and carrying out projects. These occupations can involve leading people and making many decisions. They sometimes require risk taking and often deal with business.

EDUCATION/TRAINING PROGRAM(S)—Business and Personal/Financial Services Marketing Operations; Financial Planning and Services; Investments and Securities. **RELATED KNOWLEDGE/COURSES**—**Economics and Accounting:** Knowledge of economic and accounting principles and practices, the financial markets, banking, and the analysis and reporting of financial data. **Sales and Marketing:** Knowledge of principles and methods for showing, promoting, and selling products or services. This includes marketing strategy and tactics, product demonstration, sales techniques, and sales control systems. **Mathematics:** Knowledge of arithmetic, algebra, geometry, calculus, and statistics and their applications. **English Language:** Knowledge of the structure and content of the English language, including the meaning and spelling of words, rules of composition, and grammar. **Law and Government:** Knowledge of laws, legal codes, court procedures, precedents, government regulations, executive orders, agency rules, and the democratic political process.

Sales Agents, Securities and Commodities

- ▲ Education/Training Required: Bachelor's degree
- ▲ Annual Earnings: $59,690
- ▲ Growth: 22.3%
- ▲ Annual Job Openings: 55,000
- ▲ Self-Employed: 22.4%
- ▲ Part-Time: 8.6%

Buy and sell securities in investment and trading firms and develop and implement financial plans for individuals, businesses, and organizations. Develops financial plan based on analysis of client's financial status and discusses financial options with client. Contacts exchange or brokerage firm to execute order or buys and sells securities based on market quotation and competition in market. Records transactions accurately and keeps client informed about transactions. Analyzing market conditions to determine optimum time to execute securities transactions. Reads corporate reports and calculates ratios to determine best prospects for profit on stock purchase and to monitor client account. Identifies potential clients, using advertising campaigns, mailing lists, and personal contacts, and solicits business. Prepares financial reports to monitor client or corporate finances. Informs and advises concerned parties regarding fluctuations and securities transactions affecting plan or account. Completes sales order tickets and submits for processing of client-requested transaction. Prepares documents to implement plan selected by client. Reviews all securities transactions to ensure accuracy of information and ensure that trades conform to regulations of governing agencies. Interviews client to determine client's assets, liabilities, cash flow, insurance coverage, tax status, and financial objectives. Keeps informed about political and economic trends that influence stock prices. **SKILLS—Management of Financial Resources:** Determining how money will be spent to get the work done and accounting for these expenditures. **Systems Analysis:** Determining how a system should work and how changes in conditions, operations, and the environment will affect outcomes. **Active Learning:** Understanding the implications of new information for both current and future problem-solving and decision-making. **Systems Evaluation:** Identifying measures or indicators of system performance and the actions needed to improve or correct performance relative to the goals of the system. **Persuasion:** Persuading others to change their minds or behavior. **Critical Thinking:** Using logic and reasoning to identify the strengths and weaknesses of alternative solutions, conclusions, or approaches to problems. **Judgment and Decision Making:** Considering the relative costs and benefits of potential actions to choose the most appropriate one.

GOE INFORMATION—Interest Area: 10. Sales and Marketing. **Work Group:** 10.02. Sales Technology. **Other Job Titles in This Work Group:** Advertising Sales Agents; Insurance Sales Agents; Sales Agents, Financial Services; Sales Representatives, Agricultural; Sales Representatives, Chemical and Pharmaceutical; Sales Representatives, Electrical/Electronic; Sales Representatives, Instruments; Sales Representatives, Mechanical Equipment and Supplies; Sales Representatives, Medical; Sales Representatives, Services, All Other; Sales Representatives, Wholesale and Manufacturing, Technical and Scientific Products; Securities, Commodities, and Financial Services Sales Agents. **PERSONALITY TYPE—**Enterprising. Enterprising occupations frequently involve starting up and carrying out projects. These occupations can involve leading people and making many decisions. They sometimes require risk taking and often deal with business.

EDUCATION/TRAINING PROGRAM(S)—Business and Personal/Financial Services Marketing Operations; Financial Planning and Services; Investments and Securities. **RELATED KNOWLEDGE/COURSES—Economics and Accounting:** Knowledge of economic and accounting principles and practices, the financial markets, banking, and the analysis and reporting of financial data.

Mathematics: Knowledge of arithmetic, algebra, geometry, calculus, and statistics and their applications. **Sales and Marketing:** Knowledge of principles and methods for showing, promoting, and selling products or services. This includes marketing strategy and tactics, product demonstration, sales techniques, and sales control systems. **English Language:** Knowledge of the structure and content of the English language, including the meaning and spelling of words, rules of composition, and grammar. **Cus**-tomer and Personal Service: Knowledge of principles and processes for providing customer and personal services. This includes customer needs assessment, meeting quality standards for services, and evaluation of customer satisfaction. **Clerical Studies:** Knowledge of administrative and clerical procedures and systems, such as word processing, managing files and records, stenography and transcription, designing forms, and other office procedures and terminology.

Sales Engineers

▲ Education/Training Required: Bachelor's degree
▲ Annual Earnings: $59,720
▲ Growth: 17.7%
▲ Annual Job Openings: 4,000
▲ Self-Employed: 2.7%
▲ Part-Time: 4.5%

Sell business goods or services, the selling of which requires a technical background equivalent to a baccalaureate degree in engineering. Calls on management representatives at commercial, industrial, and other establishments to convince prospective client to buy products or services offered. Assists sales force in sale of company products. Demonstrates and explains product or service to customer representatives, such as engineers, architects, and other professionals. Draws up sales or service contract for products or services. Provides technical services to clients relating to use, operation, and maintenance of equipment. Arranges for trial installations of equipment. Designs and drafts variations of standard products in order to meet customer needs. Reviews customer documents to develop and prepare cost estimates or projected production increases from use of proposed equipment or services. Draws up or proposes changes in equipment, processes, materials, or services resulting in cost reduction or improvement in customer operations. Assists in development of custom-made machinery. Diagnoses problems with equipment installed. Provides technical training to employees of client. **SKILLS—Speaking:** Talking to others to convey information effectively. **Operations Analysis:** Analyzing needs and product requirements to create a design. **Reading Comprehension:** Understanding written sentences and paragraphs in work-related documents. **Active Learning:** Understanding the implications of new information for both current and future problem-solving and decision-making. **Mathematics:** Using mathematics to solve problems. **Technology Design:** Generating or adapting equipment and technology to serve user needs. **Troubleshooting:** Determining causes of operating errors and deciding what to do about them.

GOE INFORMATION—Interest Area: 02. Science, Math, and Engineering. **Work Group:** 02.07. Engineering. **Other Job Titles in This Work Group:** Aerospace Engineers; Agricultural Engineers; Architects, Except Landscape and Naval; Biomedical Engineers; Chemical Engineers; Civil Engineers; Computer Hardware Engineers; Computer Software Engineers, Applications; Computer Software Engineers, Systems Software; Electrical Engineers; Electronics Engineers, Except Computer; Engineers, All Other; Environmental Engineers; Fire-Prevention and Protection Engineers; Health and Safety Engineers, Except Mining Safety Engineers and Inspectors; Industrial Engineers; Industrial Safety and Health Engineers; Landscape Architects; Marine Architects; Marine Engineers; Marine Engineers and Naval Architects; Materials Engineers; Mechanical Engineers; Mining and Geological Engineers, Including Mining Safety Engineers; Nuclear Engineers; Petroleum Engineers; Product Safety Engineers. **PERSONALITY TYPE—**Enterprising. Enterprising occupations frequently involve starting up and carrying out projects. These occupations can involve leading people and making many decisions. They sometimes require risk taking and often deal with business.

EDUCATION/TRAINING PROGRAM(S)—Selling Skills and Sales Operations. **RELATED KNOWLEDGE/ COURSES—Sales and Marketing:** Knowledge of principles and methods for showing, promoting, and selling products or services. This includes marketing strategy and tactics, product demonstration, sales techniques, and sales control systems. **Engineering and Technology:** Knowledge of the practical application of engineering science and technology. This includes applying principles, techniques, procedures, and equipment to the design and production of various goods and services. **Design:** Knowledge of design techniques, tools, and principles involved in production of precision technical plans, blueprints, drawings, and models. **Customer and Personal Service:** Knowledge of principles and processes for providing customer and personal services. This includes customer needs assessment, meeting quality standards for services, and evaluation of customer satisfaction. **English Language:** Knowledge of the structure and content of the English language, including the meaning and spelling of words, rules of composition, and grammar.

Sales Managers

- ▲ Education/Training Required: Work experience plus degree
- ▲ Annual Earnings: $71,620
- ▲ Growth: 32.8%
- ▲ Annual Job Openings: 21,000
- ▲ Self-Employed: 2.4%
- ▲ Part-Time: 2.6%

Direct the actual distribution or movement of a product or service to the customer. Coordinate sales distribution by establishing sales territories, quotas, and goals and establish training programs for sales representatives. Analyze sales statistics gathered by staff to determine sales potential and inventory requirements and monitor the preferences of customers. Confers with potential customers regarding equipment needs and advises customers on types of equipment to purchase. Visits franchised dealers to stimulate interest in establishment or expansion of leasing programs. Advises dealers and distributors on policies and operating procedures to ensure functional effectiveness of business. Reviews operational records and reports to project sales and determine profitability. Confers or consults with department heads to plan advertising services and secure information on appliances, equipment, and customer-required specifications. Directs clerical staff to maintain export correspondence, bid requests, and credit collections and current information on tariffs, licenses, and restrictions. Resolves customer complaints regarding sales and service. Directs product research and development. Directs conversion of products from USA to foreign standards. Inspects premises of assigned stores for adequate security exits and compliance with safety codes and ordinances. Represents company at trade association meetings to promote products. **SKILLS—Coordination:** Adjusting actions in relation to others' actions. **Speaking:** Talking to others to convey information effectively. **Monitoring:** Monitoring/Assessing your performance or that of other individuals or organizations to make improvements or take corrective action. **Time Management:** Managing one's own time and the time of others. **Active Listening:** Giving full attention to what other people are saying, taking time to understand the points being made, asking questions as appropriate, and not interrupting at inappropriate times.

GOE INFORMATION—Interest Area: 10. Sales and Marketing. **Work Group:** 10.01. Managerial Work in Sales and Marketing. **Other Job Titles in This Work Group:** Advertising and Promotions Managers; First-Line Supervisors/Managers of Non-Retail Sales Workers; First-Line Supervisors/Managers of Retail Sales Workers; Marketing Managers. **PERSONALITY TYPE—**Enterprising. Enterprising occupations frequently involve starting up and carrying out projects. These occupations can involve leading people and making many decisions. They sometimes require risk taking and often deal with business.

EDUCATION/TRAINING PROGRAM(S)—Business Administration and Management, General; Business/Commerce, General; Consumer Merchandising/Retailing Management; Marketing, Other; Marketing/Marketing Management, General. **RELATED KNOWLEDGE/COURSES—Administration and Management:** Knowledge of business and management principles involved in strategic planning, resource allocation, human resources modeling, leadership technique, production methods, and coordination of people and resources. **Sales and Marketing:** Knowledge of principles and methods for showing, promoting, and selling products or services. This includes marketing strategy and tactics, product demonstration, sales techniques, and sales control systems. **Customer and Personal Service:** Knowledge of principles and processes for providing customer and personal services. This includes customer needs assessment, meeting quality standards for services, and evaluation of customer satisfaction. **English**

Language: Knowledge of the structure and content of the English language, including the meaning and spelling of words, rules of composition, and grammar. **Mathematics:** Knowledge of arithmetic, algebra, geometry, calculus, and statistics and their applications.

Sales Representatives, Agricultural

▲ Education/Training Required: Moderate-term on-the-job training
▲ Annual Earnings: $54,360
▲ Growth: 7.5%
▲ Annual Job Openings: 24,000
▲ Self-Employed: 10.7%
▲ Part-Time: 22.3%

Sell agricultural products and services, such as animal feeds; farm and garden equipment; and dairy, poultry, and veterinarian supplies. Solicits orders from customers in person or by phone. Demonstrates use of agricultural equipment or machines. Recommends changes in customer use of agricultural products to improve production. Prepares reports of business transactions. Informs customer of estimated delivery schedule, service contracts, warranty, or other information pertaining to purchased products. Displays or shows customer agricultural-related products. Compiles lists of prospective customers for use as sales leads. Prepares sales contracts for orders obtained. Consults with customer regarding installation, setup, or layout of agricultural equipment and machines. Quotes prices and credit terms. **SKILLS—Speaking:** Talking to others to convey information effectively. **Active Listening:** Giving full attention to what other people are saying, taking time to understand the points being made, asking questions as appropriate, and not interrupting at inappropriate times. **Writing:** Communicating effectively in writing as appropriate for the needs of the audience. **Reading Comprehension:** Understanding written sentences and paragraphs in work-related documents. **Mathematics:** Using mathematics to solve problems. **Persuasion:** Persuading others to change their minds or behavior.

GOE INFORMATION—Interest Area: 10. Sales and Marketing. **Work Group:** 10.02. Sales Technology. **Other Job Titles in This Work Group:** Advertising Sales Agents; Insurance Sales Agents; Sales Agents, Financial Services; Sales Agents, Securities and Commodities; Sales Representatives, Chemical and Pharmaceutical; Sales Represen-

tatives, Electrical/Electronic; Sales Representatives, Instruments; Sales Representatives, Mechanical Equipment and Supplies; Sales Representatives, Medical; Sales Representatives, Services, All Other; Sales Representatives, Wholesale and Manufacturing, Technical and Scientific Products; Securities, Commodities, and Financial Services Sales Agents. **PERSONALITY TYPE**—Enterprising. Enterprising occupations frequently involve starting up and carrying out projects. These occupations can involve leading people and making many decisions. They sometimes require risk taking and often deal with business.

EDUCATION/TRAINING PROGRAM(S)—Business, Management, Marketing, and Related Support Services, Other; Selling Skills and Sales Operations. **RELATED KNOWLEDGE/COURSES—Sales and Marketing:** Knowledge of principles and methods for showing, promoting, and selling products or services. This includes marketing strategy and tactics, product demonstration, sales techniques, and sales control systems. **Mathematics:** Knowledge of arithmetic, algebra, geometry, calculus, and statistics and their applications. **English Language:** Knowledge of the structure and content of the English language, including the meaning and spelling of words, rules of composition, and grammar. **Economics and Accounting:** Knowledge of economic and accounting principles and practices, the financial markets, banking, and the analysis and reporting of financial data. **Customer and Personal Service:** Knowledge of principles and processes for providing customer and personal services. This includes customer needs assessment, meeting quality standards for services, and evaluation of customer satisfaction.

Sales Representatives, Chemical and Pharmaceutical

- ▲ Education/Training Required: Moderate-term on-the-job training
- ▲ Annual Earnings: $54,360
- ▲ Growth: 7.5%
- ▲ Annual Job Openings: 24,000
- ▲ Self-Employed: 10.7%
- ▲ Part-Time: 22.3%

Sell chemical or pharmaceutical products or services, such as acids, industrial chemicals, agricultural chemicals, medicines, drugs, and water treatment supplies. Promotes and sells pharmaceutical and chemical products to potential customers. Explains water treatment package benefits to customer and sells chemicals to treat and resolve water process problems. Estimates and advises customer of service costs to correct water-treatment process problems. Discusses characteristics and clinical studies pertaining to pharmaceutical products with physicians, dentists, hospitals, and retail/wholesale establishments. Distributes drug samples to customer and takes orders for pharmaceutical supply items from customer. Inspects, tests, and observes chemical changes in water system equipment, utilizing test kit, reference manual, and knowledge of chemical treatment. **SKILLS—Speaking:** Talking to others to convey information effectively. **Active Listening:** Giving full attention to what other people are saying, taking time to understand the points being made, asking questions as appropriate, and not interrupting at inappropriate times. **Reading Comprehension:** Understanding written sentences and paragraphs in work-related documents. **Persuasion:** Persuading others to change their minds or behavior. **Science:** Using scientific rules and methods to solve problems. **Critical Thinking:** Using logic and reasoning to identify the strengths and weaknesses of alternative solutions, conclusions, or approaches to problems. **Social Perceptiveness:** Being aware of others' reactions and understanding why they react as they do.

GOE INFORMATION—Interest Area: 10. Sales and Marketing. **Work Group:** 10.02. Sales Technology. **Other Job Titles in This Work Group:** Advertising Sales Agents; Insurance Sales Agents; Sales Agents, Financial Services; Sales Agents, Securities and Commodities; Sales Representatives, Agricultural; Sales Representatives, Electrical/Electronic; Sales Representatives, Instruments; Sales Representatives, Mechanical Equipment and Supplies; Sales Representatives, Medical; Sales Representatives, Services, All Other; Sales Representatives, Wholesale and Manufacturing, Technical and Scientific Products; Securities, Commodities, and Financial Services Sales Agents. **PERSONALITY TYPE—Enterprising.** Enterprising occupations frequently involve starting up and carrying out projects. These occupations can involve leading people and making many decisions. They sometimes require risk taking and often deal with business.

EDUCATION/TRAINING PROGRAM(S)—Business, Management, Marketing, and Related Support Services, Other; Selling Skills and Sales Operations. RELATED KNOWLEDGE/COURSES—Sales and Marketing: Knowledge of principles and methods for showing, promoting, and selling products or services. This includes marketing strategy and tactics, product demonstration, sales techniques, and sales control systems. **Chemistry:** Knowledge of the chemical composition, structure, and properties of substances and of the chemical processes and transformations that they undergo. This includes uses of chemicals and their interactions, danger signs, production techniques, and disposal methods. **Mathematics:** Knowledge of arithmetic, algebra, geometry, calculus, and statistics and their applications. **English Language:** Knowledge of the structure and content of the English language, including the meaning and spelling of words, rules of composition, and grammar. **Economics and Accounting:** Knowledge of economic and accounting principles and practices, the financial markets, banking, and the analysis and reporting of financial data.

Sales Representatives, Electrical/Electronic

▲ Education/Training Required: Moderate-term on-the-job training
▲ Annual Earnings: $54,360
▲ Growth: 7.5%
▲ Annual Job Openings: 24,000
▲ Self-Employed: 10.7%
▲ Part-Time: 22.3%

Sell electrical, electronic, or related products or services, such as communication equipment, radiographic-inspection equipment and services, ultrasonic equipment, electronics parts, computers, and EDP systems. Analyzes communication needs of customer and consults with staff engineers regarding technical problems. Trains establishment personnel in equipment use, utilizing knowledge of electronics and product sold. Recommends equipment to meet customer requirements, considering salable features such as flexibility, cost, capacity, and economy of operation. Negotiates terms of sale and services with customer. Sells electrical or electronic equipment such as computers, data processing and radiographic equipment to businesses and industrial establishments. **SKILLS—Persuasion:** Persuading others to change their minds or behavior. **Active Listening:** Giving full attention to what other people are saying, taking time to understand the points being made, asking questions as appropriate, and not interrupting at inappropriate times. **Instructing:** Teaching others how to do something. **Speaking:** Talking to others to convey information effectively. **Operations Analysis:** Analyzing needs and product requirements to create a design. **Negotiation:** Bringing others together and trying to reconcile differences. **Equipment Selection:** Determining the kind of tools and equipment needed to do a job.

GOE INFORMATION—Interest Area: 10. Sales and Marketing. **Work Group:** 10.02. Sales Technology. **Other Job Titles in This Work Group:** Advertising Sales Agents; Insurance Sales Agents; Sales Agents, Financial Services; Sales Agents, Securities and Commodities; Sales Representatives, Agricultural; Sales Representatives, Chemical and Pharmaceutical; Sales Representatives, Instruments; Sales Representatives, Mechanical Equipment and Supplies; Sales Representatives, Medical; Sales Representatives, Services, All Other; Sales Representatives, Wholesale and Manufacturing, Technical and Scientific Products; Securities, Commodities, and Financial Services Sales Agents. **PERSONALITY TYPE—Enterprising.** Enterprising occupations frequently involve starting up and carrying out projects. These occupations can involve leading people and making many decisions. They sometimes require risk taking and often deal with business.

EDUCATION/TRAINING PROGRAM(S)—Business, Management, Marketing, and Related Support Services, Other; Selling Skills and Sales Operations. RELATED KNOWLEDGE/COURSES—Sales and Marketing: Knowledge of principles and methods for showing, promoting, and selling products or services. This includes marketing strategy and tactics, product demonstration, sales techniques, and sales control systems. **Computers and Electronics:** Knowledge of circuit boards, processors, chips, electronic equipment, and computer hardware and software, including applications and programming. **Education and Training:** Knowledge of principles and methods for curriculum and training design, teaching and instruction for individuals and groups, and the measurement of training effects. **Economics and Accounting:** Knowledge of economic and accounting principles and practices, the financial markets, banking, and the analysis and reporting of financial data. **Mathematics:** Knowledge of arithmetic, algebra, geometry, calculus, and statistics and their applications.

Sales Representatives, Instruments

- ▲ Education/Training Required: Moderate-term on-the-job training
- ▲ Annual Earnings: $54,360
- ▲ Growth: 7.5%
- ▲ Annual Job Openings: 24,000
- ▲ Self-Employed: 10.7%
- ▲ Part-Time: 22.3%

Sell precision instruments, such as dynamometers and spring scales, and laboratory, navigation, and surveying instruments. Assists customer with product selection, utilizing knowledge of engineering specifications and catalog resources. Evaluates customer needs and emphasizes product features based on technical knowledge of product capabilities and limitations. Sells weighing and other precision instruments, such as spring scales, dynamometers, and laboratory, navigational, and surveying instruments, to customer. **SKILLS—Active Listening:** Giving full attention to what other people are saying, taking time to understand the points being made, asking questions as appropriate, and not interrupting at inappropriate times. **Persuasion:** Persuading others to change their minds or behavior. **Speaking:** Talking to others to convey information effectively. **Reading Comprehension:** Understanding written sentences and paragraphs in work-related documents. **Service Orientation:** Actively looking for ways to help people. **Instructing:** Teaching others how to do something. **Mathematics:** Using mathematics to solve problems.

GOE INFORMATION—Interest Area: 10. Sales and Marketing. **Work Group:** 10.02. Sales Technology. **Other Job Titles in This Work Group:** Advertising Sales Agents; Insurance Sales Agents; Sales Agents, Financial Services; Sales Agents, Securities and Commodities; Sales Representatives, Agricultural; Sales Representatives, Chemical and Pharmaceutical; Sales Representatives, Electrical/Electronic; Sales Representatives, Mechanical Equipment and Supplies; Sales Representatives, Medical; Sales Representatives, Services, All Other; Sales Representatives, Wholesale and Manufacturing, Technical and Scientific Products; Securities, Commodities, and Financial Services Sales Agents. **PERSONALITY TYPE—Enterprising.** Enterprising occupations frequently involve starting up and carrying out projects. These occupations can involve leading people and making many decisions. They sometimes require risk taking and often deal with business.

EDUCATION/TRAINING PROGRAM(S)—Business, Management, Marketing, and Related Support Services, Other; Selling Skills and Sales Operations. RELATED KNOWLEDGE/COURSES—Sales and Marketing: Knowledge of principles and methods for showing, promoting, and selling products or services. This includes marketing strategy and tactics, product demonstration, sales techniques, and sales control systems. **English Language:** Knowledge of the structure and content of the English language, including the meaning and spelling of words, rules of composition, and grammar. **Customer and Personal Service:** Knowledge of principles and processes for providing customer and personal services. This includes customer needs assessment, meeting quality standards for services, and evaluation of customer satisfaction. **Computers and Electronics:** Knowledge of circuit boards, processors, chips, electronic equipment, and computer hardware and software, including applications and programming. **Engineering and Technology:** Knowledge of the practical application of engineering science and technology. This includes applying principles, techniques, procedures, and equipment to the design and production of various goods and services. **Principles of Mechanical Devices:** Knowledge of machines and tools, including their designs, uses, repair, and maintenance.

Sales Representatives, Mechanical Equipment and Supplies

▲ Education/Training Required: Moderate-term on-the-job training
▲ Annual Earnings: $54,360
▲ Growth: 7.5%
▲ Annual Job Openings: 24,000
▲ Self-Employed: 10.7%
▲ Part-Time: 22.3%

Sell mechanical equipment, machinery, materials, and supplies, such as aircraft and railroad equipment and parts, construction machinery, material-handling equipment, industrial machinery, and welding equipment. Recommends and sells textile, industrial, construction, railroad, and oil field machinery, equipment, materials, and supplies and services, utilizing knowledge of machine operations. Computes installation or production costs, estimates savings, and prepares and submits bid specifications to customer for review and approval. Submits orders for product and follows up on order to verify material list accuracy and ensure that delivery schedule meets project deadline. Appraises equipment and verifies customer credit rating to establish trade-in value and contract terms. Reviews existing machinery/equipment placement and diagrams proposal to illustrate efficient space utilization, using standard measuring devices and templates. Attends sales and trade meetings and reads related publications to obtain current market condition information, business trends, and industry developments. Inspects establishment premises to verify installation feasibility and obtains building blueprints and elevator specifications to submit to engineering department for bid. Demonstrates and explains use of installed equipment and production processes. Arranges for installation and test-operation of machinery and recommends solutions to product-related problems. Contacts current and potential customers, visits establishments to evaluate needs, and promotes sale of products and services. **SKILLS—Active Listening:** Giving full attention to what other people are saying, taking time to understand the points being made, asking questions as appropriate, and not interrupting at inappropriate times. **Reading Comprehension:** Understanding written sentences and paragraphs in work-related documents. **Speaking:** Talking to others to convey information effectively. **Equipment Selection:** Determining the kind of tools and equipment needed to do a job. **Operations Analysis:** Analyzing needs and product requirements to create a design.

GOE INFORMATION—Interest Area: 10. Sales and Marketing. **Work Group:** 10.02. Sales Technology. **Other Job Titles in This Work Group:** Advertising Sales Agents; Insurance Sales Agents; Sales Agents, Financial Services; Sales Agents, Securities and Commodities; Sales Representatives, Agricultural; Sales Representatives, Chemical and Pharmaceutical; Sales Representatives, Electrical/Electronic; Sales Representatives, Instruments; Sales Representatives, Medical; Sales Representatives, Services, All Other; Sales Representatives, Wholesale and Manufacturing, Technical and Scientific Products; Securities, Commodities, and Financial Services Sales Agents. **PERSONALITY TYPE—**Enterprising. Enterprising occupations frequently involve starting up and carrying out projects. These occupations can involve leading people and making many decisions. They sometimes require risk taking and often deal with business.

EDUCATION/TRAINING PROGRAM(S)—Business, Management, Marketing, and Related Support Services, Other; Selling Skills and Sales Operations. **RELATED KNOWLEDGE/COURSES—Sales and Marketing:** Knowledge of principles and methods for showing, promoting, and selling products or services. This includes marketing strategy and tactics, product demonstration, sales techniques, and sales control systems. **Mathematics:** Knowledge of arithmetic, algebra, geometry, calculus, and statistics and their applications. **Economics and Accounting:** Knowledge of economic and accounting principles and practices, the financial markets, banking, and the analysis and reporting of financial data. **Principles of Mechanical Devices:** Knowledge of machines and tools, including their designs, uses, repair, and maintenance. **Communications and Media:** Knowledge of media production, communication, and dissemination techniques and methods. This includes alternative ways to inform and entertain via written, oral, and visual media.

Sales Representatives, Medical

- ▲ Education/Training Required: Moderate-term on-the-job training
- ▲ Annual Earnings: $54,360
- ▲ Growth: 7.5%
- ▲ Annual Job Openings: 24,000
- ▲ Self-Employed: 10.7%
- ▲ Part-Time: 22.3%

Sell medical equipment, products, and services. Does not include pharmaceutical sales representatives. Promotes sale of medical and dental equipment, supplies, and services to doctors, dentists, hospitals, medical schools, and retail establishments. Writes specifications to order custom-made surgical appliances, using customer measurements and physician prescriptions. Advises customer regarding office layout, legal and insurance regulations, cost analysis, and collection methods. Designs and fabricates custom-made medical appliances. Selects surgical appliances from stock and fits and sells appliance to customer. Studies data describing new products to accurately recommend purchase of equipment and supplies. **SKILLS— Active Listening:** Giving full attention to what other people are saying, taking time to understand the points being made, asking questions as appropriate, and not interrupting at inappropriate times. **Reading Comprehension:** Understanding written sentences and paragraphs in work-related documents. **Writing:** Communicating effectively in writing as appropriate for the needs of the audience. **Speaking:** Talking to others to convey information effectively. **Equipment Selection:** Determining the kind of tools and equipment needed to do a job. **Persuasion:** Persuading others to change their minds or behavior. **Operations Analysis:** Analyzing needs and product requirements to create a design.

GOE INFORMATION—Interest Area: 10. Sales and Marketing. **Work Group:** 10.02. Sales Technology. **Other Job Titles in This Work Group:** Advertising Sales Agents; Insurance Sales Agents; Sales Agents, Financial Services; Sales Agents, Securities and Commodities; Sales Representatives, Agricultural; Sales Representatives, Chemical and Pharmaceutical; Sales Representatives, Electrical/Electronic; Sales Representatives, Instruments; Sales Representatives, Mechanical Equipment and Supplies; Sales Representatives, Services, All Other; Sales Representatives, Wholesale and Manufacturing, Technical and Scientific Products; Securities, Commodities, and Financial Services Sales Agents. **PERSONALITY TYPE—Enterprising.** Enterprising occupations frequently involve starting up and carrying out projects. These occupations can involve leading people and making many decisions. They sometimes require risk taking and often deal with business.

EDUCATION/TRAINING PROGRAM(S)—Business, Management, Marketing, and Related Support Services, Other; Selling Skills and Sales Operations. RELATED KNOWLEDGE/COURSES—Sales and Marketing: Knowledge of principles and methods for showing, promoting, and selling products or services. This includes marketing strategy and tactics, product demonstration, sales techniques, and sales control systems. **Mathematics:** Knowledge of arithmetic, algebra, geometry, calculus, and statistics and their applications. **Engineering and Technology:** Knowledge of the practical application of engineering science and technology. This includes applying principles, techniques, procedures, and equipment to the design and production of various goods and services. **Design:** Knowledge of design techniques, tools, and principles involved in production of precision technical plans, blueprints, drawings, and models. **Economics and Accounting:** Knowledge of economic and accounting principles and practices, the financial markets, banking, and the analysis and reporting of financial data.

Sales Representatives, Wholesale and Manufacturing, Except Technical and Scientific Products

▲ Education/Training Required: Moderate-term on-the-job training
▲ Annual Earnings: $41,520
▲ Growth: 5.7%
▲ Annual Job Openings: 86,000
▲ Self-Employed: 10.7%
▲ Part-Time: 22.3%

Sell goods for wholesalers or manufacturers to businesses or groups of individuals. Work requires substantial knowledge of items sold. Contacts regular and prospective customers to solicit orders. Recommends products to customers based on customer's specific needs and interests. Answers questions about products, prices, durability, and credit terms. Meets with customers to demonstrate and explain features of products. Prepares lists of prospective customers. Reviews sales records and current market information to determine value or sales potential of product. Estimates delivery dates and arranges delivery schedules. Completes sales contracts or forms to record sales information. Instructs customers in use of products. Assists and advises retail dealers in use of sales promotion techniques. Investigates and resolves customer complaints. Forwards orders to manufacturer. Assembles and stocks product displays in retail stores. Writes reports on sales and products. Prepares drawings, estimates, and bids to meet specific needs of customer. Obtains credit information on prospective customers. Oversees delivery or installation of products or equipment. **SKILLS—Speaking:** Talking to others to convey information effectively. **Active Listening:** Giving full attention to what other people are saying, taking time to understand the points being made, asking questions as appropriate, and not interrupting at inappropriate times. **Writing:** Communicating effectively in writing as appropriate for the needs of the audience. **Persuasion:** Persuading others to change their minds or behavior. **Service Orientation:** Actively looking for ways to help people. **Active Learning:** Understanding the implications of new information for both current and future problem-solving and decision-making. **Negotiation:** Bringing others together and trying to reconcile differences.

GOE INFORMATION—Interest Area: 10. Sales and Marketing. **Work Group:** 10.03. General Sales. **Other Job**

Titles in This Work Group: Parts Salespersons; Real Estate Brokers; Real Estate Sales Agents; Retail Salespersons; Service Station Attendants; Stock Clerks, Sales Floor; Travel Agents. **PERSONALITY TYPE—Enterprising.** Enterprising occupations frequently involve starting up and carrying out projects. These occupations can involve leading people and making many decisions. They sometimes require risk taking and often deal with business.

EDUCATION/TRAINING PROGRAM(S)—Apparel and Accessories Marketing Operations; Business, Management, Marketing, and Related Support Services, Other; Fashion Merchandising; General Merchandising, Sales, and Related Marketing Operations, Other; Sales, Distribution, and Marketing Operations, General; Special Products Marketing Operations; Specialized Merchandising, Sales, and Related Marketing Operations, Other. **RELATED KNOWLEDGE/COURSES—Sales and Marketing:** Knowledge of principles and methods for showing, promoting, and selling products or services. This includes marketing strategy and tactics, product demonstration, sales techniques, and sales control systems. **Customer and Personal Service:** Knowledge of principles and processes for providing customer and personal services. This includes customer needs assessment, meeting quality standards for services, and evaluation of customer satisfaction. **English Language:** Knowledge of the structure and content of the English language, including the meaning and spelling of words, rules of composition, and grammar. **Mathematics:** Knowledge of arithmetic, algebra, geometry, calculus, and statistics and their applications. **Communications and Media:** Knowledge of media production, communication, and dissemination techniques and methods. This includes alternative ways to inform and entertain via written, oral, and visual media.

Sales Representatives, Wholesale and Manufacturing, Technical and Scientific Products

- ▲ Education/Training Required: Moderate-term on-the-job training
- ▲ Annual Earnings: $54,360
- ▲ Growth: 7.5%
- ▲ Annual Job Openings: 24,000
- ▲ Self-Employed: 10.7%
- ▲ Part-Time: 22.3%

Sell goods for wholesalers or manufacturers where technical or scientific knowledge is required in such areas as biology, engineering, chemistry, and electronics, normally obtained from at least two years of post-secondary education. SKILLS—No data available.

GOE INFORMATION—Interest Area: 10. Sales and Marketing. Work Group: 10.02. Sales Technology. Other Job Titles in This Work Group: Advertising Sales Agents; Insurance Sales Agents; Sales Agents, Financial Services; Sales Agents, Securities and Commodities; Sales Representatives, Agricultural; Sales Representatives, Chemical and Pharmaceutical; Sales Representatives, Electrical/Electronic; Sales Representatives, Instruments; Sales Representatives, Mechanical Equipment and Supplies; Sales Representatives, Medical; Sales Representatives, Services, All Other; Securities, Commodities, and Financial Services Sales Agents. PERSONALITY TYPE—No data available.

EDUCATION/TRAINING PROGRAM(S)—Business, Management, Marketing, and Related Support Services, Other; Selling Skills and Sales Operations. RELATED KNOWLEDGE/COURSES—No data available.

Secondary School Teachers, Except Special and Vocational Education

- ▲ Education/Training Required: Bachelor's degree
- ▲ Annual Earnings: $43,280
- ▲ Growth: 18.6%
- ▲ Annual Job Openings: 60,000
- ▲ Self-Employed: 0%
- ▲ Part-Time: 10.6%

Instruct students in secondary public or private schools in one or more subjects at the secondary level, such as English, mathematics, or social studies. May be designated according to subject matter specialty, such as typing instructors, commercial teachers, or English teachers. Instructs students, using various teaching methods such as lecture and demonstration. Maintains discipline in classroom. Selects, stores, orders, issues, and inventories classroom equipment, materials, and supplies. Performs advisory duties, such as sponsoring student organizations or clubs, helping students select courses, and counseling students with problems. Keeps attendance records. Participates in faculty and professional meetings, educational conferences, and teacher training workshops. Confers with students, parents, and school counselors to resolve behavioral and academic problems. Develops and administers tests. Prepares course outlines and objectives according to curriculum guidelines or state and local requirements. Evaluates, records, and reports student progress. Uses audiovisual aids and other materials to supplement presentations. Assigns lessons and corrects homework. SKILLS—Learning Strategies: Selecting and using training/instructional methods and procedures appropriate for the situation when learning or teaching new things. Speaking: Talking to others to convey information effectively. Reading Comprehension: Understanding written sentences and paragraphs in work-related documents. Instructing: Teaching others how to do something. Mathematics: Using mathematics to solve problems.

GOE INFORMATION—Interest Area: 12. Education and Social Service. Work Group: 12.03. Educational Services. Other Job Titles in This Work Group: Adult Literacy, Remedial Education, and GED Teachers and Instructors; Agricultural Sciences Teachers, Postsecondary; Anthropology and Archeology Teachers, Postsecondary; Architecture Teachers, Postsecondary; Archivists; Area, Ethnic, and Cultural Studies Teachers, Postsecondary; Art,

Drama, and Music Teachers, Postsecondary; Atmospheric, Earth, Marine, and Space Sciences Teachers, Postsecondary; Audio-Visual Collections Specialists; Biological Science Teachers, Postsecondary; Business Teachers, Postsecondary; Chemistry Teachers, Postsecondary; Child Care Workers; Communications Teachers, Postsecondary; Computer Science Teachers, Postsecondary; Criminal Justice and Law Enforcement Teachers, Postsecondary; Curators; Economics Teachers, Postsecondary; Education Teachers, Postsecondary; Educational Psychologists; Educational, Vocational, and School Counselors; Elementary School Teachers, Except Special Education; Engineering Teachers, Postsecondary; English Language and Literature Teachers, Postsecondary; Environmental Science Teachers, Postsecondary; Farm and Home Management Advisors; Foreign Language and Literature Teachers, Postsecondary; Forestry and Conservation Science Teachers, Postsecondary; Geography Teachers, Postsecondary; Graduate Teaching Assistants; Health Specialties Teachers, Postsecondary; History Teachers, Postsecondary; Home Economics Teachers, Postsecondary; Kindergarten Teachers, Except Special Education; Law Teachers, Postsecondary; Librarians; Library Assistants, Clerical; Library Science Teachers, Postsecondary; Library Technicians; Mathematical Science Teachers, Postsecondary; Middle School Teachers, Except Special and Vocational Education; Museum Technicians and Conservators; Nursing Instructors and Teachers, Postsecondary; Personal Financial Advisors; Philosophy and Religion Teachers, Postsecondary; Physics Teachers, Postsecondary; Political Science Teachers, Postsecondary; Postsecondary Teachers, All Other; others. **PERSONALITY TYPE**—Social. Social occupations frequently involve working with, communicating with, and teaching people. These occupations often involve helping or providing service to others.

EDUCATION/TRAINING PROGRAM(S)—Agricultural Teacher Education; Art Teacher Education; Biology Teacher Education; Business Teacher Education; Chemistry Teacher Education; Computer Teacher Education; Drama and Dance Teacher Education; Driver and Safety Teacher Education; English/Language Arts Teacher Education; Family and Consumer Sciences/Home Economics Teacher Education; Foreign Language Teacher Education; French Language Teacher Education; Geography Teacher Education; German Language Teacher Education; Health Occupations Teacher Education; Health Teacher Education; History Teacher Education; Junior High/Intermediate/Middle School Education and Teaching; Latin Teacher Education; Mathematics Teacher Education; Music Teacher Education; Physical Education Teaching and Coaching; Physics Teacher Education; Reading Teacher Education; Sales and Marketing Operations/Marketing and Distribution Teacher Education; Science Teacher Education/General Science Teacher Education; Secondary Education and Teaching; Social Science Teacher Education; Social Studies Teacher Education; Spanish Language Teacher Education; Speech Teacher Education; Teacher Education and Professional Development, Specific Subject Areas, Other; Teacher Education, Multiple Levels; Technology Teacher Education/Industrial Arts Teacher Education. **RELATED KNOWLEDGE/COURSES**—**Education and Training:** Knowledge of principles and methods for curriculum and training design, teaching and instruction for individuals and groups, and the measurement of training effects. **English Language:** Knowledge of the structure and content of the English language, including the meaning and spelling of words, rules of composition, and grammar. **Mathematics:** Knowledge of arithmetic, algebra, geometry, calculus, and statistics and their applications. **Therapy and Counseling:** Knowledge of principles, methods, and procedures for diagnosis, treatment, and rehabilitation of physical and mental dysfunctions and for career counseling and guidance. **Clerical Studies:** Knowledge of administrative and clerical procedures and systems, such as word processing, managing files and records, stenography and transcription, designing forms, and other office procedures and terminology. **Psychology:** Knowledge of human behavior and performance; individual differences in ability, personality, and interests; learning and motivation; psychological research methods; and the assessment and treatment of behavioral and affective disorders.

Securities, Commodities, and Financial Services Sales Agents

- ▲ Education/Training Required: Bachelor's degree
- ▲ Annual Earnings: $59,690
- ▲ Growth: 22.3%
- ▲ Annual Job Openings: 55,000
- ▲ Self-Employed: 22.4%
- ▲ Part-Time: 8.6%

Buy and sell securities in investment and trading firms or call upon businesses and individuals to sell financial services. Provide financial services such as loan, tax, and securities counseling. May advise securities customers about such things as stocks, bonds, and market conditions. SKILLS—No data available.

GOE INFORMATION—Interest Area: 10. Sales and Marketing. Work Group: 10.02. Sales Technology. Other Job Titles in This Work Group: Advertising Sales Agents; Insurance Sales Agents; Sales Agents, Financial Services; Sales Agents, Securities and Commodities; Sales Representatives, Agricultural; Sales Representatives, Chemical and Pharmaceutical; Sales Representatives, Electrical/Electronic; Sales Representatives, Instruments; Sales Representatives, Mechanical Equipment and Supplies; Sales Representatives, Medical; Sales Representatives, Services, All Other; Sales Representatives, Wholesale and Manufacturing, Technical and Scientific Products. PERSONALITY TYPE—No data available.

EDUCATION/TRAINING PROGRAM(S)—Business and Personal/Financial Services Marketing Operations; Financial Planning and Services; Investments and Securities. RELATED KNOWLEDGE/COURSES—No data available.

Security and Fire Alarm Systems Installers

- ▲ Education/Training Required: Postsecondary vocational training
- ▲ Annual Earnings: $30,490
- ▲ Growth: 23.4%
- ▲ Annual Job Openings: 4,000
- ▲ Self-Employed: 0%
- ▲ Part-Time: 2.6%

Install, program, maintain, and repair security and fire alarm wiring and equipment. Ensure that work is in accordance with relevant codes. SKILLS—No data available.

GOE INFORMATION—Interest Area: 06. Construction, Mining, and Drilling. Work Group: 06.02. Construction. Other Job Titles in This Work Group: Boat Builders and Shipwrights; Boilermakers; Brattice Builders; Brickmasons and Blockmasons; Carpenters; Carpet Installers; Ceiling Tile Installers; Cement Masons and Concrete Finishers; Commercial Divers; Construction Carpenters; Drywall and Ceiling Tile Installers; Drywall Installers; Electricians; Explosives Workers, Ordnance Handling Experts, and Blasters; Fence Erectors; Floor Layers, Except Carpet, Wood, and Hard Tiles; Floor Sanders and Finishers; Glaziers; Grader, Bulldozer, and Scraper Operators; Hazardous Materials Removal Workers; Insulation Workers, Floor, Ceiling, and Wall; Insulation Workers, Mechanical; Manufactured Building and Mobile Home Installers; Operating Engineers; Operating Engineers and Other Construction Equipment Operators; Painters, Construction and Maintenance; Paperhangers; Paving, Surfacing, and Tamping Equipment Operators; Pile-Driver Operators; Pipe Fitters; Pipelayers; Pipelaying Fitters; Plasterers and Stucco Masons; Plumbers; Plumbers, Pipefitters, and Steamfitters; Rail-Track Laying and Maintenance Equipment Operators; Refractory Materials Repairers, Except Brickmasons; Reinforcing Iron and Rebar Workers; Riggers; Roofers; Rough Carpenters; Segmental Pavers; Sheet Metal Workers; Ship Carpenters and Joiners; Stone Cutters and Carvers; Stonemasons; Structural Iron and Steel Workers; Tapers; Terrazzo Workers and Finishers; Tile and Marble Setters. PERSONALITY TYPE—No data available.

EDUCATION/TRAINING PROGRAM(S)—Electrician; Security System Installation, Repair, and Inspection Technology/Technician. **RELATED KNOWLEDGE/ COURSES**—No data available.

Security Guards

- ▲ Education/Training Required: Short-term on-the-job training
- ▲ Annual Earnings: $18,600
- ▲ Growth: 35.4%
- ▲ Annual Job Openings: 242,000
- ▲ Self-Employed: 0.1%
- ▲ Part-Time: 19.8%

Guard, patrol, or monitor premises to prevent theft, violence, or infractions of rules. Patrols industrial and commercial premises to prevent and detect signs of intrusion and ensure security of doors, windows, and gates. Operates detecting devices to screen individuals and prevent passage of prohibited articles into restricted areas. Monitors and adjusts controls that regulate building systems, such as air conditioning, furnace, or boiler. Escorts or drives motor vehicle to transport individuals to specified locations and to provide personal protection. Writes reports of daily activities and irregularities, such as equipment or property damage, theft, presence of unauthorized persons, or unusual occurrences. Answers telephone calls to take messages, answer questions, and provide information during non-business hours or when switchboard is closed. Drives and guards armored vehicle to transport money and valuables to prevent theft and ensure safe delivery. Inspects and adjusts security systems, equipment, and machinery to ensure operational use and to detect evidence of tampering. Monitors and authorizes entrance and departure of employees, visitors, and other persons to guard against theft and maintain security of premises. Answers alarms and investigates disturbances. Circulates among visitors, patrons, and employees to preserve order and protect property. Calls police or fire departments in cases of emergency, such as fire or presence of unauthorized persons. Warns persons of rule infractions or violations; apprehends or evicts violators from premises, using force when necessary. **SKILLS**—**Active Listening:** Giving full attention to what other people are saying, taking time to understand the points being made, asking questions as appropriate, and not interrupting at inappropriate times. **Critical Thinking:** Using logic and reasoning to identify the strengths and weaknesses of alternative solutions, conclusions, or approaches to problems. **Writing:** Communicating effectively in writing as appropriate for the needs of the audience. **Speaking:** Talking to others to convey information effectively. **Judgment and Decision Making:** Considering the relative costs and benefits of potential actions to choose the most appropriate one. **Monitoring:** Monitoring/Assessing your performance or that of other individuals or organizations to make improvements or take corrective action. **Social Perceptiveness:** Being aware of others' reactions and understanding why they react as they do.

GOE INFORMATION—**Interest Area:** 04. Law, Law Enforcement, and Public Safety. **Work Group:** 04.03. Law Enforcement. **Other Job Titles in This Work Group:** Animal Control Workers; Bailiffs; Child Support, Missing Persons, and Unemployment Insurance Fraud Investigators; Correctional Officers and Jailers; Criminal Investigators and Special Agents; Crossing Guards; Detectives and Criminal Investigators; Fire Investigators; Fish and Game Wardens; Forensic Science Technicians; Gaming Surveillance Officers and Gaming Investigators; Highway Patrol Pilots; Immigration and Customs Inspectors; Lifeguards, Ski Patrol, and Other Recreational Protective Service Workers; Parking Enforcement Workers; Police and Sheriff's Patrol Officers; Police Detectives; Police Identification and Records Officers; Police Patrol Officers; Private Detectives and Investigators; Sheriffs and Deputy Sheriffs; Transit and Railroad Police. **PERSONALITY TYPE**—Social. Social occupations frequently involve working with, communicating with, and teaching people. These occupations often involve helping or providing service to others.

EDUCATION/TRAINING PROGRAM(S)—Securities Services Administration/Management; Security and Loss Prevention Services. **RELATED KNOWLEDGE/ COURSES**—**Public Safety and Security:** Knowledge of relevant equipment, policies, procedures, and strategies to promote effective local, state, or national security operations for the protection of people, data, property, and institutions. **Law and Government:** Knowledge of laws, legal codes, court procedures, precedents, government regulations, executive orders, agency rules, and the democratic political process. **English Language:** Knowledge of the structure and content of the English language, including the meaning and spelling of words, rules of composition, and grammar. **Customer and Personal Service:** Knowledge of principles and processes for providing customer and personal services. This includes customer needs assessment, meeting quality standards for services, and evaluation of customer satisfaction. **Telecommunications:** Knowledge of transmission, broadcasting, switching, control, and operation of telecommunications systems.

Segmental Pavers

▲ Education/Training Required: Moderate-term on-the-job training
▲ Annual Earnings: $26,170
▲ Growth: 26.7%
▲ Annual Job Openings: 21,000
▲ Self-Employed: 20.7%
▲ Part-Time: 8.5%

Lay out, cut, and paste segmental paving units. Includes installers of bedding and restraining materials for the paving units. SKILLS—No data available.

GOE INFORMATION—Interest Area: 06. Construction, Mining, and Drilling. Work Group: 06.02. Construction. Other Job Titles in This Work Group: Boat Builders and Shipwrights; Boilermakers; Brattice Builders; Brickmasons and Blockmasons; Carpenters; Carpet Installers; Ceiling Tile Installers; Cement Masons and Concrete Finishers; Commercial Divers; Construction Carpenters; Drywall and Ceiling Tile Installers; Drywall Installers; Electricians; Explosives Workers, Ordnance Handling Experts, and Blasters; Fence Erectors; Floor Layers, Except Carpet, Wood, and Hard Tiles; Floor Sanders and Finishers; Glaziers; Grader, Bulldozer, and Scraper Operators; Hazardous Materials Removal Workers; Insulation Workers, Floor, Ceiling, and Wall; Insulation Workers, Mechanical; Manufactured Building and Mobile Home Installers; Operating Engineers; Operating Engineers and Other Construction Equipment Operators; Painters, Construction and Maintenance; Paperhangers; Paving, Surfacing, and Tamping Equipment Operators; Pile-Driver Operators; Pipe Fitters; Pipelayers; Pipelaying Fitters; Plasterers and Stucco Masons; Plumbers; Plumbers, Pipefitters, and Steamfitters; Rail-Track Laying and Maintenance Equipment Operators; Refractory Materials Repairers, Except Brickmasons; Reinforcing Iron and Rebar Workers; Riggers; Roofers; Rough Carpenters; Security and Fire Alarm Systems Installers; Sheet Metal Workers; Ship Carpenters and Joiners; Stone Cutters and Carvers; Stonemasons; Structural Iron and Steel Workers; Tapers; Terrazzo Workers and Finishers; Tile and Marble Setters. **PERSONALITY TYPE**—No data available.

EDUCATION/TRAINING PROGRAM(S)—Concrete Finishing/Concrete Finisher. **RELATED KNOWLEDGE/COURSES**—No data available.

Self-Enrichment Education Teachers

▲ Education/Training Required: Work experience in a related occupation
▲ Annual Earnings: $28,880
▲ Growth: 18.5%
▲ Annual Job Openings: 34,000
▲ Self-Employed: 48.9%
▲ Part-Time: 42.5%

Teach or instruct courses other than those that normally lead to an occupational objective or degree. Courses may include self-improvement, nonvocational, and nonacademic subjects. Teaching may or may not take place in a traditional educational institution. Conducts classes, workshops, and demonstrations to teach principles, techniques, procedures, or methods of designated subject. Plans and conducts field trips to enrich instructional programs. Orders, stores, and inventories books, materials, and supplies. Writes instructional articles on designated subjects. Maintains records such as student grades, attendance, and supply inventory. Confers with leaders of government and other groups to coordinate training or to assist students in fulfilling required criteria. Evaluates success of instruction based on number and enthusiasm of participants and recommends retaining or eliminating course in future. Plans course content and method of instruction. Selects and assembles books, materials, and supplies for courses or projects. Observes students to determine and evaluate qualifications, limitations, abilities, interests, aptitudes, temperament, and individual characteristics. Directs and supervises student project activities, performances, tournaments, exhibits, contests, or plays. Prepares outline of instructional program and lesson plans and establishes course goals. Administers oral, written, and performance tests and issues grades in accordance with performance. Presents lectures and conducts discussions to increase students' knowledge and competence. **SKILLS—Writing:** Communicating effectively in writing as appropriate for the needs of the audience. **Speaking:** Talking to others to convey information effectively. **Reading Comprehension:** Understanding written sentences and paragraphs in work-related documents. **Instructing:** Teaching others how to do something. **Active Listening:** Giving full attention to what other people are saying, taking time to understand the points being made, asking questions as appropriate, and not interrupting at inappropriate times.

GOE INFORMATION—Interest Area: 12. Education and Social Service. **Work Group:** 12.03. Educational Services. **Other Job Titles in This Work Group:** Adult Literacy, Remedial Education, and GED Teachers and Instructors; Agricultural Sciences Teachers, Postsecondary; Anthropology and Archeology Teachers, Postsecondary; Architecture Teachers, Postsecondary; Archivists; Area, Ethnic, and Cultural Studies Teachers, Postsecondary; Art, Drama, and Music Teachers, Postsecondary; Atmospheric, Earth, Marine, and Space Sciences Teachers, Postsecondary; Audio-Visual Collections Specialists; Biological Science Teachers, Postsecondary; Business Teachers, Postsecondary; Chemistry Teachers, Postsecondary; Child Care Workers; Communications Teachers, Postsecondary; Computer Science Teachers, Postsecondary; Criminal Justice and Law Enforcement Teachers, Postsecondary; Curators; Economics Teachers, Postsecondary; Education Teachers, Postsecondary; Educational Psychologists; Educational, Vocational, and School Counselors; Elementary School Teachers, Except Special Education; Engineering Teachers, Postsecondary; English Language and Literature Teachers, Postsecondary; Environmental Science Teachers, Postsecondary; Farm and

Home Management Advisors; Foreign Language and Literature Teachers, Postsecondary; Forestry and Conservation Science Teachers, Postsecondary; Geography Teachers, Postsecondary; Graduate Teaching Assistants; Health Specialties Teachers, Postsecondary; History Teachers, Postsecondary; Home Economics Teachers, Postsecondary; Kindergarten Teachers, Except Special Education; Law Teachers, Postsecondary; Librarians; Library Assistants, Clerical; Library Science Teachers, Postsecondary; Library Technicians; Mathematical Science Teachers, Postsecondary; Middle School Teachers, Except Special and Vocational Education; Museum Technicians and Conservators; Nursing Instructors and Teachers, Postsecondary; Personal Financial Advisors; Philosophy and Religion Teachers, Postsecondary; Physics Teachers, Postsecondary; Political Science Teachers, Postsecondary; Postsecondary Teachers, All Other; others. **PERSONALITY TYPE—** Social. Social occupations frequently involve working with, communicating with, and teaching people. These occupations often involve helping or providing service to others.

EDUCATION/TRAINING PROGRAM(S)—Adult and Continuing Education and Teaching. **RELATED KNOWLEDGE/COURSES—Education and Training:** Knowledge of principles and methods for curriculum and training design, teaching and instruction for individuals and groups, and the measurement of training effects. **English Language:** Knowledge of the structure and content of the English language, including the meaning and spelling of words, rules of composition, and grammar. **Administration and Management:** Knowledge of business and management principles involved in strategic planning, resource allocation, human resources modeling, leadership technique, production methods, and coordination of people and resources. **Mathematics:** Knowledge of arithmetic, algebra, geometry, calculus, and statistics and their applications. **Psychology:** Knowledge of human behavior and performance; individual differences in ability, personality, and interests; learning and motivation; psychological research methods; and the assessment and treatment of behavioral and affective disorders. **Sociology and Anthropology:** Knowledge of group behavior and dynamics, societal trends and influences, human migrations, ethnicity, and cultures and their history and origins. **Computers and Electronics:** Knowledge of circuit boards, processors, chips, electronic equipment, and computer hardware and software, including applications and programming.

Semiconductor Processors

- ▲ Education/Training Required: Associate's degree
- ▲ Annual Earnings: $26,480
- ▲ Growth: 32.4%
- ▲ Annual Job Openings: 7,000
- ▲ Self-Employed: 0%
- ▲ Part-Time: 2.7%

Perform any or all of the following functions in the manufacture of electronic semiconductors: load semiconductor material into furnace; saw formed ingots into segments; load individual segment into crystal growing chamber and monitor controls; locate crystal axis in ingot, using X-ray equipment, and saw ingots into wafers; clean, polish, and load wafers into series of special-purpose furnaces, chemical baths, and equipment used to form circuitry and change conductive properties. Measures and weighs amounts of crystal growing materials, mixes and grinds materials, and loads materials into container, following procedures. Forms seed crystal for crystal growing or locates crystal axis of ingot, using X-ray equipment, drill, and sanding machine. Aligns photo mask pattern on photoresist layer, exposes pattern to ultraviolet light, and develops pattern, using specialized equipment. Attaches ampoule to diffusion pump to remove air from ampoule and seals ampoule, using blowtorch. Places semiconductor wafers in processing containers or equipment holders, using vacuum wand or tweezers. Monitors operation and adjusts controls of processing machines and equipment to produce compositions with specific electronic properties. Manipulates valves, switches, and buttons or keys commands into control panels to start semiconductor processing cycles. Etches, laps, polishes, or grinds wafers or ingots, using etching, lapping, polishing, or grinding equipment. Operates saw to cut remelt into sections of specified size or to cut ingots into wafers. Cleans and dries materials and equipment, using solvent, etching or sandblasting equipment, and drying equipment to remove contaminants or photoresist. Studies work order, instructions, formulas, and processing charts to determine specifications and sequence of operations. Loads and unloads equipment chambers and transports finished product to storage or to area for further processing. Inspects materials, components, or products for surface defects and measures circuitry, using electronic test equipment, precision measuring instruments, and standard procedures. Counts, sorts, and weighs processed items. Stamps or etches identifying information on finished component. Main-

tains processing, production, and inspection information and reports. **SKILLS—Operation Monitoring:** Watching gauges, dials, or other indicators to make sure a machine is working properly. **Operation and Control:** Controlling operations of equipment or systems. **Science:** Using scientific rules and methods to solve problems. **Equipment Selection:** Determining the kind of tools and equipment needed to do a job. **Reading Comprehension:** Understanding written sentences and paragraphs in work-related documents. **Mathematics:** Using mathematics to solve problems. **Writing:** Communicating effectively in writing as appropriate for the needs of the audience.

GOE INFORMATION—Interest Area: 08. Industrial Production. **Work Group:** 08.03. Production Work. **Other Job Titles in This Work Group:** Bakers, Manufacturing; Bindery Machine Operators and Tenders; Brazers; Cementing and Gluing Machine Operators and Tenders; Chemical Equipment Controllers and Operators; Chemical Equipment Operators and Tenders; Chemical Equipment Tenders; Cleaning, Washing, and Metal Pickling Equipment Operators and Tenders; Coating, Painting, and Spraying Machine Operators and Tenders; Coil Winders, Tapers, and Finishers; Combination Machine Tool Operators and Tenders, Metal and Plastic; Computer-Controlled Machine Tool Operators, Metal and Plastic; Cooling and Freezing Equipment Operators and Tenders; Crushing, Grinding, and Polishing Machine Setters, Operators, and Tenders; Cutters and Trimmers, Hand; Cutting and Slicing Machine Operators and Tenders; Cutting and Slicing Machine Setters, Operators, and Tenders; Design Printing Machine Setters and Set-Up Operators; Electrolytic Plating and Coating Machine Operators and Tenders, Metal and Plastic; Electrolytic Plating and Coating Machine Setters and Set-Up Operators, Metal and Plastic; Electrotypers and Stereotypers; Embossing Machine Set-Up Operators; Engraver Set-Up Operators; Extruding and Forming Machine Operators and Tenders, Synthetic or Glass Fibers; Extruding and Forming Machine Setters, Operators, and Tenders, Synthetic and Glass Fibers; Extruding, Forming, Pressing, and Compacting

Machine Operators and Tenders; Fabric and Apparel Patternmakers; Fiber Product Cutting Machine Setters and Set-Up Operators; Fiberglass Laminators and Fabricators; Film Laboratory Technicians; Fitters, Structural Metal—Precision; Food and Tobacco Roasting, Baking, and Drying Machine Operators and Tenders; Food Batchmakers; Food Cooking Machine Operators and Tenders; Furnace, Kiln, Oven, Drier, and Kettle Operators and Tenders; Glass Cutting Machine Setters and Set-Up Operators; Graders and Sorters, Agricultural Products; Grinding and Polishing Workers, Hand; Hand Compositors and Typesetters; Heaters, Metal and Plastic; others. **PERSONALITY TYPE**—Realistic. Realistic occupations frequently involve work activities that include practical, hands-on problems and solutions. They often deal with plants, animals, and real-world materials like wood, tools, and machinery. Many of the occupations require working outside and do not involve a lot of paperwork or working closely with others.

EDUCATION/TRAINING PROGRAM(S)—Industrial Electronics Technology/Technician. **RELATED KNOWLEDGE/COURSES—Production and Processing:** Knowledge of raw materials, production processes, quality control, costs, and other techniques for maximizing the effective manufacture and distribution of goods. **Mathematics:** Knowledge of arithmetic, algebra, geometry, calculus, and statistics and their applications. **Principles of Mechanical Devices:** Knowledge of machines and tools, including their designs, uses, repair, and maintenance. **Engineering and Technology:** Knowledge of the practical application of engineering science and technology. This includes applying principles, techniques, procedures, and equipment to the design and production of various goods and services. **Computers and Electronics:** Knowledge of circuit boards, processors, chips, electronic equipment, and computer hardware and software, including applications and programming.

Set and Exhibit Designers

- ▲ Education/Training Required: Bachelor's degree
- ▲ Annual Earnings: $33,460
- ▲ Growth: 27.0%
- ▲ Annual Job Openings: 2,000
- ▲ Self-Employed: 31.9%
- ▲ Part-Time: 20.0%

Design special exhibits and movie, television, and theater sets. May study scripts, confer with directors, and conduct research to determine appropriate architectural styles. SKILLS—No data available.

GOE INFORMATION—Interest Area: 01. Arts, Entertainment, and Media. **Work Group:** 01.04. Visual Arts. **Other Job Titles in This Work Group:** Cartoonists; Commercial and Industrial Designers; Designers, All Other; Exhibit Designers; Fashion Designers; Fine Artists, Including Painters, Sculptors, and Illustrators; Floral Designers; Graphic Designers; Interior Designers; Merchandise Displayers and Window Trimmers; Multi-Media Artists and Animators; Painters and Illustrators; Sculptors; Set Designers; Sketch Artists. **PERSONALITY TYPE**—No data available.

EDUCATION/TRAINING PROGRAM(S)—Design and Applied Arts, Other; Design and Visual Communications, General; Illustration; Technical Theatre/Theatre Design and Technology. **RELATED KNOWLEDGE/COURSES**—No data available.

Set Designers

- ▲ Education/Training Required: Bachelor's degree
- ▲ Annual Earnings: $33,460
- ▲ Growth: 27.0%
- ▲ Annual Job Openings: 2,000
- ▲ Self-Employed: 31.9%
- ▲ Part-Time: 20.0%

Design sets for theatrical, motion picture, and television productions. Integrates requirements, including script, research, budget, and available locations, to develop design. Presents drawings for approval and makes changes and corrections as directed. Selects furniture, draperies, pictures, lamps, and rugs for decorative quality and appearance. Confers with heads of production and direction to establish budget and schedules and discuss design ideas. Directs and coordinates set construction, erection, or decoration activities to ensure conformance to design, budget, and schedule requirements. Assigns staff to complete design ideas and prepare sketches, illustrations, and detailed drawings of sets or graphics and animation. Examines dressed set to ensure that props and scenery do not interfere with movements of cast or view of camera. Reads script to determine location, set, or decoration requirements. Estimates costs of design materials and construction or rental of location or props. Researches and consults experts to determine architectural and furnishing styles to depict given periods or locations. Designs and builds scale models of set design or miniature sets used in filming backgrounds or special effects. Prepares rough draft and scale working drawings of sets, including floor plans, scenery, and properties to be constructed. **SKILLS—Reading Comprehension:** Understanding written sentences and paragraphs in work-related documents. **Management of Material Resources:** Obtaining and seeing to the appropriate use of equipment, facilities, and materials needed to do certain work. **Active Listening:** Giving full attention to what other people are saying, taking time to understand the points being made, asking questions as appropriate, and not interrupting at inappropriate times. **Coordination:** Adjusting actions in relation to others' actions. **Active Learning:** Understanding the implications of new information for both current and future problem-solving and decision-making. **Management of Financial Resources:** Determining how money will be spent to get the work done and accounting for these expenditures. **Critical Thinking:** Using logic and reasoning to identify the strengths and weaknesses of alternative solutions, conclusions, or approaches to problems.

GOE INFORMATION—Interest Area: 01. Arts, Entertainment, and Media. **Work Group:** 01.04. Visual Arts. **Other Job Titles in This Work Group:** Cartoonists; Commercial and Industrial Designers; Designers, All Other; Exhibit Designers; Fashion Designers; Fine Artists, Including Painters, Sculptors, and Illustrators; Floral Designers; Graphic Designers; Interior Designers; Merchandise Displayers and Window Trimmers; Multi-Media Artists and Animators; Painters and Illustrators; Sculptors; Set and Exhibit Designers; Sketch Artists. **PERSONALITY TYPE—Artistic.** Artistic occupations frequently involve working with forms, designs, and patterns. They often require self-expression, and the work can be done without following a clear set of rules.

EDUCATION/TRAINING PROGRAM(S)—Design and Applied Arts, Other; Design and Visual Communications, General; Illustration; Technical Theatre/Theatre Design and Technology. RELATED KNOWLEDGE/COURSES—Design: Knowledge of design techniques, tools, and principles involved in production of precision technical plans, blueprints, drawings, and models. **Fine Arts:** Knowledge of the theory and techniques required to compose, produce, and perform works of music, dance, visual arts, drama, and sculpture. **Building and Construction:** Knowledge of materials, methods, and tools involved in the construction or repair of houses, buildings, or other structures, such as highways and roads. **Sociology and Anthropology:** Knowledge of group behavior and dynamics, societal trends and influences, human migrations, ethnicity, and cultures and their history and origins. **English Language:** Knowledge of the structure and content of the English language, including the meaning and spelling of words, rules of composition, and grammar. **Psychology:** Knowledge of human behavior and performance; individual differences in ability, personality, and interests; learning and motivation; psychological research methods; and the assessment and treatment of behavioral and affective disorders.

Sheet Metal Workers

▲ Education/Training Required: Moderate-term on-the-job training
▲ Annual Earnings: $33,210
▲ Growth: 23.0%
▲ Annual Job Openings: 13,000
▲ Self-Employed: 2.7%
▲ Part-Time: 4.4%

Fabricate, assemble, install, and repair sheet metal products and equipment, such as ducts, control boxes, drain-

pipes, and furnace casings. Work may involve any of the following: setting up and operating fabricating machines to cut, bend, and straighten sheet metal; shaping metal over anvils, blocks, or forms, using hammer; operating soldering and welding equipment to join sheet metal parts; and inspecting, assembling, and smoothing seams and joints of burred surfaces. Sets up and operates fabricating machines, such as shears, brakes, presses, and routers, to cut, bend, block, and form materials. Selects gauge and type of sheet metal or nonmetallic material according to product specifications. Inspects assemblies and installation for conformance to specifications, using measuring instruments such as calipers, scales, dial indicators, gauges, and micrometers. Determines sequence and methods of fabricating, assembling, and installing sheet metal products, using blueprints, sketches, or product specifications. Welds, solders, bolts, rivets, screws, clips, caulks, or bonds component parts to assemble products, using hand tools, power tools, and equipment. Trims, files, grinds, deburrs, buffs, and smoothes surfaces, using hand tools and portable power tools. Installs assemblies in supportive framework according to blueprints, using hand tools, power tools, and lifting and handling devices. Lays out and marks dimensions and reference lines on material, using scribes, dividers, squares, and rulers. Shapes metal material over anvil, block, or other form, using hand tools. **SKILLS— Installation:** Installing equipment, machines, wiring, or programs to meet specifications. **Mathematics:** Using mathematics to solve problems. **Equipment Selection:** Determining the kind of tools and equipment needed to do a job. **Operation and Control:** Controlling operations of equipment or systems. **Coordination:** Adjusting actions in relation to others' actions.

GOE INFORMATION—Interest Area: 06. Construction, Mining, and Drilling. **Work Group:** 06.02. Construction. **Other Job Titles in This Work Group:** Boat Builders and Shipwrights; Boilermakers; Brattice Builders; Brickmasons and Blockmasons; Carpenters; Carpet Installers; Ceiling Tile Installers; Cement Masons and Concrete Finishers; Commercial Divers; Construction Carpenters; Drywall and Ceiling Tile Installers; Drywall Installers; Electricians; Explosives Workers, Ordnance Handling Experts, and Blasters; Fence Erectors; Floor Layers, Except Carpet, Wood, and Hard Tiles; Floor Sanders

and Finishers; Glaziers; Grader, Bulldozer, and Scraper Operators; Hazardous Materials Removal Workers; Insulation Workers, Floor, Ceiling, and Wall; Insulation Workers, Mechanical; Manufactured Building and Mobile Home Installers; Operating Engineers; Operating Engineers and Other Construction Equipment Operators; Painters, Construction and Maintenance; Paperhangers; Paving, Surfacing, and Tamping Equipment Operators; Pile-Driver Operators; Pipe Fitters; Pipelayers; Pipelaying Fitters; Plasterers and Stucco Masons; Plumbers; Plumbers, Pipefitters, and Steamfitters; Rail-Track Laying and Maintenance Equipment Operators; Refractory Materials Repairers, Except Brickmasons; Reinforcing Iron and Rebar Workers; Riggers; Roofers; Rough Carpenters; Security and Fire Alarm Systems Installers; Segmental Pavers; Ship Carpenters and Joiners; Stone Cutters and Carvers; Stonemasons; Structural Iron and Steel Workers; Tapers; Terrazzo Workers and Finishers; Tile and Marble Setters. **PERSONALITY TYPE—**Realistic. Realistic occupations frequently involve work activities that include practical, hands-on problems and solutions. They often deal with plants, animals, and real-world materials like wood, tools, and machinery. Many of the occupations require working outside and do not involve a lot of paperwork or working closely with others.

EDUCATION/TRAINING PROGRAM(S)—Sheet Metal Technology/Sheetworking. **RELATED KNOWLEDGE/COURSES—Production and Processing:** Knowledge of raw materials, production processes, quality control, costs, and other techniques for maximizing the effective manufacture and distribution of goods. **Principles of Mechanical Devices:** Knowledge of machines and tools, including their designs, uses, repair, and maintenance. **Design:** Knowledge of design techniques, tools, and principles involved in production of precision technical plans, blueprints, drawings, and models. **Computers and Electronics:** Knowledge of circuit boards, processors, chips, electronic equipment, and computer hardware and software, including applications and programming. **Building and Construction:** Knowledge of materials, methods, and tools involved in the construction or repair of houses, buildings, or other structures, such as highways and roads.

Sheriffs and Deputy Sheriffs

▲ Education/Training Required: Long-term on-the-job training
▲ Annual Earnings: $40,970
▲ Growth: 23.2%
▲ Annual Job Openings: 21,000
▲ Self-Employed: 0%
▲ Part-Time: 2.7%

Enforce law and order in rural or unincorporated districts or serve legal processes of courts. May patrol courthouse, guard court or grand jury, or escort defendants. Serves subpoenas and summonses. Executes arrest warrants, locating and taking persons into custody and issues citations. Patrols and guards courthouse, grand jury room, or assigned areas to provide security, enforce laws, maintain order, and arrest violators. Confiscates real or personal property by court order and posts notices in public places. Takes control of accident scene to maintain traffic flow, assist accident victims, and investigate causes. Investigates illegal or suspicious activities of persons. Transports or escorts prisoners or defendants between courtroom, prison or jail, district attorney's offices, or medical facilities. Questions individuals entering secured areas to determine purpose of business and directs or reroutes individuals to destinations. Maintains records, submits reports of dispositions, and logs daily activities. Arranges delivery of prisoner's arrest records from criminal investigation unit at district attorney's request. Notifies patrol units to take violators into custody or provide needed assistance or medical aid. **SKILLS—Social Perceptiveness:** Being aware of others' reactions and understanding why they react as they do. **Active Listening:** Giving full attention to what other people are saying, taking time to understand the points being made, asking questions as appropriate, and not interrupting at inappropriate times. **Speaking:** Talking to others to convey information effectively. **Judgment and Decision Making:** Considering the relative costs and benefits of potential actions to choose the most appropriate one. **Coordination:** Adjusting actions in relation to others' actions. **Reading Comprehension:** Understanding written sentences and paragraphs in work-related documents.

GOE INFORMATION—Interest Area: 04. Law, Law Enforcement, and Public Safety. **Work Group:** 04.03. Law Enforcement. **Other Job Titles in This Work Group:** Animal Control Workers; Bailiffs; Child Support, Missing Persons, and Unemployment Insurance Fraud Investigators; Correctional Officers and Jailers; Criminal Investigators and Special Agents; Crossing Guards; Detectives and Criminal Investigators; Fire Investigators; Fish and Game Wardens; Forensic Science Technicians; Gaming Surveillance Officers and Gaming Investigators; Highway Patrol Pilots; Immigration and Customs Inspectors; Lifeguards, Ski Patrol, and Other Recreational Protective Service Workers; Parking Enforcement Workers; Police and Sheriff's Patrol Officers; Police Detectives; Police Identification and Records Officers; Police Patrol Officers; Private Detectives and Investigators; Security Guards; Transit and Railroad Police. **PERSONALITY TYPE—Social.** Social occupations frequently involve working with, communicating with, and teaching people. These occupations often involve helping or providing service to others.

EDUCATION/TRAINING PROGRAM(S)—Criminal Justice/Police Science; Criminalistics and Criminal Science. RELATED KNOWLEDGE/COURSES—Public Safety and Security: Knowledge of relevant equipment, policies, procedures, and strategies to promote effective local, state, or national security operations for the protection of people, data, property, and institutions. **Law and Government:** Knowledge of laws, legal codes, court procedures, precedents, government regulations, executive orders, agency rules, and the democratic political process. **Psychology:** Knowledge of human behavior and performance; individual differences in ability, personality, and interests; learning and motivation; psychological research methods; and the assessment and treatment of behavioral and affective disorders. **Geography:** Knowledge of principles and methods for describing the features of land, sea, and air masses, including their physical characteristics, locations, interrelationships, and distribution of plant, animal, and human life. **Clerical Studies:** Knowledge of administrative and clerical procedures and systems, such as word processing, managing files and records, stenography and transcription, designing forms, and other office procedures and terminology.

Ship Carpenters and Joiners

▲ Education/Training Required: Moderate-term on-the-job training
▲ Annual Earnings: $33,470
▲ Growth: 8.2%
▲ Annual Job Openings: 161,000
▲ Self-Employed: 36.8%
▲ Part-Time: 8.1%

Fabricate, assemble, install, or repair wooden furnishings in ships or boats. Reads blueprints to determine dimensions of furnishings in ships or boats. Shapes and laminates wood to form parts of ship, using steam chambers, clamps, glue, and jigs. Repairs structural woodwork and replaces defective parts and equipment, using hand tools and power tools. Shapes irregular parts and trims excess material from bulkhead and furnishings to ensure that fit meets specifications. Constructs floors, doors, and partitions, using woodworking machines, hand tools, and power tools. Cuts wood or glass to specified dimensions, using hand tools and power tools. Assembles and installs hardware, gaskets, floors, furnishings, or insulation, using adhesive, hand tools, and power tools. Transfers dimensions or measurements of wood parts or bulkhead on plywood, using measuring instruments and marking devices. Greases gears and other moving parts of machines on ship. **SKILLS—Installation:** Installing equipment, machines, wiring, or programs to meet specifications. **Monitoring:** Monitoring/Assessing your performance or that of other individuals or organizations to make improvements or take corrective action. **Repairing:** Repairing machines or systems, using the needed tools. **Mathematics:** Using mathematics to solve problems. **Equipment Selection:** Determining the kind of tools and equipment needed to do a job.

GOE INFORMATION—Interest Area: 06. Construction, Mining, and Drilling. **Work Group:** 06.02. Construction. **Other Job Titles in This Work Group:** Boat Builders and Shipwrights; Boilermakers; Brattice Builders; Brickmasons and Blockmasons; Carpenters; Carpet Installers; Ceiling Tile Installers; Cement Masons and Concrete Finishers; Commercial Divers; Construction Carpenters; Drywall and Ceiling Tile Installers; Drywall Installers; Electricians; Explosives Workers, Ordnance Handling Experts, and Blasters; Fence Erectors; Floor Layers, Except Carpet, Wood, and Hard Tiles; Floor Sanders and Finishers; Glaziers; Grader, Bulldozer, and Scraper Operators; Hazardous Materials Removal Workers; Insulation Workers, Floor, Ceiling, and Wall; Insulation Workers, Mechanical; Manufactured Building and Mobile Home Installers; Operating Engineers; Operating Engineers and Other Construction Equipment Operators; Painters, Construction and Maintenance; Paperhangers; Paving, Surfacing, and Tamping Equipment Operators; Pile-Driver Operators; Pipe Fitters; Pipelayers; Pipelaying Fitters; Plasterers and Stucco Masons; Plumbers; Plumbers, Pipefitters, and Steamfitters; Rail-Track Laying and Maintenance Equipment Operators; Refractory Materials Repairers, Except Brickmasons; Reinforcing Iron and Rebar Workers; Riggers; Roofers; Rough Carpenters; Security and Fire Alarm Systems Installers; Segmental Pavers; Sheet Metal Workers; Stone Cutters and Carvers; Stonemasons; Structural Iron and Steel Workers; Tapers; Terrazzo Workers and Finishers; Tile and Marble Setters. **PERSONALITY TYPE**—Realistic. Realistic occupations frequently involve work activities that include practical, hands-on problems and solutions. They often deal with plants, animals, and real-world materials like wood, tools, and machinery. Many of the occupations require working outside and do not involve a lot of paperwork or working closely with others.

EDUCATION/TRAINING PROGRAM(S)—Carpentry/Carpenter. **RELATED KNOWLEDGE/COURSES—Building and Construction:** Knowledge of materials, methods, and tools involved in the construction or repair of houses, buildings, or other structures, such as highways and roads. **Design:** Knowledge of design techniques, tools, and principles involved in production of precision technical plans, blueprints, drawings, and models. **Engineering and Technology:** Knowledge of the practical application of engineering science and technology. This includes applying principles, techniques, procedures, and equipment to the design and production of various goods and services. **Principles of Mechanical Devices:** Knowledge of machines and tools, including their designs, uses, repair, and maintenance. **Mathematics:** Knowledge of arithmetic, algebra, geometry, calculus, and statistics and their applications.

Shipping, Receiving, and Traffic Clerks

▲ Education/Training Required: Short-term on-the-job training
▲ Annual Earnings: $22,710
▲ Growth: 9.3%
▲ Annual Job Openings: 133,000
▲ Self-Employed: 0%
▲ Part-Time: 9.6%

Verify and keep records on incoming and outgoing shipments. Prepare items for shipment. Duties include assembling, addressing, stamping, and shipping merchandise or material; receiving, unpacking, verifying and recording incoming merchandise or material; and arranging for the transportation of products. Examines contents and compares with records, such as manifests, invoices, or orders, to verify accuracy of incoming or outgoing shipment. Confers and corresponds with establishment representatives to rectify problems such as damages, shortages, and nonconformance to specifications. Requisitions and stores shipping materials and supplies to maintain inventory of stock. Delivers or routes materials to departments, using work devices such as hand truck, conveyor, or sorting bins. Computes amounts such as space available and shipping, storage, and demurrage charges using calculator or price list. Records shipment data such as weight, charges, space availability, and damages and discrepancies for reporting, accounting, and record-keeping purposes. Contacts carrier representative to make arrangements and to issue instructions for shipping and delivery of materials. Packs, seals, labels, and affixes postage to prepare materials for shipping, using work devices such as hand tools, power tools, and postage meter. Prepares documents such as work orders, bills of lading, and shipping orders to route materials. Determines shipping method for materials, using knowledge of shipping procedures, routes, and rates. **SKILLS—Reading Comprehension:** Understanding written sentences and paragraphs in work-related documents. **Critical Thinking:** Using logic and reasoning to identify the strengths and weaknesses of alternative solutions, conclusions, or approaches to problems. **Mathematics:** Using mathematics to solve problems. **Service Orientation:** Actively looking for ways to help people. **Active Listening:** Giving full attention to what other people are saying, taking time to understand the points being made, asking questions as appropriate, and not interrupting at inappropriate times. **Writing:** Communicating effectively in writing as appropriate for the needs of the audience.

GOE INFORMATION—Interest Area: 09. Business Detail. **Work Group:** 09.08. Records and Materials Processing. **Other Job Titles in This Work Group:** Cargo and Freight Agents; Couriers and Messengers; Mail Clerks, Except Mail Machine Operators and Postal Service; Marking Clerks; Order Fillers, Wholesale and Retail Sales; Postal Service Mail Carriers; Postal Service Mail Sorters, Processors, and Processing Machine Operators; Stock Clerks and Order Fillers; Stock Clerks—Stockroom, Warehouse, or Storage Yard; Weighers, Measurers, Checkers, and Samplers, Recordkeeping. **PERSONALITY TYPE—**Conventional. Conventional occupations frequently involve following set procedures and routines. These occupations can include working with data and details more than with ideas. Usually there is a clear line of authority to follow.

EDUCATION/TRAINING PROGRAM(S)—General Office Occupations and Clerical Services; Traffic, Customs, and Transportation Clerk/Technician. **RELATED KNOWLEDGE/COURSES—Transportation:** Knowledge of principles and methods for moving people or goods by air, rail, sea, or road, including the relative costs and benefits. **Clerical Studies:** Knowledge of administrative and clerical procedures and systems, such as word processing, managing files and records, stenography and transcription, designing forms, and other office procedures and terminology. **Production and Processing:** Knowledge of raw materials, production processes, quality control, costs, and other techniques for maximizing the effective manufacture and distribution of goods. **Mathematics:** Knowledge of arithmetic, algebra, geometry, calculus, and statistics and their applications. **Computers and Electronics:** Knowledge of circuit boards, processors, chips, electronic equipment, and computer hardware and software, including applications and programming. **English Language:** Knowledge of the structure and content of the English language, including the meaning and spelling of words, rules of composition, and grammar. **Economics and Accounting:** Knowledge of economic and accounting principles and practices, the financial markets, banking, and the analysis and reporting of financial data.

Signal and Track Switch Repairers

▲ Education/Training Required: Postsecondary vocational training
▲ Annual Earnings: $42,390
▲ Growth: 11.5%
▲ Annual Job Openings: 16,000
▲ Self-Employed: 0%
▲ Part-Time: 24.3%

Install, inspect, test, maintain, or repair electric gate crossings, signals, signal equipment, track switches, section lines, or intercommunications systems within a railroad system. Installs and inspects switch-controlling mechanism on trolley wire and switch in bed of track bed, using hand tools and test equipment. Inspects and tests gate crossings, signals, and signal equipment, such as interlocks and hotbox detectors. Inspects electrical units of railroad grade crossing gates to detect loose bolts and defective electrical connections and parts. Tests signal circuit connections, using standard electrical testing equipment. Replaces defective wiring, broken lenses, or burned-out light bulbs. Tightens loose bolts, using wrench, and tests circuits and connections by opening and closing gate. Tests air lines and air cylinders on pneumatically operated gates. Inspects batteries to ensure that batteries are filled with battery water or to determine need for replacement. Lubricates moving parts on gate crossing mechanisms and swinging signals. Maintains high-tension lines, deenergizing lines for power company as repairs are requested. Cleans lenses of lamps with cloths and solvent. Compiles reports indicating mileage or track inspected, repairs made, and equipment requiring replacement. **SKILLS—Installation:** Installing equipment, machines, wiring, or programs to meet specifications. **Troubleshooting:** Determining causes of operating errors and deciding what to do about them. **Equipment Maintenance:** Performing routine maintenance on equipment and determining when and what kind of maintenance is needed. **Repairing:** Repairing machines or systems, using the needed tools. **Quality Control Analysis:** Conducting tests and inspections of products, services, or processes to evaluate quality or performance.

GOE INFORMATION—Interest Area: 05. Mechanics, Installers, and Repairers. **Work Group:** 05.02. Electrical and Electronic Systems. **Other Job Titles in This Work Group:** Avionics Technicians; Battery Repairers; Central Office and PBX Installers and Repairers; Communication Equipment Mechanics, Installers, and Repairers; Computer, Automated Teller, and Office Machine Repairers;

Data Processing Equipment Repairers; Electric Home Appliance and Power Tool Repairers; Electric Meter Installers and Repairers; Electric Motor and Switch Assemblers and Repairers; Electric Motor, Power Tool, and Related Repairers; Electrical and Electronics Installers and Repairers, Transportation Equipment; Electrical and Electronics Repairers, Commercial and Industrial Equipment; Electrical and Electronics Repairers, Powerhouse, Substation, and Relay; Electrical Parts Reconditioners; Electrical Power-Line Installers and Repairers; Electronic Equipment Installers and Repairers, Motor Vehicles; Electronic Home Entertainment Equipment Installers and Repairers; Elevator Installers and Repairers; Frame Wirers, Central Office; Home Appliance Installers; Home Appliance Repairers; Office Machine and Cash Register Servicers; Radio Mechanics; Station Installers and Repairers, Telephone; Telecommunications Equipment Installers and Repairers, Except Line Installers; Telecommunications Facility Examiners; Telecommunications Line Installers and Repairers; Transformer Repairers. **PERSONALITY TYPE—Realistic.** Realistic occupations frequently involve work activities that include practical, hands-on problems and solutions. They often deal with plants, animals, and real-world materials like wood, tools, and machinery. Many of the occupations require working outside and do not involve a lot of paperwork or working closely with others.

EDUCATION/TRAINING PROGRAM(S)—Electrician. RELATED KNOWLEDGE/COURSES—Principles of Mechanical Devices: Knowledge of machines and tools, including their designs, uses, repair, and maintenance. **Transportation:** Knowledge of principles and methods for moving people or goods by air, rail, sea, or road, including the relative costs and benefits. **Telecommunications:** Knowledge of transmission, broadcasting, switching, control, and operation of telecommunications systems. **Public Safety and Security:** Knowledge of relevant equipment, policies, procedures, and strategies to promote effective local, state, or national security operations for the protection of people, data, property, and institutions.

Engineering and Technology: Knowledge of the practical application of engineering science and technology. This includes applying principles, techniques, procedures, and equipment to the design and production of various goods and services.

Singers

▲ Education/Training Required: Long-term on-the-job training
▲ Annual Earnings: $40,320
▲ Growth: 20.1%
▲ Annual Job Openings: 33,000
▲ Self-Employed: 25.8%
▲ Part-Time: 53.5%

Sing songs on stage, radio, or television or in motion pictures. Sings before audience or recipient of message as soloist or in group, as member of vocal ensemble. Memorizes musical selections and routines or sings following printed text, musical notation, or customer instructions. Observes choral leader or prompter for cues or directions in vocal presentation. Practices songs and routines to maintain and improve vocal skills. Interprets or modifies music, applying knowledge of harmony, melody, rhythm, and voice production, to individualize presentation and maintain audience interest. Sings a cappella or with musical accompaniment. **SKILLS—Active Listening:** Giving full attention to what other people are saying, taking time to understand the points being made, asking questions as appropriate, and not interrupting at inappropriate times. **Coordination:** Adjusting actions in relation to others' actions. **Speaking:** Talking to others to convey information effectively. **Reading Comprehension:** Understanding written sentences and paragraphs in work-related documents. **Active Learning:** Understanding the implications of new information for both current and future problem-solving and decision-making.

GOE INFORMATION—Interest Area: 01. Arts, Entertainment, and Media. **Work Group:** 01.05. Performing Arts. **Other Job Titles in This Work Group:** Actors; Choreographers; Composers; Dancers; Directors—Stage, Motion Pictures, Television, and Radio; Music Arrangers and Orchestrators; Music Directors; Music Directors and Composers; Musicians and Singers; Musicians, Instrumental; Public Address System and Other Announcers; Radio and Television Announcers; Talent Directors. **PERSONALITY TYPE**—Artistic. Artistic occupations frequently involve working with forms, designs, and patterns. They often require self-expression, and the work can be done without following a clear set of rules.

EDUCATION/TRAINING PROGRAM(S)—Jazz/Jazz Studies; Music Pedagogy; Music Performance, General; Music, General; Music, Other; Piano and Organ; Voice and Opera. **RELATED KNOWLEDGE/COURSES**—**Fine Arts:** Knowledge of the theory and techniques required to compose, produce, and perform works of music, dance, visual arts, drama, and sculpture. **English Language:** Knowledge of the structure and content of the English language, including the meaning and spelling of words, rules of composition, and grammar. **Communications and Media:** Knowledge of media production, communication, and dissemination techniques and methods. This includes alternative ways to inform and entertain via written, oral, and visual media. **Education and Training:** Knowledge of principles and methods for curriculum and training design, teaching and instruction for individuals and groups, and the measurement of training effects. **Mathematics:** Knowledge of arithmetic, algebra, geometry, calculus, and statistics and their applications.

Social and Community Service Managers

▲ Education/Training Required: Bachelor's degree
▲ Annual Earnings: $41,260
▲ Growth: 24.8%
▲ Annual Job Openings: 13,000
▲ Self-Employed: 49.4%
▲ Part-Time: 7.2%

Plan, organize, or coordinate the activities of a social service program or community outreach organization. Oversee the program or organization's budget and policies regarding participant involvement, program requirements, and benefits. **Work may involve directing social workers, counselors, or probation officers.** Confers and consults with individuals, groups, and committees to determine needs and plan, implement, and extend organization's programs and services. Determines organizational policies and defines scope of services offered and administration of procedures. Establishes and maintains relationships with other agencies and organizations in community to meet and not duplicate community needs and services. Assigns duties to staff or volunteers. Plans, directs, and prepares fundraising activities and public relations materials. Researches and analyzes member or community needs as basis for community development. Participates in program activities to serve clients of agency. Prepares, distributes, and maintains records and reports, such as budgets, personnel records, or training manuals. Coordinates volunteer service programs, such as Red Cross, hospital volunteers, or vocational training for disabled individuals. Speaks to community groups to explain and interpret agency purpose, programs, and policies. Advises volunteers and volunteer leaders to ensure quality of programs and effective use of resources. Instructs and trains agency staff or volunteers in skills required to provide services. Interviews, recruits, or hires volunteers and staff. Observes workers to evaluate performance and ensure that work meets established standards. **SKILLS—Speaking:** Talking to others to convey information effectively. **Coordination:** Adjusting actions in relation to others' actions. **Reading Comprehension:** Understanding written sentences and paragraphs in work-related documents. **Social Perceptiveness:** Being aware of others' reactions and understanding why they react as they do. **Service Orientation:** Actively looking for ways to help people. **Instructing:** Teaching others how to do something. **Writing:** Communicating effectively in writing as appropriate for the needs of the audience.

GOE INFORMATION—Interest Area: 12. Education and Social Service. **Work Group:** 12.01. Managerial Work in Education and Social Service. **Other Job Titles in This Work Group:** Education Administrators, All Other; Education Administrators, Elementary and Secondary School; Education Administrators, Postsecondary; Education Administrators, Preschool and Child Care Center/Program; Instructional Coordinators; Park Naturalists. **PERSONALITY TYPE**—Social. Social occupations frequently involve working with, communicating with, and teaching people. These occupations often involve helping or providing service to others.

EDUCATION/TRAINING PROGRAM(S)—Business Administration and Management, General; Business, Management, Marketing, and Related Support Services, Other; Business/Commerce, General; Community Organization and Advocacy; Entrepreneurship/Entrepreneurial Studies; Human Services, General; Non-Profit/Public/Organizational Management; Public Administration. **RELATED KNOWLEDGE/COURSES—Administration and Management:** Knowledge of business and management principles involved in strategic planning, resource allocation, human resources modeling, leadership technique, production methods, and coordination of people and resources. **Customer and Personal Service:** Knowledge of principles and processes for providing customer and personal services. This includes customer needs assessment, meeting quality standards for services, and evaluation of customer satisfaction. **Education and Training:** Knowledge of principles and methods for curriculum and training design, teaching and instruction for individuals and groups, and the measurement of training effects. **Personnel and Human Resources:** Knowledge of principles and procedures for personnel recruitment, selection, training, compensation and benefits, labor relations and negotiation, and personnel information systems. **English Language:** Knowledge of the structure and content of the English language, including the meaning and spelling of words, rules of composition, and grammar.

Social and Human Service Assistants

- ▲ Education/Training Required: Moderate-term on-the-job training
- ▲ Annual Earnings: $23,070
- ▲ Growth: 54.2%
- ▲ Annual Job Openings: 45,000
- ▲ Self-Employed: 0%
- ▲ Part-Time: 42.4%

Assist professionals from a wide variety of fields, such as psychology, rehabilitation, or social work, to provide client services as well as support for families. May assist clients in identifying available benefits and social and community services and help clients obtain them. May assist social workers with developing, organizing, and conducting programs to prevent and resolve problems relevant to substance abuse, human relationships, rehabilitation, or adult daycare. Visits individuals in homes or attends group meetings to provide information on agency services, requirements, and procedures. Interviews individuals and family members to compile information on social, educational, criminal, institutional, or drug history. Assists clients with preparation of forms, such as tax or rent forms. Assists in planning of food budget, utilizing charts and sample budgets. Meets with youth groups to acquaint them with consequences of delinquent acts. Observes and discusses meal preparation and suggests alternate methods of food preparation. Oversees day-to-day group activities of residents in institution. Cares for children in client's home during client's appointments. Keeps records and prepares reports for owner or management concerning visits with clients. Submits to and reviews reports and problems with superior. Informs tenants of facilities such as laundries and playgrounds. Demonstrates use and care of equipment for tenant use. Explains rules established by owner or management, such as sanitation and maintenance requirements and parking regulations. Transports and accompanies clients to shopping area and to appointments, using automobile. Consults with supervisor concerning programs for individual families. Observes clients' food selections and recommends alternate economical and nutritional food choices. Monitors free supplementary meal program to ensure cleanliness of facility and that eligibility guidelines are met for persons receiving meals. Assists in locating housing for displaced individuals. Provides information on and refers individuals to public or private agencies and community services for assistance. Advises clients regarding food stamps, child care, food, money management, sanitation, and housekeeping.

SKILLS—Social Perceptiveness: Being aware of others' reactions and understanding why they react as they do. **Service Orientation:** Actively looking for ways to help people. **Active Listening:** Giving full attention to what other people are saying, taking time to understand the points being made, asking questions as appropriate, and not interrupting at inappropriate times. **Speaking:** Talking to others to convey information effectively. **Reading Comprehension:** Understanding written sentences and paragraphs in work-related documents.

GOE INFORMATION—Interest Area: 12. Education and Social Service. **Work Group:** 12.02. Social Services. **Other Job Titles in This Work Group:** Child, Family, and School Social Workers; Clergy; Clinical Psychologists; Clinical, Counseling, and School Psychologists; Community and Social Service Specialists, All Other; Counseling Psychologists; Counselors, All Other; Directors, Religious Activities and Education; Marriage and Family Therapists; Medical and Public Health Social Workers; Mental Health and Substance Abuse Social Workers; Mental Health Counselors; Probation Officers and Correctional Treatment Specialists; Rehabilitation Counselors; Religious Workers, All Other; Residential Advisors; Social Workers, All Other; Substance Abuse and Behavioral Disorder Counselors. **PERSONALITY TYPE—**Social. Social occupations frequently involve working with, communicating with, and teaching people. These occupations often involve helping or providing service to others.

EDUCATION/TRAINING PROGRAM(S)—Mental and Social Health Services and Allied Professions, Other. **RELATED KNOWLEDGE/COURSES—Customer and Personal Service:** Knowledge of principles and processes for providing customer and personal services. This includes customer needs assessment, meeting quality standards for services, and evaluation of customer satisfaction. **Therapy and Counseling:** Knowledge of principles, methods, and procedures for diagnosis, treatment, and rehabilitation of physical and mental dysfunctions and for career counseling and guidance. **Psychology:** Knowledge of human behavior and performance; individual differences in ability, personality, and interests; learning and motivation; psychological research methods; and the assessment and treatment of behavioral and affective disorders. **Education and Training:** Knowledge of principles and methods for curriculum and training design, teaching and instruction for individuals and groups, and the measurement of training effects. **Clerical Studies:** Knowledge of administrative and clerical procedures and systems, such as word processing, managing files and records, stenography and transcription, designing forms, and other office procedures and terminology.

Social Sciences Teachers, Postsecondary, All Other

- ▲ Education/Training Required: Master's degree
- ▲ Annual Earnings: No data available.
- ▲ Growth: 23.5%
- ▲ Annual Job Openings: 184,000
- ▲ Self-Employed: 0%
- ▲ Part-Time: 32.3%

All postsecondary social sciences teachers not listed separately. **SKILLS**—No data available.

GOE INFORMATION—**Interest Area:** 12. Education and Social Service. **Work Group:** 12.03. Educational Services. **Other Job Titles in This Work Group:** Adult Literacy, Remedial Education, and GED Teachers and Instructors; Agricultural Sciences Teachers, Postsecondary; Anthropology and Archeology Teachers, Postsecondary; Architecture Teachers, Postsecondary; Archivists; Area, Ethnic, and Cultural Studies Teachers, Postsecondary; Art, Drama, and Music Teachers, Postsecondary; Atmospheric, Earth, Marine, and Space Sciences Teachers, Postsecondary; Audio-Visual Collections Specialists; Biological Science Teachers, Postsecondary; Business Teachers, Postsecondary; Chemistry Teachers, Postsecondary; Child Care Workers; Communications Teachers, Postsecondary; Computer Science Teachers, Postsecondary; Criminal Justice and Law Enforcement Teachers, Postsecondary; Curators; Economics Teachers, Postsecondary; Education Teachers, Postsecondary; Educational Psychologists; Educational, Vocational, and School Counselors; Elementary School Teachers, Except Special Education; Engineering Teachers, Postsecondary; English Language and Literature Teachers, Postsecondary; Environmental Science Teachers, Postsecondary; Farm and Home Management Advisors; Foreign Language and Literature Teachers, Postsecondary; Forestry and Conservation Science Teachers, Postsecondary; Geography Teachers, Postsecondary; Graduate Teaching Assistants; Health Specialties Teachers, Postsecondary; History Teachers, Postsecondary; Home Economics Teachers, Postsecondary; Kindergarten Teachers, Except Special Education; Law Teachers, Postsecondary; Librarians; Library Assistants, Clerical; Library Science Teachers, Postsecondary; Library Technicians; Mathematical Science Teachers, Postsecondary; Middle School Teachers, Except Special and Vocational Education; Museum Technicians and Conservators; Nursing Instructors and Teachers, Postsecondary; Personal Financial Advisors; Philosophy and Religion Teachers, Postsecondary; Physics Teachers, Postsecondary; Political Science Teachers, Postsecondary; Postsecondary Teachers, All Other; others. **PERSONALITY TYPE**—No data available.

EDUCATION/TRAINING PROGRAM(S)—Social Science Teacher Education; Social Sciences, General. **RELATED KNOWLEDGE/COURSES**—No data available.

Social Work Teachers, Postsecondary

▲ Education/Training Required: Master's degree
▲ Annual Earnings: $50,250
▲ Growth: 23.5%
▲ Annual Job Openings: 184,000
▲ Self-Employed: 0%
▲ Part-Time: 32.3%

Teach courses in social work. **SKILLS**—No data available.

GOE INFORMATION—**Interest Area:** 12. Education and Social Service. **Work Group:** 12.03. Educational Services. **Other Job Titles in This Work Group:** Adult Literacy, Remedial Education, and GED Teachers and Instructors; Agricultural Sciences Teachers, Postsecondary; Anthropology and Archeology Teachers, Postsecondary; Architecture Teachers, Postsecondary; Archivists; Area, Ethnic, and Cultural Studies Teachers, Postsecondary; Art, Drama, and Music Teachers, Postsecondary; Atmospheric, Earth, Marine, and Space Sciences Teachers, Postsecondary; Audio-Visual Collections Specialists; Biological Science Teachers, Postsecondary; Business Teachers, Postsecondary; Chemistry Teachers, Postsecondary; Child Care Workers; Communications Teachers, Postsecondary; Computer Science Teachers, Postsecondary; Criminal Justice and Law Enforcement Teachers, Postsecondary; Curators; Economics Teachers, Postsecondary; Education Teachers, Postsecondary; Educational Psychologists; Educational, Vocational, and School Counselors; Elementary School Teachers, Except Special Education; Engineering Teachers, Postsecondary; English Language and Literature Teachers, Postsecondary; Environmental Science Teachers, Postsecondary; Farm and Home Management Advisors; Foreign Language and Literature Teachers, Postsecondary; Forestry and Conservation Science Teachers, Postsecondary; Geography Teachers, Postsecondary; Graduate Teaching Assistants; Health Specialties Teachers, Postsecondary; History Teachers, Postsecondary; Home Economics Teachers, Postsecondary; Kindergarten Teachers, Except Special Education; Law Teachers, Postsecondary; Librarians; Library Assistants, Clerical; Library Science Teachers, Postsecondary; Library Technicians; Mathematical Science Teachers, Postsecondary; Middle School Teachers, Except Special and Vocational Education; Museum Technicians and Conservators; Nursing Instructors and Teachers, Postsecondary; Personal Financial Advisors; Philosophy and Religion Teachers, Postsecondary; Physics Teachers, Postsecondary; Political Science Teachers, Postsecondary; Postsecondary Teachers, All Other; others. **PERSONALITY TYPE**—No data available.

EDUCATION/TRAINING PROGRAM(S)—Clinical/Medical Social Work; Social Work; Teacher Education and Professional Development, Specific Subject Areas, Other. **RELATED KNOWLEDGE/COURSES**—No data available.

Sociologists

▲ Education/Training Required: Master's degree
▲ Annual Earnings: $54,880
▲ Growth: 17.2%
▲ Annual Job Openings: 2,000
▲ Self-Employed: 5.2%
▲ Part-Time: 18.1%

Study human society and social behavior by examining the groups and social institutions that people form, as well as various social, religious, political, and business organizations. May study the behavior and interaction of groups, trace their origin and growth, and analyze the influence of group activities on individual members. Collects and analyzes scientific data concerning social phenomena, such as community, associations, social institutions, ethnic minorities, and social change. Plans and directs research on crime and prevention, group relations in industrial organization, urban communities, and physical environment and technology. Directs work of statistical clerks, statisticians, and others. Collaborates with research workers in other disciplines. Prepares publications and reports on subjects such as social factors that affect health, demographic characteristics, and social and racial discrimination in society. Interprets methods employed and findings to individuals within agency and community. Consults with lawmakers, administrators, and other officials who deal with problems of social change. Monitors group interaction and role affiliations to evaluate progress and to determine need for additional change. Develops intervention procedures, utilizing techniques such as interviews, consultations, role-playing, and participant observation of group interaction to facilitate solution. Analyzes and evaluates data. Collects information and makes judgments through observation, interview, and review of documents. Constructs and tests methods of data collection. Develops approaches to solution of group's problems based on findings and incorporating sociological research and study in related disciplines. Develops research designs on basis of existing knowledge and evolving theory. Observes group interaction and interviews group members to identify problems and collect data related to factors such as group organization and authority relationships. **SKILLS—Writing:** Communicating effectively in writing as appropriate for the needs of the audience. **Mathematics:** Using mathematics to solve problems. **Reading Comprehension:** Understanding written sentences and paragraphs in work-related documents. **Active Learning:** Understanding the implications of new information for both current and future problem-solving and decision-making. **Critical Thinking:** Using logic and reasoning to identify the strengths and weaknesses of alternative solutions, conclusions, or approaches to problems.

GOE INFORMATION—Interest Area: 02. Science, Math, and Engineering. **Work Group:** 02.04. Social Sciences. **Other Job Titles in This Work Group:** Anthropologists; Anthropologists and Archeologists; Archeologists; City Planning Aides; Economists; Historians; Industrial-Organizational Psychologists; Political Scientists; Psychologists, All Other; Social Science Research Assistants; Social Scientists and Related Workers, All Other; Survey Researchers; Urban and Regional Planners. **PERSONALITY TYPE—**Investigative. Investigative occupations frequently involve working with ideas and require an extensive amount of thinking. These occupations can involve searching for facts and figuring out problems mentally.

EDUCATION/TRAINING PROGRAM(S)—Criminology; Demography and Population Studies; Sociology; Urban Studies/Affairs. **RELATED KNOWLEDGE/ COURSES—Sociology and Anthropology:** Knowledge of group behavior and dynamics, societal trends and influences, human migrations, ethnicity, and cultures and their history and origins. **English Language:** Knowledge of the structure and content of the English language, including the meaning and spelling of words, rules of composition, and grammar. **Administration and Management:** Knowledge of business and management principles involved in strategic planning, resource allocation, human resources modeling, leadership technique, production methods, and coordination of people and resources. **Education and Training:** Knowledge of principles and methods for curriculum and training design, teaching and instruction for individuals and groups, and the measurement of training effects. **Mathematics:** Knowledge of arithmetic, algebra, geometry, calculus, and statistics and their applications. **Psychology:** Knowledge of human behavior and performance; individual differences in ability, personality, and interests; learning and motivation; psychological research methods; and the assessment and treatment of behavioral and affective disorders.

Sociology Teachers, Postsecondary

▲ Education/Training Required: Master's degree
▲ Annual Earnings: $51,110
▲ Growth: 23.5%
▲ Annual Job Openings: 184,000
▲ Self-Employed: 0%
▲ Part-Time: 32.3%

Teach courses in sociology. Prepares and delivers lectures to students. Stimulates class discussions. Compiles, administers, and grades examinations or assigns this work to others. Compiles bibliographies of specialized materials for outside reading assignments. Serves on faculty committee providing professional consulting services to government and industry. Acts as adviser to student organizations. Conducts research in particular field of knowledge and publishes findings in professional journals. Directs research of other teachers or graduate students working for advanced academic degrees. Advises students on academic and vocational curricula. **SKILLS—Reading Comprehension:** Understanding written sentences and paragraphs in work-related documents. **Instructing:** Teaching others how to do something. **Speaking:** Talking to others to convey information effectively. **Active Learning:** Understanding the implications of new information for both current and future problem-solving and decision-making. **Active Listening:** Giving full attention to what other people are saying, taking time to understand the points being made, asking questions as appropriate, and not interrupting at inappropriate times. **Writing:** Communicating effectively in writing as appropriate for the needs of the audience. **Learning Strategies:** Selecting and using training/instructional methods and procedures appropriate for the situation when learning or teaching new things.

GOE INFORMATION—Interest Area: 12. Education and Social Service. **Work Group:** 12.03. Educational Services. **Other Job Titles in This Work Group:** Adult Literacy, Remedial Education, and GED Teachers and Instructors; Agricultural Sciences Teachers, Postsecondary; Anthropology and Archeology Teachers, Postsecondary; Architecture Teachers, Postsecondary; Archivists; Area, Ethnic, and Cultural Studies Teachers, Postsecondary; Art, Drama, and Music Teachers, Postsecondary; Atmospheric, Earth, Marine, and Space Sciences Teachers, Postsecondary; Audio-Visual Collections Specialists; Biological Science Teachers, Postsecondary; Business Teachers, Postsecondary; Chemistry Teachers, Postsecondary; Child Care Workers; Communications Teachers, Postsecondary; Computer Science Teachers, Postsecondary; Criminal Justice and Law Enforcement Teachers, Postsecondary; Curators; Economics Teachers, Postsecondary; Education Teachers, Postsecondary; Educational Psychologists; Educational, Vocational, and School Counselors; Elementary School Teachers, Except Special Education; Engineering Teachers, Postsecondary; English Language and Literature Teachers, Postsecondary; Environmental Science Teachers, Postsecondary; Farm and Home Management Advisors; Foreign Language and Literature Teachers, Postsecondary; Forestry and Conservation Science Teachers, Postsecondary; Geography Teachers, Postsecondary; Graduate Teaching Assistants; Health Specialties Teachers, Postsecondary; History Teachers, Postsecondary; Home Economics Teachers, Postsecondary; Kindergarten Teachers, Except Special Education; Law Teachers, Postsecondary; Librarians; Library Assistants, Clerical; Library Science Teachers, Postsecondary; Library Technicians; Mathematical Science Teachers, Postsecondary; Middle School Teachers, Except Special and Vocational Education; Museum Technicians and Conservators; Nursing Instructors and Teachers, Postsecondary; Personal Financial Advisors; Philosophy and Religion Teachers, Postsecondary; Physics Teachers, Postsecondary; Political Science Teachers, Postsecondary; Postsecondary Teachers, All Other; others. **PERSONALITY TYPE—** Social. Social occupations frequently involve working with, communicating with, and teaching people. These occupations often involve helping or providing service to others.

EDUCATION/TRAINING PROGRAM(S)—Social Science Teacher Education; Sociology. **RELATED KNOWLEDGE/COURSES—Education and Training:** Knowledge of principles and methods for curriculum and training design, teaching and instruction for individuals and groups, and the measurement of training effects. **Sociology and Anthropology:** Knowledge of group behavior and dynamics, societal trends and influences, human migrations, ethnicity, and cultures and their history and origins. **History and Archeology:** Knowledge of historical events and their causes, indicators, and effects on civilizations and cultures. **Psychology:** Knowledge of human behavior and performance; individual differences in ability, personality, and interests; learning and motivation; psychological research methods; and the assessment and treatment of behavioral and affective disorders. **English Language:** Knowledge of the structure and content of the English language, including the meaning and spelling of words, rules of composition, and grammar.

Solderers

> ▲ Education/Training Required: Short-term on-the-job training
> ▲ Annual Earnings: $28,490
> ▲ Growth: 19.3%
> ▲ Annual Job Openings: 51,000
> ▲ Self-Employed: 3.7%
> ▲ Part-Time: 8.6%

Solder together components to assemble fabricated metal products, using soldering iron. Melts and applies solder along adjoining edges of workpieces to solder joints, using soldering iron, gas torch, or electric-ultrasonic equipment. Grinds, cuts, buffs, or bends edges of workpieces to be joined to ensure snug fit, using power grinder and hand tools. Removes workpieces from molten solder and holds parts together until color indicates that solder has set. Cleans workpieces, using chemical solution, file, wire brush, or grinder. Cleans tip of soldering iron, using chemical solution or cleaning compound. Melts and separates soldered joints to repair misaligned or damaged assemblies, using soldering equipment. Applies flux to workpiece surfaces in preparation for soldering. Heats soldering iron or workpiece to specified temperature for soldering, using gas flame or electric current. Dips workpieces into molten solder or places solder strip between seams and heats seam with iron to band items together. Aligns and clamps workpieces together, using rule, square, or hand tools, or positions items in fixtures, jigs, or vise. Melts and applies solder to fill holes, indentations, and seams of fabricated metal products, using soldering equipment. **SKILLS—Operation and Control:** Controlling operations of equipment or systems. **Equipment Selection:** Determining the kind of tools and equipment needed to do a job. **Equipment Maintenance:** Performing routine maintenance on equipment and determining when and what kind of maintenance is needed.

GOE INFORMATION—Interest Area: 08. Industrial Production. **Work Group:** 08.03. Production Work. **Other Job Titles in This Work Group:** Bakers, Manufacturing; Bindery Machine Operators and Tenders; Brazers; Cementing and Gluing Machine Operators and Tenders; Chemical Equipment Controllers and Operators; Chemical Equipment Operators and Tenders; Chemical Equipment Tenders; Cleaning, Washing, and Metal Pickling Equipment Operators and Tenders; Coating, Painting, and Spraying Machine Operators and Tenders; Coil Winders, Tapers, and Finishers; Combination Machine Tool Operators and Tenders, Metal and Plastic; Computer-Controlled Machine Tool Operators, Metal and Plastic; Cooling and Freezing Equipment Operators and Tenders; Crushing, Grinding, and Polishing Machine Setters, Operators, and Tenders; Cutters and Trimmers, Hand; Cutting and Slicing Machine Operators and Tenders; Cutting and Slicing Machine Setters, Operators, and Tenders; Design Printing Machine Setters and Set-Up Operators; Electrolytic Plating and Coating Machine Operators and Tenders, Metal and Plastic; Electrolytic Plating and Coating Machine Setters and Set-Up Operators, Metal and Plastic; Electrotypers and Stereotypers; Embossing Machine Set-Up Operators; Engraver Set-Up Operators; Extruding and Forming Machine Operators and Tenders, Synthetic or Glass Fibers; Extruding and Forming Machine Setters, Operators, and Tenders, Synthetic and Glass Fibers; Extruding, Forming, Pressing, and Compacting Machine Operators and Tenders; Fabric and Apparel Patternmakers; Fiber Product Cutting Machine Setters and Set-Up Operators; Fiberglass Laminators and Fabricators; Film Laboratory Technicians; Fitters, Structural Metal—Precision; Food and Tobacco Roasting, Baking, and Drying Machine Operators and Tenders; Food Batchmakers; Food Cooking Machine Operators and Tenders; Furnace, Kiln, Oven, Drier, and Kettle Operators and Tenders; Glass Cutting Machine Setters and Set-Up Operators; Graders and Sorters, Agricultural Products; Grinding and Polishing Workers, Hand; Hand Compositors and Typesetters; Heaters, Metal and Plastic; others. **PERSONALITY TYPE—Realistic.** Realistic occupations frequently involve work activities that include practical, hands-on problems and solutions. They often deal with plants, animals, and real-world materials like wood, tools, and machinery. Many of the occupations require working outside and do not involve a lot of paperwork or working closely with others.

EDUCATION/TRAINING PROGRAM(S)—Welding Technology/Welder. RELATED KNOWLEDGE/COURSES—Principles of Mechanical Devices: Knowledge of machines and tools, including their designs, uses, repair, and maintenance. **Building and Construction:** Knowledge of materials, methods, and tools involved in the construction or repair of houses, buildings, or other structures, such as highways and roads. **Production and Processing:** Knowledge of raw materials, production processes, quality control, costs, and other techniques for maximizing the effective manufacture and distribution of goods. **Engineering and Technology:** Knowledge of the practical application of engineering science and technology. This includes applying principles, techniques, proce-

dures, and equipment to the design and production of various goods and services. **Chemistry:** Knowledge of the chemical composition, structure, and properties of substances and of the chemical processes and transformations that they undergo. This includes uses of chemicals and their interactions, danger signs, production techniques, and disposal methods.

Soldering and Brazing Machine Operators and Tenders

▲ Education/Training Required: Short-term on-the-job training
▲ Annual Earnings: $28,220
▲ Growth: 15.1%
▲ Annual Job Openings: 9,000
▲ Self-Employed: 0%
▲ Part-Time: 8.6%

Operate or tend soldering and brazing machines that braze, solder, or spot weld fabricated metal products or components as specified by work orders, blueprints, and layout specifications. Operates or tends soldering and brazing machines that braze, solder, or spot weld fabricated products or components. Adds chemicals and materials to workpieces or machines, using hand tools. Cleans and maintains workpieces and machines, using equipment and hand tools. Reads and records operational information on specified production reports. Examines and tests soldered or brazed products or components, using testing devices. Removes workpieces and parts from machinery, using hand tools. Loads and adjusts workpieces, clamps, and parts onto machine, using hand tools. Moves controls to activate and adjust soldering and brazing machines. Observes meters, gauges, and machine to ensure solder or brazing process meets specifications. **SKILLS—Operation Monitoring:** Watching gauges, dials, or other indicators to make sure a machine is working properly. **Operation and Control:** Controlling operations of equipment or systems. **Equipment Maintenance:** Performing routine maintenance on equipment and determining when and what kind of maintenance is needed. **Equipment Selection:** Determining the kind of tools and equipment needed to do a job. **Quality Control Analysis:** Conducting tests and inspections of products, services, or processes to evaluate quality or performance.

GOE INFORMATION—Interest Area: 08. Industrial Production. **Work Group:** 08.03. Production Work. **Other Job Titles in This Work Group:** Bakers, Manufacturing; Bindery Machine Operators and Tenders; Brazers; Cementing and Gluing Machine Operators and Tenders;

Chemical Equipment Controllers and Operators; Chemical Equipment Operators and Tenders; Chemical Equipment Tenders; Cleaning, Washing, and Metal Pickling Equipment Operators and Tenders; Coating, Painting, and Spraying Machine Operators and Tenders; Coil Winders, Tapers, and Finishers; Combination Machine Tool Operators and Tenders, Metal and Plastic; Computer-Controlled Machine Tool Operators, Metal and Plastic; Cooling and Freezing Equipment Operators and Tenders; Crushing, Grinding, and Polishing Machine Setters, Operators, and Tenders; Cutters and Trimmers, Hand; Cutting and Slicing Machine Operators and Tenders; Cutting and Slicing Machine Setters, Operators, and Tenders; Design Printing Machine Setters and Set-Up Operators; Electrolytic Plating and Coating Machine Operators and Tenders, Metal and Plastic; Electrolytic Plating and Coating Machine Setters and Set-Up Operators, Metal and Plastic; Electrotypers and Stereotypers; Embossing Machine Set-Up Operators; Engraver Set-Up Operators; Extruding and Forming Machine Operators and Tenders, Synthetic or Glass Fibers; Extruding and Forming Machine Setters, Operators, and Tenders, Synthetic and Glass Fibers; Extruding, Forming, Pressing, and Compacting Machine Operators and Tenders; Fabric and Apparel Patternmakers; Fiber Product Cutting Machine Setters and Set-Up Operators; Fiberglass Laminators and Fabricators; Film Laboratory Technicians; Fitters, Structural Metal—Precision; Food and Tobacco Roasting, Baking, and Drying Machine Operators and Tenders; Food Batchmakers; Food Cooking Machine Operators and Tenders; Furnace, Kiln, Oven, Drier, and Kettle Operators and Tenders; Glass Cutting Machine Setters and Set-Up Operators; Graders and Sorters, Agricultural Products; Grinding and Polishing Workers, Hand; Hand Compositors and Typesetters; Heaters, Metal and Plastic; others. **PERSONALITY TYPE**—Realistic. Realistic occupations frequently involve work activities that include practical, hands-on problems and solutions. They often deal with plants, animals, and real-world materials like wood, tools, and machinery. Many of the occupations require working outside and do not involve a lot of paperwork or working closely with others.

EDUCATION/TRAINING PROGRAM(S)—Welding Technology/Welder. **RELATED KNOWLEDGE/ COURSES**—**Principles of Mechanical Devices:** Knowledge of machines and tools, including their designs, uses, repair, and maintenance. **Production and Processing:**

Knowledge of raw materials, production processes, quality control, costs, and other techniques for maximizing the effective manufacture and distribution of goods. **Design:** Knowledge of design techniques, tools, and principles involved in production of precision technical plans, blueprints, drawings, and models. **Chemistry:** Knowledge of the chemical composition, structure, and properties of substances and of the chemical processes and transformations that they undergo. This includes uses of chemicals and their interactions, danger signs, production techniques, and disposal methods. **Clerical Studies:** Knowledge of administrative and clerical procedures and systems, such as word processing, managing files and records, stenography and transcription, designing forms, and other office procedures and terminology.

Soldering and Brazing Machine Setters and Set-Up Operators

▲ Education/Training Required: Moderate-term on-the-job training
▲ Annual Earnings: $28,220
▲ Growth: 15.1%
▲ Annual Job Openings: 9,000
▲ Self-Employed: 0%
▲ Part-Time: 8.6%

Set up or set up and operate soldering or brazing machines to braze, solder, heat-treat, or spot weld fabricated metal products or components as specified by work orders, blueprints, and layout specifications. Selects torch tips, alloy, flux, coil, tubing and wire, according to metal type and thickness, data charts, and records. Sets dials and timing controls to regulate electrical current, gas flow pressure, heating/cooling cycles, and shutoff. Connects, forms, and installs parts to braze, heat-treat, and spot weld workpiece, metal parts, and components. Positions, aligns, and bolts holding fixtures, guides, and stops onto or into brazing machine to position and hold workpieces. Cleans, lubricates, and adjusts equipment to maintain efficient operation, using air hose, cleaning fluid, and hand tools. Examines workpiece for defective seams, solidification, and adherence to specifications and anneals finished workpiece to relieve internal stress. Disconnects electrical current and removes and immerses workpiece into water or acid bath to cool and clean component. Operates and trains workers to operate heat-treating equipment to bond fabricated metal components according to blueprints, work orders, or specifications. Manipulates levers to synchronize brazing action or to move workpiece through brazing process. Assembles, aligns, and clamps workpieces into holding fixture to bond, heat-treat, or solder fabricated metal com-

ponents. Starts machine to complete trial run, readjusts machine, and records setup data. Fills hoppers and positions spout to direct flow of flux or manually brushes flux onto seams of workpieces. **SKILLS—Operation and Control:** Controlling operations of equipment or systems. **Quality Control Analysis:** Conducting tests and inspections of products, services, or processes to evaluate quality or performance. **Operation Monitoring:** Watching gauges, dials, or other indicators to make sure a machine is working properly. **Instructing:** Teaching others how to do something. **Installation:** Installing equipment, machines, wiring, or programs to meet specifications. **Equipment Selection:** Determining the kind of tools and equipment needed to do a job.

GOE INFORMATION—Interest Area: 08. Industrial Production. **Work Group:** 08.02. Production Technology. **Other Job Titles in This Work Group:** Aircraft Rigging Assemblers; Aircraft Structure Assemblers, Precision; Aircraft Structure, Surfaces, Rigging, and Systems Assemblers; Aircraft Systems Assemblers, Precision; Bench Workers, Jewelry; Bindery Machine Setters and Set-Up Operators; Bindery Workers; Bookbinders; Buffing and Polishing Set-Up Operators; Casting Machine Set-Up Operators; Coating, Painting, and Spraying Machine Setters and Set-Up

Operators; Coating, Painting, and Spraying Machine Setters, Operators, and Tenders; Combination Machine Tool Setters and Set-Up Operators, Metal and Plastic; Cutting, Punching, and Press Machine Setters, Operators, and Tenders, Metal and Plastic; Dental Laboratory Technicians; Drilling and Boring Machine Tool Setters, Operators, and Tenders, Metal and Plastic; Electrical and Electronic Equipment Assemblers; Electrical and Electronic Inspectors and Testers; Electromechanical Equipment Assemblers; Engine and Other Machine Assemblers; Extruding and Drawing Machine Setters, Operators, and Tenders, Metal and Plastic; Extruding, Forming, Pressing, and Compacting Machine Setters and Set-Up Operators; Extruding, Forming, Pressing, and Compacting Machine Setters, Operators, and Tenders; Forging Machine Setters, Operators, and Tenders, Metal and Plastic; Foundry Mold and Coremakers; Gem and Diamond Workers; Grinding, Honing, Lapping, and Deburring Machine Set-Up Operators; Grinding, Lapping, Polishing, and Buffing Machine Tool Setters, Operators, and Tenders, Metal and Plastic; Heat Treating Equipment Setters, Operators, and Tenders, Metal and Plastic; Heat Treating, Annealing, and Tempering Machine Operators and Tenders, Metal and Plastic; Heating Equipment Setters and Set-Up Operators, Metal and Plastic; Inspectors, Testers, Sorters, Samplers, and Weighers; Jewelers; Jewelers and Precious Stone and Metal Workers; Lathe and Turning Machine Tool Setters, Operators, and Tenders, Metal and Plastic; Log Graders and Scalers; Materials Inspectors; Mechanical Inspectors; others. **PERSONALITY TYPE**—Realistic. Realistic occupations frequently involve work activities that include practical, hands-on problems and solutions. They often deal with plants, animals, and real-world materials like wood, tools, and machinery. Many of the occupations require working outside and do not involve a lot of paperwork or working closely with others.

EDUCATION/TRAINING PROGRAM(S)—Welding Technology/Welder. **RELATED KNOWLEDGE/COURSES**—**Principles of Mechanical Devices:** Knowledge of machines and tools, including their designs, uses, repair, and maintenance. **Building and Construction:** Knowledge of materials, methods, and tools involved in the construction or repair of houses, buildings, or other structures, such as highways and roads. **Engineering and Technology:** Knowledge of the practical application of engineering science and technology. This includes applying principles, techniques, procedures, and equipment to the design and production of various goods and services. **Design:** Knowledge of design techniques, tools, and principles involved in production of precision technical plans, blueprints, drawings, and models. **Physics:** Knowledge and prediction of physical principles and laws and their inter-relationships and applications to understanding fluid, material, and atmospheric dynamics and mechanical, electrical, atomic, and sub-atomic structures and processes. **Education and Training:** Knowledge of principles and methods for curriculum and training design, teaching and instruction for individuals and groups, and the measurement of training effects.

Special Education Teachers, Middle School

▲ Education/Training Required: Bachelor's degree
▲ Annual Earnings: $40,010
▲ Growth: 24.4%
▲ Annual Job Openings: 6,000
▲ Self-Employed: 0%
▲ Part-Time: 12.9%

Teach middle school subjects to educationally and physically handicapped students. Includes teachers who specialize and work with audibly and visually handicapped students and those who teach basic academic and life processes skills to the mentally impaired. Teaches socially acceptable behavior, employing techniques such as behavior modification and positive reinforcement. Instructs students, using special educational strategies and techniques to improve sensory-motor and perceptual-motor development, memory, language, and cognition. Instructs students in academic subjects, utilizing various teaching techniques, such as phonetics, multisensory learning, and repetition, to reinforce learning. Instructs students in daily living skills required for independent maintenance and economic self-sufficiency, such as hygiene, safety, and food preparation. Plans curriculum and other instructional materials to meet student's needs, considering such factors as physical, emotional, and educational abilities. Administers and interprets results of ability and achievement tests. Confers with other staff members to plan programs designed to promote educational, physical, and social development of students. Provides consistent reinforcement to learning and continuous feedback to student. Meets with parents to provide support, guidance in using community resources, and skills in dealing with student's learning impairment. Observes, evaluates, and prepares reports on progress of students. Works with students to increase motivation. Confers with parents, administrators, testing specialists, social workers, and others to develop individual educational plan for student. Selects and teaches reading material and math problems related to everyday life of individual student. **SKILLS—Learning Strategies:** Selecting and using training/instructional methods and procedures appropriate for the situation when learning or teaching new things. **Social Perceptiveness:** Being aware of others' reactions and understanding why they react as they do. **Instructing:** Teaching others how to do something. **Active Listening:** Giving full attention to what other people are saying, taking time to understand the points being made, asking questions as appropriate, and not interrupting at inappropriate times. **Speaking:** Talking to others to convey information effectively. **Monitoring:** Monitoring/Assessing your performance or that of other individuals or organizations to make improvements or take corrective action.

GOE INFORMATION—Interest Area: 12. Education and Social Service. **Work Group:** 12.03. Educational Services. **Other Job Titles in This Work Group:** Adult Literacy, Remedial Education, and GED Teachers and Instructors; Agricultural Sciences Teachers, Postsecondary; Anthropology and Archeology Teachers, Postsecondary; Architecture Teachers, Postsecondary; Archivists; Area, Ethnic, and Cultural Studies Teachers, Postsecondary; Art, Drama, and Music Teachers, Postsecondary; Atmospheric, Earth, Marine, and Space Sciences Teachers, Postsecondary; Audio-Visual Collections Specialists; Biological Science Teachers, Postsecondary; Business Teachers, Postsecondary; Chemistry Teachers, Postsecondary; Child Care Workers; Communications Teachers, Postsecondary; Computer Science Teachers, Postsecondary; Criminal Justice and Law Enforcement Teachers, Postsecondary; Curators; Economics Teachers, Postsecondary; Education Teachers, Postsecondary; Educational Psychologists; Educational, Vocational, and School Counselors; Elementary School Teachers, Except Special Education; Engineering Teachers, Postsecondary; English Language and Literature Teachers, Postsecondary; Environmental Science Teachers, Postsecondary; Farm and Home Management Advisors; Foreign Language and Literature Teachers, Postsecondary; Forestry and Conservation Science Teachers, Postsecondary; Geography Teachers, Postsecondary; Graduate Teaching Assistants; Health Specialties Teachers, Postsecondary; History Teachers, Postsecondary; Home Economics Teachers, Postsecondary; Kindergarten Teachers, Except Special Education; Law Teachers, Postsecondary; Librarians; Library Assistants, Clerical; Library Science Teachers, Postsecondary; Library Technicians; Mathematical Science Teachers, Postsecondary; Middle School Teachers, Except Special and Vocational Education; Museum Technicians and Conservators; Nursing Instructors and Teachers, Postsecondary; Personal Financial Advisors; Philosophy and Religion Teachers, Postsecondary; Physics Teachers, Postsecondary; Political Science Teachers, Postsecondary; Postsecondary Teachers, All Other; others. **PERSONALITY TYPE—** Social. Social occupations frequently involve working with, communicating with, and teaching people. These occupations often involve helping or providing service to others.

EDUCATION/TRAINING PROGRAM(S)—Special Education and Teaching, General. **RELATED KNOWLEDGE/COURSES—Education and Training:** Knowledge of principles and methods for curriculum and training design, teaching and instruction for individuals and groups, and the measurement of training effects. **Psychology:** Knowledge of human behavior and performance; individual differences in ability, personality, and interests; learning and motivation; psychological research methods; and the assessment and treatment of behavioral and affective disorders. **Therapy and Counseling:** Knowledge of principles, methods, and procedures for diagnosis, treatment, and rehabilitation of physical and mental dysfunctions and for career counseling and guidance. **English Language:** Knowledge of the structure and content of the English language, including the meaning and spelling of words, rules of composition, and grammar. **Customer and Personal Service:** Knowledge of principles and processes for providing customer and personal services. This includes customer needs assessment, meeting quality standards for services, and evaluation of customer satisfaction.

Special Education Teachers, Preschool, Kindergarten, and Elementary School

▲ Education/Training Required: Bachelor's degree
▲ Annual Earnings: $42,110
▲ Growth: 36.8%
▲ Annual Job Openings: 15,000
▲ Self-Employed: 0%
▲ Part-Time: 12.9%

Teach elementary and preschool school subjects to educationally and physically handicapped students. Includes teachers who specialize and work with audibly and visually handicapped students and those who teach basic academic and life processes skills to the mentally impaired. Teaches socially acceptable behavior, employing techniques such as behavior modification and positive reinforcement. Instructs students in academic subjects, utilizing various teaching techniques, such as phonetics, multisensory learning, and repetition, to reinforce learning. Instructs students, using special educational strategies and techniques to improve sensory-motor and perceptual-motor development, memory, language, and cognition. Plans curriculum and other instructional materials to meet students' needs, considering such factors as physical, emotional, and educational abilities. Administers and interprets results of ability and achievement tests. Confers with other staff members to plan programs designed to promote educational, physical, and social development of students. Provides consistent reinforcement to learning and continuous feedback to student. Meets with parents to provide support, guidance in using community resources, and skills in dealing with student's learning impairment. Observes, evaluates, and prepares reports on progress of students. Works with students to increase motivation. Confers with parents, administrators, testing specialists, social workers, and others to develop individual educational plan for student. Selects and teaches reading material and math problems related to everyday life of individual student. Instructs students in daily living skills required for independent maintenance and economic self-sufficiency, such as hygiene, safety, and food preparation. **SKILLS—Learning Strategies:** Selecting and using training/instructional methods and procedures appropriate for the situation when learning or teaching new things. **Social Perceptiveness:** Being aware of others' reactions and understanding why they react as they do. **Instructing:** Teaching others how to do something. **Active Listening:** Giving full attention to what other people are saying, taking time to understand the points being made, asking questions as appropriate, and not interrupting at inappropriate times. **Monitoring:** Monitoring/Assessing your performance or that of other individuals or organizations to make improvements or take corrective action. **Speaking:** Talking to others to convey information effectively.

GOE INFORMATION—Interest Area: 12. Education and Social Service. **Work Group:** 12.03. Educational Services. **Other Job Titles in This Work Group:** Adult Literacy, Remedial Education, and GED Teachers and Instructors; Agricultural Sciences Teachers, Postsecondary; Anthropology and Archeology Teachers, Postsecondary; Architecture Teachers, Postsecondary; Archivists; Area, Ethnic, and Cultural Studies Teachers, Postsecondary; Art, Drama, and Music Teachers, Postsecondary; Atmospheric, Earth, Marine, and Space Sciences Teachers, Postsecondary; Audio-Visual Collections Specialists; Biological Science Teachers, Postsecondary; Business Teachers, Postsecondary; Chemistry Teachers, Postsecondary; Child Care Workers; Communications Teachers, Postsecondary; Computer Science Teachers, Postsecondary; Criminal Justice and Law Enforcement Teachers, Postsecondary; Curators; Economics Teachers, Postsecondary; Education Teachers, Postsecondary; Educational Psychologists; Educational, Vocational, and School Counselors; Elementary School Teachers, Except Special Education; Engineering Teachers, Postsecondary; English Language and Literature Teachers, Postsecondary; Environmental Science Teachers, Postsecondary; Farm and Home Management Advisors; Foreign Language and Literature Teachers, Postsecondary; Forestry and Conservation Science Teachers, Postsecondary; Geography Teachers, Postsecondary; Graduate Teaching Assistants; Health Specialties Teachers, Postsecondary; History Teachers, Postsecondary; Home Economics Teachers, Postsecondary; Kindergarten Teachers, Except Special Education; Law Teachers, Postsecondary; Librarians; Library Assistants, Clerical; Library Science Teachers, Postsecondary; Library Technicians; Mathematical Science Teachers, Postsecondary; Middle School Teachers, Except Special and Vocational Education; Museum Technicians and Conservators; Nursing Instructors and Teachers, Postsecondary;

Personal Financial Advisors; Philosophy and Religion Teachers, Postsecondary; Physics Teachers, Postsecondary; Political Science Teachers, Postsecondary; Postsecondary Teachers, All Other; others. **PERSONALITY TYPE—** Social. Social occupations frequently involve working with, communicating with, and teaching people. These occupations often involve helping or providing service to others.

EDUCATION/TRAINING PROGRAM(S)—Education/Teaching of Individuals with Autism; Education/Teaching of Individuals with Emotional Disturbances; Education/Teaching of Individuals with Hearing Impairments, Including Deafness; Education/Teaching of Individuals with Mental Retardation; Education/Teaching of Individuals with Multiple Disabilities; Education/Teaching of Individuals with Orthopedic and Other Physical Health Impairments; Education/Teaching of Individuals with Specific Learning Disabilities; Education/Teaching of Individuals with Speech or Language Impairments; Education/Teaching of Individuals with Traumatic Brain Injuries; Education/Teaching of Individuals with Vision Impairments, Including Blindness; Special Education and Teaching, General; Special Education and Teaching, Other. **RELATED KNOWLEDGE/COURSES—Education and Training:** Knowledge of principles and methods for curriculum and training design, teaching and instruction for individuals and groups, and the measurement of training effects. **Psychology:** Knowledge of human behavior and performance; individual differences in ability, personality, and interests; learning and motivation; psychological research methods; and the assessment and treatment of behavioral and affective disorders. **Therapy and Counseling:** Knowledge of principles, methods, and procedures for diagnosis, treatment, and rehabilitation of physical and mental dysfunctions and for career counseling and guidance. **English Language:** Knowledge of the structure and content of the English language, including the meaning and spelling of words, rules of composition, and grammar. **Customer and Personal Service:** Knowledge of principles and processes for providing customer and personal services. This includes customer needs assessment, meeting quality standards for services, and evaluation of customer satisfaction.

Special Education Teachers, Secondary School

- ▲ Education/Training Required: Bachelor's degree
- ▲ Annual Earnings: $42,780
- ▲ Growth: 24.6%
- ▲ Annual Job Openings: 8,000
- ▲ Self-Employed: 0%
- ▲ Part-Time: 12.9%

Teach secondary school subjects to educationally and physically handicapped students. Includes teachers who specialize and work with audibly and visually handicapped students and those who teach basic academic and life processes skills to the mentally impaired. Teaches socially acceptable behavior, employing techniques such as behavior modification and positive reinforcement. Confers with parents, administrators, testing specialists, social workers, and others to develop individual educational plan for student. Works with students to increase motivation. Meets with parents to provide support, guidance in using community resources, and skills in dealing with student's learning impairment. Observes, evaluates, and prepares reports on progress of students. Provides consistent reinforcement to learning and continuous feedback to student. Confers with other staff members to plan programs designed to promote educational, physical, and social development of students. Administers and interprets results of ability and achievement tests. Instructs students in academic subjects, utilizing various teaching techniques, such as phonetics, multisensory learning, and repetition, to reinforce learning. Instructs students in daily living skills required for independent maintenance and economic self-sufficiency, such as hygiene, safety, and food preparation. Selects and teaches reading material and math problems related to everyday life of individual student. Plans curriculum and other instructional materials to meet students' needs, considering such factors as physical, emotional, and educational abilities. Instructs students, using special educational strategies and techniques to improve sensory-motor and perceptual-motor development, memory, language, and cognition. **SKILLS—Learning Strategies:** Selecting and using training/instructional methods and procedures appropriate for the situation when learning or teaching new things. **Social Perceptiveness:** Being aware of others' reactions and understanding why they react as they do. **Instructing:** Teaching others how to do something. **Monitoring:** Monitoring/Assessing your performance or that of other individuals or organizations to make improvements or take corrective action. **Active Listening:** Giving full attention to what other people are saying, taking time to understand the points being made, asking questions as appropriate, and not interrupting at inappropriate times. **Speaking:** Talking to others to convey information effectively.

GOE INFORMATION—Interest Area: 12. Education and Social Service. **Work Group:** 12.03. Educational Services. **Other Job Titles in This Work Group:** Adult Literacy, Remedial Education, and GED Teachers and Instructors; Agricultural Sciences Teachers, Postsecondary; Anthropology and Archeology Teachers, Postsecondary; Architecture Teachers, Postsecondary; Archivists; Area, Ethnic, and Cultural Studies Teachers, Postsecondary; Art, Drama, and Music Teachers, Postsecondary; Atmospheric, Earth, Marine, and Space Sciences Teachers, Postsecondary; Audio-Visual Collections Specialists; Biological Science Teachers, Postsecondary; Business Teachers, Postsecondary; Chemistry Teachers, Postsecondary; Child Care Workers; Communications Teachers, Postsecondary; Computer Science Teachers, Postsecondary; Criminal Justice and Law Enforcement Teachers, Postsecondary; Curators; Economics Teachers, Postsecondary; Education Teachers, Postsecondary; Educational Psychologists; Educational, Vocational, and School Counselors; Elementary School Teachers, Except Special Education; Engineering Teachers, Postsecondary; English Language and Literature Teachers, Postsecondary; Environmental Science Teachers, Postsecondary; Farm and Home Management Advisors; Foreign Language and Literature Teachers, Postsecondary; Forestry and Conservation Science Teachers, Postsecondary; Geography Teachers, Postsecondary; Graduate Teaching Assistants; Health Specialties Teachers, Postsecondary; History Teachers, Postsecondary; Home Economics Teachers, Postsecondary; Kindergarten Teachers, Except Special Education; Law Teachers, Postsecondary; Librarians; Library Assistants, Clerical; Library Science Teachers, Postsecondary; Library Technicians; Mathematical Science Teachers, Postsecondary; Middle School Teachers, Except Special and Vocational Education; Museum Technicians and Conservators; Nursing Instructors and Teachers, Postsecondary; Personal Financial Advisors; Philosophy and Religion Teachers, Postsecondary; Physics Teachers, Postsecondary; Political Science Teachers, Postsecondary; Postsecondary Teachers, All Other; others. **PERSONALITY TYPE—**Social. Social occupations frequently involve working with, communicating with, and teaching people. These occupations often involve helping or providing service to others.

EDUCATION/TRAINING PROGRAM(S)—Special Education and Teaching, General. **RELATED KNOWLEDGE/COURSES—Education and Training:** Knowledge of principles and methods for curriculum and training design, teaching and instruction for individuals and groups, and the measurement of training effects. **Therapy and Counseling:** Knowledge of principles, methods, and procedures for diagnosis, treatment, and rehabilitation of physical and mental dysfunctions and for career counseling and guidance. **Psychology:** Knowledge of human behavior and performance; individual differences in ability, personality, and interests; learning and motivation; psychological research methods; and the assessment and treatment of behavioral and affective disorders. **English Language:** Knowledge of the structure and content of the English language, including the meaning and spelling of words, rules of composition, and grammar. **Customer and Personal Service:** Knowledge of principles and processes for providing customer and personal services. This includes customer needs assessment, meeting quality standards for services, and evaluation of customer satisfaction.

Speech-Language Pathologists

- ▲ Education/Training Required: Master's degree
- ▲ Annual Earnings: $48,520
- ▲ Growth: 39.2%
- ▲ Annual Job Openings: 4,000
- ▲ Self-Employed: 10.5%
- ▲ Part-Time: 20.8%

Assess and treat persons with speech, language, voice, and fluency disorders. May select alternative communication systems and teach their use. May perform research related to speech and language problems. Administers hearing or speech/language evaluations, tests, or examinations to patients to collect information on type and degree of impairment. Counsels and instructs clients in techniques to improve speech or hearing impairment, including sign language or lip-reading. Refers clients to additional medical or educational services if needed. Participates in conferences or training to update or share knowledge of new hearing or speech disorder treatment methods or technology. Advises educators or other medical staff on speech or hearing topics. Records and maintains reports of speech or hearing research or treatments. Evaluates hearing and speech/language test results and medical or background information to determine hearing or speech impairment and treatment. Conducts or directs research and reports findings on speech or hearing topics to develop procedures, technology, or treatments. **SKILLS—Writing:** Communicating effectively in writing as appropriate for the needs of the audience. **Reading Comprehension:** Understanding written sentences and paragraphs in work-related documents. **Instructing:** Teaching others how to do something. **Speaking:** Talking to others to convey information effectively. **Critical Thinking:** Using logic and reasoning to identify the strengths and weaknesses of alternative solutions, conclusions, or approaches to problems. **Active Learning:** Understanding the implications of new information for both current and future problem-solving and decision-making. **Learning Strategies:** Selecting and using training/instructional methods and procedures appropriate for the situation when learning or teaching new things.

GOE INFORMATION—Interest Area: 14. Medical and Health Services. **Work Group:** 14.06. Medical Therapy. **Other Job Titles in This Work Group:** Audiologists; Massage Therapists; Occupational Therapist Aides; Occupational Therapist Assistants; Occupational Therapists; Physical Therapist Aides; Physical Therapist Assistants; Physical Therapists; Radiation Therapists; Recreational Therapists; Respiratory Therapists; Respiratory Therapy Technicians; Therapists, All Other. **PERSONALITY TYPE—Social.** Social occupations frequently involve working with, communicating with, and teaching people. These occupations often involve helping or providing service to others.

EDUCATION/TRAINING PROGRAM(S)—Audiology/Audiologist and Speech-Language Pathology/Pathologist; Communication Disorders Sciences and Services, Other; Communication Disorders, General; Speech-Language Pathology/Pathologist. **RELATED KNOWLEDGE/COURSES—Therapy and Counseling:** Knowledge of principles, methods, and procedures for diagnosis, treatment, and rehabilitation of physical and mental dysfunctions and for career counseling and guidance. **Medicine and Dentistry:** Knowledge of the information and techniques needed to diagnose and treat human injuries, diseases, and deformities. This includes symptoms, treatment alternatives, drug properties and interactions, and preventive health-care measures. **English Language:** Knowledge of the structure and content of the English language, including the meaning and spelling of words, rules of composition, and grammar. **Education and Training:** Knowledge of principles and methods for curriculum and training design, teaching and instruction for individuals and groups, and the measurement of training effects. **Personnel and Human Resources:** Knowledge of principles and procedures for personnel recruitment, selection, training, compensation and benefits, labor relations and negotiation, and personnel information systems. **Administration and Management:** Knowledge of business and management principles involved in strategic planning, resource allocation, human resources modeling, leadership technique, production methods, and coordination of people and resources.

Spotters, Dry Cleaning

- ▲ Education/Training Required: Short-term on-the-job training
- ▲ Annual Earnings: $16,360
- ▲ Growth: 11.4%
- ▲ Annual Job Openings: 62,000
- ▲ Self-Employed: 11.4%
- ▲ Part-Time: 26.3%

Identify stains in wool, synthetic, and silk garments and household fabrics and apply chemical solutions to remove stain. Determine spotting procedures on basis of type of fabric and nature of stain. Inspects spots to ascertain composition and select solvent. Operates drycleaning machine. Applies chemicals to neutralize effect of solvents.

Sprays steam, water, or air over spot to flush out chemicals, dry material, raise nap, or brighten color. Cleans fabric, using vacuum or air hose. Spreads article on worktable and positions stain over vacuum head or on marble slab. Mixes bleaching agent with hot water in vats and soaks material until it is bleached. Applies bleaching powder to spot and sprays with steam to remove stains from certain fabrics which do not respond to other cleaning solvents. Sprinkles chemical solvents over stain and pats area with brush or sponge until stain is removed. **SKILLS—Equipment Selection:** Determining the kind of tools and equipment needed to do a job.

GOE INFORMATION—Interest Area: 11. Recreation, Travel, and Other Personal Services. **Work Group:** 11.06. Apparel, Shoes, Leather, and Fabric Care. **Other Job Titles in This Work Group:** Custom Tailors; Fabric Menders, Except Garment; Laundry and Drycleaning Machine Operators and Tenders, Except Pressing; Laundry and Dry-Cleaning Workers; Precision Dyers; Pressers, Delicate Fabrics; Pressers, Hand; Pressers, Textile, Garment, and Related Materials; Shoe and Leather Workers and Repairers; Shop and Alteration Tailors; Tailors, Dressmakers, and Custom Sewers; Textile, Apparel, and Furnishings Workers, All Other; Upholsterers. **PERSONALITY TYPE—**Realistic.

Realistic occupations frequently involve work activities that include practical, hands-on problems and solutions. They often deal with plants, animals, and real-world materials like wood, tools, and machinery. Many of the occupations require working outside and do not involve a lot of paperwork or working closely with others.

EDUCATION/TRAINING PROGRAM(S)—No data available. **RELATED KNOWLEDGE/COURSES— Chemistry:** Knowledge of the chemical composition, structure, and properties of substances and of the chemical processes and transformations that they undergo. This includes uses of chemicals and their interactions, danger signs, production techniques, and disposal methods. **Customer and Personal Service:** Knowledge of principles and processes for providing customer and personal services. This includes customer needs assessment, meeting quality standards for services, and evaluation of customer satisfaction. **Mathematics:** Knowledge of arithmetic, algebra, geometry, calculus, and statistics and their applications. **Public Safety and Security:** Knowledge of relevant equipment, policies, procedures, and strategies to promote effective local, state, or national security operations for the protection of people, data, property, and institutions.

Statement Clerks

- ▲ Education/Training Required: Short-term on-the-job training
- ▲ Annual Earnings: $25,350
- ▲ Growth: 8.5%
- ▲ Annual Job Openings: 69,000
- ▲ Self-Employed: 4.0%
- ▲ Part-Time: 19.1%

Prepare and distribute bank statements to customers, answer inquiries, and reconcile discrepancies in records and accounts. Compares previously prepared bank statements with canceled checks, prepares statements for distribution to customers, and reconciles discrepancies in records and accounts. Keeps canceled checks and customer signature files. Encodes and cancels checks, using machine. Takes orders for imprinted checks. Posts stop-payment notices to prevent payment of protested checks. Routes statements for mailing or over-the-counter delivery to customers. Recovers checks returned to customer in error, adjusts customer account, and answers inquiries. Matches statement with batch of canceled checks by account number. Inserts statements and canceled checks in envelopes and affixes postage or stuffs envelopes and meters post-

age. **SKILLS—Reading Comprehension:** Understanding written sentences and paragraphs in work-related documents. **Active Listening:** Giving full attention to what other people are saying, taking time to understand the points being made, asking questions as appropriate, and not interrupting at inappropriate times. **Mathematics:** Using mathematics to solve problems. **Speaking:** Talking to others to convey information effectively. **Critical Thinking:** Using logic and reasoning to identify the strengths and weaknesses of alternative solutions, conclusions, or approaches to problems.

GOE INFORMATION—Interest Area: 09. Business Detail. **Work Group:** 09.03. Bookkeeping, Auditing, and Accounting. **Other Job Titles in This Work Group:** Billing and Posting Clerks and Machine Operators; Billing,

Cost, and Rate Clerks; Bookkeeping, Accounting, and Auditing Clerks; Brokerage Clerks; Payroll and Timekeeping Clerks; Tax Preparers. **PERSONALITY TYPE**—Conventional. Conventional occupations frequently involve following set procedures and routines. These occupations can include working with data and details more than with ideas. Usually there is a clear line of authority to follow.

EDUCATION/TRAINING PROGRAM(S)—Accounting Technology/Technician and Bookkeeping. **RELATED KNOWLEDGE/COURSES—Clerical Studies:** Knowledge of administrative and clerical procedures and systems, such as word processing, managing files and records, stenography and transcription, designing forms, and other office procedures and terminology. **Mathematics:** Knowledge of arithmetic, algebra, geometry, calculus, and statistics and their applications. **Economics and Accounting:** Knowledge of economic and accounting principles and practices, the financial markets, banking, and the analysis and reporting of financial data. **Customer and Personal Service:** Knowledge of principles and processes for providing customer and personal services. This includes customer needs assessment, meeting quality standards for services, and evaluation of customer satisfaction. **Computers and Electronics:** Knowledge of circuit boards, processors, chips, electronic equipment, and computer hardware and software, including applications and programming.

Stevedores, Except Equipment Operators

- ▲ Education/Training Required: Short-term on-the-job training
- ▲ Annual Earnings: $19,440
- ▲ Growth: 13.9%
- ▲ Annual Job Openings: 519,000
- ▲ Self-Employed: 1.6%
- ▲ Part-Time: 16.2%

Manually load and unload ship cargo. Stack cargo in transit shed or in hold of ship, using pallet or cargo board. Attach and move slings to lift cargo. Guide load lift. Carries or moves cargo by hand truck to wharf and stacks cargo on pallets to facilitate transfer to and from ship. Stacks cargo in transit shed or in hold of ship as directed. Attaches and moves slings used to lift cargo. Guides load being lifted to prevent swinging. Shores cargo in ship's hold to prevent shifting during voyage. **SKILLS—Active Listening:** Giving full attention to what other people are saying, taking time to understand the points being made, asking questions as appropriate, and not interrupting at inappropriate times. **Reading Comprehension:** Understanding written sentences and paragraphs in work-related documents.

GOE INFORMATION—Interest Area: 07. Transportation. **Work Group:** 07.08. Support Work. **Other Job Titles in This Work Group:** Freight Inspectors; Railroad Yard Workers; Train Crew Members; Transportation Inspectors.

PERSONALITY TYPE—Realistic. Realistic occupations frequently involve work activities that include practical, hands-on problems and solutions. They often deal with plants, animals, and real-world materials like wood, tools, and machinery. Many of the occupations require working outside and do not involve a lot of paperwork or working closely with others.

EDUCATION/TRAINING PROGRAM(S)—No data available. **RELATED KNOWLEDGE/COURSES—Production and Processing:** Knowledge of raw materials, production processes, quality control, costs, and other techniques for maximizing the effective manufacture and distribution of goods. **Transportation:** Knowledge of principles and methods for moving people or goods by air, rail, sea, or road, including the relative costs and benefits. **Building and Construction:** Knowledge of materials, methods, and tools involved in the construction or repair of houses, buildings, or other structures, such as highways and roads.

Stock Clerks and Order Fillers

> ▲ Education/Training Required: Short-term on-the-job training
> ▲ Annual Earnings: $19,060
> ▲ Growth: 8.5%
> ▲ Annual Job Openings: 467,000
> ▲ Self-Employed: 0%
> ▲ Part-Time: 12.8%

Receive, store, and issue sales floor merchandise, materials, equipment, and other items from stockroom, warehouse, or storage yard to fill shelves, racks, tables, or customers' orders. May mark prices on merchandise and set up sales displays. SKILLS—No data available.

GOE INFORMATION—Interest Area: 09. Business Detail. Work Group: 09.08. Records and Materials Processing. Other Job Titles in This Work Group: Cargo and Freight Agents; Couriers and Messengers; Mail Clerks, Except Mail Machine Operators and Postal Service; Mark-ing Clerks; Order Fillers, Wholesale and Retail Sales; Postal Service Mail Carriers; Postal Service Mail Sorters, Processors, and Processing Machine Operators; Shipping, Receiving, and Traffic Clerks; Stock Clerks—Stockroom, Warehouse, or Storage Yard; Weighers, Measurers, Checkers, and Samplers, Recordkeeping. PERSONALITY TYPE—No data available.

EDUCATION/TRAINING PROGRAM(S)—Retailing and Retail Operations. RELATED KNOWLEDGE/COURSES—No data available.

Stock Clerks, Sales Floor

> ▲ Education/Training Required: Short-term on-the-job training
> ▲ Annual Earnings: $19,060
> ▲ Growth: 8.5%
> ▲ Annual Job Openings: 467,000
> ▲ Self-Employed: 0.1%
> ▲ Part-Time: 13.7%

Receive, store, and issue sales floor merchandise. Stock shelves, racks, cases, bins, and tables with merchandise and arrange merchandise displays to attract customers. May periodically take physical count of stock or check and mark merchandise. Receives, opens, and unpacks cartons or crates of merchandise and checks invoice against items received. Takes inventory or examines merchandise to identify items to be reordered or replenished. Requisitions merchandise from supplier based on available space, merchandise on hand, customer demand, or advertised specials. Stamps, attaches, or changes price tags on merchandise, referring to price list. Stocks storage areas and displays with new or transferred merchandise. Sets up advertising signs and displays merchandise on shelves, counters, or tables to attract customers and promote sales. Cleans display cases, shelves, and aisles. Itemizes and totals customer merchandise selection at checkout counter, using cash register, and accepts cash or charge card for purchases. Answers questions and advises customer in selection of merchandise. Cuts lumber, screening, glass, and related materials to size requested by customer. Packs customer purchases in bags or cartons. Transports packages to customer vehicle. SKILLS—Reading Comprehension: Understanding written sentences and paragraphs in work-related documents. Active Listening: Giving full attention to what other people are saying, taking time to understand the points being made, asking questions as appropriate, and not interrupting at inappropriate times. Service Orientation: Actively looking for ways to help people. Social Perceptiveness: Being aware of others' reactions and understanding why they react as they do. Mathematics: Using mathematics to solve problems.

GOE INFORMATION—Interest Area: 10. Sales and Marketing. Work Group: 10.03. General Sales. Other Job Titles in This Work Group: Parts Salespersons; Real Estate Brokers; Real Estate Sales Agents; Retail Salespersons; Sales Representatives, Wholesale and Manufacturing, Except Technical and Scientific Products; Service Station Attendants; Travel Agents. PERSONALITY TYPE—Realistic. Realistic occupations frequently involve work activities that include practical, hands-on problems and solutions. They often deal with plants, animals, and real-world materials like wood, tools, and machinery. Many of the occupations require working outside and do not involve a lot of paperwork or working closely with others.

EDUCATION/TRAINING PROGRAM(S)—Retailing and Retail Operations. **RELATED KNOWLEDGE/COURSES—Clerical Studies:** Knowledge of administrative and clerical procedures and systems, such as word processing, managing files and records, stenography and transcription, designing forms, and other office procedures and terminology. **Customer and Personal Service:** Knowl-

edge of principles and processes for providing customer and personal services. This includes customer needs assessment, meeting quality standards for services, and evaluation of customer satisfaction. **Sales and Marketing:** Knowledge of principles and methods for showing, promoting, and selling products or services. This includes marketing strategy and tactics, product demonstration, sales techniques, and sales control systems. **Mathematics:** Knowledge of arithmetic, algebra, geometry, calculus, and statistics and their applications. **English Language:** Knowledge of the structure and content of the English language, including the meaning and spelling of words, rules of composition, and grammar.

Stock Clerks—Stockroom, Warehouse, or Storage Yard

- ▲ Education/Training Required: Moderate-term on-the-job training
- ▲ Annual Earnings: $19,060
- ▲ Growth: 8.5%
- ▲ Annual Job Openings: 467,000
- ▲ Self-Employed: 0.1%
- ▲ Part-Time: 13.7%

Receive, store, and issue materials, equipment, and other items from stockroom, warehouse, or storage yard. Keep records and compile stock reports. Receives, counts, and stores stock items and records data, manually or using computer. Assists or directs workers to other stockroom, warehouse, or storage yard. Adjusts, repairs, assembles, or prepares products, supplies, equipment, or other items according to specifications or customer requirements. Examines and inspects stock items for wear or defects, reports damage to supervisor, and disposes of or returns items to vendor. Confers with engineering and purchasing personnel and vendors regarding procurement and stock availability. Purchases or prepares documents to purchase new or additional stock and recommends disposal of excess, defective, or obsolete stock. Receives and fills orders or sells supplies, materials, and products to customers. Prepares documents such as inventory balance, price lists, shortages, expenditures, and periodic reports, using computer, typewriter, or calculator. Verifies computations against physical count of stock, adjusts for errors, or investigates discrepancies. Delivers products, supplies, and equipment to designated area and determines sequence and release of backorders according to stock availability. Drives truck to pick up incoming stock or deliver parts to designated locations. Cleans and maintains supplies, tools, equipment, instruments, and storage areas to ensure compliance to safety regulations. Compares office inventory

records with sales orders, invoices, or requisitions to verify accuracy and receipt of items. Locates and selects material, supplies, tools, equipment, or other articles from stock or issues stock item to workers. Compiles, reviews, and maintains data from contracts, purchase orders, requisitions, and other documents to determine supply needs. Determines method of storage, identification, and stock location based on turnover, environmental factors, and physical capacity of facility. Packs, unpacks, and marks stock items, using identification tag, stamp, electric marking tool, or other labeling equipment. Records nature, quantity, value, or location of material, supplies, or equipment received, shipped, used, or issued to workers. **SKILLS—Mathematics:** Using mathematics to solve problems. **Reading Comprehension:** Understanding written sentences and paragraphs in work-related documents. **Writing:** Communicating effectively in writing as appropriate for the needs of the audience. **Active Listening:** Giving full attention to what other people are saying, taking time to understand the points being made, asking questions as appropriate, and not interrupting at inappropriate times. **Speaking:** Talking to others to convey information effectively.

GOE INFORMATION—Interest Area: 09. Business Detail. **Work Group:** 09.08. Records and Materials Processing. **Other Job Titles in This Work Group:** Cargo and Freight Agents; Couriers and Messengers; Mail Clerks, Except Mail Machine Operators and Postal Service; Marking Clerks; Order Fillers, Wholesale and Retail Sales; Postal Service Mail Carriers; Postal Service Mail Sorters, Processors, and Processing Machine Operators; Shipping, Receiving, and Traffic Clerks; Stock Clerks and Order Fillers; Weighers, Measurers, Checkers, and Samplers, Recordkeeping. **PERSONALITY TYPE**—Conventional. Conventional occupations frequently involve following set procedures and routines. These occupations can include working with data and details more than with ideas. Usually there is a clear line of authority to follow.

EDUCATION/TRAINING PROGRAM(S)—Retailing and Retail Operations. **RELATED KNOWLEDGE/ COURSES—Clerical Studies:** Knowledge of administrative and clerical procedures and systems, such as word pro-

cessing, managing files and records, stenography and transcription, designing forms, and other office procedures and terminology. **Mathematics:** Knowledge of arithmetic, algebra, geometry, calculus, and statistics and their applications. **Computers and Electronics:** Knowledge of circuit boards, processors, chips, electronic equipment, and computer hardware and software, including applications and programming. **Economics and Accounting:** Knowledge of economic and accounting principles and practices, the financial markets, banking, and the analysis and reporting of financial data. **English Language:** Knowledge of the structure and content of the English language, including the meaning and spelling of words, rules of composition, and grammar. **Production and Processing:** Knowledge of raw materials, production processes, quality control, costs, and other techniques for maximizing the effective manufacture and distribution of goods.

Stonemasons

▲ Education/Training Required: Long-term on-the-job training
▲ Annual Earnings: $32,470
▲ Growth: 20.8%
▲ Annual Job Openings: 2,000
▲ Self-Employed: 27.9%
▲ Part-Time: 8.7%

Build stone structures, such as piers, walls, and abutments. Lay walks, curbstones, or special types of masonry for vats, tanks, and floors. Shapes, trims, faces, and cuts marble or stone preparatory to setting, using power saws, cutting equipment, and hand tools. Mixes mortar or grout and pours or spreads mortar or grout on marble slabs, stone, or foundation. Cleans excess mortar or grout from surface of marble, stone, or monument, using sponge, brush, water, or acid. Lines interiors of molds with treated paper and fills molds with composition-stone mixture. Repairs cracked or chipped areas of ornamental stone or marble surface, using blowtorch and mastic. Drills holes in marble or ornamental stone and anchors bracket. Digs trench for foundation of monument, using pick and shovel. Removes sections of monument from truck bed and guides stone onto foundation, using skids, hoist, or truck crane. Positions mold along guidelines of wall, presses mold in place, and removes mold and paper from wall. Smoothes, polishes, and bevels surfaces, using hand tools and power tools. Finishes joints between stones, using trowel. Lays out wall pattern or foundation of monument, using straightedge, rule, or staked lines. Sets stone or marble in

place according to layout or pattern. Aligns and levels stone or marble, using measuring devices such as rule, square, and plumbline. **SKILLS—Equipment Selection:** Determining the kind of tools and equipment needed to do a job. **Operation and Control:** Controlling operations of equipment or systems. **Mathematics:** Using mathematics to solve problems.

GOE INFORMATION—Interest Area: 06. Construction, Mining, and Drilling. **Work Group:** 06.02. Construction. **Other Job Titles in This Work Group:** Boat Builders and Shipwrights; Boilermakers; Brattice Builders; Brickmasons and Blockmasons; Carpenters; Carpet Installers; Ceiling Tile Installers; Cement Masons and Concrete Finishers; Commercial Divers; Construction Carpenters; Drywall and Ceiling Tile Installers; Drywall Installers; Electricians; Explosives Workers, Ordnance Handling Experts, and Blasters; Fence Erectors; Floor Layers, Except Carpet, Wood, and Hard Tiles; Floor Sanders and Finishers; Glaziers; Grader, Bulldozer, and Scraper Operators; Hazardous Materials Removal Workers; Insulation Workers, Floor, Ceiling, and Wall; Insulation Workers, Mechanical; Manufactured Building and Mobile

Home Installers; Operating Engineers; Operating Engineers and Other Construction Equipment Operators; Painters, Construction and Maintenance; Paperhangers; Paving, Surfacing, and Tamping Equipment Operators; Pile-Driver Operators; Pipe Fitters; Pipelayers; Pipelaying Fitters; Plasterers and Stucco Masons; Plumbers; Plumbers, Pipefitters, and Steamfitters; Rail-Track Laying and Maintenance Equipment Operators; Refractory Materials Repairers, Except Brickmasons; Reinforcing Iron and Rebar Workers; Riggers; Roofers; Rough Carpenters; Security and Fire Alarm Systems Installers; Segmental Pavers; Sheet Metal Workers; Ship Carpenters and Joiners; Stone Cutters and Carvers; Structural Iron and Steel Workers; Tapers; Terrazzo Workers and Finishers; Tile and Marble Setters. **PERSONALITY TYPE**—Realistic. Realistic occupations frequently involve work activities that include practical, hands-on problems and solutions. They often deal with plants, animals, and real-world materials like wood, tools, and machinery. Many of the occupations require working outside and do not involve a lot of paperwork or working closely with others.

EDUCATION/TRAINING PROGRAM(S)—Mason/Masonry. **RELATED KNOWLEDGE/COURSES**—**Building and Construction:** Knowledge of materials, methods, and tools involved in the construction or repair of houses, buildings, or other structures, such as highways and roads. **Principles of Mechanical Devices:** Knowledge of machines and tools, including their designs, uses, repair, and maintenance. **Design:** Knowledge of design techniques, tools, and principles involved in production of precision technical plans, blueprints, drawings, and models. **Mathematics:** Knowledge of arithmetic, algebra, geometry, calculus, and statistics and their applications.

Storage and Distribution Managers

- ▲ Education/Training Required: Work experience in a related occupation
- ▲ Annual Earnings: $57,240
- ▲ Growth: 20.2%
- ▲ Annual Job Openings: 13,000
- ▲ Self-Employed: 0%
- ▲ Part-Time: 6.1%

Plan, direct, and coordinate the storage and distribution operations within an organization or the activities of organizations that are engaged in storing and distributing materials and products. Establishes standard and emergency operating procedures for receiving, handling, storing, shipping, or salvaging products or materials. Examines products or materials to estimate quantities or weight and type of container required for storage or transport. Interacts with customers or shippers to solicit new business, answer questions about services offered or required, and investigate complaints. Prepares or directs preparation of correspondence, reports, and operations, maintenance, and safety manuals. Schedules air or surface pickup, delivery, or distribution of products or materials. Interviews, selects, and trains warehouse and supervisory personnel. Examines invoices and shipping manifests for conformity to tariff and customs regulations and contacts customs officials to effect release of shipments. Reviews invoices, work orders, consumption reports, and demand forecasts to estimate peak delivery periods and issue work assignments. Supervises the activities of worker engaged in receiving, storing, testing, and shipping products or materials. Inspects physical condition of warehouse and equipment and prepares work orders for testing, maintenance, or repair. Develops and implements plans for facility modification or expansion, such as equipment purchase or changes in space allocation or structural design. Negotiates contracts, settlements, and freight-handling agreements to resolve problems between foreign and domestic shippers. Plans, develops, and implements warehouse safety and security programs and activities. Confers with department heads to coordinate warehouse activities, such as production, sales, records control, and purchasing. **SKILLS—Management of Personnel Resources:** Motivating, developing, and directing people as they work, identifying the best people for the job. **Negotiation:** Bringing others together and trying to reconcile differences. **Writing:** Communicating effectively in writing as appropriate for the needs of the audience. **Coordination:** Adjusting actions in relation to others' actions. **Monitoring:** Monitoring/Assessing your performance or that of other individuals or organizations to make improvements or take corrective action. **Operations Analysis:** Analyzing needs and product requirements to create a design. **Speaking:** Talking to others to convey information effectively.

GOE INFORMATION—**Interest Area:** 13. General Management and Support. **Work Group:** 13.01. General Management Work and Management of Support Functions. **Other Job Titles in This Work Group:** Chief Executives; Compensation and Benefits Managers; Farm, Ranch, and Other Agricultural Managers; Financial Managers; Financial Managers, Branch or Department; Funeral Directors; General and Operations Managers; Government Service Executives; Human Resources Managers; Human Resources Managers, All Other; Legislators; Managers, All Other; Postmasters and Mail Superintendents; Private Sector Executives; Property, Real Estate, and Community Association Managers; Public Relations Managers; Purchasing Managers; Training and Development Managers; Transportation, Storage, and Distribution Managers; Treasurers, Controllers, and Chief Financial Officers. **PERSONALITY TYPE**—Enterprising. Enterprising occupations frequently involve starting up and carrying out projects. These occupations can involve leading people and making many decisions. They sometimes require risk taking and often deal with business.

EDUCATION/TRAINING PROGRAM(S)—Aeronautics/Aviation/Aerospace Science and Technology, General; Aviation/Airway Management and Operations; Business Administration and Management, General; Business/Commerce, General; Logistics and Materials Management; Public Administration. **RELATED KNOWLEDGE/COURSES**—**Administration and Management:** Knowledge of business and management principles involved in strategic planning, resource allocation, human resources modeling, leadership technique, production methods, and coordination of people and resources. **Personnel and Human Resources:** Knowledge of principles and procedures for personnel recruitment, selection, training, compensation and benefits, labor relations and negotiation, and personnel information systems. **Mathematics:** Knowledge of arithmetic, algebra, geometry, calculus, and statistics and their applications. **Transportation:** Knowledge of principles and methods for moving people or goods by air, rail, sea, or road, including the relative costs and benefits. **Production and Processing:** Knowledge of raw materials, production processes, quality control, costs, and other techniques for maximizing the effective manufacture and distribution of goods.

Structural Iron and Steel Workers

- ▲ Education/Training Required: Long-term on-the-job training
- ▲ Annual Earnings: $38,950
- ▲ Growth: 18.4%
- ▲ Annual Job Openings: 12,000
- ▲ Self-Employed: 0%
- ▲ Part-Time: 4.9%

Raise, place, and unite iron or steel girders, columns, and other structural members to form completed structures or structural frameworks. May erect metal storage tanks and assemble prefabricated metal buildings. Guides structural-steel member, using tab line (rope), or rides on member in order to guide it into position. Fastens structural-steel members to cable of hoist, using chain, cable, or rope. Signals worker operating hoisting equipment to lift and place structural-steel member. Sets up hoisting equipment for raising and placing structural-steel members. Inserts sealing strips, wiring, insulating material, ladders, flanges, gauges, and valves, depending on type of structure being assembled. Cuts and welds steel members to make alterations, using oxyacetylene welding equipment. Bucks (holds) rivets while pneumatic riveter uses air-hammer to form heads on rivets. Catches hot rivets tossed by rivet heater in bucket and inserts rivets in holes, using tongs. Verifies vertical and horizontal alignment of structural-steel members, using plumb bob and level. Bolts aligned structural-steel members in position until they can be permanently riveted, bolted, or welded in place. Pulls, pushes, or pries structural-steel member into approximate position while member is supported by hoisting device. Forces structural-steel members into final position, using turnbuckles, crowbars, jacks, and hand tools. Drives drift pins through rivet holes to align rivet holes in structural-steel member with corresponding holes in previously placed member. **SKILLS**—**Coordination:** Adjusting actions in relation to others' actions. **Installation:** Installing equipment, machines, wiring, or programs to meet specifications. **Equipment Selection:** Determining the kind of tools and equipment needed to do a job. **Operation and Control:** Controlling operations of equipment or systems.

GOE INFORMATION—**Interest Area:** 06. Construction, Mining, and Drilling. **Work Group:** 06.02. Construction. **Other Job Titles in This Work Group:** Boat Builders and Shipwrights; Boilermakers; Brattice Builders; Brickmasons and Blockmasons; Carpenters; Carpet Installers; Ceiling Tile Installers; Cement Masons and Concrete Finishers; Commercial Divers; Construction Carpenters; Drywall and Ceiling Tile Installers; Drywall Installers; Electricians; Explosives Workers, Ordnance Handling Experts, and Blasters; Fence Erectors; Floor Layers, Except Carpet, Wood, and Hard Tiles; Floor Sanders and Finishers; Glaziers; Grader, Bulldozer, and Scraper Operators; Hazardous Materials Removal Workers; Insulation Workers, Floor, Ceiling, and Wall; Insulation Workers, Mechanical; Manufactured Building and Mobile Home Installers; Operating Engineers; Operating Engineers and Other Construction Equipment Operators; Painters, Construction and Maintenance; Paperhangers; Paving, Surfacing, and Tamping Equipment Operators; Pile-Driver Operators; Pipe Fitters; Pipelayers; Pipelaying Fitters; Plasterers and Stucco Masons; Plumbers; Plumbers, Pipefitters, and Steamfitters; Rail-Track Laying and Maintenance Equipment Operators; Refractory Materials Repairers, Except Brickmasons; Reinforcing Iron and Rebar Workers; Riggers; Roofers; Rough Carpenters; Security and Fire Alarm Systems Installers; Segmental Pavers; Sheet Metal Workers; Ship Carpenters and Joiners; Stone Cutters and Carvers; Stonemasons; Tapers; Terrazzo Workers and Finishers; Tile and Marble Setters. **PERSONALITY TYPE**—Realistic. Realistic occupations frequently involve work activities that include practical, hands-on problems and solutions. They often deal with plants, animals, and real-world materials like wood, tools, and machinery. Many of the occupations require working outside and do not involve a lot of paperwork or working closely with others.

EDUCATION/TRAINING PROGRAM(S)—Construction Trades, Other; Metal Building Assembly/Assembler. **RELATED KNOWLEDGE/COURSES—Building and Construction:** Knowledge of materials, methods, and tools involved in the construction or repair of houses, buildings, or other structures, such as highways and roads. **Principles of Mechanical Devices:** Knowledge of machines and tools, including their designs, uses, repair, and maintenance. **Public Safety and Security:** Knowledge of relevant equipment, policies, procedures, and strategies to promote effective local, state, or national security operations for the protection of people, data, property, and institutions. **Engineering and Technology:** Knowledge of the practical application of engineering science and technology. This includes applying principles, techniques, procedures, and equipment to the design and production of various goods and services. **Mathematics:** Knowledge of arithmetic, algebra, geometry, calculus, and statistics and their applications. **Physics:** Knowledge and prediction of physical principles and laws and their interrelationships and applications to understanding fluid, material, and atmospheric dynamics and mechanical, electrical, atomic, and sub-atomic structures and processes.

Structural Metal Fabricators and Fitters

- ▲ Education/Training Required: Moderate-term on-the-job training
- ▲ Annual Earnings: $28,000
- ▲ Growth: 19.5%
- ▲ Annual Job Openings: 20,000
- ▲ Self-Employed: 0%
- ▲ Part-Time: 2.3%

Fabricate, lay out, position, align, and fit parts of structural metal products. SKILLS—No data available.

GOE INFORMATION—**Interest Area:** 08. Industrial Production. **Work Group:** 08.03. Production Work. **Other Job Titles in This Work Group:** Bakers, Manufacturing; Bindery Machine Operators and Tenders; Brazers; Cementing and Gluing Machine Operators and Tenders; Chemical Equipment Controllers and Operators; Chemical Equipment Operators and Tenders; Chemical Equipment Tenders; Cleaning, Washing, and Metal Pickling Equipment Operators and Tenders; Coating, Painting, and Spraying Machine Operators and Tenders; Coil Winders, Tapers, and Finishers; Combination Machine Tool Operators and Tenders, Metal and Plastic; Computer-Controlled Machine Tool Operators, Metal and Plastic; Cooling and Freezing Equipment Operators and Tenders; Crushing, Grinding, and Polishing Machine Setters, Operators, and Tenders; Cutters and Trimmers, Hand; Cutting and Slicing Machine Operators and Tenders; Cutting and Slicing Machine Setters, Operators, and Tenders; Design Printing Machine Setters and Set-Up Operators; Electrolytic Plating and Coating Machine Operators and Tenders, Metal and Plastic; Electrolytic Plating and Coating Machine Setters and Set-Up Operators, Metal and Plastic; Electrotypers and Stereotypers; Embossing Machine Set-Up Operators; Engraver Set-Up Operators; Extruding and Forming Machine Operators and Tenders, Synthetic or Glass Fibers; Extruding and Forming Machine Setters, Operators, and Tenders, Synthetic and Glass Fibers; Extruding, Forming, Pressing, and Compacting Machine Operators and Tenders; Fabric and Apparel Patternmakers; Fiber Product Cutting Machine Setters and Set-Up Operators; Fiberglass Laminators and Fabricators; Film Laboratory Technicians; Fitters, Structural Metal—Precision; Food and Tobacco Roasting, Baking, and Drying Machine Operators and Tenders; Food Batchmakers; Food Cooking Machine Operators and Tenders; Furnace, Kiln, Oven, Drier, and Kettle Operators and Tenders; Glass Cutting Machine Setters and Set-Up Operators; Graders and Sorters, Agricultural Products; Grinding and Polishing Workers, Hand; Hand Compositors and Typesetters; Heaters, Metal and Plastic; others. **PERSONALITY TYPE**—No data available.

EDUCATION/TRAINING PROGRAM(S)—Machine Shop Technology/Assistant. **RELATED KNOWLEDGE/ COURSES**—No data available.

Substance Abuse and Behavioral Disorder Counselors

- ▲ Education/Training Required: Master's degree
- ▲ Annual Earnings: $29,870
- ▲ Growth: 35.0%
- ▲ Annual Job Openings: 7,000
- ▲ Self-Employed: 8.4%
- ▲ Part-Time: 20.8%

Counsel and advise individuals with alcohol, tobacco, drug, or other problems, such as gambling and eating disorders. May counsel individuals, families, or groups or engage in prevention programs. Plans and conducts programs to prevent substance abuse or improve health and counseling services in community. Supervises and directs other workers providing services to client or patient. Intervenes as advocate for client or patient to resolve emergency problems in crisis situation. Counsels clients and patients, individually and in group sessions, to assist in overcoming dependencies, adjusting to life, and making changes. Counsels family members to assist in understanding, dealing with, and supporting client or patient. Interviews clients, reviews records, and confers with other professionals to evaluate mental or physical condition of client or patient. Formulates or coordinates program plan for treatment, care, and rehabilitation of client or patient, based on social work experience and knowledge. Modifies treatment plan to comply with changes in client's status. Refers patient, client, or family to community resources to assist in recovery from mental or physical illness. Monitors, evaluates, and records client progress according to measurable goals described in treatment and care plan. **SKILLS—Social Perceptiveness:** Being aware of others' reactions and understanding why they react as they do.

Reading Comprehension: Understanding written sentences and paragraphs in work-related documents. **Critical Thinking:** Using logic and reasoning to identify the strengths and weaknesses of alternative solutions, conclusions, or approaches to problems. **Service Orientation:** Actively looking for ways to help people. **Management of Financial Resources:** Determining how money will be spent to get the work done and accounting for these expenditures. **Active Listening:** Giving full attention to what other people are saying, taking time to understand the points being made, asking questions as appropriate, and not interrupting at inappropriate times.

GOE INFORMATION—Interest Area: 12. Education and Social Service. **Work Group:** 12.02. Social Services. **Other Job Titles in This Work Group:** Child, Family, and School Social Workers; Clergy; Clinical Psychologists; Clinical, Counseling, and School Psychologists; Community and Social Service Specialists, All Other; Counseling Psychologists; Counselors, All Other; Directors, Religious Activities and Education; Marriage and Family Therapists; Medical and Public Health Social Workers; Mental Health and Substance Abuse Social Workers; Mental Health Counselors; Probation Officers and Correctional Treatment Specialists; Rehabilitation Counselors; Religious Workers, All Other; Residential Advisors; Social and Human Service Assistants; Social Workers, All Other. **PERSONALITY TYPE**—Social. Social occupations frequently involve working with, communicating with, and teaching people. These occupations often involve helping or providing service to others.

EDUCATION/TRAINING PROGRAM(S)—Clinical/ Medical Social Work; Mental and Social Health Services and Allied Professions, Other; Substance Abuse/Addiction Counseling. **RELATED KNOWLEDGE/COURSES**— **Therapy and Counseling:** Knowledge of principles, methods, and procedures for diagnosis, treatment, and rehabilitation of physical and mental dysfunctions and for career counseling and guidance. **Psychology:** Knowledge of human behavior and performance; individual differences in ability, personality, and interests; learning and motivation; psychological research methods; and the assessment and treatment of behavioral and affective disorders. **Customer and Personal Service:** Knowledge of principles and processes for providing customer and personal services. This includes customer needs assessment, meeting quality standards for services, and evaluation of customer satisfaction. **Education and Training:** Knowledge of principles and methods for curriculum and training design, teaching and instruction for individuals and groups, and the measurement of training effects. **English Language:** Knowledge of the structure and content of the English language, including the meaning and spelling of words, rules of composition, and grammar.

Surgeons

- ▲ Education/Training Required: First professional degree
- ▲ Annual Earnings: More than $145,600
- ▲ Growth: 17.9%
- ▲ Annual Job Openings: 27,000
- ▲ Self-Employed: 20.4%
- ▲ Part-Time: 7.2%

Treat diseases, injuries, and deformities by invasive methods, such as manual manipulation or by using instruments and appliances. Operates on patient to correct deformities, repair injuries, prevent diseases, or improve or restore patient's functions. Analyzes patient's medical history, medication allergies, physical condition, and examination results to verify operation's necessity and to determine best procedure. Examines patient to provide information on medical condition and patient's surgical risk. Refers patient to medical specialist or other practitioners when necessary. Conducts research to develop and test surgical techniques to improve operating procedures and outcomes. Examines instruments, equipment, and operating room to ensure sterility. Directs and coordinates activities of nurses, assistants, specialists, and other medical staff. **SKILLS—Reading Comprehension:** Understanding written sentences and paragraphs in work-related documents. **Judgment and Decision Making:** Considering the relative costs and benefits of potential actions to choose the most appropriate one. **Science:** Using scientific rules and methods to solve problems. **Critical Thinking:** Using logic and reasoning to identify the strengths and weaknesses of alternative solutions, conclusions, or approaches to problems. **Coordination:** Adjusting actions in relation to others' actions. **Writing:** Communicating effectively in writing as appropriate for the needs of the audience.

GOE INFORMATION—Interest Area: 14. Medical and Health Services. **Work Group:** 14.02. Medicine and Surgery. **Other Job Titles in This Work Group:** Anesthesiologists; Family and General Practitioners; Internists, General; Medical Assistants; Obstetricians and Gynecologists; Pediatricians, General; Pharmacists; Pharmacy Aides; Pharmacy Technicians; Physician Assistants; Physicians and Surgeons, All Other; Psychiatrists; Registered Nurses; Surgical Technologists. **PERSONALITY TYPE**—Investigative. Investigative occupations frequently involve working with ideas and require an extensive amount of thinking. These occupations can involve searching for facts and figuring out problems mentally.

EDUCATION/TRAINING PROGRAM(S)—Adult Reconstructive Orthopedics (Orthopedic Surgery); Colon and Rectal Surgery; Critical Care Surgery; General Surgery; Hand Surgery; Neurological Surgery/Neurosurgery; Orthopedic Surgery of the Spine; Orthopedics/Orthopedic Surgery; Otolaryngology; Pediatric Orthopedics; Pediatric Surgery; Plastic Surgery; Sports Medicine; Thoracic Surgery; Urology; Vascular Surgery. **RELATED KNOWLEDGE/COURSES—Medicine and Dentistry:**

Knowledge of the information and techniques needed to diagnose and treat human injuries, diseases, and deformities. This includes symptoms, treatment alternatives, drug properties and interactions, and preventive health-care measures. **Biology:** Knowledge of plant and animal organisms and their tissues, cells, functions, interdependencies, and interactions with each other and the environment. **Chemistry:** Knowledge of the chemical composition, structure, and properties of substances and of the chemical processes and transformations that they undergo. This includes uses of chemicals and their interactions, danger signs, production techniques, and disposal methods. **Administration and Management:** Knowledge of business and management principles involved in strategic planning, resource allocation, human resources modeling, leadership technique, production methods, and coordination of people and resources. **Psychology:** Knowledge of human behavior and performance; individual differences in ability, personality, and interests; learning and motivation; psychological research methods; and the assessment and treatment of behavioral and affective disorders.

Surgical Technologists

▲ Education/Training Required: Postsecondary vocational training
▲ Annual Earnings: $30,090
▲ Growth: 34.7%
▲ Annual Job Openings: 8,000
▲ Self-Employed: 0%
▲ Part-Time: 22.9%

Assist in operations under the supervision of surgeons, registered nurses, or other surgical personnel. May help set up operating room, prepare and transport patients for surgery, adjust lights and equipment, pass instruments and other supplies to surgeons and surgeon's assistants, hold retractors, cut sutures, and help count sponges, needles, supplies, and instruments. Places equipment and supplies in operating room and arranges instruments according to instruction. Maintains supply of fluids, such as plasma, saline, blood, and glucose, for use during operation. Cleans operating room. Washes and sterilizes equipment, using germicides and sterilizers. Puts dressings on patient following surgery. Aids team to don gowns and gloves. Scrubs arms and hands and dons gown and gloves. Assists team members in placing and positioning patient on table. Counts sponges, needles, and instruments before and after operation. Hands instruments and supplies to surgeon, holds retractors and cuts sutures, and performs other tasks as directed by surgeon during operation. **SKILLS—Reading Comprehension:** Understanding written sentences and paragraphs in work-related documents. **Active Listening:** Giving full attention to what other people are saying, taking time to understand the points being made, asking questions as appropriate, and not interrupting at inappropriate times. **Coordination:** Adjusting actions in relation to others' actions. **Critical Thinking:** Using logic and reasoning to identify the strengths and weaknesses of alternative solutions, conclusions, or approaches to problems. **Active Learning:** Understanding the implications of new information for both current and future problem-solving and decision-making.

GOE INFORMATION—Interest Area: 14. Medical and Health Services. **Work Group:** 14.02. Medicine and Surgery. **Other Job Titles in This Work Group:** Anesthesiologists; Family and General Practitioners; Internists, General; Medical Assistants; Obstetricians and Gynecologists; Pediatricians, General; Pharmacists; Pharmacy Aides; Pharmacy Technicians; Physician Assistants; Physicians and Surgeons, All Other; Psychiatrists; Registered Nurses; Surgeons. **PERSONALITY TYPE—Realistic.** Realistic occupations frequently involve work activities that include practical, hands-on problems and solutions. They often deal with plants, animals, and real-world materials like wood, tools, and machinery. Many of the occupations require working outside and do not involve a lot of paperwork or working closely with others.

EDUCATION/TRAINING PROGRAM(S)—Pathology/Pathologist Assistant; Surgical Technology/Technologist. **RELATED KNOWLEDGE/COURSES—Medicine and Dentistry:** Knowledge of the information and techniques needed to diagnose and treat human injuries, diseases, and deformities. This includes symptoms, treatment alternatives, drug properties and interactions, and preventive health-care measures. **Biology:** Knowledge of plant and animal organisms and their tissues, cells, functions, interdependencies, and interactions with each other and the environment. **Mathematics:** Knowledge of arithmetic, algebra, geometry, calculus, and statistics and their applications. **English Language:** Knowledge of the structure and content of the English language, including the meaning and spelling of words, rules of composition, and grammar. **Chemistry:** Knowledge of the chemical composition, structure, and properties of substances and of the chemical processes and transformations that they undergo. This includes uses of chemicals and their interactions, danger signs, production techniques, and disposal methods.

Survey Researchers

▲ Education/Training Required: Bachelor's degree
▲ Annual Earnings: $23,230
▲ Growth: 34.5%
▲ Annual Job Openings: 3,000
▲ Self-Employed: No data available.
▲ Part-Time: No data available.

Design or conduct surveys. May supervise interviewers who conduct the survey in person or over the telephone. May present survey results to client. **SKILLS**—No data available.

GOE INFORMATION—Interest Area: 02. Science, Math, and Engineering. **Work Group:** 02.04. Social Sciences. **Other Job Titles in This Work Group:** Anthropologists; Anthropologists and Archeologists; Archeologists; City Planning Aides; Economists; Historians; Industrial-Organizational Psychologists; Political Scientists; Psychologists, All Other; Social Science Research Assistants; Social Scientists and Related Workers, All Other; Sociologists; Urban and Regional Planners. **PERSONALITY TYPE**—No data available.

EDUCATION/TRAINING PROGRAM(S)—Applied Economics; Business/Managerial Economics; Economics, General; Marketing Research. **RELATED KNOWLEDGE/COURSES**—No data available.

Surveying and Mapping Technicians

▲ Education/Training Required: Moderate-term on-the-job training
▲ Annual Earnings: $28,210
▲ Growth: 25.3%
▲ Annual Job Openings: 7,000
▲ Self-Employed: 7.3%
▲ Part-Time: 4.5%

Perform surveying and mapping duties, usually under the direction of a surveyor, cartographer, or photogrammetrist, to obtain data used for construction, mapmaking, boundary location, mining, or other purposes. May calculate mapmaking information and create maps from source data such as surveying notes, aerial photography, satellite data, or other maps to show topographical features, political boundaries, and other features. May verify accuracy and completeness of topographical maps. **SKILLS**—No data available.

GOE INFORMATION—Interest Area: 02. Science, Math, and Engineering. **Work Group:** 02.08. Engineering Technology. **Other Job Titles in This Work Group:** Aerospace Engineering and Operations Technicians; Architectural and Civil Drafters; Architectural Drafters; Calibration and Instrumentation Technicians; Cartographers and Photogrammetrists; Civil Drafters; Civil Engineering Technicians; Construction and Building Inspectors; Drafters, All Other; Electrical and Electronic Engineering Technicians; Electrical and Electronics Drafters; Electrical Drafters; Electrical Engineering Technicians; Electro-Mechanical Technicians; Electronic Drafters; Electronics Engineering Technicians; Engineering Technicians, Except Drafters, All Other; Environmental Engineering Technicians; Industrial Engineering Technicians; Mapping Technicians; Mechanical Drafters; Mechanical Engineering Technicians; Numerical Tool and Process Control Programmers; Pressure Vessel Inspectors; Surveying Technicians; Surveyors. **PERSONALITY TYPE**—No data available.

Surveying Technicians

Adjust and operate surveying instruments, such as the theodolite and electronic distance-measuring equipment, and compile notes, make sketches and enter data into computers. Obtains land survey data, such as angles, elevations, points, and contours, using electronic distance measuring equipment and other surveying instruments. Compiles notes, sketches, and records of survey data obtained and work performed. Directs work of subordinate members of party, performing surveying duties not requiring licensure. **SKILLS—Mathematics:** Using mathematics to solve problems. **Reading Comprehension:** Understanding written sentences and paragraphs in work-related documents. **Writing:** Communicating effectively in writing as appropriate for the needs of the audience. **Time Management:** Managing one's own time and the time of others.

GOE INFORMATION—Interest Area: 02. Science, Math, and Engineering. **Work Group:** 02.08. Engineering Technology. **Other Job Titles in This Work Group:** Aerospace Engineering and Operations Technicians; Architectural and Civil Drafters; Architectural Drafters; Calibration and Instrumentation Technicians; Cartographers and Photogrammetrists; Civil Drafters; Civil Engineering Technicians; Construction and Building Inspectors; Drafters, All Other; Electrical and Electronic Engineering Technicians; Electrical and Electronics Drafters; Electrical Drafters; Electrical Engineering Technicians; Electro-Mechanical Technicians; Electronic Drafters; Electronics Engineering Technicians; Engineering Technicians, Except Drafters, All Other; Environmental Engineering Techni-

EDUCATION/TRAINING PROGRAM(S)—Cartography; Surveying Technology/Surveying. **RELATED KNOWLEDGE/COURSES**—No data available.

- ▲ Education/Training Required: Long-term on-the-job training
- ▲ Annual Earnings: $28,210
- ▲ Growth: 25.3%
- ▲ Annual Job Openings: 7,000
- ▲ Self-Employed: 7.3%
- ▲ Part-Time: 4.5%

cians; Industrial Engineering Technicians; Mapping Technicians; Mechanical Drafters; Mechanical Engineering Technicians; Numerical Tool and Process Control Programmers; Pressure Vessel Inspectors; Surveying and Mapping Technicians; **PERSONALITY TYPE**—Realistic. Realistic occupations frequently involve work activities that include practical, hands-on problems and solutions. They often deal with plants, animals, and real-world materials like wood, tools, and machinery. Many of the occupations require working outside and do not involve a lot of paperwork or working closely with others.

EDUCATION/TRAINING PROGRAM(S)—Cartography; Surveying Technology/Surveying. **RELATED KNOWLEDGE/COURSES—Engineering and Technology:** Knowledge of the practical application of engineering science and technology. This includes applying principles, techniques, procedures, and equipment to the design and production of various goods and services. **Mathematics:** Knowledge of arithmetic, algebra, geometry, calculus, and statistics and their applications. **Design:** Knowledge of design techniques, tools, and principles involved in production of precision technical plans, blueprints, drawings, and models. **Computers and Electronics:** Knowledge of circuit boards, processors, chips, electronic equipment, and computer hardware and software, including applications and programming. **Geography:** Knowledge of principles and methods for describing the features of land, sea, and air masses, including their physical characteristics, locations, interrelationships, and distribution of plant, animal, and human life.

Talent Directors

- ▲ Education/Training Required: Long-term on-the-job training
- ▲ Annual Earnings: $45,090
- ▲ Growth: 27.1%
- ▲ Annual Job Openings: 11,000
- ▲ Self-Employed: 23.7%
- ▲ Part-Time: 25.3%

Audition and interview performers to select most appropriate talent for parts in stage, television, radio, or motion picture productions. Auditions and interviews performers to identify most suitable talent for broadcasting, stage, or musical production. Maintains talent file, including information about personalities, such as specialties, past performances, and availability. Directs recording sessions for musical artists. Promotes record sales by personal appearances and contacts with broadcasting personalities. Negotiates contract agreements with performers. Selects performer or submits list of suitable performers to producer or director for final selection. Arranges for screen tests or auditions for new performers. **SKILLS—Speaking:** Talking to others to convey information effectively. **Negotiation:** Bringing others together and trying to reconcile differences. **Active Listening:** Giving full attention to what other people are saying, taking time to understand the points being made, asking questions as appropriate, and not interrupting at inappropriate times. **Social Perceptiveness:** Being aware of others' reactions and understanding why they react as they do. **Reading Comprehension:** Understanding written sentences and paragraphs in work-related documents.

GOE INFORMATION—Interest Area: 01. Arts, Entertainment, and Media. **Work Group:** 01.05. Performing Arts. **Other Job Titles in This Work Group:** Actors; Choreographers; Composers; Dancers; Directors—Stage, Motion Pictures, Television, and Radio; Music Arrangers and Orchestrators; Music Directors; Music Directors and Composers; Musicians and Singers; Musicians, Instrumental; Public Address System and Other Announcers; Radio and Television Announcers; Singers. **PERSONALITY TYPE**—Artistic. Artistic occupations frequently involve working with forms, designs, and patterns. They often require self-expression, and the work can be done without following a clear set of rules.

EDUCATION/TRAINING PROGRAM(S)—Cinematography and Film/Video Production; Directing and Theatrical Production; Drama and Dramatics/Theatre Arts, General; Dramatic/Theatre Arts and Stagecraft, Other; Film/Cinema Studies; Radio and Television; Theatre/Theatre Arts Management. **RELATED KNOWLEDGE/ COURSES—Fine Arts:** Knowledge of the theory and techniques required to compose, produce, and perform works of music, dance, visual arts, drama, and sculpture. **Sales and Marketing:** Knowledge of principles and methods for showing, promoting, and selling products or services. This includes marketing strategy and tactics, product demonstration, sales techniques, and sales control systems. **Personnel and Human Resources:** Knowledge of principles and procedures for personnel recruitment, selection, training, compensation and benefits, labor relations and negotiation, and personnel information systems. **Administration and Management:** Knowledge of business and management principles involved in strategic planning, resource allocation, human resources modeling, leadership technique, production methods, and coordination of people and resources. **Communications and Media:** Knowledge of media production, communication, and dissemination techniques and methods. This includes alternative ways to inform and entertain via written, oral, and visual media.

Tax Preparers

- ▲ Education/Training Required: Moderate-term on-the-job training
- ▲ Annual Earnings: $27,680
- ▲ Growth: 17.4%
- ▲ Annual Job Openings: 8,000
- ▲ Self-Employed: No data available.
- ▲ Part-Time: No data available.

Prepare tax returns for individuals or small businesses but do not have the background or responsibilities of an accredited or certified public accountant. Reviews financial records, such as income statements and documentation of expenditures to determine forms needed to prepare return. Calculates form preparation fee according to complexity of return and amount of time required to prepare forms. Computes taxes owed, using adding machine or personal computer, and completes entries on forms, following tax form instructions and tax tables. Consults tax law handbook or bulletins to determine procedure for preparation of atypical returns. Verifies totals on forms prepared by others to detect errors in arithmetic or procedure as needed. Interviews client to obtain additional information on taxable income and deductible expenses and allowances. **SKILLS—Reading Comprehension:** Understanding written sentences and paragraphs in work-related documents. **Mathematics:** Using mathematics to solve problems. **Active Listening:** Giving full attention to what other people are saying, taking time to understand the points being made, asking questions as appropriate, and not interrupting at inappropriate times. **Speaking:** Talking to others to convey information effectively. **Active Learning:** Understanding the implications of new information for both current and future problem-solving and decision-making.

GOE INFORMATION—Interest Area: 09. Business Detail. **Work Group:** 09.03. Bookkeeping, Auditing, and Accounting. **Other Job Titles in This Work Group:** Billing and Posting Clerks and Machine Operators; Billing, Cost, and Rate Clerks; Bookkeeping, Accounting, and Auditing Clerks; Brokerage Clerks; Payroll and Timekeeping Clerks; Statement Clerks. **PERSONALITY TYPE—** Conventional. Conventional occupations frequently involve following set procedures and routines. These occupations can include working with data and details more than with ideas. Usually there is a clear line of authority to follow.

EDUCATION/TRAINING PROGRAM(S)—Accounting Technology/Technician and Bookkeeping; Taxation. **RELATED KNOWLEDGE/COURSES—Mathematics:** Knowledge of arithmetic, algebra, geometry, calculus, and statistics and their applications. **Economics and Accounting:** Knowledge of economic and accounting principles and practices, the financial markets, banking, and the analysis and reporting of financial data. **Law and Government:** Knowledge of laws, legal codes, court procedures, precedents, government regulations, executive orders, agency rules, and the democratic political process. **Clerical Studies:** Knowledge of administrative and clerical procedures and systems, such as word processing, managing files and records, stenography and transcription, designing forms, and other office procedures and terminology. **English Language:** Knowledge of the structure and content of the English language, including the meaning and spelling of words, rules of composition, and grammar. **Computers and Electronics:** Knowledge of circuit boards, processors, chips, electronic equipment, and computer hardware and software, including applications and programming.

Taxi Drivers and Chauffeurs

▲ Education/Training Required: Short-term on-the-job training
▲ Annual Earnings: $17,920
▲ Growth: 24.4%
▲ Annual Job Openings: 37,000
▲ Self-Employed: 44.1%
▲ Part-Time: 21.5%

Drive automobiles, vans, or limousines to transport passengers. May occasionally carry cargo. Drives taxicab, limousine, company car, hearse, or privately owned vehicle to transport passengers. Communicates with taxicab dispatcher by radio or telephone to receive requests for passenger service. Collects and documents fees, payments, and deposits determined by rental contracts or taximeter recordings. Assists passengers in entering and exiting vehicle, assists with luggage, and holds umbrellas in wet weather. Maintains vehicle by performing such duties as regulating tire pressure and adding gasoline, oil, and water. Delivers automobiles to customers from rental agency, car dealership, or repair shop. Tests performance of vehicle accessories, such as lights, horn, and windshield wipers. Performs errands for customers, such as carrying mail to and from post office. Vacuums, sweeps, and cleans interior and washes and polishes exterior of automobile. Makes minor repairs on vehicle, such as fixing punctures, cleaning spark plugs, or adjusting carburetor. **SKILLS— Operation and Control:** Controlling operations of equipment or systems. **Service Orientation:** Actively looking for ways to help people. **Repairing:** Repairing machines or systems, using the needed tools. **Operation Monitoring:** Watching gauges, dials, or other indicators to make sure a machine is working properly. **Mathematics:** Using mathematics to solve problems. **Writing:** Communicating effectively in writing as appropriate for the needs of the audience.

GOE INFORMATION—Interest Area: 07. Transportation. **Work Group:** 07.07. Other Services Requiring Driving. **Other Job Titles in This Work Group:** Ambulance Drivers and Attendants, Except Emergency Medical Technicians; Bus Drivers, School; Bus Drivers, Transit and Intercity; Driver/Sales Workers; Parking Lot Attendants. **PERSONALITY TYPE**—Realistic. Realistic occupations frequently involve work activities that include practical, hands-on problems and solutions. They often deal with plants, animals, and real-world materials like wood, tools, and machinery. Many of the occupations require working outside and do not involve a lot of paperwork or working closely with others.

EDUCATION/TRAINING PROGRAM(S)—Truck and Bus Driver/Commercial Vehicle Operation. **RELATED KNOWLEDGE/COURSES—Transportation:** Knowledge of principles and methods for moving people or goods by air, rail, sea, or road, including the relative costs and benefits. **Customer and Personal Service:** Knowledge of principles and processes for providing customer and personal services. This includes customer needs assessment, meeting quality standards for services, and evaluation of customer satisfaction. **Geography:** Knowledge of principles and methods for describing the features of land, sea, and air masses, including their physical characteristics, locations, interrelationships, and distribution of plant, animal, and human life. **Principles of Mechanical Devices:** Knowledge of machines and tools, including their designs, uses, repair, and maintenance. **English Language:** Knowledge of the structure and content of the English language, including the meaning and spelling of words, rules of composition, and grammar. **Law and Government:** Knowledge of laws, legal codes, court procedures, precedents, government regulations, executive orders, agency rules, and the democratic political process.

Teacher Assistants

- ▲ Education/Training Required: Short-term on-the-job training
- ▲ Annual Earnings: $18,070
- ▲ Growth: 23.9%
- ▲ Annual Job Openings: 256,000
- ▲ Self-Employed: 0%
- ▲ Part-Time: 46.8%

Perform duties that are instructional in nature or deliver direct services to students or parents. Serve in a position for which a teacher or another professional has ultimate responsibility for the design and implementation of educational programs and services. Presents subject matter to students, using lecture, discussion, or supervised role-playing methods. Helps students, individually or in groups, with lesson assignments to present or reinforce learning concepts. Prepares lesson outline and plan in assigned area and submits outline to teacher for review. Plans, prepares, and develops various teaching aids, such as bibliographies, charts, and graphs. Discusses assigned teaching area with classroom teacher to coordinate instructional efforts. Prepares, administers, and grades examinations. Confers with parents on progress of students. **SKILLS—Active Listening:** Giving full attention to what other people are saying, taking time to understand the points being made, asking questions as appropriate, and not interrupting at inappropriate times. **Learning Strategies:** Selecting and using training/instructional methods and procedures appropriate for the situation when learning or teaching new things. **Speaking:** Talking to others to convey information effectively. **Instructing:** Teaching others how to do something. **Reading Comprehension:** Understanding written sentences and paragraphs in work-related documents.

GOE INFORMATION—Interest Area: 12. Education and Social Service. **Work Group:** 12.03. Educational Services. **Other Job Titles in This Work Group:** Adult Literacy, Remedial Education, and GED Teachers and Instructors; Agricultural Sciences Teachers, Postsecondary; Anthropology and Archeology Teachers, Postsecondary; Architecture Teachers, Postsecondary; Archivists; Area, Ethnic, and Cultural Studies Teachers, Postsecondary; Art, Drama, and Music Teachers, Postsecondary; Atmospheric, Earth, Marine, and Space Sciences Teachers, Postsecondary; Audio-Visual Collections Specialists; Biological Science Teachers, Postsecondary; Business Teachers, Postsecondary; Chemistry Teachers, Postsecondary; Child Care Workers; Communications Teachers, Postsecondary; Computer Science Teachers, Postsecondary; Criminal Justice and Law Enforcement Teachers, Postsecondary; Curators; Economics Teachers, Postsecondary; Education Teachers, Postsecondary; Educational Psychologists; Educational, Vocational, and School Counselors; Elementary School Teachers, Except Special Education; Engineering Teachers, Postsecondary; English Language and Literature Teachers, Postsecondary; Environmental Science Teachers, Postsecondary; Farm and Home Management Advisors; Foreign Language and Literature Teachers, Postsecondary; Forestry and Conservation Science Teachers, Postsecondary; Geography Teachers, Postsecondary; Graduate Teaching Assistants; Health Specialties Teachers, Postsecondary; History Teachers, Postsecondary; Home Economics Teachers, Postsecondary; Kindergarten Teachers, Except Special Education; Law Teachers, Postsecondary; Librarians; Library Assistants, Clerical; Library Science Teachers, Postsecondary; Library Technicians; Mathematical Science Teachers, Postsecondary; Middle School Teachers, Except Special and Vocational Education; Museum Technicians and Conservators; Nursing Instructors and Teachers, Postsecondary; Personal Financial Advisors; Philosophy and Religion Teachers, Postsecondary; Physics Teachers, Postsecondary; Political Science Teachers, Postsecondary; Postsecondary Teachers, All Other; others. **PERSONALITY TYPE—Social.** Social occupations frequently involve working with, communicating with, and teaching people. These occupations often involve helping or providing service to others.

EDUCATION/TRAINING PROGRAM(S)—Teacher Assistant/Aide; Teaching Assistants/Aides, Other. **RELATED KNOWLEDGE/COURSES—Education and Training:** Knowledge of principles and methods for curriculum and training design, teaching and instruction for individuals and groups, and the measurement of training effects. **English Language:** Knowledge of the structure and content of the English language, including the meaning and spelling of words, rules of composition, and grammar. **Mathematics:** Knowledge of arithmetic, algebra, geometry, calculus, and statistics and their applications. **Clerical Studies:** Knowledge of administrative and clerical procedures and systems, such as word processing, managing files and records, stenography and transcription, designing forms, and other office procedures and terminology. **Customer and Personal Service:** Knowledge of principles and processes for providing customer and personal services. This includes customer needs assessment,

meeting quality standards for services, and evaluation of customer satisfaction. **Psychology:** Knowledge of human behavior and performance; individual differences in ability, personality, and interests; learning and motivation; psychological research methods; and the assessment and treatment of behavioral and affective disorders.

Team Assemblers

- ▲ Education/Training Required: Moderate-term on-the-job training
- ▲ Annual Earnings: $22,260
- ▲ Growth: 5.9%
- ▲ Annual Job Openings: 283,000
- ▲ Self-Employed: 2.2%
- ▲ Part-Time: 5.9%

Work as part of a team having responsibility for assembling an entire product or component of a product. Team assemblers can perform all tasks conducted by the team in the assembly process and rotate through all or most of them rather than being assigned to a specific task on a permanent basis. May participate in making management decisions affecting the work. Team leaders who work as part of the team should be included. SKILLS— No data available.

GOE INFORMATION—**Interest Area:** 08. Industrial Production. **Work Group:** 08.03. Production Work. **Other Job Titles in This Work Group:** Bakers, Manufacturing; Bindery Machine Operators and Tenders; Brazers; Cementing and Gluing Machine Operators and Tenders; Chemical Equipment Controllers and Operators; Chemical Equipment Operators and Tenders; Chemical Equipment Tenders; Cleaning, Washing, and Metal Pickling Equipment Operators and Tenders; Coating, Painting, and Spraying Machine Operators and Tenders; Coil Winders, Tapers, and Finishers; Combination Machine Tool Operators and Tenders, Metal and Plastic; Computer-Controlled Machine Tool Operators, Metal and Plastic; Cooling and Freezing Equipment Operators and Tenders; Crushing, Grinding, and Polishing Machine Setters, Operators, and Tenders; Cutters and Trimmers, Hand; Cutting and Slicing Machine Operators and Tenders; Cutting and Slicing Machine Setters, Operators, and Tenders;

Design Printing Machine Setters and Set-Up Operators; Electrolytic Plating and Coating Machine Operators and Tenders, Metal and Plastic; Electrolytic Plating and Coating Machine Setters and Set-Up Operators, Metal and Plastic; Electrotypers and Stereotypers; Embossing Machine Set-Up Operators; Engraver Set-Up Operators; Extruding and Forming Machine Operators and Tenders, Synthetic or Glass Fibers; Extruding and Forming Machine Setters, Operators, and Tenders, Synthetic and Glass Fibers; Extruding, Forming, Pressing, and Compacting Machine Operators and Tenders; Fabric and Apparel Patternmakers; Fiber Product Cutting Machine Setters and Set-Up Operators; Fiberglass Laminators and Fabricators; Film Laboratory Technicians; Fitters, Structural Metal— Precision; Food and Tobacco Roasting, Baking, and Drying Machine Operators and Tenders; Food Batchmakers; Food Cooking Machine Operators and Tenders; Furnace, Kiln, Oven, Drier, and Kettle Operators and Tenders; Glass Cutting Machine Setters and Set-Up Operators; Graders and Sorters, Agricultural Products; Grinding and Polishing Workers, Hand; Hand Compositors and Typesetters; Heaters, Metal and Plastic; others. **PERSONALITY TYPE**—No data available.

EDUCATION/TRAINING PROGRAM(S)—No data available. **RELATED KNOWLEDGE/COURSES**—No data available.

Technical Directors/Managers

▲ Education/Training Required: Long-term on-the-job training
▲ Annual Earnings: $45,090
▲ Growth: 27.1%
▲ Annual Job Openings: 11,000
▲ Self-Employed: 23.7%
▲ Part-Time: 25.3%

Coordinate activities of technical departments, such as taping, editing, engineering, and maintenance, to produce radio or television programs. Coordinates activities of radio or television studio and control-room personnel to ensure technical quality of programs. Coordinates elements of program, such as audio, camera, special effects, timing, and script, to ensure production objectives are met. Schedules use of studio and editing facilities for producers and engineering and maintenance staff. Directs personnel in auditioning talent and programs. Operates equipment to produce programs or broadcast live programs from remote locations. Trains workers in use of equipment, such as switcher, camera, monitor, microphones, and lights. Monitors broadcast to ensure that programs conform with station or network policies and regulations. Supervises and assigns duties to workers engaged in technical control and production of radio and television programs. Observes picture through monitor and directs camera and video staff concerning shading and composition. **SKILLS—Coordination:** Adjusting actions in relation to others' actions. **Operation and Control:** Controlling operations of equipment or systems. **Equipment Selection:** Determining the kind of tools and equipment needed to do a job. **Speaking:** Talking to others to convey information effectively. **Management of Personnel Resources:** Motivating, developing, and directing people as they work, identifying the best people for the job.

GOE INFORMATION—Interest Area: 01. Arts, Entertainment, and Media. **Work Group:** 01.01. Managerial Work in Arts, Entertainment, and Media. **Other Job Titles in This Work Group:** Agents and Business Managers of Artists, Performers, and Athletes; Art Directors; Producers; Producers and Directors; Program Directors. **PERSONALITY TYPE—Realistic.** Realistic occupations frequently involve work activities that include practical, hands-on problems and solutions. They often deal with plants, animals, and real-world materials like wood, tools, and machinery. Many of the occupations require working outside and do not involve a lot of paperwork or working closely with others.

EDUCATION/TRAINING PROGRAM(S)—Cinematography and Film/Video Production; Directing and Theatrical Production; Drama and Dramatics/Theatre Arts, General; Dramatic/Theatre Arts and Stagecraft, Other; Film/Cinema Studies; Radio and Television; Theatre/Theatre Arts Management. **RELATED KNOWLEDGE/COURSES—Administration and Management:** Knowledge of business and management principles involved in strategic planning, resource allocation, human resources modeling, leadership technique, production methods, and coordination of people and resources. **Communications and Media:** Knowledge of media production, communication, and dissemination techniques and methods. This includes alternative ways to inform and entertain via written, oral, and visual media. **Telecommunications:** Knowledge of transmission, broadcasting, switching, control, and operation of telecommunications systems. **Education and Training:** Knowledge of principles and methods for curriculum and training design, teaching and instruction for individuals and groups, and the measurement of training effects. **English Language:** Knowledge of the structure and content of the English language, including the meaning and spelling of words, rules of composition, and grammar.

Technical Writers

▲ Education/Training Required: Bachelor's degree
▲ Annual Earnings: $49,360
▲ Growth: 29.6%
▲ Annual Job Openings: 5,000
▲ Self-Employed: 31.2%
▲ Part-Time: 18.5%

Write technical materials, such as equipment manuals, appendices, or operating and maintenance instructions. May assist in layout work. Organizes material and completes writing assignment according to set standards regarding order, clarity, conciseness, style, and terminology. Studies drawings, specifications, mock-ups, and product samples to integrate and delineate technology, operating procedure, and production sequence and detail. Assists in laying out material for publication. Interviews production and engineering personnel and reads journals and other material to become familiar with product technologies and production methods. Reviews published materials and recommends revisions or changes in scope, format, content, and methods of reproduction and binding. Reviews manufacturer's and trade catalogs, drawings, and other data relative to operation, maintenance, and service of equipment. Analyzes developments in specific field to determine need for revisions in previously published materials and development of new material. Selects photographs, drawings, sketches, diagrams, and charts to illustrate material. Draws sketches to illustrate specified materials or assembly sequence. Confers with customer representatives, vendors, plant executives, or publisher to establish technical specifications and to determine subject material to be developed for publication. Arranges for typing, duplication, and distribution of material. Maintains records and files of work and revisions. Observes production, developmental, and experimental activities to determine operating procedure and detail. Edits, standardizes, or makes changes to material prepared by other writers or establishment personnel. **SKILLS—Writing:** Communicating effectively in writing as appropriate for the needs of the audience. **Reading Comprehension:** Understanding written sentences and paragraphs in work-related documents. **Active Listening:** Giving full attention to what other people are saying, taking time to understand the points being made, asking questions as appropriate, and not interrupting at inappropriate times. **Active Learning:** Understanding the implications of new information for both current and future problem-solving and decision-making. **Critical Thinking:** Using logic and reasoning to identify the strengths and weaknesses of alternative solutions, conclusions, or approaches to problems.

GOE INFORMATION—Interest Area: 01. Arts, Entertainment, and Media. **Work Group:** 01.02. Writing and Editing. **Other Job Titles in This Work Group:** Copy Writers; Creative Writers; Editors; Poets and Lyricists; Writers and Authors. **PERSONALITY TYPE**—Artistic. Artistic occupations frequently involve working with forms, designs, and patterns. They often require self-expression, and the work can be done without following a clear set of rules.

EDUCATION/TRAINING PROGRAM(S)—Business/Corporate Communications; Family and Consumer Sciences/Human Sciences Communication; Technical and Business Writing. **RELATED KNOWLEDGE/COURSES—English Language:** Knowledge of the structure and content of the English language, including the meaning and spelling of words, rules of composition, and grammar. **Communications and Media:** Knowledge of media production, communication, and dissemination techniques and methods. This includes alternative ways to inform and entertain via written, oral, and visual media. **Computers and Electronics:** Knowledge of circuit boards, processors, chips, electronic equipment, and computer hardware and software, including applications and programming. **Education and Training:** Knowledge of principles and methods for curriculum and training design, teaching and instruction for individuals and groups, and the measurement of training effects. **Design:** Knowledge of design techniques, tools, and principles involved in production of precision technical plans, blueprints, drawings, and models.

Telecommunications Line Installers and Repairers

▲ Education/Training Required: Long-term on-the-job training
▲ Annual Earnings: $39,200
▲ Growth: 27.6%
▲ Annual Job Openings: 9,000
▲ Self-Employed: 0%
▲ Part-Time: 0.9%

String and repair telephone and television cable, including fiber optics and other equipment for transmitting messages or television programming. Installs terminal boxes and strings lead-in-wires, using electrician's tools. Ascends poles or enters tunnels and sewers to string lines and install terminal boxes, auxiliary equipment, and appliances according to diagrams. Repairs cable system, defective lines, and auxiliary equipment. Pulls lines through ducts by hand or with use of winch. Collects installation fees. Explains cable service to subscriber. Cleans and maintains tools and test equipment. Fills and tamps holes, using cement, earth, and tamping device. Digs holes, using power auger or shovel, and hoists poles upright into holes, using truck-mounted winch. Installs and removes plant equipment, such as callboxes and clocks. Measures signal strength at utility pole, using electronic test equipment. Connects television set to cable system, evaluates incoming signal, and adjusts system to ensure optimum reception. Computes impedance of wire from pole to house to determine additional resistance needed for reducing signal to desired level. **SKILLS—Installation:** Installing equipment, machines, wiring, or programs to meet specifications. **Repairing:** Repairing machines or systems, using the needed tools. **Troubleshooting:** Determining causes of operating errors and deciding what to do about them. **Mathematics:** Using mathematics to solve problems. **Equipment Maintenance:** Performing routine maintenance on equipment and determining when and what kind of maintenance is needed. **Active Listening:** Giving full attention to what other people are saying, taking time to understand the points being made, asking questions as appropriate, and not interrupting at inappropriate times.

GOE INFORMATION—Interest Area: 05. Mechanics, Installers, and Repairers. **Work Group:** 05.02. Electrical and Electronic Systems. **Other Job Titles in This Work Group:** Avionics Technicians; Battery Repairers; Central Office and PBX Installers and Repairers; Communication Equipment Mechanics, Installers, and Repairers; Computer, Automated Teller, and Office Machine Repairers; Data Processing Equipment Repairers; Electric Home Appliance and Power Tool Repairers; Electric Meter Installers and Repairers; Electric Motor and Switch Assemblers and Repairers; Electric Motor, Power Tool, and Related Repairers; Electrical and Electronics Installers and Repairers, Transportation Equipment; Electrical and Electronics Repairers, Commercial and Industrial Equipment; Electrical and Electronics Repairers, Powerhouse, Substation, and Relay; Electrical Parts Reconditioners; Electrical Power-Line Installers and Repairers; Electronic Equipment Installers and Repairers, Motor Vehicles; Electronic Home Entertainment Equipment Installers and Repairers; Elevator Installers and Repairers; Frame Wirers, Central Office; Home Appliance Installers; Home Appliance Repairers; Office Machine and Cash Register Servicers; Radio Mechanics; Signal and Track Switch Repairers; Station Installers and Repairers, Telephone; Telecommunications Equipment Installers and Repairers, Except Line Installers; Telecommunications Facility Examiners; Transformer Repairers. **PERSONALITY TYPE**—Realistic. Realistic occupations frequently involve work activities that include practical, hands-on problems and solutions. They often deal with plants, animals, and real-world materials like wood, tools, and machinery. Many of the occupations require working outside and do not involve a lot of paperwork or working closely with others.

EDUCATION/TRAINING PROGRAM(S)—Communications Systems Installation and Repair Technology. **RELATED KNOWLEDGE/COURSES—Telecommunications:** Knowledge of transmission, broadcasting, switching, control, and operation of telecommunications systems. **Computers and Electronics:** Knowledge of circuit boards, processors, chips, electronic equipment, and computer hardware and software, including applications and programming. **Engineering and Technology:** Knowledge of the practical application of engineering science and technology. This includes applying principles, techniques, procedures, and equipment to the design and production of various goods and services. **Principles of Mechanical Devices:** Knowledge of machines and tools, including their designs, uses, repair, and maintenance. **Mathematics:** Knowledge of arithmetic, algebra, geometry, calculus, and statistics and their applications.

Telemarketers

▲ Education/Training Required: Short-term on-the-job training
▲ Annual Earnings: $19,210
▲ Growth: 22.2%
▲ Annual Job Openings: 145,000
▲ Self-Employed: 10.7%
▲ Part-Time: 22.3%

Solicit orders for goods or services over the telephone. Contacts customers by phone, by mail, or in person to offer or persuade them to purchase merchandise or services. Delivers merchandise, serves customer, collects money, and makes change. Maintains records of accounts and orders and develops prospect lists. Sets up and displays sample merchandise at parties or stands. Orders or purchases supplies and stocks cart or stand. Distributes product samples or literature that details products or services. Arranges buying party and solicits sponsorship of parties to sell merchandise. Explains products or services and prices and demonstrates use of products. Writes orders for merchandise or enters order into computer. Circulates among potential customers or travels by foot, truck, automobile, or bicycle to deliver or sell merchandise or services. **SKILLS—Persuasion:** Persuading others to change their minds or behavior. **Speaking:** Talking to others to convey information effectively. **Social Perceptiveness:** Being aware of others' reactions and understanding why they react as they do. **Service Orientation:** Actively looking for ways to help people. **Mathematics:** Using mathematics to solve problems.

GOE INFORMATION—Interest Area: 10. Sales and Marketing. **Work Group:** 10.04. Personal Soliciting. **Other Job Titles in This Work Group:** Demonstrators and Product Promoters; Door-To-Door Sales Workers, News and Street Vendors, and Related Workers. **PERSONALITY TYPE—Enterprising.** Enterprising occupations frequently involve starting up and carrying out projects. These occu-

pations can involve leading people and making many decisions. They sometimes require risk taking and often deal with business.

EDUCATION/TRAINING PROGRAM(S)—Sales, Distribution, and Marketing Operations, General; Selling Skills and Sales Operations. RELATED KNOWLEDGE/COURSES—Sales and Marketing: Knowledge of principles and methods for showing, promoting, and selling products or services. This includes marketing strategy and tactics, product demonstration, sales techniques, and sales control systems. **Customer and Personal Service:** Knowledge of principles and processes for providing customer and personal services. This includes customer needs assessment, meeting quality standards for services, and evaluation of customer satisfaction. **Economics and Accounting:** Knowledge of economic and accounting principles and practices, the financial markets, banking, and the analysis and reporting of financial data. **English Language:** Knowledge of the structure and content of the English language, including the meaning and spelling of words, rules of composition, and grammar. **Telecommunications:** Knowledge of transmission, broadcasting, switching, control, and operation of telecommunications systems. **Communications and Media:** Knowledge of media production, communication, and dissemination techniques and methods. This includes alternative ways to inform and entertain via written, oral, and visual media. **Mathematics:** Knowledge of arithmetic, algebra, geometry, calculus, and statistics and their applications.

Tile and Marble Setters

- ▲ Education/Training Required: Long-term on-the-job training
- ▲ Annual Earnings: $35,390
- ▲ Growth: 15.6%
- ▲ Annual Job Openings: 5,000
- ▲ Self-Employed: 44.0%
- ▲ Part-Time: 8.4%

Apply hard tile, marble, and wood tile to walls, floors, ceilings, and roof decks. Positions and presses or taps tile with trowel handle to affix tile to plaster or adhesive base. Cuts and shapes tile, using tile cutters and biters. Measures and cuts metal lath to size for walls and ceilings, using tin snips. Installs and anchors fixtures in designated positions, using hand tools. Brushes glue onto manila paper on which design has been drawn and positions tile's finished side down onto paper. Mixes and applies mortar or cement to edges and ends of drain tiles to seal halves and joints. Wipes grout between tiles and removes excess, using wet sponge. Tacks lath to wall and ceiling surfaces, using staple gun or hammer. Selects tile and other items to be installed, such as bathroom accessories, walls, panels, and cabinets, according to specifications. Spreads mastic or other adhesive base on roof deck to form base for promenade tile, using serrated spreader. Measures and marks surfaces to be tiled and lays out work, following blueprints. Cuts tile backing to required size, using shears. Spreads plaster or concrete over surface to form tile base and levels to specified thickness, using brush, trowel, and screed. **SKILLS—Mathematics:** Using mathematics to solve problems. **Equipment Selection:** Determining the kind of tools and equipment needed to do a job. **Installation:** Installing equipment, machines, wiring, or programs to meet specifications. **Monitoring:** Monitoring/Assessing your performance or that of other individuals or organizations to make improvements or take corrective action.

GOE INFORMATION—Interest Area: 06. Construction, Mining, and Drilling. **Work Group:** 06.02. Construction. **Other Job Titles in This Work Group:** Boat Builders and Shipwrights; Boilermakers; Brattice Builders; Brickmasons and Blockmasons; Carpenters; Carpet Installers; Ceiling Tile Installers; Cement Masons and Concrete Finishers; Commercial Divers; Construction Carpenters; Drywall and Ceiling Tile Installers; Drywall Installers; Electricians; Explosives Workers, Ordnance Handling Experts, and Blasters; Fence Erectors; Floor Layers, Except Carpet, Wood, and Hard Tiles; Floor Sanders and Finishers; Glaziers; Grader, Bulldozer, and Scraper Operators; Hazardous Materials Removal Workers; Insu-

lation Workers, Floor, Ceiling, and Wall; Insulation Workers, Mechanical; Manufactured Building and Mobile Home Installers; Operating Engineers; Operating Engineers and Other Construction Equipment Operators; Painters, Construction and Maintenance; Paperhangers; Paving, Surfacing, and Tamping Equipment Operators; Pile-Driver Operators; Pipe Fitters; Pipelayers; Pipelaying Fitters; Plasterers and Stucco Masons; Plumbers; Plumbers, Pipefitters, and Steamfitters; Rail-Track Laying and Maintenance Equipment Operators; Refractory Materials Repairers, Except Brickmasons; Reinforcing Iron and Rebar Workers; Riggers; Roofers; Rough Carpenters; Security and Fire Alarm Systems Installers; Segmental Pavers; Sheet Metal Workers; Ship Carpenters and Joiners; Stone Cutters and Carvers; Stonemasons; Structural Iron and Steel Workers; Tapers; Terrazzo Workers and Finishers. **PERSONALITY TYPE—Realistic.** Realistic occupations frequently involve work activities that include practical, hands-on problems and solutions. They often deal with plants, animals, and real-world materials like wood, tools, and machinery. Many of the occupations require working outside and do not involve a lot of paperwork or working closely with others.

EDUCATION/TRAINING PROGRAM(S)—Building/Construction Finishing, Management, and Inspection, Other. **RELATED KNOWLEDGE/COURSES—Building and Construction:** Knowledge of materials, methods, and tools involved in the construction or repair of houses, buildings, or other structures, such as highways and roads. **Mathematics:** Knowledge of arithmetic, algebra, geometry, calculus, and statistics and their applications. **Design:** Knowledge of design techniques, tools, and principles involved in production of precision technical plans, blueprints, drawings, and models. **Principles of Mechanical Devices:** Knowledge of machines and tools, including their designs, uses, repair, and maintenance. **Physics:** Knowledge and prediction of physical principles and laws and their interrelationships and applications to understanding fluid, material, and atmospheric dynamics and mechanical, electrical, atomic, and sub-atomic structures and processes.

Tractor-Trailer Truck Drivers

- ▲ Education/Training Required: Moderate-term on-the-job training
- ▲ Annual Earnings: $32,580
- ▲ Growth: 19.8%
- ▲ Annual Job Openings: 240,000
- ▲ Self-Employed: 9.2%
- ▲ Part-Time: 9.9%

Drive tractor-trailer truck to transport products, livestock, or materials to specified destinations. Drives tractor-trailer combination, applying knowledge of commercial driving regulations, to transport and deliver products, livestock, or materials, usually over long distance. Maneuvers truck into loading or unloading position, following signals from loading crew as needed. Drives truck to weigh station before and after loading and along route to document weight and conform to state regulations. Maintains driver log according to I.C.C. regulations. Inspects truck before and after trips and submits report indicating truck condition. Reads bill of lading to determine assignment. Fastens chain or binders to secure load on trailer during transit. Loads or unloads or assists in loading and unloading truck. Works as member of two-person team driving tractor with sleeper bunk behind cab. Services truck with oil, fuel, and radiator fluid to maintain tractor-trailer. Obtains customer's signature or collects payment for services. Inventories and inspects goods to be moved. Wraps goods using pads, packing paper, and containers; secures load to trailer wall, using straps. Gives directions to helper in packing and moving goods to trailer. **SKILLS—Operation and Control:** Controlling operations of equipment or systems. **Reading Comprehension:** Understanding written sentences and paragraphs in work-related documents. **Equipment Maintenance:** Performing routine maintenance on equipment and determining when and what kind of maintenance is needed. **Writing:** Communicating effectively in writing as appropriate for the needs of the audience. **Troubleshooting:** Determining causes of operating errors and deciding what to do about them.

GOE INFORMATION—Interest Area: 07. Transportation. **Work Group:** 07.05. Truck Driving. **Other Job Titles in This Work Group:** Truck Drivers, Heavy; Truck Drivers, Heavy and Tractor-Trailer; Truck Drivers, Light or Delivery Services. **PERSONALITY TYPE—**Realistic. Realistic occupations frequently involve work activities that include practical, hands-on problems and solutions. They often deal with plants, animals, and real-world materials like wood, tools, and machinery. Many of the occupations require working outside and do not involve a lot of paperwork or working closely with others.

EDUCATION/TRAINING PROGRAM(S)—Truck and Bus Driver/Commercial Vehicle Operation. **RELATED KNOWLEDGE/COURSES—Transportation:** Knowledge of principles and methods for moving people or goods by air, rail, sea, or road, including the relative costs and benefits. **Geography:** Knowledge of principles and methods for describing the features of land, sea, and air masses, including their physical characteristics, locations, interrelationships, and distribution of plant, animal, and human life. **Principles of Mechanical Devices:** Knowledge of machines and tools, including their designs, uses, repair, and maintenance. **Law and Government:** Knowledge of laws, legal codes, court procedures, precedents, government regulations, executive orders, agency rules, and the democratic political process. **Public Safety and Security:** Knowledge of relevant equipment, policies, procedures, and strategies to promote effective local, state, or national security operations for the protection of people, data, property, and institutions.

Training and Development Managers

- Education/Training Required: Work experience plus degree
- Annual Earnings: $61,880
- Growth: 12.7%
- Annual Job Openings: 14,000
- Self-Employed: 0.5%
- Part-Time: 3.6%

Plan, direct, or coordinate the training and development activities and staff of an organization. Analyzes training needs to develop new training programs or modify and improve existing programs. Plans and develops training procedures, utilizing knowledge of relative effectiveness of individual training, classroom training, demonstrations, on-the-job training, meetings, conferences, and workshops. Formulates training policies and schedules, utilizing knowledge of identified training needs. Evaluates effectiveness of training programs and instructor performance. Develops and organizes training manuals, multimedia visual aids, and other educational materials. Coordinates established courses with technical and professional courses provided by community schools and designates training procedures. Develops testing and evaluation procedures. Confers with management and supervisory personnel to identify training needs based on projected production processes, changes, and other factors. Reviews and evaluates training and apprenticeship programs for compliance with government standards. Prepares training budget for department or organization. Trains instructors and supervisors in effective training techniques. Interprets and clarifies regulatory policies governing apprenticeship training programs and provides information and assistance to trainees and labor and management representatives. **SKILLS— Critical Thinking:** Using logic and reasoning to identify the strengths and weaknesses of alternative solutions, conclusions, or approaches to problems. **Reading Comprehension:** Understanding written sentences and paragraphs in work-related documents. **Speaking:** Talking to others to convey information effectively. **Instructing:** Teaching others how to do something. **Management of Personnel Resources:** Motivating, developing, and directing people as they work, identifying the best people for the job. **Learning Strategies:** Selecting and using training/instructional methods and procedures appropriate for the situation when learning or teaching new things.

GOE INFORMATION—Interest Area: 13. General Management and Support. **Work Group:** 13.01. General Management Work and Management of Support Functions. **Other Job Titles in This Work Group:** Chief Executives; Compensation and Benefits Managers; Farm, Ranch, and Other Agricultural Managers; Financial Managers; Financial Managers, Branch or Department; Funeral Directors; General and Operations Managers; Government Service Executives; Human Resources Managers; Human Resources Managers, All Other; Legislators; Managers, All Other; Postmasters and Mail Superintendents; Private Sector Executives; Property, Real Estate, and Community Association Managers; Public Relations Managers; Purchasing Managers; Storage and Distribution Managers; Transportation, Storage, and Distribution Managers; Treasurers, Controllers, and Chief Financial Officers. **PERSONALITY TYPE—**Enterprising. Enterprising occupations frequently involve starting up and carrying out projects. These occupations can involve leading people and making many decisions. They sometimes require risk taking and often deal with business.

EDUCATION/TRAINING PROGRAM(S)—Human Resources Development; Human Resources Management/ Personnel Administration, General. **RELATED KNOWLEDGE/COURSES—Education and Training:** Knowledge of principles and methods for curriculum and training design, teaching and instruction for individuals and groups, and the measurement of training effects. **Administration and Management:** Knowledge of business and management principles involved in strategic planning, resource allocation, human resources modeling, leadership technique, production methods, and coordination of people and resources. **Personnel and Human Resources:** Knowledge of principles and procedures for personnel recruitment, selection, training, compensation and benefits, labor relations and negotiation, and personnel information systems. **English Language:** Knowledge of the structure and content of the English language, including the meaning and spelling of words, rules of composition, and grammar. **Law and Government:** Knowledge of laws, legal codes, court procedures, precedents, government regulations, executive orders, agency rules, and the democratic political process. **Psychology:** Knowledge of human behavior and performance; individual differences in ability, personality, and interests; learning and motivation; psychological research methods; and the assessment and treatment of behavioral and affective disorders.

Training and Development Specialists

- ▲ Education/Training Required: Bachelor's degree
- ▲ Annual Earnings: $41,780
- ▲ Growth: 19.4%
- ▲ Annual Job Openings: 20,000
- ▲ Self-Employed: 2.6%
- ▲ Part-Time: 6.9%

Conduct training and development programs for employees. Develops and conducts orientation and training for employees or customers of industrial or commercial establishment. Confers with managers, instructors, or customer representatives of industrial or commercial establishment to determine training needs. Assigns instructors to conduct training and assists them in obtaining required training materials. Coordinates recruitment and placement of participants in skill training. Attends meetings and seminars to obtain information useful to train staff and to inform management of training programs and goals. Screens, hires, and assigns workers to positions based on qualifications. Refers trainees with social problems to appropriate service agency. Monitors training costs to ensure budget is not exceeded and prepares budget report to justify expenditures. Supervises instructors, monitors and evaluates instructor performance, and refers instructors to classes for skill development. Maintains records and writes reports to monitor and evaluate training activities and program effectiveness. Organizes and develops training procedure manuals and guides. Schedules classes based on availability of classrooms, equipment, and instructors. Evaluates training materials, such as outlines, text, and handouts, prepared by instructors. **SKILLS—Learning Strategies:** Selecting and using training/instructional methods and procedures appropriate for the situation when learning or teaching new things. **Writing:** Communicating effectively in writing as appropriate for the needs of the audience. **Monitoring:** Monitoring/Assessing your performance or that of other individuals or organizations to make improvements or take corrective action. **Management of Financial Resources:** Determining how money will be spent to get the work done and accounting for these expenditures. **Speaking:** Talking to others to convey information effectively. **Active Listening:** Giving full attention to what other people are saying, taking time to understand the points being made, asking questions as appropriate, and not interrupting at inappropriate times.

GOE INFORMATION—Interest Area: 13. General Management and Support. **Work Group:** 13.02. Management Support. **Other Job Titles in This Work Group:** Accountants; Accountants and Auditors; Appraisers and Assessors of Real Estate; Appraisers, Real Estate; Assessors; Auditors; Budget Analysts; Claims Adjusters, Examiners, and Investigators; Claims Examiners, Property and Casualty Insurance; Compensation, Benefits, and Job Analysis Specialists; Cost Estimators; Credit Analysts; Employment Interviewers, Private or Public Employment Service; Employment, Recruitment, and Placement Specialists; Financial Analysts; Human Resources, Training, and Labor Relations Specialists, All Other; Insurance Adjusters, Examiners, and Investigators; Insurance Appraisers, Auto Damage; Insurance Underwriters; Loan Counselors; Loan Officers; Logisticians; Management Analysts; Market Research Analysts; Personnel Recruiters; Purchasing Agents and Buyers, Farm Products; Purchasing Agents, Except Wholesale, Retail, and Farm Products; Tax Examiners, Collectors, and Revenue Agents; Wholesale and Retail Buyers, Except Farm Products. **PERSONALITY TYPE**—Social. Social occupations frequently involve working with, communicating with, and teaching people. These occupations often involve helping or providing service to others.

EDUCATION/TRAINING PROGRAM(S)—Human Resources Management/Personnel Administration, General; Organizational Behavior Studies. **RELATED KNOWLEDGE/COURSES—Education and Training:** Knowledge of principles and methods for curriculum and training design, teaching and instruction for individuals and groups, and the measurement of training effects. **Personnel and Human Resources:** Knowledge of principles and procedures for personnel recruitment, selection, training, compensation and benefits, labor relations and negotiation, and personnel information systems. **Psychology:** Knowledge of human behavior and performance; individual differences in ability, personality, and interests; learning and motivation; psychological research methods; and the assessment and treatment of behavioral and affective disorders. **English Language:** Knowledge of the structure and content of the English language, including the meaning and spelling of words, rules of composition, and grammar. **Sales and Marketing:** Knowledge of principles and methods for showing, promoting, and selling products or services. This includes marketing strategy and tactics, prod-

uct demonstration, sales techniques, and sales control systems. **Economics and Accounting:** Knowledge of economic and accounting principles and practices, the financial markets, banking, and the analysis and reporting of financial data. **Clerical Studies:** Knowledge of administrative and clerical procedures and systems, such as word processing, managing files and records, stenography and transcription, designing forms, and other office procedures and terminology.

Transportation Managers

▲ Education/Training Required: Work experience in a related occupation
▲ Annual Earnings: $57,240
▲ Growth: 20.2%
▲ Annual Job Openings: 13,000
▲ Self-Employed: 0%
▲ Part-Time: 6.1%

Plan, direct, and coordinate the transportation operations within an organization or the activities of organizations that provide transportation services. Directs and coordinates, through subordinates, activities of operations department to obtain use of equipment, facilities, and human resources. Participates in union contract negotiations and settlement of grievances. Negotiates and authorizes contracts with equipment and materials suppliers. Oversees procurement process, including research and testing of equipment, vendor contacts, and approval of requisitions. Inspects or oversees repairs and maintenance to equipment, vehicles, and facilities to enforce standards for safety, efficiency, cleanliness, and appearance. Acts as organization representative before commissions or regulatory bodies during hearings, such as those to increase rates and change routes and schedules. Oversees workers assigning tariff classifications and preparing billing according to mode of transportation and destination of shipment. Oversees process of investigation and response to customer or shipper complaints relating to operations department. Recommends or authorizes capital expenditures for acquisition of new equipment or property to increase efficiency and services of operations department. Enforces compliance of operations personnel with administrative policies, procedures, safety rules, and government regulations. Reviews transportation schedules, worker assignments, and routes to ensure compliance with standards for personnel selection, safety, and union contract terms. Conducts investigations in cooperation with government agencies to determine causes of transportation accidents and to improve safety procedures. Prepares management

recommendations, such as need for increasing fares, tariffs, or expansion or changes to existing schedules. Oversees activities relating to dispatching, routing, and tracking transportation vehicles, such as aircraft and railroad cars. Analyzes expenditures and other financial reports to develop plans, policies, and budgets for increasing profits and improving services. Confers and cooperates with management and others in formulating and implementing administrative, operational, and customer relations, policies, and procedures. **SKILLS—Coordination:** Adjusting actions in relation to others' actions. **Reading Comprehension:** Understanding written sentences and paragraphs in work-related documents. **Management of Personnel Resources:** Motivating, developing, and directing people as they work, identifying the best people for the job. **Management of Material Resources:** Obtaining and seeing to the appropriate use of equipment, facilities, and materials needed to do certain work. **Judgment and Decision Making:** Considering the relative costs and benefits of potential actions to choose the most appropriate one.

GOE INFORMATION—Interest Area: 07. Transportation. **Work Group:** 07.01. Managerial Work in Transportation. **Other Job Titles in This Work Group:** First-Line Supervisors/Managers of Transportation and Material-Moving Machine and Vehicle Operators; Railroad Conductors and Yardmasters. **PERSONALITY TYPE—** Enterprising. Enterprising occupations frequently involve starting up and carrying out projects. These occupations can involve leading people and making many decisions. They sometimes require risk taking and often deal with business.

EDUCATION/TRAINING PROGRAM(S)—Aeronautics/Aviation/Aerospace Science and Technology, General; Aviation/Airway Management and Operations; Business Administration and Management, General; Business/Commerce, General; Logistics and Materials Management; Public Administration. **RELATED KNOWLEDGE/ COURSES—Transportation:** Knowledge of principles and methods for moving people or goods by air, rail, sea, or road, including the relative costs and benefits. **Administration and Management:** Knowledge of business and management principles involved in strategic planning, resource allocation, human resources modeling, leadership technique, production methods, and coordination of people and resources. **Mathematics:** Knowledge of arithmetic, algebra, geometry, calculus, and statistics and their applications. **Economics and Accounting:** Knowledge of economic and accounting principles and practices, the financial markets, banking, and the analysis and reporting of financial data. **Personnel and Human Resources:** Knowledge of principles and procedures for personnel recruitment, selection, training, compensation and benefits, labor relations and negotiation, and personnel information systems.

Transportation, Storage, and Distribution Managers

- ▲ Education/Training Required: Work experience in a related occupation
- ▲ Annual Earnings: $57,240
- ▲ Growth: 20.2%
- ▲ Annual Job Openings: 13,000
- ▲ Self-Employed: 0%
- ▲ Part-Time: 6.1%

Plan, direct, or coordinate transportation, storage, or distribution activities in accordance with governmental policies and regulations. SKILLS—No data available.

GOE INFORMATION—Interest Area: 13. General Management and Support. **Work Group:** 13.01. General Management Work and Management of Support Functions. **Other Job Titles in This Work Group:** Chief Executives; Compensation and Benefits Managers; Farm, Ranch, and Other Agricultural Managers; Financial Managers; Financial Managers, Branch or Department; Funeral Directors; General and Operations Managers; Government Service Executives; Human Resources Managers; Human Resources Managers, All Other; Legislators; Managers, All Other; Postmasters and Mail Superintendents; Private Sector Executives; Property, Real Estate, and Community Association Managers; Public Relations Managers; Purchasing Managers; Storage and Distribution Managers; Training and Development Managers; Treasurers, Controllers, and Chief Financial Officers. **PERSONALITY TYPE—**No data available.

EDUCATION/TRAINING PROGRAM(S)—Aeronautics/Aviation/Aerospace Science and Technology, General; Aviation/Airway Management and Operations; Business Administration and Management, General; Business/ Commerce, General; Logistics and Materials Management; Public Administration. **RELATED KNOWLEDGE/ COURSES—**No data available.

- ▲ Education/Training Required: Short-term on-the-job training
- ▲ Annual Earnings: $24,090
- ▲ Growth: 14.5%
- ▲ Annual Job Openings: 39,000
- ▲ Self-Employed: 0%
- ▲ Part-Time: 31.7%

Travel Clerks

Provide tourists with travel information, such as points of interest, restaurants, rates, and emergency service. Duties include answering inquiries, offering suggestions, and providing literature pertaining to trips, excursions, sporting events, concerts, and plays. May make reservations, deliver tickets, arrange for visas, or contact individuals and groups to inform them of package tours. Provides customers with travel suggestions and information such as guides, directories, brochures, and maps. Contacts motel, hotel, resort, and travel operators by mail or telephone to obtain advertising literature. Studies maps, directories, routes, and rate tables to determine travel route and cost and availability of accommodations. Calculates estimated travel rates and expenses, using items such as rate tables and calculators. Informs client of travel dates, times, connections, baggage limits, medical and visa requirements, and emergency information. Obtains reservations for air, train, or car travel and hotel or other housing accommodations. Confirms travel arrangements and reservations. Assists client in preparing required documents and forms for travel, such as visas. Plans itinerary for travel and accommodations, using knowledge of routes, types of carriers, and regulations. Provides information concerning fares, availability of travel, and accommodations, either orally or by using guides, brochures, and maps. Confers with customers by telephone, in writing, or in person to answer questions regarding services and determine travel preferences. **SKILLS—Service Orientation:** Actively looking for ways to help people. **Active Listening:** Giving full attention to what other people are saying, taking time to understand the points being made, asking questions as appropriate, and not interrupting at inappropriate times. **Speaking:** Talking to others to convey information effectively. **Reading Comprehension:** Understanding written sentences and paragraphs in work-related documents. **Writing:** Communicating effectively in writing as appropriate for the needs of the audience. **Mathematics:** Using mathematics to solve problems. **Coordination:** Adjusting actions in relation to others' actions.

GOE INFORMATION—Interest Area: 09. Business Detail. **Work Group:** 09.05. Customer Service. **Other Job Titles in This Work Group:** Adjustment Clerks; Bill and Account Collectors; Cashiers; Counter and Rental Clerks; Customer Service Representatives; Customer Service Representatives, Utilities; Gaming Cage Workers; Gaming Change Persons and Booth Cashiers; New Accounts Clerks; Order Clerks; Receptionists and Information Clerks; Tellers. **PERSONALITY TYPE—Conventional.** Conventional occupations frequently involve following set procedures and routines. These occupations can include working with data and details more than with ideas. Usually there is a clear line of authority to follow.

EDUCATION/TRAINING PROGRAM(S)—Selling Skills and Sales Operations; Tourism and Travel Services Marketing Operations; Tourism Promotion Operations. **RELATED KNOWLEDGE/COURSES—Customer and Personal Service:** Knowledge of principles and processes for providing customer and personal services. This includes customer needs assessment, meeting quality standards for services, and evaluation of customer satisfaction. **Geography:** Knowledge of principles and methods for describing the features of land, sea, and air masses, including their physical characteristics, locations, interrelationships, and distribution of plant, animal, and human life. **Transportation:** Knowledge of principles and methods for moving people or goods by air, rail, sea, or road, including the relative costs and benefits. **Mathematics:** Knowledge of arithmetic, algebra, geometry, calculus, and statistics and their applications. **Telecommunications:** Knowledge of transmission, broadcasting, switching, control, and operation of telecommunications systems.

Treasurers, Controllers, and Chief Financial Officers

- ▲ Education/Training Required: Work experience plus degree
- ▲ Annual Earnings: $70,210
- ▲ Growth: 18.5%
- ▲ Annual Job Openings: 53,000
- ▲ Self-Employed: 1.4%
- ▲ Part-Time: 2.6%

Plan, direct, and coordinate the financial activities of an organization at the highest level of management. Includes financial reserve officers. Coordinates and directs financial planning, budgeting, procurement, and investment activities of organization. Prepares reports or directs preparation of reports summarizing organization's current and forecasted financial position, business activity, and reports required by regulatory agencies. Delegates authority for receipt, disbursement, banking, protection, and custody of funds, securities, and financial instruments. Analyzes past, present, and expected operations. Advises management on economic objectives and policies, investments, and loans for short- and long-range financial plans. Evaluates need for procurement of funds and investment of surplus. Arranges audits of company accounts. Ensures that institution reserves meet legal requirements. Interprets current policies and practices and plans and implements new operating procedures to improve efficiency and reduce costs. **SKILLS—Management of Financial Resources:** Determining how money will be spent to get the work done and accounting for these expenditures. **Judgment and Decision Making:** Considering the relative costs and benefits of potential actions to choose the most appropriate one. **Systems Analysis:** Determining how a system should work and how changes in conditions, operations, and the environment will affect outcomes. **Systems Evaluation:** Identifying measures or indicators of system performance and the actions needed to improve or correct performance relative to the goals of the system. **Mathematics:** Using mathematics to solve problems. **Critical Thinking:** Using logic and reasoning to identify the strengths and weaknesses of alternative solutions, conclusions, or approaches to problems.

GOE INFORMATION—Interest Area: 13. General Management and Support. **Work Group:** 13.01. General Management Work and Management of Support Functions. **Other Job Titles in This Work Group:** Chief Executives; Compensation and Benefits Managers; Farm, Ranch, and Other Agricultural Managers; Financial Managers; Financial Managers, Branch or Department; Funeral Directors; General and Operations Managers; Government Service Executives; Human Resources Managers; Human Resources Managers, All Other; Legislators; Managers, All Other; Postmasters and Mail Superintendents; Private Sector Ex-

ecutives; Property, Real Estate, and Community Association Managers; Public Relations Managers; Purchasing Managers; Storage and Distribution Managers; Training and Development Managers; Transportation, Storage, and Distribution Managers. **PERSONALITY TYPE—**Enterprising. Enterprising occupations frequently involve starting up and carrying out projects. These occupations can involve leading people and making many decisions. They sometimes require risk taking and often deal with business.

EDUCATION/TRAINING PROGRAM(S)—Accounting and Business/Management; Accounting and Finance; Credit Management; Finance and Financial Management Services, Other; Finance, General; International Finance; Public Finance. **RELATED KNOWLEDGE/ COURSES—Economics and Accounting:** Knowledge of economic and accounting principles and practices, the financial markets, banking, and the analysis and reporting of financial data. **Administration and Management:** Knowledge of business and management principles involved in strategic planning, resource allocation, human resources modeling, leadership technique, production methods, and coordination of people and resources. **Mathematics:** Knowledge of arithmetic, algebra, geometry, calculus, and statistics and their applications. **Law and Government:** Knowledge of laws, legal codes, court procedures, precedents, government regulations, executive orders, agency rules, and the democratic political process. **English Language:** Knowledge of the structure and content of the English language, including the meaning and spelling of words, rules of composition, and grammar.

Tree Trimmers and Pruners

- ▲ Education/Training Required: Short-term on-the-job training
- ▲ Annual Earnings: $23,950
- ▲ Growth: 16.3%
- ▲ Annual Job Openings: 11,000
- ▲ Self-Employed: 0%
- ▲ Part-Time: 25.4%

Cut away dead or excess branches from trees or shrubs to maintain right-of-way for roads, sidewalks, or utilities or to improve appearance, health, and value of tree. Prune or treat trees or shrubs using handsaws, pruning hooks, shears, and clippers. May use truck-mounted lifts and power pruners. May fill cavities in trees to promote healing and prevent deterioration. Cuts away dead and excess branches from trees, using handsaws, pruning hooks, shears, and clippers. Climbs trees, using climbing hooks

and belts, or climbs ladders to gain access to work area. Prunes, cuts down, fertilizes, and sprays trees as directed by tree surgeon. Uses truck-mounted hydraulic lifts and pruners and power pruners. Scrapes decayed matter from cavities in trees and fills holes with cement to promote healing and to prevent further deterioration. Applies tar or other protective substances to cut surfaces to seal surfaces against insects. **SKILLS—Operation and Control:** Controlling operations of equipment or systems.

GOE INFORMATION—**Interest Area:** 03. Plants and Animals. **Work Group:** 03.03. Hands-on Work in Plants and Animals. **Other Job Titles in This Work Group:** Agricultural Equipment Operators; Fallers; Farmworkers and Laborers, Crop, Nursery, and Greenhouse; Farmworkers, Farm and Ranch Animals; Fishers and Related Fishing Workers; Forest and Conservation Technicians; Forest and Conservation Workers; General Farmworkers; Grounds Maintenance Workers, All Other; Hunters and Trappers; Landscaping and Groundskeeping Workers; Logging Equipment Operators; Logging Tractor Operators; Logging Workers, All Other; Nursery Workers; Pest Control Workers; Pesticide Handlers, Sprayers, and Applicators, Vegetation. **PERSONALITY TYPE—** Realistic. Realistic occupations frequently involve work activities that include practical, hands-on problems and solutions. They often deal with plants, animals, and real-world materials like wood, tools, and machinery. Many of the occupations require working outside and do not involve a lot of paperwork or working closely with others.

EDUCATION/TRAINING PROGRAM(S)—Applied Horticulture/Horticultural Business Services, Other. **RELATED KNOWLEDGE/COURSES—Principles of Mechanical Devices:** Knowledge of machines and tools, including their designs, uses, repair, and maintenance. **Biology:** Knowledge of plant and animal organisms and their tissues, cells, functions, interdependencies, and interactions with each other and the environment. **Chemistry:** Knowledge of the chemical composition, structure, and properties of substances and of the chemical processes and transformations that they undergo. This includes uses of chemicals and their interactions, danger signs, production techniques, and disposal methods.

Truck Drivers, Heavy

- ▲ Education/Training Required: Short-term on-the-job training
- ▲ Annual Earnings: $32,580
- ▲ Growth: 19.8%
- ▲ Annual Job Openings: 240,000
- ▲ Self-Employed: 9.2%
- ▲ Part-Time: 9.9%

Drive truck with capacity of more than three tons to transport materials to specified destinations. Drives truck with capacity of more than three tons to transport and deliver cargo, materials, or damaged vehicle. Maintains radio or telephone contact with base or supervisor to receive instructions or be dispatched to new location. Maintains truck log according to state and federal regulations. Keeps record of materials and products transported. Positions blocks and ties rope around items to secure cargo for transport. Cleans, inspects, and services vehicle. Operates equipment on vehicle to load, unload, or disperse cargo or materials. Obtains customer signature or collects payment for goods delivered and delivery charges. Assists in loading and unloading truck manually. **SKILLS—Equipment Maintenance:** Performing routine maintenance on equipment and determining when and what kind of maintenance is needed. **Operation and Control:** Controlling operations of equipment or systems. **Operation Monitoring:** Watching gauges, dials, or other indicators to make sure a machine is working properly. **Reading Comprehension:** Understanding written sentences and paragraphs in work-related documents. **Writing:** Communicating effectively in writing as appropriate for the needs of the audience.

GOE INFORMATION—**Interest Area:** 07. Transportation. **Work Group:** 07.05. Truck Driving. **Other Job Titles in This Work Group:** Tractor-Trailer Truck Drivers; Truck Drivers, Heavy and Tractor-Trailer; Truck Drivers, Light or Delivery Services. **PERSONALITY TYPE—**Realistic. Realistic occupations frequently involve work activities that include practical, hands-on problems and solutions. They often deal with plants, animals, and real-world materials like wood, tools, and machinery. Many of the occupations require working outside and do not involve a lot of paperwork or working closely with others.

EDUCATION/TRAINING PROGRAM(S)—Truck and Bus Driver/Commercial Vehicle Operation. **RELATED KNOWLEDGE/COURSES—Transportation:** Knowledge of principles and methods for moving people or goods by air, rail, sea, or road, including the relative costs and benefits. **Geography:** Knowledge of principles and methods for describing the features of land, sea, and air masses, including their physical characteristics, locations, interrelationships, and distribution of plant, animal, and human life. **Principles of Mechanical Devices:** Knowledge of machines and tools, including their designs, uses, repair, and maintenance. **Clerical Studies:** Knowledge of administrative and clerical procedures and systems, such as word processing, managing files and records, stenography and transcription, designing forms, and other office procedures and terminology. **Public Safety and Security:** Knowledge of relevant equipment, policies, procedures, and strategies to promote effective local, state, or national security operations for the protection of people, data, property, and institutions. **Law and Government:** Knowledge of laws, legal codes, court procedures, precedents, government regulations, executive orders, agency rules, and the democratic political process.

Truck Drivers, Heavy and Tractor-Trailer

▲ Education/Training Required: Moderate-term on-the-job training
▲ Annual Earnings: $32,580
▲ Growth: 19.8%
▲ Annual Job Openings: 240,000
▲ Self-Employed: No data available.
▲ Part-Time: No data available.

Drive a tractor-trailer combination or a truck with a capacity of at least 26,000 GVW to transport and deliver goods, livestock, or materials in liquid, loose, or packaged form. May be required to unload truck. May require use of automated routing equipment. Requires commercial drivers' license. **SKILLS**—No data available.

GOE INFORMATION—Interest Area: 07. Transportation. **Work Group:** 07.05. Truck Driving. **Other Job Titles in This Work Group:** Tractor-Trailer Truck Drivers; Truck Drivers, Heavy; Truck Drivers, Light or Delivery Services. **PERSONALITY TYPE**—No data available.

EDUCATION/TRAINING PROGRAM(S)—Truck and Bus Driver/Commercial Vehicle Operation. **RELATED KNOWLEDGE/COURSES**—No data available.

Truck Drivers, Light or Delivery Services

▲ Education/Training Required: Short-term on-the-job training
▲ Annual Earnings: $23,330
▲ Growth: 19.2%
▲ Annual Job Openings: 153,000
▲ Self-Employed: 9.2%
▲ Part-Time: 9.9%

Drive a truck or van with a capacity of under 26,000 GVW primarily to deliver or pick up merchandise or to deliver packages within a specified area. May require use of automatic routing or location software. May load and unload truck. Drives truck, van, or automobile with capacity under three tons to transport materials, products, or people. Loads and unloads truck, van, or automobile. Communicates with base or other vehicles using telephone or radio. Maintains records such as vehicle log, record of cargo, or billing statements in accordance with regulations. Inspects and maintains vehicle equipment and supplies. Presents billing invoice and collects receipt or payment. Performs emergency roadside repairs. **SKILLS**—**Equipment Maintenance:** Performing routine maintenance on equipment and determining when and what kind of maintenance is needed. **Operation and Control:** Controlling operations of equipment or systems. **Repairing:** Repairing machines or systems, using the needed tools. **Operation Monitoring:** Watching gauges, dials, or other indicators to make sure a machine is working properly. **Reading Comprehension:** Understanding written sentences and paragraphs in work-related documents. **Writing:** Communicating effectively in writing as appropriate for the needs of the audience.

GOE INFORMATION—Interest Area: 07. Transportation. **Work Group:** 07.05. Truck Driving. **Other Job Titles in This Work Group:** Tractor-Trailer Truck Drivers; Truck Drivers, Heavy; Truck Drivers, Heavy and Tractor-Trailer. **PERSONALITY TYPE**—Realistic. Realistic occupations frequently involve work activities that include practical, hands-on problems and solutions. They often deal with plants, animals, and real-world materials like wood, tools, and machinery. Many of the occupations require working outside and do not involve a lot of paperwork or working closely with others.

EDUCATION/TRAINING PROGRAM(S)—Truck and Bus Driver/Commercial Vehicle Operation. **RELATED KNOWLEDGE/COURSES**—**Transportation:** Knowledge of principles and methods for moving people or goods by air, rail, sea, or road, including the relative costs and benefits. **Principles of Mechanical Devices:** Knowledge of machines and tools, including their designs, uses, repair, and maintenance. **Geography:** Knowledge of principles and methods for describing the features of land, sea, and air masses, including their physical characteristics, locations, interrelationships, and distribution of plant, animal, and human life. **Public Safety and Security:** Knowledge of relevant equipment, policies, procedures, and strategies to promote effective local, state, or national security operations for the protection of people, data, property, and institutions. **Clerical Studies:** Knowledge of administrative and clerical procedures and systems, such as word processing, managing files and records, stenography and transcription, designing forms, and other office procedures and terminology.

Urban and Regional Planners

- ▲ Education/Training Required: Master's degree
- ▲ Annual Earnings: $48,530
- ▲ Growth: 16.4%
- ▲ Annual Job Openings: 3,000
- ▲ Self-Employed: 3.5%
- ▲ Part-Time: 18.1%

Develop comprehensive plans and programs for use of land and physical facilities of local jurisdictions, such as towns, cities, counties, and metropolitan areas. Develops alternative plans with recommendations for program or project. Compiles, organizes, and analyzes data on economic, social, and physical factors affecting land use, using statistical methods. Recommends governmental measures affecting land use, public utilities, community facilities, housing, and transportation. Evaluates information to determine feasibility of proposals or to identify factors requiring amendment. Reviews and evaluates environmental impact reports applying to specific private and public planning projects and programs. Discusses purpose of land use projects, such as transportation, conservation, residential, commercial, industrial, and community use, with planning officials. Determines regulatory limitations on project. Advises planning officials on feasibility, cost-effectiveness, regulatory conformance, and alternative recommendations for project. Maintains collection of socioeconomic, environmental, and regulatory data related to land use for governmental and private sectors. Conducts field investigations, economic or public opinion surveys, demographic studies, or other research to gather required information. Prepares or requisitions graphic and narrative report on land use data. **SKILLS**— **Judgment and Decision Making:** Considering the relative costs and benefits of potential actions to choose the most appropriate one. **Complex Problem Solving:** Identifying complex problems and reviewing related information to develop and evaluate options and implement solutions. **Systems Analysis:** Determining how a system should work and how changes in conditions, operations, and the environment will affect outcomes. **Critical Thinking:** Using logic and reasoning to identify the strengths and weaknesses of alternative solutions, conclusions, or approaches to problems. **Reading Comprehension:** Understanding written sentences and paragraphs in work-related documents.

GOE INFORMATION—**Interest Area:** 02. Science, Math, and Engineering. **Work Group:** 02.04. Social Sciences. **Other Job Titles in This Work Group:** Anthropologists; Anthropologists and Archeologists; Archeologists; City Planning Aides; Economists; Historians; Industrial-Organizational Psychologists; Political Scientists; Psychologists, All Other; Social Science Research Assistants; Social Scientists and Related Workers, All Other; Sociologists; Survey Researchers. **PERSONALITY TYPE**—Investigative. Investigative occupations frequently involve working with ideas and require an extensive amount of thinking. These occupations can involve searching for facts and figuring out problems mentally.

EDUCATION/TRAINING PROGRAM(S)—City/Urban, Community, and Regional Planning. **RELATED KNOWLEDGE/COURSES—Mathematics:** Knowledge of arithmetic, algebra, geometry, calculus, and statistics and their applications. **Sociology and Anthropology:** Knowledge of group behavior and dynamics, societal trends and influences, human migrations, ethnicity, and cultures and their history and origins. **Law and Government:** Knowledge of laws, legal codes, court procedures, precedents, government regulations, executive orders, agency rules, and the democratic political process. **English Language:** Knowledge of the structure and content of the English language, including the meaning and spelling of words, rules of composition, and grammar. **Economics and Accounting:** Knowledge of economic and accounting principles and practices, the financial markets, banking, and the analysis and reporting of financial data. **Building and Construction:** Knowledge of materials, methods, and tools involved in the construction or repair of houses, buildings, or other structures, such as highways and roads. **Administration and Management:** Knowledge of business and management principles involved in strategic planning, resource allocation, human resources modeling, leadership technique, production methods, and coordination of people and resources.

Veterinarians

- ▲ Education/Training Required: First professional degree
- ▲ Annual Earnings: $62,000
- ▲ Growth: 31.8%
- ▲ Annual Job Openings: 2,000
- ▲ Self-Employed: 39.6%
- ▲ Part-Time: 10.5%

Diagnose and treat diseases and dysfunctions of animals. May engage in a particular function, such as research and development, consultation, administration, technical writing, sale or production of commercial products, or rendering of technical services to commercial firms or other organizations. Includes veterinarians who inspect livestock. Examines animal to detect and determine nature of disease or injury and treats animal surgically or medically. Inspects and tests horses, sheep, poultry flocks, and other animals for diseases and inoculates animals against various diseases, including rabies. Establishes and conducts quarantine and testing procedures to prevent spread of disease and compliance with governmental regulations. Participates in research projects, plans procedures, and selects animals for scientific research based on knowledge of species and research principles. Oversees activities concerned with feeding, care, and maintenance of animal quarters to ensure compliance with laboratory regulations. Exchanges information with zoos and aquariums concerning care, transfer, sale, or trade of animals to maintain all-species nationwide inventory. Trains personnel in handling and care of animals. Participates in planning and executing nutrition and reproduction programs for animals. Ensures compliance with regulations governing humane and ethical treatment of animals used in scientific research. Inspects housing and advises animal owners regarding sanitary measures, feeding, and general care to promote health of animals. Conducts postmortem studies and analysis results to determine cause of death. **SKILLS—Reading Comprehension:** Understanding written sentences and paragraphs in work-related documents. **Active Learning:** Understanding the implications of new information for both current and future problem-solving and decision-making. **Science:** Using scientific rules and methods to solve problems. **Critical Thinking:** Using logic and reasoning to identify the strengths and weaknesses of alternative solutions, conclusions, or approaches to problems. **Complex Problem Solving:** Identifying complex problems and reviewing related information to develop and evaluate options and implement solutions.

GOE INFORMATION—Interest Area: 03. Plants and Animals. **Work Group:** 03.02. Animal Care and Training. **Other Job Titles in This Work Group:** Animal Breeders; Animal Trainers; Nonfarm Animal Caretakers; Veterinary Assistants and Laboratory Animal Caretakers; Veterinary Technologists and Technicians. **PERSONALITY TYPE—** Investigative. Investigative occupations frequently involve working with ideas and require an extensive amount of thinking. These occupations can involve searching for facts and figuring out problems mentally.

EDUCATION/TRAINING PROGRAM(S)—Comparative and Laboratory Animal Medicine (Cert, MS, PhD);

Laboratory Animal Medicine; Large Animal/Food Animal and Equine Surgery and Medicine (Cert, MS, PhD); Small/Companion Animal Surgery and Medicine (Cert, MS, PhD); Theriogenology; Veterinary Anatomy (Cert, MS, PhD); Veterinary Anesthesiology; Veterinary Biomedical and Clinical Sciences, Other (Cert, MS, PhD); Veterinary Dentistry; Veterinary Dermatology; Veterinary Emergency and Critical Care Medicine; Veterinary Infectious Diseases (Cert, MS, PhD); Veterinary Internal Medicine; Veterinary Medicine (DVM); Veterinary Microbiology; Veterinary Microbiology and Immunobiology (Cert, MS, PhD); Veterinary Nutrition; Veterinary Ophthalmology; Veterinary Pathology; Veterinary Pathology and Pathobiology (Cert, MS, PhD); Veterinary Physiology (Cert, MS, PhD); Veterinary Practice; Veterinary Preventive Medicine; Veterinary Preventive Medicine Epidemiology and Public Health (Cert, MS, PhD); Veterinary Radiology; Veterinary Residency Programs, Other; Veterinary Sciences/Veterinary Clinical Sciences, General (Cert, MS, PhD); Veterinary Surgery; Veterinary Toxicology; Veterinary Toxicology and Pharmacology (Cert, MS, PhD); Zoological Medicine. RE-LATED KNOWLEDGE/COURSES—**Biology:** Knowledge of plant and animal organisms and their tissues, cells, functions, interdependencies, and interactions with each other and the environment. **Medicine and Dentistry:** Knowledge of the information and techniques needed to diagnose and treat human injuries, diseases, and deformities. This includes symptoms, treatment alternatives, drug properties and interactions, and preventive health-care measures. **English Language:** Knowledge of the structure and content of the English language, including the meaning and spelling of words, rules of composition, and grammar. **Chemistry:** Knowledge of the chemical composition, structure, and properties of substances and of the chemical processes and transformations that they undergo. This includes uses of chemicals and their interactions, danger signs, production techniques, and disposal methods. **Education and Training:** Knowledge of principles and methods for curriculum and training design, teaching and instruction for individuals and groups, and the measurement of training effects. **Mathematics:** Knowledge of arithmetic, algebra, geometry, calculus, and statistics and their applications.

Veterinary Assistants and Laboratory Animal Caretakers

▲ Education/Training Required: Short-term on-the-job training
▲ Annual Earnings: $17,470
▲ Growth: 39.8%
▲ Annual Job Openings: 8,000
▲ Self-Employed: 0%
▲ Part-Time: 38.1%

Feed, water, and examine pets and other nonfarm animals for signs of illness, disease, or injury in laboratories and animal hospitals and clinics. Clean and disinfect cages and work areas; sterilize laboratory and surgical equipment. May provide routine post-operative care, administer medication orally or topically, or prepare samples for laboratory examination under the supervision of veterinary or laboratory animal technologists or technicians, veterinarians, or scientists. Assists veterinarian in variety of animal health care duties, including injections, venipunctures, and wound dressings. Prepares examination or treatment room and holds or restrains animal during procedures. Prepares patient, medications, equipment, and instruments for surgical procedures, using specialized knowledge. Assists veterinarian during surgical procedures, passing instruments and materials in accordance with oral instructions. Inspects products or carcasses to ensure compliance with health standards when employed in food processing plant. Assists professional personnel with research projects in commercial, public health, or research laboratories. Completes routine laboratory tests and cares for and feeds laboratory animals. SKILLS—**Reading Comprehension:** Understanding written sentences and paragraphs in work-related documents. **Active Listening:** Giving full attention to what other people are saying, taking time to understand the points being made, asking questions as appropriate, and not interrupting at inappropriate times. **Speaking:** Talking to others to convey information effectively. **Social Perceptiveness:** Being aware of others' reactions and understanding why they react as they do. **Science:** Using scientific rules and methods to solve problems.

GOE INFORMATION—**Interest Area:** 03. Plants and Animals. **Work Group:** 03.02. Animal Care and Training. **Other Job Titles in This Work Group:** Animal Breeders; Animal Trainers; Nonfarm Animal Caretakers; Veterinarians; Veterinary Technologists and Technicians. PERSON-

ALITY TYPE—Realistic. Realistic occupations frequently involve work activities that include practical, hands-on problems and solutions. They often deal with plants, animals, and real-world materials like wood, tools, and machinery. Many of the occupations require working outside and do not involve a lot of paperwork or working closely with others.

EDUCATION/TRAINING PROGRAM(S)—Veterinary/Animal Health Technology/Technician and Veterinary Assistant. RELATED KNOWLEDGE/COURSES—Biology: Knowledge of plant and animal organisms and their tissues, cells, functions, interdependencies, and interactions with each other and the environment. Medicine and Den-

tistry: Knowledge of the information and techniques needed to diagnose and treat human injuries, diseases, and deformities. This includes symptoms, treatment alternatives, drug properties and interactions, and preventive health-care measures. Therapy and Counseling: Knowledge of principles, methods, and procedures for diagnosis, treatment, and rehabilitation of physical and mental dysfunctions and for career counseling and guidance. Mathematics: Knowledge of arithmetic, algebra, geometry, calculus, and statistics and their applications. English Language: Knowledge of the structure and content of the English language, including the meaning and spelling of words, rules of composition, and grammar.

Veterinary Technologists and Technicians

- ▲ Education/Training Required: Associate's degree
- ▲ Annual Earnings: $22,430
- ▲ Growth: 39.3%
- ▲ Annual Job Openings: 6,000
- ▲ Self-Employed: 0%
- ▲ Part-Time: 11.7%

Perform medical tests in a laboratory environment for use in the treatment and diagnosis of diseases in animals. Prepare vaccines and serums for prevention of diseases. Prepare tissue samples; take blood samples; and execute laboratory tests, such as urinalysis and blood counts. Clean and sterilize instruments and materials and maintain equipment and machines. SKILLS—No data available.

GOE INFORMATION—Interest Area: 03. Plants and Animals. Work Group: 03.02. Animal Care and Training.

Other Job Titles in This Work Group: Animal Breeders; Animal Trainers; Nonfarm Animal Caretakers; Veterinarians; Veterinary Assistants and Laboratory Animal Caretakers. PERSONALITY TYPE—No data available.

EDUCATION/TRAINING PROGRAM(S)—Veterinary/Animal Health Technology/Technician and Veterinary Assistant. RELATED KNOWLEDGE/COURSES—No data available.

Vocational Education Teachers, Postsecondary

- ▲ Education/Training Required: Work experience in a related occupation
- ▲ Annual Earnings: $38,540
- ▲ Growth: 23.5%
- ▲ Annual Job Openings: 184,000
- ▲ Self-Employed: 0%
- ▲ Part-Time: 42.5%

Teach or instruct vocational or occupational subjects at the postsecondary level (but at less than the baccalaureate) to students who have graduated or left high school. Includes correspondence school instructors; industrial, commercial and government training instructors; and adult education teachers and instructors who prepare

persons to operate industrial machinery and equipment and transportation and communications equipment. Teaching may take place in public or private schools whose primary business is education or in a school associated with an organization whose primary business is other than education. Conducts on-the-job training, classes, or training sessions to teach and demonstrate principles, techniques, procedures, or methods of designated subjects. Plans course content and method of instruction. Selects and assembles books, materials, supplies, and equipment for training, courses, or projects. Participates in meetings, seminars, and training sessions and integrates relevant information into training program. Recommends advancement, transfer, or termination of student or trainee based on mastery of subject. Arranges for lectures by subject matter experts in designated fields. Reviews enrollment applications and corresponds with applicants. Prepares reports and maintains records, such as student grades, attendance, training activities, production records, and supply or equipment inventories. Develops teaching aids, such as instructional software, multimedia visual aids, computer tutorials, or study materials for instruction in vocational or occupational subjects. Corrects, grades, and comments on lesson assignments. Determines training needs of students or workers. Administers oral, written, or performance tests to measure progress and to evaluate effectiveness of training. Solves operational problems and provides technical assistance with equipment and process techniques. Prepares outline of instructional program and training schedule and establishes course goals. Observes and evaluates students' work to determine progress, provide feedback, and make suggestions for improvement. Presents lectures and conducts discussions to increase students' knowledge and competence, using visual aids such as graphs, charts, videotapes, and slides. **SKILLS—Writing:** Communicating effectively in writing as appropriate for the needs of the audience. **Speaking:** Talking to others to convey information effectively. **Reading Comprehension:** Understanding written sentences and paragraphs in work-related documents. **Active Listening:** Giving full attention to what other people are saying, taking time to understand the points being made, asking questions as appropriate, and not interrupting at inappropriate times. **Instructing:** Teaching others how to do something.

GOE INFORMATION—Interest Area: 12. Education and Social Service. **Work Group:** 12.03. Educational Services. **Other Job Titles in This Work Group:** Adult Literacy, Remedial Education, and GED Teachers and Instructors; Agricultural Sciences Teachers, Postsecondary; Anthropology and Archeology Teachers, Postsecondary; Architecture Teachers, Postsecondary; Archivists; Area, Ethnic, and Cultural Studies Teachers, Postsecondary; Art, Drama, and Music Teachers, Postsecondary; Atmospheric, Earth, Marine, and Space Sciences Teachers, Postsecondary; Audio-Visual Collections Specialists; Bio-logical Science Teachers, Postsecondary; Business Teachers, Postsecondary; Chemistry Teachers, Postsecondary; Child Care Workers; Communications Teachers, Postsecondary; Computer Science Teachers, Postsecondary; Criminal Justice and Law Enforcement Teachers, Postsecondary; Curators; Economics Teachers, Postsecondary; Education Teachers, Postsecondary; Educational Psychologists; Educational, Vocational, and School Counselors; Elementary School Teachers, Except Special Education; Engineering Teachers, Postsecondary; English Language and Literature Teachers, Postsecondary; Environmental Science Teachers, Postsecondary; Farm and Home Management Advisors; Foreign Language and Literature Teachers, Postsecondary; Forestry and Conservation Science Teachers, Postsecondary; Geography Teachers, Postsecondary; Graduate Teaching Assistants; Health Specialties Teachers, Postsecondary; History Teachers, Postsecondary; Home Economics Teachers, Postsecondary; Kindergarten Teachers, Except Special Education; Law Teachers, Postsecondary; Librarians; Library Assistants, Clerical; Library Science Teachers, Postsecondary; Library Technicians; Mathematical Science Teachers, Postsecondary; Middle School Teachers, Except Special and Vocational Education; Museum Technicians and Conservators; Nursing Instructors and Teachers, Postsecondary; Personal Financial Advisors; Philosophy and Religion Teachers, Postsecondary; Physics Teachers, Postsecondary; Political Science Teachers, Postsecondary; Postsecondary Teachers, All Other; others. **PERSONALITY TYPE—** Social. Social occupations frequently involve working with, communicating with, and teaching people. These occupations often involve helping or providing service to others.

EDUCATION/TRAINING PROGRAM(S)—Agricultural Teacher Education; Business Teacher Education; Health Occupations Teacher Education; Sales and Marketing Operations/Marketing and Distribution Teacher Education; Teacher Education and Professional Development, Specific Subject Areas, Other; Technical Teacher Education; Technology Teacher Education/Industrial Arts Teacher Education; Trade and Industrial Teacher Education. **RELATED KNOWLEDGE/COURSES—Education and Training:** Knowledge of principles and methods for curriculum and training design, teaching and instruction for individuals and groups, and the measurement of training effects. **English Language:** Knowledge of the structure and content of the English language, including the meaning and spelling of words, rules of composition, and grammar. **Mathematics:** Knowledge of arithmetic, algebra, geometry, calculus, and statistics and their applications. **Clerical Studies:** Knowledge of administrative and clerical procedures and systems, such as word processing, managing files and records, stenography and transcription, designing forms, and other office procedures and termi-

nology. **Administration and Management:** Knowledge of business and management principles involved in strategic planning, resource allocation, human resources modeling, leadership technique, production methods, and coordination of people and resources.

Vocational Education Teachers, Secondary School

▲ Education/Training Required: Bachelor's degree
▲ Annual Earnings: $43,590
▲ Growth: 13.4%
▲ Annual Job Openings: 7,000
▲ Self-Employed: 0%
▲ Part-Time: 42.5%

Teach or instruct vocational or occupational subjects at the secondary school level. Instructs students, using various teaching methods, such as lecture and demonstration. Assigns lessons and corrects homework. Develops and administers tests. Prepares course outlines and objectives according to curriculum guidelines or state and local requirements. Uses audiovisual aids and other materials to supplement presentations. Evaluates, records, and reports student progress. Confers with students, parents, and school counselors to resolve behavioral and academic problems. Maintains discipline in classroom. Participates in faculty and professional meetings, educational conferences, and teacher training workshops. Selects, stores, orders, issues, and inventories classroom equipment, materials, and supplies. Keeps attendance records. Performs advisory duties, such as sponsoring student organizations or clubs, helping students select courses, and counseling students with problems. **SKILLS—Learning Strategies:** Selecting and using training/instructional methods and procedures appropriate for the situation when learning or teaching new things. **Speaking:** Talking to others to convey information effectively. **Reading Comprehension:** Understanding written sentences and paragraphs in work-related documents. **Mathematics:** Using mathematics to solve problems. **Instructing:** Teaching others how to do something.

GOE INFORMATION—Interest Area: 12. Education and Social Service. **Work Group:** 12.03. Educational Services. **Other Job Titles in This Work Group:** Adult Literacy, Remedial Education, and GED Teachers and Instructors; Agricultural Sciences Teachers, Postsecondary; Anthropology and Archeology Teachers, Postsecondary; Architecture Teachers, Postsecondary; Archivists; Area, Eth-

nic, and Cultural Studies Teachers, Postsecondary; Art, Drama, and Music Teachers, Postsecondary; Atmospheric, Earth, Marine, and Space Sciences Teachers, Postsecondary; Audio-Visual Collections Specialists; Biological Science Teachers, Postsecondary; Business Teachers, Postsecondary; Chemistry Teachers, Postsecondary; Child Care Workers; Communications Teachers, Postsecondary; Computer Science Teachers, Postsecondary; Criminal Justice and Law Enforcement Teachers, Postsecondary; Curators; Economics Teachers, Postsecondary; Education Teachers, Postsecondary; Educational Psychologists; Educational, Vocational, and School Counselors; Elementary School Teachers, Except Special Education; Engineering Teachers, Postsecondary; English Language and Literature Teachers, Postsecondary; Environmental Science Teachers, Postsecondary; Farm and Home Management Advisors; Foreign Language and Literature Teachers, Postsecondary; Forestry and Conservation Science Teachers, Postsecondary; Geography Teachers, Postsecondary; Graduate Teaching Assistants; Health Specialties Teachers, Postsecondary; History Teachers, Postsecondary; Home Economics Teachers, Postsecondary; Kindergarten Teachers, Except Special Education; Law Teachers, Postsecondary; Librarians; Library Assistants, Clerical; Library Science Teachers, Postsecondary; Library Technicians; Mathematical Science Teachers, Postsecondary; Middle School Teachers, Except Special and Vocational Education; Museum Technicians and Conservators; Nursing Instructors and Teachers, Postsecondary; Personal Financial Advisors; Philosophy and Religion Teachers, Postsecondary; Physics Teachers, Postsecondary; Political Science Teachers, Postsecondary; Postsecondary Teachers, All Other; others. **PERSONALITY TYPE—Social.** Social occupations frequently involve working with, communicating with, and teaching people.

These occupations often involve helping or providing service to others.

EDUCATION/TRAINING PROGRAM(S)—Technology Teacher Education/Industrial Arts Teacher Education. **RELATED KNOWLEDGE/COURSES**—**Education and Training:** Knowledge of principles and methods for curriculum and training design, teaching and instruction for individuals and groups, and the measurement of training effects. **English Language:** Knowledge of the structure and content of the English language, including the meaning and spelling of words, rules of composition, and grammar. **Mathematics:** Knowledge of arithmetic, algebra, geometry, calculus, and statistics and their applica-

tions. **Therapy and Counseling:** Knowledge of principles, methods, and procedures for diagnosis, treatment, and rehabilitation of physical and mental dysfunctions and for career counseling and guidance. **Psychology:** Knowledge of human behavior and performance; individual differences in ability, personality, and interests; learning and motivation; psychological research methods; and the assessment and treatment of behavioral and affective disorders. **Clerical Studies:** Knowledge of administrative and clerical procedures and systems, such as word processing, managing files and records, stenography and transcription, designing forms, and other office procedures and terminology.

Waiters and Waitresses

- ▲ Education/Training Required: Short-term on-the-job training
- ▲ Annual Earnings: $13,720
- ▲ Growth: 18.3%
- ▲ Annual Job Openings: 596,000
- ▲ Self-Employed: 0.6%
- ▲ Part-Time: 57.0%

Take orders and serve food and beverages to patrons at tables in dining establishment. Takes order from patron for food or beverage, writing order down or memorizing it. Observes patrons to respond to additional requests and to determine when meal has been completed or beverage consumed. Presents menu to patron, suggests food or beverage selections, and answers questions regarding preparation and service. Obtains and replenishes supplies of food, tableware, and linen. Computes cost of meal or beverage. Serves, or assists patrons to serve themselves, at buffet or smorgasbord table. Serves meals or beverages to patrons. Relays order to kitchen or enters order into computer. Accepts payment and returns change or refers patron to cashier. Removes dishes and glasses from table or counter and takes them to kitchen for cleaning. Prepares hot, cold, and mixed drinks for patrons and chills bottles of wine. Cleans and arranges assigned station, including side stands, chairs, and table pieces such as linen, silverware, and glassware. Prepares salads, appetizers, and cold dishes; portions desserts; brews coffee; and performs other services as determined by establishment's size and practices. Fills salt, pepper, sugar, cream, condiment, and napkin containers. Carves meats, bones fish and fowl, and prepares special dishes and desserts at work station or patron's table. Garnishes and decorates dishes preparatory to serving. **SKILLS**—**Active Listening:** Giving full atten-

tion to what other people are saying, taking time to understand the points being made, asking questions as appropriate, and not interrupting at inappropriate times. **Service Orientation:** Actively looking for ways to help people. **Mathematics:** Using mathematics to solve problems. **Monitoring:** Monitoring/Assessing your performance or that of other individuals or organizations to make improvements or take corrective action. **Social Perceptiveness:** Being aware of others' reactions and understanding why they react as they do.

GOE INFORMATION—**Interest Area:** 11. Recreation, Travel, and Other Personal Services. **Work Group:** 11.05. Food and Beverage Services. **Other Job Titles in This Work Group:** Bakers; Bakers, Bread and Pastry; Bartenders; Butchers and Meat Cutters; Chefs and Head Cooks; Combined Food Preparation and Serving Workers, Including Fast Food; Cooks, All Other; Cooks, Fast Food; Cooks, Institution and Cafeteria; Cooks, Restaurant; Cooks, Short Order; Counter Attendants, Cafeteria, Food Concession, and Coffee Shop; Dining Room and Cafeteria Attendants and Bartender Helpers; Dishwashers; Food Preparation and Serving Related Workers, All Other; Food Preparation Workers; Food Servers, Nonrestaurant; Hosts and Hostesses, Restaurant, Lounge, and Coffee Shop. **PERSONALITY TYPE**—Social. Social occupations frequently involve working with, communicating with, and teaching people. These occupations often involve helping or providing service to others.

EDUCATION/TRAINING PROGRAM(S)—Food Service, Waiter/Waitress, and Dining Room Management/Manager. RELATED KNOWLEDGE/COURSES—Customer and Personal Service: Knowledge of principles and processes for providing customer and personal services. This includes customer needs assessment, meeting quality standards for services, and evaluation of customer satisfaction. Mathematics: Knowledge of arithmetic, algebra, geometry, calculus, and statistics and their applica-

tions. English Language: Knowledge of the structure and content of the English language, including the meaning and spelling of words, rules of composition, and grammar. Sales and Marketing: Knowledge of principles and methods for showing, promoting, and selling products or services. This includes marketing strategy and tactics, product demonstration, sales techniques, and sales control systems. Psychology: Knowledge of human behavior and performance; individual differences in ability, personality, and interests; learning and motivation; psychological research methods; and the assessment and treatment of behavioral and affective disorders.

Water and Liquid Waste Treatment Plant and System Operators

- ▲ Education/Training Required: Long-term on-the-job training
- ▲ Annual Earnings: $32,560
- ▲ Growth: 18.1%
- ▲ Annual Job Openings: 6,000
- ▲ Self-Employed: 0%
- ▲ Part-Time: 1.8%

Operate or control an entire process or system of machines, often through the use of control boards, to transfer or treat water or liquid waste. Operates and adjusts controls on equipment to purify and clarify water, process or dispose of sewage, and generate power. Collects and tests water and sewage samples, using test equipment and color analysis standards. Cleans and maintains tanks and filter beds, using hand tools and power tools. Directs and coordinates plant workers engaged in routine operations and maintenance activities. Maintains, repairs, and lubricates equipment, using hand tools and power tools. Records operational data, personnel attendance, and meter and gauge readings on specified forms. Inspects equipment and monitors operating conditions, meters, and gauges to determine load requirements and detect malfunctions. Adds chemicals, such as ammonia, chlorine, and lime, to disinfect and deodorize water and other liquids. SKILLS—Operation and Control: Controlling operations of equipment or systems. Operation Monitoring: Watching gauges, dials, or other indicators to make sure a machine is working properly. Science: Using scientific rules and methods to solve problems. Reading Comprehension: Understanding written sentences and paragraphs in work-related documents. Critical Thinking: Using logic and reasoning to identify the strengths and weaknesses of alternative solutions, conclusions, or approaches to problems. Mathematics: Using mathematics to solve problems.

Quality Control Analysis: Conducting tests and inspections of products, services, or processes to evaluate quality or performance.

GOE INFORMATION—Interest Area: 08. Industrial Production. Work Group: 08.06. Systems Operation. Other Job Titles in This Work Group: Auxiliary Equipment Operators, Power; Boiler Operators and Tenders, Low Pressure; Chemical Plant and System Operators; Gas Compressor and Gas Pumping Station Operators; Gas Compressor Operators; Gas Distribution Plant Operators; Gas Plant Operators; Gas Processing Plant Operators; Gas Pumping Station Operators; Gaugers; Nuclear Power Reactor Operators; Petroleum Pump System Operators; Petroleum Pump System Operators, Refinery Operators, and Gaugers; Petroleum Refinery and Control Panel Operators; Plant and System Operators, All Other; Power Distributors and Dispatchers; Power Generating Plant Operators, Except Auxiliary Equipment Operators; Power Plant Operators; Ship Engineers; Stationary Engineers; Stationary Engineers and Boiler Operators; Wellhead Pumpers. PERSONALITY TYPE—Realistic. Realistic occupations frequently involve work activities that include practical, hands-on problems and solutions. They often deal with plants, animals, and real-world materials like wood, tools, and machinery. Many of the occupations require working outside and do not involve a lot of paperwork or working closely with others.

EDUCATION/TRAINING PROGRAM(S)—Water Quality and Wastewater Treatment Management and Recycling Technology/Technician. **RELATED KNOWLEDGE/COURSES—Chemistry:** Knowledge of the chemical composition, structure, and properties of substances and of the chemical processes and transformations that they undergo. This includes uses of chemicals and their interactions, danger signs, production techniques, and disposal methods. **Principles of Mechanical Devices:** Knowledge of machines and tools, including their designs, uses, repair, and maintenance. **Production and Processing:** Knowledge of raw materials, production processes, quality control, costs, and other techniques for maximizing the effective manufacture and distribution of goods. **Mathematics:** Knowledge of arithmetic, algebra, geometry, calculus, and statistics and their applications. **Clerical Studies:** Knowledge of administrative and clerical procedures and systems, such as word processing, managing files and records, stenography and transcription, designing forms, and other office procedures and terminology.

Weighers, Measurers, Checkers, and Samplers, Recordkeeping

- ▲ Education/Training Required: Short-term on-the-job training
- ▲ Annual Earnings: $24,690
- ▲ Growth: 17.9%
- ▲ Annual Job Openings: 13,000
- ▲ Self-Employed: 0%
- ▲ Part-Time: 16.2%

Weigh, measure, and check materials, supplies, and equipment for the purpose of keeping relevant records. Duties are primarily clerical by nature. Weighs or measures materials or products, using volume meters, scales, rules, and calipers. Compares product labels, tags, or tickets; shipping manifests; purchase orders; and bills of lading to verify that the contents, quantity, or weight of shipments is accurate. Removes products or loads not meeting quality standards from stock and notifies supervisor or appropriate department of discrepancy or shortage. Transports materials, products, or samples to processing, shipping, or storage areas manually or by using conveyors, pumps, or hand trucks. Unloads or unpacks incoming shipments or arranges, packs, or prepares materials and products for display, distribution, outgoing shipment, or storage. Fills orders for products and samples, following order tickets, and forwards or mails items. Collects and prepares product samples for laboratory analysis or testing. Maintains perpetual inventory of samples and replenishes stock to maintain required levels. Sorts products or materials into predetermined sequence or groupings for packing, shipping, or storage. Prepares measurement tables and conversion charts, using standard formulae. Computes product totals and charges for shipments, using calculator. Works with, signals, or instructs other workers to weigh, move, or check products. Communicates with customers and vendors to exchange information regarding products, materials, and services.

Operates or tends machines to clean or sanitize equipment or manually washes equipment, using detergent, brushes, and hoses. Collects fees and issues receipts for payments. Examines blueprints and prepares plans, layouts, or drawings of facility or finished products to identify storage locations or verify parts assemblies. Collects, prepares, or attaches measurement, weight, or identification labels or tickets to products. Documents quantity, quality, type, weight, and value of materials or products to maintain shipping, receiving, and production records and files. Examines products or materials, parts, and subassemblies for damage, defects, or shortages, using specification sheets, gauges, and standards charts. Counts or estimates quantities of materials, parts, or products received or shipped. **SKILLS—Operation and Control:** Controlling operations of equipment or systems. **Mathematics:** Using mathematics to solve problems. **Equipment Selection:** Determining the kind of tools and equipment needed to do a job. **Operation Monitoring:** Watching gauges, dials, or other indicators to make sure a machine is working properly. **Coordination:** Adjusting actions in relation to others' actions. **Reading Comprehension:** Understanding written sentences and paragraphs in work-related documents.

GOE INFORMATION—Interest Area: 09. Business Detail. **Work Group:** 09.08. Records and Materials Processing. **Other Job Titles in This Work Group:** Cargo and Freight Agents; Couriers and Messengers; Mail Clerks, Except Mail Machine Operators and Postal Service; Marking Clerks; Order Fillers, Wholesale and Retail Sales; Postal Service Mail Carriers; Postal Service Mail Sorters, Processors, and Processing Machine Operators; Shipping, Receiving, and Traffic Clerks; Stock Clerks and Order Fillers; Stock Clerks—Stockroom, Warehouse, or Storage Yard. **PERSONALITY TYPE**—Conventional. Conventional occupations frequently involve following set procedures and routines. These occupations can include working with data and details more than with ideas. Usually there is a clear line of authority to follow.

EDUCATION/TRAINING PROGRAM(S)—General Office Occupations and Clerical Services. **RELATED KNOWLEDGE/COURSES**—Clerical Studies: Knowledge of administrative and clerical procedures and systems, such as word processing, managing files and records, stenography and transcription, designing forms, and other office procedures and terminology. **Mathematics:** Knowledge of arithmetic, algebra, geometry, calculus, and statistics and their applications. **Production and Processing:** Knowledge of raw materials, production processes, quality control, costs, and other techniques for maximizing the effective manufacture and distribution of goods. **Transportation:** Knowledge of principles and methods for moving people or goods by air, rail, sea, or road, including the relative costs and benefits. **Design:** Knowledge of design techniques, tools, and principles involved in production of precision technical plans, blueprints, drawings, and models.

Welder-Fitters

- ▲ Education/Training Required: Long-term on-the-job training
- ▲ Annual Earnings: $28,490
- ▲ Growth: 19.3%
- ▲ Annual Job Openings: 51,000
- ▲ Self-Employed: 7.0%
- ▲ Part-Time: 2.6%

Lay out, fit, and fabricate metal components to assemble structural forms, such as machinery frames, bridge parts, and pressure vessels, using knowledge of welding techniques, metallurgy, and engineering requirements. Includes experimental welders who analyze engineering drawings and specifications to plan welding operations where procedural information is unavailable. Lays out, positions, and secures parts and assemblies according to specifications, using straightedge, combination square, calipers, and ruler. Tack-welds or welds components and assemblies, using electric, gas, arc, or other welding equipment. Cuts workpiece, using powered saws, hand shears, or chipping knife. Melts lead bar, wire, or scrap to add lead to joint or to extrude melted scrap into reusable form. Installs or repairs equipment, such as lead pipes, valves, floors, and tank linings. Observes tests on welded surfaces, such as hydrostatic, X-ray, and dimension tolerance, to evaluate weld quality and conformance to specifications. Inspects grooves, angles, or gap allowances, using micrometer, caliper, and precision measuring instruments. Removes rough spots from workpiece, using portable grinder, hand file, or scraper. Welds components in flat, vertical, or overhead positions. Heats, forms, and dresses metal parts, using hand tools, torch, or arc welding equipment. Ignites torch and adjusts valves, amperage, or voltage to obtain desired flame or arc. Analyzes engineering drawings and specifications to plan layout, assembly, and welding operations. Develops templates and other work aids to hold and align parts. Determines required equipment and welding method, applying knowledge of metallurgy, geometry, and welding techniques. **SKILLS—Mathematics:** Using mathematics to solve problems. **Equipment Selection:** Determining the kind of tools and equipment needed to do a job. **Repairing:** Repairing machines or systems, using the needed tools. **Equipment Maintenance:** Performing routine maintenance on equipment and determining when and what kind of maintenance is needed. **Quality Control Analysis:** Conducting tests and inspections of products, services, or processes to evaluate quality or performance.

GOE INFORMATION—Interest Area: 08. Industrial Production. **Work Group:** 08.03. Production Work. **Other Job Titles in This Work Group:** Bakers, Manufacturing; Bindery Machine Operators and Tenders; Brazers; Cementing and Gluing Machine Operators and Tenders; Chemical Equipment Controllers and Operators; Chemical Equipment Operators and Tenders; Chemical Equipment Tenders; Cleaning, Washing, and Metal Pickling Equipment Operators and Tenders; Coating, Painting, and Spraying Machine Operators and Tenders; Coil Winders, Tapers, and Finishers; Combination Machine Tool Operators and Tenders, Metal and Plastic; Computer-Controlled Machine Tool Operators, Metal and Plastic; Cooling and Freezing Equipment Operators and Tenders; Crushing, Grinding, and Polishing Machine Setters, Operators, and Tenders; Cutters and Trimmers, Hand; Cutting and Slicing Machine Operators and Tenders; Cutting and Slicing Machine Setters, Operators, and Tenders; Design Printing Machine Setters and Set-Up Operators; Electrolytic Plating and Coating Machine Operators and Tenders, Metal and Plastic; Electrolytic Plating and Coating Machine Setters and Set-Up Operators, Metal and Plastic; Electrotypers and Stereotypers; Embossing Machine Set-Up Operators; Engraver Set-Up Operators; Extruding and Forming Machine Operators and Tenders, Synthetic or Glass Fibers; Extruding and Forming Machine Setters, Operators, and Tenders, Synthetic and Glass Fibers; Extruding, Forming, Pressing, and Compacting Machine Operators and Tenders; Fabric and Apparel Patternmakers; Fiber Product Cutting Machine Setters and Set-Up Operators; Fiberglass Laminators and Fabricators; Film Laboratory Technicians; Fitters, Structural Metal—Precision; Food and Tobacco Roasting, Baking, and Drying Machine Operators and Tenders; Food Batchmakers; Food Cooking Machine Operators and Tenders; Furnace, Kiln, Oven, Drier, and Kettle Operators and Tenders; Glass Cutting Machine Setters and Set-Up Operators; Graders

and Sorters, Agricultural Products; Grinding and Polishing Workers, Hand; Hand Compositors and Typesetters; Heaters, Metal and Plastic; others. **PERSONALITY TYPE**—Realistic. Realistic occupations frequently involve work activities that include practical, hands-on problems and solutions. They often deal with plants, animals, and real-world materials like wood, tools, and machinery. Many of the occupations require working outside and do not involve a lot of paperwork or working closely with others.

EDUCATION/TRAINING PROGRAM(S)—Welding Technology/Welder. **RELATED KNOWLEDGE/ COURSES**—**Principles of Mechanical Devices:** Knowledge of machines and tools, including their designs, uses, repair, and maintenance. **Design:** Knowledge of design techniques, tools, and principles involved in production of precision technical plans, blueprints, drawings, and models. **Engineering and Technology:** Knowledge of the practical application of engineering science and technology. This includes applying principles, techniques, procedures, and equipment to the design and production of various goods and services. **Building and Construction:** Knowledge of materials, methods, and tools involved in the construction or repair of houses, buildings, or other structures, such as highways and roads. **Production and Processing:** Knowledge of raw materials, production processes, quality control, costs, and other techniques for maximizing the effective manufacture and distribution of goods.

Welders and Cutters

- ▲ Education/Training Required: Long-term on-the-job training
- ▲ Annual Earnings: $28,490
- ▲ Growth: 19.3%
- ▲ Annual Job Openings: 51,000
- ▲ Self-Employed: 7.0%
- ▲ Part-Time: 2.6%

Use hand welding and flame-cutting equipment to weld together metal components and parts or to cut, trim, or scarf metal objects to dimensions as specified by layouts, work orders, or blueprints. Welds metal parts or components together, using brazing, gas, or arc welding equipment. Repairs broken or cracked parts, fills holes, and increases size of metal parts, using welding equipment. Welds in flat, horizontal, vertical, or overhead position. Cleans or degreases parts, using wire brush, portable grinder, or chemical bath. Inspects finished workpiece for

conformance to specifications. Chips or grinds off excess weld, slag, or spatter, using hand scraper or power chipper, portable grinder, or arc-cutting equipment. Positions workpieces and clamps together or assembles in jigs or fixtures. Preheats workpiece, using hand torch or heating furnace. Ignites torch or starts power supply and strikes arc. Reviews layouts, blueprints, diagrams, or work orders in preparation for welding or cutting metal components. Selects and inserts electrode or gas nozzle into holder and connects hoses and cables to obtain gas or specified amperage, voltage, or polarity. Connects and turns regulator valves to activate and adjust gas flow and pressure to obtain desired flame. Selects and installs torch, torch tip, filler rod, and flux according to welding chart specifications or type and thickness of metal. Guides electrodes or torch along weld line at specified speed and angle to weld, melt, cut, or trim metal. **SKILLS—Operation Monitoring:** Watching gauges, dials, or other indicators to make sure a machine is working properly. **Operation and Control:** Controlling operations of equipment or systems. **Mathematics:** Using mathematics to solve problems. **Equipment Selection:** Determining the kind of tools and equipment needed to do a job. **Equipment Maintenance:** Performing routine maintenance on equipment and determining when and what kind of maintenance is needed.

GOE INFORMATION—Interest Area: 08. Industrial Production. **Work Group:** 08.03. Production Work. **Other Job Titles in This Work Group:** Bakers, Manufacturing; Bindery Machine Operators and Tenders; Brazers; Cementing and Gluing Machine Operators and Tenders; Chemical Equipment Controllers and Operators; Chemical Equipment Operators and Tenders; Chemical Equipment Tenders; Cleaning, Washing, and Metal Pickling Equipment Operators and Tenders; Coating, Painting, and Spraying Machine Operators and Tenders; Coil Winders, Tapers, and Finishers; Combination Machine Tool Operators and Tenders, Metal and Plastic; Computer-Controlled Machine Tool Operators, Metal and Plastic; Cooling and Freezing Equipment Operators and Tenders; Crushing, Grinding, and Polishing Machine Setters, Operators, and Tenders; Cutters and Trimmers, Hand; Cutting and Slicing Machine Operators and Tenders; Cutting and Slicing Machine Setters, Operators, and Tenders; Design Printing Machine Setters and Set-Up Operators; Electrolytic Plating and Coating Machine Operators and Tenders, Metal and Plastic; Electrolytic Plating and Coating Machine Setters and Set-Up Operators, Metal and Plastic; Electrotypers and Stereotypers; Embossing Machine Set-Up Operators; Engraver Set-Up Operators; Extruding and Forming Machine Operators and Tenders, Synthetic or Glass Fibers; Extruding and Forming Machine Setters, Operators, and Tenders, Synthetic and Glass Fibers; Extruding, Forming, Pressing, and Compacting Machine Operators and Tenders; Fabric and Apparel Patternmakers; Fiber Product Cutting Machine Setters and Set-Up Operators; Fiberglass Laminators and Fabricators; Film Laboratory Technicians; Fitters, Structural Metal—Precision; Food and Tobacco Roasting, Baking, and Drying Machine Operators and Tenders; Food Batchmakers; Food Cooking Machine Operators and Tenders; Furnace, Kiln, Oven, Drier, and Kettle Operators and Tenders; Glass Cutting Machine Setters and Set-Up Operators; Graders and Sorters, Agricultural Products; Grinding and Polishing Workers, Hand; Hand Compositors and Typesetters; Heaters, Metal and Plastic; others. **PERSONALITY TYPE—**Realistic. Realistic occupations frequently involve work activities that include practical, hands-on problems and solutions. They often deal with plants, animals, and real-world materials like wood, tools, and machinery. Many of the occupations require working outside and do not involve a lot of paperwork or working closely with others.

EDUCATION/TRAINING PROGRAM(S)—Welding Technology/Welder. **RELATED KNOWLEDGE/COURSES—Principles of Mechanical Devices:** Knowledge of machines and tools, including their designs, uses, repair, and maintenance. **Building and Construction:** Knowledge of materials, methods, and tools involved in the construction or repair of houses, buildings, or other structures, such as highways and roads. **Production and Processing:** Knowledge of raw materials, production processes, quality control, costs, and other techniques for maximizing the effective manufacture and distribution of goods. **Design:** Knowledge of design techniques, tools, and principles involved in production of precision technical plans, blueprints, drawings, and models. **Physics:** Knowledge and prediction of physical principles and laws and their interrelationships and applications to understanding fluid, material, and atmospheric dynamics and mechanical, electrical, atomic, and sub-atomic structures and processes. **Mathematics:** Knowledge of arithmetic, algebra, geometry, calculus, and statistics and their applications. **Engineering and Technology:** Knowledge of the practical application of engineering science and technology. This includes applying principles, techniques, procedures, and equipment to the design and production of various goods and services.

Welders, Cutters, Solderers, and Brazers

- ▲ Education/Training Required: Long-term on-the-job training
- ▲ Annual Earnings: $28,490
- ▲ Growth: 19.3%
- ▲ Annual Job Openings: 51,000
- ▲ Self-Employed: 7.0%
- ▲ Part-Time: 2.6%

Use hand-welding, flame-cutting, hand soldering, or brazing equipment to weld or join metal components or to fill holes, indentations, or seams of fabricated metal products. **SKILLS**—No data available.

GOE INFORMATION—Interest Area: 08. Industrial Production. **Work Group:** 08.03. Production Work. **Other Job Titles in This Work Group:** Bakers, Manufacturing; Bindery Machine Operators and Tenders; Brazers; Cementing and Gluing Machine Operators and Tenders; Chemical Equipment Controllers and Operators; Chemical Equipment Operators and Tenders; Chemical Equipment Tenders; Cleaning, Washing, and Metal Pickling Equipment Operators and Tenders; Coating, Painting, and Spraying Machine Operators and Tenders; Coil Winders, Tapers, and Finishers; Combination Machine Tool Operators and Tenders, Metal and Plastic; Computer-Controlled Machine Tool Operators, Metal and Plastic; Cooling and Freezing Equipment Operators and Tenders; Crushing, Grinding, and Polishing Machine Setters, Operators, and Tenders; Cutters and Trimmers, Hand; Cutting and Slicing Machine Operators and Tenders; Cutting and Slicing Machine Setters, Operators, and Tenders; Design Printing Machine Setters and Set-Up Operators; Electrolytic Plating and Coating Machine Operators and Tenders, Metal and Plastic; Electrolytic Plating and Coating Machine Setters and Set-Up Operators, Metal and Plastic; Electrotypers and Stereotypers; Embossing Machine Set-Up Operators; Engraver Set-Up Operators; Extruding and Forming Machine Operators and Tenders, Synthetic or Glass Fibers; Extruding and Forming Machine Setters, Operators, and Tenders, Synthetic and Glass Fibers; Extruding, Forming, Pressing, and Compacting Machine Operators and Tenders; Fabric and Apparel Patternmakers; Fiber Product Cutting Machine Setters and Set-Up Operators; Fiberglass Laminators and Fabricators; Film Laboratory Technicians; Fitters, Structural Metal—Precision; Food and Tobacco Roasting, Baking, and Drying Machine Operators and Tenders; Food Batchmakers; Food Cooking Machine Operators and Tenders; Furnace, Kiln, Oven, Drier, and Kettle Operators and Tenders; Glass Cutting Machine Setters and Set-Up Operators; Graders and Sorters, Agricultural Products; Grinding and Polishing Workers, Hand; Hand Compositors and Typesetters; Heaters, Metal and Plastic; others. **PERSONALITY TYPE**—No data available.

EDUCATION/TRAINING PROGRAM(S)—Welding Technology/Welder. **RELATED KNOWLEDGE/COURSES**—No data available.

Welders, Production

- ▲ Education/Training Required: Short-term on-the-job training
- ▲ Annual Earnings: $28,490
- ▲ Growth: 19.3%
- ▲ Annual Job Openings: 51,000
- ▲ Self-Employed: 7.0%
- ▲ Part-Time: 2.6%

Assemble and weld metal parts on production line, using welding equipment requiring only a limited knowledge of welding techniques. Welds or tack welds metal parts together, using spot welding gun or hand, electric, or gas welding equipment. Connects hoses from torch to tanks of oxygen and fuel gas and turns valves to release mixture. Ignites torch and regulates flow of gas and air to obtain desired temperature, size, and color of flame. Preheats workpieces preparatory to welding or bending, using torch. Fills cavities or corrects malformation in lead parts and hammers out bulges and bends in metal workpieces. Examines workpiece for defects and measures workpiece with straightedge or template to ensure conformance with specifications. Climbs ladders or works on scaffolds to disassemble structures. Signals crane operator to move large workpieces. Dismantles metal assemblies or cuts scrap metal, using thermal-cutting equipment such as flame-cutting torch or plasma-arc equipment. Positions and secures workpiece, using hoist, crane, wire and banding machine, or hand tools. Selects, positions, and secures torch, cutting tips, or welding rod according to type, thickness, area, and desired temperature of metal. Guides and directs flame or electrodes on or across workpiece to straighten, bend, melt, or build up metal. Fuses parts together, seals tension points, and adds metal to build up parts. **SKILLS—Operation and Control:** Controlling operations of equipment or systems. **Operation Monitoring:** Watching gauges, dials, or other indicators to make sure a machine is working properly. **Equipment Selection:** Determining the kind of tools and equipment needed to do a job. **Equipment Maintenance:** Performing routine maintenance on equipment and determining when and what kind of maintenance is needed. **Mathematics:** Using mathematics to solve problems.

GOE INFORMATION—Interest Area: 08. Industrial Production. **Work Group:** 08.03. Production Work. **Other Job Titles in This Work Group:** Bakers, Manufacturing; Bindery Machine Operators and Tenders; Brazers; Cementing and Gluing Machine Operators and Tenders; Chemical Equipment Controllers and Operators; Chemical Equipment Operators and Tenders; Chemical Equipment Tenders; Cleaning, Washing, and Metal Pickling Equipment Operators and Tenders; Coating, Painting, and Spraying Machine Operators and Tenders; Coil Winders, Tapers, and Finishers; Combination Machine Tool Operators and Tenders, Metal and Plastic; Computer-Controlled Machine Tool Operators, Metal and Plastic; Cooling and Freezing Equipment Operators and Tenders; Crushing, Grinding, and Polishing Machine Setters, Operators, and Tenders; Cutters and Trimmers, Hand; Cutting and Slicing Machine Operators and Tenders; Cutting and Slicing Machine Setters, Operators, and Tenders; Design Printing Machine Setters and Set-Up Operators; Electrolytic Plating and Coating Machine Operators and Tenders, Metal and Plastic; Electrolytic Plating and Coating Machine Setters and Set-Up Operators, Metal and Plastic; Electrotypers and Stereotypers; Embossing Machine Set-Up Operators; Engraver Set-Up Operators; Extruding and Forming Machine Operators and Tenders, Synthetic or Glass Fibers; Extruding and Forming Machine Setters, Operators, and Tenders, Synthetic and Glass Fibers; Extruding, Forming, Pressing, and Compacting Machine Operators and Tenders; Fabric and Apparel Patternmakers; Fiber Product Cutting Machine Setters and Set-Up Operators; Fiberglass Laminators and Fabricators; Film Laboratory Technicians; Fitters, Structural Metal—Precision; Food and Tobacco Roasting, Baking, and Drying Machine Operators and Tenders; Food Batchmakers; Food Cooking Machine Operators and Tenders; Furnace, Kiln, Oven, Drier, and Kettle Operators and Tenders; Glass Cutting Machine Setters and Set-Up Operators; Graders and Sorters, Agricultural Products; Grinding and Polishing Workers, Hand; Hand Compositors and Typesetters; Heaters, Metal and Plastic; others. **PERSONALITY TYPE—Realistic.** Realistic occupations frequently involve work activities that include practical, hands-on problems and solutions. They often deal with plants, animals, and real-world materials like wood, tools, and machinery. Many of the occupations require working outside and do not involve a lot of paperwork or working closely with others.

EDUCATION/TRAINING PROGRAM(S)—Welding Technology/Welder. **RELATED KNOWLEDGE/ COURSES—Principles of Mechanical Devices:** Knowledge of machines and tools, including their designs, uses, repair, and maintenance. **Production and Processing:** Knowledge of raw materials, production processes, quality control, costs, and other techniques for maximizing the effective manufacture and distribution of goods. **Building and Construction:** Knowledge of materials, methods, and tools involved in the construction or repair of houses, buildings, or other structures, such as highways and roads. **Public Safety and Security:** Knowledge of relevant equipment, policies, procedures, and strategies to promote effective local, state, or national security operations for the protection of people, data, property, and institutions. **Physics:** Knowledge and prediction of physical principles and laws and their interrelationships and applications to understanding fluid, material, and atmospheric dynamics and mechanical, electrical, atomic, and sub-atomic structures and processes. **Mathematics:** Knowledge of arithmetic, algebra, geometry, calculus, and statistics and their applications.

Welding Machine Operators and Tenders

- ▲ Education/Training Required: Moderate-term on-the-job training
- ▲ Annual Earnings: $28,220
- ▲ Growth: 15.1%
- ▲ Annual Job Openings: 9,000
- ▲ Self-Employed: 0%
- ▲ Part-Time: 2.6%

Operate or tend welding machines that join or bond together components to fabricate metal products and assemblies according to specifications and blueprints. Operates or tends welding machines that join or bond components to fabricate metal products and assemblies. Turns and presses knobs and buttons to adjust and start welding machine. Enters operating instructions into computer to adjust and start welding machine. Stops and opens holding device on welding machine, using hand tools. Reads production schedule and specifications to ascertain product to be fabricated. Positions and adjusts fixtures, attachments, or workpiece on machine, using hand tools and measuring devices. Observes and listens to welding machine and its controls to ensure welding process meets specifications. Inspects metal workpiece to ensure specifications are met, using measuring devices. Transfers components, metal products, and assemblies, using moving equipment. Cleans and maintains workpieces and welding machine parts, using hand tools and equipment. Adds chemicals or solutions to welding machine to join or bind components. Tends auxiliary equipment used in the welding process. **SKILLS—Operation and Control:** Controlling operations of equipment or systems. **Operation Monitoring:** Watching gauges, dials, or other indicators to make sure a machine is working properly. **Equipment Selection:** Determining the kind of tools and equipment needed to do a job. **Equipment Maintenance:** Performing routine maintenance on equipment and determining when and what kind of maintenance is needed. **Reading Comprehension:** Understanding written sentences and paragraphs in work-related documents. **Mathematics:** Using mathematics to solve problems. **Quality Control Analysis:** Conducting tests and inspections of products, services, or processes to evaluate quality or performance.

GOE INFORMATION—Interest Area: 08. Industrial Production. **Work Group:** 08.03. Production Work. **Other Job Titles in This Work Group:** Bakers, Manufacturing; Bindery Machine Operators and Tenders; Brazers; Cementing and Gluing Machine Operators and Tenders; Chemical Equipment Controllers and Operators; Chemi-

cal Equipment Operators and Tenders; Chemical Equipment Tenders; Cleaning, Washing, and Metal Pickling Equipment Operators and Tenders; Coating, Painting, and Spraying Machine Operators and Tenders; Coil Winders, Tapers, and Finishers; Combination Machine Tool Operators and Tenders, Metal and Plastic; Computer-Controlled Machine Tool Operators, Metal and Plastic; Cooling and Freezing Equipment Operators and Tenders; Crushing, Grinding, and Polishing Machine Setters, Operators, and Tenders; Cutters and Trimmers, Hand; Cutting and Slicing Machine Operators and Tenders; Cutting and Slicing Machine Setters, Operators, and Tenders; Design Printing Machine Setters and Set-Up Operators; Electrolytic Plating and Coating Machine Operators and Tenders, Metal and Plastic; Electrolytic Plating and Coating Machine Setters and Set-Up Operators, Metal and Plastic; Electrotypers and Stereotypers; Embossing Machine Set-Up Operators; Engraver Set-Up Operators; Extruding and Forming Machine Operators and Tenders, Synthetic or Glass Fibers; Extruding and Forming Machine Setters, Operators, and Tenders, Synthetic and Glass Fibers; Extruding, Forming, Pressing, and Compacting Machine Operators and Tenders; Fabric and Apparel Patternmakers; Fiber Product Cutting Machine Setters and Set-Up Operators; Fiberglass Laminators and Fabricators; Film Laboratory Technicians; Fitters, Structural Metal—Precision; Food and Tobacco Roasting, Baking, and Drying Machine Operators and Tenders; Food Batchmakers; Food Cooking Machine Operators and Tenders; Furnace, Kiln, Oven, Drier, and Kettle Operators and Tenders; Glass Cutting Machine Setters and Set-Up Operators; Graders and Sorters, Agricultural Products; Grinding and Polishing Workers, Hand; Hand Compositors and Typesetters; Heaters, Metal and Plastic; others. **PERSONALITY TYPE—Realistic.** Realistic occupations frequently involve work activities that include practical, hands-on problems and solutions. They often deal with plants, animals, and real-world materials like wood, tools, and machinery. Many of the occupations require working outside and do not involve a lot of paperwork or working closely with others.

EDUCATION/TRAINING PROGRAM(S)—Welding Technology/Welder. **RELATED KNOWLEDGE/COURSES—Production and Processing:** Knowledge of raw materials, production processes, quality control, costs, and other techniques for maximizing the effective manufacture and distribution of goods. **Principles of Mechanical Devices:** Knowledge of machines and tools, including their designs, uses, repair, and maintenance. **Engineering and Technology:** Knowledge of the practical application of engineering science and technology. This includes applying principles, techniques, procedures, and equipment to the design and production of various goods and services. **English Language:** Knowledge of the structure and content of the English language, including the meaning and spelling of words, rules of composition, and grammar. **Chemistry:** Knowledge of the chemical composition, structure, and properties of substances and of the chemical processes and transformations that they undergo. This includes uses of chemicals and their interactions, danger signs, production techniques, and disposal methods. **Mathematics:** Knowledge of arithmetic, algebra, geometry, calculus, and statistics and their applications. **Computers and Electronics:** Knowledge of circuit boards, processors, chips, electronic equipment, and computer hardware and software, including applications and programming.

Welding Machine Setters and Set-Up Operators

- ▲ Education/Training Required: Postsecondary vocational training
- ▲ Annual Earnings: $28,220
- ▲ Growth: 15.1%
- ▲ Annual Job Openings: 9,000
- ▲ Self-Employed: 0%
- ▲ Part-Time: 2.6%

Set up or set up and operate welding machines that join or bond together components to fabricate metal products or assemblies according to specifications and blueprints. Sets up and operates welding machines that join or bond components to fabricate metal products or assemblies. Feeds workpiece into welding machine to join or bond components. Observes and listens to welding machine and its gauges to ensure welding process meets specifications. Turns and presses controls, such as cranks, knobs, and buttons, to adjust and activate welding process. Operates welding machine to produce trial workpieces for examination and testing. Lays out, fits, or tacks workpieces together, using hand tools. Examines metal product or assemblies to ensure specifications are met. Tends auxiliary equipment used in welding process. Tests products and records test results and operational data on specified forms. Devises and builds fixtures used to bond components during the welding process. Cleans and maintains workpieces and welding machine parts, using hand tools and equipment. Adds components, chemicals, and solutions to welding machine, using hand tools. Stops and opens holding device on welding machine, using hand tools. Positions and adjusts fixtures, attachments, or workpieces on machine, using hand tools. **SKILLS—Equipment Selection:** Determining the kind of tools and equipment needed to do a job. **Quality Control Analysis:** Conducting tests and inspections of products, services, or processes to evaluate quality or performance. **Operation Monitoring:** Watching gauges, dials, or other indicators to make sure a machine is working properly. **Operation and Control:** Controlling operations of equipment or systems. **Mathematics:** Using mathematics to solve problems.

GOE INFORMATION—**Interest Area:** 08. Industrial Production. **Work Group:** 08.02. Production Technology. **Other Job Titles in This Work Group:** Aircraft Rigging Assemblers; Aircraft Structure Assemblers, Precision; Aircraft Structure, Surfaces, Rigging, and Systems Assemblers; Aircraft Systems Assemblers, Precision; Bench Workers, Jewelry; Bindery Machine Setters and Set-Up Operators; Bindery Workers; Bookbinders; Buffing and Polishing Set-Up Operators; Casting Machine Set-Up Operators; Coating, Painting, and Spraying Machine Setters and Set-Up Operators; Coating, Painting, and Spraying Machine Setters, Operators, and Tenders; Combination Machine Tool Setters and Set-Up Operators, Metal and Plastic; Cutting, Punching, and Press Machine Setters, Operators, and Tenders, Metal and Plastic; Dental Laboratory Technicians; Drilling and Boring Machine Tool Setters, Operators, and Tenders, Metal and Plastic; Electrical and Electronic Equipment Assemblers; Electrical and Electronic Inspectors and Testers; Electromechanical Equipment Assemblers; Engine and Other Machine Assemblers; Extruding and Drawing Machine Setters, Operators, and Tenders, Metal and Plastic; Extruding, Forming, Pressing, and Compacting Machine Setters and Set-Up Operators; Extruding, Forming, Pressing, and Compacting Machine Setters, Operators, and Tenders; Forging Machine Setters, Operators, and Tenders, Metal and Plastic; Foundry Mold and Coremakers; Gem and Diamond Workers; Grinding, Honing, Lapping, and Deburring Machine Set-Up Operators; Grinding, Lapping, Polishing, and Buffing Machine Tool Setters, Operators, and Tenders, Metal and Plastic; Heat Treating Equipment Setters, Operators, and Tenders, Metal and Plastic; Heat Treating, Annealing, and Tempering Machine Operators and Tenders, Metal and Plastic; Heating Equipment Setters and Set-Up Operators, Metal and Plastic; Inspectors, Testers, Sorters, Samplers, and Weighers; Jewelers; Jewelers and Precious Stone and Metal Workers; Lathe and Turning Machine Tool Setters, Operators, and Tenders, Metal and Plastic; Log Graders and Scalers; Materials Inspectors; Mechanical Inspectors; others. **PERSONALITY TYPE**—Realistic. Realistic occupations frequently involve work activities that include practical, hands-on problems and solutions. They often deal with plants, animals, and real-world materials like wood, tools, and machinery. Many of the occupations require working outside and do not involve a lot of paperwork or working closely with others.

EDUCATION/TRAINING PROGRAM(S)—Welding Technology/Welder. **RELATED KNOWLEDGE/COURSES**—**Principles of Mechanical Devices:** Knowledge of machines and tools, including their designs, uses, repair, and maintenance. **Production and Processing:** Knowledge of raw materials, production processes, quality control, costs, and other techniques for maximizing the effective manufacture and distribution of goods. **Chemistry:** Knowledge of the chemical composition, structure, and properties of substances and of the chemical processes and transformations that they undergo. This includes uses of chemicals and their interactions, danger signs, production techniques, and disposal methods. **Design:** Knowledge of design techniques, tools, and principles involved in production of precision technical plans, blueprints, drawings, and models. **Engineering and Technology:** Knowledge of the practical application of engineering science and technology. This includes applying principles, techniques, procedures, and equipment to the design and production of various goods and services.

Welding, Soldering, and Brazing Machine Setters, Operators, and Tenders

▲ Education/Training Required: Moderate-term on-the-job training
▲ Annual Earnings: $28,220
▲ Growth: 15.1%
▲ Annual Job Openings: 9,000
▲ Self-Employed: 0%
▲ Part-Time: 2.6%

Set up, operate, or tend welding, soldering, or brazing machines or robots that weld, braze, solder, or heat treat metal products, components, or assemblies. **SKILLS**—No data available.

GOE INFORMATION—**Interest Area:** 08. Industrial Production. **Work Group:** 08.02. Production Technology. **Other Job Titles in This Work Group:** Aircraft Rigging Assemblers; Aircraft Structure Assemblers, Precision; Aircraft Structure, Surfaces, Rigging, and Systems Assemblers; Aircraft Systems Assemblers, Precision; Bench Workers, Jewelry; Bindery Machine Setters and Set-Up Operators; Bindery Workers; Bookbinders; Buffing and Polishing Set-Up Operators; Casting Machine Set-Up Operators; Coating, Painting, and Spraying Machine Setters and Set-Up Operators; Coating, Painting, and Spraying Machine Setters, Operators, and Tenders; Combination Machine Tool Setters and Set-Up Operators, Metal and Plastic; Cutting, Punching, and Press Machine Setters, Operators, and Tenders, Metal and Plastic; Dental Laboratory Technicians; Drilling and Boring Machine Tool Setters, Operators, and Tenders, Metal and Plastic; Electrical and Electronic Equipment Assemblers; Electrical and Electronic Inspectors and Testers; Electromechanical Equipment Assemblers; Engine and Other Machine Assemblers; Extruding and Drawing Machine Setters, Operators, and Tenders, Metal and Plastic; Extruding, Forming, Pressing, and Compacting Machine Setters and Set-Up Operators; Extruding, Forming, Pressing, and Compacting Machine Setters, Operators, and Tenders; Forging Machine Setters, Operators, and Tenders, Metal and Plastic; Foundry Mold and Coremakers; Gem and Diamond Workers; Grinding, Honing, Lapping, and Deburring Machine Set-Up Operators; Grinding, Lapping, Polishing, and Buffing Machine Tool Setters,

Operators, and Tenders, Metal and Plastic; Heat Treating Equipment Setters, Operators, and Tenders, Metal and Plastic; Heat Treating, Annealing, and Tempering Machine Operators and Tenders, Metal and Plastic; Heating Equipment Setters and Set-Up Operators, Metal and Plastic; Inspectors, Testers, Sorters, Samplers, and Weighers; Jewelers; Jewelers and Precious Stone and Metal Workers; Lathe and Turning Machine Tool Setters, Operators, and Tenders, Metal and Plastic; Log Graders and Scalers; Materials Inspectors; Mechanical Inspectors; others. **PERSONALITY TYPE**—No data available.

EDUCATION/TRAINING PROGRAM(S)—Welding Technology/Welder. **RELATED KNOWLEDGE/COURSES**—No data available.

Writers and Authors

- ▲ Education/Training Required: Bachelor's degree
- ▲ Annual Earnings: $42,450
- ▲ Growth: 28.4%
- ▲ Annual Job Openings: 18,000
- ▲ Self-Employed: 31.2%
- ▲ Part-Time: 18.5%

Originate and prepare written material, such as scripts, stories, advertisements, and other material. **SKILLS**—No data available.

GOE INFORMATION—**Interest Area:** 01. Arts, Entertainment, and Media. **Work Group:** 01.02. Writing and Editing. **Other Job Titles in This Work Group:** Copy Writers; Creative Writers; Editors; Poets and Lyricists; Technical Writers. **PERSONALITY TYPE**—No data available.

EDUCATION/TRAINING PROGRAM(S)—Broadcast Journalism; Business/Corporate Communications; Communication Studies/Speech Communication and Rhetoric; Communication, Journalism, and Related Programs, Other; Creative Writing; English Composition; Family and Consumer Sciences/Human Sciences Communication; Journalism; Mass Communication/Media Studies; Playwriting and Screenwriting; Technical and Business Writing. **RELATED KNOWLEDGE/COURSES**—No data available.

Zoologists and Wildlife Biologists

- ▲ Education/Training Required: Doctoral degree
- ▲ Annual Earnings: $46,220
- ▲ Growth: 21.0%
- ▲ Annual Job Openings: 5,000
- ▲ Self-Employed: 4.9%
- ▲ Part-Time: 6.6%

Study the origins, behavior, diseases, genetics, and life processes of animals and wildlife. May specialize in wildlife research and management, including the collection and analysis of biological data to determine the environmental effects of present and potential use of land and water areas. Studies origin, interrelationships, classification, life histories and diseases, development, genetics, and distribution of animals. Studies animals in their natural habitats and assesses effects of environment on animals. Analyzes characteristics of animals to identify and classify animals. Collects and dissects animal specimens and examines specimens under microscope. Conducts experimental studies, using chemicals and various types of scientific equipment. Raises specimens for study and observation or for use in experiments. Prepares collections of preserved specimens or microscopic slides for species identification and study of species development or animal disease. **SKILLS**—**Science:** Using scientific rules and methods to solve problems. **Reading Comprehension:** Understanding written sentences and paragraphs in work-related documents. **Active Learning:** Understanding the implications of new information for both current and future problem-solving and decision-making. **Writing:** Communicating effectively in writing as appropriate for the needs of the audience. **Critical Thinking:** Using logic and reasoning to identify the strengths and weaknesses of alternative solutions, conclusions, or approaches to problems.

GOE INFORMATION—Interest Area: 02. Science, Math, and Engineering. **Work Group:** 02.03. Life Sciences. **Other Job Titles in This Work Group:** Agricultural and Food Science Technicians; Agricultural Technicians; Animal Scientists; Biochemists; Biochemists and Biophysicists; Biological Scientists, All Other; Biologists; Biophysicists; Conservation Scientists; Environmental Scientists and Specialists, Including Health; Epidemiologists; Food Science Technicians; Food Scientists and Technologists; Foresters; Life Scientists, All Other; Medical Scientists, Except Epidemiologists; Microbiologists; Plant Scientists; Range Managers; Soil and Plant Scientists; Soil Conservationists; Soil Scientists. **PERSONALITY TYPE—**Investigative. Investigative occupations frequently involve working with ideas and require an extensive amount of thinking. These occupations can involve searching for facts and figuring out problems mentally.

EDUCATION/TRAINING PROGRAM(S)—Animal Behavior and Ethology; Animal Physiology; Cell/Cellular Biology and Anatomical Sciences, Other; Ecology; Entomology; Wildlife and Wildlands Science and Management; Wildlife Biology; Zoology/Animal Biology; Zoology/Animal Biology, Other. **RELATED KNOWLEDGE/COURSES—Biology:** Knowledge of plant and animal organisms and their tissues, cells, functions, interdependencies, and interactions with each other and the environment. **Mathematics:** Knowledge of arithmetic, algebra, geometry, calculus, and statistics and their applications. **Chemistry:** Knowledge of the chemical composition, structure, and properties of substances and of the chemical processes and transformations that they undergo. This includes uses of chemicals and their interactions, danger signs, production techniques, and disposal methods. **Clerical Studies:** Knowledge of administrative and clerical procedures and systems, such as word processing, managing files and records, stenography and transcription, designing forms, and other office procedures and terminology. **English Language:** Knowledge of the structure and content of the English language, including the meaning and spelling of words, rules of composition, and grammar.

11-3-01

Look into Jobs ss; soces

1. Real estate sales agent
2. Home care aides
3. Social service assistant
4. pest control workers
5. Lawn service
6. bus driver
7. Janitors & cleaners
8. Immigration & custom inspector
9. storage manager
10. parking lot attendant
11. retail salesperson
12. dry-cleaning worker
13. GED & adult literacy teacher
14. correction workers
15. Taxi driver